CHESHIRE AND BURN'S
MODERN LAW OF REAL PROPERTY

First Edition	September	1925
Second Edition	September	1927
Third Edition	February	1933
Fourth Edition	July	1944
Second Impression	August	1945
Third Impression	January	1947
Fourth Impression	December	1947
Sixth Edition	September	1949
Second Impression	July	1952
Seventh Edition	September	1954
Second Impression	September	1956
Eighth Edition	March	1958
Second Impression	January	1961
Ninth Edition	March	1962
Second Impression	February	1964
Third Impression	August	1966
Tenth Edition	May	1967
Second Impression	April	1970
Eleventh Edition	April	1972
Second Impression	May	1974
Twelfth Edition	May	1976
Thirteenth Edition	August	1982
Second Impression	August	1983
Third Impression	January	1987
Fourteenth Edition	June	1988
Fifteenth Edition	July	1994
Sixteenth Edition	September	2000
Seventeenth Edition	August	2006
Eighteenth Edition	August	2011

CHESHIRE AND BURN'S

MODERN LAW OF REAL PROPERTY

Eighteenth Edition

E H BURN BCL, MA

Barrister and Honorary Bencher of Lincoln's Inn
Emeritus Student of Christ Church, Oxford
Formerly Professor of Law in The City University

J CARTWRIGHT BCL, MA

Solicitor
Student and Tutor in Law, Christ Church, Oxford
Professor of the Law of Contract, University of Oxford
Professor of Anglo-American Private Law, University of Leiden

OXFORD

UNIVERSITY PRESS

OXFORD
UNIVERSITY PRESS

Great Clarendon Street, Oxford OX2 6DP

Oxford University Press is a department of the University of Oxford.
It furthers the University's objective of excellence in research, scholarship,
and education by publishing worldwide in

Oxford New York

Auckland Cape Town Dar es Salaam Hong Kong Karachi
Kuala Lumpur Madrid Melbourne Mexico City Nairobi
New Delhi Shanghai Taipei Toronto

With offices in

Argentina Austria Brazil Chile Czech Republic France Greece
Guatemala Hungary Italy Japan Poland Portugal Singapore
South Korea Switzerland Thailand Turkey Ukraine Vietnam

Oxford is a registered trade mark of Oxford University Press
in the UK and in certain other countries

Published in the United States
by Oxford University Press Inc., New York

Fifteenth edition 1994
Sixteenth edition 2000
Seventeenth edition 2006

British Library Cataloguing in Publication Data

Data available

Library of Congress Cataloging in Publication Data

Control number: 2011933693

Typeset by Newgen Imaging Systems (P) Ltd, Chennai, India
Printed in Great Britain
on acid-free paper by
CPI Group (UK) Ltd, Croydon, CR0 4YY

ISBN 978–0–19–959340–8

3 5 7 9 10 8 6 4 2

CONTENTS

PART III ESTATES AND INTERESTS IN LAND

PART IV THE CREATION, TRANSFER AND EXTINCTION OF ESTATES AND INTERESTS IN LAND

PREFACE

In this new edition we have made some significant changes to the structure of the book in order to make it more accessible to the student who comes to the study of land law for the first time, whilst at the same time ensuring that we can retain the depth of detail of coverage which is needed by the advanced learner or the practitioner in this field.

The first chapter now gives an introduction to some of the key concepts, and to the thinking of the land lawyer, which will assist the first-time reader to understand the context of the detailed chapters which follow. It makes clear that we remain committed in this book to the approach which was set by Cheshire in his first edition in 1925: that the modern land law cannot be seen in isolation from its historical roots. There remains, therefore, in Part II the more detailed account of the historical background for the reader who wishes to pursue this further (or to dip into the detail where it becomes relevant in later chapters to understand particular points in the modern law). Part II ends with a chapter on the more modern developments and gives an outline of land transactions—in both unregistered and registered conveyancing—in the modern law which then allows the reader to move to a detailed consideration of the estates and interests in land (Part III). As in the previous edition, we have kept the detailed discussion of conveyancing until the final part (Part IV), because we believe that one can better understand the mechanisms of conveyancing once one has a clear picture of the nature of the rights which are the subject-matter of conveyancing transactions. The order in which to read the chapters is, of course, for the reader to decide (or, in the case of the student, as set by the structure of the course). But we have designed it so that in Part I the first-time reader can see the significance of property rights, and their protection both as between the parties and as against third parties (chapter 1), and can understand in particular the significance of registration of estates and interests in land (chapter 5) before later reading about, say, registration of title in detail (chapter 28) in the light of the substantive property rights (Part III).

There are also other changes of structure, which are generally designed to make it easier for the reader to find the way through the material: the old single chapter on Leases has now been divided into four separate chapters (general characteristics and creation; covenants; termination and recovery of possession; special statutory codes); and the old single chapter on transfer of estates and interests in land has now been more clearly divided into separate chapters on unregistered conveyancing and registered conveyancing. We have moved the discussion of adverse possession back into the final chapter on the extinction of estates and interests in land. And—the most significant change—we took the view that the time had come to leave to specialist books the law of planning control and compulsory purchase: there is no longer a final part on the public control over the use of land.

The most important changes in this new edition, however, are of course the changes to the text in the light of developments in the law. There are very many significant changes throughout the book to bring it—as far as possible—up to date.

The courts at all levels have developed most aspects of land law. For example, the courts from the High Court through the House of Lords (and now the Supreme Court) to the Grand Chamber of the European Court of Human Right have continued to work out the relevance of the European Convention on Human Rights to our land law in relation to such things as the exercise of the power of sale of mortgaged property without a court order, the court order for sale in favour of the trustee in bankruptcy, the landlord's claim for possession, and the loss of title through adverse possession. The House of Lords has further clarified the non-proprietary nature of a '*Bruton* tenancy'; has given guidance on easements of parking, doubting the earlier approach in the Court of Appeal; and has twice given guidance on the scope of the doctrine of proprietary estoppel (and appears to have limited the scope for the operation of estoppel to circumvent the requirements of a written contract for the sale of land). In the context of co-ownership, the House of Lords has re-assessed the approach to finding and quantifying the interests of the parties under a constructive trust: the courts at all levels have been working out the implications of this development, and at the time when this book was finalised the Supreme Court had heard (but had not yet decided) the latest appeal on this (in *Jones v Kernott*). The Supreme Court has also examined again the circumstances in which inhabitants claiming registration of greens have used the land 'as of right'; and the Court of Appeal has held that the benefit of an easement attaches to the land rather than to an estate in land; and has limited the operation of the rule in *Wheeldon v Burrows*.

Parliament has remained active in the field of land law during this period: the Commons Act 2006 and the Consumer Credit Act 2006 were passing through the legislative process at the time of the last edition; the Commons Act is still being brought progressively into force (although at a slower pace than originally planned), but the new Consumer Credit Act has now amended the 1974 Act in relation to unregulated mortgages, most notably to reform courts' powers to intervene where the relationship between the creditor and debtor is 'unfair'. We have seen the statutory demise of the tolerated trespasser; and almost the demise of the remedy of distress for rent (through Part 3 of the Tribunals, Courts and Enforcement Act 2007, but it has not yet been brought into force). The most significant general statutory change, perhaps, is the Perpetuities and Accumulations Act 2009 (significant for the practitioner, although not for the student of law for whom the law of perpetuities seems to be a closed book these days): it is a simplifying Act, but we now have the added complexity of three different perpetuity regimes, depending on whether the instrument in question took effect before 16 July 1964 (common law), after 15 July 1964 but before 6 April 2010 (Perpetuities and Accumulations Act 1964), or after 5 April 2010 (the new Act). It also abolished the rule against excessive accumulation of income, but again only after 5 April 2010. There have also been measures to provide additional protection to mortgagors against possession, including the Pre-Action Protocol for Possession Claims based on Mortgage or Home

Purchase Plan Arrears in Respect of Residential Property; and limited protection for unauthorised tenants of defaulting mortgagors through the Mortgage Repossessions (Protection of Tenants etc) Act 2010. The requirement for home information packs was immediately suspended by the new Government in 2010, and the repeal is to follow when the Localism Bill, currently passing through Parliament, is enacted—a Bill which will also introduce reforms to tenancies in the public rental sector. And the Lands Tribunal has turned into the Upper Tribunal (Lands Chamber).

Other significant changes include more measured progress towards electronic conveyancing: the Land Registry's strategic objective of the creation of a Land Register with comprehensive content and national coverage by 2012 has been replaced by the setting of annual targets for increasing the total area of freehold land which is on the register; and although there has been an extension of preparations for electronic conveyancing through pilot scheme for e-charges, and new provisions for electronic discharge or release of charges, the introduction of electronic contracts has been delayed until later in the incremental programme by which electronic conveyancing is to be introduced.

The Law Commission has again been very active, and its proposals (old and new) have met with mixed success. It seems that if one leaves a report on the shelf for a sufficiently long period, it is thought to show that the reform is no longer necessary. The Government at last decided on (and rejected in part) the 1996 Report on Responsibility for State and Condition of Property, and has also in the end decided not to take forward the implementation of the 2001 Report on Limitation of Actions. It also rejected the fundamental reforms proposed in 2006 to replace the existing forms of residential tenancies, and the new Government in 2010 further limited possible reform in the private residential sector (but has signalled a move towards more flexible residential tenancies in the public residential tenancy sector). The Law Commission produced its long-awaited Consultation Paper on easements and covenants; the final Report is promised for June 2011 and so we have unfortunately been unable to include it in this edition. We wait with interest to see whether the next edition will be able to include the enacted reforms following the final Report. Some other recent Reports, which we have been able to discuss in this book, are at the time of writing still awaiting a response from the Government: in particular, the latest proposal to replace the law on forfeiture, and the proposed new statutory scheme for cohabitants on separation (in both cases the response was promised for 'early' in 2011 but had not been published by the end of May).

In every field of the law, the enthusiast for reform, or the critic of our existing law, would do well to keep an eye on what happens elsewhere. A notable recent development, to which we have drawn attention at appropriate points in the text, is the Land and Conveyancing Reform Act 2009 in the Republic of Ireland, which has revised very significantly the Irish law (hitherto still based largely on the old law which it inherited from England before the great reforms of English land law in 1925). It has taken some different directions from those taken by English law, and so provides food for thought: for example, it has abolished feudal tenure (but retained the concept of an estate in land); abolished the rules against perpetuities and accumulations; rejected the operation of the equivalent of our section 62 of the Law of Property Act 1925 to create easements from informal permissions, and replaced the rule in *Wheeldon v Burrows*; replaced prescription at common law and by lost modern grant; replaced the rules of common law and equity in relation to the enforceability of freehold covenants and allowed the enforcement of positive as well as restrictive covenants; and prevented the operation of upwards only rent review clauses in business leases.

We would like to thank Marilyn Kennedy-McGregor, Barrister of Gray's Inn and Lincoln's Inn, for her valuable comments and advice. We would also like to thank our publishers for undertaking the compilation of the various tables and the index, and for their ready and expert help at all times.

This edition purports to state the law as it was on 28 February 2011, but, where space permitted, more recent developments have been incorporated to the end of May 2011.

EHB

JC

TABLE OF STATUTES

TABLE OF STATUTORY INSTRUMENTS

TABLE OF CONVENTIONS AND TREATIES

TABLE OF EUROPEAN SECONDARY LEGISLATION

TABLE OF OTHER NATIONAL LEGISLATION

TABLE OF CASES

ABBREVIATIONS

Statutes and Rules

AEA	Administration of Estates Act
AJA	Administration of Justice Act
CA	Companies Act
CCA	Consumer Credit Act
CLRA	Commonhold and Leasehold Reform Act
C(LR)R	Commonhold (Land Registration) Rules
CPA	Compulsory Purchase Act
CPR	Civil Procedure Rules
ECHR	Convention for the Protection of Human Rights and Fundamental Freedoms (the European Convention on Human Rights)
FA	Finance Act
HA	Housing Act
HRA	Human Rights Act
IEA	Intestates' Estates Act
ITA	Inheritance Tax Act
LA	Limitation Act
LCA	Land Charges Act
LLCA	Local Land Charges Act
LLCR	Local Land Charges Rules
LPA	Law of Property Act
LP(A)A	Law of Property (Amendment) Act
LP(MP)A	Law of Property (Miscellaneous Provisions) Act
LRA	Land Registration Act
LR(A)R	Land Registration (Amendment) Rules
LRR	Land Registration Rules
LTA	Landlord and Tenant Act
LT(C)A	Landlord and Tenant (Covenants) Act
PAA	Perpetuities and Accumulations Act
RSC	Rules of the Supreme Court
SCA	Senior Courts Act (until 1 October 2009, Supreme Court Act)
SI	Statutory Instrument
SLA	Settled Land Act

TA	Trustee Act
TCPA	Town and Country Planning Act
TLATA	Trusts of Land and Appointment of Trustees Act

Reports and Periodicals

All ER Rev	All England Law Reports Annual Review
CLJ	Cambridge Law Journal
CLP	Current Legal Problems
CLY	Current Law Yearbook
Conv (NS)	Conveyancer (New Series)
EG	Estates Gazette
EGCS	Estates Gazette Case Summaries
EGLR	Estates Gazette Law Reports
EHR	Economic History Review
Harv L Rev	Harvard Law Review
HLR	Housing Law Reports
JPL	Journal of Planning and Environment Law (until 1972, Journal of Planning and Property Law)
Jurid Soc	Juridical Society's Papers
L & TR	Landlord and Tenant Reports
L & T Rev	Landlord and Tenant Review
LJ News	Law Journal Newspaper
LQR	Law Quarterly Review
LS	Legal Studies
LSG	Law Society's Gazette
LT	Law Times
L & T Rev	Landlord and Tenant Review
MLR	Modern Law Review
NILQ	Northern Ireland Legal Quarterly
NLJ	New Law Journal
NPC	New Property Cases
OJLS	Oxford Journal of Legal Studies
P & CR	Property, Planning and Compensation Reports
RLR	Restitution Law Review
SJ	Solicitors' Journal
Yale LJ	Yale Law Journal

Books
(See detailed bibliography)

Aldridge	*Leasehold Law*
Anson	*Anson's Law of Contract*
Blackstone	Blackstone, *Commentaries on the Laws of England*
Chitty	*Chitty on Contracts*
Co Litt	*Coke's Commentary upon Littleton*
Conv Prec	Precedents for the Conveyancer
Emmet	*Emmet and Farrand on Title*
Fisher and Lightwood	*Fisher and Lightwood's Law of Mortgage*
Gale	*Gale on Easements* (18th edn)
H & B	Harpum and Bignell, *Registered Land: Law and Practice under the Land Registration Act 2002*
H & M	Hanbury and Martin, *Modern Equity*
Litt	*Littleton's Tenures*
M & B	*Maudsley & Burn's Land Law: Cases and Materials*
M & W	Megarry and Wade, *The Law of Real Property*
Maudsley	Maudsley, *The Modern Law of Perpetuities*
Morris and Leach	Morris and Leach, *The Rule against Perpetuities*
Preston and Newsom	*Preston and Newsom's Restrictive Covenants Affecting Freehold Land*
R & R	Ruoff and Roper, *Registered Conveyancing* (2003 looseleaf edn)
Snell	*Snell's Equity*
W & C	*Wolstenholme and Cherry's Conveyancing Statutes*
W & H	Whitehouse and Hassall, *Trust of Land, Trustee Delegation and the Trustee Act 2000*

Miscellaneous

CML	Council of Mortgage Lenders
CA	Court of Appeal
CP	Consultation Paper
Cty Ct	County Court
DCA	Department for Constitutional Affairs
DCLG	Department for Communities and Local Government
Defra	Department for Environment, Food and Rural Affairs

DETR   Department of the Environment, Transport and the Regions
ECtHR   European Court of Human Rights
FSA   Financial Services Authority
HL   House of Lords
LCD   Lord Chancellor's Department
MoJ   Ministry of Justice
ODPM   Office of the Deputy Prime Minister
SC   Supreme Court
UK   United Kingdom
VAT   Value Added Tax
WP   Working Paper

PART I

INTRODUCTION

The modern law of real property in England can be fully understood only by reference to its history. The land law of the twenty-first century contains structures, concepts and language that date back to the middle ages. There has never been a codification of the law in England similar to the great civil codes on the Continent.[1] The nearest we have come to a codification of the land law is in the great reforms of 1925—which, however, did not constitute a complete code, breaking with the past and laying down a new, self-contained set of legal rules and principles for land ownership and transactions relating to land. Instead, the 1925 legislation, which is still the basis of the modern land law in England, reformed and developed the law as it then stood. Even the most recent comprehensive reform of land law, the Land Registration Act 2002, has not swept away the old law but can be fully understood only by reference to it.

In this introductory Part, we first consider some fundamental matters relating to the scope of the law of real property, and, having sketched the modern scene, we then explain its origins in more detail in Part II through the historical development of land law and an overview of the methods of conveyancing adopted today. In Part III we shall move on to consider in more detail the estates and interests, legal and equitable, that are recognised in modern English land law; in Part IV we shall see in detail how those estates and interests are created, transferred and extinguished.

---

[1] Pre-eminent amongst the codes are the French *Code civil* of 1804, and the German *Bürgeliches Gesetzbuch* ('BGB') which came into force on 1 January 1900. But there are systematic civil codes throughout continental Europe—with the exception of the Scandinavian countries.

1

AN INTRODUCTION TO LAND LAW

Summary

In this book we are concerned with the law of *real property*—land law. There are a number of separate aspects to this that should first be clarified, in order that the detailed discussion in the following chapters can be understood: first, the concept of *property rights*, as opposed to purely personal rights; and then, within the law of property, how the law defines 'real property', and the meaning attributed by the law to the word 'land'. We then give an outline of the development of the modern law to illustrate the importance of setting it in its historical context; and we outline the kinds of right that are recognised in English law as real property rights—estates and interests in land—and the mechanisms by which they are created and transferred; and the interaction between land law and the law on the protection of human rights.

I PROPERTY RIGHTS

The notion of 'property', or property rights, is deceptively simple, and cannot be fully treated here.[2] We shall confine ourselves to drawing attention, by way of introduction, to matters that are relevant to an understanding of the estates and interests in land, and their creation and transfer, which are discussed in detail later.

A PROPERTY RIGHTS AND PERSONAL RIGHTS

Property rights are to be contrasted with personal rights. This contrast, in English law, can be expressed in the same essential terms as were developed in Roman law:[3] property rights are rights *in rem*; personal rights are rights *in personam*. To say that one has a property right in relation to land is to say that one has a right over, or in respect of, the land itself. A personal right, however, is a right against a person, generated by the act of the person or imposed on him by the law, but in every case the right is against—and so the correlative duty is owed by—the particular individual concerned. Obligations arising from contract, for example, are personal: the reason that the defendant is bound to the claimant is because he has (expressly or impliedly) undertaken the burden of the obligation.

B THIRD PARTIES AND PROPERTY RIGHTS

The significance of the distinction between personal rights and property rights, for our purposes, lies in the case where third parties become involved. As Lord Wilberforce said:[4]

> Before a right or an interest can be admitted into the category of property, or of a right affecting property, it must be definable, identifiable by third parties, capable in its nature of assumption by third parties, and have some degree of permanence or stability.

This emphasises the link between property rights and third parties, and the focus is on the burden of rights affecting property. A contract creates a personal relationship in law between the contracting parties, and although English law allows the *benefit* of a contractual right to be transferred by assignment,[5] a third party cannot generally be *bound* by an obligation in a contract without himself accepting it—and in that case he is bound by his own act rather than simply as successor to the original obligor under

---

[2] Lawson and Rudden, *The Law of Property* (3rd edn, 2002); Bright and Dewar, *Land Law Themes and Perspectives* (1998), chs 1 (Gray and Gray), 18 (Birks); Tee, *Land Law Issues, Debates, Policy* (2002), ch 1 (Dixon); Harris, *Property and Justice* (1996); Honoré, *Oxford Essays in Jurisprudence* (ed Guest, 1961), pp 107 ff; Rudden, *Oxford Essays in Jurisprudence* (3rd series, eds Eekelaar and Bell, 1987), pp 239 ff.

[3] Nicholas, *Introduction to Roman Law* (1962), pp 99–103; Bright and Dewar, above, p 472 (Birks).

[4] *National Provincial Bank Ltd v Ainsworth* [1965] AC 1175, 1247–8; p 943, below.

[5] Anson, ch 22. Even so, this involves a recognition of the benefit of a contractual right as having proprietary characteristics: it is a chose in action: ibid, pp 661–3; LPA 1925, s 136(1).

the contract.[6] By contrast, proprietary rights are inherently capable of both benefiting and binding parties who were not involved in their original creation. The fundamental point, therefore, is that—to take the example of land law—a property right is either the right to the land itself (in some sense, the 'ownership' of the land); or a right owned by a third party in or over that land (for example, an easement), which means that it is a right that is capable of binding the owner for the time being of the land: his acquisition of the land brings with it the burdens that are in law recognised as attaching to the land.

As we have already said, this is only an introduction—a starting-point for a further analysis of the notion of property rights as recognised by English law. In some respects the simplicity of the notion of rights in land as rights *in rem* is complicated by certain peculiarly English notions[7] of real property rights, which are explained by the historical development of the land law: in particular, by the fact that the common law does not recognise absolute property rights in land, but has developed the doctrine of *estates* in land;[8] and that equity developed the protection of property rights through the concept of the trust.[9] Not every successor in title to the land will necessarily be bound by every right attached to the land.[10] And an interest in the land can have limits on its alienability.[11] But the underlying principle still holds. The principal concern of the law of property—and in particular land law—is with what is meant by saying that a person is the 'owner' of the property; what other rights of third parties are recognised by the law as being capable of existing in or over that property; and in what circumstances a successor to the owner is bound to give effect to those third-party rights.

II REAL PROPERTY

English law draws a technical distinction between 'real property' and other property ('personal property'), a distinction grounded in history but that must still be understood in order to understand the language and concepts of modern land law.[12]

The common law devised certain forms of action to enable rights to be enforced. As we shall see later,[13] in the early law the actions by which property could be specifically

---

[6] Ibid, pp 675–6.   [7] Contrast Roman law and modern civil law systems; below, p 55.

[8] Below, pp 12–13 and Ch 2.   [9] Below, pp 14–15 and Ch 3.

[10] Below, pp 80–83, noting that an equitable estate can be characterised as a right *in personam*, since the category of persons who are bound by it are limited by the doctrine of the bona fide purchaser for value without notice. For the use of registration to supersede the doctrine of the bona fide purchaser in the modern law, see pp 21–22 and Ch 5, below.

[11] But a total restraint on alienation is inconsistent with the conception of ownership: p 621, below; *Re Brown* [1954] Ch 39, M & B p 306.

[12] Continental European systems, following Roman law, typically distinguish between 'immovable' property and 'movable' property; English law draws that distinction not in domestic law but in the context of private international law (conflict of laws): Dicey, Morris & Collins, *The Conflict of Laws* (14th edn, 2006) paras 22-004–22-007.

[13] Below, p 49.

recovered were known as the 'real actions'. But only land could be specifically recovered by such actions; a person who was dispossessed of a chattel could bring only an action for damages for the wrong committed by the dispossession, and could not recover the chattel itself.[14] Land, the subject of the 'real actions', therefore came to be known as 'real property'.

It should be noted, however, that leases were not included within 'real property', principally because the real actions were not extended to allow the recovery of the land subject to the lease, but other actions were instead given to the tenant.[15] The interest of a tenant under a lease was therefore classed as personal property, rather than real property—although because of its obvious attachment to the land it was called a 'chattel real'. But within the technical distinction of the common law between real property and personal property the leasehold estate constituted—and still today technically constitutes—an interest in personal property. Until the legislative reforms of 1925 this distinction was critical for such things as the descent of property on intestacy and the order in which assets were applied for the payment of a testator's debts.[16] However, these distinctions between real and personal property were largely eradicated by the 1925 legislation, and even though the leasehold estate is still technically not 'real property' we naturally consider it in detail in this book, of which the focus is estates and interests in land.

III THE MEANING OF LAND

Before we can consider the estates and interests that can exist in land, however, we must first explain what in law constitutes 'land'. The following is the definition for the purposes of the Law of Property Act 1925:[17]

> 'Land' includes land of any tenure, and mines and minerals, whether or not held apart from the surface, buildings or parts of buildings (whether the division is horizontal, vertical or made in any other way) and other corporeal hereditaments; also a manor, an advowson, and a rent and other incorporeal hereditaments, and an easement, right, privilege, or benefit in, over, or derived from land…

[14] Even in the modern law the normal claim for wrongful dispossession and retention of a chattel is in tort—the tort of conversion—and damages remain the primary remedy although the defendant has the choice between paying damages and returning the chattel, and a court may order the return of the chattel: Torts (Interference with Goods) Act 1977, s 3 (replacing a similar provision for the tort of detinue (now abolished) first introduced by Common Law Procedure Act 1854, s 78). Specific recovery of chattels remains, however, the exception: Bridge, *Personal Property Law* (3rd edn, 2002), pp 76–7.

[15] Below, p 58.   [16] Below, pp 117–18.

[17] S 205(1)(ix), amended by TLATA 1996, s 25(2), Sch 4. Cf the definitions in SLA 1925, s 117(1)(ix); TA 1925, s 68(6); LRA 1925, s 3(viii) (all amended by TLATA 1996, s 25(2), Sch 4); LCA 1972, s 17(1); LRA 2002, s 132(1). See also Interpretation Act 1978, s 5, Sch 1; *Starke v IRC* [1995] 1 WLR 1439. Before TLATA 1996 there was a question as to whether land included an interest under a trust for sale: see below, p 466.

A DISTINCTION BETWEEN CORPOREAL AND INCORPOREAL HEREDITAMENTS

Law is at one with the layman in agreeing that 'land' includes the surface of the earth, together with such physical things above and below it as buildings and trees, mines and minerals,[18] but it also gives the word a far wider meaning. The definition set out above from the Law of Property Act 1925 includes both 'corporeal hereditaments' and 'incorporeal hereditaments' within the meaning of 'land'. These terms call for explanation. The word 'hereditament' signifies a right that is heritable, that is capable of passing by way of descent to heirs; and our legal ancestors came to the conclusion that hereditaments may be either corporeal or incorporeal. As Blackstone said:

> Hereditaments, then, to use the largest expression, are of two kinds, corporeal and incorporeal. Corporeal consist of such as affect the senses; such as may be seen and handled by the body; incorporeal are not the object of sensation, can neither be seen nor handled, are creatures of the mind and exist only in contemplation. Corporeal hereditaments consist of substantial and permanent objects.[19]

The subject-matter of ownership may therefore consist either of physical, tangible (corporeal) things ('corporeities') or of intangible (incorporeal) things ('incorporeities'). There is nothing remarkable in this, for it is obvious that an incorporeity such as a right of way over adjacent land may be held with a house or a piece of land. What is remarkable,[20] however, is a terminology that declares that an interest in a corporeal, physical thing, is itself a corporeal *interest*, but that an interest in an incorporeal thing is an incorporeal *interest*. However, no proprietary interest can be other than a mere *right* of ownership, and no matter what the nature of its subject-matter may be, it must always be incorporeal: 'All property, of whatever kind, is an *incorporeal* right to the *corporeal* use and profit of some *corporeal* thing.'[21] It is difficult to answer the following criticism of Austin:[22]

> With us *all* rights and obligations are not *incorporeal things*; but certain rights are styled *incorporeal hereditaments*, and are opposed by that name to *hereditaments corporeal*. That is to say, *rights* of a certain species ... are absurdly opposed to the *things* (strictly so called) which are the *subjects* or *matter* of rights of another species. The word *hereditaments* is

---

[18] Below, p 159. As to waste products dumped on land, see *Rogers (Inspector of Taxes) v Longsdon* [1967] Ch 93.

[19] Blackstone, vol ii, p 17.   [20] Co Litt 6a; *Lloyd v Jones* (1848) 6 CB 81, 90.

[21] (1857) 1 Jurid Soc, p 542 (SM Leake).

[22] Austin, *Lectures on Jurisprudence* (5th edn, 1885, ed Campbell), vol i, p 362; but see Sweet's answer in *Challis's Law of Real Property* (3rd edn, 1911), pp 48–58. LPA 1925, s 1(2), pp 123–4, below, perpetuates the confusion in describing a right to, for example, an easement as an interest in land, notwithstanding that in s 205(1)(ix) (p 6, above) it includes an easement in the definition of 'land': 'An easement is that familiar creature of English land law: an estate or interest carved out of a larger estate or interest, but nevertheless constituting a hereditament in its own right. It is a burden on the servient tenement, but also "land" vested in the proprietor of the dominant tenement': *Willies-Williams v National Trust for Places of Historic Interest or Natural Beauty* (1993) 65 P & CR 359, 361 (Hoffmann LJ).

evidently taken in two senses in the two phrases which stand to denote the species of hereditaments. A corporeal hereditament is the thing itself which is the subject of the right; an incorporeal hereditament is not the subject of the right, but the right itself.

The use of this unscientific terminology need not, however, disturb us. The two things to bear in mind are: first, that whether an interest, such as a fee simple estate, exists in a corporeity or an incorporeity, it is an interest in *land*; and secondly, that the number of incorporeities recognised by English law is considerable. Blackstone described no fewer than ten *incorporeal hereditaments* some of which are no longer of practical importance.[23] The most important now are easements,[24] profits[25] and rentcharges.[26]

B FIXTURES

There is one class of corporeal things, traditionally known as *fixtures*, which are regarded as 'land' and which are sufficiently important to merit discussion.

(1) Distinction Between Land and Chattels

The primary legal meaning of 'fixtures' is objects that are so affixed to land or to a building on land as to become in fact part of it.[27] A house built into the land becomes part of the land. A chattel may be attached to an existing building in such a way as to lose the character of a chattel and become part of the building, and therefore also part of the land. The maxim is: *quicquid plantatur solo, solo cedit*; whatever is affixed to the soil accedes to the soil.

The house attached to the land[28] and the chattel attached to the building are both in law 'fixtures', but this does not reflect everyday terminology:[29]

> In ordinary language one thinks of a fixture as being something fixed to a building. One would not ordinarily think of the building itself as a fixture.

and

> The term fixture is apt to be a source of misunderstanding owing to the existence of the category of so called 'tenants' fixtures' (a term used to cover both trade fixtures and

[23] Blackstone, vol ii, c iii. The list is: advowsons, tithes, commons, ways, offices, dignities, franchises, corodies (a right to receive victuals for one's maintenance), annuities and rents. 'Whether the benefit of a restrictive covenant can be described as an incorporeal hereditament is a very doubtful question': *Earl of Leicester v Wells-next-the-Sea UDC* [1973] Ch 110, 119 (Plowman J). On franchises, see *Sevenoaks DC v Pattullo & Vinson Ltd* [1984] Ch 211 (right of market); *R (Corporation of London) v Secretary of State for the Environment, Food and Rural Affairs* [2006] UKHL 30, [2006] 1 WLR 1721 (Smithfield and Billingsgate common law markets); *Crown Estate Commissioners v Roberts* [2008] EWHC 1302 (Ch), [2008] 2 P & CR 15 (rights to wreck and several fishery).

[24] Below, pp 123, 634.   [25] Below, p 701.   [26] Below, p 124 and Ch 20.

[27] Leake, *Uses and Profits of Land* (1888), p 103.   [28] *Billing v Pill* [1954] 1 QB 70, 75.

[29] *Elitestone Ltd v Morris* [1997] 1 WLR 687, 690–1, M & B p 7; (1997) 147 NLJ 1031 (HW Wilkinson); [1997] CLJ 498 (S Bridge); [1998] Conv 418 (H Conway).

ornamental fixtures),[30] which are fixtures in the full sense of the word (and therefore part of the realty) but which may nevertheless be removed by the tenant in the course of or at the end of his tenancy. Such fixtures are sometimes confused with chattels which have never become fixtures at all.

Because of these concerns, in *Elitestone Ltd v Morris*[31] the House of Lords preferred a tripartite classification into (a) chattels, (b) fixtures and (c) objects that are 'part and parcel of the land itself'. Objects in categories (b) (which will include those chattels that have become part of a building) and (c) (which will include buildings[32]) are in law treated as being part of the land.

The question whether an object has been so affixed to a building or to land as to become part of it is sometimes difficult to answer. It is a question of law for the judge,[33] but the decision in one case is not conclusive in another, for everything turns upon the circumstances and mainly, though not decisively, upon two particular circumstances: the *degree of annexation* and the *object of annexation*.[34] We shall take these considerations separately.

(a) Degree of annexation

The general rule is that a chattel is not deemed to become part of the land unless it is actually fastened to or connected with the land or building. Mere juxtaposition or the laying of an article, however heavy, upon the land does not prima facie make it a fixture, or 'part and parcel of the land', even though it subsequently sinks into the ground. If a superstructure can be removed without losing its identity, it will not in general be regarded as part of the land. Examples are a Dutch barn, consisting of a roof resting upon wooden uprights, the uprights being made to lie upon brick columns let into the ground;[35] or a white marble statue of a Greek athlete weighing half a ton and standing on a plinth.[36] The case is the same if the posts that support the roof of a corrugated iron building are not embedded in the concrete floor, but are held in position by iron strips fixed into the floor. The concrete foundation, which of course

---

[30] Below, pp 238–9.

[31] [1997] 1 WLR 687, 691, following Woodfall, *Landlord and Tenant* (looseleaf edn), vol 1, para 13.131; followed in *Chelsea Yacht and Boat Co Ltd v Pope* [2000] 1 WLR 1941, 1944; *Wessex Reserve Forces and Cadets Association v White* [2005] EWHC 983, [2005] 3 EGLR 127 at [21].

[32] *Elitestone Ltd v Morris*, above (wooden bungalow resting only by its own weight on concrete pillars set into the ground became part and parcel of the land).

[33] *Reynolds v Ashby & Son* [1904] AC 466.

[34] *Holland v Hodgson* (1872) LR 7 CP 328, 334 (Blackburn J). See *Melluish v BMI (No 3) Ltd* [1996] AC 545 (contractual term that object shall remain a chattel not decisive: 'The concept of a fixture which remains personal or removable property is a contradiction in terms and an impossibility in law'; [1995] Ch 90, 115 (Dillon LJ in CA)). For a useful summary of the principles, see *Wessex Reserve Forces and Cadets Association v White* [2005] EWHC 983, [2005] 3 EGLR 127 at [21]–[23] (Michael Harvey QC).

[35] *Elwes v Maw* (1802) 3 East 38, 55; *Wiltshear v Cottrell* (1853) 1 E & B 674; *Deen v Andrews* (1986) 52 P & CR 17; *Hynes v Vaughan* (1985) 50 P & CR 444 (chrysanthemum growing frame and sprinkler system held not to be fixtures); *Kennedy v Secretary of State for Wales* [1996] EGCS 17 (three massive ormulu bronze chandeliers and carillon turret clock at Neo-Gothic Grade II listed Leighton Hall, Welshpool, held to be fixtures).

[36] *Berkley v Poulett* [1977] 1 EGLR 86; cf *Hamp v Bygrave* [1983] 1 EGLR 174 (stone and lead garden ornaments held to be fixtures): *Berkley v Poulett* was not cited; [1983] NZLJ 256 (HW Wilkinson).

becomes part of the land, is regarded as a separate unit from the superstructure.[37] Again, a printing machine that stands by its own weight upon the floor is not a fixture, even though the driving apparatus is attached to the building at certain points.[38] On the other hand, a chattel that is attached to land, however slightly, is prima facie to be deemed a fixture. Thus, a conservatory attached to a house is a fixture,[39] as also are doors, windows, chimney-pieces, ovens and other similar things.

Nevertheless the extent of annexation is not a decisive test. As Blackburn J said:[40]

> Perhaps the true rule is, that articles not otherwise attached to the land than by their own weight are not to be considered as part of the land, unless the circumstances are such as to shew that they were intended to be part of the land, the onus of showing that they were so intended lying on those who assert that they have ceased to be chattels; and that, on the contrary, an article which is affixed to the land even slightly is to be considered as part of the land, unless the circumstances are such as to shew that it was intended all along to continue a chattel, the onus lying on those who contend that it is a chattel.

(b) Object of annexation

The test here is to ascertain whether the chattel has been fixed for its more convenient use as a chattel, or for the more convenient use of the land or building.[41] Blackburn J gave the following example:

> Blocks of stone placed one on the top of another without any mortar or cement for the purpose of forming a dry stone wall would become part of the land, though the same stones, if deposited in a builder's yard and for convenience sake stacked on the top of each other in the form of a wall, would remain chattels.[42]

Again, a comparatively durable method of affixation will not render a chattel a fixture, if the method of annexation is necessary to its proper enjoyment as a chattel. Thus in the case of *Leigh v Taylor*[43] a tenant for life, the owner of some valuable tapestry, laid strips of wood over the drawing-room paper and fixed them to the walls with two-inch nails. Canvas was stretched over these strips, and the tapestry was fastened by tacks to the strips. It was held that the tapestry had not become a fixture. Vaughan Williams LJ said:[44]

> In my judgment it is obvious that everything which was done here can be accounted for as being absolutely necessary for the enjoyment of the tapestry, and when one arrives at that conclusion there is an end of the case.

---

[37] *Webb v Bevis Ltd* [1940] 1 All ER 247; cf *Jordan v May* [1947] KB 427 (electric lighting engine and dynamo bolted to a concrete bed. These were held to be fixtures, but not the batteries). The degree of affixation is not necessarily the same in every type of case; see, eg, *London County Council v Wilkins* [1955] 2 QB 653; affd [1957] AC 362 (wooden sectional hut).

[38] *Hulme v Brigham* [1943] KB 152.   [39] *Buckland v Butterfield* (1820) 2 Brod & Bing 54.

[40] *Holland v Hodgson* (1872) LR 7 CP 328, 335; *Bradshaw v Davey* [1952] 1 All ER 350 (yacht mooring in the Hamble River held intended to be a chattel); *Chelsea Yacht and Boat Co Ltd v Pope* [2000] 1 WLR 1941 (houseboat moored by ropes and connected to services which could be untied and disconnected without undue effort not annexed to the land; leave to appeal to HL refused: [2000] 1 WLR 2469).

[41] *Wake v Hall* (1883) 8 App Cas 195, 204.   [42] *Holland v Hodgson*, above, at 335.

[43] [1902] AC 157.   [44] In CA under the name *Re De Falbe* [1901] 1 Ch 523, 537.

The principle of this decision was adopted where a lessee had erected some oak and pine panelling and a chimney-piece;[45] and where a vendor had screwed pictures while still in their frames into the recesses in the panelling of a dining-room.[46]

On the other hand, chattels may be annexed to or placed on land in circumstances that show an obvious intention to benefit the use of the land, and if this is so they become fixtures. Examples are seats secured to the floor of a cinema hall,[47] and such objects as statues, stone seats and ornamental vases, held in position merely by their own weight, which are part of the architectural design of a house and its grounds.[48]

Similarly, a wooden bungalow resting on its own weight on concrete pillars has been held to be part of the land, whereas a greenhouse resting on its own weight on concrete dollies has been held not to be a fixture.[49] As Lord Lloyd of Berwick said:[50]

> It is obvious that a greenhouse which can be moved from site to site is a long way removed from a two bedroom bungalow which cannot be removed at all without being demolished.

In *Botham v TSB Bank plc*,[51] the Court of Appeal examined household appliances and held that baths, lavatories and bathroom fittings, as well as fitted kitchen units and sinks will usually be fixtures; but not so carpets, curtains, most light fittings and gas fires whose only connection with the building is by a pipe to the gas supply; and white goods, such as refrigerators, dishwashers and washing machines, where the degree of annexation is slight and no more than needed to allow normal use. Emphasising that the purpose of annexation is the key issue, Roch LJ said:

> If the item viewed objectively, is intended to be permanent and to afford a lasting improvement to the building, the thing will have become a fixture. If the attachment is temporary and is no more than is necessary for the item to be used and enjoyed, then it will remain a chattel.

(2) Right to Remove Fixtures

Even if a chattel is affixed to the land so as to become part of the land, the person who affixed it or his successors in title may have a right to remove it. At common law, a tenant for years and a tenant for life is entitled to remove trade, ornamental or domestic fixtures.[52] Agricultural tenants also have the right by statute to remove

---

[45] *Spyer v Phillipson* [1931] 2 Ch 183. [46] *Berkley v Poulett* [1977] 1 EGLR 86.

[47] *Vaudeville Electric Cinema Ltd v Muriset* [1923] 2 Ch 74. Cf *Lyon & Co v London City and Midland Bank* [1903] 2 KB 135.

[48] *D'Eyncourt v Gregory* (1866) LR 3 Eq 382; *Monti v Barnes* [1901] 1KB 205; cf *Berkley v Poulett*, n 46, above, where the statue was not an integral part of the design.

[49] *HE Dibble Ltd v Moore* [1970] 2 QB 181; *Hynes v Vaughan* (1985) 50 P & CR 444, n 35, above.

[50] *Elitestone Ltd v Morris* [1997] 1 WLR 687, 693.

[51] (1996) 73 P & CR D1; *Chelsea Yacht and Boat Co Ltd v Pope* [2000] 1 WLR 1941 (mooring of houseboat was not with the object of providing a permanent home, but to prevent it from being carried by the tide or the weather and to provide services to it).

[52] For the meaning of trade fixtures, ornamental fixtures and domestic fixtures, see below, pp 238–39.

agricultural fixtures.[53] As between devisee and personal representative,[54] vendor and purchaser[55] and mortgagor and mortgagee[56] there is no general right of removal, and the question of entitlement is dependent upon the question of annexation to the land.

IV DEVELOPMENT OF MODERN LAND LAW

Modern English[57] land law is based on the reforms enacted in a series of statutes that were passed in 1925 and came into force on 1 January 1926: the Settled Land Act 1925, the Trustee Act 1925, the Law of Property Act 1925, the Land Registration Act 1925, the Land Charges Act 1925 and the Administration of Estates Act 1925.

Since 1925 there has been continuous legislative activity, especially in the fields of landlord and tenant and the public control of the use of land; and the system of registration of title to land has in large part superseded earlier methods of conveyancing. But the principles of modern land law are contained in the 1925 legislation. An understanding of those principles is essential to the understanding of the modern law; at the same time, some understanding of the land law as it developed from medieval times to 1926 is essential to the understanding of the 1925 legislation.[58]

A FEUDAL BASIS OF LAND LAW.
TENURES AND ESTATES

The land law is a body of law that, while based on a feudal system imposed by the Norman Conquest, has been adapted to a succession of political and social upheavals, culminating in the welfare state of the twentieth century. It is its feudal basis that explains why, even today, land is not the subject of absolute ownership by private citizens but is formally held of the Crown—the doctrine of 'tenure'. Before 1926 there were different forms of tenure[59] by which the person who appeared to be the 'owner' of land in fact held it of a feudal superior lord, or directly of the Crown, and who was liable to lose the land if, for example, he failed to fulfil the conditions attached to his tenure. As we shall see, the 1925 reforms simplified and modernised the doctrine of tenure but did not abolish it. It is still only the Crown that can technically hold land by

---

[53] Agricultural Holdings Act 1986, s 10; Agricultural Tenancies Act 1995, s 8; below, pp 240–1.

[54] *Re Whaley* [1908] 1 Ch 615; *Re Lord Chesterfield's Settled Estates* [1911] 1 Ch 237 (ornamental wood carvings by Grinling Gibbons).

[55] *Gibson v Hammersmith & City Rly Co* (1863) 32 LJ Ch 337; *Phillips v Lamdin* [1949] 2 KB 33; below, p 982.

[56] *Vaudeville Electric Cinema Ltd v Muriset* [1923] 2 Ch 74; *Longbottom v Berry* (1869) LR 5 QB 123; cf *Gough v Wood & Co* [1894] 1 QB 713 (third party may have right of removal as against mortgagee); below, p 866.

[57] This includes Wales, but not Scotland or Northern Ireland. For the inter-relation between English and Irish land law, see Wylie, *Irish Land Law* (4th edn, 2010), ch 1.

[58] For the history, see below, Chs 2–4.   [59] Below, pp 36–47.

way of absolute ownership,[60] although this has little consequence in practice and we commonly refer to an individual as the 'owner' of the land.

What the 'owner' owns, however, is not the land itself. It is an *estate* in the land.[61] The estate is the right to 'seisin',[62] or possession, of the land for a period of time, either of uncertain duration (a freehold estate) or of a duration that is fixed or at least ascertainable from the time of its creation (a leasehold estate). Before 1926 the common law came to recognise a range of different freehold estates, not only the estate that would continue as long as the holder for the time being had any heirs to whom it could be passed (the 'fee simple'[63]—which is the nearest English approximation to absolute ownership) but also one that was limited in the range of heirs to which it could be passed (the 'fee tail') or was limited to last only for the duration of the life of the grantee (the 'life estate') or of a third party (the 'estate *pur autre vie*'). Estates could be granted under which the right to take possession was in the future, subject to some other estate owner's right to (present) possession. And so multiple estates could exist in the same land; the fee simple could be held by A, an immediate life estate in the land by B and after B's death a life estate by C; and either B or C might grant out of their own estate a leasehold estate to D for a defined number of years.

B THE SIGNIFICANCE OF POSSESSION WITHIN THE LAND LAW

The estate in the land is based on the right to seisin, or possession, of the land. We shall see that, since the enactment of the Law of Property Act 1925, the estates that can exist at common law are limited to the fee simple absolute in possession, and the term of years absolute.[64] But that Act did not change the nature of land ownership or of the doctrine of the estate. Thus from 1926 in English law the 'ownership' of land was still based on the doctrine of the estate, which is itself inextricably linked to the notion of the right to possession of the land.

This reliance on possession as the basis of land ownership resulted in the common law taking the view that the acquisition of possession of the land was itself the acquisition of a title to the land. Possession was a *root of title*. From the first day of his possession, even if he took it by dispossessing another, the possessor had full beneficial rights over the land, holding fee simple estate—although this was only a *relative* title, since if anyone could show a better right to possession, he could recover the land.[65]

Two separate issues arise from this view, taken by the common law, of the significance of possession.[66] First, if possession is a root of title, how, in practice, will a vendor of

---

[60] Known as 'demesne land': see, eg, LRA 2002, ss 79–81.　　　　[61] Below, pp 48–57.

[62] For the technical usage of 'seisin' (for freeholds) and 'possession' (for leaseholds), see below, p 48.

[63] For the meaning of 'fee simple' see below, p 151.　　　　[64] LPA 1925, s. 1(1); below, p 123.

[65] Below, pp 48–51.

[66] Possession, or the right to possession, of land also has other significance; eg in the law of tort it gives standing to sue in trespass, or in nuisance: *Powell v McFarlane* (1977) 38 P & CR 452 at 469 (Slade J); *Malory*

land establish his title to sell? Where the title to the land has not yet been registered, this remains a question even today,[67] although the modern system of registration of title, guaranteed by the State, has now resolved these difficulties.[68] Secondly, what is the significance of the loss of possession: in what circumstances does a squatter not only oust the owner from possession of his land, but also deprive him of the right any longer to claim that he is owner? This is discussed in Chapter 29, where we shall see again that, under the Land Registration Act 2002, in relation to registered land the loss of possession does not of itself give rise to a loss of title, and therefore the significance of possession, in relation to registered land, is now fundamentally changed.[69]

C COMMON LAW AND EQUITY

The development of land law is bound up with the development of equity in English law, and the modern land law cannot be understood without an appreciation of the historical distinction between the common law and equity, and the significance of equity today.

An outline of the development of the equity jurisdiction by the Chancellor, and in particular the recognition of the trust, is set out in Chapter 3.[70] Although the separate jurisdictions of the old courts (and courts of appeal) of common law and equity were united into a single court structure[71] by the Judicature Act 1873, the substantive rules of common law and equity remained distinct but were administered concurrently by the new High Court and Court of Appeal.[72] The old courts of equity had come to recognise estates and interests in land separate from the estates and interests recognised by the common law courts. In particular, equity developed the *trust* where, for example, land was conveyed to a person (the trustee) to hold on trust for another (the beneficiary) and the beneficiary was recognised as having in equity an estate in the land although at common law the estate was held by the trustee. The legal owner of the land was required by equity to give effect to the trust, and the beneficiary under the trust was regarded, in equity, as the real (beneficial) owner. Similarly, the courts of equity recognised that a person who did not have an interest in another's land at common law because, for example, the formalities required by the common law for the creation of the interest had not been complied with, had in certain circumstances an equivalent right in equity that the courts of equity would enforce. A person may therefore be the beneficiary of an equitable fee simple, or an equitable lease, or an equitable easement,

---

Enterprises Ltd v Cheshire Homes (UK) Ltd [2002] EWCA Civ 151, [2002] Ch 216; *Hunter v Canary Wharf Ltd* [1997] AC 655.

[67] Below, pp 21–2; 1043–49.   [68] Below, pp 21–2; 1079–80.
[69] Below, pp 1160–4.   [70] Below, pp 71–8.
[71] Known as the 'Supreme Court of Judicature': s 3, made up of the High Court and the Court of Appeal: s 4. 'Supreme Court' was changed to the 'Senior Courts' when the appellate jurisdiction of the House of Lords was transferred to the new Supreme Court in October 2009: Constitutional Reform Act 2005, s 26.

[72] Supreme Court of Judicature Act 1873, s 24. See now Senior Courts Act (formerly Supreme Court Act) 1981, s 49.

which the courts of equity would enforce; and after the fusion of law and equity by the Judicature Act 1873 such equitable estates and interests were recognised and enforced by all courts. We shall see that even today certain rights in land are referred to as equitable estates and interests, many of them mirroring equivalent estates and interests at common law,[73] but some of them developed by equity as independent interests where there is no corresponding common law property right.[74]

An equitable estate was not, however, as strong as a legal estate; and an equitable interest was not as strong as a legal interest. A legal estate and interest operated as a property right in the full sense—as a right *in rem*, which would bind any person who came to the land over which the estate or interest had been created.[75] An equitable estate or interest, however, was not so fully effective. It had the main characteristic of a property right in that it was capable of enduring through successive changes of ownership of the land, so as to both benefit and bind parties who were not involved in its original creation.[76] But it was defeated if a legal estate in the burdened land passed into the hands of a bona fide purchaser for value who had no notice of the prior equitable estate or interest. This 'bona fide purchaser' (as he was—and is—commonly known) took priority over the equitable owner.

This account of the distinction between estates and interests recognised at common law and in equity is not simply history. Rather, it lays the foundation for the operation of the modern land law. As we shall see, the introduction of provisions for the registration of interests in land where the title to land is itself still unregistered ('unregistered land'[77]) or for the registration of the legal title to the land ('registered land'[78]) presuppose the distinction between legal and equitable interests in land and the basic difference that legal estates and interests are generally stronger than equitable estates and interests. Registration has now been largely adopted as a substitute for the former doctrine of notice. But the core distinction between legal and equitable estates and interests remains, and even the most recent reworking of registered land in the Land Registration Act 2002 follows a scheme that is based on the old distinctions.[79]

D LEGISLATIVE REFORMS OF NINETEENTH CENTURY AND THE IMPETUS TO THE 1925 REFORMS

Legislative reform of land law has a long history. Reform with a view to simplification of the land law began in earnest after the report of the Real Property Commissioners in 1829. Although the Commissioners began their report by saying that this department of English law 'appears to come almost as near to perfection as can be expected in any human institutions',[80] they nevertheless went on to express their

---

[73] See below, pp 215–20 (equitable lease), 650–1 (equitable easement), 807–13 (equitable mortgage).
[74] See below, pp 732–41 (burden of a restrictive covenant), 909–19 (equity by estoppel).
[75] Above, p 5; below, p 80.   [76] Above, p 4.
[77] Below, pp 21; 121; Ch 27.   [78] Below, pp 21; 131; Ch 28.
[79] Below, pp 21–22; 139–40; 143–6.   [80] Real Property Commissioners' First Report, p 6.

opinion that the modes by which interests in land were created, transferred and secured had become unnecessarily defective and that they demanded substantial alteration. The result of this view was that on their recommendation a number of statutes were passed between 1832 and 1837[81] which swept away many impediments to the smooth operation of the law.

Between 1837 and 1922 the legislature became more and more active in the sphere of real property law, but most of the enactments were directed towards the simplification of conveyancing and the extension of the landowner's powers of enjoyment. No comprehensive effort was made to smooth the path by abolishing the substantive defects that had settled on the main body of the law like barnacles on the hull of a ship. Then came the war of 1914–18, and with it a general desire to set the social life of the nation in order. One of the results of this desire was to give an impetus to land legislation, and the main idea that lay at the back of the legislation was a desire to render the sale of land as rapid and simple a matter as is the sale of goods or of stocks and shares.[82] The layman knows that if he desires to transfer to another the ownership of a chattel, such as a car or a picture, the normal requirement is the making of a contract that names the parties, records their intention, describes the article to be sold and states the price to be paid. The contract for the sale of a chattel need not even be in writing but may be oral; and the moment that the contract is concluded, the property in the article, in the absence of a contrary intention, passes to the buyer.[83] At first sight it is difficult to appreciate why the same simple expedient cannot be adopted in the case of land, and not unnaturally the layman grows impatient of the long and expensive investigation required for the conveyance of a piece of land.

But the difference is inevitable, and one reason[84] is that in the great majority of cases the possessor of personal goods is their absolute owner, and therefore able to pass a title that will confer upon their deliveree an equally full and unincumbered ownership. If X is in possession of a piano, it is probable that he is its owner, and in most cases a buyer is safe in paying its value and taking delivery of possession. A seller cannot generally transfer a title greater than his own—*nemo dat quod non habet*—and if it should happen that X, instead of being the owner, is a thief or is merely holding the piano under a hire purchase agreement, then a buyer from him will not acquire ownership. But the fact remains that despite risks of this nature a buyer is generally

---

[81] Chiefly the Prescription Act 1832, Fines and Recoveries Act 1833, Real Property Limitation Act 1833, Dower Act 1833, Inheritance Act 1833 and Wills Act 1837.

[82] See Birkenhead, *Points of View* (1922), vol ii, p 34, discussing LPA 1922. As Lord Chancellor, he was responsible for the passage of this Act and, subsequently, the whole of the 1925 legislation through the House of Lords.

[83] Sale of Goods Act 1979, ss 17, 18.

[84] Another reason is that the law desires to protect the owner of land, which is often his most significant asset, against informal dealings in the land that may not be sufficiently carefully deliberated. For the aims of formality, and the formalities required for both contracts relating to, and dispositions of, interests in land, see below, pp 959–60; Ch 25.

justified in assuming that the possessor of goods is also the owner, and as a rule there is no need to go to trouble and expense in order to ascertain whether some person other than the possessor has any interest in them. It is a legitimate risk to take. But for a purchaser of land to be content with the word of the vendor and with the appearance of ownership that flows from his possession would be foolish.

Land and goods are and must ever be on a different plane. Land is fixed, permanent and vital to the needs of society, and a subject-matter in which rights may be granted to persons other than the ostensible owner. X is in possession of land and is obviously exercising all the powers of enjoyment and management that amount to the popular idea of ownership, but none the less it is by no means certain that he is entitled to dispose of the interest that he may have agreed to sell. He may be in possession under a lease for any period from one week to 999 years or more, or he may have a life interest under a family settlement; and even if he holds the fee simple it is likely that he or his predecessors have granted to third parties rights, such as mortgages, restrictive covenants and rights of way, which continue to be enforceable against the land regardless of any transfer to which it may have been subjected. So long as third parties can in this way have enforceable rights against land that outwardly appears to belong absolutely to the possessor, it is difficult, in the absence of a complete register of title, to devise a system under which conveyances of land can be conducted with the facility of sales of goods; and even then it will always be necessary for a purchaser to make careful searches and inquiries in order to see that there are no third-party rights that will bind the land after it has been transferred to him.

We may start, then, with the assumption that no effort of legislative genius can, from the point of view of simplicity and rapidity, put conveyances of land on an equal footing with sales of goods. But when the question of reforming the law came before Parliament in 1922, the result of nearly a thousand years of development from a feudal origin was that the law of real property contained so many antiquated rules and useless technicalities that additional and unnecessary impediments had arisen to hinder the transfer of land. The real property law as it existed in 1922 might justly be described as an archaic feudalistic system that, though originally evolved to satisfy the needs of a society based and centred on the land, had by considerable ingenuity been twisted and distorted into a shape more or less suitable to a commercial society dominated by money. The movement of progressive societies has been from land to money, or rather to trade, and a legal system that acquired its main features at a time when land constituted the major part of the country's wealth can hardly be described as suitable to an industrial community. To borrow the words of Bagehot directed to a different subject, the 1922 real property law might be likened to 'an old man who still wears with attached fondness clothes in the fashion of his youth; what you see of him is the same; what you do not see is wholly altered'.

To take any structure, whether it be a system of law, a constitution or a house, and for a period of some thousand years to patch it here and there in order to adapt it to new conditions, cannot fail to lead to complications of a bewildering character.

E LAW OF PROPERTY ACT 1922.
ASSIMILATION OF REAL AND PERSONAL PROPERTY

Confirmed in these views, the legislature began in 1922 to reform the law on a far more ambitious scale than had been attempted in the earlier legislative changes. Although the main purpose was to simplify conveyancing, this was pursued not merely by a simplification of the machinery of land transfer, but also by a free use of the pruning knife. In the official view, reforms were needed as a prelude to the simplification and extension of the system of registration of title.[85]

The first Act to be passed was the Law of Property Act 1922, which was described in its preamble as:

An Act to assimilate and amend the law of Real and Personal Estate, to abolish copyhold and other special tenures, to amend the law relating to commonable lands and of intestacy, and to amend the Wills Act, 1837, the Settled Land Acts, 1882 to 1890, the Conveyancing Acts, 1881 to 1911, the Trustee Act, 1893 and the Land Transfer Acts, 1875 and 1897.

The all-important fact that emerges from this descriptive title is that one main object was to 'assimilate...the law of real and personal estate'.

We shall see as we proceed that a comparison of the law relating to real and personal property respectively is, from the point of view of convenience and reason, very much to the advantage of the latter. Part I of the Act put the two forms of property as nearly as possible upon the same footing, a result that was obtained partly by abolishing the chief differences that formerly existed between the two, and partly by eliminating many of the technical anachronisms that had grown up in the land laws. In addition, the law of personal property, which thus became the dominating system, was itself amended in several particulars.

F LEGISLATION OF 1925.
CONSOLIDATING ACTS

The date at which the Act of 1922 was appointed to come into operation, however, was postponed, for the changes it made were sufficiently drastic to necessitate the redrafting and consolidation of the real property statute law from the year 1285. The Law of Property (Amendment) Act 1924 was therefore passed to facilitate the task of

---

[85] Wolstenholme and Cherry, *Conveyancing Statutes* (12th edn, 1932), vol i, p clxvi. See the speech of Sir Leslie Scott, who was Solicitor-General, introducing the Bill into the House of Commons (1922) 154 HC Debates (5th Series) 90; reproduced with annotations by B B Benas in Scott, *The New Law of Property Explained* (1925); and the valuable six *Lectures* by Sir Benjamin Cherry on *The New Property Acts* (1926), and especially his series of Questions and Answers at pp 104 ff. See also Anderson, *Lawyers and the Making of English Land Law 1832–1940* (1992).

consolidation, and then all but the transitional provisions of this Act and of the Act of 1922 were absorbed into the six statutes, passed in 1925, which are set out above.[86]

These statutes are all consolidating Acts. Where the Acts of 1922 and 1924 make no change in the old law, there is a presumption that the Acts of 1925 did not change it. But where the Acts of 1922 and 1924 do make some change, there is only a presumption that the Acts of 1925 did not change the changes made by those two Acts.[87]

G FURTHER DEVELOPMENTS IN 1996 AND 2002

The reform of the land law by the legislator did not stop in 1925. Throughout the twentieth century, and now already in the twenty-first century, there has been further legislative activity in many areas. Most has not changed the fundamental principles of the modern law set out in the 1925 legislation, but two particular developments should be noted that have changed the significance of those statutes.

In the first, the Trusts of Land and Appointment of Trustees Act 1996, legislation intervened to make significant changes to the principles by which beneficial interests can be held in land. We shall see the detail in Chapter 13, The Trust of Land. But for the present purposes we should notice that the effect of the 1996 Act was to prevent the future creation of strict settlements—which had been part of the historical structure of family land ownership in English law. The significance of the Settled Land Act 1925 was thereby considerably reduced.

Most recently, the Land Registration Act 1925 was repealed and replaced by the Land Registration Act 2002. This was not just a cosmetic change, nor simply designed to bring the former statute up to date.[88] It constituted a revision of the principles of registered conveyancing, designed to lead within the following decade to a complete register of title to every parcel of land in England and Wales, and to the introduction of electronic conveyancing.

---

[86] P 12. For a detailed commentary on the 1925 legislation, see the six volumes of Wolstenholme and Cherry, *Conveyancing Statutes* (13th edn, ed Farrand, 1972). Previous editions are valuable, as these contain the commentaries of Wolstenholme (who was responsible for drafting CA 1881 and SLA 1882) and Cherry (the property statutes of 1922 and 1925). On the 1922 Act, see Underhill, *A Concise Explanation of Lord Birkenhead's Act (the Law of Property Act 1922) in Plain Language* (1922).

[87] *Beswick v Beswick* [1968] AC 58; cf *Maunsell v Olins* [1975] AC 373, 392–3; *Farrell v Alexander* [1977] AC 59, 72, 82, 96; *Johnson v Moreton* [1980] AC 37, 56. See also *Grey v IRC* [1960] AC 1; *Lloyds Bank Ltd v Marcan* [1973] 1 WLR 339, 344; affd [1973] 1 WLR 1387; *Re Dodwell & Co Ltd's Trust* [1979] Ch 301, 308; *R v Heron* [1982] 1 WLR 451, 459; Wolstenholme and Cherry, vol 1, p 31; (1959) 75 LQR 307 (REM).

[88] The Land Charges Act 1925 was repealed and replaced by the Land Charges Act 1972, although without fundamental changes of substance. The other statutes of 1925, listed on p 12, remain in force, although all have been amended from time to time.

V OUTLINE OF RIGHTS IN LAND AND THEIR CREATION AND TRANSFER

Land law is the area of the law that defines those rights that are recognised as real property rights—estates and interests in land—and the mechanisms by which they are created and transferred. We shall see the detail later,[89] including something of how the law has developed,[90] an historical context without which the current law cannot be fully understood. At the outset, however, in order to set a framework within which the account given in the following chapters can be placed, it will be useful to give an outline of the estates and interests that are recognised in the modern law, the methods by which they may be created and transferred, and the impact on third parties of the transfer of land. The analysis of a person's claim to exercise a right against another's land generally involves these questions: what is the nature of the right that is claimed? If it is a property right, has it been created according to the requirements set for that kind of right? If so, has the claimant the benefit of the right and is the defendant subject to its burden?—that is, if the parties are not the original parties to the creation of the right in question,[91] has the benefit of the right been transferred to the claimant, and is the defendant bound by it (for example by each being the successor to the land to which the benefit or burden was attached at its creation)?

A ESTATES AND INTERESTS IN LAND

We have already noted that English law recognises both legal and equitable estates and interests in land. Since 1926 there are only two legal estates:[92] the 'fee simple absolute in possession' (the freehold estate that approximates to ownership of the land), and the 'term of years absolute' (the leasehold estate granted for a period that is defined from the outset); and a finite list of legal interests or charges in or over land,[93] the most important of which are easements and mortgages granted over legal estates in land. All other estates, interests and charges in or over land can take effect only as equitable interests:[94] this will include such things as the benefit of a trust of land; an equitable lease, an equitable easement and an equitable mortgage or charge; and a restrictive covenant or an equity by estoppel.

---

[89] See pp 119–43, below, for a short account of conveyancing in the modern law. Part III explains in detail the different estates and interests in land, and Part IV the detailed rules for the creation, transfer and extinction of those estates and interests.

[90] Below, Chs 2–5.

[91] Where the claimant and defendant are the original parties, the claim will often fall simply within the law of contract, and even a third party may be able to claim a direct right in contract under the Contracts (Rights of Third Parties) Act 1999; below, p 743.

[92] LPA 1925, s 1(1); below, p 123.   [93] Ibid, s 1(2).

[94] Ibid, s 1(3).

B CREATION OF ESTATES AND INTERESTS

We shall see that there are special rules for the creation of certain estates and interests in land. A legal estate and interest can generally be created only by deed:[95] failure to use this formality where it is required will render the transaction ineffective to create the legal estate or interest although in some circumstances the transaction may be effective to create the equivalent estate or interest in equity.[96] Furthermore, where the title to the land in or over which the estate or interest is to be created has been registered under the Land Registration Act 2002, the disposition by which the estate or interest is created must often be completed by registration, failing which it takes effect only as an equitable interest.[97]

C TRANSFER OF ESTATES AND INTERESTS

Since one of the characteristics of a property interest is that not only is its benefit transmissible but also it may burden a successor of the property to which it is attached, it is important to understand, for each of the property interests recognised by the land law, the circumstances in which its benefit and its burden may be transferred. The detail will be discussed later in relation to each separate interest,[98] but it should here be noted that a distinction is drawn according to whether the title to the land over which the interest subsists is registered or unregistered.

In unregistered land the title to the land itself is conveyed by deed; and before 1926 the question whether a disponee of the land was burdened by interests that had attached to the land before the disposition was determined by whether the interest was legal (in which case it was automatically binding) or equitable (in which case it bound the disponee unless he was a bona fide purchaser of a legal estate in the land without notice of the equitable interest).[99] Since the introduction of the register of land charges by the Land Charges Act 1925,[100] however, many third-party interests in unregistered land can be entered on the land charges register and any such interest that has not been so registered will not bind a purchaser for value of a legal estate in the land. In effect, registration in such cases takes the place of notice of the interest, as against a purchaser of the legal estate.

Where, however, the title to the land is registered under the Land Registration Act 2002,[101] the legal title itself is not transferred by the execution of a deed alone but the deed of transfer must in addition be completed by registration. All interests affecting registered land automatically bind a transferee of the land who is not a purchaser of the legal title.[102] But a purchaser of the legal title takes free of third-party rights in registered land that are not 'protected':[103] an interest can generally be protected by its

---

[95] Ibid, s 52; below, p 1001.
[96] For formality requirements and the consequences of failure to comply with them, see Ch 25.
[97] LRA 2002, s 27; below, pp 1008–9.
[98] Below, Part III.   [99] Below, pp 80–91.
[100] Now LCA 1972; below, pp 127–8, 1053–66.
[101] Formerly LRA 1925. For differences in the 1925 and 2002 Acts, see below, pp 139–41.
[102] LRA 2002, s 28; eg where the legal title is transferred by way of gift.   [103] Ibid, s 29(1).

beneficiary entering a notice on the register of title of the burdened land, but some interests are also binding on a purchaser even if they are not entered on the register ('overriding interests').[104]

VI LAND LAW AND HUMAN RIGHTS[105]

The United Kingdom has been bound by the European Convention on Human Rights[106] since 1953, but before the enactment of the Human Rights Act 1998 the only recourse was against the State, in an action brought before the European Court of Human Rights at Strasbourg.[107] Under the Human Rights Act, however, the domestic courts now have jurisdiction in relation to alleged breaches of the Convention, although the Act does not expressly create rights enforceable directly between private individuals.[108] However, it is unlawful for a public authority to act in a way that is incompatible with a Convention right,[109] and this gives private individuals directly enforceable rights against, for example, public authority landlords. Indeed, since 'public authority' includes the court, it can be argued that the court must take into account Convention

[104] LRA 2002, Sch 3 (eg certain short legal leases, certain legal easements and interests 'belonging to a person in actual occupation' of the land): below, pp 137–40, 1100–13.

[105] See generally Rook, *Property Law and Human Rights* (2001); Allen, *Property and the Human Rights Act 1998* (2005); Tee, ch 7 (Gray); (2007) 123 LQR 618 (J Howell).

[106] Convention for the Protection of Human Rights and Fundamental Freedoms, agreed at Rome by the Council of Europe (of which the United Kingdom was a founding member) on 4 November 1950, ratified by the United Kingdom on 8 March 1951 and in force from 3 September 1953. The protection of property was excluded from the Convention rights and negotiated separately in the First Protocol which was added to the Convention by agreement of the Council on 20 March 1952 and became effective on 18 May 1954: Allen, *Property and the Human Rights Act 1998* (2005), ch 1.

[107] Such recourse is still possible, and a litigant who cannot obtain an appropriate remedy in the domestic courts may seek to obtain an order from the European Court of Human Rights for compensation from the UK Government for its failure to protect his human rights in accordance with the Convention. See, eg, the litigation in *JA Pye (Oxford) Ltd v United Kingdom* [2005] 3 EGLR 1 (combined operation of Limitation Act 1980 and LRA 1925 incompatible with Article 1 of the First Protocol), reversed by the Grand Chamber [2008] 1 EGLR 111; p 1165, below; *Kay v United Kingdom* [2010] ECHR 37341/06, [2011] L & TR 1 (violation of procedural aspect (only) of Art 8 at the time of the decision in *Kay v Lambeth LBC* [2006] UKHL 10, [2006] 2 AC 465, below, p 350); [2010] Conv 498 (S Nield). On the scope of the duty of English courts to follow Strasbourg jurisprudence, see HRA 1998, s 2; *Ofulue v Bossert* [2008] EWCA Civ 7, [2009] Ch 1 at [32] (Court of Appeal), [2009] UKHL 16, [2009] 1 AC 990 at [72]-[73] (House of Lords); *Manchester City Council v Pinnock* [2010] UKSC 45, [2010] 3 WLR 1441 at [48] (Supreme Court).

[108] So-called 'horizontal effect' (contrasted with the 'vertical effect' of the enforceability of rights as against the State); see n 110, below.

[109] HRA 1998, s 6(1). For the problem of the definition of 'public authority', see *Aston Cantlow and Wilmcote with Billesley Parochial Church Council v Wallbank* [2003] UKHL 37, [2004] 1 AC 546 (PCC not a public authority and therefore had no obligation to act in accordance with Convention rights in enforcing defendants' liability to pay for chancel repairs); [2004] PL 329 (D Oliver); *R (Weaver) v London and Quadrant Housing Trust* [2009] EWCA Civ 587, [2010] 1 WLR 363 (registered social landlord was hybrid public authority: question was whether termination of tenancy was a private act within HRA 1998, s 6(5)).

rights even in disputes between private parties.[110] However, courts cannot disapply legislation that they find to be incompatible with the Convention,[111] nor require the legislature to enact amending legislation to comply with the Convention. They can, however, make a declaration that a provision of primary or subordinate legislation is incompatible with a Convention right;[112] and they must interpret primary and subordinate legislation in a way that is compliant with the Convention rights 'so far as it is possible to do so'.[113]

In recent years the Human Rights Act 1998 has been invoked in a significant number of cases involving real property rights. The Convention rights that have generally been invoked are those contained in Articles 8 and 14 of the Convention, which read as follows:

Article 8 Right to respect for private and family life
1. Everyone has the right to respect for his private and family life, his home and his correspondence.
2. There shall be no interference by a public authority with the exercise of this right except such as is in accordance with the law and is necessary in a democratic society in the interests of national security, public safety or the economic well-being of the country, for the prevention of disorder or crime, for the protection of health or morals, or for the protection of the rights and freedoms of others.

Article 14 Prohibition of discrimination
The enjoyment of the rights and freedoms set forth in this Convention shall be secured without discrimination on any ground such as sex, race, colour, language, religion, political or other opinion, national or social origin, association with a national minority, property, birth or other status.

together with Article 1 of the First Protocol, which reads:

Article 1 Protection of property
Every natural or legal person is entitled to the peaceful enjoyment of his possessions. No one shall be deprived of his possessions except in the public interest and subject to the conditions provided for by law and by the general principles of international law. The preceding provisions shall not, however, in any way impair the right of a State to enforce such laws as it deems necessary to control the use of property in accordance with the general interest or to secure the payment of taxes or other contributions or penalties.

In applying the Human Rights Act, the courts have interpreted the succession provisions of the Rent Act 1977 so as to apply to same-sex partners, in order to

---

[110] For arguments for such an indirect horizontal effect of the HRA 1998, see (2000) 116 LRQ 217 (HW Wade); against, see (2000) 116 LQR 48 (R Buxton). The debate was not settled by the House of Lords: *Campbell v MGN Ltd* [2004] UKHL 22, [2004] 2 AC 457 at [18] and has been left open by the Supreme Court: *Manchester City Council v Pinnock*, above, n 107, at [50].

[111] HRA 1998, s 4(6).   [112] Ibid, s 4(2), (4).

[113] Ibid, s 3(1). This has the effect of protecting Convention rights in litigation between purely private parties: *Ghaidan v Godin-Mendoza* [2004] UKHL 30, [2004] 2 AC 557, M & B p 109.

eliminate their discriminatory effect and so to comply with the Convention;[114] and have interpreted the provisions of the Land Registration Act 1925[115] on adverse possession in order to comply with Article 1 of the First Protocol.[116] They have also considered a number of cases in which public authorities have been alleged to have infringed Convention rights—for example in the exercise by public authority landlords of their right to possession of premises against residential occupiers;[117] but have also rejected arguments that legislation affecting property rights is subject to challenge under the Human Rights Act or is incompatible with Convention rights.[118]

---

[114] *Ghaidan v Godin-Mendoza* above, n 113; below, p 381 (HRA 1998, s 3; Art 14 of the Convention, read with Art 8).

[115] S 75; below, p 1165. LRA 2002 has a different regime for adverse possession which complies with the Convention: below, p 1166.

[116] *Beaulane Properties Ltd v Palmer* [2006] Ch 79, p 1165, below; [2005] Conv 345 (Dixon); but see *JA Pye (Oxford) Ltd v United Kingdom* [2008] 1 EGLR 111, pp 1165–6, below.

[117] Most recently in a seven-judge Supreme Court in *Hounslow LBC v Powell* [2011] UKSC 8, [2011] 2 WLR 287, following a nine-judge Supreme Court in *Manchester City Council v Pinnock* [2010] UKSC 45, [2010] 3 WLR 1441, below, p 353 (Art 8), departing from the earlier decisions of the House of Lords in *Harrow LBC v Qazi* [2003] UKHL 43, [2004] 1 AC 983, *Kay v Lambeth LBC* [2006] UKHL 10, [2006] 2 AC 465 (HRA 1998, s 6 and Art 1 of the First Protocol) and *Doherty v Birmingham CC* [2008] UKHL 57, [2009] 1 AC 367 (Mobile Homes Act 1983 and Art 8). See also *Smith v Evans* [2007] EWCA Civ 1318, [2008] 1 WLR 661 (Caravan Sites Act 1968, s 4, as amended, and Art 8).

[118] *Horsham Properties Group Ltd v Clark* [2008] EWHC 2327 (Ch), [2009] 1 WLR 1255, M&B 937, below, p 855 (mortgagee's power of sale without first obtaining court order for possession); *Lee v Leeds City Council* [2002] EWCA Civ 6, [2002] 1 WLR 1488, below, p 231 (landlord's duty to repair under LTA 1985, s 11); *R (Coombes) v Secretary of State for Communities and Local Government* [2010] EWHC 666, [2010] L & TR 29 (Protection from Eviction Act 1977, s 3, below, p 348).

PART II

THE MODERN LAW IN HISTORICAL CONTEXT

We can detect three stages in the historical development of the English real property law:

First was the purely common law system, which was designed to meet the needs of a feudal society.

Second came the equitable system that was gradually evolved in certain directions by the Chancellor with a view to adapting the common law rules to a society moved by different ideals and possessing a more commercial outlook on life.

And finally we come to the various legislative enactments by which the judge-made law of land was rendered more adequate to the needs of society.

In this Part we first sketch an outline of the historical origins of the modern law: the common law system, certain conceptions that were introduced into the law by the Chancellor in the exercise of his equitable jurisdiction, and settlements of land before 1926. We then discuss the legislative changes of 1925, 1996 and 2002 which set the framework for the modern law.

A ORIGINS OF THE MODERN LAW

Summary

2

THE COMMON LAW SYSTEM

Summary

We begin by explaining the system of land law devised by the common law. It has been substantially modified, first by equity, and then by statute, as we shall see in the following chapters. But the modern structure of land law cannot be understood without first having an understanding of the feudal origins of the common law system of land tenure, and the common law doctrine of the *estate*.

I THE DOCTRINE OF TENURE[1]

A FEUDALISM IN EUROPE

(1) Development of Continental Feudalism

The outstanding feature of the English land law and one that explains many of its peculiarities is that, at least from the time of the Norman Conquest, it fell into line with the continental systems and became and remained for several centuries intensely feudalistic. *Feudalism* itself is a word of some vagueness and ambiguity, and one that was certainly unknown to the peoples to whom it is applied. It is often thought to represent the history of Western Europe from the eighth to the fourteenth

---

[1] For the history of this doctrine, see Simpson, *A History of the Land Law* (2nd edn, 1986), pp 1 ff; Bean, *The Decline of English Feudalism* (1968), esp ch 1; Baker, *Introduction to English Legal History* (4th edn, 2002), ch 13.

century,[2] and, like the modern use of the word *capitalism*, to describe the social characteristics of the period.[3] To a lawyer, however, it represents:

> A state of society in which the main social bond is the relation between lord and man, a relation implying on the lord's part protection and defence; on the man's part protection, service and reverence, the service including service in arms. This personal relation is inseparably involved in a proprietary relation, the tenure of land—the man holds of the lord, the man's service is a burden on the land, the lord has important rights in the land.[4]

Thus it is the negation of independence. It implies subordination; it means that one man is deliberately made inferior to another.

In pre-feudal days the land of Europe was owned absolutely, though subject to custom, by persons who were grouped together in village communities and it therefore becomes a matter of interest to discover why it was that a great part of the world lapsed from a state of comparative freedom into one of servility, why landownership disappeared and land tenure took its place. The change represented a retrogressive step in the history of man, but in Europe it was one of the necessary consequences of the disruption of the Roman Empire by the barbarian invaders. The overthrow of the Roman Empire caused chaos and disorganisation in Europe and produced conditions in which it was necessary for private persons to procure for themselves a higher degree of protection than could be provided by their own unaided efforts. In those days interference with personal freedom or with the ownership of property might come from several different quarters, such as a revolt of peasants, the arrogance of a powerful neighbour, the extortion of a government or the hostility of some tribe. The only method of obtaining security was mutual support, and so individuals deliberately subordinated themselves to some magnate versed in the arts of war, and were compensated for the diminution of personal independence and the loss of landownership by acquiring the protection afforded by the forces of which he disposed. This process involved both a personal and a proprietary subordination, but it is only on the latter that we need dwell.

One of the effects of the feudalisation of Europe was that from a legal aspect land became the exclusive bond of union between persons. Individual or communal landownership was destroyed. The ownership of the whole of the land in any given district was vested in the overlord, and the persons who had formerly owned it in their own right now held it from the overlord. In return for the land that they held they were bound to render services, chiefly of a military nature, to the overlord, while the latter in his turn was bound to protect his tenants. Feudalism implied a reciprocity of rights and duties. The lord gained in dignity and became entitled to personal services, while the tenant obtained security.

This conversion from ownership to tenure began in the lower ranks of society, but quickly spread upwards until it finally embraced the greater part of the land of Western

---

[2] Pollock and Maitland, *The History of English Law Before the Time of Edward I* (2nd edn, 1898, revised 1968), vol i, p 67.

[3] Plucknett, *A Concise History of the Common Law* (5th edn, 1956), p 506.

[4] Maitland, *The Constitutional History of England* (1908), p 143.

Europe. Various reasons contributed to this extension. The general anarchy of the times, the lack of a central government sufficiently strong to ensure a well-ordered and peaceful existence, and the natural ambition of magnates to increase the extent of their possessions induced even the large landowners to put themselves and their land under the protection of someone greater than themselves.

This development took place under the Franks, and in the time of the Carolingians in the eighth and ninth centuries a still further impetus was given to the movement, for the government itself—if such a term can be applied to those times—was obliged to resort to the principle of feudalism. Administration had to be carried on somehow and taxes were difficult to collect. The solution was to farm out Crown lands to great men who paid a sum of money to the government and who in return became lords of the lands (which were called benefices) and of the persons who dwelt thereon. A little later, when military pressure from the east and the south made it imperative that society should be organised on a basis that would afford protection to the State, the device of granting benefices in return for military services, a device that was gradually failing owing to the scarcity of Crown lands, was widened in scope by an act of confiscation.

The Church had become the greatest landowner in Europe. Charles Martel, who was Mayor of the Frankish Empire in the first part of the eighth century, deliberately carried out wholesale seizures of Church property, but in AD 751 some sort of amicable arrangement was made whereby vast tracts of Church lands were granted by the ecclesiastical corporations to laymen at the request of the King. The Church ownership of the lands was recognised by the payment of an uneconomic rent to the corporations, while the tenants—and this was the significance of the transaction— became liable by virtue of their holdings to render services to the King.[5] Thus the net of feudalism spread everywhere. In this way life and government were made to depend upon the land.[6]

(2) The Manor

This can be seen by an examination of the unit of society called the manor. The grant of benefices led to the creation of great estates or manors vested in the grantees from the Crown. Topographically a manor denoted a certain area of land consisting of a number of houses, strips of arable and pasture land and waste lands, all of which were within the domain of the lord of the manor. The waste, in proportion to the cultivated land, formed by far the greater part of the manor, a fact that serves to explain the inclosures of later centuries. But we shall miss the significance of this system unless we realise that the manor was both a social and an administrative unit through the agency of which a whole country was governed. Each manor was, as it were, a small government in itself.

[5] Vinogradoff, *Cambridge Medieval History*, vol ii, 646.
[6] See, generally, *Encyclopaedia Britannica*, under the title *Feudalism*; Van Caenegem, *An Historical Introduction to Western Constitutional Law* (1995), pp 48-9, 56-61.

The central government required soldiers and money, but instead of approaching its subjects directly it looked no further than the lord of the manor. His obligation vis-à-vis the government was to supply a fully equipped fighting force, and the right that he obtained in return was that of holding his manor or group of manors immune from the legal and administrative control of the government. Thus, when the power of a central government was on the wane, it became customary to grant immunities to powerful men, which meant nothing more nor less than that the functions of government were handed over to feudal lords. As Vinogradoff wrote:[7]

> As in the later Empire, the government is obliged to have recourse to great landlords in order to carry out its functions of police, justice, military and fiscal authority. Great estates had become extra-territorial already under Roman rule in the fourth and fifth centuries, and it would be superfluous to point out how much more the governments of the barbarians stood in need of the help of great landowners.

One of the most important features of the administrative side of a Continental manor was the lord's right of jurisdiction. As the royal writ did not run within the territorial limits of a manor, the lord set up local courts of his own, and it was only in the manorial court of the defendant that a claimant was entitled to sue. Thus, to use the expressive language of Stubbs,[8] there was

> a graduated system of jurisdiction based on land tenure, in which every lord judged, taxed, and commanded the class next below him, ... in which private war, private coinage, private prisons took the place of the imperial institutions of government.

(3) Characteristics of Feudalism

By way of summary we may say that the characteristics of feudalism are the relation of lord and vassal; the principle that every person interested in land is a mere holder of it, a tenant and not an owner; the condition that this tenure shall continue to exist only so long as the tenant performs the particular services imposed upon him at the beginning of the tenure; and lastly, the recognition of a reciprocity of rights and duties. The foundation of the whole system is the fief—that is to say, the land that the inferior holds as tenant of the superior. The word *fief* becomes *feudum* in Latin, and *feud*, and later *fee* in English.

B FEUDALISM IN ENGLAND

(1) Development of English Feudalism

We now come to consider the effect that this Continental feudalism had upon the land law of England. It is not necessary to discuss here the extent to which feudalism existed in England prior to the Conquest. That a system was in vogue that bore similarities to

---

[7] Vinogradoff, *Cambridge Medieval History*, vol ii, p 651.
[8] Stubbs, *The Constitutional History of England*, vol i (1874), p 292.

Continental feudalism cannot be doubted, but the only fact that we need notice here is that the Normans applied their own ideas to the conditions prevalent in this country, and succeeded in establishing an English variety of feudalism that, though differing in many respects from that of the Continent, became a striking and universal feature of the land law. The policy of William the Conqueror left England, whatever it may have been before, a highly feudalised state. He took the line that, since the English landowners had denied his right to the Crown of England and had compelled him to assert it by force, their landed possessions became his to dispose of as he chose.[9] What he did was not so much to seize land and parcel it out among his Norman followers, as to allow all Englishmen who recognised him as King to redeem by money payments the estates that by right of conquest had momentarily passed to him.

This process of confiscation and redistribution flowed on evenly, and though it cannot be said that the redistributions amounted to direct feudal grants, there is no doubt that they came to be regarded as such when the idea of Norman feudalism took hold of men's minds. As Stubbs wrote:[10]

> After each effort the royal hand was laid on more heavily; more and more land changed owners, and with the change of owners the title changed. The complicated and unintelligible irregularities of the Anglo-Saxon tenures were exchanged for the simple and uniform feudal theory. The 1500 tenants in chief of Domesday take the place of the countless landowners of King Edward's day…It is enough for our purpose to ascertain that a universal assimilation of title followed the general changes of ownership. The King of Domesday is the supreme landlord; all the land of the nation, the old folkland, has become the King's, and all private land is held mediately or immediately of him; all holders are bound to their lords by homage and fealty, either actually demanded or understood to be demandable, in every case of transfer by inheritance or otherwise.

This English feudalism differed from the Continental variety in that all freemen were bound by the Salisbury Oath of 1086 to swear allegiance directly to the King instead of to the immediate lord from whom they held their lands; and again in the fact that William, instead of setting up great territorial jurisdictions, organised administration in such a way that he governed the country through sheriffs who were directly responsible to him. Though the Frankish system of tenure displaced the Anglo-Saxon system, the establishment of a feudal mode of government was deliberately avoided. But in respect of tenure the result was much the same as on the Continent. By a certain date, which we need not attempt to define, the doctrine of land tenure became universal in England.

(2) Land Tenure

Every acre of land in the country was held of the King. As Pollock and Maitland wrote:[11] 'The person whom we may call the owner, the person who has the right to use

---

[9] Stenton, *William the Conqueror and the Rule of the Normans* (1925), pp 494–5.
[10] Above, n 8, pp 296–7.   [11] *The History of English Law*, vol ii, p 232.

and abuse the land, to cultivate it or leave it uncultivated, to keep all others off it, holds the land of the King either immediately or mediately.'

(a) Seignories

If a tenant held immediately of the King, he was said to hold of him in chief or *in capite*. But the position might be less simple. Instead of a tenant holding directly of the King he might hold mediately, as for instance where C held of B, who held of A, who held of the King. C, who stood at the bottom of the scale, and who to a layman would look more like an owner than anybody else, was called the *tenant in demesne—tenet terram in dominico suo*. The persons between him and the King were called *mesne lords*, and their lordships were called *seignories*. A held the land, not in *demesne* but in service, since he was entitled to the services of B, and B was in a similar position, since he was entitled to the services of C. The services due from these tenants would not necessarily be of the same nature, for A might hold of the King by military service, B of A in return for a money rent, and C of B in return for some personal service. In such a case each grantee owed to his immediate grantor the service that he had agreed to render, and from this point of view the service was called *intrinsec*. Services were not merely personal, but charged on the tenement, so that if A failed in the performance of his military duties the King could distrain upon the land in the hands of C, as could A if B fell into arrears with the rent. B could agree to perform the military service in place of A, but no private arrangement of this kind could free the land from the burden. From this point of view the service was called *forinsec*, that is foreign to any bargain between other parties.[12] Of course, if, for example, A failed to perform his military service and the King proceeded against the land in C's occupation, the latter had a remedy against A, called the writ of *mesne*. A tenant came under an obligation, confirmed by the oath of fealty, to serve his lord faithfully, and the price of infidelity in this respect was the forfeiture of his fief. In particular, forfeiture ensued if he did anything to the disinherison of his lord, as, for example, if he deliberately failed to defend an action for the recovery of land brought against him by a third party.[13]

Perhaps the most striking fact about English feudalism was the universality of this doctrine of land tenure. On the Continent tenure applied only to those who held lands in return for military services,[14] but in England it applied to every holder whatever the nature of the duties that he had agreed to perform might be. Moreover, a movement began by which the number of mesne lordships was increased to a bewildering extent. As each year passed, more and more sub-tenancies were created. A, who held of the King, would transfer his land or part of it to B, and B to C, and so on, but each transfer, instead of being an out and out grant by which the transferor got rid of his entire interest, would operate as a grant of land to be held by each transferee as tenant of

---

[12] Pollock and Maitland, *The History of English Law*, vol i, p 237.

[13] For a discussion of this defunct principle, see the judgment of Denning LJ in *Warner v Sampson* [1959] 1 QB 297, 312–16.

[14] Holdsworth, *A History of English Law*, vol ii, p 199.

his immediate transferor. As a result 'innumerable petty lords sprang up between the great barons and the immediate tenant of the soil'.[15]

(b) Subinfeudation

This process, which was termed subinfeudation, was carried to such lengths that Maitland was able to discover a case where there were as many as eight sub-tenancies in the same piece of land. One explanation of this reluctance to part with one's entire interest was the economic significance of land in the centuries immediately following the Conquest. Apart from cattle, land was practically the only form of wealth. Money was scarce, and something had to take its place as a medium of exchange. This can be illustrated by the recompense usually given for services rendered.

Domestic servants in a manor were paid by a crude method of profit-sharing. As Vinogradoff wrote:[16]

> The swine-herd of Glastonbury Abbey, for instance, received one sucking-pig a year, the interior parts of the best pig and the tails of all the others which were slaughtered in the abbey. The chief scullion had a right to all remnants of viands—but not of game—to the feathers and the bowels of geese.

But the form that payment took in the case of labourers on the manorial estate, and also in the case of servants who rendered non-domestic services for a great lord, was a grant of land to be held only so long as the services were properly performed. Thus it was through one of the forms of tenure, known as tenure by sergeanty, that most needs were satisfied. Those who acted as president of a lord's court, or carried his letters, or fed his hounds, or cared for his horses, or provided him with bows and arrows, generally held land as tenants in sergeanty of the lord.[17] They would continue to hold the land as long as they served faithfully, and no longer.

(c) Statute Quia Emptores 1290

In other words, the importance of land as a means of payment made it advisable for tenants to keep as tenacious a hold upon it as possible, and, when a transfer was contemplated, to subinfeudate rather than dispose of it outright. But, for reasons into which we need not enter,[18] the practice of subinfeudation was obnoxious to the great lords, and was finally prohibited in 1290 by the Statute *Quia Emptores*.[19]

(1) Effect

This important statute altered the law in two respects:

First, it set at rest a controversy by enacting that every free man should be at liberty to alienate the whole or part of his land without the consent of his lord. If part only were conveyed, the services were to be apportioned.

---

[15] Hayes, *An Introduction to Conveyancing* (5th edn, 1840), vol i, p 9.

[16] *Villainage in England* (1892), pp 321–2.

[17] Pollock and Maitland, *The History of English Law*, vol i, p 285.

[18] See Challis, *Law of Real Property* (3rd edn, ed Sweet, 1911), pp 18–19.

[19] Holdsworth, *A History of English Law*, vol iii, p 79.

Secondly, it enacted that every alienee should hold the land of the same lord of whom the alienor previously held. The effect of this was to prevent the creation of new tenancies. The alienor dropped out, the alienee stepped into his shoes for all purposes, and thus instead of a new sub-tenancy there was the substitution of one tenant for another. If, therefore, the existence of a mesne lordship is proved at the present day, it follows that it must have been created before 1290, or created by the Crown thereafter.

(2) Limits

The statute, however, extended only to land held for a fee simple estate, the largest interest known to the law, and it never prevented the creation of a new tenure by the grant of a lesser estate, such as a fee tail or a life interest.[20]

The statute did not bind the Crown. This had two consequences.

In the first place, the privilege of unrestricted alienation did not avail tenants in chief. In their case the consent of the Crown remained necessary and in practice this was given only on the payment of a sum of money known as a fine.[21]

Secondly, the Crown was unaffected by the abolition of subinfeudation and was therefore still able to create new tenancies in respect of the fee simple.

(3) Importance

Quia Emptores was a landmark in the history of real property. Its chief virtue was that it led to the gradual disappearance of the numerous petty lordships that had arisen between the Crown and the tenant in demesne. Blackacre might no doubt have been held before 1290 by B of A, but if in course of time it passed into the hands of a succession of alienees, each one being substituted for his predecessor, it would ultimately become extremely difficult to prove the existence of A's original lordship. Thus, there was a constant tendency for seignories to become vested in the Crown, and to this extent the law was simplified.

C FORMS OF TENURE

A feature of English feudalism, and one that complicated the land law, was that there was not one common kind of tenure. We have seen how in early days, if a man wanted work of a regular nature done for him, he would generally get it done in exchange for land granted by him to the workman. Considering the diversity of personal needs that require to be satisfied, it is obvious that the services due from tenants would vary considerably in nature, importance and dignity. One tenant had to fight; another to look after a household, or to provide arms, or to pray for the soul of his overlord, or to do such agricultural work as might be demanded of him. There were vast differences between the possible services. It was considered an honourable thing to fight, but not

---

[20] For the 'fee simple', 'fee tail' and life interest see below, pp 53–4, 151, 584, 605.

[21] Challis, *Law of Real Property*, pp 14, 15. Such fines were abolished by the Tenures Abolition Act 1660.

to plough, and thus there gradually arose different forms of tenure based upon the differences in the nature of the services. The following table shows the state of affairs in the time of Edward I, when the tenures had become stabilised.

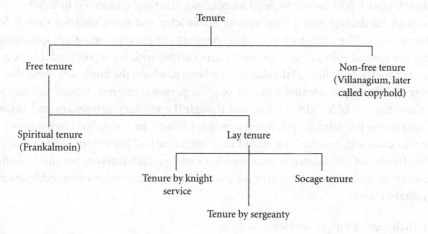

(1) Knight Service[22]

(a) Nature of knight service

The most important of the regular tenures in early days was knight service, or the tenure by which a man was obliged to render military services in return for the land that he held. Soon after the Conquest, a process set in whereby the military needs of the country were satisfied in this manner. All the land of the country was held directly of the King, and it was a practically universal rule that the tenants in chief—that is those men who held directly of the King as distinct from sub-tenants who owed their position to the practice of subinfeudation[23]—held by knight service. Each tenant in chief had to produce for 40 days in each year a definite number of fully armed horsemen. The number required in any particular case did not depend upon the extent of the tenant's land, but was arbitrarily fixed when the grant of the land was made, and, as the unit of the feudal host was a constabularia consisting of ten knights, it appears always to have been some multiple of five or ten.[24] For about a hundred years after the Conquest, the army—to the strength of about 5,000 knights—was actually raised in this way, but it was soon discovered that such a short service as forty days scarcely promoted the success of military operations, and the King began in about 1166 to exact money payments called scutage from the tenants in chief instead of requiring the production of the fixed quota of knights. But by the time of Edward I even scutage had become useless as a means of providing an army, and it can be said that thenceforth

[22] See Holdsworth, A History of English Law, vol iii, pp 37–46.   [23] Above, p 35.
[24] Round, Feudal England (1895), pp 259–60.

the tenure ceased to be military in the sense that it no longer served to supply forces for the defence of the realm.[25]

What at first sight seems remarkable is that knight service, instead of falling into oblivion after it had ceased to fulfil its original function, continued to develop, and ended by hardening into a legal system far stricter and more onerous than it had hitherto been. The explanation of this inopportune survival was that, quite apart from the duty of military service, the tenure carried with it certain feudal incidents that had such a high financial value for the lords of whom the lands were held that to foster and develop it became a matter of great personal interest. Subinfeudation led to the extension of knight service, and though the military sub-tenant had neither to fight nor to pay scutage, yet, being a military tenant, he was subject to a number of onerous claims from which he would have been free had his tenure been one of the other forms. As the matter is now merely of antiquarian interest, we must confine ourselves to the barest statement of the most valuable of the rights enforceable against a military tenant.

(b) Incidents of knight service

(1) Relief

The lord was entitled to the payment of a certain sum, called a relief, when a new tenant succeeded to the land on the death of the old tenant. Payment of the relief entitled the heir to immediate possession, but this was not so where the land was held of the King. In this case the official escheator took possession and held an inquest as to who was next heir. It was only when the heir had done homage and paid the relief that he was entitled to enter the land. This royal privilege of first possession was called primer seisin.[26]

(2) Aids

The lord was entitled to demand in three special cases that his tenants should pay him a certain sum of money called an aid. The three cases arose when the lord was imprisoned and required a ransom; when he desired to make his eldest son a knight; and when he was obliged to supply his eldest daughter with a dowry on her marriage.

(3) Escheat *propter delictum tenentis*

The commission by the tenant of a felony caused the land to escheat, that is to pass to the lord of whom it was held. Felony originally meant a breach of that faith and trust that ought to exist between lord and vassal, for example, where the tenant laid violent hands on his lord. At an early date, however, felony lost its exclusively feudal signification and came to mean in effect any serious crime such as murder. The result of this was to benefit the lords, and though it would seem incompatible with the interests of the Crown as custodian of the public peace that the land of a murderer or a thief should pass to a subject, the right of escheat was expressly confirmed by Magna

---

[25] Pollock and Maitland, *The History of English Law*, vol i, p 252.
[26] Ibid, vol i, p 311.

Carta in 1215, subject to the proviso that the land should be held by the Crown for a year and a day. Forfeiture of the land was now said to occur because the felon's blood was attainted or corrupted.[27]

(4) Escheat *propter defectum sanguinis*

This type of escheat was the right of the lord to take the land of his tenant who died intestate without leaving heirs.

(5) Wardship

The most profitable right of the lord was that of wardship. If an existing tenant died leaving as his heir a male under twenty-one or a female under fourteen, the lord was entitled to the wardship of the heir, and as a consequence was free to make what use he liked of the lands during the minority without any obligation to render an account of his stewardship. Upon reaching the prescribed age the ward might sue for *livery* or *ousterlemain*, that is, might enforce delivery of the land. For this privilege half a year's profits had to be paid, though a relief could not be demanded.

(6) Marriage

Another privilege that the lord enjoyed in respect of infant tenants was the right of marriage. As Blackstone wrote:[28]

> While the infant was in ward, the guardian had the power of tendering him or her a suitable match, without disparagement or inequality; which if the infants refused, they forfeited the value of the marriage, *valorem maritagii*, to their guardian; that is, so much as a jury would assess, or anyone would bona fide give to the guardian for such an alliance; and if the infants married themselves without the guardian's consent, they forfeited double the value, *duplicem valorem maritagii*.

(2) Tenure by Sergeanty[29]

Tenure by sergeanty was in early times, and from an economic point of view, of considerable importance, but it soon ceased to be anything more than a peculiarly dignified method of holding land. All tenures imply service of one kind or another, but the characteristic of sergeanty was that it required the tenant to perform services of an essentially personal nature. It was that particular form of landholding that was designed to supply the necessities of life. In the first place the great officials of the realm were sergeants, and as such might be required:[30]

> to carry the banner of the king, or his lance, or to lead his army, or to be his marshall, or to carry his sword before him at his coronation, or to be his sewer at his coronation or his

---

[27] Ibid, p 303; Digby, *History of the Law of Real Property* (5th edn, 1897), p 132; Holdsworth, *A History of English Law*, vol iii, p 67.

[28] Blackstone, vol ii, p 70.   [29] Holdsworth, *A History of English Law*, vol iii, pp 46 ff.

[30] Littleton, *Tenures* (1481), s 153.

carver or his butler, or to be one of his chamberlains at the receipt of his exchequer or to do other like services.

Duties of this nature came to be regarded as conferring honour and dignity, and for this reason outlasted the tenure itself, but they did not exhaust the forms of personal services that might be demanded from sergeants. A great lord would require that his accounts should be kept, his letters carried, his estates managed, armour provided, his food cooked, and so on, and he would in most cases grant lands to various sergeants to be held by them so long as the duties were faithfully performed. However, as time went on, it was realised that this was scarcely a convenient method of supplying the needs of life, and tenure by sergeanty began to decay as early as the fourteenth century. It died out altogether except in the case of those great men who performed honourable services for the King, or of humbler persons whose duty it might be to perform some small military duty, such as to supply transport. Moreover, the idea took root, and it was established by Littleton's day that the tenure could exist only between the King and his immediate tenants in chief. The tenure of the great men who performed what were regarded as honourable services came to be called *grand sergeanty*, while that of the lesser military tenants was termed *petit sergeanty*. Grand sergeanty came to be similar to knight service, while petit sergeanty, after the time of Littleton, was practically equivalent to socage.[31]

(3) Frankalmoin

Frankalmoin was the tenure by which a man made provision for the repose of his soul, and it arose where lands were granted to an ecclesiastical body on the understanding that as tenant it would say prayers and masses for the souls of the grantor and his heirs. For various reasons the tenure fell into disuse.[32]

(4) Tenures Abolition Act 1660

It is not necessary to describe these tenures further because, in 1660, a considerable simplification of the forms of landholding was effected by the legislature. The Tenures Abolition Act, which was passed in that year, abolished practically all the *free* lay tenures except socage. Tenure by knight service was abolished altogether, and sergeanty was allowed to continue only in a limited form. Formerly it had rendered the tenant liable to onerous duties similar to those that might be exacted from a knight-service tenant, but the effect of the Act was to abolish it as a separate tenure, and, where it existed, only to leave the privilege of performing those honorary services that, as we have seen, were

---

[31] Holdsworth, *A History of English Law*, vol iii, p 51. For socage, see below, p 41.

[32] The chief reason for the decline of frankalmoin tenure was that upon alienation of the land, even to another ecclesiastical body, or upon escheat of the lordship to a superior lord, the tenure was converted into socage. Moreover, no fresh grant in frankalmoin, except by the Crown, has been possible since *Quia Emptores*; Challis, *Law of Real Property*, p 11. Ecclesiastical bodies more frequently held land by one of the other tenures: Maitland, *The Constitutional History of England* (1908), p 25.

peculiar to the higher ranks of sergeants. In other words, sergeanty was converted into socage,[33] the exceptional feature of the converted land being that the tenant might in some cases substantiate his right to perform certain honorary and dignified services.

Although frankalmoin was not formally abolished by the Act of 1660, it was seldom encountered in practice.

The Act of 1660 was, then, a move in the right direction, since it simplified the system of landholding by practically reducing the former tenures to two, that is to say, to socage and copyhold,[34] though the simplification was not quite so complete as this, owing to the retention of divergent customary methods of holding land known as gavelkind, ancient demesne and borough-English.[35] Yet, even apart from these peculiar cases it is obvious that the existence from 1660 to 1925 of two separate and quite different methods by which a man might hold land, tended to increase the complexities of conveyancing and to render real property law unnecessarily difficult.

We must now briefly describe the two tenures of socage and copyhold that held the field until the legislation of 1925 abolished the latter.

(5) Socage[36]

As distinguished from knight service, socage was the species of tenure that represented the new aspect that the economic life of the country gradually assumed. It was essentially non-military and free from the worst features of knight service. At first it could not be defined in positive terms, but was described negatively as being the form of tenure that was not spiritual, military, sergeanty nor villeinage.

(a) Origin

In early days the services due in respect of the land varied considerably. The tenant might pay a nominal rent sufficient to record the fact that the lands were held of the lord, or a substantial rent equal to the economic value of the land, while sometimes his obligation would extend to the performance of agricultural services. Originally, no doubt, the *socmanni*, as they were called, belonged to the lower orders of society, but the tendency was for this mode of landholding to extend upwards, since it was free from the worst of the feudal burdens incidental to knight service and, to escape those, even the greater landowners were willing to sacrifice something of their dignity.

(b) Commutation of services

The next step was that it became usual to commute services, whatever these might have been, into money payments, and though these, when they were originally fixed, no doubt represented the economic value of the land, yet with the gradual fall in the value of money they became in course of time so insignificant in amount as scarcely to merit

---

[33] Challis, *Law of Real Property*, p 9.
[34] For copyhold, see below, p 42.
[35] Below, p 46.
[36] Holdsworth, *A History of English Law*, vol iii, pp 51 ff.

the trouble of collection.[37] Thus by 1925 it had become practically impossible to prove that A held of B in socage tenure, for the payment of rent that would have revealed the existence of the tenure had in most cases not been made for centuries. B does not lose much, for the rent is generally of little pecuniary value, and the only other event that might have benefited him before the doctrine of escheat was abolished as from 1 January 1926—namely, the death of the tenant intestate and without heirs, whereby the land would pass to B by escheat—is normally of rare occurrence. Of course the land must be held of somebody, and the rule is that, where no private person can prove his lordship, it is deemed to be held of the Crown.

So socage became the great residuary tenure. It included every tenure that was not knight service, sergeanty, frankalmoin or villeinage, and its outstanding characteristic came to be that it involved some service that was absolutely certain and fixed, and that in the vast majority of cases took the form of a money payment.[38] Though subject to aids and to relief, it was free from the onerous rights of wardship and marriage that characterised knight service. The guardian of an infant socage tenant was the nearest relative who was incapable of inheriting the land. It was enacted by the Statute of Marlborough 1267 that a guardian in socage must account for the profits of the land at the end of his stewardship, and must not give or sell the ward in marriage.

(6) Copyhold[39]

The other tenure to which as late as 1925 English land might be subject was copyhold, the modern name for the old villeinage. Although this tenure was abolished from 1 January 1926,[40] something must be said about its origin and peculiar characteristics.

(a) Origin

We see in this tenure a system of land holding that represented in modern times customs far older than feudalism, and that dated back to the primitive method of agriculture called the open field system. In remote days the actual tillers of the English soil were almost certainly members of free village communities who owned in common the land that they farmed; but after the Conquest, although they still continued to follow those precepts and habits of agriculture that had been customary for generations, they were gradually absorbed into the feudal system. An overlord had appeared, a new concept in the shape of the manor had been established, and by imperceptible degrees the humble tillers found themselves part of the manorial organisation; no longer free owners, but instead subservient to an overlord upon whose will, according to the strict letter of the law, they were absolutely dependent. Blackstone thought that the modern

---

[37] Pollock and Maitland, *The History of English Law*, vol i, p 291.

[38] Littleton, *Tenures*, s 117.

[39] Holdsworth, *A History of English Law*, vol iii, pp 491 ff; vol vii, pp 296 ff; Simpson, *A History of the Land Law*, 155 ff; Scriven, *A Treatise on the Law of Copyholds* (7th edn, ed Brown, 1896); Gray, *Copyhold, Equity and the Common Law* (1963).

[40] LPA 1922, s 128; below, p 111.

copyholders were merely serfs who by continual encroachments on their superiors had gradually established a customary right to estates that, strictly speaking, had always been held at the will of the lords.[41] In fact, however, the truth is the exact reverse, for the lords had gradually induced the belief that only by their will were these ancient owners permitted to enjoy their customary rights and estates.[42]

(b) The manor

To understand the character of copyhold tenure we must refer once more to the feudal manor that was the unit of society in mediaeval England.

A typical manor consisted of:

(1) the land belonging to the lord, which was called his demesne;

(2) the land held of the lord by free tenants whether in socage or knight service;

(3) the land held of the lord by persons called villein tenants;

(4) rights of jurisdiction exercisable by the lord over the free tenants in the Court Baron, and over the villeins in the Court Customary;

(5) waste land on which the tenants were entitled to pasture their cattle.

(1) Farm system

The first point that emerges about the villeins is that it was they who cultivated the lord's demesne, a practice that originated in what has been termed the farm system. 'Farm' in Anglo-Saxon times meant food, and the system in vogue was for the tenant, in return for his holding, to produce a farm—that is enough food to sustain his lord for some given period, say a night, a week or a fortnight.[43]

(2) Labour service system

In the thirteenth century this primitive system gave way to the labour service system,[44] which meant that the villein tenant came under an obligation, often specified in the greatest detail,[45] to cultivate by his own labour his lord's demesne. But the mere obligation to perform agricultural services does not alone suffice to distinguish a villein from a socage tenant, since a socage tenant might also be subject to the same liability. What, then, was the test of villein tenure?

(c) Test of villein tenure

One fact that might be thought at first sight to provide this test is that the villeins received no protection in the King's courts. If they were unjustifiably ejected by the lord, they could recover neither possession nor damages in the royal courts, for in

---

[41] Blackstone, vol ii, p 95.

[42] See Pollock, *The Land Laws* (3rd edn, 1896), pp 43–52, 208–9.

[43] Vinogradoff, *Villainage in England*, pp 301–2.   [44] Ibid, p 304.

[45] See, for example, Pollock and Maitland, *The History of English Law*, vol i, p 366.

the view of the latter they were nothing more than tenants at the will of the lord.[46] But, though superficially the tenure seemed precarious to the last degree, it was saved from being so because the tenants were entitled to protection from the lord's manorial court, where those rules that had been hallowed by immemorial custom within the manor were recognised and enforced. These manorial customs gradually grew into legal systems under which the rights and the duties of the tenants were defined, and the everyday events of marriage, succession, alienation and the like were regulated.[47] But the lack of a remedy in the royal courts was not a sufficient test of villeinage or no villeinage since it also affected an ordinary tenant for years.

That test is to be found, however, in the nature of the services rendered by a tenant. If a man was bound to perform agricultural services it could not be said that he was necessarily a villein tenant, but if he did not know from day to day *what* kind of work would be assigned to him, then he was looked upon as a villein tenant. In other words, the test was the uncertainty of the nature of the work. As Pollock and Maitland wrote:[48]

> When they go to bed on Sunday night they do not know what Monday's work will be; it may be threshing, ditching, carrying; they cannot tell. This seems the point that is seised by law and that general opinion of which law is the exponent: any considerable uncertainty as to the amount or the kind of the agricultural services makes the tenure unfree. The tenure is unfree, not because the tenant holds at the will of the lord, in the sense of being removable at a moment's notice, but because his services, though in many respects minutely defined by custom, cannot be altogether defined without frequent reference to the lord's will.

So, then, in the thirteenth century villeinage was that tenure in which the return made by the tenant for his holding was the performance on his lord's demesne of agricultural services uncertain in nature.

(d) Money payment system

In the fourteenth and fifteenth centuries this labour service system gave way to a money payment system under which the tenant in villeinage paid a sum of money to his lord instead of giving personal services, and the lord cultivated his demesne by hired labour.[49] This was an example of the general movement from natural husbandry to the money system, which was fostered in England by several causes, such as the growth of the wool trade with Flanders and the great increase of trade with the Continent as a result of the English occupation of Normandy and Aquitaine.[50]

(e) Villein tenure becomes copyhold

The result of the change as regards villeinage was to benefit the tenant, because the rents remained stabilised despite the gradual fall in monetary values. This transition from

---

[46] Pollock and Maitland, *The History of English Law*, vol i, p 360.
[47] Vinogradoff, *Villainage in England*, p 172.
[48] Pollock and Maitland, *The History of English Law*, vol i, p 371.
[49] Holdsworth, *A History of English Law*, vol iii, p 204.
[50] Vinogradoff, *Villainage in England*, p 180.

labour services to money payments corresponded with the transition in nomenclature from villeinage to copyhold tenure:

> With the completion of the transition from praedial services to money rents, tenure in villeinage may be said to have come to an end... The essence of villein tenure had consisted in the uncertainty of the tenant's services, and when the old agricultural services were commuted for a fixed money payment, this uncertainty passed away.[51]

The derivation of the word 'copyhold' is this: the copyhold tenant, like his predecessor the villein, held at the will of the lord; but at the same time he held on the conditions that had become fixed by the customs of his particular manor. The lord's will could not be exercised capriciously, but only in conformity with custom. He still held a court, and that court kept records of all transactions affecting the lands. These records were called the rolls of the court. When, for instance, a tenant sold his interest to a third party, the circumstances of the sale would be recorded, and the buyer would receive a copy of the court rolls in so far as they affected his holding.[52] Inasmuch as he held his estate by copy of court roll, he came to be called a copyholder.

The change from villeinage to copyhold was of far-reaching importance to the tenant. He was rid of all traces of servility; he acquired an interest that in essentials was on all-fours with interests in land held by socage tenure, and above all he obtained recognition and protection from the King's courts. This protection was assured by the end of the fifteenth century. Coke summed up the position in expressive language:[53]

> But now copyholders stand upon a sure ground, now they weigh not their lord's displeasure; they shake not at every sudden blast of wind, they eat, drink and sleep securely, only having a special care of the main chance, viz, to perform carefully what duties and services soever their tenure doth exact, and custom doth require: then let lord frown, the copyholder cares not, knowing himself safe, and not within any danger. For if the lord's anger grow to expulsion, the law hath provided several weapons of remedy; for it is at his election, either to sue a *subpoena* or an action of trespass against the lord. Time hath dealt very favourably with copyholders in divers respects.

(f) Defects of copyhold tenure

Despite the possibility of enfranchisement, a process by which copyhold might be converted into socage tenure, a great proportion of English land, even in 1925, was still copyhold. The tenure was distinguished by several defects. For instance, the customs, which represented the local law governing land of this tenure, varied considerably from manor to manor, so that it was impossible to determine the law applicable to a disputed matter without an examination of the manorial records; the form of conveyance was very different from that required in the case of socage; copyhold and socage lands were often intermixed in so confusing a fashion as to make it difficult to discriminate between them, a dilemma from which the only escape in the event of a

---

[51] Page, *The End of Villeinage*, p 83, cited Holdsworth, *A History of English Law*, vol iii, p 206.

[52] A system of registration of title thus existed long before LRA 1925. But, as we shall see, this system lapsed with the abolition of copyhold.

[53] Coke, *Compleat Copyholder* (1641), s 9.

sale was the execution of two conveyances, one appropriate for copyhold, the other for a socage holding; certain rights of the land were so burdensome to the tenant that they caused strife and ill-will; and finally, it was impossible for either the lord or the tenant, without the assent of the other, to exploit the minerals under the land.

This bare summary of the history of copyhold tenure should be enough to show that from about the beginning of the seventeenth century it was an outmoded and exceedingly inconvenient form of ordinary tenure. It served no particular social need and it certainly impeded a simplified system of conveyancing because of its frequent diversity from socage tenure. It has been rightly described as 'an anachronism and a nuisance'.[54]

(7) Customary Methods of Landholding

In addition to these regular tenures there also existed in certain districts a few customary methods of landholding under which land was subject in various respects to a number of abnormal incidents. Instances are gavelkind, borough-English and ancient demesne.

(a) Gavelkind

Gavelkind is a word that denotes the customs that have applied since the Conquest to socage land situated in Kent.[55] Such land was in certain particulars subject to different legal rules from those obtaining in other parts of the country. Thus,

(i) the land descended upon intestacy to all the sons equally;

(ii) a husband who survived his wife was entitled until his remarriage to a life estate in one-half of her land although issue of the marriage might not have been born;[56]

(iii) a widow was entitled until her remarriage to dower in one-half of her husband's land;

(iv) an infant could alienate his land by the form of conveyance known as a feoffment when he reached 15 years of age; and

(v) the land could be left by will.

(b) Borough-English

Borough-English was a custom, found in certain parts of the country, under which the land descended to the youngest son to the exclusion of all the other children.[57]

---

[54] Underhill, *A Century of Law Reform* (1911), p 310.

[55] Pollock and Maitland, *The History of English Law*, vol ii, pp 271 ff; Blackstone, vol ii, p 84; Challis, *Law of Real Property*, p 14.

[56] *Re Howlett* [1949] Ch 767.

[57] Littleton, *Tenures*, ss 165, 211; Blackstone, vol ii, p 83.

(c) Ancient demesne

Ancient demesne land was land held by freehold tenants in any manor that had belonged to the Crown in the time of Edward the Confessor or William the Conqueror.[58] The tenants in ancient demesne were subject to certain restraints and entitled to certain immunities.[59]

(8) Summary of Tenures in 1925

If we now take stock of the feudal tenures as they existed in 1925, we see that the greater part of English land was held by socage tenure, a considerable part was subject to copyhold tenure, while the remainder was held either in grand sergeanty or in frankalmoin, or was affected by the peculiar customs of gavelkind, borough-English or ancient demesne. Here was room for at least one form of simplification, and we shall see later[60] that the Law of Property Acts 1922 and 1925 seized the opportunity. They converted copyhold and ancient demesne into socage tenure; they abolished gavelkind, borough-English, and all other customary modes of descent; and they purported to abolish frankalmoin.[61] The honorary services incident to sergeanty were retained. Escheat *propter defectum sanguinis*, which was the right of a lord to take the land of his tenant who had died intestate without leaving heirs, was abolished and replaced by a right in the Crown to take the land as *bona vacantia* in the same way that it takes goods.

The result is that though the general theory of tenure is still a part of English law in the sense that only the Crown holds land absolutely, and in the case of all others land is held of a superior and is incapable of absolute ownership, yet the law of tenure is both simpler and of less significance than it was before 1926. It is simpler because there is now only one form of tenure—namely, socage. It is of less significance because all the tenurial incidents (including escheat) which might in exceptional cases have brought profit to a mesne lord have been abolished, so that there is no inducement for a private person to prove that he is the lord of land. We can, in fact, now describe the theory of tenure, despite the great part that it has played in the history of English law, as a conception of merely academic interest. It no longer restricts the tenant in his free enjoyment of the land.

---

[58] Coke, *Institutes of the Laws of England*, Part IV (1644) 269; Blackstone, vol ii, p 99; Holdsworth, *A History of English Law*, vol iii, pp 263–9; Challis, *Law of Real Property*, p 29; *Merttens v Hill* [1901] 1 Ch 842.

[59] Real Property Commissioners, Third Report, pp 12 ff; *Merttens v Hill*, above; *Iveagh v Martin* [1961] 1 QB 232.

[60] Below, p 110.   [61] As to frankalmoin, see below, p 111.

II THE DOCTRINE OF THE ESTATE[62]

A SEISIN. POSSESSION NOT OWNERSHIP

Tenure signifies the relation between lord and tenant, and what it implies is that the person whom we should naturally call the owner does not own the land, but merely holds it as tenant of the Crown or of some other feudal superior. But if he is not owner of the land, what is the nature of the interest that he holds? In statutes, in judicial decisions and in common speech he is always described as a 'landowner', but we may well ask what it is that he owns.

The doctrine of tenure as developed in England made it difficult, if not impossible, to regard either him or his lord as the owner of the land itself. The land could not be owned by the tenant, since it was recoverable by the lord if the tenurial services were not faithfully performed; it could not be owned by the lord, since he had no claim to it as long as the tenant fulfilled his duties.[63]

Quite apart from this practical difficulty, however, the truth is that English law has never applied the conception of ownership to land. 'Ownership' is a word of many meanings, but in the present context we can take it to signify a title to a subject-matter, whether movable or immovable, that is good against the whole world.[64] The holder of the title, such as the owner of a car, has a real as opposed to a personal right—he is the absolute owner. This position is illustrated by the Roman doctrine of *dominium*, under which the *dominus* was entitled to the absolute and exclusive right of property in the land. Nothing less in the way of ownership was recognised. A man had either absolute ownership or no ownership at all. Possession was regarded as fundamentally different—*nihil commune habet proprietas cum possessione*[65]—and, though it was adequately protected, the remedies available were personal, not real.

In sharp contrast to this attitude, English law, in analysing the relation of the tenant to the land, has directed its attention not to ownership, but to possession, or, as it is called in the case of land, *seisin*. All titles to land are ultimately based upon possession in the sense that the title of the man seised prevails against all who can show no better right to seisin. Seisin is a root of title.

'Seisin'…is an enjoyment of property based upon title, and is not essentially distinguishable from right. In other words, the sharp distinction between property and possession made in Roman law did not obtain in English law; seisin is not the Roman possession and right is not the Roman ownership. Both of these conceptions are represented in English law only by seisin, and it was the essence of the conception of seisin that some seisins might be better than others.[66]

---

[62] Holdsworth, *A History of English Law*, vol iii, pp 101–37; Pollock and Maitland, *The History of English Law*, vol ii, pp 2–29; Hargreaves, *Introduction to The Principles of Land Law* (4th edn, ed Grove, 1963), pp 19–25, 42–54; Simpson, *A History of the Land Law*, pp 47 ff.

[63] Hargreaves, *Introduction to the Principles of Land Law*, p 44.   [64] Above, p 4.

[65] Ownership has nothing in common with possession: Digest of Justinian, 41.2.12.1.

[66] Plucknett, *A Concise History of the Common Law* (5th edn, 1956), p 358.

This unfailing emphasis upon the concrete and obvious fact of possession will be apparent if we consider for a moment the following three topics: the remedies that lay at common law for the recovery of land, the position of a tenant who was wrongfully dispossessed, and the long-established mechanism of conveyancing.

(1) Possessory Nature of Early Actions for Recovery of Land

The English actions for the recovery of land, called in early days *real actions*, have consistently and continuously turned upon the right to possession. Moreover, their object throughout has been not to inquire whether the title to possession set up by the defendant is an absolute title good against all persons, but whether it is relatively better than any title that the claimant can establish. English land law from the earliest days was committed to the doctrine of relative titles to possession. Thus, the issue raised in the most ancient and solemn remedy, the *writ of right*, was not whether the demandant (claimant) could prove an absolute title good against third parties, but whether he or the tenant (defendant) could establish the earlier and therefore the better seisin.[67] Similarly, the possessory assizes, simpler remedies introduced by Henry II to supplement the writ of right and to rectify a recent invasion of possession, merely considered the specific question whether the demandant or his ancestor had been unjustly disseised of his free tenement by the defendant. The assize of *novel disseisin*— in other words, recent dispossession—enabled A to recover land from B on proof that he had been ejected by B. The assize of *mort d'ancestor* availed him if he could show that X, his ancestor, had died seised of his land, and that the defendant had entered upon the land on X's death.[68] The sole question in these actions was one of fact relating to seisin. Did B disseise A? Did B take the seisin held by A's ancestor?[69] If so, the court ordered restoration of the seisin, but it did not adjudge that A held an absolute title good against all adversaries. If the defendant wished to litigate the question of title further, he would be driven to issue a writ of right.[70]

At a later date the various *writs of entry* met the case where the disseisin of which the demandant complained was not so immediate, as, for example, where B, after disseising the demandant, had granted the land to Y, who had granted it to the defendant. These actions, no less than the possessory assizes, merely decided whether the better right to seisin lay in the demandant or in the defendant.

Finally, it must be observed that this mediaeval principle of relativity of titles dominated the later action of ejectment. All that the claimant needed to do was to prove that he had a better right to possession than the defendant, not that he had a better right than anybody else. If, for instance, he was ejected by the defendant, he

---

[67] Lightwood, *A Treatise on Possession of Land* (1894), pp 73–4; Plucknett, *A Concise History of the Common Law*, p 358; Simpson, *A History of the Land Law*, pp 37 ff.

[68] Sutherland, *The Assize of Novel Disseisin* (1973).

[69] Holdsworth, *A History of English Law*, vol iii, p 90; Maitland, *Forms of Action at Common Law* (1936), p 28.

[70] Plucknett, *A Concise History of the Common Law*, p 359.

would recover by virtue of his prior possession, notwithstanding that a still better right might reside in some third person.[71]

(2) Effect of Loss of Seisin on Proprietary Rights

The effects that flow from a disseisin of the tenant afford a further illustration of the crucial part played by possession in English law. It was established at an early date that the seisin wrongfully taken by the disseisor was the commencement of a fresh title and that it gave him a real, though tortious, interest, valid against all but the disseisee and his successors in title:

> Possession being once admitted to be a root of title, every possession must create a title which, as against all subsequent intruders, has all the incidents and advantages of a true title.[72]

In the view of the common law, from the first day of his possession the disseisor had full beneficial rights over the land, holding a fee simple estate that was transmissible either *inter vivos* or by will.[73] Moreover, although the disseisee had a right of action to recover the land, for a long period in our legal history his lack of possession confronted him with serious and ever-increasing difficulties as against the disseisor and his successors in title. In mediaeval days and for long afterwards, the effect of the disseisin was to deprive him of most of his beneficial rights over the land until he had vindicated his claim to seisin in the appropriate real action. His former rights were reduced to a right of entry, a reduction that entailed certain important consequences.

Thus, the disseisee lost the power of alienation, for, being dispossessed, he was unable to make the delivery of seisin essential for a conveyance of land, and a right of entry could neither be devised until 1837,[74] nor be conveyed *inter vivos* until 1845.[75]

Circumstances might well occur that would deprive him of his right of entry and leave him with a mere right of action—a *chose in action* that was equally inalienable, though it would descend to his heirs.[76] For instance, where the disseisor died while still in possession, the land passed to his heir by operation of law with the result that the interest held by him was no longer regarded as tortious. The right of entry was said to be 'tolled', taken away, by descent cast.[77]

Again, if the disseisee failed to recover seisin, his widow had no right to dower;[78] if he died heirless, the land did not in all cases escheat to his lord;[79] and if he died leaving an infant heir, his lord was not entitled to wardship.[80]

---

[71] *Asher v Whitlock* (1865) LR 1 QB 1; M & B p 251.

[72] Pollock and Wright, *An Essay on Possession in the Common Law* (1888), p 95.

[73] It was only in LRA 2002 that English land law abandoned (for registered land) the common law principle of title based on possession, and the consequential principle that the title of a disseisor could no longer be defeated by the disseisee after the period prescribed by the Limitation Acts; below pp 1160 ff.

[74] Wills Act 1837, s 3.   [75] Real Property Act 1845, s 6.

[76] Hayes, *An Introduction to Conveyancing*, vol i, p 231.

[77] The doctrine of descent cast was abolished by the Real Property Limitation Act 1833, s 39.

[78] Maitland, *Collected Papers* (ed Fisher, 1911), vol i, p 366.   [79] Ibid, pp 368–9.

[80] Ibid, p 369. On the subject generally, see Holdsworth, *A History of English Law*, vol iii, pp 91–2.

The position may be summarised in the words of Holdsworth:

The person seised has all the rights of an owner; the person disseised has the right to get seisin by entry or action; but, till he has got it, he has none of the rights as an owner. In other words, the common law recognises, not *dominium* and *possessio*, but seisin only.[81]

(3) Possession: a Root of Title for Conveyancing Purposes

The third illustration of the emphasis laid by English land law upon possession, not upon ownership, is afforded by the practice of conveyancers in unregistered land.[82] A vendor must prove to the satisfaction of the purchaser, not only that he is entitled to the land that he has agreed to sell, but also that his title is not subject to adverse claims vested in third parties. He can hardly be expected to prove that he has a title good against the whole world, for, since land is permanent and indestructible, it may well be that there exists a competing and better title created many years ago and still existing.

English land law has no doctrine akin to that of Roman law by which possession for a definite but short period had the positive effect of investing the possessor with *dominium*. As one writer has observed, the absolute ownership of a perishable chattel, such as a car, is a comparatively easy matter to prove, but 'if we were to insist upon the same fulness of ownership with regard to land we should have to trace back our title to the original grant of Paradise to Adam'.[83] What the vendor can do, however, and what he does do in practice, is to rely upon the fundamental principle that seisin is evidence of his title to the land.

With very few exceptions, there is only one way in which an apparent owner of English land who is minded to deal with it can show his right so to do; and that way is to show that he and those through whom he claims have possessed the land for a time sufficient to exclude any reasonable probability of a superior adverse claim.[84]

What, then, emerges so far is that land cannot be the subject-matter of ownership, though the person in whom its seisin is vested is entitled to exercise proprietary rights in respect of it. But again the question recurs—what is the nature of the interest held by the person seised? Is there nothing that he can be said to own? The answer made by English law is unique. The person entitled to seisin owns an abstract entity, called an *estate*, which is interposed between him and the land.[85] 'The English lawyer...first detaches the ownership from the land itself, and then attaches it to an imaginary thing that he calls an estate.'[86]

---

81 Holdsworth, *A History of English Law*, vol iii, p 95.
82 For the distinction between registered and unregistered land, see below, pp 119 ff.
83 Hargreaves, *An Introduction to the Principles of Land Law*, p 42.
84 Pollock and Wright, *An Essay on Possession in the Common Law*, pp 94–5.
85 Lawson, *The Rational Strength of English Law* (1951), p 87.
86 Markby, *Elements of Law* (1905), s 330.

B FEATURES OF THE DOCTRINE OF THE ESTATE

The estate represents the extent of the right to seisin. Thus the correct description of a tenant entitled to immediate seisin for his life is that he is 'seised of Blackacre for an estate for life'. This estate entitles its owner to exercise proprietary rights over the land for the prescribed period, subject to observance of the tenurial duties, and it may be disposed of as freely as any other subject-matter of ownership. This doctrine, as will be explained later,[87] is not confined to the case where a man is entitled to immediate seisin. If he is definitely entitled to it at some future time, he is equally the owner of an estate.

Two phenomena of great significance emerged during the development of this doctrine by the common law.

First, estates vary in size according to the time for which they are to endure. On this basis they are classified as estates of freehold and estates of less than freehold.

Secondly, several different persons may simultaneously own distinct and separate estates in the same piece of land.

These matters will now be discussed in more detail.

(1) Estates Classified According to Duration

The main classification of estates depends upon their quantification and their quantification depends upon their duration. The estate will vary in size according to the time for which it is to continue. 'Proprietary rights in land are, we may say, projected upon the plane of time.'[88] Thus a person may be entitled to seisin forever or for a lesser period.

(a) Meaning of freehold estate

Estates are sub-classified into those of freehold and those of less than freehold. Into which of these categories they fell depended in the earliest days upon the quality of the tenure by which the estate owner held his land. A tenant in knight service, sergeanty, socage or frankalmoin was called a 'freeholder', since the services due from him were free from servile incidents. He was said to have a frank tenement or freehold estate to distinguish him from a villein tenant.[89] Such was the original meaning of the expression 'freehold estate'.

But one of the characteristics of these free tenants was that the time for which they were entitled to hold the land was not fixed and certain. They invariably held

---

[87] Below, p 56.

[88] Pollock and Maitland, *The History of English Law*, vol ii, p 10. Compare the language used in the course of argument in *Walsingham's Case* (1579) 2 Plowd 547, 555: 'The land itself is one thing, and the estate in the land is another thing, for an estate in the land is a time in the land, or land for a time, and there are diversities of estates, which are no more than diversities of time, for he who has a fee simple in land has a time in the land without end or the land for time without end.'

[89] Ibid, vol ii, p 78; Holdsworth, *A History of English Law*, vol ii, p 351. For these various forms of tenure see above, pp 36–47.

either for life or for some other space of time dependent upon an event that might not happen within a lifetime, and it was this uncertainty of duration, not the quality of the services to be rendered, that gradually came to be regarded as the essential feature of a freehold estate.[90] Thus, even at the present day, an estate is freehold if its duration is uncertain; it is less than freehold if the time of its termination is fixed or capable of being fixed. The life tenant is a freeholder, but not so the tenant holding under a lease for a definite period, even though he holds for as long a period as 999 years.[91]

(b) Freeholds and non-freeholds distinguished in respect of seisin

Freehold and non-freehold estates were further distinguished in respect of seisin. At first the word 'seisin' was used to denote possession both of land and of chattels, but this usage did not last long and by the fifteenth century a man was said to be seised of land, but possessed of chattels. Later the subject-matter of seisin became even further restricted. The real actions that lay for the recovery of land, the possessory assizes and the writs of entry, were available only to freeholders, that is to tenants in fee simple, in tail and for life. These actions, as we have seen, were based entirely upon seisin and since they availed only freeholders it is not unnatural that the word 'seisin' was reserved exclusively to describe the possession of a freehold estate. Since mediaeval days it has been correct, for instance, to describe a tenant for life as seised, but a tenant for years as possessed, of the land.

(c) Tabular illustration

On the basis of duration the common law classified estates in the manner set out in the table on page 54.

(d) Freehold estates

As regards duration, the three freehold estates may be distinguished as follows:

(1) Fee simple

The fee simple[92] is the largest estate in point of duration, for, being one that is granted to a person and his heirs, it will last as long as the person entitled to it for the time being dies leaving an heir, and therefore it may last forever in the sense that it may never pass to the Crown so long as there is an heir. The word 'fee' denotes its inheritability, and the word 'simple' indicates that it is inheritable by the general heirs of the owner for the time being whether they be ascendants, descendants or collateral.

---

[90] Co Litt 43b.
[91] See, generally, Preston, *An Elementary Treatise on Estates* (2nd edn, 1820-7), vol i, c 1.
[92] Below, Ch 6.

(2) Fee tail

The fee tail,[93] which is the only other estate of inheritance, is less in quantum than the fee simple since it is inheritable only by the specified descendants of the original grantee and never by his ascendants, and also because it can descend only to his lineal issue and not to his collateral relatives. Thus it is inferior to the fee simple in the sense that it has not as great a capacity for perpetual existence. The classic formula for its creation was 'to A and the *heirs of his body*'.

(3) Life estate

The life estate[94] includes an estate that A holds for his own life and also one that he holds during the lifetime of B, this second species being called an estate *pur autre vie*.

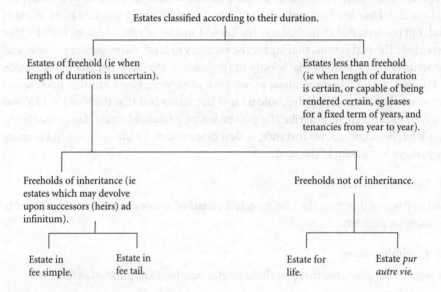

Estates classified according to their duration.

Estates of freehold (ie when length of duration is uncertain).

Estates less than freehold (ie when length of duration is certain, or capable of being rendered certain, eg leases for a fixed term of years, and tenancies from year to year).

Freeholds of inheritance (ie estates which may devolve upon successors (heirs) ad infinitum).

Freeholds not of inheritance.

Estate in fee simple.

Estate in fee tail.

Estate for life.

Estate *pur autre vie*.

(2) *Apportionment of Fee Simple*

The second phenomenon mentioned above is that the fee simple, which entitles the tenant to use the land for an infinite time, is regarded by English law as an aggregate out of which any number of smaller *and simultaneous* estates may be carved.[95] The entire subject-matter of enjoyment is apportionable among a number of persons, each of whom is the present owner of his individual portion.

> By way of illustration let us suppose that a fee simple owner desires that A shall enjoy Blackacre for life, that on A's death the right of enjoyment shall pass to B for life and that subject to these life interests the fee simple shall be vested in C.

---

[93] Below, Ch 16.
[94] Below, Ch 16.   [95] Digby, *History of the Law of Real Property*, p 270.

(a) Civil law doctrine

Every legal system that permits dispositions of this kind must necessarily particularise the legal nature of the rights, if any, vested in the successive beneficiaries, and the solution reached must depend upon whether or not the land itself is capable of ownership. It is obvious that any system of law that admits this capacity cannot regard A, B and C as simultaneous owners, for, in so far as ownership imports the right of immediate user, B and C cannot use the land at the same time as A, unless, of course, they are made joint, not as in our example successive, owners. The jurisprudential solution, therefore, if the land itself is the subject of ownership, is to insist that it can be the subject only of absolute ownership, and that where, as in the above example, there is a limitation to a succession of persons the entire and absolute ownership shall pass from one beneficiary to another upon the happening of the prescribed events. This is what is called *substitution*. Under this doctrine, if land is limited to A, then to B and then to C, the legal result is that these persons in their turn become owners of the property, each taking by substitution for the one who preceded him; each in his turn being complete owner; but each taking nothing until his turn comes.[96] B, for instance, is not even a limited owner of the land during the life of A, but on the death of the latter he becomes the absolute owner of the land for a limited time. Until his turn comes, he has no proprietary interest that he can alienate or otherwise dispose of.

This is the solution of Roman law and of certain modern legal systems[97] which regard dominium as the exclusive and unlimited right to the land itself, not merely to its user. By Roman law, A, the owner, might indeed let the land to X by *locatio conductio* or grant it to him for life by way of *usufruct*, but his ownership was affected by neither transaction. In the former case, X, if evicted, had merely a contractual right enforceable against A alone; in the latter, he acquired only a *jus in re aliena*, that is a right to use for his life land the ownership of which remained vested in A.

(b) English law doctrine

English law, however, having divorced ownership from the land itself and attached it to an imaginary thing called an *estate*, which entitles the owner to use the land for a longer or a shorter period of time, has been able to take a bolder course. Having decided that estates may vary in size according to their duration, it goes a step further and concedes that any estate, whether its duration is long or short, and whether it confers a right to immediate or to future seisin, is capable of a present existing ownership.

(c) Consequences of English law doctrine

Two results flow from this view.

---

[96] See Markby, *Elements of Law*, s 330.

[97] Typically, modern European civil systems follow the Roman model. See, eg, Bell, Boyron and Whittaker, *Principles of French Law* (2nd edn, 2008), p 269; *International Encyclopedia of Comparative Law*, vol VI, *Property and Trust*, ch 2 (Beekhuis), giving a general account of the law of property in civil law jurisdictions.

(1) Different degrees of estate ownership

First, there may be different degrees or gradations of estate ownership. The tenant in tail and the tenant for life, no less than the tenant in fee simple, are owners of their estates. As compared with the tenant in fee simple, they must, indeed, be described as *limited* owners, since their estates have not the same capacity of infinite duration. None the less they are owners, and their ownership differs from that of the tenant in fee simple only in degree—in quantity. There is no difference in kind or quality.[98]

The same remedies for the recovery of the land and the same powers of dealing with the estate by way of alienation are available, irrespective of the size of the estate. The different freehold estates, in other words, represent various grades in the hierarchy of ownership.

(2) Futurity of right to seisin not incompatible with present ownership

The second result of the English doctrine is that an estate may be the subject of a present existing ownership, even though the right of the owner to seisin is postponed to a future time. This is explicable in elementary terms.

An estate is the right to possess and use the land for the period of time for which it has been granted. In the case of the fee simple the period is infinite, since the estate is capable of perpetual existence. The entire ownership, in other words, resides in the person holding the fee simple, since he and his successors are entitled to use the land for ever. But time is divisible, and this right of perpetual user may be divided into successive periods of limited duration or, as one writer put it, into successive intervals of time.[99] One slice of the perpetual time, one slice of the entire ownership, may be given to A, another to B, and so on. Therefore, if the fee simple owner makes a grant

to A for life, then to B for life and then to C in tail,

each grantee receives at once a portion of the one uniform subject-matter, namely the right to use the land. A, B and C each hold a distinct and separate share of the identical thing. The only difference between them lies in the periods for which the user is to be enjoyed. Moreover, there is no futurity about the *ownership* of B and C. Upon the execution of the grant they become the immediate and absolute owners of an estate. It is not the right of ownership, but the right to actual seisin of the land that is future. Indeed, by virtue of their power of disposition they may exchange their property for money and so make it immediately available.[100]

---

[98] Pollock and Maitland, *The History of English Law*, vol ii, p 7. As we shall see in the following chapters (a) equity recognised the equivalent estates—and so there could be an equitable fee simple, estate tail or life estate; and (b) in 1925 the *legal* estates were limited to the fee simple absolute in possession and the term of years absolute. So in the modern law there are differences of kind or quality between a fee simple, an entail and a life interest, as regards their recognition by, respectively, the common law and equity. But the first stage in the development of the law of real property, described in the present chapter, was the recognition *by the common law* of these several estates.

[99] (1857) 1 Jurid Soc 537 (SM Leake).   [100] Ibid, 538.

(d) Advantages of English law doctrine

In conclusion, it may be said that this doctrine of the estate has given an elasticity to the English law of land that is not found in countries outside the area of the common law.[101] This is particularly true in respect of settlements, that is dispositions of property designed to provide for a succession of persons, such as the present and future members of a family. The desire to do this has dominated English real property law throughout its long history; for land, with its virtue of permanency, is an ideal source of endowment and its use for this purpose has been favoured by the courts. The aims of a settlor will be more effectively attained if he is permitted to vest a definite right of ownership in certain persons upon the occurrence of certain prescribed events in the future, as for example by directing that if a son is born to the present tenant of Blackacre, he shall, on reaching his majority, immediately acquire a definite proprietary interest, even though the present tenant is still alive. If the land itself is the subject-matter of ownership, the simultaneous existence of two or more owners, unless they are to take jointly, is, as we have seen, impossible, and therefore in countries where that concept of ownership prevails the power to create successive interests stretching into the future is necessarily restricted. But once admitted that what is owned is an imaginary thing called an estate, then it immediately becomes possible to frame elaborate and subtle schemes for the passing of the beneficial enjoyment of the land to one person after another in certain prescribed eventualities. There is room 'to deal with ownership in a more fanciful way than if it were attached to the soil'.[102]

C LEASEHOLD INTEREST.
TERM OF YEARS[103]

We shall now conclude with a short description of the leasehold interest or term of years that, quantitatively considered, is the smallest proprietary interest recognised by English law.

(1) Not a Freehold Estate

This interest, generally referred to as a term of years, arises where land has been demised, that is leased, for a definite number of years. It thus lacks the requirement of an uncertain duration, and though the period for which it is to last may be very great, such as 999 years, still it is not a freehold estate, and in the eye of the law is a smaller interest than a life estate.

---

[101] It has been described by a distinguished writer as 'one of the most brilliant feats of the English mind': Lawson, *The Rational Strength of English Law*, p 97.

[102] Markby, *Elements of Law*, s 330.

[103] Holdsworth, *A History of English Law*, vol iii, pp 213–17; vol vii, pp 238–96; Simpson, *A History of the Land Law*, pp 71–7, 92–5, 247–56.

(2) Not Real Property

Moreover it is not even real property. At an early period English law arrived at the general principle that, while land could be recovered specifically by a dispossessed tenant from a man who had ejected him, yet a person who was deprived of personal chattels could not enforce their actual recovery, but had to content himself with compensation in the shape of pecuniary damages.[104] Broadly speaking, actions fell into two classes. The real actions lay for the restitution of some object, and the personal actions for the recovery of damages. As land was the only object of which restitution in specie could be enforced, it followed that it formed the only subject matter of a real action, and it is not surprising to find the ancient lawyers seizing upon this fact and defining land as real property. Property that could be recovered in a real action was itself called real property, and thus it resulted that real property consisted solely of interests in land.

But not every interest in land could be specifically recovered, for, as we have seen, the real actions were available only to freeholders, that is only to tenants who were seised of the land. A tenant for years was possessed, not seised, and if dispossessed he could originally bring only a personal action for the recovery of damages against the grantor of his term. It is true that by the close of the Middle Ages a remedy had been introduced whereby he might recover the term itself, but nevertheless he was still regarded, and has ever since been regarded, as a non-freeholder. The doctrine of seisin was never extended to his interest, and the *possessory assizes* and the *writ of right*, which were the real actions properly so called, were never made available to him. He continued to hold merely personal property because originally his sole remedy was to bring a personal action.

At first sight this refusal of the law to regard a leaseholder's interest as real property is curious. It was not due to the unimportance or insignificance of terms of years. Such interests were on the contrary exceedingly valuable. The cause of their segregation, the reason why they were dissociated from the real actions and from feudal doctrine, was probably none other than economic pressure.[105]

At a time when investments in the modern sense of the term were unknown, one of the few methods by which a person might increase his income was to purchase a beneficial lease and take the profits of the land as interest on the money expended. Again, one of the ordinary methods of exacting security for a debt was for the debtor to lease his lands at a nominal rent to the creditor, so that the latter could obtain interest at the agreed rate out of the profits of the land without coming into conflict with the usury laws.[106] Another familiar form of investment was to purchase a wardship, which was the right to administer for one's own benefit the lands of an infant tenant

---

[104] See also above, p 6, n 14.

[105] Pollock and Maitland, *The History of English Law*, vol ii, pp 113 ff; Plucknett, *A Concise History of the Common Law*, pp 571–3.

[106] Holdsworth, *A History of English Law*, vol iii, pp 128, 215. For the significance of the usury laws in the modern law, see below, p 820.

in knight service. But if terms of years and wardships were to be effective investments, it was necessary that they should not be regarded as freehold estates in land carrying seisin, or, in more general terms, it was convenient to exclude them from the domain of strict real property law. There were several considerations that made this line of action advisable, but none was more potent than the fact that freehold estates as distinct from chattels could not be left by will. It may have been a matter of sound policy that an estate in lands should inevitably descend to the heir of the deceased tenant, but it would be poor comfort to tell a man who had invested his money in the purchase of a term of years that he had lost the right of bequeathing his money because he had converted it into land. After showing that as early as 1200 there was a large speculative traffic in wardships, Pollock and Maitland say:

> And then as to the term of years, we believe that in the twelfth century and later, this stands often, if not generally, in the same economic category. It is a beneficial lease bought for a sum of ready money; it is an investment of capital, and therefore for testamentary purposes it is *quasi catallum*.[107]

D CLASSIFICATION OF PROPERTY

(1) Real and Personal Property

The position reached by the common law was that estates of freehold represented real property law in the strict sense of that term, and as such were subject to all the consequences of feudal tenure; while on the other hand leaseholds (together with some other rights in land) were personal property and not so subject, and for this reason were neither affected by the incidents of feudalism, nor governed by the same legal rules as freeholds.

(2) Chattels Real and Personal

This position soon gave rise to a difficulty, for a term of years, no matter how it might be treated by the technique of the law, was obviously a valuable interest in land, and one that it was appropriate to bring within the province of land law. To sever its connection with the law of land merely because it was outside the scope of the real actions would have been absurd, and so the law was obliged to surmount the difficulty by the invention of a new terminology.

It was already a commonplace that the subject-matter of proprietary interests was either real property or chattels. Chattels were personal property, since they were not specifically recoverable in a real action. Leaseholds were thus subject to the law of chattels, but since they lacked the attribute of movability the obvious solution was

---

[107] Pollock and Maitland, *The History of English Law*, vol ii, p 117. *Catallum* is the mediaeval Latin word for cattle, chattels or, generally, movable goods.

to regard them as interests partly real and partly personal. Thus it was that personal property was sub-divided into chattels real and chattels personal.

> Chattels real, saith Sir Edward Coke, are such as concern or savour of the realty; as terms for years of land, wardships in chivalry,...the next presentation to a church, estates by statute merchant, statute staple,[108] *elegit*[109] or the like. And these are called real chattels, as being interests issuing out of or annexed to real estates; of which they have one quality, viz. immobility, which denominates them *real*, but want the other, viz. a sufficient legal indeterminate duration, and this want it is that constitutes them *chattels*.[110]

Thus there are two classes of chattels known to English law—chattels real as described by Coke, and chattels personal, which originally were confined to movable things, but that are now taken to comprise many forms of wealth, such as negotiable instruments, copyright, patents, trade marks, shares in a company and so on.

(3) Summary

We see, therefore, that the Law of Property as a whole falls into the following three divisions:

> The *law of real property* strictly so called, ie the rules that govern freehold interests in land—the fee simple, the entailed interest and the life interest;
>
> The law of chattels real, ie the rules that govern leaseholds;
>
> The law of pure personalty.

Of these three divisions the first and the last stand furthest apart, for the law of real property has been constructed on feudal principles, while the law of pure personalty has drawn its inspiration from a variety of non-feudal sources, such as Roman and Canon law and the customs of merchants. Midway between the two comes the law of chattels real, which Blackstone describes as having a 'mongrel amphibious nature', since it has derived its rules partly from real property law and partly from the law of pure personalty. The tendency, however, for several centuries has been to bring freeholds into conformity with chattels real, and the process of assimilation has been carried to such lengths, especially by the legislation of 1925, that we now have substantially a common and uniform system of law for real property and chattels real.[111] But, in spite of this assimilation, leaseholds today still remain personal as opposed to real property.[112]

---

[108] A tenancy by statute merchant or statute staple arose when a merchant creditor by taking advantage of the Statutes Merchant and Staple (Edward I and III) obtained seisin of his debtor's lands; see Digby, *History of the Law of Real Property*, p 282.

[109] A writ of execution by which a judgment creditor might obtain seisin of his debtor's lands. It was abolished by SCA 1981, s 141.

[110] Blackstone, vol ii, p 386.

[111] Below, pp 115 ff.

[112] Above, p 6.

3

MODIFICATION OF THE COMMON LAW BY EQUITY

Summary

In this chapter we show how equity modified and tempered the feudal principles of the common law, set out in Chapter 2, by its introduction of the 'use' and the consequent establishment of the trust concept, which is probably the most outstanding characteristic of English law. It is this concept that has produced the peculiarly English distinction between the legal and the equitable estate that forms the basis of modern conveyancing.

I DISADVANTAGES INCIDENTAL TO THE COMMON LAW TENURES

To understand the origin of uses it is necessary to examine the position of a tenant of land under the common law. Several of the disadvantages and restrictions that attached to the tenant at common law were due to the important part played by possession—seisin[1]—in the feudal system. A feature of that system was its immaturity, as regards both the interests that might be created in land and the methods by which the interests could be dealt with. Possession is an obvious fact, and in early days it was the dominating fact upon which most of the restrictive rules that came into being were founded.

Two fundamental principles that in themselves were sufficient to establish the importance of seisin were that the feudal services that in the early history of tenure were of such consequence to the lord were enforceable against the person seised and only against him; and again that it was only against the person seised that an action for the recovery of land could be brought. It was necessary that there should always be some person capable of meeting adverse claims and preserving the seisin for successors.[2] The effect of not knowing who was actually seised of land would be the loss of public and private rights in the land,[3] and therefore two inviolable rules that became established were that there must never be an abeyance of seisin, or in other words that there must be an uninterrupted tenancy of the freehold; and that every transfer of a freehold estate must be effected by an open and public delivery of seisin. Any disposition that would cloud the title to the seisin was forbidden at common law.

The following were some of the restrictions laid on the free enjoyment of a freehold estate at common law:

A CONVEYANCES WERE REQUIRED TO BE PUBLIC AND FORMAL

In a feudal society it was imperative that there should be no uncertainty as to the identity of the freehold tenant of any piece of land. A question might arise regarding the title to the land or the right of a lord to enforce the feudal dues to which he was entitled, and as both these matters could be settled only if it was known who was seised, the common law required that every transfer of a freehold estate be effected by an open and public delivery of seisin, either upon or within view of the land conveyed. The merit of this was that in the event of a dispute the actual freehold tenant would be well known to the neighbourhood. The method itself was called *feoffment with livery of seisin*, but the operative part of the transaction was the delivery, and a charter

---

[1] Above, p 48.   [2] See Co Litt 342b, Butler's note (1).
[3] Challis, *Law of Real Property* (3rd edn, ed Sweet, 1911), p 100.

of feoffment, which only served to authenticate the transaction, was not strictly necessary.[4]

There were other kinds of common law conveyance, but they were all open and public, although, when the feudal vigour began to abate, they gradually ceased to bear this characteristic.[5] It often happens that, instead of publishing his dealings with land to the world at large, an owner prefers to resort to a transaction that is secret and free from ceremony,[6] but at common law this was a desire that was unattainable, at least in the early days.

B TYPES OF INTERESTS WERE STRICTLY LIMITED

As it was essential that the seisin should not be in abeyance for an instant, but should always be vested in a freehold tenant, it followed that every conveyance of freehold had to be made to take immediate effect, so that the seisin passed at once to the grantee. This meant that many dispositions that a tenant might legitimately desire to make were rendered impossible. For example, a gift of a freehold interest that was to vest in the donee if and when he attained 21 years of age was void, since such a gift had to be completed by delivery of seisin, and if seisin were delivered at once, it would, having been parted with by the donor, be vested in nobody until the donee attained 21. If a grant were made to A for life and after his death to B when he attained 21, the grant to B failed unless he had reached that age at the death of A, because otherwise an abeyance of seisin would have occurred. Again, under a grant to A for life and after his death to the future children of B, only children who were in existence at A's death could take, for to allow later children to come in would have broken still another general principle, namely, that a transfer of a freehold interest had to be carried out by a public transaction.

Thus it is clear that the concentration of the common law upon the simple fact of possession led to extreme simplicity in the interests that might be created, and restricted within narrow bounds the limitation of future interests.[7]

C A TENANT AT COMMON LAW COULD NOT DEVISE HIS FREEHOLD ESTATE

Whatever may have been the rule in Anglo-Saxon days, one of the effects of the introduction of feudal tenure into this country was to abolish the right of leaving freeholds by will, except in a few particular localities and boroughs. To have allowed such wills would not only have diminished the lord's right of taking the land by escheat and have been a hardship to the heir, but it would have run

---

[4] Co Litt 271b, note 1.

[5] Hayes, *An Introduction to Conveyancing* (5th edn, 1840), vol i, pp 29–30. For the history of the subject, see Holdsworth, *A History of English Law*, vol iii, pp 220–46; vol vii, pp 353 ff.

[6] For the avoidance of formalities in the modern law, see below, pp 1011 ff.   [7] Below, pp 526 ff.

counter to a feudal policy that demanded that every transfer should be open and public.[8]

D A TENANT AT COMMON LAW WAS LIABLE TO CERTAIN ONEROUS FEUDAL INCIDENTS[9]

This is not the place to elaborate the burdensome nature of the tenurial dues that have already been briefly described. It must suffice to cite an expressive passage in which Blackstone sums up the position of one who held his lands in knight service:[10]

In the meantime the families of all our nobility and gentry groaned under the intolerable burthens, which (in consequence of the fiction adopted after the Conquest) were introduced and laid upon them by the subtlety and finesse of the Norman lawyers. For, besides the scutages to which they were liable in defect of personal attendance, which however were assessed by themselves in parliament, they might be called upon by the king or lord paramount for aids, whenever his eldest son was to be knighted or his eldest daughter married; not to forget the ransom of his own person. The heir, on the death of his ancestor, if of full age, was plundered of the first emoluments arising from his inheritance, by the way of relief and primer seisin; and, if under age, of the whole of his estate during infancy. And then, as Sir Thomas Smith very feelingly complains, 'when he came to his own, after he was out of wardship, his woods decayed, houses fallen down, stock wasted and gone, lands let forth and ploughed to be barren,' to reduce him still farther, he was yet to pay half a year's profit as a fine for suing out his livery; and also the price or value of his marriage, if he refused such wife as his lord and guardian had bartered for, and imposed upon him; or twice that value, if he married another woman. Add to this, the untimely and expensive honour of knighthood; to make his poverty more completely splendid. And when by these deductions his fortune was so shattered and ruined that perhaps he was obliged to sell his patrimony, he had not even that poor privilege allowed him, without paying an exorbitant fine for a licence of alienation.

There were additional disadvantages that resulted directly from the important part played by the feudal services. For example, several of the feudal dues consisted of payments that were made by the newcomer upon the death of a tenant, and, as these would never be enforceable if the lands were granted to a body that never died, the rule soon became established that lands were forfeited if they were granted to an association such as a monastery without the licence of the King and the lord paramount. Such a grant was called a *grant in mortmain*, and statutes were passed from time to time maintaining the rule as to forfeiture.[11]

Enough has now been said to show that the position of a freehold tenant at common law, as regards freedom of disposition, was not enviable. To quote Hayes:[12]

Large deductions must, therefore, be made from the praise lavished on the ancient common law, when its provisions are said to have promoted security of enjoyment, simplicity of

---

[8] Holdsworth, *A History of English Law*, vol iii, pp 75–6.   [9] Above, pp 38–9.
[10] Blackstone, vol ii, p 76.   [11] Blackstone, vol ii, p 268; below, p 1036.
[12] Hayes, *An Introduction to Conveyancing*, vol i, pp 30–1.

title and notoriety of transfer. As civilisation advanced, it proved less and less sufficient to attain those favourite objects of its founders, while it was manifestly ill-adapted to meet the growing demands of freedom and commerce. The rules of ownership and modes of assurance which we have endeavoured to explain, composed an unbending and oppressive code, utterly inadequate to the extended view and complicated interests of an intelligent and wealthy community. The progress of society called for a more pliant and liberal policy.

II DISADVANTAGES OF COMMON LAW TENURES AVOIDED BY THE DEVICE OF PUTTING LANDS IN USE

History shows us that whenever a grievance presses hard on the greater part of the population, it is not long before a remedy is discovered, and it was certainly not long before a 'more pliant and liberal policy' was introduced with regard to the rights and powers of landowners in general. But the new policy did not come from the common law. It was the sole work of the Chancellor, who made it possible by means of the protection that he gave in his court of equity to the new conception called the *use* of lands. It was due to this alone that a tenant was enabled to retain the ordinary advantages of landholding that were assured to him by the common law while escaping some of the worst disabilities of that system.

A ORIGIN AND EFFECT OF PUTTING LANDS IN USE

(1) Origin of the Use

The word 'use' is derived not from the Latin *usus* but from *opus*.[13] Maitland has shown us that before Domesday it was a common practice for one man to deal with land *ad opus*—on behalf of—another, such as where the sheriff seized lands for on behalf of the King (*ad opus domini Regis*), where a knight about to go to the Crusades conveyed his property to a friend on behalf of his wife and children, or where the vendor of an unfree tenement surrendered it to the lord to hold on behalf of the purchaser.[14] The word *opus*, which was commonly adopted in such connections, became gradually transformed into *oes*, *ues*, and thence into *use*.

If one could deal with land on behalf of, or to the use of, another for a particular purpose, the question that inevitably occurred was why one should not in a *general* way be allowed to hold land to the use of another. This is exactly what was done in

---

[13] Maitland, *Collected Papers* (ed Fisher, 1911), vol ii, p 403; Pollock and Maitland, *The History of English Law* (2nd edn, 1898), vol ii, p 228. For the origin and history of uses, see Holdsworth, *A History of English Law*, vol iv, pp 407 ff; (1965) 81 LQR 562 (Barton); Simpson, *A History of the Land Law* (2nd edn, 1986), pp 173 ff; Bean, *The Decline of English Feudalism* (1968), esp ch 3; Baker, *An Introduction to English Legal History* (4th edn, 2002), ch 14.

[14] Maitland, above, n 13.

course of time. The tenant A would transfer his land by a common law conveyance to B, who undertook to hold it on behalf of, or, adopting the correct expression, to the use of, A. In such a case B was called the *feoffee to uses*, that is the person to whom the feoffment[15] had on certain conditions been made; while A went by the name of the *cestui que use*, which meant the person on whose behalf the land was held.

The practice did not spring into life all at once, and Maitland believed that 1230 was the earliest time at which one person was holding land permanently and generally to the use of another:[16]

> In the second quarter of the thirteenth century came hither the Franciscan friars. The rule of their order prescribes the most perfect poverty: they are not to have any wealth at all....Still, despite this high ideal, it becomes plain that they must have at least some dormitory to sleep in. They have come as missionaries to the towns. The device is adopted of having land conveyed to the borough community to the use of the friars.

By the fourteenth century this device had become more extensive and there is evidence that it was a common practice for a landholder to convey his land to two or more friends *ad opus suum*—to his own use[17]—or to the use of a third person.

(2) Legal Effect of Putting Lands in Use

(a) Cestui que use lost his rights at common law

The important point to observe is the legal effect of this practice. It was to cut off the *cestui que use* in the eyes of the *common law* from all connection with the land. By an assurance operating at common law he had conveyed his estate to the feoffees to uses, and was therefore deprived of all common law rights over the land. He was nothing, the feoffees were everything; he had exchanged an actual estate for an intangible right, for instead of keeping seisin he had decided to rely upon the confidence that he had reposed in the feoffees:

> If, therefore, B [the feoffee] refused to account to his *cestui que use* A for the profits, or wrongfully conveyed the estate to another, this was merely a breach of confidence on the part of B, for which the common law gave no redress; much less did that law acknowledge any right in A to the possession or enjoyment of the land. The ordinary judicature knew no other proprietor than B; to him, and to him alone, attached the privileges and liabilities of a landholder; for *he* it was, to whom the possession was legally delivered. To have regarded A in any other light than that of a mere stranger to the soil, would have been to subvert a system raised upon investiture and tenure. It was accordingly decided at a very early period[18] that the common law judges had no jurisdiction whatever in regard to the use.[19]

---

[15] The conveyance by which the estate—the *fee*—was invested at common law.

[16] Maitland, *Equity* (rev Brunyate, 1936), p 25; and see *Collected Papers*, vol ii, p 408. A Papal Bull ordained in 1279 that a use was not property.

[17] Ibid, pp 25–6.

[18] 4 Edw 4.

[19] Hayes, *An Introduction to Conveyancing*, vol i, p 33.

If the feoffees failed or refused to carry out the directions imposed upon them,[20] or if they deliberately alienated the land for their own purposes,[21] there was no common law action by which they could be rendered liable, and as a *cestui que use* who was let into possession of the land was regarded as a mere tenant at will of the feoffees to uses, who could turn him out at any moment, and if necessary sue him in trespass.[22]

(b) Uses protected by Chancellor

This absence of all remedy seems at first sight to stultify the practice of putting lands in use, and it would have been fatal had no alternative means been discovered for protecting the *cestui que use*. But from about the year 1400 the Chancellor, early in his growing jurisdiction, stepped in and interceded on behalf of the *cestui que use*. He could not interfere with the jurisdiction of the common law courts by proceeding in a direct fashion against the land itself, because the absolute title to the land was vested in the feoffees by operation of the immutable principles enforced in those courts. His role was to see that persons acted honestly according to the precepts of good morality, and, in accordance with the principle that equity acts *in personam*, he did not hesitate to proceed against feoffees who disregarded the moral rights of the *cestui que use*. He was in a stronger position than the common law courts, for not only could he order a person to perform some definite act under pain of attachment, but his power of oral examination enabled him to discover breaches of good faith.

> The spectacle of feoffees retaining for themselves land which they had received upon the faith of their dealing with it for the benefit of others was too repugnant to the sense of justice of the community to be endured. The common law could give no remedy, for by its principles the feoffee was the absolute owner of the land. A statute might have vested, as the Statute of Uses a century later did vest, the legal title in the *cestui que use*. But in the absence of a statute the only remedy for the injustice of disloyal feoffees to uses was to compel them to convey the title to the *cestui que use* or hold it for his benefit. Accordingly the right of the *cestui que use* was worked out by enforcing the doctrine of personal obedience.[23]

In other words, the wrong that an unfaithful feoffee committed was breach of contract, but it was a breach for which at that time no remedy lay in the ordinary courts, since the general principle of the enforceability of contracts was still undeveloped. Further, it was common for a use to be declared in favour of a third party, and even if the modern doctrine of contract had been perfected, the rules as to privity of contract[24] would have precluded the grant of a remedy to the *cestui que use*.

---

[20] 3 Rot Parl 511, No 112, cited Ames (1907–8) 21 Harv L Rev 265; *Select Essays in Anglo-American Legal History* (1907-1909) vol ii, p 741.

[21] Sanders, *Uses and Trusts* (5th edn, ed Sanders and Warner, 1844), vol i, p 67.

[22] *Preston, An Elementary Treatise on Estates* (2nd edn, 1820-27), vol i, p 145.

[23] Ames, *Select Essays in Anglo-American Legal History*, vol ii, p 741.

[24] It was only in 1999 that the doctrine of privity of contract was reformed to allow a third party to enforce directly a term of a contract where the contract expressly or impliedly so provides: Contracts (Rights of Third Parties) Act 1999; below, p 743.

B CREATION OF THE DISTINCTION BETWEEN THE LEGAL AND THE EQUITABLE ESTATE

The Chancellor's intervention in this field led to the introduction into English law of what is generally described as a duality of land ownership. He did not deny that the feoffee was entitled at common law, to the exclusion of the *cestui que use*, since the land had been conveyed to him by a conveyance effective at common law. That fact was inescapable, but what the Chancellor insisted upon was that the feoffee should scrupulously observe the directions imposed upon him by the feoffor. The feoffment had not been made to him for his own benefit. In other words, while the feoffee was regarded as owner by the common law, the *cestui que use* was considered to be the true owner by equity: the former had the legal ownership, the latter the equitable ownership of the same piece of land. Thus we get the essentially English[25] distinction between the legal and the equitable estate—the legal estate recognised and protected by the common law courts, and the equitable estate recognised and protected only by the Chancellor. This is what is meant by *duality of ownership*. Writing in 1840, Hayes described the case where A had conveyed land to B to be held to the use of A, or to the use of C:[26]

> But, under the auspices of an ecclesiastical chancellor, the use, though alien to the soil, took root in our civil jurisprudence, and attained to a degree of influence and importance which at length almost superseded the ancient polity. Means were soon devised for compelling B, the owner in point of law, to keep good faith towards A or C, the owner in point of conscience. The King, in his Court of Chancery, assumed jurisdiction to extort a disclosure upon oath of the nature and extent of the confidence reposed in B, and to enforce a strict discharge of the duties of his trust. Hence Equity arose. From this period, when the right of A (or C) became cognisable in the Court of Chancery, we may speak of him as the equitable or beneficial owner, and of B as the legal owner. But in order to preserve a clear perception of the twofold character of the system, we must keep steadily in view the fact that B had still the *real* right, to be enforced, on one side of Westminster Hall, by judgment of law *in rem*, which went at once to the possession of the land itself; while A (or C) had nothing more than a mere right *in personam*, to be enforced on the other side of the Hall, by subpoena, directed against the individual trustee. The Chancery, in assuming jurisdiction over the use, left untouched and inviolate the ownership at the common law. It exercised no direct control over the land, but only coerced and imprisoned the person of the legal owner who obstinately resisted its authority. It usurped none of the powers or functions of a court of law, but, leaving to the latter the redress of wrongs done to the realty, confined

---

[25] Civil law systems traditionally cannot divide ownership in this way, and have also been hostile to the establishment of a separate 'patrimony': *International Encyclopedia of Comparative Law*, vol VI, *Property and Trust*, ch 2, paras 2.1, 2.10 (JH Beekhuis), 2.274 (FH Lawson); but many systems have now developed a 'diluted "trust" concept of a segregated ring-fenced fund (or fiduciary patrimony) immune from the claims of the owner's creditors and heirs': Underhill and Hayton, *Law relating to Trusts and Trustees* (18th edn, 2010), para 100.47. See also Recognition of Trusts Act 1987, giving effect to the Hague Convention on the Law Applicable to Trusts and on their Recognition; Underhill and Hayton, ch 25; Graziadei, Mattei and Smith, *Commercial Trusts in European Private Law* (2005).

[26] Hayes, *An Introduction to Conveyancing*, vol i, pp 33–4.

its jurisdiction to matters of trust and confidence, which could not be reached by the arm of ordinary justice.

C ADVANTAGES OF PUTTING LANDS IN USE

Some of the worst burdens incidental to tenure at common law might be avoided by the device of a use: indeed, there were at least six substantial advantages that might accrue to the *cestui que use*.

(1) Lands became Devisable

The very natural desire that the power of testamentary disposition, which already applied to goods and chattels, should be extended to land, contributed more largely than any other factor to the rapid establishment of the use. The obligation of the feoffees to administer the legal estate according to the wishes of the *cestui que use* was not confined to the latter's lifetime, and from an early date it was the usual practice for the beneficial owner to specify what the destination of the use should be after his death. In this indirect way, by making a testamentary disposition of the equitable as distinct from the legal estate, property owners became accustomed to provide for their younger sons, daughters and other relatives, to ensure the payment of their debts and to make charitable gifts.[27]

(2) Conveyances of Land Facilitated[28]

The common law principle that a conveyance should be open and public could easily be evaded by means of the use, for just as the *cestui que use* could direct what dispositions of the land should be made after his death, so he could give similar directions that would be operative during his life. A transfer of the use required no formality; the one essential was that the intention of its owner should be clearly manifested. Moreover, the system of conveyancing was radically affected as the result of an equitable doctrine that applied even where land had not deliberately been put in use. This was that a mere contract to sell a legal estate raised a use in favour of the purchaser immediately on payment of the purchase money. Such a contract was called a *bargain and sale*, and though at first it passed merely an equitable estate to the purchaser, it gained a far wider operation after the Statute of Uses in 1535 and developed into the normal method of conveying *legal* estates.[29]

---

[27] Holdsworth, *A History of English Law*, vol iv, pp 438–9. [28] Ibid, pp 424–7.

[29] For the history of the matter, see Holdsworth, *A History of English Law*, vol vii, pp 356–60. The process of development may be briefly described as follows: (1) A, having bargained and sold land to B for a fee simple estate and having received the purchase money, was implicitly seised to the use of B. (2) The Statute of Uses provided that when A stood seised to the use of B, the latter should acquire the *legal* estate (below, p 73). Had this been the only enactment, therefore, a bargain and sale after the statute would have provided a secret method of conveying *legal* estates. (3) The Statute of Enrolments, however, passed at the same time,

(3) Settlements of Land Facilitated

We have already seen[30] that the power of a landowner at common law to create future interests was so severely restricted that only the simplest forms of settlement of a legal estate were possible. This stringency was relaxed upon the introduction of uses. The use, to which the restrictive rules of common law were wholly inapplicable, conferred upon its owner an almost unrestrained liberty to specify who the future beneficiaries should be, upon what events their interests should arise, and in what order the interests should take effect. The equitable estate was, in fact, a pliable instrument, a subject-matter that could be moulded by its owner into such forms as might appear desirable to him. Thus arose what were called shifting and springing uses.[31]

(4) Avoidance of Feudal Burdens

The most oppressive of the feudal burdens to which a tenant was liable at common law[32] were those that became exigible at his death, namely, wardship, marriage, reliefs and primer seisin. No relief from these would be gained by the appointment of a sole feoffee to uses, for the latter, in his capacity as tenant at law, would be caught in the feudal net and *his* death would entitle the lord to exact such dues as might be demandable. The usual practice, therefore, was to enfeoff, not one, but several, persons as joint tenants. The rule of joint tenancy is that the share of a tenant who dies does not pass to his heir but accrues to the surviving tenants.[33] He leaves nothing for which his heir can be made to pay a relief, he leaves nobody over whom the lord can claim the right of wardship or of marriage. The one essential, therefore, was to ensure that the number of feoffees never fell below two. The death of the *cestui que use* himself, despite his position as the true beneficial owner, created no right to feudal dues, since they were the consequence of tenure, and the use 'being the creature of conscience, the offspring of moral obligation, could not be the subject of tenure'.[34] 'The lord could not look behind the feoffees; they were his tenants: it was nothing to him that they were allowing another person to enjoy land that by law was theirs.'[35]

---

enacted that no estate of *inheritance or freehold* should pass, nor should any use be raised, by a bargain and sale, unless the bargain and sale was made by deed and enrolled in one of the King's Courts of Record. (4) The last statute applied only to sales of freehold or inheritable estates. Therefore a bargain and sale of a leasehold might be made privately without enrolment. This fact was quickly appreciated (certainly before 1620), and it became usual to transfer a fee simple as follows: A bargained and sold Blackacre to B *for one year*. On payment of the purchase money A became seised to the use of B. The Statute of Uses operated upon this state of affairs and passed the legal possession to B, leaving the reversion in A. Next day A executed a deed of *release* that extinguished his reversion and consequently enlarged B's leasehold into the fee simple. This form of conveyance, which was called a *lease and release*, remained the normal method of conveyance until 1841, when it was enacted that a release alone should be as effectual as a lease and release. A simple deed of grant was substituted for a release in 1845. See (1988) 104 LQR 617 (J M Kaye), arguing that the object of the Statute of Enrolments was not to prevent secret conveyancing, but that 'it was foreseen that, without it, the Statute of Uses would have had some unfortunate effects upon security of titles'.

[30] Above, p 63. For further explanation, see below, pp 95–7.   [31] Below, p 97.
[32] Above, pp 38–9.   [33] Below, p 495.
[34] Hayes, *An Introduction to Conveyancing*, vol i, p 34.   [35] Maitland, *Equity*, p 27.

(5) Avoidance of Forfeiture and Escheat

Land held by tenure at common law was forfeited to the Crown if the tenant committed high treason, and upon his conviction or outlawry for felony it passed to the Crown for a year and a day and then escheated to the lord.[36] These unpleasant consequences were avoided, however, if a tenant, before embarking upon some doubtful enterprise, had the prescience to vest his lands in a few confidential friends. The delinquent might possibly suffer the extreme penalty, but at least his family would not be destitute.

(6) Evasion of the Mortmain Statutes

We have seen that, since those feudal dues that became exigible at the death of a tenant would be lost to the lord if land came into the hands of a body that might never die, such as a corporation, a series of Acts, generally called the Mortmain Statutes, were passed from an early date providing that land granted to a corporation without the licence of the King and lord paramount should be forfeited.[37] Uses, however, provided an obvious means of evading this prohibition, and, until the practice was finally stopped in 1392,[38] it was a common plan for a donor to enfeoff a number of persons to hold to the use of a monastery or other corporation.

D INFLUENCE OF COMMON LAW DOCTRINES ON THE USE

We should next notice how the Chancellor dealt with this new form of ownership called the use or equitable estate. It was his own creation. He had invented something hitherto unknown to the law. He was free to do what he liked with his own. In the quaint language of an old judge, the use was as clay in the hands of the potter,[39] and, as the owner of a use was in theory allowed to give any imaginable directions as to its enjoyment, the Chancellor might have allowed it to be moulded into forms entirely subversive of common law principles. There were, in fact, several forms of interests in land, unattainable at common law, which he did permit to be carved out of the use, but they were mostly confined to the realm of future interests. For example, the dispositions mentioned on page 63, which would have been void at common law, were open to a landowner if he was content to create them by way of use.

It may be said in general, indeed, that in framing rules for the governance of the use the Chancellor refused to be bound, or to let the development of the use be hampered, by any of the common law rules connected with tenure. And yet it was certainly not his policy to encourage wide deviations from the established tenets of the law. The exact contrary was the case. Having begun by affording an adequate protection to the use, he then to some extent allowed the fact that its basis rested on personal confidence to

---

[36] Challis, *Law of Real Property*, pp 33 ff.   [37] Below, p 1036.   [38] 15 Ric 2, c 5.
[39] *Brent's Case* (1583) 2 Leon 14, 16 (Manwood J).

fade into the background, and proceeded to regard it as a kind of interest in land, 'a sort of immaterialized piece of land', in which actual estates might be created just as they might be created at common law.[40]

In other words, the general policy of the Chancellor in his development of the use was to adopt the established rules of the common law. When necessary he was prepared to depart from those rules on the ground of convenience, but he usually took them as his guide. It can, indeed, be said 'that there scarcely is a rule of law or equity of more ancient origin, or which admits of fewer exceptions, than the rule that Equity followeth the law.'[41]

Thus on the death of the *cestui que use*, Equity applied the common law rules of descent; the common law rights of a husband to the wife's property after her death were extended to the equitable interest, though a wife was not entitled to dower[42] out of her husband's equitable estates until 1833; and estates, similar in extent to those possible at law, might be created in the use. As Butler noted: 'There is the same division in Equity as there is at law, of estates of freehold and inheritance, of estates of freehold only, and of estates less than freehold; of estates in possession, remainder or reversion; and of estates several and of estates undivided.'[43]

To sum up this part of the discussion we may say that a use of lands existed where the legal estate was vested in A in such circumstances that he was subject to a trust enforceable in equity to convey the legal estate to such persons, and in the meantime to apply the rents and profits in such manner, as the *cestui que use* should direct; and, failing directions, should hold the land and pay the profits to the use of the *cestui que use* himself.[44]

E THE LATER HISTORY OF USES AND THE RISE OF THE MODERN TRUST ESTATE

What, then, is the essential difference between the legal and the equitable estate? It is clear at first sight that the legal estate carries the bare technical ownership, while its equitable counterpart gives the *cestui que use* beneficial ownership. One is the kernel, the other is the nut. If land is conveyed to

A and his heirs to the use of B and his heirs,

there is no doubt that A is the true *legal* owner. But it is an unprofitable ownership, for unless he succeeds in some fraudulent enterprise he will be compelled to deal with the land as B desires. In truth, the difference goes much deeper than this, but before discussing this further we should say something of the subsequent history of uses.

---

[40] Maitland, *Equity*, p 31.   [41] Butler's note to Co Litt 250b, xvi.
[42] Above, p 50.   [43] Above, n 41.
[44] *Gilbert on Uses and Trusts* (3rd edn, ed Sugden, 1811) p 1; Fearne, *Contingent Remainders* (10th edn, ed Butler, 1844), p 291, note *h*.

(1) Statute of Uses 1535

(a) Object of statute

The equitable estate, which was the greatest achievement of the Chancellor, was not allowed to pursue its course of development undisturbed. It was assailed by the legislature under Henry VIII, who, with a view to the 'extirping and extinguishment of all such subtle practised feoffments, fines, recoveries, abuses', procured the passing of the Statute of Uses in 1535.[45] Many reasons were alleged in justification of this statute, but the real object of the King's action was to restore to something like their ancient buoyancy and dimensions the feudal dues of which the collection had been rendered so much less fruitful by the practice of conveying land to uses. The simplest remedy was to abolish uses altogether, and this the King tried to do. In 1532 a Bill was presented to Parliament in an attempt to limit the consequences of uses. This met with strong opposition, however, and Henry warned the Commons in March 1532 that he would 'search out the extremity of the law'. This he did by obtaining, in the case of *Lord Dacre* in 1535, a decision that any devise of lands by a tenant in chief who died leaving an heir under age was fraudulent. Parliament, faced with this fait accompli that undermined the title of many tenants in chief, was prevailed upon to pass the Statute of Uses.[46]

The Statute contained a very long preamble, the general object of which was to denigrate as grievances the advantages that uses conferred upon the landowning class as a whole, while keeping in the background the real purpose of the statute, which was to replenish the royal coffers. The preamble made the statute look as if it were a highly popular measure, but Maitland put the matter in its true historical setting when he wrote:[47]

> A long preamble states the evil effects of the system [of uses], and legal writers of a later day have regarded the words of this preamble as though they stated a generally admitted evil. As a matter of historical fact this is not true. The Statute of Uses was forced upon an extremely unwilling parliament by an extremely strong-willed King. It was very unpopular and was one of the excuses, if not one of the causes, of the great Catholic Rebellion known as the Pilgrimage of Grace. It was at once seen that it would deprive men of that testamentary power, that power of purchasing the repose of their souls, which they had long enjoyed. The King was the one person who had all to gain and nothing to lose by the abolition of uses.

(b) Effect of the Statute

The statute was passed, however, and its effect was to abolish the distinction between the legal and the equitable estate in the case of the passive use, that is to say where the feoffees stood seised to the use of B and were the mere passive instruments for carrying out the directions of B. A conveyance to

---

[45] 27 Hen 8, c 10.

[46] (1967) 82 EHR 673 (EW Ives); Bean, *The Decline of English Feudalism*, ch 6. For an earlier view of the origins of the Statute, see Holdsworth, *A History of English Law*, vol iv, pp 450–61; (1912–13) 26 Harv L Rev 108–27.

[47] Maitland, *Equity*, p 34; and see Froude, *History of England* (1893), vol iii, pp 91, 105, 158.

A and his heirs to the use of B and his heirs,

which before the statute would have carried only the equitable estate to B, operated after 1535 to pass the legal estate to him. This was so because the statute provided in effect that, when any person was seised of lands to the use of any other person, the *cestui que use* should be deemed to have lawful seisin of the land to the extent of his interest in the use, and the seisin that prior to the statute would have been in the feoffee to uses, A, should be deemed to be in the *cestui que use*, B. In other words, the statute brought about two results:

> First, to adopt a technical expression it *executed the use*, that is to say, it turned B's former equitable estate into a legal estate carrying common law seisin; and
>
> Secondly, the common law seisin, which would normally have been vested in A as a consequence of the conveyance, was taken away from him entirely.[48]

A was a mere nonentity, and as a general rule nothing was to be gained by conveying to A to the use of B instead of making a direct conveyance at common law to B, since in both cases B was seised of the legal estate, and by reason of that fact was in both cases subject to the dues, burdens and incapacities that had always affected an estate at common law.

(c) Advantages and disadvantages of statute

The advantages of the statute lay with the common lawyers and with the King, its disadvantages with the general class of landowners. The common lawyers profited because they acquired a profitable jurisdiction over the uses that had been turned into legal estates. The King profited because the conversion of uses into legal estates involved the abolition of the power to devise lands, and this, in itself, increased very considerably the value of the tenurial incidents.[49]

The statute was a real grievance in many ways. For one thing the common belief was that it prevented wills of land, and, though this was a misapprehension,[50] it caused such irritation[51] that it was found necessary in 1540 to pass the Statute of Wills that permitted a tenant to devise all his socage lands and two-thirds of his lands held in knight service.

It would seem, then, if we proceeded no further with the history of uses, as if Coke was right when he said that:[52]

> the makers of the statute at last resolved, that uses were so subtle and perverse, that they could by no policy or provision be governed or reformed; and therefore, as a skilful gardener will not cut away the leaves of the weeds, but extirpate them by the roots, and as a wise householder will not cover or stir up the fire which is secretly kindled in his house, but utterly put it out; so the makers of the said statute did not intend to provide a remedy and reformation by the continuance or preservation, but by the extinction and extirpation of

---

[48] Fearne, *Contingent Remainders*, p 273, Butler's note.
[49] Holdsworth, *A History of English Law*, vol iv, pp 463–4.   [50] See (1944) 7 CLJ 354 (RE Megarry).
[51] Froude, *History of England*, vol iii, p 89.   [52] *Chudleigh's Case* (1595) 1 Co Rep 113b.

uses; and because uses were so subtle and ungovernable, they have with an indissoluble knot coupled and married them to the land, which of all the elements is the most ponderous and immovable.

(d) Uses not executed by statute

This, however, was to go too far, for the Act did not entirely abolish uses. There were at least two cases in which the grantees to uses retained the legal estate and were still compelled by the Chancellor to fulfil the intention of the grantor.

First, since the statute applied only where a feoffee was seised to the use of another, it was necessarily inoperative where a term of years, as distinct from a freehold estate, was given to A to the use of B, for A was possessed, not seised, of the subject-matter.[53]

Secondly, the exclusion of the statute was admitted where an active duty was imposed upon the feoffees to uses, such as where they were directed to collect the rents and profits and to pay them to B. In these circumstances it was recognised that the legal estate must remain with the feoffees, for otherwise they could not justify their right to the rents.

In both these instances, the conscience of the feoffees to uses was affected and they came under a moral duty to deal with the legal estate on behalf of the beneficiary—in the one case to transfer the term to him, in the other to secure the rents for him—and it was a duty that was enforceable only by the Chancellor. As regards terminology, however, it became usual to describe the person whose conscience was affected in these cases as being under a *trust* to carry out the directions of the grantor.[54] The uses were not those that the statute could execute, yet they were trusts that in conscience ought to be performed.[55] The statutory abolition of the passive use, of course, was not affected by this exercise of the Chancellor's jurisdiction. It long remained true that if the fee simple were granted to A to the use of B, A was divested of the legal estate and deprived of his former functions. Nevertheless, the principle that a moral duty must be performed was developed with such insistence that the passive use was ultimately restored in the shape of the passive trust, for the courts of equity gradually extended the circumstances in which the person upon whom the statute conferred the legal estate was bound in conscience to hold it in trust for some other person in accordance with the intention of the grantor.[56]

(e) The use upon a use

A striking example of this enduring concern of Chancery with the problem of conscience is furnished by the ancient rule that there could be no use upon a use. The rule established before the statute was that if land were conveyed to

A and his heirs to the use of B and his heirs to the use of C and his heirs.

---

[53] Above, p 53.

[54] Plucknett, *A Concise History of the Common Law* (5th edn, 1956), pp 598–9.

[55] Blackstone, vol ii, p 336. [56] Plucknett, *A Concise History of the Common Law*, p 599.

it was only the use in favour of B that took effect. He acquired the equitable estate, and the second use in favour of C was ruled out as being repugnant to the first.[57] This was confirmed at common law soon after the statute in *Jane Tyrrel's Case*,[58] the result of which was that B, not A, acquired the legal estate and the limitation in favour of C was still nugatory. The repugnancy of his use with that of B was apparent, for as was said in another case, 'The use is only a liberty to take the profits, but two cannot severally take the profits of the same land, therefore there cannot be an use upon an use.'[59]

(2) Development of Modern Trust

(a) Passive use finally restored

Although it was equally apparent, as Blackstone remarks,[60] that B was never intended by the parties to have any beneficial interest in the land, the Chancery court at first came to the same conclusion and repudiated the second use.[61] Ultimately, however, and certainly by 1700, it reversed this view and restored the passive use by holding that B must be regarded as holding the legal estate in trust for C. It was against conscience for one man to retain what was clearly intended for another. The exact stages by which this result was reached are not discernible. It was long thought that *Sambach v Dalston* (or *Darston*)[62] in 1634 was the decisive authority, but research has shown that this is to go too far.[63] The importance of that decision was the refusal of the court to ignore the grantor's intention. In the actual circumstances of the case he intended to benefit not only C, but also an infant after the death of C and therefore the court directed B to make such dispositions of the land as would fulfil the whole of the grantor's design. This direction, however, did not involve the restoration of the passive use or any recognition of the modern passive trust, for B's obligation was to divest himself of the legal estate, not to retain it and hold it on behalf of C.[64]

---

[57] (1532) Bro Ab, Feoff al Uses, 40; cited Ames, *Select Essays in Anglo-American Legal History*, vol ii, p 748.

[58] (1557) 2 Dyer 155a; Digby, *History of the Law of Real Property* (5th edn, 1897), p 375. Jane bargained and sold land (above, p 69) to her son, G, and his heirs, upon the understanding that G was to hold to the use of Jane for life and thereafter to the use of himself in tail. The purchase money was paid, and therefore by implication of law Jane was seised to the use of G. The statute operated upon this use, and gave G the legal fee simple. But further uses had been declared, namely, to Jane for life and then to G in tail, and the question was whether these were valid or not. It was held that they were void.

[59] *Daw v Newborough* (1716) 1 Com 242; cited Ames, vol ii, p 748.   [60] Vol ii, p 336.

[61] *Girland v Sharp* (1595) Cro Eliz 382; Digby, *History of the Law of Real Property*, p 375.

[62] (1635) Toth 188; Nelson 30, sub nom *Morris, Lambeth et Margery v Darston*.

[63] (1958) 74 LQR 550 (JE Strathdene); Simpson, *A History of the Land Law*, p 202; see further (1957) CLJ 72 (DEC Yale); (1966) 82 LQR 215 (JL Barton), arguing that 'the trust of freehold was an accepted institution at any rate in the latter part of the sixteenth century'; and this is supported by two manuscripts: (1977) 93 LQR 33 (JH Baker).

[64] Plucknett, *A Concise History of the Common Law*, pp 601–2.

(b) Rise of modern passive trust

Eventually, however, a change in the political situation facilitated the restoration of the passive use. The passive use had been abolished in 1535 for the sole reason that the King laid the loss of his feudal revenue at its door. But towards the end of the seventeenth century a complete revolution had occurred in the political sphere. Owing to the abolition of the military tenures in 1660[65] and to the gradual fall in the value of money, the feudal dues had become of little consequence and, indeed, the royal finances had been put on a more satisfactory footing. This fact, coupled with an almost universal desire for the old liberty of action, enabled the Chancellor once more to recognise the former distinction between the legal and the equitable estate whenever the intention was that B should hold land on behalf of C. The device eventually adopted by conveyancers to make this intention effective was merely to limit a use upon a use.[66] Thus, if it was desired to create an equitable estate in favour of C, instead of adopting the pre-statute method of a conveyance to A to the use of C, all that was necessary was to add a second use and make the conveyance run to A to the use of B to the use of C. The effect of this was that the statute divested A of his interest and passed the legal estate to B, with the result that, since the second use was not executed by the statute, C was left with a mere equitable estate corresponding with the equitable estate that existed in the pre-statute days under the name of the use.

(c) Creation and terminology

Thus the old distinction was retained in spite of the statute, but both the method of creating the distinction and the terminology adopted to describe it were changed. The first use in favour of B, which was executed by the statute, was still called a use, but the second in favour of C, on which the statute did not operate, was for greater clearness always designated a 'trust'.[67]

The practice ultimately adopted was to leave A out altogether and to create the equitable estate by conveying the land

unto and to the use of B and his heirs in trust for C and his heirs.

The effect of this was that B, called the *trustee*, acquired the legal estate by virtue of the common law; but he also obtained the use, and though he was deemed to take the legal estate at common law and not under the statute, for there was no other person seised to this use,[68] yet, since a use had been declared in his favour, the rule that there could

---

[65] Above, p 40.

[66] Plucknett, *A Concise History of the Common Law*, p 602.

[67] Hayes, *An Introduction to Conveyancing*, vol i, p 54. See Holdsworth, *A History of English Law*, vol v, pp 307–9; vol vi, pp 641–4.

[68] 'The statute ought to be expounded that, where the party seised to the use and the *cestui que use* is one person, he never taketh by the statute, except there be a direct impossibility or impertinency for the use to take effect by the common law': Bacon, *Reading on the Statute of Uses*, p 440.

be no use upon a use prevented the statute from operating upon the second use and passing the legal estate to C.[69]

Thus, despite the complacent optimism of Coke, the old distinction between the legal and the equitable estate was fully restored by the early eighteenth century at the latest. In 1738, Lord Hardwicke stated the position in these words:[70]

> Yet [after 1535] the judges still adhered to the doctrine, that there could be no such thing as *an use upon an use*, but where the first use was declared, there it was executed, and must rest for that estate: therefore, on a limitation to A and his heirs, to the use of B and his heirs, in trust for D, B's estate was held there to be executed by the statute, and D took nothing.
>
> Of this construction equity took hold, and said that the intention was to be supported. It is plain B was not intended to take, his conscience was affected. To this the reason of mankind assented, and it has stood on this foot ever since, and by this means a statute made upon great consideration, introduced in a solemn and pompous manner, by this strict construction, has had no other effect than to add at most three words to a conveyance.

The last remark of the Lord Chancellor, however, though picturesque and arresting, was hardly accurate, for, as we shall see, the statute had a vital and a lasting effect in so far as it enabled a class of future interests (springing and shifting uses), hitherto unknown to the common law, to be carved out of the legal estate.[71]

III THE ESSENTIAL DIFFERENCE BETWEEN THE LEGAL AND THE EQUITABLE ESTATE

The position with regard to equitable estates remained as indicated above until 1 January 1926. If, that is to say, it was desired to create a trust estate, all that was necessary was to convey land *unto and to the use of* trustees in fee simple, in trust for the *cestui que trust*—or beneficiary, as we will designate him in the future.

The questions that now require answering are:

(1) What is the nature of trust estates, and

(2) What is the difference between them and legal estates?

A NATURE OF THE TRUST ESTATE

In the first place it may be said in a general way that the uses that continued, after and in spite of the statute, to have their old effect were simply the same original uses

---

[69] *Samme's Case* (1609) 13 Co Rep 54; *Doe d Lloyd v Passingham* (1827) 6 B & C 305; *Orme's Case* (1872) LR 8 CP 281; *Hadfield's Case* (1873) LR 8 CP 306; *Cooper v Kynock* (1872) 7 Ch App 398; *Sanders on Uses and Trusts*, vol i, p 89; Hargreaves, *An Introduction to Land Law*, pp 96–8.

[70] *Hopkins v Hopkins* (1738) 1 Atk 581, 591.   [71] Below, p 97.

appearing under the different name of trusts.[72] But this is not the whole story. As Lord Mansfield said in *Burgess v Wheate*,[73] 'An use and a trust may essentially be looked upon as two names for the same thing; but the opposition consists in the difference of the practice of the Court of Chancery.' As is inevitable in the development of any legal concept equitable interests became much more elaborate and were adapted to many more purposes than in the days before the Statute of Uses. Lord Keeper Henley said in the same case:[74]

> Geometry was the same in the time of Euclid as in that of Sir Isaac Newton, though he applied the principles and rules to effect greater discoveries and more important demonstrations...An use, say the older books, was neither *jus in re*, nor *ad rem*, but a confidence resting in privity of person and estate, without remedy but in a court of equity. What else is a trust? What other definition can be given of it? No other is attempted. But it is said since the existence of trusts (since the statute), equity has modelled them into the shape and quality of real estates, much more than it did in earlier times when they were called uses. It has made tenants by the curtesy, permitted tenants in tail to suffer common recoveries etc. And why? Because equity follows the law. And between *cestui que trust* and those claiming by, from and under him, it is equity that he should be considered as formally possessed of that estate of which he is and appears substantial owner. But this is only the effect of the equitable jurisdiction's growing to maturity, and was an accident that to a degree accompanied uses as well as trusts. Lord Bacon observes that they grew to strength and credit by degrees and as the Chancery grew more eminent.

Thus uses required that the feoffee to uses should have the fee simple estate, but trusts could be declared upon the estates of tenants in tail, for life or for years; uses were generally passive, that is the feoffee was a dormant instrument compelled by equity to obey the directions of the *cestui que use*, but later development allowed the creation of special trusts under which the trustee might be directed to perform such duties as the sale of land, the accumulation of profits, the management of estates and so on. Again, the use applied only to land, but the subject-matter of trusts has expanded to such a degree that at the present day it includes, not only every conceivable kind of property, but even objects unconnected with property. The trust, for example, has enabled unincorporated associations, such as clubs, trade unions and nonconformist bodies, which, owing to the indefinite and fluctuating character of their personnel, are not persons in the legal sense, both to own property and to fulfil the objects of their formation. The ownership of premises cannot reside in an unincorporated club, but it may be vested in a few persons, who, in the capacity of trustees, will not only have a legally protected ownership but will be amenable to the jurisdiction of the court if they fail to administer the property on behalf of the members and in accordance with the rules.[75] Then again the trust is not the only form of equitable interest known to the

[72] *Lloyd and Jobson v Spillet* (1741) 2 Atk 148 (Lord Hardwicke).   [73] (1759) 1 Eden 177, 217.
[74] Ibid, 248.
[75] See Maitland, *Collected Papers*, vol iii, pp 271–84 (*The Unincorporated Body*); pp 321–404 (*Trust and Corporation*); Warburton, *Unincorporated Associations: Law and Practice* (2nd edn, 1990); Maudsley & Burn, *Trusts and Trustees* (7th edn), pp 378-99.

law. The interest that arises in favour of a person who has made a valid contract for the purchase of land or a valid contract for a lease; the right that an owner possesses to enforce certain restrictive covenants; the interest in land retained by a person before 1926 who mortgaged the land in return for a loan of money—these are all equitable interests[76] and exhibit the one great characteristic that distinguishes them from legal estates.

B DIFFERENCE BETWEEN LEGAL AND EQUITABLE ESTATE

That brings us to the second point. What is that characteristic, or, in other words, what is the difference between the legal and the equitable estate?

As we have said, the difference is not adequately defined by the statement that the legal estate confers an empty title, while the equitable estate amounts to beneficial ownership of the land. The fundamental distinction is this: a legal estate is a right *in rem*, an equitable estate a right *in personam*, that is to say, the former confers a right enforceable against the whole world, the latter one that can be enforced only against a limited number of persons.

(1) Legal Estate

If A is entitled to the legal estate in Blackacre, then as a general rule it is true to say that, apart from some voluntary act of his own, he cannot be deprived of his rights in the land by the fraud of some third person. If, for example, the owner of a fee simple grants a legal term of years in the land to A and then sells and conveys the fee simple to X, fraudulently concealing the existence of the lease, the rights of A as the owner of a legal estate are entirely unaffected by the transaction.

Exactly the same principle applies to all legal as distinct from equitable interests.[77] For example, a landowner may allow his neighbour to enjoy a right over his land such as a right of way. If the right that is so enjoyed exhibits certain characteristics (to be described in chapter 18), it is known as an easement, and an easement is capable of being a legal interest and, if so, is permanently enforceable against all subsequent owners of the land over which it is exercisable. That land may very well be bought by a person who does not know of the right and has no reason to know of it, but nevertheless it will be binding on him. The person entitled to enjoy the right has a legal interest that can be enforced against all persons whether they know of it or not.

---

[76] Below, pp 91–3.

[77] The operation of the principles described here was modified by the introduction of the registration of estates and interests in 1925 (in both registered and unregistered land), which was taken further in relation to registered land by LRA 2002; but, as we shall see, the underlying principles, and the distinction between legal and equitable estates and interests, remains essentially unchanged: below, Ch 5.

(2) Equitable Estate

So then the legal estate, or any legal interest, is binding against all people, no matter how they have obtained what seem to be absolute and unrestricted rights over the land. But the rights conferred upon the owner of an equitable estate have never been as extensive as this, though they are enforceable against so many people that they come to look very like rights *in rem*. The general principle is that they are enforceable only against those persons who, owing to the circumstances in which they have acquired the land, ought in conscience to be held responsible. This principle derives from the consistent refusal of the Chancellor to enforce the use against a person who acquired the land from the feoffee to uses unless he was affected by the confidence that had been reposed in the original feoffee. 'As the use had its beginning in personal confidence, so its continuance, as a binding obligation on the legal owner of the land, was measured by the continuance of that confidence.'[78] The number of persons who were deemed to be affected by this confidence gradually grew in number.

(3) Extension of Enforceability of Equitable Estate

The starting point was of course that the trustee himself, or the *feoffee to uses* as he was originally called, was permanently bound to observe the trust. The first extension of this was made in 1465, when it was held that a person who bought the land from the trustee with notice of the conditions upon which the land was held was bound by the trust.[79] The next stage, reached in 1522, was that all those who came to the trustee's estate by way of succession, such as his heir or doweress, were held responsible for carrying out the trust.[80] The law, which had reached this point at the time when the Statute of Uses was passed, was adopted and carried further by the courts when equitable estates reappeared under the name of trusts. Thus it was decided by *Chudleigh's Case* in 1595[81] that a voluntary alienee from the trustee, that is to say, a person who had acquired the estate without giving valuable consideration for it, was bound by the trust even though he had no notice of its existence. Therefore a trust was enforceable both against a man who bought the land *with notice* of the trust, and against one who received it by way of gift but without notice. Again, at some date after 1660,[82] trusts were made enforceable against creditors of the trustee who had seized the trust estate with a view to obtaining satisfaction for the debts due to them.

The one person, therefore, whose conscience was unaffected and against whom the equitable estate became unenforceable was the purchaser for value of the legal estate *without notice* of the rights of the *cestui que use*. If the feoffee to uses fraudulently sold and conveyed the land to an unsuspecting purchaser, the equity of the *cestui que*

---

[78] Hayes, *An Introduction to Conveyancing*, vol i, p 42. See also Sanders, *Uses and Trusts*, vol i, pp 55–6.

[79] YB 5 Ed IV, Mich pl 16, fo 7. For the whole of this subject, see Jenks, *Modern Land Law* (1899), pp 141 ff.

[80] YB 14 Hen VIII, Mich pl 5 fo 8, cited Jenks; Maitland, *Equity*, p 117.

[81] 1 Co Rep 113b, 122b; *Mansell v Mansell* (1732) 2 P Wms 678.   [82] See Maitland, *Equity*, p 112.

use was gone so far as the land was concerned and he could not claim relief against the purchaser. Nevertheless his equity remained in full force against the fraudulent trustee:

> The *very* land was irrecoverably gone, but the use remained; and while the conscience of the person *to* whom the possession had passed was unaffected, the person *from* whom it had passed was still liable, as before, to fulfil the equities tacitly included in the use.[83]

(4) Summary

We are now in a position to summarise the essential difference between the legal and equitable estate as it stood before the reforms of 1925. We have said that a legal interest is enforceable against all the world, while an equitable interest can be enforced only against a limited number of persons. To be more precise, if an equitable interest in Blackacre was created in favour of X, the following were the persons who, if they subsequently acquired an interest in land, would take that interest subject to X's right:

(1) a person who acquired Blackacre as the heir, devisee or personal representative of the trustee;

(2) a person who had acquired the legal estate in Blackacre *without the payment of valuable consideration*, even though he had no notice of the equitable interest;

(3) a creditor of the trustee, whether with or without notice of the trust; or

(4) a person who had given valuable consideration for the legal estate in Blackacre, but who was affected by notice of the equitable interest.

An equitable interest such as a trust is, then, if we put the matter with strict regard to historical accuracy, one that can be enforced only against those particular persons, but a definition that is almost equally accurate[84] is that an equitable interest is one that is enforceable against the whole world *except a bona fide purchaser for valuable consideration of the legal estate which is subject to the equitable interest, provided that, when the purchaser acquired the legal estate, he had no notice of the equitable interest.* In the case of such a person there is no reason why equity should not allow the common law to run its normal course. Equity follows the law, and will not interfere with the law unless there is some very strong equitable ground for doing so. Where a person has paid for the interest that is secure at law, and moreover has acted honestly and diligently, there is no equitable reason for postponing him to somebody who from the point of view of equity is in no stronger position, and from the point of view of law is in a far inferior position.

The position was put very forcibly by James LJ in *Pilcher v Rawlins:*[85]

> I propose simply to apply myself to the case of a purchaser for valuable consideration, without notice, obtaining, upon the occasion of his purchase, and by means of his purchase

---

[83] Hayes, *An Introduction to Conveyancing*, vol i, p 43.   [84] But see Maitland, *Equity*, pp 120–1.
[85] (1872) 7 Ch App 259, 268, M & B p 60; below, p 90.

deed, some legal estate, some legal right, some legal advantage; and, according to my view of the established law of this court, such a purchaser's plea of a purchase for valuable consideration without notice is an absolute, unqualified, unanswerable defence, and an unanswerable plea to the jurisdiction of this court. Such a purchaser, when he has once put in that plea, may be interrogated and tested to any extent as to the valuable consideration that he has given in order to shew the *bona fides* or *mala fides* of his purchase, and also the presence or the absence of notice; but when once he has gone through that ordeal, and has satisfied the terms of the plea of purchase for valuable consideration without notice, then this court has no jurisdiction whatever to do anything more than to let him depart in possession of that legal estate, that legal right, that legal advantage that he has obtained whatever it may be. In such a case the purchaser is entitled to hold that which, without breach of duty, he has had conveyed to him.

Apparently, the only exception to this immunity enjoyed by the purchaser for value without notice arose where in fact the vendor's only title to convey the fee simple was that he was tenant for life under a settlement, but he fraudulently concealed the existence of the settlement.[86]

C THE DOCTRINE OF THE BONA FIDE PURCHASER FOR VALUE OF THE LEGAL ESTATE WITHOUT NOTICE

There thus emerged the doctrine of the bona fide purchaser for value of the legal estate without notice. Maitland called such a purchaser 'Equity's darling'.[87] This doctrine is a cardinal principle of the land law, and, although it has been shorn of much of its importance by subsequent legislation, it still remains a basis of the law and is even used as a residuary principle in unregistered land to solve problems of the enforceability of third-party rights for which statute makes no provision. We must now look at the details of the doctrine as it was devised by the courts of equity.

(1) Purchaser for Value

The purchaser[88] must have given consideration in money or money's worth[89] or marriage. Otherwise he is a donee and is bound by the equitable interest whether he has notice of it or not. The consideration need not be adequate, and may even be nominal.[90] Money's worth extends to all forms of non-monetary consideration, such as other land or chattels or stocks and shares. Marriage is limited to a future marriage; a promise in consideration of a future marriage, called an ante-nuptial agreement, is

---

[86] *Weston v Henshaw* [1950] Ch 510; see, however, *Re Morgan's Lease* [1972] Ch 1; below, p 1046, n 36.

[87] See Maitland, *Collected Papers*, vol iii, p 350.

[88] For the different meanings of 'purchaser', see *IRC v Gribble* [1913] 3 KB 212, 218; below, p 155, n 22.

[89] *Thorndike v Hunt* (1859) 3 De GF & J 563.

[90] *Bassett v Nosworthy* (1673) Cas temp Finch 102; *Midland Bank Trust Co Ltd v Green* [1981] AC 513, M & B p 72.

deemed to have been made for value,[91] but a promise made in consideration of a past marriage, called a post-nuptial agreement, is not.

A purchaser is not limited to a person who acquires the fee simple, but includes a mortgagee[92] or lessee.

(2) Legal Estate

The purchaser must normally show that he has acquired a legal estate in the land. The doctrine is based on the maxim that where the equities are equal the law prevails; and as between the beneficiary's equitable interest and the innocent purchaser's legal estate, the equities are equal, and the purchaser's legal estate prevails.

On the other hand, the purchaser of an equitable interest in land takes the land subject to existing equitable interests in the same land whether he has notice of them or not.[93] The competition here is between two equitable interests and the rule is that the first in time prevails: *qui prior est tempore potior est jure*.[94]

The purchaser for value of an equitable interest without notice, however, takes free of an *equity* or a *mere equity*.[95] An equitable interest is distinguishable from what is generally called an *equity* or a *mere equity*. This is a concept that defies precise definition, but it includes a right to enforce an equitable remedy, such as specific performance, rescission for misrepresentation or undue influence, rectification for mistake and the rights to consolidation of mortgages or to reopen a foreclosure.[96]

The defence of the purchaser for value without notice thus avails the purchaser of an equitable interest against the owner of an earlier equity, but not against the owner of an earlier equitable interest.

(3) Without Notice

(a) Actual notice

A purchaser of the land for valuable consideration from the trustee was not liable to carry out the trusts provided that he had no notice of them when he acquired the legal estate, but it is obvious that, unless a careful watch had been kept on the conduct of such a purchaser, he would have taken care not to have notice. The definition of

---

[91] *A-G v Jacobs-Smith* [1895] 2 QB 341.

[92] *Caunce v Caunce* [1969] 1 WLR 286; *Kingsnorth Finance Co Ltd v Tizard* [1986] 1 WLR 783, M & B p 216.

[93] It has, however, been held that, if B, an equitable incumbrancer for value without notice of A's prior equitable incumbrance, gets in the legal estate, he takes precedence over A, even if he then has notice; *Bailey v Barnes* [1894] 1 Ch 25; cf *McCarthy and Stone Ltd v Julian S Hodge & Co Ltd* [1971] 1 WLR 1547, M & B p 76.

[94] *Phillips v Phillips* (1861) 4 De GF & J 208, 215; *Cave v Cave* (1880) 15 Ch D 639. But see below, p 895, for the modification of this principle by LPA 1925, s 137(1).

[95] However, in registered land a mere equity has the same effect as against third parties as an equitable interest: LRA 2002, s 116(b); below, p 905.

[96] *Phillips v Phillips*, above, 218 (Lord Westbury); *National Provincial Bank Ltd v Ainsworth* [1965] AC 1175, 1238 (Lord Upjohn), 1252–3 (Lord Wilberforce); (1955) 71 LQR 480 (RE Megarry); *Shiloh Spinners Ltd v Harding* [1973] AC 691, 721 (Lord Wilberforce). See generally Ch 22 (Equities and Proprietary Estoppel).

notice was therefore made elastic. If a purchaser was diligent enough and acted in a reasonable and sensible manner, making all those investigations that the purchaser of land normally did make, then he was affected only by actual notice of trusts. If, however, he omitted to make the usual investigations then he might be affected by constructive notice.

(b) Constructive notice

Constructive notice[97] is generally taken to include two different things:[98]

(1) The notice that is implied when a purchaser omits to investigate the vendor's title properly or to make reasonable inquiries as to deeds or facts that come to his knowledge.

(2) The notice that is imputed to a purchaser by reason of the fact that his solicitor or other legal agent has actual or implied notice of some fact. This is more particularly called 'imputed notice'.[99]

Now the question is: what ought a prudent, careful person to do when purchasing an estate? The answer will afford us an insight into the equitable doctrine of notice, and at the same time will show us in what circumstances a purchaser takes an estate free from any trust or other equitable interests to which it may be subject.

It is not necessary to go back further than the Conveyancing Act 1882, in which section 3 was designed to protect purchasers against a doctrine that had been refined to the point of unfairness. The section is now re-enacted in section 199(1)(ii) of the Law of Property Act 1925, which provides that no purchaser is to be prejudicially affected by notice of any instrument, matter, fact or thing unless he actually knows of it, or unless he would have known of it had such inquiries and inspections been made as ought reasonably to have been made by him, or unless his counsel, solicitor or other agent, while carrying out that particular transaction, actually obtains knowledge of that instrument, matter, fact or thing, or would have obtained it had he made reasonable inquiries and inspections. What it comes to, then, is that a purchaser is deemed to have notice of anything that he has failed to discover because he or his agent did not investigate the title properly, or did not inquire for deeds relating to the land, or did not inspect it.

We will take these three cases separately:

(1) Notice from not investigating title

For centuries it has been regarded as essential that one who is purchasing land should investigate the title of his vendor, that is to say, should require the vendor to 'prove his title' by producing evidence to show that the interest that he has contracted to sell is vested in him, and that it is unincumbered by rights and interests enforceable against the land by

[97] Sugden, *The Law of Vendors and Purchasers of Estates* (14th edn, 1862), p 755.

[98] White and Tudor, *Leading Cases in Equity* (9th edn, ed Hewitt and Richardson, 1928), vol ii, p 172.

[99] *Kingsnorth Finance Co Ltd v Tizard* [1986] 1 WLR 783, M & B p 216. See also *Sharpe v Foy* (1868) 4 Ch App 35; *Re Cousins* (1886) 31 Ch D 671; *Woolwich plc v Gomm* (2000) 79 P & CR 61 (imputed notice under LPA 1925, s 199(1)(ii)(b)).

third parties. Under the system of unregistered conveyancing,[100] proof of the title[101] takes the form of requiring the vendor to set out the history of the land in what is called an *abstract of title* with a view to showing how the interest he has contracted to sell became vested in him, so as to prove that for a given number of years he and his predecessors have rightfully exercised dominion over the land consistent with that interest. The old rule both at law and in equity was that, if a vendor could adduce evidence of acts of ownership for a period of not less than 60 years, he had satisfied the obligation that lay upon him, and, unless anything appeared to the contrary, had proved a title that the purchaser was bound to accept. But there was no rigid rule about the length of this period, for it was useless to trace the title for 60 years unless the result was to show that the vendor was entitled to convey that interest that he had agreed to sell.[102] For example, a vendor might very well show 60 years' possession in himself, but if this possession was held under a long lease, something more was obviously required to substantiate a right to sell the fee simple. The vendor's proof must always begin with a 'good root of title', in other words, with some instrument transferring the interest that the purchaser now seeks to obtain.

The Vendor and Purchaser Act 1874 provided that in an open contract of sale, that is where no express stipulation had been entered into fixing a precise date from which title should be traced, 40 years should be substituted for the old period of 60 years. Thus under the law as it existed in 1925 a vendor who failed to persuade the purchaser to accept a shorter title was obliged to adduce evidence of acts of ownership stretching over a period of at least 40 years. This obligation was satisfied by the vendor showing what conveyances of the estate—whether inter vivos or as a result of death—had been effected, and, to take a simple illustration, if documents could be produced showing that 45 years earlier X had bought the estate for valuable consideration and then left it by will to the vendor, it was clear that the latter could make a good title.

> If, then, on the sale of a freehold in fee simple, the vendor produces the title-deeds for the last 40 years, and these show that the fee simple in the land sold has been conveyed to him, free from incumbrances, and if there be satisfactory evidence that the deeds produced relate to the land sold, and the vendor be in possession of the land and of the deeds, he has shown a good title to the land.[103]

The general obligations of a vendor in unregistered land are the same under the modern law, except that the period for which title must be traced under an open contract was reduced in 1925 from 40 to 30 years,[104] and further reduced in 1969 to 15 years.[105]

The first duty of the vendor is to prepare an abstract of title, that is a statement of the material parts of all deeds and other instruments by which the property has been

---

[100] For registered conveyancing, see below, pp 131 ff and Ch 28.
[101] For a fuller account of investigation of title, see below, pp 1042 ff.
[102] Williams, *Vendor and Purchaser* (1st edn, 1903), p 76.   [103] Ibid, 84.
[104] LPA 1925, s 44(1), in respect of contracts made on or after 1 January 1926.
[105] LPA 1969, s 23, in respect of contracts made on or after 1 January 1970. See Law Com No 9, *Interim Report on Root of Title to Freehold Land* (1967).

disposed of during the period in question, and also of all facts, such as births, deaths and marriages, which affect the ownership of the land. But in addition to producing this abstract the vendor is required to verify its contents by producing either the actual documents abstracted or the best possible evidence of the contents of those that he is not in a position to produce, and by proving facts, such as births and deaths, which are material to the title.

We can now understand what is meant by constructive notice. One object of investigating title is to discover whether the land is subject to rights vested in persons other than the vendor, and by virtue of the equitable doctrine of notice a purchaser is bound by any right that he would have discovered had he made the ordinary investigations as outlined above. Moreover, if the vendor has imposed conditions requiring a purchaser to accept a title shorter than the statutory period, the doctrine of notice is extended to rights that would have been disclosed if title had been shown for the full period.[106] The third party's rights cannot be prejudiced by an agreement between the vendor and purchaser.

In general, then, it may be said that a purchaser will be bound by equitable interests of which he may in fact be ignorant but whose existence he would have discovered had he acted as a prudent man of business, placed in similar circumstances, would have acted.[107]

(2) Notice from not inquiring for deeds

As we have just seen, the system of unregistered conveyancing requires that a person who is buying land should examine the vendor's deeds, in order both to ascertain whether a good title can be made and to ensure that no third person possesses rights enforceable against the land. It follows from this that, if a purchaser makes no inquiries for the title deeds, and allows them to remain in the possession of a third person, he will be deemed to have notice of any equitable claims that the possessor of the deeds may have against the land.[108] If, however, he makes inquiry but fails to secure their production, his liability for any equity that they would have disclosed depends upon whether or not his failure was due to his own gross negligence. If he is satisfied with an unreasonable excuse for their non-production, he is liable;[109] but if the excuse is reasonable, he may successfully shelter behind the plea of purchaser of the legal estate for valuable consideration without notice.[110]

(3) Notice from not inspecting land

A purchaser should inspect the land and make such inquiries as a reasonable purchaser would make; what those inquiries are depends on the circumstances of each individual case.[111] He will have constructive notice of any rights that are reasonably

---

[106] *Re Cox and Neve's Contract* [1891] 2 Ch 109, 117–18.   [107] *Bailey v Barnes* [1894] 1 Ch 25, 35.

[108] *Walker v Linom* [1907] 2 Ch 104.   [109] *Oliver v Hinton* [1899] 2 Ch 264, 274.

[110] *Hewitt v Loosemore* (1851) 9 Hare 449. On the subject generally, see below, pp 874 ff, especially p 875, n 499.

[111] *Midland Bank Ltd v Farmpride Hatcheries Ltd* (1980) 260 EG 493, 498, (Oliver LJ); M & B p 62.

discoverable.[112] In particular he should make inquiries of any tenant or other person in occupation of the land, since the occupation of a person is constructive notice to a purchaser of the interest of that person; indeed, not only of his interest, but of his other rights.[113] 'A tenant's occupation is notice of all that tenant's rights,[114] but not of his lessor's title or rights.'[115] This is known as the rule in *Hunt v Luck* and it was further elaborated in that case by Vaughan Williams LJ as follows:[116]

> If a purchaser or a mortgagee has notice that the vendor or mortgagor is not in possession of the property, he must make inquiries of the person in possession—of the tenant who is in possession—and find out from him what his rights are, and, if he does not choose to do that, then whatever title he acquires as purchaser or mortgagee will be subject to the title or right of the tenant in possession.

If, however, the person in occupation of the land deliberately puts the inquirer off the scent by withholding information about his interest, he will be estopped from relying on the defence that the inquirer had constructive notice arising from the occupation.[117]

---

[112] *Hervey v Smith* (1856) 22 Beav 299 (purchaser of house held to have constructive notice of equitable easement to use two chimneys for the passage of smoke from the mere fact of there being fourteen chimney pots on top of the chimney stack and only twelve flues in the house); *Kingsnorth Finance Co Ltd v Tizard* [1986] 1 WLR 783, M & B, p 216 (mortgagee held to have constructive notice of mortgagor's wife's equitable interest in matrimonial home due to (a) his agent's inspection at a time prearranged with the mortgagor and (b) his failure to make further inquiries after his agent (i) found evidence of occupation by twin 15-year-old children of the mortgagor and (ii) was informed by the mortgagor, who had described himself as single on the mortgage application form, that he was separated from his wife who was residing nearby). The decision is criticised in [1986] Conv 283 (MP Thompson); (1986) 136 NLJ 771 (P Luxton); [1986] All ER Rev 181 (PJ Clarke). See also *Northern Bank Ltd v Henry* [1981] Ir 1; *Barclays Bank plc v O'Brien* [1994] 1 AC 180, below, p 832 (bank's constructive notice that wife's suretyship agreement was induced by misrepresentation of husband).

[113] *Barnhart v Greenshields* (1853) 9 Moo PCC 18. But not of an equity to rectification of a tenancy agreement which the tenant may have against the vendor: *Smith v Jones* [1954] 1 WLR 1089, M & B p 82. Cf *Nurdin & Peacock plc v DB Ramsden & Co Ltd* [1999] 1 EGLR 119, below, p 1106, n 226.

[114] Eg, an option to purchase: *Daniels v Davison* (1809) 16 Ves 249.

[115] *Hunt v Luck* [1901] 1 Ch 45, 51 (Farwell J); approved by CA [1902] 1 Ch 428, 432. The principle is preserved by LPA 1925, s 14: *City of London Building Society v Flegg* [1988] AC 54, 80 (Lord Oliver of Aylmerton); below, p 1115.

[116] *Hunt v Luck* [1902] 1 Ch 428, 433.

[117] *Midland Bank Ltd v Farmpride Hatcheries Ltd*, above, n 111 (where a company mortgaged its property to a bank, a contractual licensee who was in occupation of a house under a licence from the company, of which he and his wife were in complete control, was held to be estopped from relying on the doctrine; he had 'set up a smoke-screen designed to hide even the possible existence of some interest in himself which could derogate from the interest of the company ostensibly conferred by the mortgage': Shaw LJ at 497); Oliver and Buckley LJJ held that the bank did not have constructive notice, because the licensee was not only in control of the company but also had been negotiating as agent on his principal's behalf. 'He does not thereby make any representation that his principal has an indefeasible title to the property offered as security... but he does at least represent that he has his principal's authority to offer the property free from any undisclosed adverse interest of his own' (Oliver LJ at 498). His failure to disclose that interest entitled the bank to assume that there was no such interest. See (1982) 132 NLJ 68 (HW Wilkinson); *Abbey National plc v Tufts* [1999] 2 FLR 399 (bank had no constructive notice of wife's credit status where bankrupt husband had fraudulently applied for loan on her behalf).

Finally, it is now clear that the rule operates to give a purchaser or mortgagee constructive notice of the interest of a person in occupation, even if the vendor or mortgagor is also in occupation.[118]

(c) Summary

In *Royal Bank of Scotland plc v Etridge (No 2)*,[119] Stuart-Smith LJ summarised constructive notice as follows:

> Where there is a standard procedure for investigating title, a purchaser is fixed with constructive notice of everything that he would have discovered if he had followed the standard procedure. The doctrine of constructive notice is, however, wider than this. It also applies whenever a party is put on inquiry as to the existence of another's rights. If he makes no inquiry he is fixed with constructive notice of whatever he would have discovered if he had made reasonable inquiry: see Law of Property Act 1925, section 199(1)(ii)(a).
>
> If he does make inquiry, the question depends in the first instance on whether he has made reasonable inquiry. If he has, and the results of his inquiries are such as would reasonably allay suspicion, then he takes free from the other's rights. If he has taken reasonable steps to allay suspicion, the question is not whether he could reasonably have done more, but whether, in the light of all the information, including the results of his inquiries, at his disposal at the time when he gave value, any suspicions have reasonably been allayed.

(4) Bona Fide

This requirement is not synonymous with absence of notice. As Lord Wilberforce said in *Midland Bank Trust Co Ltd v Green*:[120]

> The character in the law known as the bona fide (good faith) purchaser for value without notice was the creation of equity. In order to affect a purchaser for value of a legal estate with some equity or equitable interest, equity fastened upon his conscience and the composite expression was used to epitomise the circumstances in which equity would or rather would not do so. I think that it would generally be true to say that the words 'in good faith' related to the existence of notice. Equity, in other words, required not only absence of notice, but genuine and honest absence of notice. As the law developed, this requirement

---

The issues of the binding effect of a licence on a third party (below, p 930) and of the lifting of the veil of corporate personality were not raised. See (1982) 132 NLJ 68 (HW Wilkinson); [1982] Conv 67 (RE Annand); (1982) 79 LSG 464 (H Lawless and J Alder). Cf, in registered land, LRA 2002, Sch 3, para 2(b); below, p 1103.

[118] *Kingsnorth Finance Co Ltd v Tizard*, above, n 112, not following *Caunce v Caunce* [1969] 1 WLR 286; cf the position in registered land: *Hodgson v Marks* [1971] Ch 892, 934–5 and *Williams & Glyn's Bank Ltd v Boland* [1981] AC 487, M & B p 203; below, p 1106.

[119] [1998] 4 All ER 705, 718; for HL, see below, p 830. See also *Macmillan Inc v Bishopsgate Investment Trust plc (No 3)* [1995] 1 WLR 978, where Millett J said at 1000: 'In English law notice...includes not only actual notice (including 'wilful blindness' or 'contrived ignorance', where the purchaser deliberately abstains from an inquiry in order to avoid learning the truth) but also constructive notice, that is to say notice of such facts as he would have discovered if he had taken proper measures to investigate them.'

[120] [1981] AC 513, 528; below, p 1065; *Grindal v Hooper* [1999] EGCS 150 (actual notice an essential but not exclusive element of good faith).

became crystallised in the doctrine of constructive notice that assumed a statutory form in the Conveyancing Act 1882, section 3. But it would be a mistake to suppose that the requirement of good faith extended only to the matter of notice, or that when notice came to be regulated by statute, the requirement of good faith became obsolete. Equity still retained its interest in and power over the purchaser's conscience. The classic judgment of James LJ in *Pilcher v Rawlins*[121] is clear authority that it did: good faith there is stated as a separate test that may have to be passed even though absence of notice is proved. And there are references in cases subsequent to 1882 which confirm the proposition that honesty or bona fides remained something that might be inquired into.[122]

The burden of proving all the elements of the defence is on the purchaser.[123]

(5) Purchaser With Notice From Purchaser Without Notice

A bona fide purchaser for value of a legal estate without notice, who takes free from equitable interests, may nevertheless pass a good title to a purchaser who *has* notice of them.[124] Otherwise the owner of the equitable interest, by proclaiming his right, could make it difficult for the purchaser without notice to sell the land that he had purchased. There is an exception to this rule; where a trustee who is bound by equitable interests sells the trust property in breach of trust to a purchaser without notice, and then reacquires the property, he will again hold it subject to the equitable interests. He cannot take advantage of the purchaser's immunity under the doctrine.[125]

(6) Effect on Equitable Estate

In brief, then, an equitable estate is not as safe as a legal estate. An equitable owner may find himself, without any fault or negligence on his part, postponed to a third person who has obtained the legal estate in the same land, and his remedy will be reduced to that of recovering the value of the estate from the fraudulent or negligent trustee. The facts of *Pilcher v Rawlins*[126] will serve to illustrate this proposition.

> Pilcher, who was the sole surviving trustee of £8,373, which he held in trust for X for life and after his death for X's children, lent the money to Rawlins on a legal mortgage of Blackacre. This was a perfectly legitimate transaction, the effect of which was to vest the legal estate of Blackacre in Pilcher as trustee on the same trusts for X, so that until the mortgage was redeemed by Rawlins, Pilcher acquired the legal and X the equitable estate of the lands.

---

[121] (1872) 7 Ch App 259, 269, M & B p 60; above, pp 81–3.
[122] *Berwick & Co v Price* [1905] 1 Ch 632, 639; *Taylor v London and County Banking Co* [1901] 2 Ch 231, 256; *Oliver v Hinton* [1899] 2 Ch 264, 273.
[123] *Re Nisbet and Potts' Contract* [1906] 1 Ch 386, 398; *Barclays Bank plc v Boulter* [1999] 1 WLR 1919, 1924 (Lord Hoffmann).
[124] *Wilkes v Spooner* [1911] 2 KB 473, M & B p 62.
[125] *Bovey v Smith* (1682) 1 Vern 84; *Lowther v Carlton* (1741) 2 Atk 242; *Sweet v Southcote* (1786) 2 Bro CC 66; *Re Stapleford Colliery Co* (1880) 14 Ch D 432.
[126] (1872) 7 Ch App 259, M & B p 60.

Rawlins then arranged to grant a legal mortgage of Blackacre to Z in return for a loan of £10,000. As things stood this was impossible because a legal mortgage before 1926 necessitated the transfer to the lender of the legal fee simple,[127] and this was vested in Pilcher. Pilcher, however, decided to abet Rawlins in the fraudulent scheme. First of all Rawlins (who had been a solicitor) prepared an abstract of title to Blackacre that stopped short of and excluded the mortgage to Pilcher and thus made it appear that the legal fee simple was still vested in himself. Of course it was not, but at this point Pilcher came into the plot by reconveying his legal estate in Blackacre to Rawlins in consideration of a repayment of X's trust moneys. This repayment was never in fact made, but Rawlins, having thus attained the legal estate, was enabled to transfer it to Z, who paid over the £10,000. The deed of reconveyance was suppressed. When the fraud was discovered, the question was, which of the two innocent parties, X or Z, had the better right to Blackacre. It was held that, as Z had acted reasonably and honestly, the legal interest that had passed to him must prevail over the mere equitable interest vested in X. Pilcher was the sole trustee and as such had the legal estate and the title-deeds. That being so, the effect of his reconveyance was to give the legal estate to Rawlins, and, as the whole mortgage transaction was concealed, there was no document to put Z on inquiry.

D OTHER FORMS OF EQUITABLE INTERESTS

Throughout the account set out above we have principally considered one form of equitable interest, the trust, but though this is the most important species, it is not the only one. The trust, already described, is an interest that corresponds with a legal estate in the sense that just as, before 1926, there could be a legal fee simple, entailed interest or life interest, so also may there be equitable counterparts possessing the same incidents by way of equitable estates.[128] But other equitable interests may exist. The more important of these, which will require a more detailed discussion later, are the following:

(1) Estate Contract

This arises where the owner of a legal estate either agrees to convey it to the other contracting party or to create a legal estate or interest out of it in favour of that other. Thus, if A, the owner of the fee simple absolute in Blackacre, enters into a binding contract to sell it to B, or to create a term of years absolute out of it in favour of B, or to grant a legal mortgage in favour of B, or to grant a legal easement over it in favour of B, the equitable interest in the land as measured by the terms of the contract passes at once to B, although the legal estate or interest is not conveyed or created until a deed of conveyance has been executed.[129] The contract therefore, in these examples, gives rise

---

[127] Below, pp 797–800.
[128] We shall see later (below, p 123) that by the legislation of 1925 it became impossible for entailed and life interests to subsist as *legal* as distinct from equitable estates.
[129] LPA 1925, s 52, below, p 1001. In registered land, the disposition may also need to be completed by registration in order to perfect the legal title: LRA 2002, s 27, below, pp 1008–9.

to, respectively, an equitable fee simple, an equitable lease, an equitable mortgage or an equitable easement. This is an application of a general doctrine, commonly known as the doctrine of *Walsh v Lonsdale*,[130] under which a specifically enforceable contract to create or convey a legal estate or interest is treated in equity as creating the equivalent estate or interest.

(2) Restrictive Covenant

This is a covenant by which the use of the covenantor's land is restricted for the benefit of the covenantee's adjoining land, for example, where it is agreed that it shall not be used for the purpose of trade. The effect of such a covenant, if the necessary conditions are satisfied,[131] is that the covenantee acquires an equitable interest in the burdened land.

(3) Equity of Redemption

This is the right of a mortgagor to redeem the mortgaged property upon payment of all that is due by way of capital or interest.[132]

(4) Equitable Charge

This arises where, without the transfer of any definite estate, land is designated as security for the payment of a sum of money.[133] In such a case, the chargee acquires an equitable interest that entitles him to take proceedings for the sale of the land.[134]

(5) Equitable Lien

This is similar in effect to the equitable charge, and most generally arises when the vendor conveys the land to the purchaser before he has been paid. If so, he becomes entitled by operation of law to an equitable lien on the land for the amount of the unpaid purchase money that is enforceable by a sale under the direction of the court.[135]

(6) Equity by Estoppel

This right, which became fully recognised only during the twentieth century, arises, for example, where A encourages B to believe that he has or will acquire an interest in A's

---

[130] (1882) 21 Ch D 9, M & B p 30; below, pp 215–17, 978–9. [131] Below, p 732 ff.
[132] Below, pp 798–9, 814 ff.   [133] Land can be similarly charged at law. See below, pp 803, 806.
[134] Below, p 872.   [135] Below, pp 979–80.

land, and B relies on this encouragement to his detriment. A is estopped (ie prevented) from insisting on his strict legal rights where it would be unconscionable for him to do so. B has an interest[136] which in equity is enforceable against A and his successors in title.[137]

---

[136] It is an equity, rather than an equitable interest: above, p 84. However, in registered land it has the same effect as against third parties as an equitable interest: LRA 2002, s 116(a); below, p 921.

[137] Below, pp 920–2.

4

SETTLEMENTS BEFORE 1926[1]

Summary

I   **The Strict Settlement**   95
   A Form of Settlement   95
   B Disadvantages of Settlement   97
   C Statutory Reform   101

II **The Trust for Sale**   103

III **Summary of the Two Methods**
    of Settling Land before 1926   105

An owner of property may need to do more than to own it during his lifetime and then to pass it on to someone else when he dies. He may desire to create successive interests, as, for example, by giving it in his will to his widow for her life, with a remainder to the children; or by providing on a son's marriage a life interest for the son, and after the son's death for the daughter-in-law, and after her death for their children. He may even wish to found a family dynasty.

Any historical survey must begin with this latter type of settlement, which was a feature of English social life for many centuries. It was the desire of the aristocracy to order the future destiny of their land and to prevent its sale out of the family that decisively affected the form and substance of real property law. A fee simple owner made a *settlement* by which he retained the benefit of ownership during his own life, but withheld the entire ownership in the shape of the fee simple from his descendants for as long as possible by reducing them, one after the other, to the position of mere limited owners. The English doctrine of estates is ideally adapted to the achievement of this object. The fee simple of infinite duration is divisible into shorter periods of time each of which may be allotted successively to a number of persons, with the result that while these periods are running there is no person able to dispose of the entire ownership.

---

[1] Simpson, *A History of the Land Law* (2nd edn, 1986), pp 233–41; Harvey, *Settlements of Land* (1973); Bonfield, *Marriage Settlements 1601–1740* (1983); English and Saville, *Strict Settlement* (1985), which contains details of several dynastic settlements of land; and essays in Rubin and Sugarman, *Law, Economy and Society 1750-1914* (1984), pp 1–123 (Sugarman and Rubin), 124–67 (Chesterman), 168–91 (Spring) and 209–10 (English); (1988) EHR 454 (E Spring); Spring, *Law, Land and Family* (1993); (1998) 61 MLR 162 (A Pottage).

I THE STRICT SETTLEMENT

A FORM OF SETTLEMENT

(1) Settlement

Settlements in one form or another have been common since at least the early thirteenth century,[2] and indeed for some 200 years after the statute *De Donis Conditionalibus* in 1285,[3] it was possible to grant an estate tail that would descend only from heir to heir and would permanently remain inconvertible into a fee simple. Although by the end of the fifteenth century means had been contrived to cut short such an impolitic tying-up of the land, by allowing any tenant in tail in possession and of full age to bar the entail and so to acquire the fee simple,[4] the urge to keep the land in the family for as long as the law would permit still persisted, and by the time of the Restoration the general form of the *strict settlement* had been established. Suppose, for example, that a fee simple owner, A, a widower, has decided to use the land as a source of endowment for his only son B, who is about to be married, and for B's issue. In such a case the practice for several centuries was for A to execute a deed of settlement by which he limited the land to himself for life; then to B for life and then, after making provision for B's widow and younger children, to the first and every other son of B successively in tail.

Under such a settlement the desire of A to keep the land in the family is at least partly achieved, for no one will be able to acquire complete control over the land before the eldest son of B, who may bar the entail and so convert it into a fee simple as soon as he attains his majority. To create a fee simple absolute, however, the disentailment must either be effected by him after he had become entitled in possession on the deaths of A and B or, if he desired to act earlier, it must be effected with the collaboration of the present possessor. There was no difficulty, therefore, if he waited until the successive life tenants, A and B, were dead, for in that case he was tenant in tail in possession and free to act independently. But even while, say, B was tenant for life in possession, he might join as party to the disentailment and thus enable his son to acquire the fee simple absolute.

(2) Resettlement

This collaboration of life tenant in possession and tenant in tail in remainder—usually father and son—was consistently utilised by conveyancers as part of the scheme to prolong the retention of the land in the family. That scheme would, of course, succeed automatically if the eldest son or other heir in each generation refrained throughout his life from barring the entail, for in that event the entailed interest would descend in due course to his own heir. But the danger was that he would bar the entail when he

---

[2] By gifts to a person and a special class of heirs; below, p 585.
[3] Below, p 585. For the effect of this statute, see Plucknett, *Legislation of Edward I* (1949), pp 125–35.
[4] Below, p 587 (common recovery).

became entitled in possession and would then acquire and sell the fee simple. Hence the long-established practice of making a *resettlement* by which the eldest son, on the attainment of his majority, was in most cases persuaded to bar the entail with the concurrence of his father and then voluntarily to settle the fee simple thus acquired upon himself for a mere life interest with a further limitation in favour of his own sons successively in tail. This ensured that the land would remain in the family for yet another generation. If, therefore, a resettlement was effected in each generation, the land was held by a succession of limited owners and there was nobody who could claim to be owner of the fee simple.[5]

(3) Effect of Statute of Uses 1535

Settlements, as we have said, are of respectable antiquity, but at common law the opportunities of carving up the *legal* fee simple so as to anticipate events that might affect the family in the future were severely restricted, for limitations only of the simplest nature were allowed. The Chancellor, on the other hand, had never imposed restrictions upon limitations of the *equitable* estate. The use might be moulded into any form congenial to its creator and adapted to solve the uncertainties of the future. The Statute of Uses 1535,[6] therefore, played an important part in the evolution of the strict settlement, an evolution that was complete towards the end of the seventeenth century. The flexibility of the use was imparted to the legal estate by the statute. What was impossible at common law might now be achieved by a single assurance, either a grant to uses or a will. The simple expedient of vesting the legal estate in feoffees with a declaration of the uses to which they were to hold, entitled the beneficiaries to legal interests in the land, as and when their rights matured.

(a) Grant of fee simple defeasible by later events

The opportunities of a settlor were now greater. For example, the common law did not permit a person to convey a freehold estate to himself, nor did it recognise any estate limited to take effect after the grant of a fee simple.[7]

Neither of these rules, however, affected the use and they ceased to affect the legal estate into which the use was converted by the Statute of Uses, if the limitation was made by a grant to uses or by will. The normal method of creating a marriage settlement was for the settlor to grant his fee simple to feoffees to the use of himself in fee simple until the intended marriage, and thereafter to the use of himself for life with remainder to such uses in favour of his wife and issue as he might dictate. Thus, after the statute he acquired a determinable fee simple during the interval between the settlement and the marriage, but on his marriage it was displaced in favour of the subsequent limitations, which were themselves legal.[8]

---

[5] For a clear account, see Elphinstone, *Introduction to Conveyancing* (7th edn, ed Maw, 1918), pp 638 ff.

[6] Above, p 73.   [7] The fee simple is the largest estate known to the law: below, p 151.

[8] Digby, *An Introduction to the History of the Law of Real Property* (5th edn, 1897), pp 357–8.

(b) Springing and shifting uses

Again, at common law a freehold estate could not be given to a person to begin at some future date, nor was it permissible to annex to a grant a condition that the freehold should shift from the donee to another person upon the happening of a prescribed event.[9]

Yet, the Chancellor had always protected such limitations of the equitable estate and therefore when uses were by the statute converted into legal estates, a limitation to feoffees to the use of X when he married (springing use) or to the use of Y for life, but if he became insolvent then to the use of Z for life (shifting use), operated to vest a legal estate in X and Z upon the occurrence of the prescribed events.

(c) Powers of appointment

Another innovation of the Chancellor that greatly increased the pliability of settlements was the *power of appointment*. The normal procedure upon the creation of a use was for the feoffor to declare then and there the exact uses to which the land should be held. But such a definitive declaration was not essential. The feoffor might reserve to himself or to a third person a power to declare in the future what uses should arise or to revoke existing uses and substitute new ones in their place. The donee of such a power, who might be a stranger having no proprietary interest, present or future, in the land, was thus enabled before the Statute of Uses to give fresh directions as to the enjoyment of the equitable estate. If, for example, in place of an existing use in favour of A for life, he *appointed* to the use of B in tail, the original feoffees immediately stood seised to the use of B who consequently acquired an equitable estate tail. If the appointment were made after the statute, B would take a legal estate tail.

Thus, through the machinery of powers, an appointor was able to dispose of an estate that he did not own, and the legal ownership might at his instance be freely shifted and modified to suit exigencies occurring after the date of the settlement.

B DISADVANTAGES OF SETTLEMENT

A settlement of land, though it afforded a convenient means of providing for descendants and, when followed by periodic resettlements, of keeping the land in the family, suffered from three particular disadvantages. It tended to render land inalienable, it might have an adverse effect upon the prosperity of the family, and it complicated conveyancing.[10]

(1) Inalienability of the Land

The first of these dangers was inherent in the pliability that the legal estate had inherited from the use. It soon became obvious that, unless some limit of time was imposed upon the power to create future interests, an astute employment of a series

---

[9] For further discussion, see the 17th edition of this book, pp 524–5.
[10] For the conveyancing difficulties, see below, p 102.

of springing and shifting clauses might well render the fee simple inalienable for an unreasonable period. Thus, the general employment in settlements of such devices to create a series of merely limited interests, enduring far into the future, would have starved the market of land to the detriment of the community. The courts have always fought against the creation of inalienable interests and have held them void. Further, they developed what is now called the *rule against perpetuities*, which looks to the date at which a contingent interest will vest, if it vests at all, and hold it to be void as a perpetuity if the date is too remote. The common law rule, which will require detailed treatment later,[11] allowed a settlor to provide that an estate will shift to a person or spring up in his favour upon the occurrence of a prescribed contingency, but it provided that the estate should be void unless the contingency, if it ever happened at all, would necessarily happen not later than 21 years from the death of some person or persons alive when the settlement took effect.

(2) Impoverishment of the Land

(a) Effect of settlement on power of alienation

The chief defect inherent in a system of strict settlements and of periodic resettlements is that at no point of time is there any beneficiary competent to exercise many of the powers of a fee simple owner, unless a right to do so is reserved by the settlement or granted by statute. The person who under this system has every appearance of being owner is the life tenant in possession, but since his beneficial interest must necessarily determine with his death it follows that any interest granted by him must also determine at that moment. A conveyance by him purporting to pass the fee simple will at common law pass to the grantee nothing more than an estate that lasts for the length of his life—an estate *pur autre vie*[12]—and a lease for any number of years will automatically determine on his death unless saved by statute or permitted by the settlement. The grave effects resulting from this limited power of alienation, in the days when the strict settlement was the foundation of landed society, are clear. Given a system in which it was usual for a fee simple owner, in view of his approaching marriage, to limit the land to himself for life and then to his eldest son in tail, and given further the inclination to resettle the land in each generation on the eldest son for life, with remainder in tail to *his* eldest son, it is obvious what a prejudicial effect such a perpetual series of life tenants, each devoid of the power to convey the fee simple estate, must have had not only on the supply of land available for purposes of trade, but also on the prosperity of the settled land itself.

[11] Below, Ch 15 (Future Interests). The common law perpetuity rule was amended by PAA 1964, to allow 'wait and see': below, pp 558 ff; and the law of perpetuities was further simplified, and restricted to future estates and interests in property held on trust, by PAA 2009 which imposed a single mandatory perpetuity period of 125 years: below, pp 575 ff.

[12] Above, p 54.

The common practice, by which the eldest son under a strict settlement was persuaded on reaching his majority to convert his estate tail into a fee simple and then to resettle the fee simple upon himself for a mere life estate with remainder to his own issue in tail, was stigmatised as follows by a critic:[13]

> It is commonly supposed that a son acts with his eyes open and with a special eye to the contingencies of the future and of family life. But what are the real facts of the case? Before the future owner of the land has come into possession, before he has any experience of his property, or of what is best to be done, or what he can do with regard to it, before the exigencies of the future or his own real position are known to him, before the character, number and wants of his children are learned, or the claims of parental affection and duty can make themselves felt, while still very much at the mercy of a predecessor desirous of posthumous greatness and power, he enters into an irrevocable disposition by which he parts with the rights of a proprietor over his future property for ever, and settles its devolution, burdened with charges, upon an unborn heir.

Under such a system there never exists, apart from statute, a beneficial owner capable of selling or dealing with the fee simple. In the words of Sir Frederick Pollock:[14]

> The lord of this mansion is named by all men its owner; it is said to belong to him; the park, the demesne, the farms are called his. But we shall be almost safe in assuming that he is not the full and free owner of any part of it. He is a 'limited owner', having an interest only for his own life. He might have become the full owner...if he had possessed the means of waiting, the independence of thought and will to break with the tradition of his order and the bias of his education, and the energy to persevere in his dissent against the counsels and feelings of his family. But he had every inducement to let things go their accustomed way. Those whom he had always trusted told him, and probably with sincere belief, that the accustomed way was the best for the family, for the land, for the tenants and for the country. And there could be no doubt that it was at the time the most agreeable to himself.

(b) Economic disadvantages

It is clear, in fact, that an uncontrolled system of settlements and resettlements is an evil—both social and economic—to any country that tolerates it, though it was not one that was apparent to the lawyers of the early nineteenth century. Thus we find the Real Property Commissioners in their report of 1829 stating:

> The owner of the soil is, we think, vested with exactly the dominion and power of disposition over it required for the public good, and landed property in England is admirably made to answer all the purposes to which it is applicable. Settlements bestow on the present possessor of an estate the benefits of ownership, and secure the property to his posterity...In England families are preserved and purchasers always find a supply of land in the market.

This language is specious. It is true in the sense that settled land could usually be sold in fee simple, because a settlement might contain, and a well-drawn settlement would contain, powers enabling the tenant for life to deal with the land by way of sale,

---

[13] Cliffe Leslie, *Fraser's Magazine*, February 1867, cited Scrutton, *Land in Fetters* (1886), p 135.
[14] Pollock, *The Land Laws* (3rd edn, 1896), p 9.

lease, mortgage and so on.[15] If he took advantage of such a power and for example sold the land to X, the fact that he was a mere life tenant was no obstacle to the transfer of the fee simple, for the feoffees had been directed by the settlement to hold to such uses as might be appointed by the donee of the power and therefore they now held to the use of the appointee X. Thus under the Statute of Uses, X acquired a legal fee simple. But, although the land could be rendered manageable and saleable by this device, it happened only too often that powers were either omitted altogether or were too restricted in character. Speaking broadly, land was kept in families only at the expense of removing it from commerce and too often starving it of money necessary for its development and improvement. No doubt the evil was not so great under the rural conditions prevalent until the early nineteenth century, but it became urgent when the vast spread of industrialism produced a demand for coal and other minerals, and converted England from an agricultural to a trading community. To appreciate the nature of the problem it is only necessary to examine the position of a life tenant of settled land in, say, 1835. This was admirably summed up by Underhill:[16]

> Unless the will or settlement...contained express powers (which was frequently not the case) a tenant for life could neither sell, exchange, nor partition the settled property, however desirable it might be. If the estate consisted of a large tract of poor country, fruitful in dignity but scanty in rent, and specially if the portions of younger children charged on it were heavy, he too often found it a damnosa hereditas; the rents, after payment of interest on the portions, leaving a mere pittance for the unfortunate life tenant to live on, and quite disabling him from making improvements, or even keeping the property in a decent state of repair. Nay more, if he did spend money in improvements, the money was sunk in the estate to the detriment of his younger children. He could not pull down the mansion-house, however old or inconvenient it might be, nor even, strictly, make any substantial alteration in it. Unless expressly made unimpeachable for waste, he could not open new mines. But in addition to these disabilities, what pressed still more hardly upon him, and on the development of the estate generally, was his inability to make long leases.[17] Consequently when valuable minerals lay beneath a settled property, or the growth of the neighbouring town made it ripe for building sites (the rents for which would greatly exceed the agricultural rent) nothing could lawfully be done. The tenant for life could not open mines himself, even if he had the necessary capital for working them; nor, even if unimpeachable for waste, could he grant leases of them to others for a term that would repay the lessees for the necessary expenditure in pits and plant; nor could he grant building leases or sell for building purposes at fee farm rents. In some settlements powers were expressly inserted, enabling the trustees to grant such leases and to sell, exchange and partition. But frequently, especially in wills, such powers were omitted, and in such cases the only means of doing justice to the land was to apply for a private Act of Parliament authorising the trustees or life tenant to sell, exchange, partition or lease. But such Acts were expensive luxuries, only open to the rich, and beyond the means of most country gentlemen of moderate means.

---

[15] For a seventeenth-century precedent, see Holdsworth, *A History of English Law*, vol vii, p 547.

[16] Underhill, *A Century of Law Reform* (1911), pp 284–5.

[17] A tenant *in tail*, however, was empowered by the Fines and Recoveries Act 1833, s 41, to grant a lease for a term not exceeding 21 years.

C STATUTORY REFORM

(1) Before 1882

When, however, the modern industrial era set in, the legislature took the matter in hand, and in a tentative manner began to pass a series of public Acts of Parliament that enabled settled land to be dealt with in a manner likely to enhance its prosperity. A start was made in the 1840s with statutes that empowered tenants for life to borrow money for the purpose of carrying out permanent drainage improvements and to charge the loan on the inheritance. Then the Improvement of Land Act 1864 enabled a tenant for life to raise money with the consent of the Ministry of Agriculture in order to execute certain specified improvements, and to charge the loan on the corpus of the property.[18] Further examples were the Limited Owners Residences Acts 1870 and 1871, which allowed money to be raised for completing or adding to a mansion-house; and the Limited Owners Reservoirs Act 1877, which sanctioned the same method for the construction of permanent waterworks.

But in 1856 the much more important Settled Estates Act had been passed that contained the germ of all the future legislation on the subject. Its object was to facilitate leases and sales of settled estates, and after being amended by several statutes in the succeeding generation, it was replaced by the Settled Estates Act 1877. This allowed the Chancery Division of the High Court to sanction the sale, exchange or partition of the settled land, and the grant of leases of 21 years for an agricultural or occupation lease, 40 years for a mining lease, and 99 years for a building lease. It also allowed the tenant for life without resorting to the court to grant a valid lease up to a period of 21 years. So this Act made great strides towards permitting all opportunities for the proper development of the land to be seized, but its weakness was that, except in the case of short leases, its enabling powers could not be exercised without an order of the court. It had facilitated dealings, since it substituted an order of the court for a private Act of Parliament, but it stopped short of placing the powers unreservedly in the hands of the tenant for life.

About this time an agitation sprang up for the total abolition of life estates and the restriction of grants to the creation of a fee simple, the argument being that settlements, besides making conveyances difficult and costly, deprived a father of a much-needed power of control over his eldest son, and prevented an estate from being thrown on the market when its poverty made such a course desirable. For better or for worse the argument did not prevail. It was realised that settlements enabled a fair and reasonable provision to be made for all the members of a family, and therefore, while the general features of the time-honoured system were retained, a plan was evolved to prevent settled land from becoming an inert mass through lack of capital or of adequate powers of management.[19]

---

[18] Below, p 785.   [19] Underhill, *A Century of Law Reform*, pp 287–90.

(2) Settled Land Act 1882

The principle adopted by Lord Cairns and incorporated in the famous Settled Land Act of 1882 was to put the entire management of the land into the hands of the tenant for life for the time being, and to give him, at his own sole discretion and without asking the permission of the court or the trustees of the settlement, wide powers of selling, leasing, mortgaging and otherwise dealing with the property. These powers were independent of, and could not be restrained by, the settlement itself, but they were subject to certain statutory provisions designed to protect the interests of all persons entitled under the settlement, and to prevent the tenant for life from acquiring more than a life interest in the income or profits.

The objects of the Act were lucidly explained by Chitty LJ in the following words:[20]

> The object is to render land a marketable article, notwithstanding the settlement. Its main purpose is the welfare of the land itself, and of all interested therein, including the tenants and not merely the persons taking under the settlement. The Act of 1882 had a much wider scope than the Settled Estates Acts. The scheme adopted is to facilitate the striking off from the land of the fetters imposed by settlement; and this is accomplished by conferring on *tenants for life in possession*, and others considered to stand in a like relation to the land, large powers of dealing with the land by way of sale, exchange, lease and otherwise, and by jealously guarding those powers from attempts to defeat them or to hamper their exercise. At the same time the rights of persons claiming under the settlement are carefully preserved in the case of a sale by shifting the settlement from the land to the purchase money which has to be paid into court or into the hands of trustees.

The Act of 1882 was amended in small particulars by further statutes passed in 1884, 1887, 1889 and 1890, but its policy has stood the test of time, and though it was repealed and replaced by the Settled Land Act 1925,[21] its general principles still continue to govern the rights and the liabilities of a tenant for life under a strict settlement.

(a) The legal title

The third disadvantage of a settlement—its aggravation of the complexity of conveyancing—became evident when a tenant for life, by virtue of a power conferred upon him, had agreed to sell the fee simple to a purchaser. In this event, he would prove the title down to the date of the settlement in the normal fashion by tracing the history of the land back to a good root of title, in order to show that the fee simple was owned by the original settlor. So far there was nothing abnormal, but at this point arose the difficulty that the vendor himself did not own the estate that he had contracted to sell. His case would be, of course, that as tenant for life under a settlement he possessed a power, conferred upon him either by the settlement itself or after 1882 by the Settled Land Act, to convey the fee simple. The general rule on this matter is that the exercise of a power, whether it is given by act of parties or by statute, is void unless all the conditions imposed by the instrument or statute from which it derives are literally

---

[20] *Re Mundy and Roper's Contract* [1899] 1 Ch 275, 288.   [21] Below, pp 432 ff.

observed. If attention is concentrated on a sale after 1882, the governing factors in this respect were that the Act of that year empowered a tenant for life under a settlement to convey a good title to the fee simple, provided that the purchase money was paid to the trustees. In other words, before the statutory power of sale or any other statutory power was validly exercisable, it was essential that, *within the meaning of the Act,*

> the instrument under which the vendor held was a 'settlement';
>
> the vendor himself was a 'tenant for life' or one of the persons to whom the statutory powers were given;
>
> the trustees were properly appointed.

In order, therefore, to verify that these conditions were satisfied, it was necessary for the original deed of settlement and, in fact, several further deeds if there had been one or more resettlements, to be abstracted by the vendor and investigated by the purchaser. Thus, in order to satisfy himself that a good title would be made, the purchaser was confronted with the formidable task of scrutinising a series of transactions and documents stretching back perhaps for very many years.

(b) Overreaching of beneficial interests

In contrast to this complication that beset a purchaser of settled land, his position vis-à-vis the beneficial interests under the settlement was simple. This was due to the doctrine of overreaching, which originated in conveyancing practice and was adopted by the Settled Land Act 1882. The Act provided that if the purchaser paid the purchase money to at least two trustees or into Court (and not to the tenant for life) the interests of the beneficiaries under the settlement should be transferred from the land to the purchase money.[22] Thus the purchaser by virtue of the Act took the land free from the beneficial interests; and he did this even though he had notice of them and even though the interests might be legal. The conveyancing advantage to the purchaser is obvious. So far as the beneficiaries are concerned, they lose their opportunity of enjoying the land itself, but, instead, they have equivalent interests in the purchase money. A beneficial interest in a fund of £50,000 is just as valuable as the same interest in land worth £50,000; more valuable, if the money is invested more profitably; less valuable, if the land was a better investment. The question is one of choice of investment of the family capital.

II THE TRUST FOR SALE

So far we have concentrated attention upon the strict settlement. An entirely different way of applying the principle of the settlement to land was by means of a trust for sale, a method that was common in wills for some 500 years and in deeds since the early

---

[22] SLA 1882, ss 20, 22(5), 39(1).

nineteenth century.[23] By 1997, when it was replaced by the trust of land,[24] it had almost superseded the strict settlement.

If it were used to create a family settlement *inter vivos* as described in Section I, above, the transaction would fall into two parts and, though not strictly necessary, would usually be effected by two separate deeds. If, for example, it preceded the marriage of the settlor:

> The first deed in its opening clause conveyed the fee simple to the trustees upon trust (with the consent of the husband until the intended marriage, and after the marriage with the consent of the husband and wife, or of the survivor, and after the death of the survivor at the discretion of the trustees) to sell the said fee simple.
>
> The second clause of the deed directed the trustees to hold the money arising from the sale and the rents and profits accruing prior to the sale upon such trusts as were declared by a deed already engrossed and made between the same parties and on the same date as the present deed.[25]

According to the equitable doctrine of *conversion* the effect of the execution of this deed was that in the eyes of equity the land was notionally converted into money, for that doctrine, based on the principle that equity looks on that as done which ought to be done, insisted that an imperative direction to turn land into money should impress the land with the quality of money no matter how long the sale might be postponed.[26] The important point to notice, therefore, is that a trust for sale relating to the fee simple and containing a succession of beneficial limitations was a settlement of personalty, not of realty.

The second deed set out the beneficial trusts of the personalty into which the realty had already been notionally converted. It would usually provide, first, that the income, whether arising from the invested purchase money or from the rents and profits prior to the sale, should be held in trust for the husband during his life and after his death in trust for his wife if she survived him. Secondly, it would provide that after the death of the husband and wife the capital should be divided among the children or remoter issue of the marriage in such shares as the husband and wife or the survivor should appoint, and, failing appointment, among the children equally.[27]

The investigation of title upon a sale by the trustees raised none of the difficulties that, as we have already seen, formerly attended a sale by a tenant for life under a strict settlement. The legal fee simple was vested in the trustees for sale and it was from them that the purchaser took his title. His main concern was to ascertain that the settlor was entitled to the fee simple that was conveyed to the trustees for sale. As far as the interests of the beneficiaries were concerned, the purchaser took free from them if he paid the purchase money to at least two trustees. In contrast to the position under the strict settlement, overreaching under the trust for sale was automatic: no statutory

---

[23] (1929) 3 CLJ 59, 63 (JM Lightwood).   [24] TLATA 1996; below, Ch 13 (The Trust of Land).

[25] See Burnett, *The Elements of Conveyancing* (8th edn, 1952), pp 455–6.

[26] *Fletcher v Ashburner* (1779) 1 Bro CC 497. The reverse was also true.

[27] Burnett, *The Elements of Conveyancing*, pp 456–8.

intervention was necessary. The legal estate was held by the trustees for sale on trust to sell, and the beneficial interests were imposed upon the proceeds of sale or upon the rents and profits until sale. They were not upon the land. The only trust upon the land was the trust to sell. Where therefore the trustees for sale sold the land in performance of their duty to sell, the land that the purchaser took was unaffected by any trusts; the trusts were and always had been imposed upon the purchase money.

Furthermore, the purchaser was not responsible for the proper application of the money, provided that he paid it to at least two trustees. The beneficiaries must then look to the trustees and to them alone. This was not always so. In earlier days it was considered that the purchaser, since he had notice of the existence of beneficial limitations, was bound to see that the money was applied in accordance with the trust,[28] and it therefore became the usual practice to insert a clause in the first deed authorising the trustees to give the purchaser a receipt exonerating him from liability in this respect. This was made unnecessary, however, by a series of statutes dating from 1859,[29] culminating in:

> The receipt in writing of a trustee for any money...payable to him under any trust or power shall be a sufficient discharge to the person paying...the same and shall effectually exonerate him from seeing to the application or being answerable for any loss or misapplication thereof.[30]

III SUMMARY OF THE TWO METHODS OF SETTLING LAND BEFORE 1926

Before 1926 there had been evolved two methods of settling land: the strict settlement, in which the purchaser took his title from the tenant for life under the Settled Land Act 1882; and the trust for sale in which he took it from the trustees for sale. In both he might overreach the interests of the beneficiaries, even though he had notice of them. As to which was used depended on the object of the settlor. The strict settlement was appropriate where 'land was settled with the object of founding a family or continuing the possession of family estates in the line of primogeniture';[31] here the tenant for life would reside on the land and himself exercise control over it. On the other hand the trust for sale was convenient where the settled property was not to be kept in the family, but was to be treated as an investment and as a source of income for the beneficiaries. It was especially useful where the fund settled was a mixture of personalty and realty and where the ultimate object was the division of land among children equally.

In 1925, the legislature, impressed by the advantages that the trust for sale imparted to the practice of conveyancing, made it the basis of several of the reforms introduced

---

[28] Vaizey, *The Law of Settlements of Property* (1887), pp 1409–12.

[29] LP(A)A 1859, s 23; Conveyancing Act 1881, s 36; Trustee Act 1893, s 20.   [30] TA 1925, s 14(1).

[31] (1929) 3 CLJ 59, 63 (JM Lightwood).

in that year. In particular, it was by extending the machinery and principle of the trust for sale that the law relating to concurrent interests[32] was strikingly simplified.

As we shall see,[33] the simplification of settlements was continued by the Trusts of Land and Appointment of Trustees Act 1996, which replaced the dual system of strict settlement and trust for sale by a unitary trust of land that applies to both successive and concurrent interests.

B THE MODERN LAW

Summary

5

THE SIMPLIFICATION OF THE LAW: 1925, 1996 AND 2002

Summary

Even as late as the end of the war of 1914–18 there were many features of English land law that seemed unnecessarily cumbrous and antiquated to a generation that, for the moment at any rate, considered itself destined to effect a general simplification of life. There was certainly much in the fundamentals of the subject that would seem strange to an impartial critic. Land was the subject not of ownership, but of tenure; and instead of there being one common form of tenure with incidents of universal application, there were the two distinct forms, socage and copyhold, with various divergent offshoots such as gavelkind and borough-English. This division of tenures, which led to differences in the ordinary incidents of ownership and in the modes of conveyance, was complicated by a cross-division under which estates were classified as being either freehold or leasehold, and estates were recognised both at common law and in equity. The main object of the legislation of 1925 was the simplification of conveyancing, and the committee[1] that was appointed to suggest reform was instructed by its terms of reference 'to consider the present position of land transfer, and to advise what action should be taken to *facilitate and cheapen the transfer of land*'. It was found, however, that a necessary preliminary to the attainment of this object was the simplification of the law of real property. It is hardly possible to modernise a system of transfer if the subject-matter of the transfer

---

[1] Acquisition and Valuation of Land Committee, Fourth Report (1919); (1926) 74 U Pa L Rev 767, 768-69 (GC Cheshire).

is itself governed by antiquated rules. An analysis of the legislation of 1925, therefore, requires us to consider how it simplified, first the law of real property, and then the system of conveyancing. We shall, however, also see that the simplification of the law did not stop in 1925. Further significant reforms were effected by the Trusts of Land and Appointment of Trustees Act 1996, with the replacement of strict settlements and the trust for sale by the trust of land; and by the Land Registration Act 2002, which paves the way for electronic conveyancing with the reform of registration of title to land.

I SIMPLIFICATION OF THE LAW OF REAL PROPERTY IN 1925

In 1925 land was subject not to one system, but to three systems of law. This surprising result was caused by the distinction between freeholds and chattels real (leaseholds),[2] and by the existence of two forms of tenure—socage and copyhold.

The law of real property strictly so-called, which governed freehold interests in land, was still different in several respects from that which governed leaseholds. Furthermore, whether the interest enjoyed by a proprietor was a freehold or a leasehold, the land affected would be held either by socage or by copyhold tenure. This was an added complication, since in several important respects the rules governing socage and copyhold lands were divergent. The continued existence of copyhold as a distinct tenure not only disturbed the simplicity of conveyancing, but also tended to inhibit the full exploitation of the land.[3] Not only did the form of conveyance vary according to whether the land was socage or copyhold but, much more serious, there were differences in such legal incidents as the rules relating to modes of descent—the transmission of property by inheritance—and the types of interest that could be created. Indeed, in this there was not even a system of law common to all copyholds, for the actual customs upon which the legal incidents were dependent frequently varied from manor to manor.

There was thus a law of freeholds, a law of leaseholds and a law of copyholds. The obvious solution, therefore, and the one adopted by the legislature, was first to institute one common form of tenure by the abolition of copyhold; then to assimilate as far as practicable the law of real property and of chattels; finally, to abolish certain anachronisms of the common law—irritating survivals that were inimical to a simplified legal system. We shall consider these three improvements separately.

A THE REDUCTION OF TENURES TO ONE COMMON FORM

(1) Abolition of all Tenures except Socage

All previous modes of descent, whether operating by the general law or by the custom of gavelkind or borough-English or by any other custom of any county, locality or

---

[2] Above, pp 59–60.   [3] Above, p 45.

manor, were abrogated.[4] Escheat[5] *propter defectum sanguinis* was discarded and replaced by the right of the Crown to take as *bona vacantia* the interest of a tenant who died intestate and heirless.[6] The honorary services incident to tenure by sergeanty, where they still existed, were expressly reserved, but the tenure itself had already disappeared.[7] An attempt was also made to abolish frankalmoin, though whether it succeeded is doubtful. The Tenures Abolition Act 1660, which by its first section abolished knight service, provided in section 7 that nothing in the first section was to affect frankalmoin. The Administration of Estates Act 1925, instead of abolishing frankalmoin by express language, merely repealed section 7 of the Statute of 1660.[8] This repeal, however, would appear to be fruitless, for even if the seventh section had been omitted from the Statute, frankalmoin would have been unaffected by an enactment that merely abolished knight service. The matter is of little importance, for no land can be held by frankalmoin at the present day unless it has been continuously so held by the same ecclesiastical tenant since before *Quia Emptores* 1290.[9] Finally, and at long last, the decisive step was taken of abolishing copyhold tenure. As from 1 January 1926, every parcel of copyhold land was enfranchised and converted into freehold land held by socage tenure.[10]

(2) Extinguishment of Manorial Incidents

It was realised, of course, that copyhold tenure could not be dismissed in this peremptory manner, for certain manorial incidents had long been associated with it, and to extinguish without compensation incidents that possessed a money value would obviously be unjust to the beneficiary, whether lord or copyholder. The solution adopted was based upon a tripartite classification of these incidents.

(a) Extinguished at once

The first class, consisting of those that had become anachronisms, were extinguished immediately subject to a single payment of compensation.[11]

(b) Continued until 1950

The second class consisted of those incidents that still possessed a money value. These were temporarily saved,[12] but it was provided that they should be extinguished upon the payment of compensation, the amount of which was to be determined either by agreement or by the Minister of Agriculture and Fisheries at the instance of either

---

[4] AEA 1925, s 45(1)(*a*).   [5] Above, pp 38–9.   [6] AEA 1925, s 45(1)(*d*).

[7] LPA 1922, s 136.   [8] AEA 1925, Sch 2.   [9] Above, p 40, n 32.

[10] LPA 1922, Part V, ss 128–37, and Sch 2, as amended by LP(A)A 1924, s 2 and Sch 2; LPA 1922, s 189.

[11] LPA 1922, Sch 12, para 1: forfeiture for an alienation without the lord's licence; liability of the copyholder to customary suits and to do fealty; customary modes of descent or any custom relating to dower, curtesy (below, p 589) or freebench (Blackstone, vol ii, p 337).

[12] Ibid, s 128(2): *rents*; *fines* payable to the lord in certain circumstances; *reliefs* payable to the lord upon descent of the land; *heriots*, the right of the lord to seize the best beast or best chattel upon the tenant's decease; *forfeitures* for a variety of acts by the tenant; the right of the lord to fell *timber* trees.

party. The final date of extinction was to be 31 December 1935, though if by then no agreement upon the amount of compensation had been reached either party might apply to the Minister requiring the amount to be determined, provided that the application was made before 31 December 1940. Owing to the war, this was later extended to 1 November 1950.[13]

(c) Continued indefinitely

The following incidents, falling within the third class, were permanently saved and they continue to attach to the land, unless the parties agree to their extinction upon payment of compensation:[14]

(a) any commonable rights to which the tenant is entitled;[15]

(b) any right of the lord or the tenant to mines, minerals, gravel pits or quarries, whether in or under the land;[16]

(c) any rights of the lord in respect of fairs, markets or sporting;

(d) any liability for the construction, maintenance, cleansing or repair of any dykes, ditches, canals, sea or river walls, bridges, levels, ways, etc.[17]

In registered land, manorial rights are overriding interests[18] and therefore continue to bind all transferees of the land even if the rights are not entered on the register of title. However, such rights are to be removed from the category of overriding interests on 13 October 2013[19] and so will thereafter bind a disponee of the land for valuable consideration only if they have been entered on the register.[20]

Lordships of manors continue to exist;[21] they represent mesne tenure between the Crown and the freeholders. In addition to potential manorial rights, the owner is entitled to be called 'Lord of the Manor' and has the right to the manorial records, which may date from before the Norman Conquest.[22]

---

13 SI 1949 No 836.   14 LPA 1922, s 138(12).   15 Ibid, Sch 12, para 4; below, p 705.
16 Ibid, Sch 12, para 5. As to the right to work out coal in former copyhold land, see Coal Industry Act 1994, s 49.
17 Ibid, Sch 12, para 6.
18 LRA 2002, Sch 1, para 11 (first registration), Sch 3, para 11 (registered disposition of registered estate).
19 Ibid, s 117. See Land Registry Practice Guide 66, pp 5-6.
20 Ibid, s 29. On overriding interests generally, see below, pp 1100-13.
21 Manors could be registered under LRA 1925: LRR 1925, rr 50, 51; but this is no longer possible under LRA 2002. A manor which was registered under LRA 1925 may now be removed from the register on the application of the proprietor: LRA 2002, s 119. See generally Land Registry Practice Guide 22.
22 For a discussion of the contemporary significance of manors by Lord Denning who, as Master of the Rolls, had charge and superintendence of manorial documents, see *Corpus Christi College, Oxford v Gloucestershire County Council* [1983] QB 360, 364-6. In 1985, 29 Lordships were sold at public auction; the highest price paid was £21,200 for the Lordship of Codicote in Hertfordshire. This included a right to hold a fair in the manor on the Vigil and Feast of St James and the two following days: (1985) 274 EG 15.

(3) Unimportance of Doctrine of Tenure in the Modern Law

Thus, after some 900 years of development the doctrine of tenure still characterises the English law of real property. Land is still incapable of ownership by a subject. Every acre is held by a tenant, not owned, though by a gradual process of elimination the various forms of tenure that complicated the law in former days have at last been reduced to the one type—socage. And, given that there is now no distinction between different types of tenure, even the term 'socage' is hardly ever invoked. But what are the practical effects of the doctrine? Are the rights that the English tenant in fee simple enjoys any less valuable, for instance, than those of an absolute owner of land in the State of New York where all feudal tenures have been expressly abolished? Is tenure a mere name, a reminder only of the pomp and splendour of former days? The truth is, of course, that it is a mere historical survival that now has little practical effect. To have styled the tenant a landowner some centuries ago would have been inaccurate, since his very right to retain the land was conditional on his performance of the tenurial liabilities. But in course of time these liabilities have almost entirely disappeared, and it is only on the rarest occasion that anything of value can now be claimed by virtue of tenure. Even until 1926, a lord, if he were still able to establish his lordship, might be fortunate enough to derive an unearned increment under the doctrine of escheat, but he lost even this when the Administration of Estates Act 1925 provided that the land of a tenant who dies intestate without leaving near relatives shall pass to the Crown.[23] The feudal doctrine of tenure has no doubt impressed an indelible mark upon the framework of land law, but it no longer affects the tenant's rights of enjoyment. The living results of feudalism must be sought, not in the realm of tenures, but in the classification of estates[24] that is a peculiarity of English law. Apart from this 'wonderful calculus of estates', as Maitland expressed it, perhaps the sole feudal incident that is a living force at the present day consists of those rights of common that the successors of the copyhold lord and tenant may still hold in the manorial waste. To quote Maitland again:[25]

> Everyone knows that this doctrine [of tenure], however indispensable as an explanation for some of the subtleties of real property law, is, in fact, untrue. 'The first thing the student has to do is to get rid of the idea of absolute ownership.' So says Mr. Williams;[26] but we may add, with equal truth, that the second thing he has to do is to learn how, by slow degrees,

[23] Ss 45, 46(1)(vi). Escheat may, however, still exist if a trustee in bankruptcy of a landowner disclaims the land: *British General Insurance Co Ltd v A-G* [1945] LJNCCR 113; (1946) 62 LQR 223 (RE Megarry), or if a corporation (other than a company incorporated under the Companies Acts) holding real property is dissolved: *Re Sir Thomas Spencer Wells* [1933] Ch 29, 54; *Re Strathblaine Estates Ltd* [1948] Ch 228. See too (1954) 70 LQR 25 (DW Elliott); *Re Lowe's Will Trusts* [1973] 1 WLR 882, 884, where Russell LJ said: 'By a happy chance [escheat to the Crown of realty *propter defectum sanguinis*] has arisen from the past in connection with the Phoenix Inn in Stratford-on-Avon'. See also *Scmlla Properties Ltd v Gesso Properties (BVI) Ltd* [1995] BCC 793.

[24] Above, pp 48 ff.   [25] *Collected Papers*, vol i, p 196. See also Challis, *Law of Real Property*, p 3.

[26] Williams, *The Law of Real Property*, p 17.

the statement that there is no absolute ownership of land has been deprived of most of its important consequences.

If this was true in 1880 when Maitland wrote, the doctrine of tenure is even less substantial after the abolition of copyholds in 1925.

It should be observed that, although the substance has gone, the form remains. To quote Megarry J: 'Hundreds of … phrases and concepts which permeate our law will have to be remembered if reforming zeal ever proposes to sweep away the theoretical structure of tenures and estates upon which English land law rests.'[27]

There is indeed a reforming zeal at the start of the twenty-first century. The Law Commission is proposing to review feudal land law:[28]

Reform is necessary for a number of technical and practical reasons. First, it makes little sense to have a partial retention of feudal land law for 21st century land holdings. Land law has, in most major respects, moved on from ancient concepts and practices and it is inconsistent that remnants remain in operation. Secondly, the remnants that do remain cause uncertainty to members of the public, to practitioners and to the courts due to their complex and archaic nature and their incompatibility with modern case and statute law. Finally, there is an unnecessary and confusing overlap in the main area in which feudal land law finds modern expression: the treatment of ownerless land.[29]

The Commission initially sought to reform this area of the law as part of its project on Land Registration.[30] During the course of the project, however, far-ranging reform of feudal land law was postponed and 'stop-gap' measures substituted. It was felt that more time and further research was needed to understand fully both the law and the best means of reforming it and to gain the agreement of interested parties.[31] Nevertheless, the report called in very strong terms for wholesale reform to follow as 'the present law is indefensible'.[32] Feudal land law is included in the Ninth Programme of Law Reform…

However, the Law Commission has not yet been able to carry out work in this area because of the demands of other projects.[33]

---

[27] *Lowe (Inspector of Taxes) v J W Ashmore Ltd* [1971] Ch 545, 554.

[28] Law Com No 294, *Thirty-ninth Annual Report 2004–05*, para 6.24; *Modern Studies in Property Law*, vol 5 (2009), ch 4 (J Bray). The feudal system of land tenure was formally abolished in Scotland by Abolition of Feudal Tenures etc (Scotland) Act 2000 (asp 5), implementing the Scottish Law Commission's Report on Abolition of the Feudal System 1999 (Scots Law Com No 168). The modern law of immovable property in Scotland is substantially civilian in nature: Zimmermann, Visser and Reid, *Mixed Legal Systems in Comparative Perspective* (2004), pp 643–4 (K Reid and GG van de Merwe); Reid, *The Abolition of Feudal Tenure in Scotland* (2003). In Ireland, the Land and Conveyancing Law Reform Act 2009, ss 9, 10, abolish feudal tenure, but keep retain the concept of an estate in land which retains its pre-existing characteristics but without any tenurial incidents; Wiley, *Irish Land Law* (4th edn, 2010), paras 2.53-2.74.

[29] That is, the doctrines of escheat and bona vacantia.

[30] Law Com No 271, *Land Registration for the Twenty-First Century—A Conveyancing Revolution* (2001). This joint project with HM Land Registry was implemented in the Land Registration Act 2002.

[31] Ibid, para 11.27.   [32] Ibid, para 11.26.

[33] Law Com No 311, *Tenth Programme of Law Reform* (2008), para 4.1. The project will be put forward for consideration for the Eleventh Programme of Law Reform.

B THE ASSIMILATION OF REAL AND PERSONAL PROPERTY LAW

Originally, as we have seen, there were wide distinctions between the law of real and of personal property, but there has been a tendency from an early date to make both subject to the same legal rules, and in the main the rules that have been adopted are those that govern personal property. Thus the legislation of 1925 attempted to complete a process of assimilation that was already far advanced. We may see the picture more clearly if we first consider in what respects a common body of legal rules had been created before 1926, and then review the statutes in 1925 designed to procure as complete a unification as possible.

(1) Matters in which Assimilation had been Effected Before 1926

(a) Remedies for dispossession

The original rule that leaseholds, unlike freeholds, were not specifically recoverable[34] ceased to be true towards the middle of the fifteenth century, by which time the action *de ejectione firmae* was available to the lessee. The actions that lay for recovery of land were still different according as the claimant's interest was freehold or leasehold, but complete assimilation in this respect was attained in the seventeenth century, by which time the action *de ejectione firmae* had been borrowed from the law of chattels real and, under the name of the action of ejectment, had been adapted to the recovery of freeholds.[35]

(b) Power of testamentary disposition

It was always possible to bequeath leaseholds and other forms of personal property, but the feudal law would not admit a will of freeholds. A partial power of testamentary disposition over real property was obtained, however, in 1540, when the Statute of Wills permitted tenants to devise all their socage lands and two-thirds of their land held in knight service. This testamentary power was completed by the Tenures Abolition Act 1660,[36] which converted knight service tenure into free and common socage.

(c) Availability of property for creditors

At an early date leaseholds and other forms of personal property belonging to a deceased debtor constituted assets available for all creditors, but the general rule was that a fee simple estate passed directly to the heir or devisee of a deceased tenant and could not be seized by his creditors. Gradual inroads into this immunity of real property were, however, made by statute and by equity, and assimilation was almost attained in 1833, when the Administration of Estates Act made all land belonging to a deceased debtor available as assets for the one class of creditors—namely, simple contract creditors—who had not already obtained a remedy against freeholds. There

---

[34] Above, p 58.   [35] Holdsworth, *A History of English Law*, vol vii, pp 4 ff.   [36] Above, p 40.

was, however, still a difference in remedies, for to render personal property available a creditor had to proceed against the personal representatives, whereas to satisfy his claim against real property, which did not vest in the personal representatives, he had to bring a suit in equity for administration. Assimilation on this point came with the Land Transfer Act 1897, which provided that realty should vest in the personal representatives, as had always been the practice with personalty.

The law that regulated the right of a creditor to seize the land of his *living* debtor was also assimilated before 1926. At common law all the chattels, real and personal, of a judgment debtor might be seized, but there was no right to satisfaction out of his freeholds. The Statute of Westminster 1285 made half the debtor's land available for creditors, and this was extended to the whole of the land by the Judgments Act 1838.

(2) Matters in which Assimilation was Effected by the Legislation of 1925

The process of assimilation was carried further by the legislation of 1925 in the following respects.

(a) Size and nature of estates and interests

Before 1926 there was a fundamental distinction between realty and personalty with regard to the interests that might be created.

In the case of real property it has been possible for many centuries to create not only legal and equitable estates of different sizes—namely, the fee simple, the estate tail and the life estate—but also to split the full fee simple up into a series of partial and successive legal or equitable interests, as for example by a grant to A for life, then to B in tail, and then to C in fee simple.

The position with regard to personal property was different. Pure personalty (goods and money) and chattels real (such as a lease for 20 years) were *at common law* the subjects of absolute ownership only. They were outside the doctrine of estates altogether, and they could not be divided into successive interests. A grant of an existing term of years to A for life or in tail made A at common law the owner of the entire term. A gift for an hour was a gift for ever. The position *in equity* was different, for to a limited extent equity did permit successive interests to be created in personalty if the device of a grant to trustees was adopted. If the owner of a leasehold for 30 years granted it to trustees

upon trust for A for life and then upon trust for B for life,

A did not become absolute owner of the whole term as he would have done at common law, but held merely for life, while on his death B similarly became entitled to a life estate. The interests of both A and B were equitable. There was one method, however, though it was seldom used, by which even at common law an effective life estate might be given in personalty—namely, by will. Without adopting the instrument of a trust a testator might make a direct bequest of a leasehold

to A for life with a further gift to B for life,

and the bequests would be upheld. But it is important to observe that, before 1926, it was impossible to create an estate tail in leaseholds either by a direct bequest or through the instrumentality of trustees. A term of years, not being an estate of inheritance, could not be entailed.[37]

A summary of the law as it stood in 1925 is, then, that in real property there might be legal or equitable fees simple, estates tail or life interests, either alone or in succession, but that in personal property there was normally only absolute ownership, though there might be equitable and, exceptionally, legal life interests.

Assimilation, as regards both the size of the interests that could be created, and their nature when created, was, however, effected as from 1 January 1926 by the Law of Property Act 1925. In the first place this provided that personalty could be entailed.[38] The result was that the nature of the subject-matter no longer affected the quantitative interest that could be carved out of it. In realty there may be a fee simple estate, in personalty absolute ownership; while in both cases either entailed interests or life interests could validly be created. Secondly, as we shall see later,[39] entailed and life interests, whether in real or in personal property, can no longer exist as legal estates, but must always be equitable. Moreover, it is no longer possible to have a future *legal* estate in freeholds.

(b) Descent on intestacy

Perhaps the most striking difference between realty and personalty in 1925 lay in the rules that regulated their descent, or distribution upon the death of the owner intestate. The old canons of descent, based upon feudal doctrines as amended by statute, governed the descent of fee simple and entailed estates, while the Statutes of Distribution contained a different set of rules prescribing what relatives were entitled to share the leaseholds and personal chattels of the deceased. Both these systems, together with various customary modes of descent, were abolished and new distributive rules were introduced that apply to both real and personal property.[40] The old canons of descent have, however, been retained for entailed interests.

(c) Order in which assets were applied for payment of debts

It is essential that definite rules prescribe the order in which the beneficiaries under a will must be deprived of their interests for the benefit of the unpaid creditors of the testator. The rules before 1926 on this matter represented another difference between real and personal property, for they required the exhaustion of the general personal estate before recourse was had to the realty. They were replaced by new provisions in

---

[37] *Leventhorpe v Ashbie* (1635) 1 Roll Abr 831.

[38] LPA 1925, s 130 (1); below, p 599. Entails can no longer be created after 1996: TLATA 1996; below, p 605.

[39] Ibid, s 1(1)–(3); below, pp 123–4.

[40] AEA 1925, ss 45, 46, as amended by IEA 1952, Family Provision Act 1966, Law Reform (Succession) Act 1995, s 1 and Civil Partnership Act 2004. For the detail of the law of intestate succession see the 16th edn of this book, ch 26.

the Administration of Estates Act 1925 which, from this point of view, put realty and personalty on the same footing.[41]

(d) Necessity for words of limitation

A conveyance that was intended to pass the whole fee simple had under the old law to contain technical words of limitation, namely, 'to A and *his heirs*' or 'to A *in fee simple*', otherwise it operated to pass only a life estate. Such words were not necessary in the case of a transfer of leaseholds; a simple grant to A, without more, was sufficient to transfer the whole interest of the grantor. Assimilation on this point, however, was effected by the Law of Property Act 1925,[42] which provides that a conveyance of freehold land without words of limitation shall pass the whole interest held by the grantor unless a contrary intention appears in the conveyance.

(e) Method of creating legal mortgages

The method of creating a legal mortgage of the fee simple before 1926 was by a conveyance of the legal fee simple to the mortgagee with a proviso that he should reconvey the estate upon repayment of the loan; but where the subject-matter of the mortgage was a leasehold interest, the almost universal practice was for the mortgagor to grant a sub-lease of the property to the mortgagee. This particular difference between freeholds and leaseholds disappeared after 1925: the practice of conveying the fee simple was forbidden, and it was enacted that a legal mortgage of freeholds must be made by the grant of a lease, or by a legal charge that had equivalent effect.[43]

(f) Application of rule in *Dearle v Hall*

If successive assignments or mortgages of an *equitable* interest in property were made before 1926, the order in which the several assignees or mortgagees were entitled to repayment out of the property depended upon the nature of the property. If it was land, whether freehold or leasehold, they ranked for payment according to the order of time in which they had taken their assignment or mortgage; but if it was pure personalty, the rule in *Dearle v Hall*[44] applied, and the priorities were governed by the order of time in which the assignments or mortgages had been notified to the trustees of the personalty. This rule now applies to equitable interests in unregistered land, so that a later assignee who is the first to notify the estate owner of the land affected ranks prior to an earlier assignment of which he had no notice when he took his own assignment.[45]

(3) *Remaining Differences Between Realty and Personalty*

The above review of the differences between realty and personalty that were eradicated by the legislation of 1925 shows that the law relating to the two forms of property has

---

[41] AEA 1925, s 34(3), Sch 1, Part II.   [42] S 60(1); below, p 156.
[43] LPA 1925, s 85(1); below, p 803. Under LRA 2002 it is now no longer possible to create a mortgage of registered land by the grant of a lease; below, p 806.
[44] (1823) 3 Russ 1.
[45] LPA 1925, s 137; below, pp 895 ff. Priority in registered land has a different rule: below, p 897.

been assimilated as far as is possible. Certain differences must, of course, inevitably persist. For instance, easements and profits may subsist in land, but not in pure personalty; time under the Limitation Act 1980 varies according as the subject-matter is realty or personalty; the forms of disposition of interests in property are different— and so is the procedure on disposition, for investigation of title, though not usual in the case of personalty, is essential upon the transfer of an interest in land. Indeed, the very system of registration of title to estates in land emphasises the different significance of realty as compared with personalty. It would seem that most of these divergences must always in the nature of things continue to exist, since they result inevitably from the physical difference between the two forms of property.

C THE ABOLITION OF CERTAIN ANACHRONISMS

A subsidiary part of the simplification of land transfer was the abolition of certain real property rules and doctrines that, though they had originally been introduced to preserve principles of importance in feudal days, were nothing more than obstructive anachronisms in 1925. The abolitions and alterations of this character effected by the various Acts will be described later, and we shall therefore here simply list the most important:

(1) the abolition of the rule in *Shelley's Case*;[46]

(2) the indirect abolition of the old contingent remainder rules;[47]

(3) the abolition of the rule in *Whitby v Mitchell*;[48]

(4) the almost complete abolition of the old canons of descent;[49]

(5) the final abolition of the doctrine of *Dumpor's Case* so far as it related to leases;[50]

(6) the reversal of the rule that husband and wife were always one person for the purposes of the acquisition of land;[51]

(7) the abolition of special occupancy.[52]

II SIMPLIFICATION OF CONVEYANCING IN 1925, 1996 AND 2002

There are two systems of conveyancing in England and Wales today; the unregistered system, under which title to land is deduced from past transactions relating to the property, and the registered system, where the title is recorded on a national register

---

[46] Below, p 596.   [47] Below, p 620.   [48] See the 17th edn of this book, p 519.
[49] Above, p 117.   [50] Below, p 267.   [51] Below, p 1026.
[52] See the 16th edn of this book, p 294, n 19.

and is guaranteed by the State. The registered system under the Land Registration Acts 1925 and 2002 has gradually superseded the unregistered system and since 1990 has been made compulsory over the whole of England and Wales; compulsory in the sense that dealings in land must now be carried out under the new and not the old system of conveyancing.[53] A detailed discussion of both systems will be found in Part IV.[54] In this section we are concerned with a general outline of the two systems, and with a comparison of their main features from the point of view of a purchaser. As we shall see,[55] conveyancing under the unregistered system is still relevant, but it is gradually becoming obsolete: for every parcel of land, the freehold title to which has not yet been registered,[56] the next conveyance[57] will still be effected (and the title to the estate will still be investigated) under the system of unregistered conveyancing. But the title will then be placed on the register and subsequent dealings will be governed entirely by the system of registered conveyancing.

A CONTRACT BEFORE CONVEYANCE

In both unregistered conveyancing and registered conveyancing, a contract for the sale of land usually precedes the conveyance of the legal estate to the purchaser.[58] As a matter of common practice, the purchaser will make some of his inquiries in relation to the property before the contract is entered into; others in the period between the contract and the conveyance. We shall consider in detail the law and practice governing the contract, and its effect, in Chapter 24. From the outset, however, it should be realised, first, that since 1989 a contract for the sale or other disposition of land must be in writing, signed by both parties;[59] and, secondly, that the effect of a contract for the sale of land is very significant: under the doctrine of *Walsh v Lonsdale*,[60] a specifically enforceable contract to create or convey a legal estate or interest is treated in equity as creating the equivalent estate or interest. A contract for the sale of land—commonly termed an *estate contract*[61]—therefore has the effect of creating an immediate equitable interest in favour of the purchaser.

---

[53] Below, pp 131 ff.   [54] Below, Chs 27 and 28.   [55] Below, p 132.

[56] By 2010 the freehold title to 73 per cent of the area of England and Wales had been registered: below, p 132, n 125.

[57] Compulsory registration is triggered not only by the transfer of the freehold, but other dispositions, such as certain forms of mortgage, and the range of triggers may be extended: LRA 2002 ss 4, 5; below, pp 1073–5.

[58] Similarly, a contract for a lease may be made first, and then followed at a later date by a formal grant of the legal term of years absolute; below, p 210. Although it is less common, the owner of an estate in land may also contract to create an interest in it, such as an easement or a charge, the actual creation of the interest to follow later.

[59] LP(MP)A 1989, s 2 (contracts entered into after 26 September 1989). A contract entered into before 27 September 1989 was valid even if not made in writing, but would be enforceable by action only if evidenced by a signed memorandum (LPA 1925, s 40), or if there was a sufficient act of part performance by the party seeking to enforce it; below, pp 961 ff.

[60] (1882) 21 Ch D 9, M & B p 30; below, pp 215–20, 978–9.   [61] Above, p 91.

B UNREGISTERED CONVEYANCING

Under the system of unregistered conveyancing, a purchaser must make inquiries on two matters—first, that the vendor is entitled to convey the estate that he has contracted to sell, and, secondly, that there are no incumbrances in favour of third parties that will continue to affect the land after the conveyance.

The legislation of 1925 made no fundamental alteration in the practice relating to proof of title to unregistered land,[62] but devoted its main attention to the question of incumbrances. There may well be no undisclosed incumbrances, but because of the doctrine of constructive notice, a purchaser has no practical choice but to institute an expensive inquiry. Land is different from such subjects of ownership as goods, since more often than not it is affected by rights vested in parties other than the ostensible owner.

A may appear to be absolute unincumbered tenant in fee simple of Blackacre, but investigation may disclose that B has an easement of way over the land, that C has a right to prevent the erection of buildings upon it, or that D, having lent £10,000 to A, has taken a mortgage over Blackacre as security for repayment of the loan.

The power to create rights of this description in favour of third parties, and enforceable primarily against the land itself rather than against its owner, is a valuable, in fact an inevitable, feature of our social life. For the sake of brevity, we shall refer to such rights as third-party rights.

(1) Classification of Third-party Rights

In some cases (such as easements and restrictive covenants), third-party rights are a necessary local complement of land ownership; in others they originate in the financial requirements of owners (such as mortgages); while in others (such as the rights of a wife who has contributed to the purchase price where the legal estate is vested in the husband alone) they are due to the social traditions of family life. They may be conveniently divided into two categories:

(1) concurrent or successive beneficial interests in land arising either under a trust of land or a settlement, such as the wife's beneficial share in the family home, or financial provisions made for a widow and after her death for the children of the marriage;

(2) other legal or equitable interests in the land arising under some other transaction connected with the landowner's activities as a landowner or business man. Examples of this second class are easements, profits, restrictive covenants, estate contracts, mortgages and annuities.

But whatever their origin or character, it is clear that the possibility of their existence, and the risk that they may continue to bind the land after its sale, must cause a purchaser to enter into the transaction with care, and without undue haste.

---

[62] Above, pp 85 ff.

(2) Extent to which a Purchaser was Bound by Third-party Rights before 1926

The extent to which a purchaser was affected by third-party rights before 1926 depended upon the fundamental distinction between the legal and the equitable estate.[63] A bona fide purchaser for value of the legal fee simple that was subject to third-party rights was absolutely bound by them if they amounted to legal estates or interests, the question of his actual knowledge or ignorance of their existence being irrelevant. On the other hand, he was not bound by rights that were merely equitable in nature, unless he had actual or constructive notice of their existence. Thus:

> An easement in perpetuity or a lease for a definite number of years would be enforceable against even an innocent purchaser because each is a legal interest, ie a right *in rem* enforceable against the whole world. On the other hand, if a fee simple owner had made an estate contract with X (eg had contracted to sell him the legal fee simple or to grant him a lease), or if he had subjected the land to a restrictive covenant in favour of Y (such as by covenanting that he would erect no business premises), the rights thus vested in X and Y, since they are merely equitable in nature, would not bind a subsequent purchaser for value who took a conveyance of the legal estate from the fee simple owner, unless the purchaser was affected with notice.

The significant points, then, are that a purchaser had more to fear from legal than from equitable third-party rights, and conversely that the third party himself was less secure with an equitable than a legal right.

(3) Outline of Statutory Changes by Legislation of 1925 and 1996

The legislation of 1925 attempted to simplify the problem of third-party rights in the following respects:

(a) It drastically curtailed the category of legal estates and legal third-party rights. The result is that after 1925 most third-party rights are equitable.

(b) It made the legal estate the basis of conveyancing. The principal effect of this is that the legal estate can be conveyed only by its owner, not, as occurred under the former law in relation to settlements of land, by a person who had no estate in the land at all.[64]

(c) The existing system by which in certain circumstances the conveyance of a legal estate by way of sale overreached equitable third-party rights, that is it encumbered the purchase money instead of the land with their payment and relieved the purchaser of the duty to investigate them, was extended. In the result,

  (i) these rights are cleared off the land altogether if they can equally well be satisfied out of the purchase money; but

---

[63] Above, pp 78 ff.   [64] Above, pp 102–3.

    (ii) if this is not possible, then they can be registered as *land charges* in a public register, so that their owners are protected and a purchaser is warned.

Furthermore, in 1996 legislation further simplified settlements of land, and provided that no new strict settlements can be created, and that both successive and concurrent interests should take effect under a trust of land.

These statutory changes now require a little elaboration.

(a) Reduction in number of legal estates

Before 1926 any recognised estate in land might be either legal or equitable. The Law of Property Act 1925, however, reduced the possible legal estates to the fee simple absolute in possession in the case of freeholds, and the term of years absolute in the case of leaseholds.

The person in whom such an estate is vested is called the *estate owner*. All other estates, interests and charges in or over the land can exist only as equitable interests,[65] with the exception of those interests permitted to exist at law by section 1(2) of the Act.[66]

In the case of freeholds, for instance, the:

determinable fee simple,[67]

entailed interest,[68]

life interest,[69]

future interest of whatever size,[70]

can now subsist only in equity, not at law. Each one must be created behind a trust, that is the legal estate in the land affected must be held by an *estate owner* whose function it is to give effect to the equitable interest. The very terminology, indeed, is changed. The correct expression now, for instance, is 'entailed interest' not 'estate tail', and 'life interest' instead of 'life estate'.

Section 1 of the Law of Property Act 1925 runs as follows:

(1) The only estates in land which are capable of subsisting or of being conveyed or created at law are—

    (*a*) An estate in fee simple absolute in possession;[71]

    (*b*) A term of years absolute.[72]

(2) The only interests or charges in or over land which are capable of subsisting or of being conveyed or created at law are—

    (*a*) An easement, right, or privilege in or over land for an interest equivalent to an estate in fee simple absolute in possession or a term of years absolute;[73]

---

[65] LPA 1925, s 1(1)–(3).   [66] Below.   [67] Below, Ch 17.
[68] Below, Ch 16.   [69] Below, Ch 16.   [70] Below, Ch 15.
[71] Below, Ch 6.   [72] Below, Ch 8.   [73] Below, Ch 18.

(b) A rentcharge in possession issuing out of or charged on land being either perpetual or for a term of years absolute;[74]

(c) A charge by way of legal mortgage;[75]

(d) [Land tax,[76] tithe rentcharge,[77]] and any other similar charge on land which is not created by an instrument;

(e) Rights of entry exercisable over or in respect of a legal term of years absolute, or annexed, for any purpose, to a legal rentcharge.

(3) All other estates, interests, and charges in or over land take effect as equitable interests.

It will be observed that in referring in the first subsection to *estates* and in the second to *interests* the Act invented a new terminology[78] that depends upon the difference between a right to the land itself and a right to some claim against the land of another person.

To be entitled to a legal as distinct from an equitable interest in the land itself it is necessary to hold an estate, and the only estate that qualifies for this purpose is either the fee simple absolute in possession or the term of years absolute according as the subject-matter is freehold or leasehold.

On the other hand, a claim against the land of another, if falling within the five items in the Law of Property Act 1925, s 1(2), is termed an *interest* in that land, but to constitute a *legal* interest it must correspond in duration to one of the two legal estates. A person entitled in perpetuity or for 21 years to an easement, such as a right of way over Blackacre, owns a legal interest in Blackacre provided that the easement is created in the appropriate form. If he is only entitled to it for life, he is an equitable owner.

Thus, the ancient doctrine of estates under which the fee simple, the entail and the life interest were recognised as estates at common law, has been drastically abridged. There is only the one freehold estate at law—the fee simple absolute in possession. The doctrine, however, has only been 'as it were, pushed back into equity'[79] in the sense that the interests that were formerly estates at law still subsist with equal vigour as equitable interests.

(b) Legal estate as basis of conveyancing

This may be illustrated by two observations.

---

[74] Below, Ch 20. The Rentcharges Act 1977 is phasing out the creation of certain kinds of rentcharge.

[75] Below, Ch 21.

[76] Abolished by the Finance Act 1963, s 73, Sch 14, Part VI.

[77] Extinguished by the Tithe Act 1936, s 48, Sch 9 and replaced by a 60 years' redemption annuity payable to the Crown. This is a legal interest within the meaning of 'any other similar charge...' of para (d). This was itself extinguished as from 2 October 1977 by FA 1977, s 56.

[78] However, the term 'legal estate' is still used as shorthand to refer to both the two legal estates (property so-called) and legal interests and charges: LPA 1925, s 1(4).

[79] Lawson, *The Rational Strength of English Law* (1951), p 94.

(1) Powers of appointment now equitable

First, we have seen that it was a common practice before 1926 to limit land to A and B in fee simple to such uses as X might appoint, with the result that if X, who had no proprietary interest in the land, 'appointed' to the use of Y and his heirs, A and B thereupon stood seised to the use of Y and he took a *legal* fee simple under the Statute of Uses.[80] This is no longer possible. The Statute of Uses has been repealed[81] and, though land may still be limited to A and B upon such trusts as X shall appoint, this merely empowers X to dispose of the equitable interest. With very few exceptions powers are now equitable.[82]

(2) Title to legal estate alone investigated

Secondly, if a legal estate that is held in trust for beneficiaries is offered for sale, the purchaser's sole concern in the normal case is to trace the title of the vendors to the legal estate. As we have seen,[83] he is entirely unaffected by the beneficial interests, for, as long as the purchase money is paid to two trustees or to a trust corporation,[84] the beneficial interests are overreached, that is once the legal estate has been conveyed to a purchaser, they are no longer binding on the land but are transferred to the purchase money that has been paid to the trustees.[85]

(c) Strict settlements: Settled Land Act 1925

(1) Conveyancing difficulties

The policy of freeing the title to the legal estate from beneficial interests to which it may be subject, had begun in 1882 in the case of settled land. This was continued by the 1925 legislation. Furthermore the conveyancing machinery was greatly simplified. Before 1926 a strict settlement was created by a single deed that conferred legal estates and interests upon the successive beneficiaries, so that for instance the husband acquired a legal estate for life and the eldest son a legal estate tail.[86] When the tenant for life exercised, say, his statutory power of sale under the Settled Land Act 1882, his conveyance did, indeed, overreach these legal interests, but, as we have seen, the conveyancing difficulties were not inconsiderable.[87] They derived mainly from the fact that, since the fee simple was not vested in the tenant for life, his right to convey it rested solely upon the statutory powers of sale. The whole settlement required investigation, and before the purchaser was relieved from liability in respect

---

[80] Above, p 96.   [81] LPA 1922, s 207, Sch 7.
[82] LPA 1925, ss 1(7), 3 as amended by TLATA 1996, s 25(2), Sch 4. Section 205(1)(xi) contains the following definitions: 'Legal powers' include the powers vested in a chargee by way of legal mortgage or in an estate owner under which a legal estate can be transferred or created, and 'equitable powers' mean all the powers in or over land under which equitable interests or powers only can be transferred or created.
[83] Above, p 103.   [84] Below, pp 143, 145.   [85] For details, see below, pp 1068–9, 1113–22.
[86] These interests could also be equitable. After the reintroduction of the use in the form of the trust (above, pp 76–8) it was possible to create a strict settlement by the alternative method of a grant unto and to the use of trustees to hold the legal estate upon the requisite trusts, in which case the beneficiaries would be entitled to equitable interests.
[87] Above, pp 102–3.

of the beneficial limitations, he had to make sure that the statutory conditions for the exercise of the power had been satisfied.

(2) Settled Land Act 1925

These conveyancing difficulties were removed, however, by the Settled Land Act 1925. Owing to the reduction in the number of legal estates, the limited and beneficial interests arising under a strict settlement are now necessarily equitable, and the legal fee simple out of which they have been carved must, in accordance with the statutory provisions, be vested in the first tenant for life and be transferred to each subsequent tenant for life as and when he becomes entitled to possession.[88]

(3) Dual position of tenant for life

Thus the tenant for life occupies a dual position. Although he is a mere tenant for life as regards beneficial enjoyment, he is the owner of the legal fee simple for conveyancing purposes. This means that within the scope of his statutory powers he can dispose of the legal estate, whether it be the fee simple absolute in possession or the term of years absolute, so as to pass to the purchaser a title free from the rights under the settlement; but it does not mean that he becomes entitled to the capital money arising from the transaction. It is, in fact, a condition of the purchaser's immunity that the money should be paid to the trustees.

(4) Method of creating a strict settlement after 1925

In order to emphasise this separation of the legal estate from the beneficial and equitable interests and to facilitate conveyancing, a new method of creating a strict settlement, framed on the pattern of the trust for sale, was introduced by the Settled Land Act 1925. Every inter vivos settlement had to be made by two deeds. One (the *vesting deed*) vested the legal fee simple in the tenant for life, described the property and named the trustees; the other (the *trust instrument*) declared the beneficial interests of the tenant for life and the other persons entitled under the settlement.[89]

(5) Overreaching of equitable interests

The effect of a conveyance made by the tenant for life in his capacity as estate owner is to overreach the equitable interests of the beneficiaries, that is it clears them off the title to the legal fee simple and converts them into equivalent interests in the purchase money. Their fate is of no concern to the purchaser, provided that he pays the purchase money to the trustees, and not to the tenant for life. His sole object is to investigate the title to the *legal* estate. He must, therefore, trace that title down to the first vesting deed, that is he must require the vendor to show that the person who purported to vest

---

[88] Below, pp 436 ff.

[89] SLA 1925, s 4; below, pp 436–7. In the case of a settlement made by a testator, the legal estate devolved upon his executors who held it upon trust to convey it to the tenant for life. The will itself constituted the trust instrument and the executors made a *vesting assent*, corresponding to the vesting deed, in favour of the tenant for life; below, p 438.

the legal estate in the first tenant for life was in fact entitled to do so. He does not see, nor in general may he demand to see, the trust instrument. That instrument is solely the charter of the beneficiaries. The rights that it grants to the beneficiaries are still intact, still secure, but they are now transferred to the purchase money. The whole operation set in motion upon a conveyance by the tenant for life is an illustration of what is called the *curtain* principle. The vesting deed is, as it were, a curtain that veils the equitable interests.[90]

(d) Trusts of land

A major change was made by the Trusts of Land and Appointment of Trustees Act 1996.[91] The Act applies to trusts of land created before or after its commencement on 1 January 1997. Under it the dual system of strict settlement and trust for sale[92] is replaced by a trust of land that applies to both successive and concurrent interests. Existing strict settlements continue, but no new strict settlements can be created. Existing express trusts for sale, whether of successive or of concurrent interests, also continue, and may still be expressly created so as to come within the wide definition of the trust of land.[93] Trusts of concurrent interests that were implied by statute, are converted into trusts of land.[94] Under the trust of land the legal estate to the land is vested in trustees who are given all the powers of an absolute owner for the purpose of exercising their functions as trustees. The trustees have a power, but not a duty, to sell, and the interests of the beneficiaries are still overreachable on sale, as they were under the previous dual system. The doctrine of conversion[95] is abolished in respect of all trusts for sale, whenever created,[96] and consequently the interests of the beneficiaries cease to be interests in personalty and become interests in land. The Act is another and welcome measure in the long line of measures that over the centuries have sought to develop and simplify the land law; it is an important gloss on the 1925 legislation, and gives to the trustees broad and flexible powers to enable them to manage the land more effectively, and to the beneficiaries more scope in the control of those powers.

(e) Registrable third-party rights

In the case, then, of concurrent or successive beneficial interests in the land, whether arising under a strict settlement, a trust for sale, or, after 1996, a trust of land, the beneficial interests are cleared altogether off the title to the legal estate and, since they are transferred to the purchase money, no economic harm is done to their owners. Family rights and incumbrances in the nature of pecuniary claims do not therefore impede a conveyance of the legal estate. There are, however, other equitable third-party rights to which the doctrine of overreaching is necessarily inapplicable, since they are incapable of being attached to money. For instance, an estate contract or a restrictive covenant of which a purchaser has had notice must continue to affect the land after conveyance to him of the legal estate. In such cases the obvious method of

---

[90] For a detailed account, see below, pp 1117 ff.   [91] Below, Ch 13.   [92] Below, pp 471–3.
[93] Below, pp 475–8.   [94] Below, p 501.   [95] Above, p 104.
[96] Except for a trust for sale created in the will of a testator dying before 1997.

simplifying the task of the purchaser, and at the same time of protecting the equitable owner, is to require rights of this nature to be publicly recorded if they are to remain binding against purchasers. This was the policy adopted by the legislature in 1925.

Legislation enabling rights against land to be registered has long been in force, but it has appeared in successive and somewhat slow stages. Life annuities charged upon land were made registrable as far back as 1777, and the system was extended to judgments in 1838, to pending land actions in 1839, to deeds of arrangement in 1887, and to 'land charges' in 1888. These several topics are the subject of full discussion later,[97] but here we should note that a great extension of the system of registration was made by the Land Charges Act 1925. Without going into details, it may be said that almost all equitable rights against unregistered land, except those that arise under a settlement and are therefore overreachable, may be entered in one of the registers kept at the Land Charges Department of the Land Registry in Plymouth.[98] Registration of a registrable right constitutes notice of it to the whole world; failure to register it carries the penalty that it is void against a purchaser;[99] and this is so even if the purchaser has actual notice of the unregistered right. Therefore in the case of a third-party right that falls within the provisions of the Act, all now turns on registration; its owner can secure complete protection for himself by registration, while a purchaser need do no more than search at the Land Registry to discover whether the land is incumbered or not. An examination of section 2(2) of the Land Charges Act 1972[100] will show that most of the charges that are registrable are equitable. The important exception is the puisne mortgage, that is to say, a legal mortgage not protected by a deposit of documents relating to the legal estate affected.[101] A puisne mortgage, although a legal interest, does not therefore bind a purchaser for value unless registered. It is made registrable, as will be seen later, in order to comply with the post-1925 scheme for the priority of mortgages.[102]

(4) *Summary of Changes Made by Legislation of 1925*

(a) **Conveyance by estate owner**

By way of summary, it may be said, then, that one of the principal objects of the 1925 legislation was to simplify and clear the title to the legal fee simple, which is the estate that the majority of purchasers wish to obtain. As a result of the legislation the general position is now as follows:

---

[97] Below, pp 1054 ff.   [98] Land Registry Practice Guide 63.

[99] Some unregistered charges are void against a purchaser for value of any estate, legal or equitable; others are void only against a purchaser of a legal estate for money or money's worth: LCA 1972, s 4(5), (6); below, pp 1063–6.

[100] LCA 1925 has been replaced by LCA 1972 and LLCA 1975.

[101] Land charge Class C(i); below, pp 885, 1057, 1063.

[102] Below, p 883. The Matrimonial Homes Act 1967, now replaced by Family Law Act 1996 and amended by Civil Partnership Act 2004, added a new Class F land charge which does not owe its origin to equity or to common law; below, pp 522–4.

The only legal freehold estate in Blackacre is the fee simple absolute in possession. In all cases this will be vested in a definite person or body of persons called the *estate owner*. According to the circumstances the estate owner will be one of the following:

A beneficial owner entitled in his own right.

The tenant for life or 'statutory owners'[103] in the case of settled land under a settlement created before 1997.[104]

A trustee (or trustees) of land,[105] holding either for himself and one or more other persons, or as bare trustee.[106]

Personal representatives.

A mortgagor.[107]

A conveyance of the legal fee simple must be made by or in the name of the estate owner, not by anybody else. Thus the exercise of a power of appointment can no longer affect the legal estate,[108] and in the case of a strict settlement the tenant for life conveys the legal fee simple because the Settled Land Act 1925 requires that it shall be vested in him, not (as formerly) because he had a statutory power to convey what he had not got.

(b) Third-party rights

The conveyance of a legal fee simple that is subject to equitable third-party rights is considerably simplified:

(i) Concurrent or successive beneficial interests in land (whether arising under a strict settlement, a trust for sale, or, after 1996, a trust of land) continue to be overreached by the conveyance[109] and cleared off the title; they are converted into rights against the purchase money.

(ii) If such rights do not arise in that way (ie they came into existence before the creation of the settlement) but are nevertheless convertible into rights against the money, the estate owner may clear them off the title by creating a settlement for that particular purpose, called an *ad hoc* settlement.[110]

---

[103] These are the persons who take the legal fee simple in settled land when there is no person entitled to take it as tenant for life; below, p 442.

[104] Above, p 127.

[105] After 1996, under TLATA 1996. For the trust for sale before 1997, see above, p 127.

[106] A bare or naked trustee is one who holds property for the absolute benefit of a beneficiary of full age, and who himself has no beneficial interest in the property and no duty except to transfer it to its owner: *Christie v Ovington* (1875) 1 Ch D 279; and, for an example in registered land, *Hodgson v Marks* [1971] Ch 892. A bare trust did not fall either within the strict settlement or under the trust for sale before 1997: see below, p 478.

[107] In a mortgage of a legal fee simple, the mortgagor remains the estate owner of the legal fee simple, but nevertheless the mortgagee is entitled by virtue of his power of sale to convey it to a purchaser: below, pp 854–7.

[108] Save in a few exceptional cases; above, p 125, n 82.   [109] Above, p 126; below, pp 1113 ff.

[110] An ad hoc trust of land or (before 1997) an ad hoc strict settlement: below, pp 1119–21.

(iii) If the rights do not arise under a settlement and are not convertible into money, such as an estate contract or a restrictive covenant, their continued enforcement depends in general on their registration as land charges.

(c) Effect on doctrine of bona fide purchaser for value of legal estate without notice

We have already seen the curtailment of the doctrine of the bona fide purchaser[111] where overreaching operates in the case of concurrent or successive beneficial interests.[112] It has been further dramatically curtailed by the extension of the system of registration of land charges. In the case of registrable third-party rights, their enforceability no longer depends on the state of the purchaser's mind; it is the state of the register that is crucial.

The doctrine, however, continues to apply to a residual category of equitable third-party rights that are neither overreachable nor registrable. Here a purchaser is bound unless he is a bona fide purchaser of the legal estate for value without actual or constructive notice. This category is necessarily limited, because most equitable third-party rights are in practice susceptible to overreaching or registration. Certain situations where the old rules concerning notice continue to apply were contemplated by the draftsmen of the 1925 legislation, for instance, a restrictive covenant entered into before 1926.[113] But in recent years the old rules have been applied in a number of situations that were presumably not foreseen.[114]

(d) Reconciliation of family and commercial needs

One aspect of the clear-cut distinction between the legal estate and the equitable interest deserves attention. Land is employed to satisfy at least two requirements, one affecting the family of its owner, the other affecting its commercial exploitation. It must be subject to rules that facilitate its employment as a continuing source of income for the present and future members of a family, but at the same time it must be under effective administration and above all be readily transferable by way of sale, lease, mortgage and similar transactions if good estate management so demands. These two requirements, at first sight contradictory, have been reconciled by English law. The estate owner, despite the existence of family trusts, is given full powers of management and disposal in respect of the land, but he holds them as trustee for such equitable

---

[111] For the doctrine, see above, pp 83 ff.   [112] Above, pp 126–7.   [113] Below, p 740.

[114] *ER Ives Investment Ltd v High* [1967] 2 QB 379, M & B p 1074 (equity by estoppel), below, p 920; *Poster v Slough Estates Ltd* [1968] 1 WLR 1515 (right of entry to remove a fixture on termination of lease); *Shiloh Spinners Ltd v Harding* [1973] AC 691, especially at 720–1 (Lord Wilberforce), M & B p 68 (equitable right of re-entry on breach of covenant); *Midland Bank Ltd v Farmpride Hatcheries Ltd* (1980) 260 EG 493, M & B p 62 (contractual licence), above p 88, n 117. The doctrine also applies to interests which are not registrable but are overreachable but which have not in fact been overreached: *Caunce v Caunce* [1969] 1 WLR 286 (beneficial interest of wife who had contributed towards purchase price); *Kingsnorth Finance Co Ltd v Tizard* [1986] 1 WLR 783, M & B p 216, above, p 88, n 112.

beneficiaries as may exist. In this way the well-being of the land, the needs of the market and the prosperity of the family are harmonised.[115]

C REGISTERED CONVEYANCING

So far we have discussed the changes made by the 1925 legislation, which were intended to simplify the law of real property within the framework of the system of unregistered conveyancing. The intention was that the unregistered system should be replaced by a simplified system of registered conveyancing.

(1) Introduction and Extension of Registration of Title

Registration of title was introduced into England as long ago as 1862.[116] At first it was voluntary, and little used.[117] In 1897 provision was made to extend it compulsorily to areas to be defined from time to time by Orders in Council on the request of a county council,[118] but progress in this respect was slow and by the time that the Land Registration Act 1925 replaced the old statutes with a new system for registration of title as part of the great reforms of land law, only the county of London had become an area of compulsory registration. Although the 1925 Act had a renewed purpose of producing a complete register of title to land in England and Wales, the compulsion necessary to achieve this was not yet put in place: the central Government's power to initiate compulsory registration in any area was delayed for ten years;[119] and it took a further 55 years before compulsory registration was finally extended to the whole of England and Wales with effect from 1 November 1990.[120] It should be noted, however, that 'compulsory registration' does not mean that every acre of land has to be registered: only that dealings in land must now be carried out under the new and not

---

[115] Lawson, *The Rational Strength of English Law*, pp 91–2. For the balance struck by TLATA 1996 for the trust of land between the interests of beneficiaries (including their rights of occupation), the trustees' power of sale, and the protection of purchasers, see below, pp 483–8.

[116] Land Registry Act 1862, replaced by Land Transfer Act 1875. For a history of land registration before 1926, see (1972) 36 Conv (NS) 390 (HW Wilkinson); Rowton Simpson, *Land Law and Registration* (1976), pp 39–47. See also *City of London Building Society v Flegg* [1988] AC 54, 84 (Lord Oliver of Aylmerton). The Torrens system of registration of title was first introduced in South Australia by Sir Robert Torrens in 1858. It operates in many Commonwealth countries. For land registration systems in European countries, see Cooke, *The New Law of Land Registration* (2003), ch 9. Registered conveyancing must be distinguished from the system of registration of assurances practised in parts of Yorkshire which merely recorded conveyances and devises in a public register. These deeds registries are closed: LPA 1969, ss 16–22.

[117] By December 1885 only 113 titles had been registered: Rowton Simpson, *Land Law and Registration*, p 44.

[118] Land Transfer Act 1897.

[119] LRA 1925, s 120(2)(b). From 1926 until the end of 1935 the power of initiation was left in the hands of county councils, and only two took advantage of it: Middlesex, and Eastbourne and Hastings: see the 4th edn of this book (1937), pp 95–6.

[120] Registration of Title Order 1989 (SI 1989 No 1347). Earlier attempts were made to advance this plan, but all failed because of the administrative burdens involved in such an enormous task: Rowton Simpson, *Land Law and Registration*, p 49.

the old system of conveyancing, and so since 1925 the number of titles on the register has been gradually increasing. The 1925 Act[121] defined transactions with unregistered land that, in any area of compulsory registration, would require the title to be placed on the register. The triggers for compulsory registration were increased by the Land Registration Act 1997;[122] and were further increased by the Land Registration Act 2002.[123] From 2002 until 2005 the Land Registry had as a strategic objective the creation of a Land Register with comprehensive content and national coverage by 2012,[124] although this has now been replaced by the setting of annual targets for increasing the total area of freehold land that is on the register.[125] The completion of the register will require in due course the further extension of triggers for first registration, including the requirement that all land be registered, whether or not there is any disposition of it. The register must be complete in order to facilitate the full introduction of electronic conveyancing.[126]

(2) General Principles of Registered Conveyancing

Under the system of registered conveyancing contained in the Land Registration Acts 1925 and 2002 a registered title is guaranteed by the State. We have seen that the conveyancing of unregistered land depends upon the production by a vendor of a series of documents that recount previous transactions affecting the land and demonstrate to a purchaser the ability of a vendor to convey what he has agreed to convey. Title to the interest to be conveyed is thus something deduced from evidence. It has to be proved afresh each time a disposition of land is made. The conveyancing of registered land is different in principle and in practice. Once the title to land is registered, its past history is irrelevant. The title thenceforth is guaranteed by the State, and a purchaser can rely on it. Title has now become something more than evidence; in a sense, it is itself the subject-matter of the conveyance. Transfer of land becomes the substitution of one person's name for another person's name on a register. That transfer necessarily shifts the whole title registered in the former proprietor's name. Under the 1925 Act the landowner received from the registry a land certificate reproducing the relevant entries on the register, but the source of title was the register, not the land certificate, and land certificates are no longer issued under the 2002 Act.

[121] S 123: sale of freehold; grant of lease for not less than 40 years; and assignment of lease with not less than 40 years still to run.

[122] S 1: conveyance of freehold, grant of lease for more than 21 years; assignment of lease having more than 21 years still to run; assent or vesting deed of freehold or leasehold having more than 21 years still to run; first legal mortgage of freehold or leasehold having more than 21 years still to run; first legal mortgage of freehold or leasehold having more than 21 years still to run, protected by deposit of documents.

[123] S 4: the most significant change is to reduce the length of leaseholds triggering registration on grant or assignment to those granted for more than seven years, or having more than seven years still to run. For first registration under LRA 2002, see below, pp 1073 ff.

[124] Land Registry Annual Reports 2001–02, p 89; 2004–05, p 50.

[125] By 2010 the freehold title to 73 per cent of the area of England and Wales had been registered, comprising 22.5 million titles: Land Registry Annual Report 2009–10, p 12.

[126] Below, pp 141–3.

Registered conveyancing is not, however, a new system of land law. It is based on such familiar concepts as estates and interests, settlements, leases, mortgages, easements and covenants,[127] and the system introduced by the Land Registration Act 1925 was an integral part of the 1925 legislation. The Land Registration Act 2002 has made significant changes to the detail of the system contained in the 1925 Act, but the general approach remains the same. These Acts provide mechanisms for the authoritative recording of certain interests in land in a public register, the guarantee by the State of their validity and the accuracy of the record, and a system by which dealings in land can be conducted: a system of conveyancing. But what constitutes an estate or interest in land that is capable of being so recorded, is logically a prior question. The Land Registration Acts presuppose the identification and categorisation of interests in land under the general law. For this reason we shall defer a detailed consideration of the principles of registered conveyancing until we have considered the estates and interests in land recognised at law and in equity.[128] However, to complete the general picture of the 1925 reforms of land law, we shall here give an outline of the scheme as it was set out in the Land Registration Act 1925, together with a note of the significant points of comparison between that Act and the Land Registration Act 2002.

(3) Land Registration Act 1925

As we have seen, the scheme of the 1925 legislation was to reduce the number of legal estates to two: the fee simple absolute in possession and the term of years absolute;[129] and to provide simplified mechanisms to protect the holder of other rights in unregistered land. Beneficial interests under a strict settlement or trust for sale or, since 1997, a trust of land,[130] which are capable of being converted into money, could be overreached on a sale[131] of the legal estate and the beneficiary was protected by having a continuing property right in the purchase money instead of in the land. Most other property rights could be protected in unregistered land by their holder registering them as land charges, to ensure that they would remain enforceable as rights in or over the land itself even as against a transferee.[132] Those property rights that were neither overreached[133] nor capable of being registered as land charges could still bind a transferee as long as he was not a bona fide purchaser of the legal estate for value without notice (actual, imputed or constructive) of the right in question.[134]

In relation to registered land, by contrast, the Land Registration Act 1925 was designed to follow the new principles for estates and interests in land set out in the Law of Property Act 1925, but adapted to the needs of a system of registration of title.

---

[127] See *First National Bank plc v Thompson* [1996] Ch 231 (estoppel).

[128] Below, Part III.   [129] Above, p 123.   [130] Above, p 127.

[131] By at least two trustees or a trust corporation: above, p 125.   [132] Above, pp 127–8.

[133] Either because they were not overreachable (eg *ER Ives Investment Ltd v High* [1967] 2 QB 379: equity by estoppel) or because they were overreachable but not in fact overreached because the sale was by a sole trustee (eg *Kingsnorth Finance Co Ltd v Tizard* [1986] 1 WLR 783: beneficial interest under a trust for sale).

[134] Above, p 130.

The fee simple absolute in possession and the term of years absolute, the only two legal estates that could now exist, were the two estates that could be registered under separate titles.[135] Other interests were dealt with in one of three ways:

(a) by the doctrine of overreaching, which operates in registered land in the same way as in unregistered land;[136]

(b) as 'overriding interests', which bound a registered proprietor and his transferees whether or not they are entered on the register;[137]

(c) as 'minor interests', which had to be entered on the register of the land affected, if they are not to be overridden by a subsequent registered disposition of the land for value.[138]

(a) Registration and entry on the register

It is important to grasp the distinction between interests that could be *registered* under the Land Registration Act 1925, and interests that could be *entered on the register*. The former were confined to the two legal estates,[139] the titles to which were substantively registered under their own separate title numbers. Minor interests, as the name implies, were interests, lesser than registered interests, which could be protected by an entry on the register of the title affected. The entry was made on the proprietorship or charges register[140] of that title, and operated by way of an incumbrance against it.

The proper person to be registered proprietor was the person holding the legal estate under the general law: in the case of a strict settlement, this would therefore be the tenant for life, and in the case of a trust for sale (or, after 1996, a trust of land), the trustees. In these cases, warning was given to a purchaser by the entry of a *restriction* on the registered title that showed that a settlement or trust existed, without however telling him what the individual beneficial interests were. Thus the doctrine of overreaching applied to the interests of the beneficiaries, and the curtain principle was retained. 'References to trusts shall, so far as is possible, be excluded from the register.'[141]

The Land Registration Act 1925 laid down precise rules for dealings in the land, and attempted an enumeration of the powers of an owner under the Act.[142] In order to be effectual at law a disposition of registered land had to be completed by registration.

---

[135] LRA 1925, s 2(1). Not all leases were registrable: the general effect of the legislation was that only leases with more than 21 years to run could be registered: LRA 1925, s 8; other legal leases were protected by being overriding interests: below. For the suggestion that the Land Registration Acts create a statutory estate, distinct from the fee simple or term of years at common law, see below, p 158. Legal interests that could be registered in addition to those in corporeal land, were those in manors, mines and minerals, advowsons and rents (in practice, rentcharges): LRR 1925, r 50. But legal easements could only be registered as appurtenant to the registered title of the dominant tenement: LRR 1925, r 257.

[136] *City of London Building Society v Flegg* [1988] AC 54, M& B p 551 (interest of beneficiary under trust for sale overreached even though beneficiary was in actual occupation).

[137] Below, pp 138–9.   [138] Below, pp 137–8.   [139] Above.   [140] Below, pp 135–6.

[141] LRA 1925, s 74; cf s 88(1); *Abigail v Lapin* [1934] AC 491, 500.

[142] Ibid, ss 18, 21, 25, 40, 101, 104, 106, 107, 109; LRR 1925, r 74, as substituted by LRR 1997, r 2(1), Sch 1, para 18.

Thus a transfer for value of registered freehold or leasehold land had to be completed by the Registrar entering on the register the transferee as the registered proprietor[143] and until he had done this the transferor was deemed to remain the proprietor.[144] As soon as he had done this, however, the legal estate passed at once to the transferee.[145]

(b) The register

The separate register for each individual title under the Land Registration Act 1925 was divided into three parts, a property register, a proprietorship register, and a charges register.[146] It was intended that the register should 'mirror' the title, though, as we shall see, it did so in only a qualified manner. The register was originally kept on a card index system, but was gradually computerised.[147] It was a register of title, so that where there was more than one legal title subsisting in one piece of land (the obvious case is that of a registered freehold subject to a registered lease) there would be one register for each title. A copy of the various entries on the register and of the filed plan of the title, called a land certificate,[148] was given to the registered proprietor of the title, and could be retained by him or deposited in the registry. It was not, however, the certificate but the register retained in the registry that was the title.

The property register described and identified the land, and the interest in the land that was the subject-matter of the title, freehold or leasehold. As we have said already, the interest had to be legal. There might also appear on this register mention of specific benefits capable of subsisting as legal interests, such as legal easements over neighbouring land, and the effect would be to create a registered title of the same nature in them. There could also be a reference to other benefits, such as the freedom of the land from specific overriding interests.[149]

---

[143] LRA 1925, ss 19(1), 22(1). Registration was completed as of the day on which the application was delivered to the Registrar: LRR 1925, r 83(1), as substituted by LRR 1978, r 8; LR (Delivery of Applications) R 1986.

[144] Before registration, there might be a complete transfer in equity: *Mascall v Mascall* (1984) 50 P & CR 119 (intending donor executed transfer which he handed to donee together with land certificate: even though donee had not applied for registration, held to be complete gift in equity, since donor had done everything that he had to do to perfect gift: *Re Rose* [1952] Ch 499, Maudsley and Burn, *Trusts and Trustees* (7th edn, 2008), p 161). See also *E S Schwab & Co Ltd v McCarthy* (1975) 31 P & CR 196, 212; *Brown & Root Technology Ltd v Sun Alliance and London Assurance Co Ltd* [1996] Ch 51 (reversed on other grounds (1996) 75 P & CR 223).

[145] LRA 1925, ss 20(1), 23(1) as amended by FA 1975, s 52, Sch 12, para 5, which set out in detail what appurtenances passed to the transferee, and also the matters subject to which his title subsisted. See also LRR 1925, r 251.

[146] LRR 1925, r 2.

[147] LRA 1925, s 1, was amended by AJA 1982, s 66(1), to provide that the register need not be kept in documentary form.

[148] For a specimen land certificate, see M & B (7th edn, 1998) pp 105–7. Where the property was mortgaged by way of legal charge, the charge was completed by registration and a charge certificate was issued to the chargee, the land certificate being deposited at the Registry until the charge was cancelled. LRA 1925, ss 63, 65; LRR 1925, r 262 as amended by LRR 1993 (SI 1993 No 3275), r 7.

[149] LRR 1925, r 197; *Re Dances Way, West Town, Hayling Island* [1962] Ch 490.

The proprietorship register stated the nature of the title, that is, absolute, good leasehold, possessory or qualified,[150] the name, address and description of the proprietor, and also any entries that affected his right of disposing of the land. As from 1 April 2000, on first registration or following the transfer of land (freehold or leasehold), the registrar would whenever practicable enter in the register the price paid or its value, although the entry remained on the register only until a further change of proprietorship.[151] The charges register contained entries of incumbrances that burdened the land, such as restrictive covenants and mortgages.

(c) Inspection of Register

Originally, the register was accessible only to the proprietor of the land or of a registered charge, or persons authorised by them or by the court,[152] but the Land Registration Act 1988 opened it to inspection by the public.[153] It was also possible to discover whether or not a particular plot of land was registered by searching the Index Map and Parcels Index.[154]

(d) Classes of title

The purpose of the land register under the Land Registration Act 1925 was to provide an authoritative record of estates and interests in land, guaranteed by the State. In furtherance of this, the Act[155] recognised four different classes of title, which provided more or less full assurance as to the owner's title to the legal estate: absolute title, good leasehold title (for a lessee only), possessory title, and, finally, qualified title, where an application for one of the other titles could not be substantiated. The classes of title are unchanged under the Land Registration Act 2002, and are discussed in detail in the context of the new Act.[156] It suffices here to notice that an absolute title was the most frequent,[157] and that a title registered in this way could actually be improved by

---

[150] For the different classes of title, see below.

[151] LRR (No 3) R 1999 (SI 1999 No. 3462); [2000] EG 11 March p 169 (A Judge). See the Consultation Paper published by the Land Registry in 1997.

[152] LRA 1925, s 112. This corresponded broadly to the position in unregistered land, where documents of title are private, although the register of land charges is open to the public: Barnsley, *Conveyancing Law and Practice* (4th edn, ed Thompson, 1996), pp 40–2.

[153] Substituting LRA 1925, ss 112–13; *Mortgage Corpn v Halifax (SW) Ltd* The Times, 15 July 1998 (inherent jurisdiction to disclose transfer including purchase price of land). LRA 1988 was based on Law Com No 148, *Second Report on Land Registration: Inspection of the Register* (1985). See (1990) 49 EG 44 (C Coombe and H Lewis); (1990) 41 LSG 19 (EJ Pryer).

[154] LRR 1925, r 8, as amended by LRR (No 2) 1999, r 2(1), Sch 1, para 2; LR (Open Register) R 1991 (SI 1991 No 122) as amended by LRR 1999, r 2(3), Sch 3 and LRR 2000 (SI 2000 No 429), r 2(2), Sch 2; LRR 1993 (SI 1993 No 3275); LRR 1995 (SI 1995 No 1354), rr 5–7.

[155] LRA 1925, ss 4–12.   [156] Below, p 1076.

[157] On first registration of freehold land under LRA 1925, over 99 per cent of applications were registered with absolute title. The majority of the remainder relate to titles founded purely on adverse possession. See [1980] Conv, pp 7–9, 96–8, 165–7. 'Possessory titles are granted in less than one in a hundred applications for first registration. Qualified titles are virtually unknown. Good leasehold titles are common': Ruoff and Pryer, *Concise Land Registration Handbook* (1990), p 36.

registration. Any technical defect was cured, for no one could subsequently raise it, save in the exceptional case of a rectification action.[158]

(e) Rectification and indemnity

Once the title to the land had been registered under the Land Registration Act 1925, it vested in the registered proprietor, and was thenceforth guaranteed by the State. But section 82 of the Land Registration Act 1925 gave to the court and to the registrar wide powers to rectify the register where there was any error or omission. Section 83,[159] however, provided for an indemnity for those who suffered loss in certain cases by reason of such rectification or by refusal of rectification. So the system of registered conveyancing is to some extent an insurance system.[160]

(f) Protection of third party rights

We must now briefly consider the scheme of the Land Registration Act 1925 for the protection of third-party rights, and how they affected a purchaser from the proprietor of registered land.

The scheme was simple. A party who had an interest, other than a legal estate that was itself capable of substantive registration,[161] should normally protect it by an entry on the register of the title affected by it. The Land Registration Act 1925 designated such an interest a *minor interest*. There were four different forms of entry on the register,[162] each suitable to different categories of interest and different circumstances of their entry, and each having their own effect: a notice,[163] restriction,[164] caution[165]

---

[158] Below.

[159] As substituted by LRA 1997, s 2.

[160] This is discussed further in the context of the new system under LRA 2002: below, p 1081 ff. The sums paid are not significant when viewed against the Land Registry's fee income. In 2009–10 £7,782,081 was paid for 1,011 claims: Land Registry Annual Report 2009–10, p 20. The fee income in the same year was over £328 million: ibid, p 44.

[161] Ie, the fee simple or a lease for more than 21 years: above, p 134.

[162] For a more detailed discussion, see the 16th edn of this book, pp 872–6.

[163] LRA 1925, ss 48–52; LRR 1925, rr 7, 190. In most cases the entry of a notice required the land certificate to be produced to the Registry, if not already on deposit there—and so could usually be entered only with the co-operation of the owner of the land affected. The notice was entered on the charges register, and disposition of the land took effect subject to all estates, rights and claims which were protected by entry on the register, if the claim was valid and not (independently of the Act) overridden by the disposition: LRA 1925, s 52.

[164] Ibid, s 58; LRR 1925, r 6: an entry which prevents dealings in registered land until certain specified conditions or requirements have been complied with. It therefore recorded, on (normally) the proprietorship register, any impediment to the proprietor's freedom of disposal, such as the requirement to pay capital money to two trustees or a trust corporation (or into court) in the case of the restriction entered to protect the beneficial interests under a settlement or trust for sale (or, after 1996, trust of land). As with a notice, the land certificate generally had to be produced.

[165] Ibid, ss 53–6, LRR 1925, rr 6, 7. A caution against dealings was a hostile act, used to protect a claim to an interest or right over land without the need to produce the land certificate. The registered proprietor could 'warn off' the cautioner and force him either to withdraw his caution or to have the dispute about it adjudicated by the registrar or the court. If a caution was on the register (in the proprietorship register or the charges register) no dealing with the title could be registered without the registrar serving notice on the cautioner, which then served as a 'warning off' notice. For the court's exercise of its jurisdiction to order the

or inhibition.[166] The common theme, however, is that a third party who claimed an interest in the land had a means of placing his claim on the register of title itself—and therefore any purchaser[167] of the land had the opportunity, on searching the register before committing himself to the transaction,[168] to discover it.

Some minor interests were incapable of binding a purchaser even if protected by entry, but nevertheless affected the method of disposing of land. Thus, in the case of beneficial interests under a settlement or trust of land that would be overreached on a sale of the land, a restriction would be entered on the proprietorship register indicating that the proprietor of the legal title was limited in his powers, but, if the terms of the restriction were complied with, a purchaser for value was not concerned with such beneficial interests. But other minor interests such as restrictive covenants, equitable easements, legal and equitable rentcharges, and estate contracts did bind purchasers for valuable consideration, if protected by entry on the register. Conversely, a purchaser would take free from them if they were not so protected by entry; and, as in unregistered conveyancing, this was so even if he had actual notice of their existence. But no place was to be left in the system of registered conveyancing for the doctrine of notice.[169]

Such an approach, if strictly applied, would however work to protect only those persons having a right over land who had in fact made an entry on the register of the land affected. We here find one of the perennial problems of land law: finding the proper balance to strike between the need to protect a purchaser, who ought to be able to discover the rights affecting the title that he is purchasing, and the desire to protect third parties, who may often have very good reasons for not having protected their rights explicitly—for example, where the right is itself created informally in a third party who is acting without legal advice.[170] The Land Registration Act 1925 sought to strike a balance, by designating as *overriding interests* certain interests that would bind a registered proprietor and his transferee, where they had not been protected by entry on the register.[171] They were 'overriding' because they overrode, or assumed superiority over, the transferee's estate. Section 70(1) of the Act listed overriding interests, most of which were particular categories of interest in land, such as profits à prendre, legal easements, leases for not more than 21 years, local land charges, and

vacation of cautions, see the 16th edn of this book, p 874, n 3. A caution against first registration was a similar procedure to protect an interest or claim where the land was not yet registered: LRA 1925, s 53.

[166] Ibid, s 57: a hostile act which prevented any dealings with the registered land; rarely used except in the case of bankruptcy inhibitions entered by the registrar: ibid, s 61.

[167] A donee would be bound by minor interests even if they were not protected by entry: LRA 1925, ss 20(4), 23(5).

[168] Before the register became open to public inspection, the purchaser would see it because the vendor would give the purchaser authority to search the register: Barnsley, *Conveyancing Law and Practice*, p 335.

[169] *Hodges v Jones* [1935] Ch 657, 671 (Luxmoore J); *De Lusignan v Johnson* (1973) 230 EG 499; LRA 1925, s 59(6). See, however, the much criticised decisions in *Peffer v Rigg* [1977] 1 WLR 285, M & B p 222; *Lyus v Prowsa Developments Ltd* [1982] 1 WLR 1044, M & B p 223; below, p 1096, n 165. For further discussion about the extent to which the doctrine of notice is contained (or hidden) within the various categories of overriding interests under LRA 2002, see below, p 693 and 1110–11.

[170] For the informal creation of interests in land, see below, pp 1011 ff.   [171] LRA 1925, ss 3(xvi), 70.

rights acquired or being acquired under the Limitation Act. Of more significance, however was the inclusion in paragraph (g) of:[172]

> the rights of every person in actual occupation of the land or in receipt of the rents and profits thereof, save where enquiry is made of such person and the rights are not disclosed.

All overriding interests, which do not appear on the register, detract from the principle that the register should be a mirror of the vendor's title. Their existence will only be discovered by a purchaser if he resorts to the older methods of investigation. But this is particularly so in the case of paragraph (g). As Lord Denning MR said in *Strand Securities Ltd v Caswell:*[173]

> Section 70(1)(g) is an important provision. Fundamentally, its object is to protect a person in actual occupation of land from having his rights lost in the welter of registration. He can stay there and do nothing. Yet he will be protected. No one can buy the land over his head and thereby take away or diminish his rights. It is up to every purchaser before he buys to make inquiry on the premises. If he fails to do so, it is at his own risk. He must take subject to whatever rights the occupier may have. Such is the doctrine of *Hunt v Luck*,[174] for unregistered land. Section 70(1)(g) carries the same doctrine forward into registered land...

(4) The New Law: Land Registration Act 2002

The Land Registration Act 2002 repealed the 1925 Act, and replaced it with a revised scheme of registration of title to land. The new Act, together with the Land Registration Rules 2003,[175] came into force on 13 October 2003.[176] The new scheme is presented in a more coherent and logical form.[177] There are some significant changes from the 1925 Act, but the essential elements of the former scheme are still recognisable, and cases decided under the former Act may still be relevant in interpreting the new Act on points where the substance remains the same. The detail of the system of registered

---

[172] For some discussion, and a comparison with the equivalent provision under LRA 2002 (Sch 3, para 2), see below, pp 1104 ff.

[173] [1965] Ch 958, 979–80; see also Russell LJ at 984.

[174] [1902] 1 Ch 428. See above, p 88. But, as we shall see, LRA 1925, s 70(1)(g) (and its successor in LRA 2002) and the doctrine of *Hunt v Luck* are by no means identical.

[175] SI 2003 No 1417, amended by SI 2005 No 1766; SI 2005 No 1982. LRR 1925 lapsed on repeal of LRA 1925.

[176] SI 2003 No 1725. For transitional provisions, some of which operated for only limited periods after LRA 2002 came into force, see LRA 2002, s 134, Sch 12, paras 1–3 (existing entries in the register); 4 (existing cautions against first registration); 5–6 (pending applications); 7–13 (former overriding interests); 14–16 (cautions against first registration); 17 (applications under ss. 34 or 43 by cautioners); 18 (adverse possession); 19 (indemnities); 20 (implied indemnity covenants on transfer of pre-1996 leases); LRR 2003, rr 218–23 (caution against dealings); 224 (registered rentcharges); LRA 2002 (Transitional Provisions) Order 2003 (SI 2003 No 1953), arts 2–5 (general and administrative), 6–9 (disputes, objections, appeals and proceedings); 10–13 (souvenir land); 14–18 (cautions); 19 (outline applications); 20 (matrimonial home rights cautions); 21 (index of relating franchises and manors); 22–3 (compulsory first registration); 24 (land and charge certificates); 25 (obligation to make further advances); 26–7 (Forms); 28–9 (official searches and official copies); LRA 2002 (Transitional Provisions) (No 2) Order 2003 (SI 2003 No 2431) (right to repair of church chancel).

[177] LRA 1925 was the only part of the 1925 Legislation that was not drafted by Sir Benjamin Cherry.

conveyancing, as it now exists under the 2002 Act, will be considered later.[178] For the moment we shall limit ourselves to a brief summary of the key points of similarity and difference between the two Acts.

(a) Similarities between the 1925 and 2002 Acts

The fundamental principles of the scheme of registration of title, set out in the Land Registration Act 1925, are continued by the 2002 Act. The register of title is conclusive, and so the State guarantee of title remains—subject only to the powers of the court and the registrar to alter the register. Dispositions of registered land do not take effect at law until the registration requirements are met; and the new Act maintains the distinction between interests that can be registered under their own separate title numbers, and interests that should be protected by entry on the register against a registered estate. Moreover, the new scheme, like the old, admits overriding interests that bind that even though they do not appear on the register[179]—and this includes a revised version of the broad principle that used to be found in section 70(1)(g) of the 1925 Act.[180] A third party should therefore, in principle, protect his interest over a registered estate by making an entry on the register if it is to bind a purchaser; but the new Act continues to recognise the need to balance the protection of the purchaser (through a complete register that will disclose all incumbrances affecting the title) against the protection of the third party (who may have a good reason for not entering his interest on the register). No change is made to the operation of the doctrine of overreaching; and (as under the 1925 Act) the registrar is not to be affected by notice of a trust: the policy is still to keep beneficial interests off the register.

The tripartite structure of the register is unchanged. And the 2002 Act, like its predecessor, contains provisions for both voluntary and compulsory registration of title, the latter being triggered by specified events.

(b) Changes made by the Land Registration Act 2002

Although the main principles of the 1925 scheme are maintained, there are significant changes of detail in the 2002 Act.

A number of the changes are designed to make the register more complete, in two respects. In the first place, the aim is to hasten the day when all the land in England and Wales is on the register, in furtherance of which there is an increase in the number of triggers for first registration, with the promise of more to come until the register is complete. The length of leases subject to compulsory registration is reduced from twenty-one to seven years; land held by Her Majesty as demesne land now becomes registrable;[181] and there is a new law of adverse possession, which makes it much more

---

[178] Below, Ch 28.

[179] LRA 2002, Schs 1 (first registration), 3 (registered dispositions).

[180] Ibid, Sch 3, para 2 (broadly, the interest belonging to a person in discoverable actual occupation; for the detail, see below, pp 1104 ff).

[181] LRA 2002, s 79 (voluntary registration). Demesne land is held by the Crown absolutely, and therefore Her Majesty holds no estate in the land which could otherwise be registered (since an estate is necessarily held of a superior); above, pp 12–13, 47. Crown demesne land includes extensive parts of the foreshore.

difficult for a squatter to obtain title in registered land—so much so that owners of hitherto unregistered land may have an incentive to register their title voluntarily. Voluntary registration has a reduced fee.[182] In the second place, the register is to be a more complete mirror of the title to land once it has been registered: although overriding interests are still admitted, there is a decrease in their number and extent, as well as an increased effort to place incumbrances on the register so as to avoid the need to rely on overriding interests.

There are many changes designed to simplify registered conveyancing. The classes of title are redrafted; the methods of protection of minor interests are simplified (and the terminology of 'minor interests' is abandoned); the principles of rectification and indemnity are restructured (and rectification is absorbed into a wider principle of 'alteration' of the register); the principles of priority of interests are simplified; and the creation of mortgages by demise and sub-demise,[183] already obsolescent, is made obsolete.

Other changes include a new system of independent adjudication arising out of disputed applications to the registrar; and the abolition of land and charge certificates,[184] which more properly reflects the position that it is the register, rather than any document issued by the registrar, that constitutes the title to the land.

(5) The Future: Electronic Conveyancing

Many of the changes made by the Land Registration Act 2002 are designed to pave the way for the introduction of a system of paperless transfer of land by electronic conveyancing. As the Law Commission said in proposing the Bill that became the Land Registration Act 2002:[185]

> The fundamental objective of the Bill is that, under the system of electronic dealing with land that it seeks to create, the register should be a complete and accurate reflection of the state of the title of the land at any given time, so that it is possible to investigate title to land on line, with the absolute minimum of additional enquiries and inspections.

This will be the next step in the evolution of the land law of England and Wales. The Act[186] puts in place the mechanisms for fully electronic conveyancing, under which parties no longer submit documents to the Land Registry for the registrar's staff to process, but the register will be changed automatically to give effect to electronic dealings in registered land:[187]

---

[182] LR Fee Order 2009 (SI 2009 No 845), art 2, replacing similar provisions in earlier LR Fee Orders.

[183] Ie, by granting a legal lease of the property, rather than a charge over it: below, p 801.

[184] No further certificates will be issued, and if a certificate is lodged with the Land Registry it will be destroyed: LRA 2002 (Transitional Provisions) Order 2003 (SI 2003 No 1953), art 24. In its place a Title Information Document will be issued which comprises a copy of the register and a copy of the title plan. In consequence, equitable mortgages by deposit of the land certificate are no longer possible: below, p 810.

[185] Law Com No 271, Land Registration for the Twenty-First Century (2001), para 1.5.

[186] LRA 2002, Part 8; LR (Network Access) Rules 2008 (SI 2008 No 1748); LR (Electronic Conveyancing) Rules 2008 (SI 2008 No 1750). For electronic contracts, see below, p 972.

[187] Law Com No 271, para 1.12.

It is envisaged that, within a comparatively short time, it will be the only method of conducting registered conveyancing... An essential feature of the electronic system when it is fully operational is that it will be impossible to create or transfer many rights in or over registered land expressly except by registering them. Investigation of title will be almost entirely online. It is intended that the secure electronic communications network on which the system will be based, will be used to provide information about properties for intending buyers. It will also provide a means of managing a chain of transactions by monitoring them electronically. This will enable the cause of delays in any chain to be identified and remedial action encouraged. It is anticipated that far fewer chains will break in consequence and that transactions will be considerably expedited. Faster conveyancing is also likely to provide the most effective way of curbing gazumping. The process of registration under the electronic system will be initiated by solicitors and licensed conveyancers, though the Land Registry will exercise control over the changes that can be made to the register. Electronic conveyancing will not come into being as soon as the Bill is brought into force. It will be introduced over a number of years, and there will be a time when both the paper and electronic systems co-exist.

The movement towards electronic conveyancing is gaining momentum. Although the register is not yet complete, and there is no firm deadline for the Land Registry to create a complete register,[188] the Land Registry has already introduced certain electronic services, such as searches and the lodgement of electronic documents, through its 'portal', a secure website, access to which is limited to businesses who enter into a network access agreement.[189] In 2010 a consultation was launched into the rules necessary for electronic transfers, the third main element of electronic conveyancing after electronic discharges and charges, which have already been introduced.[190] The Land Registry proposes, subject to the outcome of the consultation, to introduce electronic transfers and to enlarge the scope of electronic charges to cover e-charges accompanying a transfer, as well as (as at present) stand-alone e-charges, during 2011.[191] It must, however, be noted that this will be a new system of conveyancing, not a new system of land law.[192] The estates and interests that are capable of being substantively registered or entered on the register remain those that are identified under the existing law—and in particular under the great reforms of land law that were achieved in the

[188] Above, p 132.

[189] LR (Network Access) R 2008 (SI 2008 No 1748); Land Registry Practice Guide 71. The Land Registry also operates a Business Gateway for business users: Practice Guide 71, p 2.

[190] Land Registry Annual Report and Accounts 2009–10, p 9. Electronic documents, transfers, charges and discharges are now commonly referred to as, respectively, e-documents, e-transfers, e-charges and e-discharges.

[191] Land Registry E-Conveyancing Consultation: Secondary Legislation Part 3 (March 2010), containing draft LR (Electronic Conveyancing) R 2011; available through the consultations page of the Land Registry website. The latest information on the introduction of electronic conveyancing can be found in the E-conveyancing section of that website.

[192] In introducing the Law of Property Bill 1922, Sir Leslie Scott said (above, p 18, n 85): 'The Bill is not a brand-new invention. It is not a new-fangled, ready-made scheme of law. It is not revolution, it is evolution.' Similarly, in spite of the Law Commission's Report being sub-titled *A Conveyancing Revolution*, the 2002 Act is in effect a further evolutionary stage in the development of English land law, which enables conveyancing to take advantage of information technology and develop alongside similar transactions in banking and business.

1925 legislation. However, the Land Registration Act 2002 will have significant effects on the substantive law. It will change the way in which title to land is perceived, since it is the fact of registration and registration alone that confers legal title.[193] Relativity of seisin, or possession, is no longer the test for title to land, as we shall see in Chapter 29 (Extinction of Estates and Interests in Land).

D COMPARISON OF UNREGISTERED AND REGISTERED SYSTEMS IN THE MODERN LAW

We may now compare the position of a purchaser of the legal fee simple of Blackacre under the two systems of conveyancing. Under both systems he must satisfy himself on two separate matters: first, that the vendor is entitled to convey the fee simple, and, secondly, that there are no incumbrances in favour of third parties that will continue to bind the land after the conveyance. As far as proof of title is concerned, the task of a purchaser is clearly simplified under the registered system. An investigation of the vendor's title deeds is replaced by a search of the register at the Land Registry. A comparison of third-party rights, however, is more complex, although it should be emphasised that the question whether there are third-party rights that will continue to bind the land in general arises, both in registered and unregistered land, only where the transferee is a *purchaser*: a donee is normally simply bound by all property rights, legal and equitable, that attach to the land.[194]

(1) Third-party Rights in Unregistered Land

Under the unregistered system since 1925, a purchaser must first search the Land Charges Register. He is bound by any registrable interests that have been registered at the time when he takes his conveyance from the vendor; if a registrable interest is not so registered, he takes free from it, even though he actually knows of its existence. Further, if the vendor is a tenant for life under a strict settlement or if the vendors are trustees under a trust of land, the purchaser takes free from the equitable interests of the beneficiaries under the doctrine of overreaching, as long as he pays the purchase money to at least two trustees or a trust corporation. Thirdly, a vendor is bound by certain rights that are neither registrable nor overreachable but which in the last resort can be discovered only by his own inquiries and inspection of Blackacre. These include: (a) legal third-party rights, whether he knows about them or not, for example, a legal estate, such as a lease, or a legal interest, such as a legal easement;[195] and (b) a residual category of equitable interests, unless he is a bona fide purchaser for value of the legal estate in Blackacre without actual or constructive notice, for example, a pre-1926 restrictive covenant or an equity by estoppel.[196]

---

[193] Law Com No 271, paras 1.1, 1.10; Geztler (ed), *Rationalizing Property, Equity and Trusts: Essays in Honour of Edward Burn* (2003), ch 9 (C Harpum).

[194] Above, p 83 (unregistered land); LRA 2002, s 28 (registered land).

[195] He is not bound by a puisne mortgage (a legal mortgage not protected by a deposit of documents relating to the legal estate affected) unless it is registered as a land charge; above, p 128; below, p 1063.

[196] Above, p 130, n 114.

The circumstances in which a third-party right will bind a transferee in unregistered land can be represented in outline as follows:

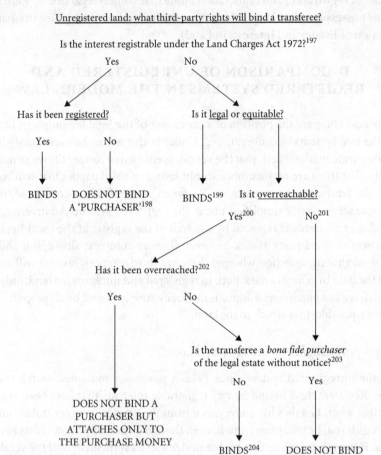

Unregistered land: what third-party rights will bind a transferee?

Is the interest registrable under the Land Charges Act 1972?[197]

Yes — No

Has it been registered? — Is it legal or equitable?

Yes — No — legal — equitable

BINDS — DOES NOT BIND A 'PURCHASER'[198] — BINDS[199] — Is it overreachable?

Yes[200] — No[201]

Has it been overreached?[202]

Yes — No

Is the transferee a *bona fide purchaser* of the legal estate without notice?[203]

No — Yes

DOES NOT BIND A PURCHASER BUT ATTACHES ONLY TO THE PURCHASE MONEY

BINDS[204] — DOES NOT BIND

(2) Third-party Rights in Registered Land

Under the registered system the position of a purchaser of Blackacre is different. On the one hand he is bound by interests that are entered on the register: if an interest is not so entered, he takes free from it even though he actually knows of its existence.

[197] Above, p 128. For details of the classes of land charge which are registrable under LCA 1972, see below, pp 1054 ff.

[198] Above, p 128; *Midland Bank Trust Co Ltd v Green* [1981] AC 513, M & B p 72, below, p 1065.

[199] Above, p 80.

[200] An interest under a strict settlement or a trust of land; above, p 127.

[201] For interests that can be neither registered under LCA 1972 nor overreached, see above, p 130, n 114.

[202] By payment of the purchase price to two trustees or a trust corporation: above, pp 103, 126–7.

[203] LPA 1925, s 199; above, pp 83 ff, 130.

[204] *Kingsnorth Finance Co Ltd v Tizard* [1986] 1 WLR 783, M & B p 216, above, p 88, n 112.

In this context an entry on the register has the same function that registration in the Land Charges Register has in unregistered conveyancing. If, however, the vendor is a tenant for life or if the vendors are trustees of land, the interests of the beneficiaries may be overreached. On the other hand a purchaser is bound by overriding interests, even though he has no knowledge of them and even though they are not entered on the register. The statutory list of overriding interests is a collection of interests that it is held desirable to be binding on a purchaser but which, for some reason or another, do not fit into the pattern of the register. They are discoverable by, but only by, the purchaser's inspection of Blackacre and by inquiries that he must make without assistance from the register. They not only include legal rights that are familiar in unregistered conveyancing, for example, legal easements and certain leases, but they also include interests belonging to a person in discoverable actual occupation of the land.[205]

The outline of the scheme of third-party rights in registered land can be summarised in the following propositions:

(1) The disposition of an estate, such as the transfer of the title to the estate, does not of itself change the priority of interests (including third-party rights), whether or not they are registered.[206]

(2) But the registered transferee *for valuable consideration* of the estate will take free of a third-party right unless it is 'protected',[207] such as by being:

(a) a registered charge, or the subject of a notice in the register;[208] or

(b) an overriding interest within Schedule 3 of the Land Registration Act 2002.[209]

(3) The transferee will also take free if the interest is *overreachable* and if he in fact overreaches it.[210]

Thus in registered conveyancing there is no residual category of equitable interests to which the doctrine of the bona fide purchaser is applicable; that doctrine has been replaced by the provisions of the Land Registration Acts for the protection of interests by notice on the register, and overriding interests. Several judges have discussed this in the context of the 1925 Act, but in terms that apply equally to the Land Registration Act 2002. Lord Wilberforce stated emphatically in *Williams & Glyn's Bank Ltd v Boland* that:[211]

the registered land system is designed to free the purchaser from the hazards of notice—real or constructive... The only kind of notice recognised is by entry on the register

---

[205] LRA 2002, Sch 3, para 2; below, p 1105.
[206] This is the 'basic rule': LRA 2002, s 28. Thus a donee of the estate is bound by all existing property rights, legal and equitable: above, p 143, n 194.
[207] LRA 2002, s 29(1).   [208] Ibid, s 29(2)(a)(i).   [209] Ibid, s 29(2)(a)(ii).
[210] By paying the purchase price to two trustees or a trust corporation: above, pp 103, 126–7, 134, n 136; *City of London Building Society v Flegg* [1988] AC 54, M& B p 551, below, p 1115.
[211] [1981] AC 487, 503.

and Plowman J in *Parkash v Irani Finance Ltd* found a claimant's reliance on the doctrine:[212]

> a little surprising, since one of the essential features of registration of title is to substitute a system of registration of rights for the doctrine of notice.

The residual category of equitable interests can exist under registered conveyancing, but any such interests that are not overriding interests must appear on the register if they are to bind a purchaser.

Third-party rights are treated differently under the two systems of conveyancing. The difference was strikingly illustrated in *Lloyds Bank plc v Carrick*,[213] where:

> Mrs Carrick, a purchaser of unregistered land from her brother-in-law, paid the purchase price in full and entered into possession of the land under an oral contract of sale. The contract, though oral, was at that time enforceable.[214] The contract was registrable as an estate contract (class C (iv)) under the Land Charges Act 1972, but had not been so registered. The vendor then charged the land to Lloyds Bank plc.

The Court of Appeal held that the bank was not bound by the rights of Mrs Carrick. The estate contract was void for non-registration against a purchaser of the legal estate for money or money's worth, even though Mrs Carrick was in possession of the land. However, if the land had been registered land under the Land Registration Act 1925, Mrs Carrick would have been in actual occupation of the land, and her rights would have been binding on the bank as an overriding interest under section 70(1)(g),[215] even though she had not protected them by an entry on the register of the vendor's title.

Commenting on the important difference between the Draconian solution in unregistered land, and the safety net of overriding interests in registered land, Morritt LJ said:[216]

> This result seems to me to be inevitable in the light of the provisions of the Land Charges Act 1972 and of the Law of Property Act 1925...However, it should be noted that the result would have been different if the title to the maisonette had been registered. In such a case the interest of Mrs Carrick, who was in possession of the maisonette and of whom no enquiry had been made, would have been an overriding interest under section 70(1)(*g*) of the Land Registration Act 1925. As such it would have been binding on the Bank....It must be for others to consider and for Parliament to decide whether this distinction between registered and unregistered land should continue.

It is this different treatment that gives rise to differences in the substance of the land law; these differences we shall consider under the various topics in which they occur.

---

212 [1970] Ch 101, 109; *Hodgson v Marks* [1971] Ch 892.   213 [1996] 4 All ER 630.
214 Under the doctrine of part performance, now abolished by LP(MP)A 1989, s 2(8); below, pp 963, 974.
215 See now LRA 2002, Sch 3, para 2.   216 [1996] 4 All ER 630, 642.

PART III

ESTATES AND INTERESTS IN LAND

In this Part we describe the estates and interests that may subsist in land in the modern law. The general arrangement is to consider, first, the estates that may subsist at common law—whether freehold (the fee simple, which in registered land may be registered as commonhold) or leasehold; secondly, the estates and interests in the land that may subsist in equity under a settlement or a trust of land; and thirdly, the interests that third parties may hold, whether at law or in equity, in or over an estate in land—easements, profits à prendre, covenants, rentcharges, mortgages and equities (including an equity arising by proprietary estoppel). A final chapter in this Part, devoted to licences, will assist in drawing the line between property rights—rights in or over the land itself—and personal rights, which we have already seen briefly in Chapter 1.

A FREEHOLD ESTATES

Summary

THE ESTATE IN FEE SIMPLE
ABSOLUTE IN POSSESSION

Summary

I DEFINITION

We must first explain the meaning of the statutory expression *fee simple* absolute in possession that, as we have seen, is the only freehold interest capable of existing as a legal estate.[1]

A FEE SIMPLE

The word *fee* had by Littleton's time, in the fifteenth century, come to denote that the estate was inheritable—that is it would endure until the person entitled to it *for the time being*, whether the original grantee or some subsequent transferee, died intestate and left no heir.[2] The word *simple* showed that the fee was one that was capable of passing to the heirs *general* and was not restricted to passing to a particular class of heirs,[3] which distinguished a fee simple from another kind of fee that used to be called a fee tail and is now called an entailed interest. This was a freehold that passed, on the intestacy of its owner, only to the particular class of lineal descendants specified in the instrument of creation.[4]

---

[1] LPA 1925, s 1(1)(a); above, p 123. For the registration of the freehold estate in land as *commonhold*, see below, Ch 7.

[2] Pollock and Maitland, *The History of English Law* (2nd edn, 1898), vol ii, p 14.

[3] Co Litt 1a, b, 18a, Blackstone, vol ii, p 105.   [4] Below, pp 584–605.

Thus if a tenant in fee simple died intestate, his estate passed to his nearest heir, who according to the circumstances might be a descendant or an ascendant, a lineal or a collateral relative. An entailed interest, on the other hand, was capable of passing only to lineal descendants, and these might, according to the terms of the instrument of creation, be either lineal descendants in general or a restricted class of descendants, such as male heirs or the issue of the tenant by a specified wife. The characteristic of general inheritability is still the attribute of a fee simple, but the significance of this is now modified by the abolition of the doctrine of heirship on intestacy except in the case of the entailed interest. The land itself no longer passes to the nearest heir but upon the death of the owner intestate is held by the administrators on trust, for distribution among the nearest relatives according to a scheme introduced by the Administration of Estates Act 1925, as amended by subsequent legislation. The relatives specified by the Act, however, comprise descendants and ascendants, both lineal and collateral, and it is therefore still true to say that a fee simple is an estate that is the subject of general inheritability.[5]

B ABSOLUTE

'Absolute' is not defined in the Law of Property Act 1925, but it clearly excludes an estate that is defeasible either by the breach of a condition or by the possibility that it may pass to some new owner upon the happening of a specified event. Preston explained *absolute* as follows:[6]

> The epithet *absolute* is used to distinguish an estate extended to any given time, without any condition to defeat, or collateral limitation to determine the estate in the mean time, from an estate subject to a condition or collateral limitation. The term absolute is of the same signification with the word pure, or *simple*, a word that expresses that the estate is not determinable by any event besides the event marked by the clause of limitation.

Thus a fee simple absolute is distinguished from a *determinable* fee simple, that is one that according to the express terms of its limitation[7] may determine by some event before the completion of the full period for which it may possibly continue.[8] If, for example, premises are limited in fee simple to an incorporated golf club 'so long as the premises are used for the purposes of the Club', the interest is a fee simple because it may possibly continue for ever, but it is not a fee simple absolute since it will cease and will return to the grantor or his successors if at some time in the future the premises are used for other purposes.

---

[5] For detail of the rules of intestate succession before 1926, see the 16th edn of this book, pp 947–50; and for the modern rules of distribution, see ibid, pp 950 ff.

[6] Preston, *An Elementary Treatise on Estates* (2nd edn, 1820–7), vol i, pp 125–6.

[7] For the meaning of 'limitation' in this context, see below, p 155.

[8] Below, p 613.

Again, the limitation of a fee simple may be accompanied by an executory limitation over which provides that if a certain event happens the estate shall pass from the grantee to another person, such as where there is a grant of Whiteacre,

to A in fee simple, but if he becomes entitled to Blackacre, then to B in fee simple.

Here the fee simple given to A is not absolute, since it is liable to be divested from him on the occurrence of the specified event. There is one exception to this rule, for section 7 of the Law of Property Act 1925 provides that a fee simple that is liable to be divested under the provisions of the Lands Clauses Acts or any similar statute is 'for the purposes of the Act' a fee simple absolute.[9] The effect of this provision is that the interest is a legal estate within section 1(1) of the Law of Property Act 1925, and not an equitable interest, which would have given rise to a strict settlement under the Settled Land Act before 1997.[10] The conditions attached to the fee simple are not affected. Statutes of this type, which enable land to be acquired for certain public purposes, generally provide expressly that if the purpose fails or is not carried out the land shall revert to the original owner or shall vest in some other person. An express provision to this effect is not, however, essential to bring a statute within the exception. It is sufficient if the implication is that the grantee shall be divested of his interest upon the fulfilment or failure of the purpose for which the land was acquired.[11]

The Law of Property Act 1925[12] also provides that a fee simple vested in a corporation shall be regarded as absolute notwithstanding its liability to determine upon the dissolution of the corporate body.

If a condition is annexed to the limitation of a fee simple providing that the grantor shall be entitled to re-enter and recover his interest if a certain event happens or does not happen, it is equally clear on general principles that the estate is not a fee simple absolute within the meaning of the description given by Preston. Nevertheless the provision of the Law of Property Act 1925 which denied the character of a legal estate to an interest

---

[9] LPA 1925, s 7(1), as amended by Reverter of Sites Act 1987, which excludes from s 7(1) the School Sites Acts, the Literary and Scientific Institutions Act 1854 and the Places of Worship Sites Act 1873. The right of reverter in those cases is now replaced by a trust of land. Where, for example, a school site ceases to be used for purposes mentioned in the School Sites Act 1841, the charitable trustees continue to hold the legal estate on a trust of land for the revertee: Reverter of Sites Act 1987, s 1, as amended by TLATA 1996, s 5, Sch 2, para 6; *Fraser v Canterbury Diocesan Board of Finance (No 2)* [2005] UKHL 65, [2006] 1 AC 377. They may apply to the Charity Commissioners to have the interests of the revertee extinguished: s 2; Charities Act 1993, s 23. A revertee in some circumstances may be entitled to compensation: s 2(4). For the difficulties caused by the original s 7(1), see Law Com No 111, *Rights of Reverter* (1981). The Act departs in a significant number of respects from the Report's recommendations. See Current Law Statutes Annotated (J Hill); [1987] Conv 408 (D Evans).

[10] Strict settlements can no longer be created after 1996: TLATA 1996, s 2(1), below, p 475.

[11] *Tithe Redemption Commission v Runcorn UDC* [1954] Ch 383 (highway vested in the local highway authority; Local Government Act 1929 held to be 'a similar statute' within LPA 1925, s 7(1)).

[12] S 7(2). As to whether the lands of a corporation upon its dissolution reverted to the donor or escheated to the lord, see Co Litt 13b; Gray, *The Rule against Perpetuities* (4th edn, 1942), ss 44–52; Challis, *The Law of Real Property* (3rd edn, ed Sweet, 1911) pp 35–6, 467–8; *Hastings Corp v Letton* [1908] 1 KB 378; *Re Woking UDC* [1914] 1 Ch 300; *Re Sir Thomas Spencer Wells* [1933] Ch 29; (1933) 49 LQR 240; (1934) 50 LQR 33 (FE Farrer); (1935) 51 LQR 347 (MW Hughes), 361 (FE Farrer).

of this nature, caused considerable difficulty. In the North West of England and in the county of Avon (and especially in Manchester and Bristol), it used to be a common practice for a purchaser of a fee simple, instead of paying the purchase money in a lump sum, to enter into a covenant to pay a perpetual annual rentcharge.[13] The payment of the rent is secured to the vendor and his successors by the reservation of either a right of entry or a right of re-entry. The former permits the vendor and his successors to enter the land at any time in the future if the annual payment falls into arrear and to hold the land as a leasehold interest until the arrears are paid.[14] The right of re-entry (which is more common in the case of a lease[15]) arises where the conveyance contains a condition that the purchaser and his successors will pay the rent and provides that the vendor shall be entitled to re-enter if this condition is broken. In this case the person entitled to the rent may either re-enter upon the land or bring proceedings for its recovery, whereupon the interest of the purchaser is forfeited and the vendor reacquires his old estate.[16]

The fact that a fee simple liable to interruption in either of these ways was not a legal estate within the meaning of the Law of Property Act 1925 operated to the prejudice of a landowner, for not only did it seem to make the land subject to the Settled Land Act and thus to require the execution of a vesting deed,[17] but it made it difficult to discover in whom the legal estate was vested.[18] In view of this, section 7 of the 1925 Act was amended in 1926 to provide that:

> a fee simple subject to a legal or equitable right of entry or re-entry is for the purposes of this Act a fee simple absolute.[19]

The word 'absolute' does not imply freedom from incumbrances. Thus a fee simple, though subject to a lien or a mortgage, whether legal or equitable, or to a mere charge, is none the less absolute.

C IN POSSESSION

Finally, to have the character of a legal estate, a fee simple absolute must be *in possession*. 'Possession' is not here confined to its popular meaning, but includes 'receipt of rents and profits or the right to receive the same'.[20] Therefore, a tenant in fee simple who has leased the land to a tenant for years is 'in possession', and therefore the owner of a legal estate, even though he is not in physical possession of the land. If, however, he is entitled to the fee simple only at some time in the future, such as in the case of a limitation:

> to A for life and then to B in fee simple,

---

[13] Below, p 781 ff.

[14] Litt s 327; Co Litt 202b; ibid, note 93 by Hargrave and Butler.   [15] Below, pp 279, 287.

[16] Litt s 325.   [17] Below, p 436.

[18] (1926) 61 LJ News 49 (FE Farrer). See also M & B p 303, n 13.

[19] LP(A)A 1926, Schedule. The rentcharge, being perpetual, is a *legal* interest under LPA 1925, s 1(2)(b), above, p 124; and under s 1(2)(e), the right of entry, being 'annexed to a legal rentcharge', is also a *legal* interest.

[20] LPA 1925, ss 205(1)(xix), 95(4); *District Bank Ltd v Webb* [1958] 1 WLR 148, M & B p 303.

A has an equitable life interest and B has an equitable fee simple. Before 1997 the land was settled land under the Settled Land Act 1925; in a grant made since then the limitation takes effect under a trust of land.[21]

II MODE OF CREATION

A WORDS OF LIMITATION

We must first distinguish between 'words of limitation' and 'words of purchase'. 'Words of limitation' indicate the size of the interest given by some instrument; they limit or define it. On the other hand, 'words of purchase' (*perquisitio*) point out, by name or description, the person who is to acquire (*perquirit*) an interest in land. A 'purchaser' in this technical sense does not denote a person who buys land, but one to whom land is expressly transferred by *act of parties*, such as by conveyance on sale, by gift or by will. If land is given 'to A and his heirs', A is a purchaser since he is personally designated as the transferee, but the words 'and his heirs' are words of limitation. They merely indicate the quantum of interest that A is to take, and give the heirs nothing by direct gift. The lands may, of course, descend to them as heirs if A dies intestate, but they will not be purchasers since the land comes to them by operation of law and not by act of parties.[22]

(1) Natural Persons

Whether a fee simple passes to a grantee or a devisee of land depends upon the words of limitation contained in the deed or will. In the case of deeds, the law was in former times extremely strict upon this point. If certain expressions were adopted, the effect was to create a fee simple; if others, a fee tail or life estate. Thus before 1882 the only way of creating a fee simple by a direct grant inter vivos was by a limitation to the grantee *and his heirs*. This expression has been common form since the birth of English law, and perhaps its original implication was that the tenant could not alienate his interest without first consulting the apparent heirs. In the thirteenth century, however, all restraints of that kind on alienation disappeared and it became settled that the expression did not confer rights of any sort upon the heir, but was used merely to show that the tenant had an estate that would endure at least as long as his heirs endured.[23]

---

[21] Below, pp 606–7.

[22] See Fearne, *Contingent Remainders* (10th edn, 1844), pp 79–80; and *IRC v Gribble* [1913] 3 KB 212, where at 218 Buckley LJ said: '"Purchaser", as it seems to me, may mean any one of four things. First, it may bear what has been called the vulgar or commercial meaning; purchaser may mean a buyer for money. Secondly, it may also include a person who becomes a purchaser, for money's worth, which would include the case of an exchange. Thirdly, it may mean a purchaser for valuable consideration, which need not be money or money's worth, but may be, say, a covenant on the consideration of marriage. Fourthly it may bear that which in the language of real property lawyers is its technical meaning, namely a person who does not take by descent.'

[23] Pollock and Maitland, *The History of English Law*, vol ii, p 13.

If, for example, in a *deed* there was a grant to:

A and his assignees; or
A for ever; or
A and his descendants; or
A and his successors,[24]

then, however untechnical the expression might be, and however obvious the intention of the parties might be to convey the fee simple, the only effect was to pass a life estate to A. This strictness was mitigated and an alternative form of words was permitted by the Conveyancing Act 1881,[25] which provided that in deeds executed after 31 December 1881, the fee simple should pass if the expression 'in fee simple' was adopted.

In the case of land *devised by will* the law was more liberal in its definition of words of limitation than it was in the case of deeds. Thus in addition to the technical expression 'and his heirs', any informal words that clearly showed that the testator intended to give the fee simple were allowed to have that effect,[26] but notwithstanding this more lenient attitude the fact remained that laxity in the use of words of limitation frequently defeated intention. Section 28 of the Wills Act 1837 therefore provided that:

> where any real estate shall be devised to any person without any words of limitation, such devise shall be construed to pass the fee simple, or other the whole estate or interest which the testator had power to dispose of by will in such real estate, unless a contrary intention shall appear by the will.

The effect of this enactment was to reverse the former law. Before 1837 the effect of using a non-technical expression was to pass only a life estate, unless an intention to pass the whole fee simple could be clearly deduced; but since 1837 the effect is to pass the entire interest that the testator happens to have in the land, unless his intention, as clearly shown by the will itself, is to give some smaller interest. The burden of proving that a smaller interest passes lies on those who maintain that hypothesis.

The rule thus introduced for wills by the Act of 1837 was extended to deeds by the Law of Property Act 1925. It provides that:[27]

> a conveyance of freehold land to any person without words of limitation,[28] or any equivalent expression, shall pass to the grantee the fee simple or other the whole interest which the grantor had power to convey in such land, unless a contrary intention appears in the conveyance.

It will be noticed that the language of this section corresponds closely with that of the Wills Act 1837.

---

[24] *Bankes v Salisbury Diocesan Council of Education Inc* [1960] Ch 631.   [25] S 51.

[26] *Jarman on Wills* (8th edn, ed Jennings and Harper, 1951), p 1802.   [27] LPA 1925, s 60(1).

[28] See [2008] Conv 129 (J Mee) for the argument that, by virtue of these words, the provision applies only if there are *no* words of limitation, and thus a limitation 'in fee simple', which is no longer covered by Conveyancing Act 1881, s 51, above n 25, since that Act was repealed by LPA 1925, can be saved only by an (unintended) interpretation of LPA 1925, s 60(4).

The position, then, at the present day, both for deeds and for wills, is that, if it is desired to confer a fee simple upon X, land may be limited 'to X in fee simple' or 'to X and his heirs'; but that, if any other expression is used, such as 'to X', or 'to X for ever', the fee simple, if owned by the person making the disposition, will pass unless the instrument clearly shows that there was no such intention.[29] In practice the words 'to X in fee simple' are used, in order to avoid the possibility of a contrary intention appearing in the instrument.[30]

A limitation before 1926, not 'to A and his heirs', but to 'A for life, remainder to his heirs' would have conferred a fee simple estate upon A under the rule known as the *Rule in Shelley's Case*. This rule, which is described below,[31] has, however, been abolished, and the effect of such a limitation now is to give a life interest to A and a fee simple estate to his heir.

(2) Corporations

Where it was desired to grant a fee simple to a corporation sole,[32] that is a body having perpetual succession and consisting of a single person, such as a bishop, the vicar of a parish, or the Public Trustee, the old law was that the grant must be made to the person in question *and his successors*, otherwise it merely operated to confer an estate for life on the actual holder of the office.[33] This rule has, however, been altered,[34] and a conveyance of freehold land in which the word 'successors' has been omitted passes to the corporation the fee simple or other the whole interest that the grantor has, unless a contrary intention appears in the conveyance.

In the case of a corporation aggregate,[35] that is a collection of several persons who are united into one body and who are followed by a perpetual succession of members, such as the mayor and corporation of a city, or a limited liability company incorporated under the Companies Act 2006, it is sufficient to grant to the corporation under its corporate name.[36]

B VOLUNTARY CONVEYANCE

If a feoffment[37] were made before the Statute of Uses to a stranger in blood without the receipt of a money consideration (ie a voluntary conveyance), and *without declaring a use* in favour of the feoffee, the rule was that the land must be held by the feoffee to the use of the feoffor.[38] The equitable interest that thus returned by implication to the feoffor was called a resulting use. The effect of the enactment by the Statute of Uses[39] that a *cestui que use* should have the legal estate was that the legal estate resulted to the feoffor.[40] In order to prevent this it became the practice in the case of such a conveyance

---

29 See, for example, *Quarm v Quarm* [1892] 1 QB 184. 30 But see above, n 28.
31 Below, p 596. 32 Below, p 1033. 33 Co Litt 8b, 94b.
34 LPA 1925, s 60(2). 35 Below, p 1033. 36 Co Litt 94b. 37 Above, p 62.
38 Sanders, *Uses and Trusts* (5th edn, ed Sandars and Warner, 1844), vol i, p 60. 39 Above, p 73.
40 Sanders, *Uses and Trusts*, vol i, p 97; *Beckwith's Case* (1589) 2 Co Rep 56b.

to declare in the deed that the land was granted 'unto and to the use of' the grantee. The repeal of the Statute of Uses by the legislation of 1925 would, in the absence of a further enactment, have restored the original rule, and it might have led practitioners to believe that the expression 'to the use of' was still necessary in order to render a voluntary conveyance effective. The Law of Property Act 1925, however, enacted that:[41]

> in a voluntary conveyance a resulting trust for the grantor shall not be implied merely by reason that the property is not expressed to be conveyed for the use or benefit of the grantee.

C REGISTERED LAND

In registered land there are two points to notice about the fee simple absolute in possession. First, where the registered proprietor transfers it inter vivos, no words of limitation are required in the transfer.[42] Secondly, as we have seen, the legal estate will not pass to the transferee until the transfer is completed by registration.[43] For this reason it has been suggested[44] that the Land Registration Acts really provide a new statutory title to land, one that is not the fee simple, but a new fee based on it. But the argument is really a verbal one as to how the consequences of registration affect the character of what is registered. Section 11 of the Land Registration Act 2002 provides that the effect of registration is to vest the freehold estate—that is, the fee simple absolute in possession[45]—in the proprietor, and so it is still, in law, the fee simple estate that he holds.

III THE LEGAL POSITION OF A TENANT IN FEE SIMPLE

A EXTENT OF OWNERSHIP

A tenant in fee simple has extensive property rights in the subject-matter of his interest. In accordance with the maxim *cujus est solum, ejus est usque ad coelum et ad inferos*,[46] the common law principle is that a tenant in fee simple is owner of

---

[41] LPA 1925, s 60(3).

[42] Below, p 1085; *A J Dunning & Sons (Shopfitters) Ltd v Sykes & Son (Poole) Ltd* [1987] Ch 287, 302.

[43] LRA 2002, s 27; above, pp 134, 140; below, pp 1008–9; replacing LRA 1925, ss 19(1), 20(1).

[44] See (1949) 12 MLR 139, 477 (AD Hargreaves); 205 (H Potter); (1947) 11 Conv (NS) 184, 232 (RC Connell); (1972) 88 LQR 93 (D Jackson); Farrand, *Contract and Conveyance* (2nd edn, 1973), pp 178–80; Barnsley, *Conveyancing Law and Practice* (4th edn, ed Thompson, 1996), pp 36–8.

[45] 'Legal estate' has the same meaning as in LPA 1925, s 1: LRA 2002, s 132(1). See also LRA 2002, s 3(1)(a). LRA 1925 referred more particularly to the proprietor having the fee simple absolute in possession vested in him: ss 5, 20(1), 69(1).

[46] 'The owner of the soil owns it up to the sky and down to the depths below': 'A colourful phrase often upon the lips of lawyers since it was first coined by Accursius in Bologna in the 13th century': *Baron Bernstein of Leigh v Skyviews and General Ltd* [1978] QB 479, 485 (Griffiths J).

everything in, on and above his land. Lord Wilberforce said:[47] 'At most the maxim is used as a statement, imprecise enough, of the extent of the rights, prima facie, of owners of land: Bowen LJ was concerned with these rights when...he said "Prima facie the owner of the land has everything under the sky down to the centre of the earth"',[48] but it has recently been applied as a useful maxim in the Supreme Court.[49] The rights are as extensive as common law and statute permit,[50] and the limitations on the rights to the airspace above the land may be more significant than the limitations on the rights to the substrata below the land.[51]

(1) In and on the Land

(a) Mines and minerals

At common law all mines and minerals that lie beneath the soil belong absolutely to the tenant in fee simple but by statute all interests in coal are vested in the Coal Authority[52] and petroleum existing in its natural condition in strata in Great Britain or beneath the territorial sea adjacent to the United Kingdom is vested in the Crown.[53] Further, the Crown is entitled to all gold and silver in gold and silver mines.[54]

(b) Chattels

In the absence of trustworthy evidence of ownership, there is a legal presumption that the fee simple owner, if in possession, is owner of chattels found on or under his land.[55]

[47] *Railways Comr v Valuer-General* [1974] AC 328, 351–2. The maxim was applied in *Grigsby v Melville* [1974] 1 WLR 80 (cellar underneath drawing-room floor); *Graystone Property Investments Ltd v Margulies* (1983) 47 P & CR 472 (void space between false ceiling and underneath of floor of flat above).

[48] *Pountney v Clayton* (1883) 11 QBD 820, 838.

[49] *Bocardo SA v Star Energy UK Onshore Ltd* [2010] UKSC 35, [2011] 1 AC 380 at [26] (Lord Hope of Craighead DPSC).

[50] 'It is quite plain that airspace is not something which even the most ingenious conveyancer of Lincoln's Inn has ever dealt with as an item of property unrelated to the ground over which it lies': *Rolfe v Wimpey Waste Management Ltd* [1988] STC 329, 357 (Harman J).

[51] *Bocardo SA v Star Energy UK Onshore Ltd*, above, n 49, at [26] (Lord Hope of Craighead DPSC; landowner's title extended down to strata through which wells, dug 800 feet to 2,800 feet below the surface, passed). For the extent of the freeholder's right to airspace, see below, p 162.

[52] Coal Industry Act 1994, replacing earlier bodies created successively by Coal Act 1938 (the Coal Commission); Coal Industry Nationalisation Act 1946 (the National Coal Board); Coal Industry Act 1987 (the British Coal Corporation).

[53] Petroleum Act 1998, s 2. See *Earl of Lonsdale v A-G* [1982] 1 WLR 887 ('mines and minerals' in 1880 conveyance held not to include oil and natural gas). However, a licence from the Crown to a third party to search and bore for and get petroleum does not dispense the licensee from obtaining a licence from the owner of the surface of the land: *Bocardo SA v Star Energy UK Onshore Ltd*, above, n 49 (on the Petroleum Production Act 1934, the predecessor to the 1998 Act).

[54] *Mines Case* (1567) 1 Plowd 310; Royal Mines Acts 1688, 1693.

[55] *South Staffordshire Water Co v Sharman* [1896] 2 QB 44; *Hannah v Peel* [1945] KB 509; *Hibbert v McKiernan* [1948] 2 KB 142; *Re Cohen* [1953] Ch 88; *City of London Corp v Appleyard* [1963] 1 WLR 982; *Moffatt v Kazana* [1969] 2 QB 152; *Parker v British Airways Board* [1982] QB 1004 especially at 1017–18 (gold bracelet found on floor in international executive lounge at Heathrow held to belong to finder); [1990]

(c) Treasure trove

The proprietary rights of the fee simple owner do not extend to treasure trove.

(1) At common law

The common law definition of treasure was stated by Chitty as follows:[56]

> Treasure trove is, where any gold or silver in coin, plate, or bullion is found concealed in a house, or in the earth, or other private place, the owner thereof being unknown, in which case the treasure belongs to the King or his grantee having the franchise of treasure trove; but if he that laid it be known or afterwards discovered, the owner and not the King is entitled to it; this prerogative right only applying in the absence of an owner to claim the property. If the owner, instead of hiding the treasure, casually lost it, or purposely parted with it,[57] in such a manner that it is evident he intended to abandon the property altogether, and did not purpose to resume it on another occasion, as if he threw it on the ground, or other public place, or in the sea, the first finder is entitled to the property as against every one but the owner, and the King's prerogative does not in this respect obtain. So that it is the hiding, and not the abandonment, of the property that entitles the King to it.

Whether a coin or object is made of silver or gold is a question of fact. It must contain a substantial proportion of gold or silver. Thus, Roman coins of the third century AD with a silver content ranging from 0.2 to 18 per cent have been held not to be treasure trove.[58]

(2) Treasure Act 1996

The Treasure Act 1996 widens the definition of treasure.[59] It is any object that is at least 300 years old when found and, if not a coin, has a metallic content of which at least 10 per cent by weight is gold or silver.

There are special rules for coins. To be treasure they must be at least 300 years old and be one of at least two coins with the same percentage of gold or silver. Alternatively, if a coin is at least 300 years old and is one of at least ten coins in the same find, it is treasure regardless of its metallic percentage. If a coin is found alone, it is not treasure. Objects found as part of the same find are also treasure; for example the pot in which the coins are found. Objects of historical or archaeological or cultural importance are

Conv 348 (DC Hoath); *Tamworth Industries v A-G* [1991] 3 NZLR 616; [1993] CLP Part I, p 81 (P Kohler). See Goodhart, *Essays in Jurisprudence and the Common Law* (1931), pp 75–90; Guest (ed), *Oxford Essays in Jurisprudence* (1961), pp 69–106 (DR Harris).

[56] *Chitty on the Prerogative*, p 152, cited *A-G v Moore* [1893] 1 Ch 676, 683; *A-G v British Museum Trustees* [1903] 2 Ch 598; *Waverley BC v Fletcher* [1996] QB 334 (mediaeval gold brooch found in park held not treasure but to belong to local authority); [1996] Conv 216 (J Stevens). On treasure generally, see Hill, *Treasure Trove in Law and Practice* (1936).

[57] On whether a possessor can divest himself of possession of a thing by its deliberate abandonment, see Pollock and Wright, *Possession in the Common Law* (1888), p 124; *Haynes' Case* (1613) 12 Co Rep 113; *Arrow Shipping Co v Tyne Improvement Comrs* [1894] AC 508, 532.

[58] *A-G of the Duchy of Lancaster v G E Overton (Farms) Ltd* [1982] Ch 277; [1980] CLJ 281 (DEC Yale); (1981) 44 MLR 178 (NE Palmer).

[59] Ss 1, 3(3); (1996) 146 NLJ 1346 (C MacMillan); [1997] Conv 273; [1998] Conv 252 (J Marston and L Ross). See also the reports of the Treasure Valuation Committee (available on the web site of the Department for Culture, Media and Sport).

not included within the statutory definition, but the Secretary of State may designate as treasure by statutory instrument any such objects that are over 200 years old.[60]

The Coroners and Justice Act 2009[61] created the office of Coroner for Treasure, who will conduct an investigation concerning objects that are reported to his or her office under the Treasure Act 1996,[62] and may conduct an investigation concerning other objects if he or she has reason to suspect that they are treasure.[63]

(d) Sea-shore

An owner of land adjoining the sea is entitled to the sea-shore[64] down to a point that is reached by an ordinary high tide, but all the shore below that is vested in the Crown or its grantee.[65]

He is also entitled to land that is added by gradual and imperceptible accretion from the sea.[66]

(e) Wild creatures

The owner's rights in respect of wild animals, such as game,[67] depend upon the circumstances. Such animals are not within the absolute ownership of any particular person. There are two exceptions: wild animals that have been tamed belong to the person who has tamed them; and animals too young to escape belong to the occupier of the land on which they are until they gain their natural liberty.[68] In other cases the tenant in fee simple or, indeed, the occupier of the land, has not an absolute, but a qualified, right of ownership over the animals within the confines of his property in the sense that the exclusive right to catch, kill and appropriate them belongs to him by

---

[60] S 2; Treasure Designation Order 2002 (SI 2002 No 2666).

[61] S 25 and Sch 4 (this section of the Act is not yet in force). The jurisdiction relating to treasure was formerly exercised by local coroners: Coroners Act 1988, s 30.

[62] It is a criminal offence not to notify the Coroner or another designated officer within 14 days of the find: Treasure Act 1996, ss 8, 8B (as amended by Coroners and Justice Act 2009, s 40; Sch 21, para 37); and the duty to notify extends also to a person who acquires property in an object which he believes or has reasonable grounds for believing is treasure: s 8A, inserted by Coroners and Justice Act 2009, s 30.

[63] Coroners and Justice Act 2009, s 26. An inquest, normally without a jury, may also be held: ibid, s 27. If, however, the Crown, or a franchisee of the Crown, disclaims any right to an object, the Coroner may no longer conduct an investigation relating to it: s 29.

[64] See *Government of Penang v Beng Hong Oon* [1972] AC 425, 435, 439.

[65] *Lowe v Govett* (1832) 3 B & Ad 863; *Blundell v Catterall* (1821) 5 B & Ald 268; *Alfred F Beckett Ltd v Lyons* [1967] Ch 449; *Crown Estate Commissioners v Roberts* [2008] EWHC 1302 (Ch), [2008] 2 P & CR 15 (insufficient evidence to rebut presumption that part of Pembrokeshire foreshore was vested in Crown; it therefore did not vest in Lord of the Manor of Trevene and of the City and Suburbs of St David's). For the rights of the public over the sea-shore, see [1974] JPL 705 (A Wharam).

[66] *Gifford v Lord Yarborough* (1828) 5 Bing 163. See *Baxendale v Instow Parish Council* [1982] Ch 14, 23; Wisdom, *Law of Watercourses* (5th edn, 1992), ch 2. The rule of accretion also applies to inland lakes: *Southern Centre of Theosophy Inc v State of South Australia* [1982] AC 706 (accretion by fluvial action and river-blown sand); (1983) 99 LQR 412 (P Jackson); [1986] Conv 255 (W Howarth).

[67] *Inglewood Investment Co Ltd v Forestry Commission* [1988] 1 WLR 1278 (game construed to mean feathered game and not deer).

[68] *Case of Swans* (1592) 7 Co Rep 15b.

reason of his interest in the land.[69] Thus, game that is killed by a trespasser belongs to the occupier of the land on which it is killed. The only exception to this principle, and one not altogether free from doubt, is that if A starts game on the land of B, and hunts it on to the ground of C and kills it there, the ownership of the game belongs to A the hunter, though of course he may be liable in trespass both to B and to C.[70]

(2) Above the Land

Although the fee simple owner does not acquire the ownership of anything that overhangs his land, such as a cornice, an illuminated advertisement, telephone wires or the bough of a tree, he can maintain an action of nuisance or of trespass against the person who allows it to be there,[71] unless it has been acquired by that person as an easement.[72] A freeholder's rights in the airspace above the property do not, however, extend to an unlimited height, but are restricted to such height as is necessary for the ordinary use and enjoyment of his land. Thus, where an aircraft flew over land for the purpose of taking an aerial photograph of a house on it, an action for trespass failed.[73] And there is also a defence under the Civil Aviation Act 1982,[74] which provides that no action shall lie in respect of trespass or nuisance by reason only of the flight of an aircraft over any property at a height that is reasonable under the circumstances, provided that certain regulations are complied with.

(3) Flying Freeholds

A fee simple can exist in an upper storey of a building, separate and distinct from the rest. As Coke said: 'A man may have an inheritance in an upper chamber though the

---

[69] *Blades v Higgs* (1865) 11 HL Cas 621, 631 (Lord Westbury LC). The Crown has a prerogative right to swans, and royal fish, eg whales and sturgeon. Any such right to other wild creatures was abolished by the Wild Creatures and Forest Laws Act 1971, s 1(1)(a).

[70] *Sutton v Moody* (1697) 1 Ld Raym 250, criticised by Lord Chelmsford in *Blades v Higgs* (1865) 11 HL Cas 621, 639. It is a criminal offence under the Protection of Badgers Act 1992 to kill badgers, and under the Wildlife and Countryside Act 1981 to kill, injure or take wild animals listed in Sch 5 (for example, swallowtail butterfly, common otter and red squirrel) and wild birds, or to disturb wild birds listed in Sch 1 while they are nesting (for example, bee-eater, chough, hoopoe, kingfisher, peregrine and barn owl). The lists of protected animals has been amended by statutory instrument: SI 1988 No 288; SI 1989 No 906; SI 1991 No 367; SI 1992 No 2350; SI 1998 No 878; SI 2007 No 1843; SI 2008 No 431. See also Wildlife and Countryside (Amendment) Act 1991. See also the Deer Act 1991; Wild Mammals Protection Act 1996. The Hunting Act 2004 makes it a criminal offence to hunt a wild mammal with a dog save in limited circumstances; *R (Jackson) v A-G* [2005] UKHL 56, [2006] 1 AC 262.

[71] *Wandsworth Board of Works v United Telephone Co* (1884) 13 QBD 904; *Lemmon v Webb* [1895] AC 1; *Gifford v Dent* [1926] WN 336; *Kelsen v Imperial Tobacco Co (of Great Britain and Ireland) Ltd* [1957] 2 QB 334; *Woollerton and Wilson Ltd v Richard Costain Ltd* [1970] 1 WLR 411; *Anchor Brewhouse Developments Ltd v Berkley House (Docklands Developments) Ltd* [1987] 2 EGLR 173 (tower cranes oversailing adjoining land held to be infringement of airspace and therefore trespass: injunction granted).

[72] *Simpson v Weber* (1925) 41 TLR 302.

[73] *Baron Bernstein of Leigh v Skyviews and General Ltd* [1978] QB 479. See McNair, *Law of the Air* (3rd edn, ed Kerr and Evans, 1964), pp 31 ff.

[74] S 76(1).

lower buildings and soil be in another.'[75] This is known as a flying freehold. Land can thus be divided horizontally as well as vertically.

A fee simple may also be[76] 'a movable fee where "the fee itself is a continuing estate, but it is an estate in land that from time to time changes its location"; as, for example, where it varies with changes of a boundary such as the foreshore.' A more sophisticated form of flying freeholds has now been created in the form of *commonhold*. This is discussed in Chapter 7.

(4) Water[77]

A landowner has certain valuable rights over water that may run through or be situated on his land.

The right of abstraction at common law, however, has been substantially modified by statute. Under the Environment Act 1995[78] the Environment Agency is responsible for running a compulsory system of licensing for the abstraction of water.

(a) Ponds and lakes

Water standing in a lake or pond is part of the land and belongs to the landowner. If it stands partly upon his land and partly upon that of another, each is probably entitled to such part as lies opposite his own bank, but only up to a point half way between his and the opposite bank.[79]

(b) Percolating water

Water percolating underneath the land and not contained in a defined channel is a common supply in which nobody has any property, but at common law it becomes the absolute property of any occupier by whom it is appropriated.[80]

If an occupier abstracts percolating water, he becomes the owner of it and may take it regardless of the consequences, whether physical or pecuniary, to his neighbours.[81] Thus he will not be liable to his neighbours, even if the effect may have been to dry up a spring or a well on their land.[82]

---

[75] Co Litt 48b; Lincoln's Inn Act 1860, which regulates flying freeholds in New Square, Lincoln's Inn. See the claim to a 'subterranean flying freehold' of a cellar in *Grigsby v Melville* [1974] 1 WLR 80, 83.

[76] *Baxendale v Instow Parish Council* [1982] Ch 14, 20 (Megarry V-C); *Welden v Bridgewater* (1592) Cro Eliz 421 (lot meadows, where two or more have a fee simple in a measured part of a meadow, but the precise part owned is determined by lots at specified times). See [1982] Conv 208 (RE Annand).

[77] See generally Waite, Jewell, Jones and Fogleman, *Environmental Law in Property Transactions* (3rd edn, 2009), ch 17; Getzler, *A History of Water Rights at Common Law* (2004); Bates, *Water and Drainage Law*.

[78] S 2, which transferred to the Environment Agency from the National Rivers Authority the functions set out in Water Resources Act 1991, ss 24–72. See also Water Act 2003.

[79] See *Mackenzie v Bankes* (1878) 3 App Cas 1324.

[80] *Ballard v Tomlinson* (1885) 29 Ch D 115, 121 (Brett MR).

[81] *Stephens v Anglian Water Authority* [1987] 1 WLR 1381, 1387 (Slade LJ); [1988] Conv 175 (M Harwood).

[82] *Acton v Blundell* (1843) 12 M & W 324; *Chasemore v Richards* (1859) 7 HL Cas 349; *Bradford Corp v Pickles* [1895] AC 587; *Rugby Joint Water Board v Walters* [1967] Ch 397; *Langbrook Properties Ltd v Surrey*

(c) Streams and rivers

The next type of case is where a river or stream runs in a *definite channel*, whether above or below the surface, though it must be noted that an underground stream does not come within this category until it is established that it follows a definite course.[83] Underground water, the course of which cannot be ascertained without excavation, ranks as percolating water. Two questions arise where a stream follows a definite course; first, the rights of the riparian owner or owners in the *bed*, secondly, their rights in the *water*.

(1) Rights in the bed

The bed of a *non-tidal* river belongs, when there is no evidence of acts of ownership to the contrary, to the owner of the land through which it flows, but when the lands of two owners are separated by a running stream, each owner is prima facie owner of the soil of the bed of the river up to the mid-point of the stream. The soil of the bed is not the common property of the two owners, but the share of each belongs to him separately, so that, if the stream becomes diverted, each owner may use his share of the bed in any way he chooses.[84] On the other hand, the bed of a *tidal* river, up to a point where the water flows and reflows regularly, belongs to the Crown unless it has been granted to a subject.[85]

(2) Rights in the water

But the water, as distinct from the bed of a river, is not the subject of absolute ownership, and, though subject to certain rights exercisable by the owners of the lands through which it flows, it does not belong to them in the ordinary sense of the term. Such a riparian owner has at common law, as a natural incident of his ownership, certain riparian rights, which have been authoritatively described as follows:[86]

> A riparian proprietor is entitled to have the water of the stream on the banks of which his property lies, flow down as it has been accustomed to flow down to his property, subject to the ordinary use of the flowing water by upper proprietors, and to such further use, if any, on their part in connection with their property as may be reasonable under the circumstances.

County Council [1970] 1 WLR 161; *Thomas v Gulf Oil Refining Ltd* (1979) 123 SJ 787; *Brace v South Eastern Regional Housing Association Ltd* (1984) 270 EG 1286; *Home Brewery Co Ltd v William Davis & Co (Leicester) Ltd* [1987] QB 339; *Palmer v Bowman* [2000] 1 WLR 842 (natural right to drain surface and percolating water onto lower neighbouring land not capable of being an easement), below, p 640, n 50.

[83] *Bleachers' Association Ltd v Chapel-en-le-Frith RDC* [1933] Ch 356; *R v Falmouth and Truro Port Health Authority, ex p South West Water Ltd* [2001] QB 445 (a watercourse does not include a river or an estuary for the purposes of Public Health Act 1936, s 259).

[84] *Bickett v Morris* (1866) LR 1 Sc & Div 47, especially at 58.

[85] *A-G v Earl of Lonsdale* (1868) LR 7 Eq 377, 388.

[86] *John Young & Co v Bankier Distillery Co* [1893] AC 691, 698 (Lord Macnaghten); *Provender Millers (Winchester) Ltd v Southampton County Council* [1940] Ch 131; *Tate & Lyle Industries Ltd v Greater London Council* [1983] 2 AC 509; *Scott-Whitehead v National Coal Board* (1985) 53 P & CR 263; [1987] Conv 368 (S Tromans); *Home Brewery Co Ltd v William Davis & Co (Leicester) Ltd* [1987] QB 339; (1987) 137 NLJ 867 (HW Wilkinson). On water pollution, see *Cambridge Water Co v Eastern Counties Leather plc* [1994] 2 AC 264 (civil liability); [1994] Conv 309 (MP Gravells); (1994) 57 MLR 799 (D Wilkinson); *Alphacell Ltd v Woodward* [1972] AC 824; *National Rivers Authority v Sir Alfred McAlpine Homes (East) Ltd* [1994] 4 All ER 286; *Environment Agency v Empress Car Co (Abertillery) Ltd* [1999] 2 AC 22 (criminal liability).

The common law may be set out in three propositions:[87]

(1) A riparian owner may take and use the water for ordinary purposes connected with his riparian tenement (such as domestic purposes or the watering of his cattle),[88] even though the result may be to exhaust the water altogether.

(2) A riparian owner may take the water for extraordinary purposes provided, first, that such user is connected with the riparian land, and, secondly, that he restores the water substantially undiminished in volume and unaltered in character. Common examples are where water is employed in the irrigation of the adjoining land or the working of a mill, for in such cases practically the same amount of water ultimately returns to the stream.[89] Manufacture, in the present connection, is prima facie an extraordinary purpose, though the ultimate solution of this question depends upon local trading conditions, and on the use to which the water of rivers is put in the adjoining district.[90]

(3) A riparian owner has no right whatever to take the water for purposes unconnected with the riparian tenement.[91] Thus it has been held that the mere possession of a mill on the bank of a stream does not entitle a waterworks company to collect the water in a reservoir for the benefit of a neighbouring town.[92]

(d) Abstraction under Water Resources Act 1991

The rights of taking water at common law have been curtailed by section 24(1) of the Water Resources Act 1991,[93] as amended and supplemented by the Water Act 2003.[94] Under the 1991 Act:[95]

no person shall

(a) abstract water from any source of supply; or

(b) cause or permit any other person so to abstract any water,

except in pursuance of a licence under this Chapter granted by the [Environment] Agency and in accordance with the provisions of that licence.

---

[87] *Attwood v Llay Main Collieries Ltd* [1926] Ch 444, 458.

[88] But not spray irrigation: *Rugby Joint Water Board v Walters* [1967] Ch 397.

[89] *Embrey v Owen* (1851) 6 Exch 353; cf *Rugby Joint Water Board v Walters*, above.

[90] *Ormerod v Todmorden Joint Stock Mill Co Ltd* (1883) 11 QBD 155, 168 (Lord Esher); see (1959) 22 MLR 35 (AH Hudson).

[91] *McCartney v Londonderry and Lough Swilly Rly Co* [1904] AC 301; *Attwood v Llay Main Collieries*, above.

[92] *Swindon Waterworks Co v Wilts and Berks Canal Navigation Co* (1875) LR 7 HL 697.

[93] Replacing the provisions of the Water Resources Act 1963, as amended. The functions were transferred to the Environment Agency by Environment Act 1995, s 2.

[94] See also report by the Department for Environment, Food and Rural Affairs, *Taking Water Responsibly* (March 1999).

[95] S 24.

The 2003 Act makes provision for different categories of licence for the abstraction of water. There is, however, an exemption for[96]

> any abstraction of a quantity of water not exceeding 20 cubic metres in any period of 24 hours, if the abstraction does not form part of a continuous operation, or of a series of operations,[97] by which a quantity of water that, in aggregate, is more than 20 cubic metres is abstracted during the period.

(e) Public rights in a river

The public have a common law right to navigation in a tidal river up to the point where the tide ebbs and flows,[98] but the non-tidal part of a river is analogous to a road running between two properties, and though the public may by dedication acquire the right of navigation on it, it must be proved in case of dispute that this has been established by long enjoyment or by Act of Parliament.[99] Such a right of navigation, if established, prevails over the ordinary rights of a riparian owner, and he cannot make any use of the bed of the river or of its water that will prejudice enjoyment by the public; he is not, for example, entitled to erect a wharf or other building on the bed so as to obstruct to the smallest extent the passage of boats.[100]

(f) Fishing

As regards the person who possesses the right of fishing in a river, a distinction must again be drawn between tidal and non-tidal rivers, for while all members of the public are entitled to fish[101] in the former up to the point where the tide ebbs and flows,[102] the right in the case of a non-tidal river belongs to the owner of the bed of the stream, or to any person who has acquired a right from or against him. It is often thought that if a river is navigable, the public have a right to fish in it, but this is not true in respect of that part of a river that lies above the flow of the tide, for the privilege of navigation

---

[96] Water Resources Act 1991, s 27(1), substituted by Water Act 2003, s 6(1).

[97] *Cargill v Gotts* [1981] 1 WLR 441 (series depends on taking, not quantity or frequency); (1981) 97 LQR 382 (P Jackson).

[98] *A-G v Tomline* (1880) 14 Ch D 58. See *Iveagh v Martin* [1961] 1 QB 232; *Evans v Godber* [1974] 1 WLR 1317; Caffyn, *The Right of Navigation on Non-Tidal Rivers and the Common Law* (2004).

[99] *Orr Ewing v Colquhoun* (1877) 2 App Cas 839.

[100] *A-G v Terry* (1874) 9 Ch App 423; *Tate & Lyle Industries Ltd v Greater London Council* [1983] 2 AC 509 (construction of ferry terminals in River Thames caused silting at jetty of plaintiffs who succeeded in claim for special damage for public nuisance). Salvage is not recoverable on a non-tidal navigable river: *The Goring* [1988] AC 831 (River Thames above Reading Bridge); [1987] CLJ 153 (DEC Yale); *Rowland v Environment Agency* [2003] EWCA Civ 1885, [2005] Ch 1 (public right of navigation on non-tidal stretch of River Thames below Cookham existing since time immemorial not extinguished by Thames Preservation Act 1885).

[101] And to take worms on the foreshore as bait in exercise of their right to fish: *Anderson v Alnwick DC* [1993] 1 WLR 1156; *Adair v National Trust for Places of Historic Interest or Natural Beauty* The Times, 19 December 1997.

[102] It is an offence under the Salmon and Freshwater Fisheries Act 1975, s 6(1) to place a net in tidal and inland waters which obstructs the passage of salmon and migratory trout: *Champion v Maughan* [1984] 1 WLR 469; *Gray v Blamey* [1991] 1 WLR 47.

does not confer a right to fish any more than the right to pass along a public highway entitles a member of the public to shoot upon it.[103] Bowen LJ said:[104]

> There is another most important matter to be recollected as regards such streams as the Thames, viz. that although the public have been in the habit, as long as we can recollect, and as long as our fathers can recollect, of fishing in the Thames, the public have no right to fish there—I mean they have no right as members of the public to fish there. That is certain law. Of course they may fish by the licence of the lord or the owner of a particular part of the bed of the river, or they may fish by the indulgence, or owing to the carelessness or good nature, of the person who is entitled to the soil, but right to fish themselves as the public they have none, and whenever the case is tried the jury ought to be told this by the judge in the most emphatic way, so as to prevent them from doing injustice under the idea that they are establishing a public right. There is no such right in law...

The position is, then, that the owner of the bed of a river is presumptively entitled to the fishing, and if, for example, the opposite banks are in different hands, each proprietor is owner of the fishing *usque ad medium filium aquae*: up to the mid-point of the water.[105] But this fishing may become separated from the ownership of the bed and be vested as an incorporeal right in the hands of another person, and when this has been done it exists either as a several fishery or as a common of fishery. Both these rights are instances of a profit à prendre.[106] A several fishery is, as was said by Lord Coleridge: 'a right to take fish *in alieno solo*,[107] and to exclude the owner of the soil from the right of taking fish himself'.[108] A right to fish in the river of another in common with the owner, or in common with others to whom the same right has been granted, is called a 'common of fishery', or 'common of piscary'.[109]

B RESTRICTIONS ON OWNERSHIP

In his account of the fee simple estate, written in 1885, Challis described the extensive powers of enjoyment available to its owner:[110]

> It confers, and since the beginning of legal history it always has conferred, the lawful right to exercise over, upon, and in respect, to the land, every act of ownership that can enter into the imagination, including the right to commit unlimited waste.[111]

---

[103] *Smith v Andrews* [1891] 2 Ch 678, 696. It is an offence to fish in such a river even though the fish are returned alive to the water: *Wells v Hardy* [1964] 2 QB 447.

[104] *Blount v Layard* [1891] 2 Ch 681n, 689.

[105] *Hanbury v Jenkins* [1901] 2 Ch 401. If he is fishing for salmon by rod and line, he is entitled to stand on his own bank or to wade out to the mid-point, and to fish as far across the river as he can reach by normal casting or spinning: *Fothringham v Kerr* (1984) 48 P & CR 173 (River Tay). See also *Welsh National Water Development Authority v Burgess* (1974) 28 P & CR 378, 383 (salmon and trout-fishing in River Dovey).

[106] Below, Ch 18.   [107] Ie, on another's land.

[108] *Foster v Wright* (1878) 4 CPD 438, 449. See *Loose v Castleton* (1978) 41 P & CR 19; *Lewis v Cavaciuti* [1993] NLJR 813 (extent of profit of piscary in River Usk).

[109] Leake, *Uses and Profits of Land* (1988), p 176; below, p 706.   [110] *Law of Real Property*, p 218.

[111] For waste, and in particular the liability of a tenant for years for waste, see below, p 234.

Challis would, no doubt, have agreed with Samuel Johnson[112] that a man cannot be allowed by society to be complete master of what he calls his own, and that he must submit to the restrictions placed by the law upon the exercise of his proprietary rights. There is little doubt, however, that the restrictions now imposed by statute upon a landowner's right to enjoy what at common law is his own would have seemed strange to both those writers. Even in Challis' time, of course, statutory interference with the freedom of a landowner was not unknown. He was required, for example, to conform with local by-laws in the erection of new buildings, and he might be compelled to demolish houses that were unfit for habitation. Later he became subject to legislation passed in the interests of the poorer sections of the community, such as the Housing Acts and the Rent Acts,[113] which further increased his burdens and circumscribed his proprietary rights. Also, Parliament has frequently authorised the compulsory purchase or redistribution of land by private and public Acts, for purposes of inclosure or the provision of docks, canals, railways, utility undertakings and public works of all kinds.[114]

But the most vigorous attack upon the right of an owner to do what he likes with his land has been made by the various Town and Country Planning Acts, which seek to prevent the social difficulties that inevitably arise if no public control is placed upon the development of land. Building operations obviously need to be controlled in the interests of the community. Land is a limited commodity, the demand for houses increases with a rising population, the profit instinct is strong, and unless something is done to curb the activities of the speculative developer certain unfortunate results must inevitably ensue. Uncontrolled development may sacrifice agricultural land and places of natural beauty, deface the countryside with unco-ordinated buildings sprawling along the main roads and causing difficulties for the sanitary and educational authorities, and in general may be effected with little thought for the amenities of the neighbourhood or for the problems that it will cause in the future. Nevertheless, there is a need to preserve a just balance between the rights of landowners and the interests of the community.

Planning law and compensation rules together have produced a situation in which the market value of land, which includes development potential in addition to the value of the land in its existing use, is affected in a striking manner. The withholding of planning permission will deprive land of development value that market demand would otherwise confer upon it. Compensation is payable only rarely for this loss of development value, except where land is compulsorily purchased.

Detailed treatment of these matters is, however, outside the scope of this book, and reference must be made to specialist works.[115]

---

[112] In a letter to Boswell, 3 February 1776.   [113] Below, Ch 11.

[114] See Blackstone, vol i, p 139; Dicey, *Introduction to the Study of the Law of the Constitution* (10th edn, ed ECS Wade, 1959) p 48.

[115] For an outline of planning control, and compulsory purchase and compensation, as they stood in 2006, see chapters 29 and 30 of the 17th edition of this book. See also the books referred to below, p 778, n 331. For *private* control of the use of neighbouring land, see below, Ch 19 (Covenants).

7

COMMONHOLD[1]

Summary

I NATURE OF COMMONHOLD

Commonhold was introduced by Part I of the Commonhold and Leasehold Reform Act 2002, which came into force on 27 September 2004. It is not a new form of tenure, but is a new form in which the *freehold* estate in *registered* land can be held. In outline, it is a means of providing for the registered freehold ownership of two or more units of land,[2] for example in a block of flats or offices. A commonhold association is the registered proprietor of the common parts, but the holder of each unit is registered as the proprietor of the freehold estate in that unit.

---

[1] Fetherstonhaugh, Sefton and Peters, *Commonhold* (2004); Cowen, Driscoll and Target, *Commonhold Law and Practice* (2005); Furber, Karas, Evans and Scott, *The Commonhold and Leasehold Reform Act 2002* (2002), ch 2; Clarke, *Commonhold: The New Law* (2002); *Clark on Commonhold: Law, Practice and Precedents*; Aldridge, *Commonhold Law*; R & R, ch 22. It appears that developers were at first slow to adopt commonhold: (2006) 156 NLJ 226 (F Larcombe); [2005] 35 EG 104 (G Fetherstonhaugh); but they then began to do so: [2006] 09 EG 173; (2005) 154 PLJ 5 (J Hopkins). For common misconceptions amongst property developers about commonhold that appear to have discouraged its use, see (2008) 158 NLJ 1137 (J Driscoll).

[2] There must be at least two units, although a unit need not contain all or any part of a building: CLRA 2002, s 11(2)(a), (4). Any commonhold property that is not comprised within a defined unit will be 'common parts': s 25(1).

II AIMS OF THE LEGISLATION INTRODUCING COMMONHOLD

The introduction of commonhold was recommended in 1987 by the Aldridge Working Group on Freehold Flats and Freehold Ownership of Other Interdependent Buildings:[3]

> The purpose of the scheme is to regulate relations between owners of separate properties that lie in close proximity to each other and are interdependent. The scheme is suitable for, but not limited to, residential property. It gives people the chance to own flats freehold, without the present drawbacks, but the scheme can also apply to offices, commercial and industrial premises and other properties.[4]

The Commonhold scheme is similar to Condominium legislation in Canada, the United States of America and, under the name of strata titles, in Australia and New Zealand.[5]

The 'present drawbacks' which the new scheme was designed to overcome are, first, the difficulty that an owner of freehold property has in enforcing a positive covenant, for example to repair or to pay service charges, against a purchaser from his original covenantor.[6] Hitherto this difficulty has been avoided by the owner of a block of flats granting *leases* of each separate unit within it. In this case any positive covenant that relates to the property is enforceable against successive owners of the unit, in accordance with the rules for the running of leasehold covenants.[7] The system of leasehold flats, however, has brought a second drawback. Many leasehold schemes were evolved in the 1930s when leases were granted for 99 years. Today a lease with less than 40 years to run is an unattractive security for a mortgagee, and so the unit in many cases becomes unsaleable. Freehold tenure (and therefore commonhold, as a form of registered freehold) has no such disadvantage.

The general scope of commonhold was outlined by Mr Aldridge himself as follows:[8]

> Like other condominium systems, [commonhold] would allow the freehold ownership of separate parts of a building. The problem of passing the benefit of positive obligations is overcome by legislation laying down the content of mutual obligations and easements, and

---

[3] Cmnd 79. The Working Group was established in 1986 by the Chairman of the Law Commission as a result of the initiative of the Lord Chancellor: p *v*.

[4] The commonhold scheme 'will be as useful for a business park or a large out-of-town shopping centre as it will for mansion flats in Kensington or leafy suburban housing estates. It could be employed for something as mundane as a shared car park': Lord Irvine of Lairg LC, Hansard, HL (series 4) vol 626, col 886 (5 July 2001). For a comparison of commonholds and leaseholds, see Cowan, Driscoll and Target, *Commonhold Law and Practice*, ch 15; Fetherstonhaugh, Sefton and Peters, *Commonhold*, para 1.3.7 (in tabular form).

[5] Cmnd 79, para 1.7. Similar legislation has been in force in Europe since the 1930s, and it has been introduced in many other parts of the world. On strata titles in Australia, see (1991) 9107 EG 92 (N Carter); and for other comparisons, see [2005] Conv 53 (CG van der Merwe and PF Smith). The suggestion that 'strata title' be introduced in England was first made in the Report of the Committee on Positive Covenants Affecting Land 1965, Cmnd 2719. For proposals to introduce 'multi-unit development' in Irish law, see [2009] Conv 21 (PF Smith).

[6] Below, pp 728 ff.   [7] Below, Ch 9.

[8] [1986] Conv 361. On the relationship between commonhold and leasehold, see (2004) 8 L & T Rev 100 (T Aldridge).

making them bind the owners for the time being of each unit for the benefit of the rest of the development. Many see the standardisation of the mutual rights and obligations as a recommendation of the system.

There would be an incorporated management association, the members of which are the owners of the freehold units. It is responsible for repairs and services and any common parts are vested in it. That structure is, of course, familiar here for leasehold flat schemes. When the commonhold is brought to an end, the owners would cease to have an exclusive interest in their respective units. They would then become equitable tenants in common of the whole property in pre-determined proportions. The legal estate would be vested in the association on trust for them. This avoids possible difficulties with the freehold ownership of blocks of air on a complete or partial destruction.

The aim of the Working Group is to recommend a property ownership system that could be freely adopted by owners or developers for all types of property: existing or new, purpose-built in separate units or converted, of any type of construction, and put to any use, whether or not residential. With the progress of compulsory registration of title, it seems to us appropriate to base a new commonhold system wholly on registration. Commonholds would only be possible with a registered title. This should ensure that they are properly constituted, and will give easy access to the basic documentation.

In 1991 the Government announced its proposals for the introduction of commonhold,[9] although the legislation was not finally enacted until 2002.[10]

III THE COMMONHOLD SCHEME

A COMMONHOLD LAND

Land is commonhold land if three conditions are satisfied:[11]

(a) the freehold estate in the land is *registered* as a freehold estate in commonhold land;

(b) the land is specified in the articles of association of a *commonhold association* as the land in relation to which the association is to exercise functions, and

---

[9] A Consultation Paper in 1990 (Cm 1345) contained a draft Bill; [1991] Conv 170 (HW Wilkinson). In 1996 the Lord Chancellor's Department issued a further Consultation Paper and draft Bill; [1997] Conv 6; (1996) IL & T Rev 3 (JC Williams); a third draft Bill published in 2000 (Cm 4843) fell when the general election of 2001 was called. See also Blundell Memorial Lecture 1991: Commonhold—Can we make it work (J Wylie and E Nugee QC); [1997] Conv 169 (L Charlebois); [1998] Conv 283 (L Crabb); [2006] Conv 14 (SMJ Wong).

[10] CLRA 2002, Part I; [2002] Conv 349 (DN Clarke); Commonhold Regulations 2004 (SI 2004 No 1829); Commonhold (LR) R 2004 (SI 2004 No 1830); Commonhold (LR) (Amendment) R 2008 and 2009 (SI 2008 No 1920, 2009 No 2024); Commonhold (Amendment) Regulations 2009 (SI 2009 No 2363). See also LCD Consultation Paper on Proposals for Commonhold Regulations 2002 and Analysis of the Responses to the Consultation Paper 2003; DCA Non-Statutory Guidance on the Commonhold Regulations 2004; Guidance on the Drafting of a Commonhold Community Statement including Specimen Local Rules 2005.

[11] CLRA 2002, s 1(1), as amended by SI 2009 No 1941.

(c) a *commonhold community statement* makes provision for rights and duties of the commonhold association and unit-holders.

B REGISTRATION OF THE TITLE TO COMMONHOLD LAND

Only freehold land, registered with absolute title,[12] can be held as commonhold land.[13] The application for registration must be made by the person who is already registered as proprietor of the land, or a person who is entitled to be registered.[14] The application for registration as commonhold must be accompanied by certain specified documents, including the certificate of incorporation and articles of association of the commonhold association, the community commonhold statement, and evidence of the consent of certain persons with an interest in the land.[15] The estate may not be registered as commonhold without the consent of anyone who is the registered proprietor of the freehold in the whole or any part of the land, or of a lease granted for more than 21 years, or the registered proprietor of a charge over it,[16] or the holder of the equivalent unregistered interests in or over the land, or the holder of a lease granted for 21 years or less that will be extinguished by virtue of the registration as commonhold.[17]

The commonhold association is registered as proprietor of the freehold estate in the common parts, and each of the unit-holders is registered as proprietor of the freehold estate in the unit.[18]

C THE COMMONHOLD ASSOCIATION

The commonhold association is a private company limited by guarantee.[19] Its purpose is to hold the registered commonhold title to the common parts of the property, and

---

[12] CLRA 2002, s 2(3)(a); for absolute title, see above, pp 136–7; below, pp 1076–7.

[13] Flying freeholds (above, p 162), certain agricultural land, and contingent estates (liable to revert or vest in another on particular events) cannot be commonhold: ibid, s 4, Sch 2.

[14] CLRA 2002, s 2(1), (3). This therefore includes a transferee of a registered estate who has not yet been registered, and a transferee of unregistered land where the estate is now to be registered for the first time. The application for first registration is completed first, before the title is then reregistered as commonhold: Land Registry Practice Guide 60, para 4.1.

[15] Ibid, s 2(2), Sch 1 as amended by SI 2009 No 1941; Commonhold Regulations 2004, reg 4; C(LR)R 2004, rr 5–7; Land Registry Practice Guide 60.

[16] Ibid, s 3.

[17] Commonhold Regulations 2004, reg 3. Registration of the freehold as commonhold extinguishes prior leases, whatever the length of the term: CLRA 2002, ss 7(3)(d), 9(3)(f). If a tenant or sub-tenant was not required to give consent, he has an action for his loss against his superior landlord or the freeholder who did give consent: s 10.

[18] CLRA 2002, s 9. The land may be registered initially as commonhold land without unit-holders being identified and registered; the applicant then continues to be registered as the proprietor of the freehold estate in the commonhold land, and the commonhold community statement does not come into effect, until at least one unit-holder becomes entitled to be registered: ibid, s 7.

[19] Ibid, s 34; Sch 3, both amended by SI 2009 No 1941.

to manage the commonhold scheme: the directors must exercise their powers so as to permit or facilitate each unit-holder to exercise his rights, and enjoy the freehold estate in his unit.[20] The unit-holders for the time being are the members of the association.[21]

In substance, therefore, the commonhold association will be responsible for the repair and maintenance of the common parts, and for giving effect to the individual parties' rights and duties in respect of the whole commonhold scheme under the commonhold community statement.

D THE COMMONHOLD COMMUNITY STATEMENT

The commonhold community statement makes provision for the rights and duties of the commonhold association, and of the unit-holders. It must take a prescribed form.[22] This is the legal heart of the commonhold scheme that, amongst other things, must define the several commonhold units,[23] make provision regulating the use of units, impose duties (on either the commonhold association or the unit-holder) in respect of the insurance, repair and maintenance of each unit,[24] and make provisions regulating the use of the common parts and imposing on the commonhold association the duty to insure, repair and maintain the common parts.[25] It may also impose duties on either the association or individual unit-holders:[26]

(a) to pay money;

(b) to undertake works;

(c) to grant access;

(d) to give notice;

(e) to refrain from entering into transactions of a specified kind in relation to a commonhold unit;

(f) to refrain from using the whole or part of a commonhold unit for a specified purpose or for anything other than a specified purpose;

(g) to refrain from undertaking works (including alterations) of a specified kind;

(h) to refrain from causing nuisance or annoyance;

(i) to refrain from specified behaviour;

(j) to indemnify the commonhold association or a unit-holder in respect of costs arising from the breach of a statutory requirement.

---

[20] Ibid, s 35.

[21] Ibid, Sch 3, paras 7, 12. The initial subscribers to the company's memorandum of association will also be members, as may any developer in respect of the scheme during the period before the commonhold was established with the registration of the unit-holders. The subscribers and any developer may resign, but the unit-holders may not: para 13; and no other person may become a member: para 10.

[22] Ibid, ss 31–33; Commonhold Regulations 2004, reg 15, Sch 3. For an example, see Cowan, Driscoll and Target, *Commonhold Law and Practice*, Appendix B.

[23] Ibid, s 11(2)(b). A plan must be included: s 11(3)(a).   [24] Ibid, s 14.

[25] Ibid, s 26. The commonhold association will in practice maintain a reserve fund, to which the unit holders are required to contribute, to provide for such expenditure: s 39. For mandatory provisions for allocation of costs between unit-holders, see s 38.

[26] Ibid, s 31(5).

In other words, it provides a complete set of rules for the enjoyment and management of the property, and covenants (both positive and negative) which bind and benefit both the unit-holders and the commonhold association that is charged with its enforcement. This set of rules, which are enforceable in the courts,[27] is designed to fulfil one of the principal aims of the introduction of commonhold: to facilitate the enforcement of covenants between freehold owners of shared property.[28]

E TRANSFER OF COMMONHOLD UNITS

Commonhold units must be freely alienable: the commonhold community statement may not prevent or restrict the transfer of a unit.[29] On a sale or gift of the registered proprietor's estate in a unit, the new unit-holder must notify the commonhold association of the transfer,[30] and he will be entitled to be registered as the proprietor.

Since the unit-holder has the benefit and burden of rights and obligations under the commonhold community statement, it is crucial—as with the rights and liabilities of a former tenant in the case of the assignment of a lease[31]—to know what rights and liabilities, if any, attach to former unit-holders, and at what moment the benefit and burden of such rights and liabilities passes to the transferee. Under the Act[32] the new unit-holder acquires the rights and duties from the moment of the transfer, and not only from the moment when he is registered as proprietor of his unit. Similarly, the former unit-holder ceases to incur any new liability or acquire any right once he has transferred his unit, even if his name still appears on the register as proprietor.

F LEASES AND CHARGES OF COMMONHOLD UNITS

The Act draws a distinction between residential and non-residential commonhold units as regards the unit-holder's power to grant leases. In the case of residential commonhold,[33] the principal restriction is that the lease must not be granted for a premium, nor for longer than seven years.[34] There is no general restriction on leasing of non-residential commonhold units, which is instead governed by the provisions of the commonhold community statement.[35]

The unit-holder is not generally restricted by the Act or by the commonhold community statement from creating, granting or transferring any other interests in the whole or part of his unit, or a charge over his unit.[36] This is particularly significant

---

[27] CLRA 2002, s 37; Commonhold Regulations 2004, reg 17.   [28] Above, p 170.
[29] CLRA 2002, s 15(2).   [30] Ibid, s 15(3).   [31] Below, pp 323 ff.   [32] CLRA 2002, s 16.
[33] A unit is residential if provision is made in the commonhold community statement for it to be used only for residential purposes, or for residential and other incidental purposes: ibid, s 17(5).
[34] CLRA 2002, s 17; Commonhold Regulations 2004, reg 11.   [35] Ibid, s 18.
[36] Regulations may, however, impose limits and require the consent of the commonhold association: ibid, s 20(3). For restrictions on the creation of interests in, and charges over, part only of a commonhold unit, see ss 21, 22.

in allowing the unit-holder to mortgage his interest. Since his interest in the unit is a freehold, not a wasting asset such as a leasehold, this therefore fulfils another principal aim of the introduction of commonhold: to facilitate the raising of funds on mortgage by owners of shared property by ensuring that it continues to constitute good security, and thereby to maintain its value as a transferable asset.[37]

G TERMINATION OF COMMONHOLD

The Act makes provision for both voluntary winding up of the commonhold association[38] and for winding-up by the court,[39] and for the registrar to make arrangements, in consequence, for the freehold estate in land to cease to be registered as a freehold estate in commonhold land.

---

[37] Above, p 170. The ability of the commonhold association to charge the common parts, of which it is the registered proprietor, is limited by CLRA 2002, ss 28, 29.

[38] CLRA 2002, ss 43 ff.   [39] Ibid, ss 50 ff.

B LEASEHOLD ESTATES

Summary

8

GENERAL CHARACTERISTICS AND CREATION OF LEASES[1]

Summary

We begin our discussion of leases with an examination of the general principles of leasehold law: in this chapter, the general characteristics of leases and the rules governing their creation; followed by a discussion of covenants in leases (Chapter 9) and the termination of leases and the recovery of possession by the landlord (Chapter 10). However, it is important to understand that that the lease may be used in significantly

---

[1] See generally Aldridge, *Leasehold Law*, Part 1, chs 1, 2; Hill and Redman's *Landlord and Tenant*, Division A; Woodfall, *Landlord and Tenant*, chs 1-6; Bright (ed), *Landlord and Tenant Law Past Present and Future* (2006); Bright, *Landlord and Tenant Law in Context* (2007); Evans and Smith, *Law of Landlord and Tenant* (6th edn, 2002); Hill and Redman, *Guide to Landlord and Tenant Law* (1999); Sparkes, *A New Landlord and Tenant* (2001); M & B, pp 324–421.

The Law Commission has published numerous reports on the law of landlord and tenant: *The Obligations of Landlords and Tenants* (Law Com No 67, 1975); *Covenants Restricting Dispositions, Alterations and Change of User* (Law Com No 141, 1985); *Forfeiture of Tenancies* (Law Com No 142, 1985); *Leasehold Conveyancing* (Law Com No 161, 1987); *Landlord and Tenant: Reform of the Law* (Law Com No 162, 1987); *Privity of Contract and Estate* (Law Com No 174, 1988); *Compensation for Tenants' Improvements* (Law Com No 178, 1989); *Distress for Rent* (Law Com No 194, 1991); *Implied Covenants for Title* (Law Com No 199, 1991); *Business Tenancies: A Periodic Review of the Landlord and Tenant Act 1954 Part II* (Law Com No 208, 1992); *Termination of Tenancies Bill* (Law Com No 221, 1994); *Responsibility for State and Condition of Property* (Law Com No 238, 1996); *Land, Valuation and Housing Tribunals* (Law Com No 281, 2003); *Renting Homes* different commercial and social contexts.[2] A lease may be a tenancy from week to week, or a term of 999 years. It may be a private residential letting, a (secure) public sector tenancy, an agricultural tenancy or a commercial letting. The application of the general principles of leasehold law will therefore in some measure reflect the context of the particular letting. But, more than that, superimposed on the general law is a large body of statutory material dealing with specialised topics that reflect these different commercial and social contexts. There are many distinct statutory codes, in various respects radically different from each other, but with the general policy of limiting the rent that a landlord can obtain, and of restricting his right to recover possession of the premises at the end of the lease; and sometimes of granting to the tenant the right to acquire an extended lease or even the freehold. An outline of these codes is given in Chapter 11.

I GENERAL CHARACTERISTICS OF A LEASE

A TERMINOLOGY

We sometimes refer to a 'lease', or a 'leasehold' estate or interest; sometimes to a 'term of years'; sometimes to a 'tenancy'. These expressions[3] are, for most practical purposes, synonymous in the sense that they all refer to the relationship between a landlord (or 'lessor') and a tenant (or 'lessee') which we shall discuss in detail in this and the

(Law Com No 284; a 'narrative report', 2003); *Renting Homes* (Law Com No 297, 2006); *Termination of Tenancies for Tenant Default* (Law Com No 303, 2006); *Housing: Proportionate Dispute Resolution* (Law Com No 309, 2008); *Housing: Encouraging Responsible Letting* (Law Com No 312, 2008).

Consultation papers have been published by
  (a) the Lord Chancellor's Department on *Distress for Rent* (2001, Cm 5096);
  (b) the Department for Transport, Local Government and the Regions on *Landlord and Tenant: Responsibility for State and Condition of Property* (2001); and on *Business Tenancies Legislation in England and Wales: The Government's Proposals for Reform* (2001); [2002] Conv 261 (R Hewitson);
  (c) the Office of the Deputy Prime Minister on *Commercial Property Leases* (2004);
  (d) the Department of the Environment on the *Reform of the Caravan Sites Act 1968* (1992); [1993] Conv 39, 111 (G Holgate); *LTA 1954 Part II* (1996); *Residential Leasehold Reform* (1999);
  (e) the Department for Communities and Local Government on *Tolerated Trespassers* (2007); and *Local decisions: a fairer future for social housing* (2010).

See also the (voluntary) Code for Leasing Business Premises 2007, [2009] 29 EG 92 (N Crosby and C Hughes); and, on 'green leases', (2008) 158 NLJ 1135 (S Bright).

Many cases on leases are reported only in the Property, Planning and Compensation Reports (until 1967, Planning and Compensation Reports; from 1968 until 1985, Property and Compensation Reports); the Estates Gazette (issued weekly); the Estates Gazette Digest (published annually until 1984) and (since 1985) the Estates Gazette Law Reports; Landlord and Tenant Reports (since 1998). Specialist periodicals are Landlord and Tenant Review (which began in 1997) and Rent Review and Lease Journal (1981).

[2] Office for National Statistics, *Social Trends 40* (2010), ch 10. For an extract from the 2004 edn, see M & B pp 326-7.

[3] And others, such as a 'letting'; or a 'demise'; cf below, p 211, n 108. A 'sub-lease', 'under-lease' or 'subtenancy' similarly refers to the relationship of landlord and tenant, but where the landlord is himself a tenant under a superior lease. See also LPA 1925, s 205(1)(xxiii).

following chapters. As we shall see, each expression may more commonly be used in certain contexts: for example, a leasehold estate that continues only from week to week may generally be referred to as a weekly *tenancy*; whereas a lease for a fixed number of years may naturally be referred to as a *term of years*. However, for the general purposes of this chapter, they may be taken to be different names for the same legal entity.[4] The interest retained by the landlord is the *reversion*.

B THE LEASE AS AN ESTATE OR INTEREST IN LAND. LEGAL AND EQUITABLE LEASES

A leasehold is capable of subsisting as a legal estate,[5] but to do so it must be created in the manner required by the law[6] and satisfy the definition of a 'term of years absolute' contained in the Law of Property Act 1925.[7] A 'term of years absolute' means a term that is to last for a certain fixed period, even though it may be liable to come to an end before the expiration of that period by the service of a notice to quit, the re-entry of the landlord,[8] operation of law,[9] or a provision for cesser on redemption (as in the case of a mortgage term[10]). It includes a term for less than a year,[11] or for one year, or for a year or years and a fraction of a year, and also a tenancy from year to year or for any other period such as a weekly or monthly tenancy. A term of years absolute is a legal estate notwithstanding that it does not entitle the tenant to enter into immediate possession, but is limited to begin at a future date. Such a lease is called a reversionary lease.[12]

The Act provides that:[13] 'A legal estate may subsist concurrently with or subject to any other legal estate in the same land in like manner as it could have done before the commencement of this Act' and it therefore follows, for example, that A, who owns the legal fee simple in Blackacre, may grant a legal lease to B, who then grants a legal sub-lease to C. In such a case three legal estates exist together in the same land.

A lease that does not satisfy the definition of a term of years absolute, or that has not been created in the required manner,[14] can take effect only as an equitable interest.[15]

---

[4] For the purpose of LPA 1925 the 'term of years' includes a term for less than a year, or from year to year (a periodic tenancy): s 205(1)(xxvii). However, other statutes might not necessarily by the use of one expression include the others; it depends on the construction of the enactment: *Re Land and Premises at Liss, Hants* [1971] Ch 986, 990 (Goulding J).

[5] LPA 1925, s 1(1)(b).   [6] Below, pp 210 ff.   [7] LPA 1925, s 205(1)(xxvii).

[8] Below, pp 279, 287.

[9] For example, where the purposes for which a term has been created are satisfied, the term merges in the reversion and ceases accordingly: LPA 1925, s 5.

[10] Mortgages by demise are no longer possible under LRA 2002: below, p 806.

[11] *Re Land and Premises at Liss, Hants* [1971] Ch 986, 991 (Goulding J); *EWP Ltd v Moore* [1992] QB 460.

[12] It must however take effect in possession within 21 years of its creation: below, pp 197–8.

[13] LPA 1925, s 1(5).   [14] *R v Tower Hamlets LBC, ex p Von Goetz* [1999] QB 1019.

[15] LPA 1925, s 1(3). For this important aspect of leases under the doctrine of *Walsh v Lonsdale*, see below, pp 215 ff.

C THE LEASE AS A CONTRACT

A lease is not only an interest in property—a legal estate or an equitable interest; it is also a contract between landlord and tenant. 'A lease is a hybrid, part contract, part property.'[16] This hybrid nature gives rise to a tension between contractual rules and property rules applicable to a lease. The courts have held that certain essential characteristics of a lease cannot be overridden by the contract between the parties.[17] However, in recent years they have emphasised the contractual nature of a lease and have sometimes applied contractual rules. A lease is now subject to the doctrine of frustration,[18] and can be terminated by the tenant in response to the repudiatory conduct of the landlord.[19] A tenancy agreement into which one party is induced to enter by the fraud of the other can be rescinded at the election of the innocent party.[20] A notice to terminate a periodic joint tenancy has been explained in contractual terms;[21] and rent is no longer conceived of as a proprietary interest but rather as a payment that a tenant is contractually bound to make to his landlord for the use of the land.[22] A person cannot grant a lease to himself because of his inability to contract with himself.[23] Terms may be implied into a lease on the same principles as other

[16] *Linden Gardens Trust Ltd v Lenesta Sludge Disposals Ltd* [1994] 1 AC 85, 108 (Lord Browne-Wilkinson). For Commonwealth approaches, see (2009) 13 L & T Rev 145 and 182 (J Brown and M Pawlowski).

[17] *Prudential Assurance Co Ltd v London Residuary Body* [1992] 2 AC 386, M & B p 358, below, p 201 (maximum duration of the term must be ascertainable at the outset: see, however, Lord Browne-Wilkinson at 397 who hoped that 'the Law Commission might look at the subject to see whether there is in fact any good reason now for maintaining a rule that operates to defeat contractually agreed arrangements between the parties'; *Mexfield Housing Co-operative Ltd v Berisford* [2010] EWCA Civ 811, [2010] 2 EGLR 137 at [54]-[55], [79]; *Joseph v Nettleton Road Housing Co-operative Ltd* [2010] EWCA Civ 228, [2010] 2 P & CR 12; [2010] Conv 461 (I Loveland); (2011) 127 LQR 31 (KFK Low); *Street v Mountford* [1985] AC 809, M & B p 383, below, p 186 (lease distinguished from (contractual) licence); *PW & Co v Milton Gate Investments Ltd* [2004] Ch 142 (it is not possible to contract out of the general rule (below, p 345) that a sub-tenancy comes to an end on determination of the head tenancy: 'a tenancy is not merely a contract: it is and it creates an estate in land': Neuberger J at 164; see, however, *Bruton v London & Quadrant Housing Trust* [2000] 1 AC 406, M & B p 348, below). See also *Linden Gardens Trust Ltd v Lenesta Sludge Disposals Ltd*, above, at 108–9 (covenant against assignment in lease, unlike similar covenant in any other contract, does not prevent the assignment taking effect because of the proprietary nature of a lease; below, p 258).

[18] *National Carriers Ltd v Panalpina (Northern) Ltd* [1981] AC 675, below, p 343.

[19] *Hussein v Mehlman* [1992] 2 EGLR 87, M & B p 343, below, p 339: Smedley QC, holding that the decisions of the House of Lords in *United Scientific Holdings Ltd v Burnley BC* [1978] AC 904 (rent review clause in lease to be interpreted on normal contractual principles) and *National Carriers Ltd v Panalpina (Northern) Ltd*, above (lease may be frustrated) have superseded the decision of the Court of Appeal in *Total Oil Great Britain Ltd v Thompson Garages (Biggin Hill) Ltd* [1972] 1 QB 318 to the effect that a lease cannot be repudiated.

[20] *Killick v Roberts* [1991] 1 WLR 1146, 1150; [1992] Conv 269 (J Martin); [1992] CLJ 21 (L Tee); cf *Islington London Borough Council v Uckac* [2006] EWCA Civ 340, [2006] 1 WLR 1303 (remedy of rescission of secure tenancy excluded by HA 1985, ss 82, 84), [2008] Conv 81 (J Morgan);

[21] *Hammersmith and Fulham LBC v Monk* [1992] 1 AC 478, below, p 338.

[22] *C H Bailey Ltd v Memorial Enterprises Ltd* [1974] 1 WLR 728, below, p 270, approved in *United Scientific Holdings Ltd v Burnley BC*, above; but cf *John Smith & Co (Edinburgh) Ltd v Hill* [2010] EWHC 1016 (Ch), [2010] 2 BCLC 556 at [23], below, p 270, n 332.

[23] *Rye v Rye* [1962] AC 496, M & B p 355: 'A man cannot make himself his own tenant': Lord Radcliffe at 512.

contracts.[24] And some of the statutory controls on unfair contract terms apply also to leases.[25] The Law Commission has also emphasised the contractual nature of residential leases.[26]

However, in *Bruton v London & Quadrant Housing Trust*[27] the House of Lords went further, and held that an agreement to grant exclusive possession[28] of a flat created a tenancy, even though the landlord housing trust had no freehold or leasehold estate out of which it could grant a leasehold estate to the tenant, but was only a licensee from the freehold owner; and this was the basis on which the tenant agreed to the arrangement. This is not simply a decision that a lease has the characteristics of a contract, creating personal obligations between the parties; but a decision that a lease can exist that is *only* personal to the parties and need not create an estate in the land at all:[29]

> The term 'lease' or 'tenancy' describes a relationship between two parties who are designated landlord and tenant. It is not concerned with the question of whether the agreement creates an estate or other proprietary interest which may be binding upon third parties. A lease may, and usually does, create a proprietary interest called a leasehold estate or, technically, a 'term of years absolute.' This will depend upon whether the landlord had an interest out of which he could grant it. Nemo dat quod non habet. But it is the fact that the agreement is a lease which creates the proprietary interest. It is putting the cart before the horse to say that whether the agreement is a lease depends upon whether it creates a proprietary interest.

This decision is surprising, and not uncontroversial.[30] It might be understood as a purposive interpretation of the meaning of a particular statutory provision: the question at issue in the case was whether the tenant could require the landlord to fulfil

---

24 *Liverpool City Council v Irwin* [1977] AC 239.

25 The Unfair Contract Terms Act 1977 does not apply to a covenant in a lease 'in so far as it relates to the creation or transfer of an interest in land': Sch 1, para 1(b); *Electricity Supply Nominees Ltd v IAF Group Ltd* [1993] 1 WLR 1059 (anti-set-off clause excluded); *Star Rider Ltd v Inntrepreneur Pub Co* [1998] 1 EGLR 53 (agreement for lease). But the Unfair Terms in Consumer Contract Regulations 1999 do apply to contracts relating to land, and therefore to a lease: *R (Khatun) v Newham LBC* [2004] EWCA Civ 55, [2005] QB 37; *Peabody Trust Governors v Reeve* [2008] EWHC 1432 (Ch), [2009] L & TR 6; Office of Fair Trading, *Guidance on Unfair Terms in Tenancy Agreements* 2005 (OFT 356). The Law Commission has proposed that the Unfair Contract Terms Act 1977 and the Unfair Terms in Consumer Contracts Regulations 1999 be replaced by a single statute that, in relation to land contracts, would apply only to consumer contracts (thereby broadly maintaining the position under the 1977 Act and the 1999 Regulations): Law Com No 293, *Unfair Terms in Contracts* (2005), paras 3.80, 4.84, 5.77.

26 Law Com No 297, *Renting Homes* (2006): see esp Part 3 (residential leases and licences to be 'occupation contracts'). This report is not to be implemented, because of the state of the housing market in the current financial climate: Law Com No 323, *Annual Report 2009-10*, paras A.24-A.25.

27 [2000] 1 AC 406, M & B, p 348; below, p 194.

28 Applying the indicia of a tenancy set out in *Street v Mountford* [1985] AC 809, M & B p 383; below, p 187.

29 [2001] 1 AC 406, 415 (Lord Hoffmann).

30 For trenchant criticism, see S Bridge in *Land Law Issues, Debates, Policy* (ed L Tee, 2002), ch 4, M & B p 351. See [1999] All ER Rev 229 (PJ Clarke); (1999) 3 L & TR 124 (M Pawlowski); (2000) 4 L & TR 119 (M Pawlowski and J Brown); (2000) 116 LQR 7 (S Bright); [2000] CLJ 25 (M Dixon); [2002] Conv 550 (M Pawlowski); [2005] Conv 114 (J-P Hinojosa). See also, for an analysis of the nature of a lease that was rejected by the House of Lords, the judgment of Millett LJ in the Court of Appeal: [1998] QB 834.

the obligation to repair the premises implied by section 11 of the Landlord and Tenant Act 1985, which applies to a 'lease of a dwelling-house granted...for a term of less than seven years'.[31] By holding that the contract constituted such a 'lease', the House of Lords ensured that landlords of such premises bear the obligation to repair, and cannot escape it by showing that they do not have a sufficient estate themselves out of which the tenant's leasehold could be granted. However, the approach taken in the case was not to restrict the decision to an interpretation of the particular statutory provision, but instead to make a general statement about the nature of a lease, applicable not only to the Landlord and Tenant Act 1985, but also to other legislation that refers to a lease or tenancy.[32]

D THE ESSENTIALS OF A LEASE

For a lease to be created, the landlord must confer on the tenant the right to exclusive possession of certain land for a term—a period that is definite or capable of definition. Discussing the case of a residential tenancy, Lord Templeman said:[33]

> where...the only circumstances are that residential accommodation is offered and accepted with exclusive possession for a term at a rent, the result is a tenancy...

If these three hallmarks—exclusive possession, for a term, at a rent—are present, then there will be a tenancy unless there are exceptional circumstances to negative it.[34] The payment of rent, though normally required under the terms of a lease, is not, however, essential.[35] We shall consider the obligation to pay rent in the context of the tenant's covenants in Chapter 9;[36] but here we consider the essential elements of a lease: the grant of exclusive possession, for a term.

---

[31] LTA 1985, s 13; below, pp 229–31.

[32] [2000] 1 AC 406, 413 (Lord Hoffmann). For discussion of the problems to which this gives rise (eg in relation to covenants under LT(C)A 1995) see (2000) 4 L & TR 119 (M Pawlowski and J Brown). However, the consequences of the decision will be limited, since a 'Bruton tenancy' (as it is now commonly called: see, eg, *Kay v Lambeth LBC* [2006] UKHL 10, [2006] 2 AC 465, M & B p 353 at [143]) does not create an estate, but only a personal relationship between the parties, and so its incidents take effect only as between the parties themselves; third parties will not be bound: *Kay v Lambeth LBC*, above; *Islington LBC v Green* [2005] EWCA Civ 56, [2005] L & TR 24 (both cases holding, on facts similar to those in *Bruton*, that the lease was not binding on the freeholder).

[33] *Street v Mountford* [1985] AC 809, 827, below, p 186.

[34] For such exceptional circumstances, see below, pp 193 ff.

[35] LPA 1925, s 205(1)(xxvii); *Ashburn Anstalt v Arnold* [1989] Ch 1, below, p 189, n 61 (occupier let into possession for business purposes under rent-free arrangement pending redevelopment; only outgoings payable during occupation; held to be a tenant); *Skipton Building Society v Clayton* (1993) 66 P & CR 223; [1993] Conv 478 (L Crabb).

Where, however, no rent is payable, a licence may be the more likely construction: *Barnes v Barratt*, above; *Onyx (UK) Ltd v Beard* [1996] ECGS 55. See also *Bostock v Bryant* (1990) 61 P & CR 23 (contribution to bills not rent); *Vesely v Levy* [2007] EWCA Civ 367, [2008] L & TR 9 (sharing of the expenses of a joint household by two friends not rent, and no intention to create landlord and tenant relationship).

[36] Below, pp 269 ff.

E THE RIGHT TO EXCLUSIVE POSSESSION

A necessary feature of a lease is that the tenant shall be given the right to exclude all other persons from the land, including the landlord.[37] This does not mean, however, that whenever a person is let into exclusive possession he necessarily becomes a tenant. It may well be that he obtains only a personal privilege in the shape of a licence that may be revoked according to the express or implied terms of the contract.[38] There are a number of reasons why it is important to determine whether a transaction creates a lease or a licence. The plethora of cases on this question in the last quarter of the twentieth century arose from the applicability of statutes (commonly referred to as the *Rent Acts*) that conferred substantial security of tenure and other rights on a residential tenant but not on a licensee.[39] Changes to the statutory regimes governing tenancies[40] have reduced the rights of tenants to the point where there is now less incentive for the owner of residential property to seek to create a licence rather than a lease.[41] However, questions may still arise in relation to the construction of occupation agreements that were entered into during the time of the Rent Acts. And the distinction between a lease and a licence is still relevant to business tenancies,[42] as well as to determine the nature, content and legal consequences more generally of agreements to occupy land.[43] Most important, however, is that a lease is generally[44]

[37] *London and North Western Rly Co v Buckmaster* (1874) LR 10 QB 70, 76.   [38] Below, pp 927 ff.

[39] In particular, Rent Act 1977; Ch 11, below. The context in which this question has arisen (statutory provisions designed to protect residential tenants) has no doubt influenced the courts' interpretation of the test to distinguish between a lease and a licence: see *Street v Mountford* [1985] AC 809, below.

[40] In particular, HA 1988 which phased out the Rent Act 1977 by introducing the assured and assured shorthold tenancy (below, pp 360 ff); and HA 1996 which further extended the application of assured shorthold tenancies (below, pp 367 ff).

[41] Below, pp 186 ff.   [42] LTA 1954 Part II; below, pp 406 ff.

[43] Eg the duty of care owed to an occupier in respect of his chattels by a licensor but not by a landlord: *Appah v Parncliffe Investments Ltd* [1964] 1 WLR 1064; the warranty of suitability of premises for their intended purpose implied into a licence: *Wettern Electric Ltd v Welsh Development Agency* [1983] QB 796; (1983) 80 LSG 2195 (HW Wilkinson): there is generally no such warranty in respect of a lease, in the absence of an express covenant by the landlord: below, p 000; the length of notice required for the termination of a licence: *Smith v Northside Developments Ltd* [1987] 2 EGLR 151; and under FA 2003, s 48(1) and (2) a lease is a stamp duty chargeable interest, but a licence to use or occupy land (or a tenancy at will) is not. Certain other differences have been removed in recent years, eg the doctrines of frustration and termination for repudiatory breach now apply to leases as well as to licences: above, p 182. It can sometimes also be necessary for the purposes of value added tax to know whether a transaction is a lease or a licence to occupy land: VAT Act 1994, s 31 and Sch 9 Part II Group 1. This provision, which implements Council Directive 77/388, must however be construed in accordance with Community law: *Sinclair Collis Ltd v Customs and Excise Commissioners* [2001] STC 989 (HL); [2003] STC 898 (ECJ); *Belgium v Temco Europe SA* [2005] STC 1451 (ECJ); *Abbey National plc v Customs and Excise Commissioners* [2006] EWCA Civ 886, [2006] 3 EGLR 153.

[44] Not, however, a 'Bruton lease': above, p 184, n 32. This is a further confusion thrown up by the House of Lords' acceptance of a 'lease' that is not an estate or interest in land. See also (2000) 4 L & TR 119 (M Pawlowski and J Brown).

capable of being enforced against third parties as a legal estate or an equitable interest, whereas generally[45] a licence is not.

In deciding whether a transaction creates a lease or a licence,[46] the test has now come full circle. In the nineteenth century the crucial issue was whether the occupier had exclusive possession of the land or not;[47] if he was in exclusive possession, other than as a freeholder or copyholder,[48] he was a tenant; if not, he was a licensee.[49] From the middle of the twentieth century the emphasis shifted from the rigid test of exclusive possession to the flexible test of the intention of the parties to be inferred from all the circumstances. For example, in *Marchant v Charters*[50] Lord Denning MR said:

> What is the test to see whether the occupier of one room in a house is a tenant or a licensee? It does not depend on whether he or she has exclusive possession or not. It does not depend on whether the room is furnished or not. It does not depend on whether the occupation is permanent or temporary. It does not depend on the label which the parties put upon it. All these are factors which may influence the decision but none of them is conclusive. All the circumstances have to be worked out. Eventually the answer depends on the nature and quality of the occupancy. Was it intended that the occupier should have a stake in the room or did he have only permission for himself personally to occupy the room, whether under a contract or not? In which case he is a licensee.

In 1985, however, the House of Lords in *Street v Mountford*[51] considered the distinction for the first time and decisively rejected the flexible test. In that case

> there was a licence agreement under which it was conceded that Mrs Mountford was given exclusive possession of furnished rooms for £37 a week. She had signed a statement at the end of the agreement that she understood and accepted that it 'does not and is not intended to give me a tenancy protected under the Rent Acts'. As Slade LJ said in the Court of Appeal: 'It was a plain expression of the intentions of both parties that what she was being given

---

[45] Unless the circumstances give rise to a constructive trust: *Ashburn Anstalt v Arnold* [1989] Ch 1, M & B pp 1097, 1104; or proprietary estoppel: below, pp 936 ff.

[46] Megarry, *The Rent Acts* (11th edn, ed Collyer and Megarry, 1988), vol 1, ch 3; Evans and Smith, *The Law of Landlord and Tenant* (6th edn, 2002), ch 3; Martin, *Residential Security* (2nd edn, 1995), pp 7–31.

[47] The giving of a right of exclusive *possession* should be distinguished from the giving of an exclusive or sole right to *use* the premises for a particular purpose that has never been held to create a tenancy: *Hill v Tupper* (1863) 2 H & C 121; *Wilson v Tavener* [1901] 1 Ch 578; *Clore v Theatrical Properties Ltd and Westby & Co Ltd* [1936] 3 All ER 483.

[48] For copyhold, see above, pp 42, 111.

[49] *Lynes v Snaith* [1899] 1 QB 486, 488 (Lawrance J: 'I think it is clear [the defendant] was a tenant at will and not a licensee; for the admissions state that she was in exclusive possession, a fact that is wholly inconsistent with her having been a mere licensee'); *Allan v Liverpool Overseers* (1874) LR 9 QB 180; *Glenwood Lumber Co Ltd v Phillips* [1904] AC 405. Cf *Taylor v Caldwell* (1863) 3 B & S 826.

[50] [1977] 1 WLR 1181, 1185. See also *Abbeyfield (Harpenden) Society Ltd v Woods* [1968] 1 WLR 374, 376 (Lord Denning MR); *Barnes v Barratt* [1970] 2 QB 657, 669 (Sachs LJ); *Shell-Mex and BP Ltd v Manchester Garages Ltd* [1971] 1 WLR 612; *Somma v Hazlehurst* [1978] 1 WLR 1014, below, p 190.

[51] [1985] AC 809, M & B p 383; [1985] All ER Rev 190 (PJ Clarke); [1985] Conv 328 (R Street); [1985] CLJ 351 (S Tromans); 48 MLR 712 (S Anderson); (1986) 130 SJ 3, 27 (PM Rank); [1986] Conv 39 (DN Clarke); [1986] Conv 344 (S Bridge); Lewison, *Lease or Licence: The Law after Street v Mountford* (1985).

was a licence rather than a tenancy. There is no plea by her of misrepresentation, undue influence or *non est factum* and no claim to rectification.'[52]

The House of Lords reversed the Court of Appeal and held that the agreement was a tenancy. Lord Templeman said:[53]

> where … the only circumstances are that residential accommodation is offered and accepted with exclusive possession for a term at rent, the result is a tenancy …
>
> Henceforth the courts which deal with these problems will, save in exceptional circumstances, only be concerned to inquire whether as a result of an agreement relating to residential accommodation the occupier is a lodger or a tenant.

The intentions of the parties as to the nature of the agreement are irrelevant; the only intention that is relevant is the intention to grant exclusive possession:

> The manufacture of a five-pronged implement for manual digging results in a fork even if the manufacturer, unfamiliar with the English language, insists that he intended to make and has made a spade.[54]

(1) Exclusive Possession

(a) Tenant or lodger

Sometimes it may be difficult to discover whether, on the true construction of an agreement, exclusive possession is conferred. As Jessel MR said:[55]

> I think it wiser and safer to say that the question whether a man is a lodger, or whether he is an occupying tenant, must depend on the circumstances of each case.

It is clear that the reservation by the landlord of the right to enter and view the state of the premises and to repair and maintain them does not derogate from the exclusive possession of the tenant. It merely serves to emphasise the fact that the occupant is entitled to exclusive possession and is a tenant.[56] It is also clear that the occupier of residential accommodation at a term for a rent is a lodger, if the landlord provides attendance or services that require the landlord or his servants to exercise unrestricted access to and use of the premises.[57] But such provision, or the lack of it, is not by itself

---

[52] (1984) 271 EG 1261, 1262.   [53] [1985] AC 809, 827.

[54] Ibid, 819. See *Antoniades v Villiers* [1990] 1 AC 417, 444 (Bingham LJ: 'The House of Lords [in *Street v Mountford*] has not, I think, held that assertions in a document that it is a licence should be ignored. It has held that the true legal nature of a transaction is not to be altered by the description the parties choose to give it. A cat does not become a dog because the parties have agreed to call it a dog. But in deciding whether an animal is a cat or a dog the parties' agreement that it is a dog may not be entirely irrelevant'). See also Lewison, *Interpretation of Contracts* (4th edn, 2007), para 9.07. In *Brooker Settled Estates v Ayers* [1987] 1 EGLR 50 O'Connor LJ said at 51: 'Lord Templeman reviewed the authorities dealing with this tortured question, and sought to introduce some order into the law for the better administration of the law and guidance of the learned judges, particularly in the county courts, who have to deal with this problem.'

[55] *Bradley v Baylis* (1881) 8 QBD 195, 218.   [56] *Street v Mountford* [1985] AC 809, 818.

[57] Ibid, 818. See also *Royal Philanthropic Society v County* [1985] 2 EGLR 109; *Brillouet v Landless* (1996) 28 HLR 836. But the fact that the occupier chooses not to avail himself of the attendance or services cannot convert a licence into a tenancy: *Uratemp Ventures Ltd v Collins* [2000] 1 EGLR 156, 157 (Peter Gibson LJ).

decisive. Lord Templeman did not say in *Street v Mountford* that the occupier was a lodger if, and only if, such attendance or services were provided.[58]

Useful guidance was given by Purchas LJ in *Crancour Ltd v Da Silvaesa*:[59]

Faced with the exercise of construing the agreement common to both appeals, for what signals should the court look in order to decide whether the occupier thereby achieved the status of tenant or whether he was merely a lodger? The speech of Lord Templeman, with which all the other noble and learned lords concurred, gives helpful indications as to those criteria which the court should ignore or, alternatively, which should not be treated as decisive. These include:

(a) the description of the agreement chosen by the parties, eg 'lease' or 'licence'—see per Lord Templeman at p 822B-C;

(b) the actual subjective intention of the parties, even if they are ad idem, see p 819F, unless they do not intend to enter into the agreement at all—see *Isaac v Hotel de Paris* [1960] 1 WLR 239, referred to at p 823E;

(c) the effects of the Rent Acts are irrelevant to the construction of the document—p 819H;

(d) the exercise or failure to exercise rights provided by the agreement by one, other or both the parties to the agreement is not of decisive importance;

(e) the court should not draw up a 'shopping list' of clauses;

(f) the court should not award marks for drafting—see p 826F.

On the other hand, so long as owner and occupier are permitted by law to reach an agreement under which the latter has the use of the premises merely as a lodger without the protection granted to a tenant, the courts must accept and enforce an agreement which achieves this objective. This proposition merely recognises that a skilful draftsman must, in appropriate circumstances, be allowed to succeed.

(b) Business tenant or licensee

The decision in *Street v Mountford*, which related to residential accommodation, has been applied also to business tenancies—and not only where the three indicia of exclusive possession and payment of rent for a term are present,[60] but even where the

---

The presence or absence of cooking facilities is not relevant: *Uratemp Ventures Ltd v Collins* [2001] UKHL 43, [2002] 1 AC 301. On the equivocal significance of the retention of keys by the landlord, see *Aslan v Murphy* [1990] 1 WLR 766, M & B p 409.

[58] *Crancour Ltd v Da Silvaesa* [1986] 1 EGLR 80, 85 (Ralph Gibson LJ); *Brooker Settled Estates Ltd v Ayers* [1987] 1 EGLR 50; *Huwyler v Ruddy* (1996) 72 P & CR D3 (provision of cleaning and linen once a week that entailed only 20 minutes' labour held to be unrestricted access).

[59] [1986] 1 EGLR 80, 88; (1987) 50 MLR 226 (AJ Waite). See also Lord Donaldson of Lymington MR in *Aslan v Murphy* [1990] 1 WLR 766, 770–1, M & B p 409.

[60] *London and Associated Investment Trust plc v Calow* [1986] 2 EGLR 80, M & B p 396; [1987] Conv 137 (S Bridge); *Dellneed Ltd v Chin* (1986) 53 P & CR 172 (Mai Toi agreement); [1987] Conv 298 (S Bridge); cf *Smith v Northside Developments Ltd* [1987] 2 EGLR 151 (oral agreement where occupier said that he 'would take unit 17 on my own' held not to be grant of exclusive possession). See also *Bracey v Read* [1962] 3 All ER 472, 475 (Cross J); *University of Reading v Johnson-Houghton* [1985] 2 EGLR 113, 116 (Leonard J: grant of right to 'gallops for racehorses at Blewbury in Berkshire' held to be a lease 'on the balance of probabilities...despite

indicium of rent is lacking.[61] In *Dresden Estates Ltd v Collinson* Glidewell LJ said[62] that the test in relation to residential premises as to whether the occupier is a tenant or a lodger:

> is of course of itself not applicable to business tenancies because there is no such person as a lodger in relation to business premises. For myself, I think that the indicia, which may make it more apparent in the case of a residential tenant or a residential occupier that he is indeed a tenant, may be less applicable or be less likely to have that effect in the case of some business tenancies.

In that case the Court of Appeal held that 'an unusual provision' in a licence agreement that reserved to the licensor of an industrial unit the right to relocate the licensee to an adjoining unit effectively deprived the licensee of the right to exclusive possession.

The decision of the Court of Appeal in *IDC Group Ltd v Clark*,[63] holding that an agreement for the occupation of business premises, which was made by a deed that was *professionally* drawn and described as a licence, was a licence and not an easement, may be significant in the construction of an agreement for business, but not for residential, accommodation. As Jonathan Parker LJ said in *Clear Channel UK Ltd v Manchester City Council*:[64]

> I find it surprising and (if I may say so) unedifying that a substantial and reputable commercial organisation...having (no doubt with full legal assistance) negotiated a

its title ['licence'] and much of its language'); [1986] Conv 275 (CP Rodgers); *Graysim Holdings Ltd v P & O Property Holdings Ltd* [1996] AC 329 (stallholder in covered market at Wallasey held to be tenant); *Hunts Refuse Disposals v Norfolk Environmental Waste Services Ltd* [1997] 1 EGLR 16 (agreement giving waste disposal firm access to part of active quarry for 21 years for disposal of waste on payment held to be licence); *Venus Investments Ltd v Stocktop Ltd* [1996] EGCS 173 (vendor of garage permitted to remain after completion under written agreement intended to create licence and not lease held to be licensee); *Clear Channel UK Ltd v Manchester City Council* [2005] EWCA Civ 1304, [2006] 1 EGLR 27, M & B p 396 (20-metre high advertising hoarding on supports that were set in one-metre deep concrete base, which covered significant area of a roundabout, but where exact site for placing bases and hoardings was undefined: licence).

61 *Ashburn Anstalt v Arnold* [1989] Ch 1, 9 (Fox LJ: 'We are unable to read Lord Templeman's speech in *Street v Mountford* as laying down a principle of "no rent, no lease"').

62 [1987] 1 EGLR 45, 47, M & B p 395; [1987] Conv 220 (PE Smith); (1987) 50 MLR 655 (S Bridge); *Esso Petroleum Co Ltd v Fumegrange Ltd* [1994] 2 EGLR 90 (three-year 'partnership licence' agreement, which reserved control to licensor over physical layout of premises and way in which the business was run, held to be licence); *National Car Parks Ltd v Trinity Development Co (Banbury) Ltd* [2001] EWCA Civ 1686, [2002] 2 P & CR 18 (agreement to operate shoppers' car park held to be licence because grantee had no right to exclude grantor). See also *London and Associated Investment Trust plc v Calow* [1986] 2 EGLR 80, 84 (Judge Baker QC: 'There might be special cases of some sort of trading properties, areas in shops and so forth, or stalls in markets, and there might be difficulties with agricultural properties, where licences are frequent'); *McCarthy v Bence* [1990] 1 EGLR 1 (joint venture in form of sharing milk arrangement held to be licence for purposes of s 2(2)(b) of the Agricultural Holdings Act 1986; agreement would not involve 'exclusive occupation', and area of land and fields available for licensee's cows might be altered from time to time by the licensor, who also enjoyed access for several purposes such as the exercise of sporting rights, felling dead elm trees, hedging and ditching and 'walking with his dog, taking his thistle spud in the thistle season to pull out thistles or doing any other minor tidying up that caught his eye'; [1991] Conv 58 (C Rodgers), 207 (M Slater)); *Wigan BC v Green & Son (Wigan) Ltd* [1985] 2 EGLR 242 ('permission to use exclusively' stalls in covered market for 'a very substantial butcher's shop' held to be tenancy).

63 (1992) 65 P & CR 179, below, p 649.   64 [2005] EWCA Civ 1304, [2006] 1 EGLR 27 at [28]–[29].

contract with the intention *expressed in the contract*... that the contract should *not* create a tenancy, should then invite the court to conclude that it did.

... [I do not] intend to cast any doubt whatever upon the principles established in *Street v Mountford*. On the other hand, the fact remains that this was a contract negotiated between two substantial parties of equal bargaining power and with the benefit of full legal advice. Where the contract so negotiated contains not merely a label but a clause that sets out in unequivocal terms the parties' intention as to its legal effect, I would in any event have taken some persuading that its true effect was directly contrary to that expressed intention.

The policies underlying the statutory regulation of business tenancies may also differ from those underlying the regulation of residential tenancies. In so far as the courts have been reluctant to allow parties to draft licences to avoid the policy of the Rent Acts[65] in relation to residential tenancies, their approach to business tenancies or licences may therefore not be so strict.[66]

(2) Sham or Genuine. Multiple Occupation

Before 1985 some landlords had drafted occupation agreements in terms designed to ensure that the premises were occupied under a licence and not under a lease. Their object was to avoid the application of the Rent Acts. Thus in *Somma v Hazelhurst*:[67]

> Mr H and Miss S each entered into separate but identical agreements with the owner of a dwelling-house to occupy a double bed-sitting room. Each agreement repeatedly proclaimed itself to be a licence and stated that the licensor was not willing to grant exclusive possession of any part of the rooms, and that the use of the rooms was to be 'in common with the licensor and such other licensees as the licensor may permit to use the said rooms'. Each occupant was severally liable for his or her rent.

The Court of Appeal held that each agreement was a licence. Cumming-Bruce LJ said:[68]

> We can see no reason why an ordinary landlord... should not be able to grant a licence to occupy an ordinary house. If that is what both he and the licensee intend and if they can frame any written agreement in such a way as to demonstrate that it is not really an agreement for a lease masquerading as a licence, we can see no reason in law or justice why they should be prevented from achieving that object. Nor can we see why their common intentions should be categorised as bogus or unreal or as sham merely on the ground that the court disapproves of the bargain.

---

[65] Below, p 359.

[66] In particular, it should be noted that the parties to a business tenancy are permitted by LTA 1954, Part II, to contract out of the provisions that are designed to protect the tenant: below, p 416.

[67] [1978] 1 WLR 1014. Followed in *Aldrington Garages Ltd v Fielder* (1978) 247 EG 557; *Sturolson & Co v Weniz* (1984) 272 EG 326. Cf *O'Malley v Seymour* (1978) 250 EG 1083; *Walsh v Griffiths-Jones* [1978] 2 All ER 1002, where the agreements were held to be sham. For a detailed review, see (1980) 130 NLJ 939, 959 (A Waite).

[68] Ibid, 1024. The HL Appellate Committee refused leave to appeal: [1978] 2 All ER 1011, 1025.

In *Street v Mountford* the House of Lords strongly disapproved of this case saying that both agreements were a sham:[69]

Although the Rent Acts must not be allowed to alter or influence the construction of an agreement, the court should, in my opinion, be astute to detect and frustrate sham devices and artificial transactions whose only object is to disguise the grant of a tenancy and to evade the Rent Acts.[70]

In *AG Securities v Vaughan* and *Antoniades v Villiers*[71] (which were heard simultaneously) the House of Lords went further and overruled *Somma v Hazelhurst*. Both cases concerned separate flat-sharing agreements, both were described as 'licences', and both denied exclusive possession (in terms drafted before *Street v Mountford*). In both cases the House of Lords reversed the Court of Appeal, holding that in the first there was a licence, and in the second a joint tenancy.

In *AG Securities v Vaughan*:

Four young men signed separate agreements on different dates with different amounts of payment. The documents were described as licences, denied exclusive possession of any

---

69 'It would have been more accurate and less liable to give rise to misunderstandings if I had substituted the word "pretence" for the references to "sham devices" and "artificial transactions"': *AG Securities v Vaughan* [1990] 1 AC 417, 462 (Lord Templeman). See also *Stribling v Wickham* [1989] 2 EGLR 35, 38 (Sir Denys Buckley). See *Snook v London and West Riding Investments Ltd* [1967] 2 QB 786, 802, where Diplock LJ defined 'this popular and pejorative word': 'If it has any meaning in law, it means acts done or documents executed by the parties to the "sham" which are intended by them to give to third parties or to the court the appearance of creating between the parties legal rights and obligations different from the actual legal rights and obligations (if any) which the parties intend to create.'

70 [1985] AC 809, 825 (Lord Templeman). Cf the similar approach in the House of Lords to tax avoidance schemes that involve 'a pre-ordained series of transactions (whether or not they include the achievement of a legitimate commercial end) into which there are inserted steps that have no commercial purpose apart from the avoidance of a liability to tax that in the absence of those particular steps would have been payable': *IRC v Burmah Oil Co Ltd* [1982] STC 30, 32 (Lord Diplock). See also *W T Ramsay v IRC* [1982] AC 300; *Furniss v Dawson* [1984] AC 474; *Craven v White* [1989] AC 398; *IRC v Fitzwilliam* [1993] 1 WLR 1189; *IRC v McGuckian* [1997] 1 WLR 991; *MacNiven v Westmoreland Investments Ltd* [2001] UKHL 6, [2003] 1 AC 311; (2001) 117 LQR 575 (Lord Templeman); *Barclays Mercantile Business Finance v Mawson* [2004] UKHL 51, [2005] 1 AC 684. See Maudsley & Burn's, *Trusts & Trustees* (7th edn, 2008), pp 32–8. In *Gisborne v Burton* [1989] QB 390, CA invoked the tax doctrine to strike down a scheme to deny a sub-tenant the protection of the Agricultural Holdings Act 1948, s 24(1); cf *Hilton v Plustitle Ltd* [1989] 1 WLR 149 (company let scheme held not to be a sham because the company tenant, rather than the occupier, performed all the obligations under the tenancy), distinguished in *Bankway Properties Ltd v Pensfold-Dunsford* [2001] EWCA Civ 528, [2001] 1 WLR 1369 (non-negotiated provision for five-fold rent increase in assured tenancy, designed to give landlord right to possession contrary to purpose of HA 1988, held unenforceable); [2001] CLJ 146 (S Bright); (2006) 10 L&T Rev 147 (M Pawlowski); *Kaye v Massbetter Ltd* (1990) 62 P & CR 558 (letting to limited company tenant with a view to excluding the Rent Acts held to be genuine); [1992] Conv 58 (P Luther); *Estavest Investments Ltd v Commercial Express Travel Ltd* [1988] 2 EGLR 91; [1991] 11 OJLS 136 (S Bright); *Belvedere Court Management Ltd v Frogmore Developments Ltd* [1997] QB 858. See also the 1986 Blundell Memorial Lecture, summarised at (1986) 83 LSG 3736 (K Lewison); (1987) 84 LSG 403 (P Freedman); (2001) 117 LQR 575 (Lord Templeman); *Rationalizing Property, Equity and Trusts* (ed Getzler, 2003), ch 7 (Lord Templeman); ch 8 (B McFarlane and E Simpson); [2008] LMCLQ 488 (J Vella).

71 [1990] 1 AC 417, M & B p 398; [1989] 1 CLJ 19 (C Harpum); (1989) 105 LQR 165 (PV Baker); (1989) Conv 128 (PF Smith); (1989) 52 MLR 408 (J Hill); [1988] All ER Rev 171 (PJ Clarke); (1992) 142 NLJ 575 (S Bright) (arguing that the co-occupants may be tenants in common; note, however, that as against the landlord, the (legal) lease must be held as a joint tenancy).

part and required the occupier to share with not more than three other persons. When there was a change, there was a pecking order for the best rooms.

The House of Lords held that the four occupiers were individual licensees, and not joint tenants. The differences of date and payment made it impossible for the four unities (of possession, interest, time and title) of a joint tenancy to exist.[72] As Lord Bridge of Harwich said:[73]

> The arrangement seems to have been a sensible and realistic one to provide accommodation for a shifting population of individuals who were genuinely prepared to share the flat with others introduced from time to time who would, at least initially, be strangers to them. There was no artificiality in the contracts concluded to give effect to this arrangement.

In *Antoniades v Villiers*:

> There were two separate agreements based on the *Somma v Hazelhurst* precedent. They were entered into by a man and a woman who wished to live together in a small flat in undisturbed quasi-connubial bliss.[74] They chose a double rather than single beds. They were to use the flat in common with the owner or other licensees permitted by him.

Unlike *AG Securities v Vaughan*, 'the two agreements were interdependent, not independent of one another. Both would have signed or neither. The two agreements must therefore be read together'.[75] The sharing term was 'contrary to the provisions of the Rent Acts and, in addition was, in the circumstances, a pretence intended only to get round the Rent Acts'.[76]

Lord Templeman set out the matters to be taken into consideration when construing one or more documents in order to decide whether a tenancy has been created:[77]

---

[72] On the four unities, see below, pp 494–5, post; cf *Mikeover Ltd v Brady* [1989] 3 All ER 618, M & B p 406 (where each of two occupants was liable for his or her own share of the payments, CA held that there was no unity of interest and therefore each had a licence). See, however, Lord Templeman in *Antoniades v Villiers* at 461 ('a tenancy remains a tenancy even though the landlord may choose to require each of two joint tenants to agree expressly to pay one-half of the rent').

AG Securities v Vaughan was followed in *Stribling v Wickham* [1989] 2 EGLR 35, M & B p 404; [1989] Conv 192 (JE Martin) (three friends signed identical agreements; on change of occupation the new occupant signed an agreement ending on expiry of agreements of the remaining occupiers; on that date all then in occupation signed new arrangements with common expiry date; CA held each occupier to have a separate licence).

[73] [1990] 1 AC 417, 454.   [74] *Street v Mountford* [1985] AC 809, 825 (Lord Templeman).

[75] [1990] 1 AC 417, 460 (Lord Templeman). Followed in *Aslan v Murphy* [1990] 1 WLR 766, M & B p 409; [1989] All ER Rev 172 (PJ Clarke); *Nicolaou v Pitt* [1989] 1 EGLR 84 ('after a certain amount of humming and hawing the owner said he did contemplate introducing a stranger into the flat. I do not believe him'. CA held that there was a tenancy, even though the flat had a spare bedroom and had been previously occupied by three persons). A clause purporting to deprive the occupier of the right to occupy between 10.30 am and 12 noon each day was held to be 'wholly unrealistic and clearly [a] pretence' in *Aslan v Murphy*, above at 773; see also *Crancour v Da Silvaesa* [1986] 1 EGLR 80, 83 ('arguably sham').

[76] Ibid, 464.   [77] Ibid, 458.

The court must consider the surrounding circumstances including any relationship between the prospective occupiers, the course of negotiations[78] and the nature and extent of the accommodation and the intended and actual mode of occupation of the accommodation.

This approach appears to resurrect some aspects of the earlier, more flexible test for distinguishing between a lease and a licence.[79]

(3) Licensee or Sub-tenant

The status of sharers of residential accommodation was further considered by the Court of Appeal in *Monmouth Borough Council v Marlog*.[80]

Mr Roberts, the secure tenant of a house, shared it with Mrs Marlog and her two children. There were three bedrooms; he occupied one, and they occupied the other two. The kitchen, bathroom and living accommodation were shared. Mrs Marlog paid a weekly rent to Mr Roberts.

The Court held that, although Mrs Marlog and her children had exclusive occupation of their two bedrooms, she was not the sub-tenant of Mr Roberts, but only his licensee, and therefore not entitled to remain as a secure tenant when Mr Roberts' tenancy from the local authority came to an end. Nourse LJ said:[81]

Where two persons move into residential premises together under a tenancy granted to one but not the other of them, each occupying a bedroom or bedrooms and the remainder of the premises being shared between them, the court will be slow to infer a common intention that the one who is not the tenant shall be the subtenant of the one who is. The natural inference is that what is intended is a contractual house-sharing arrangement under the tenancy of one of them. The inference is greatly strengthened where, as here, there is a written agreement between the landlord and the tenant and none between the tenant and the other occupant.

(4) Exceptional Circumstances

Where the occupier has the right to exclusive possession, there are certain exceptional circumstances where he may nevertheless be only a licensee. In *Street v Mountford* Lord Templeman identified as exceptional[82] those cases where:

---

[78] The negotiations, however, are of limited relevance in construing a written contract: Lewison, *Interpretation of Contracts*, para 3.08; *KPMG v Network Rail Infrastructure Ltd* [2007] EWCA Civ 363, [2008] 1 P & CR 11 (draft lease attached to agreement for lease); *Chartbrook Ltd v Persimmon Homes Ltd* [2009] UKHL 38, [2009] 1 AC 1101. On the relevance of subsequent conduct, Lord Oliver of Aylmerton said in *AG Securities v Vaughan* [1990] AC 417, 469: 'though subsequent conduct is irrelevant as an aid to construction, it is certainly admissible as evidence on the question of whether the documents were or were not genuine documents giving effect to the parties' true intentions'.

[79] See, eg, *Marchant v Charters* [1977] 1 WLR 1181, 1185 (Lord Denning MR); above, p 186.

[80] [1994] 2 EGLR 68, M & B p 406.   [81] Ibid, 70.

[82] [1985] AC 809, 826. The categories are 'illustrative and not exhaustive': *Dellneed Ltd v Chin* (1986) 53 P & CR 172, 187 (Millett J). See *Royal Philanthropic Society v County* [1985] 2 EGLR 109, where CA rejected a number of circumstances submitted to be exceptional; [1986] Conv 215 (PF Smith); *Whitbread West Pennines Ltd v Reedy* [1988] ICR 807.

(a) *the occupancy is within one of a number of special categories*, that is under a contract for the sale of land, or pursuant to a contract of employment or referable to the holding of an office.[83] The Court of Appeal has interpreted the first exception narrowly, in holding that a *potential* purchaser of a dwelling-house who entered into exclusive possession for a term at a rent under an arrangement with the ultimate intention of negotiating for its sale was a tenant;[84]

(b) *the owner has no power to grant a tenancy*.[85] This exception has been controversially whittled down by the House of Lords in *Bruton v London and Quadrant Housing Trust*.[86] In this case:

> a local authority owned a block of flats of which it had no statutory authority to grant a tenancy. It therefore entered into a licence agreement with the Housing Trust, which prohibited the Trust from granting a tenancy. The Trust then entered into a 'weekly licence agreement' with Mr Bruton, who had exclusive possession of his flat. He brought an action against the Trust for breach of repairing obligations implied by section 11 of the Landlord and Tenant Act 1985.[87]

In holding the Trust liable, the House of Lords held that, although the Trust had no estate out of which it could grant a tenancy, nevertheless the agreement satisfied the criteria of *Street v Mountford*. It was not a special circumstance that the Trust was 'a

---

[83] *Mayhew v Suttle* (1854) 4 E & B 347; *Smith v Seghill Overseers* (1875) LR 10 QB 422. Distinguish a service occupant, who is a licensee, from a service tenant, who is not. The latter is a person to whom a dwelling-house is let in consequence of his employment, but who is not required to live there for the better performance of his duties: *Torbett v Faulkner* [1952] 2 TLR 659. See *Royal Philanthropic Society v County*, above; *Norris v Checksfield* [1991] 1 WLR 1241 (semi-skilled mechanic held to be service licensee, even though he was never in a position to perform the duties required of him); *Burgoyne v Griffiths* [1991] 1 EGLR 14 (farm cottage); *South Glamorgan County Council v Griffiths* [1992] 2 EGLR 232; *Hughes v Greenwich LBC* [1994] 1 AC 170; *Surrey County Council v Lamond* [1999] 1 EGLR 32 (employer providing facility, but not imposing obligation). The occupant may also be an object of charity; *Gray v Taylor* [1998] 1 WLR 1093 (occupant of Peterborough Almshouse held to be a licensee); [1998] 2 L & TR 40.

[84] *Bretherton v Paton* [1986] 1 EGLR 172. See also *Essex Plan Ltd v Broadminster* (1988) 56 P & CR 353 (licence where occupier continued in possession after expiry of option; no exclusive possession); [1989] Conv 55 (JE Martin); cf *Heslop v Burns* [1974] 1 WLR 1241, M & B p 329, below, p 202, where Scarman LJ held that occupation prior to a contract of sale was a paradigm case of a tenancy at will; *Vandersteen v Agius* (1992) 65 P & CR 266 (occupation pursuant to sale of goodwill of osteopathy practice not an exception); *Cameron v Rolls-Royce plc* [2007] EWHC 546 (Ch), [2007] All ER (D) 397 (business tenant remaining in exclusive possession at end of lease was granted, pending negotiation for renewal, a 'licence' in substance on same terms as proposed leases: held, only licence), [2008] 08 EG 155 (S Murdoch). On purchasers in possession generally, see [1987] Conv 278 (P Sparkes).

[85] *Street v Mountford* [1985] AC 809, 821; *Camden LBC v Shortlife Community Housing Ltd* (1992) 90 LGR 358 (which contains a critique by Millett J on the exceptions); [1993] Conv 157 (DS Cowan).

[86] [2000] 1 AC 406; (1999) 3 L & TR 124 (M Pawlowski); [1998] Conv 524 (D Rook); [2000] CLJ 25 (M Dixon). The doctrine of tenancy by estoppel was held to be irrelevant; the sole issue was whether the agreement created a tenancy; above, p 183. See *Mehta v Royal Bank of Scotland* [1999] 3 EGLR 153 (licence even though the three hallmarks of *Street v Mountford* were present; ten other equally significant factors based on the parties' intentions and surrounding circumstances to be taken into account; no deliberate intention to exclude the Rent Acts); (1999) 3 L & TR 64.

[87] Below, p 229.

responsible landlord performing socially valuable functions'.[88] However, Mr Bruton had no estate binding on third parties.[89]

(c) *the circumstances show that there is no intention to create legal relationships* as, for example, 'where there has been something in the circumstances, such as a family arrangement, an act of friendship or generosity, or such like, to negative any intention to create a tenancy'.[90]

It would appear that the test of intention is relevant in deciding whether there is an intention to create a legal relationship, but irrelevant in deciding which legal relationship is created.

(5) Examples of Licences

Licences rather than leases have been created where an employer allowed his retiring servant to remain in his cottage rent free for the rest of his life;[91] where a father, wishing to provide a home for his son and daughter-in-law, allowed them to occupy a house that

---

[88] See Lord Hoffmann at 414. Cf *Westminster City Council v Clarke* [1992] 2 AC 288; [1992] Conv 112 (JE Martin), 285 (DS Cowan); [1992] All ER Rev 225 (PJ Clarke) (grant of 'licence to occupy' to occupant of single room in men's hostel run by appellant council, in pursuance of its duty to house the homeless under HA 1985, s 65(2), held to be a licence and not a secure tenancy; 'a very special case which depends on the peculiar nature of the hostel maintained by the council, the use of the hostel by the council, the totality, immediacy, and objectives of the powers exercisable by the council and the immediate restrictions imposed on Mr Clarke. The decision in this case will not allow a landlord, private or public, to free himself from the Rent Acts or from the restrictions of a secure tenancy merely by adopting or adapting the language of the licence to occupy': Lord Templeman at 302); *Parkins v Westminster City Council* [1998] 1 EGLR 22. See also HA 1985, s 79(2)(a), Sch 1, para 4, which excludes most tenancies granted in such circumstances from statutory protection. See also HA 1996, Part VII; below, p 384.

[89] Above, p 184, n 32.

[90] *Facchini v Bryson* [1952] 1 TLR 1386, 1389–90 (Denning LJ), cited *Street v Mountford* at 821. See *Booker v Palmer* [1942] 2 All ER 674; *Marcroft Wagons Ltd v Smith* [1951] 2 KB 496; *Heslop v Burns* [1974]1 WLR 1241; *Sharp v MacArthur* (1987) 19 HLR 364 (owner of flat, with empty 'For Sale' notice board prominently displayed, let defendant into possession as a favour pending sale. Held by CA to be a licence, even though defendant had exclusive possession and was given a rent book for the purpose of enabling him to obtain payment from the DHSS for outgoings for accommodation); *Carr Gomm Society v Hawkins* [1990] CLY 2811 (self-employed gardener held to be licensee of registered charity that had 60 homes in London and a continuing need to move people if necessary); *Westminster City Council v Basson* [1991] 1 EGLR 277 (girl friend who remained in exclusive possession of flat after her boy friend's tenancy had been terminated held to be licensee, even though she had received rent rebates from the council, that had made it clear that no tenancy was intended); [1992] Conv 113 (JE Martin); *Colchester BC v Smith* [1991] Ch 448, 485–6 (no intention to create legal relations where occupant's implied offer to pay reasonable rent was rejected, and where there was insistence on his occupation at his own risk and on his giving up possession at short notice if land required for other purposes). Cf *Nunn v Dalrymple* (1989) 59 P & CR 231; *Ward v Warnke* (1990) 22 HLR 496 (in both cases a family arrangement in which exclusive possession of a cottage in return for regular payments was held to be a tenancy). See also *Abbeyfield (Harpenden) Society Ltd v Woods* [1968] 1 WLR 374; *Barnes v Barratt* [1970] 2 QB 657 (house-sharing arrangement without rent or fixed term held to be licence); *Vesely v Levy* [2007] EWCA Civ 367, [2008] L & TR 9 (exclusive use and occupation of premises, rent free but sharing household expenses).

[91] *Foster v Robinson* [1951] 1 KB 149; *Binions v Evans* [1972] Ch 359, M & B p 1102 (widow of deceased employee).

he had bought in return for their promise to pay the instalments still due to a building society;[92] where a landlord allowed the daughter of his deceased employee to remain in her father's cottage rather than evict her immediately;[93] where a woman bought a house and allowed her brother to occupy it, rent free;[94] where a man aged 85 occupied a room in an old people's home;[95] where a lodger occupied a room in a self-contained residential hotel for men;[96] where 'under an informal family arrangement' a mother bought a house and allowed her son and his second wife to live there on payment of £7 a week;[97] where a gardener-handyman occupied a cottage rent and rates free;[98] where a petrol company granted what purported to be a one-year licence of a petrol filling station;[99] and where a company was permitted to sink concrete bases into the ground and to fix to them substantial advertising hoardings.[100]

F THE TERM

There is no limit of time for which a lease may be made to last; periods of 99 or 999 years are common, and longer periods are possible,[101] but a lease cannot exist for an indeterminate period, such as in perpetuity.[102]

It may be limited to certain hours of the day.[103] It may even be for a discontinuous period, for example, a single letting for three successive bank holidays. In the context of time-sharing of holiday homes, it has been held that the lease of a cottage for one week in each year for 80 consecutive years was a lease for a discontinuous period of 80 years.[104]

---

[92] *Errington v Errington and Woods* [1952] 1 KB 290.

[93] *Marcroft Wagons Ltd v Smith* [1951] 2 KB 496.

[94] *Cobb v Lane* [1952] 1 All ER 1199. See also *Heslop v Burns* [1974] 1 WLR 1241.

[95] *Abbeyfield (Harpenden) Society Ltd v Woods* [1968] 1 WLR 374.

[96] *Marchant v Charters* [1977] 1 WLR 1181. The decision was approved, but not its reasoning, in *Street v Mountford* at 824.

[97] *Hardwick v Johnson* [1978] 1 WLR 683, M & B p 1093; cf *Tanner v Tanner* [1975] 1 WLR 1346.

[98] *Scrimgeour v Waller* (1980) 257 EG 61; *De Rothschild v Wing RDC* [1967] 1 WLR 470.

[99] *Shell-Mex and BP Ltd v Manchester Garages Ltd* [1971] 1 WLR 612; *Esso Petroleum Co Ltd v Fumegrange Ltd* [1994] 2 EGLR 90, above, p 189, n 62.

[100] *Clear Channel UK Ltd v Manchester City Council* [2005] EWCA Civ 1304, [2006] 1 EGLR 27, above, p 189.

[101] The length of a lease can be significant for tax purposes, since stamp duty land tax is payable under FA 2003, Part 4 and Sch 5, on the net present value of the lease, which is the discounted aggregate of the rents payable over the whole of the term. A shorter lease with an option to renew may therefore be more tax efficient than a longer lease with a break clause: [2004] Conv 167 (M Blackwell); [2005] Conv 7 (E Slessenger).

[102] *Sevenoaks, Maidstone and Tunbridge Rly Co v London, Chatham and Dover Rly Co* (1879) 11 Ch D 625, 635–6. The effect of an instrument purporting to create a perpetual lease at a rent may perhaps be either to create a yearly tenancy or to pass the fee simple to the lessee subject to the payment of an annual rentcharge in perpetuity: *Doe d Roberton v Gardiner* (1852) 12 CB 319, 333. Contrast a perpetually renewable lease, which is converted by statute into a term of 2,000 years: below, p 198.

[103] *Graysim Holdings Ltd v P & O Property Holdings Ltd* [1996] AC 329.

[104] And not for 'a term certain exceeding 21 years' within VATA 1983, s 1, Sch 2, para 4. VAT was therefore chargeable: *Cottage Holiday Associates Ltd v Customs and Excise Comrs* [1983] QB 735. See Timeshare Act 1992; Timeshare Directive (94/47/EC); Timeshare Regulations 1997 (SI 1997 No 1081); Timeshare Act 1992

(1) The Term must be Certain. Commencement of Period

The term must be for a definite period in the sense that it must have a certain beginning[105] and a certain ending. This does not necessarily mean that the parties must immediately fix the exact date of commencement, for it is open to them to agree that the lease shall *begin* upon the occurrence of an uncertain event as, for example, upon the declaration of war by Great Britain;[106] or: 'upon possession of the premises becoming vacant'.[107]

Such an agreement, though at first conditional, becomes absolute and enforceable as soon as the event occurs.[108]

(2) Interesse Termini *Abolished*

There was a troublesome doctrine of the common law that provided, in the case of a lease not operating under the Statute of Uses, that the lessee acquired no estate in the land until he actually entered into possession. Until that time he was said to have an *interesse termini*, a mere right to take possession. This requirement of entry to perfect a lease was abolished, however, by the Law of Property Act 1925, and all terms of years absolute, created before or after the commencement of the Act, take effect from the date fixed for the commencement of the term without actual entry.[109]

(3) Reversionary Leases

A term expressed to begin from a past date[110] or, as is more usual, from the date of the lease is called a lease *in possession*. It is also possible to create a *reversionary* lease, by which the term is limited to commence at some future date.[111] Formerly such a term might be granted so as to commence at any time in the future, such as where a lease was made in 1917 to commence in 1946,[112] but a restriction was imposed upon this right by the Law of Property Act 1925, which provides that:

(Amendment) Regulations 2003 (SI 2003 No 1922); Timeshare (Cancellation Information) Order 2003 (SI 2003 No 2579); [1992] Conv 30; [1993] Conv 248 (HW Wilkinson).

[105] *Harvey v Pratt* [1965] 1 WLR 1025 (contract for lease void for failing to specify date of commencement); *Liverpool City Council v Walton Group plc* [2001] 1 EGLR 149 (uncertainty in respect of two dates six weeks apart in 999-year term could be resolved).

[106] *Swift v Macbean* [1942] 1 KB 375.

[107] *Brilliant v Michaels* [1945] 1 All ER 121. In this case, however, it was held that no final agreement had been made.

[108] Ibid, 126, citing Fry, *Specific Performance* (6th edn, 1921), p 458. [109] LPA 1925, s 149(1), (2).

[110] *James v Lock* (1977) 246 EG 395. Such a lease cannot retrospectively vest an estate in the lessee: a grant of a term of seven years from this day a year ago merely creates a term of six years from today. See *Bradshaw v Pawley* [1980] 1 WLR 10, 14.

[111] The lease must be created by deed: *Long v Tower Hamlets LBC* [1998] Ch 197; the law was different before 1926. See the detailed historical analysis by James Munby QC; [1998] Conv 229 (S Bright). See also *Wolff v Wolff* [2004] EWHC 2110 (Ch), [2004] STC 1633 (reversionary lease executed by parents in favour of daughters as part of inheritance tax saving scheme set aside for parents' mistake as to its legal effect).

[112] *Mann, Crossman and Paulin Ltd v Registrar of the Land Registry* [1918] 1 Ch 202.

A term, at a rent or granted in consideration of a fine, limited after the commencement of this Act to take effect more than 21 years from the date of the instrument purporting to create it, shall be void, and any contract made after such commencement to create such a term shall likewise be void.[113]

The first limb of this provision nullifies the creation of a reversionary lease limited to take effect more than 21 years from the date of the lease, such as a lease executed in 2011 for a term of ten years to run from 2035. The second limb nullifies a contract to create *such a term*, that is a term that will commence more than 21 years from the date of the lease by which it will eventually be created. For example, a contract, which is made in 2011 to grant a lease for ten years in 2013, the term to run from 2035, is void.[114]

Thus, the Act relates the period of 21 years to the date of the lease, not to the date of the contract. Therefore a contract in a lease for 35 years giving the tenant an option to renew it for a further period of 35 years by making a written request to this effect twelve months before the expiration of the current term, is not void, since the contractual option, if exercised, will result in a term to begin upon the execution of the second lease. It is immaterial that it will be more than 21 years before the contractual right is exercised.[115]

(4) Perpetually Renewable Leases and Other Renewal Clauses

The nearest approach to a perpetual lease before 1926 was one that was perpetually renewable; that is one in which the landlord covenanted that he would from time to time grant a new lease on the determination of the one then existing, if the tenant should so desire and should pay a fine[116] for the privilege.

Perpetually renewable leases were inconvenient[117] and were modified by the Law of Property Act 1922. A lease made after 1925 that contains a covenant that, when properly construed, provides for perpetual renewal, operates as the grant of a lease for 2,000 years.[118] A term for 2,000 years that arises as a result of this legislation is in general subject to the covenants, conditions and provisions of the original lease, but the following special incidents have been attached to it by statute:

---

[113] S 149(3). This restriction does not affect terms, such as portions terms, taking effect in equity under a settlement.

[114] *Re Strand and Savoy Properties Ltd* [1960] Ch 582, M & B p 364; *Weg Motors Ltd v Hales* [1962] Ch 49, M & B p 365; see (1960) 76 LQR, pp 352–4 (REM).   [115] *Re Strand and Savoy Properties Ltd*, above.

[116] A fine is usually the single payment of a lump sum made by the tenant, and is in addition to the rent. See also below, n 128.

[117] See remarks by Jessel MR in *Re Smith's Charity* (1882) 20 Ch D 516.

[118] Perpetually renewable leases that already existed on 1 January 1926 were converted into leases for 2,000 years calculated from the date at which the existing term began; and any perpetually renewable sub-lease granted by the tenant out of his interest was converted into a term of 2,000 years less one day: LPA 1922, s 145, Sch 15, para 1. Any fine that was due on renewal became payable as additional rent: ibid, para 12. Where a lease made after 1925 containing a covenant for perpetual renewal is converted into a term of 2,000 years, the lessor is not entitled to convert into any additional rent any fine that may have been reserved: ibid, para 5.

(a) The lessee or his successor in title may terminate the lease by giving at least ten days' written notice before any date at which, but for its conversion, it would have expired if no renewal had taken place.[119]

(b) The lessee is bound to register with the lessor every assignment or devolution of term within six months of its taking place.[120]

(c) A lessee who assigns the term to another ceases after the assignment to be liable on the covenants contained in the lease.[121]

Great care must be taken in drafting renewal clauses, since a landlord may find that a lease, though not expressly made perpetually renewable, is converted, by reason of the language used in a renewal clause, into a term that will continue for 2,000 years unless the tenant chooses to determine it sooner. This will be the case, for example, if a lease for three years contains a covenant that

> the lessor will on the request of the tenant grant him a tenancy at the same rent containing the like provisions as are herein contained including the present covenant for renewal.[122]

Such a clause contains the seeds of its own reproduction[123] in the sense that a lease granted for a second period of three years would also contain a covenant for renewal, and so on ad infinitum.

It should be noted, however, that, in construing renewal clauses, the courts lean against perpetual renewals.[124] In *Marjorie Burnett Ltd v Barclay*[125] a perpetual lease was not created where a seven-year lease contained a covenant by the landlord to grant to the tenant at his request:

> a new lease of the premises hereby demised for a further term of seven years, to commence from and after the expiration of the term hereby granted at a rent to be agreed between the parties...
>
> And such lease shall also contain a like covenant for renewal for a further term of seven years on the expiration of the term thereby granted.

Nourse J held that the second paragraph of the covenant was not part of the covenant for renewal, and the notion of a 2,000-year term was completely inimical to a lease containing provision for rent review every seven years.[126]

---

[119] LPA 1922, Sch 15, para 10(1)(i).   [120] Ibid, para 10(1)(ii).

[121] Ibid, para 11(1). Until LT(C)A 1995, below, pp 320 ff, this was an exception to the general rule that an original lessee remained liable on the covenants in a lease despite the assignment of his interest.

[122] *Parkus v Greenwood* [1950] Ch 644; *Northchurch Estates Ltd v Daniels* [1947] Ch 117; *Caerphilly Concrete Products Ltd v Owen* [1972] 1 WLR 372 at 376, M & B p 368, where Sachs LJ referred to 'an area of the law in which the courts have manoeuvred themselves into an unhappy position.... The use of a certain set of words... causes the lease to be perpetually renewable, even when no layman—at least if he has some elementary knowledge of business—would dream of granting such a lease and, if aware of the technical meaning of the particular phraseology would almost certainly be aghast at its devastating effect and refuse to sign. One reason for the courts so binding themselves is said to be that the formula is one the effect of which is well-known to trained conveyancers, and that this is advantageous, however much of a trap it may constitute for others.'

[123] An expression used by counsel in the court below: [1950] Ch 33, 34.

[124] *Marjorie Burnett Ltd v Barclay* (1980) 258 EG 642, 644 (Nourse J).

[125] Ibid; (1981) 131 NLJ 683 (HW Wilkinson), M & B p 370.   [126] Ibid, 644.

The result, then, of the legislation is that there may be a valid contract for renewal, but not for perpetual renewal. In order to keep permissible renewals within reasonable bounds, however, it was also enacted by the Law of Property Act 1922[127] that an agreement to renew for a longer period than 60 years from the end of the lease in question shall be void.

(5) Leases for Lives or until Marriage

Certain other leases were also modified by the Law of Property Act 1925.

A lease at a rent, or in consideration of a fine,[128] made:

(i) for life or lives, eg to T for life or during the lives of A and B; or

(ii) for any term of years determinable with a life or lives, eg to T for nine years or to T for 99 years, if X shall so long live; or

(iii) for any term of years determinable on the marriage of the tenant, eg to T for 20 years until T marries,

now takes effect as a lease for 90 years.[129] This lease may be terminated upon the death or the marriage, as the case may be, of the original tenant: after these events have occurred a month's notice in writing to terminate the tenancy on one of the usual quarter days[130] may be given by either side.[131]

The policy of the Act is not altogether clear. In the case of a lease for life, 90 years is chosen as a term long enough to exceed the specified life, but it is difficult to see why *all* terms determinable with life or lives should be converted into 90 years irrespective of the term actually granted:

> Why should a term of 3 years if X shall so long live automatically become a term of 90 years determinable by notice after X's death? It is possible (although one hardly dares whisper such a suggestion about the great conveyancers who drafted the statute) that it was simply a mistake.[132]

(6) Ending of Period

The date upon which a lease is to terminate is generally expressed specifically, but it is sufficient if made to depend upon some uncertain event, provided that the event occurs before the lease takes effect; as for example where lands are let to A for so many years

---

[127] Sch 15, para 7(2).

[128] See above, n 116. By statute the word includes 'a premium or foregift and any payment, consideration or benefit in the nature of a fine, premium or foregift': LPA 1925, s 205(1)(xxiii). *Skipton Building Society v Clayton* (1993) 66 P & CR 223 (transfer of freehold at two-thirds discount was 'benefit in the nature of a premium' for grant of lease-back to vendor). The rent or fine excludes beneficial tenancies for life under a settlement; these are equitable interests and subject to SLA 1925 or, after 1996, to a trust of land: *Binions v Evans* [1972] Ch 359, 366; *Ivory v Palmer* [1975] ICR 340; below, p 944, n 129.

[129] LPA 1925, s 149(6).   [130] Below, p 336.   [131] LPA 1925, s 149(6).

[132] *Bass Holdings Ltd v Lewis* (1986) unreported (Hoffmann J); affd [1986] 2 EGLR 40, M & B p 366.

as B shall fix. On the other hand a lease is void if the date of its termination remains uncertain after it has taken effect.[133] It was accordingly held in *Lace v Chantler*[134] that an agreement to let a house for the duration of the war did not create a valid tenancy.[135]

This principle, which has been judicially accepted for 500 years, was reaffirmed by the House of Lords in *Prudential Assurance Co Ltd v London Residuary Body*[136] in which the London County Council granted a lease of a strip of land fronting a road on terms that 'the tenancy shall continue until the land is required by the council for the purposes of widening the road'. The lease was held to be void for uncertainty, since it was not possible to say at the outset what the maximum duration of the lease would be.

II TENANCIES AT WILL AND AT SUFFERANCE, PERIODIC TENANCIES, AND TENANCIES BY ESTOPPEL

This section deals with various types of tenancy, apart from a lease for a fixed period of time.

A TENANCY AT WILL

A tenancy at will exists when A has possession of the land of B as tenant with B's consent, on the understanding that either A or B may terminate the tenancy when he likes. Littleton wrote:

> Tenant at will is where lands or tenements are let by one man to another, to have and to hold to him at the will of the lessor, by force of which lease the lessee is in possession. In this case

---

[133] A tenancy at will, below, is of infinite duration, but in other respects it shares the characteristics of a tenancy: *Ramnarace v Lutchman* [2001] UKPC 25, [2001] 1 WLR 1651, 1656 (Lord Millett), M & B p 329.

[134] [1944] KB 368.

[135] A conveyancing device by which the difficulty may be surmounted is to grant a lease for a fixed period determinable upon the happening of the uncertain event, eg to A for 99 years terminable on the cessation of hostilities: *Prudential Assurance Co Ltd v London Residuary Body* [1992] 2 AC 386, 389 (Lord Templeman). In *Great Northern Rly Co v Arnold* (1916) 33 TLR 114 Rowlatt J managed even to construe a lease similar to that in *Lace v Chantler* as a lease for 999 years terminable on the cessation of the 1914 War. The effect of *Lace v Chantler* was to defeat so many leases made before and during the war of 1939 that it was necessary to save them by a temporary measure, the Validation of War-time Leases Act 1944.

[136] [1992] 2 AC 386, M & B p 358; (1993) 109 LQR 93 (P Sparkes); [1993] Conv 461 (PF Smith); (1994) 57 MLR 117 (D Wilde); [1993] CLJ 26 (S Bridge); (1992) 13 LS 38 (S Bright); [1992] All ER Rev 223 (PJ Clarke); [1993] CLP Part I 69 (P Kohler). For the decision that the purported lease was valid as a periodic tenancy on the terms of the agreement in so far as they were consistent with a yearly tenancy, see below, p 205. For discussion of whether the rule in *Prudential* could be challenged under ECHR, in the context of tenants of fully mutual housing co-operatives who are excluded from the statutory protection of the assured tenancy regime under HA 1988, below, p 364, see [2010] Conv 461 (I Loveland).

the lessee is called tenant at will, because he hath no certain or sure estate, for the lessor may put him out at what time it pleaseth him.[137]

But such a tenancy equally arises when possession is held at the will of the lessee, and indeed it is important to notice that, even though a tenancy is made determinable at the will of the lessor only, it is also by implication determinable at the will of the lessee. In other words, every tenancy at will must be at the will of both parties.[138] In the words of Lord Simonds:

> A tenancy at will, though called a tenancy, is unlike any other tenancy except a tenancy at sufferance, to which it is next-of-kin. It has been properly described as a personal relation between the landlord and his tenant: it is determined by the death of either of them or by one of a variety of acts, even by an involuntary alienation, which would not affect the subsistence of any other tenancy.[139]

A tenancy at will may be created either expressly[140] or by implication, as, for example, where a tenant, with the consent of his landlord, holds over after the expiry of the lease;[141] or where he goes into possession under a contract for a lease or under a void lease;[142] or where a purchaser goes into possession prior to completion, or a prospective tenant goes into possession during negotiations for a lease.[143] These situations apart, the courts have restricted the scope of implied tenancies at will. They are now disinclined to infer such a tenancy from an exclusive possession of premises for an indefinite period.[144] As Scarman LJ said in 1974:[145]

> It may be that the tenancy at will can now serve only one legal purpose, and that is to protect the interests of an occupier during a period of transition. If one looks to the classic cases in which tenancies at will continue to be inferred, ... one sees that in each there is a transitional period during which negotiations are being conducted touching the estate or interest in the land that has to be protected, and the tenancy at will is an apt legal mechanism to protect the occupier during such a period of transition: he is there and can keep out trespassers:

---

[137] Litt, s 68.

[138] Co Litt 55a; *Fernie v Scott* (1871) LR 7 CP 202.

[139] *Wheeler v Mercer* [1957] AC 416, 427.

[140] Eg *Manfield & Sons Ltd v Botchin* [1970] 2 QB 612; *Hagee (London) Ltd v AB Erikson and Larson* [1976] QB 209.

[141] On the level of rent payable during the holding over period, see *Cathedral and Metropolitan Church of Christ Canterbury (Dean and Chapter) v Whitbread plc* (1996) 72 P & CR 9. Cf the tolerated trespasser who, before Housing and Regeneration Act 2008, s 299, Sch 11, Part 1, was a public sector tenant remaining in possession after the tenancy has been ended by a possession order, and paying for occupation, without the local authority taking any active steps to evict: below, p 385.

[142] Below, p 213.

[143] *British Railways Board v Bodywright Ltd* (1971) 220 EG 651; *Ramnarace v Lutchman* [2001] UKPC 25, [2001] 1 WLR 1651, M & B p 329, which contains a useful summary of the law. See also *City of Westminster Assurance Co Ltd v Ainis* (1975) 29 P & CR 469, below, p 296. Where the potential purchaser has exclusive possession and pays rent the result may be a (periodic) tenancy: *Bretherton v Paton* [1986] 1 EGLR 172, above, p 194, n 84 (where, however, the Court did not consider the possibility of a tenancy at will). For an order for payment for use and occupation enjoyed during the period of negotiations for a lease, where the tenant at will left without the lease being concluded, see *Mayor and Burgesses of the London Borough of Lewisham v Masterson* (1999) 80 P & CR 117.

[144] As in *Lynes v Snaith* [1899] 1 QB 486.

[145] *Heslop v Burns* [1974] 1 WLR 1241, 1253.

he is there with the consent of the landlord and can keep out the landlord as long as that consent is maintained.

Where, therefore, there is a grant of exclusive possession at a rent, a court is more likely to find that a lease has been created; and, in particular, the payment of rent by reference to a yearly (or other) period is presumptive evidence of a periodic tenancy.[146]

The tenant at will therefore holds a position somewhere between a lessee and a licensee. Like the licensee, he has no estate: no interest in the land to which his possession can be referred,[147] and therefore has no property right to assign to another, nor anything that can bind a successor of the landlord. And his 'tenancy' may be less secure than a lease, since some of statutes giving protection to tenants under residential or business leases do not apply to tenancies at will.[148] On the other hand, unlike the licensee, he has possession; and therefore as long as his tenancy at will lasts, he can maintain against third parties' actions to which that possession entitles him.[149] Moreover, despite the termination of his tenancy, a tenant at will has a right to emblements, that is a right to re-enter the land at harvest to recover the crops that he has sown.[150]

B TENANCY AT SUFFERANCE

Coke said that:

> Tenant at sufferance is he that at first comes in by lawful demise and after his estate ended continueth in possession and wrongfully holdeth over.[151]

For example, a tenant for a fixed term becomes a tenant at sufferance if he 'holds over', that is remains in possession without the consent of the landlord, after the term has come to an end. Such a person differs from a tenant at will because his holding over after the determination of the term is a wrongful act, and he differs from a disseisor (or squatter) in that his original entry upon the land was lawful.[152]

---

[146] Below, p 205.

[147] *Ramnarace v Lutchman* [2001] UKPC 25, [2001] 1 WLR 1651, M & B p 329 at [18].

[148] LTA 1954 Part II, below, p 406, does not apply to a tenancy at will: *London Baggage Co (Charing Cross) Ltd v Railtrack plc (No 2)* [2003] 1 EGLR 141. For doubts whether HA 1985 Part IV, below, p 383, applies, see *Banjo v Brent LBC* [2005] EWCA Civ 282, [2005] 1 WLR 2520 at [25]–[26], [31]–[35] (Chadwick LJ), and [40]–[43] (Buxton LJ). However, the Rent Acts did apply to a tenancy at will, and some of the modern statutory codes that replaced them similarly apply: eg assured tenancies under HA 1988, below p 360; Megarry, *Rent Acts*, vol 1, p 66; vol 3, p 72.

[149] Such as trespass: *Heslop v Burns*, above; and, presumably, nuisance: *Hunter v Canary Wharf* [1997] AC 655; *Pemberton v Southwark LBC* [2000] 1 WLR 1672 ('tolerated trespasser'; above, n 141). On the significance of possession in the modern law generally, see below, pp 1126–7.

[150] This situation, in which the land reverted to the lessor but the right to enjoyment remained in effect with the tenant, seemed unsatisfactory to the common law courts and was a further reason for the preference, if the circumstances warranted it, for holding that the tenancy at will had been converted into one from year to year: *Smith's Leading Cases* (13th edn, 1929), notes to *Clayton v Blakey* (1798) 8 Term Rep 3, vol ii, 120; below, p 205.

[151] Co Litt 57b.   [152] Co Litt 57b, and Butler's note to 270b.

A tenant at sufferance, unless he is a tenant of premises within the Rent Acts,[153] is in a precarious position. He may be ejected at any moment and has no right to emblements, while he becomes liable to statutory penalties if he remains in occupation after he should have departed. In the view of the common law tenants at sufferance came under no liability to pay rent, since it was the folly of the owners that suffered them to continue in possession after their estate had ended,[154] but under section 1 of the Landlord and Tenant Act 1730 any tenant (or any other person getting possession under or by collusion with him) who wilfully holds over after the determination of the term, and after demand made and written notice given for delivery up of possession, is liable to pay double the yearly value of the lands for the time the premises are detained. A tenant is not deemed to hold over 'wilfully' unless he is well aware that he has no right to retain possession.[155]

Similarly, by section 18 of the Distress for Rent Act 1737, a tenant holding under a periodic tenancy who gives notice to quit and who does not give up possession in accordance with his notice is liable to pay double the rent for the time he remains in possession after the notice expires. The tenant must not only become a trespasser as a result of his own notice to quit; the landlord must also treat him as such.[156] Such a person is not a tenant at sufferance, but his tenancy is statutorily prolonged at double rent.

On the other hand, a tenant at sufferance, since he is in possession, may maintain trespass against a third party or recover in an action for possession of land against a mere wrongdoer,[157] and, in unregistered land, if he remains in possession for 12 years without paying rent, he defeats the right of the landlord and of those claiming under the landlord to recover the land.[158]

C TENANCY FROM YEAR TO YEAR AND OTHER PERIODIC TENANCIES

(1) Nature

A tenancy from year to year, or another periodic tenancy such as a tenancy from week to week, or from month to month, differs from a tenancy for a fixed number of years, in that, unless terminated by a proper notice to quit, it may last indefinitely; and from a tenancy at will, in that the death of either party or the alienation of his interest by either party does not automatically terminate it. The tenancy from year to year is practically the universal form of letting in the case of agricultural land.[159]

---

[153] Megarry, *Rent Acts*, vol 1, p 66; vol 3, p 72.   [154] Cruise, Digest, Tit ix, c ii s 5.

[155] *French v Elliott* [1960] 1 WLR 40; *Dun & Bradstreet Software Services (England) Ltd v Provident Mutual Life Assurance Association* [1998] 2 EGLR 175.

[156] *Ballard (Kent) Ltd v Oliver Ashworth (Holdings) Ltd* [2000] Ch 12.

[157] *Asher v Whitlock* (1865) LR 1 QB 1, M & B p 251 (ejectment).

[158] *Re Jolly* [1900] 2 Ch 616. For registered land, see below, pp 1160 ff.

[159] It is greater than a tenancy for one year: *Bernays v Prosser* [1963] 2 QB 592. See below, p 417.

The rule in *Lace v Chantler*[160] that requires certainty of duration in the case of a lease for a fixed term applies also to a tenancy from year to year (or to any other periodic tenancy). The term, although originally indeterminate, is determinable by either party.[161] As Lord Templeman explained:[162]

> A tenancy from year to year is saved from being uncertain because each party has power by notice to determine at the end of the year. The term continues until determined as if both parties made a new agreement at the end of each year for a new term for the ensuing year. A power for nobody to determine or for one party only to be able to determine is inconsistent with the concept of a term from year to year.

(2) Creation

A tenancy from year to year, or any other periodic tenancy, may arise from express agreement, or by operation of law.

(a) Express

Where a tenancy from year to year is created by express agreement, the phrase best adopted for carrying out the intention of the parties is 'from year to year', since this enables the tenancy to be determined at the end of the first or any subsequent year.[163] But it sometimes happens that the parties by inadvertence use expressions that have the effect of creating a tenancy for at least two years, as for example, 'for one year and so on from year to year' in which case the tenancy can be determined only by notice in the second or any later year.[164]

(b) Implied

A tenancy from year to year will arise by operation or presumption of law when a person is in possession of land with the permission of the owner, not as a licensee nor for an agreed period, and rent measured by reference to a year is paid and accepted.[165] Two important cases[166] where this occurs are where either a tenant at will or a tenant at sufferance pays a yearly rent.

(1) Where a tenant at will pays a yearly rent

It has been the law from an early date that the payment and acceptance of rent is presumptive evidence of an intention by the parties to establish a yearly tenancy,

---

[160] [1944] KB 368; above, p 201.   [161] Partington, *Landlord and Tenant* (1975), p 45.

[162] *Prudential Assurance Co Ltd v London Residuary Body* [1992] 2 AC 386, 394; above, p 201.

[163] *Doe d Clarke v Smaridge* (1845) 7 QB 957. For termination of yearly or other periodic tenancies, see below, p 335.

[164] *Re Searle* [1912] 1 Ch 610; *Cannon Brewery v Nash* (1898) 77 LT 648.

[165] Similarly, a weekly or monthly rent will create a weekly or monthly tenancy: below.

[166] For the situation where the tenant under a void lease takes possession and pays rent, see *Walsh v Londsale*, below, p 215.

provided that the rent is contractually assessed on a yearly basis.[167] In 1798 Chambre J said:

> If he accepts yearly rent, or rent measured by any aliquot part of a year, the courts have said that is evidence of a taking for a year.[168]

The assessment of rent on a yearly basis is evidence of an intention to create a yearly tenancy, even though payment may fall due at more frequent intervals such as every quarter or month. If the rent is fixed by reference to some period less than a year it creates a shorter tenancy.[169] Where, for example, a lease for one year reserves a rent of £3 weekly, the tenant holds under a weekly tenancy if he remains in possession after the end of the year.[170]

But the presumption in favour of a periodic tenancy raised by the payment and acceptance of rent may be rebutted by contrary evidence, such as by proof that, unknown to the lessor, the payments have been made by a squatter who disseised the original occupier,[171] or where the tenant has a right to remain in possession as a statutory tenant of a residential letting within the Rent Act.[172] As Denning LJ said:[173]

> If the acceptance of rent can be explained on some other footing than a contractual tenancy, as, for instance, by reason of an existing or possible statutory right to remain, then a new tenancy should not be inferred.

In *Javad v Aqil*,[174] where a prospective tenant was let into possession of premises during negotiations, Nicholls LJ thought that it would be artificial to impose a periodic tenancy on the parties, and said:[175]

> They cannot sensibly be taken to have agreed that he shall have a periodic tenancy, with all the consequences flowing from that, at a time when they are still not agreed about the terms on which the prospective tenant shall have possession under the proposed lease, and when he has been permitted to go into possession or remain in possession merely as an interim measure in the expectation that all will be regulated and regularised in due course when terms are agreed and a formal lease granted.

---

[167] *Clayton v Blakey* (1798) 8 Term Rep 3.   [168] *Richardson v Langridge* (1811) 4 Taunt 128, 132.

[169] *Ladies' Hosiery and Underwear Ltd v Parker* [1930] 1 Ch 304.

[170] Ibid, 327–9; *Adler v Blackman* [1953] 1 QB 146, M & B p 330.

[171] *Tickner v Buzzacott* [1965] Ch 426. In this case, the original occupier was not a tenant at will but was holding under a lease for an unexpired period of 75 years. See too *Manfield & Sons Ltd v Botchin* [1970] 2 QB 612.

[172] *Marcroft Wagons Ltd v Smith* [1951] 2 KB 496. The same applies to renewable business tenancies: *Lewis v MTC (Cars) Ltd* [1975] 1 WLR 457, and to long leases under the Leasehold Reform Act 1967: *Baron v Phillips* (1978) 38 P & CR 91.

[173] Ibid, 506.

[174] [1991] 1 WLR 1007, M & B p 332; [1991] CLJ 232 (S Bridge); (1990) 140 NLJ 1538 (HW Wilkinson). The possibility of a licence was not raised: above, pp 193–5. See also *Cricket Ltd v Shaftesbury plc* [1999] 3 All ER 283; (1999) 143 SJ 1174 (M Draper).

[175] At 1012; *Brent LBC v O'Bryan* [1993] 1 EGLR 59.

In essence, the court must look at all the circumstances of the case and determine what is a fair inference to be drawn.[176]

(2) Where a tenant at sufferance pays a yearly rent

This is the second case in which a periodic tenancy may arise by presumption of law. A L Smith LJ explained this in *Dougal v McCarthy*:[177]

If the landlord consents to such holding over by the tenant, and the tenant consents to remain in possession as tenant, then the implication of law is, unless there is evidence to rebut it, that the tenant holds over as tenant from year to year on the terms of the old tenancy so far as they are not inconsistent with a tenancy from year to year.

The best evidence of this consent is the payment and acceptance of rent on a yearly basis. But other indications suffice. Thus in *Dougal v McCarthy*:

Premises were let at an annual rent of £140 for one year ending 1 February. The tenants remained in possession after 1 February and on 25 February they received a demand from the landlord for £35, being one quarter's rent due in advance. The tenants did not answer this demand, but wrote on 26 March intimating their intention to discontinue the tenancy.

It was held that under the circumstances the parties must be taken to have consented to a tenancy from year to year on the terms of the original lease. AL Smith LJ said:

In the present case there is a direct statement by the landlord to the tenants that he consents to their holding over, because on 25 February, three weeks after the expiration of the tenancy, he writes asking for a quarter's rent as on a fresh tenancy. For a whole month the tenants do nothing, but hold over with notice that the landlord is demanding rent from them as tenants on the terms of the agreement that expired on 1 February. Speaking for myself, I should say that the proper inference from that was that the tenants consented to hold over on the terms of the old agreement.

If, however, the contractual tenant who holds over occupies premises that are within the Rent Acts, the landlord has no alternative but to accept the rent, for the tenant becomes a 'statutory tenant' and not a tenant holding under a new contractual agreement.[178]

(3) Terms of Tenancy from Year to Year

Where a yearly tenancy arises by implication of law there is often some instrument of agreement under which the premises were formerly held, or under which it was

---

[176] *Longrigg, Burrough and Trounson v Smith* (1979) 251 EG 847 (Lord Scarman); *Cardiothoracic Institute v Shrewdcrest Ltd* [1986] 1 WLR 368; *Dreamgate Properties Ltd v Arnot* (1998) 76 P & CR 25 (new tenancy not implied after expiry of lease: demand for rent computer generated and not result of conscious decision); *London Baggage Co (Charing Cross) Ltd v Railtrack plc (No 1)* [2000] L & TR 439 (test of intention objective); *Walji v Mount Cook Land Ltd* [2002] 1 P & CR 13.

[177] [1893] 1 QB 736; *Lowther v Clifford* [1926] 1 KB 185, affd [1927] 1 KB 130.

[178] *Morrison v Jacobs* [1945] KB 577; below, p 359.

intended that they should be held. For example, there is the old lease when a tenant holds over with the consent of the landlord and, as in *Walsh v Lonsdale*,[179] there is the void lease or the contract for a lease where the parties have failed to comply with the formalities for the creation of the lease. In such a case the tenant holds the land subject to all the terms of the old or the void lease or the contract, as the case may be, where they are not inconsistent with the general nature of a yearly tenancy.

Examples of terms that in this way will be read into an implied yearly tenancy are agreements to pay rent,[180] to keep a house in repair,[181] and to keep the premises open as a shop and to promote its trade as far as possible.[182]

On the other hand, covenants by the tenant to build,[183] or to paint every three years,[184] and a covenant by the landlord giving the tenant an option to purchase the freehold at a certain price[185] are incompatible with a yearly tenancy and will not be enforced.

D TENANCY BY ESTOPPEL[186]

(1) The Doctrine

If a person purports to grant, in favour of another, a lease of land in which he has no estate, both the grantor and the grantee may be estopped from denying that a tenancy has been created.

> The estoppel arises when one or other of the parties wants to deny one of the ordinary incidents or obligations of the tenancy on the ground that the landlord had no legal estate. The basis of the estoppel is that having entered into an agreement which constitutes a lease or tenancy, he cannot repudiate that incident or obligation.[187]

There thus arises what is called a *tenancy by estoppel* that, as between the parties estopped, possesses the attributes of a true tenancy:[188]

> It is true that a title by estoppel is only good against the person estopped and imports from its very existence the idea of no real title at all, yet as against the person estopped it has all the elements of a real title.

Thus, the covenants contained in the lease are enforceable by the landlord against the tenant, and the successors in title to either party are themselves equally

---

[179] Below, p 815.   [180] *Lee v Smith* (1854) 9 Exch 662.
[181] *Cole v Kelly* [1920] 2 KB 106; *Felnex Central Properties Ltd v Montague Burton Properties Ltd* (1981) 260 EG 705.
[182] *Sanders v Karnell* (1858) 1 F & F 356.   [183] *Bowes v Croll* (1856) 6 E & B 255, 264.
[184] *Pinero v Judson* (1829) 6 Bing 206.   [185] *Re Leeds and Batley Breweries Ltd* [1920] 2 Ch 548.
[186] For a full discussion, see Spencer Bower and Turner, *Estoppel by Representation* (4th edn, 2003), paras IX.3.1–IX.3.32; (1964) 80 LQR 370 (AM Prichard). For the derivation of the word, see below, p 907.
[187] *Bruton v London & Quadrant Housing Trust* [2000] 1 AC 406, 416 (Lord Hoffmann). 'It is the fact that the agreement between the parties constitutes a tenancy that gives rise to an estoppel, and not the other way round': ibid.
[188] *Bank of England v Cutler* [1908] 2 KB 208, 234 (Farwell LJ); *Bell v General Accident Fire & Life Assurance Corp Ltd* [1998] 1 EGLR 69 (tenant by estoppel of business premises entitled to protection of LTA 1954).

estopped.[189] The estoppel does not, however, bind strangers to it; for example, the landlord cannot exercise his right to distrain goods, which are not owned by the tenant, for rent in arrear.[190]

The estoppel operates from the time when the landlord puts the tenant into possession, and continues to operate after the tenant has given up possession, unless he has been evicted by someone claiming by title paramount.[191] Thus the covenants contained in the lease are enforceable by the landlord in respect of breaches that occurred before the tenant surrendered his lease.[192] The tenant, however, can show that the landlord no longer has a title; if, for example, the landlord assigns his reversion to A and then sues the tenant for rent, the tenant can deny the landlord's title and claim that the rent is now due to A. Similarly, if the landlord's title is a lease that has expired, the tenant can withhold the rent even though no third party is claiming it.[193]

The doctrine applies to all types of tenancy.

(2) Feeding the Estoppel

A tenancy by estoppel may, however, be transformed into an effective tenancy. If the landlord later acquires the legal estate in the land, the effect is to 'feed the estoppel' and to clothe the tenant also with a legal estate. The tenant then acquires a legal tenancy and ceases to rely on the estoppel. The tenancy commenced by estoppel, but for all purposes it has now become an estate or interest.[194] Formerly this gave rise to difficulties where the landlord purchased land on mortgage. For example:

P agrees to purchase a house from V and is let into possession before completion. Though at present entitled only to an equitable interest, he purports to lease the premises to T, whereupon a tenancy by estoppel arises between these two parties. The conveyance of the legal estate to P is completed some weeks later and this is followed immediately by a mortgage of the premises to M who has agreed to advance the purchase money and who pays it direct to V.

---

[189] *Cuthbertson v Irving* (1859) 4 H & N 742. If the lessor has any legal estate in the land, though one less in extent than that which he purports to lease, there is no estoppel. The tenant acquires the interest, whatever it may be, that the lessor holds: *Hill v Saunders* (1825) 4 B & C 529. There may be an estoppel if the lessor has an equitable interest: *Universal Permanent Building Society v Cooke* [1952] Ch 95, 102.

[190] *Tadman v Henman* [1893] 2 QB 168. Section 71 of the Tribunals, Courts and Enforcement Act 2007, which provides that the common law right to distrain for arrears of rent is abolished, has not been implemented: see below, p 277.

[191] Or the equivalent, eg where the tenant, without going out of possession, recognises the title of a third person by attorning tenant to him (ie, acknowledging that he is the third party's tenant).

[192] *Industrial Properties (Barton Hill) Ltd v Associated Electrical Industries Ltd* [1977] QB 580, M & B p 337, where CA did not follow its own previous decision in *Harrison v Wells* [1967] 1 QB 263 on the ground that it was decided per incuriam; (1977) 40 MLR 718 (P Jackson); [1978] Conv 137 (J Martin).

[193] *National Westminster Bank Ltd v Hart* [1983] QB 773, M & B p 339; [1984] Conv 64 (JW Price). But if the claimant is an assignee of the reversion from the landlord the tenant must prove a valid title paramount.

[194] *Webb v Austin* (1844) 7 Man & G 701, 724 (Tindal CJ, citing Preston, *Treatise on Abstracts*); M & B p 337.

It had been held[195] that there was a *scintilla temporis*[196] between the conveyance to P (which fed the estoppel and gave T a legal tenancy) and the mortgage to M, with the result that the legal tenancy acquired by T preceded and took priority over M's mortgage.

However, in *Abbey National Building Society v Cann*[197] the House of Lords reversed this approach and held that the transactions are 'not only precisely simultaneous but indissolubly bound together', with the result that M takes free from T's tenancy.

III CREATION OF A LEASE

A CONTRACT FOR A LEASE

We shall discuss later in detail the requirements for a valid and enforceable contract for the sale or other disposition of an interest in land.[198] For a contract for a lease to be valid, there must be a final agreement on the terms of the lease,[199] that is to say, on the parties, the property, the consideration or rent, the commencement and period of the lease and any other special terms. The contract must also comply with the formalities required for a contract for the sale or other disposition of land.[200]

It is usual for a contract for the sale of land to precede the conveyance of the legal estate to the purchaser. However, this is the exception rather than the rule in the case of a lease.[201] Where there is a building lease, a contract is often made first, and then a lease is subsequently granted when the building is complete. But in most cases, the transaction is effected either by a contract for a lease, or by a lease, but not always by a combination of both.[202]

B LEASE

A lease may be brought into existence either *at law* or *in equity*.

If made in the form required by law, and if the term created satisfies the definition of a 'term of years absolute' contained in the Law of Property Act 1925,[203] it passes a legal term of years to the tenant and creates the legal relationship of landlord and tenant—either at once in the case of an immediate letting or at the agreed future

---

[195] *Church of England Building Society v Piskor* [1954] Ch 553.
[196] A 'spark of time', ie an extremely short period of time.
[197] [1991] 1 AC 56, M & B p 340; preferring *Coventry Permanent Economic Building Society v Jones* [1951] 1 All ER 901; *Security Trust Co v Royal Bank of Canada* [1976] AC 503; (1992) 108 LQR 380 (G Goldberg). See also *Walthamstow Building Society v Davies* (1989) 60 P & CR 99 (where mortgagee took a second charge to replace a first charge, held no *scintilla temporis* between discharge of first and creation of second charge during which unauthorised tenancy granted by mortgagor became binding on mortgagee).
[198] Ch 24.   [199] See eg *Fletcher v Davies* (1980) 257 EG 1149 (flat in Inner Temple).
[200] Below, pp 959 ff.
[201] See *Hollington Bros Ltd v Rhodes* [1951] 2 TLR 691, 694.   [202] Emmet, para 26.058.
[203] S 205(1)(xxvii); above, p 181.

date in the case of a reversionary lease. The formalities required to create a legal lease depend on the length of the term; and whether the title to the estate out of which it is granted is unregistered or registered.

If the formalities required to create a legal lease are not complied with, the trans-action may still create a lease in equity. In particular, although a *contract* for a lease does not operate to create the relationship of landlord and tenant at law,[204] an *equitable* term of years may pass to the person who holds under a contract for a lease.[205] As we shall see, if the contract is capable of being enforced by specific performance, then he will hold under the same terms in equity as if a lease had actually been granted to him. The relationship of landlord and tenant will be created *in equity*, and as between the parties the rights and duties of that relationship will be the same as if the lease had been granted.[206] In such a case, however, the tenant has only an equitable interest in the land.[207]

The grant of a legal lease may take the form of more or less technical language;[208] and the mere fact that an instrument is drafted as a contract does not preclude it from taking effect as an actual demise. Whether a contract operates as a lease or as only a contract depends on the intention of the parties, which must be gathered from all the circumstances. Moreover, as we shall see,[209] the courts have sometimes construed a document that purported to be the grant of a lease, but that failed to satisfy the formality requirements for the grant, as having the force of a contract between the parties and therefore effective to create a lease in equity.

(1) Formalities Necessary to Create a Legal Lease under Law of Property Act 1925

We here consider the requirements set by the Law of Property Act 1925 for the creation of a lease at common law. The further registration requirements set by the Land Registration Act 2002 in the case of certain legal leases that satisfy the Law of Property Act 1925 are considered below.[210]

(a) Lease not exceeding three years

At common law a parol (oral) lease was sufficient to create the relation of landlord and tenant in the case of corporeal hereditaments, and there was no necessity to employ

---

[204] *Borman v Griffith* [1930] 1 Ch 493, M & B p 420 (contract for lease not a 'conveyance' for the purposes of LPA 1925, ss 62, 205(1)(ii)).

[205] *National Carriers Ltd v Panalpina (Northern) Ltd* [1981] AC 675, 704 (Lord Simon of Glaisdale, citing the 12th edn of this book).

[206] *Walsh v Lonsdale* (1882) 21 Ch D 9, M & B p 30; below, p 215.

[207] For the differences between a legal lease and an equitable lease, see below, pp 217 ff.

[208] The usual words by which a lease is made are 'demise' and 'let', but any words that amount to a grant are sufficient: Woodfall, para 5.016. In early days, the language was significant in that the landlord's covenant for quiet enjoyment would only be implied if the word 'demise' was used: below, p 224, n 4. For precedents, see *Encyclopedia of Forms and Precedents*, vols 22 (business tenancies) and 23 (residential tenancies).

[209] Below, p 214.   [210] Below, pp 220 ff.

either a deed or a writing. This is still the law with regard to leases *not exceeding three years*, for the Law of Property Act 1925,[211] re-enacting in effect the Statute of Frauds 1677, provides that:

> the creation by parol of leases taking effect in possession for a term not exceeding three years (whether or not the lessee is given power to extend the term) at the best rent which can be reasonably obtained without taking a fine,

shall be valid.

Thus a mere oral lease suffices to create a *legal* term of years, provided that it is to take effect in possession, that it reserves the best rent reasonably obtainable,[212] and that it is not to last for longer than three years. A lease exceeds three years within the meaning of the Act only if it is for a definite term longer than that period. It is immaterial in such a case that it contains a provision allowing its earlier determination by notice.[213] On the other hand, a periodic tenancy for an indefinite period, such as from year to year or week to week, may be validly created by a parol lease, for, though it may continue for much longer than three years, each party has power to determine it at the end of each period.[214]

Although a lease not exceeding three years may be *created* orally, it cannot be *assigned* at law without a deed.[215]

(b) Lease exceeding three years

A lease that exceeds three years, however, will not pass a legal estate to the tenant unless it is made by deed. The history of this requirement is as follows. Section 1 of the Statute of Frauds 1677 enacted that:

> All leases...or terms of years...made or created...by parol, and not put in writing, and signed by the parties so making or creating the same, or their agents thereunto lawfully authorised by writing, shall have the force and effect of leases or estates *at will* only.

The second section excepted leases not exceeding three years at a rent of two-thirds at least of the full improved value of the land.

The next enactment was the Real Property Act 1845, section 3, which required a further formality by providing that:

> A lease, required by law to be in writing, of any tenements or hereditaments...made after the first day of October, 1845, shall be void at law unless also made by deed.

---

[211] S 54(2).

[212] *Fitzkriston LLP v Panayi* [2008] EWCA Civ 283, [2008] L & TR 26 (one-year tenancy at rent of £4,000 per annum, by document that was not properly executed as a deed, took effect at will only because not at the best rent reasonably obtainable), [2009] Conv 54 (J Brown); *Looe Fuels Ltd v Looe Harbour Commissioners* [2008] EWCA Civ 414, [2009] L & TR 3 (judge entitled to find as fact that the bargain gave the best rent that could reasonably be obtained), (2008) 12 L & T Rev 215 (B Baruch). See [2010] Conv 146 (J Brown and M Pawlowski, arguing for simplification of s 54(2)).

[213] *Kushner v Law Society* [1952] 1 KB 264.   [214] Above, p 204; below, p 335.

[215] *Crago v Julian* [1992] 1 WLR 372, M & B p 416; [1992] Conv 375 (P Sparkes); *Camden LBC v Alexandrou* (1997) 74 P & CR D33. For assignment of a lease, see below, pp 302 ff. On informal short-term leases, see [1992] Conv 252, 337 (P Sparkes).

Thus it was only in the case of leases exceeding three years that a deed became necessary, since it was these alone that had previously been 'required by law to be in writing'. A lease exceeding three years and not executed as a deed had—and still has—a greater effect than is indicated by the language of the two statutes cited but since 1845 it has never sufficed to pass to the tenant an immediate legal interest equivalent to that which the parties intended to create. The Statutes of 1677 and 1845 have been in effect re-enacted by the Law of Property Act 1925 in, respectively, the two following sections:

> 54.—(1) All interests in land created by parol and not put in writing and signed by the persons so creating the same, or by their agents thereunto lawfully authorized in writing, have, notwithstanding any consideration having been given for the same, the force and effect of interests at will only.
>
> (2) Nothing in the foregoing provisions... shall affect the creation by parol of leases taking effect in possession for a term not exceeding three years... at the best rent which can be reasonably obtained without taking a fine.

> 52.—(1) All conveyances of land or of any interest therein are void for the purpose of conveying or creating a legal estate unless made by deed.
>
> (2) This section does not apply to—
>
> (d) leases or tenancies or other assurances not required by law to be made in writing.

(2) Effect of a Lease Exceeding Three Years that is not made in Accordance with the Formalities Required by Law of Property Act 1925

In order to understand the effect under sections 52 and 54 of the Law of Property Act 1925 of a lease exceeding three years that fails to satisfy the statutory requirements, it is important to understand how the courts developed their views of a lease that failed to satisfy the statutory provisions that are reproduced in the 1925 Act. We therefore consider, first, the legal effect between 1677 and 1845 of a lease not put into writing as required by the Statute of Frauds; and, secondly, the effect since 1845 of a lease not made by deed as required by the Real Property Act of that year.

(a) Effect at common law

The Statute of Frauds said that a lease that was not put in writing should create a mere tenancy at will, and this was the view taken by the common law when a tenant did nothing more than enter into possession of the premises under a parol lease. But this was not the final word. The common law went further and presumed that a tenant who had not merely gone into possession, but had also paid rent on a yearly basis, became tenant from year to year, and that he held this yearly tenancy subject to such of the terms and conditions of the unwritten lease as were consistent with a yearly tenancy.[216]

---

[216] *Doe d Rigge v Bell* (1793) 5 Term Rep 471; *Mann v Lovejoy* (1826) Ry & M 355; *Clayton v Blakey* (1798) 8 Term Rep 3; *Richardson v Gifford* (1834) 1 Ad & El 52; *Hamerton v Stead* (1824) 3 B & C 478, 483. See above, p 208.

The provision of the Real Property Act 1845 that a lease that was not made by deed should be *void at law* was construed in the same manner. The document was void as a lease in the sense that it did not create the agreed term of years, but if the intended tenant entered into possession and paid rent at a yearly rate, he was presumed to be a yearly tenant.[217]

The above still represents the legal position at the present day *if we confine our attention to the common law*. A conveyance of land, and this includes a lease,[218] is void under section 52 of the Law of Property Act 1925 for the purpose of creating a legal estate unless made by deed (except in the case of a lease not exceeding three years), but nevertheless, if the tenant enters into possession and pays a yearly rent, he will become a yearly tenant.[219] Again, by section 54 of the 1925 Act a term exceeding three years that is not put in writing is to have the force and effect of an interest at will only, but, given the same two facts of possession and payment of a yearly rent, it also will be converted into a legal yearly tenancy. It is expressly provided that the requirements of the Act with regard to formalities shall not 'affect the right to acquire an interest in land by virtue of taking possession'.[220]

(b) Effect in equity

Equity, however, took a very different view of the effect of a lease for more than three years that was not put in writing as required by the Statute of Frauds, or that, after 1845, was not made by deed. While admitting that the statutes rendered such a lease incapable of passing the term agreed upon by the parties, courts of equity held that the abortive lease must be regarded as *a contract for a lease*, provided that the constituents of an enforceable contract were present. When this principle was devised by the courts of equity,[221] this meant that an *oral* lease followed by an act of part performance, and a *written* lease signed by the party to be charged and constituting a sufficient memorandum of the terms of the bargain, were both allowed to have the same effect as a contract for a lease, although since 1989 a contract for a lease cannot be oral but must be in writing.[222] It becomes necessary, therefore, to ascertain what the effect has always been in equity of a contract for a lease.

A contract for a lease is a contract to which the equitable remedy of specific performance is peculiarly appropriate. If a party can prove to the satisfaction of the court that such a contract has been entered into, he can bring an action for specific performance requiring the other party to execute a deed in the manner required by statute so as to create that legal term that the parties intended to create. One effect, therefore, of such a specifically enforceable contract is that the prospective tenant

---

[217] *Martin v Smith* (1874) LR 9 Exch 50; *Rhyl UDC v Rhyl Amusements Ltd* [1959] 1 WLR 465, where the lease was void for lack of compliance with the Public Health Act 1875, s 177.

[218] S 205(1)(ii).

[219] *Hutchison v B & DF Ltd* [2008] EWHC 2286 (Ch), [2009] L & TR 12 (oral agreement for lease not complying with LP(MP)A 1989, s 2).

[220] S 55(c).

[221] Under Statute of Frauds 1677, s 4; below, p 961.   [222] LP(MP)A 1989, s 2; below, p 966.

immediately acquires an equitable interest in the land in the sense that he has an equitable right to a legal estate.[223] As was said in a case prior to 1845:[224]

> The defendant was let into possession under an agreement, which gave the parties a right to go to equity to compel the execution of it by making out a formal lease.

The same view was upheld even when the Real Property Act 1845 had enacted that a lease exceeding three years made otherwise than by deed should be void at law. As Lord Chelmsford said in *Parker v Taswell*:[225]

> The legislature appears to have been very cautious and guarded in language, for it uses the expression 'shall be void at law'. If the legislature had intended to deprive such a document of all efficacy, it would have said that the instrument should 'be avoided to all intents and purposes'. There are no such words in the Act. I think it would be too strong to say that because it is void at law as a lease, it cannot be used as an agreement enforceable in Equity, the intention of the parties having been that there should be a lease, and the aid of Equity being only invoked to carry that intention into effect.

(3) *Doctrine of* Walsh v Lonsdale

(a) The doctrine

The effect of this divergence between the views of common law and equity was that, prior to the passing of the Judicature Act 1873, a lease that was not made by deed and a contract for a lease both resulted in the creation of two entirely different interests, according as the common law or the equitable doctrine was invoked. At common law the tenant acquired the interest of a tenant from year to year if he paid rent and entered into possession: in equity he was entitled to call for the execution of a legal lease and to have inserted therein all the provisions of the void lease or of the contract.

The Judicature Act, however, materially affected the position. It provided in effect that, whenever an action is brought in any court, the claimant may set up equitable claims and the defendant may raise equitable defences, and that:

> [Where] there is any conflict or variance between the rules of equity and the rules of the common law with reference to the same matter, the rules of equity shall prevail.[226]

The particular point of variance that existed in the case of a lease that was not made by deed fell to be considered in the leading case of *Walsh v Lonsdale*,[227] decided in 1882. In that case:

> the claimant agreed in writing to take a lease of a mill for seven years, and part of the agreement was that a deed should be executed containing inter alia a provision that *on any given day* the lessor might require the tenant to pay one year's rent in advance. No deed

---

[223] *Palmer v Carey* [1926] AC 703, 706.
[224] *Doe d Thomson v Amey* (1840) 12 Ad & El 476, 479 (Lord Denman CJ).
[225] (1858) 2 De G & J 559, 570.
[226] Supreme Court of Judicature Act 1873, s 25(11); now SCA 1981, s 49(1).
[227] (1882) 21 Ch D 9, M & B p 30; (1988) 8 OJLS 350 (P Sparkes).

was executed, and the claimant, who was let into possession, paid rent quarterly, but not in advance, for a year and a half. The landlord then demanded a year's rent in advance and upon refusal distrained for the amount. The claimant brought an action to recover damages for illegal distress, for specific performance of the contract for a lease and for an interim injunction to restrain the distress.

The main ground upon which he rested his claim was that, as he had been let into possession and had paid rent under a contract which did not operate as a lease, he was in the position of a tenant from year to year and held the mill upon such of the agreed terms as were consistent with a yearly tenancy. The condition making a year's rent always payable in advance was obviously inconsistent with a yearly tenancy which could be determined by half a year's notice, and for this reason it was argued that the distress was illegal.

This argument did not prevail. It was decided that a tenant who holds under a contract for a lease of which specific performance will be decreed occupies the same position *vis-à-vis the landlord*, as regards both rights and liabilities, as he would occupy if a formal lease had been executed as a deed.

If in this case a lease by deed had been executed on the lines of the contract, the defendant would have been entitled to distrain for rent not paid in advance, and the mere fact that the formal lease had not been actually made was not to prejudice his rights. Sir George Jessel MR said:

> There is an agreement for a lease under which possession has been given. Now since the Judicature Act the possession is held under the agreement. There are not two estates as there were formerly—one estate at common law by reason of the payment of the rent from year to year, and an estate in equity under the agreement. There is only one court, and the equity rules prevail in it. The tenant holds under an agreement for a lease.[228] He holds, therefore, under the same terms in equity as if a lease had been granted, it being a case in which both parties admit that relief is capable of being given by specific performance. That being so, he cannot complain of the exercise by the landlord of the same rights as the landlord would have had if a lease had been granted. On the other hand, he is protected in the same way as if a lease had been granted; he cannot be turned out by six months' notice as a tenant from year to year. He has a right to say: 'I have a lease in equity and you can only re-enter if I have committed such a breach of covenant as would, if a lease had been granted, have entitled you to re-enter according to the terms of a proper proviso for re-entry'. That being so, it appears to me that being a lessee in equity he cannot complain of the exercise of the right of distress merely because the actual parchment has not been signed and sealed.

This is the doctrine of *Walsh v Lonsdale*. It is one example of the principle that equity regards as already done what the parties to a transaction have agreed to do—a principle that is not confined to a contract for a lease, for it applies to any contract to convey or create a legal estate or an interest in land of which equity will order specific performance.[229]

---

[228] He can, however, choose to rely on his (legal) periodic tenancy if he so chooses, eg where a purchaser is bound by the legal tenancy but takes free of the equitable lease: below, p 220.

[229] Below, pp 978–9, 1012.

(b) Application of doctrine

In the context of landlord and tenant, *Walsh v Lonsdale* has been followed,[230] qualified[231] and explained[232] in later cases. It has also been applied 'once removed',[233] where V entered into a contract to sell the fee simple of land to P, who then agreed to grant a lease of the land to T. T was treated as a lessee in equity by virtue of a double application of the doctrine. T could not become a lessee at common law until a legal lease had been properly granted. As Lord Denning said:[234]

> It is quite plain that, if the lease to T was defective in point of law, nevertheless it was good in equity, and for this simple reason. There were two agreements of which specific performance would be granted. One was the agreement by V to convey to P. The other was the agreement by P to grant a lease to T. In respect of each of these agreements, equity looks upon that as done which ought to be done. It follows that, by combining the two agreements, the tenant, T, holds upon the same terms as if a lease had actually been granted by V to T. This is, of course, an extension of the doctrine of *Walsh v Lonsdale* where there was only one agreement. But I see no reason why the doctrine should not be extended to a case like the present, where there were two agreements, each of which was such that specific performance would be granted.

The doctrine is now the governing rule whenever it is necessary to ascertain the effect of a lease or contract for a lease that is not made by deed as required by the Law of Property Act 1925. As we have seen,[235] section 52(1) of the Act provides that all conveyances of land 'are void for the purpose of conveying or creating a legal estate unless made by deed', but, if a tenant has an enforceable right to call for a deed, he is, as far as his rights and liabilities in relation to the landlord are concerned, in practically the same position as if he actually had a deed.

(4) A Contract for a Lease is not Equal to a Lease

It must not, however, be concluded that a contract for a lease is as effective in all respects and against all persons as a lease. This is not so.[236] What Sir George Jessel MR meant in *Walsh v Lonsdale* was that if, in litigation between the parties, the circumstances would justify a decree for the execution of a lease by deed, then both in the Queen's

---

[230] *Lowther v Heaver* (1889) 41 Ch D 248; *Coatsworth v Johnson* (1885) 55 LJQB 220, M & B p 32; *Tottenham Hotspur Football and Athletic Co Ltd v Princegrove Publishers Ltd* [1974] 1 WLR 113; (1974) 90 LQR 149 (M Albery); *Re A Company (No 00792 of 1992), ex p Tredegar Enterprises Ltd* [1992] 29 EG 122.

[231] *Cornish v Brook Green Laundry Ltd* [1959] 1 QB 394, where it was held that it cannot be invoked if the contract to grant a term of years is subject to a condition precedent performable by the proposed tenant and not yet performed; *Shelley v United Artists Corp Ltd* [1990] 1 EGLR 103; *Mexfield Housing Co-operative Ltd v Berisford* [2010] EWCA Civ 811, [2010] 2 EGLR 137 (tenancy agreement void at law for uncertainty of term cannot be saved by *Walsh v Lonsdale*); [2010] Conv 492 (S Bridge).

[232] *Manchester Brewery Co v Coombs* [1901] 2 Ch 608, M & B p 478; *Gray v Spyer* [1922] 2 Ch 22.

[233] *Industrial Properties (Barton Hill) Ltd v Associated Electrical Industries Ltd* [1977] QB 580, M & B p 31.

[234] ibid, 598. Letters have been substituted for the names of the parties.

[235] Above, p 213.   [236] *Manchester Brewery Co v Coombs* [1901] 2 Ch 608, 617.

Bench Division and in the Chancery Division, the case must be treated as if such a lease had been granted. There are at least three points that illustrate the limitations of the doctrine, and the advantages of a lease as compared with a contract for a lease.

(a) Specific performance

First, the doctrine is excluded if the contract is one of which equity will not grant specific performance.[237] This is still a discretionary remedy and will not be granted in all cases, such as where a tenant who seeks the aid of the court will be unable to perform the covenants in the lease owing to his insolvent state, or where he has already committed a breach of covenant that would have formed part of the lease. Thus, in *Coatsworth v Johnson*:[238]

> The claimant entered into possession under an agreement that the defendant would grant him a lease for 21 years. Before any rent was due or had been paid, the defendant gave him notice to quit and evicted him on the ground that he had done that which amounted to a breach of a covenant contained in the agreement and intended to be inserted in the lease.

The claimant sued in trespass, but failed. At common law, having paid no rent, he was a mere tenant at will and as such could be evicted at the pleasure of the defendant; in equity he was precluded from obtaining a decree of specific performance, since he had broken a covenant into which he had entered.

Stamp J, in explaining that the doctrine only applies where the tenant is entitled to specific performance, said in *Warmington v Miller*:[239]

> The equitable interests which the intended lessee has under an agreement for a lease do not exist in vacuo, but arise because the intended lessee has an equitable right to specific performance of the agreement. In such a situation that which is agreed to be and ought to be done is treated as having been done and carrying with it in equity the attendant rights.

Further, specific performance will not be granted if the court has no jurisdiction to grant it. Thus a county court has such jurisdiction only where the value of the property claimed does not exceed £30,000.[240]

(b) Conveyance

Secondly, the statutory definition of 'conveyance'[241] includes a lease but not a contract for a lease. Thus, a tenant under a contract cannot claim those privileges that are granted

---

[237] For criticism of this requirement, see (1987) 7 OJLS 60 (S Gardner).

[238] (1886) 55 LJQB 220, M & B p 32; *Rouf v Tragus Holdings Ltd* [2009] EWHC 96 (Ch), [2009] All ER (D) 29 (Jan).

[239] [1973] QB 877, 887.

[240] County Courts Act 1984, s 23(d); County Courts Jurisdiction Order 1981 (SI 1981 No 1123); *Foster v Reeves* [1892] 2 QB 255; cf *Cornish v Brook Green Laundry Ltd* [1959] 1 QB 394; *Kingswood Estate Co Ltd v Anderson* [1963] 2 QB 169; *Rushton v Smith* [1976] QB 480.

[241] LPA 1925, s 205(1)(ii).

by section 62 of the Law of Property Act 1925[242] to one who takes a 'conveyance' of land.[243]

(c) Third parties

Thirdly, an equitable lease, including one created under the doctrine in *Walsh v Lonsdale*, does not affect the rights of third parties as extensively as a legal lease.

The most important consequence of this is that, since a specifically enforceable contract confers only an equitable interest on the lessee, its potency against third parties is less than that of a legal lease, as is the case with all equitable interests by comparison with legal estates and interests.[244] Writing at a time when the old general principle of notice was still applied, Maitland said:[245]

An agreement for a lease is not equal to a lease. An equitable right is not equivalent to a legal right; between the contracting parties an agreement for a lease may be as good as a lease; just so between the contracting parties an agreement for the sale of land may serve as well as a completed sale and conveyance. But introduce the third party and then you will see the difference. I take a lease; my lessor then sells the land to X; notice or no notice my lease is good against X. I take a mere agreement for a lease, and the person who has agreed to grant the lease then sells and conveys to Y, who has no notice of my merely equitable right. Y is not bound to grant me a lease.

The current position depends on whether the land is still unregistered, or is already registered, at the time when it is purchased by the third party.

(1) Unregistered land

In unregistered land a contract for a lease is an estate contract within the meaning of the Law of Property Act 1925[246] and will therefore be enforceable against a purchaser for money or money's worth of the legal estate from the landlord only if it has been registered as a land charge under the Land Charges Act 1972[247] at the Land Registry. Thus

if A takes a contract for lease from B and then B sells and conveys the land to C, A's estate contract if registered will prevail against C, but if not registered will be defeated by the conveyance, even if C actually knew that it had been made.[248]

---

[242] Below, p 654.   [243] *Borman v Griffith* [1930] 1 Ch 493, M & B p 420.

[244] Above, pp 78 ff, 143–6. In addition, privity of estate exists at common law between the landlord and the assignee from the tenant holding under a lease, but not the assignee from a person 'whose only title to call himself a lessee depends on his right to specific performance of an agreement': *Purchase v Lichfield Brewery Co* [1915] 1 KB 184, 188 (Lush J), M & B p 480. See also *Manchester Brewery Co v Coombs* [1901] 2 Ch 608, M & B p 478; (1978) 37 CLJ 98 (RJ Smith). In consequence, covenants in a lease were enforceable by and against the assignee under a lease but, until this rule was changed by statute in relation to agreements for lease created after 1995 (LT(C)A 1995, below, pp 320 ff, which defines 'tenancy' as including 'an agreement for a tenancy': s 28(1)) it was not entirely certain that the same was true for covenants in an agreement for lease.

[245] Maitland, *Equity* (1910), p 161 (revised edn, 1936), p 158.

[246] S 2(3)(iv).   [247] Formerly LCA 1925; class C(iv).

[248] LPA 1925, s 199(1)(i); *Sharp v Coates* [1948] 1 All ER 136; on appeal, [1949] 1 KB 285. See *Midland Bank Trust Co Ltd v Green* [1981] AC 513, M & B p 72; *Hollington Bros Ltd v Rhodes* [1951] 2 TLR 691, M & B p 81;

If, however, A goes into possession of the land before the sale to C and pays rent on a yearly (or other periodic) basis, he acquires a legal periodic tenancy that will be binding on C.[249] This is not affected by A's failure to register his equitable lease, although of course the basis on which A holds of C is under the terms of the periodic tenancy (which is therefore terminable accordingly[250]) rather than under the terms of the contract for lease.

(2) Registered land

Under the Land Registration Act 2002 the purchaser from the landlord will be bound by a legal lease.[251] But the purchaser for value[252] will take free of an equitable lease unless it is protected by a notice on the register or, failing that, if it takes effect as an overriding interest by virtue of the tenant being in discoverable actual occupation.[253]

(5) Registered Land. Formalities Necessary to Create a Legal Lease under Land Registration Act 2002

(a) The requirement of registration

A lease that complies with the formalities required by the Law of Property Act 1925 in order to create a legal estate will none the less not take effect at law if it is in addition required to comply with registration requirements set by the Land Registration Act 2002 but fails to do so. Under the 2002 Act the grant of a term of years absolute out of a registered estate in land is required to be completed by registration if it is a grant:[254]

(i)   for a term of more than seven years[255] from the date of the grant,

---

Markfaith Investment Ltd v Chiap Hua Flashlights Ltd [1991] 2 AC 43 ('indistinguishable from the decision of Harman J in *Hollington Bros Ltd v Rhodes*': Lord Templeman at 60). See also *Lyus v Prowsa Developments Ltd* [1982] 1 WLR 1044, below, p 1096, n 165, where a sale expressly subject to an estate contract gave rise to a constructive trust; *Ashburn Anstalt v Arnold* [1989] Ch 1, below, p 933, at 25 (Fox LJ).

[249] *Bell Street Investments Ltd v Wood* (1970) 216 EG 585. As a tenancy not exceeding three years it can take effect at law without a deed: above, pp 211–12.

[250] For example, a yearly tenancy will be terminable at the end of each year by half a year's notice: below, p 385.

[251] Either because it is registered with an individual title: below, p 1074; or because it is an overriding interest under LRA 2002, Sch 3, para 1; above, p 145; below, p 1102. An equitable lease is not included as an overriding interest within this provision because it has not been 'granted': *City Permanent Building Society v Miller* [1952] Ch 840, 852, M & B p 198 (Jenkins LJ), on equivalent wording in LRA 1925, s 70(1)(k). LRA 2002 is also more explicit than LRA 1925 in referring to a 'leasehold estate' rather than just a 'lease' in its list of overriding interests.

[252] LRA 2002, s 29; above, p 145; below, pp 1095–6.

[253] Ibid, Sch 3, para 2; below, pp 1104 ff. ('Discoverable actual occupation' is used in this book as a summary of the requirements of an overriding interest under para 2.) This provision superseded LRA 1925, s 70(1)(g). Where the tenant under an equitable lease goes into possession and pays rent, the legal periodic tenancy that thereby arises (see above) will therefore be binding as an overriding interest under Sch 3, para 1. But possession will generally constitute discoverable actual occupation and therefore give rise to an overriding interest under para 2—which will render the terms of the contract for lease itself binding on the purchaser.

[254] LRA 2002, s 27(2)(b). See also s 27(2)(c) (grant of a lease out of a registered franchise or manor).

[255] The Lord Chancellor has power to shorten the seven-year period: LRA 2002, s 5. It is intended that, when electronic conveyancing is fully implemented, the period will be reduced to three years so as to bring

(ii) to take effect in possession after the end of the period of three months beginning with the date of the grant,

(iii) under which the right to possession is discontinuous,[256]

(iv) in pursuance of Part 5 of the Housing Act 1985 (the right to buy), or

(v) in circumstances where section 171A of that Act applies (disposal by landlord that leads to a person no longer being a secure tenant).

Until the relevant registration requirements are met, it does not operate at law,[257] and therefore if it is to bind a purchaser from the landlord it requires protection by notice on the register unless it is an overriding interest by virtue of the tenant being in discoverable actual occupation.[258]

(b) Requirements as to form and content

Most leases that are required to be completed by registration must also, if granted on or after 19 June 2006, comply with requirements as to their form and content.[259] Certain prescribed clauses must be set out at the beginning of the lease, dealing with the date of the lease; the title number(s) of the property out of which the lease is granted (if already registered); the parties to the lease; the property; certain prescribed statements (if applicable[260]); the term for which the property is leased; any premium paid; a statement indicating whether or not the lease contains any prohibition or

the registration requirement into line with the rules requiring leases to be granted by deed, above, p 212; H & B, para 2.14.

Under LRA 1925, s 123, as substituted by LRA 1997, s 1, only leases granted for more than 21 years out of registered land were substantively registrable and were required to be registered. Leases for 21 years or less were overriding interests: s 70(1)(k). For further details, see the 16th edn of this book, pp 561–3. At first sight, the effect of the reduction by LRA 2002 of the length of leases required to be registered will be to render many business leases, which have generally been granted for ten or 15 years, registrable. However, the average length of a commercial lease has been reduced in recent years: Reading University Report Monitoring the 2002 Code of Practice for Commercial Leases (March 2005), discussed (2005) EG 179 (N Crosby, S Murdoch, C Hughes), 186 (M Hull); (2004) 8 L & TR 1 (J Bignell). See also above, n 101 (impact on introduction in 2003 of stamp duty land tax on length of leases).

[256] Eg a timeshare lease: above, n 104.

[257] LRA 2002, s 27(1). Under the provision formerly in force, LRA 1925, s 123A, as substituted by LRA 1997, s 1, the legal estate passed by virtue of the disposition, but became void as regards the legal estate if not registered within two months, and thereafter took effect as a contract for a lease.

[258] Ibid, s 29; Sch 3, para 2.

[259] LRR 2003, r 58A, Sch 1A, inserted by Land Registration (Amendment) (No 2) Rules 2005 (SI 2005 No 1982), r 5; Land Registry Practice Guide 64. The new rule came into force on 9 January 2006; from that date until 18 June 2006 compliance was voluntary. The new rule does not apply to leases granted in a form expressly required by an agreement entered into before 19 June 2006, by an order of the court, by or under an enactment, or by a necessary consent or licence for the grant of the lease given before 19 June 2006: ibid, r 58A(4). For the consultation leading up to the introduction of these requirements, see Land Registry Consultation Document on Presentation of Prescribed Information in Registrable Leases (September 2004); Report on Consultation (July 2005); [2006] Conv 282 (EJ Slessenger); (2004) 45 LSG 34 (J Jenkins); [2005] EG 270 (PJG Williams, K Fenn and A Colby).

[260] LRR 2003, rr 179 (dispositions in favour of a charity), 180 (dispositions by a charity), 196 (leases under the Leasehold Reform, Housing and Urban Developments Act 1993).

restriction on dispositions; any rights of renewal or surrender; restrictive covenants given in the lease by the landlord in respect of other property; easements granted or reserved by the lease; any estate rentcharge burdening the property; an application, if appropriate, for any standard form restriction that should be entered on the register; and a declaration of trust where the tenant comprises more than one person. The failure to comply with these requirements will result in the Land Registry rejecting the application for registration as defective.[261]

The purpose of these requirements is to to facilitate quicker and more accurate registration of leases, and to prepare for e-conveyancing.[262] They will also have the consequence of standardising the form of leases and thereby simplifying conveyancing.

(6) Summary

We have now reviewed the methods by which the relation of landlord and tenant may be created, and it may be helpful to summarise the present state of the law:

   (a) A lease not exceeding three years, whether by parol, in writing or by deed, confers a legal term of years upon the tenant.[263]

   (b) A lease by deed exceeding three years has the same effect,[264] if granted out of unregistered land; but if it is granted out of registered land, if the grant is for more than seven years it does not operate at law until the registration requirements are met.[265]

   (c) A lease exceeding three years that is not executed as a deed, but that complies with the formalities for a contract for the sale or other disposition of an interest in land,[266] confers an equitable term upon the tenant by virtue of the doctrine of *Walsh v Lonsdale*.[267] There may be a concurrent legal periodic tenancy by virtue of the tenant's taking possession and paying rent; but as long as the equitable term is enforceable against a purchaser from the landlord,[268] the tenant need not rely on the periodic tenancy.

   (d) A contract for a lease of any period (which, if for longer than three years, complies with the relevant formalities for land contracts[269]), if specifically enforceable, confers an equitable term on the tenant by virtue of the doctrine of *Walsh v Lonsdale*.[270]

---

[261] Land Registry Practice Guide 64, para 6; Practice Guide 49.

[262] Land Registry Consultation Document, above. See also Explanatory Note to SI 2005 No 1982.

[263] Above, pp 211–12.   [264] Above, pp 212–13.

[265] Above, p 220; and the lease must contain the prescribed clauses: above.

[266] LP(MP)A 1989, s 2; below, Ch 24.   [267] Above, p 215.

[268] By being protected (in unregistered land) by registration of the estate contract as a land charge; or (in registered land) by registration of a notice or as an overriding interest by virtue of the tenant's discoverable actual occupation: above, pp 219–20.

[269] A lease not exceeding three years need not be in writing: LP(MP)A 1989, s 2(5)(a).

[270] Whether it binds a purchaser from the landlord depends on whether it is protected by registration or as an overriding interest: above, n 268.

9

COVENANTS IN LEASES[1]

Summary

In this chapter we consider the rights and duties of the landlord and the tenant under a lease: first, the source of the parties' mutual rights and duties in covenants, implied or express, in the lease; then the remedies of the landlord, in particular, for the enforcement of the covenants; and finally the effect on the enforceability of covenants, by both landlord and tenant, of the assignment of the lease by the tenant or of the reversion by the landlord.

I RIGHTS AND DUTIES OF LANDLORD AND TENANT

The rights and the duties of a landlord and a tenant are commonly fixed by the express covenants that, having been settled by the parties, are incorporated in the lease or the contract under which the premises are held. But a contract may be silent on several matters of importance, or there may be no express agreement at all, and therefore it

---

[1] See generally Aldridge, *Leasehold Law*, Part 4; Hill and Redman's *Landlord and Tenant*, Division A, ch 9; Woodfall, *Landlord and Tenant*, chs 7–11; Crabb, *Leases Covenants and Consents* (2nd edn, 2008); Fancourt, *Enforceability of Landlord and Tenant Covenants* (2nd edn, 2006); M & B pp 421–99.

is necessary to consider, first, what the position of the parties is where there are no express covenants, and then the usual covenants common to all ordinary leases.[2]

A POSITION WHERE THERE ARE NO EXPRESS COVENANTS OR CONDITIONS

(1) Implied Obligations of the Landlord

(a) Quiet enjoyment

A covenant that the tenant shall have quiet enjoyment[3] of the premises is implied in every lease that does not expressly deal with the matter.[4] The meaning of this is that the tenant shall be put into possession[5] and that he shall be entitled to recover damages from the landlord[6] if his enjoyment is substantially disturbed by acts either of the landlord or of somebody claiming under the landlord.[7] 'It is a covenant for freedom from disturbance by adverse claimants to the property.'[8] Instances are, where the landlord, having reserved the right to work minerals under the land, so works them as to cause the land to subside;[9] or where, in a lease of shooting rights, he erects buildings so as substantially to reduce the area over which the rights are exercisable,[10] or where, with a view to getting rid of the tenant, he removes the doors and windows of the demised premises,[11] or subjects him to persistent and prolonged intimidation,[12] or

---

[2] For the application of the Unfair Contract Terms Act 1977 and the Unfair Terms in Consumer Contracts Regulations 1999 to covenants in leases, see above, p 183, n 25; cf [2006] Conv 137 (S Bright, arguing for increased protection for small business tenants).

[3] See (1976) 40 Conv (NS) 427; (1977) 40 MLR 651; [1978] Conv 419 (MJ Russell).

[4] *Markham v Paget* [1908] 1 Ch 697. In early days there was no such implication unless the word 'demise' had been used in the lease; ibid. See *Gordon v Selico Co Ltd* [1986] 1 EGLR 71, 77, where Slade LJ held that no covenants were to be implied 'where it was intended by all parties to provide a comprehensive code in regard to repair and maintenance'.

[5] *Miller v Emcer Products Ltd* [1956] Ch 304.

[6] Or an injunction in appropriate cases: cf *Lunn Poly Ltd v Liverpool & Lancashire Properties Ltd* [2006] EWCA Civ 430, [2006] 2 EGLR 29 (principles of assessment of damages under s 50 SCA 1981 in lieu of injunction). For criminal offences, see below, p 348.

[7] *Jones v Lavington* [1903] 1 KB 253; *Sanderson v Berwick-upon-Tweed Corp* (1884) 13 QBD 547, 551; *Matania v National Provincial Bank Ltd and Elevenist Syndicate Ltd* [1936] 2 All ER 633; *Sampson v Hodson-Pressinger* [1981] 3 All ER 710, 714; *Guppys (Bridport) Ltd v Brookling* (1983) 269 EG 846 (exemplary damages); *Mira v Aylmer Square Investments Ltd* [1990] 1 EGLR 45 (damages for loss of revenue from sublettings). An express right of entry in the lease must be construed consistently with the covenant for quiet enjoyment: *Yeoman's Row Management Ltd v Bodentien-Meyrick* [2002] EWCA Civ 860, [2002] 2 EGLR 39 (express covenant); and where there is a covenant to repair the landlord must take all reasonable precautions (but not all *possible* precautions) before causing a disturbance by carrying out the repairs: *Goldmile Properties Ltd v Lechouritis* [2003] EWCA Civ 49, [2003] 1 EGLR 60 (express covenants).

[8] *Hudson v Cripps* [1896] 1 Ch 265, 268 (North J).   [9] *Markham v Paget*, above, n 4.

[10] *Peech v Best* [1931] 1 KB 1 (a case, however, of an express covenant).

[11] *Lavender v Betts* [1942] 2 All ER 72.

[12] *Kenny v Preen* [1963] 1 QB 499; *Branchett v Beaney* [1992] 3 All ER 910, where CA reviewed the authorities and held that damages are not recoverable for mental distress, doubting *Sampson v Floyd* [1989] 2 EGLR 49 (constructive eviction where tenant was frightened for himself and for his wife; damages awarded

inflicts physical discomfort on him by cutting off his gas and electricity,[13] or where he erects scaffolding that obstructs access to the premises.[14] However, there is no liability under the covenant that would impose on the landlord an obligation to alter or improve the premises so as to provide adequate sound-proofing against noise penetration from his adjoining premises.[15] There is also no liability under the covenant if the act of disturbance is committed by a person claiming not under the landlord, but under a title paramount to his;[16] nor is there liability if a landlord enters into possession as a result of a court order on the ground of forfeiture of the lease, which is subsequently reversed on appeal.[17] And the tenant must expect some disruption with his enjoyment of the premises when the landlord fulfils his duty to repair.[18]

(b) Non-derogation from grant[19]

Closely related to the covenant for quiet enjoyment[20] is the landlord's implied covenant that he shall not derogate from his grant. He must not frustrate the use of the land for the purposes for which it was let;[21] or, as Bowen LJ put it, 'a grantor having given a thing with one hand is not to take away the means of enjoying it with the other'.[22] Wood V-C in one case said:

> If a landowner conveys one of two closes to another, he cannot afterwards do anything to derogate from his grant; and if the conveyance is made for the express purpose of having buildings erected upon the land so granted, a contract is implied on the part of the

for loss of lease, conveyancing costs and distress). On the recoverability of damages for mental distress for breach of contract generally, see *Farley v Skinner* [2001] UKHL 49, [2002] 2 AC 732; Anson, pp 536-8. Such conduct might however constitute a tort, such as trespass or assault; and damages may be recoverable in tort for distress: *Branchett v Beaney*, at 918. See also Protection from Harassment Act 1997, s 3 (civil remedy may include damages for anxiety).

[13] *Perera v Vandiyar* [1953] 1 WLR 672.

[14] *Owen v Gadd* [1956] 2 QB 99, a case of an express covenant, but equally applicable to an implied covenant: *Queensway Marketing Ltd v Associated Restaurants Ltd* (1984) 271 EG 1106; *Lawson v Hartley-Brown* (1995) 71 P & CR 242 (erection of scaffolding outside shop and construction of flat roof above it).

[15] *Southwark LBC v Tanner* [2001] 1 AC 1 (18 flats built at the end of First World War that had fallen short of modern standards); [2000] Conv 161 (D Rook).

[16] *Jones v Lavington* [1903] 1 KB 253. See also *Celsteel Ltd v Alton House Holdings Ltd (No 2)* [1987] 1 WLR 291 (lessor not liable on covenant for what predecessor in title had done).

[17] *Hillgate House Ltd v Expert Clothing Service & Sales Ltd* [1987] 1 EGLR 65.

[18] *Goldmile Properties Ltd v Lechouritis* [2003] EWCA Civ 49, [2003] 1 EGLR 60 (covenants to repair and to give quiet enjoyment must be construed and applied so as to coexist on a basis of parity, not priority). For covenants to repair, see below, pp 246 ff.

[19] For a comprehensive discussion, see (1964) 80 LQR 244 (DW Elliott); criticised in part, (1965) 81 LQR 28 (MA Peel); Gale, paras 3-32 to 3-52.

[20] Ibid, at 273-6.

[21] *Browne v Flower* [1911] 1 Ch 219, 225-7, where illustrations are given by Parker J.

[22] *Birmingham, Dudley and District Banking Co v Ross* (1888) 38 Ch D 295, 313; *Johnston & Sons Ltd v Holland* [1988] 1 EGLR 264, 267-8 (Nicholls LJ): 'The expression "derogation from grant" conjures up images of parchment and sealing wax, of copperplate handwriting and fusty title deeds. But the principle is not based on some ancient technicality of real property . . . it is a principle which merely embodies in a legal maxim a rule of common honesty.'

grantor to do nothing to prevent the land from being used for the purpose for which to the knowledge of the grantor the conveyance is made.[23]

In the case of leases this general principle of law becomes particularly applicable when the landlord makes an inconsiderate use of land adjacent to the tenant's holding. For example, where lands were leased to a tenant for the purpose of carrying on the business of a timber merchant, and the landlord proceeded to erect buildings on adjoining land in such a way as to interrupt the free flow of air to the tenant's drying sheds, it was held that damages were recoverable against the landlord's assigns for breach of the implied covenant.[24] And where a flat is leased in a building, the whole of which is clearly intended to be used solely by residential tenants, the landlord commits a breach of the covenant if he subsequently lets the greater part of the premises for business purposes.[25]

The covenant is enforceable against the landlord and his successors not only by the original tenant but also by those claiming under him.[26]

---

[23] *North Eastern Rly Co v Elliott* (1860) 1 John & H 145, 153.

[24] *Aldin v Latimer Clark, Muirhead & Co* [1894] 2 Ch 437; *Harmer v Jumbil (Nigeria) Tin Areas Ltd* [1921] 1 Ch 200 (landlord unable to build on land acquired after lease granted); *Port v Griffith* [1938] 1 All ER 295; *Romulus Trading Co Ltd v Comet Properties Ltd* [1996] 2 EGLR 70 (grant of adjoining premises to competing business held not to be derogation); cf *Chartered Trust plc v Davies* [1997] 2 EGLR 83 (held to be derogation where landlord failed to use his powers to prevent another tenant of his from substantially interfering with the way in which the tenant ran his business of selling puzzles and executive toys in a 'niche' shop in Bognor Regis); (1998) 148 NLJ 57 (HW Wilkinson); *Yankwood Ltd v Havering LBC* [1998] EGCS 75. See also *Lyme Valley Squash Club Ltd v Newcastle under Lyme BC* [1985] 2 All ER 405 (easement of light); *Oceanic Village Ltd v Shirayma Shokusan Co Ltd* [2001] L & TR 35 (implied term in lease of gift shop at London Aquarium restricting landlord from permitting sale of aquarium-related goods from other nearby premises); *Dorrington Belgravia Ltd v McGlashan* [2010] L & TR 3 (landlord not entitled to add further storey on roof where roof (with skylights) formed part of demised premises).

The principle is also applicable if the tenant is prevented from entering the lessor's land in order to execute essential repairs to the demised premises: *Ward v Kirkland* [1967] Ch 194, 226–7.

The Access to Neighbouring Land Act 1992 enables a person to obtain an order of the County Court for access to neighbouring land, in order to carry out works that are reasonably necessary for the preservation of his own land (land includes a party-wall: *Dean v Walker* (1996) 73 P & CR 366). The Act is based on Law Com No 151, *Rights of Access to Neighbouring Land* (1985). The Act had a chequered history: [1992] 26 EG 136 (J Adams). If the land is registered, the order is registrable by way of agreed notice under LRA 2002, s 34; LRR 2003, r 80, and cannot be an overriding interest: Access to Neighbouring Land Act 1992, s 5. In unregistered land, an access order is registrable as a writ or order under LCA 1972, s 6(1)(d), and is regarded as a pending land action under s 5(1). See Gale, paras 11–41 to 11–69.

[25] *Newman v Real Estate Debenture Corpn Ltd and Flower Decorations Ltd* [1940] 1 All ER 131; distinguished in *Kelly v Battershell* [1949] 2 All ER 830.

[26] *Molton Builders Ltd v City of Westminster LBC* (1975) 30 P & CR 182, 186 (Lord Denning MR: 'Sometimes it is rested on an implied term in the contract. But this is not correct. It is a principle evolved by the law itself').

(c) Fitness for habitation

In general, there is no implied undertaking by the landlord that the premises are or will be fit for habitation; and no covenant is implied that he will do any repairs.[27] Caveat lessee.[28] There are, however, exceptions to this rule.

(1) Furnished houses

Upon the letting of a furnished house, there is at common law an implied warranty, in the nature of a condition,[29] that the premises shall be reasonably fit for habitation at the date fixed for the commencement of the tenancy. As McCardie J said:[30]

> What is the meaning of 'fit for habitation'? The meaning of the phrase must vary with the circumstances to which it is applied. In the case of unclean furniture or defective drains or a nuisance by vermin the matter is not, as a rule, one of difficulty. The eye or the nostrils can detect the fault and measure its extent. But in the case of a house lately occupied by a person suffering from an infectious disease, the eye and other senses are of no avail. The bacilli of infection are not apparent to the eye. Yet a peril is none the less grave because it is hidden.

Thus, if the house is infested with bugs,[31] if its drainage is defective,[32] or if it has been lately occupied by a person suffering from tuberculosis,[33] the tenant is entitled to repudiate the tenancy and to recover damages. But provided that the house is fit for habitation at the beginning of the tenancy, the fact that it later becomes uninhabitable imposes no liability upon the landlord.[34]

This implied condition does not extend to unfurnished premises.[35]

---

[27] In 1996 the Law Commission made recommendations for the allocation of responsibility for the repair of property between landlord and tenant where none had been expressly made, and, in the case of residential property, for an implied term that a dwelling was fit for human habitation: Law Com No 238, *Responsibility for State and Condition of Property* (1996), Parts VII and VIII; below, p 256. However, in December 2009 the Government rejected the proposals in relation to residential property, and, whilst accepting those relating to commercial property, decided that primary legislation needed to implement them is not a priority: Law Com No 232, *Annual Report 2009-10*, para 3.2; cf Lord Chancellor's Report on the implementation of Law Commission Proposals (2011), para 47 ('The Government does not consider that the problems with the law in this area are sufficient to require legislative intervention'). In *Wettern Electric Ltd v Welsh Development Agency* [1983] QB 796 it was implied into a contractual licence of business premises that they were of sound construction and would be reasonably fit for the purposes required by the licensee; (1983) 80 LSG 2195 (HW Wilkinson); cf *Morris-Thomas v Petticoat Lane Rentals* (1986) 53 P & CR 238.

[28] *Southwark LBC v Tanner* [2001] 1 AC 1, 12 (Lord Hoffmann).

[29] For the technical difference between a 'condition', a 'warranty' and an 'intermediate' contractual term as now applied in the law of contract, see Anson, pp 145–6. The language of the older cases must be understood in the light of this.

[30] *Collins v Hopkins* [1923] 2 KB 617, 620–1.   [31] *Smith v Marrable* (1843) 11 M & W 5.

[32] *Wilson v Finch Hatton* (1877) 2 Ex D 336.   [33] *Collins v Hopkins*, above.

[34] *Sarson v Roberts* [1895] 2 QB 395.

[35] *Hart v Windsor* (1843) 12 M & W 68; *Robbins v Jones* (1863) 15 CBNS 221; *Cruse v Mount* [1933] Ch 278; *Cavalier v Pope* [1906] AC 428; *Bottomley v Bannister* [1932] 1 KB 458; *Otto v Bolton and Norris* [1936] 2 KB 46.

(2) Premises in multiple occupation

A landlord who retains control of the means of access to demised premises in a high-rise block of flats, such as lifts and staircases and other common facilities such as rubbish chutes or lighting, is under an implied duty to keep them in repair. The duty, implied into the lease at common law, is not absolute, but only a duty to take reasonable care to maintain them in a state of reasonable repair and usability.[36]

(3) Correlative obligation on landlord

A repairing covenant may be implied against a landlord where a tenant's express covenant as to internal repairs would eventually become impossible to perform in the absence of a correlative obligation on the landlord as to outside repairs. The imposition of such an obligation on the landlord is necessary in order to give business efficacy to the lease.[37]

(4) Houses let at low rent

The Landlord and Tenant Act 1985[38] provides for the protection of persons taking houses at a low rent. Where a contract is made on or after 6 July 1957 for letting for human habitation a house or part of a house at a rent not exceeding £80 a year in Greater London and £52 elsewhere, there shall be implied a condition by the landlord, notwithstanding any stipulation to the contrary, that the house is fit for human habitation at the commencement of the tenancy, and an undertaking that he will keep it so throughout the tenancy.[39] There is no such stipulation, however, if the letting is for at least three years upon the terms that the tenant will put the house into a condition reasonably fit for human habitation, and if the lease is not determinable by either party before the expiration of three years.[40]

---

[36] *Liverpool City Council v Irwin* [1977] AC 239; Anson, p 156. It was held on the facts that there was no breach of the duty. Cf *Duke of Westminster v Guild* [1985] QB 688 (no repairing covenant implied on part of landlord in respect of drains running under retained land).

[37] *Barrett v Lounova (1982) Ltd* [1990] 1 QB 348; cf *Demetriou v Poolaction Ltd* [1991] 1 EGLR 100 (business premises and no correlative obligation on the landlord); *Adami v Lincoln Grange Management Ltd* [1998] 1 EGLR 58.

[38] Ss 8–10, replacing HA 1957, ss 4, 6 and 7. See commentary on LTA 1985 in Current Law Statutes Annotated (A Arden and S McGrath).

[39] LTA 1985, s 8. In the case of a contract made before 6 July 1957 and on or after 31 July 1923, the equivalent figures are £40 for London and £26 elsewhere. In view of inflation, the section must now have remarkably little application: *Quick v Taff Ely BC* [1986] QB 809, 817 (Dillon LJ); *Issa v Hackney LBC* [1997] 1 WLR 956, 964 (Brooke LJ: Parliament's failure to increase rental values makes the implied covenant a 'dead letter'). In 1996 the Law Commission recommended that LTA 1985, ss 8–10 be repealed, and that a covenant should be implied into a lease of a dwelling-house for a term of less than seven years that the lessor will keep it fit for human habitation during the term of the lease: Law Com No 238, *Responsibility for State and Condition of Property*, below, p 256. This would have the effect of removing the present archaic rent limits. See also *Lee v Leeds City Council* [2002] EWCA Civ 6, [2002] 1 WLR 1488 at [23] (Chadwick LJ, criticising the delay in giving effect to the Law Commission's Report). However, in December 2009 the Government rejected the proposals in relation to residential property: Law Com No 232, *Annual Report 2009-10*, para 3.2.

[40] Ibid, s 8(5). The Law Commission's proposed reforms, above, n 39, would have removed this exception: Law Com No 238, para 8.40.

Whether the statutory condition has been broken is a question of fact and one not always easy to determine, but the Act provides that a house shall be deemed to be unfit for human habitation if and only if it is unreasonably defective in respect of one or more of the following matters: repair; stability; freedom from damp; internal arrangement; natural lighting; ventilation; water supply; drainage and sanitary conveniences; facilities for preparation and cooking of food and for the disposal of waste water.[41]

In the event of a breach of the implied condition, the tenant may repudiate the tenancy and recover damages for breach of the undertaking,[42] providing that the landlord had notice of the existence of the defect and failed to remedy it.[43] The landlord's obligation is restricted to cases where the house is capable of being made fit at reasonable expense for human habitation.[44]

(5) Houses let for short term

The Landlord and Tenant Act 1985[45] imposes further obligations on the landlord, where he has granted a lease of a dwelling-house after 24 October 1961 for a term of less than seven years.[46] In the case of such a lease or an agreement for a lease,[47] he is subjected to an implied covenant:

(a) to keep in repair the structure and exterior[48] of the dwelling-house[49] (including drains, gutters and external pipes); and

---

[41] Ibid, s 10. As to the test of unfitness in the case of disrepair, see *Summers v Salford Corp* [1943] AC 283, 293.

[42] *Walker v Hobbs & Co* (1889) 23 QBD 458.

[43] *Morgan v Liverpool Corp* [1927] 2 KB 131; *McCarrick v Liverpool Corp* [1947] AC 219.

[44] *Buswell v Goodwin* [1971] 1 WLR 92, 96–7; *Hillbank Properties Ltd v Hackney LBC* [1978] QB 998; [1979] Conv 414 (D Morgan); *FFF Estates Ltd v Hackney LBC* [1981] 1 All ER 32; *Phillips v Newham LBC* (1981) 43 P & CR 54; *Kenny v Kingston upon Thames Royal LBC* [1985] 1 EGLR 26; *R v Ealing London Borough* (1982) 265 EG 691.

[45] Ss 11–16, as amended by HA 1988, s 116, replacing HA 1961, ss 32, 33. See the commentary in Current Law Statutes Annotated (1985). S 11 does not bind the Crown: s 15(5). See *Department of Transport v Egoroff* [1986] 1 EGLR 89. For the Law Commission's proposal that an (excludable) covenant should be implied into other leases (retaining, however, the provisions of LTA 1985, ss 11–15), see Law Com No 238, *Responsibility for State and Condition of Property* (1996), Part VII; below, p 256.

[46] A lease is treated as one for less than seven years if, though made for that period or longer, it is determinable at the lessor's option within seven years: LTA 1985, s 13(2)(c). See *Parker v O'Connor* [1974] 1 WLR 1160; *Brikom Investments Ltd v Seaford* [1981] 1 WLR 863. For the meaning of a 'lease' within LTA 1985, s 11, see *Bruton v London & Quadrant Housing Trust* [2000] 1 AC 406, M & B p 348, above, pp 183–4.

[47] *Brikom Investments Ltd v Seaford*, above; [1981] Conv 396.

[48] *Brown v Liverpool Corp* [1969] 3 All ER 1345 (outside steps and path held to be essential part of access and therefore included): cf *Hopwood v Cannock Chase DC* [1975] 1 WLR 373 (backyard path not giving access excluded); *King v South Northamptonshire DC* [1992] 1 EGLR 53. See also *Campden Hill Towers Ltd v Gardner* [1977] QB 823 (exterior of flat not exterior of whole building). The decision was reversed by HA 1988, s 116. See also *Douglas-Scott v Scorgie* [1984] 1 WLR 716 (roof over a top-floor flat); *Irvine v Moran* [1991] 1 EGLR 261, where structure was defined as consisting of those elements of the overall dwelling-house that gave it its essential appearance, stability and shape; *Staves & Staves v Leeds City Council* (1990) 23 HLR 107; *Grand v Gill* [2011] EWCA Civ 554, [2011] 21 EG 95 (CS) at [19]–[25] (plaster part of structure).

[49] On the meaning of a dwelling-house, see *Okereke v Brent LBC* [1967] 1 QB 42.

(b) to keep in repair and proper working order[50] the installations in the dwelling-
house—

   (i) for the supply of water,[51] gas and electricity, and for sanitation (including
        basins, sinks, baths and sanitary conveniences); and

   (ii) for space heating or heating water.[52]

This implied covenant was extended by the Housing Act 1988 to include any part of
the building in which the landlord has an estate or interest, if the disrepair is such as
to affect the tenant's enjoyment of the dwelling-house or of any common parts that the
tenant is entitled to use.[53]

The duty to repair means that the tenant must show physical damage to that part of
the premises that has to be made good; it is not enough to show that it is defective or
inherently inefficient for living in or ineffective in providing the condition of ordinary
habitation.[54]

The statutory obligations do not require the landlord to reinstate the premises if
they are damaged by fire or by tempest, flood or other inevitable accident; or to effect
repairs necessitated by the tenant's failure to use the premises in a tenant-like manner.[55]
In determining the standard of repair, regard must be had to the age, character and
prospective life of the dwelling-house and to the locality.[56] The landlord is liable for
any consequential expenditure to which the tenant is put, such as redecoration or
alternative accommodation during the repairs.[57] But he is only liable for defects of

[50] But not to put in a new efficient system: *Liverpool City Council v Irwin* [1977] AC 239, 269–70 (water
closet cistern that flooded due to bad design held not to be in proper working order); nor to lag water pipes:
Wycombe Health Authority v Barnett (1982) 47 P & CR 394; nor to install a damp-course: *Wainwright v Leeds
City Council* (1984) 270 EG 1289. In relation to supply of water, gas and electricity, the duty is to ensure that
the installation is so designed and constructed as to be capable of performing its function at the start of the
tenancy, under conditions of supply that it is reasonable to anticipate will prevail; and might also require a
landlord to make necessary modifications during the tenancy to accommodate unanticipated alterations in
quantity or character of supply from external utility provider: *O'Connor v Old Etonian Housing Association
Ltd* [2002] EWCA Civ 150, [2002] Ch 295; [2003] Conv 80 (MP Thompson).

[51] *Sheldon v West Bromwich Corp* (1973) 25 P & CR 360.

[52] For a miscellany of 'severe defects' leading to repudiation of lease, see *Hussein v Mehlman* [1992] 2
EGLR 87, below, p 339.

[53] LTA 1985, s 11(1A), (1B), as added by HA 1988, s 116; *Niazi Services Ltd v van de Loo* [2004] EWCA
Civ 53, [2004] 1 WLR 1254 (covenant does not extend to installation not owned or controlled by lessor and
located in part of building in which lessor does not have estate or interest); [2004] Conv 330 (DW Potts);
[2005] Conv 123 (I Loveland).

[54] *Quick v Taff Ely BC* [1986] QB 809 (living conditions appalling due to condensation, but no damage
to walls or windows of house; *McNerny v Lambeth LBC* [1989] 1 EGLR 81; *Lee v Leeds City Council* [2002]
EWCA Civ 6, [2002] 1 WLR 1488 (rejecting arguments (i) that *Quick v Taff Ely BC* was wrongly decided; and
(ii) that the interpretation of 'repair' in LTA 1985, s 11 contained in *Quick* is incompatible with Convention
rights and so should be reinterpreted under HRA 1998, s 3); [2003] Conv 112 (PF Smith).

[55] LTA 1985, s 11(2).

[56] Ibid, s 11(3); *Newham London Borough v Patel* [1979] JPL 303; *McClean v Liverpool City Council* [1987]
2 EGLR 56; *Dame Margaret Hungerford Charity Trustees v Beazeley* [1993] 2 EGLR 143; [1994] Conv 145
(J Morgan). On whether the obligation to repair can extend to merely preventative works, see *Mason v
Totalfinaelf UK Ltd* [2003] EWHC 1604 (Ch), [2003] 3 EGLR 91 at [17]–[23].

[57] *McGreal v Wake* (1984) 269 EG 1254; *Bradley v Chorley BC* [1985] 2 EGLR 49.

which notice[58] is given, and only then if after a reasonable time, he fails to remedy the defect.[59]

The parties cannot contract out of the Act,[60] but with their consent the county court may exclude or modify the repairing obligations of the landlord if it is considered reasonable to do so.[61] It is further enacted that any covenant to repair by the tenant shall be of no effect in so far as it relates to the matters covered in the landlord's statutory obligations.[62]

Local housing authorities have wide powers under Part I of the Housing Act 2004[63] to enforce housing standards in relation to residential premises. A tenant may prefer to invoke action by the local authority rather than to enforce his rights directly under the covenant.

(6) Local authority landlord's duties under Human Rights Act 1998

Section 6(1) of the Human Rights Act 1998 provides that it is unlawful for a public authority to act in a way that is incompatible with a Convention right.[64] This imposes on a local authority landlord an obligation to take steps to ensure that the condition of a dwelling-house that it has let for social housing is such that the tenant's right to respect for private and family life[65] is not infringed.[66] Whether the condition of the dwelling-house is such that the tenant's Convention right is infringed depends on the circumstances of the particular case, having due regard to the needs and resources of the community and of individuals. However, it appears that a local authority landlord,

---

[58] *O'Brien v Robinson* [1973] AC 912; *McGreal v Wake*, above; *Al Hassani v Merrigan* [1988] 1 EGLR 93; *Passley v Wandsworth LBC* (1998) 30 HLR 165. The notice may be from a person other than the tenant: *Dinefwr BC v Jones* [1987] 2 EGLR 58; and may be by way of a valuation report sent to the landlord: *Hall v Howard* [1988] 2 EGLR 75.

[59] *Porter v Jones* [1942] 2 All ER 570 (landlord who failed for eight months from notice to remedy disrepair held liable in damages); *Morris v Liverpool City Council* [1988] 1 EGLR 47 (delay of one week for emergency repairs held unreasonable).

[60] LTA 1985, s 12(1).

[61] Ibid, s 12(2). For the extension of the obligations by express provision in the lease or by any subsequent variation of its terms, see *Palmer v Sandwell Metropolitan Borough* [1987] 2 EGLR 79.

[62] Ibid, s 11(4).

[63] This Act replaced HA 1985, Part VI, under which local authorities could require the person who has control of residential premises to make it fit for human habitation, or to carry out repairs where, even though the house was not unfit, substantial repairs were necessary to bring it up to a reasonable standard, having regard to its age, character and locality. HA 2004 provides a new system for assessing the condition of residential premises, and provides new kinds of enforcement action, to enforce housing standards: ss 1(1), (3). The condition of the premises is now assessed by reference to defined 'hazards' (to be prescribed by Regulations: see SI 2005, No 3208), to replace the former system based on the test of fitness for human habitation contained in HA 1985, s 604: s 1(2). The test of 'fitness for human habitation' under HA 1985 was the same as that under LTA 1985 s 10, but HA 2004 does not make any change to LTA 1985 in this respect.

See also Environmental Protection Act 1990, Part III (statutory nuisances). On noise, see Noise and Statutory Nuisance Act 1993; Noise Act 1996; Environment Act 1995. See Waite, Jewell, Jones and Fogleman, *Environmental Law in Property Transactions* (3rd edn, 2009); McCracken, Jones and Pereira, *Statutory Nuisance Law and Practice* (2nd edn, 2008); *Encyclopedia of Environmental Law*.

[64] For the Convention rights, and HRA 1998 in general, see above, pp 22–4.

[65] Art 8 of the Convention; HRA 1998, Sch 1; above, p 23.

[66] *Lee v Leeds City Council* [2002] EWCA Civ 6, [2002] 1 WLR 1488 at [48].

which lets a house unfit for habitation or in a state prejudicial to health, will not generally be in breach of this obligation.[67] It is clear that the Act does not impose some general and unqualified obligation on local authorities in relation to the condition of their housing stock.[68]

(7) Duty of care for safety in tort or under Defective Premises Act 1972

At common law a landlord of unfurnished premises does not owe a duty of care in tort to his tenant or the tenant's guests in respect of the state of the premises at the time when they are let, even in relation to personal injury suffered in consequence of the state of the premises. Erle CJ said in 1863:[69]

> A landlord who lets a house in a dangerous state is not liable to the tenant's customers or guests for accidents happening during the term: for, fraud apart, there is no law against letting a tumble-down house; and the tenant's remedy is upon his contract, if any.

This rule was confirmed by the House of Lords in *Cavalier v Pope*[70] and remains the position at common law.[71] However, persons, such as designers or builders, involved in the construction of premises owe a duty of reasonable care at common law to those who may reasonably be expected to be affected by their work, although the duty extends only to the physical injury or property damage suffered in consequence of the failure to take reasonable care.[72] Although, therefore, the landlord owes no duty of care at common law *as landlord* to his tenant or his guests, if the landlord is also

---

[67] 'The allocation of resources to meet the needs of social housing is very much a matter for democratically determined priorities': ibid, at [49] (Chadwick LJ, relying on *Southwark LBC v Mills* [2001] 1 AC 1, 9–10 (Lord Hoffmann)).

[68] *Lee v Leeds City Council*, above, at [49]. [69] *Robbins v Jones* (1863) 15 CB (NS) 221, 240.

[70] [1906] AC 428.

[71] *McNerny v Lambeth LBC* [1989] 1 EGLR 81; [1989] Conv 216 (PF Smith). The common law might have developed otherwise on this point, since the rule was based on certain assumptions of the law of tort that are no longer correct: in particular, the 'privity fallacy' which provided that a party, such as a landlord, who undertook contractual obligations should be liable only under the contract for the consequences of breach, and could not be liable directly to third parties in tort. This was corrected in *Donoghue v Stevenson* [1932] AC 562, but the absence of the landlord's duty in tort then was already well established. See Smith, *Liability in Negligence* (1984), p 18. Development of the common law rule is now unlikely, given its effective reversal by Defective Premises Act 1972, s 4, below. See also *Jackson v JH Watson Property Investment Ltd* [2008] EWHC 14 (Ch), [2008] 1 EGLR 33 at [52] (HH Judge Behrens QC: 'In the absence of an effective covenant to repair in the lease I do not think [the tenant] can rely on the law of nuisance to impose what is, in effect, an obligation to put right faulty construction work by [the current landlord]'s predecessor in title').

[72] *D & F Estates Ltd v Church Comrs for England* [1989] AC 177; *Murphy v Brentwood DC* [1991] 1 AC 398; *Department of the Environment v Thomas Bates & Son Ltd* [1991] 1 AC 499; *Robinson v PE Jones (Contractors) Ltd* [2011] EWCA Civ 9, [2011] BLR 206. For an exceptional case in which HL held that the duty could extend to economic loss, see *Junior Books Ltd v Veitchi Co Ltd* [1983] 1 AC 520, which was distinguished but not overruled in the later HL cases. The exclusion of economic loss (such as the cost of repair incurred by the building owner or tenant) has not been followed in Australia: *Bryan v Maloney* (1995) 182 CLR 609, distinguished and restricted in *Woolcock Street Investments Pty Ltd v CDG Pty Ltd* (2004) 216 CLR 515; nor in Canada: *Winnipeg Condominium Corp No 36 v Bird Construction Co Ltd* [1995] 1 SCR 85; (1995) 111 LQR 362 (JG Fleming); nor in New Zealand: *Invercargill City Council v Hamlin* [1996] AC 624; (1996) 112 LQR 369 (IN Duncan Wallace); (1996) 3 LS 387 (CF Stychin).

involved in the design or construction of the premises he will owe the duty *as designer* or *as builder*.[73]

Under the Defective Premises Act 1972, section 4,[74] however, the landlord's immunity under *Cavalier v Pope* is effectively removed. A landlord owes to all persons[75] who might reasonably be expected to be affected by defects[76] in the state of the premises, a duty to take reasonable care to see that they are reasonably safe from personal injury or from damage to their property. Such a duty arises when the landlord is under an obligation to the tenant for the maintenance or repair of the premises, or when he has an express or implied right[77] to enter the premises[78] in order to maintain and repair them. The duty is only owed, however, if the landlord knows or ought to have known of the defect,[79] and if the defect arises from his failure to carry out his obligation or right to maintain or repair.[80]

Furthermore, a landlord of residential property may sometimes be liable to a tenant or to third parties under section 1 of the Defective Premises Act 1972,[81] which provides that any person who takes on work[82] for or in connection with the provision of a dwelling,[83] whether by the erection, conversion or enlargement of a building, is under a duty to see that the work is done in a workmanlike or professional manner, with proper materials, and so that as regards that work the dwelling will be fit for

---

[73] *Rimmer v Liverpool City Council* [1985] QB 1, 7 (tenant injured by defective glass panel; the Defective Premises Act 1972, below, did not apply); *Targett v Torfaen BC* [1992] 3 All ER 27 (CA held that *Rimmer* was not overruled by *Murphy v Brentwood DC*, above).

[74] Replacing Occupiers' Liability Act 1957, s 4. The 1972 Act was based on Law Com No 40, *Civil Liability of Vendors and Lessors for Defective Premises* (1970). See generally Holyoak and Allen, *Civil Liability for Defective Premises*, as supplemented by (1984) 134 NLJ 347, 369, 411, 425; Speaight and Stone, *Law of Defective Premises* (1982); [1974] CLJ 307, [1975] CLJ 48, esp at 62–8 (JR Spencer); Hanbury, *Defective Premises Law and Practice* (2008).

[75] Including a tenant: *Smith v Bradford Metropolitan Council* (1982) 44 P & CR 171; *McNerny v Lambeth LBC* [1989] 1 EGLR 81; *Sykes v Harry* [2001] EWCA Civ 167, [2001] QB 1014 at [21]; and a contractual licensee: s 4(6). The Act applies to all types of tenancy: s 6(1). The damages may be reduced for the claimant's contributory negligence: *Sykes v Harry* (80 per cent reduction).

[76] There must be a defect that constitutes disrepair, and not just a defect inherent in the design of the property: *Lee v Leeds City Council* [2002] EWCA Civ 6, [2002] 1 WLR 1488 at [15], [81].

[77] *McAuley v Bristol City Council* [1992] QB 134; [1992] Conv 346 (J Martin).

[78] Including a back concrete patio: ibid.

[79] But this does not require him to have notice, actual or constructive, of the actual defect that gave rise to the injury: *Sykes v Harry*, above, at [23].

[80] This does not impose a duty to make safe something that is not in disrepair: *Alker v Collingwood Housing Association* [2007] EWCA Civ 343, [2007] 1 WLR 2230.

[81] The statutory duty under this section does not apply to dwellings built in accordance with an 'approved scheme' of purchaser protection: s 2. Schemes run by the National House-Building Council, under which the Council in effect guaranteed the building for a period of ten years from completion against defects arising from non-compliance with the Council's standard specifications, were approved until 1979, but the last approved scheme came to an end on 31 March 1979: Keating on *Construction Contracts* (8th edn, 2008), para 15–001.

[82] *Alexander v Mercouris* [1979] 1 WLR 1270; (1980) 255 EG 241 (HW Wilkinson); *Smith v Drumm* [1996] EGCS 192. 'Work' includes non-feasance: *Andrews v Schooling* [1991] 1 WLR 783.

[83] *Jacobs v Moreton* (1996) 72 BLR 92.

habitation[84] when completed. The duty is owed to the person to whose order the building is provided and to every person who acquires an interest (whether legal or equitable) in it,[85] including therefore a tenant under a legal or equitable lease, and is not limited to damages in respect of physical damage. The duty is not imposed on the landlord *as landlord*, but will apply to him if he takes on work within the meaning of the section.[86]

(2) Implied Obligations and Rights of the Tenant

(a) Obligations

(1) General

A tenant, including one from year to year,[87] is subject to an implied obligation to keep and to deliver up the premises in a tenant-like manner and to keep the fences in a state of repair.[88]

(2) Liability for waste

Tenants are also subject to the doctrine of waste,[89] though in varying degrees.

(i) Definition of waste

Waste means in general such damage to houses or land as tends to the permanent and lasting loss of the person entitled to the inheritance, and it falls into two main classes, permissive waste and voluntary waste.

Permissive waste arises from a mere act of omission, not of commission, and it is generally the result of allowing the buildings on an estate to fall into a state of decay.[90]

Voluntary waste is a wrong of commission consisting of a positive act of injury to the inheritance. It generally takes one of the following forms:

(a) *Pulling down or altering houses.*[91] If glass windows are broken or carried away, it is waste, although they may even have been put in by the tenant himself, and

---

[84] *Bole v Huntsbuild Ltd* [2009] EWCA Civ 1146, (2009) 127 Con LR 154.   [85] S 1(1).

[86] It will, however, apply to such persons as the builder and the architect.

[87] *Marsden v Edward Heyes Ltd* [1927] 2 KB 1.

[88] *Cheetham v Hampson* (1791) 4 Term Rep 318; *Goodman v Rollinson* (1951) 95 SJ 188. For the tenant of an agricultural holding, see *Wedd v Porter* [1916] 2 KB 91.

[89] In 1996 the Law Commission proposed that the law of waste be abolished as between landlord and tenant and that it, and the duty of tenant-like user, be replaced by a modern implied covenant to similar effect: Law Com No 238, *Responsibility for State and Condition of Property* (1996), Part X. However, in December 2009 the Government rejected the proposals in relation to residential property, and decided that primary legislation needed to implement those relating to commercial property is not a priority: Law Com No 232, *Annual Report 2009-10*, para 3.2; below, p 256. For the history of waste, see Holdsworth, *A History of English Law*, vol ii, pp 248–9; vol iii, pp 121–3; vol. vii, pp 275–81. See also below, pp 609–11 (liability of tenant for life for waste).

[90] Co Litt 53a, 54b.

[91] Co Litt 53a; *Marsden v Edward Heyes Ltd* [1927] 2 KB 1; *Mancetter Developments Ltd v Garmanson Ltd* [1986] QB 1212 (tenant who failed to make good holes left behind in landlord's brickwork when removing trade fixtures, held liable in damages).

so also in the case of benches, doors, furnaces and other things fixed to the land.

(b) *Opening pits or mines.*[92] It is waste to dig for gravel, lime, clay, stone and the like, unless for the repair of buildings; also to open a new mine, but not to work one that is already open.

(c) *Changing the course of husbandry.* To convert wood, meadow or pasture into arable land, or to turn arable or woodland into meadow or pasture, is technically waste. The old writers state that such acts are waste, not only because they change the course of husbandry, but also because they destroy the owner's evidence of title, for if an estate that had been conveyed as pasture were found on the next conveyance to be arable, it might cause confusion.[93] This, of course, is no longer in itself a reason for regarding such an act of conversion as waste. In fact, it is obvious that to change the system of husbandry must often have the effect of enhancing the value of land, such as, for example, where a farm situated near a large town is tilled intensively as a market garden, and though such conversion is technically waste, the rule, established since at least 1833,[94] is that it will not entitle the owner of the inheritance to recover damages unless it causes an injury to the inheritance.[95] This kind of waste is known as *ameliorating waste.*[96]

(d) *Cutting timber.* Timber trees are regarded as part of the inheritance and not part of the annual produce, and therefore it is waste to cut them, even though they are blown down by accident and have thus become what are called *windfalls.*[97] Sir George Jessel MR defined 'timber' as follows:[98]

The question of what timber is depends, first on general law, that is the law of England; and secondly, on the special custom of a locality. By the general rule of England, oak, ash and elm are timber, provided they are of the age of 20 years and upwards, provided also they are not so old as not to have a reasonable quantity of useable wood in them, sufficient... to make a good post. Timber, that is the kind of tree which may be called timber, may be varied by local custom. There is what is called the custom of the country, that is of a particular county or division of a county, and it varies in two ways. First of all, you may have trees called timber by the custom of the country—beech in some counties, hornbeam in others, and even whitethorn and blackthorn, and many other trees, are considered timber in peculiar localities—in addition to the ordinary timber trees.[99] Then

---

[92] Co Litt 53b, 54b. [93] Blackstone, vol ii, p 282.

[94] *Doe d Grubb v Earl of Burlington* (1833) 5 B & Ad 507.

[95] *Jones v Chappell* (1875) LR 20 Eq 539, 541.

[96] *Doherty v Allman* (1878) 3 App Cas 709 (tenant for 999 years improving delapidated stone buildings by converting them into dwellings); *Meux v Cobley* [1892] 2 Ch 253 (tenant of an agricultural lease for 21 years converted part of the land into a market garden and erected glass-houses on it for the cultivation of hot-house produce for the London market).

[97] *Garth v Cotton* (1753) 3 Atk 751.

[98] *Honywood v Honywood* (1874) LR 18 Eq 306, 309.

[99] Eg beech in Buckinghamshire: *Dashwood v Magniac* [1891] 3 Ch 306; birch in Yorkshire: *Countess of Cumberland's Case* (1610) Moore KB 812; willows in Hampshire: *Layfield v Cowper* (1694) 1 Wood 330.

again, in certain localities, arising probably from the nature of the soil, the trees of even 20 years old are not necessarily timber, but may go to 24 years, or even to a later period, I suppose, if necessary; and in other places the test of when a tree becomes timber is not its age but its girth.[100]

A tenant may cut and keep trees that do not fall within this definition of timber, such as larch, willows and chestnut, provided that they are ripe for felling and have not been planted for ornament, shelter or shade.[101] But only in three cases may he fell timber trees:

First, where the land is a timber estate, that is where it is cultivated merely for the produce of saleable timber and where the timber is cut periodically.[102] In such a case it is obvious that to cut the trees does not injure the inheritance, because the total value of the timber on the estate remains, roughly speaking, the same throughout, though new trees take the place of old.[103]

Secondly, where there is a local custom to cut timber periodically according to the normal and ordinary course of husbandry practised in the neighbourhood.[104]

Thirdly, every tenant for life is entitled to cut timber or other trees for three specific purposes, namely for the fuelling or repair of a house (*housebote*), for making and repairing agricultural implements (*ploughbote*) and for repairing existing walls, fences and ditches (*haybote*). These are called *estovers*.[105] He will be liable for waste, however, if he exercises these rights in an unreasonable manner, such as if he fells growing trees for fuel when there is dead wood sufficient for the purpose.

(ii) Tenants' liability for waste

A tenant *for a fixed number of years* is liable for voluntary and also for permissive waste.[106]

A tenant *from year to year* is liable for voluntary waste, but otherwise his only obligation, it would seem, is to use the premises in a 'tenantlike' manner.[107] This expression is obscure if not unintelligible,[108] and all that it means apparently is that

---

[100] If timber trees are blown down, they belong to the owner of the inheritance, but if they are dotards, ie decayed, they may be appropriated by the tenant: Co Litt 53a; *Herlakenden's Case* (1589) 4 Co Rep 62a at 63b; *Duke of Newcastle v Vane* (undated) 2 P Wms 241.

[101] *Re Harker's Will Trusts* [1938] Ch 323.

[102] *Honywood v Honywood* (1874) LR 18 Eq 306, 309.

[103] *Lloyd-Jones v Clark-Lloyd* [1919] 1 Ch 424, 436.

[104] *Dashwood v Magniac* [1891] 3 Ch 306; *Re Trevor-Batye's Settlement* [1912] 2 Ch 339.

[105] Co Litt 41b; below, p 237.

[106] *Yellowly v Gower* (1855) 11 Exch 274; *Mancetter Developments Ltd v Garmanson Ltd* [1986] QB 1212; *Dayani v Bromley LBC* [1999] 3 EGLR 144 (a detailed analysis referring to authorities from the tenth century), below, p 609.

[107] *Warren v Keen* [1954] 1 QB 15; (1954) 70 LQR 9 (REM); [1954] CLJ 71 (HWR Wade).

[108] Law Com No 238, paras 10.26–10.29, 10.31(vi).

the tenant must do such work as is necessary for his own reasonable enjoyment of the premises. Denning LJ gave some illustrations in *Warren v Keen*:[109]

> The tenant must take proper care of the place. He must, if he is going away for the winter, turn off the water and empty the boiler.[110] He must clean the chimneys, when necessary, and also the windows. He must mend the electric light when it fuses. He must unstop the sink when it is blocked by his waste. In short, he must do the little jobs about the place which a reasonable tenant would do. In addition, he must, of course, not damage the house, wilfully or negligently; and he must see that his family and guests do not damage it: and if they do, he must repair it. But apart from such things, if the house falls into disrepair through fair wear and tear or lapse of time, or for any reason not caused by him, then the tenant is not liable to repair it.

There is however some authority for the view that he must keep the premises wind and water tight in the sense that, although he is not bound to do anything of a substantial nature, he must carry out such repairs as are necessary to prevent the property from lapsing into a state of decay.[111] But the existence of this obligation was doubted by the Court of Appeal in *Warren v Keen*.

A tenant *at will* is not liable for either kind of waste, though the effect of the commission by him of any act of voluntary waste is to terminate his tenancy and to render him liable to an action of trespass.[112] A tenant *at sufferance* is liable for voluntary waste, but probably not for permissive waste.[113]

(b) Rights

(1) Estovers

As we have seen,[114] a tenant for years, notwithstanding the doctrine of waste, is entitled to take estovers from the land, that is to say, wood, including timber, for specific purposes: housebote (wood to be used either as fuel or for repair of a house); ploughbote (wood for making and repairing agricultural implements); and haybote (wood for repairing walls, fences and ditches).[115]

This right is limited by immediate necessity: a tenant cannot cut and store wood with a view to future requirements.

---

[109] Above, n 107, 20. The expression is an extension to tenants generally of the rule that the agricultural tenant must farm the land in a 'husbandlike' manner. In this context, 'husbandlike' has a definite meaning. The tenant must observe the custom of the country, ie the local usages of husbandry.

[110] Not, however, for two nights, even when the temperature fell to below 6 or 7 degrees below freezing. The test is reasonable foresight of frozen pipes in a cold climate: *Wycombe Health Authority v Barnett* (1982) 47 P & CR 394.

[111] *Ferguson v—* (1797) 2 Esp 590; *Wedd v Porter* [1916] 2 KB 91, 100.

[112] *Countess of Shrewsbury's Case* (1600) 5 Co Rep 13b.

[113] *Burchell v Hornsby* (1808) 1 Camp 360.   [114] Above, p 236.

[115] Co Litt 41b; cf below, p 608 (tenant for life).

(2) Emblements

A tenant for years is entitled at common law to emblements, that is a right to re-enter the land at harvest to recover the crops that he has sown.[116] A tenant for a fixed term of years cannot be entitled to this right, because he knows when his tenancy will end, and it his own fault if he sows crops that will not come to maturity until after that date. But there may be cases where a tenancy comes to an end unexpectedly, such as upon the sudden determination of a tenancy at will or upon the determination of the estate out of which the term has been created, in which the common law right to emblements exists. The right is obviously inconvenient to both parties, and in one type of case, that is where the landlord's estate ended prematurely, it was modified by the Landlord and Tenant Act 1851. This provided that a tenant for years at a rack rent (ie a rent that represents the full annual value of the land[117]) whose lease expired owing to the failure of his landlord's estate, should in lieu of emblements be entitled to remain in occupation until the end of the current year of tenancy.

In the case of agricultural tenancies, however, the Agricultural Holdings Act 1986[118] provides that a tenant at a rack rent, whose term ceases by the death, or the cesser of the estate, of a landlord entitled only for life or for any other uncertain interest, shall continue to hold and occupy the holding until the occupation is determined by a 12-month notice to quit, expiring at the end of a year of the tenancy. This provision has no counterpart in the Agricultural Tenancies Act 1995 in relation to a farm business tenancy.

(3) Right to remove certain fixtures

We have already seen the distinction between land and chattels, and the circumstances in which chattels can be affixed to the land so as to become part of the land.[119] One would expect that a fixture would pass to the landlord on the termination of the lease. However, this rule has been relaxed over time, and the tenant for years is now allowed to remove three particular classes of articles notwithstanding that they are fixtures in the strict sense of the term:

(i) Trade fixtures
First, it has long been the rule that during the term the tenant may remove fixtures that have been attached to the land for the purpose of carrying on his particular trade, since it is in the public interest that industry should be encouraged. Thus in *Poole's Case*[120] in 1703 it was held by Lord Holt

---

[116] Below, p 609 (tenant for life). The tenant at will is similarly entitled: above, p 203.

[117] *Re Sawyer and Withall* [1919] 2 Ch 333.

[118] S 21(1). The Act does not apply (subject to exceptions) to tenancies beginning on or after 1 September 1995, although it may still apply to tenancies entered into in succession to tenancies already governed by the 1986 Act: Agricultural Tenancies Act 1995, s 4. For further discussion of the policies underlying the Agricultural Holdings Act 1986 and the Agricultural Tenancies Act 1995, see below pp 417 ff.

[119] Above, pp 8–11.   [120] (1703) 1 Salk 368.

that during the term the soap-boiler might well remove the vats he set up in relation to trade, and that he might do it by the common law (and not by virtue of any special custom), in favour of trade and to encourage industry: but after the term they become a gift in law to him in reversion, and are not removable.

Engines for working collieries,[121] salt pans,[122] coppers and pipes erected by a brewing tenant,[123] the fittings of a public house,[124] petrol pumps installed at a wayside garage[125] and floor coverings and light fittings[126] have been held to come within the description of trade fixtures.

(ii) Ornamental and domestic fixtures

Secondly, it is now well established that during the term a tenant may remove such chattels as he has affixed to a house for either ornament or convenience, but this relaxation of the strict rule is not supported by such strong reasons as apply in the case of trade fixtures and it will not be extended. Examples of objects that have been held removable on this ground are ornamental chimney-pieces, wainscot fixed to the wall by screws, fixed water-tubs, stoves and grates, ranges and ovens. [127]

But any fixture that is in the nature of a permanent improvement and that cannot be removed without substantial damage to the house, such as a conservatory connected by a door with one of the living rooms, does not come within the exception of an ornamental fixture.[128]

Trade, ornamental and domestic fixtures must be removed before the end of the tenancy, otherwise they become a gift in law to the reversioner,[129] but a further period of grace is allowed when the tenant continues in possession after the term under a reasonable supposition of consent on the part of the landlord.[130] Where the tenant surrenders his tenancy to his landlord, he loses the right to remove these fixtures if the surrender is express, in the absence of agreement to the contrary; but he does not lose the right if the surrender is implied by operation of law, as where the lease has expired by effluxion of time and is replaced by a new lease between the same parties.[131] If tenant's fixtures are removed, the premises must be made good to the extent of being left in a reasonable condition.[132]

---

[121] *Lawton v Lawton* (1743) 3 Atk 13. Cf *Herbert v British Railways Board* (2000) 4 L & T Rev D13 (rails and sleepers removed by tenant railway board from disused railway line held to be landlord's fixtures, not tenant's).

[122] *Mansfield v Blackburne* (1840) 6 Bing NC 426.   [123] *Lawton v Lawton*, above.

[124] *Elliott v Bishop* (1854) 10 Exch 496.   [125] *Smith v City Petroleum Co Ltd* [1940] 1 All ER 260.

[126] *Young v Dalgety plc* [1987] 1 EGLR 116.

[127] See Hill and Redman, *Landlord and Tenant*, paras A[1008]–A[1022].

[128] *Buckland v Butterfield* (1820) 2 Brod & Bing 54.   [129] *Poole's Case* (1703) 1 Salk 368.

[130] *Ex p Brook* (1878) 10 Ch D 100, 109; *Leschallas v Woolf* [1908] 1 Ch 641.

[131] *New Zealand Government Property Corp v HM & S Ltd* [1982] QB 1145; [1987] Conv 253 (G Kodilinye).

[132] *Mancetter Developments Ltd v Garmanson Ltd* [1986] QB 1212 (holes left behind in landlord's brickwork).

(iii) Agricultural fixtures

The third exception relates to agricultural fixtures. Formerly, a farmer was in an unfavourable position with regard to chattels that he had fixed to his holding, because it was held in *Elwes v Maw*[133] in 1802 that, although the sole purpose of their affixation was to further and improve his agricultural operations, they could not be regarded as trade fixtures. In that case, the tenant farmer had built at his own cost a beast-house, a carpenter's shed, a fuel-house, a wagon-house and a fold-yard, each of which he removed before the end of the lease, leaving the premises in the same state as when he first became tenant. He was held liable to pay damages to the landlord. The only mitigation at common law of this rigour came in 1901, when it was decided that, although buildings put up by a farmer were not trade fixtures, glasshouses built by a market-gardener did come within this description and could be removed before the end of the tenancy.[134]

This matter has, however, been put upon a more equitable footing by a succession of statutes and the position now is as follows:

In the case of an agricultural tenancy granted before 1 September 1995 under the Agricultural Holdings Act 1986,[135] any fixture affixed to the agricultural holding by a tenant and any building erected by him on the holding, for which he is not otherwise entitled to compensation, becomes his property and is removable by him during the tenancy or within two months after its termination. After the expiration of this period the property in fixtures is no longer vested in him.[136] At least a month before the termination of the tenancy written notice of removal must be given to the landlord, who thereupon acquires an option to purchase the fixture.[137] There is no right of removal until the tenant has paid all rent and satisfied his other obligations under the tenancy.

The provisions that apply to a farm business tenancy beginning on or after 1 September 1995 under the Agricultural Tenancies Act 1995[138] are broadly similar, although somewhat more favourable to the tenant. Any fixture affixed by the tenant to the holding and any building erected by him on the holding may be removed by the tenant during the tenancy or so long as he remains in possession as tenant after its termination.[139] This is subject to exceptions, for example where the tenant was under an obligation to affix the fixture or erect the building, or where he has obtained compensation.[140] Unlike the position under the Agricultural Holdings Act 1986, the right to remove fixtures does not depend on compliance with the terms of the tenancy, nor is the tenant required to give notice of intention to remove, nor does the landlord acquire any option to purchase the fixture. The right to remove fixtures under section

---

[133] (1802) 3 East 38; *Smith's Leading Cases* (13th edn, ed Chitty, Denning and Harvey), vol ii, p 193.

[134] *Mears v Callender* [1901] 2 Ch 388.   [135] Below, p 417.

[136] Agricultural Holdings Act 1986, s 10(1), (2).

[137] Ibid, s 10(3)(b). Under s 10(5) the tenant must make good any damage done when removing the fixture. Likewise under s 8(3), (4) of the Agricultural Tenancies Act 1995, below.

[138] Below, p 420.

[139] Agricultural Tenancies Act 1995, s 8(1).   [140] Ibid, s 8(2).

8 of the 1995 Act may not be excluded, nor may the farm business tenant exercise any right to remove fixtures save that conferred by the section.[141]

The result of these developments is that if a landlord disputes the right of his tenant to remove a certain chattel from the premises, there are two separate questions to be answered. First, has the chattel become a fixture by reason of its affixation to the land? If not, no issue arises. If, however, the answer is in the affirmative, the further question arises whether it is a landlord's or a tenant's fixture, and this depends upon whether the chattel falls within one of the three categories already described.[142]

B POSITION WHERE THERE ARE EXPRESS COVENANTS AND CONDITIONS

The range of possible express covenants[143] is very wide, and so we can only mention briefly the more important covenants that find a place in a normal lease. Generally, a tenant will enter into covenants with regard to the payment of rent, rates and taxes, and the maintenance, repair and insurance of the premises; while the landlord will undertake to keep the tenant in quiet enjoyment, and may perhaps take upon himself part of the burden of repairs. The following covenants require special mention.

(1) Covenant by Tenant to Pay Rent

(a) Rent service

The rent payable by a tenant for years is properly called a rent service,[144] and though it generally consists of the payment of money, it may equally well take the form of the delivery of personal chattels,[145] such as corn, or the performance of personal services;[146] and there may even be no rent at all.[147]

(b) Certainty of rent

The rent must be certain,[148] but this does not mean that it must be certain at the date of the lease. Rent is sufficiently certain if it can be calculated with certainty at the time

---

[141] Ibid, s 8(6), (7).

[142] *Bain v Brand* (1876) 1 App Cas 762, 767 (Lord Cairns).

[143] For the modern approach to the interpretation of contracts in general, and covenants in leases in particular, *see Investors' Compensation Scheme Ltd v West Bromwich Building Society* [1998] 1 WLR 896; *Holding & Barnes plc v Hill House Hammond Ltd* [2001] EWCA Civ 1334, [2002] 2 P & CR 11. For the jurisdiction of the Upper Tribunal (formerly the Lands Tribunal) to modify a restrictive covenant in a lease of more than 40 years after the expiration of 25 years of the term, see LPA 1925, s 84(12), amended by SI 2009 No 1307; below, p 765.

[144] Below, p 269.   [145] Co Litt 142a.   [146] *Duke of Marlborough v Osborn* (1864) 5 B & S 67.

[147] LPA 1925, s.205(1)(xxvii); *Ashburn Anstalt v Arnold* [1989] Ch 1.

[148] This is an application of the general principle of contract law that the terms must be certain: Anson, pp 61–6. The cases discussed in this section therefore include, but are not limited to, those relating to rent. As will be seen from the cases discussed, questions have most commonly arisen over the certainty of rent in relation to the validity of an option to renew a lease, the validity of a rent review clause within an existing lease, below, p 243, and the rent payable on renewal of a lease.

when payment comes to be made. Thus a condition in a council tenant's rent book, providing that the rent was 'liable to be increased or decreased on notice being given' was held to be valid.[149] So also was an option to renew a lease 'at a rent to be fixed at a price to be determined having regard to the market valuation of the premises at the time of exercising the option'.[150] The parties may also provide machinery for the application of the formula, such as by directing that the rent shall be fixed by a third party;[151]and, if that machinery proves to be ineffective, the court may sometimes be able to substitute its own. In *Sudbrook Trading Estate Ltd v Eggleton*:[152]

---

[149] *Greater London Council v Connolly* [1970] 2 QB 100.

[150] *Brown v Gould* [1972] Ch 53, M & B p 371; *Smith v Morgan* [1971] 1 WLR 803 (right of pre-emption 'at a figure to be agreed upon' held to be valid); cf *King's Motors (Oxford) Ltd v Lax* [1970] 1 WLR 426 (option for lease 'at such rental as may be agreed upon between the parties' held to be void for uncertainty); *Courtney and Fairbairn Ltd v Tolaini Bros (Hotels) Ltd* [1975] 1 WLR 297 (building agreement to 'negotiate fair and reasonable contract sums' held to be void for uncertainty); *Bushwall Properties Ltd v Vortex Properties Ltd* [1976] 1 WLR 591 (contract for sale of 51½ acres of land for £50,000 payable in three unequal instalments held unenforceable because of provision that on each payment 'a proportionate part of the land shall be released'); cf *Hackney LBC v Thompson* [2001] L & TR 7 (covenant requiring transferee to 'pay a due proportion of management costs' held valid: construable as meaning an appropriate or reasonable proportion); *ARC Ltd v Schofield* [1990] 2 EGLR 52 (option to renew lease at a rent 'to be agreed between the landlord and tenant, being a fair and reasonable market rent at that time' held valid); *Corson v Rhuddlan BC* [1990] 1 EGLR 255, M & B p 374 (option to renew lease of golf course for further 21 years 'at a rental to be agreed [but not to exceed £1,150 per annum]' held valid with implication of term that rent was to be a fair rent with an upper limit of £1,150); [1990] Conv 290 (JE Martin); *Miller v Lakefield Estates Ltd* [1989] 1 EGLR 212 (option to purchase 'at a price to be agreed', but if no sale took place within six months of notice given to exercise option, then property should be sold at public auction, held valid); *Lambert v HTV Cymru (Wales) Ltd* [1998] EMLR 629 (clause obliging purchaser 'to use all reasonable endeavours to obtain rights of first negotiation from any assignee' for benefit of seller held not enforceable for lack of certainty); *King's Motors (Oxford) Ltd v Lax* was doubted in *Corson v Rhuddlan BC*; and *Smith v Morgan* was doubted in *Miller v Lakefield Estates Ltd*; *Walford v Miles* [1992] 2 AC 128, below, p 957 (agreement to continue to negotiate 'in good faith' held void for uncertainty). For the validity of an index-linked rent, see *Blumenthal v Gallery Five Ltd* (1971) 220 EG 31 (index of retail prices); *Cumshaw Ltd v Bowen* [1987] 1 EGLR 30; (1987) 132 NLJ 288 (HW Wilkinson); (1994) 138 SJ 552 (R Castle and A MacFarquhar).

[151] *Lloyds Bank Ltd v Marcan* [1973] 1 WLR 1387 (rent to be fixed by person chosen by President of the Royal Institution of Chartered Surveyors).

[152] [1983] 1 AC 444, M & B p 375; [1983] Conv 76 (K Hodkinson). Followed in *Re Malpass* [1985] Ch 42 (testamentary option to purchase farm 'at the agricultural value thereof determined for agricultural purposes . . . as agreed with the District Valuer'; the valuer declined to act). See also *Campbell v Edwards* [1976] 1 WLR 403 (valuation fixed by an agreed valuer held binding); *Trustees of National Deposit Friendly Society v Beatties of London Ltd* [1985] 2 EGLR 59 (option agreement for a new lease in favour of tenants who had carried on a business of selling model railways for 75 years 'the rent payable . . . to be the greater of £33,000 per annum exclusive or such rent as may be agreed as from the architect's certificate of completion': not void for uncertainty in regard to the date of the commencement of the term, the amount of rent and the covenants and conditions; Goulding J at 61: 'There has been such performance on the tenant's side as to justify the court in a much more liberal approach to the validity of the document than in the case of a purely executory option where nothing but perhaps a nominal consideration has been given on either side'); *R & A Millett (Shops) Ltd v Leon Allen International Fashions Ltd* [1989] 1 EGLR 138 (sub-lease rent to be 78/85ths of fair market rent as fixed in manner provided by head lease); *Harben Style Ltd v Rhodes Trust* [1995] 1 EGLR 118 (only landlord had power to apply to President of RICS for appointment of third party to determine rent; on his refusal to apply, tenant not entitled to have rent determined by court); cf *Royal Bank of Scotland v Jennings* [1997] 1 EGLR 101 (both landlord and tenant had such power); *Addin v Secretary of State for the Environment* [1997] 1 EGLR 99; *Black Country Housing Association v Shand and Shand* [1998] NPC 92 (land to be transferred at a price that reflected its use being restricted as a garden held valid).

a lease gave to the lessees an option to purchase the reversion 'at such a price not being less than £12,000 as may be agreed upon by two valuers one to be nominated by the lessor and the other by the lessees or in default of such agreement by an umpire appointed by the said valuers'. The lessor refused to appoint a valuer.

In granting specific performance of the option at 'a fair and reasonable price', the House of Lords held that, if the ineffective machinery is merely subsidiary and inessential, the court will provide its own, but it will not do so if the machinery constitutes an essential term of the contract. As Lord Fraser of Tullybelton said:[153]

> Where an agreement is made to sell at a price to be fixed by a valuer who is named, or who, by reason of holding some office such as auditor of a company whose shares are to be valued, will have special knowledge relevant to the question of value, the prescribed mode may well be regarded as essential. Where, as here, the machinery consists of valuers and an umpire, none of whom is named or identified, it is in my opinion unrealistic to regard it as an essential term. If it breaks down there is no reason why the court should not substitute other machinery to carry out the main purpose of ascertaining the price in order that the agreement may be carried out.

(c) Date of payment

The covenant should state precisely the dates at which rent is payable, but if no mention is made of the matter, payment is due at the end of each period by reference to which the rent has been assessed. Thus in the case of a yearly rent nothing need be paid until the end of each year of the term.[154] If a day for payment is fixed, it becomes due on the first moment of that day and is held to be in arrear if it is not paid by midnight.[155]

(d) Rent review clauses

Many leases today contain a rent review clause,[156] the object of which is to enable the rent to be raised[157] at regular intervals to what is then the fair market value of the property let. The clause may provide for a revision to be made every seven years or, not infrequently, every four or even three years. Institutional leases now commonly have a five-yearly review. In some leases of commercial premises granted for longer

---

[153] [1983] 1 AC 444, 483.

[154] *Coomber v Howard* (1845) 1 CB 440; *Collett v Curling* (1847) 10 QB 785.

[155] *Dibble v Bowater* (1853) 2 E & B 564.

[156] See generally Aldridge, *Leasehold Law*, paras 4.045–4.060; Reynolds and Fetherstonhaugh, *Handbook of Rent Review*; *Hill and Redman's Guide to Rent Review* (2001); Emmet, paras 26.080–26.152; Bernstein and Reynolds, *Essentials of Rent Review* (1995). There is no presumption that a rent review clause (even one incorporating an open review) ought to be exercisable by both parties: it depends on the proper construction of the clause: *Hemingway Realty Ltd v Clothworkers' Company* [2005] EWHC 299 (Ch), [2005] 2 EGLR 36.

[157] In May 2004 the ODPM issued a consultation paper, *Commercial Property Leases*, which asked whether upwards only rent reviews should be prohibited or deterred. The Reading University Report *Monitoring the 2002 Code of Practice for Commercial Leases* (March 2005), para 8.4.3, found that neither tenants nor their agents were seeking alternatives to upwards only rent reviews, and the Government is no longer pursuing this. Cf, in Ireland, Land and Conveyancing Law Reform Act 2009, s 132 (denying effect to upwards only rent review provisions).

terms, there may be a provision to allow the landlord to reduce the interval between rent reviews after, for example, the first 35 years; this 'review of reviews' operates in the same way as a rent review.[158] The clause usually lays down the administrative procedure or machinery by which the fair market rent is to be ascertained. Wide varieties of formulae are used.[159] In practice many clauses have not been well drawn,[160] and, in particular, there has been considerable litigation on the question of whether time is of the essence in construing clauses that specify time limits for the operation of the rent review procedure. In *United Scientific Holdings Ltd v Burnley Borough Council*[161] the House of Lords held that there was a presumption that time was not of the essence of the contract. Accordingly a landlord who fails to serve a notice on the tenant by a specified date may still serve a notice late and implement the rent review. Unreasonable delay, and even delay that causes hardship to the tenant, will not disentitle him from exercising his contractual right to claim a rent review that will be retrospective to the relevant date. The right continues to exist unless and until it is abrogated by mutual agreement, or discharged by termination of the contract for breach or frustration, or the landlord is estopped by words or conduct from exercising his rights.[162] The tenant, however, can serve a counter-notice making time of the essence.[163]

The presumption may be rebutted either expressly,[164] or impliedly by other provisions in the lease or by inference from surrounding circumstances; as where the

---

[158] Aldridge, *Leasehold Law*, para 4.046.

[159] For precedents, see Aldridge, *Leasehold Law*, paras P.016–P.029; Conv Prec, Part 5H, including revised model forms by the Joint Working Party of the Law Society and the Royal Institution of Chartered Surveyors (2nd edn, 1986) as Precedent 5–H5.

[160] *United Scientific Holdings Ltd v Burnley BC* [1976] Ch 128, 146 (Roskill LJ). See *London Regional Transport v Wimpey Group Services Ltd* [1986] 2 EGLR 41, 42 where Hoffmann J said: 'Rent formulae can often be expressed more simply and unambiguously in algebraic form and this case shows that a very modest degree of numeracy can save a great deal of money', and *Freehold & Leasehold Shop Properties Ltd v Friends Provident Life Office* (1984) 271 EG 451, where Oliver LJ referred to the 'somewhat Delphic pronouncement' of the definition of rent for the DH Lawrence House, Nottingham: 'It may be doubted whether the distinguished author after whom the premises were named would have approved of the obscurity of language with which the parties have chosen to veil their intentions'. See (1992) 12 LS 349 (GD Goldberg and PF Smith).
   On professional negligence in connection with a rent review clause in a commercial lease, see *County Personnel (Employment Agency) Ltd v Alan R Pulver & Co* [1987] 1 WLR 916.

[161] [1978] AC 904; [1979] Conv 10 (PF Smith); *Chichester Cathedral (Dean and Chapter) v Lennards Ltd* (1977) 35 P & CR 309; cf *Commission for the New Towns v R Levy & Co Ltd* [1990] 2 EGLR 121; *Lancecrest Ltd v Asiwaju* [2005] EWCA Civ 117, [2005] 1 EGLR 40.

[162] *Amherst v James Walker Goldsmith & Silversmith Ltd* [1983] Ch 305, 316 (Oliver LJ), 320 (Lawton LJ); cf *Barclays Bank plc v Savile Estates Ltd* [2002] EWCA Civ 589, [2003] 2 EGLR 16.

[163] *Factory Holdings Group Ltd v Leboff International Ltd* [1987] 1 EGLR 135.

[164] On the construction and effect of an express provision:
   (a) where time has been held to be of the essence, see *Drebbond Ltd v Horsham DC* (1978) 37 P & CR 237 (reference to arbitration within three months of original notice 'but not otherwise'); *Weller v Akehurst* [1981] 3 All ER 411; *Pips (Leisure Productions) Ltd v Walton* (1980) 43 P & CR 415 ('would use their best endeavours'); *Lewis v Barnett* (1981) 264 EG 1079 (notice to review 'shall be void and of no effect'); *Henry Smith's Charity Trustees v Awada Trading and Promotion Services Ltd* (1983) 47 P & CR 607 ('shall be deemed to be a market rent'); *Greenhaven Securities Ltd v Compton* (1985) 275 EG 628 (rent to be 'a sum equal to the rent payable immediately before the review date'); *Mammoth Greeting Cards Ltd v Agra Ltd* [1990] 2 EGLR 124 (rent 'shall be conclusively fixed'; 'This evinces the concept of finality': Mummery J at 125); *Norwich Union Life Insurance Society v Sketchley plc* [1986] 2 EGLR 126 ('but not otherwise'); *Chelsea*

tenant has an option to determine the lease that is linked to the rent review.[165] Where time is of the essence, the court will not intervene to impose a rent review, if notice is served out of time.[166]

The doctrine of time not being of the essence is one of substance and not of form. The fact that the time limit is to be found partly in a definition and partly in a substantive clause of the lease makes no difference.[167]

A rent review clause usually contains a formula for the assessment of the revised rent. In this context,[168] where rent has been paid and accepted up to the review date, the courts have been astute not to hold a formula void for uncertainty; they are more concerned with the amount of rent payable for the remainder of the term, and with the construction of the formula in such a way as to render the clause effective. Thus in *Beer v Bowden*[169] the court held that 'such rent as shall thereupon be agreed' should be

Building Society v R & A Millett (Shops) Ltd (1994) 67 P & CR 319 ('it shall be a condition precedent': 'clearest possible intention'); *Central Estates Ltd v Secretary of State for the Environment* [1997] 1 EGLR 239 (mutuality arising from interrelationship between break clause and relevant review period); *Banks v Kokkinos* [1999] 3 EGLR 133;

(b) where time has been held not to be of the essence, see *Amherst v James Walker* (1980) 254 EG 123 (two time-limit steps out of three stated to be 'of the essence'; held third step to be not of the essence); *Laing Investment Co Ltd v GA Dunn & Co* (1981) 262 EG 879; *Touche Ross & Co v Secretary of State for the Environment* (1982) 46 P & CR 187 (reference to surveyor 'as soon as practicable but in any event not later than three months'); *Thorn EMI Pension Ltd Trust v Quinton Hazell plc* (1983) 269 EG 414; *Starmark Enterprises Ltd v CPL Distribution Ltd* [2001] EWCA Civ 1252, [2002] Ch 306 (if lessees fail to serve counter-notice within period, 'they shall be deemed to have agreed to pay increased rent specified in the rent notice'); Emmet, para 26.144; *Taylor Woodrow Property Co Ltd v Lonrho Textiles Ltd* (1985) 52 P & CR 28; *Phipps-Faire Ltd v Malbern Construction Ltd* [1987] 1 EGLR 129; cf *Banks v Kokkinos*, above; *Power Securities (Manchester) Ltd v Prudential Assurance Co Ltd* [1987] 1 EGLR 121 (rent to be agreed between landlord and tenant within six months after end of second term; *Panavia Air Cargo Ltd v Southend-on-Sea BC* (1988) 56 P & CR 365 (if review not completed until 12 months of relevant period, rent payable during the period would be current rent increased by 25 per cent); *Kings (Estate Agents) Ltd v Anderson* [1992] 1 EGLR 121 (determination of rent (time to be of the essence) 'three months prior to commencement of second or third rent period', failure to mention fourth period); *North Hertfordshire DC v Hitchin Industrial Estate Ltd* [1992] 2 EGLR 121 (service of landlord's notice 'shall be a condition precedent'); *Richurst Ltd v Pimenta* [1993] 1 WLR 159 (acknowledgment of receipt of late service of notice held not to be agreement to extend time); [1993] Conv 382 (M Haley); *Woolwich Property Services Ltd v Capital Land Holdings Ltd* (1992) 66 P & CR 378 (effective counter-notice); *Bickenhall Engineering Co Ltd v Grandmet Restaurants Ltd* [1995] 1 EGLR 110 (rent specified by landlord should be market rent payable 'if no such counter-notice served' held not certain enough to rebut presumption); *Fordgate (Bingley) Ltd v National Westminster Bank plc* [1995] EGCS 97; *Fox & Widley v Guram* [1998] 1 EGLR 91 (extension of time limit under Arbitration Act 1996, s 12: purpose of Act to restrict power of court to extend time).

165 *United Scientific Holdings Ltd v Burnley BC* [1978] AC 904, 929 (Lord Diplock); *Al Saloom v Shirley James Travel Service Ltd* (1981) 42 P & CR 181; *Rahman v Kenshire* (1980) 259 EG 1074; *Coventry City Council v J Hepworth & Son Ltd* (1982) 265 EG 608; *Legal and General Assurance (Pension Management) Ltd v Cheshire County Council* (1983) 269 EG 40; *William Hill (Southern) Ltd v Govier & Govier* (1983) 269 EG 1168; *Edwin Woodhouse Trustee Co Ltd v Sheffield Brick Co plc* (1983) 270 EG 548; *McLeod Russel (Property Holding) Ltd v Emerson* (1985) 51 P & CR 176; *Metrolands Investments Ltd v J H Dewhurst Ltd* [1986] 3 All ER 659; *Stephenson & Son v Orca Properties Ltd* [1989] 2 EGLR 129.

166 *Weller v Akehurst* [1981] 3 All ER 411.

167 *Pembroke St Georges Ltd v Cromwell Developments Ltd* [1991] 2 EGLR 129.

168 For the general rules relating to certainty of rent, see above, pp 241 ff.

169 [1981] 1 WLR 522, M & B p 377; *Corson v Rhuddlan BC* [1990] 1 EGLR 255, 257.

construed to mean 'such fair rent as shall thereupon be agreed', and this formed the basis for the valuation of the revised rent.[170]

(e) Recovery of rent

The landlord's remedies for the recovery of rent will be considered later in this chapter.[171]

(2) Covenant by Landlord or Tenant to Repair[172]

Various expressions are used to describe the extent of the obligation imposed by a covenant to repair the premises. The following are typical examples:

> good tenantable repair;
>
> good and tenantable order and repair;
>
> well and substantially repair;
>
> perfect repair.

By the use of appropriate language, the parties can, of course, settle the standard of repair as high or as low as they choose, but it is generally admitted that such epithets as 'good', 'perfect' or 'substantial' do not increase the burden connoted by the simple word 'repair'.[173] By way of caution, it should be noticed that, if the premises are in a state of disrepair at the beginning of the lease, a covenant by the tenant to 'keep' them in repair requires him to put them into the required state at his own expense.[174]

---

[170] *Thomas Bates & Son Ltd v Wyndham's (Lingerie) Ltd* [1981] 1 WLR 505, M & B p 378; *Beer v Bowden*, above; *Lear v Blizzard* [1983] 3 All ER 662, M & B p 378, n 101; *British Railways Board v Mobil Oil Co Ltd* (1994) 68 P & CR 446 (rise in rents of comparable properties).

For rent reviews where improvements have been made to the premises, see *Ponsford v HMS Aerosols Ltd* [1979] AC 63, approving *Cuff v J & F Stone Property Co Ltd* [1979] AC 87; *Hambros Bank Executors and Trustee Co Ltd v Superdrug Stores Ltd* [1985] 1 EGLR 99; *Lear v Blizzard*, above; *Pleasurama Properties Ltd v Leisure Investments (West End) Ltd* [1986] 1 EGLR 145 (conversion of shop premises into a dolphinarium); *Brett v Brett Essex Golf Club Ltd* (1986) 52 P & CR 330; *Panther Shop Investments Ltd v Keith Pople Ltd* [1987] 1 EGLR 131; *Ravenseft Properties Ltd v Park* [1988] 2 EGLR 164; *Ipswich Town Football Club Co Ltd v Ipswich BC* [1988] 2 EGLR 146; *Laura Investment Co Ltd v Havering LBC* [1992] 1 EGLR 155 (where Hoffmann J reviewed the authorities); ibid *(No 2)* [1993] 08 EG 120; *Historic House Hotels Ltd v Cadogan* [1995] 1 EGLR 117 (improvements to be disregarded in spite of provision that premises so altered were to be comprised in lease at outset); *Ocean Accident & Guarantee Corp v Next plc* [1996] 2 EGLR 84 (tenant's fixtures not be taken into account, even if affixed by tenant under obligation in lease, unless expressly provided); cf *Daejan Properties Ltd v Mahoney* [1995] 2 EGLR 75; *Braid v Walsall MBC* (1999) 78 P & CR 94.

[171] Below, pp 269 ff.

[172] See generally West and Smith's *Law of Dilapidations* (11th edn, 2001); Williams, *Handbook of Dilapidations*; Dowding and Reynolds, *Dilapidations: The Modern Law and Practice* (4th edn, 2008). Whether the matter has been dealt with by covenant or not, the lessor is under a statutory obligation to repair a dwelling-house that has been let for less than seven years: above, p 229.

[173] *Anstruther-Gough-Calthorpe v McOscar* [1924] 1 KB 716, 722–3; but see at 731–2. A covenant to 'maintain . . . in good condition' adds a great deal to 'repair', and may extend to the general state of the premises and not just the structure: *Welsh v Greenwich LBC* [2000] 3 EGLR 41 (severe condensation and mould growth).

[174] *Payne v Haine* (1847) 16 M & W 541; *Proudfoot v Hart* (1890) 25 QBD 42; *Crédit Suisse v Beegas Nominees Ltd* [1994] 4 All ER 803; [1995] 145 NLJ 718 (HW Wilkinson).

A state of disrepair means a deterioration in the condition of the premises from a former better condition.[175]

In *Brew Brothers Ltd v Snax (Ross) Ltd*,[176] Sachs LJ set out the approach to be adopted in construing a covenant to repair:

> It seems to me that the correct approach is to look at the particular building, to look at the state that it is in at the date of the lease, to look at the precise terms of the lease, and then come to a conclusion as to whether, on a fair interpretation of those terms in relation to that state, the requisite work can fairly be termed repair. However large the covenant it must not be looked at in vacuo.[177]

(a) Extent of obligation

The extent of the obligation assumed by a covenantor who has agreed to repair the premises is that, after making due allowance for the locality, character and age of the premises at the time of the lease, he must keep them in the condition in which they would be kept by a reasonably minded owner.[178]

(1) Locality and character of premises

The locality and character of the premises are material. The essential fact to notice, however, is that it is the character of the premises and of the locality at the beginning, not at the end, of the lease that is material in this context. Thus in one case:[179]

> a new house, situated in what was then a fashionable part of London, was let in 1825 to a good class of tenant on a 95-year lease. In course of time the character of the neighbourhood deteriorated to such an extent that the only persons willing to occupy the house expected nothing more than that the rain should be kept out.

The covenantor, therefore, argued that the standard of repair required of him was to be measured by the needs and expectations of prospective tenants in 1920. The

---

[175] *Post Office v Aquarius Properties Ltd* [1987] 1 All ER 1055; *Plough Investments Ltd v Eclipse Radio and Television Services Ltd* [1989] 1 EGLR 244.

[176] [1970] 1 QB 612, 640; *Smedley v Chumley and Hawke Ltd* (1981) 44 P & CR 50, 54; *McDougall v Easington DC* [1989] 1 EGLR 93.

[177] 'I have found most assistance in the judgment of Sachs LJ... It contains a timely warning against attempting to impose the crudities of judicial exegesis upon the subtle and often intuitive discriminations of ordinary speech': *Post Office v Aquarius Properties Ltd* [1985] 2 EGLR 105, 107 (Hoffmann J).

[178] *Proudfoot v Hart* (1890) 25 QBD 42; *Lurcott v Wakely and Wheeler* [1911] 1 KB 905; *Anstruther-Gough-Calthorpe v McOscar* [1924] 1 KB 716; *Lloyds Bank Ltd v Lake* [1961] 1 WLR 884; *Firstcross Ltd v Teasdale* (1982) 47 P & CR 228; *Crédit Suisse v Beegas Nominees Ltd*, above. See also *British Glass Manufacturers' Corporation v University of Sheffield* [2003] EWHC 3108 (Ch), [2004] 1 EGLR 40 (demolition of laboratory and other buildings not a breach of repairing obligation in lease granted in 1957 for a term of 1,000 years); *Riverside Property Investments Ltd v Blackhawk Automotive* [2004] EWHC 3052 (TCC), [2005] 1 EGLR 114; *Fitzroy House Epworth Street (No 1) Ltd v Financial Times Ltd* [2005] EWHC 2391 (TCC), [2006] 1 EGLR 19 (summarising the general principles) affd on other grounds [2006] EWCA Civ 329, [2006] 1 WLR 2207.

[179] *Anstruther-Gough-Calthorpe v McOscar*, above; *Ladbroke Hotels Ltd v Sandhu* (1995) 72 P & CR 498 (repairs not limited to those necessary to maintain building for its commercial life); (1997) 147 NLJ 420 (HW Wilkinson).

argument failed. The obligation of a covenantor is neither increased nor diminished in extent by a change in the character of the neighbourhood.

(2) Age of premises

The age of a house is also material, though only in the sense that the covenantor's obligation is not to bring it up to date, but to keep it in a reasonably good condition for a building of that age. He cannot escape liability by the allegation that to keep so old a building in the covenanted condition requires renewal, not mere repairs. Repair always involves renewal. The covenant must be fulfilled, even though this necessitates the replacement of part after part until the whole is renewed.[180] The correct antithesis is between renewal and reconstruction. The former is required, the latter not. Whether the work necessary for the maintenance of a building is renewal or reconstruction is a question of degree, the test being whether the replacement affects a subordinate part or substantially the whole of the building.[181] Thus the tenant of an old house is not bound to replace defective foundations by foundations of an entirely different character;[182] but he must demolish and replace a dangerous wall if it is only a subsidiary part of the whole building.[183]

An inherent defect of design in the premises may be within the ambit of a covenant to repair, but the covenantor is not liable to remedy a design fault, unless that fault has caused or contributed to a proved state of disrepair.[184] As Foster J said:[185]

the true test is that it is always a question of degree whether that which the tenant is being asked to do can properly be described as repair, or whether on the contrary it would involve giving back to the landlord a wholly different thing from that which he demised.

[180] *Lurcott v Wakely and Wheeler* [1911] 1 KB 905, 916–17 (Fletcher-Moulton LJ).

[181] Ibid; *Sotheby v Grundy* [1947] 2 All ER 761; *Minja Properties Ltd v Cussins Property Group plc* [1998] 2 EGLR 52 (replacement of window frames held to be repair); *Creska Ltd v Hammersmith and Fulham LBC* [1998] 3 EGLR 35.

[182] *Lister v Lane and Nesham* [1893] 2 QB 212; *Sotheby v Grundy*, above; *Pembery v Lamdin* [1940] 2 All ER 434 (landlord's covenant); *Brew Bros Ltd v Snax (Ross) Ltd* [1970] 1 QB 612 (tenant's covenant).

[183] *Lurcott v Wakely and Wheeler*, above; cf *Smedley v Chumley and Hawke Ltd* (1981) 44 P & CR 50 (underpinning of foundations of recently constructed restaurant in motel complex held to be work of repair). Cf *Halliard Property Co Ltd v Nicholas Clarke Investments Ltd* (1983) 269 EG 1257 (no duty to rebuild jerry-built structure); *Post Office v Aquarius Properties Ltd* [1985] 2 EGLR 105 (remedial scheme for failure of 'kicker joint' more than repair), affd on other grounds [1987] 1 All ER 1055; *Elmcroft Developments Ltd v Tankersley-Sawyer* (1984) 270 EG 140 (defective damp course below ground level to be repaired by silicone injection); cf *Yanover v Romford Finance & Development Co Ltd* (1983) unreported but noted at (1984) 272 EG 250 (DW Williams); *Elite Investments Ltd v T I Bainbridge Silencers Ltd* [1986] 2 EGLR 43 (replacement of roof held to be repair) where the authorities are reviewed; [1987] Conv 140 (PF Smith); *New England Properties v Portsmouth News Shops* [1993] 1 EGLR 84.

[184] *Ravenseft Properties Ltd v Davstone (Holdings) Ltd* [1980] QB 12; [1979] Conv 429 (PF Smith); *Quick v Taff Ely BC* [1986] QB 809; *Post Office v Aquarius Properties Ltd* [1985] 2 EGLR 105; [1987] Conv 224 (PF Smith); *Stent v Monmouth DC* [1987] 1 EGLR 59; *Murray v Birmingham City Council* [1987] 2 EGLR 53; *Staves & Staves v Leeds City Council* [1992] 2 EGLR 36 (condensation affecting plasterwork); *Crédit Suisse v Beegas Nominees Ltd* [1994] 4 All ER 803; *Janet Reger International Ltd v Tiree Ltd* [2006] EWHC 1743 (Ch), [2007] 1 P & CR 24.

[185] *Ravenseft Properties Ltd v Davstone (Holdings) Ltd*, above, at 21. For more detailed formulations of the test, see *McDougall v Easington DC* [1989] 1 EGLR 93, 95–6 (Mustill LJ); [1990] Conv 735 (PF Smith); *Holding and Management Ltd v Property Holding and Investment Trust plc* [1990] 1 EGLR 65, 68 (Nicholls LJ).

(b) Exception of fair wear and tear

It is usual to qualify the covenant to repair by a clause to the effect that the covenantor shall not be liable for 'fair wear and tear' or (the same thing) for 'reasonable wear and tear'. The effect of these words is to exempt the covenantor from liability for damage that is due to the ordinary operation of natural causes, always presuming that he has used the premises in a reasonable manner.[186] As Tindal CJ put it in a case where a tenant had invoked such a clause:

> What the natural operation of time flowing on effects, and all that the elements bring about in diminishing value, constitute a loss that, so far as it results from time and nature, falls upon the landlord.[187]

But where the defect, though initially due to natural causes, will obviously cause further and lasting damage unless rectified, the clause will not continue to avail a covenantor who stands idly by and allows the ravages of time and nature to take their course. Talbot J made this clear in a passage later adopted by the House of Lords:

> The tenant is bound to do such repairs as may be required to prevent the consequences flowing originally from wear and tear from producing others which wear and tear would not directly produce. For example, if a tile falls off the roof, the tenant is not liable for the immediate consequences; but, if he does nothing and in the result more and more water gets in, the roof and walls decay and ultimately the top floor, or the whole house, becomes uninhabitable, he cannot say that it is due to reasonable wear and tear. . . . On the other hand, take the gradual wearing away of a stone floor or staircase by ordinary use. This may in time produce a considerable wear and tear, and the tenant is not liable in respect of it.[188]

(c) Covenant not to make improvements without consent

A covenant against the making of improvements without consent is by statute[189] subject to a proviso that consent shall not unreasonably be withheld, though the landlord is entitled to demand the payment of a reasonable sum for any damage or loss of value that may be caused to the premises or to neighbouring premises belonging to him. The word 'improvements' refers to improvements from the point of view of the tenant, and the statute applies even though what he proposes to do, for example, the demolition of part of the main structure of a building, will temporarily diminish the value of the

---

[186] *Haskell v Marlow* [1928] 2 KB 45, 59.

[187] *Gutteridge v Munyard* (1834) 1 Mood & R 334, 336. The words quoted do not appear in the report at 7 C & P 129.

[188] *Haskell v Marlow*, above, at 59. This decision was overruled by the Court of Appeal in *Taylor v Webb* [1937] 2 KB 283, but the principles laid down in this second case, after being stigmatised as inconsistent with earlier authorities by a later Court of Appeal in *Brown v Davies* [1958] 1 QB 117 were finally overruled by the House of Lords in *Regis Property Co Ltd v Dudley* [1959] AC 370, and the authority of *Haskell v Marlow* restored.

[189] LTA 1927, s 19(2). The tenant may apply to the High Court or the county court for a declaration that the landlord has unreasonably withheld his consent: LTA 1954, s 53(1)(b) as amended by County Courts Act 1984, s 148(1), Sch 2, para 23. For the application of s 19(2) see *Iqbal v Thakrar* [2004] EWCA Civ 592, [2004] 3 EGLR 21 at [26] (Peter Gibson LJ, adopting with variations the principles set out by Balcombe LJ in relation to s 19(1) in *International Drilling Fluids Ltd v Louisville Investments (Uxbridge) Ltd* [1986] Ch 513, 519–20, below, p 263); *Sergeant v Macepark (Whittlebury) Ltd* [2004] EWHC 1333 (Ch), [2004] 4 All ER 662.

premises.[190] In such a case no injury is, in theory, suffered by the landlord, since he is permitted by the statute to demand an undertaking from the tenant that the premises will be reinstated.[191]

(d) Landlord's right of entry

If the landlord is to perform his covenant to repair, he must have a right of entry to the premises. This may be expressly authorised by the terms of the lease or by statute; and if the landlord is liable to repair the premises he has an implied right to enter for a reasonable time to carry out the work.[192] Otherwise he has no right to enter during the currency of the lease,[193] because, as we have seen, the tenant has the right to exclusive possession.[194]

(e) Remedies for breach of covenant to repair

(1) Remedies of landlord

(i) Specific performance

Apart from forfeiture,[195] the usual remedy for breach of a covenant to repair is damages. The landlord may himself do the work, if the lease authorises him to enter to do repairs.[196] It used to be generally accepted that a landlord could not obtain specific performance to enforce his tenant's covenant. In *Rainbow Estates Ltd v Tokenhold Ltd*, however, it was held that the court has power to grant such a decree in appropriate circumstances. Lawrence Collins QC said:[197]

> Subject to the overriding need to avoid injustice or oppression, the remedy should be available when damages are not an adequate remedy or, in the more modern formulation,[198] when specific performance is the appropriate remedy. This will be particularly important if there is substantial difficulty in the way of the landlord effecting repairs: the landlord may not have a right of access to the property to effect necessary repairs, since (in the absence of contrary agreement) a landlord has no right to enter the premises, and the condition of the premises may be deteriorating...

---

[190] *Lambert v Woolworth & Co Ltd* [1938] Ch 883.

[191] LTA 1927, s 19(2). In 1989 the Law Commission published a Report: *Compensation for Tenants' Improvements* (No 178), which recommended that (a) the statutory scheme in Part I of the Landlord and Tenant Act 1927 for compensating tenants of business properties for improvements that they have made should be abolished; and (b) there should not be a statutory compensation scheme for residential tenants who improve their premises. The Government rejected the Report.

[192] *Saner v Bilton* (1878) 7 Ch D 815; *Mint v Good* [1951] 1KB 517.

[193] *Stocker v Planet Building Society* (1879) 27 WR 877. [194] Above, p 185.

[195] Below, p 287.

[196] *Regional Properties Ltd v City of London Real Property Co Ltd* (1979) 257 EG 64; *Stocker v Planet Building Society* (1879) 27 WR 877.

[197] [1999] Ch 64, 73–4; (1998) 148 NLJ 1475 (HW Wilkinson); [1995] Conv 495 (M Pawlowski and J Brown). In particular it should not be used to avoid the safeguards for tenants in the Leasehold Property (Repairs) Act 1938, below, p 294.

[198] For the modern law on specific performance see *Co-operative Insurance Society Ltd v Argyll Stores (Holdings) Ltd* [1998] AC 1; Anson, pp 575–81; Jones and Goodhart, *Specific Performance* (2nd edn, 1996).

It follows that not only is there a need for great caution in granting the remedy against a tenant, but also that it will be a rare case in which the remedy of specific performance will be the appropriate one: in the case of commercial leases, the landlord will normally have the right to forfeit or to enter and do the repairs at the expense of the tenant; in residential leases, the landlord will normally have the right to forfeit in appropriate cases.

(ii) Damages

Damages *at common law* for breach of a contract to repair are designed to compensate the loss caused by the breach, which will depend on the facts, although typically it has been held to vary according as the breach occurs during the tenancy or at the end of the tenancy. In the first case the measure is the amount by which the value of the reversion has diminished; but in the second case, where the premises are delivered up in disrepair, it is normally the amount that it will cost to carry out the repairs required by the covenant.[199] However, it was found that the second rule might inflict unnecessary hardship upon an outgoing tenant, since it enabled a landlord to recover substantial damages even though the performance of the covenant would have been entirely useless, such as where the premises were to be demolished, or where the failure to repair would not diminish the rent obtainable on a reletting. It was, therefore, provided by section 18 of the Landlord and Tenant Act 1927[200] that whether the breach is of a covenant to repair during the currency of a lease or to leave premises in repair at the termination of a lease: the damages

> shall in no case exceed the amount (if any) by which the value of the reversion (whether immediate or not) in the premises is diminished owing to the breach of [the] covenant or agreement.

This may be the reduction in the price at which the freehold reversion could be sold;[201] or may be the amount that it will cost within the terms of the covenant to make the house reasonably fit for the class of tenant likely to take it,[202] for example where the sale of the property unrepaired would fetch as high a price as its sale in a state of good repair, but where the tenancy relates only to a few rooms in a large building and they cannot be made fit for reletting unless the covenanted repairs are done.[203]

---

[199] *Joyner v Weeks* [1891] 2 QB 31; *Crewe Services & Investment Corporation v Silk* [1998] 2 EGLR 1; *Latimer v Carney* [2006] EWCA Civ 1417, [2007] 1 P & CR 13 at [2]. Cf *Duke of Westminster v Swinton* [1948] 1 KB 524 (premises could not be immediately put into repair); *James v Hutton* [1950] 1 KB 9 (damages for breach of covenant to restore premises, on request, to condition before licence to alter was granted, are to compensate the loss actually suffered (on facts, nominal)). The decision in *Ruxley Electronics Ltd v Forsyth* [1996] 1 AC 344 (cost of cure not awarded for breach of building contract where cost unreasonable and client had no intention to rebuild even if damages awarded) applies here by analogy (but subject to the cap imposed by LTA 1927, s 18): *PGF II SA v Royal and Sun Alliance Insurance plc* [2010] EWHC 1459 (TCC), [2010] All ER (D) 175 (Jul) at [34], [46], [65], [70].

[200] *Haviland v Long* [1952] 2 QB 80; *Mather v Barclays Bank plc* [1987] 2 EGLR 254; (1988) 104 LQR 372 (DN Clarke).

[201] *Jaquin v Holland* [1960] 1 WLR 258.   [202] *Latimer v Carney*, above, n 199.

[203] *Jones v Herxheimer* [1950] 2 KB 106; *Smiley v Townshend* [1950] 2 KB 311, 322–3; *Drummond v S & U Stores Ltd* (1980) 258 EG 1293 (where the landlord was awarded the bulk of the cost of repairs, including VAT, and a sum representing three months' loss of rent); *Culworth Estates Ltd v Society of Licensed Victuallers*

But the fact that the landlord has been able to relet it, though spending less than that amount on repairs, is an irrelevant consideration.[204] However, if the landlord has sold the premises for a price that shows that the tenant's failure to repair has not damaged the value of his reversion he can recover nothing.[205]

In one particular case the landlord is denied any right to damages. Section 18(1) of the Act provides that no damages shall be recoverable for breach of the covenant:

> if it is shown that the premises, in whatever state of repair they might be, would at or shortly after the termination of the tenancy have been or be pulled down, or such structural alterations made therein as would render valueless the repairs covered by the covenant or agreement.

Thus the Act requires the tenant to prove that the landlord had decided to demolish the premises and that this decision still held at the end of the lease. If this is shown, it is immaterial that the decision is later changed and the premises are not demolished.[206] The onus, therefore, that lies upon the tenant is to show that the demolition or structural alteration of the premises was firmly intended, not merely contemplated, by the landlord and also that the achievement of the plan was reasonably possible.[207] Damages will, however, be recoverable if the premises are demolished as a result of the tenant's breach of his covenant to repair.

(2) Remedies of tenant

The landlord is not liable on his covenant to repair until he has notice of the need to repair and has also a reasonable period in which to remedy the defect.[208] The

---

[1991] 2 EGLR 54 (damage to reversion greater than cost of carrying out necessary repairs); *Shortlands Investments Ltd v Cargill plc* [1995] 1 EGLR 51 (negative value of landlord's reversion; quantum of damages was that by which the failure to repair further diminished that value).

[204] *Jaquin v Holland*, above; *Hanson v Newman* [1934] Ch 298. Cf *Family Management v Gray* (1979) 253 EG 369; [1980] Conv 244; *Crown Estate Comrs v Town Investments Ltd* [1992] 1 EGLR 61; *Mason v Totalfinaelf UK Ltd* [2003] EWHC 1604 (Ch), [2003] 3 EGLR 91 (terminal dilapidations award cannot exceed the amount by which the disrepair diminishes the value of the premises).

[205] *Simmons v Dresden* [2004] EWHC 993 (TCC), (2004) 97 Con LR 81. The burden of proof that the value of the reversion has been diminished, and by how much, is on the landlord: ibid, at [88]; *Craven (Builders) Ltd v Secretary of State for Health* [2000] 1 EGLR 128, 131; *Crown Estate Commissioners v Town Investments Ltd* [1992] 1 EGLR 61, 64–5.

[206] *Keats v Graham* [1960] 1 WLR 30; *Salisbury v Gilmore* [1942] 2 KB 38.

[207] *Cunliffe v Goodman* [1950] 2 KB 237; *Ravengate Estates Ltd v Horizon Housing Group Ltd* [2007] EWCA Civ 1368, [2008] 1 EGCS 135 (premises 'ripe for development').

[208] *Torrens v Walker* [1906] 2 Ch 166; *McCarrick v Liverpool Corp* [1947] AC 219; *O'Brien v Robinson* [1973] AC 912 (extending the rule to implied covenant under LTA 1985, s 11, above, p 229). See also *Sheldon v West Bromwich Corp* (1973) 25 P & CR 360 (landlord liable for damage of which he ought to have recognised warning signs on inspection); *Dinefwr BC v Jones* [1987] 2 EGLR 58 ('actual notice from some responsible source'). For the landlord's liability to all persons likely to be affected by his failure to repair under Defective Premises Act 1972, s 4, see above, p 233. For the enforceability by the tenant of the landlord's covenant to repair where the covenant is expressly subject to payment of maintenance charges by the tenant, see *Bluestorm Ltd v Portvale Holdings Ltd* [2004] EWCA Civ 289, [2004] 2 EGLR 38; cf *Yorkbrook Investments Ltd v Batten* [1985] 2 EGLR 100.

notice is usually given to him by the tenant, but notice from any source is probably sufficient.[209]

The remedies of the tenant are:

(i) Specific performance

Where it is the landlord who breaks the covenant, damages may be an inadequate remedy for the tenant; and, in the case of dwellings, the Landlord and Tenant Act 1985 gives the court discretion to order specific performance of the covenant whether or not the breach relates to part of the premises let to the tenant.[210] Further, where a landlord has failed to carry out repairs within his express or implied covenant, the tenant, after giving due notice, may carry out the repairs himself and deduct the proper costs of repair from future payments of rent.[211] The right of set-off may be excluded by clear words in the lease.[212]

(ii) Damages

Damages are awarded on the same principle as for other breaches of contract: to place the tenant in the position he would have been in if the landlord's obligation to repair had been performed.[213] He may recover the cost of repairs and redecoration, the cost of reasonable alternative accommodation and of storage of furniture, and general damages for inconvenience and discomfort. In *Marshall v Rubypoint Ltd*[214] the Court of Appeal held that the tenant was entitled to recover damages for personal injury, consequential expenses and items stolen in three burglaries at his flat, due to

---

[209] *British Telecommunications plc v Sun Life Assurance Society plc* [1996] Ch 69; (1995) 145 NLJ 1793 (HW Wilkinson).

[210] Ss 17, 32(1). *Jeune v Queens Cross Properties Ltd* [1974] Ch 97 (specific performance granted before the Act); *Francis v Cowcliffe Ltd* (1976) 33 P & CR 368; *Parker v Camden LBC* [1986] Ch 162; *Posner v Scott-Lewis* [1987] Ch 25 (covenant to employ resident porter). See (1975) 119 SJ 362, (1976) 120 SJ 428 (HE Markson).

[211] *Lee-Parker v Izzet* [1971] 1 WLR 1688; (1976) 40 Conv (NS) 190 (PM Rank). See *Asco Developments Ltd v Gordon* (1978) 248 EG 683, 683, where Megarry V-C said that this right of deduction was equally applicable to arrears of rent. See also *British Anzani (Felixstowe) Ltd v International Marine Management (UK) Ltd* [1980] QB 137; *Melville v Grapelodge Developments Ltd* (1978) 39 P & CR 179; (1980) 131 NLJ 330 (PF Smith); [1981] Conv 199 (A Waite); *Muscat v Smith* [2003] EWCA Civ 962, [2003] 1 WLR 2853 (tenant entitled to set off cross-claim for unliquidated damages relating to former landlord's breaches of repairing covenant: see general discussion by Sedley LJ of right of set-off against landlords' claims for rent at [9] ff); cf *Edlington Properties Ltd v J H Fenner & Co Ltd* [2006] EWCA Civ 403, [2006] 1 WLR 1583 (claim for damages for defective construction against original landlord cannot be set off against rent due for periods following assignment by that landlord); [2006] Conv 460 (M Dixon). On set-off generally, see Derham, *The Law of Set-Off* (4th edn, 2010).

[212] *Connaught Restaurants Ltd v Indoor Leisure Ltd* [1994] 1 WLR 501 (payment of rent 'without any deduction' ambiguous and insufficient to exclude right of set-off). For the application of the Unfair Contract Terms Act 1977 and the Unfair Terms in Consumer Contracts Regulations 1999 to covenants in leases, see above, p 183, n 25.

[213] *Wallace v Manchester City Council* [1998] 3 EGLR 38; *English Churches Housing Group v Shine* [2004] EWCA Civ 434, [2005] L & TR 7 (Wallace is 'plainly the leading case on the subject': Wall LJ at [94]); *Earle v Charalambous* [2006] EWCA Civ 1090, [2007] HLR 8 (distinguishing long and short leases: 'A long-lease of a residential property is not only a home, but is also a valuable property asset. Distress and inconvenience caused by disrepair are not free-standing heads of claim, but are symptomatic of interference with the lessee's enjoyment of that asset': Carnwath LJ at [32]).

[214] [1997] 1 EGLR 69.

the landlord's failure to repair the front door to the block of flats, in one of which the tenant was living. The burglars had forced the internal front door of the flat, which was the tenant's responsibility. In holding that the loss was not too remote, and that the burglars did not break the chain of causation, Buckley J said: 'The main purpose of a front door, apart from affording access and egress, is to keep out uninvited visitors and that includes burglars.'

If the premises, to the knowledge of the landlord, had been purchased for resale or sub-letting or if the tenant was forced to sell because of the breach of covenant, then he can recover the loss in market value or of rental value as the case may be.[215]

(iii) Appointment of a receiver[216]

Where the landlord is in breach of his covenant to repair and neglects the property, the court may appoint a receiver to collect the rent and to carry out repairs 'if it is just and convenient to do so'.

(iv) Appointment of a manager: leasehold flats

The Landlord and Tenant Act 1987[217] makes special provision for tenants of residential[218] premises consisting of the whole or part of a building[219] which contains two or more flats.[220] Part II of the Act applies where the leasehold valuation tribunal is satisfied that the landlord[221] is in breach of any obligations under the tenancy that relate to the management of the premises, including their repair, maintenance and insurance.[222]

---

[215] *Calabar Properties Ltd v Stitcher* [1984] 1 WLR 287; *McGreal v Wake* (1984) 269 EG 1254; *Bradley v Chorley BC* [1985] 2 EGLR 49; (1984) 134 NLJ 379 (HW Wilkinson); *Chiodi's Personal Representatives v De Marney* [1988] 2 EGLR 64; *Wallace v Manchester City Council* [1998] 3 EGLR 38 (calculation of damages when tenant remained in occupation after breach by landlord).

See Secure Tenancies (Right to Repair Scheme) Regulations 1985 (SI 1985 No 1493), which entitles a secure tenant (below, p 383) to carry out his landlord's repairs ('other than a repair to the structure or exterior of a flat'), the cost of which may then be recouped from the landlord; cf *Lee-Parker v Izzet* [1971] 1 WLR 1688; (1986) 83 LSG 1376 (PM Rank).

[216] SCA 1981, s 37(1); *Hart v Emelkirk Ltd* [1983] 1 WLR 1289; *Daiches v Bluelake Investments Ltd* [1985] 2 EGLR 67; cf *Parker v Camden LBC* [1986] Ch 162; *Evans v Clayhope Properties Ltd* [1988] 1 WLR 358; [1988] Conv 363 (CP Rodgers); *Blawdziewicz v Diadon Establishment* [1988] 2 EGLR 52 (balance of convenience).

[217] As amended by HA 1988, Sch 13 and HA 1996, s 86. The Act implements the main recommendations of the Nugee Committee of Inquiry on the Management of Privately Owned Blocks of Flats (1985). This valuable report contains statistics about private sector flats in England and Wales in ch 3, and discusses the problems of owning a flat in ch 6. See (1988) 51 MLR 97 (ME Percival).

[218] Tenancies under LTA 1954, Part II (below, pp 406 ff) are excluded: ss 21(7), 26(1).

[219] A building means either a single building or one or more buildings where the occupants of qualifying flats in each of those buildings shares the use of the same appurtenant premises: *Long Acre Securities Ltd v Karet* [2004] EWHC 442 (Ch), [2005] Ch 61.

[220] Ss 21(2), 25(1).

[221] Or any other person (other than the landlord) by whom obligations relating to the management of the premises or any part of them are owed to the tenant under his tenancy: LTA 1987, ss 22(1)(ii), 24(2ZA), as amended by CLRA 2002, s 160. This allows tenants to apply for a new manager where an existing manager is failing properly to manage the premises. 'Landlord' also includes an RTM ('right to manage') company appointed under CLRA 2002: s 102, Sch 7, para 8.

[222] On service charges, see LTA 1987, s 24(2A); HA 1996, ss 85–88; on the determination of reasonableness of a service charge, see LTA 1985, s 19, as amended by HA 1996, s 83, and CLRA 2002, s 180, Sch 14; and on consultation with the tenant see LTA 1985, s 20 as substituted by CLRA 2002, s 151; Service Charges

The tribunal must also be satisfied that it is just and convenient to make the order in all the circumstances of the case. The tribunal then has power under Part II to appoint a manager to carry out:[223]

(a) such functions in connection with the management of the premises, or

(b) such functions of a receiver,

or both, as the tribunal thinks fit.

Part III of the Act makes provision for a person to be nominated by the tenants to acquire their landlord's interest in the premises without his consent.[224] In order to qualify under this Part, the tenants must be tenants of residential premises under a *long* lease[225] (ie a lease granted for a term exceeding 21 years[226]). On the application by not less than two-thirds[227] of the qualified tenants, the court may make an acquisition order[228] if the landlord is in breach, and is likely to continue to be in breach, of his obligations, or if the appointment of a manager under Part II has been in force for at least two years, and, in either case, the court considers it appropriate to make the order in the circumstances. Under the order the nominated person is entitled to acquire the landlord's interest on such terms as may be determined by agreement between the parties, or, in default of agreement, by a rent assessment committee.[229]

(3) Apportionment of liability

There are circumstances in which liability may be apportioned between landlord and tenant on the basis of causation; for example, where a tenant was in breach of his covenant to repair, but had a claim against the landlord in tort for nuisance

(Consultation Requirements) (England) Regulations 2003 (SI 2003 No 1987), amended by SI 2004 No 2939, SI 2006 No 5 and SI 2010 No 671; Freedman, Shapiro and Slater, *Service Charges Law and Practice* (4th edn, 2007). For a new no-fault right for tenants of certain long leases to manage the property, see CLRA 2002, Part 2; below, p 405.

[223] LTA 1987, s 24(1). If a tenant could apply for an order under s 24, he may not apply for the appointment of a receiver under SCA 1981, s 37(1), above: s 21(6). See *Howard v Midrome Ltd* [1991] 1 EGLR 58 (manager of a company owned by the tenants).

[224] Part III is disapplied where the tenants have exercised their right to manage under CLRA 2002, s 102, Sch 7, para 8; above, n 221; below, p 405.

[225] LTA 1987, s 26. A lease includes a sub-lease, and an agreement for a lease or for a sub-lease: s 59(1).

[226] Or a perpetually renewable lease, or a lease granted in pursuance of Part V of HA 1985 (the right to buy): ss 59(3), 60.

[227] LTA 1987, ss 25, 27(4), as amended by Leasehold Reform, Housing and Urban Development Act 1993, s 85. In addition, at least two-thirds of the flats in the premises must be held by qualifying tenants: LTA 1987, s 25(2)(c), as amended by Leasehold Reform, Housing and Urban Development Act 1993, s 85.

[228] LTA 1987, s 29.

[229] Ibid, s 30. See also Part IV, as amended by Leasehold Reform, Housing and Urban Development Act 1993, s 86, and CLRA 2002, s 162, under which the court may vary the terms of any long lease of a flat if they fail to make satisfactory provision for repair or maintenance, insurance, provision or maintenance of services, recovery of expenditure or computation of a service charge payable under the lease or such other matters as may be prescribed by regulations.

and negligence in respect of neglect that contributed to the damage, liability was apportioned 90 per cent to the landlord and 10 per cent to the tenant.[230]

(f) Law reform

In 1996 the Law Commission published a Report on *Landlord and Tenant: Responsibility for State and Condition of Property*,[231] which was intended to create a more coherent and principled code for regulating the responsibilities of the parties to a lease. Four discrete areas were addressed:[232]

First, the allocation of responsibility for repairs where the lease is silent; secondly, repairing obligations and fitness for human habitation in short residential leases; thirdly, the landlord's remedies for breach of repairing obligations; and finally, the law of waste. If enacted, the reforms will:

(a) ensure that someone will always be responsible for the repair of the premises, unless the parties expressly agree otherwise;[233]

(b) revive the statutory implied covenant that residential accommodation should be fit for human habitation,[234] by removing the present archaic rent limits,[235] and applying the covenant instead to all leases of residential accommodation for a term of less than seven years;

(c) confirm that specific performance is available as a remedy in actions for breach of covenant by tenants, and make the remedy available for landlords as well; and

(d) abolish the law of waste as between landlord and tenant, and replace both the duty not to commit waste and the duty of tenantlike user by a modern implied covenant to similar effect.[236]

With the exception of (b) above, these reforms are in essence a straightforward modernisation and clarification of the present law. They will not impose any obligation that the parties cannot avoid by express provision, nor will they affect existing leases or tenancies.

In December 2009 the Government rejected the Report's recommendations in relation to residential property and, although it accepted the recommendations relating to commercial property, the primary legislation needed to implement them was not considered a priority in the light of current commercial practice.[237]

---

[230] *Tennant Radiant Heat Ltd v Warrington Development Corp* [1988] 1 EGLR 41.

[231] Law Com No 238; [1996] Conv 342 (S Bridge); [1998] Conv 189 (PF Smith). Forerunners of the Report were Law Com No 67, *Obligations of Landlords and Tenants* (1975); Law Com CP No 123, *Landlord and Tenant: Responsibility of State and Condition of Property* (1992).

[232] Law Com No 239, *Thirtieth Annual Report* (1995), paras 5.10–5.11.

[233] We intend to achieve this by implying an excludable obligation to repair into every lease. This will remove the need to rely on the notoriously uncertain operation of general contractual principles to imply a term as to repair (see eg *Liverpool City Council v Irwin* [1977] AC 239; *Duke of Westminster v Guild* [1985] QB 688; and *Hafton Properties Ltd v Camp* [1994] 1 EGLR 67) [above, p 228].

[234] LTA 1985, s 8, which consolidated earlier legislation [above, p 228].

[235] £80 pa for houses in London and £52 pa elsewhere. These limits have not been changed since 1957 [above, p 228, n 39].

[236] This recommendation also applies to licences and tenancies at sufferance.

[237] Law Com No 323, *Annual Report 2009-10*, para 3.2.

(3) Covenant to Insure Against Fire

By the Fires Prevention (Metropolis) Act 1774[238] no action may be brought against any person in whose house a fire shall *accidentally* begin, though it is expressly enacted that this provision shall not defeat an agreement made between landlord and tenant. The result is that, when the property has been burnt, a landlord can maintain an action against his tenant in two cases: first, where the tenant has covenanted to repair, since his contractual liability is not excluded by the happening of an inevitable accident against which he might have expressly protected himself;[239] and secondly, where the fire has begun or been allowed to spread by reason of the negligence of the tenant or of those for whom he is responsible.[240]

But, in addition, it is usual for a tenant to covenant that he will insure the demised buildings to their full value and will keep them insured during the term, or for the landlord to covenant to insure but to have the right to charge the premiums to the tenant. There is no implied term that requires the landlord to show that the amount of the premium is fair and reasonable. He does not 'have to shop around', but must prove either that the rate of premium is representative of the market rate, or that the contract was negotiated at arm's length and in the market place, whether literal or metaphorical.[241] The omission to keep the premises insured for any period, no matter how short, and even though no fire breaks out during the period, constitutes a breach of the covenant.[242]

A covenant to insure is usually coupled with a covenant to apply any insurance moneys received in the reinstatement of the premises,[243] and this is effective unless it is impossible to rebuild. There is an implied duty to lay out the insurance moneys within a reasonable time.[244]

If the landlord himself takes out a policy without having agreed to do so, he is not liable to expend the insurance money on the reinstatement of the premises in the event of their destruction, unless the cost of the premiums is reflected in the rent.[245] Reinstatement of the premises may be impossible, for example, because of restrictions on building or compulsory acquisition of the site. In that case the insurance proceeds belong to the party who paid the premium.[246]

---

[238] S 86. The Act applies to the whole of England. As to its interpretation, see *Goldman v Hargrave* [1967] 1 AC 645; *Mason v Levy Auto Parts of England Ltd* [1967] 2 QB 530; *Reynolds v Phoenix Assurance Co Ltd* (1978) 247 EG 995.

[239] *Redmond v Dainton* [1920] 2 KB 256.   [240] *Musgrove v Pandelis* [1919] 2 KB 43.

[241] *Havenridge Ltd v Boston Dyers Ltd* [1994] 2 EGLR 73.

[242] *Penniall v Harborne* (1848) 11 QB 368 (tenant's covenant).

[243] *Lonsdale & Thompson Ltd v Black Arrow Group plc* [1993] Ch 361; [1983] All ER Rev 270 (PH Pettit).

[244] *Farimani v Gates* (1984) 271 EG 887.

[245] *Mumford Hotels Ltd v Wheler* [1964] Ch 117. Cf *Re King* [1963] Ch 459, M & B p 467; *Mark Rowlands Ltd v Berni Inns Ltd* [1986] QB 211; (1986) 83 LSG 1046 (HW Wilkinson).

[246] *Re King*, above; cf *Beacon Carpets Ltd v Kirby* [1985] QB 755.

(4) Covenant by Tenant not to Assign or Underlet or Part with Possession[247]

Unless there is a special agreement to the contrary, a tenant is free to grant his interest to a third party either by assignment or by underlease,[248] but as it is undesirable from the landlord's point of view that the premises should fall into the hands of an irresponsible person, it is usual to provide for the matter by express covenant. In this case, even though the assignment or underlease is made in breach of the covenant, it is nevertheless valid, but the breach may give rise to forfeiture or to a claim for damages.[249]

(a) Construction of covenant

The courts have always construed this covenant with great strictness, however, and have insisted that the restraint imposed upon the tenant shall not go beyond the letter of the express agreement.[250] Thus, a covenant *not to assign or underlet* is not broken by an equitable mortgage accompanied by deposit of title deeds,[251] nor by a deed of arrangement whereby the tenant constitutes himself trustee for his creditors,[252] nor by permitting another person to have the use of the premises without giving him legal possession,[253] nor in general by any transfer that is involuntary, such as one that results from the bankruptcy of the tenant.[254] A provision that 'this lease shall be non-assignable' does not embrace a sub-lease of the premises.[255] An agreement *not to sub-let* is not broken by a sub-lease of part of the premises;[256] but a covenant *not to assign or underlet any part of the premises* is broken if the tenant assigns or underlets the whole of the premises.[257]

---

[247] Crabb, *Leases: Covenants and Consents* (2nd edn, 2008).

[248] *Keeves v Dean* [1924] 1 KB 685, 691; *Leith Properties Ltd v Byrne* [1983] QB 433.

[249] *Old Grovebury Manor Farm Ltd v W Seymour Plant Sales and Hire Ltd (No 2)* [1979] 1 WLR 1397; *Governors of the Peabody Donation Fund v Higgins* [1983] 1 WLR 1091. The purported assignment of the benefit of a contractual right in breach of a non-assignment provision is ineffective; but although a lease is 'a hybrid, part contract, part property' (above, p 182), 'so far as rights of alienation are concerned a lease has been treated as a species of property' and the law has allowed the assignment to transfer the property rights although liable to forfeiture for breach of the covenant: *Linden Gardens Trust Ltd v Lenesta Sludge Disposals Ltd* [1994] 1 AC 85, 108–9 (Lord Browne-Wilkinson).

It may also constitute a breach of a restrictive covenant: below, Ch 19; or an inducement of a breach of contract by the tenant: *Hemingway Securities Ltd v Dunraven Ltd* [1995] 1 EGLR 61, [1995] Conv 416 (P Luxton and M Wilkie).

[250] *Church v Brown* (1808) 15 Ves 258, 265 (Lord Eldon); *Grove v Portal* [1902] 1 Ch 727, 731.

[251] *Doe d Pitt v Hogg* (1824) 4 Dow & Ry KB 226; below, p 810. A mortgage of registered land can no longer be made by demise or sub-demise: LRA 2002, s 23(1); there can therefore be no argument that such a mortgage constitutes a breach of a covenant against assignment or underletting.

[252] *Gentle v Faulkner* [1900] 2 QB 267.   [253] *Chaplin v Smith* [1926] 1 KB 198.

[254] *Re Riggs* [1901] 2 KB 16; *Marsh v Gilbert* (1980) 256 EG 715 (vesting in new trustee by order of court). As to whether a bequest of a leasehold interest breaks a covenant not to assign, see (1963) 27 Conv (NS) 159 (DG Barnsley).

[255] *Sweet and Maxwell Ltd v Universal News Services Ltd* [1964] 2 QB 699.

[256] *Cook v Shoesmith* [1951] 1 KB 752; *Esdaile v Lewis* [1956] 1 WLR 709.

[257] *Field v Barkworth* [1986] 1 WLR 137, approved in *Troop v Gibson* [1986] 1 EGLR 1 (landlord estopped from enforcing covenant); (1985) 129 SJ 781, 867.

A covenant *not to part with the possession of the premises or any part thereof* is not broken by the grant of a licence to place an advertisement hoarding on the wall of the demised premises, since the tenant is not thereby deprived of legal possession,[258] nor by a 'virtual assignment' under which the tenant passes by contract to a third party all the economic benefits and burdens of the lease (including the duty to collect a sub-tenant's rent as agent for the tenant) but the sub-tenant remains in possession of the premises;[259] but a covenant *not to underlet or part with possession of the premises* is broken if the tenant assigns his lease, since this involves a parting with possession.[260]

(b) Effect of breach of covenant

The result of a tenant's breach depends upon the nature of the covenant by which he has bound himself. A covenant is either absolute or qualified.[261]

(1) Absolute covenant

An absolute covenant is one that imposes an unconditional prohibition upon the tenant, there being no provision for its relaxation at the will of the landlord. In this case any assignment contrary to the terms of the covenant renders the tenant liable,[262] notwithstanding that it is in no way prejudicial to the landlord's interest.

(2) Qualified covenant

(i) Unreasonable withholding of consent by landlord

A qualified covenant, which is far more common in practice, is one that merely prohibits an assignment without the consent of the landlord. It has long been usual to qualify this type of covenant even further by a provision that the landlord's consent shall not be unreasonably withheld, and section 19 of the Landlord and Tenant Act 1927 makes this qualification inevitable by providing that:

> In all leases whether made before or after the commencement of this Act containing a covenant condition or agreement against assigning, underletting, charging or parting

---

[258] *Stening v Abrahams* [1931] 1 Ch 470; *Lam Kee Ying Sdn Bhd v Lam Shes Tong* [1975] AC 247. Whether the grant of the right to occupy premises constitutes an 'underletting' or parting with 'possession' ought to depend on whether a lease, rather than a licence, has been granted: above, pp 185 ff; *Victoria Dwellings Association Ltd v Roberts* [1947] LJNCCR 177. Cf *Doe d Pitt v Laming* (1814) 4 Camp 73, 77, doubted (on the question of whether there was not in the case a grant of exclusive possession) in *Greenslade v Tapscott* (1834) 1 Cr M & R 55, 59 (Parke B); *Akici v L R Butlin Ltd* [2005] EWCA Civ 1296, [2006] 1 WLR 201, M & B p 439 (distinction between 'parting with possession' and 'sharing possession').

[259] *Clarence House Ltd v National Westminster Bank plc* [2009] EWCA Civ 1311, [2010] 1 WLR 1216; [2010] Conv 99 (PG Turner); [2010] L&T Rev 55 (S Highmore and P Dollar).

[260] *Marks v Warren* [1979] 1 All ER 29.

[261] It may also be conditional: *Prudential Assurance Co Ltd v Mount Eden Land Ltd* [1997] 1 EGLR 37 (subject to formal execution of licence); cf *Next plc v National Farmers Union Mutual Insurance Co Ltd* [1997] EGCS 181.

[262] The sub-tenant who knowingly accepts an underlease in breach of the tenant's covenant in the lease and thereby intends to procure a breach of the covenant, can be liable in the tort of wrongful interference with contract; the remedy may be not only damages, but also an order against tenant and sub-tenant for surrender of the underlease: *Crestfort Ltd v Tesco Stores Ltd* [2005] EWHC 805 (Ch), [2005] 3 EGLR 25.

with the possession of demised premises or any part thereof without licence or consent, such covenant condition or agreement shall, notwithstanding any express provision to the contrary, be deemed to be subject to a proviso to the effect that such licence or consent is not to be unreasonably withheld.[263]

Thus, the Act requires that the grounds for the refusal of consent shall in fact be reasonable, and therefore its operation cannot be curtailed by a provision in the lease that certain specified grounds shall not be deemed unreasonable.[264] But if the lease contains a covenant that, before the tenant assigns or underlets, he must first offer to surrender his lease to the landlord, the landlord may demand surrender and so obtain the value of a premium obtainable on an assignment.[265] In relation to non-residential leases granted after 1995, however, a significant change was made by the Landlord and Tenant (Covenants) Act 1995 in relation to covenants against assignment.[266] If the landlord and tenant have agreed (whether in the lease or not, and at the time of the lease or later) any circumstances in which the landlord may withhold his consent to an assignment of the demised premises or any part of them, or any conditions subject to which any such consent may be granted, then the landlord is not to be regarded as unreasonably withholding his consent, or subjecting it to unreasonable conditions, if he withholds it or makes it conditional on that ground. This gives landlords much greater control over the assignment of leases to which it applies.

Under the Law of Property Act 1925[267] the landlord may not require the payment of a fine in return for his consent unless express provision for such a payment is contained in the lease.

The tenant must apply for consent to assign, even if it could not reasonably be refused; the landlord must be given a reasonable opportunity to consider whether to give his consent or not.[268] If the tenant assigns the premises without asking for consent, he is in breach of covenant, and liable to pay damages, and also at common

---

[263] S 19(1)(a). This section does not apply to an absolute covenant: *F W Woolworth & Co Ltd v Lambert* [1937] Ch 37, 58, 59 (Romer LJ); *Bocardo SA v S & M Hotels Ltd* [1980] 1 WLR 17, 22 (Megaw LJ); but see *Property and Bloodstock Ltd v Emerton* [1968] Ch 94, 119–20 (Danckwerts LJ); *Vaux Group plc v Lilley* [1991] 1 EGLR 60, 63 (Knox J). Nor does it apply to the lease of an agricultural holding or a farm business tenancy: s 19(4).

[264] *Re Smith's Lease* [1951] 1 All ER 346.

[265] *Bocardo SA v S & M Hotels Ltd*, above; *Adler v Upper Grosvenor Street Investment Ltd* [1957] 1 WLR 227; (1957) 73 LQR 157 (REM); *Creer v P and O Lines of Australia Pty Ltd* (1971) 45 ALJR 697; (1972) 88 LQR 317; *Allied Dunbar Assurance plc v Homebase Ltd* [2002] EWCA Civ 666, [2002] 2 EGLR 23. This surrender proviso was doubted by CA in *Greene v Church Comrs for England* [1974] Ch 467. It is registrable in unregistered land as an estate contract: LCA 1972, s 2(4): *Greene v Church Comrs for England*, above; in registered land it must be protected by a notice on the register: LRA 2002, s 29. For the position of business tenancies under LTA 1954, Part II, see *Allnatt London Properties Ltd v Newton* [1981] 2 All ER 290; [1980] Conv 418 (CG Blake); (1983) 127 SJ 855 (C Coombe).

[266] S 22, inserting new sub-ss (1A)–(1E) into LTA 1927, s 19; below, p 325.

[267] S 144; *Gardner & Co Ltd v Cone* [1928] Ch 955; *Comber v Fleet Electrics Ltd* [1955] 1 WLR 566. For the meaning of 'fine' see above, p 200, n 128. An increase in rent as a condition to giving consent is in the nature of a fine: *Jenkins v Price* [1907] 2 Ch 229. See also LTA 1927, s 19(3); *Barclays Bank plc v Daejan Investments (Grove Hall) Ltd* [1995] 1 EGLR 68.

[268] *Wilson v Fynn* [1948] 2 All ER 40.

law to the forfeiture of his interest.[269] He may, however, apply to the court for relief against such forfeiture.[270] If, on the other hand, the tenant asks for consent and the landlord refuses consent unreasonably, the tenant may proceed with the assignment without consent.[271]

(ii) Landlord and Tenant Act 1988

This 'curious little Act'[272] imposes statutory duties on a landlord in relation to applications for consent to an assignment, underletting, charging or parting with possession. It applies to applications served after 28 September 1988, and only affects qualified covenants.[273] Its object is to prevent undue delay by the landlord in dealing with a consent application by the tenant, especially where the landlord decides to refuse consent.[274]

Where the landlord receives written application for consent from the tenant,[275] he owes a duty to the tenant within a reasonable time:[276]

 (a) to give consent, except in a case where it is reasonable not to give consent,
 (b) to serve on the tenant written notice of his decision whether or not to give consent specifying in addition—
  (i) if the consent is given subject to conditions, the conditions,
  (ii) if the consent is withheld, the reasons for withholding it.

The landlord is also under a duty to forward the application to any other person whose consent to the transaction is needed, for example, to a superior landlord or to a mortgagee. In this case the superior landlord owes a similar duty.[277]

Where any duty imposed by the Act is broken, an action lies for the tort of breach of statutory duty.[278]

The burden of proof, which at common law was placed on the tenant to prove that consent cannot be unreasonably refused, is reversed by the Act in regard to all the

---

[269] *Barrow v Isaacs & Son* [1891] 1 QB 417.

[270] *Lambert v F W Woolworth & Co Ltd (No 2)* [1938] Ch 883, 893.

[271] The tenant may apply to the High Court or to the county court for a declaration that the landlord has unreasonably withheld his consent: LTA 1954, s. 53(1)(a), as amended by County Courts Act 1984, s 148(1), Sch 2, para 23.

[272] *Venetian Glass Gallery Ltd v Next Properties Ltd* [1989] 2 EGLR 42, 46 (Harman J). The Act is based on Law Com No 161, *Leasehold Conveyancing* (1987); [1989] Conv 1. See also, earlier, Law Com No 141, *Covenants Restricting Dispositions, Alterations and Change of User* (1985), paras 8.50–8.131; (1985) 135 NLJ 491, 1015 (PF Smith); [1986] Conv 240 (AJ Waite). For a general review of the Act, see [2004] Conv 453 (JA Sandham).

[273] S 1(1). It does not apply to a secure tenancy under HA 1985 or to an introductory tenancy under HA 1996: s 5(3), amended by SI 1997 No 74.

[274] See *29 Equities Ltd v Bank Leumi (UK) Ltd* [1986] 1 WLR 1490, 1494 (Dillon LJ).

[275] On what constitutes a sufficient application, see *Norwich Union Mercantile Linked Life Assurance Co Ltd v Mercantile Credit Co Ltd* [2003] EWHC 3064 (Ch), [2004] 4 ECGS 109.

[276] S 1(3); *Go West Ltd v Spigarolo* [2003] EWCA Civ 17, [2003] QB 1140 (service of request for consent is the commencement of reasonable time. The length of reasonable time depends on the circumstances and is the time reasonably required by the landlord to do the things required of him by the Act); *NCR Ltd v Riverland Portfolio No 1 Ltd* [2005] EWCA Civ 312, [2005] 2 EGLR 42.

[277] Ss 2, 3.   [278] S 4; *Berkeley Leisure Group Ltd v Lee* [1995] EGCS 162.

duties, that is as to reasonable time, reasonable conditions and reasonable refusal.[279] The Act contains no definition of reasonableness in any of its connotations.[280] These matters will still depend on the application of common law principles.[281]

(iii) Giving of consent by landlord

The 1988 Act changed the law on the giving of consent by the landlord. As Sir Richard Scott V-C said in *Norwich Union Life Insurance Society v Shopmoor Ltd*:[282]

> The Act of 1998 has altered the law in this respect. It has done so by necessary implication, although not explicitly. The landlord has a statutory duty to the tenant within a reasonable time to give consent, except in a case where it is reasonable not to give consent. In judging whether it is reasonable not to give consent, the position must, in my view, be tested by reference to the state of affairs at the expiry of the reasonable time. If, at that time, the landlord has raised no point and there is no point outstanding which could constitute a reasonable ground for refusal of consent, then it seems to me that the landlord's duty is positively, as expressed by s 1(3), to give consent.

It follows that a landlord who has not given his reasons for refusing consent within a reasonable time cannot thereafter justify his refusal of consent by putting forward any reasons, even though he had them in his mind.[283]

The landlord must give his reasons in writing; reasons given orally are not sufficient and must be confirmed in writing within the reasonable period required by the Act.

(iv) Test of reasonableness

The crucial question is—What does the law regard as a reasonable refusal? This was answered in *Houlder Bros & Co Ltd v Gibbs*,[284] where Tomlin J at first instance said:

> It is by reference to the personality of the lessee or the nature of the user or occupation of the premises that the court has to judge the reasonableness of the lessor's refusal.

---

[279] S. 1(6). Exemplary damages may be awarded: *Design Progression Ltd v Thurloe Properties Ltd* [2004] EWHC 324 (Ch), [2005] 1 WLR 1 (deliberate obstruction by the landlord frustrating the tenants' attempt to assign: £25,000); [2006] Conv 37 (T Fancourt). The Act has not changed the rule that it is not necessary for the landlord to prove that his conclusions were justified if he can show that they were reasonably reached in the circumstances: *Air India v Balabel* [1993] 2 EGLR 66; *Beale v Worth* [1993] EGCS 135.

[280] In the 1985 Report the Law Commission had recommended a 28-day period: para 8.125. On the obscure s 1(5), see (1989) 133 SJ 1277 (T Aldridge).

[281] *Midland Bank plc v Chart Enterprises Inc* [1990] 2 EGLR 59 (gap of two and a half months between application and notice of decision held unreasonable).

[282] [1999] 1 WLR 531, 545; [1998] All ER Rev 282 (PH Pettit).

[283] *Footwear Corp Ltd v Amplight Properties Ltd* [1999] 1 WLR 551, 559 (Neuberger J). See also *Dong Bang Minerva (UK) Ltd v Davina Ltd* [1995] 1 EGLR 41; *Kened Ltd and Den Norske Bank plc v Connie Investments Ltd* [1997] 1 EGLR 21; *CIN Properties Ltd v Gill* [1993] 2 EGLR 97; *Go West Ltd v Spigarolo*, above, n 276, at [40] (Munby J: where landlord has given reasons he does not require any further time, and so cannot assert that the reasonable time he requires has not yet elapsed; premature unreasonable refusal of consent therefore constituted actionable breach of duty and could not be cured by anything that happened later to render refusal reasonable).

[284] [1925] Ch 198, 209. See generally [1988] Conv 45 (G Kodilinye).

And where Sargant LJ in the Court of Appeal said:[285]

> I was very much impressed by counsel's argument that in a case of this kind the landlord's reason must be something affecting the subject matter of the contract which forms the relationship between the landlord and the tenant, and that it must not be something wholly extraneous and completely dissociated from the subject matter of the contract.

In that case it was held that it was unreasonable for a landlord, who had let Blackacre to X and Whiteacre to Y, to forbid an assignment of Blackacre by X to Y, on the ground that Y might terminate his tenancy of Whiteacre.

Although this approach has been criticised by the House of Lords on the ground that it involved adding glosses to the plain words of the covenant,[286] it has been generally followed by the Court of Appeal.[287] The question of reasonableness is essentially a question of fact depending on all the circumstances of the case;[288] and there is now more emphasis on this approach.[289] As Lord Denning MR said:[290]

> Seeing that the circumstances are infinitely various, it is impossible to formulate strict rules as to how a landlord should exercise his power of refusal. The utmost that the Courts can do is to give guidance to those who have to consider the problem. As one decision follows another, people will get to know the likely result in any given set of circumstances. But no one decision will be a binding precedent as a strict rule of law. The reasons given by the judges are to be treated as propositions of good sense—in relation to the particular case—rather than propositions of law applicable to all cases.

In *International Drilling Fluids Ltd v Louisville Investments (Uxbridge) Ltd*,[291] Balcombe LJ deduced the following propositions of law from the authorities:

(1) The purpose of a covenant against assignment without the consent of the landlord, such consent not to be unreasonably withheld, is to protect the lessor from

---

[285] [1925] Ch 575, 587; *Bromley Park Garden Estates Ltd v Moss* [1982] 1 WLR 1019 (where the object of the refusal was to promote good estate management); *Anglia Building Society v Sheffield City Council* (1982) 266 EG 311.

[286] *Viscount Tredegar v Harwood* [1929] AC 72, 78, 81.

[287] *Lee v K Carter Ltd* [1949] 1 KB 85, 96; *Swanson v Forton* [1949] Ch 143, 149; *Pimms Ltd v Tallow Chandlers in the City of London* [1964] 2 QB 547; *Bickel v Duke of Westminster* [1977] QB 517 (Orr and Waller LJJ; cf Lord Denning MR, who considered that no such rule bound the Court of Appeal); *Bromley Park Garden Estates Ltd v Moss*, above; *International Drilling Fluids Ltd v Louisville Investments (Uxbridge) Ltd* [1986] Ch 513, below.

[288] *Brann v Westminster Anglo-Continental Investment Co Ltd* (1975) 240 EG 927, 931; *Bickel v Duke of Westminster*, above, at 524 (Lord Denning MR); *West Layton Ltd v Ford* [1979] QB 593, 605 (Roskill LJ), 606 (Lawton LJ); *Ashworth Frazer Ltd v Gloucester City Council* [2001] UKHL 59, [2001] 1 WLR 2180.

[289] See eg *Leeward Securities Ltd v Lilyheath Properties Ltd* (1983) 271 EG 279, 282 (Oliver LJ); *International Drilling Fluids Ltd v Louisville Investments (Uxbridge) Ltd*, below, at 521; *Royal Bank of Scotland plc v Victoria Street (No 3) Ltd* [2008] EWHC 3052 (Ch), [2009] L&TR 17 (no rule of law that landlord could not refuse consent where he would continue to have benefit of original tenant's covenant and so could not show damage to reversion).

[290] *Bickel v Duke of Westminster* [1977] QB 517, 524, approved by HL in *Ashworth Frazer v Gloucester City Council*, above.

[291] [1986] Ch 513, 519–20; *Jaison Property Development Co Ltd v Roux Restaurants Ltd* (1996) 74 P & CR 357. See generally [1998] 2 L & TR 117 (J Brock).

having his premises used or occupied in an undesirable way, or by an undesirable tenant or assignee.

(2) As a corollary to the first proposition, a landlord is not entitled to refuse his consent to an assignment on grounds which have nothing whatever to do with the relationship of landlord and tenant in regard to the subject matter of the lease.

(3) The onus of proving that consent has been unreasonably withheld is on the [landlord].[292]

(4) It is not necessary for the landlord to prove that the conclusions which led him to refuse consent were justified, if they were conclusions which might be reached by a reasonable man in the circumstances.[293]

(5) It may be reasonable for the landlord to refuse his consent to an assignment on the ground of the purpose for which the proposed assignee intends to use the premises, even though that purpose is not forbidden by the lease.

(6) There is a divergence of authority on the question, in considering whether the landlord's refusal of consent is reasonable, whether it is permissible to have regard to the consequences to the tenant if consent to the proposed assignment is withheld.

(7) Subject to the propositions set out above, it is in each case a question of fact, depending upon all the circumstances, whether the landlord's consent to an assignment is being unreasonably withheld.

Two further propositions on a covenant against sub-letting were added by Phillips LJ in *Mount Eden Land Ltd v Straudley Investments Ltd*:[294]

(1) It will normally be reasonable for a landlord to refuse consent or impose a condition if this is necessary to prevent his contractual rights under the headlease from being prejudiced by the proposed assignment or sublease.

(2) It will not normally be reasonable for a landlord to seek to impose a condition which is designed to increase or enhance the rights that he enjoys under the headlease.[295]

[292] See LTA 1988, s 1(3)(a), above, p 261, reversing the burden of proof.

[293] The court does not apply public law principles and cannot quash a landlord's decision that leaves out of account a relevant matter: *Royal Bank of Scotland plc v Victoria Street (No 3) Ltd*, above, n 289, at [28].

[294] (1996) 74 P & CR 306, 310. These propositions also apply where there is a management scheme for enfranchisement for property enfranchised under Leasehold Reform Act 1967; *Estates Governors of Alleyn's College of God's Gift at Dulwich v Williams* [1994] 1 EGLR 112.

[295] *London & Argyll Developments Ltd v Mount Cook Land (No 1)* [2002] 50 EGCS 111 (unreasonable to impose new surety condition); *Mount Eden Land Ltd v Towerstone Ltd* [2003] L & TR 4 (guarantors required for assignee under terms of the lease: implied term that request for guarantors must be genuinely for the purpose of improving the landlords' financial security. They could not, in circumstances in which they were amply secured, request a large number of guarantors with the object of making it impossible for the tenant to comply and thus prevent an assignment); *Landlord Protect Ltd v St Anselm Development Co Ltd* [2009] EWCA Civ 99, [2009] P & CR 9 at [19] (lessor cannot normally reasonably require a guarantor of the

The essential question is: 'Has it been shown that no reasonable landlord would have withheld consent?'[296]

In considering whether the landlord's refusal of consent is reasonable, there is a divergence of authority as to whether it is permissible to have regard to the consequences to the tenant if consent is withheld. In *International Drilling Fluids Ltd v Louisville Investments (Uxbridge) Ltd*, Balcombe LJ reconciled this divergence by saying that:[297]

> while a landlord need usually only consider his own relevant interests, there may be cases where there is such a disproportion between the benefit to the landlord and the detriment to the tenant if the landlord withholds his consent to an assignment that it is unreasonable for the landlord to refuse consent.

In that case it was held that, where a user clause permitted only one specified type of use ('for any purpose other than as offices'), it was unreasonable to refuse consent to an assignment on the grounds of use (being within the only specified type of use) where the result would be that the property was left vacant and where the landlord was fully secured for payment of the rent.

Finally, even if a landlord was misled by a tenant as to the circumstances surrounding the tenant's application for a licence to assign his lease, the landlord's refusal of consent to it could be treated as unreasonably withheld, if disclosure of the full facts would not have justified refusal.[298]

(v) Examples of reasonable refusal

It has been held that a landlord has a valid reason for withholding his consent:

if the assignee's references[299] or financial standing[300] are unsatisfactory; or

if he considers that other property belonging to him will be injured by the use that the assignee intends to make of the demised premises;[301] or

---

liabilities of an assignee to undertake a liability extending beyond the period during which the term is vested in the assignee).

[296] *Kened Ltd and Den Norske Bank plc v Connie Investments Ltd* [1997] 1 EGLR 21, 25 (Millett LJ).

[297] [1986] Ch 513, 521; *Leeward Securities Ltd v Lilyheath Properties Ltd* (1983) 271 EG 279, 283 (Oliver LJ). Cf *Ponderosa International Development Inc v Pengap Securities (Bristol) Ltd* [1986] 1 EGLR 66 ('nothing like as grave a detriment as was in question in International Drilling'); *F W Woolworth plc v Charlwood Alliance Properties Ltd* [1987] 1 EGLR 53; [1987] Conv 381 (L Crabb).

[298] *Storehouse Properties Ltd v Ocobase Ltd* The Times, 3 April 1988.

[299] *Shanly v Ward* (1913) 29 TLR 714; *Rossi v Hestdrive Ltd* [1985] 1 EGLR 50. See also *Shires v Brock* (1977) 247 EG 127 (fictitious transaction by tenant in favour of nominee with first class references, the object being to give difficult landlord 'a bit of a fright'); *City Hotels Group Ltd v Total Property Investments Ltd* [1985] 1 EGLR 253 (extent of inquiries for information of tenant's capabilities); *Warren v Marketing Exchange for Africa Ltd* [1988] 2 EGLR 247 ('references of a particularly qualified and non-enthusiastic character').

[300] *Ponderosa International Development Inc v Pengap Securities (Bristol) Ltd*, above; *British Bakeries (Midlands) Ltd v Michael Testler & Co Ltd* [1986] 1 EGLR 64. Cf *NCR Ltd v Riverland Portfolio No 1 Ltd* [2005] EWCA Civ 312, [2005] 2 EGLR 42 (prospective sub-tenant's financial standing can sometimes be relevant also to consent to underletting).

[301] *Governors of Bridewell Hospital v Fawkner and Rogers* (1892) 8 TLR 637; *Sportoffer Ltd v Erewash BC* [1999] 3 EGLR 136.

if, where the lease is of a tied public-house, he fears that the value of the trade will depreciate because the assignee is a foreigner who does not intend to reside on the premises;[302] or,

if the effect of the assignment will be to nullify a collateral agreement made at the time of the lease;[303] or

if the assignment will enable the assignee to acquire a statutory tenancy protected by the Rent Acts,[304] or in due course to acquire the freehold under the Leasehold Reform Act 1967;[305] or

if the rent reserved in a proposed sub-lease is well below that obtainable in the open market, but the sub-lessee agrees to pay a large sum by way of premium;[306] or

if the assignment will embarrass the future development of the property of which the demised premises form part;[307] or

if, where there are breaches of a covenant to repair, he is not really sure that the assignee will remedy them;[308] or

if the assignment will undermine the estate management considerations for its strategic development;[309] or

if the motive of the assignee is to acquire a ransom position with regard to a proposed development by the landlord;[310] or

if the purpose of the assignment is to enable the original tenant to exercise his option to determine the lease.[311]

(vi) Discrimination

It is unlawful to discriminate against a person on grounds of disability, gender reassignment, pregnancy and maternity, race, religion or belief, sex or sexual orient-ation by not giving permission for the assignment, sub-letting or parting with possession

---

[302] *Mills v Cannon Brewery Co Ltd* [1920] 2 Ch 38; cf *Parker v Boggon* [1947] KB 346; *Rayburn v Wolf* (1985) 50 P & CR 463 (absentee American attorney resident in Washington).

[303] *Wilson v Fynn* [1948] 2 All ER 40.

[304] *Lee v K Carter Ltd* [1949] 1 KB 85; *Swanson v Forton* [1949] Ch 143; *Dollar v Winston* [1950] Ch 236; cf *Thomas Bookman Ltd v Nathan* [1955] 1 WLR 815; *Re Cooper's Lease* (1968) 19 P & CR 541; *Brann v Westminster Anglo Continental Investment Co Ltd* (1975) 240 EG 927; *West Layton Ltd v Ford* [1979] QB 593; cf *Deverall v Wyndham* [1989] 1 EGLR 57 (unreasonable).

[305] *Norfolk Capital Group Ltd v Kitway Ltd* [1977] QB 506; *Bickel v Duke of Westminster* [1977] QB 517. See also *Welch v Birrane* (1974) 29 P & CR 102; *Leeward Securities Ltd v Lilyheath Properties Ltd* (1983) 271 EG 279. For the Leasehold Reform Act 1967, see below, pp 390 ff.

[306] *Re Town Investments Ltd Underlease* [1954] Ch 301. Cf *Blockbuster Entertainment Ltd v Leakcliff Properties Ltd* [1997] 1 EGLR 28 (rent within open market band of validity).

[307] *Pimms Ltd v Tallow Chandlers in the City of London* [1964] 2 QB 547.

[308] *Orlando Investments Ltd v Grosvenor Estate Belgravia* [1989] 2 EGLR 74; [1989] Conv 371 (PF Smith); cf *Farr v Ginnings* (1928) 44 TLR 249.

[309] *Crown Estates Comrs v Signet Group plc* [1996] 2 EGLR 200 (freehold of Regent Street, London); (1999) 115 LQR 191 (L Crabb).

[310] *BRS Northern Ltd v Templeheight and Sainsbury's Supermarkets Ltd* [1998] 2 EGLR 182.

[311] *Olympia & York Canary Wharf Ltd v Oil Property Investment Ltd* (1994) 69 P & CR 43.

of premises to that person.[312] In the cases of 'small premises', these provisions do not apply, except in relation to race discrimination, if the person withholding permission, or a relative of his, resides and intends to continue to reside on the premises and there is shared accommodation.[313]

(3) Building leases

It is also provided by section 19 of the Landlord and Tenant Act 1927 that in the case of a lease for more than 40 years made in consideration of the erection or the substantial improvement, alteration or addition of buildings, the tenant may, notwithstanding a prohibition of assignment without the landlord's consent, assign the premises without such consent, provided that the assignment is made more than seven years before the end of the term, and provided that within six months after its completion it is notified in writing to the landlord.[314]

(4) Consequences of non-enforcement of covenant; the rule in *Dumpor's Case*

The rule at common law as laid down in *Dumpor's Case*[315] is that a condition is an entire and indivisible thing and therefore incapable of enforcement if the person entitled to enforce it has once allowed it to be disregarded. The effect of this doctrine was that, if a lease from A to B contained a covenant or condition against assigning without licence, and A permitted B to assign to C, A's right to stop further assignments was utterly gone. Once consent had been given to an assignment, the term became freely assignable. Again, and as a result of the same doctrine, if a lease was made to several tenants, upon condition that neither they nor any one of them should assign without a licence, a licence given to one of the tenants destroyed the condition with regard to the others. Again, if a tenant was allowed to assign part of the land leased, the condition ceased to apply to the whole of the land. This absurd doctrine was, however, abrogated by statute[316] in 1859 so far as conditions contained in leases were

---

[312] Equality Act 2010, s 34(1); see also ss 4 (protected characteristics), 13-15, 19 (definitions of direct and indirect discrimination), 32 (protected characteristics for purpose of Part 4), 38(3) ('disposal' includes assignment, etc). The 2010 Act repeals and replaces specific rules relating to race, sex and disability discrimination under Race Relations Act 1976, s 24, Sex Discrimination Act 1975, s 31 and Disability Discrimination Act 1995, s 22(4); cf *Lewisham LBC v Malcolm* [2008] UKHL 43, [2008] 1 AC 1399 (decided under the Disability Discrimination Act 1995, which did not, however, cover indirect discrimination). See also Equality Act 2010, s 34(2), (3) (prohibition on harassment of the person who applies for permission for assignment (etc) or from whom the consent is withheld, and on victimisation by not giving permission). See generally (2010) L&T Rev 134 and 173 (S Highmore).

[313] Ibid, Sch 5, para 3. 'Relative' is defined in para 3(5), and 'small premises' in para 3(3).

[314] S 19(1)(b). This section does not apply if the lessor is a Government department, a local or public authority, or a statutory or public utility company. See *Vaux Group plc v Lilley* [1991] 1 EGLR 60.

[315] (1603) 4 Co Rep 119b; *Smith's Leading Cases* (13th edn, 1929), vol i, p 35; Holdsworth, *A History of English Law*, vol vii, p 282. In *GMS Syndicate Ltd v Gary Elliott Ltd* [1982] Ch 1, Nourse J relied on *Dumpor's Case* as establishing that a landlord can in certain circumstances forfeit a lease in part only; below, p 296.

[316] LP(A)A 1859, s 1.

concerned, and the present position is regulated by the Law of Property Act 1925.[317] This provides that:

> where a licence is granted to a lessee to do any act, the licence, unless otherwise expressed, extends only—
>
>   (a) to the permission actually given; or
>
>   (b) to the specific breach of any provision or covenant referred to; or
>
>   (c) to any other matter thereby specifically authorised to be done;
>
> and the licence does not prevent any proceeding for any subsequent breach unless otherwise specified in the licence.

Moreover, where a lease contains a covenant or condition against assigning or doing any other act without licence, and a licence is granted to one or more of several lessees, or is granted in respect of part only of the property, it shall not operate to extinguish the landlord's remedy in case the covenant is broken either by the other lessees or with regard to the rest of the property.[318]

The result is that the rule in *Dumpor's Case* no longer applies to leases.

(5) The 'usual covenants'

Although there are many other covenants that may figure in a lease, those that are normally found have been mentioned. It should be noticed that, where the lease is preceded by a contract for a lease,[319] there is an implied term of the contract that it shall include the *usual covenants*. At one time it was generally considered, on the authority of *Hampshire v Wickens*,[320] that the only covenants by a tenant that could be described as 'usual' were:

> to pay rent;
>
> to pay tenant's rates[321] and taxes;
>
> to keep and deliver up the premises in repair;
>
> to allow the lessor to enter and view the state of repair;

and that the covenant for quiet enjoyment was the only usual covenant binding the landlord.

However, the list is neither fixed nor closed. The question whether particular covenants are usual is a question of fact dependent upon the circumstances of each case, which can be resolved only after considering the evidence of conveyancers, the

---

[317] S 143(1).

[318] LPA 1925, s 143(3).

[319] Above, p 210.

[320] (1878) 7 Ch D 555, 561(Jessel MR); *Charalambous v Ktori* [1972] 1 WLR 951.

[321] On rates and taxes, see Aldridge, Leasehold Law, paras 4.116–4.120.

books of precedents, the practice in the particular district and the character of the property.[322]

II REMEDIES OF THE LANDLORD FOR THE ENFORCEMENT OF THE COVENANTS

We have already noticed some of the remedies available to the landlord[323] or tenant[324] for breach of particular covenants (express or implied) in a lease. We shall here discuss in general terms the landlord's remedies for breach of covenant by the tenant. However, in so doing, the covenant to pay rent must be treated separately from all other covenants entered into by the tenant.

A COVENANT TO PAY RENT

(1) Meaning of Rent

The rent payable to a landlord by the tenant holding from him under a lease is technically called *rent service*. This must be distinguished from a *rentcharge*, which will be discussed in detail later.[325]

(a) Rent service

A brief account of the history of rent service is necessary in order to understand some of the modern features of the law of rent as between landlord and tenant—and in particular distress for rent, which is a very significant remedy available to a landlord for enforcement of the covenant to pay rent.[326]

Historically, rent service consisted of an annual return, made by the tenant in labour, money or provisions, for the land.[327] This is the rent that is due whenever a tenant holds his lands of a reversioner.[328] A reversion is the residue of the estate out of

---

[322] *Flexman v Corbett* [1930] 1 Ch 672. For usual covenants where there was a contract for a lease of garage workshops in Chelsea in 1971, see *Chester v Buckingham Travel Ltd* [1981] 1 WLR 96; (1981) 97 LQR 385 (G Woodman).

[323] Above, pp 250–2 (specific performance and damages for breach of tenant's covenant to repair).

[324] Above, pp 227 ff (repudiation and/or damages for breach of landlord's implied obligations in respect of the state of the premises); pp 252–5 (specific performance, damages, or appointment of a receiver or of a manager for breach of landlord's covenant to repair).

[325] Below, Ch 20. A third form of rent, rent-seck, no longer exists: below, p 271.

[326] The common law right to distrain for arrears of rent is to be abolished (but replaced, for commercial leases only, by a new procedure: commercial rent arrears recovery) when Part 3 of the Tribunals, Courts and Enforcement Act 2007 is brought into force: below, p 277.

[327] Gilbert, *A Treatise on Rents* (1758), p 9. For the history of the subject, see Holdsworth, *A History of English Law*, vol vii, pp 262 ff.

[328] Litt, s 213.

which the estate owner has carved a smaller estate, called a *particular estate*, in favour of another.[329]

Thus, where lands are leased at a rent for a term of years, the landlord is the *reversioner* and the rent payable by the tenant is called a *rent service*. Since, however, rent service is that rent that is due from a tenant who holds of a reversioner, it follows that rent that is reserved on the grant of an estate in fee simple cannot be a rent service, for since *Quia Emptores* 1290 such a grantee no longer holds of the grantor, but is substituted for him.[330] There is no reversion, no residue left in the grantor.

The origin of the term *rent service* lies far back in legal history. Originally the services due from a tenant took many forms, but in course of time they were commuted into fixed money payments called rents service, since they represented the services that formerly issued out of the land. If the tenant failed to perform the services or to pay the rent into which they had been commuted, the lord enjoyed of common right, that is independently of statute or agreement, the remedy of distress, a feudal institution of very ancient origin, which entitled him to seize cattle and other chattels found upon the land. This remedy existed of common right only where the distrainor had an interest in the form of a reversion in the land upon which the chattels lay, for otherwise it could hardly be said with justice that there was anything he was entitled to seize.[331]

Today rent is regarded as a contractual sum to which a landlord becomes entitled for the use of his land, and, therefore, 'the time and manner of the payment is to be ascertained according to the true construction of the contract, and not by reference to out-dated relics of medieval law'.[332] As Lord Diplock said:[333] 'The mediaeval concept of rent as a service rendered by the tenant to the landlord has been displaced by the modern concept of a payment... for the use of his land. The mediaeval concept has, however, left as its only surviving relic the ancient remedy of distress.'

(b) Rentcharge

From a rent service must be distinguished a rentcharge. This differs from rent service in that its owner has no tenurial interest in the land out of which it is

---

[329] Co Litt 22b.   [330] Above, pp 35–6.

[331] Litt, s 213; Gilbert, *A Treatise on Rents* (1758), p 9; Co Litt 78b, 142b; Bacon's *New Abridgement of the Law* under the title Rent (A) 1.

[332] *C H Bailey Ltd v Memorial Enterprises Ltd* [1974] 1 WLR 728, 732 (Lord Denning MR), approved in *United Scientific Holdings Ltd v Burnley BC* [1978] AC 904, 956 (Lord Salmon); *Homes (T & E) Ltd v Robinson* [1979] 1 WLR 452; *Bradshaw v Pawley* [1980] 1 WLR 10 (rent payable under contract from a date prior to execution of lease). Cf *John Smith & Co (Edinburgh) Ltd v Hill* [2010] EWHC 1016 (Ch), [2010] 2 BCLC 556 at [23] (Briggs J: 'Rent is not, of course, a purely contractual matter, even in the 21st century. Both the liability to pay, and the right to receive, rent continue to be incidents of interests in land, passing respectively with the lease and with the reversion, and enforceable by privity of estate, rather than merely by privity of contract'. But the action for nuisance purely for interference with rent 'is one of those medieval relics which... is best returned to the historical scrap heap'). See also *Property Holding Co Ltd v Clark* [1948] 1 KB 630, 648 (Evershed LJ); [1991] Conv 270 (RG Lee).

[333] *United Scientific Holdings Ltd v Burnley BC*, above, at 935.

payable, and having no such interest, is not entitled as of common right to the remedy of distress. It is, then, any rent *expressly* made payable out of land, other than rent payable by a tenant to a reversioner. For example, if A sells land to B in fee simple, he may agree to accept an annual sum of money from B in perpetuity instead of an immediate lump sum, and it is expressly agreed that the fee simple estate shall be charged in favour of A with a power of distress should the rent fall into arrears, the rent (whatever name may be given to it by local usage, such as quit rent, ground rent, chief rent, etc) is a rentcharge. 'It is called a rentcharge because the land for payment thereof is charged with a distresse.'[334] The circumstances in which rentcharges can now be created have been curtailed by the Rentcharges Act 1977, and most existing rentcharges are being phased out. The detail of the law of rentcharges will be considered in Chapter 20.

(c) Rent-seck

Formerly, if a rent was made payable out of a fee simple and for some reason an express power of distress was not reserved, the rent was called a *rent-seck* or dry rent—*dry* because it did not confer the power to distrain.[335]

Thus, at common law the three kinds of rent are rent service, rentcharge and rent-seck. But rents-seck have long ceased to exist, for the inability of their owners to distrain was removed by section 5 of the Landlord and Tenant Act 1730, which enacted that the owners of rents-seck, rents of assize and chief rents should have the same remedy by distress as was available to the owner of a rent service.

Lindley LJ said:

> Bearing in mind what was done by the Act of Geo II, which by section 5 gave a power of distress for all rents, there is now no magic in the word rentcharge. Whether you speak of a rentcharge or only of a rent, if it is a rent and not merely a sum covenanted to be paid, seems to me to be utterly immaterial, because under the Act of Geo II you have a power of distress in respect of it.[336]

The same remedy is given at present by the Law of Property Act 1925.[337] For the purpose of this Act, rent 'includes a rent service or a rentcharge, or other rent, toll, duty, royalty, or annual or periodical payment, in money or money's worth, reserved or issuing out of or charged upon land, but does not include mortgage interest.'[338]

We may now proceed to set out the remedies that are available to a landlord for the recovery of the rent service due to him.

---

[334] Co Litt 144a. See also *Jenkin R Lewis & Sons Ltd v Kerman* [1971] Ch 477, 484.

[335] Litt, s 218.   [336] Re *Lord Gerard and Beecham's Contract* [1894] 3 Ch 295, 313.

[337] S 121(2), which will be repealed, however, by Tribunals, Courts and Enforcement Act 2007, Sch 14, when that Act is brought into force: below, p 277.

[338] S 205(1)(xxiii).

(2) Distress[339]

The common law right of distress is to be abolished,[340] but unless and until the legislation that effects the abolition is brought into force,[341] distress remains a very valuable remedy for the landlord.

Distress, as it has existed in England since the Conquest, was originally allowed for the enforcement of a great number of services that in feudal days might be incidental to tenure, such as rent service, suit-service, heriot-service, aids, reliefs and so on,[342] but most of these are now obsolete, and practically the only purpose for which common law distress is exercisable is the recovery of rent in arrear.[343] It is not dependent on an express right of re-entry, and the landlord is entitled to exercise it unless he contracts not to do so.[344]

The value of the remedy to a landlord is that he can seize and sell the chattels found on the land and thus procure the rent without the necessity of taking legal proceedings. It is a self-help remedy[345] which operates outside the machinery of the courts except in the case of tenancies subject to the Rent Acts.

(a) The right to distrain

It is essential that the reversion should be vested in the distrainor at the time when the rent falls due and also when the distress is levied. Thus if L has assigned the reversion to X at a time when rent is due, L cannot distrain, since he no longer holds the reversion; and X is under the same disability, since he was not the reversioner at the critical moment.

(b) Time and place

Distress cannot be made until the rent is in arrear, which does not occur until the day after it is due,[346] nor can it be levied between sunset and sunrise.[347]

As a general rule the right of seizure is confined to chattels upon the actual land out of which the rent issues, but it may be extended by agreement to other premises, and

---

[339] See generally Tanney and Travers, *Distress for Rent* (2000); Rook, *Distress for Rent* (1999).

[340] Below, p 277. It is to be replaced, however, by a new procedure that will apply only to commercial leases: ibid.

[341] The Government announced on 17 March 2009 that it was reconsidering certain aspects of the enforcement procedures that are proposed to replace the remedy of distress once it is abolished, and that it was intiating a consultation exercise with a view to implementing the changes in April 2012: Hansard, HC Vol 489, col 46WS.

[342] Above, pp 38–9, 64.

[343] The common law right to recover compensation by way of distress for damage caused by trespassing livestock was replaced by a statutory provision for detention and sale: Animals Act 1971, s 7.

[344] *T & E Homes Ltd v Robinson* [1979] 1 WLR 452, 453 (Templeman LJ).

[345] At common law he could only retain the goods: a power of sale was given by the Distress for Rent Act 1689, s 1.

[346] *Duppa v Mayo* (1669) 1 Wms Saund 275; *Re Aspinall* [1961] Ch 526.

[347] *Tutton v Darke* (1860) 29 LJ Ex 271.

by the Distress for Rent Act 1737[348] goods that have been fraudulently and secretly removed by a tenant after the rent became due, in order to avoid distress, may be seized by the landlord within thirty days wherever found.

A distrainor must enter the demised premises[349] and in so doing may commit what in anyone else would be a trespass,[350] such as by entry through an unlocked door;[351] but he may neither break open a door, whether of a dwelling-house or of an outhouse,[352] nor effect an entrance through a closed but unfastened window.[353]

(c) Distrainable goods

The general rule of the common law is that all personal chattels found upon the premises out of which the rent issues, whether they belong to the tenant or to a stranger, can be distrained, but this extensive power is cut down in two ways.

(1) Privileged goods

It is outside the scope of this work to deal with this question in detail. It will suffice here to say that the following articles are absolutely privileged in the sense that they can never be seized:[354]

machinery belonging to a third person that is on an agricultural holding under a contract of hire;[355]

livestock belonging to a third person that is on an agricultural holding solely for breeding purposes;[356]

animals *ferae naturae* (wild animals) in which there is no right of property;[357]

things delivered to a person in the way of his trade, such as cloth given to a tailor to be made into a suit;

things in actual use, such as a horse drawing a cart;

things in the custody of the law, such as property already taken in execution;

---

[348] This Act is to be repealed when the Tribunals, Courts and Enforcement Act 2007 is brought into force: below, p 277.

[349] *Evans v South Ribble BC* [1992] QB 757; [1993] Conv 77 (JEM Sulek) (posting draft walking possession agreement and distress notice through letter-box in sealed envelope insufficient).

[350] *Long v Clarke* [1894] 1 QB 119, 122. [351] *Southam v Smout* [1964] 1 QB 308.

[352] *American Concentrated Must Corp v Hendry* (1893) 62 LJQB 388.

[353] *Nash v Lucas* (1867) LR 2 QB 590.

[354] For further detail, see *Smith's Leading Cases* (13th edn), vol 1, p 137 (notes on *Simpson v Hartopp* (1744) Willes 512).

[355] Agricultural Holdings Act 1986, s 18. The Act does not apply to tenancies beginning on or after 1 September 1995. In the case of a farm business tenancy the Agricultural Tenancies Act 1995 contains no restrictions on distress.

[356] Ibid, s 18.

[357] Co Litt 47a. For discussions of the acquisition and retention of property in animals ferae naturae, see *Hamps v Darby* [1948] 2 KB 311 (racing pigeons); *Kearry v Pattinson* [1939] 1 KB 471 (bees).

such tools, books, vehicles and other items of equipment as are necessary for the tenant's personal use in his employment, business or vocation;[358] and

such clothing, bedding, furniture, household equipment and provisions as are necessary for satisfying the basic domestic needs of the tenant and his family.[359]

The following things are conditionally privileged, that is to say, they can be seized only if there is not a sufficiency of other distrainable goods to be found upon the premises:

beasts of the plough;

sheep and instruments of husbandry;

the instruments of a man's trade or profession, such as the textbooks of a solicitor; and

the livestock of a third person found on an agricultural holding as a result of a contract of agistment.[360]

(2) Goods belonging to third parties

Blackburn J said:

> The general rule at common law was that whatever was found upon the demised premises, whether belonging to a stranger or not, might be seized by the landlord and held as a distress till the rent was paid or the service performed. This state of things produced no harm, because at common law the landlord not being able to sell the distress he generally gave up the goods as soon as he found they were not the tenant's, as his continuing to hold them would not induce the tenant to pay. But in the reign of William and Mary a very harsh and unjust law was passed by which the right was given to the landlord to sell any goods seized, and to apply the proceeds to the payment of the rent unless the tenant or the owner of the goods first paid it; and this held out a great temptation to a landlord to seize the goods of a stranger although he knew they were not the tenant's.[361]

This has gradually been put on a more equitable footing, and at the present day section 1 of the Law of Distress Amendment Act 1908, except in the case of certain specified goods,[362] provides a means by which a lodger or under-tenant or indeed any

---

[358] Law of Distress Amendment Act 1888, s 4; County Courts Act 1984, s 89(1), as substituted by Courts and Legal Services Act 1990, s 15(2). These provisions are to be repealed when the Tribunals, Courts and Enforcement Act 2007 is brought into force: below, p 277.

[359] Ibid.

[360] Agricultural Holdings Act 1986, s 18 (to be repealed when the Tribunals, Courts and Enforcement Act 2007 is brought into force: below, p 277). 'Agisted livestock' means livestock belonging to another person that has been taken in by the tenant of an agricultural holding to be fed at a fair price: s 18(5). If distrained because of an insufficiency of other goods the landlord cannot thereby recover more than the amount due and unpaid under the contract of agistment. For farm business tenancies, see above, n 355.

[361] *Lyons v Elliott* (1876) 1 QBD 210, 213.

[362] Ie goods belonging to the husband, wife or civil partner of the tenant; goods comprised in a settlement made by the tenant; goods of which the tenant is the reputed owner: *Perdana Properties Bhd v United Orient Leasing Co Sdn Bhd* [1981] 1 WLR 1496; and agisted livestock on an agricultural holding: Law of Distress Amendment Act 1908, s 4(1), as amended by Civil Partnership Act 2004, s 261, Sch 27; Agricultural Holdings

person not being a tenant of the premises and not having any beneficial interest in the tenancy, may avoid the seizure of his belongings. For example:

L has leased premises to T, and that X is the lodger or the under-tenant of T. If in such a case L levies a distress on any goods belonging to X for arrears of rent due from T, X may serve L with a notice declaring that:

> T has no right of property in the goods;
>
> the goods are not goods excepted from the Act;
>
> so much rent is due from X to T;
>
> future instalments will become due on stated days; and
>
> he will pay such rent to L.

With this notice, which is of no effect unless it contains the requisite written declarations,[363] X must also send an inventory of his goods. If L distrains on the goods of X after receipt of this notice and inventory, he is guilty of an illegal distress, and X may apply to a justice of the peace or to a magistrate for the restoration of his goods. The protection afforded by the Act applies only to a tenant whose rent equals the full annual value of the premises.

(d) Levying of distress

A landlord may distrain in person, or by employing a certificated bailiff who has been authorised to levy distress (either in the one particular case or in general cases) by a certificate in writing under the hand of a county court judge.[364] Such a bailiff should be provided by the landlord with a distress warrant authorising him to make the levy. The first step is to seize and impound the goods. At common law the impounding had to take place off the premises but now it is lawful to secure the goods in some part of the premises themselves.[365]

The usual practice is to leave someone in possession, but this is not essential, for goods are deemed to be impounded if 'walking possession' is taken of them, that is if they are left on the premises but periodically inspected by the bailiff.[366] If the bailiff is in walking possession of the goods and is later disbarred from entering the premises, he is not entitled forcibly to re-enter them, unless he has been expelled by force or deliberately excluded by the tenant.[367] Anyone who interferes with goods after they

---

Act 1986, s 100, Sch 14. These provisions are to be repealed when the Tribunals, Courts and Enforcement Act 2007 is brought into force: below, p 277.

[363] *Druce & Co Ltd v Beaumont Property Trust Ltd* [1935] 2 KB 257. It may be signed by an agent: *Lawrence Chemical Co Ltd v Rubenstein* [1982] 1 WLR 284. See *Rhodes v Allied Dunbar Pension Services Ltd* [1987] 1 WLR 1703.

[364] Law of Distress Amendment Act 1888, s 7; Distress for Rent Rules 1988 (SI 1988 No 2050), rr 3–5, as amended by SI 1999 No 2360, SI 2009 No 873. See also *Rhodes v Allied Dunbar Pension Services Ltd* [1989] 1 WLR 800.

[365] Distress for Rent Act 1737, s 10.

[366] *Lavell & Co Ltd v O'Leary* [1933] 2 KB 200.

[367] *Mcleod v Butterwick* [1998] 1 WLR 1603.

have been impounded is liable in treble damages for pound breach.[368] As soon as the seizure is complete, the landlord is bound to give the tenant[369] notice of the distress and of the place, if any, to which the goods have been removed,[370] and he is not at liberty to sell them until five days have elapsed since the service of the notice. Thus a tenant is allowed five days within which to pay what is due, but he is entitled to an extension of this period to 15 days if he makes a request in writing to this effect to the landlord and gives security for any additional expense that the delay may involve.[371] The sale is generally, though not necessarily, by auction, and it usually takes place on the premises unless the tenant has requested in writing that the goods shall be removed to a public auction-room. If it does not produce sufficient proceeds, no second sale is as a general rule permissible.[372]

Only six years' arrears of rent may be recovered by the remedy of distress, whether or not the lease is by deed.[373] When the demised premises consist of an agricultural holding with the Agricultural Holdings Act 1986 only one year's arrears are recoverable by this method.[374] No such restriction applies in the case of a farm business tenancy under the Agricultural Tenancies Act 1995.

(e) Amount recoverable

The tenant may set off any sums due to him from the landlord against a claim to levy distress. Otherwise a landlord would be able to recover more by distress than he could in an action for the debt.[375]

(f) Law reform

Reform of the law of distress for rent has been under active consideration for over 40 years. In 1969 the Payne Committee recommended the abolition of the 'highly complex technical and archaic law' of distress.[376] This was also the view of the Law Commission in 1991, which, however, recommended[377] that distress should not

---

[368] Distress for Rent Act 1689, s 3.

[369] Ibid., s 1; Distress for Rent Rules 1988 (SI 1988 No 2050), r 12, Appendix 2, Form 7.

[370] Distress for Rent Act 1737, s 9.   [371] Law of Distress Amendment Act 1888, s 6.

[372] *Rawlence and Squarey v Spicer* [1935] 1 KB 412.   [373] Limitation Act 1980, s 19.

[374] Agricultural Holdings Act 1986, s 16. The Act does not apply to tenancies beginning on or after 1 September 1995.

[375] *Eller v Grovecrest Investments Ltd* [1995] QB 272; *Fuller v Happy Shopper Markets Ltd* [2001] 1 WLR 1681, 1692 (Lightman J: 'a landlord is bound to take the greatest care before levying distress that there are no claims on the part of the tenant which may be available by way of equitable set-off . . . he would be well advised to give notice of his intention and invite the tenant to agree what is owing . . . the human rights implications of levying distress must be in the forefront of the mind of the landlord').

[376] *Report of the Committee on the Enforcement of Judgment Debts* (1969), Cmnd 3909, paras 912–32. See also Law Commission Interim Report, *Distress for Rent* (1966); Law Com No 68, *Rentcharges* (1975), para 94.

[377] Law Com No 194, *Distress for Rent* (1991). See [1985] Conv 451 (A Hill-Smith) and (1985) Law Notes 21 (M Maddock), arguing that distress is speedier and more comprehensive than an action for the arrears of rent. In *Wharfland v South London Co-operative Building Society Co Ltd* [1995] 2 EGLR 21, 22 Crowley QC said: 'At one stage the remedy of distress seemed to be passing out of use, but it appears that it has come back into fashion.' Cf, however, *Salford Van Hire (Contracts) Ltd v Bocholt Developments Ltd* [1995] 2 EGLR 50, 52

be abolished until improvements to the court system make the other remedies available to landlords effective alternatives to distress. In 2003 the Lord Chancellor's Department published a White Paper[378] setting out the Government's view that the current procedures for distress for rent are not an appropriate or proportionate[379] remedy and should be abolished for residential properties, but that a modified form of enforcement, with additional safeguards, should continue to be available in relation to leases of commercial premises through a new system of Commercial Rent Arrears Recovery ('CRAR'). This was implemented in Part 3 of the Tribunals, Courts and Enforcement Act 2007, which has not yet, however, been brought into force because the Government is first reconsidering certain aspects of the enforcement procedures contained in the Act.[380]

Under the new system the terminology is to be modernised: the words 'distress', 'distraint', 'execute', 'levy' and 'walking possession' will no longer be used in this context, and will be replaced by the phrase 'taking control of goods'.[381] CRAR will be available only for the collection of rent[382] that has accrued due and payable[383] under a lease[384] of commercial premises.[385] It will no longer be permitted for landlords to carry out enforcement action for themselves,[386] but they may use authorised enforcement agents[387] (without the need first to apply to court for prior authority); but they must give notice to the tenant before exercising their powers, and a period of notice must be given to the tenant before sale of the goods.[388]

(Hirst LJ: 'The remedy of distress, on the terms set out in the current legislation, appears to have outlived its usefulness as a just remedy').

[378] *Effective Enforcement* (March 2003, Cm 5744), following (in this respect) a consultation paper, *Distress for Rent* (Enforcement Review Consultation Paper 5), May 2001.

[379] For a discussion of the vulnerability of the law of distress to challenge under the ECHR, see Independent Review of Bailiff Law (the Beatson Report), June 2000, paras 2.21–2.26, summarised in *Effective Enforcement*, p 36, n 30; *Fuller v Happy Shopper Markets Ltd* [2001] 1 WLR 1681, 1692.

[380] These provisions of the Act are expected to be brought into force in April 2012: above, p 271, n 341.

[381] Tribunals, Courts and Enforcement Act 2007, s 72, Sch 12.

[382] Ibid, s 76: including interest and VAT, but excluding any sum in respect of rates, council tax, services, repairs, maintenance insurance or other ancillary matters (whether ot not called 'rent' in the lease).

[383] Ibid, s 77: regulations will specify the net minimum recoverable rent under the CRAR procedure.

[384] Ibid, s 74: legal and equitable leases are included, as well as a tenancy at will but not a tenancy at sufference; but the lease must be evidenced in writing.

[385] Ibid, s 75: the premises must be wholly commercial: none must be let under a lease or sub-lease, or occupied, as a dwelling.

[386] A provision in a contract purporting to confer on the landlord a right to seize or otherwise take control of goods to recover rent or other sums payable under a lease is void, although the contract may prevent or restrict the use of CRAR itself: ibid, s 85.

[387] Ibid, s 63(2).

[388] The details of the procedure are set out in Sch 12, including other such matters as the time limit for taking control of the goods once notice has been given, and the type and value of goods that may be taken. A range of matters, such as the periods of notice to be given, and the form of notices, are to be set out in regulations.

(3) Action for Arrears of Rent

(a) Arrears recoverable

The landlord's action for rent is a claim in debt, not a claim for damages for breach of contract, and therefore the sum due as rent can be claimed without any reduction by reference to the principle of mitigation.[389] Moreover, the normal principles of contract law apply under which a landlord can normally choose not to forfeit the lease for non-payment but keep it alive and continue to claim the rent due under the lease, unless an election to keep the contract alive would be wholly unreasonable and that damages would be an adequate remedy, or the landlord would have no legitimate interest in making such an election.[390]

Whether a lease is made by deed or not, only six years' arrears of rent are recoverable by action.[391] Thus a landlord must bring his action within six years after the rent has become due or has been acknowledged in writing to be due, or after some payment has been made by the tenant.[392] A payment of part of the rent does not entitle the landlord to sue for the remainder more than six years after it became due.[393]

But while the relation of landlord and tenant continues under a lease for a fixed term of years, the right of the landlord to recover rent is not *totally* barred by non-payment no matter how long the rent is in arrear.[394] Suppose, for example, that A holds lands of B for 99 years at £100 a year, and that A has not paid rent for 25 years. B's right to recover rent is not extinguished, but is limited to the recovery of the last six years' arrears.

The only case in which the right of a landlord is extinguished altogether occurs in unregistered land where for a period of 12 years the rent has been paid to a third person who wrongfully claims to be entitled to the reversion.[395]

(b) Inter-relation of remedies

A landlord cannot pursue the two remedies of action and distress at one and the same time. If he has levied a distress, he cannot bring an action for recovery until he has sold the distrained articles and found the purchase money insufficient to satisfy his

---

[389] *Reichman v Beveridge* [2006] EWCA Civ 1659, [2007] 1 P & CR 20 at [12].

[390] *White & Carter (Councils) Ltd v McGregor* [1962] AC 413; Anson, pp 508-9, 573-5. It would be an exceptional case, however, where a tenant could establish that this test is satisfied: *Reichman v Beveridge*, above, at [39]-[41].

[391] Limitation Act 1980, s 19. *Romain v Scuba TV Ltd* [1997] QB 887 (time limit applies to guarantor in respect of his undertaking to pay rent reserved by lease); *Tabarrok v EDC Lord & Co* The Times, 14 February 1997 (where negligent advice causes plaintiff to guarantee another's debts, time runs as soon as plaintiff suffers loss).

For the recovery of rent overpaid by the tenant whether due to mistake of fact or law, see *Kleinwort Benson Ltd v Lincoln City Council* [1999] 2 AC 349; (1999) 115 LQR 170 (JM Finnis); [1999] Conv 40 (MP Thompson); [1999] 3 L & TR 12 (C Lamont); *Nurdin & Peacock plc v D B Ramsden & Co Ltd* [1999] 1 WLR 1249, below, p 1155.

[392] Limitation Act 1980, s 29(5).   [393] Ibid, s 29(6).

[394] *Grant v Ellis* (1841) 9 M & W 113; *Archbold v Scully* (1861) 9 HL Cas 360.

[395] *Lehain v Philpott* (1875) LR 10 Exch 242; below, p 1146. Where the lease is registered, see below, p 1160.

demand.[396] If he has sued to judgment first, then, even though the judgment remains unsatisfied, he loses his remedy of distress altogether for that particular rent.[397]

(4) Forfeiture[398]

(a) Right to forfeit

(1) Distinction between covenant and condition

The breach of a covenant by a tenant does not entitle the landlord to resume possession by a re-entry upon the premises, unless the right to do so is expressly reserved in the lease. On the other hand, an undertaking by the tenant that is framed not as a mere covenant, but as a condition, carries with it at common law a right of re-entry if the condition is broken. Whether a stipulation amounts to a covenant or a condition is sometimes a question of considerable nicety, but it depends entirely upon the intention of the parties. A condition is a clause that shows a clear intention on the part of the landlord, not merely that the tenant shall be personally liable if he fails in his contractual duties, but that the landlord shall have the right to determine the lease in the event of such a failure. The tenancy is to remain conditional upon the fulfilment by the tenant of his obligations. In an early case, Bayley J said:[399]

In a lease for years no precise form of words is necessary to make a condition. It is sufficient if it appears that the words used were intended to have the effect of creating a condition. They must be the words of the landlord, because he is to impose the condition.

In this case it was 'stipulated and conditioned' in the lease that the tenant should not assign or underlet the premises, otherwise than to his wife or children, and it was held that these words were sufficient to create a condition. Mere words of agreement, however, as for example when the tenant 'agrees that he will not assign the premises without the consent of the landlord', create nothing more than a covenant.[400]

(2) Express proviso for re-entry and forfeiture of lease

It is, however, the usual practice for a lease to contain, in clear and unmistakable language, an express clause that reserves to the landlord the right of re-entry[401] if one or more of the covenants are broken, and that provides that upon re-entry the lease

---

[396] *Archbold v Scully*, above, n 394.

[397] *Chancellor v Webster* (1893) 9 TLR 568.

[398] Pawlowski, *The Forfeiture of Leases* (1993), which contains a useful overview of the whole subject in ch 1; Kenny, *Forfeiture of Tenancies* (1999).

[399] *Doe d Henniker v Watt* (1828) 8 B & C 308, 315.

[400] *Crawley v Price* (1875) LR 10 QB 302.

[401] A right of re-entry is capable of subsisting as a legal interest: LPA 1925, s 1(2)(e), and the express grant of such a right is a registrable disposition: LRA 2002, s 27(2)(e). However, where the grant of a term of years, which contains a right of entry, is completed by registration, the disposition that consists of the creation of the right of entry is also completed by registration, without any specific entry relating to it being made in the register: LRR 2003, r 77, substituted by LR(A)R 2008 (SI 2008 No 1919).

shall be forfeited.[402] The virtue of this is that the landlord,[403] if he finds himself saddled with an impecunious tenant who is a persistent defaulter in the payment of rent, may regain possession instead of being driven to constant litigation.

The following is a precedent of a proviso for forfeiture:

> Provided always that if any part of the said rent shall be in arrears for 21 days, whether lawfully demanded or not, the landlord or his assigns may re-enter upon the said premises, and immediately thereupon the said term shall absolutely determine.

(b) Effect of breach

Where the lease contains such a proviso, the effect of allowing the rent to fall into arrears for more than 21 days is to render the tenant's interest liable to forfeiture, and not automatically to cause a forfeiture. However clearly the proviso may state that the lease shall 'be void' or 'determine' on breach of condition, it has been held in a long series of decisions that its only effect is to render the lease liable to be determined at the option of the landlord.[404] It is only if he does some unequivocal act that shows his intention to end it that the lease will be terminated.[405] Thus an actual entry by the landlord[406] or the grant of a lease to a new tenant[407] works a forfeiture, but the usual practice at the present day is to sue for the recovery of possession instead of making a re-entry;[408] for, as Willes J said: 'The bringing of an action of ejectment is equivalent to the ancient entry. It is an act unequivocal in the sense that it asserts the right of possession upon every ground that may turn out to be available to the party

---

[402] See *Richard Clarke & Co Ltd v Widnall* (1976) 33 P & CR 339, where a clause in a lease under which the landlord was entitled to serve a notice to terminate in the event of a breach of covenant to pay rent was construed as a proviso for re-entry. Cf *Clays Lane Housing Cooperative Ltd v Patrick* (1984) 49 P & CR 72 (for a clause to be a forfeiture clause it must bring the lease to an end earlier than the actual termination date).

[403] Cf *Rother District Investments Ltd v Corke* [2004] EWHC 14 (Ch), [2004] 1 EGLR 47 (purchaser of head lease not entitled to re-enter and forfeit sub-lease until it became legal proprietor by registration of transfer; but as against the sub-lessee could not deny the effectiveness of purported forfeiture. Lightman J found four interrelated grounds, including (at [16]): 'as between what had been a "forfeiture by estoppel" between [purchaser] and [sub-lessee] was "fed" and became a full legal forfeiture valid against the world' when purchaser was registered as proprietor of head lease).

[404] *Davenport v R* (1877) 3 App Cas 115, 128–9. This case, and many others, refer to the lease being 'voidable' on forfeiture, but this language is misleading: the lease is not annulled ab initio. From the moment the forfeiture takes effect, the tenant's estate no longer exists and the landlord again holds his own estate as if there had been no lease. But the tenant's estate was (and remains) good up to the moment of forfeiture, so rendering his possession lawful and maintaining his liability for payment of rent; he is liable for damages or mesne profits for trespass for wrongful possession only thereafter: *Hartshorne v Watson* (1838) 4 Bing NC 178, 182–3 (Tindal CJ); *Elliott v Boynton* [1924] 1 Ch 236.

[405] *Toleman v Portbury* (1871) LR 6 QB 245, 250; *Eaton Square Properties Ltd v Beveridge* [1993] EGCS 91 (Lloyd LJ: 'it is difficult to imagine a more unequivocal act than changing the locks').

[406] See *Hone v Daejan Properties Ltd* (1976) 239 EG 427, where re-entry by a landlord who had taken an assignment of his tenant's mortgage did not effect a forfeiture. He was 'wearing two hats' (of landlord and mortgagee in possession) and that was equivocal.

[407] But not an agreement with a sub-lessee that he remain in occupation as lessee of a term of an existing sub-lease: *Ashton v Sobelman* [1987] 1 WLR 177.

[408] In the case of tenancies of residential premises a re-entry other than pursuant to a court order for possession is prohibited. See below, p 348.

claiming to re-enter.'[409] Under the Civil Procedure Rules 1998 it is the issue by the court[410] of a claim form at the request of the claimant that is equivalent to re-entry.[411] But the forfeiture does not become final until the landlord has obtained judgment for possession. Until then, for example, the covenants in a lease remain potentially good, since the forfeiture may not be established; or relief against forfeiture may be granted to the tenant, in which case the lease is re-established as from the beginning.[412] But where an application for relief is pending the position appears to be one-sided. As Stephenson LJ said:[413]

> A landlord who has unequivocally elected to determine a lease by serving a writ and forfeiting it cannot himself rely on any covenants of the lease in any shape or form, or any covenants in it, but the tenant who has not elected to determine the lease can do so.

The landlord may forfeit a lease in respect of part only of the premises where that part is physically separate and capable of being distinctly let.[414]

(c) Waiver of right to forfeit

A condition will be waived and therefore unenforceable if, after the act of forfeiture has been committed, the landlord clearly shows that he regards the tenancy as still existing. The two essentials for waiver are that:

(1) the landlord must be aware of the commission of an act of forfeiture by the tenant, and

(2) he must do 'some unequivocal act recognizing the continued existence of the lease'.[415]

---

[409] *Grimwood v Moss* (1872) LR 7 CP 360, 364.

[410] CPR, r 7.2. For possession claims generally, see below, p 346. The landlord cannot then withdraw and reinstate the lease: *GS Fashions Ltd v B & Q plc* [1995] 1 WLR 1088; and it is open to the tenant to accept the forfeiture and so terminate future rights and liabilities under the lease: *Kingston upon Thames Royal LBC v Marlow* [1996] 1 EGLR 101.

[411] Under the old law it was the service of the writ of possession: *Canas Property Co Ltd v KL Television Services Ltd* [1970] 2 QB 433; *Richards v De Freitas* (1975) 29 P & CR 1; *Ashton v Sobelman* [1987] 1 WLR 177; *Hammersmith and Fulham LBC v Top Shop Centres Ltd* [1990] Ch 237; *Capital and City Holdings Ltd v Dean Warburg Ltd* (1988) 58 P & CR 346.

[412] *Driscoll v Church Comrs for England* [1957] 1 QB 330, 339 (Denning LJ). For the effect of relief against forfeiture, see below, p 283.

[413] *Peninsular Maritime Ltd v Padseal Ltd* (1981) 259 EG 860, 866. See also *Meadows v Clerical, Medical and General Life Assurance Society* [1981] Ch 70, 75 (Sir Robert Megarry: 'The tenancy has a trance-like existence pendente lite; none can assert with assurance whether it is alive or dead'); *Associated Deliveries Ltd v Harrison* (1984) 50 P & CR 91; *Official Custodian for Charities v Mackey (No 2)* [1985] 1 WLR 1308; *Hillgate House Ltd v Expert Clothing Service & Sales Ltd* [1987] 1 EGLR 65; *Ivory Gate Ltd v Spetale* (1998) 77 P & CR 141; *Mount Cook Land Ltd v Media Business Centre Ltd* [2004] EWHC 346 (Ch), [2004] 2 P & CR 25 (discontinuance of claim terminated lease's 'shadowy state').

[414] *GMS Syndicate Ltd v Gary Elliott Ltd* [1982] Ch 1, below, p 296. See LT(C)A 1995, s 21.

For restrictions on forfeiture of a residential lease for non-payment of a service charge, see HA 1996, s 81, as amended by CLRA 2002, s 170; and for other restrictions on forfeiture of residential leases, see CLRA 2002, ss 167, 168; [2005] EG 185 (J Driscoll).

[415] *Matthews v Smallwood* [1910] 1 Ch 777, 786 (Parker J), M & B p 450; *Dendy v Nicholl* (1858) 4 CBNS 376.

Thus a merely passive attitude on his part has no effect,[416] nor does his failure to take action because he thinks that he will not be able to prove a suspected breach of covenant;[417] but on the other hand (and this applies to all conditions of forfeiture, whether in respect of the non-payment of rent or of the non-performance of other covenants), a waiver will be implied if a landlord, with knowledge of the breach:[418]

(1) demands or sues for rent,[419] or accepts payment of it notwithstanding that his acceptance is stated to be 'without prejudice',[420] or a clerk of his agents accepts it by mistake;[421] or

(2) distrains for rent whether due before or after the breach;[422] or

(3) grants a new lease to the defaulting tenant.[423]

It is a question of fact whether money has been tendered and accepted as rent,[424] and its acceptance as such is in law conclusive against the landlord. Subjective intention is irrelevant. As Lord Denning MR said: 'It does not matter that the landlords did not intend to waive. The very fact that they accepted the rent with the knowledge constitutes the waiver.' [425]

The waiver of a covenant or of a condition does not operate as a general waiver, but extends only to the particular breach in question.[426] An important distinction should be noticed between continuing and non-continuing breaches of covenant, for

---

[416] *Perry v Davis* (1858) 3 CBNS 769.　　[417] *Chrisdell Ltd v Johnson* [1987] 2 EGLR 123.

[418] *Metropolitan Properties Co Ltd v Cordery* (1979) 39 P & CR 10 (landlords' acceptance of rent for flat with knowledge, through their porters, of facts that pointed to breach of covenant held to be waiver). Cf *Trustees of Henry Smith's Charity v Willson* [1983] QB 316 (uncommunicated rent demand); *Re A Debtor (No 13A-IO-1995)* [1995] 1 WLR 1127 (demand for rent due before right to forfeit not waiver); *Official Custodian for Charities v Parway Estates Developments Ltd* [1985] Ch 151 (publication in London Gazette of compulsory liquidation held not to be imputed knowledge so as to constitute waiver); *Cornillie v Saha* (1996) 72 P & CR 147.

[419] *Dendy v Nicholl*, above; dist *Clarke v Grant* [1950] 1 KB 104. However, it has not yet been authoritatively settled at the level of CA that unequivocal demand for future rent constitutes waiver: *Greenwood Reversion Ltd v World Environment Foundation Ltd* [2008] EWCA Civ 47, [2008] HLR 31 at [26]-[27].

[420] *Segal Securities Ltd v Thoseby* [1963] 1 QB 887.

[421] *Central Estates (Belgravia) Ltd v Woolgar (No 2)* [1972] 1 WLR 1048. See also *Expert Clothing Service & Sales Ltd v Hillgate House Ltd* [1986] Ch 340, M & B p 444 (proffering of negotiating document held not to be waiver where no acceptance of rent or demand for rent involved): *Church Comrs for England v Nodjoumi* (1985) 51 P & CR 155 (service of s 146 notice held not to be waiver of right to forfeit lease on grounds other than those set out in notice); *Re National Jazz Centre Ltd* [1988] 2 EGLR 57 (mere entry into negotiations held not to be waiver).

[422] *Doe d David v Williams* (1835) 7 C & P 322.　　[423] *Ward v Day* (1864) 5 B & S 359.

[424] *John Lewis Properties plc v Viscount Chelsea* [1993] 2 EGLR 77 ('arguments very finely balanced').

[425] *Windmill Investments (London) Ltd v Milano Restaurant Ltd* [1962] 2 QB 373; see also *Bader Properties Ltd v Linley Property Investments Ltd* (1967) 19 P & CR 620, 638–41; *Central Estates (Belgravia) Ltd v Woolgar (No 2)*, above; *David Blackstone Ltd v Burnetts (West End) Ltd* [1973] 1 WLR 1487; *Welch v Birrane* (1974) 29 P & CR 102; (1988) 138 NLJ 95 (HW Wilkinson); *Van Haarlam v Kasner* [1992] 2 EGLR 59; [1993] Conv 288 (J Martin); *Iperion Investments Corp v Broadwalk House Residents Ltd* [1992] 2 EGLR 235; *Seahive Investments Ltd v Osibanjo* [2008] EWCA Civ 1282, [2009] 2 P & CR 2 (processing of cheque, where part retained in discharge of outstanding bankruptcy debt and part returned that had been tendered as outstanding rent, was not conclusive of whether payment accepted as rent).

[426] LPA 1925, s 148.

acceptance of rent[427] or the levy of distress after the breach of a continuing covenant, for example, to keep in repair the premises,[428] waives the forfeiture only up to the date of distress or payment of rent. The proviso for re-entry may be enforced if the breach subsequently continues.[429]

But once a landlord unequivocally and finally elects to treat a lease as determined, such as where he serves a writ for recovery of the land, no subsequent receipt of rent or other act will amount to waiver so as to deprive him of his right to enforce the clause of re-entry.[430]

(d) Formal demand for rent

In the precedent set out above[431] the landlord reserves a power of re-entry for non-payment of rent *whether lawfully demanded or not.* The object of inserting these words is to avoid the strictness of the common law that requires the landlord, failing a contrary agreement, to make a formal demand upon the premises themselves for the exact amount of rent due, and to make it between the hours of sunrise and sunset so as to afford the tenant an opportunity of counting out the money while light remains.[432] This common law rule has, however, been partly abrogated by a statute that enacts that, even though the formal demand has not been dispensed with in the lease, yet, if one-half year's rent is in arrear and there are not sufficient distrainable goods upon the premises and a power of re-entry has been reserved, the landlord can recover the premises by action at the end of the period fixed in the proviso for re-entry without making any formal demand of rent.[433] The restricted nature of this statutory modification makes it desirable, in the interests of a sure and speedy remedy, to obviate by express words the necessity for a formal demand.

(e) Relief against forfeiture

One of the aims of the old Court of Chancery was to prevent the enforcement of a legal right from producing hardship, and therefore, since the sole object of a right of re-entry was to give a landlord security for the rent, it was always prepared to relieve the tenant against the forfeiture, provided that he paid all that was due by way of arrears of rent, together with costs and interest. In this way, the landlord obtained all that the right

---

[427] *Thomas v Ken Thomas Ltd* [2006] EWCA Civ 1504, [2007] L & TR 21 (tenant entitled to appropriate payment to later instalments of rent, which (if accepted by landlord) waives right to foreiture for earlier unpaid instalments).

[428] *Penton v Barnett* [1898] 1 QB 276; *Cooper v Henderson* (1982) 263 EG 592 (covenant as to user); *City and Westminster Properties (1934) Ltd v Mudd* [1959] Ch 129, M & B p 452; cf *Farimani v Gates* (1984) 271 EG 887.

[429] *Doe d Hemmings v Durnford* (1832) 2 Cr & J 667; *Doe d Baker v Jones* (1850) 5 Exch 498.

[430] *Civil Service Co-operative Society Ltd v McGrigor's Trustee* [1923] 2 Ch 347; *Evans v Enever* [1920] 2 KB 315.

[431] Above, p 280.   [432] Notes to *Duppa v Mayo* (1669) 1 Wms Saund 275, 287.

[433] Common Law Procedure Act 1852, s 210 which will be repealed by Tribunals, Courts and Enforcement Act 2007, Sch 14, when that Act is brought into force: above, p 277).

of re-entry was intended to secure to him, and it would be inequitable for him to take advantage of the forfeiture.[434] However, as Arden J has said:[435]

> It can ... be seen that the discretion to grant relief is based on solid principle and not simply to be exercised in a manner that the court considers fair on the particular facts before it. Apart from history, there are, no doubt, sound reasons of policy why the discretion should be circumscribed and consistently exercised. If the courts do not uphold the terms of the lease except in limited situations, there will be a strong disincentive to landlords to invest in property and let it out on lease. By enforcing rights of property, the law promotes the use and availability of this resource within society, and property can be used, as in this case, for commercial purposes, which can serve to increase society's prosperity. Not all landlords are large corporations. The principles have been established by the higher courts and over centuries. They cannot be swept aside by this court.

Originally a tenant might petition for and obtain this relief at any time after he had been ejected under the power of re-entry, but his right has been restricted by statute. The present position depends upon sections 210–212 of the Common Law Procedure Act 1852 and section 38 of the Senior Courts Act 1981.[436] The result of these Acts is as follows.

If the landlord sues for possession and the tenant at any time before the trial pays or tenders to the landlord or pays into court the rent and arrears and costs, all further proceedings are stayed and he regains possession under the old lease.[437] It has been held, however, that there is no case for such a stay of proceedings unless six months' rent is in arrear.[438]

If the tenant does not, or cannot, take this opportunity and judgment is given against him, he may, nevertheless, apply for relief within six months after execution of the judgment.[439] If he applies within this period, the court is empowered to relieve him from the forfeiture subject to such terms and conditions as to payment of rent, costs and otherwise, as could formerly have been imposed by the old Court of Chancery. The effect of a grant of relief is that he holds the land according to the terms of the original lease without the necessity of a new lease.[440]

---

[434] *Howard v Fanshawe* [1895] 2 Ch 581, and authorities there cited; *Inntrepreneur Pub Co (CPC) Ltd v Langton* [2000] 1 EGLR 34 (possibility of successful claim by tenant to set off potential damages for breach of EC Treaty, art 85 (now art 101 TEU), in respect of challenge to beer tie not sufficient evidence of ability to pay: relief against forfeiture refused). For a solicitor's liability in negligence for failing to make application for relief from forfeiture, see *Vision Golf Ltd v Weightmans* [2005] EWHC 1675 (Ch), [2006] 1 P & CR D37.

[435] *Inntrepreneur Pub Co (CPC) Ltd v Langton*, above, at 38.

[436] Replacing Landlord and Tenant Act 1730, ss 2, 4, and Supreme Court of Judicature (Consolidation) Act 1925, s 46 respectively. Until the Constitutional Reform Act 2005 came into force, SCA 1981 was known as the Supreme Court Act. A useful summary of the law is given by Sir Nicolas Browne-Wilkinson V-C in *Billson v Residential Apartments Ltd* [1992] 1 AC 494, 510.

[437] Common Law Procedure Act 1852, s 212. For a 'trial' to come within the meaning of this section, it must be an effective trial binding on all the necessary parties: *Gill v Lewis* [1956] 2 QB 1, where judgment was signed against only one of two joint tenants.

[438] *Standard Pattern Co Ltd v Ivey* [1962] Ch 432, criticised (1962) 78 LQR pp 168–71 (REM).

[439] Common Law Procedure Act 1852, ss 210–212.　　　　　[440] SCA 1981, s 38(2).

The grant of relief within this extended time of six months, however, is a matter of discretion, the general principle being that, so far as rent is concerned, the landlord can claim nothing more than to be restored to the position that he would have occupied had the forfeiture not been incurred:

> The function of the court in exercising this equitable jurisdiction is to grant relief when all that is due for rent and costs has been paid up, and (in general) to disregard any other causes of complaint that the landlord may have against the tenant. The question is whether, provided all is paid up, the landlord will not have been fully compensated; and the view taken by the court is that if he gets the whole of his rent and costs, then he has got all that he is entitled to so far as rent is concerned, and extraneous matters of breach of covenant, and so forth, are, generally speaking, irrelevant.[441]

Even so, however, exceptional circumstances may justify the refusal of relief, such as the inordinate conduct of the tenant himself or the fact that the landlord has altered his position in the belief that the forfeiture is effective. Thus, for example, relief was refused to a tenant who did not apply until just before the six months had elapsed, by which time the landlord, after incurring expenditure upon the maintenance of the property, had 'made an arrangement' to let another party into possession.[442]

If relief is granted upon conditions to be performed within a limited time, the court has jurisdiction to extend the time if it is just and equitable to do so.[443]

Relief may be granted to the tenant where the landlord, instead of bringing an action for recovery of the land, enters into peaceable possession. In such a case the tenant cannot claim relief under the Act that only applies where the landlord sues for possession. He may, however, rely on the ancient inherent equitable jurisdiction of the court, and, provided that he acts with reasonable promptness, may obtain relief even if he brings his action more than six months after the landlord resumes possession.[444]

---

441 *Gill v Lewis* [1956] 2 QB 1, 13 (Jenkins LJ). See also *Belgravia Insurance Co Ltd v Meah* [1964] 1 QB 436.

442 *Stanhope v Haworth* (1886) 3 TLR 34.

443 *Chandless-Chandless v Nicholson* [1942] 2 KB 321.

444 *Howard v Fanshawe* [1895] 2 Ch 581; *Lovelock v Margo* [1963] 2 QB 786; *Thatcher v C H Pearce & Sons (Contractors) Ltd* [1968] 1 WLR 748 (four days over six months); *Ladup Ltd v Williams & Glyn's Bank plc* [1985] 1 WLR 851. See [1969] JPL 251–2. See also *Billson v Residential Apartments Ltd* [1992] 1 AC 494, 516, where CA held that there was no similar inherent jurisdiction in the case of relief for breach of covenant other than the covenant to pay rent; below, p 297.

For the statutory jurisdiction of the county court to grant relief, see the County Courts Act 1984, s 138, as amended by AJA 1985, s 55; High Court and County Courts Jurisdiction Order 1991, art 2 (SI 1991 No 724); *United Dominions Trust Ltd v Shellpoint Trustees Ltd* [1993] 4 All ER 310 (containing a detailed examination of the sections); (1994) 110 LQR 15 (N P Gravells); *Maryland Estates Ltd v Bar-Joseph* [1999] 1 WLR 83; *Croydon (Unique) Ltd v Wright* [2001] Ch 318 (charging order); *Bland v Ingrams Estates Ltd* [2001] Ch 767 (equitable chargee. CA discussed the relationship between County Courts Act 1984, s 138, and the inherent jurisdiction).

(f) Relief to under-lessees

Where a lease is forfeited, any under-leases created out of it automatically come to an end. But an under-lessee[445] has the same right of applying to the court for relief against forfeiture of the head lease as the tenant has under the head lease.[446] The Law of Property Act 1925,[447] provides that where a head lessor proceeds by action or otherwise to enforce a forfeiture, the court may, on the application of an under-lessee, make an order vesting the whole or any part of the property in the under-lessee 'for the whole term of the lease or any less term' upon such conditions as it thinks fit,[448] 'but in no case shall any such under-lessee be entitled to require a lease to be granted to him for any longer term than he had under his original sub-lease'.[449]

There is an important difference between relief granted to an under-lessee and relief granted to a tenant. In the case of the under-lessee a new term is created in him; the lease that has been forfeited is not revived and continued. Accordingly the rent from any under-lease is payable to the landlord between the forfeiture of the old lease and the creation of the new one.[450]

Relief is available to the mortgagee of a leasehold interest holding under a sub-demise or under a charge by way of legal mortgage.[451] An equitable chargee has no claim to relief because he is not an 'under-lessee'; nor directly under the court's inherent jurisdiction that extends only to granting relief to one entitled to possession of the land or who has a legal or equitable interest in it. However, he may obtain relief indirectly under the inherent jurisdiction by making the application for relief that the lessee could himself have made.[452] Relief is not available to a squatter who has dispossessed a lessee.[453]

---

[445] And so has a person deriving title under a lessee: LPA 1925, s 146(5)(b); *High Street Investments Ltd v Bellshore Property Investments Ltd* [1996] 2 EGLR 40 (equitable assignee); *Escalus Properties Ltd v Robinson* [1996] QB 231 (mortgagee by sub-demise).

[446] Common Law Procedure Act 1852, s 210; *Doe d Wyatt v Byron* (1845) 1 CB 623. See generally [1986] Conv 187 (S Tromans).

[447] S 146(4). This is the only part of s 146 which applies to forfeiture for non-payment of rent.

[448] See *Chatham Empire Theatre (1955) Ltd v Ultrans Ltd* [1961] 1 WLR 817 (relief granted on payment of proportionate share of rent by applicant sub-lessees).

[449] *Factors (Sundries) Ltd v Miller* [1952] 2 All ER 630; *Cadogan v Dimovic* [1984] 1 WLR 609.

[450] *Official Custodian for Charities v Mackey* [1985] Ch 168; [1985] Conv 50 (J Martin).

[451] *Belgravia Insurance Co Ltd v Meah* [1964] 1 QB 436; *Hammersmith and Fulham LBC v Top Shop Centres Ltd* [1990] Ch 237; [1989] All ER Rev 194; *Escalus Properties Ltd v Robinson*, above (relief granted retrospectively under s 146(2) to mortgagee by sub-demise); [1995] All ER Rev 334 (PJ Clarke); cf *Pellicano v MEPC plc* [1994] 1 EGLR 104 (vesting order under s 146(4) not retrospective; sub-lessee had no right to possession between date of forfeiture and grant of relief); *Barclays Bank plc v Prudential Assurance Co Ltd* [1998] 1 EGLR 44 (disclaimer of lease held not to prevent granting of relief to mortgagee as under-lessee). As to these forms of mortgage, see below, p 803.

[452] *Bland v Ingrams Estates Ltd* [2001] Ch 767; [2002] All ER Rev 737 (PH Pettit); leave to appeal to HL refused: [2003] 1 WLR 1810.

[453] *Tickner v Buzzacott* [1965] Ch 426.

B COVENANTS OTHER THAN THE COVENANT TO PAY RENT

(1) Damages or Injunction

If the tenant fails to observe any of the covenants contained in the lease, it is open to the landlord either to sue for damages for breach or to seek an injunction to restrain the breach.[454]

(2) Forfeiture

As a further safeguard to the landlord it is the common practice, just as in the case of the covenant to pay rent, to ensure the observance of all other covenants by inserting an express proviso for re-entry and forfeiture in the event of their breach. The following is a typical clause in a lease:

> If there shall be any breach or non-observance of any of the covenants by the tenant hereinbefore contained, then and in any such case the lessor may, at any time thereafter, into and upon the demised premises, or any part thereof, in the name the whole, re-enter, and the same have again, repossess and enjoy as in his former estate.[455]

In two respects, what has already been said above about forfeiture for non-payment of rent applies equally to these other covenants: that the effect of a breach is to render the lease liable to be determined by the landlord, and not to terminate it automatically; and that the right of termination is lost by any act on the part of the landlord that amounts to a waiver of the condition.[456] But until the legislature intervened, the jurisdiction of the court to relieve the tenant varied according as the forfeiture was due to non-payment of rent or to the breach of a covenant relating to some other matter. The question arose whether equity would protect a tenant against the loss of his interest

---

[454] *Coward v Gregory* (1866) LR 2 CP 153. For the landlord's remedies for breach of the covenant to repair, see above, pp 250 ff.

[455] In this case forfeiture is provided for the acts of the tenant contrary to the terms of the lease, but the landlord may also forfeit if the tenant asserts a title in himself adverse to the landlord (eg by a written declaration that he, not the landlord, is entitled to the freehold), or if he lets a stranger into possession with the intention of enabling him to set up such an adverse title. But in all cases, it is a question of fact whether the tenant's act shows an intention to deny the landlord's title: *Wisbech St Mary Parish Council v Lilley* [1956] 1 WLR 121; *Warner v Sampson* [1959] 1 QB 297; *W G Clark (Properties) Ltd v Dupre Properties Ltd* [1992] Ch 297; [1993] Conv 299 (J Martin); *British Telecommunications plc v Department of the Environment* [1996] NPC 148 (denial must be unequivocal); *Abidogun v Frolan Health Care Ltd* [2001] EWCA Civ 1821, [2002] L & TR 16 (no denial of title by submitting question of title to the court for determination. The right to forfeiture for denial of title has been said to arise by operation of law, but is better described as an implication into the lease: Arden LJ at [41]–[42]; [2001] Conv 399 (M Pawlowski). As part of its proposals to reform the law of forfeiture (below, p 300), the Law Commission has proposed that breach of the implied term that a tenant should not deny or disclaim his landlord's title should not constitute tenant default: Law Com No 303, *Termination of Tenancies for Tenant Default* (2006), paras 3.39-3.45.

[456] Above, pp 280–3.

under such a clause if, having incurred a forfeiture by breaking one of the covenants, he was prepared to put the matter right by paying all costs and compensation:[457]

> At first there seems to have been some hesitation whether this relief [grantable in the case of non-payment of rent] might not be extended to other cases of forfeiture for breach of covenants such as to repair, to insure, and the like, where compensation could be made; but it was soon recognised that there would be great difficulty in estimating the proper amount of compensation; and since the decision of Lord Eldon in *Hill v Barclay*[458] it has always been held that equity would not relieve, merely on the ground that it could give compensation, upon breach of any covenant in a lease except the covenant for payment of rent. But of course this left unaffected the undoubted jurisdiction to relieve in case of breach occasioned by fraud, accident, surprise, or mistake.

This denial of relief was maintained even though the breach, instead of causing loss to the landlord, operated to his advantage by restoring to him, at a much earlier date than he had a right to expect, premises upon which the tenant, in the expectation of continued tenure, might have already expended large sums of money. The strongest example of this was where a tenant failed to reinsure for a short time after the previous year's policy had run out. If in such a case no fire had occurred in the uninsured period the landlord had obviously lost nothing, and yet it was held in several cases that such a breach was sufficient to produce a forfeiture against which no relief could be given.[459] This particular case of forfeiture (by failure to insure) received legislative attention in 1859,[460] when relief was made possible on certain conditions, but it still remained true that the merely technical and innocuous breach of any other covenant inevitably led to the loss of his interest by the tenant if the landlord chose to take advantage of a proviso for re-entry.

The law was fundamentally changed in two respects, however, by the Conveyancing Act of 1881,[461] which first required certain conditions to be satisfied before forfeiture could be enforced, and then gave to the tenant the right to petition for relief.

These provisions were re-enacted by section 146 of the Law of Property Act 1925 and amended by three further Acts in 1927, 1938 and 1954.[462] The law now stands as follows.

(a) The statutory restriction on the landlord's right to enforce a forfeiture

(1) The notice

Section 146(1) of the Law of Property Act 1925 provides:

> A right of re-entry or forfeiture under any proviso or stipulation in a lease for a breach of any covenant or condition in the lease shall not be enforceable, by action or otherwise, unless and until the lessor serves on the lessee a notice—

---

[457] *Barrow v Isaacs & Son* [1891] 1 QB 417, 425 (Kay LJ); *Shiloh Spinners Ltd v Harding* [1973] AC 691, 722 ff.

[458] (1810) 16 Ves 402.   [459] See eg *Doe d Muston v Gladwin* (1845) 6 QB 953.

[460] LP(A)A 1859, ss 4–9; later repealed by the Conveyancing Act 1881.

[461] S 14.   [462] LTA 1927; Leasehold Property (Repairs) Act 1938; LTA 1954.

(a) specifying the particular breach complained of;[463] and

(b) if the breach is capable of remedy, requiring the lessee to remedy the breach; and

(c) in any case, requiring the lessee to make compensation in money for the breach;

and the lessee fails, within a reasonable time thereafter, to remedy the breach, if it is capable of remedy, and to make reasonable compensation in money, to the satisfaction of the lessor, for the breach.

A period of three months is normally regarded as a 'reasonable time', but in special circumstances it may be much less.[464] This statutory rule is designed to afford the tenant an opportunity of considering the matter before an action is brought against him and of making up his mind whether he can admit the breach and whether he ought to offer compensation.[465]

The section has effect notwithstanding any stipulation to the contrary.[466] The parties cannot even contract out of its requirements indirectly. Thus, where a tenant agreed to lodge a deed of surrender executed in escrow with the president of the local law society, who had authority to deliver it to the landlord if the tenant committed a breach of covenant, it was held that the deed was void as being a device to circumvent the section:[467]

A forfeiture in the guise of a surrender...remains a forfeiture for the purposes of section 146.

(2) Method of service

The notice may be served in accordance with the general provisions of section 196 of the Law of Property Act 1925 governing all notices under the Act.[468] It can be sent to 'the lessee'[469] or to 'the persons interested', and may be left at the tenant's

---

[463] The landlord is not required to give particulars of each defect: *Fox v Jolly* [1916] 1 AC 1; *Adagio Properties Ltd v Ansari* [1998] 2 EGLR 69.

[464] *Civil Service Co-operative Society Ltd v McGrigor's Trustee* [1923] 2 Ch 347; *Scala House and District Property Co Ltd v Forbes* [1974] QB 575, M & B p 434 (14 days held to be sufficient where breach of covenant against assigning or sub-letting held to be incapable of remedy); *Cardigan Properties Ltd v Consolidated Property Investments Ltd* [1991] 1 EGLR 64 (ten days to comply with insurance covenant held to be insufficient); [1991] Conv 223 (JE Martin); *Bhojwani v Kingsley Investment Trust Ltd* [1992] 2 EGLR 70; [1993] Conv 296 (JE Martin); *Courtney Lodge Management Ltd v Blake* [2004] EWCA Civ 975, [2005] 1 P & CR 17 (four working days insufficient to remedy nuisances caused by sub-underlessee).

[465] *Horsey Estate Ltd v Steiger* [1899] 2 QB 79, 91.   [466] LPA 1925, s 146(12).

[467] *Plymouth Corp v Harvey* [1971] 1 WLR 549, 554 (Plowman J); M & B p 432.

[468] S 196 also extends to notices required to be served by any instrument affecting property unless a contrary intention appears: s 196(5), but this does not impose a stringent requirement for writing where that was not required by such an instrument: *Michael Gerson (Leasing) Ltd v Greatsunny Ltd* [2010] EWHC 1887 (Ch), [2010] Ch 558.

[469] Lessee includes an under-lessee and the persons deriving title under the lessee: LPA 1925, s 146(5)(b). Where a lessee assigns his lease in breach of covenant, the assignment is effective and the notice must be served on the assignee and not on the original lessee: *Old Grovebury Manor Farm Ltd v W Seymour Plant Sales and Hire Ltd (No 2)* [1979] 1 WLR 1397; *Governors of the Peabody Donation Fund v Higgins* [1983] 1 WLR 1091; *Fuller v Judy Properties Ltd* [1992] 1 EGLR 75; [1992] Conv 343 (JE Martin); *Greenwich LBC v Discreet Selling Estates Ltd* [1990] 2 EGLR 65; [1991] Conv 222 (JE Martin) (landlord, who had served notice for breach of covenant to repair and then waived breach by acceptance of rent, need not serve a fresh notice).

address[470] or sent there by registered letter or recorded delivery.[471] The notice may also be served by affixing it to or leaving it for the tenant at the demised premises,[472] but will only be valid if it is 'required' to be served by the tenancy agreement.[473]

In the case of a covenant to repair, a right of re-entry is not enforceable unless the lessor proves that service of the notice was known either: [474]

(a) to the lessee; or
(b) to an under-lessee holding under an under-lease which reserved a nominal reversion
    only to the lessee; or
(c) to the person who last paid the rent,

and that a reasonable interval had elapsed since the time when the fact of service was *known to* such person. In this case, the sending of the notice by registered letter or recorded delivery to a person is only to be regarded prima facie as good service.[475]

(3) Contents of notice

The statutory notice need not contain a demand for compensation if the lessor does not desire to be compensated.[476] However, the statutory notice will sometimes be ineffective if it omits to require a breach to be remedied.

If a *positive* covenant has been broken, for example, a covenant to repair, that is clearly capable of remedy and accordingly the notice must require it to be remedied. In *Expert Clothing Service and Sales Ltd v Hillgate House Ltd*[477] the Court of Appeal held that, where a tenant had committed a once-and-for-all breach of a covenant to

The notice should be served on the tenant, and not on any mortgagee of the term: *Church Commissioners for England v Ve-Ri-Best Manufacturing Co Ltd* [1957] 1 QB 238, even if the mortgagee has taken possession: *Smith v Spaul* [2002] EWCA Civ 1830, [2003] QB 983. On problems with LPA 1925, s 196, see [2005] Conv 191 (E Slessenger).

[470] Even though the lessee is in prison and unlikely to receive it: *Van Haarlam v Kasner* [1992] 2 EGLR 59; and even though the recipient is suffering from mental disorder; *Tadema Holdings Ltd v Ferguson* [1999] 14 NPC 144 (notice served under HA 1988, s 13(2)); *WX Investments Ltd v Begg* [2002] EWHC 925 (Ch), [2002] 1 WLR 2849 (service deemed to have occurred on first occasion Post Office attempted to deliver, notwithstanding that it was not actually received by landlord until much later); [2003] Conv 90 (M Haley); *Beanby Estates Ltd v Egg Stores (Stamford Hill) Ltd* [2003] EWHC 1252 (Ch), [2003] 1 WLR 2064 (where notice sent by recorded delivery to addressee at place of abode, it was irrebuttably deemed to have been served). See also *C A Webber (Transport) Ltd v Railtrack plc* [2003] EWCA Civ 1167, [2004] 1 WLR 320 (*Beanby Estates* not inconsistent with HRA 1998); [2003] Conv 268 (JE Adams).

[471] Recorded Delivery Service Act 1962, s 1; [1990] Conv 147 (JE Adams).

[472] *Blunden v Frogmore Investments Ltd* [2002] EWCA Civ 573, [2002] 2 EGLR 29, [2002] Conv 312 (JE Adams).

[473] *Trustees of Henry Smith's Charity v Kyriakou* [1989] 2 EGLR 110; *Wandsworth LBC v Attwell* [1996] 1 EGLR 57.

[474] LTA 1927, s 18(2).

[475] If a tenant is making a claim under the Leasehold Reform Act 1967 (below, p 390), no proceedings to enforce any right of re-entry or forfeiture may be brought during the currency of the claim without the leave of the court, which shall not be granted unless it is satisfied that the claim was not made in good faith, ie to avoid forfeiture: ss 22, 34, Sch 3, para 4(1); *Central Estates (Belgravia) Ltd v Woolgar* [1972] 1 QB 48.

[476] *Lock v Pearce* [1893] 2 Ch 271; *Governors of Rugby School v Tannahill* [1935] 1 KB 87, M & B p 432.

[477] [1986] Ch 340, M & B p 444.

reconstruct premises by a certain date, the breach was capable of remedy even after that date. Slade LJ said:[478]

> The breach of a positive covenant (whether it be a continuing breach or a once-and-for-all breach) will ordinarily be capable of remedy. The concept of capability of remedy for the purpose of section 146 must surely be directed to the question whether the harm that has been done to the landlord by the relevant breach is for practical purposes capable of being retrieved. In the ordinary case, the breach of a promise to do something by a certain date can for practical purposes be remedied by the thing being done, even out of time.
>
> In my judgment on the remediability issue, the ultimate question for the court was this: if the section 146 notice had required the lessee to remedy the breach and the lessors had then allowed a reasonable time to elapse to enable the lessee fully to comply with the relevant covenant, would such compliance, coupled with the payment of any appropriate monetary compensation, have effectively remedied the harm which the lessors had suffered or were likely to suffer from the breach? If, but only if, the answer to this question was 'No,' would the failure of the section 146 notice to require remedy of the breach have been justifiable.

There may, however, be rare cases where the breach of a positive covenant is incapable of remedy, for example, where there is a breach of a covenant to insure at a time when the premises have already been burnt down.

Where, however, the covenant that has been broken is *negative*, there is some difficulty. At first it was held that the breach of *all* negative covenants was incapable of remedy. This 'attractive and easy ratio'[479] was, however, rejected. The matter has arisen in the Court of Appeal in different situations:

(i) Not to use premises for illegal or immoral purposes. Stigma

If, for example, the tenant has agreed not to permit the premises to be used for illegal or immoral purposes and he is convicted of using them for habitual prostitution, it may be that the landlord is already branded locally as the owner of a brothel. If so, the tenant may discontinue his immoral use of the premises, his only mode of redemption, but mere cessation will not wipe out the past and remove the stigma on the landlord's reputation. In this sense the breach is not capable of remedy. If, therefore, the landlord can show that he has suffered lasting damage of this nature, his statutory notice need not require the breach to be remedied.[480] But the position is different where the action for forfeiture is brought against the original tenant in respect of immoral user

---

[478] Ibid, 355.

[479] *Hoffman v Fineberg* [1949] Ch 245, 254 (Harman J) referring to the ratio of Mackinnon J in *Governors of Rugby School v Tannahill* at first instance [1934] 1 KB 695, 700–1. While affirming his decision, CA rejected his view that all breaches of negative covenants are irremediable: [1935] 1 KB 87, 90, 92. If it were held that breaches of negative covenants were incapable of remedy, recovery of possession by the landlord would depend solely upon whether the court would grant relief from forfeiture to the tenant.

[480] *Governors of Rugby School v Tannahill*, above; *Egerton v Esplanade Hotels, London Ltd* [1947] 2 All ER 88 (immoral use of hotel); *Hoffman v Fineberg*, above (breach of health regulations in restaurant); *Ali v Booth* (1966) 110 SJ 708; *D R Evans & Co Ltd v Chandler* (1969) 211 EG 1381 (pornographic literature); *Dunraven Securities Ltd v Holloway* (1982) 264 EG 709 (illegal pornography); *British Petroleum Pension Trust Ltd v Behrendt* (1985) 52 P & CR 117 (prostitution); *Van Haarlam v Kasner* [1992] 2 EGLR 59 (paraphernalia for spying found in flat).

permitted not by him, but by his sub-tenant or assignee. In these circumstances, it is the duty of the original tenant to take immediate steps to stop the wrongful user and also to enforce the forfeiture against the wrongdoer. It is only if he fails to do so within a reasonable time after learning the facts that the breach will be regarded as incapable of remedy.[481]

(ii) Not to assign or sub-let without consent of landlord, and other negative covenants

In *Scala House and District Property Co Ltd v Forbes*[482] the Court of Appeal held that a covenant not to assign or sub-let without the consent of the landlord is a once and for all breach that cannot be remedied, even by obtaining a surrender from the tenant of the sub-lease. 'Whatever events follow the breach they cannot wipe the slate clean.'[483] In reaching that decision Russell LJ reviewed the cases of *user* of premises in breach of covenant and said:[484]

> We have a number of cases ... in which the decision that the breach is not capable of remedy has gone upon the 'stigma' point, without considering whether a short answer might be—if the user had ceased before the section 146 notice—that it was *ex hypothesi* incapable of remedy, leaving the lessee only with the ability to seek relief from forfeiture and the writ unchallengeable as such.

However, more recent decisions of the Court of Appeal cast doubt on this decision, and its authority has been severely qualified.

In *Savva v Houssein*[485] the tenant covenanted not to display on the outside of the premises any sign or advertisement and not to make any alterations to them without the prior consent of the landlords. The tenant broke both covenants. The Court of Appeal, while leaving in place the solutions in the former two categories,[486] held that the breaches were capable of remedy. In so doing, it adopted the approach of Slade LJ in *Expert Clothing Service and Sales Ltd v Hillgate House Ltd* and considered whether the harm caused by the breaches was remediable rather than whether the breach itself could be remedied. There was nothing in the statute, nor in logic, which required different considerations between a positive and a negative covenant, although it might be right to differentiate between particular covenants. The test was one of effect. If a

---

[481] *Glass v Kencakes Ltd* [1966] 1 QB 611; *Patel v K&J Restaurants Ltd* [2010] EWCA Civ 1211, [2011] L & TR 6 (reasonable grounds for suspicion as result of telephone call from police). These difficulties will be avoided if the statutory notice requires the tenant to remedy the breach if it is capable of remedy. The landlord can then claim in his action (1) that the breach is incapable of remedy, or (2) if it is capable of remedy that it has not been remedied: at 629–30.

[482] [1974] QB 575, M & B p 434, (1973) 89 LQR 460 (PVB); (1973) 37 Conv (NS) 455 (D Macintyre); *Billson v Residential Apartments Ltd* [1992] 1 AC 494 (where Sir Nicolas Browne-Wilkinson V-C doubted whether breach of covenant not to make alterations without prior consent of landlord was irremediable).

[483] Ibid, 591 (James LJ).

[484] Ibid, 588. For criticism of some of the reasoning in this decision, see *Expert Clothing Service and Sales Ltd v Hillgate House Ltd* [1986] Ch 340, 364, M & B p 437, n 231 (O'Connor LJ).

[485] [1996] 2 EGLR 65, M & B p 437; (1997) 1 L & TR 70 (J Brown and R Doddridge).

[486] See *Expert Clothing Service and Sales Ltd v Hillgate House Ltd*, above, at 358; *Savva v Houssein* [1996] 2 EGLR 65, 66.

breach had been remedied then it must have been capable of being remedied.[487] As Staughton LJ said:[488]

> In my judgment, except in a case of breach of a covenant not to assign without consent, the question is: whether the remedy referred to is the process of restoring the situation to what it would have been if the covenant had never been broken, or whether it is sufficient that the mischief resulting from a breach of the covenant can be removed. When something has been done without consent, it is not possible to restore the matter wholly to the situation which it was in before the breach. The moving finger writes and cannot be recalled. This is not to my mind what is meant by a remedy, it is a remedy if the mischief caused by the breach can be removed. In the case of a covenant not to make alterations without consent or not to display signs without consent, if there is a breach of that, the mischief can be removed by removing the signs or restoring the property to the state it was in before the alterations.

In *Akici v L R Butlin Ltd*[489] the Court of Appeal went further. Holding that the breach of a covenant against parting with possession of the premises is capable of remedy, Neuberger LJ accepted that *Scala House* might be binding authority on whether the breach of a covenant against assignment can be remedied, but said that it should not be given any wider authority:

> Unless there is some binding authority, which either calls into question the conclusion or renders it impermissible, both the plain purpose of section 146(1) and the general principles laid down in two relatively recent decisions in this court, namely the *Expert Clothing* and *Savva* cases[490] point strongly to the conclusion that, at least in the absence of special circumstances, a breach of covenant against parting with possession or sharing possession, falling short of creating or transferring of legal interest, are breaches of covenant which are capable of remedy within the meaning of section 146.
>
> The only authority which could be cited to call that conclusion into question is the *Scala House* case itself, but that does not deter me from my conclusion. First, it was only concerned with underletting; secondly, the reasoning of the leading judgment in the case is, at least in part, demonstrably fallacious and inconsistent with common sense and many other authorities; thirdly, it has been overtaken and marginalised by the *Expert Clothing* and *Savva* cases; fourthly, there is no reason of logic or principle why the reasoning or conclusion in the *Scala House* case should be extended to apply to a breach which falls short of creating a legal interest.

There must be some doubt whether *Scala House* will survive, even in the context of covenants against assignment.

As regards the details that must be brought to the knowledge of the tenant, the notice must be sufficiently precise to direct his attention to the particular things of which the landlord complains, so that he may understand with reasonable certainty what he is required to do and may be in a position to put matters right before the action

---

[487] [1996] 2 EGLR 65, 67.　　　　[488] Ibid, 66.

[489] [2005] EWCA Civ 1296, [2006] 1 WLR 201 at [73]–[74], M & B, p 439; [2006] Conv 382 (PF Smith); [2006] All ER Rev 270 (PH Pettit); [2006] JBL 830 (NP Gravells, considering how far the decision in *Akici* already achieves objectives of the Law Commission's proposals for reform (below, p 300)).

[490] Above.

is brought.[491] If, for example, the tenant holds six houses from the landlord and he is merely notified that he has broken his covenant to repair, the notice will be bad as not indicating which of the houses are involved.

(4) Exceptional case of covenant to repair

Where a landlord sues for damages or to enforce a forfeiture in respect of a covenant to keep or put the premises in repair,[492] he is subject to a further statutory restriction under the Leasehold Property (Repairs) Act 1938.[493] This Act applies to premises, other than an agricultural holding, which have been let for a period of not less than seven years, of which at least three years remain unexpired. The landlord must serve on the tenant a notice under section 146 of the Law of Property Act 1925 not less than one month before the commencement of the action, and inform him in that notice of his right to serve a counter-notice.[494] The tenant may within 28 days of receiving the notice serve a counter-notice on the landlord claiming the benefit of the Act.

The effect of a counter-notice is that no proceedings whatsoever may be taken by the landlord for the enforcement of any right of re-entry or forfeiture, or for the recovery of damages, in respect of a breach of the repairing covenant, unless he first obtains the leave of the court. But as soon as the lease has less than three years to run, there is no longer any need to apply for this leave.[495] The circumstances in which leave is to be given are specifically enumerated by the statute.[496] At this stage of the proceedings the landlord need only show a prima facie case of a breach by the tenant.[497]

The Act applies where the landlord is claiming forfeiture or damages, but not where he is claiming for a contract debt. A claim for expenses incurred in the preparation and the service of a section 146 notice is a claim for a contract debt and therefore no

---

[491] *Fletcher v Nokes* [1897] 1 Ch 271, 274; approved *Fox v Jolly* [1916] 1 AC 1; *John Lewis Properties plc v Viscount Chelsea* [1993] 2 EGLR 77.

[492] An obligation to cleanse is not an obligation to repair: *Starrokate Ltd v Burry* (1982) 265 EG 871.

[493] S 1(1); as extended by LTA 1954, s 51(1).

[494] S 1(4); *Middlegate Properties Ltd v Messimeris* [1973] 1 WLR 168; *BL Holdings Ltd v Marcolt Investments Ltd* (1978) 249 EG 849. See *Swallow Securities Ltd v Brand* (1983) 45 P & CR 328 (where a landlord failed in his attempt to circumvent the requirement of serving a notice).

[495] *Baker v Sims* [1959] 1 QB 114.

[496] Leasehold Property (Repairs) Act 1938, s 1(5): (a) where substantial damage has been caused, or will be caused if breach not remedied; (b) where an immediate remedy is required for giving effect to any enactment, by-law or order of a local authority respecting the safety, repair, maintenance or sanitary condition of the house; (c) where the tenant does not occupy the whole of the house and the breach is injurious to the other occupant; (d) where the cost of repair is relatively small as compared with the much greater expense that a postponement will involve; or (e) where it is 'just and equitable' that leave should be given. It is sufficient to give the court jurisdiction if the landlord proves any one of these five grounds: *Phillips v Price* [1959] Ch 181. And he must prove it on the balance of probabilities: *Associated British Ports v C H Bailey plc* [1990] 2 AC 703; [1990] CLJ 401 (S Bridge); [1990] Conv 305 (PF Smith). The relevant date for proving one or more of the s 1(5) grounds is the date of the application for leave to bring forfeiture proceedings: *Landmaster Properties Ltd v Thackeray Property Services Ltd* [2003] EWHC 959 (QB), [2003] 2 EGLR 30 (leave granted under s 1(5)(e) where premises destroyed by fire before the hearing, but tenant's breach of covenant to repair was a direct cause of vandalism and arson).

[497] *Sidnell v Wilson* [1966] 2 QB 67; *Land Securities plc v Receiver for Metropolitan Police District* [1983] 1 WLR 439 (Scotland Yard).

leave to enforce it under the Act is required.[498] There are conflicting decisions at first instance as to whether this extends to a case where the lease contains a covenant that the landlord can enter and carry out repairs at the tenant's expense, if the tenant fails to do them, and that the tenant will reimburse his proper expenditure. The better view is that an action for the recovery of the cost of repair is an action for debt and therefore no leave of the court is required under the Act.[499]

(b) Suspension of covenant

There may exist lawful excuses for the non-performance of a covenant in a lease. If so, the lease is not forfeitable; the covenant is merely suspended, but the lease remains valid. Lord Russell of Killowen recognised (obiter) that there may be excuses for the non-performance of a building covenant short of full frustration:[500]

> It may well be that circumstances may arise during the currency of the term which render it difficult, or even impossible, for one party or the other to carry out some of its obligations as landlord or tenant, circumstances which might afford a defence to a claim for damages for their breach, but the lease would remain.

This dictum was applied in *John Lewis Properties plc v Viscount Chelsea*[501] where a tenant was unable to perform a covenant to demolish and rebuild property owing to his inability to obtain planning permission, which had become necessary on its subsequent listing as a Grade II building.

(c) Statutory right of tenant to claim relief

(1) Power of court to grant or refuse relief

After requiring the above preliminaries from a lessor before he can enforce a forfeiture the Act of 1925 then provides that, when the lessor is proceeding by action[502] or entry to recover the premises, the lessee may apply to the court for relief,[503] and the court may, after reviewing the circumstances of the case and the conduct of the parties, refuse such relief, or grant it upon such terms as to costs, expenses, damages, compensation, penalty, etc, as seem fit.[504] This application must be made by all the tenants if the premises are held by joint lessees.[505] Where the court grants relief, the effect is as if the

---

[498] *Bader Properties Ltd v Linley Property Investments Ltd* (1967) 19 P & CR 620; *Middlegate Properties Ltd v Gidlow-Jackson* (1977) 34 P & CR 4.

[499] *Hamilton v Martell Securities Ltd* [1984] Ch 266; *Jervis v Harris* [1996] 1 All ER 303; [1997] Conv 299 (R Hewitson). See also *SEDAC Investments Ltd v Tanner* [1982] 1 WLR 1342; (1984) 134 NLJ 791 (HW Wilkinson); [1986] Conv 85 (PF Smith).

[500] *Cricklewood Property and Investment Trust Ltd v Leighton's Investment Trust Ltd* [1945] AC 221, 233–4; so also Lord Goddard at 244.

[501] [1993] 34 EG 116 (25 Cadogan Gardens, 'once described as the most wonderful house in the world'); [1995] Conv 74 (J Morgan). Frustration was not pleaded; below, p 343.

[502] Such an action is a pending land action under LCA 1972, s 17(1) and is registrable under s 5; and, in the case of registered land, is required to be protected by a notice under LRA 2002, s. 87; H & B, paras 10.102–10.105; *Selim Ltd v Bickenhall Engineering Ltd* [1981] 1 WLR 1318.

[503] He may apply as soon as the s 146 notice has been served: *Pakwood Transport Ltd v 15 Beauchamp Place Ltd* (1977) 36 P & CR 112.

[504] LPA 1925, s 146(2).   [505] *T M Fairclough and Sons Ltd v Berliner* [1931] 1 Ch 60.

lease had never been forfeited.[506] If the relief is granted upon terms to be performed by the tenant in the future, the order for relief falls to the ground if they are not performed; but, until the time comes for performance, the tenant who remains on the premises is there not as a tenant under the lease, but as a tenant at will or on sufferance.[507] The court has jurisdiction to extend the time.[508]

Further, where the tenant has underlet the premises, if the court grants relief to the tenant, the effect is to revive the under-lease in its entirety. In a case, however, where part of the demised premises had been underlet by the tenant, and where those premises were physically separated and the breach of covenant was committed by the under-lessee on his part of the property only, it was held that relief could be granted to the tenant without reviving the under-lease.[509]

Attempts have been made to specify the principles upon which this relief should be granted or withheld,[510] but the House of Lords has held that though such statements are useful and may reflect the judicial view for normal cases, yet the discretion given by the statute is so wide that it is better not to lay down rigid rules for its exercise.[511] Although the court will rarely exercise its discretion in favour of a lessee who knowingly suffers premises to be used for immoral purposes, it may nevertheless do so where there are special mitigating circumstances.[512]

(2) Time of application

After the statutory notice under section 146 has been served, the tenant may apply for relief under subsection (2). He may do so not only where the landlord proceeds

---

[506] *Dendy v Evans* [1910] 1 KB 263; *Meadows v Clerical, Medical and General Life Assurance Society* [1981] Ch 70; *Hynes v Twinsectra Ltd* [1995] 2 EGLR 69.

[507] *City of Westminster Assurance Co Ltd v Ainis* (1975) 29 P & CR 469.

[508] *Chandless-Chandless v Nicholson* [1942] 2 KB 321; *Starside Properties Ltd v Mustapha* [1974] 1 WLR 816.

[509] *GMS Syndicate Ltd v Gary Elliott Ltd* [1982] Ch 1, relying on *Dumpor's Case* (1603) 4 Co Rep 119b, above, p 267. For an under-lessee's independent right to claim relief, see below.

[510] Eg *Rose v Hyman* [1911] 2 KB 234.

[511] *Hyman v Rose* [1912] AC 623, 631 (Lord Eldon LC); *Southern Depot Co Ltd v British Railways Board* [1990] 2 EGLR 39; *Darlington BC v Denmark Chemists Ltd* [1993] 1 EGLR 62.

[512] *Borthwick-Norton v Romney Warwick Estates Ltd* [1950] 1 All ER 798; *Borthwick-Norton v Dougherty* [1950] WN 481; *Central Estates (Belgravia) Ltd v Woolgar (No 2)* [1972] 1 WLR 1048; *Burfort Financial Investments Ltd v Chotard* (1976) 239 EG 891; *British Petroleum Pension Trust Ltd v Behrendt* (1985) 52 P & CR 117; *Ropemaker Properties Ltd v Noonhaven Ltd* [1989] 2 EGLR 50; (1989) 139 NLJ 1747 (HW Wilkinson); *Patel v K&J Restaurants Ltd* [2010] EWCA Civ 1211, [2011] L & TR 6 (immoral user by sub-tenant: tenant's own breaches not wilful and to grant vacant possession to freeholder would be out of all proportion). See also *Earl Bathurst v Fine* [1974] 1 WLR 905 (relief refused to unsatisfactory tenant, where personal qualifications were important); *Southern Depot Co Ltd v British Railways Board* [1990] 2 EGLR 39 (relief granted despite wilful breaches involving 'a thoroughly deceptive course of conduct' towards the landlord); *Mount Eden Land Ltd v Towerstone Ltd* [2003] L & TR 4 (relief refused where assignee had failed to provide guarantors as required by the lease and had failed to tell landlord that (a) it had taken possession under assignment for which consent had not been given, (b) part of premises were occupied by others ('deliberate and reprehensible' silence), and (c) one of its directors was a discharged bankrupt (a 'lack of frankness'); and it had not been shown that the tenant could not find alternative premises); *Mount Cook Land Ltd v Hartley* [2000] EGCS 26 (relief granted where landlord was using the breach of covenant against underletting as an opportunity to seize a valuable asset, and the landlord would have had to give consent to the underletting if it had been applied for).

by action, but also where he peaceably re-enters without a court order. The latter was decided by the House of Lords in *Billson v Residential Apartments Ltd*,[513] as a result of a purposive interpretation of the opening words of the section: 'Where a lessor is proceeding, by action or otherwise, to enforce such a right of re-entry or forfeiture.'

Before *Billson*, these words had been construed to mean that the tenant could only apply for relief during the time when *the lessor is proceeding*, and that, once the lessor had recovered possession, it would be too late. The House of Lords has now held that the effect of the subsection is that the tenant may apply for relief if the landlord *proceeds or has proceeded* to forfeit by action or otherwise. Accordingly, the tenant may apply where the landlord has peaceably re-entered without first obtaining a court order.[514]

Where the landlord proceeds by action, the tenant must apply before the landlord has entered into possession pursuant to a final judgment; but where the landlord forfeits by peaceable re-entry, there is no time limit. In deciding whether to grant relief, the court will take into account all the circumstances, including delay on the part of the tenant.[515]

(3) Under-lessees

The jurisdiction of the court to relieve an under-lessee, or a person deriving title under him,[516] against a forfeiture due to the under-lessor's failure to pay rent[517] is equally exercisable where the failure relates to some other covenant.[518] This is so, even though the nature of the breach, for example, the bankruptcy of a publican, precludes the under-lessor from applying for relief.[519] It is a jurisdiction that should be sparingly exercised.[520]

(4) Inherent equitable jurisdiction

The Court of Appeal in *Billson*[521] first decided that there was no statutory jurisdiction to grant relief against forfeiture and then held by a majority that it had no inherent equitable jurisdiction either. The section was an exhaustive provision. As Sir Nicolas Browne-Wilkinson V-C said:[522] 'If Parliament intended the court to be able to grant

---

[513] [1992] 1 AC 494, M & B p 453; [1992] CLJ 216 (S Bridge); [1992] Conv 273 (PF Smith); (1992) 02 EG 154 (P Dollar and C Peet).

[514] An application for relief was subsequently refused: *Billson v Residential Apartments Ltd (No 2)* [1993] EGCS 155.

[515] [1992] 1 AC 494, 539–40, 543–4.

[516] *Re Good's Lease* [1954] 1 WLR 309; as for example, a mortgagee by legal charge: *Grand Junction Co Ltd v Bates* [1954] 2 QB 160.

[517] Above, p 286.   [518] LPA 1925, s 146(4).

[519] LP(A)A 1929, s 1.

[520] *Creery v Summersell and Flowerdew & Co Ltd* [1949] Ch 751; *Hill v Griffin* [1987] 1 EGLR 81; *Duarte v Mount Cook Land Ltd* [2002] L & TR 21 (relief granted where landlord was extremely anxious to have sub-tenant as its direct tenant, and had used forfeiture as a negotiating tactic for grant of a new lease).

[521] [1992] 1 AC 494, above.

[522] Ibid, 517. The equitable jurisdiction is available in cases of non-payment of rent: above, p 285. CPR PD 55A, para 2.4 requires a landlord of a residential tenancy to notify any person entitled to relief against forfeiture of whom he is aware.

relief even when the landlord is *not* proceeding to enforce his rights but has enforced them, what was the reason for including in section 146(2) and (4) the limitation that the powers of relief could be exercised only when the landlord is proceeding?'

The House of Lords did not refer to this equitable jurisdiction, since it had reversed the Court of Appeal and held that it had statutory jurisdiction to grant relief.

(5) Decorative repairs

A special rule was introduced by section 147 of the Law of Property Act 1925 for covenants relating to the internal decorative repair of a house. Where a statutory notice has been served by the landlord indicating a breach of such a covenant, the court, after reviewing all the circumstances and in particular the length of the term, may wholly or partially relieve the tenant from liabilities for such repairs. But this power to set a covenant aside is not exercisable when a tenant, having expressly agreed to put the property in a decorative state of repair, has never performed the covenant, nor is it to apply to anything that is necessary for keeping the property in a sanitary condition or in a state that makes it fit for human habitation.

(d) Exceptions to the statutory requirements

The particular subsections of the Act already considered are general in nature and would, without more, apply to every covenant contained in a lease, but there are three covenants for the breach of which a lessor need not serve the statutory notice as a preliminary to enforcing the forfeiture, and in respect of which relief is not grantable. The covenants so excepted are the following.

(1) Covenant to pay rent[523]

(2) Covenant for inspection in mining lease

If a mining tenant, under obligation to pay royalties according to the quantity of minerals mined, breaks the covenant by which he has agreed to give access to his books, accounts, records, weighing machines or other things, or to the mine itself, forfeiture may be enforced without service of the statutory notice and no relief can be granted.[524]

(3) Condition of forfeiture on the bankruptcy of tenant or where lease is taken in execution

It is common to provide in a lease that the premises shall be forfeited to the lessor if the tenant becomes bankrupt[525] or if his interest is taken in execution. There are certain classes of property in which it is vital to the landlord that he should recover his property in either of these events, and where the lease relates to such property the Act provides that the statutory provisions shall be excluded. The following are the leases concerned:[526]

---

[523] LPA 1925, s 146(11); above, pp 279 ff.   [524] Ibid, s 146(8)(ii).
[525] But not if his surety does: *Halliard Property Co Ltd v Jack Segal Ltd* [1978] 1 WLR 377.
[526] LPA 1925, s 146(9).

(a) agricultural or pastoral land,

(b) mines or minerals,

(c) a house used or intended to be used as a public-house or beer shop,

(d) a house let as a dwelling-house, with the use of any furniture, books, works of art, or other chattels not being in the nature of fixtures,

(e) any property with respect to which the personal qualifications of the tenant are of importance[527] for the preservation of the value or character of the property, or on the ground of neighbourhood to the lessor,[528] or to any person holding under him.

In such a lease, then, the lessor can proceed to enforce a forfeiture as soon as the bankruptcy occurs, and the tenant has no claim to relief.

If the demised land is not within one of the classes enumerated above, the extent to which the statutory provisions concerning notice and relief apply depends upon whether the lessee's interest is sold, or is not sold, for the benefit of his creditors within one year from the bankruptcy or taking in execution. The two rules on the matter, which are designed to enable the trustee in bankruptcy to decide whether he will disclaim the lease or use it for the benefit of the creditors, are as follows:[529]

(a) If the interest is sold within the year, the statutory provisions apply without any limit of time. This means, in the case of bankruptcy, that if the trustee in bankruptcy is able to sell the tenant's interest under the lease within the year for the benefit of the creditors, then, despite proceedings for forfeiture, he can apply for relief even after the year has elapsed, and the court may grant the application and confirm the title of the purchaser.

(b) If the interest is not sold within the year, the statutory provisions apply only during that year, ie, although the landlord cannot take steps to regain possession during that period without serving the statutory notice and without the risk of defeat by a successful application for relief, yet, after the year has elapsed, his right to recover the premises is absolute. No notice need be served; no relief can be granted.[530]

In practice, however, leases do not usually contain a proviso for forfeiture on the bankruptcy of the tenant, except in the five cases enumerated above, since it is troublesome for the landlord to be deprived of his rent until a decision has been reached by the trustee, and if he accepts rent falling due after the date of bankruptcy the forfeiture is thereby waived.[531]

---

[527] *Earl Bathurst v Fine* [1974] 1 WLR 905.

[528] *Hockley Engineering Co Ltd v V & P Midlands Ltd* [1993] 1 EGLR 76.

[529] LPA 1925, s 146(10). Any wider equitable jurisdiction is ousted by s 146(10): *Official Custodian for Charities v Parway Estates Developments Ltd* [1985] Ch 151; *Billson v Residential Apartments Ltd* [1992] 1 AC 494, above, p 297.

[530] *Civil Service Co-operative Society v McGrigor's Trustee* [1923] 2 Ch 347, 355; *Horsey Estate Ltd v Steiger* [1899] 2 QB 79; *Gee v Harwood* [1933] Ch 712; affd as *Pearson v Gee and Braceborough Spa Ltd* [1934] AC 272.

[531] *Doe d Gatehouse v Rees* (1838) 4 Bing NC 384.

(e) Law reform

In recent years there have been several proposals to reform the law of forfeiture, none of which has yet been implemented.[532]

In 1985 the Law Commission[533] said that the law of forfeiture was 'complex and confused; its many features fit together awkwardly; and it contains a number of uncertainties, anomalies and injustices'. It identified two major defects.

First,[534] the doctrine of re-entry under which a landlord forfeits a tenancy by re-entry upon the property let, and the tenancy terminates on the date on which re-entry takes place. As a result, the obligations that the tenancy imposes upon the tenant terminate also at that time. So, although the tenant may remain in possession for several months afterwards, he is not obliged to pay rent or to perform any of his other covenants unless he is granted relief, in which case the tenancy is taken never to have ended at all, and his liability revives retrospectively.

Secondly,[535] in relation to relief against forfeiture, there are two almost entirely separate regimes, one for cases involving non-payment of rent and the other for all other cases. There are also uncertainties, including the fact that the courts' ancient equitable jurisdiction to grant relief exists, though to an extent not altogether certain, side by side with their statutory powers.

The Law Commission's Report in 1985 recommended that the present law of forfeiture, both statutory and non-statutory, be swept away, and with it the doctrine of re-entry, to be replaced by a scheme under which there would be no distinction between termination for non-payment of rent and termination for other reasons, and under which the tenancy would continue in force until the date on which the court orders that it should terminate. The court would have power to make a *termination order* that could be applied for only on the occasion of a *termination order event*: (a) breach of covenant by the tenant; or (b) disguised breach of covenant (that is, broadly, a breach by the tenant of an obligation imposed on him otherwise than by covenant); or (c) insolvency of the tenant. The order may be either *absolute* (to terminate the tenancy unconditionally on a date specified) or *remedial* (to terminate the tenancy on a date specified unless the tenant takes remedial action by that time). In both cases the court may grant or refuse to grant the order according to a discretion exercisable within guidelines.[536] Finally, the tenant would be given a new right to terminate the tenancy in cases of default on the part of the landlord.[537] The right is analogous to the landlord's right to terminate, and the tenant exercising this right is given a right to claim damages from the landlord for the loss of his tenancy.[538]

Subsequent proposals for reform have built upon the 1985 Report. In 1994 the Law Commission published a further Report, which was in effect a republication

---

[532] For a general overview, see Law Commission CP No 174, *Termination of Tenancies for Tenant Default* (2004), paras 1.16 ff.

[533] Law Com No 142, *Forfeiture of Tenancies* (1985), para 3.2; [1986] Conv 165 (PF Smith); [1987] LSG 1042 (J Cherryman).

[534] Ibid, paras 3.3–3.10.   [535] Ibid, paras 3.11–3.13, 3.16.   [536] Ibid, paras 3.25–3.71.

[537] Termination is now possible at common law: *Hussein v Mehlman* [1992] 2 EGLR 87, below, p 339.

[538] Law Com No 142, paras 3.72–3.93.

of the 1985 Report,[539] together with minor amendments and a draft Termination of Tenancies Bill. This was however limited to the *landlord's* termination order scheme; the Law Commission found that there was no consensus on its proposals for a tenant's termination order scheme and therefore shelved that part of the 1985 proposals in order to facilitate the implementation of the other elements of the proposals.[540] However they were still not implemented. After further consideration and discussion with Government departments and property professionals, in 1998 the Law Commission published a consultative document[541] in which it provisionally concluded that, although the common law doctrine of re-entry should be abolished, there should be a new statutory right of re-entry so that, in appropriate cases, the landlord would be able to terminate a tenancy by physical re-entry without the need for court proceedings. This proposal stemmed from the view that the landlord's ability to determine a tenancy in appropriate circumstances without recourse to the courts is an effective management tool, and fears that its abolition might have an adverse effect on the commercial property sector and on the availability of rented property.[542] Although the Law Commission's consultation exercise led it to conclude that this proposal should be finalised and implemented, there was further delay. Finally, a new Consultation Paper[543] was published in 2004, which again made proposals for the abolition of the remedy of forfeiture, building on the original 1985 Report but with modifications to take into account significant developments since the earlier proposals.[544]

The final Report was published in 2006,[545] and recommends the replacement of the current law of forfeiture with a statutory scheme under which a landlord may terminate a tenancy on the sole ground of *tenant default*—broadly defined to include the breach of any of the tenant's express or implied covenants under the lease (including breach by a former tenant, or breach by a guarantor of the tenant's obligations) unless the parties agreed to exclude the covenant from the operation of the termination scheme. No right of re-entry need be expressly reserved in a lease, but the landlord must normally, at the time the tenancy begins, give the tenant an explanatory statement about the landlord's right to terminate the lease. The termination action may be taken by making a *termination claim* through the

---

[539] Law Com No 221, *Termination of Tenancies Bill* (1994). Appendix C contains an updated summary of the law of forfeiture and its defects.

[540] Ibid, para 1.13: 'reforms to cure the evident defects in the law of forfeiture should take precedence over implementing proposals for innovation, for which there has been no great support ... It would not be helpful for the landlords' termination order scheme to be unnecessarily embroiled in controversy'.

[541] *Termination of Tenancies by Physical Re-entry*; (1998) 2 L & TR 24 (M Pawlowski); Law Com No 250, *Thirty-Second Annual Report 1997* (1998), paras 5.3–5.5; Law Com No 258, *Thirty-Third Annual Report 1998* (1999), paras 5.5–5.6.

[542] Law Com No 250, above, para 5.3.

[543] CP No 174, *Termination of Tenancies for Tenant Default*; (2004) 154 NLJ 113 (S Bridge); (2004) 8 L & T Rev 32, 119 (M Pawlowski).

[544] In particular, the new Civil Procedure Rules and the Human Rights Act 1998: ibid, paras 1.31–1.32. The Law Commission began again with a Consultation Paper, because of the lack of consultation responses by participants and advisers currently involved in the property industry, given the length of time since the original consultation: ibid, para 1.30.

[545] Law Com No 303, *Termination of Tenancies for Tenant Default*; (2007) 157 NLJ 54 (S Bridge); (2007) 11 L & T Rev 140 (J Bignell), 145 (S Bridge).

courts or—except in certain defined circumstances[546]—a *summary termination procedure* may be used, which may result in termination of the tenancy without any reference to the courts. But the landlord must in all cases first issue a written *tenant default notice* in a prescribed form to the tenant and others with qualifying interests in the property (such as sub-tenants and chargees) particularising the default, and specifying any remedial action that may be required (including compensation), and the period within which the landlord may take termination action on the ground of the default. The orders available to the court are a termination order (terminating the tenancy together with any interest derived from it), a remedial order (requiring the tenant to take specified action to remedy the tenant default), an order for sale of the tenant's interest in the demised premises and (where two or more persons constitute the tenant or hold a qualifying interest) a joint tenancy adjustment order. Two further orders (a transfer order and a new tenancy order) can only be made on the application of a holder of a qualifying interest. Where the summary termination procedure applies, the tenancy (and any interests derived from it) automatically terminates one month after the landlord's summary termination notice was served, but the tenant may apply to court to challenge the termination during that period (and has a further six months after the termination to make a further challenge).

The Law Commission has said:[547]

> The scheme is designed to encourage the negotiated settlement of disputes at an early stage. Where differences are irreconcilable, the scheme offers a court-based procedure, building on the Civil Procedure Rules' central principles of advancing the interests of justice and the efficient use of court resources. The scheme addresses the interests of relevant third parties (notably those with mortgages over the property) by requiring that they are served with notice of the dispute and by entitling them to intervene. The scheme makes available a wide range of orders, including a new type of order that the tenancy be sold and the proceeds distributed. An expeditious extra-judicial procedure is provided for landlords in cases where a tenant would have no defence to a court action (for example, because he or she has abandoned the premises).

The Government has not yet indicated whether it will accept the report, but is undertaking work to study and consider it, and aims to respond early in 2011.[548]

III THE EFFECT OF ASSIGNMENT ON COVENANTS[549]

A covenant in a lease is prima facie a contract binding only on the landlord and the tenant—the actual contracting parties. Within the law of contract a general exception

---

[546] Not (inter alia) where anyone is lawfully residing in the premises, or the unexpired term of the tenancy exceeds 25 years, or the default is the breach of a repairing covenant in a tenancy of seven years or more (and the unexpired term of the tenancy is three years or more).

[547] Law Com No 306, *Annual Report 2006-07*, para 3.47.

[548] Report of the Lord Chancellor to Parliament on the implementation of Law Commission Proposals (2011), para 24. The response had not yet been published at the end of May 2011.

[549] Holdsworth, *A History of English Law*, vol vii, pp 287–92; Fancourt, *Enforceability of Landlord and Tenant Covenants* (2nd edn, 2006).

to this doctrine of privity of contract was made only as late as 1999.[550] But at an early stage it was seen that to enforce privity of contract was highly undesirable in the case of leases, since both parties had transmissible interests the value of which depended largely upon the obligations that each had assumed. Thus mediaeval land law, although it never lost sight of the general principle that a stranger to a contract cannot sue or be sued upon it, did recognise that covenants contained in a lease might have a wider operation than ordinary contracts. As Holdsworth remarked, 'they were regarded in a sense as being annexed to an estate in the land, so that they could be enforced by anyone who took that estate in the land.' [551]

Our question here is in what circumstances persons other than the original landlord and tenant can sue or be sued upon the covenants.[552] Two events may occur—an assignment of the term by the tenant and an assignment of the reversion by the landlord.[553] In each case the question is whether the benefit and burden of the covenants pass to the assignee. In short, do the covenants run with the land and with the reversion? Four cases, therefore, fall to be considered:

(1) The tenant assigns his interest to A. Can A enforce the covenants inserted in the lease in favour of the original tenant? *Does the benefit of these covenants run with the land?*

(2) The tenant assigns his interest to A. Can A be sued on the covenants inserted in the lease in favour of the landlord? *Does the burden of the covenants entered into by the original tenant run with the land?*

(3) The landlord assigns his interest, that is the reversion, to Z. Can Z enforce the covenants inserted in the lease in favour of the original landlord? *Does the benefit of the covenants run with the reversion?*

(4) The landlord assigns his reversion to Z. Can Z be sued upon the covenants inserted in the lease in favour of the tenant? *Does the burden of the original landlord's covenants run with the reversion?*

We must first notice that the Landlord and Tenant (Covenants) Act 1995 radically changed the law.[554] It is not retrospective,[555] but provides a new statutory code for covenants in leases granted after 1995. The existing law, which is an amalgam of rules laid down by common law and statute, continues in force where the lease was granted before 1996. The effect therefore is that we now have two separate sets of rules for the

---

[550] Contracts (Rights of Third Parties) Act 1999, below p 743; Law Com No 242, *Privity of Contract: Contracts for the Benefit of Third Parties* (1996); Anson, ch 21.

[551] Holdsworth, *A History of English Law*, vol iii, p 158.

[552] We are generally concerned here only with the enforceability between landlord (and his successors) and tenant (and his successors). For circumstances in which a covenant can benefit and burden a sub-tenant as against the head landlord, see below, pp 316–17, 323 and 738.

[553] For the meaning of assignment, see below, p 316.

[554] (1996) 59 MLR 78 (M Davey); [1996] CLJ 313 (S Bridge); [1996] Conv 432 (P Walter); (1996) 49 CLP Part I 95 (A Clarke). In *First Penthouse Ltd v Channel Hotels & Properties (UK) Ltd* [2003] EWHC 2713 (Ch), [2004] 1 EGLR 16 at [43] Lightman J said: 'The 1995 Act is the product of rushed drafting, and its provisions create exceptional difficulties.'

[555] Except for ss 17–20 which apply to all leases whenever granted; below, p 319.

enforcement of covenants in leases; and that the existing rules will continue in force for many years to come; for example, covenants in a lease granted in 1990 for 99 or 999 years will attract those rules for decades or even centuries.

A COVENANTS IN LEASES GRANTED BEFORE 1996

(1) Covenants Touching and Concerning the Land

Before dealing with the four cases given above, we must describe what is meant by covenants that *touch and concern the land demised*, for under the law as it applies to leases granted before 1996 it is only these, as distinct from covenants merely affecting the person, that are capable of running either with the land or with the reversion.

From the present point of view all covenants fall into one or other of two classes, being either personal to the contracting parties, or such as touch and concern the land.

The time-honoured[556] expression 'touching and concerning the land' was replaced in the Law of Property Act 1925[557] by the phrase *having reference to the subject-matter of the lease*. This affords a clue to the meaning of what is at first sight a little vague. If the covenant has direct reference to the land, if it lays down something that is to be done or is not to be done upon the land, or—and perhaps this is the clearest way of describing the test—*if it affects the landlord in his normal capacity as landlord or the tenant in his normal capacity as tenant*, it may be said to touch and concern the land. Lord Russell CJ said:[558]

> The true principle is that no covenant or condition that affects merely the person, and that does not affect the nature, quality, or value of the thing demised or the mode of using or enjoying the thing demised, runs with the land.

Bayley J at an earlier date asserted the same principle:[559]

> In order to bind the assignee, the covenant must either affect the land itself during the term, such as those that regard the mode of occupation, or it must be such as per se, and not merely from collateral circumstances, affects the value of the land at the end of the term.

If a simple test is desired for ascertaining into which category a covenant falls, it is suggested that the proper inquiry should be whether the covenant affects either the landlord qua landlord or the tenant qua tenant. A covenant may very well have reference to the land, but, unless it is reasonably incidental to the relation of landlord and tenant, it cannot be said to touch and concern the land so as to be capable of running with it or with the reversion.[560]

---

[556] A 'somewhat archaic expression': *Cardwell v Walker* [2003] EWHC 3117 (Ch), [2004] 2 P & CR 9 at [41] (Neuberger J).

[557] Ss 141, 142.   [558] *Horsey Estate Ltd v Steiger* [1899] 2 QB 79, 89.

[559] *Mayor of Congleton v Pattison* (1808) 10 East 130, 135.

[560] Cited with approval in *Hua Chiao Commercial Bank Ltd v Chiaphua Industries Ltd* [1987] AC 99, 107, M & B p 464 (Lord Oliver of Aylmerton); and in *Breams Property Investment Co Ltd v Stroulger* [1948] 2 KB 1, 7 (Scott LJ). See also formulations of the test by Sir Nicolas Browne-Wilkinson V-C in *Kumar v Dunning* [1989] QB 193, 204; and by Lord Oliver of Aylmerton in *P & A Swift Investments v Combined English Stores Group plc* [1989] AC 632, 642, M & B pp 463–4; and generally [1989] 47 LSG 24, 48 LSG 22 (J Adams and H Williamson).

(a) Examples of covenants touching and concerning the land

Tested by this principle the following covenants have been held to touch and concern the land:

Covenants by the tenant:

to pay rent or taxes;[561]

to repair or leave in repair;[562]

to spend a stated yearly sum on repairs, or in default to pay to the landlord the difference between this sum and the amount actually expended;[563]

to lay dung on the land annually;[564]

to renew tenant's fixtures;[565]

to reside on a farm during the term;[566]

to insure the premises against fire;[567]

by a publican tenant to buy all beer from the landlord;[568]

not to assign or underlet without the landlord's consent;[569]

not to allow a third party, X, to be concerned in the conduct of the business carried on at the demised premises.[570]

Covenants by the landlord:

to renew the lease;[571]

to supply the demised house with good water;[572]

not to build on adjoining land so as to depreciate the amenity of the demised land;[573]

to erect a new building in place of an old one;[574]

to keep a housekeeper to act as servant of the lessee;[575]

not to serve a notice to quit for three years, unless he requires the premises for his own occupation;[576]

---

[561] *Parker v Webb* (1693) 3 Salk 5. Cf a premium payable by instalments: *Hill v Booth* [1930] 1 KB 381. A covenant by a surety guaranteeing the tenant's rent also touches and concerns the land: *Kumar v Dunning*, above.

[562] *Martyn v Clue* (1852) 18 QB 661.

[563] *Moss' Empires Ltd v Olympia (Liverpool) Ltd* [1939] AC 544.

[564] *Sale v Kitchingham* (1713) 10 Mod Rep 158.   [565] *Williams v Earle* (1868) LR 3 QB 739.

[566] *Tatem v Chaplin* (1793) 2 Hy Bl 133.   [567] *Vernon v Smith* (1821) 5 B & Ald 1.

[568] *Clegg v Hands* (1890) 44 Ch D 503; *Caerns Motor Services Ltd v Texaco Ltd* [1994] 1 WLR 1249 (solus agreement to purchase products held to touch and concern).

[569] *Goldstein v Sanders* [1915] 1 Ch 549.

[570] *Lewin v American and Colonial Distributors Ltd* [1945] Ch 225, 236.

[571] *Muller v Trafford* [1901] 1 Ch 54; *Weg Motors Ltd v Hales* [1961] Ch 176; affd [1962] Ch 49.

[572] *Jourdain v Wilson* (1821) 4 B & Ald 266.

[573] *Ricketts v Enfield (Churchwardens)* [1909] 1 Ch 544.

[574] *Easterby v Sampson* (1830) 6 Bing 644.

[575] *Barnes v City of London Real Property Co* [1918] 2 Ch 18.

[576] *Breams Property Investment Co Ltd v Stroulger* [1948] 2 KB 1.

to accept a surrender of the lease.[577]

Covenant by a third party:

to guarantee the tenant's performance of his obligations.[578]

(b) Examples of personal covenants

On the other hand personal, or collateral, covenants do not touch and concern the land, since they have no direct reference to the subject-matter of the lease. The word *collateral*, admittedly ambiguous in this context, indicates a covenant relating to a matter not normally relevant to the relationship of landlord and tenant. For example, a covenant by either party to pay a sum of money to the other is merely collateral,[579] unless it is inextricably bound up with other covenants that touch and concern the land.[580] Thus a covenant by a tenant, in furtherance of his express undertaking to repair, to expend £500 yearly upon repairs, or to pay the landlord the difference between this amount and what is actually expended, is not a bare obligation personal to the contracting parties. It touches and concerns the land, since it is part and parcel of the repairing covenant.[581]

In *Thomas v Hayward*,[582] where the landlord of a public house had covenanted that he would not open another beer or spirit house within half a mile of the demised premises, the question arose whether this covenant could be enforced by an assignee of the tenant. It was held that it could not, because it was collateral in the sense that it did not oblige the landlord to do or to refrain from doing anything on the demised premises. On the other hand a covenant by the tenant of a public house to conduct the business in such a manner as to afford no ground for the suspension of the licence, was held to touch and concern the land, since it concerned the manner in which the covenantor was to use the premises as tenant.[583]

A covenant that entitles the tenant to purchase the fee simple at a given price at any time during the term, affects the parties as vendor and purchaser, not as landlord and tenant. It is collateral to the lease and as such it cannot run as a matter of course

---

[577] *System Floors Ltd v Ruralpride Ltd* [1995] 1 EGLR 48; *Harbour Estates Ltd v HSBC Bank plc* [2004] EWHC 1714 (Ch), [2005] Ch 194 (an unusually framed clause that allowed the first tenant and only a limited group of assigns, if permitted, to break (ie terminate) the lease: benefit passed to assignee with the term under LPA 1925, s 63).

[578] *Kumar v Dunning* [1989] QB 193; [1988] CLJ 180 (C Harpum); approved *P & A Swift Investments v Combined English Stores Group plc* [1989] AC 632, 637 (Lord Templeman: 'A surety for a tenant is a quasi tenant who volunteers to be a substitute or twelfth man for the tenant's team and is subject to the same rules and regulations as the player he replaces. A covenant that runs with the reversion against the tenant runs with the reversion against the surety'); *Milverton Group Ltd v Warner World Ltd* [1995] 2 EGLR 28, 31. See also *Coronation Street Industrial Properties Ltd v Ingall Industries plc* [1989] 1 WLR 304 (covenant by surety of tenant to accept new lease replacing lease granted to tenant, where that lease was disclaimed by liquidator on tenant's insolvency, held to touch and concern).

[579] *Re Hunter's Lease* [1942] Ch 124. The tenant's covenant to pay rent of course touches and concerns the land: above.

[580] *Moss' Empires Ltd v Olympia (Liverpool) Ltd*, above; *Boyer v Warbey* [1953] 1 QB 234.

[581] Ibid.   [582] (1869) LR 4 Exch 311.

[583] *Fleetwood v Hull* (1889) 23 QBD 35.

with the land or with the reversion as being one that touches and concerns the land.[584] Nevertheless, if it does not infringe the rule against perpetuities,[585] its effect is to confer upon the tenant an equitable interest in the land[586] that, like any other piece of property, is freely assignable unless the terms of its grant show that it is personal to him. Therefore, the option will pass on an assignment of the demised land and will be enforceable by an assignee of the tenant against the landlord; and if protected by registration or as an overriding interest[587] it will be enforceable against an assignee of the reversion.[588]

It has also been held that a covenant by the tenant to pay to the landlord a substantial security deposit on the terms that it would be repayable at the end of the lease if there was no breach of the tenant's covenants did not touch and concern the land.[589] The obligation was entered into with the landlord as payee rather than as landlord.[590]

Finally, a covenant may be personal to one party but not to the other, for example, the benefit of a term expressed to be personal to an original tenant may nevertheless bind an assignee of the reversion.[591]

(2) Running of Covenants at Common Law and by Statute

We can now take up the four cases indicated above and determine in what circumstances the covenant will run in each case. The rules depend partly upon the common law as enunciated in 1583 in *Spencer's Case*[592] and partly upon statutes. The statutes that formerly regulated the matter were the Grantees of Reversions Act, passed in 1540[593] after the dissolution of the monasteries, and the Conveyancing Act 1881,[594] but these were both repealed and replaced by the Law of Property Act 1925.[595]

(a) Benefit of covenant given to original tenant runs with land

The tenant assigns his interest to A. Can A enforce the covenants that were inserted in the lease in favour of the original tenant? The rule even at common law is that the benefit of the covenants runs with the land, enabling an assignee (A) from the tenant to sue the landlord on any covenants that touch and concern the land demised and that enure for the benefit of the tenant, such as a covenant by the landlord to supply the demised

---

[584] A right of pre-emption over adjoining land is also collateral: *Collison v Lettsom* (1815) 6 Taunt 224; *Charles Frodsham & Co Ltd v Morris* (1972) 229 EG 961.

[585] Above, pp 574 (PAA 1964), 577 (PAA 2009, for instruments taking effect after 5 April 2010).

[586] *London and South Western Rly Co v Gomm* (1882) 20 Ch D 562; below, p 984.

[587] In registered land, by notice on the register or by discoverable actual occupation: below, pp 1097 ff; in unregistered land, by registration as an estate contract: below, p 1054.

[588] *Griffith v Pelton* [1958] Ch 205, explaining *Woodall v Clifton* [1905] 2 Ch 257; *Re Button's Lease* [1964] Ch 263. See generally (1958) 74 LQR 242 (WJ Mowbray).

[589] *Hua Chiao Commercial Bank Ltd v Chiaphua Industries Ltd* [1987] AC 99, M & B p 464.

[590] Ibid, 107 (Lord Oliver of Aylmerton).

[591] *System Floors Ltd v Ruralpride Ltd* [1995] 1 EGLR 48.

[592] (1583) 5 Co Rep 16a, M & B p 465.　　　　　　　[593] 32 Hen 8, c 34, s 1.

[594] Ss 10, 11.　　　　　　　[595] Ss 141, 142.

premises with pure water. The authority for this rule is *Spencer's Case*, in the fourth resolution of which the court, dealing with a covenant for quiet enjoyment, said:

> for the lessee and his assignee hath the yearly profits of the land, which shall grow by his labour and industry for an annual rent; and therefore it is reasonable when he hath applied his labour and employed his cost upon the land, and be evicted (whereby he loses all), that he shall take such benefit of the demise and grant, as the first lessee might . . .

(b) Burden of covenant given by original tenant runs with land

The tenant assigns his interest to A. Can A be sued upon the covenants that were inserted in the lease in favour of the landlord? The common law answers this also in the affirmative, provided that the covenant touches and concerns the land, for it was said in *Spencer's Case* that:

> When the covenant extends to a thing *in esse*, parcel of the demise, the thing to be done by force of the covenant is *quodammodo* annexed and appurtenant to the thing demised, and shall go with the land and shall bind the assignee, although he be not bound by express words.

It is true that the judgment drew a distinction between a covenant that referred to something '*in esse*', already in existence (such as to repair an existing wall), and one that related to a thing not in existence at the time of the lease (such as a covenant to build a new wall), and laid down that though the former would bind assignees in all cases, the latter would not do so unless the original tenant had covenanted for himself *and his assigns*.

This distinction rested upon no solid basis but, though adversely criticised,[596] it remained law until 1926. It was abolished by section 79 of the Law of Property Act 1925, which provides that:

(1) A covenant relating to any land of a covenantor or capable of being bound by him, shall, unless a contrary intention is expressed,[597] be deemed to be made by the covenantor on behalf of himself his successors in title and the persons deriving title under him or them, and, subject as aforesaid, shall have effect as if such successors and other persons were expressed.

This subsection extends to a covenant to do some act relating to the land, notwithstanding that the subject-matter may not be in existence when the covenant is made.

(2) For the purposes of this section in connexion with covenants restrictive of the user of land 'successors in title' shall be deemed to include the owners and occupiers for the time being of such land.

This section, however, applies only to covenants made on or after 1 January 1926.[598] In the case of a lease executed before 1926, the burden of a covenant relating to

---

[596] *Minshull v Oakes* (1858) 2 H & N 793. See Behan, *The Use of Land as Affected by Covenants* (1924), pp 75 ff.

[597] Ie unless an indication to the contrary is found in the instrument, and this may be expressed or implied: *Re Royal Victoria Pavilion, Ramsgate* [1961] Ch 581, 589, M & B p 762.

[598] S 79 does not, however, apply to covenants in leases granted after 1995: LT(C)A 1995, s 30(4)(a); below, pp 321 ff.

something not in existence will not run with the land unless it was expressly imposed upon the tenant *and his assigns.*

(c) Benefit of covenant given to original landlord runs with reversion

The landlord assigns his interest, that is the reversion, to Z. Can Z enforce the covenants that were inserted in the lease in favour of the original landlord? The rule at common law is that the grantee of a reversion can sue upon an implied covenant, that is one that automatically results from the relationship of landlord and tenant (such as a covenant to pay rent), but he cannot sue upon express covenants contained in the lease.[599] The difficulty is said to be that in the case of a reversion there is no corporeal thing to which the covenant can be regarded as annexed, such as there is where the land is assigned.[600]

A mitigation of this strict rule of the common law became urgent when the monasteries were dissolved by Henry VIII in 1539, because, if the law had not been altered, it would have precluded the grantees of the monastic lands from enforcing against existing tenants the express covenants in leases granted by the monasteries before their dissolution. Hence the Grantees of Reversions Act 1540, which, though designed merely to accommodate grantees of monastic lands, soon came to be regarded as having universal application and as laying down the law for assignees of reversions in general. This statute, which remained the only law on the subject until the Conveyancing Act 1881,[601] enacted that assignees of reversions should have the same right of enforcing forfeitures, and the same right of suing for a breach of any covenant, as the original lessors.

Both these statutes have been repealed, and the right of an assignee of a reversion to enforce the covenants now rests upon section 141 of the Law of Property Act 1925, which, in a section that applies to all leases whether made before or after the Act[602] provides that:

(1) Rent reserved by a lease, and the benefit of every covenant or provision therein contained, having reference to the subject-matter thereof,[603] and on the lessee's part to be observed or performed, and every condition of re-entry and other condition therein contained, shall be annexed and incident to and shall go with the reversionary estate in the land, or in any part thereof, immediately expectant on the term granted by the lease, notwithstanding severance of that reversionary estate, and without prejudice to any liability affecting a covenantor or his estate.[604]

(2) Any such rent, covenant or provision shall be capable of being recovered, received, enforced and taken advantage of, by the person from time to time entitled, subject to the term, to the income of the whole or any part, as the case may require, of the land leased.

(3) Where that person becomes entitled by conveyance or otherwise, such rent, covenant or provision may be recovered, received, enforced or taken advantage of by him

---

[599] Platt, *A Practical Treatise on the Law of Covenants* (1829), p 531; *Wedd v Porter* [1916] 2 KB 91, 100–1.

[600] Eg *Smith's Leading Cases* (13th edn), vol i, pp 61–2.

[601] S 10.

[602] S 141 does not, however, apply to covenants in leases granted after 1995: LT(C)A 1995, s 30(4)(b); below, pp 321 ff.

[603] Ie, touching and concerning the land demised: above, p 304.

[604] *London and County (A & D) Ltd v Wilfred Sportsman Ltd* [1971] Ch 764, M & B p 469.

notwithstanding that he becomes so entitled after the condition of re-entry or forfeiture has become enforceable, but this subsection does not render enforceable any condition of re-entry or other condition waived or released before such person becomes entitled as aforesaid.

(1) Form of lease

One result of this enactment, which provides, repeating the Conveyancing Act 1881, that 'rent reserved by a lease,[605] and the benefit of every covenant or provision therein contained' shall pass with the reversion, is to abolish the old construction that was put upon the Grantees of Reversions Act 1540, to the effect that the assignee of a reversion could not sue upon the covenants unless the original lease was under seal, and replace it with the rule that the assignee can sue if the lease is in writing or if the tenancy is the result of a written agreement for a lease.[606] The same is the case if a parol lease is made for a period not exceeding three years[607] or where the assignment is effective only to transfer the title to the landlord in equity.[608]

(2) Breach of covenant committed before assignment

The Court of Appeal has held that, under this section of the Act, the assignee of the reversion is the only person entitled to sue the tenant for any breach of covenant, whether of a continuous nature or not and even though committed before the date of the assignment:[609]

> The expression 'go with' must be intended to add something to the concept involved in the expression 'annexed and incident to' and in my view connotes the transfer of the right to enforce the covenant from the assignor to the assignee with the consequent cessation of the right of the assignor to enforce the covenant against the tenant.

So, where arrears of rent have accrued before the landlord has assigned his reversion, it is the assignee who is entitled to sue for them; he may, however, assign his right to collect those arrears to his predecessor and still retain his right to forfeit the lease for non-payment of rent.[610]

(d) Burden of covenant given by original landlord runs with reversion

The landlord assigns his reversion to Z. Can Z be sued upon the covenants that were inserted in the lease in favour of the tenant? There was no right of action against Z at common law, but the Grantees of Reversions Act 1540 enacted that a lessee and

---

[605] 'Lease' includes 'an under-lease or other tenancy': s 154.

[606] *Rickett v Green* [1910] 1 KB 253, M & B p 480; *Rye v Purcell* [1926] 1 KB 446; *Boyer v Warbey* [1953] 1 QB 234, M & B p 481; [1978] 37 CLJ 98 (RJ Smith).

[607] See M & B pp 476–82; Smith, *Property Law* (6th edn, 2009), pp 441–3.

[608] *Scribes West Ltd v Relsa Anstalt (No 3)* [2004] EWCA Civ 1744, [2005] 1 WLR 1847 (transfer of legal title, not yet registered).

[609] *Re King* [1963] Ch 459, 497 (Diplock LJ), M & B p 467 (covenant to repair and reinstate); *London and County (A & D) Ltd v Wilfred Sportsman Ltd* [1971] Ch 764, M & B p 469 (covenant to pay rent); *Arlesford Trading Co Ltd v Servansingh* [1971] 1 WLR 1080; *Electricity Supply Nominees Ltd v Thorn EMI Retail Ltd* [1991] 2 EGLR 46.

[610] *Kataria v Safeland plc* [1998] 1 EGLR 39. For post-1995 tenancies under LT(C)A 1995, see s 3(3), where the position is the same.

his assigns should have the same remedy against the assignees of the lessor as the original lessee would have had against the lessor. This enactment was attended by certain difficulties, which are no longer of interest since they were removed by the Conveyancing Act 1881[611] in a section now replaced by section 142(1) of the Law of Property Act 1925, and applicable to all leases whenever made:[612]

> The obligation under a condition or of a covenant entered into by a lessor[613] with reference to the subject-matter of the lease shall, if and as far as the lessor has power to bind the reversionary estate immediately expectant on the term granted by the lease, be annexed and incident to and shall go with that reversionary estate, or the several parts thereof, notwithstanding severance of that reversionary estate, and may be taken advantage of and enforced by the person in whom the term is from time to time vested by conveyance, devolution in law, or otherwise; and, if and as far as the lessor has power to bind the person from time to time entitled to that reversionary estate, the obligation aforesaid may be taken advantage of and enforced against any person so entitled.

The word 'covenant' as used in this section is not confined to its strict meaning of a contract under seal, but includes any promise touching and concerning the land[614] that is contained in a tenancy agreement made otherwise than by deed.[615]

(1) Breach of covenant committed before assignment

Section 142 differs in one respect from its counterpart, section 141. It does not contain subsections corresponding to subsections (2) and (3) of section 141. As a result of the omission, it has been held that, although a tenant can sue the assignee of the reversion for breach of a repairing covenant that occurred before the assignment, because the property is still in disrepair, he cannot sue him for consequential damages flowing from the breach.[616]

(2) Severance of reversion

One particular difficulty that arose under the Grantees of Reversions Act was that, owing to its indivisible nature, a condition could not be enforced by an assignee of *part* of the reversion. If the reversion was severed, the condition could not be apportioned. The statutory rule now, however, is that, where such a severance has taken place, every condition contained in the lease is apportioned and remains annexed to the severed parts of the reversion.[617] The tenancy itself, however, is not severed, with the result

---

[611] S 11.

[612] S 142 does not, however, apply to covenants in leases granted after 1995: LT(C)A 1995, s 30(4)(b); below, pp 321 ff.

[613] The obligation may be expressed in a side letter: *System Floors Ltd v Ruralpride Ltd* [1995] 1 EGLR 48; *Lotteryking Ltd v AMEC Properties Ltd* [1995] 2 EGLR 13; cf s 141, where the covenant must be contained in the lease: *Weg Motors Ltd v Hales* [1962] Ch 49, 73.

[614] *Davis v Town Properties Investment Corp Ltd* [1903] 1 Ch 797.

[615] *Weg Motors Ltd v Hales* [1962] Ch 49.

[616] *Duncliffe v Caerfelin Properties Investment Corp Ltd* [1989] 2 EGLR 38; [1990] Conv 127 (JE Martin). For another difference between the sections, see *City and Metropolitan Properties Ltd v Greycroft Ltd* [1987] 1 WLR 1085, below, p 315.

[617] LPA 1925, s 140(1); replacing LP(A)A 1859, s 3, and Conveyancing Act 1881, s 12.

that there is still a single tenancy, even though the reversion has been severed.[618] If the owner of a severed part of the reversion determines the tenancy by a notice to quit,[619] the tenant is permitted within one month to determine the whole tenancy by serving notice on the owner in whom the rest of the reversion is vested.[620]

(3) Essentials of Enforceability

Two points of considerable importance should be noted on the subject of covenants that run with the land or the reversion in leases granted before 1996.

(a) Privity of contract or estate

First, the enforcement of covenants between two parties depends upon the existence between them of either privity of contract or privity of estate.

We have seen[621] that a lease is a contract, as well as an interest in property. *Privity of contract* denotes the relationship that exists between the landlord and the tenant by virtue of the contract, and under it each party[622] is entitled by the law of contract to enforce those covenants contained in the contract of which he has the benefit, and bound by those covenants of which he has the contractual burden. This relationship continues to subsist between the landlord and tenant despite an assignment of their respective property interests in the lease.[623] The covenants in a contract for a lease, which is not completed by the grant of a lease, will similarly be enforceable between the parties under the general law of contract.

Privity of estate describes the relationship between two parties who respectively hold the same legal estates as those created by the lease. This is the position where one holds the original reversion and the other the original term, or rather, the whole of what is left of the original term. Thus there is privity of estate between the landlord and an assignee from the tenant of the residue of the term; also between the tenant and an assignee of the reversion; also between an assignee of the reversion and an assignee of the residue of the term. In the absence of assignment, therefore, there is privity both of contract and of estate between the original landlord and tenant.[624]

---

[618] LPA 1925, s 140(2). The severance must be genuine, and not, eg, where the landlord conveys part of the reversion to bare trustees for himself: *Persey v Bazley* (1983) 47 P & CR 37.

[619] See, eg, *Smith v Kinsey* [1936] 3 All ER 73.

[620] *Jelley v Buckman* [1974] QB 488; *Nevill Long & Co (Boards) Ltd v Firmenich & Co* (1983) 47 P & CR 59.

[621] Above, pp 182 ff.

[622] In relation to the leases we are here considering (leases granted before 1996), only the parties themselves acquired original contractual rights; cf Contracts (Rights of Third Parties) Act 1999, under which the benefit of a term in a contract (including a lease) may now in certain circumstances be enforced by a person who is not a party to it: below, p 743.

[623] The benefit of contractual rights may be assigned at law under LPA 1925, s 136, but then the assignor will lose the right to enforce them. The burden of contractual rights cannot be assigned, but can be novated. See generally Anson, ch 21.

[624] *Bickford v Parson* (1848) 5 CB 920, 929. See also Platt, *A Treatise on the Law of Leases* (1847), vol ii, p 351: 'Privity of estate is the result of tenure; it subsists by virtue of the relation of landlord and tenant, and follows alike the devolution of the reversion, and of the term'; *City of London Corp v Fell* [1994] 1 AC 458, 464, M & B p 471.

There is privity of estate only between the parties holding the *legal* estates created by the original lease. There is therefore no privity between persons who have entered into a contract for a lease[625] or between their assigns;[626] nor between the landlord and one who has only contracted to take an assignment from a tenant.[627] Such situations therefore raise certain difficulties in relation to the enforcement of covenants. Since the benefit of a covenant can be assigned at law, the courts had little difficulty in holding that the benefit of a covenant in a contract for a lease could pass to the assignee of the reversion;[628] and it appears that the benefit will also run by virtue of Law of Property Act 1925, section 141, which has been interpreted as applying to contracts for a lease as well as to leases.[629] Similarly, the benefit of the landlord's covenant is capable of assignment with the assignment of the benefit of the contract for a lease; and it appears that the burden of the landlord's covenant in a contract for a lease should pass to the assignee of the reversion under Law of Property Act 1925, section 142.[630] However, it has been held that the burden of covenants in an equitable lease does not run with the land,[631] although there are later dicta to the effect that the rules relating to the running of covenants in leases should be the same, whether the lease that has been assigned is legal or equitable.[632] Whatever the proper legal analysis of this proposition,[633] it is submitted that the better view is that the court should hold that the assignee of an equitable lease, and that the equitable assignee of a legal lease, should be both bound by and able to enforce the covenants.[634]

We shall see that there are no such problems in relation to covenants in equitable leases granted after 1995, since the Landlord and Tenant (Covenants) Act 1995 treats equitable leases and equitable assignments in the same way as their legal counterparts.[635]

(1) Original tenant always liable to original landlord

There are certain important rules that flow from this general principle. Thus:

---

[625] Which can take effect as an equitable lease under the doctrine of *Walsh v Lonsdale* (1882) 21 Ch D 9, above, p 215.

[626] *Purchase v Lichfield Brewery Co* [1915] 1 KB 184, M & B p 480.

[627] An equitable assignment; *Cox v Bishop* (1857) 8 De GM & G 815, M & B p 480; *Friary, Holroyd, and Healey's Breweries Ltd v Singleton* [1899] 1 Ch 86.

[628] *Manchester Brewery Co v Coombs* [1901] 2 Ch 608, M & B p 478, applying the doctrine of *Walsh v Lonsdale* (1882) 21 Ch D 9, above, p 215.

[629] Above, p 310.

[630] Above, p 311: both ss 141 and 142 refer to a 'lease', which is defined in LPA 1925, s 154, as including 'an under-lease or other tenancy'.

[631] *Purchase v Lichfield Brewery Co*, above, which was a case, however, of assignment by mortgage.

[632] *Boyer v Warbey* [1953] 1 QB 234, 246 (Denning LJ), M & B p 481.

[633] The 'fusion of law and equity': Denning LJ in *Boyer v Warbey*, above; or, more particularly, an application of the doctrine of *Walsh v Lonsdale*: *Manchester Brewery Co v Coombs*, above; *Industrial Properties (Barton Hill) Ltd v Associated Electrical Industries Ltd* [1977] QB 580; Smith, *Property Law*, pp 441–2; [1978] CLJ 98 (RJ Smith).

[634] The technical case for extending this to the equitable assignee of the legal lease is more problematic than the case of the equitable lease: Smith, *Property Law*, pp 442–3.

[635] S 28(1); below, p 321.

It is perfectly settled by a multitude of decisions that, notwithstanding an assignment of his lease, the lessee continues liable on the personal privity of the contract to the payment of the rent and the performance of the covenants during the whole term; although the lessor concur in the assignment, or, by acceptance of rent or otherwise, recognise the assignee as his tenant.[636]

This continuing liability of the original tenant for all breaches of covenant throughout the duration of the lease, even after he has assigned it, is a hazard for the tenant.[637] Several cases have highlighted this, and in one of them:[638]

> a warehouse was let for 21 years at a rent of £17,000 a year, subject to a rent review at the end of 14 years. The original tenant assigned the lease and in the following year the landlord and the assignee agreed a revised rent of £40,000 a year. When the assignee failed to pay the rent for two quarters, the tenant was held liable to pay the £20,000 then outstanding.

Harman J said:[639]

---

[636] Platt, *A Treatise on the Law of Leases* (1847), vol ii, pp 352–3; *Warnford Investments Ltd v Duckworth* [1979] Ch 127, 137. Distinguish, however, the liability of a lessee who acquires a statutory term of 2,000 years under the provisions for converting perpetually renewable leases; above, p 198.

[637] The original tenant is released if the landlord unconditionally releases the assignee by accord and satisfaction: *Deanplan Ltd v Mahmoud* [1993] Ch 151; (1993) 143 NLJ 28 (HW Wilkinson); cf *Sun Life Assurance Society plc v Tantofex (Engineers) Ltd* [1999] 2 EGLR 135; *City of London Corp v Fell* [1994] 1 AC 458 (where lease, assigned by original lessee, had run its term and had been extended under Landlord and Tenant Act 1954, original lessee's obligations held to cease on completion of term); [1994] CLJ 28 (S Bridge); [1994] Conv 247 (M Haley); cf *Herbert Duncan Ltd v Cluttons* [1993] QB 589; [1993] Conv 164 (PF Smith). See also *Norwich Union Life Insurance Society v Low Profile Fashions Ltd* [1992] 1 EGLR 86; [1992] CLJ 425 (S Bridge) (no duty of care on landlord to ensure solvency of assignee when consenting to assignment, and no equitable principle that obliges landlord to sue assigns and his surety before original tenant); *Becton Dickinson UK Ltd v Zwebner* [1989] QB 208, 217 (original tenant entitled to be indemnified by solvent guarantor of later assignee). *Re A Debtor (No 21 of 1995)* [1995] NPC 170. Other defences available are fraught with difficulty:
(a) surrender and regrant: *Jenkin R Lewis Ltd v Kerman* [1971] Ch 477; [1995] Conv 124 (A Dowling); *Friends' Provident Life Office v British Railways Board* [1995] 2 EGLR 55;
(b) release by accord and satisfaction: *Deanplan Ltd v Mahmoud* [1993] Ch 151; [1993] 143 NLJ 23 (HW Wilkinson); *Allied London Investments Ltd v Hambro Life Assurance Ltd* [1984] 1 EGLR 16; *Mytre Investments Ltd v Reynolds* [1995] 3 All ER 588; *March Estates plc v Gunmark Ltd* [1996] 2 EGLR 38;
(c) disclaimer by liquidator or trustee in bankruptcy: *Hindcastle Ltd v Barbara Attenborough Associates Ltd* [1997] AC 70; [1997] Conv 24 (T Taylor); *Scottish Widows plc v Tripipatkul* [2003] EWHC 1874 (Ch), [2004] 1 P & CR 29. See generally [1996] CLJ 313 at 319 (S Bridge); *Groveholt Ltd v Hughes* [2005] EWCA Civ 897, [2005] 2 BCLC 421.

[638] *Centrovincial Estates plc v Bulk Storage Ltd* (1983) 46 P & CR 393; [1984] Conv 443 (P McLoughlin). The other cases are *Allied London Investments Ltd v Hambro Life Assurance Ltd* [1985] 1 EGLR 45; *Selous Street Properties Ltd v Oranel Fabrics Ltd* (1984) 270 EG 643 (tenant liable for rent increase under review clause where landlord permitted improvements otherwise forbidden by terms of original lease); *Thames Manufacturing Co Ltd v Perrotts (Nichol & Peyton) Ltd* (1984) 50 P & CR 1; *GUS Property Management Ltd v Texas Homecare Ltd* [1993] 2 EGLR 63.

For the continuing liability of a surety for the original lessee, see *P & A Swift Investments v Combined English Stores Group plc* [1989] AC 632; *Becton Dickinson UK Ltd v Zwebner* [1989] QB 208; *Johnsey Estates Ltd v Webb* [1990] 1 EGLR 80. For his liability to an assignee of the lessee, see *Cerium Investments Ltd v Evans* [1991] 1 EGLR 80. And for release of a surety by variation, see *Metropolitan Properties Co (Regis) Ltd v Bartholomew* [1996] 1 EGLR 82; *Howard de Walden Estates Ltd v Pasta Place Ltd* [1995] 1 EGLR 79.

[639] Ibid, 396; Jackson and Wilde, *Reform of Property Law* (1997), p 73 (S Bright); *Beegas Nominees Ltd v BHP Petroleum Ltd* [1998] 2 EGLR 57; *Metropolitan Properties Co (Regis) Ltd v Bartholomew*, above.

Each assignee is the owner of the whole estate and can deal with it so as to alter it or its terms. The estate as so altered then binds the original tenant, because the assignee has been put into the shoes of the original tenant and can do all such acts as the original tenant could have done.

In *Friends' Provident Life Office v British Railways Board*,[640] however, the Court of Appeal rejected this approach and held that:

If the contract in the original lease itself provides for some variation in the future of the obligations to be performed by the tenant (for example by a rent review clause), the original tenant may be bound to perform the obligations as so varied, even though the variations occur after the assignment of the lease—this will depend on the construction of the relevant covenant(s) in the original lease.

Although the point does not often arise, the landlord is in the same position as the tenant. He remains personally liable on his covenants in the lease even after he has assigned his reversion.[641] Likewise he remains liable to the tenant, even after the tenant has assigned his lease.[642]

(2) Assignee liable and entitled only in respect of matters occurring while he holds the land

Again, as the liability of an assignee of the tenant is based upon the privity[643] of estate between him and the landlord or the latter's assignee, it follows that the tenant's assignee cannot be liable for a breach of covenant committed before he took the estate under the assignment,[644] and cannot sue the landlord for breaches committed prior to that time. Lastly, and consistently with the same principle, an assignee ceases to be liable for breaches occurring after he has assigned his interest to a third party, for such a reassignment destroys the privity of estate that previously existed.[645] He is liable, however, even for these subsequent breaches, if he expressly covenants with the landlord at the time of taking the assignment that he will perform the terms of the lease.[646] Moreover, in any event, he remains liable after reassignment for any breaches that occurred while the tenancy was vested in him.[647]

---

[640] [1995] 2 EGLR 55, 60 (Sir Christopher Slade). See also his other three propositions. Beldam LJ thought at p 59 that *Centrovincial* might be justified on the ground that the original covenant contained a promise to pay not only the original but also the reviewed rent.

[641] *Stuart v Joy* [1904] 1 KB 362, M & B p 474; (1996) 59 MLR 79, 83 (M Davey).

[642] *City and Metropolitan Properties Ltd v Greycroft* [1987] 1 WLR 1085, M & B p 469 (tenant who assigned lease at reduced value because of landlord's breach of covenant to repair held able to recover damages from landlord after assignment); [1987] Conv 374 (PF Smith); *Celsteel Ltd v Alton House Holdings Ltd (No 2)* [1987] 1 WLR 291, 296.

[643] *Purchase v Lichfield Brewery Co* [1915] 1 KB 184, M & B p 480.

[644] *Grescot v Green* (1700) 1 Salk 199.   [645] *Paul v Nurse* (1828) 8 B & C 486.

[646] *J Lyons & Co Ltd v Knowles* [1943] 1 KB 366; *Estates Gazette Ltd v Benjamin Restaurants Ltd* [1994] 1 WLR 1528.

[647] *Harley v King* (1835) 2 Cr M & R 18; cf *Richmond v Savill* [1926] 2 KB 530.

(3) Implied indemnity by assignee

It will thus be seen that, where one of the tenant's covenants has been broken after an assignment of the term, the landlord has the option of suing either the original tenant on the contract or the particular assignee who had the estate when the breach occurred, but although this joint liability undoubtedly exists, the assignee in possession is the principal debtor, while the original tenant occupies the position of a surety.[648] Nevertheless the continuing liability of the original tenant is an obvious menace to him, and it became the invariable practice for every assignee expressly to covenant to indemnify his assignor against future breaches of the provisions contained in the lease. This is no longer necessary, for it is now enacted that every assignment for valuable consideration[649] shall be deemed to include a covenant by the assignee that he will pay all rent falling due in the future and will perform all the covenants, agreements and conditions binding upon the original tenant. This implied covenant of indemnity binds all persons, such as later assignees, deriving title under the assignee.[650] To take an example:

L leases land to T. Later successive assignments of the land are made first to U, then to V, and finally to W. If L sues T for the breach committed by W of some condition contained in the lease, the implied covenant of indemnity entitles T to make U a party to the action. Similarly U can join V, and V can join W as a party. In this way judgment can be given against the person who has actually committed the breach.[651]

(b) Assignment

(1) Whole interest must be transferred. Assignee and sub-tenant

The second observation is that the rules laid down above with regard to the running of covenants apply only where there has been an assignment in the proper sense of that term, for it is only then that privity of estate exists between the reversioner and the person who is in occupation of the land. The term 'assignee' is very comprehensive: it applies to all persons who take the estate either by act of party[652] or by act of law, such as the executors of a tenant or assignee, and persons taking the premises by way of execution for debt, but in the eyes of the law no person occupies the position of

---

[648] *Humble v Langston* (1841) 7 M & W 517, 530.

[649] On valuable consideration, see *Johnsey Estates Ltd v Lewis & Manley (Engineering) Ltd* [1987] 2 EGLR 69.

[650] LPA 1925, s 77(1)(c) (repealed only in relation to post-1995 tenancies by LT(C)A 1995, s 30(2), (3), Sch 2); Sch 2, Part IX; and in registered land, LRA 2002, s 134(2), Sch 12, para 20, replacing LRA 1925, s 24 (whether or not there is valuable consideration). The implied statutory covenant is one of indemnity, not guarantee: *Scottish & Newcastle plc v Raguz* [2003] EWCA Civ 1070, [2004] L & TR 11; see also [2008] UKHL 65, [2008] 1 WLR 2494 at [72] (Lord Walker); and may be excluded by an express term of the contract: *Re Healing Research Trustee Co Ltd* [1992] 2 All ER 481. For a later assignee's obligation at common law to indemnify the original lessee for breaches of covenant in the lease committed during his own tenancy, see *Moule v Garrett* (1872) LR 7 Exch 101; Goff and Jones, para 15–006.

[651] As to the nature of this covenant, see *Butler Estates Co Ltd v Bean* [1942] 1 KB 1. See also *Re Mirror Group (Holdings) Ltd* (1992) 65 P & CR 252 (original lessee cannot compel his assignee to enforce the benefit of its own indemnity covenant against an ultimate assignee if the latter has reassigned the lease).

[652] *Old Grovebury Manor Farm Ltd v W Seymour Plant Sales and Hire Ltd (No 2)* [1979] 1 WLR 1397; above, p 289, n 469.

assignee of the land unless he takes the *identical term* that the tenant had, and also takes the *whole of that term*.[653]

Thus if the tenant, on making what purports to be an assignment of his term, reserves to himself a reversion, no matter how small it may be—as where he assigns the remainder of his lease less one day—the transaction amounts to a sub-lease and not to an assignment. In such a case there is neither privity of contract nor privity of estate between the superior landlord and the sub-tenant, and therefore neither of them can sue or be sued *at law* upon the covenants of the lease,[654] though as we shall see later the sub-tenant may be liable under the equitable doctrine of *Tulk v Moxhay* on purely negative covenants.[655] But there is no magic in words. If one has acquired an interest in the tenancy and a question arises with regard to his position, the first point that falls to be considered is whether he has taken the whole of the tenant's interest. Thus where the tenant executes a deed couched in the form of a sub-lease, which purports to sub-let the property for the whole of the remainder of his term or for a longer period, the transaction amounts to an assignment.[656]

Although there is no privity of estate between landlord and sub-tenant, nevertheless the sub-tenant may be able to enforce a covenant that touches and concerns the land against the landlord. In *Caerns Motor Services Ltd v Texaco Ltd*[657] L granted a lease to T and T then sub-let to S. S could enforce the benefit of any landlord covenants that touched and concerned the land against L, despite the absence of privity of contract. This is because the benefit of such covenants was annexed under section 78 of the Law of Property Act 1925 and could be enforced by a person with a derivative interest.[658]

(2) Identical interest must be transferred

The other point, as we have observed, is that if there is to be an assignment, the assignee must take the identical interest that the assignor possessed. If, for example, a tenant

---

[653] Platt, *A Treatise on the Law of Leases*, vol ii, pp 419–20.

[654] *South of England Dairies Ltd v Baker* [1906] 2 Ch 631, M & B p 476.

[655] Below, p 732; *Hemingway Securities Ltd v Dunraven Ltd* [1995] 1 EGLR 61 (enforceability of restrictive covenant against sub-letting). The burden of a restrictive covenant in the head lease is binding on the sub-tenant in unregistered land if he has actual, imputed or constructive notice of it (which he will have, having being entitled to call for sight of the head lease before signing the under-lease: *Gosling v Woolf* [1893] 1 QB 39, below, p 1047): LPA 1925, s 199(1)(ii). A restrictive covenant between lessor and lessee is not registrable as a Class D(ii) land charge: LCA 1972, s 2(5)(ii). In registered land it is binding automatically: LRA 2002, ss 29(2)(b), 30(2)(b); H & B, para 9.8. For restrictive covenants in post-1995 leases, see below, p 323.

[656] *Beardman v Wilson* (1868) LR 4 CP 57; *Hallen v Spaeth* [1923] AC 684; *Milmo v Carreras* [1946] KB 306, M & B p 476 (sub-lease for a term longer than that of lease is an assignment of the lease); *Parc Battersea Ltd v Hutchinson* [1999] 2 EGLR 33 (oral sub-lease effective as assignment by operation of law).

[657] [1994] 1 WLR 1249; Law Com No 242, *Privity of Contract: Contracts for the Benefit of Third Parties* (1996), para 2.11(iii). See also Contracts (Rights of Third Parties) Act 1999, under which, in relation to covenants entered into by L on or after the Act came into force, S may have a direct right against L under s 1; below, p 743. See the remarks of the Parliamentary Secretary of the Lord Chancellor's Department in the Standing Committee Proceedings in HL on 15 July 1999. See also (2000) 4 L & TR D10 (DR Perks).

[658] *Smith and Snipes Hall Farm Ltd v River Douglas Catchment Board* [1949] 2 KB 500 (lessee able to enforce annexed freehold covenant on the wording of s 78). As it is clear that s 78 applies to leases as well as to freeholds, S must be able to enforce the covenant against L.

deposits his lease with X by way of mortgage, X obtains a mere equitable right to the land and not the legal term to which the tenant was entitled. Therefore, whether he goes into possession or not, he can neither sue nor be sued on the covenants.[659] A similar result again follows where a person obtains a title in unregistered land under the Limitation Act against the tenant. In *Tichborne v Weir*:[660]

In 1802 D leased land to B for 89 years.

In 1836 G seized the land and remained in possession of it until 1876, paying D the rent which had been fixed by the lease of 1802.

In 1876 G by deed assigned all his interest to the defendant, who remained in possession until 1891, paying the same rent to the plaintiff, who had succeeded to D.

The original lease between D and B contained a covenant by B to keep the premises in repair, and the plaintiff now sued the defendant for breach of that covenant. The right of the original covenantor B to his tenancy of the land had been extinguished by lapse of time when the defendant came to the land in 1876, but the question that arose was whether the defendant was an assignee of B through G. It was clear, if the identical lease that was vested in B had passed to G and from him to the defendant, that the latter would be liable as assignee on the repairing covenant, and it was strenuously argued that the effect of the Real Property Limitation Act 1833, which was the statute then in force, was to transfer the term from B to G.

It was held that the only effect of the statute was to extinguish B's right of recovering the land and not to convey what he had to G. It therefore followed that the defendant was not liable on the repairing covenant, because, not possessing the very estate to which it was attached, he was not an assignee. But the limits of the decision must be noted. It was said by a learned Irish judge:[661]

It appears to me to decide only this, that the Statute of Limitations operates by way of extinguishment, and not by way of assignment of the estate, which is barred; and that a person who becomes entitled to a leasehold interest by adverse possession for the prescribed period is not liable to be sued *in covenant as assignee* of the lease, unless he has estopped himself from denying that he is assignee.

So, in the first place, the decision will not apply where the occupier of the land has estopped himself from denying that he holds on all the terms of the original lease,[662] but although this point was pressed in *Tichborne v Weir*, it was held that the terms under which the defendant paid rent did not warrant the conclusion that he stood for all purposes in the shoes of the original tenant B.[663] But where a lease contains a proviso that the rent shall be reduced by half if all the covenants are duly observed, and

---

[659] *Cox v Bishop* (1857) 8 De GM & G 815, M & B p 480. He may, however, be liable under the doctrine of *Tulk v Moxhay*, below, pp 732 ff.

[660] (1892) 67 LT 735, M & B pp 272, 759, followed in *Taylor v Twinberrow* [1930] 2 KB 16.

[661] *O'Connor v Foley* [1906] 1 IR 20, 26 (Fitzgibbon LJ).

[662] See, eg, *Rodenhurst Estates Ltd v Barnes Ltd* [1936] 2 All ER 3.

[663] For another instance, see *Official Trustee of Charity Lands v Ferriman Trust Ltd* [1937] 3 All ER 85.

an adverse possessor avails himself of the privilege, he is estopped from denying that he is subject to the burden of the lease.[664]

Secondly, the case only goes to show that an adverse possessor cannot be sued in covenant as assignee. When we come to deal with equitable doctrines, we shall see that he is liable on such negative covenants as create an equitable burden on the estate he takes.[665]

(4) Statutory Protection for Former Tenants

Sections 17 to 20 of the Landlord and Tenant (Covenants) Act 1995 impose restrictions on the liability of a former tenant and his guarantor after assignment of the tenancy. The restrictions apply to *all* tenancies, whether created before or after the Act.

(a) Restriction on liability for fixed charge[666]

Under section 17, a former tenant (and his guarantor) is not liable for a 'fixed charge', unless the landlord serves a prescribed notice[667] informing him that the charge is now due and that the landlord intends to recover a specified sum and, where payable, interest. The notice must be served within six months of the charge becoming due.

A fixed charge is defined as rent, service charge or any liquidated sum payable in the event of failure on breach of a covenant in the lease.

The object of the section is to give protection to former tenants against a landlord who allows arrears of payment to accumulate without their knowledge.

(b) Right to overriding lease[668]

Sections 19 and 20 entitle the tenant (or his guarantor), who has made full payment of a fixed charge under section 17, to 'have the landlord under that tenancy grant him an overriding lease of the premises demised by the tenancy'.[669] The effect is to insert a lease between the interest of the landlord and that of a defaulting assignee.

It will be for a term equal to the remainder of the term of the relevant tenancy[670] plus three days,[671] and on essentially the same terms.

---

[664] *Ashe v Hogan* [1920] 1 IR 159.

[665] *Re Nisbet and Potts' Contract* [1905] 1 Ch 391, M & B pp 273, 759; below, p 739.

[666] See Fancourt, *Enforceability of Landlord and Tenant Covenants* (2nd edn, 2006), ch 20.

[667] LT(C)A 1995 (Notices) Regulations 1995 (SI 1995 No 2964), Schedule Form 1; *Cheverell Estates Ltd v Harris* [1998] 1 EGLR 27 (where guarantor is to be sued, notice need not also be served on former tenant as well); *Commercial Union Life Assurance Co Ltd v Moustafa* [1999] 2 EGLR 44 (notice is properly served if sent to intended recipient at his last residential address, whether it was received by that recipient or not). *Scottish & Newcastle plc v Raguz* [2008] UKHL 65, [2008] 1 WLR 2494 (sum to be specified in notice is the sum of rent currently payable, not unquantified sum that would become quantified and accordingly payable at some unknown date in the future). The amount recoverable may be less than the amount specified in the notice under s 17(4); *Kellogg v Tobin* [1999] L & TR 513; [1999] EG 25 May p 152 (D Stevens) (former tenants must receive notices from landlord in order to obtain indemnity).

[668] Fancourt, *Enforceability of Landlord and Tenant Covenants*, ch 22.

[669] S 19(1). Failure of the landlord to grant the lease within a reasonable time renders him liable in tort for breach of statutory duty: ss 19(6)(a), 20(3).

[670] Ie the lease to which the overriding lease is immediately in reversion and under which the tenant defaulted.

[671] S 19(2)(a).

Thus, if L has granted a lease to T, who then assigns it to A, T, who has paid the fixed charge to L, is entitled to call upon L to grant him an overriding lease. This makes T the landlord of A and gives him control over A for the duration of the lease; he can pursue remedies directly against A for breach of covenant or forfeit his lease, and thus either take possession himself or assign it to a more attractive and solvent assignee.

A claim to an overriding lease must be made in writing within 12 months of the date of payment of the fixed charge.[672] In order to be enforceable against a successor in title of the landlord, it must be registered under the Land Charges Act 1972, if it is unregistered land, or protected by a notice, if it is registered land, as if it were an estate contract. It cannot be an overriding interest under paragraph 2 of Schedule 1 or Schedule 3 of the Land Registration Act 2002.[673] It is expressly provided that an overriding lease will be binding on a mortgagee of the landlord.[674]

(c) Restriction on liability for post-assignment variation[675]

As we have seen, the Court of Appeal considered the effect of post-assignment variation in *Friends' Provident Life Assurance v British Railways Board*[676] a week after the passing of the Landlord and Tenant (Covenants) Act 1995 and declined to follow the reasoning in *Centrovincial Estates plc v Bulk Storage Ltd*.[677] Section 18 is anticipated by the protection given to the tenant in that case.[678] Under the section a former tenant or his guarantor are not liable to pay any amount that is solely attributable to a relevant variation of a tenant covenant by the landlord and the assignee effected after the assignment.

A relevant variation is one where the landlord either has the absolute right to refuse to allow it, or would have had such a right if the former tenant had sought a variation immediately before he assigned the tenancy but, between then and the time of the variation, the tenant covenants had been varied so as to deprive the landlord of his rights.[679]

B COVENANTS IN LEASES GRANTED AFTER 1995

(1) Introduction

We have seen the hazards that beset a tenant who has assigned his lease if it was originally granted before 1996. These were exacerbated by the recession of the late 1980s and early 1990s.

The Landlord and Tenant (Covenants) Act 1995, which came into effect on 1 January 1996, radically changed the law and provides a new code for covenants in leases granted after 1995. It follows the Law Commission Report of 1988[680] (with substantial

---

[672] S 19(5).
[673] S 20(6), as amended by LRA 2002, s 133, Sch 11, para 33.   [674] S 20(4).
[675] Fancourt, *Enforceability of Landlord and Tenant Covenants*, ch 21.
[676] [1995] 2 EGLR 55, in which reference is made to s 18; above, p 315.
[677] (1983) 46 P & CR 393; above, p 315.
[678] Nothing in the section applies to any variation effected before 1996: s 18(6).
[679] S 18(4). See [1996] CLJ 313 (S Bridge) at pp 317, 335.
[680] Law Com No 174, *Privity of Contract and Estate* (1988). See Aldridge, *Privity of Contract: Landlord and Tenant (Covenants) Act 1995* (1995).

amendments introduced during the debate in the House of Lords), which sets out the principles of the legislation:[681]

> First, a landlord or tenant of property should not continue to enjoy rights nor be under any obligation arising from a lease once he has parted with all interest in the property.
>
> Secondly, all the terms of the lease should be regarded as a single bargain for letting the property. When the interest of one of the parties changes hands, the successor should fully take his predecessor's place as landlord or tenant, without distinguishing between the different categories of covenant.

The Bill, as amended during the debates in the House of Lords, was the result of a concordat reached between the United Kingdom's major property organisations; the British Property Federation (for the landlord) and the British Retail Consortium (for the tenant). Without it the Bill would not have been passed. At the same time, the opportunity was taken to extend the original object and to enact a code that would contain complete provisions for the running of covenants in a lease.

The essence of the change is that the contractual liability of original tenants and landlords after they have assigned their interests is terminated, and that all landlord and tenant covenants, other than those that are expressed to be personal,[682] are enforceable and binding upon successors in title of the original parties. Accordingly the principles of privity of contract and privity of estate no longer apply, and sections 78, 79, 141 and 142 of the Law of Property Act 1925[683] cease to have effect in the new statutory code.[684]

(2) Terminology

The code is new, and so is the terminology. The leases to which the Act applies are called 'new tenancies', to be distinguished from other tenancies.[685] However some leases granted after 1995 are not new tenancies; for example, where a lease is granted as a result of an option or a right of first refusal that was granted before 1996, even though it was exercised after 1995.[686]

A tenancy includes a sub-tenancy and an agreement for a tenancy but not a mortgage term, thereby avoiding any technical difficulties that have arisen in connection with pre-1996 agreements for leases.[687]

---

[681] Ibid, para 4.1.

[682] A covenant is not personal if it would endure throughout the term and be binding on the landlord's successors in title, even though the liability of one particular landlord's liability under the covenant is limited to the period during which it holds the reversion: *London Diocesan Fund v Phithwa* [2005] UKHL 70, [2005] 1 WLR 3956 at [27] (Lord Nicholls of Birkenhead). For a personal covenant, see *BHP Petroleum Great Britain Ltd v Chesterfield Properties Ltd* [2001] EWCA Civ 1797, [2002] Ch 194 (landlord's obligations, contained in agreement for lease and expressed to be personal to the landlord, to remedy defects in building within specified period).

[683] Above, pp 308, 309, 311, 317. Sections 78 and 79 continue to apply in the running of freehold covenants: below, Ch 19.

[684] LT(C)A 1995, s 30(4).   [685] S 1(1). The word 'old' is not used for pre-1995 tenancies.

[686] Ss 1(6), (7), 28(1).

[687] S 28(1); above, pp 312–13. Agreements for tenancies must comply with the formalities of LP(MP)A 1989, s 2, below, p 966.

Covenants are either 'landlord covenants' or 'tenant covenants' that fall to be complied with by the landlord or tenant of premises demised by the tenancy. It is immaterial whether or not the covenant has reference to the subject matter of the tenancy and whether the covenant is implied or imposed by law.[688]

(3) Anti-avoidance Provisions[689]

The anti-avoidance provisions are widely drawn. Section 25(1) makes void any agreement to the extent that

(a) it would . . . have effect to exclude, modify or otherwise frustrate the operation of any provision of this Act, or

(b) it provides for—
    (i) the termination or surrender of the tenancy, or
    (ii) the imposition on the tenant of any penalty, disability or liability, in the event of the operation of any provision of this Act.

However, paragraph (a) does not limit the parties' freedom to define the scope of their obligations at the outset of the tenancy, and therefore does not prevent a landlord from defining his liability as being limited to the period when he holds the reversion. In *London Diocesan Fund v Phithwa*[690] a lease contained a covenant in the following terms: 'The landlord covenants with the tenant as follows (but not, in the case of Avonridge Property Co Ltd only, so as to be liable after the landlord has disposed of its interest in the Property) . . .' The House of Lords held[691] that this provision did not frustrate the operation of the Act, and was therefore effective. Lord Nicholls of Birkenhead said:[692]

> Section 25 is of course to be interpreted generously, so as to ensure the operation of the Act is not frustrated, either directly or indirectly. But there is nothing in the language or scheme of the Act to suggest the statute was intended to exclude the parties' ability to limit liability under their covenants from the outset in whatever way they may agree. An agreed limitation of this nature does not impinge upon the operation of the statutory provisions.

It is, however, always possible for one party to a tenancy to release the other from a covenant.[693]

---

[688] S 2(1). S 2(2), as amended by SI 1996 No 2325, art 5, Sch 2, excludes covenants under HA 1985, ss 35, 155; Sch 6A, para 1; Housing Associations Act 1985, Sch 2, paras 1, 3; HA 1996, ss 11, 13; *First Penthouse Ltd v Channel Hotels (UK) Ltd* [2003] EWHC 2713 (Ch), [2004] 1 EGLR 16 (obligations to grant sub-lease and pay commission held not to be tenant covenants).

[689] Fancourt, *Enforceability of Landlord and Tenant Covenants*, ch 23.

[690] [2005] UKHL 70, [2005] 1 WLR 3956; [2007] Conv 1; [2006] All ER Rev 264 (PH Pettit). The case is also known in some reports as *Avonridge Property Co Ltd v Mashru* ([2006] 1 P & CR 25; [2006] L & TR 4). Avonridge was the appellant and Mashru the respondent before the House of Lords. Cf *Good Harvest Partnership LLP v Centaur Services Ltd* [2010] EWHC 330 (Ch), [2010] Ch 426 (provision requiring guarantor of tenant's obligations to enter into further guarantee where lease assigned would frustrate operation of s 24(2) LT(C)A 1995, contrary to s 25(1)(a)); [2010] Conv 318 (P Clark), 427 (E Slessenger); questioned but applied in *K/S Victoria Street v House of Fraser (Stores Management) Ltd* [2010] EWHC 3006 (Ch), [2010] 44 EGCS 125).

[691] Lord Walker of Gestingthorpe dissenting.   [692] At [18].

[693] LT(C)A 1995, s 26(1)(a).

(4) Transmission of Benefit and Burden of Covenants[694]

The requirement of touching and concerning[695] does not feature in the running of new covenants. The Act provides for the automatic running of *all* landlord and tenant covenants, unless they are (in whatever terms) expressed to be personal to any person. Section 3(1) provides:

> The benefit and burden of all landlord and tenant covenants of a tenancy—
>
> (a) shall be annexed to the whole, and to each and every part, of the premises[696] demised by the tenancy and of the reversion in them, and
> (b) shall in accordance with this section pass on an assignment of the whole or any part of those premises or of the reversion of them.

(a) Assignees and sub-tenants

The running of the covenants is still limited to cases of assignment.[697] As far as sub-tenancies are concerned, section 3(5) expressly preserves the equitable doctrine that any landlord and tenant covenant that is restrictive of the user of land: 'shall, as well as being capable of enforcement against an assignee, be capable of being enforced against any other person who is the owner or occupier of any demised premises[698] to which the covenant relates, even though there is no express provision in the tenancy to that effect'. The effect is that such a restrictive covenant in the head tenancy binds any sub-tenant automatically.[699]

However, *Caerns Motor Services Ltd v Texaco Ltd*[700] would be decided differently. In a new tenancy the sub-tenant could not enforce any covenant in the head lease against the landlord. Section 78 of the Law of Property Act 1925 does not apply to new tenancies and the effect of that section is not replicated in the Act.[701]

Where, however, the Contracts (Rights of Third Parties) Act 1999 applies, a sub-tenant may be able to enforce covenants in a lease against the landlord.[702]

---

[694] Fancourt, *Enforceability of Landlord and Tenant Covenants*, chs 11–13.   [695] Above, p 304.

[696] The wording of annexation is taken from the formula in *Rogers v Hosegood* [1900] 2 Ch 388, after some discussion of a looser formula in the House of Lords debate.

[697] Above, p 316.

[698] *Oceanic Village Ltd v United Attractions Ltd* [2000] Ch 234 ('any demised premises' refers only to premises demised by the lease in question, and not to all premises demised by the landlord, if only to have conformity with s 3(2) and (3) where 'any demised premises' can only refer to the premises comprised in the relevant lease).

[699] Law Com No 242, *Privity of Contract: Contracts for the Benefit of Third Parties* (1996), para 2.11(iii). See also Emmet, para. 26.265. For the mechanisms by which a restrictive covenant in a lease binds a sub-tenant, see above, p 318, n 659.

[700] [1994] 1 WLR 1249, above, p 317.

[701] LT(C)A 1995, s 30(4); s 15. For the transmission of rights of re-entry, see s 4. A landlord's right of re-entry is not a landlord covenant. In pre-1996 leases, the right passed with the reversion under LPA 1925, s 141. Since this section does not apply to new tenancies, a specific provision is necessary. S 3(7) abolishes as far as necessary the rule in *Spencer's Case* (1583) 5 Co Rep 16a, above, p 308.

[702] The Act allows a third party (such as a sub-tenant in relation to the head lease) to enforce a term in the contract if it was the contracting parties' express or implied intention that he should, and as long as he was expressly identified in the contract by name or as a member of a class or by description, even if he was not yet in existence when the contract was entered into: s 1; below, p 743. On the Act generally, see Anson, pp 624-35.

(b) Enforcement of covenants by persons other than landlord and tenant

Section 15 of the Act makes special provision for mortgagees of the reversion and of the tenancy. The benefit and burden of the landlord and tenant covenants run, if the mortgagee is in possession of the reversion or of the premises.[703]

(5) Release of Tenant Covenants on Assignment

Section 5 is the centre piece of the Act. Under it a tenant, who has assigned the premises, is automatically released from his tenant covenants as from the date of the assignment. He also ceases to be entitled to the benefit of the landlord covenants.[704] This automatic release and cessation also applies where only part of the premises is assigned; the release and cessation are effective only to the extent that the covenants fail to be complied with in relation to the part assigned.[705]

This statutory rule is not retrospective; the release is from future liability for breach of covenant. Thus, the tenant remains liable for any breach of covenant committed before assignment;[706] but he also retains his right to sue the landlord for breaches of landlord covenants committed before assignment.[707] However, as has been well said:[708]

> The relative purity of the Law Commission proposals has been tainted by the Parliamentary process, and the euphoria of the tenant on being rid of privity of contract liability will soon be dampened by acquaintance with the other secrets of the Act. Although the assigning tenant is released from the covenants on assignment, it is almost certain that the *quid pro quo* for release will be a requirement to guarantee the liability of the immediate assignee.

And it is to that guarantee that we must now turn.

(6) Authorised Guarantee Agreement (AGA)

An authorised guarantee agreement is an agreement whereby a tenant who has assigned his new tenancy to A, guarantees to his landlord the performance of tenant covenants by A.[709] It guarantees the performance by A only, and does not extend to the breach of covenants by B to whom A subsequently assigns the tenancy.[710] The landlord may, however, be able to enter into an AGA with B when A assigns the tenancy to B.

(a) Conditions of entering into agreement

Under section 16(2) of the Act an AGA is only effective if:

(a) under it the tenant guarantees the performance of the relevant covenant to any extent by the assignee; and

(b) it is entered into in the circumstances set out in subsection (3); and

---

[703] So too where a landlord grants a further lease of his reversionary interest in the premises, for example, in the case of an overriding lease under s 19; above, p 319.

[704] For a similar release of a guarantor and to the same extent, see s 24(2).

[705] LT(C)A 1995, s 5(3).   [706] Ibid, s 24(1).   [707] Ibid, s 24(4).

[708] [1996] CLJ 313, 337 (S Bridge).   [709] LT(C)A 1995, s 16.   [710] Ibid, s 16(4).

(c) its provisions conform with subsections (4) and (5).[711]

Subsection (3) defines the circumstances as follows:

(a) by virtue of a covenant against assignment (whether absolute or qualified) the assignment cannot be effected without the consent of the landlord under the tenancy or some other person;[712]

(b) any such consent is given subject to a condition (lawfully imposed[713]) that the tenant is to enter into an agreement guaranteeing the performance of the covenant by the assignee; and

(c) the agreement is entered into by the tenant in pursuance of that condition.

(b) Consent and reasonableness

As to whether a landlord, when giving consent to an assignment, may lawfully make it conditional on the tenant entering into an AGA, depends, first, on the type of tenancy. Residential new tenancies, which are defined as being 'a lease by which a building or part of a building is let wholly or mainly as a single private residence'[714] continue to be governed by section 19 of the Landlord and Tenant Act 1927, which, as we have seen, implies into a covenant by a tenant not to assign without the landlord's consent a proviso that the consent of the landlord shall not be unreasonably withheld.[715] There is nothing in the Landlord and Tenant (Covenants) Act 1995 to suggest that it is always reasonable for the landlord of a residential new tenancy to make consent to an assignment conditional on the tenant entering into an AGA. Accordingly, the onus is on the landlord to prove that refusal to consent is reasonable within section 1(6) of the Landlord and Tenant Act 1988,[716] and, as was said in *International Drilling Fluids Ltd v Louisville Investments (Uxbridge) Ltd*,[717] each case turns on its own facts. In the case of a tenancy containing an *absolute* covenant not to assign, however, the landlord has an absolute discretion as to whether or not to give his consent, and so it will always be lawful to make the consent conditional on the tenant entering into an AGA.[718]

The position is different, however, if the new tenancy does not come within the definition of a residential tenancy.[719] Here section 22 of the 1995 Act adds a new

[711] Ibid, above. Under s 16(5) the liability of the tenant may be as a principal debtor or as a guarantor, in which case the rules of law relating to guarantees apply: s 16(8). On disclaimer of the tenancy, see s 16(5), (7). See also *Shaw v Doleman* [2009] EWCA Civ 279, [2009] 2 P & CR 12 (guarantor remained liable under terms of AGA, read with Insolvency Act 1987, s 178(4), where assignee became insolvent and ceased itself to be liable because lease was disclaimed).

[712] For example, a head landlord.

[713] *Wallis Fashion Group Ltd v CGU Life Assurance Ltd* [2000] 2 EGLR 49 (where an assignment of a lease requires the landlord's consent, and the alienation covenant is silent as to whether he can demand an AGA, the landlord can only refuse consent if it is reasonable to do so: LTA 1927, s 19(1). Therefore a landlord can only 'lawfully impose' an AGA condition in the alienation provisions of a new lease granted under LTA 1954, Part II if it is qualified as being enforceable 'where reasonable').

[714] LTA 1927, s 19(1E)(a).   [715] Above, p 259.

[716] Above, p 261.   [717] [1986] Ch 513, 521, above, p 263.

[718] Emmet, para 26.320.

[719] An agricultural tenancy is also outside s 19: Agricultural Holdings Act 1986; and so too is a farm business tenancy: Agricultural Tenancies Act 1995.

section 19(1A) to the Landlord and Tenant Act 1927,[720] by providing that a landlord may specify in advance the conditions subject to which consent may be granted. A condition to the effect that a tenant must enter into an AGA comes within the amended section 19 and will be 'lawfully imposed'.

The new section 19(1A) of the 1927 Act[721] provides that where the parties specify in their AGA

(a) any circumstances in which the landlord may withhold his licence or consent to an assignment of the demised premises of any part of them, or

(b) any conditions subject to which any such licence or consent may be granted,

then the landlord—

(i) shall not be regarded as unreasonably withholding his licence or consent to any such assignment if he withholds it on the ground (and this is the case) that any such circumstances exist, and

(ii) if he gives such licence or consent subject to any such conditions, shall not be regarded as giving it subject to unreasonable conditions.

However, if these predetermined circumstances or conditions are not purely factual, but are at the discretion of the landlord or any other person, then the agreement must either state that the discretion is to be exercised reasonably, or give to the tenant an unrestricted right to have its exercise reviewed by an independent third party, whose determination is to be conclusive.

The agreement specifying these terms need not be set out in the new tenancy itself and may be made at any time before the tenant makes application for consent to the assignment.

(c) Statutory protection for former tenants

Sections 17 to 20 of the Act,[722] which impose restrictions on the liability of a former tenant or his guarantor for a fixed charge, for post-assignment variations and for his right to the grant of an overriding lease, have already been set out in connection with covenants in pre-1996 leases to which the restrictions also apply.

(7) Excluded Assignments

Section 11 of the Act excludes two cases of assignment in which the tenant is not released from liability. First, where the tenant assigns his tenancy in breach of his covenant not to assign; and secondly, where the assignment is by operation of law. Examples of the latter are an assignment on the death of a tenant when the tenancy

---

[720] Above, p 259.

[721] *Legends Surf Shops plc v Sun Life Assurance Society plc* [2005] EWHC 1438 (Ch), [2005] 3 EGLR 43 (whether landlord could insist on personal guarantees in AGA where former tenant in administrative receivership).

[722] Above, p 319.

will vest in his personal representatives; on the death of a joint tenant of a legal estate, when it vests in the other joint tenant; on the bankruptcy of an individual tenant, when it vests in his trustee in bankruptcy; and on registration of a squatter as the new proprietor of a registered estate.[723]

The effect of an excluded assignment is to defer the release to the next assignment that is not an excluded assignment.[724]

(8) Release of Landlord Covenants on Assignment

There are two separate situations to consider: where the landlord is released and where a former landlord is released.

(a) Release of landlord

Unlike the tenant, the landlord is not automatically released from the landlord covenants when he assigns his reversion. If he were, a tenant would have no way of vetting the landlord's assignee and preventing assignment to a man of straw. Instead, he must apply to the tenant to be released under section 6 of the Act. He can do this by serving a notice on him under section 8 of the Act,[725] informing him of the assignment and requesting the release of the covenants. The notice must be served either before or within four weeks from the date of the assignment. If the tenant either consents or fails to object within this strict time limit, the landlord is released. If the tenant objects, he must serve a counter-notice objecting to the release within four months of the service of the notice on him. If he does so, the landlord may then apply to the county court for a declaration that it is reasonable for the covenant to be released. If the covenant is released, then the landlord ceases to be bound by the landlord covenants and loses their benefit.

Similarly, when the landlord assigns part of the reversion, the release relates to the covenants only to the extent that they fall to be complied with in relation to that part of the demised premises.

(b) Release of former landlord

If the landlord fails to apply for release within the four-month period, or fails in his application, he is nevertheless entitled under section 7 to make a further application when the reversion is next assigned.

---

[723] Law Com No 271, *Land Registration for the Twenty-First Century* (2001), para 14.71, n 242; H & B, paras 31.2, 31.3.

[724] LT(C)A 1995, s 11(5). The implied indemnity covenants given by an assignee to a tenant on assignment with regard to future performance of the covenants in a lease under LPA 1925, s 77(1)(c) and (d) and LRA 1925, s 24(1)(b) and (2) (now LRA 2002, s 134(2), Sch 12, para 20), above, p 316, are repealed by the Act in respect of new tenancies: s 30(2),(3), Sch 2.

[725] S 27; SI 1995 No 2964, Sch, Forms 3–6. S 8 allows the landlord to obtain release only of 'landlord covenants': ie, a covenant that is capable of binding the person from time to time entitled to the reversion. It does not apply to a covenant entered into by a landlord but expressed to be personal to him: *BHP Petroleum Great Britain Ltd v Chesterfield Properties Ltd* [2001] EWCA Civ 1797, [2002] Ch 194.

(9) Joint Liability under Covenants

As a result of the provisions of the Act, a situation may arise where two or more persons are bound by the same covenant. Under section 13(1) they are jointly and severally liable under the covenant; the Civil Liability (Contribution) Act 1978 applies for the purposes of contribution between the joint covenantors.

For example, in the context of the release of landlord covenants:

One landlord (A) may assign his interest to B and decide to serve no notice on the tenant, with the result that his liability continues. B may in turn decide to assign to C, serving notice on him. If the tenant takes no action and the property is assigned to C, B escapes liability. At that point, C is fully liable to comply with the landlord's covenants, and he is jointly and severally liable with A.[726]

---

[726] Law Com No 174, *Privity of Contract and Estate* (1988). A similar joint liability may arise in the context of tenant covenants: for example, where a tenant assigns the whole of the demised premises in breach of assignment (an excluded assignment), above, p 326; or where a tenant assigns part of the demised premises, where no apportionment has occurred. For apportionment of liability, see LT(C)A 1995, ss 9 and 10; [1986] CLJ 313, 343 (S Bridge).

10

TERMINATION OF LEASES AND RECOVERY OF POSSESSION BY THE LANDLORD[1]

Summary

We have already seen in Chapter 9 one remedy that can be invoked by the landlord for breach of the tenant's covenants: forfeiture of the lease. We here consider more generally the grounds on which a lease may be terminated by the landlord, or by the tenant, or by operation of law, together with the circumstances in which the landlord can recover possession of the premises.

---

[1] See generally Aldridge, *Leasehold Law*, Part 6; Hill and Redman's *Landlord and Tenant*, Division A, ch 14; Woodfall, *Landlord and Tenant*, chs 17, 19.

I TERMINATION OF A LEASE

A lease may be terminated on various grounds. The lease may provide for its own termination without fault of either party—for example, by allowing either party to serve on the other a notice[2] to terminate; and by being of its very nature limited in time by reference to the term granted.[3] The conduct of one party in breach of his obligations under the lease may be accepted by the other as grounds to terminate, either under an express provision contained in the lease,[4] or under general principles of law.[5] The parties may agree to terminate the lease during its currency,[6] or circumstances may occur that are not provided for in the lease but that have the effect in law of terminating the lease.[7] And sometimes statute provides a particular mechanism for termination.[8]

We have seen[9] that a lease is both a contract and an estate or interest in land. The rules for termination generally follow from one or other of these characteristics.[10] It should be noted from the outset, however, that the common law rules, in so far as they give the landlord the right to terminate, are in many cases limited by statutory rules designed to protect the tenant. In this Chapter we shall notice some of these statutory rules, applicable to the termination of leases in general, but in Chapter 11 we shall discuss the statutory protections afforded to particular types of tenancy.

A EFFLUXION OF TIME

In principle there is no need for a notice to quit in the case of a lease for a definite term,[11] since the tenancy terminates automatically upon the expiration of the agreed period. However, the scope of this rule has been drastically restricted by legislation, since in certain types of tenancy there is no automatic cessation of the tenancy (or, in some cases, a new tenancy automatically arises) upon the expiration of the period

---

[2] A notice is commonly referred to as a 'notice to quit', particularly where given by a landlord; a notice given by the tenant is often the exercise of its right under the terms of the lease to 'break' the term. We shall however see that a 'notice to quit' can operate in different ways: below, p 331.

[3] For the different operation of termination by effluxion of time in fixed-term and periodic tenancies, however, see below, pp 330–1, 335.

[4] Eg re-entry and forfeiture by the landlord under an express provision in the lease: below, p 339.

[5] Eg acceptance by the landlord or the tenant of the other's repudiation, under general contractual principles: below, p 339.

[6] Surrender: below, p 340.   [7] Frustration: below, p 343; merger: below, p 342.

[8] Eg enlargement under LPA 1925, s 153: below, p 343. For termination by disclaimer of the lease as onerous property by the tenant's liquidator or trustee in bankruptcy, see Insolvency Act 1986, ss 178, 179, 182, 315, 317, 321; *Christopher Moran Holdings Ltd v Bairstow* [2000] 2 AC 172.

[9] Above, p 182.

[10] Eg the contractual doctrines of frustration and repudiation have been applied in recent years to leases; whereas the doctrine of merger follows from the nature of a lease as an estate in land as well as being a consequence of the principle that one cannot contract with oneself.

[11] Nor where there is a condition in the lease that provides for its automatic determination: *Graves v Graves* [2007] EWCA Civ 660, [2008] HLR 10 (condition that lease would come to end if housing benefit not payable); [2008] Conv 70 (J Brown).

for which it was granted. These cases, discussed in more detail in Chapter 11, are the following:

private residential lettings;[12]

public sector housing (secure tenancies);[13]

long tenancies;[14]

business tenancies;[15] and

agricultural tenancies.[16]

In the result there are relatively few cases in which effluxion of time has its normal effect.

B TERMINATION BY NOTICE

If the lease so provides, and subject to any restriction by statute in the case of particular types of tenancy,[17] the lease may be terminated by notice by either the landlord or the tenant.[18] A notice operates differently in terminating a tenancy for a fixed period, and a periodic tenancy, but in both cases there is an overriding protection for the tenant of a dwelling.

(1) Special Rule in Case of Lease of a Dwelling

In the case of premises let as a dwelling, the Protection from Eviction Act 1977[19] provides that no notice by a landlord or a tenant shall be valid unless it is given not less than four weeks before the date on which it is to expire. The notice must be in writing and contain such information as may be prescribed by the Secretary of State.[20] The

---

[12] Below, p 358.   [13] Below, p 383.   [14] Below, p 389.
[15] Below, p 406.   [16] Below, p 417.   [17] Above; Ch 11.

[18] A termination clause will benefit and bind the assignees of the original parties, unless it is expressed to be personal: *Harbour Estates Ltd v HSBC Bank plc* [2004] EWHC 1714 (Ch), [2005] Ch 194, above, p 306, n 577 (pre-1996 lease); *Brown & Root Technology Ltd v Sun Alliance and London Assurance Co Ltd* [2001] Ch 733 (tenant's option to break expressed to be personal); LT(C)A 1995, ss 2(1), 3(1), (6), above, p 323. A break clause that is defined as exercisable by only the original tenant cannot be construed as allowing that tenant to exercise the break clause after he has assigned the lease: *Aviva Life and Pensions UK Ltd v Linpac Mouldings Ltd* [2010] EWCA Civ 395, [2010] L & TR 10 (Etherton LJ at [45]: such a clause 'would be extraordinary, even if technically possible'). For the operation of LPA 1925 s 196 (above, p 289) to notices required to be served by an instrument affecting property, see *Michael Gerson (Leasing) Ltd v Greatsunny Ltd* [2010] EWHC 1887 (Ch), [2010] Ch 558.

[19] S 5(1)(b), replacing a similar provision in Rent Act 1957, s 16. This section only applies where the true relation between the parties is that of landlord and tenant: *Alliance Building Society v Pinwill* [1958] Ch 788 (mortgagor/mortgagee); *Crane v Morris* [1965] 1 WLR 1104 (tenancy at will); *Peckham Mutual Building Society v Registe* (1980) 42 P & CR 186 (mortgagor/mortgagee). However, s 5(1A), inserted by HA 1988, s 32(2), applies the same rule to a periodic licence to occupy premises as a dwelling: s 5(1A). Four weeks is also the minimum notice for a residential contract in respect of a caravan: Caravan Sites Act 1968, s 2.

[20] Protection from Eviction Act 1977, s 5(1)(a): Notices to Quit (Prescribed Information) Regulations 1988 (SI 1988 No 2201), Sch. This includes notifying the tenant that the landlord cannot evict him without

common law rule[21] applies in this context and the provision is satisfied by a notice given on one day to expire that day four weeks hence.[22]

(2) Notice to Terminate a Tenancy for a Fixed Period

Since the notice is a unilateral act performed in the exercise of a contractual right, it must conform strictly to the terms of the contract.[23] The onus of proving its validity lies upon the person by whom it is given.[24] Its validity depends on three matters in particular.

(a) Must indicate correct day

First, it is void unless it either names the correct date for the termination of the tenancy[25] or uses a formula from which the correct date is ascertainable with certainty. A familiar example of the latter is when the notice requires the yearly tenant to quit the premises: 'at the expiration of the year of your tenancy, which shall expire next after the end of one half-year from the service of this notice'.[26]

This rigid rule has been relaxed, however, where the date in the notice is one that no reasonable tenant could possibly have supposed was the date correctly intended by the landlord. Thus, where by a clerical error a notice served in 1974 referred to a 1973 date instead of a 1975 date, Goulding J held the notice valid. The general test is:[27] 'is

---

first obtaining a court order for possession: below, p 348. Even if the notice is ineffective as a notice to quit under the 1977 Act, if given by the tenant it can still be evidence of the tenant's intention to surrender the lease: *Ealing Family Housing Association Ltd v McKenzie* [2003] EWCA Civ 1602, [2004] L & TR 15; *Lewisham LBC v Lasisi-Agiri* [2003] EWHC 2392 (Ch), [2003] 45 EGCS 175; *Laine v Cadwallader* (2001) 33 HLR 36 (depositing keys through letterbox amounted to offer by tenant to surrender tenancy).

[21] Below, p 334.   [22] *Schnabel v Allard* [1966] 3 All ER 816.

[23] *Dagger v Shepherd* [1946] KB 215, 220; *Hankey v Clavering* [1942] 2 KB 326, 330; *Hexstone Holdings Ltd v AHC Westlink Ltd* [2010] EWHC 1280 (Ch), [2010] 2 EGLR 13 (break clause can be validly exercised only by tenant and not another party, such as tenant's parent company, who has no authority to act on the tenant's behalf). Cf *Brown & Root Technology Ltd v Sun Alliance and London Assurance Co Ltd* [2001] Ch 733 (break clause personal to original tenant who had assigned lease but not yet registered the transfer: still exercisable because, on proper construction, right to exercise break clause ceased only after there had been a legal assignment); *Prudential Assurance Co Ltd v Exel UK Ltd* [2009] EWHC 1350 (Ch), [2010] 1 P & CR 7 (notice given by only one of two joint tenants: invalid). For service of a notice affecting land where intended recipient is dead, see LP(MP)A 1994, s 17; [1995] Conv 476 (L Clements).

[24] *Lemon v Lardeur* [1946] KB 613; *Lemmerbell Ltd v Britannia LAS Direct Ltd* [1998] 3 EGLR 67 (wrong person identified in notice); [2004] Conv 361 (JL Diamond and JA Sandham).

[25] *Hankey v Clavering*, above; *Keepers and Governors of John Lyon Grammar School v Secchi* [1999] 3 EGLR 49.

[26] *Addis v Burrows* [1948] 1 KB 444. See (1974) 38 Conv (NS) 312.

[27] *Carradine Properties Ltd v Aslam* [1976] 1 WLR 442, 444, approved and followed by CA in *Germax Securities Ltd v Spiegal* (1978) 37 P & CR 204 (where the clerical error was not in the operative part of the notice, and was clear from association of the notice with a covering letter from the landlord); (1977) 40 MLR 490 (PF Smith). See also *Safeway Food Stores Ltd v Morris* (1980) 254 EG 1091 (notice, which failed to identify subsidiary part of property necessarily enjoyed with main part of it, held to apply to whole); *Crawford v Elliott* [1991] 1 EGLR 13; *Divall v Harrison* [1992] 2 EGLR 64 (notice that failed to identify correct landlord held invalid); *Trafford MBC v Total Fitness (UK) Ltd* [2002] EWCA Civ 1513, [2003] 2 P & CR 2.

the notice quite clear to a reasonable tenant reading it? Is it plain that he cannot be misled by it?' A gloss was put on this test in *Land v Sykes*,[28] where Scott LJ held that it was 'subject perhaps to the qualifications that the reasonable tenant reading the notice is to be taken to have had the knowledge of the surrounding facts and circumstances that the actual landlord and tenant enjoyed'.

In *Mannai Investment Co Ltd v Eagle Star Life Assurance Co Ltd*,[29] the House of Lords, by a majority of three to two, approved this 'ordinary commonsense interpretation of what people say'. In that case a tenant served a notice purporting to operate a break clause in a lease by specifying 12 January 1995, instead of 13 January 1995, as the date for expiry. Holding that the notice was valid, Lord Steyn said:[30]

> In determining the meaning of the language of a commercial contract, and unilateral contractual notices, the law therefore generally favours a commercially sensible construction. The reason for this approach is that a commercial construction is more likely to give effect to the intention of the parties. Words are therefore interpreted in the way in which a reasonable commercial person would construe them. And the standard of the reasonable commercial person is hostile to technical interpretations and undue emphasis on niceties of language.

Lord Hoffmann added the graphic comment:[31]

> I propose to begin by examining the way we interpret utterances in everyday life. It is a matter of constant experience that people can convey their meaning unambiguously although they have used the wrong words. We start with an assumption that people will use words and grammar in a conventional way but quite often it becomes obvious that, for one reason or another, they are not doing so and we adjust our interpretation of what they are saying accordingly. We do so in order to make sense of their utterance: so that the different parts of the sentence fit together in a coherent way and also to enable the sentence to fit the background of facts which plays an indispensable part in the way we interpret what anyone is saying. No one, for example, has any difficulty in understanding Mrs Malaprop. When she says 'She is as obstinate as an allegory on the banks of the Nile', we reject the conventional or literal meaning of allegory as making nonsense of the sentence and substitute 'alligator' by using our background knowledge of the things likely to be found on the banks of the Nile and choosing one which sounds rather like 'allegory'.

---

[28] [1992] 1 EGLR 1, 3 (9 ft by 200 ft strip not material in context of 290 acre farm).

[29] [1997] AC 749; [1987] Conv 326 (PF Smith); (1999) 115 LQR 389 (M Robinson); [1998] CLJ 29 (L Tee). Followed in *Garston v Scottish Widows' Fund and Life Assurance Society* [1998] 1 WLR 1583, 1585 (Nourse LJ: 'In the company of "the man on the Clapham Omnibus", "the officious bystander", and "the man skilled in the art", there has now been added "the reasonable recipient", a formidable addition to the imagery of our law'). See also *York v Casey* [1998] 2 EGLR 25; *Investors' Compensation Scheme Ltd v West Bromwich Building Society* [1998] 1 WLR 896; *Havant International Holdings Ltd v Lionsgate (H) Investment Ltd* [2000] L & TR 297 (lessee's break notice mistakenly given by director of associated company having very similar name held valid); *Peer Freeholds Ltd v Clean Wash International Ltd* [2005] EWHC 179 (Ch), [2005] 1 EGLR 47. On interpretation generally: Anson, pp 166–70; Lewison, *Interpretation of Contracts* (4th edn, 2007).

[30] Ibid, 771.   [31] Ibid, 774.

Commenting on these two speeches, Neuberger J said in *Proctor & Gamble Technical Centres Ltd v Brixton plc*:[32]

> like Lord Hoffmann, Lord Steyn did not give a green light to inaccurate and sloppily drafted notices. The test, even in relation to the construction of notices, is relatively strict.

(b) Must be unconditional

Secondly, a notice to quit must be unconditional. It must be expressed in such decisive and unequivocal terms, that the person to whom it is directed can entertain no reasonable doubt as to its intended effect. In particular, although no precise form is required, 'there must be plain unambiguous words claiming to determine the existing tenancy at a certain time'.[33] Thus a notice given by a tenant would be ineffective if it expressed his intention to quit the premises on 25 March unless he was unable to obtain alternative accommodation.

Where, however, the naming of a certain day for the termination of the tenancy is followed by an intimation that the lease shall continue if the other party assents to certain terms, as for example to an increase[34] or diminution[35] of rent, the courts are inclined to treat the document as a valid notice accompanied by an offer of a new tenancy capable of acceptance or refusal by the other party.

Similarly, the courts will treat as valid a notice that gives only a long-stop date for termination. In *Dagger v Shepherd*,[36] for example, the question arose whether a notice, given on 21 December, directing the tenant to quit the premises 'on or before the 25th March next', was valid and effective. It was objected by the tenant that the notice was void for uncertainty, since he was left in doubt as to its intended effect. In his submission the document contained nothing more than a statement that the tenancy was to end on some unspecified date between 21 December and 25 March. The court, however, rejected this submission. It construed the document as an irrevocable notice to quit on 25 March in any event, but followed by an offer to accept the termination of the tenancy at an earlier date at which the tenant might elect to give up possession. Similarly, a notice to quit 'by' a certain day is valid.[37] And, where the landlord has a right to determine a lease by giving to the tenant 'not less than three months' notice', a notice to vacate the premises 'within a period of three months from the date of the service of the notice' is valid. Nourse LJ said:[38]

> If someone is required to vacate premises within or during a specified period, he will comply with the requirement by walking out of the door either before, or on, the stroke of midnight on the last day of that period.

---

[32] [2002] EWHC 2835 (Ch), [2003] 2 EGLR 24 at [35].
[33] *Gardner v Ingram* (1889) 61 LT 729, 730 (Lord Coleridge).
[34] *Ahearn v Bellman* (1879) 4 Ex D 201; but Lord Esher vigorously dissented.
[35] *Bury v Thompson* [1895] 1 QB 696.   [36] [1946] KB 215.
[37] *Eastaugh v Macpherson* [1954] 1 WLR 1307.
[38] *Manorlike Ltd v Le Vitas Travel Agency and Consultancy Services Ltd* [1986] 1 All ER 573.

(c) Must relate to whole of premises

Thirdly, a notice to quit given by a landlord must relate to the whole of the premises. It is void if it directs the tenant to surrender possession of part only of what he holds, unless this is permitted by the lease itself or by statute.[39]

Such a statutory power is vested in the landlord of an agricultural holding if he requires part of the land for certain purposes, such as the erection of cottages or the provision of allotments, specified by the Agricultural Holdings Act 1986.[40] If, however, he takes advantage of this power, the tenant may treat the notice as a notice to quit the entire holding.[41]

(3) Notice to Terminate a Yearly or Other Periodic Tenancy

As we have seen,[42] a periodic tenancy is one that is renewed at the end of each period unless determined by notice to quit. As Lord Templeman said:[43]

> The term continues until determined as if both parties made a new agreement at the end of each year for a new term for the ensuing year.

In the case of a periodic tenancy, therefore, a notice to quit does not involve the premature termination of the term, but causes the tenancy to terminate at the end of a period—therefore, by effluxion of time—without being renewed.[44]

(a) Tenancies from year to year

(1) Half a year's notice necessary

A tenancy from year to year does not expire at the end of the first or any subsequent year, but continues until it is determined at the end of a year by a notice served by either the landlord or the tenant.[45] It has been the rule since the reign of Henry VIII that not less than half a year's notice is necessary, unless a different agreement has been made by the parties.

---

[39] *Re Bebington's Tenancy* [1921] 1 Ch 559. The actual decision is now out of date owing to LPA 1925, s 140(1), (2).

[40] S 31. The Act does not apply to tenancies beginning on or after 1 September 1995: below, p 417. In the case of a farm business tenancy (from 1 September 1995), any notice to quit part that is permitted by the lease must be in writing and be given at least 12 months but less than 24 months before the date on which it is to take effect: Agricultural Tenancies Act 1995, ss 6, 7, which apply only to tenancies for more than two years or for year to year. In the latter case the notice must take effect at the end of the year of the tenancy.

[41] S 32.   [42] Above, p 204.

[43] *Prudential Assurance Co Ltd v London Residuary Body* [1992] 2 AC 386, 394. See also *Hammersmith and Fulham LBC v Monk* [1992] 1 AC 478, 490 (Lord Bridge of Harwich), below, p 338.

[44] *Newlon Housing Trust v Alsulaimen* [1999] AC 313 (notice to quit therefore not a disposition of property for the purposes of Matrimonial Causes Act 1973).

[45] See *Youngmin v Heath* [1974] 1 WLR 135 (personal representative of deceased weekly tenant liable for rent until notice to quit given).

It is well established what is meant by 'half a year'. If the tenancy began on one of the usual quarter days,[46] it means the interval between a quarter day and the next quarter day but one, notwithstanding that, measured by days, such a period may not amount to half a year.[47] Thus in a Lady Day tenancy notice to quit will be good if given on or before Michaelmas Day, though the actual period is five days short of 182. If the tenancy began at some day falling between two quarter days, then the length of notice must be 182 days at least.[48]

(2) Exceptions

There are two exceptions to the rule requiring half a year's notice.

(i) Contrary agreement

First, where the parties have made a different arrangement:

> I know of nothing which prevents parties, in entering into an agreement for a tenancy from year to year, from stipulating that it should be determinable by a notice to quit shorter than the usual six months' notice; or that the notices to quit to be given by the landlord and the tenant respectively should be of unequal length; or that the tenancy should be determinable by the one party only by notice to quit and by the other party either by notice to quit or in some other way.[49]

Any such agreement must not be repugnant to the nature of a yearly tenancy. Thus a term under which neither of the parties may determine, or under which only one of them may determine, is inconsistent with the concept of a yearly tenancy,[50] and will be struck out, thereby enabling a landlord to terminate on giving the appropriate notice.

(ii) Agricultural holding

Secondly, it is provided by statute in the case of an agricultural holding that, notwithstanding any express stipulation to the contrary, a notice to quit shall be invalid if it purports to terminate the tenancy before the expiration of 12 months from the end of the current year of the tenancy.[51]

(3) Notice to expire at end of current year

A yearly tenancy is terminable only at the end of the current year, and therefore a notice, given for example by the landlord, must require the tenant to quit the holding on that date—no earlier, no later. Literally interpreted, the end of the current year is midnight of the day prior to the anniversary of the day on which the tenancy began.

---

[46] Lady Day (25 March); Midsummer Day (24 June); Michaelmas (29 September); Christmas (25 December).

[47] *Right d Flower v Darby and Bristow* (1786) 1 Term Rep 159.

[48] 1 Wms Saunders 276 C; *Sidebotham v Holland* [1895] 1 QB 378, 384.

[49] *Allison v Scargall* [1920] 3 KB 443, 449 (Salter J).

[50] *Prudential Assurance Co Ltd v London Residuary Body* [1992] 2 AC 386, 394, above, p 201 (reversing *Re Midland Rly Co's Agreement* [1971] Ch 725); *Doe d Warner v Browne* (1807) 8 East 165; *Cheshire Lines Committee v Lewis & Co* (1880) 50 LJQB 121.

[51] Agricultural Holdings Act 1986, s 25(1); below, p 419.

For example, if a yearly tenancy began on 29 September,[52] its current period ends each year on 28 September. In strictness, therefore, a notice given, say, by the landlord, must direct the tenant to quit on 28 September and it must reach the tenant at least half a year before that day. A notice, for example, that is not served upon him till after 25 March, and that directs him to quit on the next ensuing 28 September is bad, and he will be entitled to remain until 28 September in the following year.

After some hesitation, however, the courts extended the strict meaning of the expression 'end of the current year' to include the anniversary of the day on which the tenancy began. 'A notice to quit at the first moment of the anniversary,' said Lindley LJ, 'ought to be just as good as a notice to quit on the last moment of the day before.'[53] A notice, therefore, given not later than Lady Day, will be good if it purports to terminate a Michaelmas tenancy on 29 September.[54]

(b) Other periodic tenancies

Similar rules apply in the case of other periodic tenancies. Subject to the statutory rule in the case of premises let as a dwelling,[55] the length of the notice must be not less than the length of the tenancy; for example, at least seven days' notice is necessary to terminate a weekly tenancy, and the notice must purport to terminate the tenancy at the end of the current period.[56] In computing the period of seven days or other appropriate period, the day of expiry but not the day of service is included. Thus, a tenancy that began on a Saturday may be terminated by a notice to quit given on a Saturday, notwithstanding that this does not give the tenant seven clear days' notice. In *Lemon v Lardeur*,[57] a tenant who held on a four-weekly tenancy was given 'a month's notice as from 1 August, 1945, to vacate' the premises. No evidence was given of the date on which the tenancy began. The notice was invalid, for, since it had not been shown that 1 August was the first day of one of the four-weekly periods, it was impossible to ascertain whether the month's notice would expire at the end of the current period.

---

[52] There is a presumption that a tenancy from a named date commences on the first moment of the day following: *Ladyman v Wirral Estates Ltd* [1968] 2 All ER 197. The presumption was rebutted in *Whelton Sinclair v Hyland* [1992] 2 EGLR 158 (application of presumption would have left premises undemised for one day, where parties were mistaken as to correct date of renewed lease under Landlord and Tenant Act 1954); *Meadfield Properties Ltd v Secretary of State for the Environment* [1995] 1 EGLR 39 (term expressed as 'from 24 June 1984 until 24 December 2003' held to include both specified days).

[53] *Sidebotham v Holland* [1895] 1 QB 378, 383.

[54] Ibid; *Crate v Miller* [1947] KB 946 (dealing with the analogous case of a weekly tenancy); *Yeandle v Reigate and Banstead BC* [1996] 1 EGLR 20. Where notice is given in months, the period of notice ends on the day of the month that bears the same number as that on which the notice was given. February, having only 28 or 29 days, is an exception: *Dodds v Walker* [1981] 1 WLR 1027; *E J Riley Investments Ltd v Eurostile Holdings Ltd* [1985] 1 WLR 1139.

[55] Protection from Eviction Act 1977, s 5(1); above, p 331.

[56] *Lemon v Lardeur* [1946] KB 613; *Queen's Club Gardens Estates Ltd v Bignell* [1924] 1 KB 117; *Bathavon RDC v Carlile* [1958] 1 QB 461. The payment period of a week is not necessarily the appropriate test in the case of a licence: in that case, the test is: what is the reasonable period in all the circumstances of the case? *Smith v Northside Developments Ltd* (1987) 283 EG 1211; [1992] Conv 263 (E Cooke).

[57] [1946] KB 613.

These rules may be varied by the parties. Subject to the statutory rule that four weeks' notice is necessary to terminate a lease of premises let as a dwelling,[58] the length of the notice and the date at which it may be given are matters upon which the parties may make what arrangement they like.[59]

(c) Termination of joint periodic tenancy

A notice to quit given by one of two joint landlords[60] or by one of two joint tenants is effective to determine a periodic tenancy,[61] even though the other joint owner does not concur.[62] In *Hammersmith and Fulham LBC v Monk*[63] the House of Lords held that this was so, in spite of the law that a single joint tenant cannot exercise a break clause in a lease,[64] surrender the term, make a disclaimer, exercise an option to renew the lease or apply for relief against forfeiture. Lord Bridge of Harwich said:[65]

> All these positive acts which joint tenants must concur in performing are said to afford analogies with the service of notice to determine a periodic tenancy, which is likewise a positive act. But this is to confuse the form with the substance. The action of giving notice to determine a periodic tenancy is in form positive; but both on authority and on the principle so aptly summed up in the pithy Scottish phrase 'tacit relocation' the substance of the matter is that it is by his omission to give notice of termination that each party signifies the necessary positive assent to the extension of the term for a further period.

---

[58] Protection from Eviction Act 1977, s 5(1); above, p 331.

[59] *Land Settlement Association Ltd v Carr* [1944] KB 657. As regards the actual decision in this case, see Agricultural Holdings Act 1986, s 2(1). See also *Harler v Calder* [1989] 1 EGLR 88.

[60] *Doe d Aslin v Summersett* (1830) 1 B & Ad 135; *Parsons v Parsons* [1983] 1 WLR 1390 (two of four joint tenants); criticised in [1983] Conv 194 (F Webb). For a similar rule in licences, see *Annen v Rattee* (1985) 273 EG 503; [1985] Conv 218 (J Martin).

[61] A break clause in a fixed term tenancy, by contrast, cannot be exercised by only one of two joint tenants: *Prudential Assurance Co Ltd v Exel UK Ltd* [2009] EWHC 1350 (Ch), [2010] 1 P & CR 7.

[62] The giving of a notice is not an exercise of any function relating to land subject to the trust under which the joint owners hold their respective interests, and therefore there is no requirement for one to consult the other under TLATA 1996, s 11 (below, p 484): *Notting Hill Housing Trust v Brackley* [2001] EWCA Civ 601, [2001] 3 EGLR 11; [2004] Conv 370 (S Pascoe). Nor is the failure to consult a breach of trust: *Crawley BC v Ure* [1996] QB 13. For problems that can arise for the remaining tenant when one joint tenant under a secure tenancy, in ignorance of the law, gives notice to quit intending simply to bring her own liability to an end but to safeguard the position of the other joint tenant, see *Bradney v Birmingham City Council* [2003] EWCA Civ 1783, [2004] HLR 27; see also *Harrow LBC v Qazi* [2003] UKHL 43, [2004] 1 AC 983; (2004) 120 LQR 398 (S Bright). Cf (2006) 10 L&T Rev 147 (M Pawlowski, discussing scheme comprising grant of periodic tenancy to landlord and another, and notice to quit by landlord (in capacity as a joint tenant), as way of avoiding normal limitations on termination by landlord).

[63] [1992] 1 AC 478; [1992] Conv 279 (S Goulding); CLJ 218 (L Tee); 108 LQR 375 (J Dewar); *Crawley BC v Ure* [1996] QB 13 (no obligation on one joint tenant to consult other joint tenant before serving notice); *Burton v Camden LBC* [2000] 2 AC 399, below, p 495 (deed of release by one joint tenant); *Osei-Bonsu v Wandsworth LBC* [1999] 1 WLR 1011. For discussion of possible challenges to the rule in *Hammersmith v Monk* based on the ECHR, see [2005] Conv 123 (I Loveland); *McCann v United Kingdom* [2008] 2 EGLR 45 (held by ECtHR that art 8 (right to respect for a person's home: above, p 23; below, p 350) was violated by notice to quit and possession proceedings by public authority landlord against one joint tenant where the other joint tenant (his wife) signed notice terminating tenancy without realising that it would extinguish the husband's right to live in the house).

[64] *Hounslow LBC v Pilling* [1993] 1 WLR 1242.   [65] At 490.

C FORFEITURE

The landlord's remedy of forfeiture, which has the effect of terminating the lease, has been discussed already.[66]

D REPUDIATION

A contract may be terminated by one party's acceptance of the other's repudiatory breach.[67] Although it used to be said that a repudiatory breach of a lease is not possible,[68] it has been held more recently that it is. In *Hussein v Mehlman*,[69] there was a miscellany of serious breaches of the implied covenant to repair (one of which 'vitiated the central purpose of the contract of letting'[70]) by the landlord who persistently attempted to evade compliance with his covenant. It was held that the tenant had accepted the landlord's repudiation by vacating the premises and returning the keys.

The judge[71] held that in a line of nineteenth-century cases it had been 'treated as axiomatic that a contract of letting could be terminated by the innocent party without notice if the other party failed to fulfil a fundamental term of the contract', but this case also forms part of the modern approach under which the lease is seen as a contract as much as an estate or interest in land.[72] Whether a breach of covenant by landlord or tenant justifies the other terminating the lease must therefore depend upon the application of the normal principles of contract law.[73] However, it is important to note that the landlord cannot, by appealing to a contractual analysis in order to obtain termination of the lease for the tenant's repudiatory breach, avoid the

---

[66] Above, pp 279 ff (forfeiture for breach of covenant to pay rent); pp 287 ff (forfeiture for breach of other covenants). For proposals to reform the law of forfeiture, see above, pp 300–2.

[67] Anson, ch 15.

[68] *Total Oil Great Britain Ltd v Thompson Garages (Biggin Hill) Ltd* [1972] 1 QB 318, 324; rejected in Australia in *Progressive Mailing House Pty Ltd v Tabili Pty Ltd* (1985) 157 CLR 17; [1986] Conv 262 (J Carter and J Hill); (1988) Monash LR 83 (J Effron). It was, however, clear that a *contract* for a lease could be terminated by acceptance of a repudiatory breach, on normal contractual principles: *Sweet & Maxwell Ltd v Universal News Services Ltd* [1964] 2 QB 699.

[69] [1992] 2 EGLR 87, M & B p 343; [1993] CLJ 212 (C Harpum); [1993] Conv 71 (S Bright); [1995] Conv 379 (M Pawlowski). See also *W G Clark (Properties) Ltd v Dupre Properties Ltd* [1992] Ch 297 (tenant's disclaimer of a lease a repudiation); *Kingston upon Thames Royal LBC v Marlow* [1996] 1 EGLR 101, 102 (Simon Brown LJ: tenant's acceptance of landlord's wrongful claim to forfeit would be acceptance of repudiation by landlord); *Chartered Trust plc v Davies* [1997] 2 EGLR 83 (landlord's failure to prevent nuisance constituted repudiatory breach of covenant against derogation from grant or of quiet enjoyment); *Nynehead Developments Ltd v Fibreboard Containers Ltd* [1999] 1 EGLR 7 (landlord's breaches not repudiatory); *Petra Investments Ltd v Jeffrey Rogers plc* (2000) 81 P & CR 21 (no breach, so no repudiation).

[70] Ibid, 90 (Stephen Sedley QC).

[71] Ibid, 89, drawing also on the development by which a lease can now in principle be frustrated: below, p 343.

[72] Above, p 182.

[73] *Nynehead Developments Ltd v Fibreboard Containers Ltd*, above; [1999] Conv 150 (M Pawlowski and J Brown); *Dominion Corporate Trustees Ltd v Debenhams Properties Ltd* [2010] EWHC 1193 (Ch), [2010] 23 EGCS 106.

limitations on the forfeiture of leases put in place by Parliament for the protection of tenants.[74]

E SURRENDER

Surrender occurs where the tenant yields up his estate to the landlord and the landlord accepts it. Termination by surrender is distinct from termination by notice, because a notice to quit served in accordance with the provisions of a lease does not require the consent of the other party to be effective, whereas a surrender by the tenant constitutes the premature determination of the tenancy and is ineffective without the landord's consent given at the time of surrender.[75]

In the case of a joint tenancy, a surrender is not effective unless made by all tenants.[76]

(1) Express Surrender

The express surrender of a lease not exceeding three years must be made by deed.[77] If an express surrender is not made by deed, but complies with the formalities required for a contract for the sale or other disposition of land[78] and is made for value (for example, where the landlord releases the tenant's arrears of rent), it is effective in equity as a contract to surrender the lease.[79]

(2) Surrender by Operation of Law

If, however, the intention of the parties as inferred from their conduct is that the lease should be yielded up,[80] surrender results by operation of law without the necessity either

---

[74] LPA 1925, s 146; *Abidogun v Frolan Health Care Ltd* [2001] EWCA Civ 1821, [2002] L & TR 16 at [48]–[49] (Arden LJ: 'the right to bring the lease to an end by accepting repudiation is, in my judgment, a forfeiture' within s 146), at [52] (Buxton LJ).

[75] *Barrett v Morgan* [2000] 2 AC 264, 272 (Lord Millett, listing four major differences between surrender and termination by notice to quit).

[76] *Leek and Moorlands Building Society v Clark* [1952] 2 QB 788; *Greenwich LBC v McGrady* (1982) 46 P & CR 223, 224. For the effect of surrender by a tenant on his sub-tenant's estate, see below, pp 342, 345; *Bromley Park Garden Estates Ltd v George* [1991] 2 EGLR 95; *Barrett v Morgan*, above, at 272.

[77] LPA 1925, s 52. This will be so even if the lease was for a period not exceeding three years, and could therefore be created orally; the exception in s 54(2) applies only to the *creation* of a lease: *Crago v Julian* [1992] 1 WLR 372, M & B p 416, above, p 212.

[78] Below, Ch 24.

[79] *Tarjomani v Panther Securities Ltd* (1982) 46 P & CR 32, 37–8 (Peter Gibson J, doubting whether the doctrine of *Walsh v Lonsdale*, above, p 215, applies to a contract to surrender). It is not an actual surrender as required by Landlord and Tenant Act 1954, s 24(2): ibid.

[80] *John Laing Construction Ltd v Amber Pass Ltd* [2004] 2 EGLR 128 (if there is no prescribed process, the tenant yields up when, objectively, his acts manifest a clear intention to terminate the tenancy, and the landlord can, if he wants to, occupy the premises without difficulty or objection: at [45]).

of writing or a deed.[81] This doctrine rests upon the principle of estoppel. Peter Gibson J said:[82]

> In my judgment, it is indeed estoppel that forms the foundation of the doctrine. The doctrine operates when the tenant is a party to a transaction that is inconsistent with the continuation of his tenancy, but in my judgment the conduct of the tenant must unequivocally amount to an acceptance that the tenancy has been terminated. There must be either relinquishment of possession and its acceptance by the landlord or other conduct consistent only with the cesser of the tenancy, and the circumstances must be such as to render it inequitable for the tenant to dispute that the tenancy has ceased.[83]

It operates where the owner of a particular estate, such as a tenant for years, is a party to some transaction that would not be valid if his estate continued to exist.[84] If, for example, the landlord grants to him a new lease that is to begin during the currency of the existing lease, the latter is implicitly surrendered and the tenant is estopped from disputing the validity of the new lease.[85] But it must amount to more than a mere variation of the terms of an existing tenancy,[86] and in particular, an agreed increase in rent does not necessarily amount to an implied surrender.[87] Implied surrender does not depend on the subjective intention of the parties and may even take place in spite of the intention of one of them.[88] The burden of proof lies on the party asserting the surrender, who must show that the parties' conduct unequivocally amounts to an acceptance that the tenancy has ended.[89]

---

[81] LPA 1925, s 52(2)(c).

[82] *Tarjomani v Panther Securities Ltd*, above, at 41. Followed in *Mattey Securities Ltd v Ervin* [1988] 34 EG 91 (payment of rent); *McDougalls Catering Foods Ltd v BSE Trading Ltd* [1997] 2 EGLR 65. See also *Chamberlaine v Scally* [1992] EGCS 90. For operation of estoppel in the creation of a tenancy, see above, p 208.

[83] It may be the landlord who does the disputing. See *Proudreed Ltd v Microgen Holdings plc* [1996] 1 EGLR 89, 90 (Schiemann LJ: 'The circumstances must be such as to render it inequitable for the tenant to dispute that the tenancy has ceased, or such as to render it inequitable for the landlord to dispute that the tenancy has ended'); *Bellcourt Estates Ltd v Adesina* [2005] EWCA Civ 208, [2005] 2 EGLR 33 (no unequivocal act by landlord to show it had accepted surrender: 'the parties must have acted towards each other in a way that is inconsistent with the continuation of the tenancy. That imposes a high threshold': Peter Gibson LJ at [30]).

[84] *Allen v Rochdale BC* [2000] Ch 221 (Council, holding freehold as trustee, in which it also held leasehold interest as local education authority, sold part of freehold: implied surrender only in relation to the part sold).

[85] *Lyon v Reed* (1844) 13 M & W 285; *Fenner v Blake* [1900] 1 QB 426; *Knight v Williams* [1901] 1 Ch 256. To produce a surrender, the new lease must be effective, not, eg, one that is beyond the powers of the lessor: *Barclays Bank Ltd v Stasek* [1957] Ch 28.

[86] *Smirk v Lyndale Developments Ltd* [1975] Ch 317, 339 (Lawton LJ); *Bush Transport Ltd v Nelson* [1987] 1 EGLR 71 (oral agreement).

[87] *Jenkin R Lewis & Son Ltd v Kerman* [1971] Ch 477; *Take Harvest Ltd v Liu* [1993] AC 552. See also *J W Childers Trustees v Anker* [1996] 1 EGLR 1 (addition to premises); *Friends' Provident Life Office v British Railways Board* [1995] 2 EGLR 55; cf *Francis Perceval Saunders' Trustees v Ralph* (1993) 66 P & CR 335 (addition of tenant); [1995] Conv 124 (A Dowling).

[88] *Artworld Financial Corp v Safaryan* [2009] EWCA Civ 303, [2009] L & TR 20.

[89] Ibid; this is the same as looking for acts significantly beyond anything consistent with the continued existence of the tenancy: ibid, at [15]. See also *Phene v Popplewell* (1862) 12 CBNS 334 (act amounting to taking of possession or that would otherwise be a trespass).

Other examples of implied surrender occur, if:

possession is delivered by the tenant to the landlord and accepted by the latter.[90] The delivery of the keys to the landlord is commonly regarded as a symbolic delivery of possession; and where the circumstances show that they were handed over by the tenant and accepted by the landlord with the intention of bringing the tenancy to an end then it is sufficient to do so;[91]

the tenant is permitted to remain in occupation of the premises as a licensee paying no rent;[92]

the landlord grants a new lease to a third party, or accepts a third party as the new tenant, with the assent of the existing tenant;[93]

the tenant has been absent from the premises for a substantial period and owes a substantial amount of rent;[94]

the tenant has served on the landlord a notice to terminate the tenancy with effect from a date on which she then moves to a new flat, owned by the same landlord, and the landlord terminates her rent account for the first flat and opens a new account for the second flat, even though the tenant's husband remains in the old flat.[95]

F MERGER

The term of years and the reversion are concurrent interests that cannot be held by one and the same person at the same time. If, therefore, they become united in one person in the same right,[96] as for example where the landlord conveys the fee simple to the tenant, the term is at common law immediately destroyed. It is said to be 'merged', that is sunk or drowned in the greater estate.[97] It will be explained later, however, that in

---

[90] *Dodd v Acklom* (1843) 6 Man & G 672; *Phene v Popplewell* (1862) 12 CBNS 334. See *Chamberlaine v Scally* [1992] EGCS 90 (no unequivocal conduct that was inconsistent with continuance of existing tenancy; tenant's belongings and two cats still on premises, which she visited to attend to them); cf *Brent LBC v Sharma* (1993) 25 HLR 2570.

[91] *Bolnore Properties Ltd v Cobb* (1996) 75 P & CR 127, 133 (Millett LJ). See *Filering Ltd v Taylor Commercial Ltd* [1996] EGCS 95 (surrender only reason for handing over keys); cf *Oastler v Henderson* (1877) 2 QBD 575 (keys taken in order to try to re-let); *Relvok Properties Ltd v Dixon* (1972) 25 P & CR 1 (in order to change locks to improve security); *Proudreed Ltd v Microgen Holdings plc* [1996] 1 EGLR 89 (keys accepted for six days, but surrender intended only when new lease granted); *John Laing Construction Ltd v Amber Pass Ltd* [2004] 2 EGLR 128 (retention of keys by tenant did not signify any rights in respect of the tenancies).

[92] *Foster v Robinson* [1951] 1 KB 149; *Scrimgeour v Waller* (1980) 257 EG 61; *Tarjomani v Panther Securities Ltd* (1982) 46 P & CR 32.

[93] *Wallis v Hands* [1893] 2 Ch 75; *Metcalfe v Boyce* [1927] 1 KB 758.

[94] *Preston BC v Fairclough* (1982) 8 HLR 70 (test not satisfied).

[95] *Ealing Family Housing Association Ltd v McKenzie* [2003] EWCA Civ 1602, [2004] L & TR 15 (landlord treated tenant's husband as an illegal occupier from that date, showing that it regarded the tenancy as terminated).

[96] *Allen v Rochdale BC* [2000] Ch 221 at [4] (freehold held by Council in capacity as trustee; leasehold as local education authority: no merger).

[97] Blackstone, vol ii, p 177.

equity the union of a smaller and a greater estate in one person does not always result in merger.[98]

G ENLARGEMENT

A tenant may by deed enlarge his lease into a fee simple under the Law of Property Act 1925.[99] Before the enlargement can be effected, however, the following conditions must exist:

(i) The term must originally have been created for not less than 300 years, and at the time of the proposed enlargement there must be at least 200 more years to run.

(ii) There must be no trust or right of redemption[100] still existing in favour of the reversioner.

(iii) The term must not be one that is liable to be determined by re-entry for condition broken.

(iv) There must be no rent of any money value.[101]

A fee simple, so acquired by enlargement, is subject to all the same covenants, provisions and obligations as the lease would have been subject to if it had not been so enlarged.[102]

As we shall see, this statutory power provides a possible, but untried, method of making the burden of positive covenants run with freehold land.[103]

H FRUSTRATION

In *National Carriers Ltd v Panalpina (Northern) Ltd*,[104] the House of Lords, by a majority of four to one, held that the doctrine of frustration is applicable to leases. In so doing, it reconsidered its former opinions in *Cricklewood Property and Investment Trust Ltd v Leighton's Investment Trust Ltd*,[105] in which Viscount Simon LC and Lord Wright were of opinion that the doctrine could apply; the second Lord Russell of Killowen and Lord Goddard that it never could, and Lord Porter reserved his opinion. The effect of the decision is unlikely to produce any dramatic change, and as Lord Hailsham of St Marylebone LC said:[106]

---

[98] Below, p 1124.

[99] S 153, as amended by TLATA 1996, s 25(1), Sch 3, para 4(16). See (1958) 22 Conv (NS) 101 (TPD Taylor).

[100] Ie, under a mortgage. See below, p 814.

[101] *Re Chapman and Hobbs* (1885) 29 Ch D 1007; *Re Smith and Stott* (1883) 29 Ch D 1009n.

[102] LPA 1925, s 153(8); below, p 731.   [103] Below, p 731.

[104] [1981] AC 675; (1981) 131 NLJ 189 (HW Wilkinson). For the doctrine generally, see Anson, ch 14, esp pp 496–8.

[105] [1945] AC 221.   [106] [1981] AC 675, 688.

It is the difference immortalised in *HMS Pinafore* between 'never' and 'hardly ever', since both Viscount Simon and Lord Wright conceded that, though they thought the doctrine applicable in principle to leases, the cases in which it could properly be applied must be extremely rare.

As a result of this decision,[107] it is no longer necessary for this purpose to draw the anomalous distinctions between:[108]

  (i) a lease and a licence. Hitherto frustration has been applicable to a licence, as in *Krell v Henry*[109] and the other Coronation cases, where an agreement to let a room for the purpose of viewing the coronation procession of Edward VII was frustrated when the procession was cancelled owing to the illness of the King;

 (ii) a lease and a contract for a lease. In *Rom Securities Ltd v Rogers (Holdings) Ltd*[110] Goff J had assumed, without deciding, that frustration was applicable to a contract for a lease;

(iii) the charter of a ship by demise[111] and a demise of land, for example a short lease of an oil storage tank and a demise charter for the same term of an oil tanker to serve such a storage tank, and a supervening event then frustrating the demise charter and equally affecting the use of the storage tank.

In the *National Carriers* case the House of Lords held unanimously that a ten-year lease of a warehouse was not in fact frustrated when it was made unusable for 20 months by the closing of an access street to it. Previous cases are also examples of a lease not being frustrated.

In the *Cricklewood* case itself, a building lease for 99 years from May 1936 was not frustrated by war-time legislation prohibiting building. It has also been held that a tenant must continue to pay his rent notwithstanding that the premises are utterly destroyed by fire,[112] or by a hostile bomb,[113] or are requisitioned by the Crown acting

---

[107] The third Lord Russell of Killowen, with filial piety, dissented; and followed the views of the second Lord Russell and Lord Goddard in the *Cricklewood* case. For him also 'the second answer of the Pinafore's captain on the subject of mal de mer is to be preferred to his first'. He was prepared to accept the doctrine where the lease is merely incidental to an overall commercial adventure, or where the subject-matter has totally disappeared. Lord Simon of Glaisdale noted at 701 that the majority decision had a theoretical anomaly of its own: that a conveyance of freehold cannot be frustrated, but a lease of 999 years can; but it would be only in exceptional circumstances that a lease for as long as 999 years would be susceptible of frustration.

For the effect of the unforeseen event of 'mountainous inflation and the pound dropping to cavernous depths' on the construction of the terms of a covenant in a lease, see *Staffordshire Area Health Authority v South Staffordshire Waterworks Co* [1978] 1 WLR 1387; *Pole Properties Ltd v Feinberg* (1981) 43 P & CR 121. See also *Graves v Graves* [2007] EWCA Civ 660, [2008] HLR 10 (CA held assured shorthold tenancy terminated under implied condition, so not necessary to consider whether judge correct to hold it was void for mistake or discharged by frustration); [2008] Conv 70 (J Brown).

[108] [1981] AC 675, 701 (Lord Simon of Glaisdale).   [109] [1903] 2 KB 740.

[110] (1967) 205 EG 427.

[111] *Blane Steamships Ltd v Minister of Transport* [1951] 2 KB 965; Law Reform (Frustrated Contracts) Act 1943, s 2(5)(a).

[112] *Matthey v Curling* [1922] 2 AC 180.

[113] *Redmond v Dainton* [1920] 2 KB 256; *Denman v Brise* [1949] 1 KB 22.

under statutory powers or under the prerogative,[114] even though the Crown itself is the landlord.[115]

Similarly, a covenant to repair imposes an absolute obligation for the non-performance of which the covenantor remains liable, notwithstanding that owing to some extraneous cause beyond his control, such as the refusal of the authorities to grant him a building licence[116] or the requisitioning of the premises,[117] he is unable to execute the necessary work.[118]

I EFFECT OF TERMINATION OF HEAD TENANCY ON SUB-TENANCY

At common law the general rule is that, when the head tenancy comes to an end, any sub-tenancy derived out of it also automatically and simultaneously comes to an end. This general rule applies without question when the head tenancy comes to an end by effluxion of time, by a landlord's notice to quit or by forfeiture.[119] It is equally beyond question that the general rule does not apply in cases of surrender[120] or merger.

The general rule also applies when the notice to quit is served by the head tenant.[121]

If the sub-tenancy is determined, the sub-tenant may, however, be protected by statute, for example under the Rent Act 1977.[122] If it is determined by forfeiture, he may apply to the court for relief.[123]

---

[114] *Whitehall Court Ltd v Ettlinger* [1920] 1 KB 680. But see the Landlord and Tenant (Requisitioned Land) Act 1942, which allows a tenant to disclaim a lease if the land is requisitioned by the Crown.

[115] *Crown Lands Comrs v Page* [1960] 2 QB 274.

[116] *Eyre v Johnson* [1946] KB 481.

[117] *Smiley v Townshend* [1950] 2 KB 311. But the Landlord and Tenant (Requisitioned Land) Act 1944 relieves the tenant of liability for damages to the land during the period of requisition.

[118] *John Lewis Properties plc v Viscount Chelsea* [1993] 2 EGLR 77 (excuse for non-performance short of full frustration).

[119] *Pennell v Payne* [1995] QB 192, 197 (Simon Brown LJ). See *Barrett v Morgan* [2000] 2 AC 264 (notice to quit served by landlord by pre-arrangement with head tenant effective to terminate both head tenancy and sub-tenancy; it was not to be construed as a surrender that would have preserved the sub-tenancy); *PW & Co v Milton Gate Investments Ltd* [2003] EWHC 1994 (Ch), [2004] Ch 142 (where Neuberger J held that as a matter of law, it was not possible to contract out of the general rule in *Pennell v Payne*).

[120] *Mellor v Watkins* (1874) LR 9 QB 400. But the *Mellor v Watkins* principle and the *Pennell v Payne* principle have no relevance to a 'Bruton tenancy', above, pp 183–4, because it is not a derivative estate and therefore cannot bind the freeholder if the licence of the party who granted the Bruton tenancy is terminated: *Kay v Lambeth LBC* [2006] UKHL 10, [2006] 2 AC 465 at [140]–[147] (Lord Scott of Foscote).

[121] *Pennell v Payne*, above; [1995] Conv 263 (P Luxton and M Wilkie).

[122] S 137(2); *Keepers and Governors of the Free Grammar School of John Lyon v James* [1996] QB 163; *Basingstoke and Deane BC v Paice* [1995] 2 EGLR 9 (HA 1985, s 79(1)).

[123] Above, p 295.

J TERMINATION OF TENANCY AT WILL

A tenancy at will may be expressly terminated at any time by either party. The strict rules that govern a notice to quit do not, however, apply in this case, for, as has been said by Tindal CJ:

> Anything that amounts to a demand of possession, although not expressed in precise and formal language, is sufficient to indicate the determination of the landlord's will.[124]

Thus a declaration that the landlord will take steps to recover possession unless the tenant complies with certain conditions, determines the tenancy if the conditions are not accepted.[125]

The tenancy is also implicitly determined if the landlord does acts inconsistent with its continuance, such as if he alienates the reversion or removes material, such as stones, from the land.[126] Implicit determination also occurs if the tenant does acts incompatible with his limited rights, such as if he commits waste or assigns the land to a stranger.[127]

The death of either party also determines the tenancy.

A premature determination is not allowed to prejudice the rights of either party. If the tenant quits before the day on which his rent is due, he does not escape liability;[128] while if he has sown crops he has a right at common law to re-enter and reap them if the landlord determines the tenancy before they are ripe.[129]

II RECOVERY OF POSSESSION BY THE LANDLORD

Even if the lease has been terminated on one of the grounds described in the previous section, the landlord may still need to take positive steps to recover possession of the premises. For example, the landlord may have lawfully terminated the lease but the tenant is refusing to leave; or the tenant may have given notice to quit, but a member of the tenant's family is still on the premises. We shall see in the next chapter that certain special rules have been laid down by statute to protect tenants holding under certain special types of lease, and that this sometimes extends to requiring the landlord to obtain a court order in order to terminate the tenancy, as well as to recover possession of the premises. In this section, however, we notice the general rules applicable to a landlord's attempt to recover possession of premises, whether against the former tenant or against another person present on the premises.

---

124 *Doe d Price v Price* (1832) 9 Bing 356, 358.
125 Ibid; *Fox v Hunter-Paterson* [1948] 2 All ER 813.
126 *Doe d Bennett v Turner* (1840) 7 M & W 226.   127 *Pinhorn v Souster* (1853) 8 Exch 763, 772.
128 Cruise, Digest, Tit ix, c 1, s 13.   129 Co Litt 55b; above, p 203.

A RE-ENTRY BY THE LANDLORD

We have already seen that the landlord's right to re-enter the premises in the event of breach of covenant by the tenant will commonly be reserved by the lease, and that at common law re-entry is a means by which forfeiture of the lease may be effected; but that the usual practice is for the landlord to sue for possession, rather than to exercise his right of re-entry, in order to forfeit the lease.[130] Once the lease has been terminated, however—for example, by the expiry of a fixed term, or by notice to quit—at common law the landlord has the right to enter and retake possession.[131] This can be a useful right, allowing the landlord quickly and efficiently to recover possession in order to use the premises himself or to relet them, although the landlord may still prefer to seek a court order that will delay matters but in a clear case may be relatively speedy.[132] Where the landlord has a right to possession, the court has a duty to make an order to enforce it, subject to any inherent or statutory power to defer the landlord's taking possession.[133] The right of the landlord to retake possession without a court order is however restricted by statute in the case of a lease of a dwelling; and the unlawful eviction or harassment of a residential occupier constitutes a criminal offence.[134]

---

[130] Above, p 279. In the case of a tenancy of residential premises, re-entry without a court order is prohibited: below. The Law Commission has proposed that the doctrine of re-entry be abolished, and replaced by a new scheme for termination of a tenancy for tenant default that may involve either a termination claim in court, or a summary termination procedure without recourse to the court: Law Com No 303, *Termination of Tenancies for Tenant Default* (2006); above, p 301.

[131] *Sheffield Corporation v Luxford* [1929] 2 KB 180, 184; *Jones v Savery* [1951] 1 All ER 820, 822.

[132] The procedure for a claim for the recovery of possession of land (including a claim brought by a landlord against a tenant or sub-tenant, or former tenant or sub-tenant, or against a trespasser) is set out in CPR Part 55. Default judgment cannot be given even if the defendant does not acknowledge service or file a defence: CPR, r 55.7(4), although where the tenant has no real prospect of defending the landlord's claim to possession, summary judgment can be given as long as it is not a claim for possession of residential premises against a tenant or a person holding over after the end of his tenancy whose occupancy is protected within the meaning of the Rent Act 1977 or HA 1988: CPR, r 24.3(2)(a)(ii). Cf, however, *Manchester CC v Pinnock* [2010] UKSC 45, [2010] 3 WLR 1441, below, p 353, at [63] ('some of the provisions of CPR 55, which appear to mandate a summary procedure in some types of possession claim, may present difficulties in relation to cases where article 8 [ECHR] claims are raised'). There is an accelerated procedure for claims for possession of property let on an assured shorthold tenancy: CPR, Part 55, Section II. For such tenancies, see below, pp 367 ff. See also Pre-action Protocol for Possession Claims based on Rent Arrears (which applies to residential possession claims by social landlords (such as local authorities, Registered Social Landlords and Housing Action Trusts) and private registered providers of social housing that are based solely on claims for rent arrears).

[133] *Sheffield Corporation v Luxford*, above; *Jones v Savery*, above. Under HA 1980, s 89, the court has power in most cases to postpone the giving up of possession for only 14 days after its order or (if it appears to the court that exceptional hardship would be caused by requiring possession to be given up by that date) up to six weeks.

[134] Below.

B LEASES OF DWELLINGS. REQUIREMENT OF COURT ORDER TO RECOVER POSSESSION

Where premises have been let as a dwelling, and the tenancy has come to an end but the occupier continues to reside in the premises or part of them, it is not lawful for the owner to enforce his right to recover possession of the premises without a court order.[135] This rule is subject to certain exceptions, for example where the tenant or licensee shares accommodation with the owner or occupies it for a holiday, or where it has been granted in order to provide accommodation for asylum-seekers.[136] Similarly, the right of re-entry or forfeiture of a lease of premises let as a dwelling cannot be enforced without court proceedings while any person is residing in the premises or part of them.[137]

C CRIMINAL OFFENCES OF UNLAWFUL EVICTION AND HARASSMENT

There are several criminal offences relating to the entry onto premises or harassment of occupiers of them, even where the entry is effected by the owner of premises in order to enforce his right to possession against a person who has no right to possession.

It is an offence of *unlawful eviction* for any person unlawfully to deprive the residential occupier of his occupation of the premises, or any part thereof, or to attempt to do so, unless he proves that he believed, and had reasonable cause to believe, that the occupier had ceased to reside.[138] Furthermore, it is an offence of *harassment*[139] for any person, with the intention[140] of causing a residential occupier to give up the occupation of all or part of the premises or to refrain from exercising any of his rights, to do

---

[135] Protection from Eviction Act 1977, s 3, as amended by HA 1988, s 30. 'Occupier' means any person lawfully residing in the premises or part of them at the termination of the former tenancy: s 3(2). The provision applies to licences, as well as to leases: s 3(2A), (2B). S 3 is compatible with ECHR: *R (Coombes) v Secretary of State for Communities and Local Government* [2010] EWHC 666, [2010] L & TR 29.

[136] Ibid, s 3A, inserted by HA 1988, s 31, and amended by Immigration and Asylum Act 1999, s 169(1), Sch 14; Immigration, Asylum and Nationality Act 2006, s 43; SI 2005 No 1379. Certain statutorily protected tenancies, including assured tenancies, protected tenancies under the Rent Act 1977, tenancies under L & TA 1954, Part II, agricultural holdings and farm business tenancies, are excluded and governed by their own particular rules: s 8(1).

[137] Protection from Eviction Act 1977, s 2; *Patel v Pirabakaran* [2006] EWCA Civ 685, [2006] 1 WLR 3112 ('let as a dwelling' means 'let wholly *or partly* as a dwelling' and so applies to premises let for mixed residential and business purposes, an interpretation that is compliant with the ECHR).

[138] Protection from Eviction Act 1977, s 1(2). See also Criminal Law Act 1977, s 6 (offence of using or threatening violence for the purpose of securing entry into premises).

[139] Protection from Eviction Act 1977, s 1(3), amended by HA 1988, s 29(1). See also Protection from Harassment Act 1997, s 1 (general criminal offence of harassment; actionable in damages by the victim: s 3); *Daiichi Pharmaceuticals UK Ltd v Stop Huntingdon Animal Cruelty* [2003] EWHC 2337 (QB), [2004] 1 WLR 1503 (interlocutory injunction refused to corporate claimants but granted to individual claimants on behalf of themselves and employees of claimant companies).

[140] '"Intention" in this context meaning with the purpose or motive of causing the occupier to give up occupation of the premises': *R v Burke* [1991] 1 AC 135, 147 (Lord Griffiths).

acts[141] likely to interfere with the peace or comfort of the occupier or members of his household, or persistently to withdraw services reasonably required for the occupation of the premises as a residence. These offences are not aimed solely at, but will include, acts done by landlords. However, the Housing Act 1988 introduced a further offence of harassment, directed at the conduct of landlords and their agents. This offence[142] is committed where the landlord or his agent commits acts of harassment similar to those set out above, but it suffices that the landlord (or agent, as the case may be) knows or has reasonable cause to believe that his conduct is likely to cause the occupier to give up occupation or refrain from exercising his rights. In this offence specific intent is not required, and it is therefore easier to prove. Prosecutions for these offences can be brought by the victim, the police or the local authority, although in practice the police refer complaints to the local authority.

D DAMAGES FOR UNLAWFUL EVICTION OR HARASSMENT

Section 27 of the Housing Act 1988 confers a civil action for damages against the landlord[143] for unlawful eviction or harassment causing the occupier to give up occupation. The measure of damages is the difference in value (if any[144]) between the landlord's interest in the building subject to the occupier's rights and not so subject.[145] Although the liability is said to be in the nature of a tort,[146] in substance it is calculated to expropriate the landlord's notional gain from his wrongful conduct.[147] Where section 27 is not satisfied, remedies in the general law of contract or tort are likely to be available to the occupier for the acts of harassment. These remedies are available in addition to the statutory remedy, but damages may not be awarded twice for the same loss.[148]

---

[141] It is not necessary for an act by the defendant to be an actionable civil wrong in order to be an offence under s 1(3): *R v Burke*, above (preventing tenant from using shared bathroom and lavatories, and disconnecting front door bell).

[142] Protection from Eviction Act 1977, s 1(3A), inserted by HA 1988, s 29(2).

[143] Only the landlord is liable: *Sampson v Wilson* [1996] Ch 39.

[144] *Melville v Bruton* (1996) 29 HLR 319 (no damages where no difference in value because other tenants not evicted).

[145] HA 1988, s 28; *Tagro v Cafane* [1991] 1 WLR 378 (£31,000); *Jones v Miah* [1992] 2 EGLR 50 (£8,000); *Haniff v Robinson* [1993] QB 419 (£26,000). For county court decisions on the measure of damages, see the monthly issues of *Legal Action*. For reduction of the damages because of the tenant's conduct or refusal to accept reinstatement in the premises, see s 27(8); and for the landlord's defence that he reasonably believed that the tenant had ceased to reside, see s 27(8); *Osei-Bonsu v Wandsworth LBC* [1999] 1 WLR 1011; *Kalas v Farmer* [2010] EWCA Civ 108, [2010] HLR 25.

[146] HA 1988, s 27(4)(a).

[147] *Sampson v Wilson* [1996] Ch 39, 49 (Sir Thomas Bingham MR): the formula is 'very apt to prevent the landlord profiting from his "Rachmannite" activities'.

[148] HA 1988, s 27(4), (5).

E IMPACT OF THE HUMAN RIGHTS ACT 1998 ON THE LANDLORD'S CLAIM FOR POSSESSION

In recent years the question has been asked whether the Human Rights Act 1998 has an impact on the landlord's right to possession on termination of the lease. In 2003, in *Harrow London Borough Council v Qazi*,[149] the House of Lords by a bare majority gave an emphatic negative answer to this question. In 2006, in *Kay v Lambeth London Borough Council*,[150] the House, again by a bare majority but of a seven-judge court, substantially reaffirmed its decision in *Qazi*, and this was broadly followed in 2008 in *Doherty v Birmingham City Council*.[151] However, in 2010, in *Manchester City Council v Pinnock*[152] a nine-judge Supreme Court undertook a general review of those and other cases, in particular in the light of the developing jurisprudence of the European Court of Human Rights in this area. The decision in *Pinnock* was followed by a seven-judge Supreme Court in 2011, in *Hounslow LBC v Powell*.[153] In *Pinnock* the Supreme Court departed from the earlier decisions of the House of Lords, and the position is now therefore to be examined on the basis of these latest decisions, although it can be best understood in light of an outline of the development of the law through the decisions in *Qazi* and *Kay*.

We have seen[154] that, under the Act, it is unlawful for a public authority to act in a way that is incompatible with 'Convention rights'—certain rights under the European Convention on Human Rights.[155] The question that has arisen is whether the exercise by a public authority landlord[156] of its right to possession of premises against a residential occupier—a former tenant or another member of his family still living on the premises—is subject to the Convention rights, and in particular the

---

[149] [2003] UKHL 43, [2004] 1 AC 983; [2004] Conv 406 (J Howell); (2004) 120 LQR 398 (S Bright); [2004] PL 594 (I Loveland).

[150] [2006] UKHL 10, [2006] 2 AC 465; [2006] All ER Rev 260 (PH Pettit); [2006] Conv 294 (S Bright), 526 (D Hughes and M Davis); [2006] CLJ 696 (A Goymour).

[151] [2008] UKHL 57, [2009] 1 AC 367; [2008] Conv 437 (GLlH Griffiths); [2009] Conv 396 (I Loveland); (2009) 4 EHRLR 495 (I Loveland); [2010] Conv 57 (M Davis and D Hughes). See, however, Lord Mance at [132] and Lord Walker at [107]-[108].

[152] [2010] UKSC 45, [2010] 3 WLR 1441.   [153] [2011] UKSC 8, [2011] 2 WLR 287.

[154] Above, pp 22–4.

[155] S 6. The court may grant such relief or remedy, or make such order, within its powers as it considers just and appropriate: s 8(1).

[156] 'Public authority' under HRA 1998, s 6, includes the court: s 6(3)(a). For further discussion of the extent to which the Act applies in disputes between private parties see above, p 23. However, in *R (Gangera) v Hounslow LBC* [2003] EWHC 794 (Admin), [2003] HLR 68 at [48]–[49] Moses J firmly rejected the argument that s 6 and art 8 imposed on the court the duty to adjudicate on the compatibility of a order for possession in every case, even those in which the landlord was a private person: such an argument 'would fundamentally transform our law as to enforcement of property rights into one where such rights could only be enforced when the court thinks it justifiable to seek possession and proportionate to make an order'. See also *Harrow LBC v Qazi*, above, at [108]–[109] (Lord Millett), and at [143] (Lord Scott of Foscote). In *Kay v Lambeth LBC*, above, the application to private landlords of the principles enunciated in *Qazi* and *Kay* was left open by Lord Bingham of Cornhill at [28], Lord Nicholls of Birkenhead at [61] and Lord Hope of Craighead at [64]; and in *Manchester CC v Pinnock*, above, the Supreme Court declined at [50] to address the question until it arises in a case in which it has to be determined.

'right to respect for...his home' under article 8.1 of the Convention; and therefore whether the court in hearing a claim for possession should make an assessment of the compatibility of the claim to possession on the facts of the case with the occupant's rights under article 8.2.[157]

In *Harrow London Borough Council v Qazi*:[158]

the defendant, together with his wife, had occupied a house under a secure joint tenancy[159] granted by the local authority. His wife left, and gave notice to quit that terminated the tenancy.[160] The local authority sought possession.

The House of Lords held that, although the defendant was a trespasser, he was occupying a house as his 'home' within the meaning of article 8.1 of the Convention. However, by a majority of three to two, the House went on to hold that, since English domestic law in these circumstances gave the authority an unqualified right to possession, article 8.2 did not apply. Lord Scott of Foscote said:[161]

If Mr Qazi has no contractual or proprietary right under the ordinary law to resist the council's claim for possession, and it is accepted he has not, the acceptance by the court of a defence based on article 8 would give him a possessory right over 31 Hutton Lane that he would not otherwise have. It would deprive the council of its right under the ordinary law to immediate possession. It would constitute an amendment of the domestic social housing legislation. It would give article 8 an effect it was never intended to have and that it has never been given by the Strasbourg tribunals responsible for implementing the Convention.

However, after the decision of the House of Lords in *Qazi*, the European Court of Human Rights held in *Connors v United Kingdom*[162] that article 8 of the Convention was violated where a local authority obtained, and executed, an order for summary possession of land occupied by gypsies under a licence that had been terminated, and who therefore had in domestic law no answer to the claim for immediate possession. It was held that the eviction was not attended by the requisite procedural safeguards— the requirement to establish proper justification for the serious interference with the

---

[157] Articles 8.1 and 8.2 are set out above, p 23.   [158] Above.   [159] Below, p 383.

[160] *Hammersmith and Fulham LBC v Monk* [1992] 1 AC 478; above, p 338.

[161] [2003] UKHL 43, [2004] 1 AC 983 at [151]. See also Lord Hope of Craighead at [74], [84], and Lord Millett at [103], [109]. Lord Bingham of Cornhill and Lord Steyn dissented vigorously; see Lord Steyn at [27]: 'It would be surprising if the views of the majority on the interpretation and application of art 8...withstood European scrutiny....it empties art 8(1) of any or virtually any meaningful content. The basic fallacy in the approach is that it allows domestic notions of title, legal and equitable rights, and interests, to colour the interpretation of art 8(1). The decision of today does not fit into the new landscape created by the 1998 Act.' The general rule stated in *Qazi* was applied in *Newham LBC v Kibata* [2003] EWCA Civ 1785, [2004] 1 FLR 690; *Bradney v Birmingham City Council* [2003] EWCA Civ 1783, [2004] HLR 27; *Hounslow LBC v Adjei* [2004] EWHC 207 (Ch), [2004] 2 All ER 636; *McCann v Birmingham City Council* [2004] EWHC 2156 (Admin), [2005] 1 P & CR DG5 (proceedings for judicial review).

[162] (2005) 40 EHRR 9. The decision of the House of Lords in *Qazi* was not cited. See also *Blečić v Croatia* (2005) 41 EHRR 13 (tenant lost flat in Croatia in consequence of absence abroad during Balkan war: art 8 ECHR engaged, but interference with rights was justified. See, however, (2006) 43 EHRR 48, where Grand Chamber held that since termination of tenancy occurred before ECHR entered into force in Croatia, it had no jurisdiction).

occupier's rights—and so could not be regarded as justified by (within the meaning of article 8.2) a 'pressing social need' or proportionate to the legitimate aim being pursued.

In the light of the decision in *Connors*, in *Kay v Lambeth London Borough Council*[163] the House of Lords reviewed its own decision in *Harrow London Borough Council v Qazi*. By a decision of four to three, it reaffirmed its earlier decision with only minor qualifications. There was agreement amongst their Lordships that a possession order made by a court in respect of a defendant's home will be an interference with the right to respect for his home, and therefore article 8 of the Convention will normally be engaged where a public authority landlord seeks possession. There was also agreement that, if the ratio of *Qazi* was that the enforcement of a right to possession in accordance with the domestic law of property can *never* be incompatible with article 8, it must now be modified in the light of the decision in *Connors*. However, there was disagreement over the circumstances in which a defendant can challenge the claim to possession on the basis of the Convention. The minority would have held that the defendant must be given a fair opportunity to contend that the excepting conditions of article 8.2 have not been met on the facts of the case, and that if he so pleads, it is for the public authority to establish that the conditions have been met—even though in the overwhelming majority of cases the authority will be able to do so without difficulty.[164] The majority of the House, however, held that the defendant's right, under the Convention and therefore under the Human Rights Act 1998, to challenge the claim to possession is not based on his individual personal circumstances, or the particular facts of the case. The challenge can be only to the compatibility with the Convention of the domestic rules under which the possession order is sought.[165]

---

[163] [2006] UKHL 10, [2006] 2 AC 465. Two appeals were consolidated: *Kay v Lambeth LBC* and *Leeds City Council v Price*.

[164] See at [29] (Lord Bingham of Cornhill), at [56] (Lord Nicholls of Birkenhead) and at [176] (Lord Walker of Gestingthorpe).

[165] See at [109]–[110] (Lord Hope of Craighead). At [110] Lord Hope said that if the right to recover possession is unqualified, a county court may refrain from proceeding to summary judgment and making the possession order only in two situations (which in the following cases became know as 'gateways' (a) and (b)): '(a) if a seriously arguable point is raised that the law that enables the court to make the possession order is incompatible with article 8, the county court in the exercise of its jurisdiction under the Human Rights Act 1998 should deal with the argument in one or other of two ways: (i) by giving effect to the law, so far as it is possible for it do so under s 3, in a way that is compatible with art 8 , or (ii) by adjourning the proceedings to enable the compatibility issue to be dealt with in the High Court; (b) if the defendant wishes to challenge the decision of a public authority to recover possession as an improper exercise of its powers at common law on the ground that it was a decision that no reasonable person would consider justifiable, he should be permitted to do this provided again that the point is seriously arguable' (that is an application of the normal principles of judicial review). See also *Doherty v Birmingham City Council* [2008] UKHL 57, [2009] 1 AC 367. *Kay* was followed in, inter alia, *Liverpool CC v Doran* [2009] EWCA Civ 146, [2009] 1 WLR 2365; *Taylor v Central Bedfordshire Housing* [2009] EWCA Civ 613, [2010] 1 WLR 446 and *Barber v Croydon LBC* [2010] EWCA Civ 51, [2010] HLR 26. For the later proceedings in relation to the *Kay* case before the ECtHR, see *Kay v United Kingdom* [2010] L & TR 1 (violation of procedural aspect (only) of art 8); [2010] Conv 498 (S Nield).

In *Manchester City Council v Pinnock*[166] the Supreme Court, in a single judgment of the Court, preferred the approach of the minorities in *Qazi* and *Kay* and therefore departed from their earlier decisions.[167] The case concerned a tenancy granted by a local authority that had become a 'demoted tenancy' under the Housing Act 1996[168] and of which the local authority sought possession. However, the Court made clear that its discussion applied equally to other social landlords to the extent that they are public authorities under the Human Rights Act 1998.[169] Their discussion was not limited to the demoted tenancies regime and the facts of the case, but began with two broader questions:[170]

> This appeal gives rise to four main issues, of increasing specificity. The first is whether the jurisprudence of the European Court of Human Rights ('EurCtHR') requires that, before making an order for possession of property that consists of a person's home pursuant to a claim made by a local authority (or other public authority), a domestic court should be able to consider the proportionality of evicting that person from his home under article 8, and, in the process of doing so, to resolve any relevant factual disputes between the parties.... The second issue...is what this conclusion means in practice in relation to claims for possession, and related claims, in relation to residential property.

The Court answered the first question in the affirmative. The jurisprudence of the European Court of Human Rights established that:[171]

(a) Any person at risk of being dispossessed of his home at the suit of a local authority should in principle have the right to raise the question of the proportionality of the measure, and to have it determined by an independent tribunal in the light of article 8, even if his right of occupation under domestic law has come to an end.[172]

(b) A judicial procedure that is limited to addressing the proportionality of the measure through the medium of traditional judicial review (ie one that does not permit the court to make its own assessment of the facts in an appropriate case) is inadequate as it is not appropriate for resolving sensitive factual issues.[173]

(c) Where the measure includes proceedings involving more than one stage, it is the proceedings as a whole that must be considered in order to see if article 8 has been complied with.[174]

---

[166] [2010] UKSC 45, [2010] 3 WLR 1441.

[167] Ibid, at [49]. The judgment of the Court was given by Lord Neuberger.   [168] Below, p 386.

[169] [2010] UKSC 45, [2010] 3 WLR 1441, at [3]. This distinguishes the case where the person seeking possession is a private landlowner: ibid, at [4].

[170] Ibid, at [21]. The third issue was whether the demoted tenancy regime could properly be interpreted so as to comply with the requirements of art 8, or whether at least some aspects of that regime are incompatible with the occupiers' art 8 Convention rights; and the fourth issue was how the appeal should be disposed of in the light of the answers on the first three issues.

[171] Ibid, at [45].

[172] *McCann v United Kingdom* [2008] 2 EGLR 45 at [50]; *Ćosić v Croatia* [2009] ECHR 28261/06, at [22]; *Zehentner v Austria* [2009] ECHR 20082/02, at [59]; *Paulić v Croatia* [2009] 3572/06, at [43], and *Kay v UK* [2010] ECHR 37341/06, [2011] L & TR 1, at [73]-[74].

[173] *Connors v UK* (2005) 40 EHRR 9, at [92]; *McCann v UK*, above, at [53]; *Kay v UK*, above, at [72]-[73].

[174] *Zehentner v Austria*, above, at [54].

(d) If the court concludes that it would be disproportionate to evict a person from his home notwithstanding the fact that he has no domestic right to remain there, it would be unlawful to evict him so long as the conclusion obtains—for example, for a specified period, or until a specified event occurs, or a particular condition is satisfied.

Although it cannot be described as a point of principle, it seems that the EurCtHR has also franked the view that it will only be in exceptional cases that article 8 proportionality would even arguably give a right to continued possession where the applicant has no right under domestic law to remain.[175]

Although the Supreme Court is not bound to follow decisions of the European Court of Human Rights,[176] English domestic law had already been developing in the direction of the European jurisprudence[177] and the final step should be taken to prefer the minority view in *Qazi* and *Kay*:[178]

if our law is to be compatible with article 8, where a court is asked to make an order for possession of a person's home at the suit of a local authority, the court must have the power to assess the proportionality of making the order, and, in making that assessment, to resolve any relevant dispute of fact.

It may well be rare, however, for a court to decide that the possession order, when made in accordance with domestic law, will be disproportionate and therefore contrary to article 8. However, this should not be put in the terms that it will only be in 'very highly exceptional cases' that it will be appropriate for the court to consider a proportionality argument:[179]

We would prefer to express the position slightly differently. The question is always whether the eviction is a proportionate means of achieving a legitimate aim. Where a person has no right in domestic law to remain in occupation of his home, the proportionality of making an order for possession at the suit of the local authority will be supported not merely by the fact that it would serve to vindicate the authority's ownership rights. It will also, at least normally, be supported by the fact that it would enable the authority to comply with its duties in relation to the distribution and management of its housing stock, including, for example, the fair allocation of its housing, the redevelopment of the site, the refurbishing of sub-standard accommodation, the need to move people who are in accommodation that now exceeds their needs, and the need to move vulnerable people into sheltered or warden-assisted housing. Furthermore, in many cases…other cogent reasons, such as the need to remove a source of nuisance to neighbours, may support the proportionality of dispossessing the occupiers.

…[T]o require the local authority routinely, from the outset, to plead and prove that the possession order sought is justified would, in the overwhelming majority of cases, be burdensome and futile. In other words, the fact that the authority is entitled to possession

---

[175] *McCann v UK* 47, above, at [54]; *Kay v UK*, above, at [73].   [176] See also above, p 22, n 107.

[177] *Doherty v Birmingham City Council*, above, n 165.

[178] [2010] UKSC 45, [2010] 3 WLR 1441 at [49].

[179] Ibid, at [51]-[54]; followed in *Hounslow LBC v Powell* [2011] UKSC 8, [2011] 2 WLR 287.

and should, in the absence of cogent evidence to the contrary, be assumed to be acting in accordance with its duties, will be a strong factor in support of the proportionality of making an order for possession. But, in a particular case, the authority may have what it believes to be particularly strong or unusual reasons for wanting possession—for example, that the property is the only occupied part of a site intended for immediate development for community housing. The authority could rely on that factor, but would have to plead it and adduce evidence to support it.

Unencumbered property rights, even where they are enjoyed by a public body such as a local authority, are of real weight when it comes to proportionality. So, too, is the right—indeed the obligation—of a local authority to decide who should occupy its residential property. As Lord Bingham said in *Harrow v Qazi*:[180]

'[T]he administration of public housing under various statutory schemes is entrusted to local housing authorities. It is not for the court to second-guess allocation decisions. The Strasbourg authorities have adopted a very pragmatic and realistic approach to the issue of justification.'

Therefore, in virtually every case where a residential occupier has no contractual or statutory protection, and the local authority is entitled to possession as a matter of domestic law, there will be a very strong case for saying that making an order for possession would be proportionate. However, in some cases there may be factors that would tell the other way.

Turning to the second question—what the conclusion on the first question means in practice in relation to claims for possession, and related claims, in relation to residential property[181]—the Supreme Court drew a distinction between the case where the domestic regime gives the landlord a right to possession only where it is *reasonable* to make the order, and the case where under domestic law the landlord has an *unqualified* right to an order for possession. In the former case, it is highly unlikely, as a practical matter, that it could be reasonable for a court to make an order for possession in circumstances in which it would be disproportionate to do so under article 8.[182] In each case the statutory regime must be considered, and further cases were due to be heard by the Court on claims for possession in different circumstances,[183] but the Court gave general guidance in the following terms:[184]

First, it is only where a person's 'home' is under threat that article 8 comes into play, and there may be cases where it is open to argument whether the premises involved are the defendant's home (eg where very short-term accommodation has been provided). Secondly, as a general rule, article 8 need only be considered by the court if it is raised in the proceedings by or on behalf of the residential occupier. Thirdly, if an article 8 point is raised, the court should initially consider it summarily, and if, as will no doubt often be the case, the court is satisfied

---

180 [2003] UKHL 43, [2004] 1 AC 983 at [25].

181 Above, p 353.

182 [2003] UKHL 43, [2004] 1 AC 983 at [55]-[56]. This is the case in, eg, a secure tenancy under HA 1985, s 84; below, p 385.

183 Ibid, at [58]-[59]. *Pinnock* was a relatively unusual case of a demoted tenancy that is governed by special provisions under HA 1996, s 143D(2); below, p 386. Guidance on the form and content of the proportionality review in the more common circumstances of an introductory tenancy under HA 1996 (below, p 387) and the homelessness regime was given in *Hounslow LBC v Powell* [2011] UKSC 8, [2011] 2 WLR 287.

184 Ibid, at [61]-[64].

that, even if the facts relied on are made out, the point would not succeed, it should be dismissed. Only if the court is satisfied that it could affect the order that the court might make should the point be further entertained.

Fourthly, if domestic law justifies an outright order for possession, the effect of article 8 may, albeit in exceptional cases, justify (in ascending order of effect) granting an extended period for possession, suspending the order for possession on the happening of an event, or even refusing an order altogether.

Fifthly, the conclusion that the court must have the ability to assess the article 8 proportionality of making a possession order in respect of a person's home may require certain statutory and procedural provisions to be revisited. For example, section 89 of the [Housing Act 1980] limits the period for which a possession order can be postponed to 14 days, or, in cases of 'exceptional hardship', 42 days. And some of the provisions of CPR 55, which appear to mandate a summary procedure in some types of possession claim, may present difficulties in relation to cases where article 8 claims are raised. Again, we say no more on the point, since these aspects were not canvassed on the present appeal to any significant extent....[185]

Sixthly, the suggestions put forward on behalf of the Equality and Human Rights Commission, that proportionality is more likely to be a relevant issue 'in respect of occupants who are vulnerable as a result of mental illness, physical or learning disability, poor health or frailty', and that 'the issue may also require the local authority to explain why they are not securing alternative accommodation in such cases' seem to us well made.

---

[185] See now *Hounslow LBC v Powell*, above, at [57]-[64]: the court could not read down the strong statutory language of HA 1980, s 89, so as to postpone the execution of an order for possession for longer than the statutory maximum, but (Lord Hope at [63]) 'section 89 ... does not, of course, take away from the court its ordinary powers of case management. It would be perfectly proper for it, for example, to defer making the order for possession pending an appeal or to enable proceedings to be brought in the administrative court which might result in a finding that it was not lawful for a possession order to be made .... An adjournment would also be a permissible exercise of the court's discretion if more information was needed to enable it to decide what order it should make'. No evidence had been put before the Court to show that in practice the maximum period of 42 days is insufficient to meet the needs of cases of exceptional hardship, and since 'this is an area of law where the judgment of Parliament as to what was necessary to achieve its policy of restricting the discretion of the court in the case of non-secure tenancies should be respected, unless it was manifestly without reasonable foundation' (at [64]), a declaration of incompatibility was refused.

11

STATUTORY CODES FOR
SPECIAL LEASES

Summary

I	**Private Residential Lettings**	358	B	Landlord and Tenant Act 1954, Part I. Local Government and Housing Act 1989	398
	A Assured Tenancy	360			
	B Assured Shorthold Tenancy	367			
	C Control of Rent	369	C	Leasehold Reform, Housing and Urban Development Act 1993	400
	D Security of Tenure	371	D	'Right to Manage'	405
II	**Public Sector Housing. Secure Tenancy**	383	IV	**Business Tenancies**	406
	A Definition of a Secure Tenancy	383		A The Qualifying Tenancy	407
	B No Control of Rents	384		B Exclusions	409
	C Security of Tenure	385		C Security of Tenure and Rent	409
	D Demoted Tenancy	386	V	**Agricultural Tenancies**	417
	E Introductory Tenancy	387		A Agricultural Holdings	417
	F Succession	388		B Farm Business Tenancies	420
	G Right to Buy	389	VI	**Residential Flats. Tenants' Rights of First Refusal**	424
III	**Long Tenancies**	389			
	A Leasehold Reform Act 1967	390	VII	**Law Reform**	425

Land in overcrowded England is a scarce commodity that all need but many cannot afford to own. The forces of supply and demand, if left unchecked, would give landlords a bargaining superiority over their tenants that modern ideas of social justice have been unwilling to accept. As Lord Denning said:[1]

> No bargain will be upset which is the result of the ordinary interplay of forces. There are many hard cases which are caught by this rule. Take the case of a poor man who is homeless. He agrees to pay a high rent to a landlord just to get a roof over his head. The common law will not interfere. It is left to Parliament.

---

[1] *Lloyds Bank Ltd v Bundy* [1975] QB 326, 336.

In consequence, ever since the First World War, legislation has been used to redress the balance in favour of the tenant.[2] Restrictions have been imposed on the level of rent chargeable and the landlord's common law right to recover possession. With changes in Government the tide of protection has ebbed and flowed—most particularly in relation to residential tenancies, where the policy in favour of social protection has most commonly been seen to outweigh the policy of freedom of contract.[3] The high water-mark of residential tenants' rights in the private sector was the Labour Government's Rent Act of 1974. However, the Conservative Governments between 1979 and 1997 reduced the tenant's protection very significantly, through the Housing Acts of 1980, 1988 and 1996; and the Labour Governments from 1997 showed no sign of a return to the extreme protective measures of the mid-1970s. The Coalition Government that took office in 2010 regards the private rented sector as already governed by a well-established legal framework and will not introduce further regulation.[4] But the need for protection of some kind is today generally accepted and it is highly unlikely that landlord and tenant will ever be restored to their nineteenth-century freedom of contract.

Statutory protection was at first afforded only to tenants who held periodic tenancies or short leases of unfurnished residential premises;[5] but protection has been extended to most residential lettings by private landlords who do not themselves reside in the same house,[6] while different systems of control have been devised for public sector housing,[7] long leaseholders,[8] business tenants,[9] and agricultural holdings.[10] The result of somewhat haphazard historical development is that there are today many distinct statutory codes of protection, in various respects radically different from each other. The detailed provisions of this legislation are extremely complex and the subject matter of a number of specialised works. What follows is only an outline of how the various codes operate.

I PRIVATE RESIDENTIAL LETTINGS[11]

Statutory control of residential lettings dates back to 1915, but almost all the provisions now in force will be found in the Rent Act 1977 and the Housing Act 1988, as amended by the Housing Act 1996 and other legislation.

---

[2] See *Johnson v Moreton* [1980] AC 37, 65 (Lord Simon of Glaisdale); *R v Secretary of State for the Environment, Transport and the Regions, ex p Spath Holme Ltd* [2001] 2 AC 349, 378–9 (Lord Bingham of Cornhill).

[3] For an overview, see Megarry, *Rent Acts* (11th edn, 1988), Introductory Survey, esp pp 1–3.

[4] Below, p 427. There are, however, proposals for reform in the field of social housing: below, p 427. A summary of the Government's housing policy can be viewed on the Housing pages of the DCLG website, www.communities.gov.uk.

[5] Increase of Rent and Mortgage Interest (War Restrictions) Act 1915.   [6] Rent Act 1977; HA 1988.

[7] HA 1985, Part IV; below, p 383.

[8] LTA 1954, Part I; Local Government and Housing Act 1989; Leasehold Reform Act 1967; Leasehold Reform, Housing and Urban Development Act 1993; CLRA 2002, Part 2; below, pp 389 ff.

[9] LTA 1954, Part II; below, p 406.

[10] Agricultural Holdings Act 1986; Agricultural Tenancies Act 1995; below, p 417.

[11] Megarry, *Rent Acts*, vol 3; Hill and Redman's *Landlord and Tenant*, Division C; Woodfall, *Landlord and Tenant*, chs 23, 24; Martin, *Residential Security* (2nd edn, 1995); Rodgers, *Housing Law Residential*

A tenancy falling within the Rent Act 1977 is known as a 'protected tenancy'. Tenants under protected tenancies are given security of tenure by the mechanism of the 'statutory tenancy'—a status of irremovability that attaches to a tenant remaining in occupation after his protected tenancy has come to an end and that cannot be terminated by the landlord except by an order of the court made upon limited and specified grounds. For the purposes of rent regulation, both protected and statutory tenancies are termed 'regulated tenancies' and are subject to machinery for determining a 'fair rent' which is the maximum that the tenant can be required to pay. 'Fair rent' does not simply mean a 'reasonable rent', but takes as its starting point the open market rent for the premises in their current state,[12] although it is usually lower than the open market rent because it must be assumed that the demand for similar dwellings in the locality is not substantially greater than the supply.[13]

One consequence of the expansion of the rental market following the Housing Act 1988 has been to reduce the gap between supply and demand, and therefore to increase the open market rental value of premises. This has led to a corresponding increase in 'fair rents', but to avoid hardship to tenants the growth in 'fair rents' is controlled by a cap on the maximum permitted rent rise.[14]

The philosophy behind the Housing Act 1988 was that the reduction of security and rent control would increase the supply of rented accommodation by encouraging owners to let. The effect of the 1988 Act was to phase out the regulated tenancy (and also the 'restricted contract', an inferior form of protection under the Rent Act 1977 applying primarily to tenants of resident landlords). The operation of the Rent Act 1977 has been much reduced in that, subject to narrow exceptions,[15] no new protected tenancies may be granted after 15 January 1989, the date upon which the 1988 Act came into operation. Tenancies created before that date continue to enjoy the protection of the Rent Act 1977,[16] but the 1988 Act hastens their termination by diminishing the succession rights that previously existed on the death of a protected or statutory tenant.

The key concepts of the Housing Act 1988 are the 'assured tenancy' and its variant the 'assured shorthold tenancy'. The basic principle of security of tenure remains, but

---

Security and Enfranchisement (2002); Evans and Smith, Law of Landlord and Tenant (6th edn, 2002), Part D.

[12] Spath Holme Ltd v Greater Manchester and Lancashire Rent Assessment Committee (1995) 28 HLR 107; Curtis v London Rent Assessment Committee [1999] QB 92.

[13] Rent Act 1977, s 70(2). Certain other matters are also to be disregarded: ibid, s 70(3), amended by HA 1980, Sch 26.

[14] Rent Acts (Maximum Fair Rent) Order 1999 (SI 1999 No 6) caps the increase by reference to the increase in the UK Retail Prices Index plus 7.5 per cent (first applications after the Order comes into force) or 5 per cent (any subsequent applications). A challenge to the Order was rejected in R v Secretary of State for the Environment, Transport and the Regions, ex p Spath Holme Ltd [2001] 2 AC 349. For an account of the background to the Order, see at 378–80 (Lord Bingham of Cornhill, pointing out that the earlier reluctance of rent officers and rent assessment committees properly to operate the provisions of Rent Act 1977, s 70, when combined with the expansion of the rental market, and therefore higher open market rents, after HA 1988, led to 'very sharp and unexpected increases in the rent payable' under regulated tenancies). See also DETR Consultation Paper, Limiting Fair Rent Increases (1998), paras 2.3–2.5.

[15] HA 1988, s 34; Laimond Properties Ltd v Al-Shakarchi (1998) 30 HLR 1099.

[16] See, eg, Whitehouse v Lee [2009] EWCA Civ 375, [2009] 2 EGLR 75 (tenancy granted in 1963; possession order under Rent Act 1977, s 98, refused against tenants, now aged 79 and 75).

the grounds for possession are strengthened and there are only very limited rights of succession and rent control. In order to dissuade landlords from evicting Rent Act tenants unlawfully in order to get the benefit of the new Housing Act regime, the 1988 Act strengthened the Protection from Eviction Act 1977 by extending criminal and civil liability for unlawful eviction and harassment.[17]

The Housing Act 1996 gave landlords further incentive to let by removing some of the restrictive conditions formerly necessary for the creation of the less secure shorthold tenancy. The broad effect of the 1996 Act is that most assured tenancies granted after its commencement are shorthold tenancies.

The account that follows deals only with assured and assured shorthold tenancies under the Housing Act 1988 as amended. Much of the Rent Act case law, however, remains relevant, as many provisions of the 1988 Act are modelled on those of the 1977 Act, in particular in relation to the conditions for protected status, the exceptions to protection and the grounds for possession.

It appears, however, that the Housing Acts 1988 and 1996 have not had the effect of increasing the pool of private rented accommodation.[18]

A ASSURED TENANCY[19]

(1) Definition

By section 1 of the Housing Act 1988, a tenancy under which a dwelling-house is let as a separate dwelling is an assured tenancy if and so long as:

(a) the tenant or each of joint tenants is an individual; and

(b) the tenant or at least one of joint tenants occupies the dwelling-house as his only or principal home; and

(c) the tenancy is not one that cannot be an assured tenancy by virtue of the exclusions in Schedule 1[20] or by virtue of section 1(6).[21]

Further, the tenancy cannot be assured unless it was entered into on or after the commencement of the 1988 Act on 15 January 1989.[22]

Each part of the definition will now be examined.

---

[17] Above, p 348.

[18] The percentage of households renting privately fell from 20 per cent in 1971 to 10 per cent in 1995. Between 1995 and 2008 the proportion remained between 9 per cent and 11 per cent, but increased to 13 per cent in 2009 (a shift from owner occupiers with a mortgage, which decreased from 39 per cent in 2008 to 37 per cent in 2009): Office for National Statistics, *General Lifestyle Survey 2009 Overview* (2011), p 3.

[19] Bridge, *Assured Tenancies* (1999).   [20] Below, p 364.

[21] This excluded tenancies granted to homeless persons by private landlords by arrangement with the local authority. It was repealed by HA 1996, Sch 19, Pt 8. HA 1996, Pt VII, made new provision for homelessness.

[22] HA 1988, Sch 1, para 1.

(a) Dwelling-house...let as a separate dwelling

Every word of this phrase has been the subject of judicial interpretation and the last five words are among the most litigated on the statute book.

(1) Dwelling-house

A 'dwelling-house', which may be a house or part of a house, includes a flat and even an hotel,[23] but the premises must be structurally suitable for occupation as a residence and must have some degree of permanence.[24] Caravans are therefore not normally within the definition and their occupants are protected, if at all, by different legislation.[25]

(2) Let

The use of the word 'let' connotes the relationship of landlord and tenant. Contractual licensees are therefore not within the Act.[26]

The most common examples of residential licensees are lodgers (who lack exclusive possession because the owner provides attendance or services that require him to exercise unrestricted access to the premises[27]) and the 'service occupant' (the employee who is required by his contract of employment to occupy a particular dwelling for the better performance of his duties[28]). Caretakers occupying flats in blocks or office buildings usually come within this category. Agricultural workers in tied cottages also do so, but they are now subject to a separate code under the Rent (Agriculture) Act 1976. But a service occupant must be distinguished from a 'service tenant', that is a person to whom a dwelling-house is let in consequence of his employment, but who is not required to live there for the better performance of his duties.[29] Service tenants are within the Housing Act 1988, although the Act contains a special provision to enable the employer to recover possession from a tenant who has left his service.[30]

(3) As

The requirement that the house must be let *as* a separate dwelling means that one has regard to the purpose for which it was let, which will not necessarily be the same as the purpose for which it is actually being used. If a lease contains a covenant confining the use of the premises to business purposes, the tenancy will not be protected merely

---

[23] *Luganda v Service Hotels Ltd* [1969] 2 Ch 209.

[24] See *Elitestone Ltd v Morris* [1997] 1 WLR 687(chalet part of realty), M & B p 7; *Chelsea Yacht and Boat Co Ltd v Pope* [2000] 1 WLR 1941 (houseboat moored by ropes and connected to services that could be untied and disconnected without undue effort not part of the land, and therefore not occupied as a dwelling for HA 1988 which only applies to the letting of land). In November 2005, ODPM issued a Consultation Paper on security of tenure and additional contract rights of occupants of residential boats and long-term moorings. The summary of responses was published in May 2006, proposing only non-legislative measures. For fixtures generally, see above, pp 8 ff.

[25] Caravan Sites Act 1968, Part I, and Mobile Homes Act 1983; *R v Rent Officer of Nottinghamshire Registration Area, ex p Allen* (1985) 52 P & CR 41.

[26] For the distinction between a lease and a licence, see above, pp 185 ff.

[27] See *Street v Mountford* [1985] AC 809; above, p 186.

[28] *Norris v Checksfield* [1991] 1 WLR 1241.

[29] *Royal Philanthropic Society v County* [1985] 2 EGLR 109.   [30] HA 1988, Sch 2, Ground 16.

because the tenant in fact uses them as a dwelling.[31] If there is no specific user covenant in the lease, the question will turn upon the use contemplated by the parties at the time of the letting,[32] and if they had no particular use in mind, it will depend upon the nature of the premises and their de facto use at the time when the question arises for decision.

(4) A

The house (or part of a house) must be let as a single dwelling. A house let to one person as a number of separate dwellings in multiple occupation is not protected.[33] Similarly, where the owner of a house in Oxford let it to a college for the purpose of enabling it to grant sub-tenancies or licences of rooms to undergraduates, the Court of Appeal held that a letting for the purpose of permitting a number of people the exclusive use of particular rooms was not a letting of the house as a single dwelling.[34]

(5) Separate

The requirement that the premises be let as a separate dwelling would, if unqualified, exclude all cases where the tenant shares some living accommodation, either with another tenant or with his landlord.[35] This was in fact the position before 1949, by which time the courts had evolved a great deal of learning on what constituted sharing and what amounted to 'living accommodation'. Now, however, the tenant who shares with another tenant nevertheless has an assured tenancy,[36] while a tenant who shares with his landlord is normally excluded by the resident landlord exception.[37]

(6) Dwelling

The word 'dwelling' has its ordinary meaning of premises used for normal domestic purposes such as cooking, feeding and sleeping, of which sleeping seems to be the most important.[38] If premises are let partly as a dwelling and partly for business purposes (as in the common case of a shop with living accommodation above) the tenancy will be subject only to the code governing business tenancies[39] and not come within the Housing Act 1988 at all.[40]

---

[31] *Wolfe v Hogan* [1949] 2 KB 194.   [32] Ibid.

[33] *Horford Investments Ltd v Lambert* [1976] Ch 39.

[34] *St Catherine's College v Dorling* [1980] 1 WLR 66.

[35] *Neale v Del Soto* [1945] KB 144; *Goodrich v Paisner* [1957] AC 65.

[36] HA 1988, s 3.   [37] Ibid, Sch 1, para 10. See below, p 364.

[38] *Wright v Howell* (1947) 92 SJ 26; *Palmer v McNamara* [1991] 1 EGLR 121; *Westminster City Council v Clarke* [1992] 2 AC 288. Cooking facilities need not be available: *Uratemp Ventures Ltd v Collins* [2001] UKHL 43, [2002] 1 AC 301.

[39] See below, p 406.

[40] HA 1988, Sch 1, para 4. Unless the business element is *de minimis*: *Lewis v Weldcrest Ltd* [1978] 1 WLR 1107.

(b) The tenant is an individual

This part of the definition makes it clear that a corporate tenant cannot have an assured tenancy. It has long been established that a 'company let' cannot attract security of tenure under the Rent Act 1977 because that Act, although not expressly requiring the tenant to be an 'individual', imposes a residence requirement[41] that corporate tenants cannot satisfy.[42] The courts have been reluctant to regard company lettings as shams even where the mechanism has clearly been adopted solely as a device to avoid statutory protection,[43] although it remains possible that a letting to a company could be construed as a letting to the individual who occupies.[44]

(c) Occupation as only or principal home

The purpose of the Housing Act 1988 and its predecessors is to protect a tenant in the occupation of his home, not to confer rights on those who do not occupy, because they have sub-let[45] or for some other reason. The occupation requirement of the 1988 Act may be best understood by first considering the authorities under the Rent Act 1977, which remain to a great extent relevant. The rule under section 2 of the 1977 Act is that the tenant must occupy the dwelling-house as his residence. Clearly he need not be there all the time, so long as he preserves a sufficient intention to return and leaves some visible indication of continued occupation. In other words, he must establish the necessary intention to possess (*animus possidendi*) and factual possession (*corpus possessionis*).[46] The presence of the tenant's furniture and effects, his wife[47] or other member of his family are the usual ways in which the latter requirement is satisfied while the tenant is away on business, at sea or in prison.[48] A tenant who has sub-let part of the premises continues to satisfy the requirement so long as he resides in the other part.

The 'only or principal home' requirement of the assured tenancy is stricter. Although a tenant who has two homes is not excluded, he can only have an assured tenancy in relation to his principal home. This is a question of fact. The requirement is the same as that which applies to public sector secure tenants under the Housing Act 1985.[49] Decisions concerning secure tenancies may thus afford guidance.[50] In the case of joint

---

[41] Rent Act 1977, s 2.

[42] *Hiller v United Dairies (London) Ltd* [1934] 1 KB 57; *Firstcross Ltd v East-West (Export/Import) Ltd* (1980) 41 P & CR 145.

[43] *Hilton v Plustitle Ltd* [1989] 1 WLR 149; *Kaye v Massbetter Ltd and Kanter* (1990) 62 P & CR 558.

[44] See *Gisborne v Burton* [1989] QB 390 (tax doctrine of 'artificial transaction' applicable in landlord and tenant context); cf *Belvedere Court Management Ltd v Frogmore Developments Ltd* [1997] QB 858.

[45] *Ujima Housing Association v Ansah* (1997) 30 HLR 831.

[46] *Brown v Brash and Ambrose* [1948] 2 KB 247; *Skinner v Geary* [1931] 2 KB 546. This is a question of fact and degree. For the meaning of possession (both animus and corpus), see below, p 1135.

[47] Occupation by the tenant's spouse or civil partner satisfies the requirement even if the tenant does not intend to return: Family Law Act 1996, s 30(4)(a), as amended by Civil Partnership Act 2004, s 82, Sch 9.

[48] *Brown v Brash and Ambrose*, above. [49] S 81.

[50] See *Peabody Donation Fund Governors v Grant* (1982) 264 EG 925; *Crawley BC v Sawyer* (1987) 20 HLR 98. See also, on the Leasehold Reform Act 1967, *Dymond v Arundel-Timms* [1991] 1 EGLR 109.

tenants, only one need occupy as his only or principal home.[51] Hence assured status is not lost if the tenants are a married couple who separate. As in the case of the Rent Act 1977, occupation by the tenant's spouse or civil partner (where there is no joint tenancy) will satisfy the requirement.[52]

(2) The Exceptions

The Act contains a fairly long list of exceptions.[53] Only the more important ones will be considered here.

(a) Houses let by an exempted body

Tenancies granted by certain specified bodies, which include local authorities, development corporations and housing action trusts are not assured.[54] They are instead subject to the code of protection for public sector housing now found in the Housing Act 1985.[55] Exemption from the Housing Act 1988 (and from the public sector code) has been conferred upon fully mutual housing associations,[56] educational institutions and similar bodies who let premises to students,[57] and upon Crown lettings.[58] Other housing associations are not, however, exempted.

(b) Lettings by resident landlords

A tenancy is not assured if the dwelling forms part of a building[59] (other than a purpose-built block of flats) in which the landlord was also residing when the tenancy began and in which he has since continued to reside.[60]

This exception was introduced by the Rent Act 1974 and is hedged about with qualifications of great complexity that can only be explained (though not excused) by its legislative history. Until 1974 the law took no account of whether or not the landlord resided on the premises. Instead, there was a general exception for furnished lettings. The furnished tenancy exception was socially controversial because it was comparatively easy and inexpensive for a landlord to provide enough furniture to prevent the tenant from acquiring security of tenure.[61] This was hard on the many persons

---

[51] HA 1988, s 1.

[52] Family Law Act 1996, s 30(4)(b), as amended by Civil Partnership Act 2004, s 82, Sch 9. The exception extends to former spouses or civil partners, cohabitants or former cohabitants who have obtained occupation orders: ibid, ss 35(13), 36(13). The court may order the transfer of the tenancy on divorce, or on the separation of cohabitants; see below, p 366.

[53] See HA 1988, Sch 1 as amended.   [54] Ibid, para 12.   [55] See below, p 383.

[56] A housing association whose rules restrict membership to persons who are tenants or prospective tenants of the association and preclude the granting or assignment of tenancies to persons other than members: Housing Associations Act 1985, s 1(2); HA 1988, s 45(1); *Mexfield Housing Co-operative Ltd v Berrisford* [2010] EWCA Civ 811, [2010] 2 EGLR 137; *Joseph v Nettleton Road Housing Co-operative Ltd* [2010] EWCA Civ 228, [2010] 2 P & CR 12; [2010] Conv 461 (I Loveland).

[57] HA 1988, Sch 1, para 8; HA 1985, Sch 1, para 10.

[58] Ibid, para 11 (no exemption for Crown Estate Commissioners or Duchies of Lancaster or Cornwall).

[59] See *Bardrick v Haycock* (1976) 31 P & CR 420; *Griffiths v English* (1982) 261 EG 257.

[60] HA 1988, Sch 1, para 10.   [61] See *Woodward v Docherty* [1974] 1 WLR 966.

(including a substantial proportion of recent immigrants and single-parent families) who had to take furnished accommodation because they could not find or afford any other. On the other hand, there is a need for a pool of short-term accommodation that would dry up if all tenants were given full protection. The Rent Act 1974 compromised by abolishing the furnished lettings exception and trying to preserve the pool of short-term accommodation by introducing an exception for resident landlords.

The 1988 Act deals in two ways with the amount of residence that a landlord must put in to keep his tenant within the exception. In the first place, it provides that the landlord, or at least one of joint landlords, must occupy as his only or principal home.[62] Secondly, the Act specifies periods of non-residence that may be overlooked, such as up to six months for a purchaser landlord to move in and up to two years after a landlord has died and while the premises are vested in his estate.[63]

Finally, where the landlord is not only resident but also shares accommodation with the tenant, the tenancy is excluded from the requirements of the Protection from Eviction Act 1977 relating to notices to quit and recovery of possession by court order.[64]

(c) Holiday lettings

These are outside the Housing Act 1988[65] or any other system of control.[66] The lack of statutory definition of 'holiday' has facilitated attempts to avoid the Act. In the leading case of *Buchmann v May*[67] there was a three-month letting in Norbury to an Australian with a temporary visitor's permit, who had already occupied under a series of short lettings. The document, signed by her, stated that the letting was 'solely for the purpose of the tenant's holiday in the London area'.

The Court of Appeal held that where the tenancy is stated to be for a holiday, the onus is on the tenant to establish that the document is a sham or the result of mistake or misrepresentation, but added that the court would be astute to detect a sham if evasion was suspected. On the facts, the tenant failed.

(d) Tenancies at a low rent

Tenancies under which no rent is payable[68] or, if entered into on or after 1 April, 1990 (when domestic rating was abolished), at a rent not exceeding £1,000 a year in Greater London or £250 elsewhere[69] are excluded. Tenancies entered into before that date are excluded if the current rent is less than two-thirds of the rateable value on 31 March 1990.[70] The effect of these provisions is to exclude tenants under leases, usually for long terms such as 99 years, which have been granted at a low or 'ground' rent in return for payment of a substantial premium. Such tenants are, from an economic point of view,

---

62 HA 1988, Sch 1, para 10(1)(b). See above, p 363.   63 Ibid, paras 17, 20.
64 Above, p 348; Protection from Eviction Act 1977, s 3A, inserted by HA 1988, s 31.
65 HA 1988, Sch 1, para 9.   66 Protection from Eviction Act 1977, s 3A; above, n 64.
67 [1978] 2 All ER 993.   68 HA 1988, Sch 1, para 3.
69 Ibid, para 3A, inserted by References to Rating (Housing) Regulations 1990 (SI 1990 No 434).
70 Ibid, para 3B.

owner-occupiers, and the machinery of the 1988 Act is not appropriate for them. As we shall see, they have substantial protection under other statutory codes.[71]

(e) Tenancies at a high rent

Tenancies granted on or after 1 April 1990 cannot be assured if the current rent exceeds a figure which is now set at £100,000 a year.[72] At this level there is no hardship in allowing a free market. Tenancies granted prior to that date, before the abolition of domestic rating, are excluded if the property (or such part as is subject to the tenancy) had a rateable value on 31 March 1990 exceeding £1,500 in Greater London or £750 elsewhere.[73]

(3) Implied terms of the assured tenancy

The most important implied term relates to assignment and sub-letting. In the case of an assured periodic tenancy, there is an implied term that the tenant shall not assign, sub-let or part with possession (in whole or in part) without the landlord's consent.[74] Section 19 of the Landlord and Tenant Act 1927,[75] implying that the landlord's consent shall not be unreasonably withheld, is excluded.

No such term is implied in the case of a periodic tenancy (which is not a statutory periodic tenancy[76]) if there is an express term either prohibiting or permitting assignment and so forth (absolutely or conditionally).[77] In the case of an express conditional prohibition, section 19 of the 1927 Act will apply.

Nor is such a term implied in the case of a fixed-term assured tenancy, where the general law on assignment and sub-letting (including section 19 of the 1927 Act) applies. It should be noted that the court has power to order the transfer of an assured tenancy to the other spouse, civil partner of cohabitant on divorce, on making a property adjustment order with respect to a civil partnership, or on separation of cohabitants.[78]

In the case of all assured tenancies there is an implied term that the tenant shall afford the landlord access for doing repairs that the landlord is entitled to execute.[79]

The jurisdiction of the rent assessment committee to vary the terms of a statutory periodic tenancy is dealt with below.[80]

---

[71] See below, p 389.

[72] HA 1988, Sch 1, para 2, as substituted by References to Rating (Housing) Regulations 1990 (SI 1990 No 434), and raised from £25,000 to £100,000 by Assured Tenancies (Amendment) (England) Order 2010 (SI 2010 No 908); *R v London Rent Assessment Panel, ex p Cadogan Estates Ltd* [1998] QB 398. 'Rent' does not include any sum payable by the tenant as is expressed (in whatever terms) to be payable in respect of rates, council tax, services, management, repairs, maintenance or insurance, unless it could not have been regarded by the parties to the tenancy as a sum so payable: ibid.

[73] Ibid, Sch 1, para 2A.   [74] Ibid, s 15.   [75] See above, p 259.   [76] See below, p 369.

[77] HA 1988, s 15(3)(a). Nor is such a term implied where a premium is payable on the grant or renewal of the tenancy: s 15(3)(b).

[78] Family Law Act 1996, Sch 7, as amended by Civil Partnership Act 2004, s 82, Sch 9.

[79] HA 1988, s 16.   [80] See below, p 370.

B ASSURED SHORTHOLD TENANCY

An assured shorthold tenancy is one that is within the definition of an assured tenancy, as discussed above, and that satisfies further conditions. In the case of tenancies granted before 28 February 1997 (when the amending provisions of the Housing Act 1996 came into operation) the conditions were as follows:[81]

(a) it is a fixed-term tenancy granted for a term certain of not less than six months; and

(b) the landlord has no power to determine[82] the tenancy at any time earlier than six months from the beginning of the tenancy; and

(c) a notice in prescribed form[83] was served by the prospective landlord on the prospective tenant[84] before the assured tenancy was entered into, stating that the tenancy was to be a shorthold tenancy.[85]

Subject to certain exceptions,[86] failure to satisfy the three conditions resulted in the creation of an assured tenancy, so long as section 1 of the 1988 Act was satisfied.

The attraction of the assured shorthold tenancy to landlords is that they may recover possession more easily than in the case of an assured tenancy because of the availability of a special mandatory ground of possession applicable only to assured shorthold tenancies. This ground, which is available in addition to the grounds that apply to assured tenancies generally, is explained below.[87] The other distinction between assured tenancies and assured shorthold tenancies is that a greater degree of rent control applies to assured shortholds.[88]

The Housing Act 1996 gave landlords further inducement to let by providing that assured tenancies granted on or after 28 February 1997 are shortholds unless they fall within certain narrow exceptions. In other words, the shorthold is the norm and positive steps must be taken to create a full assured tenancy, which is the converse of the previous position. The simple definition is that an assured tenancy entered into after the 1996 Act is an assured shorthold unless it falls within the exceptions mentioned below.[89] Thus there is no minimum term, no prohibition on landlord's

---

[81] HA 1988, s 20(1). See also s 20(3) (anti-avoidance).

[82] The existence of a right of re-entry is not treated as a power to determine the tenancy; ibid, s 45(4). Forfeiture is not a means of determining assured tenancies; see below, p 372.

[83] The question is whether the notice is substantially to the same effect as the prescribed form in accomplishing the statutory purpose of telling the proposed tenant the special nature of an assured shorthold tenancy, even if it is wrong in some detail: Assured Tenancies and Agricultural Occupancies (Forms) Regulations 1988, SI 1988 No 2203, reg 2; *Ravenseft Properties Ltd v Hall* [2001] EWCA Civ 2034, [2002] 1 EGLR 9.

[84] Or the tenant's authorised agent: *Yenula Properties Ltd v Naidu* [2002] EWCA Civ 719, [2002] 3 EGLR 28.

[85] See *Panayi v Roberts* [1993] 2 EGLR 51. The court has no power to dispense with this requirement.

[86] HA 1988, s 20(4) (where prior assured shorthold); s 34(2) (where prior shorthold tenancy under Rent Act 1977); s 39(7) (succession on death of shorthold tenant under Rent Act 1977).

[87] Ibid, s 21; below, p 377.   [88] Below, p 370.

[89] HA 1996, s 96, inserting s 19A into the 1988 Act. A statutory periodic tenancy arising under s 5 of the 1988 Act at the end of a fixed term falling within s 19A is also shorthold, as explained below.

break clauses, periodic tenancies are included, and there is no need to serve prior notice on the prospective tenant. The tenant no longer has a warning as to the nature of the tenancy. As explained below, the tenant is protected by the rule that possession cannot be recovered during the first six months.

The main exceptional cases where a full assured tenancy may still be created are as follows.[90]

    (a) *Excluded by notice* Where the prospective landlord serves notice on the prospective tenant before the tenancy is entered into, stating that the tenancy is not to be shorthold; or, where the landlord serves a notice on the tenant after an assured tenancy has been entered into, stating that it is no longer shorthold.

    (b) *Excluded by tenancy provision* Where the tenancy itself contains a provision to the effect that it is not shorthold.

    (c) *Successor to Rent Act tenant* An assured tenancy arising under section 39 of the 1988 Act in favour of a successor to a deceased Rent Act tenant (whose tenancy was not a protected shorthold) takes effect as a full assured tenancy.

    (d) *Tenancies replacing non-shortholds* Where immediately before[91] the grant of a tenancy the tenant (alone or jointly with others) had a full assured tenancy, then the new tenancy is also a full assured tenancy, if granted by the same landlord (or one of the joint landlords). There is no requirement that the premises be the same. The replacement tenancy will, however, be a shorthold if the tenant serves a prescribed form notice before the grant of the replacement tenancy stating that the new tenancy is to be shorthold.

As it is now possible to grant a shorthold informally, for example a weekly or monthly periodic tenancy, the Act[92] provides a means for the tenant to acquire a written statement of the terms of the tenancy. A tenant who has an assured shorthold granted on or after 28 February 1997 may by notice in writing require the landlord to provide a written statement of any of the following terms that is not already evidenced in writing:

    (a) the date the tenancy began or, if it is a statutory periodic tenancy, the date it arose;

    (b) the rent and the dates on which it is payable;

    (c) any term providing for rent review;

    (d) the length of the term if it is a fixed term.

---

[90] HA 1996, Sch 7, inserting Sch 2A into the 1988 Act. Other exceptions relate to assured agricultural occupancies, tenancies that transfer from the secure to the assured regime when the landlord ceases to be a local authority, and assured tenancies arising on termination of long leaseholds.

[91] See *Dibbs v Campbell* [1988] 2 EGLR 122 (no assured tenancy immediately before the grant where effectively surrendered).

[92] HA 1996, s 97, inserting s 20A into the 1988 Act.

Such a statement is not conclusive evidence of what was agreed. A landlord who fails to comply without reasonable excuse is liable to a fine.

Further protection was given to assured shorthold tenants by the Housing Act 2004,[93] under which tenancy deposit schemes were introduced to safeguard tenancy deposits and facilitate the resolution of disputes relating to deposits.

The result of the 1996 Act is that most private landlords will create only assured shortholds, while full assured tenancies continue to be granted by 'social landlords' such as housing associations.[94] Thus the private rental sector has been substantially deregulated.

C CONTROL OF RENT

Rent control under the 'fair rent' system of the Rent Act 1977[95] took the form of keeping the rent below market levels. In order to encourage letting, the philosophy of the Housing Act 1988 is to impose a form of rent control that seeks merely to prevent excessive rents and does not prohibit the recovery of a market rent. Unlike the Rent Act 1977, the payment of a premium on the grant or assignment of an assured tenancy is not prohibited.

(1) Fixed-term Assured Tenancy

The rent control scheme of the 1988 Act does not apply to such a tenancy during the period of the fixed term. The rent under such a tenancy is that which the parties have agreed. It may be increased if there is a rent review clause (or by agreement).

(2) Periodic Assured Tenancy and Statutory Periodic Assured Tenancy

As will be explained below,[96] the scheme of the Housing Act 1988 is that a periodic assured tenancy continues until a ground for possession becomes available, and cannot be terminated by a landlord's notice to quit. The security mechanism for a fixed-term assured tenancy is that, on expiry of the fixed term, a statutory periodic assured tenancy arises, which continues until a ground for possession becomes available and

---

[93] Ss 212-215. The landlord cannot issue a notice under HA 1988, s 21, to recover possession of the property if he is in default in relation to the tenancy deposit scheme: s 215.

[94] If the landlord is (a) a non-profit registered provider of social housing, or (b) a profit-making registered provided of social housing and the dwelling-house is social housing, or (c) a registered social landlord, the landlord may apply to a county court for a demotion order under HA 1998, s 6A, inserted by Anti-social Behaviour Act 2003, s 14(4) (and amended by SI 2010 No 866, Sch 2, para 64), under which the assured tenancy is terminated and replaced by a demoted assured shorthold tenancy. This demoted tenancy lasts for at least one year: HA 1988, s 20B, inserted by Anti-social Behaviour Act 2003, s 15(1); and during the demotion period the landlord can obtain an order for possession without having to establish grounds: HA 1988, s 21, as amended by Anti-social Behaviour Act 2003, s 15(2). For demotion orders in relation to secure tenancies under HA 1985, see below, p 386.

[95] Above, p 359. [96] Below, p 372.

cannot be ended by a landlord's notice to quit. In both of these cases section 13 of the 1988 Act provides a means of increasing the rent.[97]

The landlord may serve on the tenant a notice in prescribed form proposing a new rent to take effect at the beginning of a new period of the tenancy specified in the notice.[98] Except in the case of a statutory periodic tenancy, the increase cannot take effect within a year of the commencement of the tenancy. If the rent has already been increased under this procedure, no further increase can take effect within a year of the date on which the previous increase took effect. Subject to these two rules, the Act provides that the increased rent cannot take effect within certain minimum periods from the date of service of the notice, such as six months in the case of a yearly tenancy.[99]

The rent specified in the landlord's notice will take effect unless the tenant refers the notice to a rent assessment committee before the beginning of the new period specified in the notice.[100] Alternatively, the rent may be varied by agreement without following these procedures.[101]

If the tenant refers the landlord's notice to a rent assessment committee, the committee will determine the rent that the dwelling 'might reasonably be expected to be let in the open market by a willing landlord under an assured tenancy'.[102] In assessing the market rent, certain matters must be disregarded, such as any increase in value attributable to relevant improvements by the tenant[103] or any decrease in value attributable to a breach of covenant by the tenant, such as a failure to repair.[104] The rent determined by the committee takes effect from the beginning of the new period specified in the landlord's notice (unless the parties agree otherwise), although a later date may be substituted if it appears that the earlier date would cause undue hardship to the tenant.[105]

(3) Assured Shorthold Tenancy

The procedures described above can apply to assured shorthold tenancies provided they are periodic.[106] Shorthold tenancies granted before the operation of the Housing Act 1996 were normally fixed-term,[107] and, accordingly, outside these provisions unless

---

[97] Any rent review clause in the original assured tenancy, even if expressed to continue to apply after the expiry of the assured tenancy, is excluded from the new tenancy and is of no effect. It is replaced by the statutory rent review procedure under s 13: *London District Properties (Management) Ltd v Goolamy* [2009] EWHC 1367 (Admin), [2010] 1 WLR 307.

[98] HA 1988, s 13(2), as amended by SI 2003 No 259.

[99] Ibid, s 13(2), (3), as amended by SI 2003 No 259.   [100] Ibid, s 13(4).   [101] Ibid, s 13(5).

[102] Ibid, s 14(1). An assessment above the statutory maximum rent for assured tenancies will take the tenancy out of assured status; *R v London Rent Assessment Panel, ex p Cadogan Estates Ltd* [1998] QB 398 (then, the limit was £25,000; it is now £100,000: above, n 72).

[103] But not improvements made to the premises by the tenant under an earlier lease that was not itself an assured tenancy: *Hughes v Borodex Ltd* [2010] EWCA Civ 425; [2010] 1 WLR 2682.

[104] Ibid, s 14(2). The default must be that of the present tenant: *N & D (London) Ltd v Gadsdon* [1992] 1 EGLR 112.

[105] Ibid, s 14(7).   [106] Ibid, s 14(9), inserted by HA 1996, s 104, Sch 8.   [107] Above, p 367.

they had become statutory periodic tenancies on expiry of the fixed term. There is no requirement of a minimum six-month fixed term in the case of assured shortholds granted after the commencement of the 1996 Act. Thus the provisions discussed in (b) above are now of wider application.

The 1988 Act provides a further procedure that is applicable only to assured shorthold tenancies, and that enables the tenant to refer the rent initially agreed to a rent assessment committee.[108] This differs from the procedure already discussed, which merely facilitates a review of the rent after it has operated for a certain period. A shorthold tenant may apply by notice in prescribed form for a determination by the committee, which will then determine the rent that 'the landlord might reasonably be expected to obtain under the assured shorthold tenancy'.[109] This procedure may be invoked only once, and is not available in the case of a statutory periodic tenancy that has arisen on the expiry of a fixed-term shorthold tenancy.[110] In the case of an assured shorthold granted on or after 28 February 1997 the tenant may refer the rent under this procedure only within the period of six months from the beginning of the tenancy.[111]

The committee is not to make a determination unless it considers that there is a sufficient number of similar dwellings in the locality let on assured tenancies (whether or not shorthold), and that the agreed rent is significantly higher than the rent that the landlord might reasonably be expected to be able to obtain.[112] The committee has no power to increase the rent. The effect of these limitations is that the tenant will not succeed if there are insufficient comparables nor if the rent is insufficiently excessive. His lack of security of tenure may in any event make him reluctant to apply.

If the committee does determine the rent, it takes effect from such date as it directs, not being earlier than the date of the application.[113]

Finally, information as to rents that have been the subject of applications to rent assessment committees is publicly available, to assist in the establishment of comparables.[114]

D SECURITY OF TENURE

An assured tenancy may be terminated only in the manner laid down by the Housing Act 1988, as amended by the Housing Act 1996. As in the case of the Rent Act 1977, it is clear from the mandatory wording of the Act that the parties cannot contract out of security of tenure.[115] If, however, the tenancy has ceased to be assured, as where the

---

[108] HA 1988, s 22.   [109] Ibid, s 22(1).   [110] Ibid, s 22(2).

[111] Ibid, s 22(2)(aa), inserted by HA 1996, s 100.   [112] Ibid, s 22(3).

[113] Ibid, s 22(4). Any excess is irrecoverable from the tenant. The landlord cannot serve a notice of increase under s 13 within a year of this date.

[114] Ibid, s 42.

[115] *Bankway Properties Ltd v Pensfold-Dunsford* [2001] EWCA Civ 528, [2001] 1 WLR 1369 (provision for five-fold rent increase, designed to give landlord right to possession, held unenforceable as being an improper attempt to evade the mandatory scheme for security of tenure: Arden LJ at [56]; or as being inconsistent with

tenant no longer occupies as his only or principal home, the landlord may terminate it by any methods that are available under the general law.

(1) Periodic Assured Tenancy

In the case of a periodic tenancy, section 5 of the 1988 Act provides that service of a notice to quit by the landlord shall be of no effect.[116] Such a tenancy may be terminated by a tenant's notice to quit[117] or by the excecution of a court order based on a ground for possession, as explained below.

(2) Fixed-term Assured Tenancy

Such a tenancy may be terminated by 'surrender or other action on the part of the tenant'.[118] The 'other action' would include the operation of a break clause (a provision permitting premature termination of a fixed term) by the tenant. The landlord cannot terminate the tenancy except by a court order based on a ground for possession or, 'in the case of a fixed-term tenancy that contains a power for the landlord to determine the tenancy in certain circumstances, by the exercise of that power'.[119] It is further provided that, unless the tenancy is terminated by the tenant or by a court order, the tenant is entitled to remain after termination of the fixed term as a statutory periodic tenant.[120] This will occur, for example, where the fixed term ends by expiry or is determined by the exercise of a break clause by the landlord. The provisions relating to forfeiture are obscurely drafted, but the position has been held to be as follows. The reference in section 5 to ending the tenancy by the exercise of a landlord's power to determine it does not include forfeiture,[121] which is not, therefore, an available method of terminating an assured tenancy.[122] A notice under section 146 of the Law of Property Act 1925[123] would be ineffective, and the concept of relief from forfeiture does not apply. A landlord who would have had grounds for forfeiture may, however, be able to invoke a statutory ground for possession. Only certain grounds are available during the currency of a fixed term,[124] and the terms of the tenancy must provide for

the statutory purpose of security of tenure that the parties, by choosing to contract in the form of an assured tenancy under HA 1988, had incorporated into their agreement: Pill LJ at [70]).

[116] See *Love v Herrity* [1991] 2 EGLR 44.

[117] Notice by one of joint tenants will suffice; *Hammersmith and Fulham LBC v Monk* [1992] 1 AC 478, above, p 338.

[118] HA 1988, s 5(2).

[119] Ibid, s 5(1). See *Aylward v Fawaz* (1996) 29 HLR 408. For the termination of an assured tenancy and its replacement by a demoted assured shorthold tenancy, see above, p 369, n 94.

[120] HA 1988, s 5(2). For the avoidance of doubt, a statutory periodic tenancy arising after the commencement of HA 1996 on the termination of an assured tenancy that was not a shorthold will not itself be a shorthold: HA 1996, Sch 7, para 8.

[121] Ibid, s 45(4).   [122] *Artesian Residential Investments Ltd v Beck* [2000] QB 541.

[123] See above, p 288.

[124] The available grounds are the mandatory Grounds 2 and 8 and the discretionary grounds other than Grounds 9 and 16. These are explained below, pp 373–81.

termination on the ground in question (whether by forfeiture, notice or otherwise).[125] It appears that the forfeiture clause or other terminating provision in the tenancy need not refer specifically to the grounds for possession, although the safest course would be to make specific reference.

Where a statutory periodic tenancy arises on termination of the fixed term, it can be ended only by the tenant[126] or by a court order based on a ground for possession, as described in (a) above. The periods of this tenancy are the same as those for which rent was last payable under the fixed term. The other terms (including rent) are the same as those of the fixed term immediately before it ended.[127] The implied terms relating to assignment and sub-letting and the procedure for increasing the rent have already been discussed.[128] Either party may seek a variation in the terms of the tenancy (other than rent) by serving a notice proposing different terms on the other party. If the other party does not accept the new terms he may refer the notice to a rent assessment committee, which will determine whether those terms or some other terms might reasonably be expected in an assured periodic tenancy of the dwelling-house in question.[129]

(3) The Grounds for Possession

The court may make an order for possession that, when executed,[130] determines the assured tenancy, only if the judge is satisfied of the existence of one of the grounds for possession specified in the Act.[131] In some cases the establishment of a statutory ground for possession concludes the matter. An order for possession is then mandatory.[132] In other cases, the judge may not make such an order unless he considers it reasonable to do so.[133] The requirement gives the judge a wide discretion, enabling him to consider all relevant circumstances at the date of the hearing. There are 18 grounds for possession, eight mandatory and ten discretionary. In addition, there is the special mandatory ground that applies only to assured shorthold tenancies.[134] The position as to termination during the currency of a fixed-term assured tenancy has already been discussed.[135] Where a fixed-term tenancy has come to an end, execution of the possession order operates to terminate also any statutory periodic tenancy that has arisen.[136]

---

[125] HA 1988, s 7(6). See (1989) 139 NLJ 326 (C Rodgers).

[126] As in the case of any tenancy of premises let as a dwelling, the tenant must give four weeks' notice: Protection from Eviction Act 1977, s 5, above, p 331; *Laine v Cadwallader* (2001) 33 HLR 36.

[127] HA 1988, s 5(3).   [128] See s 15 (assignment etc), above, p 366, and s 13 (rent), above, p 370.

[129] HA 1988, s 6.

[130] Ibid, s 5(1)(a), amended by Housing and Regeneration Act 2008, Sch 11, para 6, to avoid the possibility of a former tenant being a 'tolerated trespasser' if the court's order is not executed: below, p 385 (cf, however, *Knowsley Housing Trust v White* [2008] UKHL 70, [2009] 1 AC 636, where HL decided that, by contrast with a secured tenancy under HA 1985 (below, p 385), an assured tenancy under HA 1988 subject to a suspended possession order ended only when possession was given up).

[131] As to consent orders, see *Baygreen Properties Ltd v Gil* [2002] EWCA Civ 1340, [2002] 3 EGLR 42.

[132] HA 1988, Sch 2, Part I.   [133] Ibid, Sch 2, Part II.   [134] Ibid, s 21, below.   [135] Above.

[136] HA 1988, s 7(7), amended by Housing and Regeneration Act 2008, Sch 11, para 7; see above, n 130.

In order to invoke a ground for possession, the landlord must serve a notice[137] in prescribed form under section 8 of the 1988 Act, specifying the ground or grounds relied on.[138] He must then begin proceedings within the time limits laid down by section 8, which vary according to the ground in question.[139]

Compensation is payable where the landlord recovers possession but it later appears that he obtained the order by misrepresentation or concealment of material facts.[140]

(a) Mandatory grounds

The following grounds are those upon which the court must order possession.

(1) Ground 1: landlord occupied or intends to occupy

This ground applies either where the landlord (or at least one of joint landlords) occupied the dwelling as his only or principal home at some time before the beginning of the tenancy or, without any such condition, the landlord (or at least one of joint landlords) requires the dwelling as his, his spouse's, or his civil partner's[141] only or principal home. In the latter case the landlord must not have acquired the reversion for money or money's worth. In the former case there is no requirement that the landlord intends to occupy. In both cases the ground is available only if the landlord gave written notice no later than the beginning of the tenancy that possession might be recovered on this ground, although the court may dispense with this requirement if of the opinion that it is just and equitable to do so.[142]

(2) Ground 2: mortgagee's power of sale

Where the landlord mortgaged the property before granting the tenancy, this ground is available where the mortgagee requires possession in order to exercise the power of sale. Written notice[143] must have been given before the beginning of the tenancy, unless the court dispenses with the requirement, as in the case of Ground 1.

Where the mortgage was granted after the tenancy, the mortgagee's power of sale can be exercised only subject to the tenancy,[144] and so this ground is not available. A tenancy granted after the mortgage will be binding on the mortgagee only if the mortgagor's leasing power under section 99 of the Law of Property Act 1925[145] has not been excluded, or if he has consented to the grant or accepted the tenant. It is in these cases that Ground 2 is relevant. Where the tenancy is not binding on the mortgagee, the latter may recover possession under the general law without regard to the Housing

---

[137] The court may dispense with this requirement (except in the case of Ground 8) if it considers it just and equitable to do so: ibid, s 8(1)(b). *Kelsey Housing Association v King* (1995) 28 HLR 270.

[138] The statutory grounds need not be set out verbatim in the notice but the substance must be fully set out; *Mountain v Hastings* (1993) 25 HLR 427 (Ground 8).

[139] The time limits have been amended by s 151 of HA 1996. The main effect is to enable proceedings based on Ground 14 to be commenced more speedily.

[140] HA 1988, s 12.   [141] As amended by Civil Partnership Act 2004, s 81, Sch 8.

[142] See *Boyle v Verrall* [1997] 1 EGLR 25; *Mustafa v Ruddock* (1998) 30 HLR 495.

[143] It appears that the notice in question must have been a notice under Ground 1.

[144] See p 854, below; *Barclays Bank plc v Zaroovabli* [1997] Ch 321.   [145] See p 843, below.

Act 1988,[146] although the landlord could not do so. If the subject of the mortgage is the assured tenancy itself, the mortgagee's right to possession is not affected by the Housing Act 1988.[147]

(3) Ground 3: out-of-season lettings

This ground applies to a fixed-term tenancy not exceeding eight months where the dwelling has been occupied for a holiday within the 12-month period before the beginning of the tenancy. The landlord must have given written notice to the tenant no later than the beginning of the tenancy that possession might be recovered on this ground. The effect of this ground is that landlords may let holiday accommodation out of season and be able to recover possession when the property is again required for holiday lettings, which, as has been seen, cannot be assured tenancies.[148]

(4) Ground 4: vacation lettings of student accommodation

This is based on the same principle as Ground 3. Student lettings themselves cannot be assured.[149] If the landlord wishes to utilise the accommodation in the vacation, possession may be recovered on this ground when the property is again required for student lettings. The vacation letting must be for a fixed term not exceeding 12 months, the dwelling must have been subject to an excluded student letting during the twelve-month period before the beginning of the tenancy, and written notice must have been given to the tenant no later than the beginning of the tenancy that possession might be recovered on this ground.

(5) Ground 5: occupation by minister of religion

This ground applies to a dwelling that is held for the purposes of being available as a residence for a minister of religion, where the court is satisfied that the dwelling is now required for that purpose. Notice must have been given to the tenant not later than the beginning of the tenancy that possession might be recovered on this ground.

(6) Ground 6: intention to demolish or reconstruct

A landlord[150] who intends to demolish or reconstruct the whole or a substantial part of the dwelling or to do substantial works may invoke this ground, which is based on one of the business tenancy grounds in the Landlord and Tenant Act 1954.[151] The landlord will not succeed if the work could reasonably be done without the tenant giving up possession. The tenant may, for example, be willing to take an assured tenancy of a reduced part of the dwelling or to give the landlord access and facilities, where the nature of the work is such that either course would be practicable.

---

[146] See, on the Rent Act 1977, *Britannia Building Society v Earl* [1990] 1 WLR 422.   [147] S 7(1).
[148] See p 365, above.   [149] See p 364, above.
[150] Or, where the landlord is a non-profit registered provider of social housing, registered social landlord or charitable housing trust, or (where the dwelling-house is social housing) a profit-making registered provider of social housing, if the superior landlord intends to demolish or reconstruct the premises: as amended by SI 2010 No 866, Sch 2, para 72.
[151] S 30(1)(f), below, p 412.

This ground is available only to the original landlord or a successor who acquired the reversion other than for money or money's worth. In other words, he must not have purchased the property subject to the tenancy.

Where Ground 6 is established, the landlord must pay reasonable removal expenses to the tenant.[152]

(7) Ground 7: death of periodic tenant

Where a periodic assured tenant dies without leaving a spouse or civil partner who is qualified to succeed to the assured tenancy,[153] it devolves under his will or intestacy and becomes subject to termination by Ground 7. The landlord must begin proceedings not later than 12 months after the death or after the date on which the court considers that the landlord became aware of it. If the landlord does not act in time, the tenancy will continue until some other ground for possession becomes available, provided the beneficiary satisfies the conditions required for an assured tenancy. If he does not, the tenancy may be terminated by a notice to quit, without recourse to Ground 7.

Ground 7 does not apply to a fixed-term assured tenancy. On the death of the tenant such a tenancy will pass under his will or intestacy and will continue assured if the beneficiary satisfies the conditions required for an assured tenancy. A statutory periodic tenancy will then arise at the end of the fixed term, which will be subject to Ground 7 on the tenant's death. If the beneficiary does not satisfy the conditions required for an assured tenancy, the tenancy will terminate on expiry of the fixed term.

(8) Ground 8: two months' rent unpaid[154]

There are three grounds for possession relating to rent, one mandatory and two discretionary.[155] Ground 8 applies where the arrears exist both at the date of service of the notice of proceedings under section 8[156] and at the date of the hearing. The amount of arrears necessary to establish the ground varies according to how frequently the rent is payable under the tenancy, but broadly at least two months' rent must be unpaid. The rent must be 'lawfully due', which will not be the case, for example, so far as it exceeds any figure determined by a rent assessment committee.[157]

As the ground is mandatory, the court has no power to suspend or postpone the order subject to conditions as to payment.[158] If, however, the tenant pays the arrears before

---

[152] HA 1988, s 11.   [153] See p 381, below.
[154] Reduced from three months by HA 1996, s 101.   [155] Grounds 10 and 11, below.
[156] Above, p 374. See *Mountain v Hastings* (1993) 25 HLR 427; *Marath v MacGillivray* (1996) 28 HLR 484.
[157] HA 1988, ss 14, 22; see pp 370, 371, above. Other examples would include non-compliance with Landlord and Tenant Act 1987, ss 47, 48 (duty to provide information to tenant). The rent 'lawfully due' is the rent after deduction of the amount of any equitable set-off: *Baygreen Properties Ltd v Gil* [2002] EWCA Civ 1340, [2002] 3 EGLR 42.
[158] Ibid, s 9(6). See *North British Housing Association Ltd v Matthews* [2004] EWCA Civ 1736, [2005] 1 WLR 3133 (court has power to adjourn before being 'satisfied' (by judgment, given in a perfected order of the court) that the landlord is entitled to possession, but such adjournment can be granted in order to enable tenant to reduce arrears of rent below Ground 8 threshold only in exceptional circumstances and

the hearing, Ground 8 will no longer apply.[159] The discretionary grounds applicable to rent may still apply, and so the landlord should include these in his section 8 notice.

(9) Assured shorthold tenancy

Section 21 provides a further mandatory ground that is confined to assured shorthold tenancies. Where the tenancy has ended and no further tenancy is in existence other than a statutory periodic tenancy, the court must make a possession order if the landlord has given the tenant not less than two months' notice in writing[160] stating that he requires possession.[161] The court cannot stay or suspend the order.[162] The notice may be given on or before the day on which a fixed-term tenancy ends, although the order cannot be made before the fixed term has ended.[163]

Where a fixed-term tenancy has already become a statutory periodic tenancy before the notice is served, the date specified in the landlord's notice cannot be earlier than the earliest date upon which the tenancy could have been ended[164] by notice to quit.

In the case of a shorthold granted on or after 28 February 1997, a possession order may not be made so as to take effect earlier than six months after the beginning of the tenancy.[165] Where the tenancy is a 'replacement tenancy', coming into being at the end of an assured shorthold with the same parties and premises, the six-month period runs from the beginning of the original tenancy. Thus a landlord who renews the shorthold or does not act to prevent a statutory periodic tenancy arising on termination of a fixed-term shorthold is not prejudiced. These provisions thus provide minimum security to shorthold tenants in the light of the fact that the former requirement of a fixed term of at least six months does not apply to shortholds granted after the commencement of the 1996 Act. However short the term, the landlord cannot regain possession for at least six months.

(b) Discretionary grounds

The grounds discussed below are those upon which the court may make an order for possession if it considers it reasonable to do so.[166] In the case of these discretionary

---

cannot be used to defeat the policy of the Act); [2005] EG 165 (S Murdoch). See also *Floyd v S* [2008] EWCA Civ 201, [2008] 1 WLR 1274 (arrears not referable to defendant's alleged disability: possession order not discriminatory under Disability Discrimination Act 1995).

[159] An uncleared cheque delivered to the landlord or his agent at or before the hearing and that is accepted by him, or that he is bound by earlier agreement to accept, is to be treated as payment at the date of delivery provided the cheque is subsequently paid at first presentation; and an adjournment is appropriate to see if the cheque will clear: *Day v Coltrane* [2003] EWCA Civ 342, [2003] 1 WLR 1379; [2004] Conv 152 (J Morgan).

[160] HA 1988, s 21(1), as amended by HA 1996, s 98.

[161] A notice of proceedings under s 8 is not required; *Panayi v Roberts* [1993] 2 EGLR 51.

[162] HA 1988, s 9(6). An accelerated possession procedure is available: CPR, Part 55, Section II.

[163] See *Lower Street Properties Ltd v Jones* (1996) 28 HLR 877 (landlord may not start proceedings before expiry of notice).

[164] But for s 5(1), which prohibits termination by a landlord's notice to quit.

[165] HA 1988, s 21(5), inserted by HA 1996, s 99. The proceedings may be commenced within this period. This restriction does not apply to a demoted assured shorthold tenancy: HA 1988, s 21(5A), as inserted by Anti-social Behaviour Act 2003, s 15(2); p 369, n 94, above.

[166] Ibid, s 7(4).

grounds the court may adjourn the proceedings or stay or suspend execution of the order or postpone the date of possession for such period as it thinks just.[167] In such a case the court will impose conditions as to the payment of any rent arrears or such other conditions as it thinks fit. Where the tenant complies with the conditions, the possession order may be discharged.

(1) Ground 9: alternative accommodation

The court can make an order for possession if it is satisfied that 'suitable alternative accommodation' is available for the tenant or will be available for him when the order takes effect. Alternative accommodation is suitable if (as will normally be the case) the tenant will have an assured tenancy or equivalent security of tenure,[168] and if the premises are reasonably suitable to the means of the tenant and the needs of his family as regards proximity to place of work, extent and character.[169] Although the alternative accommodation must be suitable for the tenant and his family, it need not be as pleasant and commodious as the existing premises.[170] The test is suitability to the means and needs of the tenant and not comparison with what the tenant has got.[171] Indeed, landlords would seldom in practice offer alternative accommodation if it had to be in all respects equivalent to the existing premises. Furthermore, the rent may be higher than that of the existing premises. If the tenant has the means to pay, the accommodation will nevertheless be suitable.[172] It should however be observed that although comparisons with the existing premises and rent are not admissible on the question of suitability, they are nevertheless matters that the judge may take into account in deciding whether or not it is reasonable to make an order for possession.[173]

An ingenious piece of judicial interpretation has made the 'alternative accommodation' provision a means of regaining possession of parts of the premises that the tenant has sub-let. We have seen that as long as the tenant himself resides somewhere on the premises as his only or principal home, he may sub-let the rest and retain his assured tenancy of the whole.[174] An assured tenant may thus be able to make more out of sub-lettings of parts than he pays his landlord for the whole premises.

---

[167] HA 1988, s 9. As to the mandatory grounds, see HA 1980, s 89 (fourteen days or up to six weeks if exceptional hardship).

[168] Ibid, Sch 2, Part III, para 2. A tenancy subject to Grounds 1–5 or an assured shorthold will not suffice. Whether a residential property owned by the tenant but let out to another person will be 'suitable alternative accommodation' depends on whether it is reasonable to expect the tenant to take steps to recover possession of it: *Amrit Holdings Co Ltd v Shahbakhti* [2005] EWCA Civ 339, [2005] L & TR 18.

[169] HA 1988, Sch 2, Part III, para 3. See *Siddiqui v Rashid* [1980] 1 WLR 1018, in which a room in a house in Luton (where the tenant worked) was held to be a suitable alternative to a room in Islington, where the tenant had cultural, social and religious connections. The Rent Act cases discussed in this section remain authoritative, as Ground 9 is closely modelled on the equivalent Rent Act provisions.

[170] *Hill v Rochard* [1983] 1 WLR 478 (proximity to sport, entertainment and recreation not relevant).

[171] *Warren v Austen* [1947] 2 All ER 185.   [172] *Cresswell v Hodgson* [1951] 2 KB 92.

[173] *Warren v Austen*, above; *Redspring Ltd v Francis* [1973] 1 WLR 134 (relevance of environmental factors).

[174] For terms as to sub-letting, see above, p 366.

But the landlord may be able to put an end to this situation by offering the tenant as 'alternative accommodation' a tenancy of the part of the premises that he is actually occupying, and on this ground seeking an order for possession of the whole.[175] As the tenant is voluntarily confining himself to the part in question, it is difficult for him to say that it is not suitable to his needs. The end result is that the tenant obtains a new tenancy of his part, while the landlord takes over his sub-tenants.

Finally, a landlord who recovers possession under Ground 9 must pay reasonable removal expenses to the tenant.[176]

(2) Ground 10: some rent unpaid

This ground applies where some rent lawfully due was unpaid at the date on which the possession proceedings were begun and was in arrears at the date of service of the notice under section 8.[177] Unlike mandatory Ground 8, the rent need not be unpaid at the date of the hearing, and may be less than two months in arrears. The possibility of suspension or postponement of the order has been dealt with.[178] It is most unlikely that an immediate possession order will result from an isolated breach.

(3) Ground 11: persistent delay in paying rent

Persistent delay in paying rent that is lawfully due is a ground for possession even if there are no arrears on the date on which possession proceedings are begun. Again, the court may suspend or postpone the execution of the order, subject to conditions.[179]

(4) Ground 12: other breaches

Breach of any obligation of the tenancy other than non-payment of rent affords a ground for possession. Where the breach is not serious or can be remedied, the order is likely to be refused or suspended, as is also the case with the following grounds.

(5) Ground 13: condition of the dwelling-house

This ground applies where the dwelling (or common parts) has deteriorated owing to the act, neglect or default of the tenant or other person residing in the tenant's dwelling. If the guilty party is the tenant's lodger or sub-tenant, the ground applies only if the tenant has not taken reasonable steps to remove him.

(6) Ground 14: nuisance or annoyance or certain criminal offences

It is a ground for possession if the tenant or any person residing in or visiting the dwelling has been guilty of conduct causing or likely to cause a nuisance or annoyance to a person residing, visiting or otherwise engaging in a lawful activity in the locality, or has been convicted of using the dwelling-house or allowing it to be used for immoral or illegal purposes,[180] or of an arrestable offence committed in, or in the locality of, the

---

[175] *Mykolyshyn v Noah* [1970] 1 WLR 1271; cf *Yoland Ltd v Reddington* (1982) 263 EG 157.

[176] HA 1988, s 11.   [177] Above, p 374.   [178] Above, p 376–7.

[179] HA 1988, s 9. Ground 11 is modelled on the business tenancy ground in LTA 1954, s 30(1)(b).

[180] See *Abrahams v Wilson* [1971] 2 QB 88 (possession of drugs).

dwelling-house.[181] The degree of control that the tenant could have exercised over the person in question will be taken into account in deciding whether it is reasonable to make an order.[182] In deciding whether to grant a possession order on Ground 14 the court must give particular consideration to the actual or likely effect that the nuisance or annoyance has had or could have on others.[183]

(7) Ground 14A: domestic violence

This ground was introduced by section 149 of the Housing Act 1996. It may be used only where the landlord is a non-profit registered provider of social housing, a registered social landlord (primarily a housing association) or a charitable housing trust, or a profit-making registered provider of social housing.[184] The ground applies where the dwelling was occupied by a married couple, a couple who are civil partners, or a couple living together as husband and wife or as civil partners,[185] one or both of whom is the tenant, and one partner has left the dwelling because of the violence or threats of violence by the other towards that partner or a member of the family[186] of that partner who was residing with that partner immediately before he or she left.[187] The court must be satisfied that the partner who has left is unlikely to return.

(8) Ground 15: condition of furniture

Deterioration in the condition of furniture provided under the tenancy owing to ill-treatment by the tenant or any other person residing in the dwelling is a ground for possession. Where the person responsible is the tenant's lodger or sub-tenant, the ground applies only if the tenant has not taken reasonable steps to remove him.

(9) Ground 16: tenant ceasing to be in landlord's employment

This ground for possession lies only against a 'service tenant', that is a person to whom the premises were let in consequence of his employment.[188] The court may make an

---

[181] This ground, substituted by HA 1996, s 148, replaces a similar but narrower ground. Proceedings based on Ground 14 may be commenced more speedily than those based on other grounds; HA 1988, s 8(4), as amended by HA 1996, s 151.

[182] *West Kent Housing Association Ltd v Davies* (1999) 31 HLR 415.

[183] HA 1988, s 9A, inserted by Anti-social Behaviour Act 2003, s 16(2); *London Quadrant Housing Trust v Root* [2005] EWCA Civ 43, [2005] L & TR 23 (tenant's partner ran business of repairing and scrapping cars at the premises; garden and surrounding areas were littered with general debris, especially car parts; partner had terrorised the neighbours and also the landlord's representatives by his intimidation and threats; 'there is a limit to which the courts can be willing to tolerate behaviour of this kind out of the kindness of their hearts to a woman and three children when their neighbours have suffered as much as they have on this occasion': Brooke LJ at [30]).

[184] Amended by SI 2010 No 866, Sch 2, para 74.

[185] As amended by Civil Partnership Act 2004, s 81, Sch 8.

[186] As defined by HA 1996, s 62. See also HA 1988, s 8A, introduced by s 150 of the 1996 Act, relating to the service of the s 8 notice (above, p 374) on the partner who has left.

[187] The violence need not, however, have taken place while the couple were living together at the property: *Metropolitan Housing Trust v Hadjazi* [2010] EWCA Civ 750, [2010] HLR 39.

[188] See above, p 361.

order for possession if the tenant has ceased to be in the landlord's employment, whether or not the premises are needed for another employee.

(10) Ground 17: grant of tenancy induced by false statement

This ground, introduced by section 102 of the Housing Act 1996 and modelled on Ground 5 of the Housing Act 1985 (secure tenancies),[189] applies when the landlord was induced to grant the tenancy by a false statement made knowingly or recklessly by the tenant (or one of joint tenants) or a person acting at the tenant's instigation.[190]

(4) Succession to an Assured Tenancy

Section 17 of the 1988 Act creates succession rights to an assured periodic tenancy (including a statutory periodic tenancy). In its original drafting it provided that on the death of a sole[191] tenant under such a tenancy, the tenancy vests in the tenant's spouse provided that the spouse was occupying as his or her only or principal home immediately before the death. 'Spouse' includes a person living with the tenant as his or her wife or husband.[192] No minimum period of cohabitation is specified. Cases arose in which the issue was whether a same-sex partner could succeed to a tenancy under this provision. In construing a similar provision in the Rent Act 1977,[193] the House of Lords first held that the words 'living with the...tenant as his or her wife or husband' were gender-specific, connoting a relationship between a man and a woman and therefore could not include a same-sex relationship.[194] However, in *Ghaidan v Godin-Mendoza*[195] the House reviewed this in the light of the requirement of the Human Rights Act 1998[196] that, so far as it is possible to do so, legislation must be read and given effect in a way that is compatible with Convention rights, and held that the Rent Act provision could be construed as extending to same-sex partners so as to eliminate its discriminatory effect[197] on such persons without contradicting the underlying social policy of the Rent Act.[198] The decision in *Ghaidan v Godin-Mendoza*

---

[189] Below, p 385. In practice this ground is rarely used by a private landlord but is more likely to be provable where false statements have been made in order to influence the way in which a public sector or social landlord allocates its housing: [2005] 25 EG 191 (S Murdoch).

[190] *Merton LBC v Richards* [2005] EWCA Civ 639, [2005] HLR 44 (secure tenancy under HA 1985).

[191] On the death of a joint tenant, the other joint tenant will take by survivorship, and no further succession will be possible: HA 1988, s 17(2), below.

[192] HA 1988, s 17(4).

[193] Sch 1, para 2, as substituted by HA 1980, s 76, and amended by HA 1988, s 39, Sch 4, Pt I, para 2.

[194] *Fitzpatrick v Sterling Housing Association Ltd* [2001] 1 AC 27. The Rent Act 1977 also allowed succession by a member of the tenant's 'family', and it was held that this was capable of a construction that included the same-sex partner.

[195] [2004] UKHL 30, [2004] 2 AC 557; [2005] PL 23 (A Young). The original tenant in the *Fitzpatrick* case, above, died in 1994, before the coming into force of the Human Rights Act 1998.

[196] S 3.   [197] ECHR, art 14, as read with art 8; above, p 23.

[198] Lord Millett dissented on the question of whether it was proper to construe the Rent Act provision by 'adopting an interpretation of the existing legislation which it not only does not bear but which is manifestly inconsistent with it': at [101]. He drew attention (at [96]) to the fact that Parliament was already considering corrective legislation in the Civil Partnership Bill.

has since been applied to similar language in section 17 of the Housing Act 1988,[199] but the section was itself amended by the Civil Partnership Act 2004[200] to provide explicitly that the succession right extends also to a surviving civil partner and a person living with the tenant as if they were civil partners.[201]

In the unlikely event of more than one claimant, only one can be the successor. Failing agreement, the county court will decide the matter.[202] Where succession rights are established, the tenancy will not devolve under the tenant's will or intestacy.[203] It appears that these provisions apply also to a shorthold periodic tenancy although in such a case the succession right would be of minimal value.[204]

Succession can occur only once, because section 17 applies only where the deceased tenant was not himself a successor.[205] On the death of the successor a mandatory ground for possession becomes available.[206]

These succession rights do not apply on the death of a tenant holding under a fixed-term assured tenancy.[207] If the beneficiary who acquires the tenancy on the death satisfies the assured tenancy requirements, the tenancy will continue to be assured.[208] If the beneficiary does not qualify as an assured tenant (for example because he does not occupy as his only or principal home), the tenancy will terminate under the general law at the end of the term.

Where there is no person who qualifies to be a successor on the death of an assured periodic tenant, the tenancy will devolve as part of the deceased tenant's estate, but a mandatory ground for possession is available.[209]

---

[199] *Nutting v Southern Housing Group Ltd* [2004] EWHC 2982 (Ch), [2005] 2 P & CR 14; however, the claim failed: the relationship must be openly and unequivocally displayed to the outside world; and 'without a lifetime commitment at least at some point in the relationship there is no sufficient similarity to marriage': Evans-Lombe J at [17]. Cf *Westminster City Council v Peart* (1992) 24 HLR 389 (for a couple to be 'living together as man and wife' it is necessary to show that the parties have a settled intention to be so regarded).

[200] S 81, Sch 8.

[201] A civil partnership is a relationship between two people of the same sex ('civil partners') which has been formalised by registration: Civil Partnership Act 2004, s 1. It remains to be seen what the courts will require to be satisfied that same-sex cohabitants are living together 'as if they were civil partners' without having entered into a civil partnership; cf *Nutting v Southern Housing Group Ltd*, above. See also [2005] Conv 318 (M Davis and D Hughes); *Souter v McAuley* 2010 SLT (Sh Ct) 121 ('the relationship beween the parties [which had lasted six years] having been sexual in nature' they were entitled to be regarded as a cohabiting couple within Matrimonial Homes (Family Protection) (Scotland) Act 1981, s 18 ('if...two persons of the same sex are living together as if they were civil partners')); *Savage v Purches* 2009 SLT (Sh Ct) 36 at [9] ('the relationship was intimate': Family Law (Scotland) Act 2006).

[202] HA 1988, s 17(5).   [203] Ibid, s 17(1).

[204] See *Lower Street Properties Ltd v Jones* (1996) 28 HLR 877.

[205] HA 1988, s 17(1)(c). 'Successor' has an extended meaning, including, for example, the survivor of joint tenants or a person who inherited a fixed-term assured tenancy by will or intestacy: s 17(2), (3).

[206] Ground 7, above, p 376.   [207] Nor does Ground 7 apply.

[208] If a statutory periodic tenancy subsequently arises, there can be no succession rights under s 17 on the tenant's death (see s 17(2)), and Ground 7 will be available.

[209] Ground 7, above, p 376. The tenancy ceases to be assured if the person entitled to it does not occupy, in which case it may be terminated by notice to quit.

(5) Sub-tenants

The Housing Act 1988 applies between tenant and sub-tenant in the same way as between landlord and tenant. The question to be considered here is whether the sub-tenant has any security of tenure against the head landlord when the tenancy terminates. In addition to any rights he may have at common law,[210] he will retain security if he falls within section 18 of the 1988 Act. This section protects only lawful sub-tenants (whose presence does not constitute a breach of a covenant against sub-letting) and who qualify as assured tenants against their immediate landlord. Its effect is that, on termination of the superior tenancy (in any way), the sub-tenant becomes assured tenant of the superior landlord.[211] There is no requirement that the mesne landlord should have had an assured tenancy, and it seems unlikely that this could have been the case. If the mesne landlord was not also occupying as his only or principal home, he would not have satisfied the residence requirement of an assured tenancy,[212] whereas if he was occupying part as his only or principal home, the sub-tenancy would not have been assured because of the resident landlord exception.[213]

II PUBLIC SECTOR HOUSING.
SECURE TENANCY[214]

Until the Housing Act 1980 the residential tenants of landlords in the public sector (by far the most numerous category of tenants) were altogether excluded from statutory protection. They may now enjoy a 'secure tenancy', which is modelled upon the Rent Act protected tenancy with certain variations and modern improvements. The provisions are now found in the Housing Act 1985.[215]

A DEFINITION OF A SECURE TENANCY

A secure tenancy is a tenancy:

   (i)   under which a dwelling-house is let as a separate dwelling;[216]

---

210 Above, p 286.

211 Unless the landlord's interest is such that the tenancy cannot be assured, for example where the superior landlord is the Crown: HA 1988, s 18(2).

212 Above, p 363.   213 Above, p 364.

214 Hill and Redman's *Landlord and Tenant*, Division D; Woodfall, *Landlord and Tenant*, ch 25; Hughes and Lowe, *Public Sector Housing Law* (3rd edn, 2000); Evans and Smith, *Law of Landlord and Tenant*, ch 16.

215 Part IV. See also Part V and Leasehold Reform, Housing and Urban Development Act 1993, Part II (the right to buy), below, p 389. For reforms which are expected to be made by the Localism Bill, which is passing through Parliament during 2011, see below, p 427.

216 HA 1985, s 79. Certain licences are included: s 79(3), (4).

(ii) in respect of which the interest of the landlord belongs to one or other of a list of 'public sector' bodies such as local authorities, development corporations and housing action trusts;[217]

(iii) in respect of which the tenant is an individual who occupies the house as his only or principal home or, where the tenancy is a joint tenancy, each of the joint tenants is an individual and at least one of them occupies the house as his only or principal home;[218]

(iv) that does not fall within any of the exceptions listed in the Housing Act 1985.

The first of these conditions reproduces part of the definition of a protected or assured tenancy in the private sector. The second mirrors (with certain exceptions) the list of tenancies excluded from the definition of a protected or assured tenancy on account of the identity of the landlord.[219] The third is the same as the conditions as to occupation that apply to assured tenancies.[220] The list of exceptions has some common ground with the exceptions for protected and assured tenancies (incuding long tenancies,[221] student lettings,[222] business tenancies,[223] farm business tenancies and agricultural holdings,[224] tenancies for asylum-seekers[225]) but also includes important arrangements that exist only in the public sector, such as the provision of accommodation for homeless persons under Part VII of the Housing Act 1996,[226] lettings of 'short-life' premises acquired for development,[227] the provision of temporary accommodation for persons who have come to the area to seek employment[228] and lettings to local authority or other public sector employees.[229]

B NO CONTROL OF RENTS

There is no control of the rents that may be charged in the public sector in any way analogous to the machinery provided by rent officers and rent assessment committees in the private sector.

---

[217] HA 1985, s 80, as amended by HA 1988, s 83; SI 2008 No 3002, Sch 1, para 10; SI 2010 No 866, Sch 2, para 19.

[218] Ibid, s 81. Ss 80 and 81 have an 'ambulatory' effect in that occupiers may pass in or out of 'secure' status, depending on either a change of landlord or a change in the tenant's own circumstances: *Kay v Lambeth LBC* [2004] EWCA Civ 926, [2005] QB 352 at [53] (Auld LJ). But a secure tenancy for the purpose of HA 1985, s 79 is one in which there is a direct landlord and tenant relationship between a landlord, satisfying the landlord condition in s 80, and a tenant, satisfying the tenant condition in s 81: ibid, at [67]. It most probably does not include a tenancy at will: *Banjo v Brent LBC* [2005] EWCA Civ 292, [2005] 1 WLR 2520 at [25]–[26], [31]–[35] (Chadwick LJ), and [40]–[43] (Buxton LJ).

[219] Rent Act 1977, ss 14–16; HA 1988, Sch 1, para 12.

[220] Above, p 363.   [221] HA 1985, Sch 1, para 1.   [222] Ibid, para 10.   [223] Ibid, para 11.

[224] Ibid, para 8, as substituted by the Agricultural Tenancies Act 1995.

[225] Ibid, para 4A, inserted by Immigration and Asylum Act 1999, s 169(1), Sch 14.

[226] Ibid, para 4, substituted by HA 1996, s 216, Sch 17. Homeless persons are not excluded in all cases. See *Westminster City Council v Clarke* [1992] 2 AC 288; above, p 195, n 88.

[227] Ibid, para 3.   [228] Ibid, para 5.   [229] Ibid, para 2.

C SECURITY OF TENURE

The mechanism for giving security of tenure in the public sector resembles that which applies to assured tenancies in the private sector.[230] The scheme of the Act is that the landlord cannot recover possession without obtaining a court order based on one of the grounds for possession.[231] Thus a periodic tenancy cannot be terminated by notice to quit[232] unless a ground for possession is available. Where the tenancy is for a fixed term, a periodic tenancy automatically arises on its expiry,[233] which cannot be terminated without a ground for possession. A similar principle applies to the forfeiture of a fixed-term tenancy: on termination by forfeiture a periodic tenancy arises, which again cannot be terminated without a ground for possession.[234] There is a list of cases in which orders for possession may be made, and the order has the effect of terminating the tenancy when the order is executed.[235]

Several of the grounds upon which orders for possession may be made are the same or similar to the grounds upon which the court may make such an order in the private sector. Non-payment of rent or breach of covenant,[236] nuisance or annoyance to neighbours or visitors,[237] neglect of the premises,[238] furniture[239] or common parts, and inducement of the tenancy by a false statement made knowingly or recklessly

---

[230] Above, p 371. For the position of sub-tenants, see *Basingstoke and Deane BC v Paice* [1995] 2 EGLR 9.

[231] HA 1985, s 82(1), amended by Anti-social Behaviour Act 2003, s 14. It is otherwise if the tenancy is not secure: *Sevenoaks DC v Emmott* (1979) 39 P & CR 404. S 82 impliedly removes any right of the landlord to bring a secure tenancy to an end by the private law remedy of rescission (eg for misrepresentation): *Islington LBC v Uckac* [2006] EWCA Civ 340, [2006] 1 WLR 1303.

[232] Except by the tenant: *Hammersmith and Fulham LBC v Monk* [1992] 1 AC 478.

[233] HA 1985, s 86.

[234] Ibid, ss 82(3), 86(1)(b). The ground for forfeiture will not necessarily constitute a ground for possession.

[235] Ibid, s 82(2), substituted by Housing and Regeneration Act 2008, s 14(1), to reverse the previous law under which a former secure tenant was a 'tolerated trespasser' if he remained in possession and the court's order was not executed: *Thompson v Elmbridge BC* [1987] 1 WLR 1425; *Burrows v Brent LBC* [1996] 1 WLR 1448; DCLG Consultation, *Tolerated trespassers* (2007). In *Knowsley Housing Trust v White* [2008] UKHL 70, [2009] 1 AC 636 HL declined to reconsider the earlier cases on tolerated trespassers in relation to secured tenancies (including its own earlier decision in *Burrows v Brent LBC*), but noted that the law had now been changed by the 2008 Act: see at [92]-[93] (Lord Neuberger of Abbotsbury); confirmed by SC in *Austin v Southwark LBC* [2010] UKSC 28, [2010] 3 WLR 144.

[236] Ibid, Sch 2, Part 1, Ground 1.

[237] Ibid, Ground 2, as amended by HA 1996, s 144. In deciding whether to grant a possession order on Ground 2 the court must give particular consideration to the actual or likely effect that the nuisance or annoyance has had or could have on others: HA 1985, s 85A, inserted by Anti-social Behaviour Act 2003, s 16(1); *Manchester City Council v Higgins* [2005] EWCA Civ 1423, [2006] 1 All ER 841 (judge wrong to suspend possession order, which was necessary and proportionate under ECHR in order to protect the rights and freedoms of neighbours where tenant showed no remorse for son's bullying towards neighbour and her mentally disabled sons). For other provisions concerning anti-social behaviour in relation to public sector and social housing, see Anti-social Behaviour Act 2003, ss 12 and 13, inserting into HA 1996 new ss 218A (anti-social behaviour: landlords' policies and procedures) and 153A–153E (injunctions against anti-social behaviour); and ss 14 and 15 (demoted tenancies), below.

[238] Ibid, Ground 3.   [239] Ibid, Ground 4.

by the tenant[240] are examples. A new 'domestic violence' ground was added by the Housing Act 1996.[241] There are also other grounds special to public sector dwellings, for example where the dwelling has features designed to make it suitable for occupation by a physically disabled person and such a person no longer resides in the dwelling-house.[242] In such a case suitable alternative accommodation must be available for the tenant.[243]

It should be noted that all the grounds for possession are to some degree discretionary; for secure tenancies there are no mandatory grounds for possession comparable to those in relation to assured tenancies.[244] In most cases the court must be satisfied not only that a ground for possession has been made out, but also that it is reasonable to make the order, although there are four grounds (overcrowding, proposed demolition of the premises, proposed disposal under a redevelopment scheme and conflict with purposes of a charity landlord) where there is no requirement of reasonableness, but the court must still be satisfied that there is suitable alternative accommodation for the tenant.[245]

D DEMOTED TENANCY

The Anti-social Behaviour Act 2003 introduced the 'demoted tenancy'. If the landlord is a local housing authority or a housing action trust, or a private registered provider of social housing or a registered social landlord, it may apply to a county court for a 'demotion order'. The court may make an order if the tenant, or a person residing in or visiting the dwelling-house, has engaged in or threatened to engage in certain forms of anti-social behaviour, or the use of the premises for unlawful purposes,[246] and if the court is satisfied that it is reasonable to make the order.[247] The effect of the order is that the secure tenancy is terminated and replaced by a demoted tenancy,[248] which lasts for

---

[240] HA 1985, Ground 5, amended by HA 1996, s 146; *Merton LBC v Richards*[2005] EWCA Civ 639, [2005] HLR 44. This does not cover the case where a false statement was made by the current tenant's predecessor in title: *Islington LBC v Uckac* [2006] EWCA Civ 340, [2006] 1 WLR 1303; [2008] Conv 81 (J Morgan).

[241] S 145, introducing Ground 2A; amended by Civil Partnership Act 2004, s 81, Sch 8.

[242] HA 1985, Sch 2, Part III, Ground 13. Cf *Freeman v Wansbeck DC* [1984] 2 All ER 746.

[243] See *Enfield LBC v French* (1984) 49 P & CR 223; *Wandsworth LBC v Fadayomi* [1987] 1 WLR 1473 (wife's position).

[244] Above, p 374.

[245] HA 1985, s 84(2); Sch 2, Part II as amended by Housing and Planning Act 1986, s 9(1). See also *Manchester City Council v Romano* [2004] EWCA Civ 834, [2005] 1 WLR 2775 (relevance of tenant's disability, under Disability Discrimination Act 1995 [replaced now by Equality Act 2010], in deciding whether reasonable to order possession on ground of nuisance or annoyance to neighbours).

[246] HA 1996, s 153A or 153B, inserted by Anti-social Behaviour Act 2003, s 13; *Manchester City Council v Higgins*, above; [2006] Conv 85 (S Bright); cf *Moat Housing Group-South Ltd v Harris* [2005] EWCA Civ 287, [2006] QB 606.

[247] HA 1985, s 82A, inserted by Anti-social Behaviour Act 2003, s 14, and amended by SI 2010 No 866, Sch 2, para 20.

[248] If the landlord is a private registered provider of social housing or a registered social landlord, the demoted tenancy takes effect as a demoted assured shorthold tenancy under HA 1988, s 20B, inserted by Anti-social Behaviour Act 2003, s 15 and amended by SI 2010 No 866, Sch 2, para 65; above, p 369, n 94.

at least one year and during the demotion period the landlord can obtain an order for possession without having to establish grounds.[249]

The purpose of these provisions is to encourage landlords not to seek possession immediately in all cases of anti-social behaviour:[250]

Demoted tenancies have been designed to be both a warning and a last chance. We want to encourage landlords to use them instead of seeking suspended or outright possession orders. Demotion is not a soft option. As well as being a warning and an incentive to behave, it is a real sanction. The tenant, through his or her actions, has lost security; we want him to understand that this may have serious consequences. Tenants need to understand that when they are considering how to conduct themselves in the first instance.

E INTRODUCTORY TENANCY

The Housing Act 1996[251] introduced the introductory tenancy regime, which a local authority may elect to operate. While such an election is in force, any new periodic tenancy (or licence) that would otherwise have qualified as secure takes effect as introductory for a trial period of one year. The Housing Act 2004[252] permits landlords to extend the trial period by six months. During the trial period the landlord may terminate the tenancy by obtaining a court order. No ground for possession needs to be established, nor has the court any discretion to refuse the order,[253] but the landlord must state its reasons, as to which the tenant may request that the landlord review its decision.[254] If not ended during the trial period, the introductory tenancy becomes secure at the end of that period.

Otherwise, it takes effect as a demoted tenancy under HA 1996, ch 1A, inserted by Anti-social Behaviour Act 2003, s 14(5), Sch 1: HA 1985, s 82A(8). The procedure for obtaining possession under HA 1996, s 143D(2), is compatible with ECHR, art 8, since the County Court judge who is invited to make an order for possession can consider whether it is proportionate to make the order sought: *Manchester CC v Pinnock* [2010] UKSC 45, [2010] 3 WLR 1441 at [104].

[249] In the case of a demoted tenancy under HA 1996, ch 1A, however, the tenant may request a review by the landlord of its decision: ibid, s 143F. For the procedure to be followed in such a review, see Demoted Tenancies (Review of Decisions) (England) Regulations 2004 (SI 2004 No 1679).

[250] Lord Bassam of Brighton, Hansard HL (Series 5), vol 653, col 1805 (23 October 2003) (Report stage).

[251] Part V, ss 124–143. The tenancy will not be introductory if granted to a tenant who, immediately beforehand, was a secure tenant of the same or another dwelling-house.

[252] S 179, inserting ss 125A and 125B into HA 1996, with effect for introductory tenancies entered into on or after the section came into force (6 June 2005: SI 2005 No 1451). The landlord must give reasons: s 125A(5), and the tenant can request a review by the landlord of its decision: s 125B. See also Introductory Tenancies (Review of Decisions to Extend a Trial Period) (England) Regulations 2006 (SI 2006 No 1077).

[253] *Manchester City Council v Cochrane* [1999] 1 WLR 809.

[254] For the procedure to be followed in a review, including a requirement that the review be undertaken by a person who was not involved in the decision to apply for an order for possession, see Introductory Tenants (Review) Regulations 1997 (SI 1997 No 72). The regime for possession in introductory tenancies complies with ECHR because the court's powers of review can extend to reconsidering the facts found by the local authority, or considering facts that have arisen since the issue of proceedings; and it is open to the court to consider whether the procedure for seeking a possession order has been lawfully followed having regard to the defendant's art 8 ECHR rights: *Hounslow LBC v Powell* [2011] UKSC 8, [2011] 2 WLR 287 at

F SUCCESSION

As in the case of the private sector, the Housing Act 1985 confers certain rights of succession to the secure tenancy. As with an assured tenancy, succession can occur once only.[255] The successor must have occupied the dwelling-house as his only or principal home[256] at the time of the tenant's death,[257] and must either be the tenant's spouse or civil partner, or another member of his family. In the latter case he must have resided with the tenant for the period of 12 months ending with the tenant's death,[258] although not necessarily in the same dwelling.[259] If there is more than one claimant, the landlord selects the successor in default of agreement.[260] The Housing Act contains a definition of 'family',[261] which includes persons who live together as husband and wife[262] and, after it was amended by the Civil Partnership Act 2004,[263] same-sex partners who live together 'as if they were civil partners'.[264]

---

[53], [56], following the decision in *Manchester CC v Pinnock* [2010] UKSC 45, [2010] 3 WLR 1441 (demoted tenancies).

[255] HA 1985, s 87. The succession provisions do not infringe ECHR arts 8 and 14: *R (Gangera) v Hounslow LBC* [2003] EWHC 794 (Admin), [2003] HLR 68. Succession rights exist also in the case of demoted tenancies, below: HA 1996, s 143H, inserted by Anti-social Behaviour Act 2003, s 14(5), Sch 1 and amended by Civil Partnership Act 2004, Sch 8, para 55; and introductory tenancies, below: HA 1996, s 131, amended by SI 2005 No 3336, art 20.

[256] See *Peabody Donation Fund Governors v Grant* (1982) 264 EG 925.

[257] The death of only one of two joint tenants does not constitute the death of 'the tenant': *Solihull MBC v Hickin* [2010] EWCA Civ 868, [2010] 1 WLR 2254 (second joint tenant not living in the property so on death of resident joint tenant it ceased to be secure and had been determined by notice to quit: another resident member of family could not succeed to it).

[258] HA 1985, s 87; amended by Civil Partnership Act 2004, s 81, Sch 8. 'Residing with' is narrowly construed: *Freeman v Islington LBC* [2009] EWCA Civ 536, [2010] HLR 6.

[259] *Waltham Forest LBC v Thomas* [1992] 2 AC 198.   [260] HA 1985, s 89(2).

[261] Ibid, s 113; amended by Civil Partnership Act 2004, s 81, Sch 8. A minor may be the successor: *Kingston upon Thames BC v Prince* [1999] 1 FLR 593; but the legal estate must be held on trust for the minor: *Newham LBC v R* [2004] EWCA Civ 41; (2004) 148 SJLB 113; (2004) 8 L & T Rev 61 (M Pawlowski). The definition of 'family' is exhaustive, and should not be interpreted more widely under HRA 1998, s 3: *Wandsworth LBC v Michalak* [2002] EWCA Civ 271, [2003] 1 WLR 617. 'Child' does not include a foster child; and the exclusion of foster children is compliant with ECHR: *Sheffield CC v Wall* [2010] EWCA Civ 922, [2010] HLR 47.

[262] See *Westminster City Council v Peart* (1991) 24 HLR 389.

[263] S 81, Sch 8. The definition in HA 1980, s 50(3) (the predecessor of HA 1985, s 113) was originally interpreted as not including same-sex partners: *Harrogate BC v Simpson* [1986] 2 FLR 91. Although the term 'family' in the Rent Act 1977 was held to be capable of a construction that included a same-sex partner (*Fitzpatrick v Sterling Housing Association Ltd* [2001] 1 AC 27), that Act contained no definition of 'family', thus permitting a more flexible approach. However, the decision in *Ghaidan v Godin-Mendoza* [2004] UKHL 30, [2004] 2 AC 557, above, p 381, would equally apply to the original language of HA 1985, and therefore allow it to be interpreted as extending to same-sex partners even without the amendment of the Civil Partnership Act 2004.

[264] For a couple to be 'living together as man and wife' it is necessary to show that the parties have a settled intention to be so regarded: *Westminster City Council v Peart* (1992) 24 HLR 389. For the meaning of living together 'as' civil partners, see above, p 382, n 201.

that 'different considerations of equity' applied to flats,[293] although it is not easy to guess what these could be. However, the sale of flats on long leases has continued to be a widespread practice, being considered a more profitable proposition than letting them on regulated or assured tenancies.[294] Steps have, however, been taken in recent years to increase the rights of long leaseholders of flats. Qualifying leaseholders may acquire a new extended lease or may collectively acquire the freehold of the block under the Leasehold Reform, Housing and Urban Development Act 1993, discussed below.[295] And the introduction of the system of commonhold, discussed in Chapter 7, has extended the freehold ownership of flats.

(d) Rateable value

Formerly the Act did not apply if the rateable value of the house exceeded certain limits or, after the abolition of domestic rating, if the premium paid for the lease exceeded a specified figure.[296] Tenants of houses previously so excluded have now been given the right to acquire the freehold by the Leasehold Reform, Housing and Urban Development Act 1993.[297] As will be explained below, the price to be paid by such tenants is assessed in a manner more favourable to the landlord.

(e) Qualifying period

Until it was amended by the Commonhold and Leasehold Reform Act 2002, the 1967 Act contained a qualifying condition that the tenant must have been occupying the house or some part of it in right of his tenancy as his only or main residence for a particular period.[298] Now, however, the residence test has been largely abolished,[299] and in most cases the only question is whether the tenant has held his tenancy for a qualifying period—which is now two years.[300] This therefore enables non-resident

[293] *Leasehold Reform in England and Wales* (1966) Cmnd 2916, para 8. For the White Paper's statement on the consideration of equity applicable to houses, see below, p 397.

[294] Above, pp 358 ff. The market in short lettings has, by contrast, been substantially deregulated and therefore made more accessible to landlords who wish to retain short-term control of their properties, through the extended use of shorthold tenancies, especially after HA 1996: ibid.

[295] Below, p 400.   [296] Leasehold Reform Act 1967, s 1(1)(a), as amended.

[297] S 63, introducing s 1A(1) of the 1967 Act.

[298] Leasehold Reform Act 1967, s 1(1); originally the last five years or for five out of the last ten years; in both cases 'five' was reduced to 'three' by HA 1980, s 141, Sch 21. The residence test involved difficult questions of fact and degree: *Poland v Earl Cadogan* [1980] 3 All ER 544; *Dymond v Arundel-Timms* [1991] 1 EGLR 109. For further discussion, see the 16th edn of this book, pp 536–7.

[299] CLRA 2002, s 138; [2010] Conv 444 (J Morgan). The residence requirement (now reduced to the last two years, or two years in the last ten years) is retained for tenancies of a house to which LTA 1954, Part II applies (business tenancies, below, p 406; *Smith v Titanate Ltd* [2005] 2 EGLR 63, Cty Ct). The right for business tenants to enfranchise is further restricted by CLRA 2002, s 140, inserting s 1(1ZC) into Leasehold Reform Act 1967 (in particular, only leases granted for a term exceeding 35 years can now be enfranchised). The residence requirement is also retained to prevent a non-resident landlord of the house, who has sub-let the premises in parts under long leases of flats to which Leasehold Reform, Housing and Urban Development Act 1993 applies, above, pp 400 ff, from making a windfall profit at the freeholder's expense through acquiring the freehold: CLRA 2002, s 138(2), inserting s 1(1ZB) into Leasehold Reform Act 1967; *Earl Cadogan v Search Guarantees plc* [2004] EWCA Civ 969, [2004] 1 WLR 2768.

[300] CLRA 2002, s 139.

tenants, such as companies, to exercise the right to acquire the freehold.[301] The removal of the residence requirement has made it necessary to deal explicitly with the case were there are two or more long tenancies in respect of the same house (for example, if there is both a long tenancy and a long sub-tenancy). In such a case, the superior tenant has no right under the 1967 Act as long as the inferior tenancy subsists.[302]

(2) Enfranchisement Procedure

A tenant exercises his rights under the Act by serving upon his landlord a notice in the prescribed statutory form, stating that he desires to acquire the freehold or an extended lease.[303] In particular, the notice must make it clear whether he wants the one or the other. A notice claiming the freehold or an extended lease in the alternative is invalid.[304] The effect of service of the notice is to create rights and obligations that have the same effect as a contract between landlord and tenant, registrable as if it were an estate contract[305] under which the one is bound to grant and the other to take the freehold or an extended lease, as the case may be, on the terms laid down by the Act.[306] The landlord can oppose enfranchisement or extension if the house is reasonably required for occupation as the only or main residence of the landlord or an adult member of his family.[307]

(3) Freehold or Extended Lease

(a) Freehold

A tenant who claims the freehold is entitled to have it conveyed to him free of incumbrances.[308] Any intermediate leasehold interests will be merged in the freehold and there are provisions for dividing up the purchase money between the freeholder and intermediate leaseholders according to the value of their respective interests.[309]

The effect of enfranchisement is of course ordinarily to extinguish the covenants between landlord and tenant in the lease and thereby to deprive the landlord of all rights that he may have had under the lease to control the use, appearance or state

---

[301] *Hareford Ltd v Barnet LBC* [2005] 2 EGLR 72 (Cty Ct).

[302] CLRA 2002, s 138(2), inserting s 1(1ZA) into Leasehold Reform Act 1967.

[303] For the position where there is a claim to forfeiture, see Sch 3, para 4(1); *Central Estates (Belgravia) Ltd v Woolgar* [1972] 1 QB 48.

[304] *Byrnlea Property Investments Ltd v Ramsay* [1969] 2 QB 253. The prescribed form has since been amended. See *Speedwell Estates Ltd v Dalziel* [2001] EWCA Civ 1277, [2002] 1 EGLR 55 (certain omissions did not invalidate notice, on construction under *Mannai Investment Co Ltd v Eagle Star Life Assurance Co Ltd* [1997] AC 749, above p 333; other omissions however rendered notice invalid). On irregularities in a tenant's notice, see *Malekshad v Howard de Walden Estates Ltd (No 2)* [2003] EWHC 3106 (Ch), [2004] 1 WLR 862; *Earl Cadogan v Strauss* [2004] EWCA Civ 211, [2004] 2 P & CR 16.

[305] Leasehold Reform Act 1967, s 5(1), (5). Protection is (in unregistered land) by registration as a land charge; or (in registered land) by registration of a notice. It cannot take effect as an overriding interest: ibid, s 5(5).

[306] Ibid, ss 8(1), 14 (1).   [307] Ibid, s 18. Compensation is payable.

[308] Ibid, s 8(1).   [309] Ibid, Sch 1.

of repair of the house. The Act did, however, provide for exceptional cases in which the former landlord was allowed to retain limited 'powers of management'.[310] This exception was intended to apply to substantial residential estates that were held from one landlord where the Secretary of State for the Environment certified that it was in the general interest 'in order to maintain adequate standards of appearance and amenity and regulate development in the area' that the landlord should retain some control. Applications for the Minister's certificate had to be made before 1 January 1970.[311] If the certificate was granted, the landlord could apply to the High Court for approval of a scheme giving him the appropriate powers.

(b) Extended lease

A tenant who claims an extended lease is entitled to the grant of a new tenancy, in substitution for the existing tenancy, for a term expiring 50 years after the term date of the existing tenancy[312] and on terms as to rent that will be considered in the next paragraph.

Compared with the freehold, the extended tenancy is weak, although it has recently been made more attractive. Until reforms introduced by the Commonhold and Leasehold Reform Act 2002,[313] the extended lease carried no further rights, either to claim the freehold or to another extension, and the tenant under the extended tenancy had no security of tenure after the expiry of his term. However, although there can be no further extension of the lease,[314] the restriction on the tenant claiming the freehold has been removed;[315] and some security of tenure is now afforded to the leaseholder under an extended lease.[316]

Furthermore, the landlord may at any time from 12 months before the commencement of the last 50 years of the term apply to the court for an order terminating the tenancy (on payment of compensation) if he can show that he intends to demolish or reconstruct the whole or a substantial part of the house and premises.[317]

---

[310] Ibid, s 19.

[311] For houses that became enfranchisable only by virtue of the increases in rateable value limits effected by HA 1974, s 118, the date was 31 July 1976. For houses brought within the 1967 Act by Leasehold Reform, Housing and Urban Development Act 1993, the landlord's application must be made within two years of the coming into force of the 1993 Act.

[312] Leasehold Reform Act 1967, s 14(1). This option is not available to tenants given enfranchisement rights by Leasehold Reform, Housing and Urban Development Act 1993 or HA 1996.

[313] S 143, amending s 16 of the 1967 Act in relation to all tenancies, whether extended before or after the amendment comes into force: s 143(3).

[314] Leasehold Reform Act 1967, s 16(1)(b).

[315] CLRA 2002, s 143(1)(a), deleting s 16(1)(a) and amending s 16(4) of the 1967 Act.

[316] Ibid, s 143(2), inserting s 16(1B) into the 1967 Act, applying Local Government and Housing Act 1989, Sch 10, below, p 398, whether or not the extended lease would otherwise fulfil the low rent qualifying condition of that Schedule. LTA 1954, Part II continues, however, to be excluded: Leasehold Reform Act 1967, s 16(1)(c).

[317] Leasehold Reform Act 1967, s 17.

(4) Terms of acquisition

(a) Extended Lease

The rent for the new substituted tenancy is the old rent for the remainder of the old term and then, for the 50-year extension, a 'modern ground rent' representing the letting value of the site without including anything for the value of the buildings on the site, calculated at the date when the extension commences, with a review after 25 years.[318]

(b) Freehold

The Act now contains three different methods of calculating the price that the tenant must pay for the freehold. The first, contained in the original Act, now applies to houses of a rateable value on 31 March 1990 of less than £500 (£1,000 in Greater London). The second, introduced by the Housing Act 1974, applies to houses of which the rateable value exceeds those figures but does not exceed £750 (£1,500 in Greater London).[319] The third applies to high-value houses brought within the 1967 Act by the Leasehold Reform, Housing and Urban Development Act 1993 and to houses brought within the 1967 Act by the Housing Act 1996 where the tenancy fails the 'low rent' test.

Under the original scheme, the price of the freehold is the price that it would fetch if sold in the open market by a willing seller subject to the lease, on the assumption that the lease had already been extended by 50 years in accordance with the Act,[320] but without regard to any enhanced bid that might be expected from the tenant himself or a member of his family.[321] In practice, therefore, the price will be the capitalised value of the rent payable under the lease as extended together with the value (if any) of the reversion. In the case of a lease that still has a very long time to run, the calculation is comparatively easy because the reversion has no value. No one will give anything simply for the right to possession of a property in 90 years' time. The value is therefore simply a capitalisation of the rent. Thus the freehold reversion upon a lease of a house at a ground rent of £20 a year with 70 years unexpired is likely to be worth today about eight years' purchase or £160. On the other hand, as the term date approaches, the reversion begins to acquire some value. However, because of the deemed extension, there will always be at least 50 years to run. If the reversion does have any value, this must be added to the value of the right to receive the rent for the rest of the term. If the parties cannot agree on the value, it must be determined by the Leasehold Valuation Tribunal.[322]

The terms upon which the freehold can be acquired are perhaps the most controversial feature of the Leasehold Reform Act 1967. The effective disregard of the

---

[318] Leasehold Reform Act 1967, s 15(2).

[319] Below, p 397. For houses built after the abolition of domestic rating, see below.

[320] Leasehold Reform Act 1967, s 9(1). See also Leasehold Reform Act 1979, protecting a tenant against artificial inflation of the price he has to pay; the Act negatives the effect of the device considered by HL in *Jones v Wrotham Park Settled Estates* [1980] AC 74.

[321] HA 1969, s 82.

[322] Leasehold Reform Act 1967, s 21(1), as amended by HA 1980.

value of the reversion to the building means that the terms can be highly advantageous to the tenant whose lease has a short period left unexpired. This method of calculation was intended to give effect to the Government's declaration in the White Paper that 'the price of enfranchisement must be calculated in accordance with the principle that in equity the bricks and mortar belong to the qualified leaseholder and the land to the landlord'.[323] The word 'equity' is clearly used in the sense of social justice and not in any sense that would have been recognised by Lord Eldon. Even so, it is not easy to understand. It is presumably intended to reflect the situation on the grant of a building lease, when the landlord reserves a rent that reflects the value of the land alone and the builder is able to dispose at a profit of the building that he has erected.[324] At this stage, however, the reversion is so remote that the question of whether it should in equity be a reversion in the land alone or the land and building is entirely academic; in either case it will have no value. But the position is very different when the lease is approaching its end, as was the case with many Victorian building leases at the time when the Act was passed. At this point the reversion has a value that is enhanced by the fact that it includes the house as well as the land and a person who bought the reversion would have paid a price that reflected this enhanced value. A purchaser of the residue of the term will have paid a price that was correspondingly lower in order to allow for the fact that he was buying a wasting asset. The 'equity' of the Act deprives the landlord of part of the value of his reversion and gives the tenant a windfall gain. It can be justified only on the general ground that it is desirable to enrich tenants at the expense of their landlords.[325]

It was no doubt for these reasons that a different method of calculating the price was applied to the more expensive houses that were brought within the scope of the Act by the Housing Act 1974. In the case of houses that had a rateable value on 31 March 1990 of between £500 and £750 (the figures are £1,000 and £1,500 in Greater London) the price is calculated upon a set of assumptions that result in the tenant paying more or less the market value of the reversion, including the reversion to the building as well as the site.[326] Instead of assuming a 50-year extension, as in the case of low rateable value properties, it is assumed that the tenant has the right to remain at the end of his contractual term as an assured tenant under the Housing Act 1988.[327] Unlike the low rateable value properties, the fact that the tenant himself might make an enhanced bid is not to be disregarded. The price, therefore, includes the value of the rent for the

---

[323] *Leasehold Reform in England and Wales* (1966, Cmnd 2916), para 4.   [324] Above, p 389.

[325] A claim that the Act contravened ECHR was rejected in *James v United Kingdom* (1986) 8 EHRR 123 (trustees of the Grosvenor Estate in Mayfair compelled under 1967 Act to sell 80 houses to long-lease tenants at a loss of £2,529,903). See also *Di Palma v United Kingdom* (1988) 10 EHRR 149.

[326] Leasehold Reform Act 1967, s 9(1A); *Shalson v Keepers and Governors of John Lyon School* [2003] UKHL 32, [2004] 1 AC 802; *Fattal v Keepers and Governors of John Lyon School* [2004] EWCA Civ 1530, [2005] 1 WLR 803 (leave to appeal refused by HL: [2005] 1 WLR 1285). This method applies also to leases of houses built after the abolition of domestic rating if the premium paid for the lease exceeds a limit based on a mathematical formula. Otherwise the original method applies: Local Government and Housing Act 1989, s 149 and SI 1990 No 434. See generally [1998] 14 EG 122 (C Boston).

[327] Formerly the assumption was that the tenant had security under Part I of LTA 1954.

residue of the contractual term, the value of the market rent for the dwelling-house (not just the site) during continuation under the 1988 Act, the value of the reversion to the site and building subject to these rights, and an addition to reflect the higher bid a sitting tenant would make.

It became apparent that a tenant of a high rateable value property could achieve a substantial reduction in the price by first extending the lease for 50 years under the 1967 Act prior to enfranchising.[328] This effectively gave the tenant the benefit of the formula applicable to low rateable value properties, and thereby diminished the value of the reversion. This was prohibited by the Housing and Planning Act 1986, under that it is assumed, for the purpose of calculating the price, that the tenant has no right to an extension, and that, where the lease has been extended, that it will end on the original term date.[329]

In the case of high-value houses brought within the 1967 Act by the Leasehold Reform, Housing and Urban Development Act 1993, the price of the freehold is calculated on a basis similar to the second method described above, but with certain modifications that operate in the landlord's favour.[330] For example, there is no assumption that the tenant has any statutory right to remain in possession at the end of the tenancy. This, accordingly, increases the value of the freehold. Further, compensation is payable to the landlord if the enfranchisement causes the value of his other property to diminish.[331] This third method applies also to houses brought within the 1967 Act by the Housing Act 1996, where the tenancy fails the 'low rent' test.[332]

B LANDLORD AND TENANT ACT 1954, PART I. LOCAL GOVERNMENT AND HOUSING ACT 1989

Part I of the Landlord and Tenant Act 1954 gave security of tenure to long leaseholders who, at common law, would have been obliged to give up possession on the ground that their leases had terminated by effluxion of time. In effect, it allowed them to remain in possession as Rent Act statutory tenants. In the case of long leases entered into on or after 1 April 1990 or those created before that date but still existing on 15 January 1989, Part I of the 1954 Act is replaced by a new regime under the Local Government and Housing Act 1989.[333] Under this system the leaseholder becomes entitled to an assured tenancy on termination of the long lease. Even after the Housing Act 1996, the entitlement is to a full assured tenancy as opposed to an assured shorthold.[334] Only the new rules will be examined in this section. Nowadays, however, long leaseholders

---

[328] *Mosley v Hickman* (1986) 52 P & CR 248.

[329] S 23, amending s 9 of the 1967 Act, but not retrospectively; further amended by CLRA 2002, ss 143(4), 180; Sch 14.

[330] S 9(1C) of the 1967 Act, introduced by s 66 of the 1993 Act, and as further amended by CLRA 2002, ss 145–147, inserting also ss 9(1D) and 9(1E) into the 1967 Act.

[331] S 9A, introduced by s 66 of the 1993 Act. See [1996] 50 EG 93 (J Briant).

[332] S 9(1C), as amended by HA 1996, Sch 9, para 2(4); repealed (but without retrospective effect) by Housing and Regeneration Act 2008, Sch 16; SI 2009 No 2096, arts 2(c), 3(1).

[333] S 186 and Sch 10.   [334] HA 1988, Sch 2A, para 6, introduced by HA 1996, Sch 7; above, p 360.

of houses will usually also be entitled to the more attractive privileges of the Leasehold Reform Act 1967,[335] while long leaseholders of flats have been given enhanced rights by the Leasehold Reform, Housing and Urban Development Act 1993.[336]

(1) The Qualifying Tenancy

The 1989 Act protects the tenant if he holds under a long tenancy at a low rent[337] and if he satisfies the 'qualifying condition'.[338] This requires him to show that, if the tenancy had not been at a low rent, it would for the time being qualify as an assured tenancy under the Housing Act 1988. Thus the premises must have been let as a separate dwelling,[339] they must fall within the appropriate limits of rent or rateable value,[340] the tenant must have been occupying them wholly or in part as his only or principal home,[341] and so forth. The crucial moment when the qualifying condition must be satisfied is on 'the term date',[342] that is the date on which the tenancy would expire at common law.

(2) Security of Tenure

At common law the landlord would be entitled to possession on the term date. But the 1989 Act provides that he shall be entitled to possession only if he can show the existence of certain specified grounds.[343] These grounds are broadly similar to those upon which a court may make an order for possession under the Housing Act 1988.[344] If the landlord is unable to prove the existence of any of the statutory grounds, the tenant is entitled to an assured tenancy.[345] Possession may thereafter be recovered under the Housing Act 1988 grounds for possession.

The machinery by which the Act provides security of tenure is rather different from that applicable to ordinary short protected tenancies. The Act artificially prolongs the existence of the long tenancy until it has been determined in accordance with a complicated procedure of notices, counter-notices and (if necessary) applications to the county court. While thus prolonged, the tenancy remains 'property', capable of vesting in the tenant's trustee in bankruptcy.[346] If the landlord wishes to retake

---

[335] Above, p 390.   [336] Below, p 400.

[337] As defined in Sch 10, para 2. For tenancies granted on or after 1 April 1990, the rent must not exceed £1,000 a year in Greater London or £250 elsewhere. A rateable value formula applies to those granted before that date.

[338] HA 1988, Sch 10, para 1.   [339] Above, p 361.

[340] Defined in HA 1988, Sch 1. For tenancies granted on or after 1 April 1990, the requirement is that the premium paid for the tenancy did not exceed a limit based on a mathematical formula: Local Government and Housing Act 1989, Sch 10, para 1(2A).

[341] Above, p 363.   [342] Local Government and Housing Act 1989, Sch 10, para 3.

[343] Ibid, para 5.

[344] For example, breach of covenant, nuisance or annoyance, redevelopment, or requirement for occupation by landlord or family.

[345] Local Government and Housing Act 1989, Sch 10, paras 4, 9.

[346] De Rothschild v Bell [2000] QB 33 (LTA 1954, Part I).

possession, he must serve the appropriate notice on the tenant at least six months but less than 12 months in advance, stating the ground upon which he claims that he is entitled to possession.[347] If the tenant replies with a counter-notice electing to remain in possession, or simply stays there and continues to fulfil the 'qualifying condition',[348] the landlord must apply to the court for an order for possession.[349] If he is successful, the tenancy will of course come to an end. If he is unsuccessful, or if he did not want to retake possession in the first place, he may terminate the long tenancy by a notice proposing an assured monthly periodic tenancy.[350] Such a notice must specify the date upon which the long tenancy is to come to an end. Except in the case of a notice served after an unsuccessful application for possession, the notice must also be given at least six months but less than one year in advance. The notice must also propose the terms of the new assured tenancy. If these are not agreed, they must be settled by an application to the rent assessment committee.[351] The committee will assess the open market rent and, if other terms are disputed, the terms that might reasonably be expected to be found in an assured monthly periodic tenancy of the dwelling-house (not being an assured shorthold).[352]

C LEASEHOLD REFORM, HOUSING AND URBAN DEVELOPMENT ACT 1993

Long leases of flats have been a source of dissatisfaction to tenants for two reasons. First, they are wasting assets that in time become unsaleable. Secondly, the tenants have insufficient control over the level of service charges and the standard of maintenance. We have seen that flat-dwellers have no rights of enfranchisement under the Leasehold Reform Act 1967.[353]

The Leasehold Reform, Housing and Urban Development Act 1993 sought to improve the position of long leaseholders of flats by giving them a collective right to acquire the landlord's interest in the building. It should be appreciated that this Act does not enable a leaseholder to acquire the freehold of his *flat*, as the system of commonhold tenure does.[354] Also, such a leaseholder is given an individual right to an extended lease of his flat. Contracting out of either of these rights is prohibited.[355] Significant amendments were made to the 1993 Act by the Commonhold and Leasehold Reform Act 2002, which further improved the leaseholder's position.

---

[347] Local Government and Housing Act 1989, Sch 10, para 4.   [348] Ibid, para 1, above.
[349] Ibid, para 13.   [350] Ibid, para 4.   [351] Ibid, para 10.
[352] Ibid, para 11. An interim monthly rent may be fixed during the statutory continuation of the long tenancy; ibid, para 6.
[353] The tenants of flats (including, but not limited to, long leaseholders) were first given limited rights to acquire the landlord's interest, by way of a right of first refusal on disposal by the landlord, under LTA 1987, amended by HA 1996, ss 89–91 and Sch 6; below, p 424.
[354] Above, Ch 7.   [355] Leasehold Reform, Housing and Urban Development Act 1993, s 93.

(1) Conditions for Enfranchisement

The 2002 Act relaxed the conditions for enfranchisement. Formerly, only tenants of flats under a long lease (granted for a term exceeding 21 years) at a low rent,[356] or a 'particularly long' term if not at a low rent,[357] qualified for enfranchisement; and a proportion of the qualifying tenants had to satisfy a residence condition.[358] Now, however, a 'qualifying tenant'[359] is any person who is the tenant of the flat[360] under a long lease—still defined[361] primarily as a term exceeding 21 years—but without restriction as to the level of rent and without any residence condition.[362] The premises must still be a self-contained building or a self-contained part[363] of a building containing at least two flats held by qualifying tenants, and such tenants must hold at least two-thirds of the total number of flats in the premises.[364] The right to enfranchisement is excluded if there is a resident landlord and the premises contain no more than four units,[365] or if more than 25 per cent of the internal floor area (disregarding common parts) is non-residential.[366] Until 2002 the mixed-use exclusion was defined as applying where more than 10 per cent was non-residential, thus excluding from the operation of the Act a building consisting of a row of flats above shops, but the new definition is likely to bring some such properties within the scope of collective enfranchisement.

(2) Procedure

Under amendments to the 1993 Act made by the Commonhold and Leasehold Reform Act 2002[367] (but still not yet, because of their complexity, brought into force), the

---

[356] Ibid, s 8, as amended by HA 1996, s 105. The requirement of low rent related to the first year of the lease. For leases granted on or after 1 April 1990 the limits were £1,000 per annum in Greater London or £250 elsewhere. In other cases the limit was based on the letting value or the rateable value.

[357] Ibid, s 8A, inserted by HA 1996, s 106, Sch 9. 'Particularly long' meant, primarily, a term exceeding 35 years.

[358] Ibid, s 6: occupation of the flat as the tenant's only or principal home for the last 12 months or for periods amounting to three years in the last ten years. Occupation by a company or other artificial person did not suffice.

[359] Ibid, s 5. Business leases are excluded: s 5(2)(a). The 1993 Act does not apply to tenants holding directly of the Crown, but for the application of the provisions of the 1993 Act to Crown leaseholders, see above, p 391, n 279.

[360] Defined ibid s 101; *Slamon v Planchon* [2004] EWCA Civ 799, [2005] Ch 142 (meaning of resident landlord exemption).

[361] Ibid, s 7.   [362] CLRA 2002, ss 117, 120.

[363] *41-60 Albert Palace Mansions (Freehold) Ltd v Craftrule Ltd* [2011] EWCA Civ 185, [2011] NPC 23 ('self-contained part' can be a part of the building that could itself also be sub-divided into smaller self-contained parts).

[364] Leasehold Reform, Housing and Urban Development Act 1993, s 3, as amended by HA 1996, s 107, to include premises owned by multiple freeholders.

[365] Ibid, s 4(4). 'Resident landlord' is defined in s 10, amended (and narrowed) by CLRA 2002, s 118; and 'unit' in s 38.

[366] Ibid, s 4(1), as amended by CLRA 2002, s 115; *Indiana Investments Ltd v Taylor* [2004] 3 EGLR 63 (Cty Ct; non-residential portion was 24.11126 per cent).

[367] Ss 121–123 and Sch 8.

right to collective enfranchisement can be exercised only by a 'RTE company',[368] a private company limited by guarantee that has as its object (or one of its objects[369]) the exercise of the right to collective enfranchisement of the premises, which has among its participating members qualifying tenants of at least one-half of the flats contained in the premises.[370]

The statutory procedure requires the RTE company to serve a notice on the landlord, who must respond by counter-notice.[371] The purpose of the counter-notice by the landlord is meant[372] 'to define the basic issues before proceedings start, and the landlord should not be entitled then to depart from that position and keep other matters up its sleeve'.

In outline, the RTE company's notice must provide the landlord with information such as the names of the qualifying tenants and must propose a purchase price. The landlord's counter-notice must state whether he accepts the right to enfranchise and whether the price is acceptable. If the right is denied, the matter will be resolved by the court.[373] If the landlord accepts the right but rejects the proposed price, his counter-notice must include a counter-offer.

The landlord may defeat the claim by applying to court and establishing an intention to redevelop the whole or a substantial part of the premises. This course is open to him only if at least two-thirds of all the long leases of flats in the premises are due to end within five years from the date of the tenants' notice.[374]

The RTE company must grant a lease back to the former landlord of any flats subject to secure tenancies. This lease will be for 999 years at a peppercorn rent. The former landlord may also require such a lease of non-residential units or flats having no qualifying tenant.[375]

---

[368] Leasehold Reform, Housing and Urban Development Act 1993, s 13(2)(b), amended by CLRA 2002, s 121. Formerly the qualifying tenants themselves gave the notice to exercise the right to enfranchise, and could choose whom to nominate as 'nominee purchaser', to conduct the proceedings arising out of the initial notice and to take the conveyance of the freehold under s 15 of the 1993 Act. The 'RTE' company is so-called because it exercises the Right To collective Enfranchisement: 1993 Act, s 4A(1)(b); cf 'RTM company' which exercises the 'right to manage' under CLRA 2002, s 71.

[369] It may have other objects, including the right to manage the premises: below, p 405. The same company could therefore be both the RTM company and the RTE company in relation to the same premises.

[370] If there are only two qualifying tenants, both must be participating members: 1993 Act, s 13(2ZA), inserted by CLRA 2002, s 121. All qualifying tenants must be given the opportunity to participate: s 12A (inserted by CLRA 2002, s 123: a change from the previous law, under which a group of at least two-thirds of the qualifying tenants, of at least one-half of the total number of flats, could give the notice without involving the others).

[371] Leasehold Reform, Housing and Urban Development Act 1993, ss 13, 21. By s 28, the RTE company's notice may be withdrawn before a binding contract is made. Leasehold Reform (Collective Enfranchisement) (Counter-notices) (England) Regulations 2002 (SI 2002 No 3208); *7 Strathay Gardens Ltd v Poinstar Shipping & Finance Ltd* The Times 10 January 2005.

[372] *Bishopsgate Foundation v Curtis* [2004] 3 EGLR 57 at [13] (Cty Ct: Judge Cooke).

[373] Leasehold Reform, Housing and Urban Development Act 1993, s 22.   [374] Ibid, s 23.

[375] Ibid, s 36, Sch 9. Likewise a flat occupied by a resident landlord (ie where the right to enfranchise is not excluded because the premises contain more than four units: s 4).

It will be appreciated that, after enfranchisement, the tenants (via the RTE company) will be responsible for the management of the premises.

Where it is necessary for the maintenance of standards of appearance and amenity of an estate, the former landlord may be permitted to retain limited control over an enfranchised building by means of a management scheme along the lines of section 19 of the Leasehold Reform Act 1967.[376]

(3) The Price[377]

The tenants must pay the market value[378] of the landlord's interest, which includes the capitalised value of the rents for the residue of the leases and the value of the reversion on expiry of the leases, allowing for the tenants' rights to remain in possession (ie as assured tenants), but disregarding the right to enfranchise or to extend the lease. If the landlord does not take a lease of any non-qualifying parts, the value of the reversion to these parts must be included. In addition, except in relation to any lease that has more than 80 years still to run, the tenants must pay half of the 'marriage value'[379] of the landlord's and tenants' interests. This means that the landlord can share in the increased value accruing to the tenants as a result of their ability to acquire new long leases from the RTE company without paying a premium.[380] The price must also include any compensation payable to the landlord on account of loss or damage to his other property as a result of the enfranchisement.

(4) Extended Lease

The 1993 Act also confers on long leaseholders individual rights to a new lease of their flats, on payment of a premium. Again, the Commonhold and Leasehold Reform Act 2002 made significant amendments that have enhanced the rights of leaseholders. As with the right to collective enfranchisement,[381] the 2002 Act has removed both the 'low rent' requirement and the residence condition that used to apply to the right to a

[376] Ibid, s 69. The landlord must apply to a leasehold valuation tribunal for approval within two years of the coming into force of s 70. The time limits were modified by HA 1996, s 118, where properties become newly enfranchisable.

[377] Ibid, Sch 6, as amended by HA 1996, s 109 and CLRA 2002, ss 126–128 and Sch 8 (Sch 8 is not yet in force: above, p 401). Only an outline can be given here. Failing agreement, the price will be determined by a leasehold valuation tribunal; s 24. On the meaning of 'agreed', see *Pleadream Properties Ltd v 5 Felix Avenue London Ltd* [2010] EWHC 3048 (Ch), [2011] L & TR 20.

[378] Before the amendments made by CLRA 2002, the valuation was made on the date when the interest to be acquired by the tenants was agreed or otherwise determined by a leasehold valuation tribunal. Under CLRA 2002, it is the date on which the notice to exercise the right to enfranchise is given by the RTE company.

[379] Leasehold Reform, Housing and Urban Development Act 1993, Sch 6, para 4, amended by CLRA 2002, ss 127, 128.

[380] *McHale v Earl Cadogan* [2010] EWCA Civ 1471, [2011] 05 EG 106. In calculating the landlord's interest the 'hope value' in respect of non-participating tenants wishing to obtain new leases of their flats in the open market can be taken into account: *Earl Cadogan v Pitts* [2008] UKHL 71, [2010] 1 AC 226.

[381] Above, p 401.

new lease. Now the only condition is that the leaseholder must have been a qualifying tenant under a long lease of the flat for the last two years before exercising the right to the new lease.[382] This greatly extends the scope of operation of the 1993 Act.[383] The statutory procedure requires a tenant's notice and a landlord's counter-notice.[384] The tenant's rights may be assigned along with the lease of the flat, but cannot be exercised during the currency of any claim to acquire the freehold of the block.[385] Where the original lease is due to end within five years from the date of the tenant's notice, the landlord may defeat the right to a new lease by applying to court and establishing his intention to redevelop the premises in which the flat is contained.[386]

A qualifying tenant is entitled, on payment of premium, to a new lease at a peppercorn rent for a term expiring 90 years after the term date of his existing lease.[387] This lease, which replaces the existing lease, is otherwise on the same terms as the original lease, but excluding any express renewal right or option to purchase.[388] The tenant is not entitled to any security of tenure (ie as an assured tenant) at the end of the new lease, but the new lease may itself be renewed under the statutory procedure.[389]

The premium that the tenant must pay for the new lease is the aggregate of (a) the diminution in the value of the landlord's interest in the flat (on the assumption that the tenant had no enfranchisement or extension rights, but not disregarding his right to the existing and extended tenancy), (b) the landlord's share (50 per cent) of the 'marriage value', and (c) any compensation payable to the landlord on account of loss or damage to his other property as a result of the grant of the new lease.[390]

---

[382] Leasehold Reform, Housing and Urban Development Act 1993, s 39, amended by CLRA 2002, ss 130, 131. 'Qualifying tenant' and 'long lease' are given the same definition as for the right to collective enfranchisement: primarily, a term exceeding 21 years, but excluding a business lease: ibid, ss 5, 7, incorporated by s 39(3).

[383] *Maurice v Hollow-Ware Products Ltd* [2005] EWHC 815 (Ch), [2005] 2 EGLR 71 (tenant of block of 28 flats, which were sub-let, entitled to new lease in respect of each of the flats); *Howard de Walden Estates Ltd v Aggio* [2008] UKHL 44, [2009] 1 AC 39.

[384] Leasehold Reform, Housing and Urban Development Act 1993, ss 42, 45. See *Cadogan v Morris* (1998) 77 P & CR 336 (unrealistic proposal by tenant on price can invalidate notice); *9 Cornwall Crescent London Ltd v Kensington and Chelsea Royal LBC* [2005] EWCA Civ 324, [2006] 1 WLR 1186 (no such rule as regards landlord's counter-notice); (2005) 155 NLJ 942 (J Driscoll); *Lay v Ackerman* [2004] EWCA Civ 184, [2005] 1 EGLR 139 (misdescription of landlord did not invalidate notice, on construction under *Mannai Investment Co Ltd v Eagle Star Life Assurance Co Ltd* [1997] AC 749, above, p 333); cf *Burman v Mount Cook Land Ltd* [2001] EWCA Civ 171,2 [2002] Ch 256 (counter-notice did not contain matters required by the Act and so could not be construed under *Mannai* to be valid).

[385] Ibid, s 54.

[386] Ibid, s 47; *Majorstake Ltd v Curtis* [2008] UKHL 10, [2008] 1 AC 787 at [39] ('premises in which the flat is contained' must be an objectively recognisable physical space, something that the landlord, the tenant, the visitor, the prospective purchaser would recognise as 'premises': flat and flat immediately below, which landlord proposed to combine into single duplex apartment, not 'premises').

[387] Ibid, s 56.　　　　　　　　　　[388] Ibid, s 57.　　　　　　　　　　[389] Ibid, s 59.

[390] Ibid, Sch 13, as amended by HA 1996, s 110 and CLRA 2002, ss 134–136. Only an outline is given here. For 'marriage value', see above, p 403.

The landlord may subsequently terminate the new lease if he satisfies the court of his intention to redevelop the premises in which the flat is contained.[391] In such a case he must pay compensation to the tenant based on the open market value of the new lease.[392]

It is likely in practice that this right to a new lease will be more attractive to tenants than the collective right to acquire the freehold of the block, not least because the conditions are easier to satisfy.

D 'RIGHT TO MANAGE'

We have seen that many amendments were made by the Commonhold and Leasehold Reform Act 2002 to the existing provisions for enfranchisement of long leases and the rights of long leaseholders to new or extended leases, and that the general purpose of the Act was to enhance tenants' rights. The Act also introduced an entirely new provision: the right[393] for long leaseholders, who have a greater present interest in the state of the premises than the landlord, to acquire and exercise the right to manage their premises. It may well be that the very existence of such a right will act as an inducement for landlords to exercise their own management functions in such a way as to avoid a claim by the tenants to take over the management, but the exercise of the right does not depend on the tenants' showing any failing on the part of the landlord.

Many of the provisions regarding the right to manage are similar to those elsewhere in the 2002 Act that modified existing legislation on long leases, and in particular the Leasehold Reform, Housing and Urban Development Act 1993. The right to manage applies only to a self-contained building or part of a building that contains two or more flats held by qualifying tenants, where the total number of flats held by such tenants is not less than two-thirds of the total number of flats contained in the premises.[394] A 'qualifying tenant' is any person who is the tenant of the flat under a long lease—defined primarily as a term exceeding 21 years—but without restriction as to the level of rent and without any residence condition.[395] The right to manage must be acquired and exercised through an 'RTM company', which has among its participating members qualifying tenants of at least one-half of the flats contained in the premises.[396]

---

[391] Ibid, s 61. The application may be during the 12 months ending with the original term date or during the period of five years ending with the term date of the new lease.

[392] Ibid, Sch 14.

[393] The parties cannot contract out of the 'right to manage' provisions: CLRA 2002, s 106.

[394] CLRA 2002, s 72(1). The right to manage is excluded if there is a resident landlord and the premises contain no more than four units, or if more than 25 per cent of the internal floor area (disregarding common parts) is non-residential: ibid, s 72(6) and Sch 6, paras 1, 3. These are the new rules also for enfranchisement under the 1993 Act; above, p 401.

[395] Ibid, ss 75–77; business tenancies are excluded. Again, this follows the definition of 'qualifying tenant' for the purposes of the 1993 Act.

[396] Ibid, ss 71(1), 73, 74, 79. All qualifying tenants must be given the opportunity to participate: s 78. Cf the RTE company for the purpose of exercising the right to collective enfranchisement under the 1993 Act.

The RTM company must serve a notice on the landlord claiming to acquire the right to manage, and the landlord must serve a counter-notice either accepting or denying the company's right.[397] Once the company has acquired the right to manage,[398] it takes over all the management functions that the landlord formerly had under the lease: functions with respect to services, repairs, maintenance, improvements, insurance and management.[399] The terms of the lease on these matters are overridden.[400] The company has the right to any uncommitted service charges that have already been collected by the landlord,[401] and has the right to collect service charges from the tenants thereafter.[402]

IV BUSINESS TENANCIES[403]

Protection is necessary for business tenants principally because a tenant with an established business is in a vulnerable position. If he has built up a goodwill attaching to the premises, such as that of a successful shopkeeper, he may suffer a severe loss of custom if he is required to remove elsewhere at the end of his tenancy. Furthermore, he will often have adapted the premises at his own cost to the needs of his particular business, so that removal would involve him in considerable further outlay. A landlord may therefore be able to extract a higher rent from his sitting tenant than he would obtain by letting the premises to a new tenant in the open market. Parliament thought it unfair that the landlord should be able to force the tenant to pay this additional rent merely to preserve goodwill and improvements[404] created by his own effort and expense. The need to protect the tenant became more acute after the Second World War, when bomb damage had caused a shortage of business accommodation and a consequent increase in the landlord's bargaining power. The provisions for security of tenure and rent control are now contained in Part II of the Landlord and Tenant Act

---

[397] CLRA 2002, ss 79–81, 84. The company bears the landlord's reasonable costs: s 88. In the case of a dispute the matter is resolved by a leasehold valuation tribunal: s 84(3).

[398] The right to manage is registrable as a notice in registered land: CLRA 2002, s 104 (amending LRA 1925, s 49); LRA 2002, s 32; R & R, para 26.027.

[399] CLRA 2002, s 96. Functions concerning only part of the premises not held under a lease by a qualifying tenant, and functions relating to re-entry or forfeiture, are excluded.

[400] Ibid, s 96(4).   [401] Ibid, s 94.

[402] The landlord must also contribute to the service charges in certain cases where the premises contain excluded units and the landlord has the right to service charges from his tenant: ibid, s 103.

[403] Aldridge, *Leasehold Law*, Part 1, ch 4, Part 5, ch 1; Hill and Redman's *Landlord and Tenant*, Division B; Woodfall, *Landlord and Tenant*, ch 22; Aldridge, *Letting Business Premises* (8th edn, 2004); Lewison, *Drafting Business Leases* (7th edn, 2006); Tromans, *Commercial Leases* (1996); Reynolds and Clark, *Renewal of Business Tenancies* (3rd edn, 2007); Williams, Brand and Hubbard, *Handbook of Business Tenancies*; Haley, *Statutory Regulation of Business Tenancies* (2000); Hewitson, *Business Tenancies* (2005); Evans and Smith, *Law of Landlord and Tenant* (6th edn, 2002), Part E. See Code for Leasing Business Premises (2002, available at www.leasingbusinesspremises.co.uk); N Crosby and C Hughes, *Monitoring the 2007 Code for Leasing Business Premises* (2009, available at www.communities.gov.uk) which concluded that awareness of the code of practice is not high, especially among small tenants and small landlords.

[404] As to compensation for improvements, see LTA 1927, Part I.

1954, as amended by Part I of the Law of Property Act 1969 and the Regulatory Reform (Business Tenancies) (England and Wales) Order 2003.[405]

A THE QUALIFYING TENANCY

A tenancy qualifies for the protection of Part II of the Landlord and Tenant Act 1954 if the property comprised in the tenancy 'is or includes' premises that are occupied by the tenant 'and are so occupied for the purposes of a business carried on by him or for those and other purposes'.[406] There are some features of this definition that require closer examination.

(1) 'Is or includes premises…occupied by the tenant…'

A tenant will enjoy the protection of the Act if he occupies any part of the property comprised in his lease for the purposes of his business, although his protection extends only to what the Act defines as his 'holding'. This means the part of the property occupied by the tenant himself (whether for business or other purposes) or by a person employed in his business.[407] Thus the tenant of a shop with a flat above who carries on business in the shop and lives in the flat, or sub-lets it to an assistant or manager working in the shop will enjoy protection in respect of the whole premises. If he has sub-let the flat to someone who does not work in the shop, the tenancy will be within the Act but his 'holding' will be the shop alone.[408] If he has sub-let the whole premises, his tenancy will not be protected at all, although that of the sub-tenant probably will be. Difficult questions can arise as to the meaning of 'occupation'. Where the tenant maintains a presence on the premises but his business in reality involves no more than the receipt of income from sub-tenants, he will not be protected. Thus the operator of a market hall who had sub-let the market stalls was not entitled to a renewal even though he was occupying the common parts, which alone could be the 'holding'.[409]

---

[405] SI 2003 No 3096, which came into force on 1 June 2004. The reforms introduced by the 2003 Regulations amended many details of the Act while leaving the fundamentals undisturbed, largely following the recommendations of the Law Commission: Law Com No 208, *Business Tenancies* (1992); [1993] Conv 334 (M Haley). See also Department of the Environment, Transport and the Regions' Consultation Paper, *Business Tenancies Legislation in England and Wales* (2001). Regulatory Reform Orders are made under the Regulatory Reform Act 2001 and are designed to remove burdens on businesses. See [2006] Conv 137 (S Bright), advocating improved protection for the Small Business Tenant.

[406] LTA 1954, s 23(1). The definition includes a tenancy by estoppel: *Bell v General Accident Fire & Life Assurance Corp Ltd* [1998] 1 EGLR 69.

[407] Ibid, s 23(3). Occupation or the carrying on of a business by a company in which the tenant has a controlling interest are treated as occupation or the carrying on of a business by the tenant: LTA 1954, s 23(1A), (1B), inserted by SI 2003 No 3096. See *Pointon York Group plc v Poulton* [2006] EWCA Civ 1001, [2007] 1 P & CR 6 (right to occupy parking spaces under easement (below, p 648) could be 'premises' which were 'occupied' for the purposes of the business on the dominant tenement).

[408] *Narcissi v Wolfe* [1960] Ch 10.

[409] *Graysim Holdings Ltd v P & O Property Holdings Ltd* [1996] AC 329; [1997] Conv 119 (S Higgins). Where the sub-letting is of a residential premises covered by the Rent Acts, or is a residential licence, rather

It was left open whether the tenant was outside the 1954 Act or was a business tenant with no right of renewal (in which case the statutory termination procedure would nevertheless apply). The former approach seems preferable.

(2) 'Occupied for the purposes of a business'

'Business' is very widely defined, to include a 'trade, profession or employment' and, rather curiously, '*any* activity carried on by a body of persons, whether corporate or unincorporate'. Thus the tenancy of a members' tennis club has been held within the Act, because playing tennis is undoubtedly an activity and it was carried on by a body of persons.[410] For an individual, on the other hand, activity is not enough. It must be a 'trade, profession or employment'. Accordingly a tenant who ran a free Sunday school in a disused shop was held to be outside the definition.[411]

Under the Housing Act 1988, where the key phrase is 'let as a separate dwelling', attention is concentrated on the purpose for which the premises were let rather than the purpose for which they are actually being used.[412] The business code, on the other hand, is more concerned with actual user at the time when the question has to be decided.[413] Prima facie, the fact that the tenant is carrying on business upon the premises is enough. But in some cases the fact that the business user is in breach of covenant will exclude the application of the Act.[414] And there is nothing in the Act to restrict the landlord's common law right to forfeit the tenancy for breach of covenant.[415]

(3) 'Or for those and other purposes'

The tenant need use only a part of the premises for the purposes of his business, or he may use the same part for business purposes some of the time and other purposes at other times. If the premises are used partly for business and partly for residential purposes, residential security is excluded and only the Landlord and Tenant Act 1954

---

than a tenancy, it might be possible for the tenant still to be in occupation but only if it retains such use and control of the sub-occupied parts as can be regarded as business occupation: [2005] 20 EG 259 (S Murdoch); *Lee-Verhulst (Investments) Ltd v Harwood Trust* [1973] QB 204; *Smith v Titanate Ltd* [2005] 2 EGLR 63 (Cty Ct).

[410] *Addiscombe Garden Estates Ltd v Crabbe* [1958] 1 QB 513; *Hawkesbrook Leisure Ltd v Reece-Jones Partnership* [2003] EWHC 3333 (Ch), [2004] 2 EGLR 61 (non-profit-making company managing sports grounds).

[411] *Abernethie v A M and J Kleiman Ltd* [1970] 1 QB 10; see also *Lewis v Weldcrest Ltd* [1978] 1 WLR 1107 (taking lodgers).

[412] Above, p 361.

[413] The critical dates are the contractual term date (because unless the premises are then being used for business purposes the term will not be artificially prolonged: *Esselte AB v Pearl Assurance plc* [1997] 1 WLR 891, below, p 411) and the date when a notice to determine the tenancy is served: *Cheryl Investments Ltd v Saldanha* [1978] 1 WLR 1329, 1337 (Geoffrey Lane LJ).

[414] LTA 1954, s 23(4); see *Bell v Alfred Franks and Bartlett Co Ltd* [1980] 1 WLR 340.

[415] Ibid, s 24(2).

applies.[416] But the business user must be significant 'and not merely ancillary to the residential user' such as maintaining a study where one can work in the evenings or at weekends.[417]

B EXCLUSIONS

Expressly excluded from the protection of the Act are short fixed-term lettings not exceeding six months,[418] tenancies excluded by agreement,[419] and certain other tenancies such as agricultural holdings, farm business tenancies, and mining leases.[420] Although not expressly excluded, the Act does not apply to tenancies at will, even if expressly created,[421] nor to licences. With respect to the latter, the effect of the decision in *Street v Mountford*[422] must be considered.[423]

C SECURITY OF TENURE AND RENT

The Act gives a business tenant security of tenure by providing, first, that his tenancy (whether periodic or for a term certain) cannot be terminated except by the notice procedure laid down by the Act, and secondly, that upon the termination of his tenancy the tenant shall be entitled as of right to the grant of a new tenancy unless the landlord can establish one of a list of specified grounds of opposition.

(1) Termination Procedure

A business tenancy can be terminated only in accordance with the provisions of the Act.[424] Until then, the tenancy continues, whatever its term might be. At common law, if a tenant for a term certain at an annual rent holds over after the end of the term and rent continues to be paid at the old rate, the normal inference is that he is holding over as a tenant from year to year.[425] But a business tenant who stays after the term date is not holding over. There can be no inference of a tenancy from year to year because the old tenancy has not yet come to an end. In the case of a tenancy granted before the Landlord and Tenant (Covenants) Act 1995,[426] the original tenant who has assigned the tenancy during the contractual term is not liable for the defaults of the assignee

---

[416] HA 1988, Sch 1, para 4.

[417] *Cheryl Investments Ltd v Saldanha*, above.

[418] LTA 1954, s 43(3).   [419] Ibid, s 38A; below, p 416.

[420] Ibid, s 43(1), as amended by the Agricultural Tenancies Act 1995. Tenancies of public houses are no longer excluded: Landlord and Tenant (Licensed Premises) Act 1990.

[421] *Manfield & Sons Ltd v Botchin* [1970] 2 QB 612.   [422] [1985] AC 809, M & B p 383; above, p 186.

[423] See *University of Reading v Johnson-Houghton* [1985] 2 EGLR 113; *London & Associated Investment Trust plc v Calow* (1986) 53 P & CR 340, M & B p 396; *Dellneed Ltd v Chin* (1986) 53 P & CR 172; *Dresden Estates Ltd v Collinson* [1987] 1 EGLR 45, M & B p 395; *Vandersteen v Agius* (1992) 65 P & CR 266; above, p 188.

[424] LTA 1954, s 24(1). For the procedure to be followed, see CPR Part 56, PD; (2004) 154 NLJ 1620 (D Mo).

[425] Above, p 204.   [426] Above, p 314, n 637.

during the statutory continuation period.[427] The landlord may, however, ensure that guarantors remain liable during the continuation period by appropriate wording in the guarantee, whether the tenancy was granted before or after the 1995 Act.

(a) Termination by landlord

The landlord may terminate the tenancy by a notice in a prescribed form, specifying the date of termination.[428] This must be at least six months but not more than 12 months after service of the notice and not earlier than the date on which the tenancy would have terminated, or could have been terminated, at common law.[429] A landlord's notice to terminate is commonly known as a 'section 25 notice'.

The notice must state whether the landlord is opposed to the grant of a new tenancy to the tenant; and, if he is so opposed, the statutory grounds for his opposition or, if he is not so opposed, his proposals for the property, rent and other terms of the new tenancy.[430] Until the reform of the 1954 Act effected by the 2003 Regulations, the tenant was required to serve a counter-notice within two months if he wished to resist the landlord's claim to terminate the tenancy, and then to make application to the court for a new tenancy not less than two months nor more than four months after the service of the section 25 notice. These requirements constituted something of a trap for tenants, who could find that the failure to take the required steps within the strict time limits had resulted in their losing all their rights.[431] No counter-notice is now required.[432] Instead, the landlord may apply to the court for an order for termination of the tenancy, as long as neither he nor the tenant has yet made application to the court for a new tenancy,[433] and as long as he applies before the date specified for termination in his section 25 notice.[434] The court will order the termination of the current tenancy, but in order to resist the grant of a new tenancy, the landlord must satisfy the court of one or more grounds of opposition; failing that, the court will order the grant of a new tenancy.[435] Alternatively, before the date specified for termination, the tenant may himself make an application to the court for a new tenancy.[436]

---

[427] *City of London Corp v Fell* [1994] 1 AC 458.

[428] LTA 1954, s 25(1).   [429] Ibid, s 25(2).

[430] Ibid, s 25(6), (7), (8), substituted by SI 2003 No 3096. For the construction of notices in the light of the principles set out in *Mannai Investment Co Ltd v Eagle Star Life Assurance Co Ltd* [1997] AC 749, see *Barclays Bank plc v Bee* [2001] EWCA Civ 1126, [2002] 1 WLR 332.

[431] See, eg, *Beanby Estates Ltd v Egg Stores (Stamford Hill) Ltd* [2003] EWHC 1252 (Ch), [2003] 1 WLR 2064 (s 25 notice, sent by recorded delivery, deemed by LTA 1927, s 23 to have been served on posting, not receipt, so application to court out of time).

[432] The abolition was proposed by Law Com No 208, *Business Tenancies* (1992), para 2.39. The original LTA 1954, s 29(2) was replaced by SI 2003 No 3096, reg 5.

[433] LTA 1954, s 29(2), (3), substituted by SI 2003 No 3096. On the application for a new tenancy, see below.

[434] Ibid, s 29A, inserted by SI 2003 No 3096. The parties may agree to extend the period before it expires: s 29B.

[435] Ibid, s 29(2), substituted by SI 2003 No 3096. If the court orders that the current tenancy be terminated without the grant of a new tenancy, the termination takes effect three months after the proceedings have been finally disposed of: ibid, s 64.

[436] Ibid, s 24(1). The time limit is set out in s 29A, inserted by SI 2003 No 3096. The parties may agree to extend the period before it expires: s 29B.

(b) Termination or request for renewal by tenant

A tenant who simply wants to go out of possession can terminate his contractual tenancy in any way open to him at common law.[437] If the tenancy cannot be terminated, the tenant may nevertheless serve a notice on the landlord to indicate that he does not wish it to continue under the Act.[438] The Act has no further scope for application if the tenant simply ceases to occupy before the contractual termination date.[439] If the tenant ceases to occupy during the continuation period, the tenancy will continue until terminated by notice by either party.[440] Where the tenant desires a renewal, he may take the initiative by serving a notice requesting the grant of a new tenancy, provided he holds under a tenancy for a term of years certain exceeding one year, or a term of years certain and thereafter from year to year.[441] This notice is the counterpart of the landlord's section 25 notice. Like the section 25 notice, it must specify the date on which the current tenancy is to terminate, and it is subject to the same time limits.[442] A landlord who wishes to oppose the grant of a new tenancy may serve a counter-notice stating his grounds of opposition within two months of the tenant's notice,[443] but whether he does so or not, the tenant will lose his right to a new tenancy unless he follows up his notice by an application to the court before the date specified in his request for the beginning of a new tenancy.[444]

(c) Who is the landlord?

The scheme of the Act contemplates an exchange of notices followed by negotiations for a new tenancy and, if necessary, the adjudication of the court, between landlord and tenant. 'Tenant', however, includes a sub-tenant;[445] the immediate landlord of the tenant carrying on the business may himself hold only a leasehold interest. But there is little point in the grant of a new tenancy by a 'landlord' whose own interest in the premises is shortly about to expire. The Act deals with this problem by disregarding altogether a landlord who has himself only a short remaining leasehold interest. For the purposes of the Act, the 'landlord' must be the owner of the fee simple or a leasehold interest that will not come to an end within 14 months by effluxion of time

---

[437] Ibid, s 24(2); *Bentley & Skinner (Bond St Jewellers) Ltd v Searchmap Ltd* [2003] EWHC 1621 (Ch), [2003] 2 P & CR DG18 (grant of new lease operated by reason of estoppel as a surrender of the old lease); [2004] Conv 61 (M Haley).

[438] Ibid, s 27(1), (2).

[439] Ibid, s 27(1A), inserted by SI 2003 No 3096 to confirm the decision in *Esselte AB v Pearl Assurance plc* [1997] 1 WLR 891; [1998] Conv 218 (M Haley).

[440] See ibid, ss 24(3), 27(2).   [441] Ibid, s 26(1).

[442] Ibid, s 26(2). The tenant cannot operate the s 26 procedure when exercising a break clause; *Garston v Scottish Widows' Fund and Life Assurance Society* [1998] 1 WLR 1583.

[443] Ibid, s 26(6).

[444] Ibid, s 29A, inserted by SI 2003 No 3096. The parties may agree to extend the period before it expires: s 29B. The tenant's notice has the effect of terminating the current tenancy immediately before the date specified in his request: ibid, s 26(5), and is subject to the rule that once an application has been made to the court for a new tenancy, the old tenancy continues until three months after the proceedings have been finally disposed of: s 64.

[445] Ibid, s 69(1).

and in respect of which no notice to terminate has been served under the Act.[446] If the immediate landlord does not fulfil these conditions, the competent landlord for the purposes of the Act will be the next superior landlord who does.

(2) The Grounds of Opposition

The Act specifies seven grounds upon which a landlord may oppose the grant of a new tenancy.[447] These may be briefly summarised as follows: (a) the tenant's failure to repair, (b) persistent delay in paying rent, (c) other misbehaviour by the tenant, (d) alternative accommodation available, (e) that the tenant is, in relation to the landlord, a sub-tenant of part of the property originally let and that the landlord could realise a better rent by reletting the property as a whole, (f) the landlord's intention to demolish or reconstruct the premises, and (g) the landlord's intention to occupy the premises himself, either for the purposes of his business or of a business of a company in which he has a controlling interest,[448] or as a residence. The last two grounds are in practice the most frequently relied upon and the only ones upon which any further comment will be made.

(a) Intention to demolish or reconstruct

The burden is upon the landlord to establish the necessary intention at the time of the hearing.[449] 'Intention' involves more than thinking that demolition or reconstruction would be desirable. The landlord must be able to show that he means business. As Lord Asquith said:[450]

> An 'intention'…connotes a state of affairs which the party 'intending' … does more than merely contemplate: it connotes a state of affairs that, on the contrary, he decides, so far as in him lies, to bring about, and which, in point of possibility, he has a reasonable prospect of being able to bring about, by his own act of volition… The term 'intention' [is] unsatisfied if the person professing it has too many hurdles to overcome, or too little control of events… [The scheme must have] moved out of the zone of contemplation—out of the sphere of the tentative, the provisional and the exploratory—into the valley of decision.

The landlord may therefore have to satisfy the court that his scheme of redevelopment is commercially viable, that he has the means to carry it through and the necessary planning permissions and other consents, or a reasonable prospect[451] of obtaining them. His motive, however, is not relevant.[452]

---

[446] LTA 1954, s 44(1), substituted by LPA 1969, s 14(1).   [447] Ibid, s 30(1)(a)–(g).

[448] Ibid, s 30(1A), (1B), inserted by SI 2003 No 3096.

[449] *Betty's Cafés Ltd v Phillips Furnishing Stores Ltd* [1959] AC 20. This means the substantive trial of the landlord's objection, not a summary judgment hearing, at which the question is rather whether the landlord has a real prospect of forming, and proving that it has formed, the necessary intention by the anticiapted future trial date: *Somerfield Stores Ltd v Spring (Sutton Coldfield) Ltd (in administration) (No 2)* [2010] EWHC 2084 (Ch), [2010] 47 EG 142.

[450] *Cunliffe v Goodman* [1950] 2 KB 237, 253–4.

[451] '"Reasonable prospect" is a low threshold, not to be equated with probability': *Dogan v Semali Investments Ltd* [2005] EWCA Civ 1036, [2005] 3 EGLR 51 at [35] (Mance LJ).

[452] See *Turner v London Borough of Wandsworth* (1994) 69 P & CR 399.

The landlord must also show that he could not reasonably carry out his work of demolition or reconstruction without obtaining possession of the holding.[453] 'Possession' in this context means legal possession, not merely physical occupation of the premises. Thus a landlord who has reserved a right to enter and do works upon the premises may be entitled to go into occupation for a lengthy period without ousting his tenant from legal possession.[454] Such a right will prevent him from opposing the grant of a new tenancy in similar terms. Even if the lease does not include such rights of entry, the tenant may be able to preserve his right to a new lease by offering to include them. The Act provides that the landlord cannot oppose the grant of a new tenancy on this ground, if the tenant agrees to the inclusion of terms giving the landlord reasonable access and other facilities and the work could then be carried out without obtaining possession and without interfering 'to a substantial extent or for a substantial time' with the use of the holding for the purposes of the tenant's business.[455] Similarly, the tenant may be entitled to claim a new tenancy of 'an economically separable part'[456] of the holding, if possession of the rest and (if necessary) access and facilities over the part retained would be reasonably sufficient to enable the landlord to carry out his work.[457]

(b) Intention to use for own business or residence

Again the burden is upon the landlord to establish the necessary intention at the time of the hearing.[458] He must show that he has a reasonable prospect of achieving his genuine intention to occupy for business within a reasonable time, but he is not required to establish that the business is likely to be successful.[459] The Act provides, however, that the landlord cannot rely upon this ground if his own interest has been purchased or created less than five years before 'the termination of the current tenancy'.[460] The purpose of this provision, as in the case of the parallel provision in the Housing Act 1988,[461] is to prevent persons wanting premises with vacant possession from buying them over the heads of sitting tenants and then opposing their normal security of tenure on the ground that they are required for the landlord's own use.

---

[453] LTA 1954, s 30(1)(f).   [454] *Health v Drown* [1973] AC 498.

[455] LTA 1954, s 31A(1)(a), inserted by LPA 1969, s 7(1). See *Cerex Jewels Ltd v Peachey Property Corp plc* (1986) 52 P & CR 127; *Romulus Trading Co Ltd v Trustees of Henry Smith's Charity* (1989) 60 P & CR 62.

[456] Defined in LTA 1954, s 31A(2).

[457] LTA 1954, s 31A(1)(b). On the other hand, if the landlord wants to use the whole holding for the purposes of the work, the tenant cannot argue that the landlord could do as well or better by using only a part. See *Decca Navigator Co Ltd v Greater London Council* [1974] 1 WLR 748.

[458] See *Westminster City Council v British Waterways Board* [1985] AC 676. His intention must be fixed and settled; there must be some substance to it and it must be more than short-term: *Patel v Keles* [2009] EWCA Civ 1187, [2010] Ch 332 (landlords had no settled intention to sell but were highly likely to sell after two years: no sufficent intention for ground (g)).

[459] *Dolgellau Golf Club v Hett* (1998) 76 P & CR 526.

[460] LTA 1954, s 30(2).   [461] HA 1988, Sch 2, Ground 1. See also Ground 6.

(3) Compensation

A tenant who is unable to obtain a new tenancy because the landlord can establish one of the grounds of opposition listed above as (e), (f) or (g) is entitled to be paid compensation for disturbance.[462] If his business has been carried on at the premises (whether by himself or a predecessor) for more than 14 years, the compensation will be twice the rateable value of the premises. Otherwise it will be the rateable value.[463] A tenant need not go to court and lose merely in order to claim his compensation. If the landlord states in his section 25 notice, or his counter-notice opposing the tenant's request for a new tenancy, that he intends to rely on grounds (e), (f) or (g), the tenant will be entitled to his compensation if he makes no application to court, or makes one and later withdraws it.[464]

The court may also order the landlord to pay compensation to the tenant where the court makes an order for termination of a tenancy without granting a new tenancy, or refuses to grant of a new tenancy, or where the tenant quits the holding, and it subsequently appears that the order was obtained (or the court was induced to refuse the grant, or the tenant was induced to quit) by misrepresentation or the concealment of material facts.[465]

(4) Terms of the New Tenancy

If the parties cannot agree on the terms of the new tenancy, they must be fixed by the court. The court has a discretion in fixing the length of the term but it must not exceed 15 years.[466] Other terms (apart from rent) must be fixed by having regard to the terms of the current tenancy and to 'all relevant circumstances'.[467] This means in practice that the court will follow the terms of the current tenancy unless there is a good reason for not doing so. In O'May v City of London Real Property Co Ltd[468] the current tenancy made the landlord responsible for repair and services, the tenant paying a fixed service charge. The House of Lords refused to alter the tenancy to make the tenant liable for repairs and the full cost of services, paying a correspondingly lower rent, because the effect would be to transfer the risk of indeterminate financial burdens to the tenant.

---

[462] LTA 1954, s 37. For contracting out under s 38(3), see *Bacchiocchi v Academic Agency Ltd* [1998] 1 WLR 1313.

[463] Ibid, s 37(2) and (3); Local Government and Housing Act 1989, Sch 7; LTA 1954 (Appropriate Multiplier) Order 1990 (SI 1990 No 363).

[464] Until the Act was amended by LPA 1969 the tenant had to go to court.

[465] LTA 1954, s 37A, added by SI 2003 No 3096; *Inclusive Technology v Williamson* [2009] EWCA Civ 718, [2010] 1 P & CR 2 (true statement later false when landlord changed his mind but did not inform tenant); [2010] Conv 256 (G Griffiths)

[466] Ibid, s 33, amended by SI 2003 No 3096.

[467] Ibid, s 35. Amendments to ss. 34 and 35 by LT(C)A 1995, Sch 1, paras 3 and 4, reflect the changes made by that Act to the liability of original tenants; above, p 321.

[468] [1983] 2 AC 726. See also *Cairnplace Ltd v CBL (Property Investment) Co Ltd* [1984] 1 WLR 696 (guarantor term imposed).

(5) Rent

The rent under the new tenancy is that which the premises could command if let in the open market, but disregarding any effect on the rent of the fact that the tenant or his predecessors in title have been in occupation, or any goodwill attaching to the holding on account of the tenant's business, or any improvements made during the current tenancy or in certain cases in previous tenancies within the past 21 years.[469] When the court has to determine the rent, it will usually do so after hearing the evidence of expert surveyors, giving their opinions of the letting value of the premises supported by evidence of lettings of comparable properties in the same area. It may be questioned whether the court's function could not be better performed by a body that was itself expert in these matters, such as the Upper Tribunal (Lands Chamber).

Until 1970, the tenant continued to be liable only for the rent under the old tenancy until it was duly terminated in accordance with the Act and the new tenancy had begun. In the absence of contrary agreement, the old tenancy could not terminate until three months after the proceedings for the grant of the new tenancy had been finally disposed of.[470] In times of inflation, when the difference between the old rent and the new might be very considerable, it was therefore greatly in the tenant's interest to prolong the proceedings (and his tenancy) as much as possible. Time might be gained by taking fine points on the validity of the section 25 notice and similar procedural matters, while even an unsuccessful appeal to the House of Lords might be financed out of the difference in rents. This situation led to an amendment in 1969.[471] In a rising market, the interim rent will commonly be more than the current rent; but in a falling market it could be lower. Accordingly, the 2003 Regulations introduced a further amendment to allow the application to be made by either the landlord or the tenant,[472] and also made other changes to the rules governing the interim rent. Now the application cannot be made more than six months after the termination of the tenancy,[473] and the interim rent becomes payable from the earliest date that could have been specified in the landlord's section 25 notice, or the earliest date that could have been specified in the tenant's request for a new tenancy, depending on whether the assessment is initiated by the landlord's or the tenant's notice.[474] Where the landlord is not opposed to the grant of the new tenancy, the interim rent is normally the rent payable at the commencement of the new tenancy.[475] Where, however, the landlord is opposed, the interim rent is that which it is reasonable for the tenant to pay while

---

[469] LTA 1954, s 34, amended by LPA 1969, s 1.   [470] Ibid, s 64. See above, p 410.

[471] LPA 1969, s 3(1), inserting LTA 1954, s 24A. See *Stream Properties Ltd v Davis* [1972] 1 WLR 645.

[472] SI 2003 No 3096, substituting LTA 1954, s 24A; Law Com No 208, *Business Tenancies* (1992), above, n 405, para 2.63.

[473] LTA 1954, s 24A(3), substituted by SI 2003 No 3096.

[474] Ibid, s 24B. Under the original s 24A, introduced by LPA 1969, the interim rent was payable from the date of termination actually specified in the section 25 notice or in the tenant's request for a new tenancy, or the date of the application to fix the interim rent, whichever was the later.

[475] Ibid, s 24C. This is adjusted if the rent under the new tenancy would have been substantially different if it had been assessed at the date when the interim rent first becomes payable (ie the market conditions change substantially during the interim period), or if the terms of the new tenancy differ to such an extent

the old tenancy continues.[476] This will generally be lower than the rent that would be payable under statutory renewal of the tenancy, for two reasons. First, it is fixed upon the assumption that a new tenancy from year to year is being granted, the rent for such a tenancy normally being less than that of a tenancy for a fixed term. Secondly, the court must 'have regard' to the rent payable under the existing tenancy in determining the interim rent.[477] In a rising market this usually has the effect of reducing the interim rent below a market rent in order to provide a 'cushion' for the tenant against the shock of a steep increase if a market rent were to be imposed.[478]

(6) Contracting Out

Until 1970 the parties could not by agreement exclude the provisions of the Act.[479] Although landlords could avoid the Act by granting terms not exceeding six months or licences,[480] it was found that this prohibition discouraged landlords from letting premises that they intended eventually to use themselves or redevelop. Whatever the terms of the letting, the protected tenant will be entitled to at least six months' notice to terminate[481] and can usually prolong his tenancy for several months more by an unsuccessful application for a new tenancy.[482] When it finally expires, he may delay the landlord still further by compelling him to commence proceedings for possession. Many landlords therefore preferred to leave their building temporarily empty. The Law of Property Act 1969 introduced an amendment allowing the parties to agree to exclude the Act if their agreement was approved by the court, which would have to be satisfied that the tenant understood his position and had not been oppressed or overborne.[483] This was further relaxed under the 2003 Regulations: the parties may now agree that the provisions of the 1954 Act giving security of tenure shall be excluded, or that the tenancy shall be surrendered on a specified date, or in specified circumstances, and there is no longer a requirement that the parties apply to court for approval of their agreement.[484] However, this applies only where the tenancy is 'for a term of years certain';[485] and the agreement is void unless the landlord has served on the tenant a notice (in the form, or substantially in the form,[486] prescribed), normally

---

that the rent under it is substantially different from the rent that would otherwise have been assessed had the terms remained as under the old tenancy: s 24C(3).

[476] Ibid, s 24D(1).   [477] Ibid, s 24A(3).

[478] See *English Exporters (London) Ltd v Eldonwall Ltd* [1973] Ch 415; *Charles Follett Ltd v Cabtell Investments Co Ltd* [1987] 2 EGLR 88. In a falling market, it would similarly cushion the landlord.

[479] LTA 1954, s 38(1); *Allnatt London Properties Ltd v Newton* [1984] 1 All ER 423 (effect of s 38(1) on 'offer to surrender' clause), above, p 260.

[480] Above p 409.   [481] Above p 410.   [482] Above p 411.

[483] LTA 1954, s 38(4), inserted by LPA 1969, s 5.   [484] [2008] Conv 281 (M Haley).

[485] *Newham LBC v Thomas-Van Staden* [2008] EWCA Civ 1414, [2009] 1 EGLR 21 (lease for defined period but to include 'any period of holding over or extension... whether by statute or at common law or by agreement' not for term of years certain); [2009] Conv 177 (E Slessenger); [2009] L&T Rev 54 (A Colby).

[486] *The Chiltern Railway Co Ltd v Patel* [2008] EWCA Civ 178, [2008] 2 P & CR 12.

at least 14 days before they enter into the agreement, and the tenant must sign a declaration that he has received the notice and accepts its consequences.[487]

V AGRICULTURAL TENANCIES[488]

Some statutory protection for tenant farmers was introduced soon after the First World War,[489] but this was greatly strengthened and improved during and after the Second World War as part of the general effort made to increase home food production at the time. The principle upon which the legislation was based was that tenant farmers needed security of tenure to encourage them to spend money on improving the land and buying stock and other capital equipment. This principle is reflected in the Agricultural Holdings Act 1986, but has been departed from in the 'farm business tenancy' code introduced by the Agricultural Tenancies Act 1995. The purpose of the 1995 Act was to encourage new lettings of farmland by removing security of tenure and to encourage diversity in the use of the land. The Agricultural Holdings Act 1986 applies to tenancies granted before 1 September 1995;[490] the Agricultural Tenancies Act 1995 applies to tenancies granted on or after that date.

A AGRICULTURAL HOLDINGS[491]

(1) The Agricultural Holding

The key concept in the Agricultural Holdings Act 1986 is the 'agricultural holding'. This is defined as[492] 'the aggregate of the land (whether agricultural land or not) comprised in a contract of tenancy that is a contract for an agricultural tenancy'. A contract for an agricultural tenancy is one where, having regard to the terms of the tenancy, the actual or contemplated use of the land at the date of the contract or subsequently and any other relevant circumstances, substantially the whole of the land is let for use as agricultural land.[493] 'Agriculture' is very widely defined[494] and there is no minimum

---

[487] LTA 1954, s 38A. The parties can agree to waive the fourteen-day period, but then the tenant's declaration has to be in the form of a statutory declaration. The form of notice is set out at SI 2003 No 3096, Sch 1, and the requirements of a valid agreement (including the prescribed forms of declaration) in Sch 2. But it is not sufficient that the landlord's wife will occupy the premises to carry on her own business: *Zafiris v Liu* [2005] EWCA Civ 1698, [2006] 1 P & CR 26.

[488] Aldridge, *Leasehold Law*, Part 1, ch 5, Part 5, ch 3; Hill and Redman's *Landlord and Tenant*, Division F; Woodfall, *Landlord and Tenant*, ch 21.

[489] Agricultural Holdings Act 1923.

[490] For special cases where the 1986 Act applies to tenancies on or after that date, see Agricultural Tenancies Act 1995, s 4, as amended by SI 2006 No 2805, art 12.

[491] Muir Watt and Moss, *Agricultural Holdings* (14th edn, 1998); *Scammell and Densham's Law of Agricultural Holdings* (9th edn, 2007); Evans and Smith, *Law of Landlord and Tenant*, ch 26.

[492] Agricultural Holdings Act 1986, s 1(1).   [493] Ibid, s 1(2). S 1(3) deals with change of user.

[494] Ibid, s 96(1).

size for an agricultural holding. 'Agricultural land' means land that is not merely used for agriculture but is 'so used for the purposes of a trade or business'.[495] Provided the use is agricultural, the business need not be,[496] but non-commercial agricultural use does not qualify.

(2) Security of Tenure

(a) The deemed yearly tenancy

The Act confers security of tenure by limiting the circumstances in which a landlord can validly serve a notice to quit. Prima facie this machinery can operate only on periodic tenancies, because only in such cases is a notice to quit necessary to terminate the tenancy. But the Act deals with this problem in sweeping fashion by providing that tenancies for an interest less than a tenancy from year to year take effect as if they were yearly tenancies,[497] while a tenancy for a term certain of two years or upwards (unless a notice to quit has been served) thereafter continues as a yearly tenancy.[498] Licences to occupy the land for any period also take effect as tenancies from year to year.[499] Thus most agricultural tenancies granted before 1 September 1995, whatever their express terms, are deemed to be or become yearly tenancies.

It will be noticed, however, that there is a curious gap in these provisions. A tenancy for a term certain that is more than a year but less than two is not converted into a yearly tenancy. It therefore expires by effluxion of time and the security of tenure machinery cannot apply to it.[500] Furthermore, the Act contains an express exception in the case of a letting or licence 'in contemplation of the use of the land only for grazing or mowing (or both) during some specified period of the year'.[501] The owner of a country house who had some surplus fields could therefore let them to a neighbouring farmer for grazing for up to 364 days at a time[502] without committing himself to the security of tenure provisions of the Act. Finally, the security provisions do not protect sub-tenants against the head landlord.[503]

---

[495] Agricultural Holdings Act 1986, s 1(4). See *Brown v Teirnan* [1993] 1 EGLR 11.

[496] *Rutherford v Maurer* [1962] 1 QB 16 (grazing horses of a riding school).

[497] Agricultural Holdings Act 1986, s 2(1). See *Calcott v J S Bloor (Measham) Ltd* [1998] 1 WLR 1490.

[498] Ibid, s 3(1). Subject to an exception in s 5, it is not possible to contract out of this provision.

[499] Ibid, s 2(2); *Bahamas International Trust Co Ltd v Threadgold* [1974] 1 WLR 1514 (exclusive occupation necessary). See also *McCarthy v Bence* [1990] 1 EGLR 1, discussing the effect on this subsection of *Street v Mountford* [1985] AC 809, above, p 186.

[500] *Gladstone v Bower* [1960] 2 QB 384; *Keen v Holland* [1984] 1 WLR 251. Nor is it protected as a business tenancy: *EWP Ltd v Moore* [1992] QB 460.

[501] Agricultural Holdings Act 1986, s 2(3).

[502] *Reid v Dawson* [1955] 1 QB 214; *Scene Estate Ltd v Amos* [1957] 2 QB 205; *Stone v Whitcombe* (1980) 40 P & CR 296; *Watts v Yeend* [1987] 1 WLR 323.

[503] See, however, *Gisborne v Burton* [1989] QB 390 (sub-tenant treated as tenant under 'artificial transaction' doctrine); cf *Barrett v Morgan* [2000] AC 264 (notice to quit served on tenant by head landlord effective to terminate sub-tenancy also), above, p 345.

(b) The notice to quit

At common law a yearly tenancy may be terminated by at least six months' notice expiring on the anniversary of the tenancy.[504] For an agricultural holding the notice period is extended to one year.[505] The common law requirement that the notice must terminate on the anniversary is retained. It may therefore be up to two years before a notice to quit can expire.

(c) Validity of notice to quit

A notice to quit an agricultural holding can operate effectively in only two kinds of circumstances. The first is when the landlord at the time of service can rely upon one of eight specified grounds.[506] The second is when the local Agricultural Land Tribunal consents to the operation of the notice after it has been served.[507] This consent also may be given only upon certain specified grounds, for example that greater hardship would be caused by withholding than by giving consent. Compensation is payable except in default cases.

The grounds upon which a notice may be served and operate without further consent include bad husbandry; failure to pay rent or to remedy remediable breach; irremediable breach of covenant; bankruptcy; and death of the tenant or sole surviving tenant.

The last of these is important because it is the only ground that (unless the tenant is a company) must become available sooner or later. Its significance was reduced when the Agriculture (Miscellaneous Provisions) Act 1976 gave certain members of the deceased tenant's family a right to succeed to the tenancy. These succession rights, however, have now been largely confined to tenancies granted before 12 July 1984.[508]

(d) Notice procedure

A tenant who has been served with a notice to quit and wishes to invoke the security of tenure provisions of the Act must serve a counter-notice.[509] If the notice does not purport to have been given on one of the permitted grounds, he must simply claim the protection of the relevant section whereby the Tribunal's consent is required.[510] If the notice relies on certain of the permitted grounds, the tenant's notice must claim

---

[504] Above, p 335.

[505] Agricultural Holdings Act 1986, s 25(1). Contracting out is not permitted; cf *Elsden v Pick* [1980] 1 WLR 898 (waiver). This applies to notices given by the tenant, as well as by the landlord.

[506] Ibid, Sch 3. The 1986 Act is not contrary to the ECHR in distinguishing between different grounds of termination, and in providing different routes for challenging a notice to quit for different grounds of termination: *Lancashire County Council v Taylor* [2005] EWCA Civ 284, [2005] 1 WLR 2668.

[507] Ibid, ss 26, 27.

[508] Ibid, s 34. Where succession rights are available, they apply also on the tenant's retirement.

[509] It is not possible to deprive the tenant by contract of his right to serve a counter-notice: *Johnson v Moreton* [1980] AC 37. See also *Featherstone v Staples* [1986] 1 WLR 861.

[510] Agricultural Holdings Act 1986, s 26(1). See *Crawford v Elliott* [1991] 1 EGLR 13. The inclusion of a dwelling on the holding does not make s 5 of the Protection from Eviction Act 1977 applicable; *National Trust for Places of Historic Interest or Natural Beauty v Knipe* [1998] 1 WLR 230.

an arbitration on whether the appropriate ground existed.[511] There are stringent time limits for these notices and the tenant may lose all protection if they are not correctly served.[512]

(3) Rent

The rent for an agricultural holding is, in the absence of agreement, fixed by an arbitrator as the rent at which, at the next termination date, the holding might reasonably be expected to be let by a prudent and willing landlord to a prudent and willing tenant, taking into account the current level of rents for comparable lettings (as to which any scarcity element must be disregarded).[513] Certain matters must be disregarded, including the fact that the tenant is in occupation, any improvements he has made and any deterioration for which he is responsible.[514] The rent may be reviewed (by agreement or arbitration) at intervals of not less than three years.[515]

B FARM BUSINESS TENANCIES[516]

The steady decline in tenant farming led Parliament to deregulate agricultural lettings and return in substance to freedom of contract. The Agricultural Tenancies Act 1995, which applies to lettings on or after 1 September 1995, introduces the concept of the farm business tenancy. The policy of the Act is to encourage new lettings and to facilitate diversification into non-agricultural business use such as, for example, the provision of golfing or equestrian facilities.[517] Although the 1995 Act regulates the form and duration of notices to quit, it does not confer security of tenure. This is a radical departure from the previous legislation, although it must be said that many agricultural tenants before the 1995 Act did not enjoy security of tenure because of the loopholes in the previous legislation.[518] The farm business tenant will, however, be entitled to compensation for improvements on quitting. It is still too early to say whether the 1995 Act will reverse the decline in tenant farming.

---

[511] Agricultural Holdings Act 1986, ss 83, 84 (amended by SI 2006 No 2805); Agricultural Holdings (Arbitration on Notices) Order 1987 (SI 1987 No 710), Part III. But a notice containing statements that the landlord knows to be false is of no effect: *Rous v Mitchell* [1991] 1 WLR 469.

[512] As in *Magdalen College, Oxford v Heritage* [1974] 1 WLR 441.

[513] Agricultural Holdings Act 1986, s 12, amended by SI 2006 No 2805, art 3.

[514] Ibid, Sch 2, paras 1–3.   [515] Ibid, para 4. See *Mann v Gardner* (1990) 61 P & CR 1.

[516] Rodgers, *Agricultural Law* (3rd edn, 2008); Sydenham and Mainwaring, *Farm Business Tenancies—The Agricultural Tenancies Act 1995* (1995); Scammell and Densham's *Law of Agricultural Holdings* (9th edn, 2007); Muir Watt and Moss, *Agricultural Holdings* (14th edn, 1998); Evans and Smith, *Law of Landlord and Tenant*, ch 27.

[517] See [1995] Conv 445 (S Bright); [1996] Conv 164 (C Rodgers) and 243 (J Bishop).

[518] Above, p 418 (for example, fixed terms of between one and two years).

(1) The Farm Business Tenancy

The farm business tenancy is defined in section 1 of the 1995 Act as a tenancy that meets the business conditions together with either the agriculture condition or the notice conditions of the section, and is not excluded by section 2.[519] Genuine licences fall outside the Act, as do tenancies at will, but sub-lettings are included.[520]

The 'business conditions' are that all or part of the land is farmed for the purpose of a trade or business, and has been so farmed since the beginning of the tenancy.[521] The 'agriculture condition' is that the character of the tenancy is primarily or wholly agricultural, having regard to the terms of the tenancy, the use of the land, the nature of any commercial activities carried on on the land,[522] and any other relevant circumstances. The 'notice conditions' are that, on or before the 'relevant day',[523] the landlord and tenant gave each other a written notice identifying the land to be comprised in the tenancy and stating that the person giving the notice intends the tenancy to be and remain a farm business tenancy, and that, at the beginning of the tenancy, its character was primarily or wholly agricultural, having regard to the terms and any other relevant circumstances.

It will be seen that there are thus two kinds of farm business tenancy. Where the notice conditions are not satisfied, the tenancy ceases to be a farm business tenancy if its character ceases to be primarily or wholly agricultural. Where the notice conditions are satisfied, the tenancy will remain within the 1995 Act even if diversification into a non-agricultural business causes it to cease to be primarily or wholly agricultural, provided that at least part continues to be farmed for the purpose of a trade or business. In such a case the non-agricultural business will not result in the acquisition of security of tenure under the Landlord and Tenant Act 1954, Part II.[524] Thus the notice conditions should be complied with if the landlord wishes to protect himself against the possibility of the tenancy moving into the 1954 Act. Presumably, such a transfer may occur even if the notice conditions have been complied with, if, without any breach of the terms of the tenancy, all farming activity is discontinued.

---

[519] A tenancy beginning before 1 September 1995 is excluded, and also one that, although beginning on or after that date, falls within the Agricultural Holdings Act 1986 pursuant to the transitional provisions in s 4 of the 1995 Act.

[520] See s 38(1).

[521] By s 1(6), there is a rebuttable presumption that the second condition is established if the first is proved.

[522] By s 1(8), activities in breach of the terms of the tenancy must be disregarded unless the landlord has consented or acquiesced or his predecessor in title has consented.

[523] By s 1(5), this is the beginning of the tenancy or the day the parties entered into any instrument creating the tenancy, whichever is the earlier. By s 1(6), the notice must not be included in the instrument creating the tenancy.

[524] Farm business tenancies are excluded from the business tenancy code by s 43(1)(aa) of the 1954 Act, inserted by Agricultural Tenancies Act 1995, s 40, Sch, para10(b).

(2) Termination of the Tenancy

Although the farm business tenant enjoys no security of tenure, the common law rules as to termination are modified to some extent. A fixed term of two years or less will terminate by expiry or, whatever its duration, may be terminated by forfeiture in the ordinary way. Nor does the 1995 Act regulate the termination by notice to quit of periodic tenancies that are for periods other than from year to year.

The 1995 Act does, however, provide a special code for the termination of a farm business tenancy that is for a fixed term of more than two years or that is a yearly tenancy. A fixed term of more than two years does not terminate by expiry but continues as from its term date as a tenancy from year to year unless either party has given a written notice at least 12 months before the term date of his intention to terminate.[525] In such a case the tenancy will end on the term date. Where the tenancy continues, it does so on the terms of the original fixed term, so far as applicable to a yearly tenancy.

In the case of a yearly tenancy (either originally granted or arising after a fixed term, as described above) a notice to quit is invalid unless it is in writing, is to take effect at the end of a year of the tenancy, and is given at least 12 months before the date on which it is to take effect.[526] Where a farm business tenancy for a fixed term of more than two years contains a provision permitting the service of a notice to quit the whole or part during the fixed term (a 'break clause'), the notice is valid only if in writing and if given at least 12 months before the date on which it is to take effect.[527] Presumably, where such a notice is validly served, no yearly tenancy will arise under section 5(1) of the Act.

These modifications of the common law termination rules apply notwithstanding any contrary provision in the tenancy.[528] Where the statutory rules as to the form and duration of a notice are complied with, the tenancy will end as if terminated in the ordinary way at common law, without any right of renewal. This absence of any necessity for the landlord to establish a specified ground for possession is a significant distinction from the scheme of the Agricultural Holdings Act 1986.

(3) Rent

The initial rent is that which is agreed by the parties. The 1995 Act provides a statutory framework for subsequent rent review that operates, notwithstanding any agreement to the contrary, unless the document creating the tenancy (a) expressly states that the rent is not to be reviewed, or (b) provides for review by or to a specified amount or (so long as not upwards only) in a manner that does not involve the exercise of any judgment or discretion (such as an index-linked review), or (c) does not contain any

---

[525] Agricultural Tenancies Act 1995, s 5(1), as amended by SI 2006 No 2805, Sch 2, para 1.
[526] Ibid, s 6(1), as amended by SI 2006 No 2805, Sch 2, para 1. The notice may be given before the end of a fixed term, to end the yearly tenancy on the first anniversary of the term date: s 6(2).
[527] Ibid, s 7, as amended by SI 2006 No 2805, Sch 2, para 1.   [528] Ibid, ss 5(4), 6(1), 7(1).

provision that precludes a reduction in the rent during the tenancy and either expressly excludes the rent review provisions of the Act or makes provision for rent review by an independent expert whose decision is final.[529] Thus the parties have considerable freedom in setting the terms of rent review as long as they do not provide for upwards-only reviews.

Subject to the above exception, either party to a farm business tenancy may give the other a written 'statutory review notice', requiring that the rent to be payable from the 'review date' shall be referred to arbitration. This review date must be at least 12 months but less than 24 months after the day on which the notice is given. Unless the parties have otherwise agreed in writing, the review date must be an anniversary of the beginning of the tenancy and must not be within a period of three years from the beginning of the tenancy or from any previous review (by arbitration or agreement).[530]

After the notice has been served, the parties are free to agree on the machinery for rent review (for example, review by an expert), but in default of agreement an arbitrator will be appointed.[531] Where the rent is referred to arbitration, the arbitrator may increase or reduce the rent, or direct it to continue unchanged. The rent properly payable is the rent at which the holding might reasonably be expected to be let on the open market by a willing landlord to a willing tenant, taking into account the terms of the tenancy and other relevant factors. Certain matters are to be disregarded, such as any increase in the rental value due to any tenant's improvement that he was not obliged by the tenancy to provide and for which he has received no consideration or compensation, any decrease in the rental value due to any deterioration or damage caused or permitted by the tenant, and any effect on the rent of the fact that the tenant is a sitting tenant.[532]

(4) Compensation for Improvements

The absence of security of tenure is to some extent mitigated by the provisions of the 1995 Act allowing compensation for improvements when the farm business tenancy ends. Thus the tenant may acquire funds for relocation. When the tenant quits, he is entitled to compensation from the landlord in respect of any physical improvement made by him on the holding (such as a building) and of any 'intangible advantage' obtained by him for the holding (such as an unimplemented planning permission).[533] Although a compensation regime existed under the earlier legislation, the latter aspect

---

[529] Ibid, s 9, as amended by SI 2006 No 2805, art 14(1)(b).

[530] Ibid, s 10. The parties may agree in writing that the intervals between review shall be greater or less than three years.

[531] Ibid, s 12. Either party may, at any time during the period of six months ending with the review date, apply to the President of the Royal Institution of Chartered Surveyors for the appointment of an arbitrator.

[532] Ibid, s 13.

[533] Ibid, ss 15, 16. No compensation is payable if the improvement is removed or the intangible advantage does not remain attached to the holding. Where planning permission has been implemented, the tenant will be able to claim for any improvements made as a result.

was new in 1995. The landlord must have given written consent to the making of the improvement or the application for planning permission.[534] The compensation is generally the amount equal to the increase in the value of the holding at the end of the tenancy attributable to the improvement or to the securing of planning permission.[535] The compensation provisions apply notwithstanding any agreement to the contrary.[536] The right of a farm business tenant to remove fixtures has already been discussed.[537]

VI RESIDENTIAL FLATS. TENANTS' RIGHTS OF FIRST REFUSAL

The Landlord and Tenant Act 1987, Part I,[538] introduced a right for certain tenants of flats to have the first refusal on their immediate landlord's disposal of his interest in the property. The general principle was not to deprive the unwilling landlord of his interest, as in the case of a tenant's right of enfranchisement of a long lease;[539] nor to require the landlord to accept a lower price from a tenant than he would be willing to accept on a sale to a third party. It was simply to give the sitting tenants preferential treatment over a third party purchaser, as part of a broader recognition of the stake that residential tenants have in their flats. Certain problems were discovered in the workings of the 1987 Act, including the fact that some landlords appeared to seek to avoid the proper exercise of their rights by their tenants, and the provisions were amended and strengthened by the Housing Act 1996.[540]

The right is given to 'qualifying tenants' of flats:[541] tenants holding under tenancies other than protected shorthold or assured tenancies,[542] business tenancies to which Part II of the Landlord and Tenant Act 1954 applies,[543] and tenancies terminable on cessation of the tenant's employment. It therefore includes, although it is not limited to, residential tenants holding under a long lease. As long as the premises consist of the whole or part of a building, and contain two or more flats held by qualifying tenants

---

[534] Agricultural Tenancies Act 1995, ss 17, 18. Disputes are to be referred to arbitration: s 19.

[535] Ibid, ss 20, 21. The parties may, however, agree to limit the compensation payable: s 20(4A), inserted by SI 2006 No 2805, art 16. The procedure for claims (which must be made within two months of termination) and for arbitration in the absence of agreement is laid down by s 22.

[536] Ibid, s 26.   [537] Above, p 240.

[538] Implementing recommendations of the Committee of Inquiry on the *Management of Privately Owned Blocks of Flats* (1985). For other recommendations, implemented by other Parts of the 1987 Act, see above, pp 254–5.

[539] Above, pp 389 ff.

[540] Ss 89–92 and Sch 6. The Act was described as 'ill-drafted, complicated and confused' by Sir Nicolas Browne-Wilkinson in *Denetower Ltd v Toop* [1991] 1 WLR 945, 952. See also *Mainwaring v Trustees of Henry Smith's Charity* [1998] QB 1, 17–18, 20. HA 1996 introduced into the 1987 Act a new s 10A which makes it a criminal offence for the landlord to fail to comply with the requirements of Part I.

[541] LTA 1987, s 3, as amended by HA 1988, s 119, Sch 13.   [542] Above, p 358.

[543] Above, p 406.

(who together hold more than half of the total number of flats in the premises),[544] the landlord[545] must not make a 'relevant disposal'[546] affecting the premises without first serving on the qualifying tenants a notice offering to enter into the transaction in question with them.[547] The offer need not be accepted by all the qualifying tenants, but acceptance will be effective and will irrevocably bind the landlord if it is made by at least a requisite majority. The tenants who accept the landlord's offer nominate a person to enter into the transaction with him.[548]

If the landlord makes a relevant disposal to a third party without complying with the requirements of the Act, the qualifying tenants are entitled to compel the third party to dispose of the premises to them, on the same terms as the landlord's disposal to him.[549] In effect, therefore, the third party is bound by the tenants' right of first refusal.[550]

VII LAW REFORM

We have seen that in recent years there have been many significant reforms of the special rules relating to security of tenure and control of rent: for example, the extension of the scope of assured shorthold tenancies by the Housing Act 1996;[551] the introduction of introductory tenancies by the Housing Act 1996,[552] and demoted tenancies by the Anti-social Behaviour Act 2003;[553] significant changes to long leaseholders' rights made by the Commonhold and Leasehold Reform Act 2002;[554] and amendment of the rules relating to business tenancies made by the Regulatory Reform (Business Tenancies) (England and Wales) Order 2003.[555]

---

[544] LTA 1987, s 1(2). The Act does not apply to premises of which more than half of the floor area (disregarding common parts) is occupied or intended to be occupied otherwise than for residential purposes: ibid, s 1(3).

[545] The landlord may be the freeholder or a leaseholder. If he is a leaseholder holding under a lease for less than seven years, or terminable by the landlord within seven years, the superior landlord is also to be regarded as the qualifying tenant's landlord for the purposes of the Act.

[546] Defined as (with certain exclusions) the disposal of any estate or interest (legal or equitable) in the premises: LTA 1987, s 4. It includes a contract to make such a disposal: LTA 1987, s 4A, inserted by HA 1996, s 89(1).

[547] LTA 1987, s 1(1). The requirements of the offer notice are set out in ss 5–5E, as substituted by HA 1996, s 92(1), Sch 6.

[548] Ibid, s 6. 'Requisite majority' is defined in s 18A, inserted by HA 1996, s 92(1), Sch 6: qualifying tenants of constituent flats with more than 50 per cent of the available votes. Procedures for the subsequent stages of the process are set out at ss 6–10, as substituted by HA 1996, s 92 (1), Sch 6.

[549] Ibid, ss 11–12D, as substituted by HA 1996, s 92(1), Sch 6.

[550] It takes effect, however, as a direct right under the terms of the statute, rather than by the third party being bound by a pre-existing right of pre-emption. The prospective purchaser of premises to which the Act applies may serve notices on the tenants to ensure that rights of first refusal do not arise that could be enforced against him: ibid, s 18.

[551] Above, p 367.   [552] Above, p 387.   [553] Above, p 386.
[554] Above, pp 393, 400, 401, 403 and 405.   [555] Above, p 407.

The Law Commission has also undertaken a significant research project with a view to the modernisation and simplification of housing tenure, and made further, far-reaching proposals for reform that have not, however, been accepted by the Government.

In 2006 the Law Commission published its final report on *Renting Homes*.[556] This report made radical proposals to abolish many of the existing forms of tenancy (secure tenancies, assured tenancies, assured shorthold tenancies, introductory tenancies, demoted tenancies and various varieties of common law tenancies) and replace them with two new types of tenancy contract: a secure contract, modelled on the present public sector secure tenancy, and a standard contract, broadly modelled on the present assured shorthold tenancy but without the present rule that the court cannot order possession before the end of the first six months of the period of the tenancy.[557] Subject to certain exceptions from the new scheme,[558] all agreements, whether tenancies or licences, which confer on an individual a right to occupy premises as a home would be occupation contracts. Any category of landlord would be able to use either contract type, although councils and registered social landlords would normally be required to use the secure contract, and contracts entered into by private landlords would be standard contracts unless the landlord gives the contract-holder a notice specifying that it is a secure contract. There would be model forms of contract, prescribed by the Secretary of State (or, in Wales, the National Assembly), incorporating particular categories of term, which would then not be subject to the regulations on unfair contract terms,[559] although landlords would not be required to use the model contracts. Every landlord would, however, be required to provide the contract-holder with a written statement of the contract. Certain fundamental terms would be mandatory in all contracts, however, such as landlords' repairing obligations and the prohibition of certain defined conduct by contract-holders. There would be new provisions for variation and termination of the occupation contracts, and a simplification of the landlord's grounds for possession.

In addition, in 2007 the Law Commission published its report on *Encouraging Responsible Renting*,[560] which proposed a stronger system of self-regulation of landlords in the private rented sector.[561]

---

[556] Law Com No 297, following upon Law Com No 284, Narrative Report on *Renting Homes* (2003); CP No 162, *Renting Homes 1: Status and Security* (2002); CP No 168, *Renting Homes 2: Co-occupation, Transfer and Succession* (2002).

[557] Above, p 377.

[558] Business tenancies, Rent Act 1977 tenancies, long tenancies and agricultural tenancies, which are covered by other legislation, would be excluded; as would certain contracts excluded on social policy grounds (such as tenancies or licences where no rent or other consideration is payable, holiday lets, accommodation shared with the landlord) and special rules would apply to accommodation for the homeless and supported accommodation.

[559] Such as the Unfair Terms in Consumer Contracts Regulations 1999; above, p 183.

[560] Law Com No 312.

[561] See also Law Com No 309, *Housing: Proportionate Dispute Resolution* (2008), which recommended a range of reforms in relation to housing disputes. Some recommendations were accepted by the Government in 2009, others rejected: Law Com No 323, *Annual Report 2009-2010*, paras 3.22-3.24.

The Government in 2009 rejected the fundamental reforms contained in *Renting Homes* because of the upheaval it would entail for tenants and landlords, but accepted the principle that, in the private sector, there should be mandatory written agreements; and adopted an alternative to the Law Commission's proposals in *Encouraging Responsible Renting* for regulation of the private rented sector, but accepted in principle the recommendation that letting agents be subject to a formal and mandatory regulatory structure.[562] However, reform of this area of the law is not in line with the deregulatory priorities of the Coalition Government that took office in 2010, and that Government has no plans to implement the Law Commission's recommendations by amending the regulations governing private landlords or by further regulating the sector.[563]

There are, however, proposals for the reform of social housing. In November 2010 the Government issued a consultation paper[564] that, in relation to forms of tenure, proposes:[565]

to allow greater flexibility to both local authority and registered provider landlords, enabling them to offer lifetime security where it is needed, but to set shorter terms where that makes more sense.

We are introducing a new more flexible affordable rent tenancy. It will be offered by registered providers (typically housing associations) to new tenants at a rent higher than social rent and at a maximum of 80 per cent of local market rents that will be reviewed after an agreed period of time.

We will introduce legislation to:

- Create a new local authority flexible tenancy with a minimum fixed term of two years. This will be in addition to, rather than replacing, secure and introductory tenancies.
- Protect the rights of existing secure and assured tenants.
- Provide local authority flexible tenants with similar rights to secure tenants, including the right to exchange.
- Provide that all new secure and flexible tenancies include a right to one succession for spouses and partners, but give landlords the flexibility to grant whatever additional succession rights they choose.
- Place a new duty on local authorities to publish a strategic policy on tenancies.
- Allow the Secretary of State to direct on the content of a tenancy standard.

Through a new tenancy standard, we will then provide significantly increased freedom to all social landlords on the tenancies they can grant, subject to appropriate parameters on which this consultation seeks views.

The Government proposes to introduce these reforms through the enactment of the Localism Bill, which was published in December 2010 and will be passing through Parliament during 2011.

---

[562] Law Com No 316, *Annual Report 2008-09*, paras 2.18-2.14.

[563] Lord Chancellor's *Report to Parliament on the Implementation of Law Commission Proposals* (2011), para 56.

[564] *Local decisions: a fairer future for social housing*, available in the Housing section of the DCLG web site, www.communities.gov.uk.

[565] Ibid, p 9.

C EQUITABLE BENEFICIAL INTERESTS IN LAND

Summary

In this section we consider those estates and interests in the land that may subsist in equity under a settlement or a trust of land: equitable *beneficial* interests in the land. Before 1926 a range of interests could be held at law in the land. In addition to the fee simple absolute and the leasehold estate, this included such things as concurrent interests (tenancies in common, as well as joint tenancies), entailed interests and life interests. Under section 1 of the Law of Property Act 1925, however, the only legal estates that can subsist at law are now the fee simple absolute in possession and the term of years absolute, which we have discussed in the earlier sections of this Part. All other beneficial estates and interests in land can subsist only in equity. These are the beneficial interests we shall consider in this section.

In Chapters 12 and 13 we first consider the *legal framework* within which equitable beneficial interests have been held in land since 1925: until 1996, within a strict settlement or a trust for sale; and since 1997 within a trust of land. Strict settlements under the Settled Land Act 1925 can no longer be created, but those that already existed in 1996 remain in place, and so the discussion of strict settlements is not simply a matter of history although, as so often, the modern law is also better understood in the context of its historical development.

In Chapters 14 to 17 we then consider the different *substantive forms* of equitable beneficial interest that can be held within that legal framework: concurrent beneficial interests, future interests, entailed interests, life interests, and certain determinable interests.

12

THE STRICT SETTLEMENT AND THE TRUST FOR SALE BEFORE 1997

Summary

The evolution of the strict settlement and the trust for sale has already been described in the historical introduction.[1]

The system of settlements was radically changed as from 1 January 1997, when the Trusts of Land and Appointment of Trustees Act 1996 came into operation. Thereafter no new strict settlements can be created, existing trusts for sale are retrospectively modified, and a new trust of land is invented.

Since strict settlements created before 1997 continue to exist, it is still important to understand their continuing operation. And an understanding of the trust for sale as it existed before 1997 is also important in order to understand fully the changes made by the 1996 Act in introducing the trust of land. In this Chapter we shall discuss the strict settlement and the trust for sale before 1997, and in Chapter 13 the trust of land that arises under the Trust of Land and Appointment of Trustees Act 1996 and applies to all settlements thereafter.

The general idea of a settlement is to create, by either deed or will, out of real or personal property, a series of beneficial interests in favour of a succession of persons.

---

[1] Above, Ch 4.

Before 1997 there were two methods of settling land: either by strict settlement under the Settled Land Act 1925, or by trust for sale under the Law of Property Act 1925.[2] They were mutually exclusive. Indeed it was expressly enacted that the statutory definition of a settlement contained in the Settled Land Act 1925 should not apply to land held upon trust for sale.[3]

It is vital to distinguish the two methods of settlement. The chief practical importance of the distinction is that, on conveyance, title to settled land must be made by the tenant for life, since the legal estate is vested in him, while title to land held on trust must be made by the trustees. The result of a mistake in this regard is troublesome and expensive, since a purchaser who takes a conveyance from the trustees when the instrument is a settlement, or from the tenant for life when it is a trust for sale, does not acquire the legal estate. It should be remembered that a purchaser, who takes a conveyance from the correct vendor, takes the land free from the interests of the beneficiaries under the settlement, provided that he pays the purchase money to at least two trustees or to a trust corporation. The interests of the beneficiaries are transferred from the land to the purchase money and are *overreached*.[4]

Of these two methods of settling land we shall discuss first the strict settlement under the Settled Land Act 1925. Even before 1997, however, mainly due to considerations of taxation, the strict settlement had become less widely used. In particular, the classic strict settlement, which was created on the occasion of a marriage so as to provide for all members of the family and thereby to keep the land as far as possible within the family,[5] was unlikely to be created. The trust for sale was mainly used for family settlements, whether created inter vivos or by will; and furthermore its conveyancing machinery was extended by the 1925 legislation to concurrent interests[6] and intestacy.[7]

I THE STRICT SETTLEMENT

A THE DEFINITION OF A SETTLEMENT UNDER THE SETTLED LAND ACT 1925

The word *settlement* properly so called connotes succession. Its normal meaning is any instrument or series of instruments by which successive interests are carved out of realty or personalty and under which, in the case of land, there will usually be at any given time some person entitled in possession to a beneficial interest for life. But the Settled Land Act 1925 was not limited to cases where there was a succession properly so called. Its further aim was to facilitate dealings wherever the disposition of the land was inhibited by some impediment affecting its title.

---

[2] See Harvey, *Settlements of Land* (1973).   [3] SLA 1925, s 1(7).

[4] Above, pp 103, 126. For a full discussion of overreaching, see below, pp 1068–9, 1113–22.

[5] Above, pp 95–6. For a detailed account see Cheshire, *Modern Real Property* (10th edn, 1967), pp 126–31.

[6] Below, Ch 14.   [7] For a detailed account, see the 16th edn of this book, ch 26.

Minority affords a simple illustration. If a favourable offer has been made for the purchase of land to which a minor is entitled in fee simple under a will, the rule that no person under 18 years of age can hold a legal estate,[8] and so the minor cannot execute a valid conveyance, will cause the loss of a profitable bargain, unless some way out of the impasse can be found. But the difficulty disappears if the will is regarded as a 'settlement' and if a person of full age is designated to exercise the statutory power of sale.

In a case of this nature there is, of course, no settlement and no tenant for life as usually understood, but any device that renders the statutory powers exercisable in respect of the minor's land is an undoubted advantage to all concerned. What the Act did, therefore, with the object of rendering an absolute title easily transferable despite the existence of what would normally be inhibitory factors, was to define 'settlement' in broad terms so as to include a number of cases where there was no succession in the ordinary sense, and also, where necessary, to grant the statutory powers to a person who according to ordinary language is not a tenant for life. In fact, not only was the statutory definition of a 'settlement' very wide, but wherever there is a settlement within the meaning of the Act and no tenant for life properly so called, and therefore no person normally competent to exercise the statutory powers, one of two things will occur: either a person will be designated by the Act as entitled to exercise the powers; or the powers will be exercisable by trustees, who in this context are called 'statutory owners'.[9]

A settlement for the purposes of the Act exists in each of the following cases, as long as it was created before 1 January 1997:[10]

(1) Succession

Where land stands limited in trust for any persons by way of succession.

This refers to the normal case where land was limited to a series of persons by way of succession, such as to A for life, remainder to B for life, remainder to C in fee simple.[11]

---

[8] LPA 1925, s 1(6). For the age of majority, see below, p 1019. For the terminology of 'minor' or 'infant' in relation to settled land, see below, p 434, n 16.

[9] Below, p 442.   [10] SLA 1925, s 1; TLATA 1996, s 2.

[11] It need not be expressly limited. The trust could arise by operation of law, such as where there is a constructive trust under which the court gives protection to a licensee for the period of his life: *Bannister v Bannister* [1948] 2 All ER 133, M & B p 1101; *Binions v Evans* [1972] Ch 359, M & B p 1102 (Lord Denning MR dissented on this point at 366); below, p 935; *Ungurian v Lesnoff* [1990] Ch 206, esp at 224; [1990] CLJ 25 (M Oldham); [1990] Conv 223 (P Sparkes); [1991] Conv 596 (J Hill); *Costello v Costello* (1994) 70 P & CR 297; [1994] Conv 391 (MP Thompson). See also *Ivory v Palmer* [1975] ICR 340, 347 (Cairns LJ: '*Binions v Evans* stretched to the very limit the application of the Settled Land Act'); (1977) 93 LQR 561 (JA Hornby); *Dent v Dent* [1996] 1 WLR 683 (where the agreement was construed as an irrevocable licence and not a SLA settlement); [1996] All ER Rev 258 (PJ Clarke). See Harvey, *Settlements of Land*, pp 54, 82 ff; Emmet, para 23.004; (1977) 93 LQR 561 (JA Hornby); Law Com No 118, *Trusts of Land* (1989), para 4.2. On avoidance of an unintentional creation of a strict settlement in this situation, see *Griffiths v Williams* (1977) 248 EG 947, M & B p 1061; below, p 940; [1978] Conv 250. For similar problems arising in connection with settlements on

(2) Extended Meaning of Settlement

We now come to six cases where an extended meaning is given to the word 'settlement'.

(i) *Entailed interest* Where land stands limited in trust for any person in possession for an entailed interest whether or not capable of being barred or defeated.

(ii) *Base or determinable fee*[12] Where land stands limited in trust for any person in possession for a base or determinable fee or any corresponding interest in leasehold land.

Under (i) and (ii), where the possessor is a tenant in tail or tenant of a base fee, the instrument of creation is a settlement, and the tenant holds the land under a settlement.

(iii) *Limitation subject to gift over* Where land stands limited in trust for any person in possession for an estate in fee simple or for a term of years absolute subject to an executory gift over on failure of issue or in any other event.

Thus, where a house was devised to A in fee simple subject to a condition that he reside and provide a home for X there, and if he breaks this condition, then devise over to B in fee simple, the will was a settlement and A became tenant for life within the meaning of the Act.[13]

(iv) *Minor* Where land stands limited in trust for any person in possession being a minor, for an estate in fee simple or for a term of years absolute.

A conveyance that purports to grant a fee simple absolute to a minor cannot take effect according to its terms, for a minor is incapable of holding a legal estate.[14] Instead, the conveyance, if executed before 1 January 1997,[15] operated as an agreement by the grantor to execute a settlement by means of a vesting deed in favour of trustees (statutory owners),[16] and a trust instrument in favour of the minor.

(v) *Springing interests* Where land stands limited in trust for any person to take effect as a fee simple or term of years absolute on the happening of some event.

---

divorce, see *Morss v Morss* [1972] Fam 264; *Martin v Martin* [1978] Fam 12; [1978] Conv 229 (P Smith). See also *Allen v Allen* [1974] 1 WLR 1171 (trust for sale).

[12] Including a fee determinable by condition: SLA 1925, s 117(1)(iv).

[13] *Re Richardson* [1904] 2 Ch 777.   [14] LPA 1925, s 1(6); below, p 1019.

[15] Settlements under this head will cease to exist by 31 December 2015 at the latest (18 years afer the last date on which SLA 1925 could still create a new settlement.

[16] SLA 1925, s 27(1); below, p 442. SLA 1925 refers to an 'infant' rather than a minor. Under Family Law Reform Act 1969, s 12, 'A person who is not of full age may be described as a minor instead of as an infant', and most, but not all, statutes now refer accordingly to 'minors'. However, the terminology of 'infant' in SLA 1925 was not amended. In this book the term 'minor' is generally used, in accordance with modern usage: below, p 1018.

If, for example, a fee simple estate was limited in trust for the two sons of X, who attain the age of 18 years, the first son to reach that age becomes absolutely entitled to a half share, but also entitled to the fee simple in the entirety of the land contingent on the death of his brother before reaching his majority.[17] This is one of the cases where, pending the occurrence of the contingency, the powers are exercisable by the statutory owners.[18]

(vi) *Family charges* Where land stands charged, whether voluntarily (that is not for valuable consideration) or in consideration of marriage or by way of family arrangement,[19] with the payment of any rentcharge for the life of any person, or any lesser period,[20] or of any sums for the portions, advancement, maintenance or otherwise for the benefit of any persons.[21]

If, for example, A charged his fee simple absolute with an annuity for his wife and capital sums for his children, the instrument that created the charge is a 'settlement', and, although the rentchargor, A, is not a tenant for life, he is given the powers of a tenant for life by section 20(1)(ix) of the Settled Land Act 1925. Strictly speaking, therefore, he should execute a vesting deed and appoint trustees. If he does so, he may sell the fee simple under the Act, and overreach the rentcharges so as to make them recoverable from the trustees to whom payment will have been made. If, however, the purchaser is willing to buy subject to the charges, A is permitted by the Law of Property (Amendment) Act 1926 to sell as absolute owner without the necessity of executing a vesting deed. Section 1(1) of this Act provides:

> Nothing in the Settled Land Act 1925 shall prevent a person on whom the powers of a tenant for life are conferred by section 20(1)(ix) from conveying or creating a legal estate subject to a prior interest as if the land had not been settled land.

(3) Compound Settlement

It follows from the account given above that a settlement may consist of a number of instruments. This will occur, for example, where lands, which in the first place have been settled on A for life with remainder in tail to his eldest son, are resettled on A for life, remainder (subject to the charges created by the original settlement) to the eldest son for life, with remainder over. In this case the two settlements may be read as one, together called a *compound settlement*,[22] and the Act provides that the word *settlement* shall be construed as referring to such compound settlement where it exists.[23]

---

[17] *Re Bird* [1927] 1 Ch 210.   [18] SLA 1925, s 23.

[19] Presumably 'family arrangement' in this context includes an arrangement made not voluntarily, but for valuable consideration; cf *Williams v Williams* (1867) 2 Ch App 294, 301.

[20] Ch 20; below, p 779.   [21] SLA 1925, s 1(1)(v); *Re Austen* [1929] 2 Ch 155.

[22] *Re Ogle's Settled Estates* [1927] 1 Ch 229, 232–3.   [23] SLA 1925, s 1(1)(i), proviso.

B THE MACHINERY OF A SETTLEMENT AFTER 1925

We have already seen that, in order to emphasise the separation of the legal estate from the equitable interests of the beneficiaries, and also to facilitate a conveyance of the legal estate, the Settled Land Act 1925 introduced a new method for the creation of a settlement by providing that:[24]

> Every settlement of a legal estate in land inter vivos shall, save as in this Act otherwise provided, be effected by two deeds, namely, a vesting deed and a trust instrument and if effected in any other way shall not operate to transfer or create a legal estate.[25]

This method must now be examined in more detail. We shall first consider the machinery of settlements in unregistered land, which will have been the original method of creation of most settlements that remain in existence today. Then we shall consider briefly the impact of registration of title on settled land.

(1) Settlement Inter Vivos

(a) The vesting deed

The function of the vesting deed is to vest the legal fee simple in the person who for the time being is to have the actual enjoyment of the land, or, if he is a minor or otherwise legally incapable, then to vest it in a person who is denominated a *statutory owner*.[26] The virtue of thus passing the legal fee simple to a person who is beneficially entitled to some lesser interest is that, should he later desire, in the interests of the beneficiaries generally, to dispose of the fee simple by way of sale, lease or otherwise under one of the powers conferred upon him by the Settled Land Act 1925, he can produce a document that not only shows that the legal estate is vested in him, but also certifies the facts essential to a valid exercise of the statutory power.

This vesting deed, then—called the *principal vesting deed*—conveys to the tenant for life or the statutory owner the whole legal estate that is held upon trust for persons by way of succession. It is a short document and must contain the following statements and particulars:[27]

(i)   a description, either specific or general, of the settled land;

---

[24] Above, p 126.

[25] SLA 1925, s 4(1). In the case of registered land, a disposition does not operate at law until the registration requirements are met: LRA 2002, s 27(1); below, p 1093.

[26] Ibid, ss 23, 26, 117(1)(xxvi).

[27] Ibid, s 5(1). SLA, Sch. 1, Form No 2 contained a precedent of a vesting deed. The Schedule was repealed by Statute Law Repeals Act 2004, s 1, Sch 12, following a recommendation of the Law Commission on the ground that the guidance contained in such forms, necessary in 1925 when the SLA was new, is no longer necessary as there are now modern precedents in relation to the dwindling number of strict settlements in existence: Law Com No 285: *Statute Law Revision: Seventeenth Report* (2003). For precedents, see *Encyclopaedia of Forms and Precedents*, vol 40(3) (2006), part 1.

(ii) a statement that the settled land is vested in the person or persons to whom it is conveyed or in whom it is declared to be vested upon the trusts from time to time affecting the settled land;

(iii) the names of the trustees of the settlement;

(iv) a statement of any powers, over and above those conferred upon every tenant for life by the Act, which it is desired to give to the tenant for life under the settlement;

(v) the name of any person entitled to appoint new trustees of the settlement.

If after the execution of a principal vesting deed more land is acquired that is to become subject to the settlement, it is conveyed to the tenant for life by what is called a *subsidiary vesting deed*.[28]

(b) The trust instrument

At the same time a second deed, called the trust instrument, is executed that:[29]

(i) declares the trusts affecting the settled land;

(ii) appoints trustees of the settlement;

(iii) contains the power, if any, to appoint new trustees of the settlement;

(iv) sets out, either expressly or by reference, any powers intended to be conferred by the settlement in extension of those conferred by the Act;

(v) bears any ad valorem stamp duty that may be payable in respect of the settlement.

Thus it is the trust instrument that declares the trusts upon which the legal estate is to be held. If we look at the vesting deed alone, the tenant for life seems to be fully entitled to sell the fee simple. So he is. An intending purchaser need not look beyond the deed, but at the same time such a person is told in the vesting deed that the land is held upon trust and that there are trustees, and this knowledge places upon him the obligation to pay the purchase money, not to the tenant for life, but to the trustees. If he does this, his obligations are at an end, and it is no concern of his what is done with the money. But we need to look at the trust instrument, since it records the equitable interests that it is the object of the settlement to confer upon the beneficiaries. The property comprised in the settlement, whether it remains in the form of land or is sold and converted into money, is actually enjoyed by the persons who are described in, and upon the conditions that are prescribed by, the trust instrument. We must not be misled by the vesting deed into thinking that the tenant for life, who is thereby declared to be the fee simple owner, can sell the whole estate and pocket the proceeds.

---

[28] Ibid, s 10.

[29] Ibid, s 4(3). SLA, Sch. 1, Form No 3 contained a precedent of a trust instrument. The Schedule was repealed by Statute Law Repeals Act 2004, s 1, Sch 12: above, n 26.

(2) Settlement by Will

The rule that an inter vivos settlement must be created by two contemporaneous deeds called the principal vesting deed and the trust instrument, applied differently to a settlement by will. In this case the legal estate devolved upon the personal representatives of the settlor, who held it upon trust to convey it to the person entitled to the tenancy for life under the will.[30] This conveyance could be made by a *vesting assent*, that is by an assent in writing but not under seal.[31] The vesting assent then corresponds to the vesting deed that forms part of a settlement inter vivos, and the will itself is deemed to be the trust instrument.

(3) Effect of Machinery

(a) Legal estate separated from equitable interests

As a result of this machinery, the legal estate conveyed to the tenant for life by the vesting deed is kept rigorously separate from the equitable interests of the beneficiaries that are created by and contained in the trust instrument. Throughout the duration of the settlement, and however long that duration may be, the legal estate must and will be vested in a person or persons competent to deal with it as permitted by the Act. If no vesting deed has been executed, the tenant for life or statutory owner[32] can require the trustees of the settlement to repair the omission.[33] Normally, the legal estate will remain with the first tenant for life until his death, though in certain exceptional circumstances, such as where his equitable life interest is forfeited under the terms of the settlement, it will pass to the trustees. On his death it will devolve on the trustees who will as soon as practicable convey it by a vesting assent to the person next entitled.[34]

(b) Evasion of Act prevented

The evasion of the statutory requirement of a vesting deed is prevented by section 13 of the Settled Land Act 1925.[35] This provides that where a tenant for life or statutory owner has become entitled to have a vesting deed or assent executed in his favour, then, until such an instrument has in fact been executed, no disposition of the land made inter vivos by any person shall operate to pass a legal estate, unless it is made in favour of a purchaser having no notice that the tenant for life or statutory owner has become so entitled. Such a purported disposition operates as a contract to convey the legal estate as soon as the vesting deed has been executed.[36]

---

[30] Ibid, s 6.   [31] Ibid, s 8(1).   [32] Below, p 442.   [33] SLA 1925, s 9(2).
[34] Below, p 1053, n 78.   [35] SLA 1925, s 13, as amended by LP(A)A 1926, Sch.
[36] It should be protected by (in registered land) entry of a notice in the register, or by (in unregistered land) registration as a land charge: below, p 982.

There is an exception, however, in favour of personal representatives, for they are allowed to sell settled land in the ordinary course of administration even though no vesting deed has been executed when their title accrues.[37]

(c) Where vesting deed not necessary

There are three cases in which there is no necessity for a vesting deed:

(1) Where land ceases to be settled

If, for example, a tenant in tail in possession of settled land, free from any trusts or incumbrances, bars the entail before a vesting deed is executed in his favour, he thereby terminates the settlement, and can make title as a fee simple owner.[38]

(2) Where beneficiaries terminate settlement

Beneficiaries, if of full age, may terminate the settlement and so avoid the necessity for a vesting deed. If, for example, an owner devised his residence to his wife for life with remainder to his children in fee simple, the widow becomes tenant for life on his death and, as such, entitled to a vesting deed. Instead, however, she may surrender her life interest to the remaindermen in fee, and then all the parties can create a trust for sale—or, since 1997, a trust of land—with themselves as trustees, the income until sale and the ultimate proceeds to be held on trusts corresponding to those of the settlement.

(3) Where land is subject to family charges

If the land has become settled merely because it has been voluntarily subjected to family charges,[39] the tenant for life, as we have seen, is allowed by the Law of Property (Amendment) Act 1926 to convey a legal estate subject to the charges without being required to procure the execution of a vesting deed.[40]

(4) Settlements in Registered Land

Although most settlements that exist today may have been created when the land was unregistered and not yet subject to compulsory registration,[41] a transfer of the legal estate will now require the title to be registered;[42] and dispositions thereafter will be subject to the principles of registered land.[43]

The application of the principles of registered land to settlements under the Settled Land Act 1925 is governed by Schedule 7 of the Land Registration Rules 2003.[44] The legal estate in the settled land must be registered in the name of the tenant for life or

---

[37] SLA 1925, s 13.   [38] *Re Alefounder's Will Trusts* [1927] 1 Ch 360.   [39] SLA 1925, s 20(1)(ix).
[40] Above, p 435.   [41] Above, p 131.
[42] LRA 2002, s 4(1)(a), expressly including a transfer by means of a vesting assent.   [43] Ibid, s 27.
[44] Ibid, s 89; LRR 2003, r 186, Sch 7; H & B, paras 13.42, 13.43.

statutory owner,[45] and the beneficial interests under the settlement must be protected by the entry of a restriction on the register:[46] they cannot be protected by entry of a notice in the register,[47] nor can they take effect as overriding interests, even where the beneficiaries are in actual occupation.[48] The restrictions, which are designed to ensure that any sale by the tenant for life complies with the requirements of overreaching,[49] are binding on the registered proprietor during his life but do not affect a disposition by his personal representatives.[50]

Thus, if X is the tenant for life and Y and Z are the trustees of a settlement, X will be the registered proprietor of the fee simple of the settled land and the register will contain a dual restriction, first preventing the registration of any disposition not authorised by the Settled Land Act 1925, and then preventing the registration of any disposition under which capital money arises unless the money is paid to Y and Z or into court.[51] By this means, the beneficial interests of a strict settlement are protected without their details being brought onto the register. There is still a curtain, and a purchaser who complies with the restrictions will overreach the beneficial interests in the same way that he would overreach them in the case of unregistered land.

C THE TENANT FOR LIFE

(1) Definition of Tenant for Life

A tenant for life is defined as follows in section 19(1) of the Settled Land Act 1925:[52]

---

[45] LRR 2003, Sch 7, para 1. The transfer of registered land into a settlement, and the transfer of the settled land on the succession of a new tenant for life, must contain provisions that mirror those of the vesting deed in unregistered land: (a) that the property is vested on trust (identifying the trust deed or will); (b) the names of the trustees; (c) the name of the person entitled to appoint new trustees; and (d) powers, additional to those conferred by SLA 1925, conferred by the trust deed or will on the tenant for life: ibid, paras 4(1), 6(1), 12(1).

[46] Ibid, paras 2, 3. The restriction must be in one of three forms (G, H or I) specified in Sch 4 (as substituted by SI 2008 No 1919, r 4(6), Sch 4), depending on whether the tenant for life or statutory owners are registered proprietor, and whether there are trustees of the settlement.

[47] LRA 2002, s 33(a)(ii).

[48] Ibid, Sch 1, para 2; Sch 3, para 2(a). This was also the position under LRA 1925, s 86(2); (1958) 22 Conv (NS) 14 at 23–4 (FR Crane). Law Com No 158, Third Report on Land Registration (1987), para 2.69 recommended that interests under settlements should be capable of being overriding interests; and so did Law Com No 254, Land Registration for the 21st Century: A Consultative Document (1998), para 5.63.

[49] Below, p 1117.

[50] LRR 2003, Sch 7, para 3(3). When the settlement ends on the death of the proprietor, the personal representatives must apply for cancellation of the restriction, but the Registrar does not investigate whether the personal representatives are acting correctly and within their powers: ibid, para 12(2), (3).

[51] Ibid, Sch 4, Form G (as substituted by SI 2008 No 1919).

[52] Re Jefferys [1939] Ch 205 (an annuitant is not a tenant for life); Re Carne's Settled Estates [1899] 1 Ch 324 ('to occupy the land rent free so long as she might wish to do so' held to be a tenant for life); Ayer v Benton (1967) 204 EG 359; Re Catling [1931] 2 Ch 359 (wife as tenant at a nominal annual sum, the tenancy not to be determined so long as she made the property her principal place of residence; held not to be a tenant for life; and indeed there was no settlement); Re Waleran Settled Estates [1927] 1 Ch 522 (a term to a woman 'for 99 years if she should so long live' held to be a tenant for life); Re Ogle's Settled Estates [1927] 1 Ch 229, above, p 435; Re Cayley and Evans' Contract [1930] 2 Ch 143; Re Gallenga Will Trusts [1938] 1 All ER 106.

The person of full age who is for the time being beneficially entitled under a settlement to possession of settled land for his life is for the purposes of this Act the tenant for life of that land and the tenant for life under that settlement.

He is deemed to be such, notwithstanding that the land or his estate therein is charged with the payment of incumbrances.[53] If two or more persons are jointly entitled to possession they together constitute the tenant for life.[54]

(a) Persons with powers of tenant for life

There are several cases where land is settled in the sense that it is subject to a 'settlement' within the statutory meaning of that word,[55] and yet there is no tenant for life as defined in section 19. A tenant in tail in possession is a simple example of the situation.[56] The Act takes care to ensure that wherever there is a 'settlement' there shall always be some person with the *powers* of a tenant for life. In the first place, section 20 provides that the following persons shall have the powers of a tenant for life and shall be included in the expression 'tenant for life'.[57]

(i) A tenant in tail, including both a tenant after possibility[58] and one who is by Act of Parliament restrained from barring his estate tail, but excluding a tenant in tail whose land has been bought with money provided by Parliament in consideration of public services.

(ii) A person entitled to land for an estate in fee simple or for a term of years absolute, subject to a gift over on failure of his issue or in any other event.[59]

(iii) A person entitled to a base[60] or a determinable fee[61] or a corresponding interest in leaseholds.

(iv) A tenant for years determinable on life, not holding merely under a lease at a rent.

We have seen that leases *at a rent* for a term of years determinable at the death of the tenant are now converted into terms for 90 years,[62] and that such a person cannot have the powers of a tenant for life,[63] but this conversion does not operate where such a term takes effect under a settlement. For example, a devisee to whom lands are given for 30 years if he should so long live has the powers of a tenant for life.

(v) A tenant *pur autre vie*[64] not holding merely under a lease at a rent.[65]

(vi) A tenant for his own or any other life, or for years determinable on life, whose interest is liable to cease in any event during that life, or is subject to a trust for accumulation of income.

---

[53] SLA 1925, s 19(4).   [54] Ibid, s 19(2).   [55] Above, pp 432–5.   [56] Above, p 433.
[57] SLA 1925, s 117(1)(xxviii).   [58] Below, p 591.
[59] But a gift over on failure of issue becomes incapable of taking effect as soon as there is any issue who attains 18: LPA 1925, s 134(1), as amended by Family Law Reform Act 1969, s 1(3), Sch 1.
[60] Below, p 603.   [61] Below, p 613 ff.   [62] LPA 1925, s 149(6), above, p 200.
[63] *Re Catling* [1931] 2 Ch 359.   [64] Below, p 607.   [65] *Re Johnson* [1914] 2 Ch 134.

For example, a devise to A so long as he shall live on the estate for at least three months in each year, with a gift over to B upon failure to observe this condition, makes A tenant for life within section 20.[66]

(vii) A tenant by the curtesy.[67]

(viii) A person entitled to the *income* of land under a trust for payment of it to him during his own or any other life,[68] or until sale of the land, or until some event (eg bankruptcy) terminates his interest. But if the land is subject to a trust of land,[69] the person so entitled does not have the powers of a tenant for life.

(ix) A person beneficially entitled to land for an estate in fee simple or for a term of years absolute subject to any estates, interests, charges or powers of charging, subsisting or capable of being exercised under a settlement.

If, for example, lands are settled on A for life with remainder in fee simple to his eldest son B, with powers for A to charge the land with portions for his younger children, then B, on the death of A, will hold the fee simple subject to any such charges that may have been created. He is tenant for life under the above clause and as such can deal with the estate, notwithstanding the charge to which it is subject.[70]

(b) Statutory owners

Comprehensive though this list is, it still fails to provide for the case of every settlement. For example, a settlement within the meaning of the Settled Land Act 1925 exists if land is limited in trust for any person in fee simple contingently upon the happening of some event,[71] or when the person entitled in possession is entitled only to a *part* of the income from the trust[72] or where no person is entitled to any of its income at all as in the case of a discretionary strict settlement where the trustees are directed to pay the income to such members of a class of persons as they may think fit.[73] In none of these cases is the beneficiary a tenant for life or a person who has the powers of a tenant for life. The Act, therefore, provides that where such a situation arises the legal estate shall be vested in statutory owners—that is to say:

(a) any person of full age on whom they are conferred by the settlement; and

(b) in any other case the trustees of the settlement.[74]

---

[66] *Re Paget* (1885) 30 Ch D 161.   [67] Below, p 589.
[68] *Re Llanover Settled Estates* [1926] Ch 626.   [69] Amended by TLATA 1996, Sch 3, para 2(8).
[70] He also has the option under LP(A)A 1926, s 1(1), above, p 435, of conveying the legal estate to a purchaser subject to the charge, provided that the purchaser is agreeable.
[71] *Re Bird* [1927] 1 Ch 210; above, pp 434–5.   [72] *Re Frewen* [1926] Ch 580.
[73] *Re Gallenga Will Trusts* [1938] 1 All ER 106.   [74] SLA 1925, ss 23, 117(1)(xxvi).

Further, where the person who would otherwise be a tenant for life is a minor, the legal estate and statutory powers are vested during the minority of the minor in:

(a) a personal representative, if the settled land is vested in him and no vesting instrument has yet been executed; and

(b) in every other case, the trustees of the settlement.[75]

(2) Powers of Tenant for Life

In accordance with the policy that has prevailed since the Settled Land Act 1882, the person vested with the legal estate, normally the tenant for life in actual possession, is empowered by the Settled Land Act 1925 to manage and even to dispose of the fee simple, an aspect of his position that must now be developed in some detail. The general policy is that he shall have many of the powers of dealing with the land that are available to an estate owner entitled beneficially in his own right, but subject to this overriding proviso, that any gain accruing from the exercise of a power shall be held on trust for the equitable beneficiaries according to the limitations of the settlement. To this end the Act confers upon the tenant for life the right to exercise any of the following powers:

(a) Powers exercisable by tenant for life

(1) Powers to sell or exchange

The tenant for life

> may sell the settled land, or any part thereof, or any easement, right or privilege of any kind over or in relation to the land.[76]

Every sale must be made for the best consideration in money that can reasonably be obtained,[77] but instead of being made in return for a lump sum it may be made in consideration, wholly or partly, of a rent payable yearly or half-yearly and secured upon the land sold. Such a rent may be perpetual or terminable, and in the latter case—when it will cease to be payable after a certain number of years—it must be treated partly as principal and partly as interest, and the part constituting principal must be dealt with as capital money. The interest accruing on the principal sum must be accumulated by way of compound interest and added each year to capital.[78] The rent must be the best that can reasonably be obtained, though for a period not exceeding five years from the sale it may be nominal.[79] The statutory remedies for the recovery of a rentcharge given by the Law of Property Act 1925[80] lie for recovery of the rent.[81]

---

[75] Ibid, s 26; below, pp 455–8. For the terminology of 'minor' or 'infant' in relation to settled land, see above, p 434, n 16.

[76] Ibid, s 38(i).   [77] Ibid, s 39(1); *Wheelwright v Walker* (1883) 31 WR 912.   [78] Ibid, s 39(2).

[79] Ibid, s 39(3).   [80] S 121; below, p 787.   [81] LP(A)A 1926, Sched.

It is also provided that where the land is sold to any company incorporated by special Act of Parliament or by any order having the force of an Act of Parliament, the purchase money may consist, either wholly or partially, of fully-paid securities of any description of the purchasing company.[82]

The tenant for life may make an exchange of the whole or part of the land, or of any easement, right, or privilege over it, for other land or for an easement, right, or privilege over other land, and he may pay or accept money in order to render the exchanges equal in value.[83]

When a sale or exchange is made, the tenant for life is permitted to except the mines and minerals, and in such a case to reserve for the settled land all proper rights and powers incidental to mining purposes.[84]

The powers of sale and exchange are exercisable with regard to any principal mansion-house that stands on the settled land, but in two cases mere notice to the trustees of the proposed transaction[85] does not suffice, and the tenant for life must first obtain either the consent of the trustees or an order of the court:

(i) where the settlement existed before 1926, and does not expressly dispense with the necessity for such consent or order; and

(ii) where the settlement came into operation after 1925, but contains a provision that such consent or order is necessary.

The court must determine as a fact whether any particular house is a principal mansion-house,[86] but it is enacted that a house that is usually occupied as a farmhouse, or which, together with its pleasure-grounds and park and lands, does not exceed 25 acres in extent, is not a principal mansion-house within the meaning of the Act and can in all cases be disposed of without the consent of the trustees.[87]

(2) Power to grant leases

The tenant for life may lease the whole or part of the land or any easement, right, or privilege incidental thereto for any purpose whatever, whether involving waste or not, for any of the following maximum periods:[88]

(a) 999 years for a building lease;

(b) 100 years for a mining lease;

(c) 999 years for a forestry lease;

(d) 50 years for any other kind of lease.[89]

---

[82] SLA 1925, s 39(5). [83] Ibid, ss 38(iii), 40. [84] Ibid, s 50.
[85] Below, p 450. [86] Re Feversham Settled Estate [1938] 2 All ER 210.
[87] SLA 1925, s 65. [88] Ibid, s 41.
[89] Law Reform Committee 23rd Report, The Powers and Duties of Trustees (1982, Cmnd 8733), para 8.6 recommended that this period be increased to 99 years.

When any of the above leases is made:

(i) the tenant for life must give one month's notice in writing to the trustees;[90]

(ii) he must procure the best rent reasonably obtainable;[91] and

(iii) the lease must be by deed and must contain a covenant by the lessee for payment of the rent, and a condition allowing the tenant for life to re-enter if the rent is not paid within a specific time not exceeding 30 days.

The deed must be so framed that the lessee will take possession within 12 months, but if the land is already leased to a third person, then, provided that such existing lease has no more than seven years to run, it is lawful to grant a reversionary lease to take effect in possession when the existing one determines.[92]

Without any notice to the trustees, a lease may be granted for a term not exceeding 21 years at the best rent that can reasonably be obtained without a fine, provided that the lessee is made impeachable for waste.[93] If the lease does not exceed three years, it may be made by writing without a deed, but the lessee must enter into a written agreement to pay the rent.[94]

As in the case of the power of sale, the tenant for life may lease the land and reserve the minerals,[95] and if he desires to lease the principal mansion-house, he must obtain the consent of the trustees in the cases that have been specified above.[96]

Special provisions are inserted in the Act with regard to building, mining and forestry leases:

(i) Building leases

A building lease[97] must be made partly in consideration of the lessee or some other person erecting new or additional buildings or improving or repairing buildings, and partly in consideration of the payment of rent. A peppercorn or nominal rent may be reserved for the first five years of the term.[98] A lease is valid although it does not specify a definite time within which the building or rebuilding shall begin.[99]

(ii) Mining leases

As regards minerals the rule at common law was that a tenant for life unimpeachable for waste[100] could *open* and work mines and retain the whole profits, though this right can no longer be exercised without the permission of the local planning authority, since it involves a material change in the use of land (and therefore 'development') within the meaning of the Town and Country Planning Act 1990.[101] A tenant for life impeachable for waste cannot *open* mines, but he can continue to work to his own profit those

---

[90] SLA 1925, s 101.

[91] Ibid, s 42(1)(ii); *Re Morgan's Lease* [1972] Ch 1; (1971) 87 LQR 338 (DW Elliott). As to whether a tenant for life has power to insert a rent review clause in the lease, see [1979] Conv 258 (M Dockray); Law Reform Committee 23rd Report, above, para 8.4, recommended that this doubt be removed.

[92] Ibid, s 42(1)(i).   [93] For the meaning of waste, see above, p 234.   [94] SLA 1925, s 42(5)(ii).

[95] Ibid, s 50.   [96] Ibid, s 65, above, p 444.   [97] Above, p 389.   [98] SLA 1925, s 44.

[99] *Re Grosvenor Settled Estates* [1933] Ch 97.   [100] For the meaning of waste, see above, p 234.

[101] S 55(1). For planning control, see Ch 29 of the 17th edn of this book.

that have already been lawfully opened by a predecessor.[102] These rules were varied by the Settled Land Act 1925. If the tenant for life is impeachable for waste in respect of minerals, three-quarters of the rent arising from a mining lease becomes capital; if unimpeachable, one-quarter becomes capital and the residue goes to him as income.[103] A tenant for life who is impeachable for waste under the settlement is not impeachable in respect of mines that have been lawfully opened by a predecessor, and therefore he is entitled to three-quarters of the rents.[104] These rules with regard to minerals have lost much of their importance since the passing of the Coal Industry Nationalisation Act 1946, but they are still material, for 'minerals' include 'all substances in, on or under the land, obtainable by underground or by surface working'.[105]

(iii) Forestry lease

A forestry lease is defined by the Act as a 'lease to the Forestry Commissioners for any purpose for which they are authorised to acquire land by the Forestry Act [1967]',[106] but this is now to be construed as a reference to the Secretary of State, in whom the former powers of the Commissioners to acquire land are now vested.[107] In a forestry lease the rent may be nominal for any period not exceeding the first ten years or may be made to vary according to the value of the timber cut in any one year, and any other provisions may be made for the sharing of the profits of the user of the land between the tenant for life and the Secretary of State.[108]

(3) Power to raise money by the grant of a legal mortgage of the settled land

A capital sum of money may be raised by mortgage in order to meet an expense that is connected with the settled land or desirable in the interests of its prosperity. There are nine different purposes specified by the Act for which a tenant for life may raise money in this manner, but as five of these are connected with the conversion of copyhold into socage[109] and perpetually renewable leases into long terms, it is only necessary to notice that a mortgage of the legal estate is permissible when the object is:[110]

(a) The discharge of an incumbrance on the settled land.

If, for example, different parts of the land are subject to three separate mortgages, the tenant for life may grant a new mortgage of the entire land to another mortgagee and use the money to pay off the three original debts.[111]

---

[102] *Re Hall* [1916] 2 Ch 488.
[103] SLA 1925, s 47. These provisions may be displaced by the settlement: s 48.
[104] *Re Chaytor* [1900] 2 Ch 804; *Re Fitzwalter* [1943] Ch 285.   [105] SLA 1925, s 117(1)(xv).
[106] Ibid, s 117(1)(x); Forestry Act 1967, Sch 6, para 5.
[107] Forestry Act 1967, s 50, Sch 6, para 5; s 49(1). In this capacity the Secretary of State for Environment, Food and Rural Affairs is the successor in England to the Minister of Agriculture, Fisheries and Food, referred to in the Forestry Act. The National Assembly for Wales has responsibility for forestry in Wales: SI 1999 No 672, art 2, Sch 1.
[108] SLA 1925, s 48.   [109] Above, p 111.
[110] SLA 1925, s 71. See also Leasehold Reform Act 1967, s 6(5); CLRA 2002, s 109(4)(b).
[111] *Re Clifford* [1902] 1 Ch 87.

The incumbrance must be permanent, thus excluding any annual sum payable only during a life or for a term of years.[112]

  (b) Payment for any improvement authorised by the Settled Land Act 1925 or by the settlement.

This is a valuable power that was introduced in 1925. A tenant for life may spend existing capital money on carrying out any of the improvements authorised by the Act.[113]

  (c) Equality of exchange.

  (d) Payment of the costs of any transaction effected under (a) to (c) above.

A legal mortgage by the tenant for life may take the form either of a charge by deed by way of legal mortgage or (in unregistered land) of a long lease,[114] and a tenant for life who grants a mortgage term for any of the above four purposes is not subject to those provisions of the Settled Land Act[115] which in a normal case restrict the length of lease that may be made.[116]

This must be distinguished from the case where the tenant for life borrows money for his own purposes by mortgaging his beneficial interest, such as his equitable life interest.[117]

(4) Power to effect improvements

The tenant for life is empowered to effect certain authorised improvements on the land and to have the cost defrayed out of capital.[118] Moreover, his right to this payment, unlike the practice prevailing before 1926, is no longer conditional on his submitting a scheme of operations to the trustees or to the court before the work is done.[119] The Act authorises 34 specific improvements that are classified into three categories according to the permanence or impermanence of their results:[120]

Part I improvements comprise 25 different works that clearly increase the permanent capital value of the land, such as drainage, irrigation, bridges, defences against water, the provision of farmhouses and cottages for labourers and the rebuilding of the mansion house.

Part II improvements are those, the lasting value of which is more doubtful, such as the erection of houses for land agents, the repair of damage due to dry rot or boring for water.

Part III improvements are those whose value is transitory, as, for example, the installation of a heating or electric power apparatus for buildings, the wiring of a house for electricity or the purchase of moveable machinery for farming or other purposes.

---

112 SLA 1925, s 71(2).   113 Ibid, s 83, below.
114 Below, pp 803 ff. A mortgage of registered land can no longer be made by demise: below, p 806.
115 Above, p 444.   116 SLA 1925, s 71(3).   117 Below, p 811.
118 SLA 1925, s 83.   119 Ibid, s 84(1).
120 Ibid, Sch. 3. For the significance of this classification, see below, p 461 ff.

(5) Power to accept leases of other land

A new power was introduced by the Settled Land Act 1925 allowing the tenant for life to accept a lease of any other land[121] or of mines and minerals, or of any easement, right or privilege, 'convenient to be held or worked with or annexed in enjoyment to the settled land', and there is no limit to the length of the term that he may so accept.[122]

(6) Miscellaneous powers

There are several miscellaneous powers that the tenant for life is entitled to exercise, including the following:

(i) Power to contract

Power to contract to make any sale, exchange, mortgage, charge or other disposition authorised by the Act.[123] The transaction must be in conformity with the Act at the time of the performance of the contract. Thus in the case of a contract for a lease the lease must satisfy the requirement that the rent must be the best reasonably obtainable when the lease is granted.[124] Such contracts are enforceable by and against every successor in title of the tenant for life.[125]

(ii) Power to grant options

Power to grant, by writing, with or without consideration, an option to purchase or take a lease of settled land, or any easement, right, or privilege over it.[126] The price or rent must be the best reasonably obtainable and must be fixed when the option is granted.[127] The option must be made exercisable within an agreed number of years not exceeding ten.

(iii) Power to accept surrender of leases

Power to accept, with or without consideration, a surrender of any lease of settled land.[128]

(iv) Power to grant land for public purposes

Power, if the result will be for the general benefit of the settled land, to make grants or leases at a nominal price or rent for certain public and charitable purposes, for example, the grant of land not exceeding one acre for a village institute or a public library.[129]

---

[121] This includes a power to accept an extended lease under Leasehold Reform Act 1967, s 6(2)(a); above, p 395.

[122] SLA 1925, s 53.   [123] Ibid, s 90.   [124] Re Rycroft's Settlement [1962] Ch 263.

[125] SLA 1925, s 90(2).   [126] Ibid, s 51.

[127] Re Morgan's Lease [1972] Ch 1; Law Reform Committee 23rd Report, The Powers and Duties of Trustees (1982), para 8.10 recommended that the tenant for life should be given the power to grant an option at a price to be fixed at the time of the exercise of the option.

[128] SLA 1925, s 52.   [129] Ibid, s 55.

(v) Power to provide land for working classes
Power to grant or lease a restricted amount of land at a nominal price or rent for the purpose of providing allotments or dwellings for the working classes.[130]

(vi) Power to sell timber
Power with the consent of the trustees or under an order of the court for a tenant for life who is impeachable for waste to sell timber that is ripe and fit for cutting, provided, however, that three-quarters of the net proceeds become capital money and one-quarter becomes income.[131]

(vii) Power to sell heirlooms
Power under an order of the court to sell heirlooms, but in such a case the money arising from the sale becomes capital money, which in this case may be spent on the purchase of other heirlooms.[132]

(viii) Power to appoint agents
Power to appoint agents, subject to certain restrictions; and to remunerate them and to reimburse their expenses.[133]

(ix) Power to insure
Power to insure under the terms of the Trustee Act 1925, section 19.[134]

(7) Power to effect any transaction under order of court

'Any transaction' within the powers of an absolute owner may be sanctioned by the court if this will be for the benefit of the settled land or the beneficiaries, even though it is a transaction not otherwise authorised by the Act or the settlement.[135] Thus approval was given to a scheme to raise money out of capital to enable the tenant for life to continue to reside in the mansion house;[136] and it has been held that the court has jurisdiction to authorise the tenant for life to vary the beneficial interest of an ascertained beneficiary of full age and capacity, even if that beneficiary did not consent.[137] Moreover the width of the definition of 'transaction' enables the court to alter the beneficial interests under the settlement. This was commonly done for the purpose of saving estate duty on the

---

[130] Ibid, s 57(2).   [131] Ibid, s 66.   [132] Ibid, s 67.

[133] Ibid, s 107(1A)(a) and (b), inserted by TA 2000, s 40(1), Sch 2, Pt II, para 17. The exercise of this power is subject to the duty of care under TA 2000, s 1 and Sch 1: ibid, s 107(1A)(d).

[134] Ibid, s 107(1A)(c), inserted by TA 2000, s 40(1), Sch 2, Pt II, para 17. The exercise of this power is subject to the duty of care under TA 2000, s 1 and Sch 1: ibid, s 107(1A)(d). TA 1925 s 19 was substituted by TA 2000, s 34(1).

[135] Ibid, s 64(1). 'Transaction' is defined in s 64(2) as amended by Settled Land and Trustee Acts (Court's General Powers) Act 1943, s 2. *Re White-Popham Settled Estates* [1936] Ch 725; *Re Scarisbrick Re-Settlement Estates* [1944] Ch 229; *Re Earl of Mount Edgcumbe* [1950] Ch 615; *Re Simmons* [1956] Ch 125; *Re Rycroft's Settlement* [1962] Ch 263; *Raikes v Lygon* [1988] 1 WLR 281.

[136] *Re Scarisbrick Re-Settlement Estates*, above.

[137] *Hambro v Duke of Marlborough* [1994] Ch 158; [1994] Conv 492 (E Cooke) (Blenheim Parliamentary Estates).

death of beneficiaries, and the jurisdiction was largely superseded by that given to the court under the Variation of Trusts Act 1958.[138] Both jurisdictions still remain.

(b) Notice, consent or court order

As a general rule a tenant for life need not obtain the consent of the trustees to his exercise of a power, but if he intends to sell, exchange, mortgage or charge the land, to make a lease exceeding 21 years or to grant an option to purchase or to take a lease of the land, he must notify the trustees of his intention at least one month before he completes the transaction.[139] Except in the case of a proposed mortgage or charge, it is permissible, indeed usual, to give a general notice, that is one that states his intention to grant, for example, leases from time to time, without mentioning any specific lease already arranged.[140] There are, however, as we have seen, several cases in which something more than notice is required, and it may be helpful to restate these in summary form:

First, an order of the court must be obtained before the tenant for life may:

(i) grant more than the amount of land specified in the Act for providing allotments or dwellings for the working classes;[141]

(ii) buy or sell heirlooms;[142]

(iii) grant building or mining leases for terms longer than those specified in the Act.[143]

Secondly, *either* an order of the court *or* the consent of the trustees must be obtained before the tenant for life may:

(i) sell or lease the principal mansionhouse in the cases specified above;[144]

(ii) sell the timber in the event of his being impeachable for waste.[145]

Thirdly, there are two cases in which the tenant for life must obtain the consent in writing of the trustees, namely, before he:

(i) compromises or otherwise settles any claim or dispute relating to the settled land;[146]

(ii) releases, waives or modifies a right imposed on other land for the benefit of the settled land, such as an easement or a covenant.[147]

---

[138] See generally H & M, ch 22; Harris, *Variation of Trusts* (1975), pp 19–22.

[139] SLA 1925, s 101(1). Law Reform Committee 23rd Report, para 8.9, recommended that on receipt of the notice the trustees should require the tenant for life to submit to them a valuation, so that they may control the transaction more effectively.

[140] Ibid, s 101(2).   [141] Ibid, s 57(2).   [142] Ibid, s 67.

[143] Ibid, s 46.   [144] Ibid, s 65; above, p 444.   [145] Ibid, s 66.

[146] Ibid, s 58(1).   [147] Ibid, s 58(2).

(3) Position of Tenant for Life

(a) Additions to and reductions from powers

Such, then, are the powers conferred upon the tenant for life by the Act, but it must be remembered that nothing prevented additional powers being given to him by the settlement, for it is expressly provided[148] that when a settlor authorises the exercise of any powers additional to or larger than those enumerated above, they shall operate in exactly the same manner and with the same results as if they had been permitted by the Act. Thus a settlement may allow the tenant for life:

(i) to grant a lease to take effect in possession not later than three years after its date;

(ii) to use as income the whole of the rent reserved on a mining lease; or

(iii) to raise money on mortgage for the purchase of a dwelling house.[149]

In fact all the powers given by a settlement are expressly preserved, for it is provided that nothing in the Act shall take away, abridge or prejudicially affect any power under the settlement that is exercisable by the tenant for life or by the trustees with the consent of the tenant for life.[150] If, however, there is any conflict between the Act and the settlement, the Act prevails, and any power (not being a mere power of revocation or appointment[151]) conferred on the trustees becomes exercisable by the tenant for life as an additional power.[152]

Such a conflict occurs, for example, if the settlement empowers the tenant for life to sell with the consent of a third person, for such a conditional power is inconsistent with the unfettered power of sale given by the Act.[153] Though a settlor is allowed to confer upon the tenant for life the right to exercise powers additional to those permissible under the statute, any provisions inserted in the settlement with a view to cutting down the statutory powers are void. Section 106 of the Settled Land Act 1925 provides:

If in a settlement, will, assurance, or other instrument...a provision is inserted:

(a) purporting or attempting, by way of direction, declaration, or otherwise, to forbid a tenant for life or statutory owner to exercise any power under this Act, or his right to require the settled land to be vested in him; or

(b) attempting, or tending, or intended, by a limitation, gift, or disposition over of settled land, or by a limitation, gift, or disposition of other real or any personal property, or by the imposition of any condition, or by forfeiture, or in any other manner whatever, to prohibit or prevent him from exercising, or to induce him to abstain from exercising, or to put him

---

[148] Ibid, s 109.

[149] For an example of such an express power, see *City of London Building Society v Flegg* [1988] AC 54.

[150] SLA 1925, s 108(1).

[151] Such as where land is limited upon such trusts as T shall appoint, and subject thereto to A for life. Here, T's power to revoke the life interest and to appoint new interests remains exercisable by him: Wolstenholme and Cherry, *Conveyancing Statutes* (13th edn, 1972), vol 3, p 222.

[152] SLA 1925, s 108(2).　　　　　[153] *Re Jefferys* [1939] Ch 205; (1939) 55 LQR 22 (HP).

into a position inconsistent with his exercising, any power under this Act, or his right to require the settled land to be vested in him;

that provision, as far as it purports, or attempts, or tends, or is intended to have or would or might have, the operation aforesaid, shall be deemed to be void.[154]

A condition that is sometimes inserted in settlements requiring the tenant for life to reside on the settled land will serve to illustrate the application of this section. Suppose that land is settled on X for life with a proviso that if he does not reside on the settled land for at least three months in each year he shall forfeit his interest. Such a clause is void so far as it 'tends' to hinder or obstruct the exercise by X of his statutory powers. This, of course, is its natural tendency, for if he sells or leases the estate he must necessarily infringe the condition as to residence. It is a deterrent of this nature that is within the mischief of the section, and therefore, notwithstanding a disposition of the land under his statutory powers, his life interest in the income remains intact.[155] If, on the other hand, there is no question of the exercise of the powers, his failure to satisfy the condition operates as a forfeiture of his interest.[156] If it has never been his intention to exercise the powers, it cannot be said that the condition has in any way hampered his freedom of action.

Another example of the operation of the section is this:

If the settlor vests a fund of money in the trustees, with authority to apply the income upon the maintenance of the estate and to pay any surplus not required for that purpose to the tenant for life, X, the prospect of losing this income might tend to dissuade X from exercising his power of sale. As a general rule, therefore, if X sells the land he still remains entitled to the income for life.[157]

(b) Non-assignability of powers

Again, as long as the land remains settled, the powers of a tenant for life are indestructible in the sense that they are not capable of assignment or release, but remain exercisable by him notwithstanding any assignment by operation of law or otherwise of his beneficial interest under the settlement.[158] Thus:

If land stands settled on A for life, remainder to B for life with remainder over, and B sells his reversionary life interest for value to X, the statutory power to grant leases after the death of A is exercisable by B, for the design of the Act is to enable a tenant for life to exercise his powers whether he has disposed of his beneficial interest or not.[159]

---

[154] *Re Aberconway's Settlement Trusts* [1953] Ch 647.
[155] *Re Paget's Settled Estates* (1885) 30 Ch D 161; *Re Patten* [1929] 2 Ch; *Re Orlebar* [1936] Ch 147.
[156] *Re Acklom* [1929] 1 Ch 195; *Re Haynes* (1887) 37 Ch D 306; *Re Trenchard* [1902] 1 Ch 378.
[157] *Re Ames* [1893] 2 Ch 479; *Re Herbert* [1946] 1 All ER 421; cf *Re Burden* [1948] Ch 160; *Re Aberconway's Settlement Trusts*, above; [1954] CLJ 60 (RN Gooderson).
[158] SLA 1925, s 104(1).
[159] *Re Barlow's Contract* [1903] 1 Ch 382; *Earl of Lonsdale v Lowther* [1900] 2 Ch 687.

In such a case as this B could not formerly exercise his powers without the consent of his assignee for value, X, but the necessity for such consent was removed by the Act.[160] The rights of the assignee are, however, protected, for whatever interest he had in the property originally assigned to him he has a corresponding interest in any money, securities or land into which that property may have been converted as a result of the exercise of some power.[161] Moreover, notice of an intended transaction must be given to him.[162]

If, however, it is shown to the satisfaction of the court that a tenant for life has by reason of bankruptcy, assignment, incumbrance, or otherwise ceased to have a substantial interest in the settled land, and has unreasonably refused to exercise the statutory powers, an order may be made authorising the trustees of the settlement to exercise the powers in his name.[163] The mere fact that he has grossly neglected the land and has allowed it to become derelict does not justify the making of an order. The court must be satisfied that there has been an unreasonable refusal to exercise the powers.[164]

Although any attempted assignment of the powers by the tenant for life is void, it is provided that if the life interest, with the intention of causing its extinction, is surrendered to the remainderman or reversioner next entitled under the settlement, the statutory powers shall cease to be available to the tenant for life and shall be exercisable as if he were dead.[165] For example, if a tenant for life becomes bankrupt and the trustee sells his life interest to the tenant in tail in remainder,[166] or if a father surrenders his life interest to the tenant in tail in remainder, the statutory powers become exercisable by the tenant in tail.

(c) Fiduciary nature of powers

(1) Tenant for life a trustee

Finally, it must be observed that the tenant for life, though he is given an almost unfettered liberty to exercise the statutory powers, is at the same time constituted trustee for all interested parties. Section 107(1) of the Settled Land Act 1925 provides that:[167]

A tenant for life or statutory owner shall, in exercising any power under this Act, have regard to the interests of all parties entitled under the settlement, and shall, in relation to the exercise thereof by him, be deemed to be in the position and to have the duties and liabilities of a trustee for those parties.

---

[160] SLA 1925, s 104(4).   [161] Ibid, s 104(4)(a).   [162] Ibid, s 104(4)(c).

[163] Ibid, s 24(1). This section does not apply to a statutory owner: *Re Craven Settled Estates* [1926] Ch 985.

[164] *Re Thornhill's Settlement* [1940] 4 All ER 83; affd [1941] Ch 24.

[165] SLA 1925, s 105(1); LP(A)A 1926, Sch. A remainderman or reversioner does not qualify if there is an intervening limitation that may take effect: *Re Maryon-Wilson's Instruments* [1971] Ch 789.

[166] *Re Shawdon Estates Settlement* [1930] 1 Ch 217; affd [1930] 2 Ch 1.

[167] Re-enacting s 53 of SLA 1882; *Re Pelly's Will Trusts* [1957] Ch 1, 18.

Several judicial pronouncements have placed those duties on a high level. It has been said that the duty to 'have regard to the interests of all parties' requires the tenant for life to consider all the interests in the widest sense, not merely pecuniary interests, but even the aspirations and sentiments of the family.[168] Lord Esher said:

> He must take all the circumstances of the family, and of each member of the family who may be affected by what he is about to do; he must consider them all carefully, and must consider them in the way that an honest outside trustee would consider them; then he must come to what, in his judgment, is the right thing to do under the circumstances—not the best thing, but the right thing to do.[169]

Nevertheless, having regard to the deliberate policy of the Act in conferring upon the tenant for life virtually the status of absolute owner, this super-imposed trusteeship is somewhat abnormal, for in the nature of things it must inevitably be 'a highly interested trusteeship'.[170] The mere imposition of a trust is insufficient to ensure that powers, so freely confided to the judgment of the tenant for life, will not be exercised from motives of selfishness and personal aggrandisement. A tenant for life, who, with the object of securing a larger income in order to meet his debts or to indulge expensive tastes, or to relieve himself from the cares of management, or because he is hostile to the remainderman, sells land that will obviously be of far greater value in a few years' time, owing perhaps to rapidly changing conditions in the neighbourhood, can scarcely be described as acting 'as an upright independent and righteous man would act in dealing with the affairs of others',[171] and yet none of these facts alone is sufficient to render him liable, provided that he obtains the best price reasonably obtainable and otherwise observes the requirements of the Act.[172]

The Court may, however, intervene upon clear proof that the tenant for life has exercised a power with the sole object of conferring some benefit upon himself or upon some relative other than the remainderman, as, for example, where he accepts a bribe from a lessee,[173] where he makes an unsuitable investment,[174] or where a widow entitled for life as long as she does not remarry makes a lease to her second intended husband in order to ensure her continued occupation of the premises.[175]

---

[168] *Re Marquis of Ailesbury's Settled Estates* [1892] 1 Ch 506, 536 (Lindley LJ); and see generally Bowen LJ's judgment. 'He must act as an upright, independent and righteous man would act in dealing with the affairs of others': Fry LJ at 546.

[169] *Re Earl of Radnor's Will Trusts* (1890) 45 Ch D 402, 417.

[170] *Re Stamford and Warrington* [1916] 1 Ch 404, 420 (Younger J). TA 2000 extended the powers of the tenant for life in relation to the employment and remuneration of agents, and insurance, subject however to the duty of care under TA 2000, s 1 and Sch 1: SLA 1925, s 107(1A), inserted by TA 2000, s 40(1), Sch 2, Pt II, para 17; above, p 449.

[171] Above, n 168.

[172] Cf the remarks of Pearson J in *Wheelwright v Walker* (1883) 23 Ch D 752, 761–2. See too *England v Public Trustee* (1967) 205 EG 651 where Sellers LJ suggested that SLA 1925 should be amended to provide that notice of an intended sale by the tenant for life should be given to the other beneficiaries under the settlement.

[173] *Chandler v Bradley* [1897] 1 Ch 315.   [174] *Re Hunt's Settled Estates* [1906] 2 Ch 11.

[175] *Middlemas v Stevens* [1901] 1 Ch 574.

(2) Acquisitions by tenant for life

Subject to certain restrictions, a tenant for life may deal with the settled land for his own purposes. When a tenant for life exercises his statutory powers, he is normally dealing with persons who have no connection with the estate, but it may happen that in his private capacity and not as tenant for life he wishes to exercise one of the powers in favour of himself. The possibility of such a dealing between him and the settled estate was first allowed to a restricted extent by the Settled Land Act 1890, but his freedom in this respect was extended by the Act of 1925, which provides that any disposition of the settled land may be made to him, that capital money may be advanced on mortgage to him, and that land may be bought from or exchanged with him.[176]

Since a person cannot negotiate a transaction with himself, it is provided that in all such cases the trustees shall have all the powers of a tenant for life in reference to negotiating and completing the transaction, and the right to enforce any covenants entered into by the tenant for life.[177] Where the tenant for life is himself one of the trustees, he should be a conveying party as well as the person in whose favour the conveyance is made.[178]

D THE TRUSTEES OF THE SETTLEMENT

(1) Definition of Trustees

Section 30(1) of the Settled Land Act 1925 gives a list of five different classes of persons competent to act as trustees of the settlement and arranges them in a binding order of priority as follows:[179]

   (i) The persons who, under the settlement, are trustees with power to sell the settled land.

   A power given to trustees to sell settled land is in fact abortive, since the Act provides that it shall be exercisable not by them, but by the tenant for life.[180] The only effect is to make the persons to whom it is given trustees of the settlement.

  (ii) The persons who are declared by the settlement to be trustees thereof for the purposes of the Settled Land Act.

   These persons will normally constitute the trustees, for an express reservation of the power of sale contemplated by the first paragraph will rarely occur in practice.

---

[176] SLA 1925, s 68(1).   [177] Ibid, s 68(2).
[178] Re Pennant's Will Trusts [1970] Ch 75.   [179] SLA 1925, s 30(1)(i)–(v).   [180] Ibid, s 108(2).

(iii) The persons who, under the settlement, are trustees with a power or duty to sell[181] any *other* land comprised in the settlement that is subject to the same limitations as the land that is being dealt with.

(iv) The persons who, under the settlement, are trustees with a *future* power or duty to sell the settled land.[182]

If, for example, a testator devises his land to his wife for life and after her death to X and Y upon trust to sell the fee simple, then, failing persons qualified under the first three paragraphs, X and Y will be the trustees of the settlement during the wife's life.

(v) The persons appointed by deed by the beneficiaries, provided that the beneficiaries are of full capacity and entitled to dispose of the whole equitable interest in the settled land.

Where a settlement was created by will, or arose by reason of an intestacy, and there were no trustees, the personal representatives of the deceased were trustees of the settlement until others were appointed; but if there was only one personal representative, not being a trust corporation, he had to appoint an additional trustee to act with him.[183]

If at any time there are no trustees as defined above, or if for any reason it is expedient that new trustees should be appointed, the court may appoint fit persons to hold the office.[184]

(2) Compound Settlement

(a) Definition

Where land is settled by a series of separate instruments, the instruments together form one settlement that is called a *compound settlement*.[185] The commonest example of this occurs in the case of a resettlement, which, as we have seen, involves three instruments, that is the original settlement, the disentailment and the resettlement.[186] The principle that the several instruments may be regarded as constituting one settlement becomes important when the tenant for life, in exercise of his statutory power of sale, desires to convey the fee simple to the purchaser free from the limitations of the various instruments.

(b) Conveyance by tenant for life

If, after a resettlement, a sale is effected by the father as first tenant for life he can execute the conveyance in any one of three capacities:

(i) He may convey as tenant for life under the original settlement.

---

181   As amended by TLATA 1996, s 25(1), Sch 3, para 2(9)(b).   182   Ibid.
183   SLA 1925, s 30(3).   184   Ibid, s 34.
185   *Re Ogle's Settled Estates* [1927] 1 Ch 229, 233–4 (Romer J).   186   Above, pp 95–6.

The merit of this is that his conveyance overreaches the limitations of both settlements, and if the purchase money is paid to the trustees of the original settlement the purchaser acquires a title free from the rights of the beneficiaries. The disadvantage is that the tenant for life, since he is acting under the original settlement, cannot avail himself of any additional powers that may have been reserved by the deed of resettlement.

(ii) He may convey as tenant for life under the resettlement.

The position here is reversed, for although he can exercise any additional powers, he cannot convey a title free from the rights of beneficiaries that have been created by the original settlement. Conveyancers sought before 1926 to overcome this difficulty by reciting in the resettlement that the life interest resettled upon the father was 'in restoration and by way of confirmation of' his life interest under the original settlement, but it was only on the eve of a statutory amendment of the law[187] that this device was held to be effective.[188] It had previously been held that 'when once conveyancers have in fact transmuted the old body into a new body, they cannot claim to have retained the old body, whatever incantations they may use in the process'.[189]

(iii) He may convey as tenant for life under the compound settlement.

This plan combines the advantages of the two preceding methods, since the tenant for life can exercise additional powers given by the resettlement and can overreach, within the statutory limits,[190] the limitations of both settlements. Under the old law, however, this method was often open to a fatal objection, for its efficacy depends upon the existence of compound trustees, and before the legislation of 1925, it frequently happened that there were no such trustees. If compound trustees had not been appointed in the original settlement it was impossible to rectify the omission in the resettlement, and, unless all the beneficiaries were of full age (an improbable event), it was necessary to incur the expense of making an application to the court.

(c) Compound trustees

The difficulty that there may be no compound trustees was avoided by the legislation of 1925 which is retrospective and to the following effect:

(i) trustees under an instrument that is a settlement are trustees also of a settlement constituted by that instrument and any subsequent instruments, ie the original trustees are trustees of any compound settlement that later comes into being;[191]

(ii) trustees under a resettlement, where there are no trustees under the original settlement, are trustees of the compound settlement;[192]

---

[187] Below.   [188] *Parr v A–G* [1926] AC 239 (18 December 1925).
[189] *A-G v Parr* [1924] 1 KB 916, 931 (Atkin LJ); *Re Constable's Settled Estates* [1919] 1 Ch 178.
[190] Below, p 1118.   [191] SLA 1925, s 31.
[192] Ibid, as added by LP(A)A 1926, Sch.

(iii) where a resettlement states that a life interest limited to a tenant for life is *in restoration or confirmation* of his interest under the original settlement, he is entitled as of his former interest, and can exercise the statutory powers both under the original settlement and under the resettlement.[193]

(3) Protection of Trustees

It is not the policy of the legislature to subject the trustees of the settlement to a strict liability for the acts of the estate owner. The Settled Land Act 1925 therefore protects them in certain circumstances, and they now enjoy a greater measure of immunity than under the Act of 1882. Thus they are not liable for giving any consent or for not bringing any action that they might have brought, and, in the case of a purchase of land with capital money or in the case of a lease of the settled land by the tenant for life, they are not bound to investigate the propriety of the disposition.[194] Again, they are not liable for having delivered documents of title to the tenant for life, though they are responsible for securities representing capital money.[195] In short, the role of the trustees is to manage and protect the money that is paid to them.[196]

E CAPITAL MONEY

(1) Definition of Capital Money

In several cases the exercise of a statutory power will result in the payment of money to the trustees; this is called *capital money*. And so:

(i) money that becomes due on the sale of the land or of heirlooms;[197]

(ii) fines paid by lessees in consideration of obtaining a tenancy;[198]

(iii) three-quarters or one-quarter (as the case may be) of a mining rent;[199]

(iv) three-quarters of the money arising from the sale of timber by a tenant for life who is impeachable for waste;[200]

(v) consideration paid for an option to purchase or take a lease of the settled land;[201]

---

[193] SLA 1925, s 22(2); *Re Cradock's Settled Estates* [1926] Ch 944.

[194] Ibid, s 97.   [195] Ibid, s 98(3).

[196] It must, however, be remembered that, in exercising their functions the trustees of the settlement have (except as limited by SLA 1925 or by the trust instrument) the general powers and duties of trustees, including the duty of care under TA 2000, s 1 and Sch 1. TA 2000, s 40(1), Sch 2, para 12 repealed SLA 1925, s 96, which had provided that each trustee was answerable only for what he actually receives, notwithstanding his signing any receipt for conformity, and he was not answerable for the acts and defaults of his co-trustees or for any loss not due to his own wilful default.

[197] SLA 1925, s 67(2).   [198] Ibid, s 42(4).   [199] Ibid, s 47; above, p 446.

[200] Ibid, s 66(2).   [201] Ibid, s 51(5).

(vi) damages or compensation received by the tenant for life in respect of a breach of covenant by his lessee or grantee;[202] and

(vii) money raised by a mortgage of the land for the purposes authorised by the Act,[203]

are all examples of capital money.[204] The expression also covers money arising otherwise than under the Act that ought to be treated as capital,[205] such as money paid under a fire insurance policy that the tenant for life was under an obligation to maintain.

(2) Application of Capital Money

As regards the manner in which capital money must be disposed of, the first point is that if raised for some particular purpose, it must be applied accordingly. Thus, money that has been borrowed on mortgage in order to carry out some specific improvement on the land must be so spent. If, however, the money has not been raised for some particular object, but arises, for example, from the sale of the land, it must be applied in one or more of the modes set out in the Settled Land Act 1925.[206] In addition to any special mode permitted by the settlement itself, 21 different modes were originally indicated by the Act.[207] A few of the more important methods will be noted here.

(a) Investment

Wide investment powers are usually included in most modern trusts so that the trustees may make any investment that they could make if they were the absolute owners of the trust. However, the trustees of older trusts may not have been given these powers, in which case their powers are governed by the Trustee Act 2000,[208] which also gives trustees a 'general power of investment': the power to make any kind of investment that they could make if they were absolutely entitled to the assets of the trust, with certain exceptions and always subject to the provisions of the trust instrument. Capital money arising under the settlement is paid to the trustees or into court at the option of the tenant for life, and the investment is made in the name or under the control of the trustees and (subject to the directions contained in the settlement) according to the discretion of the trustees. In exercising the power to invest or apply capital money, the

---

202 Ibid, s 80(1).

203 Ibid, s 71; above, p 446.

204 Similarly, ibid, ss 52, 54(4), 55(2), 56(4), 57(3), 58–61.

205 Ibid, s 81.

206 Ibid, s 73(1).

207 Three have since been repealed: Statute Law Repeals Act 1969, s 1, Sch, Part III; Statute Law Repeals Act 1998, s 1, Sch 1, Part II. Others have been added, not by amendment of SLA itself, but in particular enactments; eg Leasehold Reform Act 1967, s 6(5); Leasehold Reform, Housing and Urban Development Act 1993, ss 9(4), 40(5), Sch 2 para 6; CLRA 2002, s 109(4)(a). The provisions relating to investment were replaced by TA 2000: below.

208 Part II, replacing narrower provisions of Trustee Investments Act 1961; SLA 1925, s 73(1)(i), substituted by TA 2000, s 40(1), Sch 2, Pt II, para 9. See generally H & M paras 18–005 to 18–023; Snell, para 29–007; Law Com No 172, *Trustees' Powers and Duties* (1999), Part II, which recommended the reform of the 1961 Act.

trustees must, so far as practicable, consult the tenant for life and, so far as consistent with the general interest of the settlement, give effect to his wishes. The money, either before or after investment, represents the land from which it originated, and it is held in trust for the same persons for whom the land was held under the settlement and for the same interests, so that, for example, the income arising from the investments is paid to the tenant for life in the same way as the annual profits of the land would have been paid prior to its sale.[209]

(b) Charge on sale of settled land

When the settled land is sold in fee simple or for a term having at least 500 years to run, a sum not exceeding two-thirds of the purchase money may be allowed to remain on mortgage of the land sold.[210]

(c) Purchase of land

Capital money may also be expended in the purchase of land or of mines or minerals convenient to be worked with the settled land, provided that the interest so bought is either the fee simple or a leasehold having at least 60 more years to run.[211] Again, it may be used to finance a person who has agreed to take a lease or grant for building purposes of the settled land, advances being made to him on the security of an equitable mortgage of his building agreement.[212]

(d) Improvements

Lastly, capital money may be used in payment for any improvement authorised by the Settled Land Act 1925.

(1) Payment for improvement

The procedure that governs payment varies according as the capital money is in the hands of the trustees or in court. In the former case the trustees, unless ordered by the court, must not pay for the improvement until they have obtained from a competent engineer or able practical surveyor, employed independently of the tenant for life, a certificate certifying that the improvement has been properly executed and declaring the amount that ought to be paid.[213] Where the capital money is in court, the court may, on a report or certificate of the Secretary of State for Environment, Food and Rural Affairs, or of a competent engineer or able practical surveyor, approved by it, or

---

[209] SLA 1925, s 75, as amended by TA 2000, s 40(1), Sch 2, Pt II, para 10. See *Re Cartwright* [1939] Ch 90. Delegation by the trustees of their power of investment cannot circumvent their duty to consult the tenant for life: ibid, s 75(4B).

[210] Ibid, s 75A, inserted by by TA 2000, s 40(1), Sch 2, Pt II, para 11, replacing TA 1925, s 10(2). The power is exercisable by the tenant for life or statutory owner with the consent of the trustees, subject to the consent of any person required by the trust instrument. The mortgagor must covenant to insure any buildings comprised in the mortgage security.

[211] Ibid, s 73(1)(xi) and (xii).

[212] Ibid, s 73(1)(xviii).

[213] Ibid, s 84(2).

on such other evidence as it may think sufficient, make what order it thinks fit for the application of the money in payment of the improvement.[214]

(2) Repayment of cost

In cases where the work done is not of lasting value it is economically sound that the tenant for life should ultimately restore the amount expended to capital by the creation of a sinking fund out of income, and it is with this object in view that the Act classifies the authorised improvements into the three categories that have already been mentioned.[215] The position is this:

Part I improvements The tenant for life cannot be required to set up a sinking fund.

Part II improvements Before meeting the cost out of capital, the trustees *may* if they think fit, and must if so directed by the court, require that the money shall be repaid to them out of the income of the settled land by not more than 50 half-yearly instalments.[216]

Part III improvements The trustees *must* require the whole cost to be paid out of income in the manner mentioned above.[217]

The court, when in possession of the capital money, is in the same position as the trustees with regard to requiring repayment of the money, except that it is not bound to require repayment in 25 years.

The effect of an order requiring repayment by instalments is that the settled land becomes subject to a yearly rentcharge that takes effect as if it were limited by the settlement prior to the estate of the tenant for life.[218] If, however, the subject matter of the settlement is agricultural land used as such for the purposes of a trade or business,[219] capital money may be applied in the execution of any improvements specified in the Agricultural Holdings Act 1986,[220] without any provision being made for the replacement of the cost out of income.[221] How prejudicial this may be to remaindermen is evident from the inclusion in the specified improvements of the execution of running repairs other than those that the tenant is under an obligation to carry out.[222] In the case of a farm business tenancy of settled land, capital money may be applied in the payment of the landlord's expenses in the making of any physical improvement on the holding or the payment of statutory compensation for any tenant's improvement.[223] The Agricultural Tenancies Act 1995 is silent on whether such expenditure is repayable out of income. It appears, therefore, that this aspect is governed by section 84 of the Settled Land Act 1925.

---

[214] Ibid, s 84(3), amended by SI 2002 No 794.

[215] Ibid, Sch 3; above, p 447. Law Reform Committee 23rd Report, above, para 8.4 said that the provisions of this Schedule 'undoubtedly require modernisation'.

[216] Ibid, s 84(2)(a).   [217] Ibid, s 84(2)(b).

[218] Ibid, s 85.   [219] Agricultural Holdings Act 1986, s 1(4).   [220] Ibid, Sch 7.

[221] Ibid, s 89(1), as amended by TLATA 1996, s 25(2), Sch 4.

[222] *Re Duke of Northumberland* [1951] Ch 202; *Re Sutherland Settlement Trusts* [1953] Ch 792; *Re Lord Brougham and Vaux's Settled Estates* [1954] Ch 24.

[223] Agricultural Tenancies Act 1995, s 22.

The power under the Agricultural Holdings Act 1986 to pay for improvements out of capital was not exercisable by trustees for sale without regard to their duty to preserve the capital.[224] Trustees of a trust of land have the powers of an absolute owner in relation to the land, but must have regard to the rights of the beneficiaries and to general rules such as the duty to hold the balance between income and capital beneficiaries.[225]

II THE TRUST FOR SALE BEFORE 1997

An alternative method of settling land before 1997 was to adopt the device of a trust for sale.

In general this arose where land was transferred by deed or will to trustees with an imperative direction that they were to effect a sale and to hold the proceeds of sale upon certain specified trusts. The manner of its formation has already been described,[226] though it should be recalled that owing to the doctrine of conversion in equity, the land notionally became money, with the result that the interests of the beneficiaries were in the proceeds of sale and not in the land,[227] and were automatically overreached on a sale of the land by the trustees for sale.[228]

It is essential to define a trust for sale. As we have seen, the strict settlement and the trust for sale were mutually exclusive, and successive or limited interests in land created a settlement under the Settled Land Act 1925, unless the land was held upon trust for sale.[229]

A THE DEFINITION OF A TRUST FOR SALE

Until it was amended by the Trusts of Land and Appointment of Trustees Act 1996,[230] the definition in section 205(1)(xxix) of the Law of Property Act 1925 read as follows:

'Trust for sale', in relation to land, means an immediate binding trust for sale, whether or not exercisable at the request or with the consent of any person, and with or without a power or discretion to postpone the sale.

We must consider the meaning of the words 'trust', 'immediate', and 'binding'.

---

[224] *Re Wynn* [1955] 1 WLR 940; *Re Boston's Will Trusts* [1956] Ch 395.
[225] TLATA 1996, s 6(1), (5), (6), below, p 479.
[226] Above, pp 103–5.
[227] See *Irani Finance Ltd v Singh* [1971] Ch 59, 80 (Cross LJ); below, pp 465 ff.
[228] Above, pp 104–5; below, pp 1068–9, 1114–17.   [229] SLA 1925, s 1(7); above, p 432.
[230] TLATA 1996, s 25(1), Sch 4 repealed the words 'binding' and the phrase 'with or without a power or discretion to postpone the sale'.

(1) Trust

An instrument did not create a trust for sale unless it contained a direction imposing a duty upon the trustees to sell. A *duty* to sell must always be distinguished from a *power* to sell. A trust is obligatory upon the trustee, a power leaves it to his discretion whether he will sell or not. It was, indeed, enacted that a disposition coming into operation after 1925 that directed that the trustees should *either retain or sell* land should constitute a trust for sale with power to postpone the sale,[231] but, apart from this statutory provision, whether an instrument created a trust or conferred a power was a question that could be answered only by construing its terms. What was in form a trust for sale might be nothing more than a discretionary power; what was in form a power might, when properly construed, be an imperative trust.[232] The distinction is of great importance in conveyancing, for if what was given to the trustees was a mere power of sale, there was no trust for sale but the land was settled land within the meaning of the Settled Land Act 1925; and the power of sale was exercisable not by them but by the tenant for life.[233] The trustees became trustees within that Act, and the proper person to make title was the tenant for life.[234]

(2) Immediate

The word 'immediate' did not mean that the land must be sold at once, for power to postpone the sale was implied in every case, unless a contrary intention appeared.[235] Its significance was to distinguish a trust for sale from a *future* trust for sale. A future trust was not immediately effective, and where it was imposed upon land, the trustees became trustees for the purposes of the Settled Land Act, not trustees for sale.[236] Thus, if land was devised to a wife for life and after her death upon trust for sale, the land *during her life* was settled land and was governed by the Settled Land Act.[237]

---

[231] LPA 1925, s 25(4).

[232] *Re Newbould* (1913) 110 LT 6 (Swinfen Eady LJ): cf *Re White's Settlement* [1930] 1 Ch 179. For the distinction between a power and a trust, see H & M, paras 2-021 to 2-027, ch 6; Maudsley and Burn, *Trusts and Trustees* (7th edn, 2008), pp 43 ff; *Farwell on Powers* (3rd edn, 1916); Maclean, *Trusts and Powers* (1989); *Thomas on Powers* (1998)

[233] SLA 1925, s 108(2).

[234] Ibid, ss 30(1)(i), 108, 109; above, p 455. The position before 1926 involved a conflict of powers, since the tenant for life had a statutory, the trustees an express, power of sale. SLA 1882, s 56 provided that in such a case the tenant for life should be unfettered in the exercise of the power, and that the trustees should not sell without his consent.

[235] LPA 1925, s 25(1).   [236] SLA 1925, s 30(1)(iv).

[237] *Re Jackson's Settled Estate* [1902] 1 Ch 258; *Re Hanson* [1928] Ch 96; *Re Herklots' Will Trusts* [1964] 1 WLR 583; *Re Nierop's Will Trusts* (Ch D, 23 April 1986), discussed in *Williams on Wills* (7th edn, 1995), pp 1008, 1174-8 (trust to sell with consent of beneficiary combined with trust to permit beneficiary to reside while property remains unsold qualified as trust for sale).

(3) Binding

In its natural meaning 'binding trust' is tautologous. A trust is different from a power because it is obligatory, not discretionary: the trustees are bound to sell the land ultimately, though the actual time of the sale is left to their discretion. A trust that imposes a duty upon the trustees as distinct from one that gives them a mere power may rightly be described as binding. Yet the word was inserted in a statutory definition and the courts searched for a secondary meaning. Romer J suggested that, if it was not surplusage, the object of its insertion might be to emphasise the exclusion of a revocable trust for sale.[238] The cases in which the word was discussed were concerned with the situation where settled land had been resettled by way of trust for sale before the Settled Land Act settlement had been exhausted, and the judges sought to find a solution in the word 'binding' to the problem of whether the unexhausted settlement had precedence over the trust for sale or vice versa.

In Re Leigh's Settled Estates:[239]

> X was tenant in tail of settled land which was subject to an equitable jointure rentcharge in favour of her mother. In 1923 X disentailed and conveyed the fee simple, still subject to the charge, to trustees upon trust for sale. The question arose whether in 1926 the land was settled land or whether it was held upon trust for sale.

It was clearly settled land[240] unless the conveyance made by X in 1923 was an 'immediate binding trust for sale' within the meaning of the Law of Property Act 1925. Tomlin J held that the land remained settled land and was not subject to a binding trust for sale, since in his opinion the word 'binding' was not used to indicate that the trustees for sale were bound to sell sooner or later but referred to the interests that would be bound, that is overreached, when the trustees conveyed. To be 'binding', the trust must enable the trustees to execute a conveyance that would bind the whole subject matter of the settlement, that is interests prior to the trust as well as those arising under its provisions. This test was not satisfied in the present case, for a conveyance in 1923 could not overreach the widow's prior equitable charge. To do this it would be necessary to obtain the additional powers of overreaching by creating an ad hoc trust for sale,[241] and this could only be done by replacing the trustees by a trust corporation or by having them approved by the court.[242]

This restricted view of the scope of the ordinary trust for sale was implicitly[243] and expressly rejected.[244] In Re Parker's Settled Estates[245] Romer J came to the conclusion

---

[238] Re Parker's Settled Estates [1928] Ch 247, 261.   [239] [1926] Ch 852.
[240] SLA 1925, s 1(1)(v).   [241] LPA 1925, s 2(2); below, pp 1119 ff.
[242] After the trustees had been approved by the court Tomlin J upheld the trust for sale: Re Leigh's Settled Estates (No 2) [1927] 2 Ch 13.
[243] Re Ryder and Steadman's Contract [1927] 2 Ch 62 (land vested in X, Y and Z as tenants in common subject to an equitable jointure rentcharge in favour of A. CA held that after 1925 X, Y and Z held on a statutory trust for sale although they could not overreach A's prior equitable interest).
[244] Re Parker's Settled Estates [1928] Ch 247; see (1928) 65 LJ News 248, 272, 293 (JML).
[245] Above.

that there could be a binding trust for sale notwithstanding that the trustees for sale were unable to overreach all charges having, under the settlement, priority to the trust for sale. He then held, however, that land could not be described as held upon trust for sale so as to take it out of the Settled Land Act unless the *whole legal estate* was vested in the trustees. He was of the opinion that if there were prior *equitable* interests the trust for sale excluded the Settled Land Act, since the whole legal estate was in the trustees; but if there were prior *legal* estates or interests then the trust for sale was not sufficient to exclude that Act, since the *whole* legal estate was not in the trustees. In *Re Parker's Settled Estates* there was a prior legal term of years to secure portions and accordingly the land remained settled land.[246]

B THE DOCTRINE OF CONVERSION

As we have seen, the doctrine of conversion applied as soon as a trust for sale came into operation.[247] As a result of this doctrine, the interests of the beneficiaries under the trust became automatically interests in the proceeds of the sale of land and not in the land itself. Cross LJ said:[248]

The whole purpose of the trust for sale is to make sure, by shifting the equitable interests away from the land and into the proceeds of sale, that a purchaser of the land takes free from the equitable interests. To hold these to be equitable interests in the land itself would be to frustrate this purpose. Even to hold that they have equitable interests in the land for a limited period, namely, until the land is sold, would, we think, be inconsistent with the trust for sale being an 'immediate' trust for sale working an immediate conversion, which is what the Law of Property Act 1925 envisages (see section 205(1)(xxix)).[249]

A simple example of the effect of the doctrine is that, where a testator had left all his personal estate to P and all his real estate to R, an interest under a trust for sale passed to P and not to R.[250] The full logic of the doctrine of conversion was not, however, applied by the courts. There were various situations where an interest under a trust for sale was treated as if it were an interest in land. Thus, a beneficiary under a trust for sale could, with the consent of the other beneficiaries, if he and they were all adult and of sound mind, terminate the trust and call for a transfer of the land itself;[251] he was a

---

246 See also *Re Norton* [1929] 1 Ch 84, (1929) 67 LJ News 24 at 44 (JML). Romer J held that there was no binding trust for sale since the trustees could not call for the legal estate from personal representatives due to a prior *equitable* charge: SLA 1925, s 7(5); *Re Beaumont Settled Estates* [1937] 2 All ER 353; *Re Sharpe's Deed of Release* [1939] Ch 51.

247 Above, p 104; (1971) 34 MLR 441 (SM Cretney); [1971] CLJ 44 (MJ Prichard); [1978] Conv 194 (H Forrest); [1981] Conv 108 (AE Boyle); [1986] Conv 415 (J Warburton); M & B (6th edn, 1992), pp 292–301. See generally (1984) 100 LQR 86 (S Anderson); Law Com No 181, *Trusts of Land* (1989), paras 3.4–3.7.

248 *Irani Finance Ltd v Singh* [1971] Ch 59, 80. For a critical analysis of the statutory provisions on overreaching and its relationship to the doctrine of conversion, see [1990] CLJ 277 (C Harpum).

249 Above, p 462. See *City of London Building Society v Flegg* [1988] AC 54, 82, where Lord Oliver of Aylmerton quoted Cross LJ verbatim as 'a useful general analysis'. The case is discussed below, p 1115.

250 *Re Kempthorne* [1930] 1 Ch 268; *Re Newman* [1930] 2 Ch 409; *Re Cook* [1948] Ch 212.

251 *Saunders v Vautier* (1841) 4 Beav 115, below, p 581.

'person interested' who might apply to the court for an order relating to the land under section 30 of the Law of Property Act 1925;[252] in the case of a statutory trust for sale, he had a right to be consulted by the trustees as to the exercise of their powers over the land;[253] and, within the discretion of the court, he might be protected from eviction from the land by the holder of the legal estate.[254]

The nature of a beneficiary's interest also arose in the context of the interpretation of a statute. The question was whether a reference in a statute to 'land' included an interest under a trust for sale. Sometimes the statute dealt expressly with the point; as in the Limitation Act 1980, where land included 'an interest in the proceeds of the sale of land held upon trust for sale'.[255] Even though the Law of Property Act 1925 contains no such provision, it was held that a contract for the sale of a beneficial interest under a trust for sale was a contract for the sale of 'land or any interest in land' within section 40 and so required a memorandum for its enforceability.[256] Similarly, under the Land Registration Act 1925, a beneficiary was held to be a person interested in land within section 54(1) and thereby entitled to lodge a caution to protect his interest as a minor interest;[257] and also to have 'an interest subsisting in reference to' registered land for the purpose of an overriding interest under section 70(1)(g).[258] The latter point was decided by the House of Lords in *Williams & Glyn's Bank Ltd v Boland*,[259] where it was held unanimously that the wife's interest was valid; her interest under the trust for sale was capable of existing as an overriding interest.[260] It was 'an interest subsisting in reference to' registered land. Lord Wilberforce said that: 'to describe the interests of spouses in a house jointly bought to be lived in as a matrimonial home as merely an interest in proceeds of sale, or rents and profits until sale is just a little unreal'.[261]

C THE POWERS OF THE TRUSTEES FOR SALE

The powers of the trustees for sale were set out in the Law of Property Act 1925.

---

[252] Below, p 469.   [253] LPA 1925, s 26(3); below, p 469.

[254] *Bull v Bull* [1955] 1 QB 234 (order for possession refused); *Cook v Cook* [1962] P 235; *Gurasz v Gurasz* [1970] P 11; cf *Barclay v Barclay* [1970] 2 QB 677 (order for possession granted).

[255] S 38(1); these words were repealed by TLATA 1996, s 25(2), Sch 4, para 1.

[256] *Cooper v Critchley* [1955] Ch 431; (1955) 71 LQR 177 (REM); *Steadman v Steadman* [1974] QB 161, 167. S 40 has been repealed in respect of contracts entered into after 26 September 1989: LP(MP)A 1989, s 2(8), below, p 966. The replacement s 2(6) expressly includes 'any interest in or over the proceeds of sale of land'. Cf *Re Rayleigh Weir Stadium* [1954] 1 WLR 786 (such a contract held not registrable under LCA 1925, where the definition of land expressly excludes an undivided share in land s 17(1)). See also *Cedar Holdings Ltd v Green* [1981] Ch 129.

[257] S 3(xv); *Elias v Mitchell* [1972] Ch 652; cf *Lynton International Ltd v Noble* (1991) 63 P & CR 452 (contractual right to share in proceeds of sale).

[258] Above, p 139; below, pp 1105–7.

[259] [1981] AC 487, 507; below, p 1106.

[260] Her interest could not be valid as a minor interest, since it had not been so protected on the register. Her only hope was in the safety-net provision of s 70(1)(g).

[261] [1981] AC 487, 507. See also Ormrod LJ in CA [1979] Ch 312, 316, describing the docrine as 'in effect a legal fiction, at least in so far as the implied trusts are concerned'.

(1) Postponement of Sale

Under section 25 a power to postpone a sale was implied in every trust for sale unless a contrary intention appeared, and the trustees were not liable for an indefinite postponement in the absence of an express direction to the contrary.[262] A disregard of such an express direction did not, however, prejudice a purchaser of a legal estate, for he was not to be concerned with directions that relate to postponement.[263] The power to postpone must, like any other power given to trustees, be exercised unanimously by them;[264] if there was disagreement between the trustees for sale, the court might at its discretion direct them to carry out the sale.[265]

(2) Management and Sale

The power of postponement might lead to the land remaining unsold for a considerable period, and it was essential that during the interval between the creation of the trust and the actual sale, the trustees should possess powers of disposition and management. These were given to them in abundance by the Law of Property Act 1925.

(a) Settled Land Act powers

Despite the fundamental distinction between a settlement and a trust for sale, it was provided by section 28 of the Law of Property Act 1925 that the trustees for sale, in relation to the land and the proceeds of sale, should have all the powers both of a tenant for life and of trustees of a settlement under the Settled Land Act 1925.[266] Thus, for example, they might grant leases, raise money on mortgage for improvements and, so long as they retained some land, might invest the proceeds of sale in the purchase of other land.[267] It was further provided by the same section that they should have the powers of management that were exercisable by trustees under section 102 of the Settled Land Act 1925 during the minority of a tenant for life of *settled* land.[268] Although, in the case of settled land, these powers given by section 102 were exercisable only during the minority of the tenant for life, they might be exercised by trustees for sale whether there was a minority or not.[269]

---

[262] LPA 1925, s 25(1), (2); *Re Rooke* [1953] Ch 716 (direction by testator to sell farm 'as soon as possible after my death' held to be contrary intention); *Re Atkins' Will Trusts* [1974] 1 WLR 761.

[263] Ibid, s 25(2).

[264] *Re Roth* (1896) 74 LT 50; *Re Hilton* [1909] 2 Ch 548; *Re Mayo* [1943] Ch 302; cf *Re 90 Thornhill Rd, Tolworth, Surrey* [1970] Ch 261 (sale not ordered under SLA 1925, s 93 when joint tenants for life disagreed as to the exercise of the power of sale). A power to act by a majority may be given in the trust deed, but it will be strictly construed: *Re Butlin's Settlement Trusts* (1974) 118 SJ 757; see also [1976] Ch 251, 253, 259.

[265] LPA 1925, s 30; below, pp 469, 489.

[266] Ibid, s 28(1), as amended by LP(A)A 1926, s 7. For the SLA powers, see above, pp 443–50.

[267] *Re Wakeman* [1947] Ch 607; *Re Wellsted's Will Trusts* [1949] Ch 296.   [268] Below, p 1025.

[269] *Re Gray* [1927] 1 Ch 242.

(b) Delegation

In many cases the trustees for sale would not wish themselves to exercise the powers that were given to them by section 28. Section 29(1), therefore, provided that while the land remained unsold they might revocably and in writing delegate from time to time the *powers of leasing, of accepting surrenders of leases, and of management* to any person of full age (not merely being an annuitant), who was beneficially entitled in possession to the net rents and profits for his life or for any less period.[270] He must exercise the powers so delegated only in the names and on behalf of the trustees.[271] They were not liable for his acts or defaults. He alone was personally liable and in relation to the exercise of a power was deemed to be in the position of a trustee.[272] Thus, pending sale, the welfare of the land might be entrusted to the person most anxious to promote it. It must be noticed, however, that only those powers that were set out in section 29 might be delegated. The legal estate remained in the trustees for sale, and only they could convey the fee simple. That was the basis of their trust.

(c) Consents

The exercise of their powers by the trustees for sale, including that of sale itself, might be made subject to the consent of any persons.[273]

If the consent of not more than two persons was required, a purchaser[274] must ascertain that the requirement had been satisfied. If, however, the consent of more than two persons was required his obligation was satisfied if any two of the persons specified gave their consent.[275] If the person whose consent was required was not sui juris or became subject to a disability, his consent, in favour of a purchaser, should not be deemed to be required. But in the case of a minor the trustees should obtain the consent of his parent or guardian, and in the case of a mental patient that of the receiver.[276]

(d) Curtailment of powers

As we have seen, the powers of a tenant for life under the Settled Land Act 1925 could not be cut down by any provisions inserted in the settlement.[277] There is no similar provision in the Law of Property Act 1925 for the curtailment of the powers of trustees for sale. Indeed their power of sale could be restricted by the imposition of a requirement of consent and the power to postpone sale might be excluded by a

---

[270] LPA 1925, s 29(1); *Stratford v Syrett* [1958] 1 QB 107; *Napier v Light* (1974) 236 EG 273.

[271] Ibid, s 29(2).   [272] Ibid, s 29(3).

[273] If they refuse to give it, any person interested may apply to the court for an order of sale: LPA 1925, s 30; *Re Beale's Settlement Trusts* [1932] 2 Ch 15.

[274] As defined by LPA 1925, s 205(1)(xxi).   [275] Ibid, s 26(1).

[276] Ibid, s 26(2) as amended by the Mental Health Act 1959, s 149, Sch 7.

[277] SLA 1925, s 106; above, p 451.

contrary intention. Apart from these cases, however, it would appear that the powers of trustees for sale, like those of a tenant for life, were irreducible.[278]

(e) Consultation

We must now consider how far the trustees for sale were required to observe the wishes of the beneficiaries. Under a statutory trust for sale[279] it was their duty, so far as practicable, to consult the persons of full age for the time being beneficially interested in possession in the rents and profits of the land until sale, and, so far as was consistent with the general interest of the trust, to give effect to the wishes of such persons, or, in the case of dispute, of the majority according to the value of their combined interests. A purchaser was not, however, concerned to see that this provision had been complied with.[280] It did not apply to express trusts for sale, unless a contrary intention appeared in the instrument creating the trust. Thus a settlor or testator might either give the trustees for sale complete freedom of discretion or compel them to consult the beneficiaries; but in the case of a statutory trust for sale there must be consultation.[281]

(f) Application to court

Finally, if the trustees for sale refused to sell or to exercise any of the powers conferred on them by sections 28 and 29 of the Law of Property Act 1925 or if any requisite consent could not be obtained, any person interested might apply to the court under section 30 for an order directing the trustees to act accordingly, and the court might make such order as it thought fit.[282] The court had the widest possible discretion under this section, and would take into account all the circumstances of the case. In order to qualify as a person interested, the applicant must have some proprietary interest in the land.[283]

The powers of the court under section 30 were entirely discretionary. In exercising this discretion the court had regard to the underlying purpose of the trust for sale and would not order a sale if some purpose of the trust remained to be discharged. Thus

---

[278] See *Re Davies' Will Trusts* [1932] 1 Ch 530 (life interest to nephew 'so long as he shall reside upon and assist in the management of the farm' held not forfeitable by exercise of powers inconsistent with such condition. The decision related to statutory trusts for sale under LPA 1925, s 35, but the principle would appear to apply to express trusts for sale as well; [1978] Conv 229 (P Smith)).

[279] Below, p 470.

[280] LPA 1925, s 26(3), as substituted by LP(A)A 1926, Sched (1973) 117 SJ 518 (AM Prichard).

[281] If the trustees failed to consult the beneficiaries it might be a breach of trust; *Re Jones* [1931] 1 Ch 375, 377 (Bennett J); *Crawley BC v Ure* [1996] QB 13 (notice to quit given to landlord by one joint tenant without consultation with other joint tenant not a 'positive' act for which consultation was necessary, and therefore, not a breach of trust).

[282] See *Dennis v McDonald* [1981] 1 WLR 810, 819 (Purchas J); affd [1982] Fam 63 (where an order for sale was refused, but one co-owner was ordered to pay an occupation rent to the other co-owner); *Bernard v Josephs* [1982] Ch 391, 411 (Kerr LJ); Law Com No 181, *Trusts of Land* (1989), paras 12.6–12.13.

[283] *Stevens v Hutchinson* [1953] Ch 299, 305 (chargee); *Re Solomon* [1967] Ch 573 (trustee in bankruptcy); see also *First National Securities Ltd v Hegerty* [1985] QB 850; *Harman v Glencross* [1986] Fam 81 (judgment creditor under Charging Orders Act 1979, s 3 (5)). For an application by a trustee in bankruptcy, see Insolvency Act 1986, s 336 and the 14th edn of this book, p 231.

the court would refuse a sale on an application by A, if he had covenanted to sell only with the consents of B and C.[284] And likewise the court would refuse a sale where land had been acquired with some particular purpose in mind, such as the joint occupation of a house and that purpose still subsisted.[285]

> Thus, if the purpose was that the house should be the matrimonial home, then so long as that purpose is still alive, the court will not allow the husband or the wife arbitrarily to insist on a sale. But if the parties are divorced and in consequence the contemplated purpose is dead, then the trust for sale will take effect, subject always to the discretion of the court to postpone it.[286]

Litigation was mainly concerned with the matrimonial or quasi-matrimonial home, where, on the breakdown of the relationship, A wanted the house to be sold in order to realise his or her share of the proceeds of sale, and B wanted it to be retained as accommodation for himself or herself and the children, if any.

In the matrimonial homes[287] cases the main question was whether the marriage still subsisted in law[288] or in fact.[289] The court had regard to all the circumstances of the case, and, in particular, to the provision of a home for young and dependent children. Other factors to be taken into account included the conduct of the parties, their financial circumstances and the contribution that each has made to the acquisition of the property. Where children were concerned, however, there were conflicting approaches in the Court of Appeal. In *Re Evers' Trust*[290] the underlying purpose of the trust was to provide a *family* home, so that a sale would not be ordered while that purpose still existed; in *Re Holliday*[291] the purpose of the trust was to provide a *matrimonial* home and the interests of the children were only to be taken into account 'so far as they affect the equities in the matter as between the two persons entitled to the beneficial interests in the property'. It has been suggested that the conflict was really a matter of language rather than substance.[292]

D STATUTORY TRUSTS FOR SALE

A trust for sale might either be created expressly by act of parties or be imposed by statute. The following is a summary of the circumstances in which a statutory trust

---

284 *Re Buchanan-Wollaston's Conveyance* [1939] Ch 738; *Re Citro* [1991] Ch 142, M & B p 537; cf *Abbey National plc v Moss* [1994] 1 FLR 307.

285 *Bull v Bull* [1955] 1 QB 234; cf *Barclay v Barclay* [1970] 2 QB 677.

286 *Bedson v Bedson* [1965] 2 QB 666, 678 (Lord Denning MR).

287 See generally Cretney and Masson, *Principles of Family Law* (6th edn, 1996), pp 162–8; M & B (6th edn, 1992), pp 238–58.

288 *Jones v Challenger* [1961] 1 QB 176.

289 *Rawlings v Rawlings* [1964] P 398; *Re Solomon* [1967] Ch 573; *Bernard v Josephs* [1982] Ch 391 (cohabitees).

290 [1980] 1 WLR 1327.

291 [1981] Ch 405. The final judgment was delivered on the day after *Re Evers' Trust* was heard, and neither case refers to the other. See (1980) 77 LSG 288 (AJ Oakley and D Marks); [1981] Conv 79 (A Sydenham); (1981) 97 LQR 200 (C Hand); (1982) 98 LQR 519 (F Webb); [1984] Conv 103 (MP Thompson).

292 *Cousins v Dzosens* The Times, 12 December 1981. See also *Chhokar v Chhokar* [1984] FLR 313.

for sale was imposed by the 1925 legislation in pursuance of its policy to simplify conveyancing by separating the legal estate from the equitable interests:

   (i) Where an estate owner died intestate.[293]

   (ii) Where property vested in trustees by way of security became discharged from the debtor's right of redemption.[294]

If, for example, trust money had been invested in a mortgage of a legal estate and the right of the mortgagor to redeem the land had been extinguished under the Limitation Act 1980[295] or by a foreclosure order,[296] the land, being thus subjected to a trust for sale, was regarded as converted into money and it would pass as such under a beneficiary's will.

In the following cases an express trust for sale was usually created, but, if not, a statutory trust for sale arose automatically.

   (iii) Where land was devised or conveyed to two or more persons as tenants in common.[297]

   (iv) Where land was devised or conveyed beneficially to two or more persons as joint tenants.[298]

   (v) Where a legal estate was conveyed to a minor jointly with one or more persons of full age other than trustees or mortgagees.[299]

   (vi) Where the trustees of a *personalty* settlement or trustees for sale of land purchased land in virtue of a power contained in the settlement.[300] The effect of this, having regard to the doctrine of conversion, was that the land remained money in the eyes of equity and thus the original character of the settlement was preserved.

III DEFECTS IN THE DUAL SYSTEM OF SETTLEMENTS

The criticism of the existing system of settlements made by the Law Commission in its Reports on *Trusts of Land*[301] and *Overreaching: Beneficiaries in Occupation*[302] was summarised in the Notes on Clauses to the Trusts of Land and Appointment of Trustees Bill (HL) as follows:

   21. The Law Commission criticised the existing law on three grounds:

     (a) it is unnecessarily complex, and the provisions governing strict settlements particularly so;

---

[293] AEA 1925, s 33(1).
[294] LPA 1925, s 31(1).
[295] Below, p 837.
[296] Below, p 863.
[297] LPA 1925, s 34(2), (3); below, p 502.
[298] Ibid, s 36(1); below, p 505.
[299] Ibid, s 19(2); below, p 1020.
[300] Ibid, s 32(1). The statutory trust could be excluded by a contrary intention.
[301] Law Com No 181 (1989).
[302] Law Com No 188 (1989).

(b) it is ill-suited to the conditions of modern property ownership, and the imposition of a trust for sale in all cases of conveyance to more than one person particularly so;

(c) it is liable to give rise to unforeseen conveyancing complications.

22. The complexity of the existing law was the main criticism. The Commission argued that the existence of a dual system with two different ways of creating successive interests is unnecessarily complicated, given the very limited difference in substance between the two systems. It argued further that the machinery of the Settled Land Act is in any event unnecessarily complex and cumbersome for its purpose, requiring both a vesting deed and a trust instrument for its creation (and thus requiring a string of subsidiary vesting deeds where additional land is brought into the settlement or a new principal vesting deed where land is brought into a settlement presently containing only capital money); requiring special personal representatives to deal with settled land where the settlement still subsists after the death of a tenant for life (and thus requiring those responsible for administering the estate to distinguish between land which ceased to be settled on the deceased's death and that which remains settled); requiring complicated and detailed provisions for strict settlements to come about in such cases as a conveyance to a minor; and giving priority to the lesser-used and more complicated Settled Land Act regime (so that an unwary grantor or testator, or one acting without legal advice, is likely to create a strict settlement inadvertently if he wishes to include any element of successive ownership in his disposition).

23. The Commission also criticised the co-ownership trust for sale as being an inappropriate legal vehicle for modern home ownership. At the time of the 1925 property legislation, owner-occupation of dwellings in England and Wales was far less usual than it is today (the proportion of owner-occupied dwellings growing from 7% in 1914 to 43% in 1938 and 66% by 1992), and where it did exist, it was much less likely that a house would be purchased in joint names. The sort of co-ownership envisaged by the 1925 legislation would have tended to arise in other contexts, for example property left by a testator to his children in equal shares, where a sale would be the most likely outcome. In contrast, under modern conditions most co-ownership of property involves a shared home, and the imposition in such circumstances of a duty to sell (albeit with an implied power to postpone sale) seemed to the Law Commission to be inconsistent with the interests and intentions of the majority of owners who buy a house to use, not purely to hold it pending sale as an investment asset.

24. The Commission considered the unsuitability of the trust for sale to be compounded by the doctrine of conversion, it being even more artificial to treat a person with a half-share in his house as having an interest only in the proceeds of sale and not in the house itself. The courts have made efforts to reduce this artificiality by developing the principle of 'collateral purpose' (that is the purpose of providing a family home, collateral to the principal purpose of sale) under which the court may refuse to order a sale in the case of dispute, and have done the same with the doctrine of conversion: this has, however, had the unfortunate result that in some cases an interest under a trust for sale will count as an interest in land while in others it will not, and it may not be clear which is to apply, since there are conflicting Court of Appeal authorities.

25. The Commission's third main head of criticism was the tendency of the existing dual system to cause conveyancing difficulties, particularly arising from 'imperfect' or

'inadvertent' strict settlements, where in some cases involving more informal personal rights of occupation it may not be apparent even with the benefit of legal advice that a settlement has been created until after the conveyance. Particular problems may arise where there is no vesting deed, resulting in 'paralysis' of the conveyance, or where the conveyance is taken from the wrong person (that is from the tenant for life rather than the trustees).

In the next chapter we shall consider the reforms made by the Trusts of Land and Appointment of Trustees Act 1996, which were designed to address the defects of the old system of settlements and trusts for sale.

13

THE TRUST OF LAND

Summary

I THE TRUST OF LAND

The Trusts of Land and Appointment of Trustees Act 1996, which came into force on 1 January 1997, changed the structure of settlements.[1] The object of the Act is to replace the two methods of settling land,[2] the strict settlement and the trust for sale, by a single system—the *trust of land*, modelled on the trust for sale—which can be used as the framework for the creation not only of successive beneficial interests but also of concurrent interests in land.

---

[1] For commentaries on the Act, see TLATA Bill (House of Lords) *Notes on Clauses*; Whitehouse and Hassall, *Trusts of Land, Trustee Delegation and the Trustee Act 2000* (2001) (a very useful commentary that is referred to throughout this chapter); Barraclough and Matthews, *The Trusts of Land and Appointment of Trustees Act 1996* (1996); Kenny and Kenny, *The Trusts of Land and Appointment of Trustees Act 1996* (1997) (with the principal sections of the 1925 legislation as amended, and Law Com No 181, *Trusts of Land* (1988)); Sydenham and Sydenham, *Trusts of Land—The New Law* (1996). See also Emmet, ch 22; R & R, ch 37; [1996] Conv 401 (AJ Oakley); 411 (N Hopkins); (1998) 61 MLR 56 (LM Clements); [1999] Liverpool LR 21(1), pp 97–121 (M Draper).

[2] See Ch 12, Section I (strict settlement); Section II (pre-1997 trust for sale), above, pp 431 ff. For criticism of the dual system, see above, pp 471–3.

No new strict settlement can be created or be deemed to be made after 1996, but existing strict settlements remain, and, where a settlement already existed before 1997, any later resettlement creates a new strict settlement. However, a trust for sale created before 1997 takes effect as a trust of land. Unlike a strict settlement, a trust for sale can still be created after 1996 but with important modifications.

A NO NEW STRICT SETTLEMENTS AFTER 1996

No new strict settlements can be created under the Settled Land Act 1925 after 1996.[3] Schedule 1 to the Trusts of Land and Appointment of Trustees Act 1996 provides for certain situations where the Settled Land Act 1925 imposed a strict settlement. As from 1 January 1997 a trust of land is imposed instead where:

(i) an attempt is made to convey a legal estate to a minor alone, or to two or more minors; or to a minor or two or more minors and to another person, or other persons who are not of full age;[4]

(ii) land is charged voluntarily, or in consideration of marriage, or by way of family arrangement, with the payment of a rentcharge for the life of a person or a shorter period;[5]

(iii) land is held on charitable, ecclesiastical or public trusts;[6]

(iv) an attempt is made to grant an entailed interest (in which case the property is held in trust absolutely for the grantee);[7] and

(v) a settlement ceases to be a settlement because no property is subject to it (any property that is, or later becomes, subject to it is held in trust for those entitled under the settlement).

B MEANING OF TRUST OF LAND

The definition of a trust of land is widely drawn so as to include all types of trust, however and whenever created. Section 1 of the Act provides:

(1) (a) 'trust of land' means (subject to subsection (3)) any trust of property which consists of or includes land, and

(b) 'trustees of land' means trustees of a trust of land.

(2) The reference in subsection (1)(a) to a trust—

(a) is to any description of trust (whether express, implied, resulting or constructive[8]), including a trust for sale[9] and a bare trust,[10] and

---

[3] TLATA 1996, s 2(1).   [4] Below, p 1023.   [5] Above, p 435.   [6] Below, p 1037.
[7] Above, p 434.
[8] For such trusts in the cases of co-ownership, see below, p 512. On resulting trusts and registered land, see [1999] Conv 382 (D Wilde).
[9] Below, p 476.   [10] Below, p 478.

(b) includes a trust created, or arising, before the commencement of this Act.

(3) The reference to land in subsection (1)(a) does not include land which (despite section 2) is settled land or which is land to which the Universities and College Estates Act 1925 applies.

We must first consider the trust for sale and the bare trust as examples of a trust of land.

(1) Trust for Sale

(a) Definition

The definition of a trust for sale has been amended retrospectively and now reads as follows:[11]

'Trust for sale', in relation to land, means an immediate trust for sale, whether or not exercisable at the request or with the consent of any person: 'trustees for sale' mean the persons (including a personal representative) holding land on trust for sale.

(b) Express trust for sale as a trust of land

After 1996 a trust for sale can still be expressly created, but it takes effect as a trust of land. It has been suggested that it may be desirable to create an express trust for sale where there is a trust in the residue clause of a will, or where there is a conveyance to co-owners.[12] In any event section 1 of the Act ensures that if a trust for sale is created in ignorance of the new legislation it will be valid under it.

Before 1997, section 25 of the Law of Property Act 1925 gave to trustees for sale the power to postpone sale indefinitely, unless a contrary intention was expressed in the trust instrument.[13] After 1996 this power still exists but under section 4(1) cannot be excluded by the settlor. The sale can only be postponed if the trustees for sale unanimously decide to exercise the power;[14] if they are not unanimous, then the land must be sold.[15]

An express trust for sale created before 1997 becomes a trust of land. There are, however, differences between a trust for sale created before 1997, and a trust for sale created after 1996. The trustees under a pre-1997 trust for sale retain the *duty* to sell

[11] LPA 1925, s 205(1), as amended by TLATA 1996, s 25(2), Sch 4. For the original definition in LPA 1925, which included the word 'binding' between 'immediate' and 'trust', as well as the words 'and with or without a power at discretion to postpone the sale' at the end , see above, p 461. The apparent tautology of the requirement that the trust be 'binding' caused difficulty: above, pp 464–5; trusts are by their very nature binding. It may be necessary to interpret 'binding' when deciding whether there is a pre-existing strict settlement before 1997, but this will be very rare.

[12] W & H, paras 2.26, 2.159, 6.41; Sydenham and Sydenham, *Trusts of Land*, para 3.8.3; [1998] Conv 84 (R Mitchell), doubting whether a trust for sale should continue to be used in a will.

[13] Above, p 467. S 25 was repealed by TLATA 1996, s 25(2), Sch 4.

[14] *Re Mayo* [1943] Ch 302 (where the power to retain required unanimity). Charitable trustees may act by a majority: *Re Whiteley* [1910] 1 Ch 600, 607.

[15] Subject to an order of the court under TLATA 1996, ss 14 and 15, below, pp 488–90.

imposed on them by the settlor, but this duty is subject to the mandatory power to postpone sale indefinitely. Presumably, if the trustees retain this duty, there will have to be a sale if they do not unanimously exercise their discretion to postpone it. Further, their duty to sell does not prevent them from delegating the duty, since they have a statutory power to delegate their functions under the trust.[16] And finally the settlor or surviving settlors may, if they wish, opt into the consultation provisions of section 11 by an irrevocable deed executed after 1996.[17]

(c) Implied trust for sale as a trust of land

All trusts for sale that are implied by statute, including those arising before 1997, are converted into trusts of land by section 5(1) of the Act.

Schedule 2 identifies these former statutory trusts for sale. Statutory provisions throughout the 1925 legislation have been amended so as to replace the duty to sell by a power to sell and a power to retain. Schedule 2 refers to:

(a) Mortgaged property held by trustees after redemption barred.[18]

(b) Land purchased by trustees of personal property.[19]

(c) Dispositions to tenants in common.[20]

(d) Joint tenancies.[21]

(e) Intestacy.[22]

(f) Reverter of sites.[23]

(d) Doctrine of conversion

Before 1997 the doctrine of conversion applied as soon as a trust for sale came into operation; the interests of the beneficiaries were thus automatically interests in the proceeds of sale of land and not in the land itself. As we have seen,[24] this doctrine gave rise to difficulties and in certain situations it was found undesirable to apply its full logic. As Lord Wilberforce said in *Williams & Glyn's Bank Ltd v Boland*:[25] 'To describe the interests of spouses in a house jointly bought to be lived in as a matrimonial home as merely an interest in proceeds of sale, or rents and profits until sale, is just a little unreal.'

Section 3 of the Act abolished the doctrine retrospectively, and the interests of beneficiaries under a trust for sale of land are now interests in the land itself. This has felicitous consequences for their rights of occupation[26] and for the powers of the court to resolve disputes.[27]

---

[16] S 9, below, pp 481–3.   [17] S 11(3), (4), below, p 484.   [18] LPA 1925, s 31; above, p 471.
[19] Ibid, s 32, above, p 471.   [20] Ibid, s 34, below, p 501.   [21] Ibid, s 36, below, p 503.
[22] AEA 1925, s 33.   [23] Reverter of Sites Act 1987, s 1; above, p 153, n 9.
[24] Above, pp 465–6.   [25] [1981] AC 487, 507.
[26] Below, p 485.   [27] Below, p 488.

The doctrine is not abolished where a trust is created by a will, if the testator died before 1997.[28]

(2) Bare Trusts

A bare trust arises when a trustee holds property on trust for an adult beneficiary absolutely.[29] He must permit the beneficiary to occupy the property and he must obey instructions about its disposition. The beneficiary can call for an outright conveyance of the legal estate at any time. A bare trustee into whose name an absolute owner transfers property is sometimes called a nominee.[30]

Before 1997 bare trusts fell outside the dual system of strict settlement and trust for sale. This caused difficulty, especially in that interests under a bare trust could not be overreached. After 1996 bare trusts come within the definition of a trust of land,[31] and are therefore overreachable.

(3) The Trust of Land in Registered Land

In registered land the legal estate must be registered in the name of the trustees (not exceeding four in number),[32] and the beneficial interests under the trust must be protected by the entry of a restriction on the register.[33] The application for the entry of a restriction may be made by the trustees as registered proprietors, or by any person with the proprietor's consent or who has a sufficient interest in the making of the entry—including a beneficiary under the trust.[34] The beneficial interests cannot be protected by a notice in the register;[35] but, unlike beneficial interests under a strict settlement,[36] they can be overriding interests under Schedules 1 and 3 of the Land Registration Act 2002 where the beneficiary is in discoverable actual occupation of the land.[37] The interests may, however, be overreached by the payment of the purchase money to two trustees or to a trust corporation.[38]

---

[28] TLATA 1996, s 3(2). See also s 25(5). The side heading of s 3 is misleading. The doctrine still subsists, eg, in specifically enforceable contracts for the sale of land: (1997) 113 LQR 207, 209 (PH Pettit); W & H, para 2.23.

[29] H & M, para 2-034.

[30] To be distinguished from the situation where trustees vest securities in a nominee to facilitate dealings with shares; here the nominee is in effect an agent of the trustees.

[31] TLATA 1996, s 1(2)(a), above, p 475.

[32] The transfer or grant of unregistered land for the purpose of constituting the trust (other than a bare trust) triggers compulsory first registration: LRA 2002, s 4(7); Law Com No 271, *Land Registration for the Twenty-First Century* (2001), p 466.

[33] LRA 2002, ss 40–47; LRR 2003, rr. 91–99, as amended by SI 2005 No 1766 and SI 2008 No 1919. The standard forms of restriction are LRR 2003, Sch 4, substituted by SI 2008 No 1919, r 4(6), Sch 4: Forms A (sole proprietor), B (trustees as proprietor) and C (personal representatives); R & R, ch 37; H & B, paras 10.72 ff; Land Registry Practice Guide 19, section 4.

[34] LRA 2002, s 43(1); LRR 2003, r 93.   [35] Ibid, s 33(a)(i).   [36] Above, pp 439–40.

[37] Below, p 1105; *Williams & Glyn's Bank Ltd v Boland* [1981] AC 487, M & B p 203 (under LRA 1925, s 70(1)(g)).

[38] Below, pp 486–7, 1114–17; *City of London Building Society v Flegg* [1988] AC 54, M & B p 551 (LRA 1925, s 70(1)(g)).

II FUNCTIONS OF TRUSTEES OF LAND

A GENERAL POWERS[39]

Before 1997 section 28 of the Law of Property Act 1925 gave to trustees for sale 'all the powers of a tenant for life and the trustees of a settlement under the Settled Land Act 1925'.[40] This section is repealed and replaced by section 6 of the Trusts of Land and Appointment of Trustees Act 1996, which applies to all trusts of land whether arising before or after the commencement of the Act. The scope of the new section is much wider than its predecessor and is designed 'to make the scheme of powers as broadly based and as flexible as possible.'[41]

Section 6(1) provides that:

> For the purpose of exercising their functions as trustees, the trustees of land have in relation to the land subject to the trust, all the powers of an absolute owner.

Functions include both powers and duties of trustees. The trustees of land have no duty to sell, unless they are trustees for sale, when the duty is combined with a mandatory power to postpone sale.[42]

There are, however, limitations on the exercise by the trustees of their general powers. Even though they enjoy all the powers of an absolute owner, section 6(6) provides that they shall not exercise them in contravention of, or of any order made in pursuance of, any other enactment or any rule of law or equity. In other words, they are subject when exercising their functions to the normal fiduciary duties of trustees.[43] These were spelt out by Megarry V-C in *Cowan v Scargill*:[44]

> The starting point is the duty of trustees to exercise their powers in the best interest of the present and future beneficiaries of the trust, holding the scales impartially between different classes of beneficiaries. This duty of the trustees towards their beneficiaries is

---

[39] Trustees are usually appointed by the settlor when creating the trust; in default the court may appoint them. New or additional trustees may be appointed by the persons nominated to do so by the instrument creating the trust or, in default by the existing trustee(s). See Trustee Act 1925, ss 34–43, as amended by TLATA 1996, s 25(1) Sch 3, paras 3(9)–(14); LPA 1925, s 24, as substituted by TLATA 1996, s 25(1), Sch 3, para 4(1), (7); TLATA 1996 Part II: ss 19 (appointment and retirement of trustee at instance of beneficiaries); 20 (appointment of substitute for trustee who lacks capacity, as amended by Mental Capacity Act 2005, s 67, Sch 6, para 42); 21 (supplementary). See generally Maudsley and Burn, *Trusts and Trustees* (7th edn, 2008), ch 13; H & M, ch 17; W & H, ch 3; Law Com No 260 (1999).

In respect of deaths after 1996, the provisions of Part I of the Act relating to trustees apply to personal representatives, other than ss 10 (below p 483), 11 (below, p 484) and 14 (below, p 488); s 18.

[40] Above, p 467; TLATA 1996, s 25(2), Sch 4.

[41] Law Com No 181, paras 10.4–10.5; [1998] Conv 178 (G Ferris and G Battersby).

[42] TLATA 1996, s 4, above, p 476.

[43] See *Avis v Turner* [2007] EWCA Civ 748, [2008] Ch 218 (power to postpone sale in *express* trust for sale is conferred by s 4 TLATA, not s 6(1), so court order to exercise power is not subject to restriction in s 6(6), (7)). See also s 6(8) (trustees acting pursuant to another enactment may not in acting under TLATA 1996, s 6, contravene restriction, limitation or condition of that other enactment).

[44] [1985] Ch 270, 287.

paramount. They must, of course, obey the law; but subject to that, they must put the interests of their beneficiaries first.

Moreover, in exercising their powers the trustees must have regard to the rights of the beneficiaries;[45] and since 1 February 2001 trustees of land have been subject to the general duty of care owed by trustees under section 1 of the Trustee Act 2000.[46]

The exercise of the powers only applies in relation to the land subject to the trust. The trustees therefore have no power to enlarge the investment powers that they have under the trust.[47]

Finally, section 6 specifically mentions

(a) the power to acquire land under the power conferred by section 8 of the Trustee Act 2000;[48] that is to acquire freehold or leasehold land in the United Kingdom as an investment, for occupation by a beneficiary or for any other reason. In relation to land in England and Wales, this confers a power to acquire only a legal estate: there is no power to acquire an equitable interest in the land, although such a power could be included expressly in the instrument creating the trust.

(b) the power to transfer the land to the beneficiaries when all are of full age and capacity, even though they have not required the trustees to do so.[49]

B EXCLUSION AND RESTRICTION OF POWERS

The powers given under section 6 may be excluded or restricted by the disposition creating the trust. Section 8(1) provides:[50]

> Sections 6 and 7[51] do not apply in the case of a trust of land created by a disposition in so far as provision to the effect that they do not apply is made by the disposition.

This is an important new provision that may have an unintended consequence. On the face of it a settlor could by express words take away the power of the trustees to sell or otherwise dispose of the land and tie it up for a long period in conformity with the rule against perpetuities.[52] If this were possible, it would be contrary to the statutory

---

[45] TLATA 1996, s 6(5).

[46] Ibid, s 6(9), inserted by TA 2000, s 40(1), Sch 2, para 45(3); H & W, paras 2.53–2.55, ch 10; H & M, para 17–003. For the application of the duty of care, see W & H, ch 10; Maudsley and Burn, *Trusts and Trustees*, pp 686–91.

[47] Above, pp 459–60, above. An application to court under the Variation of Trusts Act 1958 is necessary; above, pp 449–50.

[48] TLATA 1996, s 6(3), amended by TA 2000, s 40(1), Sch 2, para 45(1). See TLATA 1996, s 17(2), for the treatment of the proceeds of sale of land subject to the trust.

[49] TLATA 1996, s 6(2). On the power of the trustees to partition the land, see s 7, replacing LPA 1925, s 28(3), without change of substance.

[50] W & H, paras 2.68–2.76. S 8(1) does not apply to charitable, ecclesiastical or public trusts.

[51] S 7 deals with partition by trustees, below, pp 506–7.

[52] Below, Ch 15. In relation to instruments taking effect on or after 6 April 2010, there is a fixed perpetuity period of 125 years: Perpetuities and Accumulations Act 2009; below, p 575.

policy of unrestricted alienation by the tenant for life under a strict settlement,[53] and of only partial and indirect restriction on trustees for sale.[54] It is also inconsistent with the rule that a restraint on alienation is contrary to public policy.[55]

C DELEGATION BY TRUSTEES

Under section 29 of the Law of Property Act 1925[56] trustees for sale were empowered to delegate revocably their powers of leasing, accepting surrenders of leases and management to any person of full age for the time being beneficially entitled in possession to the net rents and profits of the land during his life or for any less period. The duty to sell could not be delegated. The trustees were not liable for the acts or defaults of the delegate, but the delegate was, in relation to the exercise of the power by him, deemed to be in the position, and to have the duties and liabilities, of a trustee.

This section has been repealed by the Trusts of Land and Appointment of Trustees Act 1996,[57] and replaced by a wider provision for delegation by the trustees acting together.[58] Section 9(1) provides that:

The trustees of land may, by power of attorney[59] delegate to any beneficiary or beneficiaries[60] of full age and beneficially entitled to an interest in possession in land subject to the trust any of their functions as trustees which relate to the land.[61]

The powers of delegation under this section are wider than those under section 29 of the Law of Property Act 1925 in that sale and mortgage can now be delegated. Further changes to the powers of delegation have also been made by the Trustee Delegation Act 1999[62] and the Trustee Act 2000.

We must notice several points of detail. Where there is more than one trustee of land, the delegation must be made by all the trustees jointly. If a trustee wishes

---

[53] SLA 1925, s 106, above, p 451.

[54] LPA 1925, s 26(3), replaced by TLATA 1996, s 11(1)(a) (duty to consult); LPA 1925, s 26(1), replaced by TLATA 1996, s 11(1)(b) (to give effect to wishes of beneficiaries), below, p 484.

[55] Re Brown [1954] Ch 39, M & B p 306 (in the context of a conditional fee simple). See Emmet, para 22.019; [1997] Conv 263 (G Watt) (suggesting that the court might make an order under TA 1925, s 57, which enables trustees to carry out any disposition or transaction where expedient).

[56] Above, p 468. Any delegation made before 1997 under s 29 is not affected; TLATA 1996, s 9(9).

[57] TLATA 1996, s 25(2), Sch 4. See W & H, paras 2.77–2.99.

[58] It seems that the power to delegate under s 9 cannot be excluded: Kenny and Kenny, para 47-11.

[59] It cannot be an enduring power or lasting power of attorney under Mental Capacity Act 2005: s 9(6), amended by Mental Capacity Act 2005, s 67(1), Sch 6, para 42; below, p 1031.

[60] For the definition of a beneficiary, see s 22(1): 'In this Act "beneficiary", in relation to a trust, means any person who under the trust has an interest in property subject to the trust (including a person who has such an interest as a trustee or a personal representative).' This does not include a beneficiary who has an interest only by reason of being a trustee or personal representative; nor an annuitant: ibid, s 22(2), (3). For a detailed analysis, see W & H, paras 4.1–4.8.

[61] See ss 6 and 7, above, pp 479–80.

[62] Law Com No 220, *Delegation by Individual Trustees* (1994); W & H, Part II.

to delegate his own functions, he must do so under section 25 of the Trustee Act 1925.[63]

Since the delegation must be unanimous, it follows that a delegation may be revoked by any one of the trustees. It is also automatically revoked where there is a change of trustees, or where a beneficiary delegate ceases to be beneficially entitled.[64]

The delegation may be for any period or it may be indefinite.[65] It must be made by power of attorney, and therefore executed as a deed by the donor of the power.[66] Detailed protection is given to a purchaser from an attorney by section 9(2) as follows:

> Where trustees purport to delegate to a person by a power of attorney under subsection (1) functions relating to any land and another person in good faith deals with him in relation to the land, he shall be presumed in favour of that other person to have been a person to whom the functions could be delegated unless that other person has knowledge at the time of the transaction that he was not such a person.

Protection is also given to a later purchaser from the original purchaser:

> And it shall be conclusively presumed in favour of any purchaser whose interest depends on the validity of that transaction that that other person dealt in good faith and did not have such knowledge if that other person makes a statutory declaration to that effect before or within three months after the completion of the purchase.

If the trustees refuse to delegate their functions, an application may be made to court under section 14 of the Trust of Land and Appointment of Trustees Act[67] by any person with an interest, for example a beneficiary under the trust who wishes a delegation to be made to him.

Finally, we must consider the position of the delegate beneficiary. He has the same duties and liabilities as a trustee, but he cannot sub-delegate, nor can he receive capital money.[68] As originally drafted[69] the Act provided that the liability of the trustees for any act or default of a beneficiary was limited: it arose if, and only if, the trustees did not exercise reasonable care in deciding to delegate the relevant function to the beneficiary. Since 1 February 2001, however,[70] the duty of care under the Trustee Act 2000[71] applies to trustees of land in deciding whether to delegate any of their functions under section 9 of the 1996 Act, and, if the delegation is not irrevocable, as long as the delegation continues. In the latter case, the trustees must keep the delegation under review, and

---

[63] As substituted by Trustee Delegation Act 1999, s 5(1). For delegation of general powers by trustees, see TA 2000, Part IV, which creates a new statutory regime. For delegation by trustees of land who are also beneficiaries, see Trustee Delegation Act 1999, ss 1 and 2. See generally Maudsley and Burn, *Trusts and Trustees*, pp 754–62; H & M, paras 20-012 to 20-021; W & H, chaps 7, 8 and 12.

[64] TLATA 1996, s 9(3), (4).   [65] Ibid, s 9(5).

[66] On powers of attorney generally, see Cretney and Lush, *Lasting and Enduring Powers of Attorney* (6th edn, 2009).

[67] Below, p 488.   [68] TLATA 1996, s 9(7).

[69] Ibid, s 9(8); repealed by TA 2000, s 40(1), (3), Sch 2, para 46, Sch 4, Pt II.

[70] Ibid, s 9A, inserted by TA 2000, s 40(1), Sch 2, para 47. Delegations effected before 1 February 2001 are not affected: ibid, s 9A(7).

[71] S 1; above, p 480.

consider in appropriate circumstances whether to exercise any power of intervention they may have (including intervention by giving directions to the beneficiary or by revoking the delegation). It is still provided that the liability of the trustees for any act or default of the beneficiary is limited to the case where they fail to comply with the duty of care; and it appears that this imposes on the trustee liability for his own breach of the duty of care, not vicarious liability for the act or default of the beneficiary.[72]

III BENEFICIARIES UNDER A TRUST OF LAND

Sections 10 to 13 of the Trusts of Land and Appointment of Trustees Act 1996 are mainly concerned with the rights of beneficiaries under a trust of land and with the duties owed to them by their trustees.

A CONSENTS

Section 10[73] of the Act is based on section 26 of the Law of Property Act 1925, which has been repealed.[74] Settlors may wish to make the sale of trust land dependent on the consent of the interest in possession beneficiary who will then be able to enjoy the use of the land and prevent the trustees from selling it over his head and thereby overreaching his interest. Section 10(1) provides that:

> If a disposition creating a trust of land requires the consent of more than two persons to the exercise by the trustees of any function relating to the land, the consent of any two of them to the exercise of the function is sufficient in favour of a purchaser.

This sub-section[75] protects a purchaser from any requirement in the trust instrument to obtain more than two consents to a disposition, but the trustees remain under a duty to obtain all the specified consents; if they do not, they are liable for breach of trust. Sub-section (3) provides that, where the consent of a minor is required, then in favour of a purchaser the minor's consent is not required, but the trustees are under a duty to obtain the consent of a parent who has parental responsibility for him or a guardian on his behalf.[76]

---

[72] TLATA 1996, s 9A(6); W & H, para 2.99. Before TLATA 1996 was enacted, the Law Commission had proposed that the liability should be extended to cover all the acts or defaults of the beneficiary: Law Com No 181, *Trusts of Land* (1988), para 11.3. See generally W & H, paras 2.93–2.98.

[73] W & H, paras 2.100–2.106.   [74] Above, p 468. TLATA 1996, s 25(2), Sch 4.

[75] S 10(1) does not apply to charitable, ecclesiastical or public trusts: s 10(2).

[76] It was not thought necessary to reproduce the provision of LPA 1925, s 26(2) relating to consent on behalf of a mentally incapacitated beneficiary.

B CONSULTATION WITH BENEFICIARIES

Section 11 of the Trusts of Land and Appointment of Trustees Act 1996[77] is based on section 26(3) of the Law of Property Act 1925, which has been repealed and extends to express trusts a rule that applied before 1997 to implied trusts for sale only.[78] It applies to trusts expressly created after 1996 unless excluded by the disposition; it also applies to implied trusts, whenever arising. As far as pre-1997 express trusts for sale are concerned, the section does not apply unless it is included by a deed made by the settlor or surviving settlors after 1996. It does not apply to trusts created by will before 1997.[79]

Such a deed opting into the section is irrevocable, and binds not only the beneficiary but also his successors in title.[80]

The wording of section 11(1) is as follows:

The trustees of land shall in the exercise of any function[81] relating to land subject to the trust—

(a) so far as practicable, consult the beneficiaries of full age and beneficially entitled to an interest in possession in the land, and

(b) so far as consistent with the general interest of the trust, give effect to the wishes of those beneficiaries, or (in case of dispute) of the majority (according to the value of their combined interests).

There are no cases on the interpretation of the words 'so far as practicable' in this context,[82] nor on 'so far as consistent with the general interest of the trust'. If the trustees fail to consult the beneficiaries, they may be liable for breach of trust.[83]

---

[77] W & H, paras 2.107–2.119.   [78] Above, p 469. TLATA 1996, s 25(2), Sch 4.
[79] TLATA 1996, s 11(2)–(4).   [80] Ibid, s 11(4).
[81] The giving of a notice to quit by one of joint tenants under a lease is not an exercise of any function relating to land subject to the trust: *Notting Hill Housing Trust v Brackley* [2001] EWCA Civ 601, [2001] 3 EGLR 11.
[82] Cf, discussing such language in regulations under the Industrial Relations Act 1971, *Dedman v British Building & Engineering Appliances Ltd* [1974] 1 WLR 171, 179 (Scarman LJ: 'The word "practicable" is an ordinary English word of great flexibility: it takes its meaning from its context. But, whenever used, it is a call for the exercise of common sense, a warning that sound judgment will be impossible without compromise. Sometimes the context contemplates a situation rarely to be achieved, though much to be desired: the word then indicates one must be satisfied with less than perfection: see, for example, its use in section 5 of the Matrimonial Property Act 1970. Sometimes, as is submitted in the present case, what the context requires may have been possible, but may not for some reason have been "practicable". Whatever its context, the quality of the word is that there are circumstances in which we must be content with less than 100%: and it calls for judgment to determine how much less').
[83] *Re Jones* [1931] 1 Ch 375, 377; *Crawley BC v Ure* [1996] QB 13, above, p 469, n 281.

C RIGHTS OF OCCUPATION

Section 12 of the Trusts of Land and Appointment of Trustees Act 1996[84] gives to a beneficiary who is beneficially entitled to an interest in possession in land the right to occupy trust land. Section 13 provides that the trustees may exclude, restrict or impose conditions on such occupation.[85]

Before 1997 there were difficulties concerning the occupation of beneficiaries under a trust for sale, especially where the beneficiaries were co-owners under an implied trust. This was due to the doctrine of conversion under which the interests of beneficiaries under a trust for sale were in the proceeds of sale and not in the land itself. As we have seen, the courts regarded the doctrine as artificial.[86]

In *Bull v Bull*,[87] for example, a mother and son were equitable tenants in common of residential accommodation and the son was trustee of the legal estate that he held upon an implied trust for sale in favour of his mother and himself. The question was whether the son could obtain vacant possession against his mother. In holding that the son failed, Lord Denning MR treated the mother as having an interest in land, and a right to occupy it. The doctrine of conversion has been abolished[88] retrospectively, and the matter is now regulated by sections 12 and 13.

Under section 12(1):

A beneficiary who is beneficially entitled to an interest in possession in land subject to a trust of land is entitled by reason of his interest to occupy the land at any time if at that time—

(a) the purposes of the trust include making the land available for his occupation (or for the occupation of beneficiaries of a class of which he is a member or of beneficiaries in general), or

(b) the land is held by the trustees so as to be so available.

No right to occupy arises if the land is 'either unavailable or unsuitable for occupation' by the beneficiary in question. The term 'unsuitable' was added in order to ensure that a right to occupy does not arise where premises are empty (and therefore not 'unavailable' for occupation) but it would be inappropriate for the particular beneficiary to occupy them; for example, where the land is a working farm but the beneficiary is not, and has no intention of becoming, a farmer.[89]

---

84 [1998] CLJ 123 (DG Barnsley).

85 W & H, paras 2.120–2.138; [1997] Conv 254 (JG Ross Martyn); [2006] Conv 54 (S Pascoe).

86 Above, p 466.

87 [1955] 1 QB 234; cf *Barclay v Barclay* [1970] 2 QB 677 (express testamentary trust for sale of bungalow intended to be sold and the proceeds divided). Before 1926 the answer depended very much on the discretion of the trustees: (1955) 19 Conv (NS) 146, 147 (FR Crane).

88 TLATA 1996, s 3, above, p 477.

89 TLATA Bill (House of Lords) Notes on Clauses, para 129; *Chan Pui Chun v Leung Kam Ho* [2002] EWCA Civ 1075, [2003] 1 FLR 23 at [100]–[103].

Section 13 gives to the trustees of land the power to exclude or restrict the right to occupy conferred by section 12. This power arises where two or more beneficiaries are entitled to occupy land; the trustees may exclude or restrict the right of one or more beneficiaries in favour of another beneficiary, but may not exclude the rights of occupation of all the beneficiaries.[90] They may not unreasonably exclude any beneficiary's entitlement to occupy, or restrict any such entitlement to an unreasonable extent.

Section 13(3) enables the trustees to impose conditions on occupation by a beneficiary. Guidelines are set out in sub-section (4) and particular examples of conditions in sub-section (5). Sub-section (4) specifies matters to which the trustees must have regard in exercising their powers to exclude or restrict the right to occupy; these include the intentions of the creator of the trust, the purposes for which the land is held, and the circumstances and wishes of the beneficiaries who are, or would be but for restriction or exclusion, entitled to occupy the land. Sub-section (5) lists particular conditions that the trustees may impose on a beneficiary. The list is not exhaustive; it includes conditions requiring him to pay outgoings or other expenses in respect of the land; or to assume some other obligation, such as to ensure that planning requirements are complied with.

Sub-section (6) provides for the payment of compensation to an excluded beneficiary.[91] A beneficiary already in occupation cannot be excluded unless he consents or the court has given approval.

IV PROTECTION OF PURCHASERS

Purchasers[92] are protected by the doctrine of overreaching and also by limitations on powers and consent requirements.

A OVERREACHING

The main object of the doctrine is a compromise between, on the one hand, the interest of the public in securing that land held in trust is freely marketable and, on

---

[90] *Rodway v Landy* [2001] EWCA Civ 471, [2001] Ch 703 (partition of property jointly owned by two medical practitioners prohibited by National Health Service Act 1977, but order made under TLATA 1996, s 13, to effect de facto partition by excluding one of the practitioners from one part of the property, and the other practitioner from the remainder of the property. The section prohibits only exclusion of the beneficiaries collectively: Peter Gibson LJ at [32]–[33]).

[91] On the circumstances in which a beneficiary in occupation can be required to pay an occupation rent to an excluded beneficiary, either under TLATA 1996, s 13(6), or under the general principles of equitable accounting, see below, pp 494–5.

[92] A purchaser has the same meaning as in Part I of the Law of Property Act 1925: TLATA 1996, s 23(1): ie a person who acquires an interest in or charge on property for money or money's worth, and in reference to a legal estate includes a chargee by way of legal mortgage: LPA 1925, s 205(1)(xxi).

the other hand, the interests of beneficiaries in preserving their rights under the trust. The overreaching provisions under section 2(1) of the Law of Property Act 1925 are routinely amended by the Trusts of Land and Appointment of Trustees Act 1996, and continue to operate in relation to trusts of land.[93] They are improved in that bare trusts are included in the definition of a trust of land by section 1(2)(a) and interests under them are now overreachable.[94]

B LIMITATION ON POWERS AND CONSENT REQUIREMENTS

Further detailed protection is given to a purchaser by section 16 of the Trusts of Land and Appointment of Trustees Act 1996. This section applies only to unregistered land.[95] A purchaser of registered land is left to rely on restrictions that must be placed on the register.[96]

Section 16 provides that a purchaser of unregistered land from trustees 'need not be concerned to see' that they have:

(i) had regard to the rights of beneficiaries in exercising their general powers under section 6(5);[97]

(ii) obtained the consent of beneficiaries before partition of land under section 7(3);[98]

(iii) consulted the beneficiaries and given effect to their wishes in exercising powers under section 11.[99]

A purchaser needs, however, to be concerned in cases where he has actual notice that:

(i) the trustees are exercising their general powers in contravention of sections 6(6) (the exercise of powers that are in contravention of any other enactment or any rule of law or equity)[100] or 6(8) (in contravention of a limitation on powers conferred by any other enactment).[101] An example would be where absolutely entitled beneficiaries call for the trust land to be conveyed to them, but the trustees in breach of trust convey the land to a third party. The conveyance is valid in the absence of actual notice on the part of the purchaser;

(ii) the trustees are exercising powers that are limited by section 8.[102] Here the trustees are under a duty to take all reasonable steps to bring the limitation to the notice of a purchaser; if they do not, a purchaser without actual notice takes free from the limitation;

---

[93] Below, p 1114. [94] Above, p 478.
[95] TLATA 1996, s 16(7). See [1998] Conv 168, 179–88 (G Ferris and G Battersby); [2005] Conv 140 (S Pascoe, suggesting amendments to s 16).
[96] Above, p 478, n 33. [97] Above, p 480. [98] Above, pp 506–7. [99] Above, pp 484.
[100] Above, p 479. [101] Above, p 479, n 43. [102] Above, p 480.

(iii) the trustees convey land to beneficiaries where the beneficiaries are not absolutely entitled. Here the purchaser is protected if he has no actual notice of the trustees' mistake and has obtained a deed executed by the trustees that they are discharged from the trust.

C DEED OF DISCHARGE

Where a strict settlement comes to an end, the trustees should execute a deed of discharge; but there was no similar provision in relation to land held on trust for sale before 1997. Section 16(4) of the Trusts of Land and Appointment of Trustees Act 1996 introduced a deed of discharge in relation to trusts of unregistered land.[103] Where trustees of land convey land to persons whom they believe to be beneficiaries absolutely entitled to the land and of full age and capacity, the trustees must execute a deed of discharge, which declares that they are discharged from the trust; and, if they fail to do so, the court may make an order requiring them to do so.

Section 16(5) provides that a subsequent purchaser of land, to which the deed of discharge relates, is entitled to assume that, as from the date of the deed, the land is not subject to the trust, unless he has actual notice that the trustees were mistaken in their belief.

V POWERS OF THE COURT

A GENERAL

Section 14 of the Trusts of Land and Appointment of Trustees Act 1996[104] replaced section 30 of the Law of Property Act 1925,[105] and gives to the court wider powers to interfere with the trustees' exercise of any of the trust powers, to dispense with their

---

[103] In registered land the purchaser is protected by the restriction required to be placed on the register: above, p 478, n 33. When registering the disposition of a registered estate, the registrar must cancel the restriction if he is satisfied that the estate is no longer subject to the trust of land: LRR 2003, r 99. For applications to cancel or withdraw a restriction, see ibid, rr 97 and 98 (the latter as substituted by SI 2008 No 1919, Sch 1, para 37).

[104] W & H, paras 2.139–2.164. S 14 also applies in relation to a trust of proceeds of sale: s 17(1). Where the issue is the sale of a matrimonial home, as between husband and wife the claim should be heard by the court with jurisdiction in relation to ancillary relief under the Matrimonial Causes Act 1973, which overrides TLATA 1996: *Tee v Tee* [1999] 2 FLR 613; even where the spouses are co-owners with a third party: *Laird v Laird* [1999] 1 FLR 791. Cf *Miller Smith v Miller Smith* [2009] EWCA Civ 1297, [2010] 1 FLR 1402 at [18] (confronted with an application under TLATA between separated spouses, the court should embark upon the discretionary exercise by asking itself whether the issue raised by the application can reasonably be left to be resolved within an application for ancillary relief following divorce. It is in principle much more desirable that an issue about sale of the home should be resolved within an application for ancillary relief). However, the jurisdictions under TLATA and the Children Act 1989 are concurrent: *White v White* [2003] EWCA Civ 924, [2004] 2 FLR 321 at [27] (Arden LJ).

[105] Above, pp 469–70; TLATA 1996, s 25(2), Sch 4.

obligation to obtain any consents[106] or to consult, or to regulate occupation of land by the beneficiaries. Section 15 sets out the matters to which the court must have regard in determining an application under section 14.[107]

An application may be made by a trustee;[108] an interest in possession beneficiary; a remainderman (whether vested or contingent); a discretionary beneficiary; the secured creditor of a beneficiary;[109] and trustees (and beneficiaries) of a sub-trust (because the 'interest' does not have to be owned beneficially).

There was a considerable body of case law on section 30 of the Law of Property Act 1925, decisions that were influenced by the primacy of the trustees' *duty* to sell. The courts invented the doctrine of a secondary or collateral purpose to help them to decide whether that primary purpose could be displaced. They could then exercise their discretion as to whether to make an order for sale or not. As the Law Commission Report said: 'there is something odd about a doctrine whose essential purpose is so obviously the circumvention of an inconvenient position'.[110]

Section 15(1) puts on a statutory footing the criteria that the courts developed for settling disputes over trusts for sale under section 30 of the Law of Property Act 1925. They include:

(a) the intentions of the person or persons (if any) who created the trust,[111]

(b) the purposes for which the property subject to the trust is held,[112]

(c) the welfare of any minor who occupies or might reasonably be expected to occupy any land subject to the trust as his home, and

(d) the interests of any secured creditor of any beneficiary.

---

106 *Abbey National plc v Powell* (1999) 78 P & CR D 16.

107 The sections apply to all applications whether made before or after the commencement of the Act.

108 But not a trustee in bankruptcy: s 15(4); below, p 490. See *Oke v Rideout* [1998] CLY 4876 (resulting trust).

109 Before 1997 the courts had treated a secured creditor in the same way as a trustee in bankruptcy, and therefore entitled to an order for sale save in exceptional circumstances: *Lloyds Bank plc v Byrne & Byrne* [1993] 1 FLR 369. Now, however, although 'to put it at its lowest, it does not seem to me unlikely that the legislature intended to relax the fetters on the way in which the court exercised its discretion ... and so as to tip the balance somewhat more in favour of families and against banks and other chargees': *Mortgage Corp v Shaire* [2001] Ch 743, 760, M & B p 543 (Neuberger J); yet a 'powerful consideration is and ought to be whether the creditor is receiving proper recompense for being kept out of his money, repayment of which is overdue': *Bank of Ireland Home Mortgages Ltd v Bell* [2001] 2 FLR 809 at [31] (Peter Gibson LJ). See also *First National Bank plc v Achampong* [2003] EWCA Civ 487, [2004] 1 FCR 18 at [62]; [2003] Conv 314 (MP Thompson); *Edwards v Lloyds TSB Bank plc* [2004] EWHC 1745 (Ch), [2005] 1 FCR 139 at [30].

110 Law Com No 181, para 12.3.

111 This refers only to the *common* intention of *all* those who created the trust, and only those held at the time the trust was created: *White v White* [2003] EWCA Civ 924, [2004] 2 FLR 321 at [22]–[23] (Arden LJ).

112 Cf *R v Modjidi* [2010] EWCA Crim 829, [2010] 1 WLR 2096 at [26] (provision of express declaration of trust could be overridden to allow sale on application of one co-owner against whom confiscation order has been made under Proceeds of Crime Act 2002 and who has no other means of satisfying the order, taking into account the confiscation order, the policy of the 2002 Act and the likelihood that if an order for sale were not made an enforcement receiver would be appointed who would sell the property).

The court is also required to have regard to the circumstances and wishes of any beneficiaries who are of full age and entitled in possession to property subject to the trust, or, in the case of dispute, of the majority (according to the value of their interests), except in the case of occupation disputes where regard is to be had to the circumstances and wishes of each of the beneficiaries entitled to occupy.[113] The court will also be able to take into account any other matters that it considers to be relevant.

These criteria are not exhaustive, and there is no guide as to the priorities to be accorded to each of them.[114] The relevance of the welfare of any minor as an independent criterion is welcome and comes after uncertainty in the case law on it under section 30.

However, it is clear that section 15 has changed the law.[115] In consequence, the old authorities on section 30 of the Law of Property Act 1925 must be treated with caution, and in many cases they are unlikely to be of great, let alone decisive, assistance.[116]

B BANKRUPTCY

There are different considerations where the application is made by the trustee in bankruptcy of a bankrupt who is beneficially interested in land held in trust. The application must be made to the court that has jurisdiction in the bankruptcy proceedings. Section 335A(2) of the Insolvency Act 1986[117] sets out an exhaustive list of criteria:[118]

On such an application the court shall make such order as it think just and reasonable having regard to—

(a) the interests of the bankrupt's creditors;

---

[113] And also save where the trustees wish to transfer the land to such beneficiaries pursuant to s 6(2).

[114] *White v White*, above, at [26] (Arden LJ). See *Bank of Ireland Home Mortgages Ltd v Bell* [2001] 2 FLR 809 at [24]–[32], considering, inter alia, value of beneficiary's equity (nil) compared with interest of chargee; purpose of occupation as family home (already ended once husband left); welfare of minor (only a slight consideration where son not far short of 18); beneficiary's poor health (a reason for postponing, not refusing, sale): sale ordered; [2001] All ER Rev 262 (PJ Clarke); *First National Bank plc v Achampong* [2003] EWCA Civ 487, [2004] 1 FCR 18 at [65] (sale ordered); *Edwards v Lloyds TSB Bank plc* [2004] EWHC 1745 (Ch), [2005] 1 FCR 139 (sale postponed for five years until youngest child reached full age).

[115] *Mortgage Corpn v Shaire* [2001] Ch 743, 758–60, M & B p 543 (Neuberger J), giving eight reasons to support this; [2002] Conv 329 (MP Thompson); [2000] Conv 315 (S Pascoe); [2001] CLJ 43 (M Oldham); [2001] All ER Rev 258 (PJ Clarke).

[116] [2001] Ch 743, 761.

[117] As added by TLATA 1996, s 25(1), Sch 3, para 23 and amended by Civil Partnership Act 2004, s 261(1), Sch 27, para 118. The section is retrospective. See [2006] Conv 157 (P Omar) on the paramount status of creditors in proceedings involving recovery of the family home.

[118] For pre-1996 cases on which the criteria are based, see *Re Solomon* [1967] Ch 573; *Re Turner* [1974] 1 WLR 1556; *Re McCarthy* [1975] 1 WLR 807; *Re Densham* [1975] 1 WLR 1519; *Re Bailey* [1977] 1 WLR 278; *Re Lowrie* [1981] 3 All ER 353, M & B p 541; *Re Citro* [1991] Ch 142, 159, M & B p 537. See also *Abbey National plc v Moss* [1994] 1 FLR 307; [1994] Conv 331 (DN Clarke); (1995) 111 LQR 72 (N Hopkins).

(b) where the application is made in respect of land which includes a dwelling house which is or has been the home of the bankrupt or the bankrupt's spouse or civil partner or former spouse or former civil partner—

    (i) the conduct of the spouse, civil partner, former spouse or former civil partner, so far as contributing to the bankruptcy,

    (ii) the needs and financial resources of the spouse, civil partner, former spouse or former civil partner, and

    (iii) the needs of any children; and

(c) all the circumstances of the case other than the needs of the bankrupt.

Where, however, an application is made after one year from the vesting of the bankrupt's estate in a trustee, the court must assume that the interests of the creditors outweigh all other considerations, unless the circumstances of the case are exceptional.[119] By delaying the sale, protection is given to the family to enable it to make arrangements either for alternative accommodation or for the buying out of the bankrupt's interest in the property.

---

[119] *Re Citro* [1991] Ch 142, M & B p 537; (1991) 107 LQR 177 (SM Cretney); [1991] CLJ 45 (JC Hall); [1991] Conv 302 (AMM Lawson); (1992) 15 MLR 284 (D Brown) (inability to buy alternative home and disruption of children's schooling held not to be exceptional circumstances: 'they are those melancholy consequences of debt and improvidence': Nourse LJ at 157); *TSB Bank plc v Marshall* [1996] 1 FLR 258. Cf *Re Mott* [1987] CLY 212, M & B p 540 ('it would be difficult to imagine a more extreme case of hardship than this one': Hoffmann J); *Judd v Brown* [1998] 2 FLR 360 (cancer); *Re Raval* [1998] 2 FLR 718 (mental illness of wife); *Claughton v Charalambous* [1999] 1 FLR 740 (60-year-old with chronic disease, who had great difficulty in walking in house adapted to her needs); *Re Bremner* [1999] 1 FLR 912 (wife needed to care for 79-year-old bankrupt with only six months to live); *Barca v Mears* [2004] EWHC 2170 (Ch), [2005] 2 FLR 1 (requirements of child with special educational needs not, on the facts, exceptional circumstances); [2005] Conv 161 (M Dixon); *Nicholls v Lan* [2006] EWHC 1255 (Ch), [2007] 1 FLR 744 (long-term chronic schizophrenia). See *Re Bennett* [2000] EGCS 41, applying the same test for exceptional circumstances as was applied in pre-1996 Act decisions. It may, however, be arguable that the approach to 'exceptional circumstances' adopted in *Re Citro* is not consistent with the ECHR, and there needs to be a shift in emphasis to recognise that although, in the general run of cases, the creditors' interests will outweigh all other interests, a court may find, on proper consideration of the facts of a particular case, it is one of the exceptional cases in which that proposition is not true: *Barca v Mears*, above, at [33]–[42] (Nicholas Strauss QC); [2005] Conv 161, 165–7 (M Dixon); [2010] Conv 352 (A Baker). See, however, *Hosking v Michaelides* [2006] BPIR 1192 at [70]; *Donohoe v Ingram* [2006] EWHC 282 (Ch); [2006] 2 FLR 1084 at [19]-[22]; *Nicholls v Lan*, above, at [41]-[48], [2007] Conv 78 (M Pawlowski) (Paul Morgan QC: 'the way in which s 335A operates in the present case is that the court is required to perform a balancing exercise and to decide what is "just and reasonable" and, amongst the circumstances that are to be taken into account, are the interests of the creditors and the needs of someone like [the wife who jointly owned the property, and who suffered from long-term chronic schizophrenia]. For my part, I do not see that the statutory test, leading to a balancing exercise, is inconsistent with the qualified nature of the rights enshrined in Art 8 and in Art 1 of the First Protocol. Indeed, it might be contended that s 335A precisely captures what is required by Art 8 and Art 1 of the First Protocol.') Note now the general change in approach to the application of ECHR to possession claims in *Manchester CC v Pinnock* [2010] UKSC 45, [2010] 3 WLR 1441, above, pp 353–6).

14

CONCURRENT INTERESTS[1]

Summary

As we have already observed,[2] the 1925 legislation used the statutory trust for sale to solve the conveyancing problems that arose before 1926 from the holding of concurrent interests. And since 1997 the trust for sale has been replaced by the trust of land.[3] The trust of land is now therefore the legal framework within which successive[4] and concurrent interests in land can be held. In this chapter, we consider the forms of concurrent interest in land recognised by the law.

I CONCURRENT OWNERSHIP AT LAW AND IN EQUITY

A SEVERAL AND CONCURRENT OWNERSHIP

Several and concurrent ownership must first be distinguished. The owner of an interest in land may be entitled to possession either alone or in conjunction with other persons,

---

[1] See generally Thompson, *Co-ownership* (1988); Smith, *Plural Ownership* (2005); M & B ch 7.
[2] Above, pp 462 ff.
[3] Above, Ch 13.
[4] Except successive interests under SLA 1925 which already existed when TLATA 1996 came into force on 1 January 1997, and to which SLA 1925 continues to apply: above, p 475.

and in both cases he may be entitled to take possession either now or at some time in the future. If he is entitled in his own right without having any other person joined with him in point of interest, he is said to hold in severalty; but where he and other persons have simultaneous interests in the land, they are said to hold concurrently, or in co-ownership, and to have concurrent interests. In other words, land may be the subject of several, that is separate, ownership, or of co-ownership.

B CO-OWNERSHIP AT LAW AND IN EQUITY

The forms of co-ownership that are discussed in the following section were originally recognised by both the common law and equity. However, as we shall see, the 1925 legislation made fundamental changes in the principles applicable to concurrent interests, so that in the modern law the basis on which concurrent interests may be held in the legal estate—only under a joint tenancy—is different from the basis on which equitable beneficial concurrent interests may be held—under either a joint tenancy or a tenancy in common. We must first explain the characteristics of, and the differences between, the various forms of concurrent ownership, drawing on both older authorities and examples from the modern law in order to do so. Thereafter we shall consider how they are treated in the law today.

II FORMS OF CONCURRENT OWNERSHIP

At common law there were four possible forms of co-ownership, one of which, tenancy by entireties, is now defunct;[5] while another, coparcenary, seldom arises.[6] The two found in practice are joint tenancy and tenancy in common.

A JOINT TENANCY

A joint tenancy arises whenever land is conveyed or devised to two or more persons without any words to show that they are to take distinct and separate shares, or, to use technical language, without words of severance.[7] If an estate is given, for instance, to:

A and B in fee simple,

without the addition of any restrictive, exclusive or explanatory words, the law gives effect to the whole of the grant by creating an equal estate in them both.[8] From the point of view of their interest in the land they are united in every respect. But if the

---

[5] For a discussion, see the 11th edn of this book, p 338.

[6] Coparcenary arises where an entailed interest descends to female heirs jointly. For discussion, see the 17th edn of this book, pp 462-3. See also below, p 589.

[7] Litt s 277; Blackstone, vol ii, p 179.   [8] Blackstone, vol ii, p 180.

grant contains words of severance showing an intention that A and B are to take separate and distinct interests, such as where there is a grant to:

A and B equally,[9]

the result is the creation not of a joint tenancy, but of a tenancy in common.

The two essential attributes of a joint tenancy that must be kept in mind in order to understand the purpose of the legislation of 1925 in reforming the law of co-ownership, are the absolute unity that exists between joint tenants, and the right of survivorship.

(1) Unity between Joint Tenants

There is, to use the language of Blackstone,[10] a thorough and intimate union between joint tenants. Together they form one person. This unity is fourfold, consisting of unity of title, time, interest and possession. All the titles are derived from the same grant and become vested at the same time;[11] all the interests are identical in size; and there is unity of possession, since each tenant 'holds the whole yet holds nothing': *totum tenet et nihil tenet*. Each holds the whole in the sense that in conjunction with his co-tenants he is entitled to present possession and enjoyment of the whole; yet he holds nothing in the sense that he is not entitled to the exclusive possession of any individual part of the whole.[12] Unity of possession is a feature of all forms of co-ownership. For this reason one co-owner cannot, as a general rule, maintain an action of trespass against the other or others, but can do so only if the act complained of amounts either to an actual ouster, or to a destruction of the subject matter of the tenancy.[13] Nor is one co-owner in sole occupation normally required to pay rent to another co-owner,[14] unless he has excluded or ousted him from possession,[15] or where the trustees exercise their

---

[9] Below, p 496.   [10] Blackstone, vol ii, p 182.

[11] In the case of a grant to uses (above, p 96), the fact that the interests vested at different times did not prevent the creation of a joint tenancy, eg under a grant to X and Y to the use of all the sons of A born within the lifetime of the settlor, sons born after the time of the grant became joint tenants with those alive at the time of its execution.

[12] By Littleton's time the expression *totum tenet et nihil tenet* had become *per my et per tout*, which in Blackstone's view (vol ii, p 182) meant that each tenant was seised 'by the half or moiety and by all'. *My*, however, did not mean half, but was an early form of the French word *mie* (a (bread-) crumb: used figuratively to mean a fragment, or part).

[13] Blackstone, vol ii, p 183; *Martyn v Knowllys* (1799) 8 Term Rep 145; *Murray v Hall* (1849) 7 CB 441; *Stedman v Smith* (1857) 8 E & B 1; *Wilkinson v Haygarth* (1847) 12 QB 837.

[14] *M'Mahon v Burchell* (1846) 2 Ph 127; *Jones v Jones* [1977] 1 WLR 438. See also *Chhokar v Chhokar* [1984] FLR 313, M & B p 217; *Wright v Johnson* [2001] EWCA Civ 1667, [2002] 2 P & CR 15 (one co-owner led other to believe that she could reside rent-free). Rent received by one co-owner from a stranger will be shared with another co-owner.

[15] *Dennis v McDonald* [1981] 1 WLR 810 (ousted mistress); affd [1982] Fam 63 (application under LPA 1925, s 30); above, p 469; *Bernard v Josephs* [1982] Ch 391; cf *Stott v Ratcliffe* (1982) 126 SJ 310; *Harvey v Harvey* [1982] Fam 83 (application under Matrimonial Causes Act 1973, s 25); [1982] Conv 305 (J Martin). The rule of ouster has not always been applied in matrimonial cases where application was made under the Married Women's Property Act 1882, s 17. See *Bedson v Bedson* [1965] 2 QB 666 (rent of £1 a week ordered); *Leake v Bruzzi* [1974] 1 WLR 1528; *Suttill v Graham* [1977] 1 WLR 819; [1978] Conv 161 (FR Crane); (1978) 97 Law Notes 78 (A Treleaven).

power under section 13 of the Trusts of Land and Appointment of Trustees Act 1996 to exclude the entitlement of a beneficiary with an interest in possession to occupy the land,[16] or where it is otherwise necessary in order to do equity between the parties.[17]

It is, however, possible for A and B to transfer their legal estate to A alone. Lord Nicholls of Birkenhead said:[18]

> The legal concept relied upon ... is that a joint tenant, as distinct from a tenant in common, has nothing to transfer to the other tenant, because each already owns the whole. I have to say that this esoteric concept is remote from the realities of life.

(2) Right of Survivorship

The second characteristic that distinguishes a joint tenancy is the right of survivorship, or *jus accrescendi*, by which, if one joint tenant dies without having obtained a separate share in his lifetime, his interest is extinguished and accrues to the surviving tenants whose interests are correspondingly enlarged.[19] For example:

> A and B may be joint tenants in fee simple, but the result of the death of B is that his interest totally disappears and A becomes owner of the land.

There are cases, however, where the right of survivorship does not benefit both tenants equally, for if there is a grant to

> A and B during the life of A

and A dies first, there is nothing that can accrue to B.[20]

---

[16] Above, pp 485–6.

[17] The general equitable jurisdiction ('equitable accounting') was well established before TLATA 1996, and represented a general loosening of the earlier strict requirement of 'ouster'; see, eg, *Re Pavlou* [1993] 1 WLR 1046, 1050 (Millett J: equitable accounting as between trustee in bankruptcy of co-owner not in occupation, and the other co-owner in occupation; but 'if a tenant in common leaves the property voluntarily, but would be welcome back and would be in a position to enjoy his or her right to occupy, it would normally not be fair or equitable to the remaining tenant in common to charge him or her with an occupation rent which he or she never expected to pay'); *Byford v Butler* [2003] EWHC 1267 (Ch), [2004] 1 FLR 56 (wife in occupation entitled against co-owner's trustee in bankruptcy to contribution to interest payments she had made on mortgage, but trustee entitled to set-off for occupation rent). In *Stack v Dowden* [2007] UKHL 17, [2007] 2 AC 432 at [94] Baroness Hale of Richmond said that ss 12-15 TLATA 1996 had in this context *replaced* the old doctrines of equitable accounting, and that now the (broader) statutory criteria of s 15 TLATA should be applied (including the welfare of a minor in occupation), although the results may often be the same; see also *Murphy v Gooch* [2007] EWCA Civ 603, [2007] 2 FLR 934 at [10]-[14]. Cf, however, *French v Barcham* [2008] EWHC 1505 (Ch), [2009] 1 WLR 1124 (ss 12-15 of TLATA 1996 do not provide an exhaustive regime for compensation for exclusion of a beneficiary from occupying land; where s 13(6) does not apply (eg where trustee in bankruptcy holds interest under trust but has no right of occupation) the court can order payment of compensation in its general equitable jurisdiction). See generally [2009] Conv 378 (S Bright).

[18] *Burton v Camden LBC* [2000] 2 AC 399, 404. Similarly, one joint tenant may release his interest to the other: ibid, 405.

[19] Litt s 280; Co Litt 181a; Blackstone, vol ii, p 183. The extinction of the deceased tenant's share and the corresponding enlargement in the other tenants' share is, however, a 'disposition' of it on his death for the purposes of the charge to inheritance tax: ITA 1984, s 3; McCutcheon, *Inheritance Tax* (5th edn, 2009), para 8-134; HM Revenue and Customs, Inheritance Tax Manual, para IHTM15012.

[20] Co Litt 181b. Since 1925, however, such an interest can arise only in equity: LPA 1925, s 1(3); above, pp 123–4.

B TENANCY IN COMMON

(1) Creation of Tenancy in Common

A tenancy in common arises

(i) where land is limited to two or more persons with words of severance showing an intention, even in the slightest degree,[21] that the donees are to take separate shares, or

(ii) where equity treats what is at law a joint tenancy as a tenancy in common,[22] or

(iii) where land was originally held by joint tenants but their joint tenancy has since been severed.[23]

The following expressions have at one time and another been construed as words of severance sufficient to create a tenancy in common:

equally to be divided;

to be divided;

in equal moieties;

equally;

amongst;

share and share alike.

So, also, if land is devised to A and B on condition that they pay in equal shares ten shillings a week to X during his life, this imposition of an equal burden on both donees shows that what would normally be a joint tenancy is to be a tenancy in common.[24]

The expression 'jointly and severally', which is a contradiction in terms, has been solved by the court holding that the first word prevails in a deed (thus creating a joint tenancy), but the last in a will.[25] Similarly, the words in a deed 'to hold in fee simple as beneficial joint tenants in common in equal shares' have been held to create a joint tenancy rather than a tenancy in common.[26]

(2) Differences Between Tenancy in Common and Joint Tenancy

There is a fundamental distinction between tenancy in common and joint tenancy.

(a) Unity

In the first place, that intimate union that exists between joint tenants does not necessarily exist in a tenancy in common. In a tenancy in common the one point in

---

[21] *Robertson v Fraser* (1871) 6 Ch App 696, 699; cf *Re Osoba* [1979] 1 WLR 247, 260.

[22] Below, pp 497–9.   [23] Below, pp 507–11.   [24] *Re North* [1952] Ch 397.

[25] *Slingsby's Case* (1587) 5 Co Rep 18b.

[26] *Joyce v Barker Bros (Builders) Ltd* (1980) 40 P & CR 512; cf *Martin v Martin* (1987) 54 P & CR 238, where similar words in a deed were held to create a tenancy in common. The second inconsistent clause constituted a severance of the joint tenancy and the creation of a tenancy in common; [1987] Conv 405 (JE Adams).

which the tenants are united is the right to possession.[27] They all occupy the whole, and if there are two tenants in common, A and B, A has an equal right with B to the possession of the whole land. But their union may stop at that point, for they may each hold different interests, such as where one has an equitable fee simple, the other a life interest; or where one is entitled to a two-thirds share, and the other to one third; and they may each hold under different titles, such as where one has bought and the other has succeeded to his share.[28] Each has a *share* in the ordinary meaning of that word. His share is undivided in the sense that its boundary is not demarcated, but nevertheless his right to a definite share exists.

(b) Survivorship

The second characteristic, and it is really the complement of the first, is that the *jus accrescendi* has no application to tenancies in common, so that, when one tenant dies, his share passes to his personal representatives, and not to the surviving tenant.[29] In the words of Challis:[30]

A tenancy in common, though it is an ownership only of an undivided share, is, for all practical purposes, a sole and several tenancy or ownership; and each tenant in common stands, towards his own undivided share, in the same relation that, if he were sole owner of the whole, he would bear towards the whole.

(3) *Equity Prefers Tenancy in Common to Joint Tenancy*

From early times the right of survivorship caused a divergence of views between common law and equity. Common law favoured joint tenancies because they inevitably led to the vesting of the property in one person through the operation of the doctrine of survivorship, and thus facilitated the performance of those feudal dues that were incident to the tenure of land.[31] But a tenancy in common never involved this right of survivorship, and the courts of equity inclined to construe a concurrent holding of property as a tenancy in common. Equity aims at equality, a feature that is conspicuous for its absence if the survivor becomes the absolute owner of the land. This preference of equity for a tenancy in common has been shown in four cases:

(a) Where joint purchasers of land provide purchase money in unequal shares

When purchasers take a conveyance to themselves in fee simple, they become joint tenants at law. Equity follows the law and does not treat the purchasers as being tenants in common, unless it can be inferred that they did not intend to take jointly.[32] Though this is not the only circumstance that will raise the inference, it is established that

---

[27] Co Litt 189a. [28] Blackstone, vol ii, p 191. [29] Ibid, p 194.
[30] *Law of Real Property*, p 368. [31] Above, pp 64–5.
[32] *Lake v Gibson* (1729) 1 Eq Cas Abr 290; *Lake v Craddock* (1732) 3 P Wms 158; White and Tudor, *Leading Cases in Equity*, vol ii, p 881.

purchasers who contribute the money in unequal proportions are to be regarded as tenants in common of the land conveyed.[33]

(b) Where money is advanced on mortgage by two or more persons

Where two or more persons advance money, either in equal or in unequal shares, and take a mortgage of land from the borrower to themselves jointly, *at law* they are joint tenants, so that the land and the right to the money belong absolutely to the survivor. The rule *in equity*, however, that prevails over the rule at law, is that they are tenants in common, and that the survivor is a trustee for the personal representatives of the deceased mortgagees.[34]

(c) Where land is bought by partners

In the leading case of *Lake v Craddock*,[35] where five persons joined in buying some waterlogged land with a view to its improvement by drainage, the court laid down the general rule that persons who make a joint purchase for the purposes of a joint undertaking or partnership, either in trade or in any other dealing, are to be treated in equity as tenants in common. This is, however, subject to contrary agreement by the partners:[36]

> it is necessary to disentangle two separate concepts, even if they bear upon one another. One is whether the property was partnership property.[37] If it was, then there is a strong presumption that the right of survivorship was not intended to apply.[38] The maxim is *ius accrescendi inter mercatores locum non habet*,[39] or the right of survivorship has no place among merchants. The other however is whether the partners nevertheless agreed to vary the normal rule of partnership property, in favour of their own autonomous consent to their being beneficial joint tenants with the standard consequence of that arrangement.

---

[33] *Robinson v Preston* (1858) 4 K & J 505; *Lake v Craddock*, above; White and Tudor, vol ii, p 882.

[34] *Petty v Styward* (1631) 1 Eq Cas Abr 290; *Steeds v Steeds* (1889) 22 QBD 537; White and Tudor, *Leading Cases in Equity* (9th edn, 1928), vol ii, pp 882–5. To ensure that a purchaser was not concerned with the separate interests of the lenders it became common practice to insert a *joint account clause* in a mortgage to trustees, which declared that upon the death of one of the mortgagees the receipt of the survivor should be a sufficient discharge for the money, and that the survivor should be able to reconvey the land without the concurrence of the personal representatives of the deceased trustee. The position was made clearer by the LPA 1925, s 111 (re-enacting Conveyancing Act 1881, s 61) that applies to all mortgages and not only those by trustees, provides that where there is a mortgage for the payment of money and either the sum advanced is expressly stated to be advanced by more persons than one on a joint account, or a mortgage is made to them jointly the money lent shall, as *between the mortgagees and the mortgagor*, be deemed to belong to the mortgagees on a joint account, and the survivor shall be able to give a complete discharge for the money, notwithstanding any notice to the payer of a severance of the joint account. However, evidence is admissible to show that, despite the presence of a joint account clause, it was intended that the money should belong to the lenders as tenants in common: *Re Jackson* (1887) 34 Ch D 732.

[35] (1732) 3 P Wms 158.

[36] *Bathurst v Scarborow* [2004] EWCA Civ 411, [2005] 1 P & CR 4 at [44] (Rix LJ); *Barton v Morris* [1985] 1 WLR 1257.

[37] Partnership Act 1890, ss 20, 21.   [38] *Elliot v Brown* (1791) 3 Swan 489n.   [39] Co Litt 182a.

(d) Where joint purchasers of land hold it for their individual business purposes

In *Malayan Credit Ltd v Jack Chia-MPH Ltd*, where it was held that business tenants who had paid rent and service charges in agreed proportions were tenants in common, Lord Brightman said:[40]

> Their Lordships do not accept that the cases in which joint tenants at law will be presumed to hold as tenants in common in equity are as rigidly circumscribed as the plaintiff asserts. Such are not necessarily limited to purchasers who contribute unequally, to co-mortgagees and to partners. There are other circumstances in which equity may infer that the beneficial interest is intended to be held by the grantees as tenants in common. In the opinion of their Lordships, one such case is where the grantees hold the premises for their several individual business purposes.

Despite these exceptional cases, the fundamental rule is that whenever land is granted or devised to two or more persons simply and without words of severance, the donees become joint tenants holding a single title, interest and possession, and when one dies his interest is extinguished and passes to the survivor or survivors.

(4) Determination of Tenancy in Common

The three methods by which a tenancy in common is determined and converted into separate ownership are (a) partition, (b) sale, and (c) the acquisition by one tenant, whether by grant or by operation of law, of the shares vested in his co-tenants.

III CONCURRENT INTERESTS IN THE MODERN LAW

The object of the legislation of 1925 was to simplify conveyances of land and, where this simplicity could not otherwise be attained, to make radical alterations in the pre-1926 law. The law relating to concurrent interests was a subject that called for considerable alteration. If conveyancing is to be a simple matter, one primary essential is that the legal estate to be acquired by a purchaser should be vested in an easily ascertainable person and not distributed among a number of persons whose titles will each require to be investigated.

A CONVEYANCING DIFFICULTIES BEFORE 1926

The principal difficulty before 1926 arose from the fact that at common law the title to property could be held either as a joint tenancy, or as a tenancy in common.

---

[40] [1986] AC 549, 560.

(1) Joint Tenancy

Joint tenancy does not raise difficulties in this respect, for although several persons are interested in the land, there is only one title to be deduced, and if the purchaser is satisfied as to the validity of the deed or the will under which the tenancy stands limited, he is not concerned further with the tenants except to see that they are parties to the deed of sale.

(2) Tenancy in Common

In tenancy in common, however, the case is different, for the existence of a number of persons interested in the land, each of whom, as we have seen, is entitled to a separate share, raised a serious hindrance to simplicity of transfer. An analogous difficulty occurs in the case of a strict settlement where the beneficial title is distributed among a number of persons *in succession*, but we have seen that this plurality of interests is not allowed to hinder conveyancing, since the tenant for life is treated as the fee simple owner for purposes of transmission, and the interests of the various beneficiaries are not allowed to affect a purchaser.[41] The conveyancing problem raised by a number of successive interests is in fact comparatively simple, because the tenant for life is obviously marked out as the person to act as an intermediary for passing the legal estate.

But if land can be held by tenants in common, there is no one person in whom the legal estate can appropriately be vested, since all the tenants have the equal right to present enjoyment, so that tenancy in common is a greater hindrance to simplicity of transfer than a settlement. The complication in such a case is that the separate title of each tenant must be investigated.

> Lastly, all this confusion is 'worse confounded' by concurrent ownership in tenancy in common. Here is an example that recently came before me in my official capacity. A man by his will devised his freeholds to the use of his wife for life, and after her death to the use of his children in fee simple. He had ten children; one of them died during the widow's life, leaving a similar will, seven children, and a widow. This is quite a simple example; yet the result is that a house worth about £150 per annum is (the widow being dead) now vested (not merely in equity but at law) in seventeen persons in the following proportions:
>
> (1) Each of the nine living children of the testator or their assigns: 7/70
>
> (2) Each of the seven children of the deceased child, subject to the prior life interest of their mother: 1/70
>
> Moreover, several of the parties have mortgaged their shares, and in the result when the great expense of proving the title of each of the seventeen has been paid, a very small balance will remain for distribution. Thus, tenancy in common is (having regard to the Settled Land Acts) a far greater detriment to the proper management of land than settlements (which are popularly debited with this sin), and introduces infinitely greater difficulty with

---

[41] Above, p 126.

regard to its sale, as not only must the parties be unanimous, but the title of each of them has to be deduced.[42]

B SCHEME OF THE 1925 LEGISLATION AND THE TRUSTS OF LAND AND APPOINTMENT OF TRUSTEES ACT 1996

In order to overcome such difficulties, the Law of Property Act 1925 revolutionised the law relating to tenancies in common.

The object was to enable land that is subject to such tenancies to be sold without casting upon the purchaser any obligation to consider the titles or the beneficial rights of the tenants.[43]

(1) Tenancies in Common

(a) Legal tenancies in common abolished

The first step in the attainment of the object of the legislation was the enactment that:

a legal estate is not capable of subsisting or of being created in an undivided share in land.[44]

This means that there can never be a legal tenancy in common, that is, a tenancy in common of a legal estate.

(b) Legal estate held on trust

It was then enacted that:

An undivided share in land shall ... only take effect behind a trust of land.[45]

The effect is that the legal estate must be held by trustees holding as legal joint tenants upon trust. This may be an express trust. But if no express trust is created, then an implied trust is imposed by statute. Until 1997 the trust mechanism used was that of a trust for sale. As we have seen,[46] all concurrent interests created after 1996 come within the new scheme for the trust of land. If an express trust for sale was created before 1997, it now comes within the definition of a trust of land, still with a duty to sell but now with a mandatory power to postpone the sale;[47] and the implied trust for sale is converted into a trust of land.[48]

(c) Legal joint tenancy cannot be severed

The corner-stone of this new structure is the vesting of the legal estate in joint tenants as trustees of land and, since it is essential to the success of the scheme that

---

42 Acquisition and Valuation of Land Committee, Fourth Report (1919), p 30 (Sir Arthur Underhill).
43 See *City of London Building Society v Flegg* [1988] AC 54, 77 (Lord Oliver of Aylmerton).
44 LPA 1925, s 1(6). The 1925 legislation refers to 'undivided share' not to 'tenancy in common'.
45 SLA 1925, s 36(4), as amended by TLATA 1996, s 25(1), Sch 3, para 2(1), (11) (replacing 'trust for sale' by 'trust of land').
46 Above, pp 476–7.   47 TLATA 1996, s 4.   48 Ibid, s 5, Sch 2, para 3.

this legal joint tenancy should remain intact until terminated by sale, it was enacted that:

> no severance of a joint tenancy of a legal estate, so as to create a tenancy in common in land, shall be permissible.[49]

The basic effect of the scheme is that the legal estate is held by trustees of land who hold it as legal joint tenants, but who are unable to sever; and, as in the case of all settlements by way of trust, the beneficial interests exist in equity behind the trust. The beneficial interests may be held as a joint tenancy, or as a tenancy in common; but, on the sale of the legal estate by the trustees, a purchaser is not concerned with these equitable beneficial interests and takes free from them. They are overreached, provided that the purchase money is paid to at least two trustees or to a trust corporation; the beneficiaries then have corresponding rights in the purchase money.[50]

(d) Effect of failure to create a trust

If the correct method of a conveyance upon trust is not adopted, the Law of Property Act 1925 contains a number of provisions designed to ensure that, no matter what form the transaction may have taken, the effect shall be exactly the same as if the tenancy in common had been properly limited behind a trust. There appear to be two normal cases, namely a direct conveyance of the legal estate to tenants in common, and a devise to tenants in common.

(1) Conveyance

With regard to a conveyance, section 34(2)[51] of the Law of Property Act 1925 provides that:

> where [after 1925] land is expressed to be conveyed to any persons in undivided shares and those persons are of full age, the conveyance shall ... operate as if the land had been expressed to be conveyed to the grantees, or, if there are more than four grantors, then to the first four named in the conveyance, as joint tenants in trust for the persons interested in the land.

Thus, if land is conveyed in fee simple to A, B, C, D and E in equal shares, A, B, C and D become joint tenants of the legal estate, while all five are entitled under the trust as equitable tenants in common.

(2) Devise

A devise to two or more persons in undivided shares operates to vest the legal estate in the personal representatives of the testator for the persons interested in the land, but in either case the land is held on trust and not (even before it was provided that after 1996 no new settlements could be created[52]) as settled land.[53]

---

[49] LPA 1925, s 36(2). For severance, see below, pp 507–11.
[50] Above, pp 486–7; below, pp 1068–9, 1114–17.
[51] As amended by TLATA 1996, s 5, Sch 2, para 3(1), (2), (6).   [52] Above, p 475.
[53] LPA 1925, s 34(3), as amended by TLATA 1996, s 5, Sch 2, para 3(1), (3), (6); Sch 4.

(e) Settlement

As regards settlements, section 36(4) of the Settled Land Act 1925[54] provides that a tenancy in common shall not be capable of creation except under a trust instrument or under the above provisions of the Law of Property Act 1925, and shall then take effect under a trust of land. Thus if it is desired to settle land on A and B for their lives in equal shares, with remainder to C in fee simple, the legal estate must be vested in the trustees of land.

If beneficiaries under a pre-1997 settlement become entitled in possession to the land, for example, where in a devise

to X for life, remainder to X's children equally during their lives

X dies leaving three children, the legal fee simple that was formerly held by X as tenant for life must be vested in the trustees of the settlement and held by them in trust for X's children.[55] The settlement within the meaning of the Settled Land Act 1925 comes to an end and is replaced by a trust of land.

(f) Defect in scheme of Law of Property Act 1925

The policy of the Law of Property Act 1925 was clearly to subject all forms of co-ownership to a trust for sale,[56] except those that are within the Settled Land Act 1925. It seems doubtful, however, whether the language of these enactments covers all cases in which a tenancy in common may arise, as for example when two persons buy land and contribute the purchase price in unequal shares.[57] This was the position in *Bull v Bull*,[58] where:

a mother and son bought a house as a home for themselves, the conveyance being made to the son only, who had provided the greater part of the purchase price. In an action in which the issue was the validity of a notice to quit served on the mother, the Court of Appeal, citing section 36(4) of the Settled Land Act 1925, held that the parties were tenants in common in equity, and that the legal estate vested in the son upon the statutory trusts for sale.

This decision, though expedient, was difficult to fit into the words of the legislation. There was nothing that could constitute a trust instrument within the meaning of section 36(4) of the Settled Land Act 1925; and the land was not 'expressed to be conveyed' to persons in undivided shares as required by section 34(2) of the Law of Property Act 1925. It seems, then, that the courts would readily impose a trust for sale if this fulfilled the intention of the parties.

---

[54] As amended by TLATA 1996, s 25(1), Sch 3, para 2(1), (11).   [55] SLA 1925, s 36(1), (2), (3).
[56] And now, since 1997, a trust of land under TLATA 1996.   [57] Above, p 497.
[58] [1955] 1 QB 234, followed in *Cook v Cook* [1962] P 181; affd [1962] P 235. See too *Re Buchanan-Wollaston's Conveyance* [1939] Ch 217; affd [1939] Ch 738, where a conveyance to purchasers as joint tenants (who contributed unequally) was treated as coming within LPA 1925, s 36(1); *Williams & Glyn's Bank Ltd v Boland* [1979] Ch 312, 329; affd [1981] AC 487 (where a matrimonial home, to whose purchase both spouses contributed, was conveyed to one spouse only).

This technical difficulty still remains after 1996, since the opportunity was not taken to amend section 34(2) of the Law of Property Act in the Trust of Land and Appointment of Trustees Act 1996.

(g) Advantages of scheme

We now examine the effect of the statutory trust of land that arises in these various cases from the point of view, first, of a purchaser of the land, secondly, of the beneficiaries.

(1) Advantage to purchaser

The advantage to the purchaser is that he is no longer compelled to investigate the title of each tenant in common. He is concerned only with the legal estate held by the joint tenants upon trust, since the rights of the persons beneficially entitled exist merely as equitable interests behind the trust, and they are overreached upon a conveyance of the land by the trustees, provided that the purchase money is paid to at least two trustees or to a trust corporation. It is a matter of indifference, therefore, that some of the tenants in common are minors, or that some of them are unwilling to acquiesce in the sale. Although the trustees are required, so far as practicable, to consult, and give effect to the wishes of the beneficiaries entitled in possession, or in the case of a dispute, of the majority in terms of value, yet it is expressly enacted that it shall be no concern of a purchaser to see that this requirement has been complied with.[59]

(2) Advantage to tenants in common

The advantage to the tenants in common is that, no matter how numerous they may be, a sale of the land effected is always possible without difficulty or undue expense. They are not prejudiced economically by the loss of their rights in the land itself, for they have corresponding rights in the money arising from the sale. Thus if A is entitled under the tenancy in common to a half share in the land, and B and C are entitled to a quarter share each, the duty of the trustees is to ensure that A, B and C receive the purchase money in the same proportions. They need not sell at once, nor indeed at any time, for they may instead of selling, partition the land among the persons beneficially entitled.[60] The tenants in common can still deal with their equitable interests as freely as (before 1925) they could have dealt with their legal interests. If A, B and C are tenants in common and C sells his equitable interest to D, the legal joint tenancy remains vested in the trustees upon the trust for A, B and D.

(2) Joint Tenancies

Certain consequential changes were also effected by the reforms of 1925 and 1996 in joint tenancies, and the law relating to this matter varies according as the land is, or is not, settled within the meaning of the Settled Land Act 1925.

---

[59] TLATA 1996, s 11(1), 16(1), above, pp 484, 487, replacing LPA 1925, s 26(3).
[60] Ibid, s 7, replacing LPA 1925, s 28(3), below, pp 506–7.

(a) Settled land

If two or more persons are beneficially entitled for their lives under a strict settlement created before 1997, such as where land was devised to X and Y for their lives with remainder to Z in fee simple,[61] they together constitute the tenant for life within the meaning of the Settled Land Act and there is no question of any trust for sale.[62] They are invested with the legal estate, and it is their function to make title upon a sale or other disposition of the land.

(b) Joint tenants beneficially entitled

In the second case, however, where the land is not settled, but is *beneficially* limited for a legal estate to joint tenants, for example, where a father conveys Blackacre to his two sons in fee simple without words of severance, the *legal* estate is held upon trust in like manner as if the persons beneficially entitled were tenants in common.[63] Thus if land is granted to A, B and C jointly in fee simple, A, B and C become joint tenants of the legal estate upon trust for themselves as equitable joint tenants. Both a legal and an equitable joint tenancy are automatically and inescapably brought into existence. A, B and C are trustees of the legal estate[64] and can therefore make title, but they are joint beneficiaries with regard to the equitable interests. They may postpone the sale of the land, indefinitely, but if there is a matter of dispute, any one of them may apply to the court under section 14 of the Trusts of Land and Appointment of Trustees Act 1996.[65]

(c) Determination of joint tenancy

A joint tenancy may be determined altogether (that is determination of both the legal and equitable joint tenancy); or a joint tenant, while retaining the legal joint tenancy, may sever it on its equitable side so as to create an equitable tenancy in common.

(1) Determination of legal and equitable joint tenancy

A joint tenancy is determined altogether by any one of the following methods.

(i) Sale of the legal estate

If A and B sell in their capacity as trustees of land,[66] their conveyance passes the legal fee simple to the purchaser freed from their rights as joint tenants. The purchaser is not

---

[61] See also *Re Gaul and Houlston's Contract* [1928] Ch 689; devise to X and Y in fee simple, subject to a charge, created voluntarily, of £1,000 in favour of Z. Thus, the land was settled by virtue of SLA 1925, s 1(1) (v); above, p 435.

[62] SLA 1925, s 19(2).

[63] LPA 1925, s 36(1), as amended by TLATA 1996, s 5, Sch 2, para 4(1), (2), (4).

[64] They must not exceed four in number: TA 1925, s 34, as amended by TLATA 1996, s 25(1), Sch 3, para 3(9). See (1926) 42 LQR 478, 480 (RR Formoy).

[65] Above, p 488.

[66] If any of the trustees or beneficiaries refuse to agree to a sale, the other(s) may apply to the court: TLATA 1996, s 14; above, p 489.

concerned with these rights, since they exist behind the trust and are merely equitable in nature, and will be overreached.[67]

A trust cannot be exercised unless there are at least two trustees, but the Law of Property (Amendment) Act 1926 provides that a surviving joint tenant, who is solely and *beneficially* entitled to the land, may deal with the legal estate as if it were not held on a trust.[68] Thus if land is held in fee simple by a husband and wife jointly, the wife, on the death of her husband, can pass a good title to a purchaser of the legal estate without appointing another trustee in place of her husband.[69]

Such a conveyance, however, is not without its dangers, for a deceased tenant, without the knowledge of the survivor, may have severed his interest, a fact that will not appear on the vendor's abstract of title to the legal estate on which, in unregistered land, a purchaser must rely in order to investigate the vendor's title.[70] It used to be felt, therefore, that the only sure method of overreaching any equitable interest that may have arisen by virtue of severance was for the survivor to reconstitute the trust by appointing a new trustee. But this is no longer necessary. The Law of Property (Joint Tenants) Act 1964,[71] which is retrospective to 1 January 1926, provides that:

> the survivor of two or more joint tenants shall, in favour of a purchaser of the legal estate, be deemed to be solely and beneficially interested if the conveyance includes a statement that he is so interested.[72]

This provision is not, however, to apply if a memorandum of severance has been endorsed on or annexed to the conveyance by which the legal estate was vested in the joint tenants; or if a receiving order, or a petition for such an order, has been registered under the Land Charges Act 1972.[73]

The 1964 Act applies only to unregistered land.[74] Where title to land is registered, a joint proprietor restriction should be entered on the register.[75]

(ii) Partition

If all the joint tenants are of full age, as beneficial owners they may partition the land between themselves, whereupon the legal joint tenancy will be converted into separate

---

[67] Above, pp 486–7; below, pp 1068–9, 1114–17.   [68] Sched, amending LPA 1925, s 36.

[69] According to *Re Cook* [1948] Ch 212, this would be the position apart from the Act of 1926, since, on the death of the husband the entire interest in the land, both legal and equitable, vests in the wife. The trust ceases, since she is now owner and cannot be trustee for herself.

[70] Below, p 1042.

[71] See Wolstenholme and Cherry, vol 2, pp 149–51; Barnsley, *Conveyancing Law and Practice* (4th edn, 1996), pp 315–17; (1964) 28 Conv (NS) 329; (1966) 30 Conv (NS) 27 (P Jackson); (1980) LSG 1473, 1475 (PH Kenny and A Kenny).

[72] S 1(1), as amended by LP(MP)A 1994, s 2(2), Sch 2.

[73] LP (Joint Tenants) A 1964, s 1(1), proviso. Registration constitutes notice of the order or petition to the purchaser.

[74] Ibid, s 3, as amended by LRA 2002, Sch 11, para 5.

[75] This is not, however, necessarily as effective as the 1964 Act: [2004] Conv 41 (E Cooke), proposing amendments to LRA 2002 to bring registered land into line with unregistered land. For restrictions generally in registered land, see above, p 478; below, pp 1099–100.

ownership. Apart from this, however, section 36(1) of the Law of Property Act 1925[76] provides, as we have seen, that where a legal estate is beneficially limited to persons as joint tenants it shall be held on trust *in like manner as if the persons beneficially entitled were tenants in common*. Section 7 of the Trusts of Land and Appointment of Trustees Act 1996 provides that, where the beneficiaries of full age are absolutely entitled in undivided shares to land subject to the trust, the trustees may, with the consent of each of those beneficiaries, partition the land or any part of it and provide by way of mortgage or otherwise for the payment of any equality money.[77]

If the trustees or any of the beneficiaries refuse to agree to a partition, any beneficiary may apply to the court under section 14 of the Act. The court may then make such order as it thinks fit, for example an order for sale. If the beneficiaries are of full age and capacity and absolutely entitled to the land, the trustees may insist that they accept a conveyance of the land.[78]

(iii) Release

Where land is held by A and B as joint tenants, it is open to either of them to release his interest to the other, whereupon the alienee will become sole and several owner.[79] An agreement for such a release must satisfy the requirements for a contract for the sale or other disposition of land.[80]

(2) Determination of equitable joint tenancy. Severance

Since 'each joint tenant stands, in all respects, in exactly the same position as each of the others',[81] it follows that anything that creates a distinction between them severs the tenancy and converts it into a tenancy in common.[82] Five methods of severance were established before 1926:

(a) alienation by one joint tenant;

(b) acquisition by one tenant of a greater interest than that held by his co-tenants;

(c) mutual agreement;[83]

(d) any course of dealing sufficient to intimate that the interests of all were mutually treated as constituting a tenancy in common;[84] and

---

[76] As amended by TLATA 1996, s 5, Sch 2, para 4(1), (3), (4).

[77] Replacing LPA 1925, s 28(3). See *Re Gorringe and Braybon Ltd's Contract* [1934] Ch 614n; *Re Brooker* [1934] Ch 610.

[78] TLATA 1996, s 6(2).

[79] LPA 1925, s 36(2), as amended by TLATA 1996, s 5, Sch 2, para 4(1), (3), (4).

[80] Below, Ch 24; *Cooper v Critchley* [1955] Ch 431.

[81] Challis, *Law of Real Property* (3rd edn, 1911), p 367. See Law Commission WP No 94, *Trusts of Land* (1985), paras 16.11–16.14; below, p 508, n 85.

[82] Where the parties expressly create a beneficial joint tenancy, the shares of the tenants in common on severance are equal, even if they contributed unequally to the purchase price; where they do not, the beneficiaries may claim shares proportionate to their contributions: *Goodman v Gallant* [1986] Fam 106; [1986] Conv 205 (S Juss).

[83] *Williams v Hensman* (1861) 1 John & H 546 at 557; *Burgess v Rawnsley* [1975] Ch 429, M & B p 570.

[84] *Williams v Hensman*, above, at 557 (Page Wood V-C).

(e) where one joint tenant criminally kills another joint tenant.

In 1925 an additional method was added:[85]

(f) written notice under section 36(2) Law of Property Act 1925.

(a) Alienation by a joint tenant

Although during the continuance of the tenancy one joint tenant holds nothing separately from his fellows, there is a general rule to the effect that *alienatio rei praefertur juri accrescendi*[86]—alienation of the property takes priority over the right of survivorship—and accordingly it has long been the law that one joint tenant can alienate his share to a stranger. The effect of such alienation, whether by way of sale or mortgage,[87] is to convert the joint tenancy into a tenancy in common, since the alienee and the remaining tenant or tenants hold by virtue of different titles and not under that one common title that is essential to the existence of a joint tenancy.

> If A and B are joint tenants in fee simple and A makes a grant in fee simple to X, the result is that B and X hold the lands as tenants in common, in equal undivided shares. If A, B and C are joint tenants in fee simple and A makes a grant to X in fee simple, X is tenant in common with B and C, though as between themselves the latter continue to hold as joint tenants.[88]

Severance may also be effected by involuntary alienation, as where a joint tenant is adjudicated bankrupt and his interest vests in his trustee in bankruptcy.[89]

Owing to the doctrine of survivorship, no severance results from a disposition by will—*jus accrescendi praefertur ultimae voluntati*: the right of survivorship takes priority over the last will.[90]

---

[85] Law Commission WP No 94, *Trusts of Land* (1985) suggested that the only means of severance should be by notice in writing (para 6.12); and that it should be possible to sever by will (para 16.14). As to whether beneficial joint tenancies should be abolished, see [1987] Conv 29, 225 (MP Thompson) in favour; 273 (AM Prichard) against. See also [1995] Conv 105 (L Tee).

[86] Co Litt 185a.

[87] *Cedar Holdings Ltd v Green* [1981] Ch 129, 138 (Buckley LJ); *First National Securities Ltd v Hegerty* [1985] QB 850 (joint tenancy held to be severed where husband purported to mortgage jointly owned property by forging wife's signature); *Ahmed v Kendrick* (1987) 56 P & CR 120 (severance where husband sold jointly owned house by forging wife's signature on both contract and registered transfer); *Edehomo v Bowling & Co Solicitors* [2011] EWHC 393 (Ch), [2011] 21 EG 96 at [22] (husband's forgery of wife's signature on contract sufficient to sever); cf *Penn v Bristol and West Building Society* [1995] 2 FLR 938 (no severance where purchaser colluded in forgery by husband joint tenant of his wife's signature on the conveyance); *Monarch Aluminium v Rickman* [1989] CLY 1526 (charging order nisi held to be severance).

[88] Litt s 292.

[89] *Re Dennis* [1996] Ch 80; [1995] All ER Rev 292 (SM Cretney); *Re Gorman* [1990] 1 WLR 616; *Re Pavlou* [1993] 1 WLR 1046; cf *Re Palmer* [1994] Ch 316 (insolvency administration order); [1995] Conv 68 (M Haley); [1995] CLJ 52 (L Tee); Emmet, paras 11.104-11.105.

[90] Blackstone, vol ii, pp 185–6. The instructions to a solicitor, during the lifetime of the joint tenants, to prepare mutual wills dealing with the property can however be sufficient then to sever the joint tenancy: *Re Woolnough* [2002] WTLR 595. And a variation of the dispositions of the deceased's property on his death, made by beneficiaries of the estate for the purposes of inheritance tax (ITA 1984, s 142), may include the severance of a joint tenancy and the redirection of the deceased tenant's interest so as to avoid the consequences of the doctrine of survivorship: McCutcheon, *Inheritance Tax*, para 8–134.

(b) Acquisition of larger interest by a joint tenant

A joint tenancy is also severed if one of the joint tenants subsequently acquires an interest greater in quantum than that held by his co-tenants. This destruction of the unity of interest may result from the act of the parties or by operation of law. As an instance of the former: if A and B are joint tenants for life and A purchases the fee simple in reversion, the joint tenancy is severed: A holding an undivided half in fee simple and B an undivided half for life.[91]

Again, A may release his interest to B and so terminate the tenancy by vesting the whole ownership in B.[92]

A case in which a greater interest than that held by his co-tenants is cast upon a joint tenant by operation of law occurs where the reversion in fee descends to one of the joint tenants.[93]

(c) Mutual agreement

The joint tenants may sever their joint tenancy by mutual agreement, which need not be specifically enforceable. The significance of the agreement is not that it binds the parties, but that it serves as an indication of a common intention to sever.[94]

(d) Course of dealing

A course of dealing need not amount to an agreement, express or implied, for severance. Lord Denning said:[95]

> It is sufficient if there is a course of dealing in which one party makes clear to the other that he desires that their shares should no longer be held jointly but be held in common. I emphasise that it must be clear to the other party.

Thus, it was held that there was severance where one joint tenant negotiates with another for some rearrangement of interest, even though the negotiations break down.[96]

---

91 Co Litt s 182b; *Wiscot's Case* (1599) 2 Co Rep 60b.   92 *Re Schär* [1951] Ch 280.

93 Cruise, *Digest*, Tit xviii, c ii, s 7. Contrary to the view of the majority of the Court of Appeal, it is submitted that the two methods of severance already discussed avail a husband or wife in respect of the matrimonial home: *Bedson v Bedson* [1965] 2 QB 666, 688–91 (Russell LJ, dissenting, who said that the majority view was 'without the slightest foundation in law or equity'); (1966) 82 LQR 29 (REM). The view of Russell LJ was preferred by Plowman J in *Re Draper's Conveyance* [1969] 1 Ch 486, 494, M & B p 568; and by Lawton LJ in *Harris v Goddard* [1983] 1 WLR 1203, 1208.

94 *Burgess v Rawnsley* [1975] Ch 429, 445 (Sir John Pennycuick), M & B p 570; *Hunter v Babbage* (1994) 69 P & CR 548 (draft agreement); cf *Edwards v Hastings* [1996] NPC 87 (agreement to sever conditional on sale of family home).

95 *Burgess v Rawnsley*, above, at 439.

96 Ibid. See also *Re Draper's Conveyance* [1969] 1 Ch 486, M & B p 568; below, p 510; *Greenfield v Greenfield* (1979) 38 P & CR 570 (conversion of house jointly owned by brothers into two self-contained maisonettes occupied separately held not to be severance); *Barton v Morris* [1985] 1 WLR 1257 (inclusion of jointly owned property as a partnership asset in the partnership accounts for tax purposes held not to be severance); *Re Gore and Snell v Carpenter* (1990) 60 P & CR 456 (negotiations between husband and wife with a view to settling claim for ancillary relief in divorce proceedings held not to be severance in absence of a final agreement between them).

The onus of proving severance under this heading is on the party who desires to establish it.[97]

(e) By homicide

This occurs where one joint tenant criminally kills another joint tenant. No one may benefit in law from his own crime, so that there is necessarily a severance that prevents the killer from taking any beneficial interest by survivorship. In *Re K*, where a matrimonial home was owned jointly by the killer and his victim, it was held to have been rightly conceded that there was a severance of the joint tenancy, so that the beneficial interest (subject to relief under the Forfeiture Act 1982) vested in the deceased and the survivor as tenants in common.[98]

(f) Written notice under section 36(2) Law of Property Act 1925

The Law of Property Act 1925 added a new and very useful method of severance. Section 36(2)[99] provides:

> where a legal estate (not being settled land) is vested in joint tenants beneficially, and any tenant desires to sever the joint tenancy in equity, he shall give to the other joint tenants a notice[100] in writing of such desire or do such other acts or things as would, in the case of personal estate, have been effectual to sever the tenancy in equity, and thereupon the land shall be held in trust on terms which would have been requisite for giving effect to the beneficial interests if there had been an actual severance.

It should be noted that the statute refers to the case where the legal estate in land is not settled land, but is vested in joint tenants who also hold beneficially under a joint tenancy. It does not cover severance of a joint tenancy in chattels; nor, at least if it is strictly construed, where the beneficial joint tenants are different persons from the legal owner(s), such as where A holds the legal title on trust for A and B as beneficial joint tenants, or where A and B hold the legal title on trust for C and D. But it clearly covers the case where land is limited to A, B and C as joint tenants, which creates both

---

[97] *Re Denny* (1947) 177 LT 291; *McDowell v Hirschfield Lipson* [1992] 2 FLR 126.

[98] *Re K* [1985] Ch 85; affd [1986] Ch 180; Maudsley and Burn, *Trusts and Trustees* (7th edn, 2008), pp 302–7. There was previously no English authority on the point. See *Schobelt v Barber* (1966) 60 DLR (2d) 519 and *Re Pechar* [1969] NZLR 574, where it was held that the law imposes a constructive trust of one undivided half share for the benefit of the next of kin of the deceased other than the killer.

[99] As amended by TLATA 1996, s 5, Sch 2, para 4(1), (2), (4). *Re Draper's Conveyance* [1969] 1 Ch 486, M & B p 568 (issue of summons held to amount to notice in writing under s 36(2)); (1968) 84 LQR 462 (PVB). Cf *Harris v Goddard* [1983] 1 WLR 1203 (wife's prayer in a divorce petition for a property adjustment order to be made in respect of the former matrimonial home held not to be notice); [1984] Conv 148 (S Coneys); *Grindal v Hooper* [1999] EGCS 150 (notice of severance effective, even though not endorsed on conveyance). Whether a unilateral act not amounting to notice under s 36(2) can effect severance is a matter of dispute: *Burgess v Rawnsley* [1975] Ch 429, M & B p 570; [1976] CLJ 20 (DJ Hayton); (1977) 41 Conv (NS) 243 (SM Bandali).

[100] *Re 88 Berkeley Road, London NW9* [1971] Ch 648 (notice properly served if sent by recorded delivery, even if not received by addressee: LPA 1925, s 196(4)); *Kinch v Bullard* [1999] 1 WLR 423 (severance although wife posted notice to husband but destroyed it before he received it); [1999] Conv 60 (M Percival); [1998] All ER Rev 261 (PJ Clarke).

a legal and an equitable joint tenancy. If C dies without having dealt with his interest, A and B retain the legal estate as trustees, and hold the equitable interest under the doctrine of survivorship, freed from the interest of C. But if in his lifetime C gives notice in writing of his desire to sever, his equitable joint tenancy becomes an equitable tenancy in common, and A and B hold the legal estate upon trust for themselves as equitable joint tenants and the personal representatives of C. The equitable tenancy in common will continue to exist until the sale is carried out, or the shares become vested in one person, or partition is effected.

(3) Sale by Two Trustees and by One Trustee Only

We are now in a position to summarise the difference between a sale by at least two trustees of land that is beneficially co-owned and a sale by one of them only.

(a) Sale by two trustees

Where the sale is made by at least two trustees or a trust corporation the interests of the beneficiaries are overreached, provided that the purchaser pays the purchase money to the trustees.[101] And this is so whether or not the beneficial co-owners are occupying the land.

This is the same for both unregistered and registered land.

(b) Sale by only one trustee

Where, however, the sale is made by only one trustee, the overreaching provisions do not apply. It is then necessary to consider separately the position where the land is unregistered and where it is registered.

(1) Unregistered land

This was first illustrated by *Caunce v Caunce*,[102] where

> a husband and wife agreed that the wife would make a capital payment towards the purchase of a house, that the husband would pay the instalments to the building society, and that the conveyance would be in their joint names. The house was conveyed to the husband alone, however, and without the wife's knowledge he further charged it in favour of Lloyds Bank. On the husband's bankruptcy, one question was whether the bank took subject to, or free from, the wife's equitable interest. Stamp J held that the bank took free, as a bona fide purchaser of a legal estate for value without notice.

Thus, in that situation, whether or not a purchaser is bound by the interest of the beneficial co-owner depends upon the application of the old doctrine of the bona fide

---

101 Above, pp 486–7; below, pp 1068–9, 1114–17.

102 [1969] 1 WLR 286. The actual decision was disapproved in *Williams & Glyn's Bank Ltd v Boland* [1981] AC 487, where Lord Scarman said at 511 that he 'was by no means certain that *Caunce v Caunce* was correctly decided.' So too Russell LJ in *Hodgson v Marks* [1971] Ch 892, 924–5. It was not followed in *Kingsnorth Finance Co Ltd v Tizard* [1986] 1 WLR 783, above, p 88, n 112.

purchaser without notice.[103] If the bank had had notice, actual or constructive, of the wife's interest, the mortgage would have been subject to it.

(2) Registered land

If the title to the land is registered, notice plays no part. If a restriction has been entered in the register, it will preclude the registration of the purchaser as proprietor if the terms of the restriction have not been complied with.[104] If no restriction has been entered, registration of the purchaser as proprietor will give him priority over the beneficiary's interest unless it takes effect as an overriding interest by virtue of the beneficiary being in discoverable actual occupation of the land.[105]

The comparable case to *Caunce v Caunce* in registered land is *Williams & Glyn's Bank Ltd v Boland*,[106] where the House of Lords held that the bank was bound by the wife's overriding interest; she had not protected it by an entry on the register, but was in actual occupation when the mortgage was executed.

IV ESTABLISHING THE BENEFICIAL INTERESTS

A EXPRESS, CONSTRUCTIVE AND RESULTING TRUSTS

We have seen that, in the modern law, the legal estate, whether registered or unregistered, can be held by a number of persons (not exceeding four); but that they must hold under a joint tenancy since legal tenancies in common have not been permitted since 1926. Establishing the legal title is therefore relatively straightforward. Establishing the beneficial interests can be more difficult. Once it is found that any number of persons concurrently own the property in equity, they may hold under either a beneficial joint tenancy or a beneficial tenancy in common. However, we must now consider how the beneficial interests are to be established. The principles discussed in this section apply generally to the establishment of concurrent interests in equity, although they are most commonly encountered in relation to interests in the family home. Later we shall consider certain rules that are peculiar to the case of the family home.[107]

If a number of persons wish to own property jointly they may do so by creating an *express* trust of land, under which it is conveyed to trustees (who may be themselves), who become joint tenants of the legal estate upon trust for themselves, as either equitable

---

[103] Above, pp 83 ff.

[104] LRA 2002, s 41(1). In the case of a sole registered proprietor the appropriate restriction is Form A: LRR 2003, r 91, Sch 4 (as substituted by SI 2008 No 1919, r 4(6), Sch 4); the proprietor of land held on trust is required to apply for the restriction to be entered: LRR 2003, r 94(1), (2), but the beneficiary also has a sufficient interest to make application: ibid, r 93(a).

[105] Ibid, Sch 3, para 2.   [106] Above, n 102; a decision on LRA 1925, s 70(1)(g).

[107] Below, pp 519 ff.

joint tenants or equitable tenants in common. The terms of the trust may declare not only the nature of the equitable beneficial interests, but also the quantum of the interest that each partner is to own.[108] In registered land the required forms of transfer contain provision for a declaration of trust where there is more than one transferee.[109] But in some cases it may not be so simple. Where the legal estate is held by more than one person, the legal joint tenants necessarily hold on trust,[110] but whether in equity they hold as joint tenants or as tenants in common, and (if tenants in common) the quantum of the beneficiaries' respective shares, may not be declared. Further, the legal estate in the property may be conveyed to *one* party, but the beneficial interest is to be shared between (for example) the legal owner and his cohabiting partner, although there is no formal declaration of trust. The first question in this latter type of case is whether each of the parties has an interest in equity (that is, whether the sole legal owner holds on trust for himself and his partner rather than simply as sole beneficial owner); if so, the second question is whether the beneficial interests under the trust are held as joint tenants or as tenants in common, and (if tenants in common) what is the quantum of their respective shares. The House of Lords has made clear that, in the absence of an express declaration of trust, the starting point is that the equitable title matches the legal title:[111]

> Just as the starting point where there is sole legal ownership is sole beneficial ownership, the starting point where there is joint legal ownership is joint beneficial ownership. The onus is upon the person seeking to show that the beneficial ownership is different from the legal ownership. So in sole ownership cases it is upon the non-owner to show that he has any interest at all. In joint ownership cases, it is upon the joint owner who claims to have other than a joint beneficial interest.

The approach to be adopted in this area has been developed through a series of decisions, but particularly significant in the case of the sole legal owner are the decisions of the House of Lords in *Lloyds Bank plc v Rosset*,[112] and of the Court of

---

108 Fraud or mistake apart, this is conclusive: *Pettitt v Pettitt* [1970] AC 777, 813; *Goodman v Gallant* [1986] Fam 106; cf *City of London Building Society v Flegg* [1988] AC 54. For a detailed declaration of trust (and the subsequent waiver of rights of contribution to expenses incurred in relation to the property), see *Wade v Grimwood* [2004] EWCA Civ 999, [2004] 2 P & CR DG20.

109 See, eg, LRR 2003, r 206, Sch 1, Form TR1 (as substituted by SI 2008 No 1919, r 4(2), Sch 2, para 1), below, p 1087, where at para 10 the transferees must choose between three possibilities: 'they are to hold the property on trust for themselves as joint tenants'; 'they are to hold the property on trust for themselves as tenants in common in equal shares'; and 'they are to hold the property on trust … [*Complete as necessary*]'. 'The purpose of this is not to give the registrar notice of the trusts under which the land is held, but simply to enable us to decide whether we need to enter a form A restriction [above, n 104]. It also serves as a memorandum of the trusts on which the property is held. Although details of the trusts will not appear on the register': Land Registry Practice Guide 24, para 5.4. For the use of this form to declare a trust as a joint tenancy, see *Bathurst v Scarborow* [2004] EWCA Civ 411, [2005] 1 P & CR 4 at [8]-[10], [55].

110 Above, pp 501, 505.

111 *Stack v Dowden* [2007] UKHL 17, [2007] 2 AC 432 at [56] (Baroness Hale of Richmond). See also at [4] (Lord Hope of Craighead).

112 [1991] 1 AC 107; (1990) 106 LQR 539 (J Davies); [1990] Conv 314 (MP Thompson); [1991] CLJ 38 (M Dixon); (1991) 54 MLR 126 (S Gardner); [1998] Conv 202 (V Riniker); (1998) 18 LS 369 (S Wong). For the 'theoretical underpinning of this area of the law, and its development since those issues were considered by

Appeal in *Oxley v Hiscock*;[113] and in the case where the legal estate is held by two persons, the more recent decision of the House of Lords in *Stack v Dowden*.[114]

(1) Legal Estate Held by One Person: Finding a Trust

In *Lloyds Bank plc v Rosset* the House of Lords set out two bases on which a constructive trust could be found, where there is no declaration of trust to satisfy the formality requirements of section 53 of the Law of Property Act 1925. On either basis, the trust[115] arises from a combination of an agreement to share, coupled with reliance on that agreement by the party claiming a share.

First, the question is whether:[116]

> independently of any inference to be drawn from the conduct of the parties in the course of sharing the house as their home and managing their joint affairs, there has at any time prior to acquisition, or exceptionally at some later date, been any agreement, arrangement or understanding reached between them that the property is to be shared beneficially. The finding of an agreement or arrangement to share in this sense can only, I think, be based on evidence of express discussions between the partners, however imperfectly remembered and however imprecise their terms may have been.

There need have been no discussion about the value of the respective beneficial shares; the quantification of the parties' interests can be decided as a separate matter.[117] However, an excuse as to why the property has not been put into joint names may be treated as an expression of a common intention to share.[118] But before the agreement to share gives rise to a constructive trust, the partner asserting a claim to a beneficial interest against the partner entitled to the legal estate must show that he or she has acted to his or her detriment or significantly altered his or her position in reliance on the agreement.[119] The requirement of detrimental reliance is shown by significant contributions in money or money's worth, which need not be direct,[120] but not by activities that any wife would do, such as decorating and supervising builders.[121]

---

this House in *Pettitt v Pettitt* [1970] AC 777; *Gissing v Gissing* [1971] AC 886 and *Lloyds Bank plc v Rosset* [1991] 1 AC 107' see the opinion of Lord Walker in *Stack v Dowden* at [15] ff.

[113] [2004] EWCA Civ 546, [2005] Fam 211; (2004) 120 LQR 541 (S Gardner); [2005] Conv 79 (M Dixon), 496 (MP Thompson).

[114] [2007] UKHL 17, [2007] 2 AC 432.

[115] Lord Bridge referred to this giving rise to a constructive trust *or a proprietary estoppel*: [1991] 1 AC 107, 132. The link between constructive trust and proprietary estoppel in this context is discussed further below, pp 1015–16.

[116] [1991] 1 AC 107, 132 (Lord Bridge of Harwich).

[117] *Oxley v Hiscock* [2005] Fam 211, at [40] (Chadwick LJ).

[118] *Eves v Eves* [1975] 1 WLR 1338; *Grant v Edwards* [1986] Ch 638.

[119] *Lloyds Bank plc v Rosset* [1991] 1 AC 107, 132.

[120] *Grant v Edwards*, above; *Eves v Eves*, above; *Hammond v Mitchell* [1991] 1 WLR 1127 (unpaid assistance in business); [1992] Conv 218 (A Lawson); (1993) 56 MLR 224 (P O'Hagan).

[121] *Lloyds Bank plc v Rosset*, above.

Secondly, in the absence of any express common intention, the House of Lords suggested that a common intention could be implied from the conduct of the parties, such as the direct contributions to the purchase price (either initially or by payment of mortgage instalments) by the partner who is not the legal owner. However, it was said that it was 'at least extremely doubtful whether anything less will do.'[122] The denial of any interest to a wife who has made substantial indirect contributions seems harsh, was not supported by authority, and has now been disapproved.[123] The court is to take a broader view of the parties' conduct in order to ascertain their intentions:[124]

> The parties' whole course of conduct in relation to the property must be taken into account in determining their shared intentions as to its ownership.

It should be noted, however, that for a common intention to be inferred from the parties' conduct, it must be communicated between the parties. Conduct by one party that was not known by the other cannot be evidence of their common intention.[125]

If there is no common intention, either express or implied, to found a constructive trust, then it might be expected that the court should consider whether there is a resulting trust.[126] The parties' agreement should be given priority; but if there is no agreement, one can fall back on the resulting trust: where one partner contributes part of the purchase money, in the absence of contrary intention there is a presumption of

---

122 [1991] 1 AC 107, 133.

123 See *Gissing v Gissing* [1971] AC 886 (contributions must be 'referable' to the costs of acquisition); *Stack v Dowden*, above, n 114, at [26] (Lord Walker of Gestingthorpe), [63] (Baroness Hale of Richmond); *Abbott v Abbott* [2007] UKPC 53, [2008] 1 FLR 1451 at [19] (Baroness Hale of Richmond: 'The law has indeed moved on since [*Rosset*]'). See also *Holman v Howes* [2007] EWCA Civ 877, [2008] 1 FLR 1217 (no common intention to share beneficially); *James v Thomas* [2007] EWCA Civ 1212, [2008] 1 FLR 1598 (no common intention to share); *Morris v Morris* [2008] EWCA Civ 257, [2008] Fam Law 521 (no common intention to share); *Parris v Williams* [2008] EWCA Civ 1147, [2009] 1 P & CR 9 (express common intention under *Lloyds Bank plc v Rosset*: no need for 'bargain' by which claimant had agreed to do something in return for interest; *Oxley v Hiscock* and other recent cases not cited); *Webster v Webster* [2008] EWHC 31 (Ch); [2009] 1 FLR 1240 (claim for beneficial joint tenancy, but no common intention to share); *Hapeshi v Allnatt* [2010] EWHC 392 (Ch), [2010] All ER (D) 144 (Jan) (common intention to share where claimant's name could not appear on legal title because vendor local authority would not allow it).

124 *Abbott v Abbott*, above, n 123, at [19] (Baroness Hale of Richmond); [2007] Conv 456 (M Dixon); (2008) 124 LQR 209 (R Lee). For further discussion of this test in relation to the valuation of the parties interests once the trust is established, see below, p 517.

125 *Lightfoot v Lightfoot-Brown* [2005] EWCA Civ 201, [2005] 2 P & CR 22 (repayment of mortgage by one party, not known to the other, was not evidence of common intention). At [27] Arden LJ said: 'Chadwick LJ [in *Oxley v Hiscock*] did not dispense with the requirement for communication of the common intention when determining whether a common intention constructive trust had arisen. Indeed, the concept of communication of common intention has much in common with the manifestation of intention. An intention to share a beneficial interest in property has to be manifested to give rise to a rival obligation.... The need for communication was only held to be unnecessary in the *Oxley* case in respect to the size of the parties' beneficial interest.' Intention is tested objectively from the other party's perspective: *Gissing v Gissing*, above, n 123, at 906.

126 It is not, however, clear what room there is left for the application of the resulting trust analysis in the light of the approach in *Stack v Dowden*, at least if the courts are prepared to *impute* an intention to the parties, as well as to infer it: below, p 517.

a resulting trust in equity under which the other, as purchaser, holds the property on trust for them both to the extent of their respective contributions.[127]

(2) Valuing the Interests under the Trust

The valuation of the parties' respective interests under the constructive trust[128] is a separate matter that has recently been examined by both the Court of Appeal and the House of Lords. If the parties, in forming their agreement to share the property, also agreed what their interests should be, that will be conclusive.[129] However, where there is no evidence of an agreement on the value of the interests, the court must determine the parties' intention as to their respective interests, although there has been some controversy over the appropriate test for determining the intention.

In a case in which the legal estate was held by one person, but the intention to create a trust in favour of beneficial co-owners had been established on the facts, Chadwick LJ, settling a certain conflict in earlier decisions,[130] said in *Oxley v Hiscock*:[131]

> It must now be accepted that (at least in this court and below) the answer is that each is entitled to that share which the court considers fair having regard to the whole course of dealing between them in relation to the property. And, in that context, 'the whole course of dealing between them in relation to the property' includes the arrangements which they make from time to time in order to meet the outgoings (for example, mortgage contributions, council tax and utilities, repairs, insurance and housekeeping) which have to be met if they are to live in the property as their home.

---

[127] See eg *Gissing v Gissing* [1971] AC 886. The value of the share depends on the (direct) contributions made at the time of acquisition: *Curley v Parkes* [2004] EWCA Civ 1515, [2005] 1 P & CR DG 15; [2005] Conv 79 (M Dixon). Equality Act 2010, s 199 (when brought into force) will abolish the (rebuttable) presumption of advancement that a beneficial gift was intended where the *husband* provides the purchase money. This presumption might otherwise rebut the presumption of the resulting trust, although even before the enactment of the Equality Act it appeared that the presumption of advancement was already of little weight: *Pettitt v Pettitt* [1970] AC 777; *Falconer v Falconer* [1970] 1 WLR 1333.

[128] In the case of a resulting trust, the value of the parties' interests is fixed by reference to the contribution, and no separate question of valuation arises. This further explains why the constructive trust (based on the parties' agreement, both as to existence and as to valuation) should be considered ahead of the resulting trust.

[129] *Oxley v Hiscock* [2004] EWCA Civ 546, [2005] Fam 211 at [69]; *Wright v Johnson* [2001] EWCA Civ 1667, [2002] 2 P & CR 15 at [16]; *Crossley v Crossley* [2005] EWCA Civ 1581 [2006] 1 FCR 655.

[130] Especially *Springette v Defoe* (1992) 65 P & CR 1; *Midland Bank plc v Cooke* [1995] 4 All ER 562; (1996) 112 LQR 378 (S Gardner); (1996) 55 CLJ 194 (M Oldham); [1997] Conv 66 (M Dixon); (1997) 60 MLR 420 (P O'Hagan); *Drake v Whipp* [1996] 1 FLR 826; [1997] Conv 467 (A Dunn). See also *Stokes v Anderson* [1991] 1 FLR 391; *Huntingford v Hobbs* [1993] 1 FLR 736; *McHardy & Sons v Warren* [1994] 2 FCR 1247; *Le Foe v Le Foe* [2001] 2 FLR 970.

[131] At [69]. Applied in *Cox v Jones* [2004] EWHC 1486 (Ch), [2004] 2 FLR 1010; [2005] Conv 168 (R Probert) (25 per cent share for partner who contributed nothing to cost of the purchase of house, and a very small amount on works done on it, but forewent income from her practice as barrister, and 'her real contribution was the large amounts of time and energy she put in' during the building works: at [79]); *Supperstone v Hurst* [2005] EWHC 1309 (Ch), [2006] 1 FCR 352 (having made statement to the husband's creditors that she and her husband were equal beneficial owners in the property, wife could not obtain a determination from the court that her interest exceeded 50 per cent, in litigation between herself and trustee for those creditors).

This allows the court to take into account the facts at the time of the hearing[132] in order to decide what appears to be a fair share, although the relevant facts are still those that concern the parties' 'course of dealing in relation to the property'. It is linked to the property itself. But the valuation is not to be imputed artificially back to the parties' intention at the moment of acquisition when the court does not think that the parties at that moment had any particular intention as to the valuation of their shares.[133]

However, the formulation by Chadwick LJ has been doubted in so far as it might suggest that the court is to look for what is *fair* rather than what the parties might have *intended*. A preferred formulation, which emphasises the courts' search for the intention of the parties, is:[134]

If the question really is one of the parties' 'common intention', we believe that there is much to be said for adopting what has been called a 'holistic approach' to quantification, undertaking a survey of the whole course of dealing between the parties and taking account of all conduct which throws light on the question what shares were intended.

Even this test is not, however, without difficulty, since it has been said that the court is looking not only for actual intentions but also for inferred *or imputed* intention. In *Stack v Dowden* Baronness Hale of Richmond said:[135]

The search is to ascertain the parties' shared intentions, actual, inferred or imputed, with respect to the property in the light of their whole course of conduct in relation to it.

There can be a rather fine line between determining the 'imputed intention' of the parties and what the court thinks would be fair in all the circumstances of the case, unless one bases the imputation on a hypothetical negotiation between the actual parties, rather than on what reasonable parties would have agreed.[136] The Court of Appeal has rejected the suggestion that Baroness Hale's statement should be taken as enabling courts to find, by way of 'imputation', an intention where none was expressly uttered nor inferentially formed.[137]

[132] For the argument that this allows the trust to be 'ambulatory' in the sense that the parties' intentions may change over time, see *Stack v Dowden* [2007] UKHL 17, [2007] 2 AC 432 at [62]; and see also *Jones v Kernott* [2010] EWCA Civ 578, [2010] 1 WLR 2401 (no sufficient evidence of intention that beneficial joint tenancy should change over the 12 years from parties' separation to time when one party later sought to sever it; appeal to the Supreme Court heard May 2011).

[133] *Oxley v Hiscock*, above n 129, at [71]: 'in the absence of evidence that they gave any thought to the amount of their respective shares, the necessary inference is that they must have intended that question would be answered later on the basis of what was then seen to be fair', rejecting the approach taken in *Midland Bank plc v Cooke*, above.

[134] Law Com No 278, *Sharing Homes* (2002), para 4.27, preferred to the formulation in *Oxley v Hiscock* in *Stack v Dowden* [2007] UKHL 17, [2007] 2 AC 432 at [61] (Baroness Hale of Richmond) and [144]-[145] (Lord Neuberger). Baroness Hale said at [61]: 'For the court to impose its own view of what is fair upon the situation in which the parties find themselves would be to return to the days before *Pettitt v Pettitt* [1970] AC 777 without even the fig leaf of section 17 of the [Married Women's Property Act] 1882'.

[135] Above, n 134, at [60].

[136] Ibid, at [125]-[127] (Lord Neuberger dissenting, and rejecting vigorously the proposition that intention for the purposes of finding a constructive trust can be imputed).

[137] *Jones v Kernott*, above, n 132, at [77] (Rimer LJ); see also Wall LJ at [55]-[58]; [2010] Conv 324 (S Bridge); (2011) 127 LQR 13 (S Gardner and KM Davidson).

In *Stack v Dowden*[138] the House of Lords gave guidance on the factors that can be relevant to determine whether, in the case of joint legal owners, a party satisfies the burden of proving that he or she has in equity a greater share than the presumed joint beneficial tenancy:[139]

In law, 'context is everything' and the domestic context is very different from the commercial world. Each case will turn on its own facts. Many more factors than financial contributions may be relevant to divining the parties' true intentions. These include: any advice or discussions at the time of the transfer which cast light upon their intentions then; the reasons why the home was acquired in their joint names; the reasons why (if it be the case) the survivor was authorised to give a receipt for the capital moneys; the purpose for which the home was acquired; the nature of the parties' relationship; whether they had children for whom they both had responsibility to provide a home; how the purchase was financed, both initially and subsequently; how the parties arranged their finances, whether separately or together or a bit of both; how they discharged the outgoings on the property and their other household expenses. When a couple are joint owners of the home and jointly liable for the mortgage, the inferences to be drawn from who pays for what may be very different from the inferences to be drawn when only one is owner of the home. The arithmetical calculation of how much was paid by each is also likely to be less important. It will be easier to draw the inference that they intended that each should contribute as much to the household as they reasonably could and that they would share the eventual benefit or burden equally. The parties' individual characters and personalities may also be a factor in deciding where their true intentions lay. In the cohabitation context, mercenary considerations may be more to the fore than they would be in marriage, but it should not be assumed that they always take

---

[138] [2007] UKHL 17, [2007] 2 AC 432; [2007] CLJ 517 (A Cloherty and D Fox); (2007) 123 LQR 511 (W Swadling); [2007] Conv 352 (M Dixon), 354 (M Pawlowski); [2007] All ER Rev 242 (PJ Clarke); (2008) 71 MLR 120 (N Piska); [2008] CLJ 265 (Sir Terence Etherton); (2008) 124 LQR 422 (S Gardner); [2009] Conv 309 (M Harding); *Modern Studies in Property Law*, vol 5 (2009), ch 9 (N Piška); (2011) 31 LS 175 (N Hopkins). Lord Neuberger dissented on the reasoning, arguing (1) that the approach should not differ in principle in 'the apportionment of the beneficial interest as between legal co-owners, whether in a sexual, platonic, familial, amicable or commercial relationship. In each type of case, one is concerned with the issue of the ownership of the beneficial interest in property held in the names of two people, who have contributed to its acquisition, retention or value': at [107]; and (2) that where the only evidence about the parties' intentions at the time of acquisition of property in joint names is the extent of each party's contribution to the purchase price, the beneficial ownership will be held in the same proportions as the contributions to the purchase price (ie an analysis that begins from the resulting trust basis): at [110]. See also, after the decision in *Stack v Dowden: Adekunle v Ritchie* [2007] 2 P & CR DG20 Leeds County Court, August 17, 2007; discussed as *Ritchie v Ritchie* in [2007] Conv 456 (M Dixon) (presumption of equal shares rebutted); *Laskar v Laskar* [2008] EWCA Civ 347, [2008] 1 WLR 2695 (presumption of equal shares rebutted: purchase of property primarily as investment, in spite of family relationship: Neuberger LJ at [17]), [2008] Conv 441 (N Piska); *Fowler v Barron* [2008] EWCA Civ 377, [2008] 2 FLR 831 (presumption of equal shares not rebutted), [2008] Conv 451 (N Piska); *Q v Q* [2008] EWHC 1874 (Fam), [2009] 1 FLR 395 (presumption of equal shares rebutted), [2009] Conv 145 (M Pawlowski); *Jones v Kernott*, above, n 132 (equitable joint tenancy not rebutted by change of circumstances over 12 years since parties' separation during which one party remained in occupation and paid for all outgoings and maintenance). Where the legal estate is held by two persons but a *third* person claims to have a beneficial interest, he will have to establish both a trust in his favour and his share, in a similar manner to the cases involving a single legal owner (above, p 514), since the presumption from the legal title is that he has no beneficial interest: *Hapeshi v Allnatt* [2010] EWHC 392 (Ch), [2010] All ER (D) 144 (Jan); cf *City of London Building Society v Flegg* [1988] AC 54.

[139] Ibid, at [69]-[70] (Baroness Hale of Richmond).

shall make such order under the 1996 Act as it thinks just and reasonable, having regard to various factors including the interests of A's creditors and the needs of B and any children. Where, however, the application is made more than one year after the vesting of A's estate in the trustee in bankruptcy, the court shall assume, save in exceptional circumstances, that the interests of A's creditors outweigh all other considerations.[167]

The statutory right of occupation is registrable in unregistered land as a Class F land charge.[168] In the case of registered land, it may be protected by the entry of a notice;[169] it is not an overriding interest, even if B is in actual occupation.[170] If there are two or more dwelling-houses subject to right of occupation, B may register a charge, or notice, against only one at any one time.[171]

B may register the charge without notifying A of the registration, and thus cause difficulty where A later enters into a contract to sell the dwelling-house in ignorance of the registration. Further, B may register after A has contracted to sell and thus make it impossible for A to perform the contract, at the cost of substantial damages for its breach.[172]

Before the Family Law Act 1996, no statutory occupation rights were conferred on persons other than spouses. The 1996 Act conferred limited rights on former spouses, cohabitants and former cohabitants. As we have seen, the Civil Partnership Act 2004 extends the general statutory occupation rights to civil partners, and similarly the 2004 Act confers limited rights on former civil partners, and extended the definition of cohabitants.[173] These rights are not capable of protection by registration. A former spouse or civil partner with no right to occupy (or whose right derives from an equitable interest only) may apply for an occupation order in relation to the former matrimonial or civil partnership home for a specified period not exceeding six months (although this may be extended).[174] A cohabitant or former cohabitant may similarly apply for an occupation order in relation to the home where the parties live or lived together.[175] These provisions are without prejudice to the right of a former spouse or civil partner, cohabitant or former cohabitant who has an equitable interest to apply

---

[167] Insolvency Act 1986, s 336, amended by Civil Partnership Act 2004, s 82, Sch 9, Pt 2, para 21; above, p 490.

[168] LCA 1972, s 2(7). Such a registration (and its registered land equivalent) entitles the spouse or civil partner to be given notice of any proceedings by a mortgagee, Family Law Act 1996, s 56. For the right to be made a party to any action to enforce the mortgage, see s 55.

[169] Family Law Act 1996, s 31(10).   [170] Ibid.   [171] Ibid, Sch 4, para 2.

[172] *Watts v Waller* [1973] QB 153; *Wroth v Tyler* [1974] Ch 30; (1974) 38 Conv (NS) 110, (1975) 39 Conv (NS) 78 (DJ Hayton); (1974) CLP 76 (DG Barnsley).

[173] Civil Partnership Act 2004, s 82, Sch 9, Pt 1, para 13(1), (2)(a), amending the definition of 'cohabitants' in Family Law Act 1996, s 62, to read 'two persons who are neither married to each other nor civil partners of each other but are living together as husband and wife or as if they were civil partners', repealing a different form of words ('two persons who, although not married to each other, are living together as husband and wife or (if of the same sex) in an equivalent relationship') substituted by Domestic Violence, Crime and Victims Act 2004, s 3 but never brought into force.

[174] Family Law Act 1996, s 35.

[175] S 36. By s 62, 'cohabitants' were then a man and woman who live together as husband and wife.

for an occupation order under section 33 of the 1996 Act. This section, which has already been discussed in relation to spouses and civil partners, applies also where a former spouse or civil partner, cohabitant or former cohabitant is entitled to occupy the home by reason of some beneficial interest, contract or enactment. In such a case he or she may apply for an occupation order against the other party and may, for example, secure the eviction of the other party, although such an exclusion order is regarded as drastic.[176]

V PARTY WALLS

We must finally examine the effect of the legislation of 1925 upon party-walls. According to Fry J the term 'party wall' may mean:[177]

(a) a wall of which two adjoining owners are tenants in common; or

(b) a wall divided vertically into two strips, one-half of the thickness belonging to each of the neighbouring owners; or

(c) a wall belonging entirely to one owner, but subject to an easement in the other to have it maintained as a dividing wall; or

(d) a wall divided vertically into two equal strips, each strip being subject to a cross-easement in favour of the owner of the other.

It may be said that *most* of the party walls in this country come within the first class, that is are held by the adjoining owners as tenants in common, and in view of this it is clear that the effect of the statutory alterations relating to concurrent interests would have been absurd had special provisions for party walls not been added. The effect would have been to render the majority of such walls subject to a trust for sale!

The Law of Property Act 1925[178] therefore provided that a wall that before 1926 would have been held by tenants in common shall be regarded as severed vertically as between the respective owners, and that the owner of each part shall have such rights to support and user over the other part as he would have had as tenant in common under the old law. In other words, most party walls now fall within the last class enumerated by Fry J.

---

[176] *Chalmers v Johns* [1999] 1 FLR 392. S 33 also enables an applicant with no interest in the home to obtain an order against an 'associated person'. This expression is defined in s 62(3) and includes engaged couples and those who have entered into a civil partnership agreement. Orders may be made under ss 37 and 38 in relation to a home occupied by parties neither of whom is entitled to occupy by virtue of any beneficial interest, contract or enactment.

[177] *Watson v Gray* (1880) 14 Ch D 192, 194–5. See generally Rudall, *Party Walls* (3rd edn, 1922).

[178] LPA 1925, s 38, Sch 1, Part V; see also s 187(2).

The Party Wall etc Act 1996[179] provides for the building of and work relating to party walls and structures close to the boundary. It gives rights to carry out work in three situations: where there is no existing party structure; where there is an existing party structure; and where excavation or construction within three metres of a neighbour's building is proposed.[180] In all three cases there is a notice and counter notice procedure, and disputes are to be settled by an agreed surveyor. The Act extends with some modifications the scheme of the London Building Acts (Amendment) Act 1939 to the whole of England and Wales as from July 1997. It does not affect matters of ownership of a party wall.

---

[179] [1996] Conv 326 (JE Adams); (1998) 142 SJ 772 (G Powell); Bickford-Smith and Sydenham, *Party Walls—Law and Practice* (3rd edn, 2009). On party walls and arbitration, see (2005) 115 NLJ 866 (P Aliker).

[180] Ss 1, 2 and 6 (which account for the 'etc').

15

FUTURE INTERESTS.
THE RULES AGAINST
PERPETUITIES AND
ACCUMULATIONS OF INCOME

Summary

I   FUTURE INTERESTS AND
THE PROBLEM OF PERPETUITY

A   FUTURE INTERESTS

It is important to begin by understanding what is meant by a future interest. The fee simple absolute in possession will continue into the future so long as the holder for the time being has heirs who can inherit it. In a certain way, therefore, one can predict that in the future the fee simple will become vested in others, by transmission either inter vivos on death, but the interest that they will inherit is the estate that presently exists. It is not a future interest. And where the fee simple owner has granted a lease, the gift would be void. There is no living person within 21 years of whose death A's child is certain to marry, if at all. Of course a living child of A must marry, if at all, within that *child's* lifetime. That is logical (and obvious). But logically also, the first child of A to marry may be a future born child of A, if A has no married child and is alive at the date of the gift. A focus on the logical and biological *relationship* between the vesting and living people is the simplest way to understand the rule. Many millions of persons are 'lives' in the sense that they are alive, but only those persons, within 21 years of whose death the interest must vest, if at all, are the *measuring lives*, and it is only possible to discover who they are after an examination of the *relationship* between the time of vesting and the living persons. A gift:

> to the first great-great-grandchild of A to go for a walk with X

is valid. It must vest, if at all, in X's lifetime. Application of the rule has led to a number of innocent-looking limitations being held void because of the theoretical possibility of the happening of the practically impossible, such as an old lady of 70 having further children.[28] To an ordinary person such freakish possibilities would be incomprehensible. The special situations have to be learned and recognised from the cases.

The inquiry, then, in cases governed by the common law rule is to determine whether the interest in question is certain to vest in interest, if it vests at all, within a life in being plus 21 years, plus a period of gestation if gestation in fact takes place. For the purposes of the rule, conception is treated as equivalent to birth.[29] Thus a child, whether a beneficiary or not, who is *en ventre sa mère*[30] at the time when the instrument of gift takes effect may constitute a life in being,[31] and a child *en ventre sa mère* at the end of the perpetuity period may qualify as a beneficiary under the limitation.[32]

The test for certainty of vesting is made as of the date when the instrument comes into effect, that is if the instrument is a deed, when the deed is executed; if it is a will, when the testator dies. Or, to put the rule another way, an interest is void if it might by any possibility vest outside the period of a life in being plus 21 years. A number of points arising out of the rule will now be examined.

(a) Vesting

The rule is concerned with the time of vesting in interest. An interest is vested where:

---

28 *Jee v Audley* (1787) 1 Cox Eq Cas 324; *Re Dawson* (1888) 39 Ch D 155; *Ward v Van der Loeff* [1924] AC 653. *Re Sayer's Trusts* (1868) LR 6 Eq 319; *Re Deloitte* [1926] Ch 56; *Figg v Clarke* [1997] 1 WLR 603 (1963 settlement; capital gains; CGTA 1979, s 54(1)); [1997] Conv 237 (I Ferrier).

29 *Re Stern* [1962] Ch 732, 737.

30 'In simple English, it is an unborn child inside the mother's womb': *Royal College of Nursing of the United Kingdom v Department of Health and Social Security* [1981] AC 800, 802 (Lord Denning MR). For the effect on the rule against perpetuities of delayed posthumous births by means of sperm banks or other devices, see (1979) 53 ALJ 311 (C Sappideen). See also Human Fertilisation and Embryology Act 1990, as amended by Human Fertilisation and Embryology (Deceased Fathers) Act 2003 and Human Fertilisation and Embryology Act 2008; Law Com CP No 133, *The Rules against Perpetuities and Excessive Accumulations* (1993), paras 2.16, n 30; 2.21, n 45; 5.79.

31 *Long v Blackall* (1797) 7 Term Rep 100; *Re Wilmer's Trusts* [1903] 2 Ch 411.

32 Gray, *The Rule against Perpetuities*, s 220; Challis, *Law of Real Property*, p 182.

(a) the person (or persons) entitled to take are ascertained;

(b) the interest is ready to take effect in possession immediately, subject only to any prior interest.

Thus, in a conveyance

to A for life with remainder to B in fee simple,

B's remainder is vested. It would be contingent if the remainderman were not ascertained, as where the remainder was:

to A's eldest child living at his death; or

to the survivor of B and C; or

to B (an infant) if he attains the age of 21; or

to B if he is called to the Bar,

or any other contingency. But the prospect of a life tenant in remainder surviving a life tenant in possession is not regarded as a contingency. Thus, in

to A for life with remainder to B for life with remainder to C in fee simple if he survives A

A's death is not a contingency; it is a certainty, and B has a vested life estate in remainder. If B wishes to sell his remainder, its value will of course vary according to the statistical likelihood of his surviving A. C's remainder is contingent on his surviving A, because the limitation expressly so provides.

The rule against perpetuities is not concerned with the time at which an interest may vest *in possession*. It is necessary to examine the language of the instrument to determine the time at which the interest will vest. Further, the rule is not concerned with the duration of interests, the time for which they may continue. Thus:

to A for life and after his death to the first of A's children to attain the age of 21 in fee simple. A is alive and has infant children.

This interest will vest in *interest* when the first of A's children attains the age of 21. That interest will vest in *possession* when A dies. The fact that the interest of A's child, being a fee simple, may last forever is immaterial. That interest is alienable, and the freedom of disposition of the property is not restricted in any way.

It is sometimes said also that the rule against perpetuities does not apply to vested gifts. This is a truism. The requirement of the rule is that the interest must vest, if at all, within the period. If the interest is vested, no question arises. The rule is concerned with interests that are contingent, not vested.

(b) Requirement of certainty. Remorseless construction

The common law rule against perpetuities requires that the interest must be absolutely certain to vest, *if at all*, within the perpetuity period. This does *not* mean that the interest must be certain to vest; for we are dealing with contingent interests, and there is no such thing as a contingency that is certain to occur. It is sometimes easier to look at the alternative formulation of the rule, and say that the interest is void if by any possibility it *might vest outside the period*.

The requirement of certainty of vesting, if at all, within the period means what it says. If there is any possible way, however freakish and unlikely, in which the interest might vest outside the period, the interest is void. And possibilities that are known to be not only freakish and unlikely, but also those that are physically impossible, such as that a woman over 70 may have a baby,[33] have been allowed to render gifts void. Further, the lawyers of olden days were so concerned at the possibility of the appearance of a perpetuity, that it became established that the language of the limitation must be remorselessly construed; the fact that the settlor or testator obviously did not intend the interest to fail to comply with the perpetuity rule is ignored. Lord Selborne LC said in 1880:[34]

> You do not import the law of remoteness into the construction of the instrument, by which you investigate the expressed intention of the testator. You take his words, and endeavour to arrive at their meaning, exactly in the same manner as if there had been no such law, and as if the whole intention expressed by the words could lawfully take effect.

and Gray:[35]

> Its object is to defeat intention. Therefore every provision in a will or settlement is to be construed as if the rule did not exist, and then to the provision so construed the rule is to be remorselessly applied.

The rule is applied in relation to the facts existing at the time when the instrument comes into effect. Invalidity is unaffected by the fact that, as the facts *subsequently* work out, the interest does in fact vest within the period. There is no wait and see at common law. That principle will be discussed in connection with the 1964 Act.[36]

Much of the difficulty in applying the rule stems from the fact that interests have been held void by reason of the possibility of an occurrence that would not normally be foreseen. These points will be demonstrated by a number of illustrations below. It is thought better to take the illustrations together, because more than one important point is demonstrated in each case.

(c) The perpetuity period. Measuring lives

To be valid at common law, an interest must be certain to vest, if at all, within the perpetuity period of a life or lives in being plus 21 years. Once the time of vesting is ascertained, the problem is to determine whether that vesting event must occur, if at all, within the period of a life or lives in being plus 21 years. This is what was meant by saying, above, that it is necessary to understand the *relationship* between the lives

---

[33] *Jee v Audley* (1787) 1 Cox Eq Cas 324; *Re Dawson* (1888) 39 Ch D 155; *Ward v Van der Loeff* [1924] AC 653. Developments in assisted reproductive technology in the modern era have made such possibilities appear less obviously 'physically impossible'.

[34] *Pearks v Moseley* (1880) 5 App Cas 714, 719.   [35] S 629.   [36] Below, p 560.

and the vesting. Which lives? Anybody: so long as that (living) person's relationship with the vesting is such as to enable it to be known with certainty that the vesting must occur, if at all, within 21 years of the dropping of that life. As has been said:[37]

> What one is really looking for at common law is some life in existence at the commencement of the period which shows, in the light of the circumstances existing at that date, that the interest must vest in time. In other words, one is looking for a life that will show the gift to be valid and one rejects all others as irrelevant. ... The search, at common law, is for a life in being at the commencement of the period which is (i) certain and identifiable and (ii) so related to the vesting contingency that the gift must vest if at all within twenty-one years of its termination. A life that does not satisfy these requirements can be of no assistance in determining the validity of the gift at common law and is therefore rejected as irrelevant (or simply not considered at all).

Some simple illustrations will explain.

(1) When no lives have been expressly selected

1. *To the first child of A to attain the age of 21 years.* This is valid, because it is absolutely certain that A's first child will attain the age of 21 years, if he or she ever does, within 21 years of the death of A. We will see that the rule assumed that it was possible for a man or woman to have a child at any age, however advanced, but A cannot procreate children after his death.[38] A's is the measuring life. Of course, if A were dead, his living children are certain to attain the age of 21, if they ever do, within their own lifetimes. Theirs would then be the measuring lives.

2. *To the first child of A to marry.* A is alive and has unmarried children. This is void.[39] It is not certain that A's first child to marry will do so within 21 years of the death of any person now living. The first child to marry *may* do so within 21 years of the death of A, or Mrs A, or A's parents or A's neighbours, but he or she may not. Of course, each of A's children living at the date of the gift must marry, if at all, within their own lifetimes, but the first child to marry may be future born, and may marry more than 21 years after the death of A, Mrs A, the children alive at the date of the gift, A's parents or A's neighbours. The gift is void. There is no measuring life. Of course, if A were dead at the date of the gift, the gift would be valid. Any child of A is certain to marry, if at all, during that child's lifetime. The children's would be the measuring lives.

---

[37] (1965) 81 LQR 106, 107 (DE Allan); Maudsley, pp 94–5. See also (1981) 97 LQR 593 (RL Deech); below, p 565, n 192.

[38] Human Fertilisation and Embryology Act 1990, s 29(3B), inserted by Human Fertilisation and Embryology (Deceased Fathers) Act 2003, s 1(2) (embryo brought about by using the sperm of a man after his death, or using the sperm of a man before his death but placed in the woman after his death, can be treated as child of the man for purposes of entry in register of births, but for no other purposes).

[39] Similarly, a gift to the first child of A to attain the age of 22 years was void prior to 1926; the gift was saved by LPA 1925, s 163; below, p 538.

It will be noticed that the limitation in *Re Villar* was that the estate was to be finally distributed at the end of 'the period of restriction'. The final vesting would necessarily take place 20 years from the death of the survivor of persons living at the death of the testator, which must necessarily be within the period. But if the testator makes a gift

> to such of my lineal descendants as shall be living 20 years from the death of the survivor of my friends X, Y and Z,

then, unless the court construes the language of the gift as intending to restrict the vesting to those descendants who vest within 20 years from the death of the survivor, the gift is void. All lineal descendants could claim at any time in the future. Measuring lives are nominated. But there is no *relationship* between the lives and the vesting.

(3) Human lives

The lives must be those of human beings, and not 'of animals or trees in California'.[44]

(4) No lives specified

If no lives are specified, an absolute period of 21 years, and no longer, is allowed.[45] In *Re Hooper*,[46] a gift:

> for the upkeep of certain monuments so far as the trustees legally can do so,

was upheld for a period of 21 years.

(2) Illustrations of the Operation of the Rule. Remorseless Application

A number of cases will now be examined as illustrations of the common law perpetuity rule at work. In each case, the language of the instrument should be examined in order to see when the interest is limited to vest, and then the *relationship* between the time of vesting and the lives of living people should be examined to see if the vesting is certain to occur, if at all, within 21 years of the death of some person now living.

(a) Standard illustrations of void gifts

Limitations were held void where a gift was to vest:

> when a candidate for the priesthood 'comes forward from St Saviour's Church, St Albans;'[47]

or,

> when a house ceases to be maintained as a dwelling place;[48]

or,

---

[44] *Re Kelly* [1932] IR 255 (Meredith J).
[46] [1932] 1 Ch 38.
[48] *Kennedy v Kennedy* [1914] AC 215.

[45] *Palmer v Holford* (1828) 4 Russ 403.
[47] *Re Mander* [1950] Ch 547.

where an advowson was devised to the first or other son of A that should be bred a clergyman and be in Holy Orders;[49]

or,

where there was a gift by will of an annuity of £100 to be provided to the Central London Rangers on the appointment of the next lieutenant-colonel.[50]

In each of these cases it will be seen that the time of vesting is in no way related to the lives of living people. The vesting may occur on the day after the instrument came into force. But it may not. All living people may be dead before the interest vests. This is unlikely, but we are concerned with what *might* happen, not with what is likely to happen, and we do not wait at common law to see what does happen.

(b) Vesting postponed to a date later than 21 years

The most common cause of invalidity in the older cases was the selection of an age of vesting greater than the age of 21. The child of A is certain to attain the age of 21 within 21 years of A's death. But the child of A is not certain to attain the age of 22 (or more commonly 25) within 21 years of the death of any living person. In order to avoid the necessity of holding such gifts void, section 163 of the Law of Property Act 1925 provided that:

Where in a will, settlement or other instrument the absolute vesting either of capital or income of property, or the ascertainment of a beneficiary or class of beneficiaries, is made to depend on the attainment by the beneficiary of members of the class of an age exceeding twenty-one years, and thereby the gift to that beneficiary or class or any member thereof, or any gift over, remainder, executory limitation, or trust arising on the total or partial failure of the original gift, is, or but for this section would be, rendered void for remoteness, the will, settlement, or other instrument shall take effect for the purposes of such gift, gift over, remainder, executory limitation, or trust as if the absolute vesting or ascertainment aforesaid had been made to depend on the beneficiary or member of the class attaining the age of twenty-one years, and that age shall be substituted for the age stated in the will, settlement, or other instrument.

It will be seen that the age was only to be reduced to 21 years where the gift would thereby be validated. Section 163 was repealed by the Perpetuities and Accumulations Act 1964[51] in respect of dispositions to which the Act applies.

(c) Leach's caricature cases

The trouble with the perpetuity rule was that, because of its remorseless application, it rendered void a number of perfectly reasonable dispositions, in cases in which the

---

[49] *Proctor v Bishop of Bath and Wells* (1794) 2 Hy Bl 358.

[50] *Re Lord Stratheden and Campbell* [1894] 3 Ch 265. Other illustrations are: *Edwards v Edwards* [1909] AC 275 (when the coal under certain land is exhausted); *Re Wood* [1894] 3 Ch 381 (when a gravel pit is worked out); *Re Engels* [1943] 1 All ER 506 (after termination of the present war with Germany); *Re Fry* [1945] Ch 348, 352 (when an unborn person, ascertainable within the perpetuity period, takes the testator's surname); *Re Jones* [1950] 2 All ER 239 ('upon the realization of my foreign estate'); *Re Flavel's Will Trusts* [1969] 1 WLR 444 (fund to provide superannuation benefits for present and past employees of a company).

[51] Below, p 569.

settlor's or testator's intention could have been achieved if the draftsman had been competent.[52] Professor Barton Leach listed and named a number of such situations.[53]

(1) The magic gravel pits

This situation may arise when a testator assumes that his estate will be administered by his personal representatives within a reasonably short time, and then his will is drafted in such a way that a contingent interest may, beyond all reasonable expectation, vest outside the perpetuity period. Thus, in *Re Wood*:[54]

> a testator, who was a gravel contractor, directed his trustees 'to carry on my said business of a gravel contractor until my gravel pits are worked out' and then to sell them and to divide the proceeds among his issue 'then living'. At the date of the will it was clear that the testator knew that the gravel pits would soon be worked out, and they were in fact worked out within six years of his death.

It was held that the gift was void because there was a possibility that the gravel pits might not have been worked out within the perpetuity period of 21 years. As has been said, 'like the widow's curse, the gravel pits might have replenished themselves for ever—or at least for more than twenty-one years'.[55]

(2) The unborn widow(er)

Gifts to children may fail because of the possibility that a mother (or father) who is now married may lose her husband (or wife) by death or divorce, and then may marry again, his second wife being someone who is now unborn. Thus, in *Re Frost*[56] there was a gift to:

> Emma, a spinster, for life, and after her death to any husband she may marry for his life, and then to each of their children as shall be living at the death of the survivor of Emma and such husband.

The gift to the children was void. It was contingent on the children surviving Emma and her husband. Emma was unmarried at the date of the gift, and might marry a husband who was unborn at that date. If he then survived Emma by more than 21 years, the interests of the children would not vest within 21 years of Emma's death. The result would have been the same even if Emma had been married at the date of the gift.

Re Frost must be contrasted with *Re Garnham*,[57] where there was a gift:

---

52 (1952) 68 LQR 35, 36 (W Barton Leach); Maudsley, pp 37–8.
53 (1938) 51 Harv L Rev 1329; (1952) 65 Harv L Rev 721; (1952) 68 LQR 35, 44.
54 [1894] 2 Ch 310; affd [1894] 3 Ch 381. See also *Re Lord Stratheden and Campbell* [1894] 3 Ch 265, above, n 50 (a perpetual lieutenant-colonel); *Re Atkins' Will Trusts* [1974] 1 WLR 761 (contingency was that of a bank complying with its duty to sell land within the period. Held to be valid as there was no reason to assume that the bank would commit a breach of trust).
55 Morris and Leach, p 74.
56 (1889) 43 Ch D 246.
57 [1916] 2 Ch 413.

to Thomas, a bachelor, for life, then to any woman he may marry for life, and then to the children of Thomas at 21.

The gift was held to be valid. The interests of the children vested in *interest* on the death of Thomas, and not, as in *Re Frost*, on the death of the *survivor* of Emma and her husband.

(3) The fertile octogenarian

The common law recognised no upper (or lower) limit of age at which a living person was supposedly capable of reproduction; and this led to the necessity to hold void a number of dispositions in which there was no physical possibility of the interest vesting outside the period, and no thought or expectation that there might be a problem. The leading case is *Ward v Van der Loeff*:[58]

> By his will the testator devised his residuary estate upon trust for his widow for life and then, in the events which happened, upon trust for the children of his brothers and sisters.
>
> By a codicil he declared that his widow's life interest should be terminable on her remarriage, unless such remarriage should be with a natural born British subject; and that, on her death or remarriage, the trustees should hold the residuary estate upon trust for such of the children of his brothers and sisters as should attain the age of 21 (or, being daughters, attain that age or marry). The widow married a Dutchman.
>
> At the date of the testator's death, his parents were both alive, aged 66. Two brothers and two sisters were alive, each of whom was over 30 and had infant children, one of whom was born after the remarriage of the widow.

The House of Lords held that the gift in the codicil was void, because a future born niece or nephew might have attained the age of 21 outside the period. The living nieces and nephews would attain that age, if at all, in their own lifetimes. And future born children of the testator's brothers and sisters living at the time would also attain that age, if at all, within 21 years of the death of their parents (the living brothers and sisters of the testator). But if the testator's parents were still alive, they might have another child, a new brother or sister to the testator. Everyone else might die, and then that child might have a child that might attain the age of 21 more than 21 years after the death of any person living at the date of the testator's death. The rule relating to class gifts, as will be seen, is that the gift to the class is valid only if its exact composition must be known within the period. The result was that the gift in the codicil failed.[59]

For all its complications, this case reduces itself to an illustration of the simple proposition, discussed above, that a gift to the grandchildren of living persons is void.[60] It illustrates dramatically the application of the rule of remorseless construction. What

---

[58] [1924] AC 653.

[59] But the story had a happier ending. The House of Lords further held that (i) the codicil did not revoke the gift in the will, by applying the doctrine of dependent relative revocation and (ii) the gift in the will itself was valid. That was saved by the interrelation of the class closing rules and the perpetuity rule, as a result of which the child who was born after the remarriage of the widow was excluded. See below, p 543; Maudsley, pp 54–6.

[60] One of the grandparents in fact died before the litigation. But that of course made no difference.

would the testator have said if he had been asked the question: By 'children of my brothers and sisters', do you mean the children of your *living* brothers and sisters,[61] or do you wish to include the children of a future brother or sister to which your 66-year-old mother might give birth after your death? It will be seen that the Perpetuities and Accumulations Act 1964 enacted the permissible periods of reproduction for males and females.[62]

(4) The precocious toddler

Logically, the presumption of fertility attributed to the old should equally affect the young. Whether it must be presumed that no person can be too young to beget children was canvassed in *Re Gaite's Will Trusts*[63] but was not determined. On the facts of that case, the argument in favour of such a presumption rested upon the possibility that within the short space of five years after the settlor's death a child might be born to his widow, already 65 years old, and might then marry and have issue. The judge evaded the question of physical impossibility by holding that such a hypothetical marriage, contracted by a person under 16 years of age contrary to the Age of Marriage Act 1929,[64] was a legal impossibility. And the court will not take into account an event that presupposes a contravention of statute or a breach of trust.[65]

(3) Gifts to a Class

(a) General

(1) Meaning of gift to a class

Lord Selborne said in *Pearks v Moseley*:[66]

A gift is said to be to a class of persons when it is to all those who shall come within a certain category or description defined by a general or collective formula, and who, if they take at all, are to take one divisible subject in certain proportionate shares.

There is a gift to a class if the limitation is:

to all the children of A who shall attain 21.

On the other hand, a gift of:

£2,000 to each of the daughters of B,

is not a class gift.[67]

---

[61] In which case the gift would have been valid. In CA Atkin LJ would have upheld the codicil on the ground that this was the testator's obvious intention: *Re Burnyeat* [1923] 2 Ch 52, 70.

[62] Below, p 559.

[63] [1949] 1 All ER 459. [64] Now the Marriage Act 1949, s 2.

[65] *Re Atkins' Will Trusts* [1974] 1 WLR 761. [66] (1880) 5 App Cas 714, 723.

[67] *Wilkinson v Duncan* (1861) 30 Beav 111.

(2) Vesting of interest of member of class

For the purpose of determining whether an individual member of a class has a vested interest, each member of the class obtains a vested interest on satisfying the necessary qualifications. Thus in a gift:

> to A for life and after his death to such of his children as shall attain 25,

each child of A obtains a vested interest on reaching that age. The significance of this vesting is that the child's interest is then indefeasible. If his interest vests and he then dies before A, the child's estate will claim. If however he dies at the age of 24, it will have no claim. The interest of a child of A who attains 25 is said to be vested 'subject to open'; that is to say, subject to open and admit future born children of A. Thus if A has three children and all have attained 25, they all have vested interests. But if A then has three more children, the interest of the three eldest will be reduced from one third each to one sixth; and will increase again if any of the younger children dies under the age of 25.

(3) Requirement that interest of each member vest within period

However, for the purpose of determining the validity of a gift on the ground of remoteness, the rule is that the gift to a class is only valid if the interest of every possible member of the class must vest, if at all, within the perpetuity period. If the interest of even one potential member could possibly vest outside the period, the *whole* gift fails. Those whose interests have already vested take nothing.[68] 'The vice of remoteness affects the class as a whole, if it may affect an unascertained number of its members.'[69] In other words, a class gift cannot be partially good, partially bad.

Suppose, for instance, that a testator leaves his residuary estate:

> to such of the children of A who shall marry.

If A survives the testator, the whole gift is void. Even if, when the testator dies, A already has children who must therefore marry, if at all, within their own lifetimes, there is no certainty that all his children who marry will do so within the perpetuity period. For A may have a future born child who marries more than 21 years after the death of lives in being. The whole gift, however, would be valid if it were expressed to be to the *living* children of A who marry; or if, when the testator dies, A were dead and therefore unable to have further children.[70]

---

[68] *Leake v Robinson* (1817) 2 Mer 363.

[69] *Pearks v Moseley* (1880) 5 App Cas 714, 723 (Lord Selborne).

[70] The gift would also be saved if one of the children of A were married when the testator dies. This would have the effect of bringing into operation the class-closing rules, and of artificially closing the class at the date of the gift, to include only those children of A who were alive at that time. They must marry, if at all, within their own lifetimes. For these rules and the interrelation between them and the rule against perpetuities, see below.

(b) Class closing rules[71]

(1) Rule in *Andrews v Partington*

Rules of construction, sometimes known as the rule in *Andrews v Partington*,[72] have developed, which have the effect of determining which members of a class can take. They have the effect of artificially closing the class, and of excluding members who would otherwise have taken. They are rules of construction only, and defer to a contrary intention; and the courts in recent years, it seems, are more ready than previously to find that intention.[73]

A class is artificially closed under these rules in order to allow the trustees to make a distribution[74] when one member of the class attains a vested interest and is entitled to be paid. Let us consider the position of trustees where there is a gift 'to such of the children of A who shall attain 21'; and when A's eldest child, X, becomes 21, there is a brother, Y, aged 11 and a sister, Z, aged one. X asks the trustees for payment; what are they to pay to him? If A is still alive, there is danger in paying to X a one-third share, because future born children of A would reduce X's entitlement. So the class closing rules, for the convenience of the administration of the trust, say that the trustees may calculate X's share by providing for only those children of A who have been born. His future born children are excluded. Y and Z can claim their shares when they attain 21. This is very convenient for the trustees and for X, Y and Z; but inconvenient for any future born children of A.

The key to understanding when the class closes is to appreciate that it closes when the time for distribution arises; when, that is the first claimant becomes entitled to be paid. Thus, in an immediate gift to a class, such as 'to the children of A', that class closes to include those alive at the date of the gift. If vesting is postponed, for example, 'to such of the children of A who shall attain 21', the class closes when the first child of A becomes 21. If it is an interest in remainder, for example, 'to X for life, remainder to the children of A who shall attain 21', the class closes when X has died and when the first child of A has attained 21, whichever event happens last, because that is the time at which the first member of the class becomes entitled to be paid. There is an exception to these rules where there is an immediate gift and no existing claimant. Thus if there is a gift to the children of A and A has no children, the class remains open to include all A's children.[75]

---

71 For a full discussion of these rules see (1954) 70 LQR 61 (JHC Morris); [1958] CLJ 39 (SJ Bailey); Morris and Leach, pp 109–25; Maudsley, pp 17–25.

72 (1791) 3 Bro CC 401.

73 *Re Bleckly* [1951] Ch 740; *Re Cockle's Will Trusts* [1967] Ch 690; *Re Kebty-Fletcher's Will Trusts* [1969] 1 Ch 339; *Re Harker's Will Trusts* [1969] 1 WLR 1124; *Re Henderson's Trusts* [1969] 1 WLR 651; (1970) 34 Conv (NS) 393 (JG Riddall); *Re Edmondson's Will Trusts* [1972] 1 WLR 183; *Re Deeley's Settlement* [1974] Ch 454; *Re Chapman's Settlement Trusts* [1977] 1 WLR 1163; [1978] Conv 73 (FR Crane); *Re Clifford's Settlement Trusts* [1981] Ch 63; *Re Tom's Settlement* [1987] 1 WLR 1021; *Re Drummond* [1988] 1 WLR 234; [1988] Conv 427 (P Luxton).

74 The rules apply to all forms of property, and to settlements as well as to wills.

75 *Weld v Bradbury* (1715) 2 Vern 705; *Re Ransome* [1957] Ch 348, 359 (Upjohn J).

(2) Inter-relation between class-closing and perpetuity rules

We have seen that the purpose of the class-closing rules is to simplify the administration of a trust by enabling the trustees to make payment to beneficiaries as soon as they have become entitled. Essentially the rules have nothing to do with the rule against perpetuities. But it will be appreciated that there may be situations in which the rules interact, as for instance where there is a gift to a class in which the interests of some of the members must vest within the perpetuity period, but there is a possibility that those of others may vest outside it, with the result that the whole gift is void under the rule against perpetuities. But if the class-closing rules happen to exclude all the members whose interests would invalidate the gift, then it will be valid. Thus if there was a gift 'to the children of A who shall attain 25', that was void. But, if at the date of the gift there was a child of A who was already twenty-five, the class-closing rules operate to include only those children of A who are alive at the date of the gift; and they will clearly attain 25, if at all, within their own lifetimes. The gift is therefore valid.[76] Further, to return to our earlier example[77] of a gift 'to such of the children of A who shall marry': we saw that this is void, if A is alive at the date of the gift. If, however, one of the children of A is then married, the gift is valid.[78]

(4) Powers of Appointment

We now deal with a number of situations in which it is necessary to apply special rules. The first of these situations concerns powers of appointment.

Before stating the law on this, however, we must first explain the nature of powers of appointment.

(a) Definition and terminology

A power of appointment gives to the donee of the power the right to effect dispositions of property that he does not own, and in which he may have no interest at all.[79] Thus, property may be given by a testator on trust:

> to my widow for life and after her death to such of our children and in such shares as she shall in her absolute discretion appoint.

Or the power of appointment may be given to the trustees; or to one who holds no legal or equitable interest in the property, such as where the testator gives property:

> to my widow for life and after her death to such of my nieces and nephews as my brother, X, in his absolute discretion shall appoint.

---

[76] *Picken v Matthews* (1878) 10 Ch D 264. [77] Above, p 542.

[78] See [1988] Conv 339 (P Sparkes and R Snape), arguing that the rules should be applied during the 'wait and see' period.

[79] Powers of appointment were unknown at common law, but originated with uses in equity. See Co Litt 237a; *Gilbert on Uses and Trusts* (3rd edn, 1811), p xxxix, 158 n; Hayes, *Introduction to Conveyancing* (5th edn, 1840), vol 1, p 70. On powers generally, see *Farwell on Powers* (3rd edn, 1916); H & M, ch 6; Maclean, *Trusts and Powers* (1989); *Thomas on Powers* (1998).

As regards terminology, when A gives X the right to exercise a power of appointment, A is called the *donor*; X the *donee* or *appointor*; the person in whose favour the appointment is made is termed the *appointee*; and when the donee exercises the power he is said to make an appointment.

(b) General and special powers

Powers of appointment may be either general, or special. If the appointor is authorised to appoint in favour of anybody in the world, including himself, without being required to obtain the consent of another person, he is said to have a *general power*, but if he may appoint only to the members of a restricted class, as for instance, 'amongst the children of A', he has a *special power*, and the persons whom he may select to take the property are called the *objects* of the power.

(c) Powers and the rule against perpetuities

A power of appointment may infringe the rule against perpetuities in two respects, for either its *creation* or its *exercise* may be too remote.

To give a person a general power is in effect to give him the absolute fee, for it entitles him to vest the whole fee in any person in the world, including himself, and therefore it does not tend to the creation of remote interests: 'He has an absolute disposing power over the estate, and may bring it into the market whenever his necessities or wishes may lead him to do so...The donee may sell the estate the next moment.'[80] On the other hand, the grant of a special power has an immediate tendency to be a perpetuity, for, since the objects in whose favour it is exercisable are restricted, it imposes from the moment of its creation a retriction upon the free disposability of the land.[81] It is important to notice, however, that a general power exercisable jointly by two or more persons or by one person with the consent of another is a special power for the purposes of the rule against perpetuities, the view taken by the law being that a power that cannot be exercised without the concurrence of two minds is not equivalent to property.[82]

(1) General powers

(i) Validity of creation

A general power to appoint by deed, or either by deed or by will, is void unless it will become effectively exercisable, if at all, within the perpetuity period. At the date when the instrument of creation takes effect, it must be possible to say that within that period the donee will be ascertainable, the event upon which the power is to arise

---

[80] Sugden, *Powers* (8th edn), pp 395–6, cited Morris and Leach, p 148.

[81] Co Litt 272a, Butler's note.

[82] *Re Churston Settled Estates* [1954] Ch 334; *Re Earl of Coventry's Indentures* [1974] Ch 77. This is an example of a power that is intermediate or hybrid in the sense that it conforms neither to special nor general powers. For an account, see Morris and Leach, *The Rule against Perpetuities* (2nd edn), pp 136–8; Fourth Report of Law Reform Committee 1956 (Cmnd 18), paras 44–6. See *Re Lawrence's Will Trusts* [1972] Ch 418, where that category is discussed by Megarry J.

will have occurred and any condition precedent to the right of exercise will have been satisfied.

On this basis, each of the following powers is void:

A power given to the survivor of two living persons and their children.[83]

A power to arise upon the general failure of the issue of a marriage.[84]

A power given to an unborn person upon his marriage.[85]

If a general power to appoint by deed, or either by deed or by will, is exercisable within the perpetuity period, it is not rendered objectionable by the fact that it may possibly be exercised after the period has expired, as may well happen, for instance, if it is given to the unborn child of a living person. By virtue of the power, such a donee ascertained within due limits acquires an unrestricted right of alienation, and as in the case of any absolute owner he is free to decide when he will exercise that right.[86]

On the other hand, a general testamentary power, that is one that is exercisable only by will, though it will vest in the donee, if at all, within the perpetuity period, is void if it may be exercised beyond that period. The reason is that the property is tied up during the lifetime of the donee in the sense that he possesses no right of alienation until his death. Therefore, such a power is void if, as in the case of one given to the unborn child of a living person, it may be exercisable at too remote a time.[87]

(ii) Validity of appointment

The donee of a general power, since he can appoint to anybody in the world, including himself, has complete and absolute freedom of disposition, and therefore for the purpose of testing the validity of his appointments the perpetuity period is reckoned from the exercise of the power, not from its creation.

This rule applies whether the general power is exercisable inter vivos, or whether it is a general testamentary power, exercisable only by will. It is arguable that the validity of an appointment made under a general testamentary power should be subject to the restrictions imposed on special powers, discussed below, on the ground that the disposition of the property is restricted during the lifetime of the donee. However, the donee has complete power of disposition on death, and the restriction imposed during the donee's lifetime is not thought to be a substantial breach of perpetuity policy. This view was confirmed, as we shall see, by the Act of 1964.

(2) Special powers

(i) Validity of creation

As regards the validity of its creation, a special power is subject to the following rule:

---

[83] *Re Hargreaves* (1889) 43 Ch D 401.
[84] *Bristow v Boothby* (1826) 2 Sim & St 465. Prima facie, 'issue' includes descendants of every degree.
[85] *Morgan v Gronow* (1873) LR 16 Eq 1 (in the case of the original appointment).
[86] *Re Fane* [1913] 1 Ch 404, 413.
[87] *Wollaston v King* (1869) LR 8 Eq 165; *Morgan v Gronow*, above.

A special power which, according to the true construction of the instrument creating it, is capable of being exercised beyond lives in being and 21 years afterwards is, by reason of the rule against perpetuities, absolutely void.'[88]

As in the case of a general power, a special power is too remote in its creation if the donee may not be ascertained or if the condition precedent to its exercise may not have occurred within lives in being and 21 years afterwards. But in the case of a special power there is the further requirement that the objects must be ascertainable within the same period. The difference in this respect between the two classes of powers may be illustrated by a power, to be exercised by deed, given to an unborn person.

A special power to this effect, as, for instance, one conferred by settlement upon the eldest son of X, a bachelor, to appoint to his children, is void ab initio.[89] At the time of the settlement, it can no doubt be said that the appointor will be ascertained, if at all, within 21 years from the death of the life in being, X; but it cannot be said that the children in whose favour alone the appointment may be made will be ascertainable, if at all, within the same period. In other words, the occasion upon which the power is to become operative may be too remote.[90]

On the other hand, as we have seen, a general power to the same effect exercisable by deed is valid. The donee, being ascertainable within the perpetuity period, has complete control over the property and, once ascertained, is in the same position as if he were already its absolute owner.[91]

Provided that a special power is so limited that it cannot be *exercised* beyond the perpetuity period, it is immaterial that under its terms an appointment may possibly be made that will be too remote, as in the case, for instance, of a devise:

to X for life, remainder to such of his issue as he shall by will appoint.[92]

At the date of such a devise, it is impossible to say whether the perpetuity rule will be transgressed or not, but this uncertainty does not invalidate the power. The appointments will fail only if in fact they are too remote.[93] The question is not what may be done, but what in fact is done. In other words this is an exceptional case at common law where it is necessary to wait and see what happens.

(ii) Validity of appointment

Presuming now that the power itself is valid in the sense that it is exercisable only within the perpetuity period, it remains to consider the test that governs the validity of appointments in fact made. It differs radically from that applicable to a general power.

In the case of a special power, the disposition of the property remains controlled by the donor; the donee has power only to appoint to a limited class. As Lord Romer said:

---

88 *Re De Sommery* [1912] 2 Ch 622, 630 (Parker J).
89 *Wollaston v King* (1869) LR 8 Eq 165.   90 Gray, *The Rule against Perpetuities*, ss 475, 477.
91 *Bray v Bree* (1834) 2 Cl & Fin 453.
92 *Slark v Dakyns* (1874) 10 Ch App 35; *Re Vaux* [1939] Ch 465, 472.
93 *Re Fane* [1913] 1 Ch 404, 413–14.

'It is as though the settlor had left a blank in the settlement which [the donee] fills up for him if and when the power of appointment is exercised.'[94] The rule therefore is that, for the purposes of the perpetuity rule, the appointment that is in fact made must be 'read back' into the instrument that created the power; and the perpetuity period is reckoned from the time when the instrument came into operation.

Thus, in *Whitby v Von Luedecke*:[95]

> A settlement made in 1844, upon the marriage of H and W, limited land to W for life and after her death to such of her children as she should appoint. The terms of her appointment were that the income of the land should be divided equally between her two daughters, X and Y, during their respective lives, but that upon the death of one it should pass in its entirety to the survivor.

It was held that the gift to the survivor was void. It was a contingent gift, and the event upon which it was to vest—the death of one of the daughters—would not necessarily occur within 21 years from the deaths of H and W who constituted the sole lives in being when the special power was created in 1844.

The rule that the appointment ultimately made must be regarded as having been made in the original instrument of creation, merely ensures that the donee of the power shall not grant interests that the donor himself could not have granted. It is permitted, however, to read and construe the appointments in the light of the circumstances existing at the time when they are intended to take effect, not at the time when the power was created.[96]

Thus in *Re Paul*,[97] a disposition was saved by the application of the rule:

> A testator died in 1895, leaving a share in his residuary estate to his daughter, Mrs A, for life and after her death as she should appoint among her children. She made an appointment in 1919 to her son on attaining the age of 25 years. The son was then 18. The appointment was read back into the will as an appointment by Mrs A to her son at an age which he must attain, if at all, within 21 years of Mrs A's death. It was therefore valid.

(5) Effect of Infringement on Subsequent Interests[98]

Where one of a series of limitations is void for perpetuity, the question arises as to the effect of that void limitation upon the other limitations that are not in themselves void. The obvious solution would seem to be to ignore the void limitation, and to let

---

[94] *Muir (or Williams) v Muir* [1943] AC 468, 483.

[95] [1906] 1 Ch 783; *Re Legh's Settlement Trusts* [1938] Ch 39. W, however, might have achieved her object by making the interest in the entire income vested instead of contingent. An appointment of one-half to X for life with remainder to Y for life, and of one-half to Y for life with remainder to X for life, would have been valid. The rule against perpetuities is, indeed, of a highly technical nature; see (1952) 68 LQR 47–9 (WB Leach). See also *Re Brown and Sibly's Contract* (1876) 3 Ch D 156.

[96] Gray, *The Rule against Perpetuities*, s 523; *Wilkinson v Duncan* (1861) 30 Beav 111; *Von Brockdorff v Malcolm* (1885) 30 Ch D 172; *Re Thompson* [1906] 2 Ch 199; *Re Paul* [1921] 2 Ch 1.

[97] Above.   [98] See (1950) 10 CLJ 392 (JHC Morris); (1950) 14 Conv (NS) 148 (AKR Kiralfy).

the valid limitations take effect as if the void limitation never existed. But the matter is not so simple.[99]

(a) Where subsequent limitation is subject to a void contingency

Where the subsequent limitation is itself subject to a void contingency, whether the same as or different from that of the earlier void limitation, the subsequent limitation is of course void. Thus a limitation:

> to A for life with remainder to such of his grandchildren as shall marry, but if no grandchildren of A shall marry, then to the children of B [who is alive] absolutely.

The gift to the children of B is void. Those who qualify may include future born children of B; and the takers will not be ascertained until it is known whether any of A's grandchildren marry, and that may not be known until a time outside the perpetuity period.

If the gift over had been to the living (or named) children of B for their lives, the gift over would be valid; for the gift over in those circumstances must vest, if at all, within the lifetime of those living children of B. The contrary was, however, held in *Re Hewett's Settlement*:[100]

> In a marriage settlement, life interests were given to the husband and wife, and after their deaths the property was to be divided between such of their children as should attain the age of 25, and 'if there should be no child of the marriage who should attain twenty-five' then on trust for the testator's three sisters, Helga, Hilda and Hulda.

The gift to the sisters was held to be void. Such a result could only be reached by failing to appreciate that the gift must vest in the sisters, if at all, during their own lifetimes. They were therefore the lives in being in relation to the gift to themselves; and the fact that that intermediate gift was void should have been treated as irrelevant.

(b) Intention that subsequent limitation should take effect only after termination of prior void limitation

In *Re Abbott*,[101] Stirling J said, in a famous dictum:

> It is settled that any limitation depending or expectant upon a prior limitation which is void for remoteness is invalid. The reason appears to be that the persons entitled under the subsequent limitation are not intended to take unless and until the prior limitation is exhausted; and as the prior limitation which is void for remoteness can never come into operation, much less be exhausted, it is impossible to give effect to the intentions of the settlor in favour of the beneficiaries under the subsequent limitation.

[99] Many questions of this type are settled in the United States by the application of the doctrine of 'infectious invalidity'. Under this doctrine, the invalidity of an important part of a limitation may cause the whole limitation to be held void. The justification is that, if the testator's plan is so changed by the invalidity of one part, then he may well prefer to rely on the intestacy provisions instead.

[100] [1915] 1 Ch 810; *Re Thatcher's Trusts* (1859) 26 Beav 365, 369; *Re Hubbard's Will Trusts* [1963] Ch 275; *Re Buckton's Settlement Trusts* [1964] Ch 497.

[101] [1893] 1 Ch 54, 57.

There is little to be said in support of this proposition. But some cases can only be supported on this ground. In *Re Backhouse*:[102]

> A picture was bequeathed for a series of life interests, some of which were void for perpetuity, with an ultimate gift to the testator's right heirs. This last gift was in favour of persons who would be ascertained at the testator's death, and would therefore vest at that time. Even so, it was held void on the ground that it was subsequent to the prior void limitations.

The modern and better view is that the subsequent limitation, valid in itself, should be accelerated so as to take effect in the place of the earlier void limitation.

(c) Later limitation not dependent

Where an interest is created that will not take effect in possession until a future date, but must vest in interest within the perpetuity period, and its possessory enjoyment is not dependent on the exhaustion of the precedent interests, it will be unaffected by remoteness in any of the antecedent interests.[103] This is illustrated by *Re Coleman*:[104]

> A testator left his residuary estate on discretionary trusts to H for life; after H's death upon similar discretionary trusts for any widow who might survive him; and after the death of such widow upon trust (not discretionary) for the children of H at 21 in equal shares.

By virtue of the discretionary trusts, the trustees were empowered to make payments of income to H or his widow. But this trust in the widow's case was void, for H might marry a woman born after the testator's death, and if so the discretion of the trustees, which was a condition precedent to her right to an interest, might be exercisable beyond the perpetuity period. Nevertheless, it was held that the limitation to the children was valid. The interests of the children would necessarily vest, if at all, within 21 years of H's death. Their interests were not dependent on the validity of the discretionary power to pay income to the widow.

(d) Divestment on occurrence of void condition

Where a testator or settlor gives property to A either immediately or at some future date which is not too remote, but so frames his trusts that the interest of A may be displaced by the exercise of some power or discretion, the interest of A will be unaffected by any invalidity of that power or discretion on the ground of remoteness.[105]

In one case, for example, a testator allocated a fund to be used at the discretion of trustees upon the maintenance of a mansion house so long as any person entitled to the house under a strict settlement should be under 21 years of age, 'and subject thereto' upon trust for A absolutely. The discretionary trust for the maintenance of the

---

[102] [1921] 2 Ch 51.
[103] *Re Hubbard's Will Trusts*, above, 85–7. *Re Backhouse*, above, however, is inconsistent with this proposition.
[104] [1936] Ch 528; followed in *Re Allan* [1958] 1 WLR 220.
[105] *Re Hubbard's Will Trusts* [1963] Ch 275, 287 (Buckley J).

house was admittedly too remote, but it was held that the trust in favour of A was an independent limitation and was valid.[106]

The destination of the property affected by a remote limitation differs according as the disposition is made by deed or by will. In the former case it results to the settlor. In the case of a will, it goes to the residuary legatee or devisee, but to the persons entitled as on an intestacy of the testator if there is no residuary gift or if the residue itself is the subject matter of the limitation. If the void limitation is effected by the exercise of a special power of appointment, the property concerned passes to the persons entitled in default of appointment.

(6) Alternative Limitations

Where a settlor makes the vesting of a future gift dependent upon two alternative events, one of which is too remote and the other not, the gift is allowed to take effect if the event which is not too remote is the one that actually happens.[107] This doctrine provides an exception to the rule that possible, not actual, events are alone considered, for the court waits to see which of the two events in fact occurs.[108] Thus in the early case of *Longhead v Phelps*[109] a marriage settlement declared that certain trusts should arise:

if H should die without issue male *or* if such issue male should die without issue.

The latter contingency was obviously too remote, for whether H's male issue died without themselves leaving issue might not necessarily be known within 21 years of the death of any person living at the date of the testator's death, but in fact he died without male issue and it was held that the trusts were valid. In a more recent case[110] a testator created a trust to take effect:

upon the decease of my last surviving child *or* the death of the last surviving widow or widower of my children as the case may be whichever shall last happen.

Here again the last contingency was too remote, since one or more of the children might marry a person born after the testator's death, but it was held that the trust would be valid if the first contingency in fact happened, that is if all the widows and widowers were dead when the last surviving child died.

The courts, however, have consistently held that this indulgence will not be shown to the valid gift unless the settlor has himself expressly and distinctly designated the two alternative contingencies.[111] If vesting is in terms made dependent upon a single

---

[106] *Re Canning's Will Trusts* [1936] Ch 309; see also *Re Abbott* [1893] 1 Ch 54. The difficulties arising from this doctrine of dependency no longer affect instruments taking effect after 15 July 1964; PAA 1964, s 6; below, p 573.

[107] *Longhead v Phelps* (1770) 2 Wm Bl 704; *Leake v Robinson* (1817) 2 Mer 363; *Re Curryer's Will Trusts* [1938] Ch 952; Gray, *The Rule against Perpetuities*, ch ix.

[108] Morris and Leach, pp 181–4.   [109] (1770) 2 Wm Bl 704.

[110] *Re Curryer's Will Trusts* [1938] Ch 952.

[111] *Re Bence* [1891] 3 Ch 242; *Miles v Harford* (1879) 12 Ch D 691, 702 (Jessel MR).

event that in fact includes two contingencies, one too remote the other not too remote, the future gift is void, although the contingency that actually happens is the one that satisfies the perpetuity rule. The court will not split the expression used by the settlor, ie will not separate and state in an alternative form the two events that the expression in fact includes. By way of illustration we may refer once more to *Proctor v Bishop of Bath and Wells*.[112] In that case the fee simple was devised:

> to the first or other son of A that should be bred a clergyman, and be in Holy Orders, but in case he should have no such son, then to B in fee simple.

It is clear on analysis that the event upon which the gift to B was dependent included two contingencies, namely:

(a) failure of A to leave sons;

(b) failure of any son to take Holy Orders.

A gift to B to take effect if A left no sons would obviously be valid, but though A did in fact die childless, it was held that B was not entitled to the fee simple. If the description of the event had been alternative, instead of single, in point of expression, all would have been well; that is if the testator had expressly stated that the fee simple was to vest in B:

> if A had no son *or* if he had no son who should take Holy Orders,

B's claim would have been upheld, since it was the first contingency that in fact happened. What the court refused to do was to redraft in an alternative form the single expression appearing in the will. In cases of this kind the court does not concentrate upon implementing the testator's intention, for a man who says that an estate is to go over to B if none of A's sons becomes a clergyman obviously means it to go over if A never has a son. Whether the intention will prevail is purely a question of words: 'You are bound to take the expression as you find it, and if, giving the proper interpretation to that expression, the event may transgress the limit, then the gift over is void.'[113]

(7) Exceptions to the Rule against Perpetuities

(a) Limitations after entailed interests

A tenant in tail can bar his own and all subsequent interests. The rule, therefore, is that no limitation after an entailed interest is void for remoteness, provided that the subsequent limitation must vest, if at all, at or before the end of the perpetuity period. There is in fact no perpetuity.[114]

---

[112] (1794) 2 Hy Bl 358; above, p 538.

[113] *Miles v Harford* (1879) 12 Ch D 691, 703 (Jessel MR).

[114] *Nicolls v Sheffield* (1787) 2 Bro CC 215; *Heasman v Pearse* (1871) 7 Ch App 275.

(b) Contracts and options[115]

'It is settled beyond argument that an agreement merely personal, not creating any interest in land, is not within the rule against perpetuities.'[116] Therefore, it is not void simply because the obligation it creates may last for an indefinite time.[117] For example, in *Walsh v Secretary of State for India*[118] the East India Company entered into a covenant in 1770 by which they promised to pay a certain sum of money if, at any time after 1794, they should cease to have a military force in their pay and service in the East Indies. It might have been centuries before such a state of things occurred, and in point of fact it was nearly a century, but nevertheless the court upheld the validity of the obligation.

It is equally well settled at common law that even a contract that creates an interest in land remains binding upon the parties themselves, notwithstanding that it may be enforceable beyond the perpetuity period. So long as privity of contract exists, there is no room for the rule against perpetuities. Thus in *Hutton v Watling*[119] a written agreement by which X sold his business to Y stipulated that Y should have the option, exercisable at any time in the future, to purchase the premises in which the business was carried on. An action by Y for specific performance brought seven years later was met by the plea that the stipulation was void for remoteness. The plea failed. In such a case, Y is entitled not only to recover damages from X,[120] but also to a decree of specific performance if the land is still retained by X, for 'specific performance is merely an equitable mode of enforcing a personal obligation with which the rule against perpetuities has nothing to do'.[121]

But once the promisee seeks to enforce the promise against a third person, the position is changed. We now pass from the law of contract to the law of property, with the result that such an option as that in *Hutton v Watling* or an option given to a lessee to purchase the reversion, since it creates an executory interest in land, cannot be enforced against third persons who later acquire the promisor's land unless it is confined within the perpetuity period.[122] Thus where a railway company sold land to one Powell subject to a right of repurchase if at any time thereafter the land was required for the railway, it was held that the right was unenforceable against the appellant, to whom Powell's heir had sold the land.[123]

Jessel MR said:

If then the rule as to remoteness applies to a covenant of this nature, this covenant clearly is bad as extending beyond the period allowed by the rule. Whether the rule applies or not

---

[115] (1954) 18 Conv (NS) 576 (JHC Morris and WB Leach).

[116] *South Eastern Rly Co v Associated Portland Cement Manufacturers (1900) Ltd* [1910] 1 Ch 12, 33 (Farwell J).

[117] *Witham v Vane* (1883) 32 WR 617; Challis, *Law of Real Property*, p 440.

[118] (1863) 10 HL Cas 367.   [119] [1948] Ch 26; affd on other grounds [1948] Ch 398.

[120] *Worthing Corp v Heather* [1906] 2 Ch 532.

[121] *Hutton v Watling* [1948] Ch 26. 36 (Jenkins J). This rule was reversed by PAA 1964, s 10, in the case of instruments taking effect after 15 July 1964: below, p 573; but options are not subjected to the perpetuity rule under PAA 2009 in the case of instruments taking effect after 5 April 2010: below, pp 576–7.

[122] *Woodall v Clifton* [1905] 2 Ch 257; *London and South Western Rly Co v Gomm* (1882) 20 Ch D 562; *Griffith v Pelton* [1958] Ch 205.

[123] *London and South Western Rly Co v Gomm*, above.

depends upon this as it appears to me—does or does not the covenant give an interest in the land? If it is a bare or mere personal contract it is of course not obnoxious to the rule, but in that case it is impossible to see how the present appellant can be bound. He did not enter into the contract, but is only a purchaser from Powell who did. If it is a mere personal contract it cannot be enforced against the assignee. Therefore the company must admit that it somehow binds the land. But if it binds the land it creates an equitable interest in the land. The right to call for a conveyance of the land is an equitable interest or equitable estate.

Thus, an option to call for a lease of land exemplifies this principle and is void if it is exercisable beyond the perpetuity period, but it has long been recognised that an option given to a tenant to *renew* his existing lease is entirely unaffected by the rule against perpetuities.[124]

(c) Certain easements and mortgages

A further illustration of the principles laid down by Jessel MR is that the grant of an easement to arise in the future may be void on the ground of remoteness, as for example where it entitles the grantee to use the drains and sewers 'now passing *or hereafter to pass*' under a private road.[125]

The rule against perpetuities has no application to mortgages, and therefore a postponement of the right of redemption for longer than the perpetuity period is not void for remoteness,[126] though it may be void on other grounds.[127]

(d) Certain rights of entry

The rule affects certain rights of entry, but not others.

(1) Forfeiture of lease

The right usually reserved to a lessor to enter upon the land and to terminate the lease if the tenant commits a breach of covenant[128] is not subject to the rule.[129]

(2) Enforcement of rentcharge

There are three situations to consider in relation to the enforcement of a rentcharge.

First, the owner of a rentcharge, that is a person, other than a reversioner, entitled to the payment of an annual sum of money out of land,[130] is empowered by the Law of Property Act 1925,[131] in the event of non-payment to enter upon the land and to recover the money due either by levying distress or by leasing the land to a trustee

---

[124] *Woodall v Clifton*, above, at 265, 268; *Weg Motors Ltd v Hales* [1961] Ch 176; affd [1962] Ch 49.

[125] *Dunn v Blackdown Properties Ltd* [1961] Ch 433; (1961) 25 Conv (NS) 415 (G Battersby); *Newham v Lawson* (1971) 22 P & CR 852; *McGrath v Parkside Hotels Ltd* [2011] EWHC 143 (Ch). The right may however be construed as an immediate right that has not yet been exercised, and not as a future right: *SE Rly Co v Associated Portland Cement Manufacturers (1900) Ltd* [1901] 1 Ch 12; cf *Sharpe v Durant* [1911] WN 158. See Morris and Leach, pp 228–31.

[126] *Knightsbridge Estates Trust Ltd v Byrne* [1939] Ch 441, 463; affd [1940] AC 613.

[127] Below, p 818.   [128] Above, pp 279, 287.

[129] *Re Tyrrell's Estate* [1907] 1 IR 292, 298 (Walker LC).   [130] Below, p 786.   [131] S 121.

until all arrears have been paid. The Act puts this right of entry, together with its attendant remedies, outside the rule against perpetuities.[132]

If the instrument creating the charge expressly empowers the creditor to enter the land and to determine the fee simple estate of the debtor for non-payment of rent, or to enter and enforce some covenant other than that to pay the sum due, it is doubtful whether such a power is excluded from the perpetuity rule by virtue of the Act.[133]

Secondly, a rentcharge is sometimes created merely by way of indemnity against another rentcharge.[134] If, for instance, an estate that as a whole is subject to a rentcharge is being sold off in lots, it is a common practice to throw the burden of the charge entirely upon one lot. In practice the purchaser of that lot then gives the purchasers of the other lots an indemnity rentcharge issuing out of his land, so that if they as purchasers of parts of the whole land are compelled by the rent-owner to pay the charge, they will have a right to reimburse themselves out of the lot on which it has been thrown.

The former doubt whether the law of remoteness applied to such cases was dispelled by the Law of Property Act 1925, which provides that rentcharges created only by way of indemnity against other rentcharges and powers to distrain or to take possession of land affected by such rentcharges, shall be excluded from the operation of the rule against perpetuities.[135]

Thirdly, if a fee simple is sold in return for a perpetual annual rentcharge, the right of entry or re-entry that accrues to the vendor in the event of non-payment,[136] although exercisable for an unlimited period, does not withdraw the land from commerce and therefore is unaffected at common law by the rule against perpetuities.[137]

(3) Condition broken

A right of entry for condition broken attached to a fee simple is void if it is exercisable beyond the perpetuity period.[138]

(e) Accumulative trust of income for the purpose of paying debts

The rule does not apply to a trust directing that income shall be accumulated with a view to the payment of the settlor's debts, or for the discharge of incumbrances charged upon the land, for such a trust, though capable of enduring for an indefinite time, may be determined at any moment either by the beneficiaries paying the debts and freeing the land, or by the creditors enforcing their claims by the seizure of the

---

[132] S 121(6) (repealed by PAA 2009 in relation to instruments taking effect after 5 April 2010, since such rights of entry are no longer within the rule under the 2009 Act: below, p 575).

[133] See Morris and Leach, p 218. The doubt has been removed by PAA 1964, s 11, which, however, is not retrospective; see below, p 574.

[134] Below, p 781.

[135] LPA 1925, s 162(1)(a) (repealed by PAA 2009 in relation to instruments taking effect after 5 April 2010, since such rentcharges are no longer within the rule under the 2009 Act: below, p 576).

[136] Above, p 154; below, p 781.   [137] Cf *Keppell v Bailey* (1834) 2 My & K 517, 528–9 (Lord Brougham).

[138] *Re Hollis' Hospital Trustees and Hague's Contract* [1899] 2 Ch 540; LPA 1925, s 4(3) (the closing words of which are repealed by PAA 2009 in relation to instruments taking effect after 5 April 2010, since such rights of entry are no longer within the rule under the 2009 Act: below, p 576); below, p 619.

land.[139] Nor does the rule apply to a trust under which money is to be accumulated for the reduction of the National Debt.[140]

(f) Pension and superannuation funds

If there were no specific exemption for pension and superannuation funds, they would become void after the end of the perpetuity period, because interests in the fund might vest at too remote a time.[141] Under the common law rule, the trust fund would have been wholly void unless expressly limited to the perpetuity period. In order to avoid this problem, the Pension Schemes Act 1993 makes express provision for all qualifying occupational pension schemes to be exempt from the rule.[142]

(g) Administrative powers of trustees

The former rule was that administrative powers given to trustees, such as a power to sell or lease land, or to receive remuneration for their services, were void if they were capable of being exercised at too remote a time, notwithstanding that they were attached to a trust that itself was not too remote. This may be illustrated by *Re Allott*:[143]

> A testator left his mines to trustees upon trust to pay annuities to his daughters out of the profits. He directed that if a daughter married, and was survived by her husband, such survivor should be entitled for his life to her annuity.
>
> After the testator's death, a deed of family arrangement was entered into which incorporated the trusts of the will and which inter alia gave the trustees powers to grant leases not exceeding 99 years.

The life interest given to any surviving husband was valid despite the fact that he might be a person not born at the date of the execution of the deed. His life interest would necessarily arise, if it ever arose at all, immediately on the death of his wife. Nevertheless, the power of leasing was void, since it might be exercised, and so create a fresh interest, more than 21 years after the dropping of the lives in being if the husband lived so long.

The effect of administrative powers is not to tie up the property, but to facilitate its management, and therefore the Law Reform Committee recommended that they should be excluded from the perpetuity rule provided that the trusts to which they

---

[139] *Tewart v Lawson* (1874) LR 18 Eq 490; *Lord Southampton v Marquis of Hertford* (1813) 2 Ves & B 54.

[140] Superannuation and Other Trust Funds (Validation) Act 1927, s 9.

[141] *Re Flavel's Will Trusts* [1969] 1 WLR 444.

[142] S 163; Personal and Occupational Pension Schemes (Perpetuities) Regs 1990 (SI 1990 No 1143). For a perceptive criticism, see (1995) Private Client Business, pp 133–45, 223–32 (G Thomas). See also *Air Jamaica Ltd v Charlton* [1999] 1 WLR 1399; [2000] Conv 170 (C Harpum). S 163 of the 1993 Act is repealed by PAA 2009 in relation to instruments taking effect after 5 April 2010, since pension schemes are no longer within the rule under the 2009 Act: below, p 576.

[143] [1924] 2 Ch 498.

are ancillary are valid and subsisting. This recommendation was accepted by the Perpetuities and Accumulations Act 1964, in the only section that is retrospective. It provided that:[144]

> The rule against perpetuities shall not operate to invalidate a power conferred on trustees or other persons to sell, lease, exchange or otherwise dispose of property for full consideration, or to do any other act in the administration (as opposed to the distribution) of any property, and shall not prevent the payment to trustees or other persons of reasonable remuneration for their services.

It should be noticed that it is only *administrative* powers that are exempt from the rule against perpetuities. The rule applies to beneficial powers such as powers of appointment,[145] powers of distribution under a discretionary trust and powers of maintenance and advancement.[146]

(h) Certain limitations to charities

An interest given to a charity, like any other gift, is void unless it will vest within the perpetuity period.[147] On the other hand, a limitation transferring property from one charity to another upon a certain contingency is valid, although the contingency may not occur until some indefinite time in the future. Provided that the interest of the first charity will begin within the perpetuity period, it is immaterial that the second charity may not take until a remote date. Thus in *Re Tyler*,[148] where a testator bequeathed £42,000 to the London Missionary Society with a gift over to the Blue Coat School if the Society failed to keep his family vault in repair, it was held that the gift over was valid. Had the gift over been, not to another charity, but to private persons, it would have been void.[149]

A gift to a charity is not void as a perpetuity merely because it creates an interest that may remain subject to the charitable trust for an indefinite period.[150]

---

[144] S 8(1). If a power has been created before the commencement of the Act, ie 16 July 1964, this section is applicable, provided that the exercise is effected after that date: s 8(2).

[145] Above, p 544.

[146] *Pilkington v IRC* [1964] AC 612; *Re Hastings-Bass* [1975] Ch 25 (statutory power of advancement under TA 1925, s 32).

[147] *Chamberlayne v Brockett* (1872) 8 Ch App 206; *Re Lord Stratheden and Campbell* [1894] 3 Ch 265; *Re Mander* [1950] Ch 547.

[148] [1891] 3 Ch 252; following *Christ's Hospital v Grainger* (1849) 1 Mac & G 460. For a criticism of this decision see Gray, *The Rule against Perpetuities*, 603.

[149] *Re Talbot* [1933] Ch 895; *Re Bland-Sutton's Will Trusts* [1951] Ch 485; revsd in part [1952] AC 631.

[150] *Chamberlayne v Brockett* (1872) 8 Ch App 206, 211; *Goodman v Saltash Corpn* (1882) 7 App Cas 633, 650, 651; *Re Bowen* [1893] 2 Ch 491, 494.

C THE RULE APPLICABLE TO INSTRUMENTS TAKING EFFECT AFTER 15 JULY 1964 BUT BEFORE 6 APRIL 2010: THE PERPETUITIES AND ACCUMULATIONS ACT 1964[151]

The Perpetuities and Accumulations Act 1964 came into operation on 16 July 1964.[152] It can be regarded as achieving two things: first, it provided a number of specific solutions to specific problems created by the common law rule,[153] and secondly, it altered the whole basis of operation of the perpetuity rule, by introducing the principle of 'wait and see'. 'Wait and see' is applicable, in the place of the common law rule requiring certainty of vesting, to dispositions that fail to comply with the common law rule. The draftsman expected the question of the validity of a disposition to be determined by the application first of the common law rule; if valid, all is well; if void, the disposition may be saved by the application of 'wait and see'. It will be seen, when section 3 is discussed, that this method has caused a number of unnecessary difficulties. It would have been preferable to abolish the common law rule, and to replace it by 'wait and see'. This step was finally taken by the Perpetuities and Accumulations Act 2009, but only in relation to instruments taking effect after 5 April 2010.[154] The perpetuities regime provided for by the 1964 Act therefore continues to apply to instruments taking effect before 6 April 2010.[155]

The sections of the 1964 Act will be examined in order.

(1) Section 1. The Perpetuity Period

As an alternative to the common law period during which it is permissible to suspend the vesting of interests, section 1 allows the settlor to specify a fixed period of years not exceeding 80.[156] This provision was intended to provide a more attractive option

---

[151] See generally Morris and Leach, Supplement; (1964) 80 LQR 486 (JHC Morris and HWR Wade); Wolstenholme and Cherry, Conveyancing Statutes, 13th edn, vol 2, pp 135 ff; Maudsley, chs 4, 5 and 6; [1965] CLJ 232 (SJ Bailey).

[152] The Act applies where there is a disposition contained in an instrument. On disposition, see Re Thomas Meadows & Co Ltd and Subsidiary Companies (1960) Staff Pension Scheme Rules [1971] Ch 278; and on instrument, see Re Holt's Settlement [1969] 1 Ch 100 (court order approving an arrangement under the Variation of Trusts Act 1958 constitutes an instrument).

[153] Ss 1, 2, 5, 6 and 7.　　　　　　　　　　　　　　　　　　　　　　[154] Below, p 575.

[155] Only one provision of PAA 2009 is retroactive: s 12 (where instrument specifies a perpetuity period by reference to lives and trustees believe it is difficult or not reasonably practicable to ascertain whether the lives have ended and therefore whether the perpetuity period has ended); above, p 536. Where the trustees execute a deed substituting a perpetuity period of 100 years under that section, the provisions of PAA 1964, no longer apply to the instrument: PAA 2009, s 12(2).

[156] PAA 1964, s 1(1); Re Green's Will Trusts [1985] 3 All ER 455 (period specified as 'from the date of my death to the 1st day of January 2020' held valid as being 'unambiguously identified' or 'made clear' as a period of 43½ years from the testator's death on 1 February 1976 to 1 January 2020). This provision does not apply to certain options to acquire an interest in land; s 9(2), below, p 564.

than the royal lives clause[157] in cases where, as is usual with discretionary trusts, the settlor or testator intended to lay down the period of duration of a trust; and it has had that effect.

It must be emphasised that this alternative period must be expressly specified in the instrument. And, in order to be valid under the common law rule, the vesting of interests under the trust must be related to the period selected. Thus, it is a valid specification of the alternative period of years if the settlor or testator provides for a 'trust period' of 80 years (or smaller period) during which the trustee can exercise various discretionary powers, with a provision that the trust assets vest in identifiable beneficiaries at the conclusion of the period. The vesting is then related to the alternative perpetuity period. But a disposition would be void under the common law rule if the gift was not related to the alternative period. There is no 'wait and see' period of 80 years. Thus, either of the two following dispositions would be void under the rule:

> to such of the issue of X as may be living at the expiration of 80 years after X's death. The period was not specified.

> to the lineal issue of X. I specify the period of 80 years as the perpetuity period applicable to this disposition. The period was specified, but the vesting was not related to the period.

In each case, the gift being void, the 'wait and see' provisions of section 3 will apply. Those beneficiaries whose interests in fact vest within 21 years of the dropping of the survivor of the *statutory* measuring lives will take.

The donor of a special power may provide that the perpetuity period applicable to the limitations shall be a fixed number of years not exceeding 80. Such period will, of course, begin to run from the effective creation of the power, and it cannot be extended by the donee when he makes an appointment.[158]

(2) Presumptions as to Fertility

The rule at common law that a person of whatever age must be regarded as capable of having children[159] has been abolished in the case of instruments taking effect after 15 July 1964.

Under the Act it is to be presumed in any proceedings that a male can beget a child at, but not under, the age of 14 years; and that a female can have a child at, but not over, the age of 55 years.[160] In the case of a living person, however, evidence may be given to rebut these presumptions, by showing that he or she will not be able to have a child at the time in question.[161]

The Act extends these presumptions to the possibility that a person will at any time have a child by adoption, legitimation or other means.[162] If a person is adopted or

---

[157] Above, p 536.   [158] PAA 1964, s 1(2).
[159] Above, pp 540–1.   [160] PAA 1964, s 2(1)(a).   [161] Ibid, s 2(1)(b).
[162] See also Family Law Reform Act 1969, s 15 (reference to child or other person in dispositions made after 1969 include reference to illegitimate child, etc; there are corresponding provisions for legitimated and adopted persons: Legitimacy Act 1976, s 5(2); Adoption Act 1976, s 39); Family Law Reform Act 1987, s 1(1) (in dispositions after 3 April 1988, references to any relationship between two persons is (unless contrary

legitimated, the question arises whether or not he will take as a 'child' of an adopting or legitimating parent under a gift to that person's 'children'. The rule prior to the coming into force of the Children Act 1975 was that an adopted or legitimated child took under such a disposition if he had been adopted or legitimated *before* the instrument came into effect.[163] Under the Children Act 1975, which applies to instruments coming into effect after 1 January 1976, such a person can take whether the adoption or legitimation was before or after the date of the instrument.[164]

A further question arises in relation to the presumption in section 2 of the Perpetuities and Accumulations Act 1964 to the effect that a woman over the age of 55 is incapable of giving birth to a child. A woman over that age might, of course, adopt or legitimate a child.[165] For the purpose of the perpetuity rule, however, the presumption remains.[166] If property has been distributed on the basis of the presumption, and a woman does give birth to, or adopt, or legitimate, a child inconsistently with it, the High Court is empowered to make such order 'so far as may be just', for placing the beneficiaries in the position they would have held had the presumption not been applied.[167]

(3) Uncertainty as to Remoteness. Section 3. Wait and See

It has been seen that a disposition is void under the common law rule unless it is certain to vest, if at all, within 21 years of the death of some person living at the date when the instrument comes into effect. The disposition is void even though it is 99 per cent certain that it will vest, if at all, within the period. And the void disposition is not helped by the fact that it *does in fact vest* within the period. We saw that a gift to the first child of A to marry is void under the common law rule. It is immaterial that, at the date of the gift, three of A's children are engaged to be married, and do in fact marry on the following Saturday.

Factors like these brought the rule into disrepute. The Law Reform Committee[168] examined the problem and accepted the very convincing argument that, instead of basing the decision on the certainty of vesting as seen from the date when the instrument came into effect, it would be very much better to wait and see whether it did in fact vest within the period. If it did vest within the period, it was valid. If it did not, it was void.

This solution is deceptively simple. Two important principles have to be observed if 'wait and see' is to be made to work.

---

intention) construed on basis that it is immaterial whether or not a person's parents have or had been been married to each other at any time).

163 Adoption Act 1958, s 16; Legitimacy Act 1926, s 3.

164 Adoption Act 1976, s 39. On legitimation, see Legitimacy Act 1976, s 5, Schs. 1 and 2.

165 Or even give birth to a child.

166 PAA 1964, s 2(4). As it does also in relation to an adoption after the date of the instrument: Adoption Act 1976, s 42(5) and above, n 162. For a precedent authorising trustees to assume that no child will be born to a woman over the usual age of child-bearing, see Conv Prec 11-C3.

167 Ibid, s 2(2).   168 Fourth Report, 1956 (Cmnd 18).

The first principle is that, if 'wait and see' is applied, that is, if validity is to be determined by waiting to see whether the disposition vests within the period of a life in being plus 21 years, it is essential to specify which lives are to be used to measure the period of a life in being plus 21 years. Otherwise, it is not known how long to wait and see.[169] The Act introduces a comprehensive list of lives to be used to measure the period of waiting and seeing. The list will be examined in detail below.[170]

The second principle is that, once 'wait and see' is enacted, the common law rule becomes irrelevant, and should be abolished. The common law rule becomes irrelevant, because it is no longer relevant to know whether or not a disposition complies with the common law rule. If an interest *must* vest, if at all, within the period, then it *will* vest, if at all, within the period. To say that it *must* vest, if at all, says nothing; the trustees still have to wait until the interest vests before paying out the money to the beneficiaries. Compare two dispositions:

(a) to the first child of A to attain the age of 21. A is alive and has a child aged 16.
(b) to the first great-grandchild of A to attain the age of 21. A is alive and has a great-grandchild aged 16.

The first disposition is valid under the common law rule. The trustees wait for five years to see if the child attains the age of 21, and then pay out the money.

The second disposition is void under the common law rule. So, under the Act, the trustees wait and see whether the first great-grandchild attains the age of 21 within the period.

There is no difference between these cases in the era of 'wait and see', and they should both be solved on the principle of 'wait and see'.

If the Act had *replaced* the common law rule by 'wait and see', the whole of the learning on the common law rule would have disappeared. It is impossible, however, to ignore it, because the list of measuring lives in section 3 fails to include *all* the lives that could be used to determine validity at common law. There are situations in which the disposition may be valid at common law, using the common law lives, but not so if the measuring lives listed in section 3 are used. Illustrations are cases where the settlor or testator has selected his own lives; these are omitted from the list in section 3. There are other cases of which the following may be taken as an example:

to the first of A's lineal descendants to go for a walk with X.

This would be valid at common law. But X is not included in the statutory list. If the walk takes place more than 21 years after the death of the survivor of the persons in

---

[169] It seems that the Law Reform Committee did not consider this question, nor did many jurisdictions that have selected wait and see; (1965) 81 LQR 106 (DE Allan); Maudsley, Appendix D. But the draftsman came to the rescue. In 1987 the American Uniform Act of Perpetuities adopted a period of 90 years as the wait and see period, in preference to a life in being and 21 years: (1987) 21 *Real Property, Probate & Trust Journal* 569; [1987] CLJ 234 (LW Waggoner).

[170] S 3(5); below, p 566.

the statutory list, it will be void under the 'wait and see' provision but valid under the common law.

There seems to be no point in preserving all the old learning on the common law rule to deal with situations of this type. But that is what happened. It is necessary therefore to understand both the common law and the 'wait and see' principle. Simple alterations to the Act would make this unnecessary.[171]

Section 3 provides that,[172] where an interest would be void under the common law rule on the ground that it might vest outside the common law perpetuity period, the disposition shall be treated as not subject to the rule, until it becomes established that the vesting can only occur *outside* the period. Sub-section (4) provides that where the section applies, the perpetuity period shall be measured by the lives of the persons listed in sub-section (5), plus 21 years.[173] In other words, if the disposition is void under the common law rule, using either the common law lives plus 21 years or, if so specified, the specified period not exceeding 80 years, the interest will be treated as valid (unless it becomes clear that the interest will *not* vest within the period) during a period measured by the *statutory* lives plus 21 years. In short, if the disposition is void under the common law rule, there is 'wait and see' for a period measured by the statutory lives plus 21 years.

As a result of the 1964 Act, for instruments to which it applies there are no less than three perpetuity periods and two basic doctrines.[174] This reinforces the argument made above that the common law rule should have been abolished and replaced by 'wait and see'. There would then have been one period, one doctrine, and one set of lives.[175] Illustrations of the working of the principle of 'wait and see' will be delayed until the statutory lives have been examined.

(a) Each part of limitation a separate disposition

In the application of the 'wait and see' principle, each distinct part of a limitation is treated by the Act as a separate disposition. For instance:

> A testator devises land to A for life, remainder to his widow for life, remainder to such of the children of A as are alive at the death of the widow; but if there be no such children, then to the first son of X to marry.

In such a case, the gift to the children of A and the gift to the first son of X to marry are distinct dispositions subject to different waiting periods.

[171] Maudsley, Appendix E. PAA 2009 applies 'wait and see' for a new single perpetuity period of 125 years, and abandons any reliance on the common law rule, but only in relation to instruments taking effect after 5 April 2010: below, p 575.

[172] Apart from ss 4 and 5.

[173] See ss 1 (80-year period), above, p 558; 9(2) (21-year period in connection with options to purchase).

[174] Ie, certainty of vesting and 'wait and see'.

[175] Or two, if the 80-year period were applicable for 'wait and see'.

(b) Special power of appointment

The 'wait and see' principle applies equally to the validity of appointments made by the exercise of a special power:

> Suppose that a testator, who dies in 1965, devises land to A, a bachelor, for life, remainder to such of his issue as he shall by will appoint. A appoints in favour of his infant daughter, X *on her marriage*. A dies in 1975.

At common law the appointment is too remote.[176] Under the Act, it is valid provided that the daughter marries within 21 years after A's death.

(c) Intermediate income

One problem raised by these provisions is the destination of the intermediate income during the waiting period.[177] The general rule, subject to certain exceptions, is that, although the vesting contingency may ultimately never be satisfied, a contingent gift carries the income arising from the corpus, except so far as such income has been otherwise disposed of by the donor.[178] Suppose, for example, that a testator bequeaths the residue of his estate to his grandchild, X, upon her marriage and that she is an infant and unmarried at the time of the testator's death. In these circumstances, the income is accumulated during her infancy and the trustees may use it for her maintenance and education,[179] and may make advances to her out of capital,[180] but at her majority the income becomes and remains payable to her even though she may never marry.[181]

The rights of the beneficiaries in such a case, however, are subject to the perpetuity rule, the effect of which varies according as the disposition falls to be determined by the common law or by the Act of 1964:

> Suppose, for instance, that a will bequeaths the residue of the estate to the daughters of X when they marry, and that X is childless at the time of the testator's death.

At common law the bequest is void ab initio. It is impossible to say at the time when the will takes effect that, if any daughters born to X marry, they will do so within 21 years from her death.

But under the statutory 'wait and see' provisions the gift is not void ab initio. It is void only if at the end of 21 years from the death of the last of the statutory lives none of X's daughters, if any, has married. The destination of the income of the corpus during this waiting period therefore presents a problem. If a daughter is born to X, is she to receive the benefit of the income although the bequest may ultimately become void for remoteness? The recommendation of the Law Reform Committee that such should be the rule[182] was accepted by the Act of 1964, which provides that when it becomes established that the

---

[176] Compare the example, discussed above, p 547.   [177] See Morris and Leach, pp 93–5.

[178] See eg LPA 1925, s 175(2).

[179] Trustee Act 1925, s 31(1)(i); 31(2). For dispositions taking effect after 1969 the age of majority has been reduced to 18: Family Law Reform Act 1969, s 1, Schs 1, 3, para 5.

[180] Ibid, s 32.   [181] Ibid, s 31(1)(ii).   [182] Para 22 (1956 Cmnd 18).

vesting of a gift must occur, if at all, after the end of the perpetuity period, 'the validity of anything previously done in relation to the interest disposed of by way of advancement, application of intermediate income or otherwise' shall not be affected.[183]

(d) General powers of appointment

A general power of appointment that may possibly be exercised beyond the perpetuity period, and that is therefore void at common law,[184] is to be treated as valid until it is established that it will not in fact be exercised at too remote a time.[185] If, for instance, it is exercisable only by will and is given to the unborn child of X, it will be valid if the donee is born and dies within 21 years after X's death; if it is exercisable by deed, or either by deed or by will, but only on the marriage of the unborn child, it will be valid if the marriage occurs within the same period.

(e) Any power, option or other right

In a more comprehensive section, the Act deals separately with the remote exercise of 'any power, option or other right'. It provides that a power, option or other right is no longer to be rendered void merely because it may possibly be exercised at too remote a time. It will be void only if it is not in fact fully exercised within the perpetuity period:[186] for instance, a special power granted by a deed of settlement to the eldest son of X, a bachelor, is void ab initio at common law;[187] but under the Act it is not void unless exercised beyond the perpetuity period calculated from the date of the settlement. On the other hand, if the exercise of a special power satisfies the test of remoteness prescribed by this subsection, the question whether the appointed interests are too remote is governed, as we have seen, by an earlier sub-section.[188]

The reference in this enactment to an 'option' means, inter alia, that a right conferred by contract upon one person to purchase the land of another at some unspecified time in the future is no longer void ab initio,[189] but void only if it is not in fact exercised within the perpetuity period.

But, except where the option is one that entitles a tenant to purchase his landlord's reversion, which is exercisable throughout the continuance of the lease however long this may be,[190] the only period applicable to an option to acquire for valuable consideration any interest in land is 21 years.[191]

---

[183] PAA 1964, s 3(1).   [184] Above, p 545.   [185] PAA 1964, s 3(2).
[186] Ibid, s 3(3). It will be noticed that a general power is caught by this sub-section as well as by sub-section (2).
[187] Above, pp 546–8.   [188] PAA 1964, s 3(1); see the example given above, p 563.
[189] As under the common law, *London and South Western Rly Co v Gomm* (1882) 20 Ch D 562; above, pp 553–4; *Dunn v Blackdown Properties Ltd* [1961] Ch 433; above, p 554.
[190] PAA 1964, s 9(1); below, p 574.   [191] Ibid, s 9(2).

(4) Duration of the Waiting Period. The Statutory Lives

(a) General

Before examining the statutory list of measuring lives, three important preliminary points need to be made. First, as explained above, there is the obvious point that it is impossible to wait and see for lives in being plus 21 years unless it is known whose lives are to be used for the period of waiting and seeing. Those lives need to be known exactly and precisely; otherwise difficult questions will be asked when the period comes to an end. And, for the convenience of the trustees administering the fund, it is more important to have the lives specified at the time when the intrument comes into operation. Otherwise, they will have to add new 'lives' as the years go by.

The second point is that the common law lives will not do. The common law lives, as has been seen, are those within 21 years of whose death the interest must vest, if it vest at all. They are, in other words, the lives that validate the gift. There are no other common law lives additional to the validating lives.[192] The 'wait and see' system cannot work if only the common law validating lives are used; one could only wait and see where the disposition was already valid. As Professor Allan said: 'There would never be any occasion for waiting and seeing at all.'[193]

Thirdly, it is necessary to consider who the measuring lives ought to be for 'wait and see'. The common law lives are irrelevant, and have nothing to do with the choice. The basic question under 'wait and see' is to ask: if that person does in fact live to a date within 21 years of the actual time of vesting, would it be sensible policy that that person should be used as a life that validates the gift?

For example, a settlor creates a trust under which interests are given to such of the grandchildren of A as shall marry. A is alive and has infant children. The gift is void at common law. If a grandchild of A should marry within 21 years of the death of A, or of Mrs A, or of any of the living children of A, or of the settlor, *should* each or any of those lives be used for the purpose of validating the gift? The statutory lives have

---

[192] Above, p 533. A different view is expressed in many of the books, and, in most detail, in (1964) 80 LQR 496 (JHC Morris and HWR Wade). It is there suggested that the common law lives are persons whose lives may or may not validate the interest. It is necessary to ascertain who the lives are, and the test is said to be whether there is a causal relationship between the lives and the vesting. Some lives that are causally connected will validate the interest, but others may not. It is further suggested that this principle is the one that should have been used for the measuring lives applicable to 'wait and see'.

The problem is to determine who those lives are. Causal connection is too uncertain. The standard example that is usually taken is that of a gift to the grandchildren of A who is still alive. The article in 80 LQR seems to suggest that the grandparent is a measuring life because he is causally connected, and so are his living children. It is suggested however that the living grandchildren themselves are inappropriate. It is difficult to see how the grandparent is causally connected with the vesting, because the vesting might occur at any time quite independently of the life or death of the grandparent. On the other hand, the living grandchildren would appear to be measuring lives because it is the continuance of their lives that causes the vesting to occur.

For a detailed discussion of this controversy, see Maudsley pp 87–109; (1981) 97 LQR 593 (RL Deech); (1986) 102 LQR 250 (J Dukeminier).

[193] (1965) 81 LQR 109.

been selected on that basis. In such a case they would indeed be A, Mrs A, A's living children and the settlor.

(b) Statutory lives

(1) Definition

The statutory lives are defined in section 3(5) as follows:

(a) The person by whom the disposition is made, if made by deed, even though he himself takes no interest in the property.[194]

(b) Any of the following persons in whose favour the disposition is made, namely:
    (i) In the case of a class gift, any member or potential member of the class.[195]

A person is a member of the class if he has satisfied all the conditions that entitle him to an interest; he is a potential member if he has satisfied only some of the conditions but may in time satisfy the remainder.[196] If, for instance, there is a gift by will to such of the daughters of X as may marry and if at the time of the testator's death X has an unmarried daughter, she constitutes a life. She has satisfied the condition relating to birth and there is a possibility that she may later marry.

    (ii) In the case of an individual disposition to a person subject to certain conditions, any person as to whom some of the conditions are satisfied and the remainder may in time be satisfied.[197]

This would be the position, for instance, if in the last illustration the gift had been to the first granddaughter of X to marry, and if at the time of the testator's death a granddaughter had been born but was not yet married.

    (iii) The above two provisions apply equally to special powers of appointment.[198] If, for instance, the power is conferred by will and is exercisable in favour of any of the issue of X, descendants of X alive at the testator's death constitute statutory lives.

    (iv) The person on whom any power, option or other right is conferred.[199]

Trustees who possess a special power of appointment, for instance, fall within this category.

(c) In certain circumstances, the parents and grandparents of the designated beneficiaries also constitute persons whose lives are relevant in the present context. The Act provides in section 3(5) that:

> The persons capable of ranking as 'statutory lives' shall include a person having a child or grandchild who would be a life in being under the rules (b)(i) to (iv) given above; and also

---

[194] PAA 1964, s 3(5)(a).　　　　[195] Ibid, s 3(5)(b)(i).　　　　[196] Ibid, s 15(3).
[197] Ibid, s 3(5)(b)(ii).　　　　　　　　　　　　　　　　　　[198] Ibid, s 3(5)(b)(iii) and (iv).
[199] Ibid, s 3(5)(b)(v). For a view that this relates only to the *validity* of the power, and not to appointments made under the power, see Maudsley, pp 133–7.

(c) Class exclusion provisions

We have already seen that at common law a class gift cannot be partly good, partly bad. If some members of the class may possibly fail to satisfy the vesting contingency within the perpetuity period, the whole gift fails even in respect of those members whose interests are already vested.[223]

The Act however abolishes this rule and in its place provides that the disposition shall take effect in favour of those members who acquire vested interests within the perpetuity period to the exclusion of those who fail to qualify within that time. This policy applies to two distinct cases.

First, it applies where the only cause of failure at common law is that some members of the class may not be ascertainable within the perpetuity period. In such a case, the Act provides that, unless their interests are saved by virtue of the 'wait and see' provision, those members shall be excluded from the class.[224]

> Suppose, for instance, that a disposition is made by will to X, a bachelor, for life, remainder to such of his children as may marry. Suppose further that X dies leaving a married son and an unmarried daughter.

If the daughter marries within 21 years after the death of the last of the statutory lives, her interest is saved by the 'wait and see' provisions; if she is still a spinster at the expiry of that time, she is excluded from the class. In the latter event, the gift, which would have been wholly void at common law, takes effect in favour of the son.

The second case is where neither the 'wait and see' principle nor the age reduction provisions will save the gift, as may occur if the attainment by the members of the class of an age exceeding 21 is part of the vesting contingency. The following is an example of such a case:

> A bequest to X, a bachelor, for life, remainder to such of his children as marry and attain the age of 25 years. X dies leaving a married daughter aged 19 and a son aged 3.

The inability of the son to reach the prescribed age within the perpetuity period that ends 21 years from the death of the last of the statutory lives, may no doubt be rectified under the age reduction provisions.[225] But the marriage contingency remains, for whether this is satisfied may not be established until too remote a time. If in fact he marries within 21 years after the death of the last of the statutory lives, the 'wait and see' rule will operate to validate the whole gift. If not, then the daughter becomes the sole beneficiary, for the effect of the Act of 1964 is to exclude the son from the class of designated beneficiaries.[226]

(6) General and Special Powers of Appointment

We have already discussed the importance of the distinction between general and special powers of appointment in the context of the doctrine of remoteness.[227] We

---

[223] Above, p 542.   [224] PAA 1964, s 4(4).
[225] Above, p 569.   [226] PAA 1964, s 4(3).   [227] Above, pp 544 ff.

have also seen that it is sometimes difficult to determine whether a so-called 'hybrid' power is to be classed as general or special.[228] This difficulty is removed by the Act of 1964 which defines what powers shall be treated as special powers for the purposes of the rule against perpetuities, but only for those purposes. By virtue of this enactment a power is to be treated as a special power, unless:

(a) in the instrument creating the power it is expressed to be exercisable by one person only, and

(b) it could, at all times during its currency when that person is of full age and capacity, be exercised by him so as immediately to transfer to himself the whole of the interest governed by the power without the consent of any other person or compliance with any other condition, not being a formal condition relating to the mode of exercise of the power.[229]

The result is that the only general power is one under which 'there is a sole donee who is at all times free without the concurrence of any other person to appoint to himself'.[230]

Thus, for instance, a power is to be regarded as a special power if it is exercisable by the donee jointly with other persons or only with the consent of other persons; or exercisable in favour of any persons alive at the donee's death; or exercisable in favour of any person except the donee. On the other hand, a power to appoint to any person in the world except X should be classified as general.[231]

But the general testamentary power, that is one unrestricted in respect of objects but exercisable only by will,[232] is treated as exceptional by the Act. Under the existing case law, such a power is regarded as special so far as the validity of its creation is concerned;[233] but as general when the question is whether an appointment is too remote.[234] The perpetuity period runs from the date of the instrument of creation in the former case, in the latter from the date of the appointment. To classify such a power as general in respect of the appointments is illogical since, unlike the case where exercise by deed is permissible, the donee is in no sense the virtual owner of the property. Any transfer of the ownership to himself is necessarily ineffective until after his death. Nevertheless, it was felt to be unwise to revise a rule that had obtained for some 70 years, and one upon which conveyancing precedents in constant use had been based. Therefore, the distinction between the validity of the power itself and the validity of appointments is retained by the Act.[235]

The expression 'power of appointment' includes any discretionary power to transfer a beneficial interest in property without the furnishing of consideration.[236] It ranks as a special power.

[228] Above, p 545, n 82.   [229] PAA 1964, s 7.
[230] Fourth Report of Law Reform Committee (1956 Cmnd 18), para 47.
[231] Morris and Leach, p 137.   [232] Above, p 546.
[233] *Wollaston v King* (1869) LR 8 Eq 165; *Morgan v Gronow* (1873) LR 16 Eq 1; above, p 546.
[234] *Rous v Jackson* (1885) 29 Ch D 521.   [235] PAA 1964, s 7, proviso.   [236] Ibid, s 15(2).

(7) Extended Scope of the Rule: Possibilities of Reverter and Contracts for the Purchase of Land

The scope of the rule against perpetuities was enlarged in two respects by the Act of 1964. It was extended to possibilities of reverter and analogous possibilities, a matter that is dealt with in a later chapter;[237] and its effect upon certain contracts for the purchase of land was expanded.

We have seen that at common law a contract for the purchase of land, since it creates an equitable interest in favour of the promisee, is not enforceable by or against third parties if it is too remote; but that it remains enforceable without any limit of time between the parties themselves, since the rule against perpetuities is not concerned with personal obligations.[238] The second limb of the common law rule, however, was abolished by the 1964 Act, which provided in effect that where a disposition, made inter vivos and creating proprietary rights capable of transfer, would be void for remoteness as between persons other than the original parties, it should be void as between the person by whom it was made and the person in whose favour it was made or any successor of his.[239]

(8) Effect of an Infringement of the Rule upon Subsequent Interests

The Law Reform Committee, after castigating the doctrine of dependency, recommended that[240]

> no limitation which itself complies with the rule should be invalidated solely by reason of being preceded by one or more invalid limitations, whether or not it expressly or by implication takes effect after or subject to, or is dependent upon, any such invalid limitations.

The Act of 1964 dealt with this recommendation in the following terms:[241]

> A disposition shall not be treated as void for remoteness by reason only that the interest disposed of is ulterior to and dependent upon an interest under a disposition which is so void, and the vesting of an interest shall not be prevented from being accelerated on the failure of a prior interest by reason only that the failure arises because of remoteness.

Thus each limitation in a chain of limitations must be considered separately according to its own intrinsic validity and without regard to the remoteness of its predecessors. An interest that is already vested or that will necessarily vest, if at all, within the perpetuity period takes effect according to its individual terms.

---

[237] Below, p 619. [238] Above, p 553–4.

[239] S 10. See (1964) 80 LQR pp 524–5 (JHC Morris and HWR Wade). This was reversed again by PAA 2009 to take contracts and options out of the scope of the rule against perpetuities with effect from 6 April 2010, but the rule under PAA 1964 remains for instruments executed between 16 July 1964 and 5 April 2010.

[240] Para 33 (1956 Cmnd 18). [241] S 6.

It will be noticed that the concluding words of the enactment do not direct that the ulterior interest *shall* be accelerated, that is allowed to take effect immediately upon the failure for remoteness of the prior interest, but that such failure *shall not prevent* acceleration. The reason for this negative approach is that there may be other obstacles to acceleration. If, for example, the interest that fails is followed by a contingent interest, which in turn is followed by a vested interest, the latter is not accelerated until it is established whether or not the contingent interest will take effect.[242]

(9) Exceptions to the Rule

The exceptions to the rule recognised by the common law were affected in three respects.

(a) Administrative powers

First, as we have already seen, the administrative powers of trustees are excluded from the rule even in respect of instruments taking effect before 16 July 1964.[243]

(b) Option to purchase leasehold reversion

Secondly, an option to acquire for valuable consideration an interest reversionary (whether directly or indirectly[244]) upon a lease, was wholly exempted from the rule regardless of the length of the lease, provided that it is exercisable only by the lessee or his successors in title, and provided that it is not exercisable later than one year after the end of the lease.[245]

(c) Remedies for recovery of rentcharge

Thirdly, the former doubt as to the ambit of section 121 of the Law of Property Act 1925[246] was removed. It was provided by the 1964 Act that the perpetuity rule should not apply to any powers or remedies for recovering or compelling the payment of an annual sum to which that section relates, or otherwise becoming exercisable or enforceable on the breach of any condition or other requirement relating to that sum.[247]

---

[242] *Re Townsend's Estate* (1886) 34 Ch D 357.

[243] PAA 1964, s 8(1); above, p 556.

[244] Ie if the lease is a head lease, the freehold; or if it is a sub-lease, either the freehold or a superior lease: [1965] CLJ 232, 240 (SJ Bailey).

[245] Ibid, s 9(1).   [246] Above, p 554.

[247] PAA 1964, s 11(1).

only in so far as it exceeds the appropriate statutory period.[280] The excess alone is void.[281] So if accumulation is ordered for the life of a person other than the settlor (which is not one of the statutory periods), it will be good for 21 years.[282]

If the person entitled to property under a trust is a minor, there is a statutory power given to the trustees to maintain the minor out of the income, and to accumulate any surplus income during the remainder of the minority.[283] Where, in accordance with the directions of a settlor, income has been accumulated for one of the statutory periods, and at the termination of that period the beneficiary is a minor, so that a further accumulation may be necessary, the two accumulations are not to be counted together and so held to amount to an infringement of the Act.[284]

(4) Rule in Saunders v Vautier

In the case of instruments taking effect after 15 July 1964, the presumption that no woman over 55 years of age can have a child, introduced by the Act of 1964,[285] applies to the right of beneficiaries to put an end to accumulations.[286] That right is defined in *Saunders v Vautier*[287] and later cases and is as follows: Where there is a gift of capital and income to a beneficiary absolutely, but subject to a trust that the income is to be accumulated beyond the time of his majority, he may, on reaching it, stop the accumulation and insist that the capital and accumulated income be paid to him forthwith. Once the property belongs to him absolutely, his free enjoyment of it cannot be fettered. This right, however, will not avail existing beneficiaries if it is possible that further beneficiaries may come into existence, and before 16 July 1964 the possibility that a woman over 55 years of age might have children sufficed to exclude the rule in *Saunders v Vautier*.[288]

(5) Exceptions to the Rule Against Accumulations

Section 164 of the Law of Property Act 1925 set out certain exceptions to the rule against accumulations.[289] If a settlor directs income to be accumulated for any of the following purposes, the direction will be valid although it may exceed the statutory periods.

---

[280] What is the appropriate period raises a difficult question of construction that must be determined according to the language of the instrument and the facts of the case: *Re Watt's Will Trusts* [1936] 2 All ER 1555, 1562, a test described by Upjohn J as 'artificial and difficult': *Re Ransome* [1957] Ch 348, 361.

[281] For the destination of the excessive accumulation, see eg *Green v Gascoyne* (1864) 4 De GJ & Sm 565.

[282] *Longdon v Simson* (1806) 12 Ves 295; *Griffiths v Vere* (1803) 9 Ves 127. See also *Re Ransome*, above.

[283] TA 1925, s 31.

[284] LPA 1925, s 165; *Re Maber* [1928] Ch 88.   [285] Above, p 559.

[286] PAA 1964, s 14.

[287] (1841) 4 Beav 115; *Wharton v Masterman* [1895] AC 186; Morris and Leach, pp 289–95; Fourth Report of Law Reform Committee (1956 Cmnd 18) para 14.

[288] *Re Deloitte* [1926] Ch 56.

[289] Re-enacting Accumulations Act 1800, s 2.

(a) Payment of debts

Provisions for the payment of the debts of any person need not be confined within one of the six periods.[290]

(b) Raising of portions

Provisions for raising portions for any children or remoter issue of the grantor, settlor or testator, or for any children or remoter issue of a person taking any interest under the settlement, or for a person to whom any interest is thereby limited,[291] are excepted from the Act.[292]

The reason appears to be that unless such accumulations were permissible, it would be necessary for large owners to sell part of their estates in order to make provision for their younger children. It must be noted, however, that this exception allows a latitude that may largely result in all the inconveniences that were felt or apprehended under the common law, because, by a skilfully drawn will, every purpose aimed at by Mr Thellusson could be accomplished.[293] But on the whole the courts have construed this enactment (which repeats the corresponding section of the Thellusson Act) in such a way as to render a flagrant evasion of the spirit of the statute impossible. Thus, an accumulation for the purpose of creating a fund out of which it would be possible to pay portions is not within the exception.[294] Again, an accumulation of the whole of a testator's property with a view to swelling a portions fund has been held void.[295]

Lord Cranworth said in *Edwards v Tuck*:[296]

a direction to accumulate all a person's property to be handed over to some child or children when they attain twenty-one can never be said to be a direction for raising portions for the child or children; it is not raising a portion at all, it is giving everything. 'Portion' ordinarily means a part or a share, and although I do not know that a gift of a whole might not, in some circumstances, come under the term of a gift of a portion, yet I do not think it comes within the meaning of a portion in this clause of the Act which points to the raising of something out of something else for the benefit of some children or class of children...If every direction for accumulation for a child was a portion, the intention of the Legislature, which was to prevent accumulations, such accumulations being most frequently directed for the benefit of children, would be entirely defeated.

(c) Timber or wood

The Act does not apply to any provision respecting the accumulation of the produce of timber or wood.[297]

The probable explanation of this exception is that timber is not usually regarded as annual income, but merely as a resource for some particular occasion, so that a

---

[290] LPA 1925, s 164(2)(i).

[291] Ie, the interest need not be carved out of the precise property, the income of which is to be accumulated.

[292] LPA 1925, s 164(2)(ii).

[293] Fearne, *Contingent Remainders*, p 541, note by Preston.

[294] *Re Bourne's Settlement Trusts* [1946] 1 All ER 411.   [295] *Wildes v Davies* (1853) 1 Sm & G 475.

[296] (1853) 3 De GM & G 40, 58.   [297] LPA 1925, s 164(2)(iii).

direction concerning its accumulation, provided that it conforms to the rule against perpetuities,[298] does not in effect withdraw income from the owner of the estate.[299]

B THE RULE APPLICABLE TO INSTRUMENTS TAKING EFFECT AFTER 5 APRIL 2010

The Perpetuities and Accumulations Act 2009 has repealed the statutory provisions that restricted the accumulation of income,[300] and thereby restored the position at common law before the passing of the Thelusson Act to the effect that the only restriction on accumulations is that set by the rule against perpetuities.[301] The abolition of the rule against accumulations only applies to instruments taking effect after 5 April 2010.[302] The perpetuity rule that will apply to accumulations after that date is the rule that is also set by the 2009 Act for instruments taking effect after 5 April—the single period of 125 years (with 'wait and see').[303] However, the Act makes special provision for accumulation for charitable trusts, where (unless the provision is made by a court or the Charity Commission) the accumulation period is generally restricted to 21 years.[304]

---

[298] *Ferrand v Wilson* (1845) 4 Hare 344.   [299] Fearne, *Contingent Remainders*, p 537, Butler's note.
[300] PAA 2009, s 13, repealing LPA 1925, ss 164–166 and PAA 1964, s 13.   [301] Above, p 577.
[302] PAA 2009, s 15(1); SI 2010 No 37, art 2.   [303] Ibid, ss 5, 7; above, p 575.
[304] Ibid, s 14. The period is extended where the instrument provides for the accumulation to last until the death of the settlor or one of the settlors: s 14(5); and the effect of a period longer than 21 years being specified is that the duty or power to accumulate ceases to have effect at the end of the period: s 14(3); and future income is distributed to the person who would have been entitled to it, or is applied for the purposes for which it would have had to be applied, if there had been no duty or power to accumulate: s 14(6).

16

ENTAILED INTERESTS AND LIFE INTERESTS

We have seen[1] that the fee simple, the fee tail and the life estate were the three estates recognised by the common law as estates of freehold. Before 1926 all three estates could exist as legal estates in the land, although the fee tail and the life estate were limited, as compared with the fee simple that was unlimited.[2] Since 1925, however, when the Law of Property Act provided that the only legal freehold estate is the fee simple absolute in possession,[3] the fee tail (or entailed interest) and the life interest can exist only in equity. In this chapter we consider briefly these two estates, including such aspects of their history as may be necessary to understand their operation in the modern law.

I ENTAILED INTERESTS

The entailed interest was once of great significance in family settlements but the last century and a half marked its decline. We shall see that before 1926 it was recognised as a legal estate; thereafter it could exist only as an equitable interest; and finally since 1997 no new entailed interests can be created. However, given that existing entailed interests still continue to exist, we shall here give an account of their nature in the

---

[1] Above, pp 53–4.   [2] Above, p 54.

[3] LPA 1925, s 1(1); above, p 123; Ch 6. The other legal estate is the term of years absolute, which is not a freehold estate: above, pp 57, 123; Ch 8.

modern law—which, as so often, can be understood only by first understanding their historical development.

A HISTORY

(1) Conditional Fee

The estate known to the common law as the conditional fee was the precursor of the estate tail. About the year 1200 it was becoming a common practice to limit lands to a man and a special or restricted class of his heirs, such as:

to a man and 'the heirs of his body'; or

to a husband and wife and the heirs springing from their marriage; or

to a woman and the heirs of her body—a form of gift that was called a *maritagium*.[4]

As the object of such a gift was to provide for a man's descendants, it was understood that if the donee or one of his issue to whom the land descended died without leaving any heirs of the class specified in the instrument of creation, the estate, being no longer required for the maintenance of the family, should revert to the donor, and should not, like a fee simple, pass to the general heirs of the donee.[5] The courts, however, motivated probably by a desire to render land freely alienable and to this end to prevent it from being irrevocably ear-marked for a particular family, took an entirely different view of the matter, and held that if a grant were made to A and the heirs of his body, or to him and any similarly restricted class of heirs, A could make an out-and-out alienation of his estate, binding on his own heirs and on the donor, as soon as a child of the class indicated was born to him. They said that the effect of such a gift was to confer upon A a conditional fee, that is to say, an absolute fee simple, conditional however upon the birth of issue capable of inheriting the estate according to the terms of the original gift. Once the condition had been satisfied, even though the child died the next minute, A was in as favourable a position as if the lands had originally been granted to him in fee simple, since at common law a condition once performed is completely gone; but if the condition was not fulfilled by the birth of issue, then on A's death the estate reverted to the donor and his heirs.[6]

(2) Statute De Donis Conditionalibus 1285

The rule set out above, which meant in effect that the donee could alienate the land and thus defeat both the right of his issue to succeed to the estate and the right of

[4] Holdsworth, *A History of English Law*, vol iii, pp 74, 111; Plucknett, *Legislation of Edward I* (1949), pp 125–31.

[5] If the gift took the form of what was called *liberum maritagium*, the rule was that after the land had descended three times there should no longer be any reverter to the donor and his heirs. Thus, the third heir became entitled in fee simple; Plucknett, pp 126–9.

[6] Pollock and Maitland, *The History of English Law*, vol ii, pp 16–19; Co Litt 19a; Challis, *Law of Real Property* (3rd edn, 1911), pp 263–8.

the donor to take the estate back if issue already born should die, was not popular. As early as 1258 there was an outcry against a doctrine that ran so contrary to the expressed intention of donors, and the result was the passing in 1285 of the famous Statute *De Donis Conditionalibus*.[7] This enacted that the intention of the donor, as it was manifestly expressed in the original gift, should thenceforth be observed, so that those to whom the land was given should have no power to alienate it, but that it should pass to their issue, or to the giver or his heirs if such issue failed, either by an absolute default of issue or, after the birth of issue, by its subsequent extinction.[8]

The result of this statute was the appearance of a new kind of fee or inheritable estate, called a fee tail, or in Latin *feodum talliatum*, and so called because the quantum of the estate was 'cut down' in the sense that, unlike the case of the fee simple, the right to inherit was restricted to the class of heirs specially mentioned in the gift, and was not available to the heirs-general of the donee.[9] The land could not be disposed of by the tenant in tail, it could not be seized in satisfaction of his debts after it had come into the hands of his successors, and it was not forfeitable for treason or felony—a fact that, in those disturbed times, was regarded by the Crown as a serious defect.[10] Special remedies were given to the issue and to the donor for the recovery of the land in case the form of the original gift was not observed.[11]

There was thus set up an entailed interest in the true sense of that term, that is to say, an interest in land that was bound to descend from one generation to another to the issue of the tenant, and that could not be removed from the family so long as any lineal heirs of the class specified were in existence. It was an unbarrable entail, since neither the right of the issue to succeed, nor the right of the donor and his heirs to take on failure of issue, could be barred or taken away.[12] This state of affairs continued for some 200 years after the Statute *De Donis*, but the statute, instead of being a blessing calculated to ensure the stability of families, proved to be one of the most mischievous institutions in the realm. Blackstone has described some of its effects:[13]

> Children grew disobedient when they knew they could not be set aside; farmers were ousted of their leases made by tenants in tail; for, if such leases had been valid, then, under colour of long leases, the issue might have been virtually disinherited; creditors were defrauded of their debts, for if tenant in tail could have charged his estate with their payment, he might also have defeated his issue, by mortgaging it for as much as it was worth; innumerable latent entails were produced to deprive purchasers of the lands they had fairly bought, of suits in consequence of which our ancient books are full; and treasons were encouraged, as estates

---

[7] 'On conditional gifts': Statute of Westminster II (1285), set out in full, Digby, *History of the Law of Real Property* (5th edn, 1897), p 226.

[8] See Challis, *Law of Real Property*, p 228.   [9] Litt, s 18; Challis, p 60.

[10] First Report of Real Property Commission, 1829, p 22.

[11] Called respectively the *writ of formedon in the descender* and the *writ of formedon in the reverter*; Holdsworth, *A History of English Law*, vol ii, p 350.

[12] It appears that this was not the intention of the draftsman of the statute. What was intended was that the land should be inalienable only until the third heir had entered, after which it could be alienated out of the family: Plucknett, *Legislation of Edward I*, pp 131–5.

[13] *Commentaries*, vol ii, p 116.

H and W;[29] but if H and W were persons who might not lawfully marry (such as by reason of consanguinity) the limitation made them joint tenants for life with separate inheritances.[30] That means that if H died first and had issue, W became sole tenant for life, but that on the death of W the issue of H took one half and the issue of W the other half as tenants in common in tail.[31] The result would be the same if, though capable of marrying, H and W did not actually marry.

After what has been said it will be sufficient to give the appropriate words of limitation for granting the remaining species of entailed interests:

(1) In tail male special

Grant to:

A and his heirs male which he shall beget on the body of his wife X;

or to:

A and X and the heirs male of their two bodies.[32]

(2) In tail female special

This arises from the same limitation as that just described, with the substitution of female for male.[33]

(c) Interests in tail after possibility of issue extinct

An entailed interest special might by implication of law give rise to an *entailed interest after possibility of issue extinct*. If lands were given to a man and his wife, or to the man or to the wife solely, in special tail, and one of them, or the designated spouse, died before issue had been born, the survivor is termed a *tenant in tail after possibility*; and likewise if one died leaving issue, but the other survived the issue.[34] In both these cases, owing to the premature death of one of the persons from whose body the appropriate heirs were to proceed, it was impossible that any person should become entitled to succeed to the interest in accordance with the terms of the original gift. The possibility of the right class of heirs coming into being no longer exists, and therefore the survivor is said to be a tenant after possibility. Such a person is virtually in the position of a tenant for life and he is not entitled to bar the entail.[35] He is given the statutory powers of a tenant for life by the Settled Land Act 1925.[36]

(2) *Words of Limitation*

We have now to consider what words of limitation had to be used in order to create an entailed interest. Owing to the way in which the matter was dealt with by the Law

---

[29] Co Litt 20b; 25b.
[30] Litt s 283; *Preston on Estates*, vol ii, p 417.
[31] Co Litt 182a.
[32] Litt s 25.
[33] For the whole of this section, see Challis, *Law of Real Property*, pp 290–5.
[34] Litt s 32.
[35] Fines and Recoveries Act 1833, s 18.
[36] SLA 1925, s 20(1)(i); *Hambro v The Duke of Marlborough* [1994] Ch 158; above, p 441; below, p 607.

of Property Act 1925, it is unfortunately necessary to discuss the rules that obtained under the previous law. The examples that have been given above of the various classes of entailed interests indicate the general nature of the proper words of limitation, and a short treatment of the subject will suffice here.

(a) Words of limitation before 1926

(1) Creation by deed

The first point is to ascertain the proper words of limitation necessary before 1926 for the creation of an entailed interest by *deed*.

(i) Word 'heirs'

The requirement of common law here was that the word *heirs* must be used and not such analogous expressions as *seed, offspring, descendants, issue* and so on.[37] The effect of a grant, for example, to 'A and his issue' was to confer upon A a mere life estate.

(ii) Words of procreation

The next requirement was that some expression denoting that the inheritance was to pass to the direct descendants of A should be used, and the surest phrase for this purpose was *of his body*. A grant to 'A and the heirs of his body' always conferred an entailed interest on A, but common law, though insisting upon the use of the word *heirs*, was not so exacting with regard to this second requirement, and was satisfied with any words that expressly or by implication showed that the heirs were to issue from the body of A. Thus such expressions as:

> of his flesh,
>
> from him proceeding, or
>
> which he shall beget of his wife,

were sufficient for the purpose.[38]

Before 1 January 1882, if the appropriate words of limitation as set out above were not adopted in a deed, the result was to confer a life estate upon the grantee, but the Conveyancing Act 1881[39] provided that in deeds executed after that date it should be sufficient to use the words *in tail* instead of *heirs of the body*, and the words *in tail male* or *in tail female* instead of *heirs male* or *heirs female of the body*.[40]

(2) Creation by will

Greater latitude of terminology was, however, open to testators. It is more difficult to lay down hard and fast rules as to what words would, and what words would not, have created a certain interest when they were used in a testamentary as distinct from an inter vivos instrument, because the general principle of construction for wills is that the intention of the testator must be ascertained and given effect to, no matter what

---

[37] Co Litt 20a, b; Blackstone, vol ii, p 115.   [38] Co Litt 20b.

[39] S 51. LPA 1925, s 60(4)(b), (c), repealed by TLATA 1996, s 25(2), Sch 4.

[40] For criticism, see Challis, *Law of Real Property*, pp 297–8.

language he may have adopted. It is clear that less formal language would create an entailed interest in a will than in a deed, and in fact any expressions that indicated an intention to give the devisee an estate of inheritance, descendible to his lineal as distinct from his collateral heirs, conferred an entailed interest upon him.[41]

Thus devises to:

A and his seed;[42]

A and his offspring;[43]

A and his family according to seniority;[44]

A and his issue;[45]

A and his posterity;[46]

have all, at one time or another, been held capable of passing an entailed interest when such a construction was consistent with the intention of the testator.

(3) Executory instruments

The same rule of construction was applied in the case of executory instruments inter vivos, that is in instruments that did not finally express the limitations in technical language, but indicated their general nature and left the settlor's intention to be carried out by apt phraseology. If 'marriage articles', for example, by which an intending husband and wife specified in general the terms upon which they were willing to enter into a marriage settlement, provided for the limitation of an interest to the 'issue' of the husband and wife, the presumed intention would be carried out in the formal settlement by the grant of an entailed interest to the first son of the marriage, with remainders in tail to the other children.[47]

(4) The rule in *Wild's Case*

A devise 'to A and his children' requires particular attention because of the rule in *Wild's Case*[48] laid down in 1599.[49] The rule was that where realty was devised to 'A and his children', and A had no child *at the time of the devise*, the word children was prima facie construed as a word of limitation, with the result that A acquired an estate tail. There was some justification for this. The testator clearly intended children to take in any event, but since they were not in existence they could take nothing except through A and he could transmit to them nothing unless he was given an estate of inheritance.[50]

---

[41] *Jarman on Wills*, p 1825.

[42] Co Litt 9b.

[43] *Young v Davies* (1863) 2 Drew & Sm 167.

[44] *Lucas v Goldsmid* (1861) 29 Beav 657.

[45] *Oxford University v Clifton* (1759) 1 Eden 473.

[46] *Wild's Case* (1599) 6 Co Rep 16b.

[47] *A-G v Bamfield* (1703) Freem Ch 268.

[48] (1599) 6 Co Rep 16b.

[49] See below, p 596, n 64.

[50] *Radcliffe v Buckley* (1804) 10 Ves 195, 202 (Sir William Grant MR).

The rule, however, was not inflexible and it was disregarded by the courts where it would operate to defeat the intention of the testator as gathered from other passages in the will.[51]

(b) Words of limitation after 1925 but before 1997

(1) Formal words

We are now left with this question: what words were necessary and sufficient to create an entailed interest in the case of a deed or will that came into operation after 1925, but before 1997?[52] Section 130(1) of the Law of Property Act 1925 provided:

> An interest in tail ... (in this Act referred to as 'an entailed interest') may be created by way of trust in any property, real or personal, but only by the like expressions as those by which before [1926] a similar estate tail could have been created by deed (not being an executory instrument) in freehold land.

The result is that the law on the subject became more inflexible than it was before 1926. The strict requirements of the common law applicable to deeds were extended to wills. Thus, in both instruments the limitation must be to 'A in tail', or to 'A and the heirs of his body', except that in the last case any expressions will suffice that, without expressly saying 'of the body', indicate that the heirs are to issue from the body of A. The only exception to this rule is that a direction that personal property should be enjoyed with land in which an entailed interest had already been created was sufficient to create a corresponding entailed interest in the personal property.[53]

Informal expressions contained in the instrument that would not have been sufficient in a deed before 1926 to create an entailed interest, though they would have been sufficient in a will or executory instrument, no longer sufficed to create an entailed interest.[54] If, for example, a testator who died after 1925 devised land to 'A and his issue', an interest in tail did not pass to A.

(2) Informal words

The question that then arises is—what interest did pass to A when informal expressions such as 'issue', 'seed', 'descendants' or 'children' were contained in a conveyance or in a devise of land?[55] The Act purported to provide an answer in section 130(2):

> Expressions contained in an instrument coming into operation after [1925], which, in a will, or executory instrument coming into operation before [1926], would have created an entailed interest in freehold land, but would not have been effectual for that purpose in a deed not being an executory instrument, shall ... operate in equity, in regard to property real or personal, to create absolute, fee simple or other interests corresponding to those

---

[51] *Byng v Byng* (1862) 10 HL Cas 171, 178; *Grieve v Grieve* (1867) LR 4 Eq 180.

[52] LPA 1925, s 130(1)–(3), (4) were repealed by TLATA 1996, s 25(2), Sch 4. Since 1997 no entailed interests can be created, below, p 605.

[53] LPA 1925, s 130(3).   [54] *Re Brownlie* [1938] 4 All ER 54.

[55] See (1938) 6 CLJ 67 (SJ Bailey); (1947) 9 CLJ 46 (RE Megarry); 185 (SJ Bailey); 190 (JHC Morris).

which, if the property affected had been personal estate, would have been created therein by similar expressions before [1926].

The first point to notice is that this sub-section is not concerned with those formal expressions that would have been effectual in a deed before 1926 to create an estate tail in land. A gift of personality to A and the heirs of his body or to A in tail formerly gave A the absolute ownership of the property,[56] but after 1925, by virtue of section 130(1),[57] it gave him an entailed interest. What we are concerned with here are informal expressions, and we are told that if they appear in a grant or a devise of land operating after 1925 and before 1997, the donee was to acquire in the land the interest that he would have acquired in personality had the same expression been contained in a gift of personality. The question then is, what interest passed under a gift of personality, in the following typical cases:

To A and his issue;

To A for life and then to his issue;

To A and his descendants;

To A and his children.

Find this and we know what interest was taken if the same expressions were adopted in a grant or devise of land.

The primary difficulty is that, since the effect of such informal expressions has always varied according as they appear in deeds or in wills, it is not obvious whether the rules for deeds or for wills were to be adopted. Presumably the solution was that a devise containing informal expressions was to have the effect that had always been allowed to a bequest containing the like expressions, and that a grant inter vivos was to have the effect that had always been attributed to a corresponding gift by deed of personality.

Let us examine only *bequests* of personality, for it is unlikely in practice that any but formal expressions would be found in a conveyance inter vivos.[58] No unqualified rule can be laid down, however, with regard to the quantum of interest that passed under any particular expression, for since the object in each case is to ascertain and to implement the intention of the testator, what always has to be done is to construe the will as a whole. Strictly speaking, the only correct answer to make to the question, 'What interest is taken under a gift of personality to A and his issue?' is, 'That interest which the testator intended to give'. Certain canons of construction, however, became established that covered most of the expressions found in practice.

---

[56] *Chatham v Tothill* (1771) 7 Bro PC 453; *Portman v Viscount Portman* [1922] 2 AC 473; Hawkins and Ryder, *Construction of Wills* (1965), pp 254–5.

[57] Above, p 594.

[58] For the effect of gifts by deed containing informal expressions, see (1938) 6 CLJ 81 (SJ Bailey).

(i) To A and his issue

The primary canon of construction was that a gift of personalty *to A and his issue* showed an intention on the part of the testator that the issue alive when the will comes into operation should take the property jointly with A.[59] Thus, in an immediate gift A and his issue (if any) living at the testator's death would take in joint tenancy; and in a deferred gift, issue subsequently born before the period of distribution would be admitted along with them; and if no issue had come into existence before the period of distribution, A would take the whole.[60]

(ii) To A for life and then to his issue

Again, if there was a bequest to A for life and after his death to his issue, A took merely a life interest and the property was ultimately divided among the issue born during his life.[61] Nevertheless this principle of construction that admitted issue as beneficiaries in the instances given was displaced if it appeared from the will as a whole that the testator meant to make A sole and absolute owner.

(iii) To A and his descendants

The word 'issue' has consistently been held to mean prima facie descendants of every degree,[62] and it therefore seems to follow that a gift of personalty *to A and his descendants* is construed, in the absence of a contrary intention, in the same way as a gift to A and his issue.[63] The descendants alive at the death of the testator took the absolute ownership jointly with A.

(iv) To A and his children

A gift of personalty *to A and his children* was prima facie regarded as a gift to A and the children concurrently, so that A and his children alive at the testator's death took the property as joint tenants, or, if there were no children living at that time, A took the whole absolutely.[64]

(c) Rule in *Shelley's Case*

Finally, we must mention briefly the Rule in *Shelley's Case*,[65] which, though it was abolished by the Law of Property Act 1925,[66] still applies to instruments coming into operation before 1926.[67]

---

[59] *Re Hammond* [1924] 2 Ch 276.

[60] Hawkins and Ryder, *Construction of Wills*, pp 241–2.

[61] *Knight v Ellis* (1789) 2 Bro CC 570; *Jarman on Wills* (6th edn), p 1200.

[62] Hawkins and Ryder, p 148.   [63] (1938) 6 CLJ p 75 (SJ Bailey).

[64] Hawkins and Ryder, pp 260–2. The rule in *Wild's Case* as stated above, p 593, never applied to personalty.

[65] See Challis, *Law of Real Property*, pp 152 ff; Cheshire, 11th edn of this book, pp 198–202; [1981] Conv 128 (JS Coote).

[66] S 131, as amended by TLATA 1996, s 25(2), Sch 3, para 4(14).

[67] *Re Routledge* [1942] Ch 457 (testator died in 1874); *Re Williams* [1952] Ch 828 (testator died in 1921).

(1) The rule

This was a rule of law applicable to both deeds and wills, which provided that if in the same instrument an estate of *freehold* was limited to A, with remainder, either immediately or after the limitation of an intervening estate, *to the heirs* or *to the heirs of the body* of A, the remainder, though importing an independent gift to the heirs as original takers, conferred the fee simple in the first case, and the fee tail in the second case, upon A, the ancestor.[68] Thus the effect of a grant:

> to A for life, remainder to his heirs,

was to give A the fee simple; and the effect of a grant:

> to A for life, remainder to the heirs of his body,

was to give A an estate tail.

The interest that in terms was given to the heirs and that in most cases the donor, especially when he was a testator, meant the heirs to have, was in the eye of the law given to A. So A could dispose of the estate and thereby defeat his heir, who would take only if A died intestate still owning the estate.

Thus the operation of the rule was two-fold: it denied to a remainder the effect of a gift to the 'heirs', and it attributed to the remainder the effect of a gift to A.[69] In fact, the legal effect of such a limitation was the direct opposite of what would naturally be expected, and it nearly always operated to defeat the intention of a testator.[70]

Another and more technical way of stating the rule is as follows: where the ancestor by any gift or conveyance takes an estate of freehold, and in the same gift or conveyance an estate is limited, either mediately or immediately to his heirs, in fee or in tail, in such cases 'the heirs' are words of limitation of the estate and not words of purchase. We have already considered the distinction between words of limitation and words of purchase.[71] Thus, if land was given:

> to A for life, remainder to the heirs of his body,

what the Rule in *Shelley's Case* declared was that the words 'heirs of his body' were not words of purchase pointing out the heir as a person entitled to a definite interest in the land, but were words of limitation employed to mark out the extent of the interest given to A. Had the words 'heirs of his body' been regarded as words of purchase, they would have indicated that the estate was given to the person who was found to be heir on the death of A. In other words, this person would have claimed the estate as having been given to him by the original conveyance. The result, in fact, was the same as if the grant had been:

> to A and the heirs of his body,

---

[68] Hayes, *Introduction to Conveyancing*, vol i, p 542; *Preston on Estates*, vol i pp 263–4.
[69] Ibid, p 534.
[70] For the feudal reasons for this rule, see *Van Grutten v Foxwell* [1897] AC 658, 668.
[71] Above, p 155.

but it is essential to notice that the Rule in *Shelley's Case* operated only where there were in terms two estates given, ie a freehold to the ancestor, A, and then a remainder to the heirs, for example:

> to A for life and after his death to the heirs of his body.

It is true that a limitation *to A and his heirs* or *to A and the heirs of his body* gives A a fee simple in the first case and a fee tail in the second case, but these results do not ensue from *Shelley's Case*. The law had been so established at a far earlier date.[72]

(2) Abolition of the rule

The Rule in *Shelley's Case* was abolished by section 131 of the Law of Property Act 1925 for all instruments coming into operation after 1925. Accordingly, where there is a limitation to:

> A for life and then to his heirs; or to
>
> A for life and then to the heirs of his body,

the effect is to restrict A's interest to a life interest, and to appropriate a definite interest to the heir or to the heir of the body of A. The heir is ascertained in accordance with the canons of descent that obtained before 1926,[73] and he takes the interest by way of purchase. What interest he takes is perhaps a little doubtful, but presumably in all cases he takes the fee simple or otherwise the whole interest that the donor had power to convey, unless a contrary intention appears in the deed or will.[74]

The result, then, of the abolition of the Rule in *Shelley's Case* upon the creation of an entailed interest after 1925 until 1996, seems to be this:

(i)   A gift to A for life, remainder to the heirs of his body would no longer vest an entailed interest in A, despite the enactment that such an interest may be created by the like expressions as those by which before 1 January 1926 a similar estate tail could have been created by deed.[75]

(ii) A gift to A for life, remainder to the heirs of his body would be effectual to vest a definite interest in the *heir*, although such would not have been the result of a similar conveyance by deed under the old law.

C ENTAILED INTERESTS AFTER 1925

After 1925 an entailed interest can no longer subsist as a legal estate. It is necessarily an equitable interest.[76] The only possible methods by which it could be created after 1925,

---

[72] If, for example, lands had been given 'to W and her heirs for her and their use and benefit absolutely and for ever', the Rule in *Shelley's Case* would not have applied: *Re McElligott* [1944] Ch 216; (1938) 54 LQR 70 (AD Hargreaves).

[73] Above, p 117.

[74] LPA 1925, s 60(1); Wills Act 1837, s 28; above, p 156. The rule before the Wills Act 1837 was that a devise to the *heirs of the body* of a person conferred an estate tail (*Mandeville's Case* (1328) Co Litt 26(b), and the question whether the fee simple could pass under s 28 of the Wills Act does not seem to have arisen.

[75] Above, p 594.   [76] LPA 1925, ss 1, 130.

The expression 'base fee' shall mean exclusively that estate in fee simple into which an estate tail is converted where the issue in tail are barred, but persons claiming estates by way of remainder or otherwise are not barred.

It is a less valuable fee simple than a fee simple absolute, since it will last only as long as there are in existence descendants who would have inherited the entailed interest had it never been barred; while a fee simple absolute continues as long as there exist any persons who are heirs, whether lineal or collateral, of the owner. In the example given above, if the eldest son of A, having barred the entail in his father's lifetime, conveys the interest so acquired to X and then dies without having issue, the base fee held by X ceases, and passes to the second son by way of remainder. On the other hand, had the interest conveyed to X been a fee simple absolute, the death of the eldest son without issue would have made no difference to the perpetual nature of X's interest.

A base fee, however, may be converted, or will automatically become enlarged, into a fee simple absolute in any one of the following ways.

(i) Union of base fee with remainder or reversion in fee
Suppose there is a limitation to:

A for life, remainder to B in tail, remainder to C in tail, remainder to B in fee simple.

B creates a base fee in himself by executing a disentailing deed during the life of A and without his consent. The remainderman C dies in the lifetime of B without having issue. The position now is that both the base fee and the fee simple absolute in remainder are united in B without there being any intermediate estate between them, and the Fines and Recoveries Act provides that whenever this occurs the base fee shall be enlarged into as great an estate as the tenant in tail could have created had he been in possession at the time of disentailment.[97] In plain language, it is enlarged into a fee simple absolute.

(ii) Fresh disentailing deed
If a tenant in tail in remainder creates a base fee, he can convert it into a fee simple absolute by executing a fresh disentailing deed with the consent of the protector.[98] But if the protector no longer exists, such as where the tenant for life under a strict settlement dies, the tenant can enlarge the base fee, whether he has parted with it or not, by himself executing a fresh disentailing deed.[99]

(iii) Lapse of time
A base fee becomes valid against remaindermen and reversioners if any person takes possession under the disentailing assurance, and if he or any other person remains in possession by virtue of that assurance[100] for 12 years from the time when the tenant in

---

[97] Fines and Recoveries Act 1833, s 39.
[98] Ibid, s 35.
[99] Ibid, s 19; *Bankes v Small* (1887) 36 Ch D 716.
[100] *Mills v Capel* (1875) LR 20 Eq 692.

tail would have been entitled to possession and therefore free to effect a complete bar of his own accord.[101]

(iv) Devise

The owner of a base fee *in possession* is now permitted to enlarge the base fee into a fee simple absolute by will.[102]

(3) Unbarrable entailed interests

Two classes of tenants in tail are unable to disentail their estates, namely a tenant in tail after possibility[103] and a tenant in tail to whom or to whose ancestors an estate has been granted by Parliament as a reward for services rendered, if the statute by which the grant is made has expressly prohibited the right of disentailment. Examples are the Bolton, the Marlborough and the Wellington estates.[104]

(3) Entailed Interests may be Disposed of by Will

Prior to 1926 a tenant in tail could not devise his estate, and if he died without having disentailed, it passed by descent to the appropriate class of heirs. The Law of Property Act 1925, however, provides that in a will *executed* on or after 1 January 1926 a testator of full age may devise or bequeath all property of which he is tenant in tail *in possession* at the time of his death, and all money subject to be invested in the purchase of property, of which if it had been so invested he would have been tenant in tail in possession at his death.

The tenant has power to dispose of the estate: 'in like manner as if, after barring the entail, he had been tenant in fee simple or absolute owner thereof for an equitable interest at his death',[105] and therefore the effect produced by the will is similar to that produced by a disentailing deed. But to guard against a disentailment by inadvertence, it is provided that no will shall be sufficient to dispose of the estate unless it refers specifically either to the property entailed, or to the instrument creating the entail or to entailed property generally, and therefore a mere general devise or bequest has no effect for the purpose.[106]

This power of disposition is also conferred by the Act[107] upon the owner of a base fee *in possession* provided that he is in a position to enlarge the base fee into a fee simple absolute. This position arises where a tenant in tail in remainder, having barred

---

[101] Limitation Act 1980, s 27. This section also applies to a disentailing assurance that, owing to some defect such as the lack of a deed, fails to bar the tenant's *issue*.

[102] LPA 1925, s 176(1), (3); below.   [103] Fines and Recoveries Act 1833, s 18; above, p 591.

[104] Former examples were the Abergavenny, Shrewsbury and Arundel estates, but these have now been statutorily freed from restraints upon alienation. See also SLA 1925, s 23(2); *Hambro v Duke of Marlborough* [1994] Ch 158.

[105] LPA 1925, s 176(1).

[106] Ibid. The word *specifically* was interpreted in a liberal sense by Vaisey J in *Acheson v Russell* [1951] Ch 67. For a criticism of the decision, see (1950) 66 LQR 449 (REM).

[107] LPA 1925, s 176(3).

the entail without the consent of the tenant for life as protector, becomes entitled to possession upon the death of the tenant for life. In such a case, as we have already seen, the owner of the base fee may bar the entail and enlarge the base fee into a fee simple absolute in possession by executing a fresh disentailing assurance. The extension of this principle made by the Law of Property Act 1925 is that the owner may *devise* the base fee so as to pass a fee simple absolute to the devisee provided that the will refers specifically either to the base fee or to the instrument by which it was acquired. But he has no such testamentary power unless he is in possession of the base fee or of its rents and profits. It will thus be seen that the power to execute a fresh disentailing assurance given by the Fines and Recoveries Act is wider than the power of testamentary disposition given by the Law of Property Act, since the former can be exercised by the tenant in tail even after he has conveyed the base fee to a purchaser and has lost all right to possession of the land.[108]

D NO NEW ENTAILED INTERESTS AFTER 1996

The Trusts of Land and Appointment of Trustees Act 1996[109] does not affect existing entailed interests, but after 1996 any attempt to create an entailed interest operates as a declaration of trust in favour of the grantee absolutely. Thus, if X purports to grant a freehold in tail to Y, Y is entitled to a fee simple absolute in possession, and, if he is an adult, can call for a transfer of the property from the trustees.[110] Further, if X purports to grant a freehold to Y for life, remainder to Z in fee tail, a trust of land arises under which Y has a life interest and Z a fee simple absolute in remainder. Any attempt by X to declare himself a tenant in tail is ineffective.

II LIFE INTERESTS

A LIFE INTERESTS IN THE MODERN LAW

The modern life interest differs fundamentally from that found in the days of feudalism. In those days, when lands were granted not in return for a rent nor by way of settlement, but on the condition that the tenant should render services of a military nature to the grantor, the tenant was given an interest merely for his life, because, although he was known to the lord and was a man in whose fidelity and courage the lord trusted, yet the character of his eldest son was an unknown factor, and it would have been foolish for a grantor to have tied his hands by pledging himself in advance to accept the son as a new tenant on his father's death. So in the twelfth century the life estate was the greatest interest that anyone would have had in land, and it arose when

---

[108] *Bankes v Small* (1887) 36 Ch D 716.   [109] S 2, Sch 1, para 5.
[110] *Saunders v Vautier* (1841) 4 Beav 115.

a feudal grant was made by a lord to a tenant.[111] At first the grantee did not possess the free power of alienation, since to have permitted this would have prejudiced the lord's right to make the new tenant, on the death of the old, pay a sum (a relief[112]) for the privilege of obtaining the land. Moreover, a tenant possessed of a free power of alienation might cause irreparable injury by granting the land to a personal enemy of the lord. But the restraints on alienation gradually disappeared, and it was recognised by the Statute *Quia Emptores* 1290[113] that a feudal tenant could grant his interest to whom he pleased.[114] By degrees it was also recognised that the feud was an inheritable interest that would descend to the heirs-general of the tenant, and that therefore would endure as long as there were any such heirs in existence. An estate greater than a life estate thus became known to the law, and an interest that could endure only for life, as distinguished from a fee simple that might endure for ever, was added to the list of possible estates. In the words of Hayes:[115]

> Some time elapsed after the feudal relation began to be known in Europe, before the right of inheritable succession was fully conceded. In its primitive state the possession was held at pleasure, or for a short term only: afterwards, the tenure was for life, the lord resuming the land on the death of the tenant, and granting it out anew. But at length the son of the tenant was permitted to succeed: an indulgence which was followed by the extension of the grant, first to the tenant and his issue (i.e. in fee tail) and finally to him and his heirs (i.e. in fee simple, expressed in legal phraseology by the word fee, without more), the law marking out a course of descent, which, enlarging by degrees, embraced his relations, lineal and collateral, male and female.

But though after the establishment of the fee simple it became possible and indeed common to create a life estate with peculiar incidents of its own, the object of this practice was materially different from that which underlies the life interest found in more modern conveyancing. The estate in those days was granted, generally by the rich ecclesiastical corporations, in return for an annual rent, and was the result of a purely business transaction analogous to the modern lease for a term of years. The tenant resembled the modern tenant farmer, except that he held for life instead of from year to year or for a fixed number of years, and although he was said to have a *lease*, the interest vested in him was a freehold interest and not a term of years.

In the modern law, however, the life interest serves a very different purpose, typically as part of the settlement of family interests in property—either under a strict settlement or (in the case of a life interest created after 1996[116]) under a trust of land. This aspect of the nature of a life interest became more important in the nineteenth century, when the Settled Land Act 1882 gave to a tenant for life powers that extended

---

[111] Above, p 32.   [112] Above, p 38.
[113] Above, p 35.
[114] For the growth of the power of alienation, see Holdsworth, *A History of English Law*, vol iii, pp 73 ff; Plucknett, *A Concise History of the Common Law* (5th edn, 1956), pp 35 ff; Simpson, *A History of the Land Law* (2nd edn, 1986), pp 51–6.
[115] Hayes, *Introduction to Conveyancing* (5th edn, 1840), vol i, pp 7–8.   [116] Above, p 475.

beyond those that he had as the owner of a mere life interest.[117] The crucial question at the present day therefore is not whether a claimant may enjoy the land for his life, but whether before 1997 he had the powers of a tenant for life under the Settled Land Act 1925, or after 1996 the powers delegated to him by the trustees of land under the Trusts of Land and Appointment of Trustees Act 1996.[118]

Another common example of a life interest today occurs where there is an intestacy, and the surviving spouse or civil partner is given a life interest in half the residuary estate of the deceased under the Administration of Estates Act 1925.[119]

B CLASSES OF LIFE INTERESTS

A life interest is a freehold interest—generally called a *mere freehold* to distinguish it from fees simple and entails, which are estates of inheritance. After 1925 it can no longer exist as a legal estate, and is necessarily equitable.[120] It may be limited to endure for the life either of the tenant himself or of some other person, in which latter case it is called an interest *pur autre vie*.

(1) Estate for Life of Tenant

An interest for the life of the tenant himself may be created expressly by a settlement, made either by deed or by will, but may also arise by implication of law in the case of the tenant in tail after possibility,[121] or by operation of law where a husband becomes tenant by the curtesy in the entailed lands of his deceased wife.[122] If his interest was created before 1997, the interest for life will be held under a settlement under the Settled Land Act 1925 unless it was created under an express trust for sale.[123] If created after 1996, the interest must be held under a trust of land.[124]

(2) Estate pur autre vie

The interest *pur autre vie* is the lowest estate of freehold known to the law, and is not as great as an interest for the life of the tenant himself. It arises in two ways. The first is where there is an express limitation to A for the life of B. Such a limitation may be made, like an ordinary lease for years, in return for a rent, or as part of a settlement of land. A is called the *tenant pur autre vie*, and B the *cestui que vie*.[125] Secondly, if a

---

[117] Above, p 102.

[118] See the problems that arise where the court seeks to protect a contractual licensee for the remainder of his or her life; above, p 433, n 11; below, p 944.

[119] S 46, amended by Intestates Estates Act 1952, and further amended by Civil Partnership Act 2004, s 71, Sch 4, Pt 2, para 7.

[120] LPA 1925, s 1(3); above, p 124.   [121] Above, p 591.   [122] Above, p 589.

[123] Above, p 433.   [124] Above, p 475.   [125] Litt s 56; Co Litt 41b.

person B, who is entitled to an estate for his own life assigns his interest to A, the effect is that A becomes the tenant *pur autre vie*.[126]

From the point of view of rights and liabilities, a tenant *pur autre vie* is in the same position as an ordinary tenant for life. Thus, at common law, he was entitled to the rents and profits of the land during the continuance of his interest and to cut timber within the limits of estovers, while on the negative side he is liable for waste to the same extent as if he were holding for his own life.[127] Unless holding merely under a lease at a rent, he may exercise any of the wide powers conferred by the Settled Land Act 1925.[128] No matter how the interest arises, he possesses an absolute power of alienation during his life,[129] and after his death his alienee is entitled to hold for the rest of the *cestui que vie*'s life.[130] In the absence of such alienation the interest passes on the death of the tenant to his devisee,[131] or, if he has made no will, to the persons who are entitled to take his property under the rules that govern intestacy.[132] Prior to the legislation of 1925 there were certain peculiar rules that governed the devolution of an interest *pur autre vie*, but these have been abolished.[133]

In view of the danger that a tenant *pur autre vie* may be tempted to conceal the death of the *cestui que vie*, the Cestui que Vie Act 1707 provides that a person entitled to the land upon the termination of the life interest may, after swearing an affidavit that he believes the *cestui que vie* to be dead, obtain an order from the High Court for the production of the *cestui que vie*. If the order is not complied with, the *cestui que vie* is taken to be dead and the person next entitled to possession may enter upon the lands.

C THE RIGHTS AND OBLIGATIONS OF A TENANT FOR LIFE

Under the common law a tenant for life entitled in possession could take the annual profits, but must not take or destroy anything that is a permanent part of the inheritance. He was entitled to fruits of all kinds, but must leave unimpaired the source of the fruits. He had certain positive rights, and one negative duty, which is prescribed by the doctrine of *waste*. The object of these rules was to maintain a balance between the interests of the tenant for life and those in reversion or remainder.

Although the interest of a tenant for life is now necessarily equitable, these common law rules still apply, except in so far as they are varied by the instrument creating his interest.[134]

---

[126] Co Litt 41b. For example, the mortgage of an equitable life interest under a settlement; below, p 811.

[127] Below, p 609 (waste). For estovers, see above, p 236.

[128] SLA 1925, s 20(1)(v); he is not so entitled if he is the assignee of a tenant for life holding under a settlement; above, p 452.

[129] Co Litt 41b.   [130] *Dale's Case* (1590) Cro Eliz 182.

[131] Wills Act 1837, s 3.

[132] AEA 1925, s 46.   [133] Ibid, s 45(1)(a); for the old law, see Challis, *Law of Real Property*, pp 358 ff.

[134] *Re Harker's Will Trusts* [1938] Ch 323; but see (1938) 2 Conv (NS) 233 (H Potter). In the case of a tenant for life under the Settled Land Act 1925, we have seen that there are also detailed statutory provisions relating to his powers: above, pp 443 ff.

(1) Emblements

There is little that need be said of his positive rights. The profits that arise from the land, whether they arise continuously, periodically or occasionally, belong to him. A particular hazard, however, that confronts him is that after he has sown crops his tenancy may end unexpectedly before they are ripe, such as by the death of a *cestui que vie*. In this event, he is entitled to re-enter the land at harvest time and to reap what he has sown. This is known as the right to *emblements*.[135] It is enforceable, however, only in respect of crops such as corn, hemp, flax and potatoes, which bear an annual fruit.[136] One crop only can be taken,[137] and the right does not extend to seeds that do not produce a crop within a year of sowing, such as young fruit trees or the second crop of clover.[138]

The right can be exercised only if the estate comes to an end unexpectedly without any fault on the part of the tenant for life, and therefore, if it is forfeited in his lifetime owing to the breach of some condition, or if, being a determinable interest, it is brought to an end by the happening of the terminating event—such as by the remarriage of a woman who is tenant *durante viduitate* (as long as she remains a widow)—the crops belong to the reversioner.[139]

(2) Waste

The position of the tenant for life on the negative side is governed by the common law doctrine of waste as enlarged by statute and equity. We have already seen the definition of waste in relation to the liability for waste of the tenant for years.[140]

At common law, tenants for life or years whose tenancies arose by operation of law, such as the doweress or tenant by the curtesy, were liable for waste; but no liability arose in the case of tenancies, whether for life or years, created by act of parties, for the courts were disinclined to excuse the folly of the lessor in not imposing an express restraint upon the tenant.[141] This, however, was altered by the Statute of Marlborough[142] in 1267, which provided as follows:

> Fermors,[143] during their terms, shall not make waste, sale, nor exile of house, woods, nor of anything belonging to the tenements that they have to ferm, without special licence had by writing of covenant, making mention that they may do it.

This reference to a 'special licence' recognised, therefore, that a tenant for life might be expressly permitted to do acts that would normally constitute waste without incurring liability,[144] and from this point of view it led to the emergence of two classes

---

135 Co Litt 55b. The right of the tenant for years to emblements has been replaced by a statutory right; above, p 238.

136 Co Litt 55b; Blackstone, vol ii, p 122.   137 *Graves v Weld* (1833) 5 B & Ad 105.

138 Ibid.   139 Co Litt 55b; *Oland's Case* (1602) 5 Co Rep 116a.   140 Above, p 234.

141 *Countess of Shrewsbury's Case* (1600) 5 Co Rep 13b.

142 52 Hen. 3, c 23. Also called Marlbridge. See *Dayani v Bromley LBC* [1999] 3 EGLR 144, above, p 236.

143 'Fermor' includes everybody holding for life or years.

144 *Woodhouse v Walker* (1880) 5 QBD 404, 406–7.

of tenants for life, namely those impeachable for waste, and those unimpeachable for waste.

(1) Tenant impeachable

A tenant who is impeachable is liable for the commission of voluntary waste,[145] but is not liable for permissive waste[146] unless the settlor has imposed upon him an obligation to keep the property in repair.[147]

Where such an obligation is imposed, an action lies against the tenant or against his personal representative, on the general equitable principle that a person who accepts a benefit must also shoulder the burden.[148]

Where, however, the property that is settled upon the tenant consists of leaseholds, he is bound to perform any covenants, such as a covenant to repair, contained in the lease under which the property is held. Thus, if a house that is held by a testator on a long lease is bequeathed to A for life, A must take the burden with the benefit, and instead of throwing the financial burden upon the testator's estate must meet the cost of performing the covenants out of his own pocket.[149]

(2) Tenant unimpeachable

If, as is nearly always the case under a settlement, a tenant for life is unimpeachable, he is not liable either for voluntary or for permissive waste, and at common law may fell timber or open new mines and deal with the produce as absolute owner.[150]

(3) Equitable waste

Equity, however, set its face against an abuse of this immunity and the rule has long been that any tenant who commits wanton or extravagant acts of destruction, will be restrained by injunction and ordered to rehabilitate the premises. Lord Campbell said:[151] 'Equitable waste is that which a prudent man would not do in the management of his own property.' Examples of the application of this rule occur where the tenant dismantles a mansion or other house,[152] cuts saplings at unreasonable times,[153] or fells timber that has been planted for the ornament or shelter of the mansion house and its grounds.[154] It is difficult to decide whether timber is ornamental or not, but the question depends upon whether the person who carried out the planting intended the trees to be ornamental, and not upon the personal opinion of the court or anybody else.[155]

---

[145] Co Litt 53a.

[146] *Re Cartwright* (1889) 41 Ch D 532; *Re Parry and Hopkin* [1900] 1 Ch 160; *Woodhouse v Walker*, above.

[147] *Woodhouse v Walker*, above.

[148] *Jay v Jay* [1924] 1 KB 826, 829.   [149] *Re Betty* [1899] 1 Ch 821; *Woodhouse v Walker*, above.

[150] *Lewis Bowles' Case* (1615) 11 Co Rep 79b; Tudor, *Leading Cases on Real Property* (4th edn, 1898), p 153.

[151] *Turner v Wright* (1860) 2 De GF & J 234, 243.   [152] *Vane v Lord Barnard* (1716) 2 Vern 738.

[153] *Brydges v Stephens* (1821) 6 Madd 279.   [154] *Downshire v Sandys* (1801) 6 Ves 107.

[155] *Weld-Blundell v Wolseley* [1903] 2 Ch 664.

Wanton acts of destruction of the kinds specified are said to constitute equitable waste because prior to the Judicature Act 1873 they could be remedied only in a court of equity; but section 135 of the Law of Property Act 1925 now provides that a tenant for life has no right to commit equitable waste unless an intention to confer such right appears in the instrument of creation.

A tenant *pur autre vie* is liable for waste to the same extent as a tenant for his own life,[156] but a tenant in tail after possibility of issue extinct[157] incurs no liability by the commission of voluntary or of permissive waste.[158]

Where an act of waste has been committed, the remainderman or reversioner may sue for an account in the Chancery Division, or bring an action in the Queen's Bench Division, either for conversion in respect of any things that may have been severed, or for money had and received as a result of their sale, or for the recovery of damages; and he may sue in either Division for an injunction.

---

156 Co Litt 41b; *Seymor's Case* (1612) 10 Co Rep 95b, 98a.   157 Above, p 591.

158 *Williams v Williams* (1810) 12 East 209.

17

DETERMINABLE INTERESTS AND INTERESTS UPON CONDITION SUBSEQUENT

Summary

I   DETERMINABLE INTERESTS

A   DEFINITION AND TERMINOLOGY

A determinable interest is one that may come to an end before the completion of the maximum period designated by the grantor. For example, the first clause in a deed of settlement, made by a man in view of his approaching marriage, would typically provide that the settlor shall hold the land in trust for himself in fee simple *until the solemnisation of the intended marriage*. In such a case the maximum interest taken by the settlor is a fee simple, but it is a modified, not an absolute fee, since it will not run its full course if the terminating event—the marriage—supervenes:

> A *direct* limitation marks the duration of estate by the life of a person; by the continuance of heirs; by a space of precise and measured time; making the death of the person in the first example; the continuance of heirs in the second example; and the length of the given space in the third example, the boundary of the estate or the period of duration.
>
> A *collateral* [ie determinable] limitation, at the same time that it gives an interest which may have continuance for one of the times, in a direct limitation, may, on some event which it describes, put an end to the right of enjoyment *during the continuance of that time*.[1]

---

[1] *Preston on Estates* (2nd edn, 1820), vol i, p 42, cited Challis, *Law of Real Property* (3rd edn, 1911), pp 252–3.

Much confusion of terminology is apparent among the writers on this subject. Thus Preston, in the above quotation, speaks of *collateral* limitations; Littleton describes the terminating event as a *condition in law*, while most of the other early writers adopt the expression *conditional limitations*. The words *collateral* and *conditional*, however, besides being obscure, are used in many different senses, and the modern practice is to describe this particular species of modified interest as a determinable interest, and the limitation by which it is created as a determinable limitation.[2]

B DETERMINABLE FEE SIMPLE

The older writers deal fully with determinable fees simple, and the classic example is that given by Blackstone, who stated that the effect of a grant to A and his heirs, *tenants of the manor of Dale*, is to give A and his heirs a fee simple that will be defeated as soon as they cease to be tenants of that manor. In such a case there resides in the grantor and his heirs a *possibility of reverter*,[3] since there is a possibility that the terminating event will occur and so cause the estate to revert.[4]

Another example of a determinable fee is afforded by *Re Leach*,[5] where freeholds were devised: 'upon trust to pay the rents to Robert until he should assign, charge or otherwise dispose of the same, or become bankrupt'. It was held that Robert took an equitable fee simple that would determine if one of the specified events occurred in his lifetime, but that would become absolute if he died without their having occurred.

Determinable fees disappeared from practical conveyancing, however (and gave way to shifting future estates operating under the Statute of Uses[6]) after it was decided that the fee simple in the case of a determinable limitation could not be made to pass to a stranger on the occurrence of the terminating event. The common law has never allowed a fee to be limited after a fee simple. As was said by Lord Cairns in *The Buckhurst Peerage Case*:[7]

> There is no instance in the books that we are aware of in which a fee simple, or a fee tail qualified in the way that I have mentioned, as by the addition of the words 'lords of the manor of Dale', is followed by a remainder to other persons upon the first takers ceasing to be lords of the manor.

Thus at the present day, if it is desired to make a fee simple pass from the grantee to some other person when a given event does or does not happen, the limitation will take the form of the grant of an equitable future interest.

(1) Settled Land

The uncertain duration of a determinable fee does not impede its effective disposition. If it was created before 1997, the instrument by which it is limited constitutes a settlement for the purposes of the Settled Land Act 1925;[8] the person entitled to possession is a

---

² Challis, pp 253–4.   ³ Blackstone, vol ii, p 109.   ⁴ Co Litt 18a.   ⁵ [1912] 2 Ch 422.
⁶ Above, pp 73, 96–7.   ⁷ (1876) 2 App Cas 1, 23.   ⁸ S 1(1)(ii)(c); above, p 434.

tenant for life, and as such he may convey the land by way of sale, mortgage or lease under his statutory powers.[9] When a person is granted a determinable fee after 1996, the land is held on trust under the Trusts of Land and Appointment of Trustees Act 1996, with the grantor as trustee.[10]

(2) Rule against Perpetuities

The matter aroused considerable controversy, but in one case it was decided that the possibility of reverter arising on the grant of a determinable fee simple was subject to the rule against perpetuities.[11] This view was adopted by the Perpetuities and Accumulations Act 1964,[12] and has been continued by the Perpetuities and Accumulations Act 2009.[13] Thus, if the terminating event in fact occurs at a time that complies with the perpetuity rule,[14] the reverter will take effect. Otherwise, it will be void and the determinable fee will become absolute.

(3) Resulting Trust

An interest analogous to a possibility of reverter arises where a testator gives *personalty* to trustees upon trust to pay the income to a corporation or other body until some event occurs that may not occur within the perpetuity period. In such a case, the occurrence of the event raises a resulting trust in favour of the person entitled to the undisposed residue of the testator's estate. Formerly, a resulting trust of this nature was exempt from the rule against perpetuities,[15] but it has been subjected to the rule by the Acts of 1964 and 2009.[16]

C DETERMINABLE LIFE INTEREST

There may be a limitation of a determinable *life* interest:

> If a man grant an estate to a woman *dum sola fuit*, or *durante viduitate*, or *quamdiu se bene gesserit*, or to a man and a woman during the coverture, or so long as such a grantee dwell in such a house,... or for any like incertaine time, which time, as Bracton saith, is *tempus*

---

[9] Above, pp 443 ff.

[10] TLATA 1996, s 25(1), Sch 3, para 2(1), (2), excluding a fee simple absolute within LPA 1925, s 7, above, p 153.

[11] *Hopper v Liverpool Corp* (1943) 88 SJ 213 (limitation of a house in fee simple so long as it shall be used as a news room and coffee room). On the subject generally, see Morris and Leach, *The Rule against Perpetuities* (2nd edn, 1962), pp 209–18.

[12] S 12(1)(a).   [13] S 1(2), (7)(a).

[14] For an instrument taking effect after 15 July 1964 but before 6 April 2010, the rule under PAA 1964, above, pp 558–74 (ie if the instrument fails to satisfy the common law rule because the interest is not certain to vest, if at all, not later than 21 years after a life in being, then either a fixed period not exceeding 80 years if so specified by the settlor, or 'wait and see' whether the interest in fact vests within the period of 21 years after statutory lives or lives specified in the instrument); after 5 April 2010, the single fixed perpetuity period of 125 years under PAA 2009, s 5, above, pp 575–7.

[15] *Re Randell* (1888) 38 Ch D 213; *Re Blunt's Trusts* [1904] 2 Ch 767; *Re Chardon* [1928] Ch 464; *Re Chambers' Will Trusts* [1950] Ch 267.

[16] PAA 1964, s 12(1)(b); PAA 2009, s 1(7)(b).

indeterminatum: in all these cases if it be of lands or tenements, the lessee hath in judgment of law an estate for life determinable.[17]

The *protective trust* is a common example of a determinable life interest. Its basis is a life interest subject to an executory gift over upon the happening of a certain event such as bankruptcy or attempted alienation. The gift over may be in favour of other members of the family, but today it is more commonly in favour of trustees to hold upon discretionary trusts for a class that includes the tenant for life and members of his family; and the latter is the basis of the protective trust adopted by section 33 of the Trustee Act 1925. It is now common practice, in drafting settlements, to give a protected life interest to a beneficiary, especially if the beneficiary is a minor, or if there is some doubt as to the beneficiary's financial stability. The protected life interest is followed by discretionary trusts stating how the trustees may deal with the income of the property if the interest of the beneficiary is determined. These trusts used to be set out in detail, but this is no longer necessary since section 33 provides that a mere declaration directing income to be held on *protective trusts* shall confer certain discretionary powers upon the trustees.[18] The statutory effect of using the expression is that the interest of the beneficiary automatically determines if he or she attempts to alienate or charge it or becomes bankrupt,[19] and the trustees at their discretion may apply the income during the rest of his or her life for the maintenance or support, or otherwise for the benefit, of any one or more of the following persons: the spouse or civil partner, and the children or remoter issue of the beneficiary, or, if there is no spouse or civil partner or issue, the persons who, if the beneficiary were dead, would be entitled to the trust property or its income.

In cases of a determinable life interest the grantee takes an interest that may endure for life, or may determine sooner by the occurrence of the terminating event. It differs from a determinable fee in that it may be followed by a gift over to a third party that may validly take effect when the event occurs.[20]

D DETERMINABLE TERM OF YEARS

Lastly, a *term of years* may be made determinable upon the happening of some uncertain event before the period of the term has expired.

Lord Templeman said in *Prudential Assurance Co Ltd v London Residuary Body*:[21]

---

[17] Co Litt 42a.

[18] Amended by Civil Partnership Act 2004, s 261(1), Sch 27, para 6. See generally H & M, ch 7; Snell, paras 22-006 to 22-008; (1957) 21 Conv (NS) 110; 323 (LA Sheridan).

[19] If, by virtue of a power contained in the settlement, the husband makes an advancement to an infant beneficiary, this is a disposition that will cause his life interest to be forfeited: *Re Shaw's Settlement* [1951] Ch 833.

[20] Blackstone, vol ii, p 155.

[21] [1992] 2 AC 386, 395; above, p 201. Though determinable, such a lease can still exist as a legal estate.

A lease can be made for five years subject to the tenant's right to determine if the war ends before the expiry of five years. A lease can be made from year to year subject to a fetter on the right of the landlord to determine the lease before the expiry of five years unless the war ends. Both leases are valid because they create a determinable certain term of five years.

II INTERESTS UPON CONDITION SUBSEQUENT

A GENERAL NATURE AND EFFECT

(1) Definition

An interest upon condition subsequent arises where a qualification is annexed to a conveyance by which it is provided that, in case a particular event does or does not happen, or in case the grantor or the grantee does or omits to do a particular act, the interest shall be defeated.[22] Examples of such interests taken from the Law Reports are:

> grant to trustees in fee simple on condition that, if the land granted shall ever be used for other than hospital purposes, it shall revert to the heirs of the grantor;[23]
>
> devise in fee simple to the council of a school on condition that the council shall publish annually a statement of payments and receipts;[24]
>
> devise of land to J 'on condition that he never sells out of the family';[25]
>
> devise to A for life provided that he makes the mansion-house his usual common place of abode and residence;[26]
>
> devise to A for life on condition that he assumes the name and arms of the testator within 12 months.[27]

In all cases of this type a *right of re-entry* vests in the grantor, his heirs and assignees. The exercise of the right of re-entry determines the estate of the grantee.

In principle, therefore, a fee simple subject to a condition subsequent should be classified as an equitable interest, not as a legal estate, for since it may be defeated by a re-entry before its full course is run it can hardly be described as 'absolute'. Nevertheless, for reasons already explained,[28] it has been given the status of a legal estate by the Law of Property (Amendment) Act 1926,[29] in words that are wide enough to include any right of re-entry. They state that:

---

[22] Litt s 325; Cruise, *Digest*, Tit xiii, c 1. This must be distinguished from a condition *precedent* where the qualification provides that the interest will not *commence* until the occurrence of some event, eg a grant to A if he becomes a barrister; above, p 532.

[23] *Re Hollis' Hospital Trustees and Hague's Contract* [1899] 2 Ch 540.

[24] *Re Da Costa* [1912] 1 Ch 337.   [25] *Re Macleay* (1875) LR 20 Eq 186.

[26] *Wynne v Fletcher* (1857) 24 Beav 430.

[27] *Re Evans's Contract* [1920] 2 Ch 469.   [28] Above, pp 153–4.

[29] LPA 1925, s 7(1), as amended by LP(A)A 1926, Sch; M & B p 303, n 13.

a fee simple subject to a legal or equitable right of entry or re-entry is for the purposes of [the Law of Property Act 1925] a fee simple absolute.

In registered land, such a fee simple is capable of registration and the right of entry must be noted on the register.[30]

(2) Distinction between Interest upon Condition and Determinable Interest

There is a fundamental and somewhat subtle distinction[31] between limitations upon condition and determinable limitations. Some writers contend that the distinction is a mere matter of words. On this basis the effect of such expressions as *until, so long as, whilst, during,* is to create a determinable interest; while such phrases as *on condition that, provided that, if, but if it happen that,*[32] will raise an interest upon condition. But the distinction goes deeper than this. We must differentiate between a limitation properly so called, and a condition.

A limitation is a form of words that creates an estate and denotes its extent by designating the event upon which it is to commence and the time for which it is to endure.[33] It marks the utmost time for which the estate can continue. It appears in two forms. A direct limitation marks the time by denoting the size of the estate in familiar terms, eg by using such expressions as 'for life' or 'in fee simple'; a determinable limitation gives an interest for one of the times possible in a direct limitation, but also denotes some event that may determine the estate during the continuance of that time. In the simple example of a grant to A and his heirs, tenants of the manor of Dale, the terminating event is incorporated in, and forms an essential part of, the whole limitation, and if the estate expires because the tenancy of Dale is no longer in A's family, it is none the less considered to have lasted for the period originally fixed by the limitation. So in general the province of a limitation is to fix the period for the commencement and the duration of an estate, and to mark its determinable qualities.[34]

A condition, on the other hand, specifies some event that, if it takes place during the time for which an estate has already been limited to continue, will defeat that estate:

---

[30] R & R, para 7.004; an expressly granted legal right of entry must be completed by registration: LRA 2002, s 27(1), (2)(e), (4), Sch 2, para 7; an equitable right of entry will need to be protected by a notice in the register if it is to have priority over a registrable disposition made for valuable consideration: ibid, s 29.

[31] It has been referred to as 'extremely artificial' by Pennycuick V-C in *Re Sharp's Settlement Trusts* [1973] Ch 331, 340; and as 'little short of disgraceful to our jurisprudence' by Porter MR in *Re King's Trusts* (1892) 29 LR IR 401, 410.

[32] See Sanders, *Uses and Trusts* (5th edn, 1844), vol i, p 156; *Sheppard's Touchstone* (8th edn, 1826), 122; *Bacon's New Abridgement* (7th edn, 1832), under the title *Condition (A)*; Challis, *Law of Real Property*, p 283.

[33] *Sheppard's Touchstone*, 117; Blackstone, vol ii, p 155; *Preston on Estates*, vol i, p 40; see also above, p 155.

[34] Fearne, *Contingent Remainders* (10th edn, 1844), p 11, Butler's note.

'And here is condition, because there is not a new estate limited over but the estate to which it is annexed is destroyed.'[35]

In short, if the terminating event is an integral and necessary part of the formula from which the size of the interest is to be ascertained, the result is the creation of a determinable interest; but if the terminating event is external to the limitation, if it is a divided clause from the grant, the interest granted is an interest upon condition.[36]

(3) Effect of Distinction

Outwardly a condition resembles a determinable limitation, for the difference between a grant:

> to a woman for life, but if she remarries then her life interest shall cease,

and a grant:

> to a woman during widowhood,

is not apparent at first sight. The natural inference is that the legal effect must be the same in each case. Nevertheless, certain practical distinctions between the two limitations existed at common law and to a diminished degree still exist.[37] The present position appears to be as follows.

(a) Determination

A determinable interest comes to an end automatically upon the occurrence of the terminating event, as for example upon the remarriage of a woman to whom an estate has been granted during her widowhood. This is inevitable, for according to the limitation itself, that is according to the words fixing the space of time for which the widow's right of enjoyment is to continue, her interest ceases with her remarriage and nothing remains to be done to defeat her right. There can, indeed, be no question of defeating what has already come to an end.[38]

The effect of a condition operating by way of re-entry, on the other hand, is to defeat an interest *before* it has reached the end of the period for which it has been limited. The interest becomes voidable upon the breach of the condition. It does not become void unless and until the grantor, his heir or assignee re-enters upon the land.[39]

---

[35] *Serjeant Rudhall's Case* (1586) Sav 76, cited *Re Hollis' Hospital Trustees and Hague's Contract* [1899] 2 Ch 540, 549.

[36] Fearne, p 11, note (h); vol ii, s 36 (Smith, *An Original View of Executory Interests*); Challis, *Law of Real Property*, p 260.

[37] 'Although in some respects a condition and a limitation may have the same effect, yet in English law there is a great distinction between them': *Re Moore* (1888) 39 Ch D 116, 129 (Cotton LJ).

[38] *Preston on Estates*, vol i, p 47; Challis, *Law of Real Property*, p 219; *Re Evans's Contract* [1920] 2 Ch 469, 472.

[39] Co Litt 218a. At common law, the seisin transferred by livery cannot be divested without its actual resumption by re-entry: Co Litt 214b.

(b) Rule against perpetuities

The rule against perpetuities applies both to conditions subsequent and to a possibility of reverter arising on the grant of a determinable fee.

The position as regards common law conditions was established long before the rule came into existence, and the old authorities never doubted that a right of entry was enforceable at any distance of time by the grantor or his heirs.[40] But, after several dicta in favour of subjecting conditions to the rule,[41] the point was finally decided to that effect[42] and was later confirmed by the Law of Property Act 1925,[43] and is also applied by the Perpetuities and Accumulations Act 2009.[44]

As we have already seen, a possibility of reverter appertaining to a determinable fee simple has been subjected to the rule by the Perpetuities and Accumulations Acts 1964 and 2009.[45]

(c) Assignability

At common law, a right of entry affecting a fee simple was neither devisable nor alienable inter vivos, and benefited only the grantor and his heirs.[46] This, however, is no longer the position. The Wills Act 1837 allows a testator to devise 'all rights for condition broken and other rights of entry',[47] and the Law of Property Act 1925 deals with their assignment inter vivos by providing that:

> All rights and interests in land may be disposed of, including ... a right of entry, into or upon land whether immediate or future, and whether vested or contingent.[48]

Whether a possibility of reverter is on the same footing in both these respects is not so clear. It has, indeed, been held that it may be disposed of by a testator since it is covered by the words of the Wills Act cited above.[49] But its assignment inter vivos presents some difficulty. In the view of the common law, what was left in the grantor of a determinable interest was not an estate but a possibility that he might acquire an estate at a future time. Such a *bare possibility*, as it was called, was not assignable at common law,[50] but it seems a reasonable assumption that it now falls within the wide language quoted above from the Law of Property Act 1925.

---

[40] Challis, *Law of Real Property*, pp 187 ff.

[41] *Re Macleay* (1875) LR 20 Eq 186; *London and South Western Rly Co v Gomm* (1882) 20 Ch D 562, 582; *Dunn v Flood* (1883) 25 Ch D 629.

[42] *Re Hollis' Hospital Trustees and Hague's Contract* [1899] 2 Ch 540; *Re Da Costa* [1912] 1 Ch 337. A contrary view was expressed by Palles CB in *A-G v Cummins* [1906] 1 IR 406, and his view has prevailed in Northern Ireland: *Walsh v Wightman* [1927] NI 1.

[43] S 4(3).   [44] S 1(4).   [45] PAA 1964, s 12(1)(a); above, p 573; PAA 2009, s 1(7); above, p 576.

[46] Fearne, *Contingent Remainders*, Butler's note, p 381.   [47] S 3.

[48] LPA 1925, s 4(2)(b).

[49] *Pemberton v Barnes* [1899] 1 Ch 544, where it was held that the possibility of reverter arising upon the grant of a determinable fee in copyholds was within the Act.

[50] As to the three different meanings of the word *possibility*, see Challis, *Law of Real Property*, p 76, note.

(d) Void conditions

As will be seen in the next section, a condition attached to any limitation of property may prove to be void for a variety of reasons. A condition subsequent that is thus invalidated is totally cancelled, and the limitation takes effect as if it had not been imposed;[51] but a determinable interest fails altogether if the possibility of reverter is invalidated, for to treat it as absolute would be to alter its quantum as fixed by the limitation.[52]

(e) Interest followed by remainder

At common law, a remainder might be limited to take effect after a determinable life estate, but not after a life estate that was defeasible by a condition subsequent. If, for example, there were a feoffment:

> to A during widowhood and then to B for life,

the remainder to B was valid, since by force of the limitation itself it took effect upon the natural determination of the particular estate. But had the limitation been:

> to A, a widow, for life on condition that if she remarried then to B for life,

B's remainder would have come into conflict with three rules of ancient origin: a remainder was not allowed to cut short a particular estate;[53] none but the grantor and his heirs could exercise a right of re-entry; and in any event, the effect of re-entry was to defeat all the estates that depended upon the original livery of seisin.[54]

The matter has long been of only historical interest, for a settlor, minded to impose such a condition upon a widow's interest, could at an early date frame his limitation as a shifting use, and can now effect the same result by way of a future interest under a trust.

B VOID CONDITIONS

There are three types of conditions subsequent that are void when annexed to the grant of an estate or interest.

(1) Conditions Repugnant to the Interest Granted[55]

A condition that is repugnant to the interest to which it is annexed is void.[56] For example, a condition attached to the grant of a fee simple that the grantee shall always

---

[51] *Re Wilkinson* [1926] Ch 842, 846; *Re Croxon* [1904] 1 Ch 252. If the illegal condition is *precedent*, the gift fails entirely.

[52] *Re Moore* (1888) 39 Ch D 116. If, however, a possibility of reverter or a condition subsequent is void under the rule against perpetuities, the interest of the grantee becomes absolute: PAA 1964, s 12; PAA 2009, s 10.

[53] See the 17th edn of this book, p 514.

[54] Fearne, *Contingent Remainders*, pp 261–2, 381, note; *Preston on Estates*, vol i, pp 50 et seq.

[55] For a trenchant criticism of this doctrine, see (1943) 59 LQR 343 (GL Williams).

[56] *Re Dugdale* (1888) 38 Ch D 176; *Bradley v Peixoto* (1797) 3 Ves 324.

let the land at a definite rent, or cultivate it in a certain manner or be deprived of all power of sale, is void on the ground of its incompatibility with the complete freedom of enjoyment, disposition and management that the law attributes to the ownership of such an estate.[57] It is not permissible to grant an interest and then to provide that the incidents attached to it by law shall be excluded. The most important examples of repugnant conditions that arise in practice are those designed to prohibit alienation or to exclude the operation of the bankruptcy laws.

(a) Conditions against alienation

(1) Total restraints

In accordance with the cardinal principle that the power of alienation is necessarily and inseparably incidental to ownership, it has been held in a long line of decisions that if an *absolute* interest is given to a donee—whether it be a fee simple, a fee tail, a life interest or any other interest, and whether in possession or to vest in the future—any restriction that *substantially* takes that power away is void as being repugnant to the very conception of ownership.[58] Therefore, a condition[59] that the donee:

shall not alienate at all;[60] or

shall not alienate during a particular time, such as the life of a certain person,[61] or during his own life;[62] or

shall alienate only to one particular person,[63] or to a small and diminishing class of persons, such as to one of his three brothers;[64] or

shall not adopt some particular mode of assurance such as a mortgage,[65] or shall not bar an entail,[66]

is void.

(2) Partial restraints

A restraint that is partial, however, and that therefore does not substantially deprive the owner in fee of his power of alienation, is valid. Thus it has been held that a condition is valid that restrains the owner from alienating to a specified person[67] or to anyone except a particular class of persons, provided, however, that the class is not

---

[57] *Jarman on Wills* (8th edn, 1951), p 1477.

[58] Cf the position of a tenant for life under SLA 1925 the exercise of whose powers cannot be prohibited or limited, s 106; above, p 451. But restraints even of a general nature may be valid in the case of a determinable interest: *Re Dugdale*, above; *Re Leach* [1912] 2 Ch 422; above, p 613; and this is the basis of the protected life interest under TA 1925, s 33; above, p 615.

[59] But a *covenant* against alienation is not repugnant: *Caldy Manor Estate Ltd v Farrell* [1974] 1 WLR 1303.

[60] Litt, s 360; Co Litt 206b, 223a; *Re Dugdale*, above.   [61] *Re Rosher* (1884) 26 Ch D 801.

[62] *Corbett v Corbett* (1888) 14 PD 7.

[63] *Muschamp v Bluet* (1617) J Bridg 132; *Re Cockerill* [1929] 2 Ch 131.

[64] *Re Brown* [1954] Ch 39, M & B p 306.   [65] *Ware v Cann* (1830) 10 B & C 433.

[66] *Mildmay's Case* (1605) 6 Co Rep 40a; *Mary Portington's Case* (1613) 10 Co Rep 35b; *Dawkins v Lord Penrhyn* (1878) 4 App Cas 51.

[67] Co Litt 223a.

too restricted.[68] But when does a restraint cease to be total? In the case of *Re Macleay*,[69] where there was a devise:

> to my brother J on the condition that he never sells out of the family,

the condition was held by Jessel MR to be valid, though some doubt has been cast on the correctness of this decision by a later case.[70]

The difficulty is to ascertain the principle upon which such restraints have been permitted, for they would seem to be just as repugnant to ownership as a total restraint. It may be that the courts, losing sight of the fundamental doctrine of repugnancy, have unintentionally and unwittingly allowed the necessities of public policy to engraft certain exceptions on the main rule.[71]

(b) Conditions excluding operation of bankruptcy laws

Just as the donee of property cannot be deprived of the normal rights of ownership, so also is it impossible to render his interest immune from involuntary alienation for insolvency or bankruptcy.[72] It is not permissible, for example, to annex to the grant of a life interest a condition that it shall not be liable to seizure for debt. Thus in *Graves v Dolphin*:[73]

> a testator directed his trustees to pay £500 a year to his son for life, and declared that it should not on any account be subject or liable to the debts, engagements, charges or incumbrances of his son, but that it should always be payable to him and to no other person. The son became bankrupt, and it was held that the annuity became the property of his creditors.

But, as we have seen in discussing the protective trust,[74] there is no objection to the grant by one person to another of an interest that is to determine upon the bankruptcy of the grantee. Lord Eldon, adverting to the distinction between a determinable limitation and a limitation upon condition, made this clear 200 years ago:

> A disposition to a man until he shall become bankrupt, and after his bankruptcy over, is quite different from an attempt to give to him for his life, with a proviso that he shall not sell or alien it. *If that condition is so expressed as to amount to a limitation*, reducing the interest short of a life interest, neither the man nor his assignees can have it beyond the period limited.[75]

The distinction at first sight seems fine and far from obvious, but in fact it is fundamental. In one case the only interest passing under the limitation is an interest *until* the donee becomes bankrupt; in the other, an absolute interest is first limited for

---

[68] *Doe d Gill v Pearson* (1805) 6 East 173 ('except to four sisters or their children').

[69] (1875) LR 20 Eq 186.

[70] *Re Rosher* (1884) 26 Ch D 801. But the restriction was placed only on a sale, and it was to endure only for the life of J. See too *Re Brown* [1954] Ch 39; (1954) 70 LQR 15 (REM).

[71] *Re Rosher* (1884) 26 Ch D 801, 813.

[72] *Re Machu* (1882) 21 Ch D 838; *Re Dugdale* (1888) 38 Ch D 176.　　[73] (1826) 1 Sim 66.

[74] Above, p 615.

[75] *Brandon v Robinson* (1811) 18 Ves 429, 432, 433–4; *Re The Trusts of the Scientific Investment Pension Plan* [1999] Ch 53. See TA 1925, s 33, as to these protected life interests; above pp 614–15.

life, and then an attempt is made to remove one of the incidents, namely liability for debts, to which all absolute interests are subject.

Thus, if husband and wife both bring property into a marriage settlement, the wife's property may be limited to the husband until he becomes bankrupt and then over to the trustees. But the husband cannot settle his own property upon himself in the same manner, for this would be a fraud on the bankruptcy laws.[76] On the other hand, it has long been recognised that a settlor may protect himself against other forms of alienation, voluntary and involuntary. Thus a man may settle his own property upon himself until he attempts to assign, charge or incumber it, or until he does something that makes it liable to be taken in execution by a particular creditor, and if so over to another person. The limitation over, once it has taken effect, is not avoided by the subsequent bankruptcy of the settlor.[77]

(2) Conditions Contrary to Public Policy

Any condition that has a tendency to conflict with the general interest of the community, even though it will not necessarily do so, is void.[78]

The following categories include the types of condition that most frequently occur.

(a) Conditions in restraint of marriage

The law as to the validity of conditions in restraint of marriage differs according as the gift is of real or of personal property.

(1) Personalty

The rules governing personalty have come to us from Roman Law through the ecclesiastical courts and the Court of Chancery. They are marked by numerous and fine distinctions, and in the words of a learned judge are 'proverbially difficult';[79] but it is sufficient for our purposes to say that a condition in total restraint of marriage is void, while one in partial restraint is good, provided that it is reasonable from the point of view of public policy.[80]

For example, a condition that a person shall not marry a named person,[81] a Papist,[82] a Scotchman,[83] or a domestic servant[84] have been held to be valid, but a condition that he shall not marry at all is void. But a partial restraint is not upheld unless there is a bequest over to another person in default of compliance with the condition. In

---

[76] *Mackintosh v Pogose* [1895] 1 Ch 505, 511; *Re Brewer's Settlement* [1896] 2 Ch 503; *Re Burroughs-Fowler* [1916] 2 Ch 251. This principle is retained by TA 1925, s 33(3).

[77] *Brooke v Pearson* (1859) 27 Beav 181; *Re Detmold* (1889) 40 Ch D 585.

[78] *Egerton v Earl Brownlow* (1853) 4 HL Cas 1; *Re Wallace* [1920] 2 Ch 274.

[79] *Re Hewitt* [1918] 1 Ch 458, 463 (Younger J).

[80] *Re Lanyon* [1927] 2 Ch 264. A determinable gift, however, is valid: *Re Lovell* [1920] 1 Ch 122.

[81] *Re Bathe* [1925] Ch 377.   [82] *Duggan v Kelly* (1848) 10 I Eq R 473.

[83] *Perrin v Lyon* (1807) 9 East 170.

[84] *Jenner v Turner* (1880) 16 Ch D 188. It is not certain, however, whether this example and those given in the preceding two notes would nowadays be treated as void for uncertainty; see below, pp 626–8.

the absence of such a bequest, the condition is treated as ineffectual on the ground that it has merely been imposed *in terrorem*, that is, as a threat calculated to secure compliance by the donee.[85] A condition, however, is valid that restrains a *second* marriage, either of a man or of a woman.[86] Similarly, a condition requiring consent to marriage is not invalid.[87]

(2) Realty

The rules relating to real estate, on the other hand, are both few and simple. While a condition in general restraint of marriage if attached to a gift of personalty is void, in the case of realty it is not automatically void, but only if there is an intention to promote celibacy. Thus in *Jones v Jones*[88] a man devised land to three women during their lifetime, and added:

> provided the said Mary...shall remain in her present state of single woman, otherwise... if she shall bind herself in wedlock, she is liable to lose her share of the said property immediately, and her share to be possessed and enjoyed by the other mentioned parties, share and share alike.

It was held that the condition was valid since its object was not to prevent her from marrying but to provide for her whilst unmarried.[89]

The *in terrorem* doctrine does not apply to realty,[90] and it may be said that a condition in partial restraint of marriage attached to real estate is always good,[91] and that one in total restraint *may* be good. However, a general restraint cannot be imposed upon a tenant in tail, since it is incompatible with and repugnant to an interest that is expressly made descendible to the heirs born of the marriage of the donee.[92]

(b) Conditions encouraging separation and divorce

Similarly conditions designed to encourage the separation or divorce of a married couple are invalid as being contrary to public policy;[93] but where the parties are already separated, a limitation to a woman with a condition that the interest shall cease if she and her husband live together again, is valid as constituting a maintenance of the wife while she is unprovided for, unless there is evidence showing that the donor's object is to induce her not to return to her husband.[94]

---

[85] *Re Whiting's Settlement* [1905] 1 Ch 96; *Re Hewett* [1918] 1 Ch 458; *Leong v Chye* [1955] AC 648.

[86] *Allen v Jackson* (1875) 1 Ch D 399.   [87] *Re Whiting's Settlement*, above.

[88] (1876) 1 QBD 279.

[89] As to the admissibility of any evidence of the donor's intention, see *Re Johnson's Will Trusts* [1967] Ch 387.

[90] *Jenner v Turner* (1880) 16 Ch D 188, 196 (Bacon V-C).   [91] *Re Bathe* [1925] Ch 377.

[92] *Earl of Arundel's Case* (1575) 3 Dyer 342b.

[93] *Re Moore* (1888) 39 Ch D 116; distinguished *Re Thompson* [1939] 1 All ER 681; *Re Caborne* [1943] Ch 224; *Re Johnson's Will Trusts* [1967] Ch 387; *Re Hepplewhite's Will Trusts*, The Times, 21 January 1977.

[94] See *Re Lovell* [1920] 1 Ch 122.

(c) Conditions affecting parental duties

A condition designed to separate a parent from his child, even where the parents are divorced, is contrary to public policy:[95] likewise a condition designed to interfere with the performance of parental duties.[96] But the operation of this principle was restricted by the House of Lords in *Blathwayt v Baron Cawley*,[97] where a condition that divested property if a child became a Roman Catholic was argued to be void on the ground that it would hamper parental duties in religious instructions. This argument was rejected by Lord Wilberforce: 'To say that any condition which in any way might affect or influence the way in which a child is brought up, or in which parental duties are exercised, seems to me to state far too wide a rule.'

(d) Conditions restricting freedom of religion

Conditions restricting the beneficiaries' freedom of religion have frequently been encountered. Sometimes they have failed on the ground of uncertainty,[98] but they have never been held to be contrary to public policy.[99] In *Blathwayt v Baron Cawley*[100] the House of Lords held that a condition in a will under which a beneficiary would forfeit his interest if he should 'be or become a Roman Catholic' was not invalid. Although conceptions of public policy move with the times, it is not against public policy for an adherent of one religion to distinguish in disposing of his property. To invalidate such conditions would go far beyond the mere avoidance of discrimination on religious grounds:

> To do so would bring about a substantial reduction of another freedom, firmly rooted in our law, namely that of testamentary disposition. Discrimination is not the same thing as choice: it operates over a larger and less personal area, and neither by express provision nor by implication has private selection yet become a matter of public policy.[101]

(e) Conditions affecting race

The Equality Act 2010, replacing the Race Relations Act 1976, has no application to conditions imposed by settlors and testators. There is little authority on the point, which has mainly arisen in connection with charitable trusts, but it appears that it is not contrary to public policy for a settlor to discriminate on these grounds.[102]

---

[95] *Re Sandbrook* [1912] 2 Ch 471 (condition held void that divested property if the donees 'should live with or be or continue under the custody, guardianship or control of their father'). See also *Re Piper* [1946] 2 All ER 503.

[96] *Re Borwick* [1933] Ch 657 (condition held void that divested a gift if the infant donee during minority became a Roman Catholic, for this tended to influence the parent in the discharge of his duty of religious instruction). But see now *Blathwayt v Baron Cawley* [1976] AC 397.

[97] Above.   [98] *Clayton v Ramsden* [1943] AC 320, below, p 627.

[99] Even in the case of charitable trusts. See *Re Lysaght* [1966] Ch 191, where discrimination against Jews and Roman Catholics was merely 'undesirable'. The Race Relations Act 1976 did not apply to religion as such, although the position of the Jewish religion was unclear. The Equality Act 2010 includes religion or belief as a protected characteristic, but does not apply to conditions imposed by settlors and testators.

[100] [1976] AC 397.   [101] [1976] AC 397, 426 (Lord Wilberforce); cf (2011) 31 OJLS 303 (M Harding).

[102] Underhill and Hayton, *Law relating to Trusts and Trustees* (18th edn, 2010), para 11.111.

(f) Other conditions

We have seen that any condition having a tendency to conflict with the general interest of the community is void. Thus in *Egerton v Earl Brownlow*[103] lands were devised to Lord Alford for 99 years if he should so long live, and then to the heirs male of his body, with a proviso that if Lord Alford should not in his lifetime acquire the dignity of Duke or Marquis of Bridgewater, the estates should pass from his heirs male immediately on his decease. After great conflict of opinion the condition was held invalid by the House of Lords as being contrary to public policy. But there were special considerations applicable to that case. For example, since the rank to be obtained was among the highest in the peerage, and one that conferred legislative rights and imposed legislative duties upon the holder, there was a danger that efforts to obtain the qualifying position would be pushed so far as to come into conflict with the general interests of the community. These special considerations were recognised in a later case, where a limitation that property should go to a certain person provided that he acquired the title of baronet was held to be capable of taking effect upon the fulfilment of the condition.[104] Unlike a peerage, no legislative powers and duties would be involved, thus the public interest could not be affected. But conditions forbidding entry into the naval or military services could affect the public interest, and have been accordingly held void.[105]

Difficulty has been encountered in the past with 'name and arms clauses', whereby settlors attempt to ensure that the beneficiary adopts the settlor's name and coat of arms. In addition to problems of certainty,[106] such clauses were at one time held to be contrary to public policy on the ground that, in the case of a married woman beneficiary, the taking of another name might lead to dissension between husband and wife. But it was held by the Court of Appeal in *Re Neeld*,[107] overruling many previous decisions, that such clauses are not contrary to public policy.

(3) Uncertain Conditions

A condition subsequent, designed to defeat a vested estate, is void if it is uncertain either in expression or in operation. It must be possible, not only to affirm with precision exactly what the words imposing the condition mean, but also to ascertain

---

[103] (1853) 4 HL Cas 1.

[104] *Re Wallace* [1920] 2 Ch 274 (baronetcy is 'a barren title': Warrington LJ at 289). The condition here was precedent, but a condition, if contrary to public policy, is invalid whether precedent or subsequent. The *effect* of invalidity, however, is different; below, p 629.

[105] *Re Beard* [1908] 1 Ch 383.   [106] Below.

[107] [1962] Ch 643.

with certainty the circumstances that will cause a forfeiture.[108] In a well-known passage Lord Cranworth stated the position as follows:[109]

> I consider that, from the earliest times, one of the cardinal rules on the subject has been this: that where a vested estate is to be defeated by a condition on a contingency that is to happen afterwards, that condition must be such that the court can see from the beginning, precisely and distinctly, upon the happening of what event it was that the preceding vested estate was to determine.

Several cases have been concerned with conditions designed to secure the observance by a donee of a particular religion, such as by requiring him 'to be a member of' or 'to conform to'[110] the Church of England, or not to marry any person 'not of Jewish parentage and of the Jewish faith'.[111] Such phrases are shrouded in uncertainty and are generally held to be ineffective. Of those, for example, who profess membership of the Church of England, many are devout observers of its practice and doctrines, but the conduct of countless others affords little evidence of any religious conviction. Faith varies infinitely in degree, and, even if it were possible to do so, a donor does not normally specify the exact degree that will satisfy his anxiety.[112] Again, whether a person 'conforms to' a particular religion defies any certain answer.[113] Does, for example, conformity to the Church of England necessitate attendance at religious services? If so, how regular must the attendance be? On the other hand, a condition for the forfeiture of an interest if the donee should 'become a convert to the Roman Catholic religion' has been upheld, for such a conversion requires the performance of certain definite acts.[114] The court can, therefore, say with certainty what has to be done and whether it has in fact been done.

---

[108] *Re Sandbrook* [1912] 2 Ch 471, 477 (Parker J); *Re Murray* [1955] Ch 69, 77–8 (Lord Evershed MR). A less strict test applies in the case of a condition precedent, where even conceptual uncertainty may not defeat it: *Re Allen* [1953] Ch 810. Lord Denning MR in *Re Tuck's Settlement Trusts* [1978] Ch 49, 60, described this distinction as a 'deplorable dichotomy', serving only to defeat the settlor's intention; Maudsley & Burn, *Trusts & Trustees* (7th edn, 2008), p 668. But the distinction was acknowledged by the House of Lords in *Blathwayt v Baron Cawley* [1976] AC 397, 425. An example is *Re Barlow's Will Trusts* [1979] 1 WLR 278, Maudsley & Burn, *Trusts & Trustees*, p 104 (option to purchase a painting at a low price from the testatrix's estate on satisfying the description 'any members of my family and any friends of mine' upheld as a valid condition precedent). See Underhill and Hayton, paras 8.96–8.100; [1980] Conv 263 (L McKay).

[109] *Clavering v Ellison* (1859) 7 HL Cas 707, 725.

[110] *Re Tegg* [1936] 2 All ER 878.

[111] *Clayton v Ramsden* [1943] AC 320; *Re Moss's Trusts* [1945] 1 All ER 207; *Re Tarnpolsk* [1958] 1 WLR 1157; *Re Krawitz's Will Trusts* [1959] 1 WLR 1192. Cf *Blathwayt v Baron Cawley* [1976] AC 397; *Re Tuck's Settlement Trusts*, above (marriage to an 'approved wife' of Jewish blood and faith not uncertain as condition precedent); *Re Tepper's Will Trusts* [1987] Ch 358 (gift by a devout and practising Jewish testator to children provided that 'they shall not marry outside the Jewish faith': Scott J was reluctant to find the condition subsequent void for uncertainty and adjourned the case for further evidence of the Jewish faith as practised by the testator and his family; [1987] All ER Rev 260 (CH Sherrin)).

[112] *Re Donn* [1944] Ch 8.   [113] *Re Tegg*, above.

[114] *Re Evans* [1940] Ch 629; *Blathwayt v Baron Cawley*, above.

Many other examples might be given of uncertain conditions. For example, provisions that an interest should be forfeited if the donee(s) have 'in any way associated, corresponded or visited with any of my present wife's nephews or nieces',[115] or have 'social or other relationship with' a named person,[116] have been held void, since it is impossible to say with reasonable certainty that of the many connections included in the words 'association' or 'relationship' offend the prohibition.

Again, a condition that property shall be enjoyed by a beneficiary 'only so long as she shall continue to reside in Canada' is too vague to be enforced, for there are many forms and degrees of residence and it is impossible to say precisely which of them fall under the ban.[117] But the law does not exact too high a standard of certainty. The condition need not be clear beyond all possible doubt. In one case a requirement of 'taking up permanent residence in England' was held to be sufficiently certain, since the word 'permanent' postulates an intention to live in a place for life as opposed to living there temporarily or for a fixed period.[118]

In several cases decided between 1945 and 1960, courts of first instance, in disregard of what had been conveyancing practice for at least a century, showed a surprising tendency to stigmatise as void for uncertainty clauses in a will or settlement providing for the forfeiture of an interest given to X upon his failure to assume the surname and arms of Y. It has been held more than once, for example, that to decree forfeiture, if X 'disuses' the surname Y, does not show with sufficient precision what degree of disuser he must avoid.[119]

The Court of Appeal overruled these decisions, however, on the ground that they imposed an unreasonably rigorous test of certainty:[120]

Each of us has a surname, and it seems to me altogether fanciful to suggest that there is any real ambiguity in a requirement that I should adopt and use a surname in place of that which I at present have: for the requirement does no more nor less than postulate that I should thereafter use the new surname, just as I at present use my existing name. Equally, as it seems to me, there is no real ambiguity in a divesting provision expressed to take effect if I should at any time 'disuse' or 'discontinue to use' the surname that I have adopted.[121]

---

[115] *Jeffreys v Jeffreys* (1901) 84 LT 417.

[116] *Re Jones* [1953] Ch 125.

[117] *Sifton v Sifton* [1938] AC 656. See also *Re Brace* [1954] 1 WLR 955, when a condition requiring the donee 'to provide a home for' X was held to be so vague as to be unintelligible.

[118] *Re Gape* [1952] Ch 743. Compare *Bromley v Tryon* [1952] AC 265, when it was held that a condition for forfeiture if a beneficiary became entitled to specified settled land 'or the bulk thereof' was not void for uncertainty, since 'bulk' meant anything over half.

[119] *Re Bouverie* [1952] Ch 400 at 404 (Vaisey J).

[120] *Re Neeld* [1962] Ch 643. We have seen that the Court of Appeal also held that a name and arms clause is not contrary to public policy; above, p 000. See too *Re Neeld (No 3)* [1969] 1 WLR 988.

[121] [1962] Ch 643, 667 (Lord Evershed). See also at 679 (Upjohn LJ) and at 682 (Diplock LJ), as to disuser.

(4) Effect of Void Conditions

If realty is conveyed to a person on a condition that is void, then, in the case of a condition precedent, the conveyance is void, and the interest does not arise;[122] but where a gift is subject to several conditions, some of which are valid and others void, the valid conditions are severable from the others, which alone are to be disregarded.[123] In the case of a condition subsequent the condition alone is void, and the donee takes an absolute interest in the property free from the restrictive clause.[124]

---

[122] A bequest of *personalty* subject to an illegal condition precedent is void if the condition is *malum in se*, ie wrong in itself, but if the condition is only *malum prohibitum*, ie indifferent in itself but made unlawful by statute, the bequest takes effect unfettered by the condition: *Re Elliott* [1952] Ch 217; *Re Piper* [1946] 2 All ER 503. See (1955) 19 Conv (NS) 176 (VTH Delany).

[123] *Re Hepplewhite's Will Trusts*, The Times, 21 January 1977.

[124] Co Litt 206a; *Re Croxon* [1904] 1 Ch 252; *Re Turton* [1926] Ch 96 (impossible condition). This is also the case with personalty. But in the case of a determinable interest, we have seen that the whole interest fails if the determining event is unlawful: *Re Moore* (1888) 39 Ch D 116; above, p 620.

D OTHER LEGAL AND EQUITABLE INTERESTS IN LAND

We have seen in the previous sections of this Part the estates, freehold and leasehold, that are recognised in modern English land law, and the various forms of equitable beneficial interest that can exist in land. In this section our concern is with rights *in alieno solo*, that is where one has some property right that is enforceable against the land of another: easements and profits à prendre, freehold covenants, rentcharges and mortgages. These rights may sometimes exist as legal interests in the land against which they are exercisable; sometimes they exist only as equitable interests—and, as we shall see, owing to its historical origins the restrictive covenant is capable of being enforced against third parties only in equity, and never at law. However, they merit discussion together because they are all proprietary interests in the land, conferring a lesser interest than the right to the use of the land itself.

Easements, profits, covenants, rentcharges and mortgages are all interests that are recognised and protected by the law in order to make the land more useful, whether for the benefit of the landowner against whose estate the interest is enforceable (such as a mortgage, enabling the landowner to charge his estate in order to facilitate the raising of a loan), or for the benefit of neighbours (such as freehold covenants and easements, which allow a measure of private control of the use of land—the restriction of the modes of use of a plot of land, or the grant to the neighbouring owner of positive rights over it, in order to safeguard the rights of the neighbour and thereby to enhance its value, whether in financial or non-financial terms).

In the final chapter of this section we consider equities, including the equity arising under the doctrine of proprietary estoppel, which appears now to have acquired a status equivalent to an equitable interest in the land. We reserve for the final section of this Part the subject of *licences*, which might also be said to confer an interest enforceable against the land of another, but where the nature of the right is not (in general, at least) proprietary—and therefore does not generally rank as a legal or equitable interest in the land.

18

EASEMENTS AND PROFITS

Summary

I	**Easements and Profits as Property Rights**	**633**	B Classes of Profits à Prendre	704
			C Legal and Equitable Profits à Prendre	712
II	**Easements**	**634**	D Acquisition of Profits à Prendre	712
	A Nature of Easements	634	E The Running of the Benefit and the Burden of a Profit à Prendre	715
	B Easements Distinguished from Other Rights	649	F Extinguishment of Profits à Prendre	715
	C Legal and Equitable Easements	650		
	D Acquisition of Easements	651	IV **Rights in the Nature of Easements and Profits à Prendre Acquired by Fluctuating and Undefined Classes of Persons**	**717**
	E Extent of Easements	686		
	F The Running of the Benefit and the Burden of an Easement	690		
	G Remedies for Infringement of an Easement	694	A Rights in the Nature of Easements	717
	H Extinguishment of Easements	696	B Rights in the Nature of Profits à Prendre	720
III	**Profits à Prendre**	**701**	V **Law Reform**	**723**
	A Nature of Profits à Prendre	701		

I EASEMENTS AND PROFITS AS PROPERTY RIGHTS

In the curious language of English law, easements and profits à prendre are *incorporeal hereditaments:*[1] incorporeal, or intangible, heritable interests in land that were recognised historically by the common law. They are incorporeal in the sense that, unlike the freehold or leasehold estate, they do not constitute rights to the land itself, but only rights over or in respect of the land.[2]

---

[1] Above, pp 7–8. 'An easement is...that familiar creature of English land law: an estate or interest carved out of a larger estate or interest, but nevertheless constituting a hereditament in its own right': *Willies-Williams v National Trust* (1993) 65 P & CR 359, 361 (Hoffmann LJ).

[2] In this respect—as, indeed, in many respects—the law of easements and profits follows closely the Roman law of *servitudes*, which were classified as incorporeal property rights, by contrast with the corporeal

Easements and profits are property rights: they attach to the land[3] in respect of which the right is exercisable (generally referred to as the *servient tenement*) so as to burden it in the hands of successive owners.[4] However, like corporeal estates and interests, easements and profits may exist at law or in equity,[5] and therefore, as in the case of all property rights, the circumstances in which the successor is burdened by the right will vary according to whether the right is legal or equitable.[6] As we shall see,[7] a legal easement or profit must satisfy the formality requirements prescribed by the law—it must be created by deed, and in certain cases, if it exists in relation to registered land, it must also be registered; and it can exist only for the same periods as those for which a legal estate can exist. Thus a legal easement or profit may exist in fee simple, or for a term of years absolute. But an easement or profit for any other period, for example, for life, or one created otherwise than by deed, can exist only in equity.

II EASEMENTS[8]

A NATURE OF EASEMENTS

An easement is a privilege without a profit,[9] that is to say, it is a right attached to one particular piece of land that allows the owner of that land (the dominant owner) either

property rights of the landowner: Gaius, *Institutes*, Book II, paras 12–14; although of course all property rights, whether of ownership or less than ownership, are really incorporeal rights over the corporeal property: Nicholas, *Introduction to Roman Law* (1962), p 107. Modern legal systems based on the civil law have retained the term 'servitude': eg French (*servitude*), Italian (*servitù*), Spanish (*servidumbre*) and Scots law (servitude). Servitude is a word that is occasionally adopted by English judges: eg *Dalton v Angus & Co* (1881) 6 App Cas 740, 796, (Lord Selborne); but it is not admitted as a term of art in English law, where the term 'easement' was generally adopted in the common law: 'Our law seems to look at these rights from the stand-point of the person who enjoys them, not from that of the person who suffers by their exercise. They are not "servitudes", they are "easements", "profits", "commodities"': Pollock and Maitland, *The History of English Law* (2nd edn, 1898), vol ii, p 145.

[3] In *Wall v Collins* [2007] EWCA Civ 444, [2007] Ch 390, CA held that the benefit of an easement attaches to the land rather than to an estate in the land (and so the benefit of an easement granted in favour of a tenant under a 999-year lease was not lost when the tenant later acquired the freehold and the lease merged into the freehold). For criticism, see Law Com CP No 186, *Easements, Covenants and Profits à Prendre* (2008), paras 5.72–5.5.86 (provisionally proposing a reversal of the decision in relation to termination of leaseholds); [2007] Conv 465 (T Ward); [2009] Conv 437, 438 (M Dixon); Gale, para 1-32. Cf [2010] Conv 300 (A Lyall) (supporting *Wall v Collins* and suggesting that land registration, and Land Registry Practice, have wrongly given rise to the notion that easements and profits are attached to estates rather than being appurtenant to land).

[4] As we shall see, an easement must exist also for the benefit of a particular piece of land—the 'dominant tenement': below, p 636; although a profit may exist either for the benefit of a dominant tenement, or 'in gross'—for the benefit of the person who holds the right, who can alienate it independently of land.

[5] Below, pp 650–1, 712.   [6] Below, pp 691, 715.   [7] Below, pp 652, 713.

[8] See generally Gale, *Law of Easements* (18th edn, 2008); Jackson, *Law of Easements and Profits* (1978); Sara, *Boundaries and Easements* (4th edn, 2007); Emmet, paras 17.050–17.106.

[9] *Hewlins v Shippam* (1826) 5 B & C 221; Termes de la Ley, 'Easement'. For the nature of a profit, by contrast with an easement, see below, p 703.

to use the land of another person (the servient owner)[10] in a particular manner, such as by walking over it or depositing rubbish on it, or to restrict its use by that other person to a particular extent, but that does not allow him to take any part of its natural produce or its soil.[11]

Thus an easement may be either positive or negative.[12] It is positive if it consists of a right to do something upon the land of another, as, for example, to walk or to place erections such as signboards on the land. A negative easement, on the other hand, does not permit an act, but imposes a restriction on the use that another person may make of his land. For example, the easement of light signifies that the servient owner must not build so as unreasonably to obstruct the flow of light; and an easement of support implies that the servient owner must not interfere with his own land or building so as to disturb that of his neighbour.

A question that not infrequently arises is whether some right exercisable over the land of another is an easement or a right of a different nature. It is a question of crucial importance, since the validity and enforceability of the right, both against the original owner of the land and against his successors in title, depends upon the proper characterisation of the right. An easement confers no right to possession of the land affected: it merely imposes a particular restriction upon the proprietary rights of the owner of the servient land; a right that entitles one person to possession of the land of another may therefore be a lease, or a licence, but it cannot be an easement.[13]Similarly, a limited right that in other respects bears some similarity to an easement,[14] but that the law does not regard as an easement, may give its holder a mere personal right against the landowner who gave it to him—and therefore, being a purely personal or contractual right, will not benefit or bind the parties' successors. A right cannot be given the status of an easement at the free will of the parties who create it, since no right over land will be regarded as an easement unless it possesses certain characteristics that the law has determined. This being so, the first task must be to discover what those characteristics are.

---

[10] English law here takes the language from Roman law, which referred to the owner of the dominant land (*praedium dominans*) and of the servient land (*praedium serviens*): Buckland, *Textbook of Roman Law* (3rd edn, 1963), p 259. It was Bracton in the thirteenth century who borrowed the language and some of the rules of Roman law. The lawyers did not begin to speculate on the characteristics of easements until the start of the nineteenth century. Gale, writing in 1839, started the modern law. It was the industrial revolution that caused the growth of large towns and manufacturing industries that brought into prominence such easements as ways, watercourses, light and support. So too, after the end of the Second World War, reconstruction and development have given rise to a large number of cases on the subject. For a detailed discussion of the older cases, see Gale, *A Treatise on the Law of Easements* (12th edn, 1950). See also Holdsworth, *An Historical Introduction to the Land Law* (1927), pp 101–2, 265–7.

[11] *Manning v Wasdale* (1836) 5 Ad & El 758.   [12] *Dalton v Angus* (1881) 6 App Cas 740, 821.

[13] The Law Commission has provisionally proposed that the fact that the dominant owner obtains exclusive possession of the servient land should not, without more, preclude the right from being an easement: Law Com CP No 186, *Easements, Covenants and Profits à Prendre* (2008), para 3.55; below, p 723. See also below, pp 646–8 (car parking).

[14] M & B pp 617–9.

(1) Characteristics of Easements

If an interest is to be an easement it must possess the four following characteristics.[15]

(a) There must be a dominant and a servient tenement[16]

The very nature of an easement, as being a right enforceable against another's land, requires that there shall be a tenement over which it is exercisable, the *servient tenement*, but in addition to this the law requires that there shall be another tenement, the *dominant tenement*, for the benefit of which the easement exists. To adopt legal phraseology an easement must be appurtenant or attached to land. If X, the owner of Blackacre, has acquired a right of way over the adjoining tenement Whiteacre, he is entitled to an easement of way not because he is X, but because he is the fee simple owner of Blackacre. The easement exists because Blackacre exists.[17]

It follows from this that there cannot be an easement *in gross*,[18] an easement that is independent of the ownership of land by the person who claims the right. Of course a person who does not own a yard of property may be granted a privilege to pass over Whiteacre, but though this may give him a personal right it certainly does not entitle him to an easement. It amounts to a licence confined in its effect to the actual parties.[19]

(b) An easement must accommodate the dominant tenement

It is a fundamental principle that an easement must not only be appurtenant to a dominant tenement, but must also be connected with the normal enjoyment of that tenement.[20] There must be a direct *nexus* between the enjoyment of the right and the user of the dominant tenement.[21] This requirement has been stated in various ways. An easement must be connected with the enjoyment of the dominant tenement and must be for its benefit.[22] It must have some natural connection with the estate, as being for its benefit.[23] The incident sought to be annexed, so that the assignee of the land

---

[15] *Re Ellenborough Park* [1956] Ch 131, M & B p 620; (1964) 28 Conv (NS) 450 (MA Peel).

[16] Holdsworth, *A History of English Law*, vol vii, pp 324 ff.

[17] *Rangeley v Midland Rly Co* (1868) 3 Ch App 306, 311; *Ackroyd v Smith* (1850) 10 CB 164,188; *Hawkins v Rutter* [1892] 1 QB 668.

[18] *Ackroyd v Smith*, above; *Weekly v Wildman* (1698) 1 Ld Raym 405; *London and Blenheim Estates Ltd v Ladbroke Retail Parks Ltd* [1994] 1 WLR 31 (right intended as easement and attached to servient tenement before dominant tenement identified held not to be an easement); *Voice v Bell* (1993) 68 P & CR 441. A profit à prendre may exist in gross: below p 702. In the USA both easements and profits may be in gross. See American Law Institute *Restatement of the Law, Third, Property (Servitudes)* (2000), and generally (1980) 96 LQR 557 (MF Sturley), criticising the rule; (1982) 98 LQR at 305 (S Gardner); *Jobson v Record* (1997) 75 P & CR 375 ('a right of way granted for the benefit of a defined area of land may not be used in substance for accommodating another area of land' at 378 (Morritt LJ)).

[19] Below, Ch 23.

[20] *Ackroyd v Smith* (1850) 10 CB 164.

[21] *Re Ellenborough Park* [1956] Ch 131, 174.

[22] *Gale on Easements* (12th edn), p 20; *Clapman v Edwards* [1938] 2 All ER 507.

[23] *Bailey v Stephens* (1862) 12 CBNS 91, 115 (Byles J). Cf *Stroude v Beazer Homes Ltd* [2005] EWHC 2686 (Ch), [2006] 2 EGLR 115 (right of access under TCPA 1990, s 106, agreement for purposes of constructing

may take advantage of it, must be beneficial to the land in respect of the ownership.[24] However, there is no test of real or appreciable benefit to the dominant tenement that has to be passed before a right claimed can be said to 'accommodate' it or to establish the necessary connection or nexus between the right and the dominant tenement.[25]

To take a simple example, a right of way in order to rank as an easement need not lead right up to the dominant tenement, but it must at least have some natural connection with it.[26] You cannot, said Byles J, have a right of way over land in Kent appurtenant to an estate in Northumberland,[27] for a right of way in Kent cannot possibly be advantageous to Northumberland land.[28] We may expand the statement of the principle:

> a right enjoyed by one over the land of another does not possess the status of an easement unless it accommodates and serves the dominant tenement, and is reasonably necessary for the better enjoyment of that tenement, for if it has no necessary connection therewith, although it confers an advantage upon the owner and renders his ownership of the land more valuable, it is not an easement at all, but a mere contractual right personal to and only enforceable between the two contracting parties.[29]

Whether the necessary nexus exists depends on the nature of the dominant tenement and the nature of the right alleged. If, for example, the dominant tenement is a residential house and if there is annexed to it a right to use an adjoining garden for purposes of relaxation and pleasure, this is a clear case where the right is sufficiently connected with the normal enjoyment of the house to rank as an easement.[30] The fact that the right enhances the value of the dominant tenement is a relevant, but not a decisive, consideration.[31] The principle is perhaps best illustrated by *Hill v Tupper*,[32] where the facts were as follows:

> A canal company leased land adjoining the canal to Hill and gave him the 'sole and exclusive right' to let out pleasure boats on the canal. Tupper, an innkeeper, disregarded

---

highway capable of benefiting land even though the highway, when constructed, would be public and not private).

24 Ibid. See also *Clos Farming Estates v Easton* [2002] NSWCA 389 at [30]-[34] (Stantow JA: right to enter servient land to carry out viticulture work, and to harvest grapes, not an easement).

25 *Polo Woods Foundation v Shelton-Agar* [2009] EWHC 1361 (Ch), [2010] 1 P & CR 12 at [53].

26 *Todrick v Western National Omnibus Co Ltd* [1934] Ch 561; *Birmingham, Dudley and District Banking Co v Ross* (1888) 38 Ch D 295, 314; *Pugh v Savage* [1970] 2 QB 373 (intervening land between dominant and servient tenements).

27 *Bailey v Stephens* (1862) CBNS 91.

28 *Todrick v Western National Omnibus Co Ltd* [1934] Ch 561,580 (Romer LJ).

29 Cited with approval in *Re Ellenborough Park* [1956] Ch 131, 170. For a qualification, see *Polo Woods Foundation v Shelton-Agar* [2009] EWHC 1361 (Ch), [2010] 1 P & CR 12 at [39] (Warren J: 'reasonably necessary' does no more than emphasise that the right must be connected with the normal enjoyment of the property. 'It was not being used in the sense that the person claiming the right has to show a need without which the dominant tenement cannot be reasonably enjoyed. ... The phrase is simply another way of referring to the requirement that the enjoyment of the right must benefit the dominant tenement or the owner of it in his capacity as owner rather than just personally').

30 *Re Ellenborough Park* [1956] Ch 131.   31 Ibid, 173.

32 (1863) 2 H & C 121, M & B p 620; cf *Moody v Steggles* (1879) 12 Ch D 261, M & B p 626 (right to advertise public house on servient land situated in front of it held to be an easement).

this privilege by himself letting out boats for fishing purposes. Hill thereupon brought an action in his own name against Tupper, his alleged cause of action being a disturbance of his easement to put boats on the canal.

It was held that the right conferred upon Hill by the contract with the company was not an easement but a mere licence personal to himself, since it was acquired in order to exploit an independent business enterprise, not to accommodate the riparian land as such.[33] The right was not beneficial to the land as land; rather, the land was required for the exploitation of the right. However, it is clear that an easement may exist for the purpose of the business carried on on the dominant tenement. In *Moody v Steggles* Fry J said:[34]

> It is said that the easement in question relates, not to the tenement, but to the business of the occupant of the tenement, and that therefore I cannot tie the easement to the house. It appears to me that that argument is of too refined a nature to prevail, and for this reason, that the house can only be used by an occupant, and that the occupant only uses the house for the business that he pursues, and therefore in some manner (direct or indirect) an easement is more or less connected with the mode in which the occupant of the house uses it.

The principle that the right must accommodate the dominant tenement applies equally to profits appurtenant,[35] and may be illustrated by the remark of Coke[36] that the right of cutting turfs for fuel cannot be claimed as appurtenant to land, but only to a house, because the use of fuel has no connection with land as such. In *Bailey v Stephens*:[37]

> A, who was seised in fee of a piece of land called Bloody Field, claimed the right to enter an adjoining close for the purpose of cutting down, carrying away and converting to his own use the trees and wood growing there. It was held that, as the wood was not employed for the beneficial enjoyment of Bloody Field, it was not connected with it and so was not a valid profit.

(c) Dominant and servient owners must be different persons

If one person owns two adjoining properties which, physically speaking, are separate properties, any rights that he may have been in the habit of exercising over one or other of them, such as by passing over one to reach the highway, are not easements (though

---

[33] *Re Ellenborough Park*, above, at 175. The alleged right was also asserted as a monopoly: ibid; ie, an exclusive right to use the canal for the purpose and the action was to exclude others from its use, which is not of the character of an easement. Cf the problem of exclusive user: below, p 646. Contrast the Pennsylvanian case of *Miller v Lutheran Conference and Camp Association* 331 Pa 241 (1938), Aigler, Smith and Tefft, *Cases on Property* (1960), vol ii, p 212, where a somewhat similar right was treated as an easement in gross capable of assignment.

[34] (1879) 12 Ch D 261, 266.

[35] Below, p 702; *Polo Woods Foundation v Shelton-Agar* [2009] EWHC 1361 (Ch), [2010] 1 P & CR 12.

[36] *Tyrringham's Case* (1584) 4 Co Rep 36b; below, p 707.

[37] (1862) 12 CBNS 91.

they are often called 'quasi-easements'), because they derive from his ownership not of the quasi-dominant land, but of the quasi-servient land itself.[38] Fry LJ said:[39]

Of course, strictly speaking, the owner of two tenements can have no easement over one of them in respect of the other. When the owner of Whiteacre and Blackacre passes over the former to Blackacre, he is not exercising a right of way in respect of Blackacre; he is merely making use of his own land to get from one part to another.

Thus, if X is the owner of two separate tenements and he lets one of them to a tenant, the latter cannot acquire by prescription an easement over the other, for his occupation is in the eyes of the law the occupation of his landlord, a person who cannot acquire an easement against himself.[40] As will be seen later, however, the right to light is exceptional in this respect.[41]

If the principle were otherwise and if rights exercised by a person over one of two properties both owned by him were to be treated as easements, they would necessarily remain vested in him after a sale of the quasi-servient tenement. They would also pass without express mention to a purchaser of the quasi-dominant tenement. But these consequences do not follow. To quote an old case:

JS had a close, and a wood adjoining to it, and time out of mind a way had been used over the close to the wood to carry and re-carry. He granted the close to one, and the wood to another. The question was, if the grantee of the wood shall have the way? And it was adjudged he should not, for the grantor by the grant of the close had excluded himself of the way, because it was not saved to him; and he himself could not use it, no more can his grantee.[42]

Therefore, when a large estate is split up and sold to different purchasers, any quasi-easements that were enjoyed by the former owner should be expressly reserved to the purchaser of the quasi-dominant tenement.[43]

(d) A right over land cannot amount to an easement unless it is capable of forming the subject-matter of a grant

As we shall see, apart from statute, every easement must originate in a grant, either express, implied or presumed. It follows from this that no right can have the status of an easement unless it is the possible subject-matter of a grant.[44] This characteristic has three aspects.

---

[38] *Bolton v Bolton* (1879) 11 Ch D 968.

[39] *Roe v Siddons* (1888) 22 QBD 224, 236; and see *Metropolitan Rly Co v Fowler* [1892] 1 QB 165; *Derry v Sanders* [1919] 1 KB 223.

[40] *Warburton v Parke* (1857) 2 H & N 64; *Gayford v Moffatt* (1868) 4 Ch App 133. A tenant may, however, grant an easement, for a period not exceeding that of his lease, in favour of another tenant of the same landlord.

[41] Below, p 602.   [42] *Dell v Babthorpe* (1593) Cro Eliz 300.

[43] *Wheeldon v Burrows* (1879) 12 Ch D 31, 49; below, pp 662–6.

[44] *Potter v North* (1669) 1 Wms Saund 347, in argument; *Goodman v Saltash Corpn* (1882) 7 App Cas 633, 654; *Dalton v Angus & Co* (1881) 6 App Cas 740, 795; *Chastey v Ackland* (1895) 11 TLR 460; *Harris v De Pinna* (1886) 33 Ch D 238, 262; *Bryant v Lefever* (1879) 4 CPD 172, 178.

(1) Certainty of description

The nature and extent of the right must be capable of reasonably exact description.[45] If it is so vague or so indeterminate as to defy precise definition, it cannot rank as an easement. This requirement, which is common to all forms of grant, is especially important in the present context, for a right over the land of another is allowed to ripen into an easement if it has been enjoyed for a long time without any interruption by the servient owner, but this necessarily implies that there should be something definite capable of interruption.[46]

A right to the flow of light to a particular window satisfies the test of certainty, for not only does the light pass over the servient tenement along a defined channel, but it can be interrupted by an obstruction placed across its line of approach.[47] Again, it has been held that a *jus spatiandi*, that is a right to wander at large over the servient tenement, is sufficiently determinate to constitute an easement if it is limited to a particular house or group of houses and is exercisable over an adjoining garden.[48] So also the right to a flow of air can subsist as an easement if it is claimed in respect of some definite channel, such as a ventilator in a building,[49] but not if what is claimed is that the current of air flowing indiscriminately over the entire servient tenement shall not be interrupted.[50]

In *Harris v De Pinna*,[51] where a claim to the general flow of air was made, Bowen LJ said:

> It would be just like amenity of prospect,[52] a subject-matter which is incapable of definition. So the passage of undefined air gives rise to no rights and can give rise to no rights for the best of all reasons, the reason of common sense, because you cannot acquire any rights against others by a user which they cannot interrupt.

---

[45] On whether it might be easier to satisfy the test in the case of an express grant than in a claim to an easement by prescription, see *Jackson v Mulvaney* [2002] EWCA Civ 1078, [2003] 1 WLR 360 at [10]-[15], [23], M & B p 625; *Batchelor v Marlow* [2001] EWCA Civ 1051, [2003] 1 WLR 764 at [4]-[6]; *Moncrieff v Jamieson* [2007] UKHL 42, [2007] 1 WLR 2620 at [59], M & B p 631.

[46] *Webb v Bird* (1862) 13 CBNS 841, 843; *Lawrence v Fen Tigers Ltd* [2011] EWHC 360 (QB), [2011] All ER (D) 96 (Mar) (the law does not recognise an easement of noise).

[47] *Harris v De Pinna* (1886) 33 Ch D 238, 259.

[48] *Re Ellenborough Park* [1956] Ch 131 (express grant); *Jackson v Mulvaney*, above, (implied grant or prescription).

[49] *Cable v Bryant* [1908] 1 Ch 259, M & B p 644, n 72.

[50] *Webb v Bird*, above; *Bryant v Lefever* (1879) 4 CPD 172. See also *Palmer v Bowman* [2000] 1 WLR 842 (no easement of unquantified right by owner of higher land to have main water pass by natural flow onto lower neighbouring land); above, p 163, n 82; (2000) 150 NLJ 311 (HW Wilkinson).

[51] (1886) 33 Ch D 238, 262. This may, however, be enforceable under the doctrine of non-derogation from grant. See *Aldin v Latimer Clark, Muirhead & Co* [1894] 2 Ch 437; above, p 226; *Lyme Valley Squash Club Ltd v Newcastle under Lyme BC* [1985] 2 All ER 405 (easement of light); below, p 659, n 182.

[52] *Bland v Mosely* (1587) cited in 9 Co Rep 58a. But a right to a prospect or view over neighbouring land may be framed as a restrictive covenant enforceable under the doctrine of *Tulk v Moxhay*; below, p 732. See *Wakeham v Wood* (1981) 43 P & CR 40; *Gilbert v Spoor* [1983] Ch 27; below, p 769, n 272.

And in *Hunter v Canary Wharf Ltd*,[53] Lord Hoffmann combined the concept of certainty and propinquity. In deciding that there could not be an easement for the reception of television waves from a distant transmitter, he said:

It was well settled [in *Dalton v Angus*[54]] that one could not prescribe for a right to an uninterrupted view or to a flow of air otherwise through a defined aperture or channel. Lord Blackburn...said that allowing the prescription of a right to a view would impose a burden 'on a very large and indefinite area.' Rights of light, air and support were strictly a matter between immediate neighbours. The building entitled to support, the windows entitled to light and the apertures entitled to air would be plain and obvious. The restrictions on the freedom of the person erecting the building would be limited and precise.

(2) Capable grantee

A claimant to an easement must be a person capable of receiving a grant, that is he must be a definite person or a definite body such as a corporation. Thus a claim put forward by a vague fluctuating body of persons, such as the inhabitants of a village, will not be sustainable as an easement.[55]

(3) Capable grantor

The same principle demands that the servient owner should have been lawfully entitled to grant the right claimed to be an easement. Thus a claim[56] against a company incorporated by statute will fail upon proof that the grant was ultra vires.[57]

(2) Examples of Easements

(a) List of easements not closed

Such, then, are the essential characteristics of easements, and it is important that they should be borne in mind, for otherwise certain judicial statements that new kinds of rights *in rem* cannot be created at will may be misunderstood. Thus Lord Brougham said:[58]

There are certain known incidents to property and its enjoyment, among others, certain burdens wherewith it may be affected, or rights which may be created and enjoyed over it by parties other than the owner.... But it must not therefore be supposed that incidents of a novel kind can be devised and attached to property at the fancy or caprice of any owner;...great detriment would arise and much confusion of rights, if parties were allowed to invent new modes of holding and enjoying real property, and to impress upon

---

53 [1997] AC 655, 709, M & B p 643; (1997) 113 LQR 515 (P Cane); [1997] CLJ 483 (J O'Sullivan); [1997] Conv 145 (PR Ghandi).

54 (1881) 6 App Cas 740, 824.

55 But a local customary right may be established; below, pp 717 ff.

56 *Paine & Co Ltd v St Neots Gas and Coke Co* [1939] 3 All ER 812.

57 *Mulliner v Midland Rly Co* (1879) 11 Ch D 611.

58 *Keppell v Bailey* (1834) 2 My & K 517, 535. See also *Hill v Tupper* (1863) 2 H & C 121, 127–8 (Pollock CB).

their land and tenements a peculiar character, which should follow them into all hands, however remote.

This means not that an easement of a kind never heard of before cannot be created, but that a new species of incorporeal hereditament or a new species of burden cannot be brought into being and given the status and legal effect of an easement. In other words, if a right exhibits the four characteristics described above, it is an easement that will run with the dominant and against the servient tenement, even though its object may be to fulfil a purpose for which it has not hitherto been used; but if it lacks one or more of those characteristics, it may, indeed, be enforceable between the parties who create it, but it cannot, like an easement, be enforceable by or against third parties.[59]

One of the main purposes of law is to keep pace with the requirements of society and to adapt itself to new modes of life and new business methods, a fact that was present in the mind of Lord St Leonards when he said:

The category of servitudes and easements must alter and expand with the changes that take place in the circumstances of mankind.[60]

Thus in a case where an easement was claimed to place stores and casks upon land reclaimed from the sea, the Privy Council said:

The law must adapt itself to the conditions of modern society and trade, and there is nothing in the purposes for which the easement is claimed inconsistent in principle with a right of easement as such.[61]

(b) Examples

The following list of easements, which begins with the most important kinds and which, of course, is not exhaustive, will illustrate their variety:

(1) Way

Rights of way, whether for general or special purposes, and whether exercisable in all modes or limited to a carriage way, bridle way, foot way or a way for cattle.[62]

(2) Light

A right that the light flowing over adjoining land to a window shall not be unreasonably obstructed.[63]

---

[59] *Re Ellenborough Park* [1956] Ch 131, 140–1.   [60] *Dyce v Lady Hay* (1852) 1 Macq 305.

[61] *A-G of Southern Nigeria v John Holt & Co* [1915] AC 599, 617; *Simpson v Godmanchester Corp* [1896] 1 Ch 214, 219; *Dowty Boulton Paul Ltd v Wolverhampton Corp (No 2)* [1976] Ch 13, 23 (Russell LJ: 'A tendency in the past to freeze the categories of easements has been overtaken by the defrosting operation in *Re Ellenborough Park*').

[62] There must be sufficient certainty about the route of the way, although this may be implied or one party (eg the party whose grant gave rise to the need for the way) may have the right to choose the route: *Pearson v Spencer* (1861) 1 B.& S 571 QBD, affd (1863) 3 B & S 761; see [2009] Conv 93 (T Braithwaite) discussing the authorities in relation to imperfect express grants, implied grants and ways of necessity.

[63] See generally *Colls v Home and Colonial Stores Ltd* [1904] AC 179, M & B p 728, below, pp 680–2.

(3) Water and other services

Rights in connection with water, such as a right to the uninterrupted passage of water over adjoining land,[64] or a right to enter upon adjoining land to divert the course of a stream for irrigation purposes, or a right to pollute a river or to discharge water onto the land of another.[65] Similarly, rights to other services, such as gas or electricity,[66] or to allow drainage from the dominant tenement over the servient tenement.[67]

(4) Support

A right to the support of buildings by adjoining land or buildings. Though a landowner has a natural right to have his *land* supported by adjoining land, a right to have *buildings* supported can be claimed only if it has actually been acquired as an easement.[68]

(5) Fencing

A right to have a fence maintained by an adjoining owner. This has been recognised by the Court of Appeal as 'a right in the nature of an easement'. As Lord Denning said in *Crow v Wood*:[69]

> It is not an easement strictly so called because it involves the servient owner in the expenditure of money. It was described by Gale as a 'spurious kind of easement'.[70] But it has been treated in practice by the courts as being an easement...[71]
>
> It seems to me that it is now sufficiently established—or at any rate, if not established hitherto, we should now declare—that a right to have your neighbour keep up the fences is a right in the nature of an easement which is capable of being granted by law so as to run with the land and to be binding on successors. It is a right which lies in grant.[72]

(6) Miscellaneous easements

The easements set out above are those most commonly found in practice, but we may add examples of some variations and extensions of these interests:[73]

64 *Rance v Elvin* (1985) 50 P & CR 9; below, p 644, n 86.

65 A landowner may have certain natural rights in respect of water; above, p 163; below, p 650.

66 *Coopind (UK) Ltd v Walton Commercial Group Ltd* [1989] 1 EGLR 2451 ('right to receive supply of water gas electricity and heat'); *Duffy v Lamb* (1997) 75 P & CR 364 (right to uninterrupted passage of electricity held to be easement).

67 *Atwood v Bovis Homes Ltd* [2001] Ch 379, M & B p 724; *Green v Lord Somerleyton* [2003] EWCA Civ 198, [2004] 1 P & CR 33.

68 The leading case is *Dalton v Angus & Co* (1881) 6 App Cas 740. See also *Rees v Skerrett* [2001] EWCA Civ 760, [2001] 1 WLR 1541 (demolition of adjoining terraced house in breach of easement exposing common wall; damage caused by wind suction within scope of the right of support, and so actionable in nuisance). For the relationship between the easement of support and the claim to protection against the effects of the weather, see *Phipps v Pears* [1965] 1 QB 76, M & B p 641, and the discussion below, p 645, n 89.

69 [1971] 1 QB 77 at 84, M & B p 645. See (1971) 87 LQR 13 (PV Baker).

70 Gale, *Law of Easements* (11th edn), p 432. See too *Lawrence v Jenkins* (1873) LR 8 QB 274, 279 (Archibald J). Cf *Hilton v Ankesson* (1872) 27 LT 519.

71 See *Jones v Price* [1965] 2 QB 618, 633 (Willmer LJ), 639 (Diplock LJ); *Egerton v Harding* [1975] QB 62.

72 It may also be acquired (1) as an easement by prescription: *Lawrence v Jenkins* (1873) LR 8 QB 274: *Jones v Price* [1965] 2 QB 618; (2) by custom: *Egerton v Harding*, above.

73 For further examples, see Gale, paras 1–73 to 1–77.

    (i)   Right to hang clothes on a line passing over neighbouring soil.[74]

    (ii)   Right to run telephone lines over neighbouring land.[75]

    (iii)   Right to use a close for the purpose of mixing muck and preparing manure thereon for the use of an adjoining farm.[76]

    (iv)   Right to fix a signboard to the walls of another's house.[77]

    (v)   Right of a landowner to use a particular seat in a parish church.[78]

    (vi)   Right to nail trees to a wall.[79]

    (vii)   Right to lay stones upon adjoining land to prevent sand from being washed away by the sea.[80]

    (viii)   Right to store casks and trade produce on a neighbour's land.[81]

    (ix)   Right to use a lavatory situated on the servient tenement.[82]

    (x)   Right to use a letter-box.[83]

    (xi)   Right to use an airfield.[84]

    (xii)   Right to park a car anywhere on the forecourt of a block of flats.[85]

(c) New easements

New easements may arise, but no right that fails to exhibit the four characteristics described above can exist as an easement. Whether or not a new right, complying with the accepted requirements of an easement, will be judicially recognised or not is difficult to forecast.

There are, however, three situations in which such recognition is unlikely to be granted.

(1) Expenditure by, or other positive on, servient owner

First, where the owner of the servient tenement would be under a duty to spend money or to fulfil some other positive obligation.[86] There is only one right in this category, that

---

[74] *Drewell v Towler* (1832) 3 B & Ad 735.

[75] *Lancashire and Cheshire Telephone Exchange Co v Manchester Overseers* (1884) 14 QBD 267.

[76] *Pye v Mumford* (1848) 11 QB 666.

[77] *Moody v Steggles* (1879) 12 Ch D 261, M & B p 626; *William Hill (Southern) Ltd v Cabras Ltd* [1987] 1 EGLR 37.

[78] *Mainwaring v Giles* (1822) 5 B & Ald 356; *Brumfitt v Roberts* (1870) LR 5 CP 224; *Re St Mary's Banbury* [1986] Fam 24; affd [1987] Fam 136.

[79] *Hawkins v Wallis* (1763) 2 Wils 173.   [80] *Philpot v Bath* (1905) 21 TLR 634.

[81] *A-G of Southern Nigeria v John Holt & Co (Liverpool) Ltd* [1915] AC 599; *Smith v Gates* (1952) 160 EG 512 (right to keep chicken coops on a common).

[82] *Miller v Emcer Products Ltd* [1956] Ch 304, M & B p 628.

[83] *Goldberg v Edwards* [1950] Ch 247, M & B p 768.

[84] *Dowty Boulton Paul Ltd v Wolverhampton Corpn (No 2)* [1976] Ch 13.

[85] *Newman v Jones* (22 March 1982, unreported); *London and Blenheim Estates Ltd v Ladbroke Retail Parks Ltd* [1992] 1 WLR 1278, 1288; *Handel v St Stephens Close Ltd* [1994] 1 EGLR 70; *Moncrieff v Jamieson* [2007] UKHL 42, [2007] 1 WLR 2620 at [137]. See further below, pp 647–8.

[86] *Regis Property Co Ltd v Redman* [1956] 2 QB 612 (covenant to supply hot water and central heating, involving the performance of services, not an easement); *Rance v Elvin* (1983) 49 P & CR 65 (right to metered water supply paid for by servient owner held not to be an easement, even though dominant owner agreed

of fencing, where the servient owner is under a duty to take positive steps to maintain the fence, including the expenditure of money. As we have seen, its exceptional nature is recognised by the Court of Appeal.[87] There may also be cases where the parties have expressly or impliedly agreed that the servient owner shall bear the burden; as in *Liverpool City Council v Irwin*[88] where a local authority, which owned a high-rise block of flats, let them to tenants. Easements of access over the common parts of the building retained by the local authority (the servient owner) were implied in favour of the tenants. The local authority was held liable, as on an implied contract, to maintain those parts.

(2) Negativity

Secondly, where the easement is negative, in the sense that it gives the owner of the dominant tenement a right to stop his neighbour doing something on his (the neighbour's) own land. This has long been recognised in the cases of the easements of light and support. But in *Phipps v Pears*,[89] where the premises had been exposed to damp and frost owing to the demolition of an adjacent house, the Court of Appeal

to reimburse water charges); (1985) 50 P & CR 9 (CA held that the right was to the uninterrupted passage of water, and not to its supply; it was therefore an easement, and the servient owner was liable in restitution to reimburse; [1985] CLJ 458 (AJ Waite); *Coopind (UK) Ltd v Walton Commercial Group Ltd* [1989] 1 EGLR 241 (right to receive a supply of gas under service roads retained by lessors held to extend to right to lay new gas main); *Cardwell v Walker* [2003] EWHC 3117 (Ch), [2004] 2 P & CR 9 (control of electricity supply by recording meters changed to issue of tokens available for sale by servient owners; held unrestricted easement of passage of electricity unchanged). See also *William Old International Ltd v Arya* [2009] EWHC 599 (Ch), [2009] 2 P & CR 20 (servient owner's obligation is only negative, and does not extend to duty to enter into contractual and proprietary relations with a third party).

[87] *Jones v Price* [1965] 2 QB 618; *Crow v Wood* [1971] 1 QB 77, M & B p 710.

[88] *Liverpool City Council v Irwin* [1977] AC 239; *King v South Northamptonshire DC* [1992] 1 EGLR 53; [1992] Conv 347 (JE Martin); *Duke of Westminster v Guild* [1985] QB 688 (tenant as dominant owner of right of drainage held to be liable for repairs). See also *Stokes v Mixconcrete (Holdings) Ltd* (1978) 38 P & CR 488; *Holden v White* [1982] QB 679 (servient owner owed no duty of care at common law to milkman injured by disintegrating manhole cover on private footpath giving access to terraced house, nor under Occupiers' Liability Act 1957. See now Occupiers' Liability Act 1984, in effect reversing the decision); *McGeown v Northern Ireland Housing Executive* [1995] 1 AC 233 (public right of way).

[89] [1965] 1 QB 76, M & B p 670, criticised in (1964) 80 LQR 318 (REM); (1964) 27 MLR 614; (1965) 28 MLR 264 (HW Wilkinson), and supported (1964) 27 MLR 768 (JF Garner). Followed in *Marchant v Capital and Counties Property Co Ltd* (1982) 263 EG 661, (1983) 267 EG 843 (award under London Building Acts (Amendment) Act 1939). Under Building Act 1984, ss 81, 82(1)(b), replacing Public Health Act 1961, s 29(5), a local authority may serve a notice on anyone demolishing a building, requiring him to weatherproof any surface of adjacent buildings exposed by the demolition.

In *Sedgwick Forbes Bland Payne Group Ltd v Regional Properties Ltd* [1981] EGD 44, 56 it was suggested that a right to protection against the weather by a *roof* might be an easement, thereby limiting *Phipps v Pears* to an easement of protection against the weather in the vertical plane. Cf *Rees v Skerrett* [2001] EWCA Civ 760, [2001] 1 WLR 1541 (where the adjacent buildings were not free-standing; on demolition, right of support was infringed: at [15]; above, p 643, n 68; and there was also a breach of the duty of care to take steps to waterproof wall after demolition: at [27]. The case would now be governed by Party Wall etc Act 1996: at [34]); [2002] Conv 237 (TH Wu). On party walls, see above, p 524. On negative easements generally, see (1998) 18 LS 510 (I Dawson and A Dunn).

held that there was no easement of protection against the weather. Lord Denning said:[90]

> A right to protection from the weather…is entirely negative. Seeing that it is a negative easement, it must be looked at with caution. Because the law has been very chary of creating any new negative easements…. If such an easement were to be permitted, it would unduly restrict your neighbour in his own enjoyment of his own land.

It is, however, possible for such rights to be framed as restrictive covenants that may be enforceable under the doctrine of *Tulk v Moxhay*.[91] And the law of tort might sometimes provide a remedy to the person whose property is damaged by exposure to the weather, even if no easement is infringed.[92]

(3) Exclusive or joint user

Finally, no right will be recognised as an easement that is in effect a claim to exclusive possession of the servient tenement. In *Copeland v Greenhalf*,[93] it was held that a wheelwright had no easement to store and repair an unlimited number of vehicles on a strip of his neighbour's land. In the words of Upjohn J:[94]

> I think that the right claimed goes wholly outside any normal idea of an easement, that is, the right of the owner or the occupier of a dominant tenement over a servient tenement. This claim really amounts to a claim to a joint user of the land by the defendant. Practically, the defendant is claiming the whole beneficial user of the strip of land on the south-east side of the track there; he can leave as many or as few lorries there as he likes for as long as

---

[90] At 83.   [91] Below, p 732.

[92] *Rees v Skerrett*, above: at [36] Lloyd J noted that 'as regards the law of negligence and nuisance developments since 1965, especially *Leakey v National Trust for Places of Historic Interest or Natural Beauty* [1980] QB 485, show that the balance between the position of those who are neighbours (both in fact and in law) is now to be drawn differently in these areas of law. Moreover, it is not a question of preventing a man from pulling down his house altogether, any more than a right of support prevents demolition….Rather, it is a question of requiring him, if and when he does demolish the house, to provide substitute protection, to the extent that this can be done by works which in all the circumstances it is reasonable to expect him to undertake.' Where there *is* a right of support that is infringed, damages may be claimed in tort for the consequential exposure: *Bradburn v Lindsay* [1983] 2 All ER 408; [1984] Conv 54 (P Jackson); [1987] Conv 47 (AJ Waite); *Brace v South East Regional Housing Association Ltd* (1984) 270 EG 1286. For the use of the tort of nuisance generally to remedy infringements of a easements, see below, p 694.

[93] [1952] Ch 488, M & B p 626; *Ward v Kirkland* [1967] Ch 194; cf *Wright v Macadam* [1949] 2 KB 744, M & B p 665 (right to store domestic coal in shed held to be an easement), which was not cited in *Copeland v Greenhalf*. See also *Grigsby v Melville* [1972] 1 WLR 1355; affd [1974] 1 WLR 80, M & B p 628 (claim to exclusive right of storage in cellar under drawing-room floor); *Thomas W Ward Ltd v Alexander Bruce (Grays) Ltd* [1959] 2 Lloyd's Rep 472 (right to ground ships on silt in defendant's dock in course of claimant's business as shipbrokers held not to be an easement: 'it involves an almost complete exclusion of the alleged servient owner': Harman LJ at 477); *Hanina v Morland* (2000) 97 (47) LSG 41 (use of adjoining roof for entertaining, sunbathing and generally as extension of living room held to be exclusive user and therefore no easement); *P & S Platt Ltd v Crouch* [2003] EWCA Civ 1110, [2004] 1 P & CR 18 (right to moor boats on land adjacent to Norfolk Broads capable of being an easement, and not a sufficiently substantial interference with reasonable user of land by defendants to prevent it being an easement); *Jackson v Mulvaney* [2002] EWCA Civ 1078, [2003] 1 WLR 360 (easement of use of communal garden, but no right to maintain flowerbed in a particular position within the garden).

[94] [1952] Ch 488, 498.

he likes; he may enter on it by himself, his servants and agents to do repair work thereon. In my judgment, that is not a claim which can be established as an easement. It is virtually a claim to possession of the servient tenement, if necessary to the exclusion of the owner; or, at any rate, to a joint user, and no authority has been cited to me which could justify the conclusion that a right of this wide and undefined nature can be the proper subject-matter of an easement. It seems to me that to succeed, this claim must amount to a successful claim of possession by reason of long adverse possession.[95]

Upjohn J here spoke in terms of 'joint user', 'whole beneficial user' and 'virtually a claim to possession' of the land over which the easement was claimed. Given that the exercise of any easement involves some limitation of the servient owner's rights over his own land, this suggests that the question of whether the user claimed is capable of constituting an easement is really one of degree. As Romer LJ said in *Miller v Emcer Products Ltd*,[96] where a right to use a lavatory situated on the servient tenement was held to be an easement:

It is true that during the times when the dominant owner exercised the right the owner of the servient tenement would be excluded, but this in greater or less degree is a common feature of many easements (for example, rights of way) and does not amount to such an ouster of the servient owner's rights as was held by Upjohn J to be incompatible with a legal easement in *Copeland v Greenhalf*.

However, certain statements in the House of Lords in *Moncrieff v Jamieson*[97] have left some doubt about the appropriate test. Lord Scott of Foscote said:[98]

I would, for my part, reject the test that asks whether the servient owner is left with any reasonable use of his land, and substitute for it a test which asks whether the servient owner retains possession and, subject to the reasonable exercise of the right in question, control of the servient land.

This question has arisen in connection with the right to park vehicles. In *Newman v Jones*[99] it was held that a right for a landowner to park a car anywhere in a defined area nearby was capable of existing as an easement; and the mere risk of there being not enough space for all to park simultaneously was not a reason for denying that any rights at all exist. Nor may it be an objection that charges are made by the

---

95 Below, Ch 29. See (1968) Conv (NS) 270 (MJ Goodman); [1994] Conv 196 (H Wallace).

96 [1956] Ch 304 at 316, M & B p 628; (1956) 72 LQR 172 (REM).

97 [2007] UKHL 42, [2007] 1 WLR 2620, M & B p 631; [2008] Conv 244 (M Haley); (2008) 158 NLJ 239 (A Samuels); Gale, paras 1.68, 9.100–9.103.

98 Ibid at [59]. Cf Lord Neuberger of Abbotsbury at [143]: 'I see considerable force in the views expressed by Lord Scott in paras 57 and 59 of his opinion, to the effect that a right can be an easement notwithstanding that the dominant owner effectively enjoys exclusive occupation, on the basis that the essential requirement is that the servient owner retains possession and control. If that were the right test, then it seems likely that *Batchelor v Marlow* [2003] 1 WLR 764 [below, n 102] was wrongly decided. However, unless it is necessary to decide the point to dispose of this appeal, I consider that it would be dangerous to try and identify degree of ouster is required to disqualify a right from constituting a servitude or easement, given the very limited argument your Lordships have received on the topic.'

99 High Court (Chancery Division), 22 March 1982.

servient owner, whether for the parking itself or for the general upkeep of the park. In *London and Blenheim Estates Ltd v Ladbroke Retail Parks Ltd*[100] Judge Paul Baker QC said:

> The essential question is one of degree. If the right granted in relation to the area over which it is to be exercisable is such that it would leave the servient owner without any reasonable use of his land, whether for parking or anything else, it could not be an easement though it might be some larger or different grant.[101]

This test was applied by the Court of Appeal in *Batchelor v Marlow*,[102] which held that the exclusive right to park six cars for nine and a half hours every working day was not capable of being an easement.

In *Moncrieff v Jamieson*,[103] however, Lord Scott of Foscote doubted whether *Batchelor v Marlow* was correctly decided:

> I can think of no reason why, if an area of land can accommodate nine cars, the owner of the land should not grant an easement to park nine cars on the land. The servient owner would remain the owner of the land and in possession and control of it. The dominant owner would have the right to station up to nine cars there and, of course, to have access to his nine cars. How could it be said that the law would recognise an easement allowing the dominant owner to park five cars or six or seven or eight but not nine? I would, for my part, reject the test that asks whether the servient owner is left with any reasonable use of his land, and substitute for it a test which asks whether the servient owner retains possession and, subject to the reasonable exercise of the right in question, control of the servient land.

However, this was an obiter dictum,[104] and unless and until *Batchelor v Marlow* is overruled by the Supreme Court it remains binding on courts up to the level of the Court of Appeal.[105]

---

[100] [1992] 1 WLR 1278, 1288; affd [1994] 1 WLR 31, M & B p 629; [1994] CLJ 229 (S Bridge); *Handel v St Stephens Close Ltd* [1994] 1 EGLR 70; (1994) 144 NLJ 579 (HW Wilkinson); [1996] 16 LS 51 (P Luther).

[101] For example, a lease, for which exclusive possession would be necessary; above, p 185; or, in the case of long user rather than express grant, a claim to title by adverse possession, although the regular parking of cars without taking further steps (such as enclosing the parking area) is unlikely to constitute the taking of possession: *Simpson v Fergus* (1999) 79 P & CR 398; *Central Midlands Estates Ltd v Leicester Dyers Ltd* [2003] 2 P & CR DG1. See also *Pointon York Group plc v Poulton* [2006] EWCA Civ 1001, [2007] 1 P & CR 6 (where easement of parking is established, the right to occupy parking spaces could be 'premises' that were 'occupied' for the purposes of the business on the dominant tenement under LTA 1954, s 23).

[102] [2001] EWCA Civ 1051, [2003] 1 WLR 764. However, the parties there agreed on the application of Judge Baker's test in *London & Blenheim Estates*.

[103] [2007] UKHL 42, [2007] 1 WLR 2620 at [59]-[60]. See also Lord Neuberger of Abbotsbury at [143], above, n 98.

[104] The question for decision in *Moncrieff v Jamieson* was whether (under Scots law) a servitude right to park was capable of being constituted as ancillary to a servitude right of vehicular access.

[105] Gale, para 9.102, n 266. See also Law Com No 186, *Easements, Covenants and Profits à Prendre* (2008), paras 3.45–3.52.

B EASEMENTS DISTINGUISHED FROM OTHER RIGHTS

Having seen something of the nature of easements, we may notice other rights of a somewhat similar nature from which they must be distinguished.[106]

(1) Licences

A licence is created in favour of B if, without being given any legal estate or interest, he is permitted by A to enter A's land for an agreed purpose. It is an authority that justifies what would otherwise be a trespass.

We shall discuss in Chapter 23 the categories of licence and the different rules that are applicable to each of them.[107] Here it is sufficient to note the most significant difference between a licence and an easement: the former is normally only a purely personal right, which may be revocable, and does not of itself bind a purchaser from the licensor who created the licence.[108] However, an easement is a property right, of necessity annexed to a dominant tenement, and capable of binding the successor in title of the first servient owner who granted it, and being enforced by the successor in title of the first dominant owner. Moreover, as a property right, an easement is not revocable unilaterally by the grantor or his successors.

The distinction was illustrated in *IDC Group Ltd v Clark*,[109] where an agreement, which was made by deed and described as a licence, provided for a fire escape route through a party wall between two adjoining properties; the parties to the deed were expressed to include their respective successors and assigns. The Court of Appeal held that the deed, being professionally drawn and described as a licence, created personal and not property rights, and was therefore a licence. The licensees could therefore not require the current owner, a successor in title of the original licensor, to unblock the fire escape route.

(2) Local Customary Rights

Indefinite and fluctuating classes of persons, such as the inhabitants of a village, may be entitled to exercise over another's land rights that, if the matter rested between the servient owner and a definite dominant owner, would properly be termed easements. Illustrations from the cases are:

(a) where the inhabitants of a village pass across another's land on their way to church,[110] or

(b) where the fishing inhabitants dry their nets on certain property.[111]

---

[106] For the difference between an easement and a profit, see below, p 703.

[107] For the difference between a licence and a lease, see above, pp 185 ff.

[108] We shall see that certain licences are irrevocable, such as a contractual licence that can be enforced according to the contractual terms: below, p 929. And certain licences might give rise to proprietary rights capable of binding third parties, such as through the doctrine of proprietary estoppel: below, p 936. But the starting point for the analysis of a licence is that it is a purely personal right.

[109] [1992] 1 EGLR 187; above, p 189.

[110] *Brocklebank v Thompson* [1903] 2 Ch 344.

[111] *Mercer v Denne* [1905] 2 Ch 538.

Such rights are not easements, for an easement lies in grant, and a vague and fluctuating body of persons such as fishing inhabitants is not a legal person, and is therefore incapable of taking under a grant. If, therefore, they are to be established, some other title than grant must be shown, and this, as we shall see later, is what the law calls *custom*.[112]

(3) Natural Rights

This is an expression often used to describe a right that is one of the ordinary and inseparable incidents of ownership, though its exercise requires an adjacent owner to forbear from doing something on his own land that otherwise he would be free to do. The epithet 'natural' serves to distinguish such rights from easements, which do not automatically accompany ownership but must be acquired by grant, either express, implied or presumed.[113] Thus an owner has a natural right to so much support from his neighbour's land as will support his own land, unincumbered by buildings, at its natural level;[114] and a riparian owner is entitled to demand that other riparian owners shall not divert the natural course of the stream.[115] Such natural rights differ from easements in at least two respects—their existence does not depend upon some form of grant, and they cannot be extinguished by unity of seisin.[116]

(4) Public Rights

Public rights are rights that anyone may exercise as a member of the public. Main examples are the right to pass along a public highway,[117] or to fish in the sea or to navigate over the foreshore.[118] These rights exist by virtue of the general law and do not require a dominant tenement.

C LEGAL AND EQUITABLE EASEMENTS

An easement is capable of subsisting as a legal interest. It will be legal if (i) it is held 'for an interest equivalent to an estate in fee simple absolute in possession or a term

---

[112] Below, pp 717–19.　　　　　　　　　　[113] *Backhouse v Bonomi* (1861) 9 HL Cas 503.

[114] Ibid; *Midland Bank plc v Bardgrove Property Services Ltd* [1991] 2 EGLR 283; *Holbeck Hall Hotel Ltd v Scarborough BC* [1997] 2 EGLR 213 (rvsd on the question of liability in tort [2000] QB 836).

[115] Above, pp 163 ff.　　　　　　　　　[116] For extinguishment of easements, see below, p 696.

[117] *Halsbury's Laws of England* (4th edn), vol 21 (2004), paras 1–11 (meaning of 'highway' etc), 197–9 (extent of public right of highway); Sauvain, *Highway Law* (4th edn, 2009). The legislation relating to highways is consolidated in Highways Act 1980 as amended.

[118] Above, p 166.

of years absolute',[119] and (ii) is created by statute, deed or prescription,[120] and (iii) in the case of the express[121] grant or reservation of an easement over registered land, it is completed by registration.[122] If it does not satisfy these requirements, then it may be an equitable easement: for example, if it is for the life of the grantee (even if it is created by deed), or if it is created informally,[123] or by a contract to grant a legal easement.[124] The grant of an easement implied under the doctrine of *Wheeldon v Burrows*[125] into a contract, rather than into a deed, must also therefore create an equitable easement.

This distinction is important in relation to the enforceability of the easement against third parties. This is discussed in detail below.[126]

D ACQUISITION OF EASEMENTS

The basic principle is that every easement must have had its origin in grant.[127]

All the methods of acquisition except one are traceable to a grant that has been or that might have been made, and the one exception—statute—is not of frequent occurrence. It may facilitate exposition to set the subject out in tabular form.

The figures in parentheses denote the order of treatment in the following pages.

---

[119] LPA 1925, s 1(2)(a). This defines the possible extent of a legal easement but does not require it to be attached to an equivalent estate in land: *Wall v Collins* [2007] EWCA Civ 444, [2007] Ch 390 at [15] (Carnwath LJ: 'all that matters is that the grantee has an interest at least co-extensive with the period of the easement'); cf, however, above, p 643, n 3.

[120] Below, pp 652 ff.

[121] The registration requirement applies only to easements created by *express* grant or reservation. This does not therefore include easements created by implied grant or reservation, or prescription (below, pp 659, 666). For these purposes an easement created by the operation of LPA 1925, s 62, below, p 654, is not an express grant and therefore does not require to be registered: LRA 2002, s 27(7).

[122] LRA 2002, s 27(2)(d). A notice of the interest must be entered in the register of the title of the servient tenement and (if the dominant tenement is also registered) the proprietor of the dominant tenement must be entered in the register as proprietor of the easement: ibid, Sch 2, para 7. It should be noted that the express grant of a legal easement is a registrable disposition regardless of the duration of the grant: and so even if granted for the benefit of a lease for seven years or less that is not itself required to be registered, the easement must still be registered: H & B, para 8.14.

[123] Below, p 653.

[124] *McManus v Cooke* (1887) 35 Ch D 681; below, p 653.

[125] (1879) 12 Ch D 31, below, p 662.

[126] Below, pp 691 ff.

[127] *Angus & Co v Dalton* (1877) 3 QBD 85, 102 (Cockburn CJ).

(1) Acquisition by Statute

Modern examples[128] of easements created by statute are to be found in local Acts of Parliament. Statutory rights similar to easements are also created by general Acts and are sometimes called statutory easements.[129]

A landowner may acquire an easement to enter upon his neighbour's land in order to carry out maintenance work to his own property.[130] Where an easement has not been aquired, the Access to Neighbouring Land Act 1992[131] enables him to obtain an order of the court if the neighbour refuses access. An application for an access order is regarded as a pending land action.[132] In unregistered land a pending land action must be registered in the register of pending actions[133] if it is to bind a purchaser without express notice of it.[134] In registered land it must be protected by notice and cannot be an overriding interest.[135] An access order may be registered in the register of writs and orders affecting land[136] or, in the case of registered land, protected by the entry of an agreed notice against the affected title.[137] It cannot be an overriding interest.[138]

(2) Acquisition by Express Grant

(a) Creation

(1) At common law

An easement is an incorporeal hereditament[139] and therefore, in accordance with the historic rule of the common law, it must be granted by deed. This rule is now contained

---

[128] A former example was an Inclosure Act that discharged land from rights of common and distributed it in plots among a number of absolute owners; easements of way over adjoining plots were frequently reserved to the respective owners. See 17th edn of this book, pp 653–5. Inclosure was abolished by Commons Act 2006, s 48.

[129] Jackson, ch 12; (1956) 20 Conv (NS) 208 (JF Garner); Gale, paras 1–119 to 1–128.

[130] *Ward v Kirkland* [1967] Ch 184, above, p 226, n 24.

[131] The Act was based on the Law Com No 151, *Rights of Access to Neighbouring Land* (1985), but had a chequered history: [1992] 26 EG 136 (J Adams). See Gale, paras 11–41 to 11.69; Jackson, pp 108–9. See CPR, r 56.4(c); PD, para 11.

[132] Access to Neighbouring Land Act 1992, s 5(6).   [133] LCA 1972, s 1(1)(b).   [134] Ibid, s 5(7).

[135] LRA 2002, s 87(1), (3).   [136] LCA 1972, s 6.   [137] LRA 2002, s 34; LRR 2003, r 80(c).

[138] Ibid, s 87(1), (3); Access to Neighbouring Land Act 1992, s 5(5), as substituted by LRA 2002, s 133, Sch 11, para 26(1), (4).

[139] Above, p 633.

in section 52(1) of the Law of Property Act 1925:[140]

> All conveyances of land or of any interest therein are void for the purpose of conveying or creating a legal estate[141] unless made by deed.

(2) In equity

At common law, a grant of an easement, made orally or by writing not executed as a deed, creates only a licence.[142] But this may create an equitable easement where equity acts on the principle that what ought to be done must be regarded as actually done—a view that has given us the doctrine of *Walsh v Lonsdale*.[143] If the grant satisfies the formalities required for a contract for the sale or other disposition of an interest in land and is for value, equity will treat this as a contract to grant a legal interest in land, and if the agreement is specifically enforceable, it will then treat the situation as if the grant by deed had already been made.[144] The leading case on the subject is *McManus v Cooke*.[145]

> Between adjoining properties, belonging respectively to X and Y, there was a high party wall of unnecessary width. It was orally agreed between X and Y that in order to give more space to each owner the wall should be pulled down by X and replaced by one which was lower and thinner, the work to be at their joint expense. It was also agreed orally that each of the parties should erect a lean-to skylight, and that both of these should rest on the new wall and incline upwards and outwards to the respective houses. X duly carried out his part of the work, but Y, instead of building a lean-to skylight on his side, built one so shaped that part of it showed above the wall and in consequence obstructed the access of light to X's skylight. X sued for an injunction to restrain Y from maintaining an erection which infringed the agreement.

Kay J decided in favour of the claimant X on the ground that, although the parties' agreement that each should have an easement of light over the other's land was not effective at law for lack of a deed, it was effective to create an easement in equity. The case was decided in the context of the formality requirements for contracts that existed before 27 September 1989, under which an oral contract was sufficient to create an interest in land, but could not be enforced without a written memorandum or part performance by the claimant. Kay J found that, although there was no written memorandum of the contract to grant an easement, there was the requisite part performance. For contracts entered into after 26 September 1989 the agreement to grant an easement, if it is to have the effect of creating an equitable easement, must be

---

[140] To be effective as a legal easement the grant must also be for an interest equivalent to a fee simple absolute or a term of years absolute; and (if granted over registered land) completed by registration: above, pp 650–1.

[141] A legal easement is a 'legal estate' within this definition: LPA 1925, s 1(4).

[142] *Wood v Leadbitter* (1845) 13 M & W 838, M & B p 1083; *Fentiman v Smith* (1803) 4 East 107, below, pp 926–7. For the creation of an easement through the doctrine of proprietary estoppel, see *ER Ives Investment Ltd v High* [1967] 2 QB 379, below, p 920; *Crabb v Arun DC* [1976] Ch 179, below, p 914.

[143] Above, pp 215 ff; below, p 978.

[144] *May v Belleville* [1905] 2 Ch 605.

[145] (1887) 35 Ch D 681.

in writing and signed by both dominant and servient owners, otherwise there is no contract at all.[146]

(3) Identification of dominant tenement

If the dominant tenement has not been clearly described by the parties, the court will identify it by construing the instrument that created the easement.[147]

(b) Express reservation

If the owner of two adjoining properties desired, upon the sale of one of them, to retain rights over that one, he could do so at common law either by way of *exception* from the grant or by way of *reservation*.[148] However, the only things that could be excepted were specific parts of the land, such as timber and minerals; and the word 'reservation' was only appropriate where services, such as the payment of rent, were to be rendered for the tenure of land.[149] If the vendor sought to retain an easement, therefore, it was formerly necessary either that the conveyance of the land should be executed by the *grantee* (whereupon the easement would arise by way of regrant from him),[150] or that the conveyance should be made to him to the *use* that the vendor should enjoy the easement and subject thereto *to the use* of the purchaser in fee simple.[151]

With the repeal of the Statute of Uses the latter method is now impossible, and the former is unnecessary, since section 65(1) the Law of Property Act 1925 provides that

> a reservation of a legal estate shall operate at law without any execution of the conveyance by the grantee of the legal estate out of which the reservation is made, or any regrant by him.

Such a reservation, however, still operates by way of regrant. Thus, where an easement is reserved by a vendor of land, the terms of the reservation in cases of doubt are to be construed against the purchaser and not against the vendor.[152]

It is also provided by section 65(2) that:

> a conveyance of a legal estate expressed to be made subject to another legal estate not in existence immediately before the date of the conveyance shall operate as a reservation unless a contrary intention appears.[153]

(c) Section 62 of the Law of Property Act 1925

(1) The section

It is of the greatest practical importance to observe that, owing to section 62 of the Law of Property Act 1925, a grant of land may have a far-reaching, and sometimes an

---

[146] Below, p 966.   [147] Below, p 686, n 371.
[148] *Durham and Sunderland Rly Co v Walker* (1842) 2 QB 940.
[149] Leake, *Uses and Profits of Land* (1888), p 265.   [150] *Wickham v Hawker* (1840) 7 M & W 63.
[151] Conveyancing Act 1881, s 62(1).
[152] *Johnstone v Holdway* [1963] 1 QB 601; *St Edmundsbury and Ipswich Diocesan Board of Finance v Clarke (No 2)* [1975] 1 WLR 468, M & B p 651.
[153] *Wiles v Banks* (1983) 50 P & CR 80 (conveyance 'subject to a right of way').

unexpected, effect upon the creation of easements. This section provides that unless a contrary intention is expressed in the conveyance:

> A conveyance of land shall be deemed to include and shall by virtue of this Act operate to convey, with the land, all buildings, erections, fixtures, commons, hedges, ditches, fences, ways, waters, watercourses, liberties, privileges, easements, rights, and advantages whatsoever, appertaining or reputed to appertain to the land or any part thereof, or, at the time of conveyance, demised, occupied, or enjoyed with, or reputed or known as part or parcel of or appurtenant to the land or any part thereof.[154]

The object of this section is to ensure that a grantee, without inserting numerous descriptive terms, usually called *general words*, in the conveyance, shall automatically[155] acquire the benefit not only of easements and other rights appurtenant to the land in the strict sense, but also of quasi-easements and other privileges that have hitherto been enjoyed in respect of the land. Easements already appurtenant to the land conveyed continue in favour of the grantee, but the statutory words are so sweeping and comprehensive that the conveyance, unless expressly limited in its operation, may have an effect far wider than the grantor intends. The effect indeed may be catastrophic in the sense that privileges that have hitherto been enjoyed by the permission of the grantor in respect of the land conveyed, a permission that could at any moment have been revoked, may acquire the status of permanent easements as a result of the conveyance.

> Suppose, for example, that A, the owner of two adjoining closes, Blackacre and Whiteacre, leases Blackacre to X, and as a friendly act allows X to use a path over Whiteacre as a short cut to the main road and also to store his coal in a shed on Whiteacre. Later A either sells or conveys the fee simple of Blackacre to X or renews X's lease of Blackacre.

In this case at the time of the conveyance there is a 'privilege ... enjoyed with the land' conveyed. The statute therefore comes into operation, and the effect of the conveyance, unless it expresses a contrary intention, is that a right of way over Whiteacre and a right to use the shed become appurtenant to Blackacre.[156]

> Again, if B, the owner of a mansion and park, allows Y, the tenant of the lodge at one of the gates, to use the main drive as a means of access to the neighbouring village, and later sells and conveys the fee simple of the lodge to him, a similar result follows. Y acquires an easement of way over the drive.[157]

---

[154] S 62(1), re-enacting Conveyancing Act 1881, s 6(1).

[155] Easements created by s 62 are commonly classified as created by express grant, rather than by implied grant, since the words are deemed by the statute to be written into the conveyance. However, such easements are not treated as expressly granted for the purpose of the registration requirement under LRA 2002, s 27(2)(d): ibid, s 27(7).

[156] *International Tea Stores Co v Hobbs* [1903] 2 Ch 165; *Wright v Macadam* [1949] 2 KB 744, M & B p 665.

[157] *International Tea Stores Co v Hobbs* [1903] 2 Ch 165,172; *Goldberg v Edwards* [1950] Ch 247, M & B p 668.

The permissive nature of the privilege enjoyed prior to the conveyance is quite irrelevant in these cases. The question is not whether the grantee had an enforceable right to enjoy the privilege, but, whether it was in fact enjoyed by him as occupant of the land prior to the conveyance.[158]

(2) Limits of the section

In spite of the wide wording of section 62, there are strict limits to its operation:

(i) Conveyance

The section does not operate unless there has been a 'conveyance' of land, a word that by statute includes 'a mortgage, charge, lease, assent, vesting declaration, vesting instrument, disclaimer, release and every other assurance of property or of an interest therein by any instrument, except a will'.[159]

This definition does not include an oral lease.[160] Nor does it include a contract for a lease or for the sale of land, since an assurance is 'something which operates as a transfer of property'[161] and a mere contract has no such operation, notwithstanding that under the doctrine of *Walsh v Lonsdale*[162] it is for many purposes as effective as a lease.[163]

The right must not only be enjoyed prior to the conveyance, it must also be enjoyed with the land[164] at the time of the conveyance. Megarry V-C said in *Penn v Wilkins:*[165]

> Section 62 was apt for conveying existing rights, but it did not resurrect mere memories of past rights. And likewise the section is not concerned with future rights.

---

[158] *Wright v Macadam* [1949] 2 KB 744, 750–1; *Phipps v Pears* [1965] 1 QB 76, M & B p 670. For a critical attitude to this effect of s 62(1), see *Wright v Macadam*, above, at 755 (Tucker LJ); *Green v Ashco Horticulturist Ltd* [1966] 1 WLR 889, 896 (Cross J); [1998] Conv 115 (L Tee). In Ireland, the Land and Conveyancing Reform Act 2009, s 71(3), now provides that the equivalent provision to s 62 LPA 1925 'does not on a conveyance of land... (i) create any new interest or right or convert any quasi-interest or right existing prior to the conveyance into a full interest or right, or (ii) extend the scope of, or convert into a new interest or right, any licence, privilege or other interest or right existing before the conveyance', confirming the decision of the Irish Supreme Court in *William Bennett Construction Ltd v Greene* [2004] 2 ILRM 96: see Wiley, *Irish Land Law* (4th edn, 2010), para 6.71. The Law Commission has also provisionally proposed that s 62 should no longer have the effect of transforming precarious benefits into legal easements: Law Com CP No 186, *Easements, Covenants and Profits à Prendre* (2008), para 4.104; below, p 723.

[159] LPA 1925, s 205(1)(ii).   [160] *Rye v Rye* [1962] AC 496, M & B p 355.

[161] *Re Ray* [1896] 1 Ch 468, 476.   [162] Above, pp 215 ff.

[163] *Borman v Griffith* [1930] 1 Ch 493, M & B p 420.

[164] Enjoyment is not synonymous with user: *Re Yateley Common, Hampshire* [1977] 1 WLR 840, 850. See *MRA Engineering Ltd v Trimster Co Ltd* (1987) 56 P & CR 1 (rights of access granted to an existing tenant held not to pass under s 62 on sale of freehold after surrender of the lease); *Re St Clement's, Leigh-on-Sea* [1988] 1 WLR 720.

[165] (1974) 236 EG 203 (passage of sewage that ceased many years before conveyance not covered by s 62). *Nickerson v Barraclough* [1981] Ch 426; *Payne v Inwood* (1996) 74 P & CR 42 at 47 (Roch LJ: 'section 62 cannot create new rights where there has been no actual enjoyment of a facility by the owner or occupier of the dominant tenement over the servient tenement'); [1997] Conv 453 (MP Thompson).

A right that is enjoyed with only part of the land conveyed may nevertheless benefit the whole. Thus in *Graham v Philcox*[166] the purchaser of the freehold of a converted coach house was also the tenant of a first floor flat in it that had the benefit of a right of way. The Court of Appeal held that, under section 62, the benefit of the right of way enured to the whole of the building. In effect the section operated to enlarge the extent of an existing easement.

(ii) Nature of right

No right will be conveyed by virtue of the Act, however, unless it is a right known to the law.[167] Lord Denning MR said in *Phipps v Pears:*[168]

> A fine view, or an expanse open to the winds, may be an 'advantage' to a house, but it would not pass under section 62. Whereas a right to use a coal shed or to go along a passage would pass under section 62. The reason being that these last are rights known to the law, whereas the others are not. A right to protection from the weather is not a right known to the law. It does not therefore pass under section 62.

And it must not be a right that the grantor at the time of the grant had no power to grant;[169] nor one that is merely a matter of personal contract;[170] nor one the enjoyment of which could only be expected to be temporary.[171]

(iii) Diversity of ownership or occupation

The section will not operate unless, as in the examples given above, there has been some diversity of ownership or occupation of the two closes prior to the conveyance.[172]

If, for example, the grantor, the common owner or occupier of Blackacre and Whiteacre, has been in the habit of passing over Blackacre in order to reach the highway, his conveyance of Whiteacre does not entitle the grantee to invoke the statute and to establish a right of way over Blackacre. What the grantor was accustomed to do

---

166 [1984] QB 747, M & B p 715, following *Wright v Macadam*, above; [1985] Conv 60 (P Todd); [1985] CLJ 15 (S Tromans).

167 *International Tea Stores Co v Hobbs* [1903] 2 Ch 165, 172; *Goldberg v Edwards* [1950] Ch 247; *Ward v Kirkland* [1967] Ch 194; *Green v Ashco Horticulturist Ltd* [1966] 1 WLR 889; *Phipps v Pears* [1965] 1 QB 76; *Crow v Wood* [1971] 1 QB 77.

168 Above, at 84.

169 *Quicke v Chapman* [1903] 1 Ch 659.

170 *Regis Property Co Ltd v Redman* [1956] 2 QB 612 (tenant's right to receive limited supply of hot water and central heating under contract with landlord).

171 *Wright v Macadam* [1949] 2 KB 744, 751 (Jenkins LJ), citing Cotton LJ in *Birmingham, Dudley and District Banking Co v Ross* (1888) 38 Ch D 295, 307; *Green v Ashco Horticulturist Ltd*, above, at 897; *Hair v Gillman* [2000] 3 EGLR 74, 76, where Chadwick LJ identified 'the distinction between a right that is temporary, in the sense that it is merely precarious, so that it can be withdrawn at any time, and a right that is temporary in the sense that, to the knowledge of the parties, it will only be capable of being enjoyed for some limited period because of the nature of the property over which it is enjoyed.' The former can become an easement under s 62; the latter cannot.

172 *Sovmots Investments Ltd v Secretary of State for the Environment* [1979] AC 144, 169, 176, M & B p 673, approving *Long v Gowlett* [1923] 2 Ch 177, M & B p 670. See *Ward v Kirkland* [1967] Ch 184, 227–31; *Wright v Macadam* [1949] 2 KB 744, 748; *Squarey v Harris-Smith* (1981) 42 P & CR 118 (Oliver LJ). For criticism of the rule, see Jackson, pp 100–3; (1966) 30 Conv (NS) 342–8; [1978] Conv 449 (P Smith); and in favour [1979] Conv 113 (C Harpum).

was attributable to his general rights as the occupying owner of both closes, not to a privilege deriving from his occupation of Whiteacre, as distinct from his occupation of Blackacre.[173] Approving what has come to be called the rule in *Long v Gowlett*, Lord Wilberforce said in *Sovmots Investments Ltd v Secretary of State for the Environment*:[174]

> When land is under one ownership one cannot speak in any intelligible sense of rights, or privileges, or easements being exercised over one part for the benefit of another. Whatever the owner does, he does as owner and until a separation occurs, of ownership, or at least of occupation, the condition for the existence of rights, etc, does not exist.

In order to substantiate his claim, the grantee would have to bring himself within the doctrine of an implied grant under the rule in *Wheeldon v Burrows*.[175]

In *P & S Platt Ltd v Crouch*,[176] however, the Court of Appeal held that section 62 can operate to create an easement where there is no prior diversity of occupation of the dominant and servient tenements, in a case where the easement is continuous and apparent. In that case:

> the defendants owned a hotel, a house in the grounds of the hotel, and a separate plot of land adjacent to the Norfolk Broads where river moorings were used for the benefit of the hotel guests. Signs at the river side made clear that the moorings were for the use of hotel guests only, and the hotel's web site advertised the availability of the moorings. The claimant purchased the hotel, but not the other properties. It was held that it had acquired the right to the moorings, for the benefit of the hotel, as an easement by virtue of section 62.

If confirmed, this decision will be a significant exception to the rule in *Long v Gowlett*.[177]

(iv) Subject to contrary intention

Section 62 applies only if and as far as a contrary intention is not expressed in the conveyance, and has effect subject to the terms of the conveyance;[178] it is also subject to the circumstances existing at the time of the grant.[179] In determining this, however, evidence of the contractual negotiations is not normally admissible.[180]

Enough has now been said to show that a grantor, who retains property adjoining that granted, or a landlord about to renew a lease, should be extremely vigilant to ensure that

---

[173] *Long v Gowlett*, above, at 200–1. The right to light, however, stands on a different footing: ibid, at 202–3, citing *Broomfield v Williams* [1897] 1 Ch 602.

[174] [1979] AC 144, 169.　　　　　　　　　　　　　　　　　　[175] Below, p 662.

[176] [2003] EWCA Civ 1110, [2004] 1 P & CR 18 at [47] (Peter Gibson LJ) and [59] (Longmore LJ); M & B p 675.

[177] *Sovmots Investments Ltd v Secretary of State for the Environment*, above, was not cited. It is significant in using one of the criteria for the application of the rule in *Wheeldon v Burrows* ('continuous and apparent') without the further requirement that the right be necessary for the reasonable enjoyment of the dominant tenement; below, p 662, n 207.

[178] LPA 1925, s 62(4).

[179] *Selby DC v Samuel Smith Old Brewery (Tadcaster) Ltd* [2001] 1 EGLR 71, 75 (per Chadwick LJ).

[180] *P & S Platt Ltd v Crouch*, above, at [37]-[39] (Peter Gibson LJ) and [52]-[56] (Longmore LJ); see generally *Chartbrook Ltd v Persimmon Homes Ltd* [2009] UKHL 38, [2009] 1 AC 1101; Anson, pp 167–8.

any advantages or privileges being enjoyed in respect of the land are either revoked or expressly excepted from the conveyance, unless he wishes them to continue.[181]

If an intention is shown in the preliminary contract of sale that a certain privilege shall not pass to the purchaser, the vendor is entitled to insert a clause in the deed of conveyance restrictive of the operation of the statute.[182] Moreover, in such a case he is entitled to have the conveyance rectified if, owing to the common mistake of the parties, it does not include a restrictive clause of this nature.[183]

(3) Acquisition by Implied Grant[184]

An owner, as we have seen, cannot have an easement over his own land.[185] Where, however, he has been accustomed to using one part in a particular manner, as for example by crossing a field to reach the highway, his practice is conveniently described as the exercise of a *quasi-easement*. If he later severs his ownership by granting part only of the land to another, such a quasi-easement is capable of ripening by implication into an easement properly so called in favour either of the land granted or the land retained.

The principle of this mode of creation is that although there has been no express mention of an easement in the grant of the land, yet it may very well be that the common intention of the parties cannot be carried out unless some particular easement is deemed to arise by implication.

The premises for the application of the doctrine are, first, that A, the owner of two separate tenements, has been in the habit of enjoying certain quasi-easements over one of them; and secondly, that the common ownership of A has been severed. Thus, if A sells the quasi-servient tenement, certain easements may be implied in his favour over the part sold (*implied reservation*); if he sells the quasi-dominant tenement, certain easements may be implied against him and in favour of the purchaser (*implied grant*); while the question of implication may also arise when he disposes of both the tenements to different persons. We shall now consider these three cases separately.

---

[181] See Standard Conditions of Sale (4th edn, 2003), Condition 3.4 (not included in 5th edn, 2011); Wilkinson, *Standard Conditions of Sale of Land* (4th edn, 1990), pp 29–33.

[182] *Squarey v Harris-Smith* (1981) 42 P & CR 118 (where a standard condition that the purchaser should not acquire any rights that would restrict the free use of the vendor's other land for building was held to negative the operation of s 62); cf *Lyme Valley Squash Club Ltd v Newcastle under Lyme BC* [1985] 2 All ER 405, in which *Squarey v Harris-Smith* was not cited, and the opposite conclusion reached; [1985] Conv 243. See also *William Hill (Southern) Ltd v Cabras Ltd* [1987] 1 EGLR 37; *Pretoria Warehousing Co Ltd v Shelton* [1993] EGCS 120; [1996] Conv 238 (A Dowling); *Millman v Ellis* (1995) 71 P & CR 158 (grant of narrower easement not necessarily a contrary intention); [1995] Conv 346 (J West); *Selby DC v Samuel Smith Old Brewery (Tadcaster) Ltd* [2001] 1 EGLR 71.

[183] *Clark v Barnes* [1929] 2 Ch 368.

[184] See generally Farrand, *Contract and Conveyance* (2nd edn, 1973), pp 382–90.

[185] Above, pp 638–9.

(a) Implied reservation. Common owner sells quasi-servient tenement

The law is disinclined to imply easements in favour of a grantor. The reason is not difficult to find. In the case of a grant of land the law is guided by two principles: the words of a deed must be construed as far as possible in favour of the grantee;[186] and the grantor cannot derogate from his own absolute grant by claiming rights over the thing granted.[187] If the grantor intends to retain a right over the land, it is his duty to reserve it expressly in the grant.[188] As a general rule there will be no implication in his favour.[189]

(1) Easements of necessity

There are exceptions to this rule, the most obvious of which is the way of necessity. This arises where land that is entirely surrounded by other land is segregated by the common owner, and retained by him. In such a case a way is implied in favour of the grantor.[190] However, the implication of a reservation of a way of necessity is based not on public policy, but on an implication from the circumstances of the grant of the land,[191] and so no right of way will be implied, even where the retained land thereby becomes landlocked, where the grant is to an associated company and the grantor could at that time expect to be able to enjoy rights of access even though they would not be legally enforceable.[192]

The extent of the implied right is strictly limited and depends upon the mode of enjoyment of the surrounded land prevailing at the time of the grant.[193] The way may be used for any purpose that is essential to maintain that mode of enjoyment; it may not be used for other purposes. Thus where at the time of the grant the surrounded close was used only for agricultural purposes, it was held that the grantor was not entitled to carry over it timber and other materials.[194]

---

[186] *Neill v Duke of Devonshire* [1882] 8 App Cas 135, 149 (Lord Selborne). Cf Lewison, *Interpretation of Contracts*, para 7.08, noting that this *contra proferentem* rule of construction is not always applied consistently, particularly in the modern cases.

[187] *Suffield v Brown* (1864) 4 De GJ & Sm 185 (Lord Westbury). See generally (1964) 80 LQR 244 (DW Elliott). The rule may be varied by contract; see Standard Conditions of Sale (4th edn, 2003), para 3.4 (not included in 5th edn, 2011).

[188] *Wheeldon v Burrows* (1879) 12 Ch D 31, 49 (Thesiger LJ). The precise nature of the reserved right need not, however, be spelt out expressly: *Hall v Moore* [2009] EWCA Civ 201, [2009] 2 EGLR 31 at [7].

[189] Ibid; *Aldridge v Wright* [1929] 2 KB 117; *Liddiard v Waldron* [1934] 1 KB 435; *Re Webb's Lease* [1951] Ch 808, M & B p 682. This paragraph was cited with approval by Cazalet J in *Peckham v Ellison* (2000) 79 P & CR 276, 285.

[190] *Union Lighterage Co v London Graving Dock Co* [1902] 2 Ch 557, 573; *Pinnington v Galland* (1853) 9 Exch 1; *Sweet v Sommer* [2004] EWHC 1504 (Ch), [2004] 4 All ER 288 (retained land to be regarded as landlocked where access could be obtained only over the property granted or by destruction of a physical barrier on the retained land (a building) the continued existence of which was obviously contemplated by the parties); affd on other grounds [2005] EWCA Civ 227, [2005] All ER (D) 162 (Mar).

[191] *Nickerson v Barraclough* [1981] Ch 426, below, p 661; *Adealon International Corp Pty Ltd v Merton LBC* [2007] EWCA Civ 362, [2007] 1 WLR 1898 at [11].

[192] *Adealon International Corp Pty Ltd v Merton LBC*, above, n 191; M & B p 685.

[193] *London Corp v Riggs* (1880) 13 Ch D 798, M & B p 680.

[194] Ibid; *Serff v Acton Local Board* (1886) 31 Ch D 679.

(2) Easements of common intention

Easements will also be implied in favour of the grantor as may be necessary to give effect to the common intention of grantor and grantee as for example where mutual easements of support are implied on the conveyance of one of two adjacent buildings supported by each other.[195] There may be other cases where such easements will be implied in favour of a grantor without express reservation,[196] but the scales are heavily weighted against him. The necessary inference from the circumstances must be that he was intended to retain the precise easement that he claims.[197]

(b) Implied grant. Common owner sells quasi-dominant tenement

The law is much more inclined to imply easements in favour of the grantee than in favour of the grantor.

(1) Easements of necessity

As we have seen, easements of necessity may be impliedly reserved in favour of a grantor over the quasi-servient tenement that he has granted. Consistently with the principle that a grantor may not derogate from his grant, the law more readily implies easements in favour of the grantee of the quasi-dominant tenement; a fortiori an easement of necessity will be implied in his favour.[198]

In *Nickerson v Barraclough*,[199] the Court of Appeal rejected an argument that, if the implied grant of a way of necessity has been negated by an express contrary provision, such a grant may nevertheless be implied under a rule of public policy that 'no transaction should, without good reason, be treated as effectual to deprive land of a suitable means of access'.[200] Brightman LJ said:[201]

> The doctrine of way of necessity is not founded upon public policy at all but upon an implication from the circumstances ... There would seem to be no particular reason to father the doctrine ... upon public policy when implication is such an obvious and convenient candidate for paternity.

The Court of Appeal held that a way of necessity could only exist in association with a grant of land, and depended on the intention of the parties and the implication from the circumstances that, unless some way was implied, the land would be inaccessible.

---

[195] *Richards v Rose* (1853) 9 Exch 218; *Shubrook v Tufnell* (1882) 46 LT 886.

[196] *Re Webb's Lease* [1951] Ch 808, 816–17, 823.

[197] Ibid, 828 (easement not implied); *Peckham v Ellison*, above (easement implied, having regard to length of user of path by dominant owner and disclosure of existence of right to servient owner at time of purchase); [1999] Conv 353 (L Fox).

[198] See *Liverpool City Council v Irwin* [1977] AC 239, above, p 645; cf *Manjang v Drammeh* (1990) 61 P & CR 194 (PC held no easement of necessity where available access by water across the River Gambia 'albeit perhaps less convenient than access across *terra firma*'); *MRA Engineering Ltd v Trimster Co Ltd* (1987) 56 P & CR 1 (no easement of necessity because access on foot was 'merely difficult and inconvenient'; land was not inaccessible or useless without right of way claimed).

[199] [1981] Ch 426 reversing Megarry V-C [1980] Ch 325; (1982) 98 LQR 11 (P Jackson). For a comparative study of legal solutions on access to landlocked land, see (1982) 10 Syd LR 39 (AJ Bradbrook).

[200] [1980] Ch 325, 334 (Megarry V-C).   [201] [1981] Ch 426, 440.

Public policy could not help the court to ascertain that intention;[202] it could only require the court to frustrate that intention where a contract was against public policy.

(2) Easements of common intention

Similarly the law more readily implies easements of common intention in favour of the grantee. Lord Parker of Waddington said:[203]

> The law will readily imply the grant or reservation of easements as may be necessary to give effect to the common intention of the parties to a grant of real property, with reference to the manner or purposes in and for which the land granted ... is to be used. But it is essential for this purpose that the parties should intend that the subject of the grant ... should be used in some definite and particular manner. It is not enough that the subject of the grant should be intended to be used in a manner which may or may not involve this definite and particular use.

In *Wong v Beaumont Property Trust Ltd*:[204]

> three cellars in Exeter were let by B's predecessor in title to W's predecessor in title for the purpose of being used as a Chinese restaurant. By certain statutory regulations no premises could be used for this purpose unless they were provided with a ventilation system. In the circumstances, it was impossible to install this without affixing a duct to the outside walls of B's superjacent building.

The Court of Appeal granted a declaration that W was entitled to an easement of necessity,[205] and was entitled to construct and maintain the duct.

(3) Easements within the rule in *Wheeldon v Burrows*[206]

The rule was laid down in an obiter dictum by Thesiger LJ in *Wheeldon v Burrows*, which has been accepted as a correct statement of the law, that:

> on the grant by the owner of a tenement of part of that tenement as it is then used and enjoyed, there will pass to the grantee all those continuous and apparent easements (by which, of course, I mean quasi-easements), or, in other words, all those easements which are necessary to the reasonable enjoyment of the property granted,[207] and which have been

---

[202] Eveleigh LJ at 383 thought that in a rare case public policy might help.

[203] *Pwllbach Colliery Co Ltd v Woodman* [1915] AC 634, 646; cf *Stafford v Lee* (1992) 65 P & CR 172.

[204] [1965] 1 QB 173, M & B p 660; *Stafford v Lee* (1992) 65 P & CR 172; *Mobil Oil Co Ltd v Birmingham CC* [2001] EWCA Civ 1608, [2002] 2 P & CR 14; *Davies v Bramwell* [2007] EWCA Civ 821, [2008] 1 P & CR DG2.

[205] The court classified this as an easement of necessity, but this must be an error. 'An easement is surely not an "easement of necessity" merely because it is necessary to give effect to the intention' (1964) 80 LQR 322 (REM). But the two headings may overlap: see *Nickerson v Barraclough* [1980] Ch 325, 332.

[206] *Wheeldon v Burrows* (1879) 12 Ch D 31, 49, M & B p 656. The case itself was a decision on implied reservation. In Ireland, Land and Conveyancing Law Reform Act 2009, s 40, abolished the rule in *Wheeldon v Burrows* and replaced it with a statutory provision based more closely on the doctrine of non-derogation from grant: Wiley, *Irish Land Law*, para 6.68.

[207] At 58 Thesiger LJ appears to treat these as two alternative requirements, and not, as here, synonymous. See *Ward v Kirkland* [1967] Ch 194, 224 (Ungoed-Thomas J); M & B p 658; *Squarey v Harris-Smith* (1981)

and are at the time of the grant used by the owner of the entirety for the benefit of the part granted.

This rule is also a rule of intention, based on the proposition that a grantor may not derogate from his grant:[208]

He cannot grant or agree to grant land and at the same time deny to the grantee what is at the time of the grant obviously necessary for its reasonable enjoyment.

Thus, for example, it has been law since 1663 that a person who grants a house in which there are windows cannot build on his own adjoining land so as to obstruct the light.[209] It also follows that the rule cannot apply in the case of a compulsory purchase of land; that would mean substituting for the intention of a reasonable voluntary grantor the unilateral, opposed, intention of the acquirer.[210]

It was held by the Court of Appeal in *Kent v Kavanagh* that the rule in *Wheeldon v Burrows* does not apply where there is already diversity of occupation between the dominant and servient tenements.[211] This is a rather literal and strict reading of Thesiger LJ's judgment, set out above, and it has the effect of restricting the operation of the rule in *Wheeldon v Burrows* and therefore placing more emphasis on the operation of section 62 of the Law of Property Act 1925 as a basis for the implied grant of easements.[212] But it has the result that the rule is inapplicable where the freeholder, who has already granted a lease of part of his property (but without granting an easement over the retained land to the tenant) later transfers the freehold of the leased part to the tenant. Chadwick LJ said:[213]

The two propositions[214] which, together, comprise the rule (or rules) in *Wheeldon v Burrows* are confined, in their application, to cases in which, by reason of the conveyance (or lease), land formerly in common ownership ceases to be owned by the same person.

42 P & CR 118, 124 (Oliver LJ: a right of way was necessary to the reasonable enjoyment of land 'having regard to the purpose for which, in the contemplation of both parties, it was sold', but any implied right was excluded by a condition of sale incorporated into the contract); (1967) 83 LQR 240 (AWB Simpson); *Wheeler v J J Saunders Ltd* [1996] Ch 19, 30 (Peter Gibson LJ); [1995] Conv 239 (MP Thompson); [1995] All ER Rev 311 (PJ Clarke).

208 *Sovmots Investments Ltd v Secretary of State for the Environment* [1979] AC 144, 168 (Lord Wilberforce); (1977) 41 Conv NS 415 (C Harpum).

209 *Palmer v Fletcher* (1663) 1 Lev 122; *Phillips v Low* [1892] 1 Ch 47.

210 *Sovmots Investments Ltd v Secretary of State for the Environment*, above, at 168–9. Cf *Kent v Kavanagh* [2006] EWCA Civ 162, [2007] Ch 1 (statutory obligation to convey freehold to tenant under Leasehold Reform Act 1967, above, p 390, does not of itself exclude the rule in *Wheeldon v Burrows* because (unlike in the compulsory purchaser legislation) ss 5(3) and 22(2) of the 1967 Act provide for the rights, obligations and remedies to be the same as under a contract freely entered into).

211 [2006] EWCA Civ 162, [2007] Ch 1, M &B p 658; [2006] All ER Rev 252 (PJ Clarke).

212 This preference for s 62 is emphasised further if s 62 can operate where there is no diversity of occupation but the (quasi-)easement is continuous and apparent: *P & S Platt Ltd v Crouch* [2003] EWCA Civ 1110, [2004] 1 P & CR 18, above, p 658.

213 Ibid, at [43], [45].

214 Ie, the principle set out above from Thesiger LJ's judgment, together with the second proposition that if the grantor intends to retain a right over the land, it is his duty to reserve it expressly in the grant: *Wheeldon v Burrows* (1879) 12 Ch D 31, 49; above, p 660.

It is in cases of that nature that, in order to give effect to what must be taken to be the common intention of the grantor and the grantee, the conveyance (or lease) will operate as a grant (for the benefit of the land conveyed) of such easements over the land retained by the grantor as are necessary to the reasonable enjoyment of the land conveyed. But, because the principle is founded on the common intention of the parties, the easements necessary to the reasonable enjoyment of the land conveyed are those which reflect (and, following separation of ownership, are needed to give effect to) the use and enjoyment of the land conveyed at the time of the conveyance and while that land and the retained land were in the common ownership of the grantor.

...It seems to me an unnecessary and artificial construct to hold that the grantor, as common owner and the landlord of the land conveyed, is himself using the rights over the retained land which his tenant enjoys under the lease.

However, the implication of an easement can also be negatived by contrary intention: the rule in *Wheeldon v Burrows* only operates to the extent that it is not inconsistent with the intentions of the parties, which may be inferred from the circumstances.[215]

It will be noticed that, unlike section 62 of the Law of Property Act 1925, the rule in *Wheeldon v Burrows* is limited to continuous and apparent easements.[216] Strictly speaking a continuous easement is one, such as the right to light, the constant enjoyment of which does not, as in the case of a right of way, require the active intervention of the dominant owner. The word 'continuous', however, is not in this context to be taken in its strict sense but rather in the sense of permanence. The two words 'continuous' and 'apparent' must be read together and understood as pointing to an easement that is accompanied by some obvious and permanent mark on the land itself, or at least by some mark that will be disclosed by a careful inspection of the premises.[217] Examples are:

  (i) watercourses consisting of some actual construction such as pipes;[218]

  (ii) a made road;[219]

  (iii) light flowing through windows;[220]

  (iv) drains that can be discovered with ordinary care.[221]

A right of way is not necessarily such a quasi-easement as will pass under the rule in *Wheeldon v Burrows*. To do so it must be apparent. There is no difficulty where there

---

[215] *Selby DC v Samuel Smith Old Brewery (Tadcaster) Ltd* [2001] 1 EGLR 71, 74 (Peter Gibson LJ).

[216] For an illuminating discussion of the origins of the words 'continuous' and 'apparent' in the French Civil Code, adopted first by Gale and then later by Thesiger LJ in *Wheeldon v Burrows*, see (1967) 83 LQR 240 (AWB Simpson).

[217] *Pyer v Carter* (1857) 1 H & N 916, 922, adopting *Gale on Easements*; *Ward v Kirkland* [1967] Ch 194 (right to enter neighbour's land to repair and maintain a wall held to be not continuous and apparent; it was, however, held to be an easement created under LPA 1925, s 62; above, p 654).

[218] *Watts v Kelson* (1871) 6 Ch App 166; *Schwann v Cotton* [1916] 2 Ch 120; affd [1916] 2 Ch 459.

[219] *Brown v Alabaster* (1887) 37 Ch D 490.   [220] *Allen v Taylor* (1880) 16 Ch D 355.

[221] *Pyer v Carter*, above.

is a definite made road over the quasi-servient tenement to and for the apparent use of the quasi-dominant tenement. Such will clearly pass upon a severance of the common tenement.[222] But the existence of a formed road is not essential, and if there are other indicia that show that the road was being used at the time of the grant for the benefit of the quasi-dominant tenement and that it is necessary for the reasonable enjoyment of that tenement,[223] it will pass to a purchaser of the latter.[224] Thus:

> A man built four cottages on his own land and left a strip between the rear of the cottages and the boundary of his land in order to afford a back means of access to the main highway. It was held that the quasi-easement of way was sufficiently continuous and apparent to pass under the present doctrine, for at the time of the grant the strip, though not formed into a made road, was worn and marked with rough tracks, so that no one seeing it could doubt that it was used as a way to the cottages.[225]

This doctrine of *Wheeldon v Burrows* has been shorn of much of its importance by section 62 of the Law of Property Act 1925,[226] but it still remains available in those cases where section 62 is inapplicable, either because there has been no diversity of occupation prior to a conveyance,[227] or because there has been no 'conveyance' as defined by the Act.[228] Thus in *Borman v Griffith*:[229]

> X, who owned a large park containing two houses, The Gardens and The Hall, agreed in writing to lease The Gardens to the claimant for seven years. A drive ran from the public road to The Hall, passing en route close to The Gardens. There was no separate drive for The Gardens, but at the time of the agreement X was constructing, and he later completed, an unmetalled way which ran from the back door of the house to the public road. The agreement reserved no right of way to the claimant, but he constantly used The Hall drive in preference to the unmetalled way. Later, the defendant took a lease from X of The Hall and the rest of the park, and began to obstruct the claimant in his use of the drive. In the ensuing action the claimant claimed to be entitled to a right of way over the drive.

The question, therefore, was whether the claimant had acquired the quasi-easement that the common owner of the whole land had exercised over the drive when passing from The Gardens to the public road. There was clearly no easement of necessity, since

---

[222] *Brown v Alabaster*, above; *Davies v Sear* (1869) LR 7 Eq 427.

[223] 'Necessary' must not be confused with 'necessity' (see 'easements of necessity', above, p 661). A way of necessity is one without which the property cannot be used at all, but 'necessary' in the present connection indicates that the way conduces to the reasonable enjoyment of the property. This note was cited with approval by Peter Gibson LJ in *Wheeler v JJ Saunders Ltd* [1996] Ch 19, 31.

[224] *Hansford v Jago* [1921] 1 Ch 322; *Borman v Griffith* [1930] 1 Ch 493, 499. This paragraph was cited with approval in *Ward v Kirkland* [1967] Ch 194, 225.

[225] *Hansford v Jago* [1921] 1 Ch 322.   [226] Above, p 654.

[227] On whether diversity of ownership or occupation is still a requirement for s 62, see *P & S Platt Ltd v Crouch* [2003] EWCA Civ 1110, [2004] 1 P & CR 18, above, p 658.

[228] Above, p 656; *Donaldson v Smith* [2007] 1 P & CR DG2 (appropriation and appointment of property between beneficiaries of a settlement by the trustees, but no conveyance executed to transfer legal title). Where the grant is implied into a contract, rather than a conveyance, it must necessarily create only an equitable easement: above, p 653. S 62, however, is wider, in that the right need not be 'continuous and apparent', nor 'necessary to the reasonable enjoyment of the property granted'.

[229] [1930] 1 Ch 493, M & B p 420; *Horn v Hiscock* (1972) 223 EG 1437.

the unmetalled way provided a means of approach to the outside world. It was equally clear that section 62 was inapplicable to a contract for a lease. Nevertheless it was held that an easement of way had arisen by implication in favour of the claimant according to the doctrine of *Wheeldon v Burrows*. Thus, under that doctrine a grantee acquires those easements to which he has an implied contractual right; but under section 62 of the Law of Property Act 1925, the conveyance may vest in him an easement to which he has no contractual right whatsoever.[230]

(c) Contemporaneous sales to different persons

Where, instead of a sale of part of the land and a retention by the common owner of the other part, there have been simultaneous sales effected of separate but *contemporaneous* conveyances to different persons, all those continuous and apparent quasi-easements that were in use at the time of the sales pass by implication with the respective parts.[231] In other words, when the sales are by the same vendor and take place at one and the same time, the rights of each of the purchasers are exactly the same as if the common owner had sold the dominant part and kept the rest of the land.

Thus in *Schwann v Cotton*[232] where a testator devised Blackacre to X and Whiteacre to Y, it was held that a right to the free passage of water that flowed through an underground pipe running across Blackacre to Whiteacre passed by implication to the devisee of Whiteacre.

If the sales are not simultaneous, the later purchaser is in the same position as his vendor. So if the vendor first sells the quasi-servient tenement, he will not, in the absence of an express reservation, be entitled to easements over the part sold, except a way of necessity where one exists, nor will a subsequent purchaser from him be in any better position;[233] but if the vendor first sells the quasi-dominant tenement, the purchaser can enforce quasi-easements against a subsequent purchaser of the quasi-servient tenement to the same extent as he could have done against the vendor.

(4) Acquisition by Presumed Grant or Prescription

Proof of the existence of an easement may be based upon a mere presumption that at some time in the past it has been granted by deed. There are three possible methods by which a claimant may avail himself of this presumption, for he may plead prescription:

(i) at common law; or

---

[230] (1952) 15 MLR pp 265–6 (AD Hargreaves).

[231] *Allen v Taylor* (1880) 16 Ch D 355; *Swansborough v Coventry* (1832) 9 Bing 305; *Barnes v Loach* (1879) 4 QBD 494; *Schwann v Cotton* [1916] 2 Ch 120; affd 459; *Hansford v Jago* [1921] 1 Ch 322. See also *Donaldson v Smith*, above, n 228 (appointment of property by trustees to two groups of beneficiaries made four months apart but following an earlier appropriation of the property between the beneficiaries: appointments regarded as part and parcel of a single transaction).

[232] Above.

[233] *Murchie v Black* (1865) 19 CBNS 190.

(ii) under the doctrine of lost modern grant; or

(iii) under the Prescription Act 1832.

Each method is based upon identical reasoning. The established principle is that an easement must be created by deed of grant, since incorporeal hereditaments lie in grant.[234] On the other hand, it is obviously undesirable that one should be deprived of an easement long and continuously enjoyed merely because its formal creation by deed is incapable of proof. Therefore, the law is prepared to infer from this long enjoyment that all those acts were done that were necessary to create a valid title.[235] In this way, a claim, founded upon actual enjoyment without interruption by the servient owner, is referred to a lawful origin.

(a) Nature of user

Long enjoyment, however, is not in itself sufficient to raise the presumption of a grant. It must be of a particular nature, and this is so whether an easement is claimed by prescription at common law, or under the doctrine of lost modern grant or under the Prescription Act 1832. As we shall see, the user must be as of right and continuous, and only a grant in fee simple will be presumed.

All forms of prescription ultimately depend on the acquiescence of the servient owner. Why should long user confer a right protected by the courts? The answer is, that if the servient owner has allowed somebody to exercise an easement over his land for a considerable period and if he has omitted to prevent such exercise when he might very well have done so, it is only reasonable to conclude that the privilege has been rightfully enjoyed, for otherwise some attempt to interfere with it would long ago have been made by any owner who possessed even a modicum of common sense. Fry J said in *Dalton v Angus & Co*:[236]

> In my opinion, the whole law of prescription and the whole law that governs the presumption or inference of a grant or covenant rest upon acquiescence. The courts and the judges have had recourse to various expedients for quieting the possession of persons in the exercise of rights that have not been resisted by the persons against whom they are exercised; but in all cases it appears to me that acquiescence and nothing else is the principle upon which these expedients rest. It becomes then of the highest importance to consider of what ingredients acquiescence consists... I cannot imagine any case of acquiescence in which there is not shewn to be in the servient owner:
>
> (1) a knowledge of the acts done;
>
> (2) a power in him to stop the acts or to sue in respect of them; and
>
> (3) an abstinence on his part from the exercise of such power.

---

[234] Above, p 652.

[235] In accordance with the maxim *omnia praesumuntur rite et sollemniter esse acta. Philipps v Halliday* [1891] AC 228, 231; *Foster v Warblington UDC* [1906] 1 KB 648, 679.

[236] (1881) 6 App Cas 740, 773. Lord Penzance (at 803) was 'in entire accord with' Fry J, and Lord Blackburn (at 823) described it as 'a very able opinion'. Thesiger LJ had used very similar language to that of Fry J in *Sturges v Bridgman* (1879) 11 Ch D 852, 863.

Since the doctrine of prescription depends on acquiescence by the servient landowner, however, an inquiry into the state of mind of the owner of the dominant tenement is irrelevant.[237]

(1) User as of right

This stress upon the element of acquiescence gives the clue to the kind of user required for a prescriptive title. In technical language, it must be *user as of right*,[238] or, to use the expression taken by Coke from Bracton,[239] *longus usus nec per vim, nec clam, nec precario*. The servient owner cannot be said to have acquiesced in an easement that has been enjoyed *vi, clam* or *precario* (by force, by stealth or by permission).

Thus, if the dominant owner has used coercion, or if his user is contentious in the sense that the servient owner continually and unmistakably protests against it, there is, clearly no acquiescence, and the user, being *vi*, that is by force, will not avail the claimant.[240] Again, there is no acquiescence if the user has been *clam*, that is by stealth, for a man cannot assent to something of which he is ignorant, and the law allows no prescriptive right to be acquired where there has been any concealment or where the enjoyment has not been open.[241] It must always be found that the servient owner had actual or constructive knowledge of the enjoyment upon which the claimant relies.[242] Lastly, where the user has been *precario*, that is where it is enjoyed by the permission of the servient owner and the permission is one which he may withdraw at any moment, it cannot be said that he has acquiesced in the existence of the easement as a matter of right. To ask permission is to acknowledge that no right exists. In this case an explanation of the user is forthcoming, and an irrevocable right to the perpetual enjoyment of the easement is not consistent with the explanation. What a claimant must show is that he claims the privilege not as a thing permitted to him from time

---

[237] *R v Oxfordshire CC, ex p Sunningwell Parish Council* [2000] 1 AC 335, 355-6; *London Tara Hotel Ltd v Kensington Close Hotel Ltd* [2010] EWHC 2479 (Ch), [2010] 45 EGCS 92 at [47].

[238] *Gardner v Hodgson's Kingston Brewery Co Ltd* [1903] AC 229, M & B p 689; *Tickle v Brown* (1836) 4 Ad & El 369; *Healey v Hawkins* [1968] 1 WLR 1967, M & B p 692.

[239] Co Litt 113b. The use of the noun *precarium* was taken by Bracton from Roman law, but not in the same sense as it was used there: *R (Beresford) v Sunderland City Council* [2003] UKHL 60, [2004] 1 AC 889 at [57]-[58] (Lord Rodger of Earlsferry).

[240] *Eaton v Swansea Waterworks Co* (1851) 17 QB 267; *Dalton v Angus & Co* (1881) 6 App Cas 740, 786; *Hollins v Verney* (1884) 13 QBD 304, 307; *Smith v Brudenell-Bruce* [2002] 2 P & CR 4 at [12] (Pumfrey J): 'a user ceases to be user 'as of right' if the circumstances are such as to indicate to the dominant owner, or to a reasonable man with the dominant owner's knowledge of the circumstances, that the servient owner actually objects and continues to object and will back his objection either by physical obstruction or by legal action'.

[241] *Union Lighterage Co v London Graving Dock Co* [1902] 2 Ch 557, M & B p 703, in which a dock-owner's claim to an easement of support by means of invisible rods sunk under the adjoining land was disallowed; *Dalton v Angus & Co* (1881) 6 App Cas 740, 827; *Wilsons Brewery v West Yorkshire Metropolitan County Council* (1977) 34 P & CR 224; *Liverpool Corp v H Coghill & Son Ltd* [1918] 1 Ch 307 (injurious substances discharged into the public sewer at night for more than 20 years); *Scott-Whitehead v National Coal Board* (1987) 53 P & CR 263; *Barney v BP Truckstops Ltd* [1995] NPC 5 (drain used for sewage).

[242] *Lloyds Bank Ltd v Dalton Ltd* [1942] Ch 466; *Davies v Du Paver* [1953] 1 QB 184, M & B p 701; cf *Dance v Triplow* [1992] 1 EGLR 190 (where the claimants 'failed to prove both their unwillingness to tolerate the interruption and some word or act making that clear to the defendant': Glidewell LJ); [1992] Conv 197 (J Martin).

to time by the servient owner, but as a thing that he has a right to do. For example, a woman relied upon 60 years' user of a cartway from her stables through the yard of an adjoining inn, but on it appearing that she had paid 15s each year for this privilege, it was held by the House of Lords that the user, being *precario*, was not *as of right*.[243]

Thus a common method of preventing user from developing into a right is to exact a small periodical payment, and although in such a case there is in one sense a right to enjoy what has been paid for, yet it does not amount to a right to a permanent easement, but at the most to a right to damages for breach of contract.[244]

Where, however, user was pursuant to an express licence that was strictly personal to one particular owner of the dominant tenement, user by his successor may not be impliedly licensed and so may constitute the basis of a claim to a prescriptive right.[245]

(2) User must be continuous

In addition to being *as of right*, user must also be continuous, though the continuity varies according to the nature of the right in question. For example, a right of way from the nature of the case admits only of occasional enjoyment, and therefore if it is used as and when occasion demands, the requirement of continuity is satisfied.[246] But so far as a discontinuous easement, such as a right of way, is concerned, it is impossible to define what in every case constitutes sufficient continuity of user. Every case must depend upon the exact nature of the right claimed, and all that can be said is that the user must be such as to disclose to the servient owner the fact that a continuous right to enjoyment is being asserted and that therefore it ought to be resisted if it is not to ripen into a permanent right.[247] It has been suggested that toleration by the alleged servient owner of a particular user is not to be equated to acquiescence, and therefore a prescriptive claim cannot be based on such user.[248]

Toleration, however, is not inconsistent with user as of right,[249] and the question in each case is whether the use is such as 'to bring home to the mind of a reasonable person that a continuous right of enjoyment is being asserted. If it is and the owner of

[243] *Gardner v Hodgson's Kingston Brewery Co Ltd* [1903] AC 229, M & B p 689; [1998] Conv 442, 448 (E Simpson); *Diment v N H Foot Ltd* [1974] 1 WLR 1427 (agent's knowledge); *Patel v W H Smith (Eziot) Ltd* [1987] 1 WLR 853; *R (Beresford) v Sunderland City Council*, above, where HL considered the meaning of *nec precario* in a claim to a town or village green within Commons Registration Act 1965, s 22 (and in the prescription of easements generally).

[244] Ibid, at 231. For the effect of mistake on user as of right, see *Bridle v Ruby* [1989] QB 169, where CA held that a right of way was acquired under the doctrine of lost modern grant even though there was a mistaken view of both parties as to existing rights. See too *Thomas W Ward Ltd v Alexander Bruce (Grays) Ltd* [1959] 2 Lloyd's Rep 472, where Harman LJ also reviewed *Earl de la Warr v Miles* (1881) 17 Ch D 535 and *Chamber Colliery Co v Hopwood* (1886) 32 Ch D 549; *Hamilton v Joyce* [1984] 3 NSWLR 279; [1986] Conv 356 (AH Hudson).

[245] *London Tara Hotel Ltd v Kensington Close Hotel Ltd*, above, n 237.

[246] *Dare v Heathcote* (1856) 25 LJ Ex 245.

[247] *Hollins v Verney* (1884) 13 QBD 304, 315. In that case a right of way was claimed for the purpose of removing wood cut upon adjoining land, but the evidence showed that the right had been exercised only on three occasions at intervals of 12 years. The Court of Appeal held that there had not been sufficient continuity of enjoyment.

[248] *Patel v W H Smith (Eziot) Ltd* [1987] 1 WLR 853.

[249] *R v Oxfordshire CC, ex p Sunningwell Parish Council* [2000] 1 AC 335, 358 (Lord Hoffmann).

the allegedly servient tenement knows or must be taken to know of it and does nothing about it the right is established. It is no answer for him to say, "I 'tolerated' it." '[250]

The right that is claimed on the ground of its continuous and uninterrupted exercise for a period of time need not have been exercised by the same person throughout the whole period: it is sufficient that it has been exercised by the successive owners of the estate in the dominant tenement to which the easement is appurtenant. Nor need it continue to be exercised in precisely the same manner; thus, where the dominant and servient owners agreed upon a variation of the route of a right of way for their own convenience, it was held that the user of the substituted route was substantially an exercise of the old right.[251]

(3) User in fee simple

Since the basis of a prescriptive claim is immemorial user, an easement can be prescribed for only in respect of a fee simple estate. The rule is absolute that an easement claimed either by prescription at common law, or under the doctrine of a lost grant or under the Prescription Act 1832 must be claimed in favour of the fee simple estate in the dominant tenement.[252] An easement may be granted expressly for a lesser interest than a fee simple, but it cannot arise by virtue of a presumed grant. A tenant for years, no matter what the length of his lease may be, cannot for example acquire a right of way over the adjoining land of his lessor.[253] He may, however, acquire by prescription an easement against the land of a stranger, though if he does so it enures for the benefit of the fee simple and does not cease with the cessation of his leasehold interest.[254] Furthermore, if the *servient* tenement is occupied by a tenant at the beginning of the period of user, the claim for an easement by prescription depends on whether the freehold owner could take steps to prevent the user during the tenancy, which is likely to turn on the terms of the tenancy. If so, it depends on whether (and, if so, when) the freeholder had actual or imputed knowledge of the user by the owner of the dominant tenement.[255] But if the user begins against a fee simple owner who subsequently lets the servient tenement, then it is necessary to ask whether the owner had actual or imputed knowledge at or before the date of the grant. If so, then, regardless of the terms of the

---

[250] *Mills v Silver* [1991] Ch 271, 288 (Parker LJ), M & B p 690.

[251] *Davis v Whitby* [1974] Ch 186, M & B p 705; *Payne v Shedden* (1834) 1 Mood & R 382; *Property Point Ltd v Kirri* [2009] EWHC 2958 (Ch), [2009] 47 EGCS 133 (requirement to access through third party's land for part of the 20-year period did not prevent easement by lost modern grant).

[252] *Bright v Walker* (1834) 1 Cr M & R 211, 221 (prescription at common law); *Wheaton v Maple & Co* [1893] 3 Ch 48; *Kilgour v Gaddes* [1904] 1 KB 457, 466, M & B p 693 (Prescription Act 1832); *Simmons v Dobson* [1991] 1 WLR 720, M & B p 695 (lost modern grant), criticised [1992] Conv 107 (P Sparkes); [1992] CLJ 222 (C Harpum), following (1958) 74 LQR 82 (VTH Delany); and *China Field Ltd v Appeal Tribunal (Buildings)* [2009] 5 HKC 231 (Lord Millett, Court of Final Appeal, Hong Kong) noted at [2010] Conv 176 (M Merry).

[253] *Gayford v Moffatt* (1868) 4 Ch App 133; *Kilgour v Gaddes*, above.

[254] *Wheaton v Maple & Co*, above, at 63; *Pugh v Savage* [1970] 2 QB 373.

[255] *Williams v Sandy Lane (Chester) Ltd* [2006] EWCA Civ 1738, [2007] 1 EGLR 10 at [24] (Chadwick LJ), M & B p 696; *Llewellyn v Lorey* [2011] EWCA Civ 37, [2011] All ER (D) 53 (Feb).

tenancy, the owner is likely to be said to have acquiesced in it; but, if not, the position of the freeeholder is the same as if the grant had predated the user.[256]

Owing to the wording of the Prescription Act 1832, however, the right to light is an exception to these rules.[257]

(b) Methods of prescription

We must now discuss the three methods of prescription.

(1) Prescription at common law[258]

At common law a prescriptive title to an easement may be founded upon long enjoyment. This, however, immediately raises the question—how long must the enjoyment have lasted before a grant in his favour will be presumed? The conclusion reached by the courts was that the right must have been enjoyed from *time immemorial*, that is to say, 'from time whereof the memory of men runneth not to the contrary'.[259]

This designation of what is generally termed *legal memory* is vague and unsatisfactory, and so the courts solved the difficulty in a rough and ready fashion by fixing some date at which the memory of man was supposed to begin. They did not choose a date at random, but took as their guide the statutes that from time to time restricted the period within which actions for the recovery of land had to be brought. At first those statutes, instead of fixing a given number of years, made the period of limitation run from particular dates or events, such as from the last return of King John into England. The last statute that adopted this plan was the Statute of Westminster in 1275, which fixed the first year of the reign of Richard I (1189) as the period of limitation for the recovery of land by a writ of right. These statutes were, of course, not concerned with prescription, but the courts, from time to time, adopted the various statutory dates as the time at which *legal memory* was to be taken as beginning. Thus, after the Statute of Westminster, a prescriptive claim to an easement had to be based on an enjoyment carried back to 1189. Unfortunately, this policy of keeping in line with successive statutes of limitation was not maintained: when the legislature set up a different principle in 1623[260] by enacting that actions for the recovery of land must be brought within a fixed number of years (20 years for the action of ejectment), the courts failed to restrict *legal memory* to the same period.[261] So, absurd though it is, 1189 is today still considered to be the time from which a claimant who is prescribing at common law must prove enjoyment of the easement. The result has been the adoption of what Cockburn CJ described as a 'somewhat startling rule'[262] since, in order to lighten the burden of a claimant, the courts are willing to presume that enjoyment has lasted from 1189 if proof is given of an actual enjoyment from as far back as living witnesses can

---

[256] Ibid.   [257] Below, p 680.
[258] For the history of prescription, see Holdsworth, *A History of English Law*, vol vii, pp 343 ff.
[259] Co Litt 170.   [260] Following 32 Hen. 8, c 2.
[261] See the judgment of Cockburn CJ in *Bryant v Foot* (1867) LR 2 QB 161, 180–1, M & B p 687.
[262] Ibid.

speak.[263] A lifetime's enjoyment or even a shorter period raises the presumption that the enjoyment has stretched back to the reign of Richard I.[264]

This presumption cannot, however, prevail where, as in the majority of cases, it can be shown that there was a time after 1189 when the easement could not possibly have existed.[265] This almost precludes prescription at common law in the case of easements appurtenant to buildings, such as a right to light, for proof that the building did not exist in the time of Richard I must inevitably defeat the claim.[266]

(2) Prescription under lost modern grant

The 'lost modern grant' represents the second stage in the history of acquisition by presumed grant. If protection was to be given to easements that were fortified by long enjoyment, but for the grant of which no deed could be produced, something had to be done to circumvent the rule that a prescriptive claim at common law failed if it was shown that the easement must have come into existence at some time later than 1189. Determined to support ancient user at all costs, judicial astuteness evolved the very questionable theory[267] of the lost modern grant. After actual enjoyment of an easement has been shown for a reasonable length of time, the court presumes that an actual grant was made at the time when enjoyment began, but that the deed has been lost. The justification for this is that if a claimant, despite his inability to prove enjoyment back to 1189 or to produce a deed of grant, has clearly exercised the easement for (say) the last 60 years, it is possible that at some time an actual grant was made to him or his predecessor, and that it was subsequently lost. Therefore, since long enjoyment must be upheld, the only course open to the court is to leave it to the jury to presume that the grant was in fact made.

The virtue of this theory is that it avoids the disaster that overtakes common law prescription when it is shown that the easement could not have existed (say) in 1750, for it does not matter what the state of affairs was then if you rely on a grant made some years later.

Cockburn CJ said:[268]

> Juries were first told that from user, during living memory or even during twenty years, they might presume a lost grant or deed;[269] next they were recommended to make such presumption; and lastly, as the final consummation of judicial legislation, it was held that a jury should be told, not only that they might, but also that they were bound to presume

---

[263] First Report of Real Property Commissioners (1829), p 51.

[264] *Bailey v Appleyard* (1838) 8 Ad & El 161, 166. See *Darling v Clue* (1864) 4 F & F 329, 334 (Willes J): 'At common law twenty years uninterrupted user as of right will be prima facie evidence of the right liable to be rebutted.' See also *Bealey v Shaw* (1805) 6 East 208, 215 (Lord Ellenborough).

[265] *Hulbert v Dale* [1909] 2 Ch 570, 577.

[266] *Bury v Pope* (1588) Cro Eliz 118; *Norfolk v Arbuthnot* (1880) 5 CPD 390; First Report of Real Property Commissioners, p 51.

[267] *Bryant v Foot* (1867) LR 2 QB 161, 181 (Cockburn CJ).   [268] Ibid; M & B p 687.

[269] Here the courts acted by analogy to the Limitation Act 1623: *Bright v Walker* (1834) 1 Cr M & R 211, 217 (Parke B).

the existence of such a lost grant, although neither judge nor jury, nor anyone else, had the shadow of a belief that any such instrument had ever really existed.

So the lost grant fiction rested and still rests upon the basis of long user, and though in theory the user is merely presumptive evidence, in practice and effect it is decisive. The common law presumption of user since 1189 was only a presumption of fact, which the defendant could rebut by showing some date after 1189 when the easement could not have been exercised. The doctrine of the lost modern grant is, in substance, a presumption of law.[270] At the present day it is the last expedient of a claimant who finds himself unable to rely upon prescription at common law or upon the provisions of the Prescription Act 1832.[271]

The general rule is that 20 years' enjoyment is enough to raise the presumption of a lost modern grant.[272]

The same kind of user must be shown as in the case of prescription at common law, so that if it is *vi, clam* or *precario* the doctrine will not be invoked by the court.[273] Again, in accordance with general principles, it must be clear that there was some person or body of persons to whom the grant might have been made;[274] that there was a fee simple owner capable of executing the grant;[275] and that the right claimed was one that might have been the subject matter of a grant.[276]

In *Tehidy Minerals Ltd v Norman*,[277] the Court of Appeal, after reviewing the difference of judicial opinion in *Angus v Dalton*,[278] decided that the presumption of a lost modern grant cannot be rebutted by evidence that no such grant was in fact made. If, for example, a claim to an easement of support in respect of a house were made, it might be a simple matter to prove that no grant had ever been executed, but it would not be a good reason for refusing to apply the doctrine. The doctrine is plainly a fiction; it is a means to an end, and the end is that some technical ground may be found for upholding a right that has been openly enjoyed.

---

[270] *Tehidy Minerals Ltd v Norman* [1971] 2 QB 528, below.

[271] *Hulley v Silversprings Bleaching and Dyeing Co Ltd* [1922] 2 Ch 268; see eg *Hulbert v Dale* [1909] 2 Ch 570, M & B p 696; *Healey v Hawkins* [1968] 1 WLR 1967, M & B p 692; *Ward (Helston) Ltd v Kerrier DC* (1981) 42 P & CR 412 (easement); *Tehidy Minerals Ltd v Norman*, above (profit à prendre); *Mills v Silver* [1991] Ch 271, M & B p 690; *Simmons v Dobson* [1991] 1 WLR 720, M & B p 695; *Bowring Services Ltd v Scottish Widows' Fund & Life Assurance Society* [1995] 1 EGLR 158 (presumption failed because of custom of City of London that a man may rebuild upon ancient foundations to what height he pleases); *Smith v Brudenell-Bruce* [2002] 2 P & CR 4.

[272] *Bryant v Foot* (1867) LR 2 QB 161, 181 (Cockburn CJ); *Tehidy Minerals Ltd v Norman*, above (period of 21 years 8½ months).

[273] Above, p 668; *Hanna v Pollock* [1900] 2 IR 664, 671; *Partridge v Scott* (1838) 3 M & W 220; *Oakley v Boston* [1976] QB 270. Even an unsolicited permission prevents a claim for an easement arising under the doctrine of lost modern grant because it is inconsistent with any claim to user as of right: *Odey v Barber* [2006] EWHC 3109 (Ch), [2008] Ch 175 at [74], M & B p 693.

[274] *Tilbury v Silva* (1890) 45 Ch D 98, 122.

[275] *Daniel v North* (1809) 11 East 372; *Oakley v Boston*, above.

[276] *Bryant v Lefever* (1879) 4 CPD 172.   [277] [1971] 2 QB 528, M & B p 697.

[278] (1877) 3 QBD 85; on appeal (1878) 4 QBD 162; affd as *Dalton v Angus & Co* (1881) 6 App Cas 740. The views are summarised in *Tehidy Minerals Ltd v Norman*, above, at 547.

A lost grant will not be presumed, however, if, during the period of user, there was no person capable of making the grant,[279] or if such a grant would have been in contravention of a statute.[280] Buckley LJ said:[281]

> In our judgment *Angus v Dalton* decides that, where there has been upwards of 20 years' uninterrupted enjoyment of an easement, such enjoyment having the necessary qualities to fulfil the requirements of prescription, then unless, for some reason such as incapacity on the part of the person or persons who might at sometime before the commencement of the 20-year period have made a grant, the existence of such a grant is impossible, the law will adopt a legal fiction that such a grant was made, in spite of any direct evidence that no such grant was in fact made.
>
> If this legal fiction is not to be displaced by direct evidence that no grant was made, it would be strange if it could be displaced by circumstantial evidence leading to the same conclusion, and in our judgment it must follow that circumstantial evidence tending to negative the existence of a grant (other than evidence establishing impossibility) should not be permitted to displace the fiction.

(3) Prescription under the Prescription Act 1832

The two chief objects of the Prescription Act were to shorten the time of legal memory, and to make it impossible in actions brought under the Act for a claim to be defeated by proof that at some point of time later than 1189 the easement could not have existed. For these purposes the Act separates the right to light from all other easements, and deals with each class in a different manner.

(i) Easements other than light

(1) *20- and 40-year periods*

Section 2 enacts, in effect, that where an easement has been actually enjoyed without interruption for 20 years, it shall not be defeated by proof that it commenced later than 1189, but it may be defeated in any other way possible at common law.

Thus a claimant who relies on the Act is unaffected by the doctrine of legal memory, but he may still be met by the defences admissible in a case where common law prescription is pleaded, such as that the right is not the possible subject matter of a

---

[279] *Oakley v Boston* above (incumbent of glebe land held to be capable grantor with consent of Ecclesiastical Commissioners).

[280] *Neaverson v Peterborough RDC* [1902] 1 Ch 557. Cf *Bakewell Management Ltd v Brandwood* [2004] UKHL 14, [2004] 2 AC 519 (driving over common land without lawful authority under LPA 1925, s 193(4), but user would not have been illegal if the landowner had consented: right of way could be acquired by prescription, thus rendering s 68 of Countryside and Rights of Way Act 2000 otiose: it was consequently repealed by Commons Act 2006, s 51); [2004] Conv 517 (C McNall); (2004) 148 SJ 455 (S Bickford-Smith and C Lamont); (2005) 121 LQR 200 (M Templeman); [2004] All ER Rev 240 (PJ Clarke). Cf, however, *Williams v Sandy Lane (Chester) Ltd* [2006] EWCA Civ 1738, [2007] 1 EGLR 10 at [50], (Chadwick LJ): 'It is no answer to a prescriptive claim to assert that the user upon which the claimant relies is unlawful. Public policy does not prevent conduct that is unlawful (in the sense that it is tortious or in breach of contract) or that is illegal (in a criminal sense) from leading to the acquisition of property rights—see the observations of Lord Scott of Foscote in *Bakewell Management Ltd v Brandwood* at [46].'

[281] *Tehidy Minerals Ltd v Norman*, above, at 552.

grant;[282] or that the user is not as of right, that is it has been *vi, clam* or *precario*.[283] The same section goes on to enact that an easement that has been enjoyed without interruption for 40 years shall be deemed absolute and indefeasible unless it appears that it was enjoyed by some consent or agreement expressly given by deed or writing.

The advantage derived from enjoyment for the longer of these periods will be explained below.[284]

(2) Next before some suit or action

The two periods specified do not mean *any* period of 20 or 40 years, but the period *next before some suit or action* wherein the claim is brought into question.[285] Thus, the claimant must prove uninterrupted enjoyment for the period that immediately precedes and that terminates in an action.[286] Until then the prescriptive right is said to be inchoate. For example:

suppose that a claimant proves that he and his predecessors in title have enjoyed a right of way over adjoining lands for more than a hundred years, except for a short period of 18 months 12 years ago, when he happened to be seised in fee simple of both tenements. Although this is a case where the court will still presume a lost modern grant,[287] a claim under the Act will fail, because during part of the *last* 20 years he has enjoyed the privilege not as the owner of an easement over the land of another, but as the owner of the servient tenement.[288]

(3) Without interruption

It is essential that the enjoyment for the period of 20 or 40 years should be uninterrupted, but the Act provides that nothing is to be deemed a statutory interruption unless it has been submitted to or acquiesced in by the dominant owner for one year after he had notice of the interruption and of the person responsible for it.[289]

'Interruption' means some overt act, such as the obstruction of a right of way, which shows that the easement is disputed.[290] Thus:

if A has regularly passed over a track on B's land for 25 years and is then sued in trespass by B, his user of the way for the 20 years next preceding the action will entitle him to judgment. If, however, before his right has been contested, he submits to or acquiesces in an interruption that continues for one year, his previous enjoyment for 25 years becomes unavailing to him and he must start it afresh in order to satisfy the statute.

---

[282] *Staffordshire & Worcestershire Canal Navigation Proprietors v Birmingham Canal Navigation Proprietors* (1866) LR 1 HL 254, 278.

[283] Above, p 668.   [284] Below, p 677.   [285] Prescription Act 1832, s 4.

[286] *Jones v Price* (1836) 3 Bing NC 52; *Parker v Mitchell* (1840) 11 Ad & El 788; *Hyman v Van den Bergh* [1907] 2 Ch 516; affd [1908] 1 Ch 167, M & B p 703; *Newnham v Willison* (1987) 56 P & CR 8 (interruption lasting more than one year before action brought); [1989] Conv 357 (JE Martin).

[287] Cf *Hulbert v Dale* [1909] 2 Ch 570, M & B p 696.

[288] *Bright v Walker* (1834) 1 Cr M & R 211, 219.

[289] S 4.

[290] *Carr v Foster* (1842) 3 QB 581 (Parke B).

The crucial question, therefore, is—what amounts to submission or acquiescence? This is a question of fact dependent upon the circumstances, but the test that should be applied seems a little obscure.

> Suppose, in the case above, that B erects a fence across the track over which A has been passing for 25 years and that A, though he protests violently and threatens legal proceedings, lets 13 months elapse without forcing the issue by a positive act of resistance.[291]

Does his protest suffice to negative his submission to or acquiescence in the interruption? It has been held that he need not go so far as to remove the obstruction or to take legal proceedings. It is said to be enough that he communicates to the servient owner, with sufficient force and clarity, his opposition to the interruption.[292] This vague test is hardly satisfactory. Strictly speaking, no doubt, submission or acquiescence is a state of mind, but if a dissident state of mind, without any positive act of resistance, is sufficient, what certainty will remain in the title to the servient tenement? A single protest will remain effective after the year has elapsed and the statutory rule that interruption for a year shall defeat a claimant will be deprived of its intended force. The weight of judicial opinion, however, is disinclined to regard inactivity by the dominant owner for longer than a year after the interruption and after his protest as necessarily fatal to his claim.[293]

An interruption that occurs after the enjoyment of an easement has persisted for 19 years and a fraction of a year will not avail the servient owner, provided that the dominant owner sues to vindicate his right within a year afterwards.[294] The interruption is not yet an interruption within the meaning of the statute. Nevertheless, the acquisition of an easement requires enjoyment for the full period of 20 years immediately preceding an action, and therefore if the servient owner brings an action before the period has elapsed he will be entitled to a declaration that no easement exists, notwithstanding the deficiency of the interruption.[295]

(4) User as of right

The nature of the enjoyment necessary for the statutory periods must be similar to that required at common law, that is to say, it must be *as of right*.[296] This is so even where user has been shown for the full period of 40 years. The Act does not mean that easements enjoyed for 40 years otherwise than by written permission are in all

---

[291] Cf *Davies v Du Paver* [1953] 1 QB 184, M & B p 701.

[292] *Bennison v Cartwright* (1864) 5 B & S 1; *Glover v Coleman* (1874) LR 10 CP 108.

[293] *Davies v Du Paver*, above (where, however, that view was not shared by Singleton LJ); *Ward v Kirkland* [1967] Ch 194.

[294] *Flight v Thomas* (1841) 8 Cl & Fin 231.   [295] *Reilly v Orange* [1955] 2 QB 112, M & B p 704.

[296] *Tickle v Brown* (1836) 4 Ad & El 369, 382; *Bright v Walker* (1834) 1 Cr M & R 211; *Lyell v Hothfield* [1914] 3 KB 911; *Smith v Brudenell-Bruce* [2002] 2 P & CR 4 (20 years' uninterrupted enjoyment, but not as of right). The fact that the user was illegal under LPA 1925, s 193(4), but would not have been illegal if the landowner had consented, does not prevent the user being as of right: *Bakewell Management Ltd v Brandwood* [2004] UKHL 14, [2004] 2 AC 519; above, p 674, n 280.

circumstances indefeasible, but only if their enjoyment has been open and notorious. Lord Macnaghten gave a warning against reading too much into the Act:

> The Act was passed, as its preamble declares, for the purpose of getting rid of the inconvenience and injustice arising from the meaning which the law of England attached to the expressions 'time immemorial' and 'time whereof the memory of man runneth not to the contrary'. The law as it stood put an intolerable strain on the consciences of judges and jurymen. The Act was an Act 'for shortening the time of prescription in certain cases'. And really it did nothing more.[297]

This enables us to appreciate the significance of enjoyment for the longer period of 40 years. A hasty reading of section 2 might suggest that a right enjoyed for 40 years is indefeasible unless it can be proved that it was enjoyed by virtue of a written grant. But this is not so. In the case of enjoyment for the *shorter* period the claim cannot be met by the objection that enjoyment originated subsequently to 1189, but it can be met and defeated by any one of the common law defences, namely:

(a) that the right claimed lacks one or more of the characteristics essential to an easement;[298] or

(b) that the right in question, though enjoyed for 20 years, is prohibited by law, such as because a grant would have been ultra vires the grantor[299] or the grantee;[300] or

(c) that the user was not as of right,[301] ie that it was forcible, or secret, or enjoyed by permission *whether written or oral*.[302]

Next, a claim to an easement based upon 40 years' enjoyment can likewise be defeated upon the first two grounds, and also by proof that the user was forcible or secret or enjoyed by *written* permission. What is not sufficient to nullify a user lasting for this longer period is the oral permission of the servient owner. On general principles user that is precarious in any sense cannot give rise to an easement, but the statute, by enacting that user for 40 years is not to be considered precarious unless enjoyed by written permission, has, in the case of this longer period, given a special and restricted meaning to 'precarious' if the claim is based

---

[297] *Gardner v Hodgson's Kingston Brewery Co Ltd* [1903] AC 229, 236, M & B p 689.

[298] *Mounsey v Ismay* (1863) 3 H & C 486.

[299] *Rochdale Canal Co v Radcliffe* (1852) 18 QB 287, 315; *Staffordshire & Worcestershire Canal Navigation Proprietors v Birmingham Canal Navigation Proprietors* (1866) LR 1 HL 254, 278; *Housden v Conservators of Wimbledon and Putney Commons* [2008] EWCA Civ 200, [2008] 1 WLR 1172 at [66] (Mummery LJ, obiter: 'with considerable reluctance, I am compelled by precedent to the conclusion that the judges in the *Staffordshire* case were unanimous ... in holding that, in a s 2 case, even a 40-year period of user could be defeated by showing that it was ultra vires the owner of the servient tenement to grant the easement claimed. The three judges must, I think, have proceeded on the basis that the opening words of s 2, which are absent from s 3, control the whole section. They apply the common law presumption of grant to both the shorter and the longer period of user'); [2009] CLJ 40 (S Bridge); [2009] Conv 349 (N Piska).

[300] *National Guaranteed Manure Co v Donald* (1859) 4 H & N 8.   [301] Above, pp 668–9.

[302] *Burrows v Lang* [1901] 2 Ch 502.

on statutory prescription.[303] The difference, then, between the two periods is that an oral consent may defeat enjoyment for 20 years, but not enjoyment for 40 years.

The circumstances when this may do so have been elucidated by the courts. It is clear that permission of any sort, whether written or oral, is fatal to a claim based upon prescription at common law, however long the enjoyment may have lasted. The case of a claim based on the statutory periods, however, depends upon whether the permission is given during or at the beginning of the period of user. If permission is given from time to time *during* the 20 or 40 years, the user becomes *precario* and this is fatal to the claim.[304] On the other hand, if the permission is given at the *beginning* of the period of user and extends over the whole period[305] (ie a permission given more than 20 or 40 years ago and not since renewed), then, if it is written, it is fatal to a claim based upon either of the statutory periods, and, if oral, it is only fatal to a claim based upon the 20-year period.

Goff J said in *Healey v Hawkins*:[306]

> In principle it seems to me that once permission has been given, the user must remain permissive and not be capable of ripening into a right save where the permission is oral and the user has continued for 40…years, unless and until, having been given for a limited period only, it expires or, being general, it is revoked, or there is a change in circumstances from which revocation may fairly be implied.…
>
> Of course, when the user has continued for 40…years a prior parol consent affords no answer, because it is excluded by the express terms of section 2 of the Prescription Act, but, even so, permission given during the period will defeat the claimant because it negatives user as of right. That is, in my judgment, the explanation of the distinction drawn by the House of Lords in *Gardner v Hodgson's Kingston Brewery* between antecedent and current parol consents.

Oral permission given within the period will also negative user *as of right*, where the user continues on a common understanding that the user is and continues to be permissive.[307]

(5) Disabilities

Another difference between the two statutory periods is that certain disabilities of the servient owner, which obstruct a claim based on 20 years' user, do not affect a claimant who has enjoyed an easement for 40 years.

The Act provides that a right, even though enjoyed for the statutory periods, shall not ripen into a legal easement if the servient owner has been under certain disabilities. The time during which such person may have been 'an infant, idiot, non

---

[303] *Gardner v Hodgson's Kingston Brewery Co Ltd* [1901] 2 Ch 198, 214; for the facts, see above, pp 668–9. The annual payment of 15s had been orally fixed some 60 years before the action. That was held, however, to be no evidence that an oral agreement granting the easement had in fact been made.

[304] *Gardner v Hodgson's Kingston Brewery Co Ltd* [1903] AC 229, M & B pp 689, 700.

[305] Whether it does so depends on the circumstances: *Gaved v Martyn* (1865) 19 CBNS 732; *Healey v Hawkins* [1968] 1 WLR 1967, M & B p 692. See (1968) 32 Conv (NS) 40 (PS Langan).

[306] [1968] 1 WLR 1967, 1973.

[307] *Jones v Price & Morgan* (1992) 64 P & CR 404. For unsolicited permission for the purposes of the claim to a lost modern grant, see *Odey v Barber* [2006] EWHC 3109 (Ch), [2008] Ch 175; above, n 273.

compos mentis…or tenant for life',[308] or during which an action has been pending and diligently prosecuted, is excluded by section 7 from the period of 20 years, though it begins to run again *at the point where it was interrupted* as soon as the disability is removed. Suppose, for example, that

the claimant began to exercise the right in 1972, when the servient owner was the fee simple owner. In 1977 the latter became tenant for life under a settlement, but on his death in 1989 his successor came to the estate as tenant in fee simple. The claimant has exercised the right continuously from 1972 until 2006, when the action is brought. 5 of these 34 years preceded the disability of a tenancy for life and 17 came afterwards. The 12 years during which the disability lasted must of course be excluded, but the question is whether the claimant may add the periods of 5 and 17 years together and allege enjoyment for the statutory period; or whether he will be defeated by his inability to show enjoyment for the last 20 years.

He will not be defeated, for the rule is that a claimant must show 20 years' enjoyment either:

(i)   wholly before the disability if it still exists at the time of the action, or

(ii) partly before or partly after, if the disability has ended.[309]

Except for that of a tenancy for life, these disabilities do not affect a claim based on 40 years' enjoyment;[310] this is to say, an uninterrupted user as of right for so long will confer an absolute title, no matter what the position of the servient owner may have been. Section 8, however, provides that where the servient tenement has been held during the whole or any part of the 40 years for a term of life or for a term of years exceeding three years, the period during which such term lasted shall be excluded in the computation, provided that the claim is resisted by the reversioner within three years of the determination of the term.[311]

A curious feature of these rules is that the deduction of the time during which the servient tenement has been held by a tenant for a term exceeding three years only affects the computation of the longer period of 40 years. Thus an easement of way may be acquired by 20 years' user, though for the greater part of that time the servient tenement has been in the hands of a tenant.[312]

None of the disabilities applies to the easement of light.

---

[308] The text of s 7 also counts a *femme couvert* (married woman) as under a similar disability, although Law Reform (Married Women and Tortfeasors) Act 1935, s 1(a) overrode this by providing that a married woman shall be capable of acquitting, holding and disposing of any property in all respects as if she were a *femme sole*. The language of the Prescription Act has not been amended to substitute the terminology, used in modern Acts, of 'minor' (rather than *infant*) or 'lacking mental capacity' (rather than *idiot* or *non compos mentis*): below, pp 1019, 1028.

[309] Cf *Clayton v Corby* (1842) 2 QB 813.   [310] S 7.

[311] The section is in words restricted to ways and watercourses, but there is reason to believe that the word 'convenient' has crept into the section instead of 'easement'; see *Wright v Williams* (1836) Tyr & Gr 375, 380; *Laird v Briggs* (1880) 50 LJ Ch 260, 261 (Fry J).

[312] *Palk v Shinner* (1852) 18 QB 568.

(ii) Easement of light

As the Act treats this particular easement quite differently from all others, it is necessary to cite the section dealing with it in full:[313]

> When the access and use of light to and for any dwelling house, workshop or other building[314] shall have been actually enjoyed therewith for the full period of twenty years without interruption, the right thereto shall be deemed absolute and indefeasible, any local usage or custom to the contrary notwithstanding,[315] unless it shall appear that the same was enjoyed by some consent or agreement expressly made or given for that purpose by deed or writing.

(1) User need not be as of right

We have seen that where a claim to any other easement is made under the Act, it must clearly appear that the enjoyment has been *as of right*, and the reason is that the statutory words *claiming right thereto* have been construed as equivalent to the common law expression *as of right*. Since these words, however, are omitted from the section dealing with light, it follows that in the case of this particular easement a fresh mode of creation has been statutorily introduced.[316] All that the claimant need show, if he claims not at common law but under the Act, is actual user and absence of written agreement,[317] but the user must have continued for the period of 20 years next before the action in which the claim is brought into question. In other words, the right is not absolute and indefeasible after 20 years' user, but remains merely inchoate until it has

---

[313] S 3. Bickford-Smith and Francis, *Rights of Light: The Modern Law* (2nd edn, 2007); Ellis, *Rights to Light* (1989); *Colls v Home and Colonial Stores Ltd* [1904] AC 179, M & B p 728,

[314] *Clifford v Holt* [1899] 1 Ch 698 (church); *Hyman v Van den Bergh* [1908] 1 Ch 167 (cowshed); *Allen v Greenwood* [1980] Ch 119, M & B p 731 (greenhouse). The quantity of light to which the owner of the dominant tenement is entitled is 'what is required for the ordinary purposes of inhabitancy or business of the tenement according to the ordinary notions of mankind': *Colls v Home & Colonial Stores Ltd* [1904] AC 179, 204 (Lord Davey); *Midtown Ltd v City of London Real Property Co Ltd*, above (substantial diminution in amount of natural light to an office building was an interference amounting to a nuisance, even though all rooms were habitually lit by artificial light whenever used). In *Allen v Greenwood* it was held that a right to a specially high degree of light may be acquired by prescription. Goff LJ left open the question whether a right to light would include the properties of the sun in relation to solar heating. See [1979] Conv 298 (FR Crane); [1984] Conv 408 (AH Hudson). See also *Carr-Saunders v Dick McNeil Associates Ltd* [1986] 1 WLR 922 (dominant owner's right under s 3 is for access of light to the building as a whole and not to any particular room).

[315] *Bowring Services Ltd v Scottish Widows' Fund & Life Assurance* [1995] 1 EGLR 158 (custom of City of London).

[316] *Scott v Pape* (1886) 31 Ch D 554, 571 (Bowen LJ).

[317] *Truscott v Merchant Taylors' Co* (1856) 11 Exch 855; *Frewen v Philipps* (1861) 11 CBNS 449; *Colls v Home and Colonial Stores Ltd* [1904] AC 179, 205; *Kilgour v Gaddes* [1904] 1 KB 457. The written agreement need not refer expressly to light; 'the phrase "expressly made or given for that purpose" can be satisfied by an express provision in the relevant document that, on its true construction according to normal principles, has the effect of rendering the enjoyment of light permissive or consensual, or capable of being terminated or interfered with by the adjoining owner, and is therefore inconsistent with the enjoyment becoming absolute and indefeasible after 20 years': *RHJ Ltd v FT Patten (Holdings) Ltd* [2008] EWCA Civ 151, [2008] Ch 341 at [44] (Lloyd LJ). See also *G & S Brough Ltd v Salvage Wharf Ltd* [2009] EWCA Civ 21, [2010] Ch 11 (by written agreement claimant had not abandoned rights to light but merely agreed not to enforce them).

been established in legal proceedings.[318] To defeat a claim to light, based upon user for the statutory period, the servient owner must produce an express agreement by deed or writing that shows that the user has been permissive during the last 20 years.[319] Thus, for example, user of light for 20 years is not dismissed as precarious, merely because it has been enjoyed under an oral permission extending over the whole period.[320] Even the payment of rent by the dominant owner under an oral agreement will not prevent the acquisition of the easement,[321] unless some receipt or acknowledgment has been given that can be construed as a written agreement.

(2) Interruption

A right to light cannot, of course, be acquired if its enjoyment has been effectively interrupted within the meaning of the Prescription Act, that is if there has been some adverse act by the servient owner that has lasted for at least one year.[322] In this type of easement, the adverse act must in the nature of things take the form of some physical structure, such as a hoarding, so sited as to obstruct the flow of light to the dominant tenement. An alternative to this cumbrous and unsightly method, however, was introduced by the Rights of Light Act 1959,[323] which enables the access of light to be notionally obstructed by the registration of a notice as a local land charge.

A notice in the prescribed form must be submitted to the local authority by the servient owner,[324] and it must state that its registration is intended to represent the obstruction to the access of light that would be caused by an opaque structure of certain specified dimensions, whether of unlimited height or not, erected upon the servient tenement.[325] The notice must also be accompanied by a certificate from the Upper Tribunal[326] certifying either that adequate notice of the proposed registration has been given to all persons likely to be affected, or that the case is one of exceptional urgency and that therefore registration for a limited time is essential.[327] The notice, if not cancelled, expires one year after registration or, where

---

[318] *Hyman v Van den Bergh* [1907] 2 Ch 516; affd [1908] 1 Ch 167, M & B p 703. The reason is that the third section, cited above, must be read in connection with the fourth section that requires the period to be *next before* some action.

[319] *Foster v Lyons & Co* [1927] 1 Ch 219; *Willoughby v Eckstein* [1937] Ch 167; *Midtown Ltd v City of London Real Property Co Ltd* [2005] EWHC 33 (Ch), [2005] 1 EGLR 65.

[320] *Mallam v Rose* [1915] 2 Ch 222.   [321] *Plasterers' Co v Parish Clerks' Co* (1851) 6 Exch 630.

[322] Above, p 675.

[323] As amended by LLCA 1975, s 17, Sch 1. The Act embodies the recommendations of the Harman Committee on Rights of Light, 1958 (Cmnd 473); [1959] CLJ 182 (HWR Wade). See *Hawker v Tomalin* (1969) 20 P & CR 550, 551 (Harman J).

[324] Ie, the owner of a legal fee simple or of a term of years absolute of which at least seven years remain unexpired, or the mortgagee in possession of such a fee or term: Rights of Light Act 1959, s 7(1).

[325] Rights of Light Act 1959, s 2(1), (2); Tribunal Procedure (Upper Tribunal) (Lands Chamber) Rules 2010 (SI 2010 No 2600), replacing Lands Tribunal Rules 1996 (SI 1996 No 1022); LLCR 1977 (SI 1977 No 985), r 10, amended by SI 2009 No 1307, Sch 2, para 20.

[326] Formerly the Lands Tribunal: SI 2009 No 1307, Sch 1, para 35.

[327] Ibid, s 2(3). 938 definitive and 211 temporary certificates were issued between 1959 and 1980; see (1978) 122 SJ 515, 534; (1981) 259 EG 123 (WA Greene).

accompanied by a certificate of exceptional urgency, at the end of the period specified in the certificate.[328]

For the purpose of determining whether a right to light has been acquired either at common law or under the Prescription Act, the access of light to the dominant tenement is to be treated as obstructed by a registered notice to the same extent and with the like consequences as if the structure specified in the application for registration has in fact been erected;[329] and any right of action that the dominant owner would have had in that event is available by reason of the notice.[330] In order to obviate the difficulties that may arise where the right is interrupted after it has been enjoyed for 19 years and a fraction,[331] the Act provides in effect that the enjoyment by the dominant owner of the flow of light shall be notionally prolonged for one year if he sues for cancellation of the notice.[332]

(3) Not limited to prescription in respect of fee simple

Owing to the wording of the Prescription Act 1832 the right to light is an exception to the rule that an easement can be prescribed for only in respect of a fee simple.[333] It is peculiar in two respects:

First, the fee simple estate of a landlord is bound by an easement of light acquired over the land while in the occupation of a tenant.[334] Suppose, for example, that:

> A, the fee simple owner of Blackacre, leases it to a tenant for 25 years. During the tenancy, X, the owner of an adjoining house, builds a window overlooking Blackacre and enjoys access of light to it for 20 years. A right to light is thereby acquired that is enforceable against A, his tenant and all successors in title of Blackacre.

Secondly, if two tenements are held by different lessees under a common landlord, and one lessee enjoys the use of light over the other tenement for the necessary period, he and his successors acquire an indefeasible right to the light not only against the other tenant, but also against the common landlord and all succeeding owners of the servient tenement.[335]

(c) Common law not displaced by Prescription Act 1832

The Act is only supplementary to the common law—it provides an additional method of claiming easements, but leaves the other two methods untouched. If, for example, the claimant is unable to show enjoyment for the statutory period of the last 20 years, as will happen if there has been unity of possession for part of that period, he may

---

[328] Ibid, s 3(2); *Bowring Services Ltd v Scottish Widows' Fund & Life Assurance Society* [1995] 1 EGLR 158 (calculation of date from which time runs).

[329] Rights of Light Act 1959, s 2(1).   [330] Ibid, s 3(3).   [331] Above, p 676.

[332] Rights of Light Act 1959, s 3(4). See [2009] Conv 474 (M Barnes and J Bignell), criticising the difference in this respect between a notional obstruction by registration of a notice and a physical obstruction, and suggesting that s 3(4) may result from a misconception of the law when it was introduced at a late stage in the passing of the 1959 Act.

[333] Above, p 670.   [334] *Simper v Foley* (1862) 2 John & H 555.

[335] *Morgan v Fear* [1907] AC 425, M & B p 732; *Willoughby v Eckstein* [1937] Ch 167, 170.

either prescribe at common law or invoke the doctrine of a lost modern grant.[336] Normally, he will rely on the Act. Failing this, he will base his case on prescription at common law; and, failing that, he will plead a lost modern grant, but only if driven to it, for, as Lord Lindley said, 'that doctrine only applies where the enjoyment cannot be otherwise reasonably accounted for'.[337]

(d) Reform of the law on prescription

In *Tehidy Minerals Ltd v Norman* Buckley LJ said:[338]

> The co-existence of three separate methods of prescribing is, in our view, anomalous and undesirable, for it results in much unnecessary complication and confusion. We hope that it may be possible for the Legislature to effect a long-overdue simplification in this branch of the law.

(1) Law Reform Committee report on acquisition of easements and profits by prescription

In 1966 the Law Reform Committee[339] recommended the abolition of the prescriptive acquisition of easements and of profits à prendre;[340] in the former case by a majority of eight to six, in the latter unanimously. The Committee also, however, considered the ways in which prescriptive acquisition—if it should be retained for easements—should operate, and was unanimous on the new system to be adopted.

The main recommendations, in outline, were:

(1) All existing methods of acquisition of easements and profits by prescription should be abolished. This recommendation included the abolition of prescription at common law and under the doctrine of a lost modern grant, and the repeal of the Prescription Act 1832.[341]

---

[336] See *Hulbert v Dale* [1909] 2 Ch 570, argument of counsel at 573.

[337] *Gardner v Hodgson's Kingston Brewery Co Ltd* [1903] AC 229, 240. The three alternative claims were pleaded together in *Bailey v Stephens* (1862) 12 CBNS 91; *Norfolk v Arbuthnot* (1880) 5 CPD 390; *Wheaton v Maple & Co* [1893] 3 Ch 48; *Roberts & Lovell v James* (1903) 89 LT 282. See too *Pugh v Savage* [1970] 2 QB 373.

[338] [1971] 2 QB 528, 543.

[339] Fourteenth Report (1966) Cmnd 3100. See Jackson, ch 15; (1967) 30 MLR 189 (HW Wilkinson).
In 1971 Law Commission WP No 36, *Rights Appurtenant to Land*, suggested that 'easements and covenants should be assimilated along lines hitherto regarded as appropriate to easements' (para 9) and, in relation to prescription, 'as at present advised we are inclined to agree in principle with the majority, but only on the basis that some alternative to prescription can be found. In the meantime it will be assumed that prescription will continue' (para 99). It should be reformed along the lines recommended by the Law Reform Committee (Proposition 10).
For further criticism of the Prescription Act 1832, see Holdsworth, *An Historical Introduction to the Land Law* (1927), pp 284–6; Holdsworth, *A History of English Law*, vol vii, pp 350–62; Simpson, *A History of the Land Law* (2nd edn, 1986), pp 266–9; Underhill, *A Century of Law Reform* (1911), p 308. New Zealand's Property Law Act 2007 provides for the abolition of the acquisition of easements and profits by prescription (s 179). In Ireland, Land and Conveyancing Reform Act 2009, s 34, abolishes prescription at common law and by lost modern grant and allows acquisition of legal easements and profits by prescription only on registration of a court order; Wiley, *Irish Land Law*, paras 6.107–6.111.

[340] Ibid, paras 32, 98.   [341] Paras 40, 98, 99(1)–(3).

(2) The following method should be adopted, if it were decided to substitute a new system for easements only:[342]

    (a) The prescriptive period should be a period in gross of 12 years (ie, it need not be 'next before action brought').[343]

    (b) There should be no 'disabilities'.[344]

    (c) An easement should be capable of being acquired against the owner of a limited interest in the servient land so as to subsist as long as that servient owner's interest subsists.[345] Prescription by the owner of a limited interest in the dominant land should continue, as at present, in favour of the freeholder.[346] A tenant should be able to prescribe against his landlord and vice versa.[347]

    (d) Enjoyment:

        (i) by force should not count in favour of the dominant owner;[348]

        (ii) must have been actually known to the servient owner or ought reasonably to have been known to him;[349]

        (iii) must be of such a kind and frequency as would only be justified by the existence of an easement;[350]

        (iv) by consent or agreement, whether written or oral, should not count. If so enjoyed for one year or more, the consent, like an interruption, would prevent earlier enjoyment being added to later enjoyment for the purpose of making up the required total of 12 years. A consent that is indefinite in duration should operate for one year.[351]

    (e) Notional interruption, on the lines of the Rights of Light Act 1959, should be extended to easements generally; this should be by registration against the dominant land in the local land charges register after notice given. Interruption, notional or actual, should endure for 12 months in order to be effective.[352]

    (f) An easement, acquired by prescription, should be lost by 12 years' continuous non-user.[353]

(3) The Committee was unanimous about provisions to facilitate, subject to compensation where appropriate, the acquisition of easements of support for buildings by land or for buildings by buildings.[354]

(4) Shelter of building by an adjoining building should be treated in the same way as support.[355]

---

[342] Para 99(6).
[343] Paras 41–3. Prescription Act 1832, s 4.
[344] Para 44. Prescription Act 1832, ss 7, 8.
[345] Paras 47–9.
[346] Para 50.
[347] Para 51.
[348] Para 57.
[349] Para 58.
[350] Para 59.
[351] Paras 61–3.
[352] As at present. Prescription Act 1832, s 4. Paras 64–9, 75.
[353] Para 81.
[354] Paras 89–95, 99(8)–(11).
[355] Paras 96, 99(12); *Phipps v Pears* [1965] 1 QB 76, M & B p 641, above, p 657.

(5) The Lands Tribunal should be empowered to discharge easements or substitute more convenient ones, subject to payment of compensation where appropriate.[356]

(2) Law Commission proposals in relation to registered land

In 1998 the Law Commission provisionally recommended[357] that the acquisition of easements or profits à prendre in registered land should be possible only under the Prescription Act 1832. To allow the doctrine of lost modern grant to continue would involve inventing a concept of 'a lost modern registration',[358] and any such concept would undermine the primary objective of ensuring the registration of rights that are expressly created.

However, this proposal was abandoned by the Law Commission in its final Report,[359] and was therefore not implemented in the Land Registration Act 2002.[360]

(3) Law Commission consultation paper on easements, covenants and profits à prendre

In 2008, as part of it's wider consideration of possible reforms in the law of easements, the Law Commission[361] provisionally proposed that the current law of prescriptive acquisition of easements (at common law, by lost modern grant and under the Prescription Act 1832) be abolished with prospective effect.[362] The Commission invited views as to whether the current law should be abolished without replacement (that is the outright abolition of the prescriptive acquisition of easements),[363] but provisionally proposed a new statutory scheme for prescription[364] under which it would be possible to claim an easement by prescription on proof of 20 years' continuous qualifying use; the qualifying use must continue to within 12 months of application being made to the registrar for entry of a notice on the register of title, and must be without force, without stealth, and without consent,[365] and must not be use that is contrary to law unless the

---

[356] Paras 97, 99(13). In 2009 the Lands Tribunal was abolished and replaced by the Upper Tribunal (Lands Chamber): SI 2009 No 1307, art 2; SI 2010 No 2600.

[357] Law Com No 254, paras 10.79–10.94, 10.108–10.112. [358] Ibid, para 10.89.

[359] Law Com No 271, *Land Registration for the Twenty-First Century* (2001), para 1.19. The Law Commission decided that (1) there was not a compelling case for the reform of the law of prescription in the context of registered land alone; (2) it was already undertaking a comprehensive review of easements and land obligations (below) which would include prescription, and it seemed better to 'view prescription as a totality'; and (3) some of the conveyancing concerns that informed the earlier proposals were addressed in more direct ways in the Bill—in particular, by limiting the circumstances in which easements can be overriding interests: ibid, paras 8.65–8.66.

[360] Bridge, *Prescriptive Acquisition of Easements: Abolition or Reform?* in Cooke (ed) *Modern Studies in Property Law*, vol 3 (2005), p 3.

[361] CP No 186, paras 4.151–4.256; for the other proposals for reform, see below, pp 723–5.

[362] Para 4.174.

[363] Paras 4.175–4.193; it also asks whether, even if prescription is not abolished outright, certain easements (such as negative easements) should no longer be capable of prescriptive acquisition: paras 4.184-4.186

[364] Paras 4.194–4.221.

[365] Thus limiting the right to prescription by the current rule that the use must not be *vi, clam* or *precario*; above, p 668.

use can be rendered lawful by the dispensation of the servient owner.[366] Such a new scheme might be possible only in relation to registered land, and the registration of a prescriptive easement might be subject to the servient owner's right of veto.[367]

The Law Commission has indicated that it hopes to publish a final report and draft Bill in 2011.[368]

E EXTENT OF EASEMENTS

In ascertaining the nature and extent of an easement, the principles to be applied vary with the method of its creation. Willes J said in *Williams v James*:[369]

> The distinction between a grant and prescription is obvious. In the case of proving a right by prescription the user of the right is the only evidence. In the case of a grant the language of the instrument can be referred to, and it is of course for the court to construe that language; and in the absence of any clear indication of the intention of the parties, the maxim that a grant must be construed most strongly against the grantor must be applied.[370]

(1) Express Grant

It follows that, if the easement is created by express grant, the question is one of construing the terms of the grant,[371] and, in cases of difficulty, the physical circumstances of the property must be considered. Thus, in determining whether the grant or reservation of

---

[366] Thus retaining the effect of the decision in *Bakewell Management Ltd v Brandwood* [2004] UKHL 14, [2004] 2 AC 519, above, p 674, n 280.

[367] Paras 4.222-4.232. The right of veto follows the model for registration of an adverse possessor as proprietor under LRA 2002; below, p 1161. For provisional proposals in relation to unregistered land, see paras 4.251–4.256.

[368] Law Com No 323, *Annual Report 2009-10*, para 2.61. See also *Housden v Conservators of Wimbledon and Putney Commons* [2008] 1 WLR 1172 at [72] (Mummery LJ): 'I wish the Law Commission well in its deliberations. It is better equipped than the courts to recommend improvements in this area of the law, though prescription is low down in the priorities for law reform.' For further criticism of the role of prescription in the creation of easements in the modern law see [2007] Conv 133 (F Burns); S Bridge, *Prescriptive Acquisition of Easements: Abolition or Reform?* in Cooke (ed) *Modern Studies in Property Law*, vol 3 (2005), p 3.

[369] (1867) LR 2 CP 577, 581.

[370] Cf Lewison, *Interpretation of Contracts*, para 7.08, noting that this *contra proferentem* rule of construction is not always applied consistently, particularly in the modern cases.

[371] For the modern approach to interpretation of contracts and other written documents, see *Investors' Compensation Scheme Ltd v West Bromwich Building Society* [1998] 1 WLR 896, above, p 333, applied to the interpretation of an express grant of an easement in *Mobil Oil Co Ltd v Birmingham City Council* [2001] EWCA Civ 1608, [2002] 2 P & CR 14 at [24] and [62]; *Partridge v Lawrence* [2003] EWCA Civ 1121, [2004] 1 P & CR 176 at [28]; *Brooks v Young* [2008] EWCA Civ 816, [2008] 3 EGLR 27 at [12]; Lewison, *Interpretation of Contracts*, ch 2. The construction of a grant will take into account the normal customs of conveyancing; eg the grant of a right to light, in the absence of more specific provision, will be taken to be a grant of the degree of light that satisfies the test of Lord Davey in *Colls v Home & Colonial Stores Ltd* [1904] AC 179, 204, above, p 680, n 314; *Frogmore Developments Ltd v Shirayama Shokusan Co Ltd* [2000] 1 EGLR 121, 124 (Neuberger J). Where title to the dominant and/or servient tenement is passed by an assent pursuant to a will, it is legitimate to read the assent and the will together: *Thompson v Bee* [2009] EWCA Civ 1212, [2010] Ch 412 (assent silent but will provided for 'right of way ... for all purposes connected with' the property).

'a right of way' is a right exercisable on foot only or with vehicles and, if so, what kind of vehicles, the condition of the way itself and the nature of the dominant tenement may be taken into account.[372] An unrestricted right of way may not be confined to the use of the dominant tenement contemplated by the parties at the time of the grant. Thus, where an unrestricted right of way was granted as appurtenant to a house, and the house was subsequently converted into an hotel, its owner became entitled to a right of way for the general purposes of the hotel.[373] But a grant of an unrestricted right of way does not authorise excessive use that would be an unreasonable interference with the rights of others entitled to use it.[374] And the dominant owner may not generally extend the scope of an easement, such as a right of way, by extending the dominant tenement, although it is always a matter of construction of the grant as to what constitutes the dominant tenement,[375] and a matter of interpretation of the facts as to whether the

[372] *Cannon v Villars* (1878) 8 Ch D 415, 420; *St Edmundsbury and Ipswich Diocesan Board of Finance v Clark (No 2)* [1975] 1 WLR 468, M & B p 716; *United Land Co v Great Eastern Rly Co* (1875) 10 Ch App 586; *Robinson v Bailey* [1948] 2 All ER 791 (right of way to building plot held to include business user); *Jalnarne Ltd v Ridewood* (1989) 61 P & CR 143 (right of way held to permit its use by juggernaut lorries and customers in vans and cars for access to dominant tenements subsequently used for motorcar dealing, frozen food business and snooker club with bar); *Soames-Forsythe Properties Ltd v Tesco Stores Ltd* [1991] EGCS 22 ('full and free right of way on foot only' from supermarket to car park held to include right for customers to use supermarket trolleys on it); [1992] Conv 199 (J Martin); *London and Suburban Land and Building Co (Holdings) Ltd v Carey* (1991) 62 P & CR 480 (express grant of a right of way to commercial premises did not imply a right to unload from the access way onto the dominant tenement); *CP Holdings v Dugdale Real Property* [1998] NPC 97 (unrestricted right of way over disused railway line; servient owner reopening line held not able to lower level crossing barriers thereby causing temporary but lengthy queues); *Brooks v Young* [2008] EWCA Civ 816, [2008] 3 EGLR 27 (right of way over footpath along the side and across the rear of the adjoining end-of-terrace property 'at all times' and 'for all proper purposes connected with the reasonable enjoyment of the property' not limited to occasions where use of front door was not reasonably practicable); *Waterman v Boyle* [2009] EWCA Civ 115, [2009] 2 EGLR 7 (right to park is capable of being implied into a right of vehicular access, but only if it is reasonably necessary for the exercise or enjoyment of that right, and there is no express right to park; *Moncrieff v Jamieson* [2007] UKHL 42, [2007] 1 WLR 2620, above, p 648, is an exceptional case).

[373] *White v Grand Hotel, Eastbourne, Ltd* [1913] 1 Ch 113, M & B p 711; *Kain v Norfolk* [1949] Ch 163; *Bulstrode v Lambert* [1953] 1 WLR 1064; *Keefe v Amor* [1965] 1 QB 334, M & B p 712; *McIlraith v Grady* [1968] 1 QB 468 (a right to 'pass and repass over and along' included a right to vehicles to stop for a reasonable time and unload); See also *Minor v Groves* (1997) 80 P & CR 136 (dominant owner limited in user to extend with right of way; occasional technical trespasses caused by side of vehicles intruding into airspace of servient tenement did not give rise to a right over it).

[374] *Jelbert v Davis* [1968] 1 WLR 589, M & B p 714; (1968) 112 SJ 172 (SM Cretney) (right to be used 'in common with all other persons having the like right'); *Rosling v Pinnegar* (1986) 54 P & CR 124 (access to Hammerwood Park, near East Grinstead, built by Latrobe, American architect of the White House); cf *National Trust for Places of Historic Interest or Natural Beauty v White* [1987] 1 WLR 907 (access to Figsbury Ring, near Salisbury); *White v Richards* (1993) 68 P & CR 105; *Gardner v Davis* [1998] NPC 123 (extent of sewage easement unreasonable); *Thompson v Bee*, above, n 371 (right of way 'for all purposes' may cover change of use of dominant tenement from agricultural to residential, but does not authorise excessive use where dominant tenement would be developed by building three houses).

[375] *Johnstone v Holdway* [1963] 1 QB 601, M & B p 717 (extrinsic evidence admissible where dominant tenement not identified in deed); *Shannon Ltd v Venner Ltd* [1965] Ch 682; *Land Reclamation Co Ltd v Basildon DC* [1979] 1 WLR 106, 110; *Scott v Martin* [1987] 1 WLR 841 (plan used to explain 'private road'); *Hamble Parish Council v Haggard* [1992] 1 WLR 122 at 130 (Millett J: 'I have to put myself into the shoes of the notional judge visiting the site with the conveyance in one hand and gazing about him to identify on the

exercise of the right of way by the owner is in substance for the dominant tenement or for other land that he owns.[376]

(2) Implied Grant

If the easement is created by implied grant, we have already seen that where it is implied in favour of the grantor, an easement of necessity is strictly limited to the circumstances of the necessity prevailing at the time of the grant.[377] In the case of an easement implied in favour of the grantee, the grantee must establish that the parties intended that the subject of the grant should be used in some definite and particular manner; the law will then imply the grant of such easements as may be necessary to give effect to it.[378] Where the easement is implied under the rule in *Wheeldon v Burrows*,[379] the extent of the easement will depend on the scope of the continuous and apparent user at the time of the grant.

(3) Prescription

The extent of a prescriptive easement is commensurate with its user.[380] Once the purposes for which it has been used during the period of its acquisition have been determined by evidence, the scope of the easement is defined. However, a question may arise as to whether the easement extends to a change in user of the dominant tenement. In considering such a case, the courts consider (i) whether the new user constitutes a radical change in the character or a change in the identity of the

ground those features that would enable him to ascertain the extent of the dominant land'); *West v Sharp* (2000) 79 P & CR 327. Cf, on the question of identification of the land benefited by a restrictive covenant, the judgment of Upjohn J in *Newton Abbott Co-operative Society Ltd v Williamson and Treadgold Ltd* [1952] Ch 286, below, p 754.

[376] *Harris v Flower* (1904) 74 LJ Ch 127, 132 (Romer LJ: 'If a right of way be granted for the enjoyment of Close A, the grantee, because he owns or acquires Close B, cannot use the way in substance for passing over Close A to Close B'), followed in *Bracewell v Appleby* [1975] Ch 408; cf *Nickerson v Barraclough* [1980] Ch 325, 336 (such a right held to be usable as access where Close A is itself used as access to Close B at time of grant). See also *Jobson v Record* (1997) 75 P & CR 375; *Alvis v Harrison* (1991) 62 P & CR 10, 15–16; *Peacock v Custins* [2002] 1 WLR 1815 (easement did not extend to access to field adjacent to dominant land); *Das v Linden Mews Ltd* [2002] EWCA Civ 590, [2002] 2 EGLR 76 (right of way over carriageway to dominant tenement did not extend to access to parking area not comprised within the dominant tenement); [2003] Conv 127 (E Paton and G Seabourne); *Massey v Boulden* [2002] EWCA Civ 1634, [2003] 1 WLR 1792 at [38], [45] (the 'critical question' is whether the use is more than merely ancillary to the use made for the benefit of the dominant tenement); *Macepark (Whittlebury) Ltd v Sargeant* [2003] EWHC 427 (Ch), [2003] 1 WLR 2284 (use more than merely ancillary to the right of access to the dominant land); [2004] All ER Rev 242 (PJ Clarke).

[377] Above, p 661.

[378] *Milner's Safe Co Ltd v Great Northern and City Rly Co* [1907] 1 Ch 208; *Stafford v Lee* (1992) 65 P & CR 172; *Chaffe v Kingsley* [2000] 1 EGLR 104. For changes in intensity of use of the dominant tenement, see *McAdams Homes Ltd v Robinson*, [2004] EWCA Civ 214, [2005] 1 P & CR 30.

[379] Above, p 662; *Donaldson v Smith* [2007] 1 P & CR DG 2.

[380] *Dewan v Lewis* [2010] EWCA Civ 1382, [2010] All ER (D) 125 (Dec) (user over prescription period included access by foot, vehicles and horseback, but not driving cattle).

dominant tenement, as opposed to a mere change or intensification in its use; and (ii) whether the new user results in a substantial increase or alteration in the burden on the servient land.[381] The burden upon the servient tenement must not be increased by reason of a radical change in the character of the dominant tenement.[382] For example, a right of way that has been used to carry agricultural produce to a farm cannot lawfully be used to meet the requirements of a factory into which the farm is later converted.[383] But if the character or nature of the user remains constant, there is no objection to an increase in its intensity.[384] A right of way appurtenant to a golf club, for example, is not misused merely because the membership of the club has greatly increased.[385]

(4) Servient Owner's Remedies for Excessive User by Dominant Owner

The normal remedy by which the servient owner can restrain excessive user by the dominant owner is an injunction. He may not normally obstruct the user altogether.[386] However, where the good user cannot be severed from the excessive user, the remedy may be to stop the whole user.[387]

[381] *Atwood v Bovis Homes Ltd* [2001] Ch 379, M & B p 724; [2000] All ER Rev 238 (PJ Clarke); (2001) 151 NLJ 1307 (HW Wilkinson) (prescriptive easement to drain surface water); *McAdams Homes Ltd v Robinson* [2004] EWCA Civ 214, [2005] 1 P & CR 30 at [50] (Neuberger LJ) (easement of drainage implied under the rule in *Wheeldon v Burrows*; there should be little difference between easements by prescription and implied easements as regards changes of user: at [22]); Gale, paras 1.133–1.135.

[382] *Wimbledon and Putney Commons Conservators v Dixon* (1875) 1 Ch D 362; *Ward (Helston) Ltd v Kerrier DC* (1981) 42 P & CR 412.

[383] *Williams v James* (1867) LR 2 CP 577, 582 (Willes J); *Loder v Gaden* (1999) 78 P & CR 223.

[384] *British Railways Board v Glass* [1965] Ch 538, M & B p 719 (Lord Denning MR dissenting); (1965) 87 LQR 17 (REM); *Woodhouse & Co Ltd v Kirkland (Derby) Ltd* [1970] 1 WLR 1185 (considerable increase in number of customers using right of way held to be 'mere increase in user and not a user of a different kind or for a different purpose'); *Giles v County Building Constructors (Hertford) Ltd* (1971) 22 P & CR 978 (erection of seven modern dwelling units in place of two houses held to be 'evolution rather than mutation'); *Cargill v Gotts* [1981] 1 WLR 441 (drawing of extra water from neighbour's millpond for agricultural purposes held to be mere increase in user), above, p 166. Cf *Atwood v Bovis Homes Ltd*, above (easement to discharge surface water not lost, where there was radical change of user of dominant tenement but no material effect on volume of water discharged).

[385] *British Railways Board v Glass* [1965] Ch 538, 568 (Davies LJ).

[386] *Hamble Parish Council v Haggard* [1992] 1 WLR 122, 134.

[387] Ibid; *Cawkwell v Russell* (1956) 22 LJ Ex 34; *Ashdale Land & Property Co Ltd v Maioriello* [2010] EWHC 3296 (Ch), [2011] 07 EG 102 (right of way, limited to agricultural purposes, in fact used for access to site that was being developed into gipsy caravan site in breach of planning permission and ignoring injunctions. Dominant owner, who had no serious intention to use his land for agricultural purposes, had taken 'a calculated risk that planning consent would be forthcoming and that the owner of the right of way could be persuaded to enlarge the right. The gamble has seriously backfired': Field J at [32]).

F THE RUNNING OF THE BENEFIT AND THE BURDEN OF AN EASEMENT

An easement will be binding on the original grantor in favour of the original grantee as a matter of contract. However, as an incorporeal hereditament,[388] a legal easement is capable of binding the owner for the time being of the servient tenement, in favour of the owner for the time being of the dominant tenement, as a matter of property. So too an equitable easement is capable of binding and benefiting the successors in title of the original parties. The circumstances in which the benefit and the burden will run vary according to whether the easement is legal or equitable, and whether the land is registered or unregistered.

(1) The Benefit

The benefit of an easement, whether legal or equitable, will pass on a conveyance of the dominant tenement by virtue of section 62 of the Law of Property Act 1925.[389] In the case of registered land, under the Land Registration Act 2002[390] first registration with absolute title vests the estate in the proprietor together with all interests subsisting for the benefit of the estate,[391] and therefore easements that benefited the land before it was registered continue to benefit it after registration. And a disposition of a registered estate takes effect with the benefit of rights that are appurtenant to that estate,[392] thus transferring those benefits that attached to the estate immediately before the transfer. However, the benefit of a legal easement will often be entered on the register of the dominant tenement. The policy of the new scheme for registration introduced by the 2002 Act is that, as far as possible,[393] the register should reflect rights such as legal easements, and there are provisions permitting entries of expressly granted legal easements to be made on first registration,[394] and requiring[395] or permitting[396] entries of such easements on their later creation.

---

[388] Above, pp 633–4.

[389] Above, p 655; unless a contrary intention is expressed in the conveyance: s 62(4). 'Conveyance' is drafted sufficiently widely to include a transfer of registered land: s 205(1)(ii); but does not include a contract to sell: above, p 656. The benefit of an existing easement can therefore pass on a contract only if expressly provision is made in the contract.

[390] LRA 1925, ss 19(3), 22(3), used to provide explicitly that the general words implied by LPA 1925, s 62, applied also to dispositions of a registered estate. The provisions of LRA 2002 have the same general effect as the 1925 Act as regards the passing of benefits appurtenant to registered titles: R & R, para 3.008.01.

[391] LRA 2002, ss 11(2) (freehold), 12(3) (leasehold).   [392] R & R, para 3.008.01.

[393] There is no requirement of entry in the register where the easement is legal but not expressly granted (ie, it is created by prescription, by implied grant or under LPA 1925 s 62: LRA 2002, s 27(7)), or is equitable.

[394] LRR 2003, r 33(1); H & B, para 2.34.

[395] LRA 2002, s 27(2)(d); Sch 2, para 7(2)(b) (where the grant is out of a registered estate).

[396] LRR 2003, r 73A, substituted for the original r 73 by LR(A)R 2008, SI 2008 No 1919, Sch 1, para 24 (where the grant is over an unregistered legal estate).

(2) The Burden

(a) Registered land

Under the Land Registration Act 1925 easements enjoyed a privileged position. Under section 70(1)(a) all legal easements were overriding interests, and therefore bound all successors of the servient tenement without requiring to be protected by notice on the register. There was some doubt about the intended scope of that provision as regards equitable easements, but in *Celsteel Ltd v Alton House Holdings Ltd*[397] Scott J held that it extended to

> all equitable easements other than such as by reason of some other statutory provision or applicable principle of law, could obtain protection otherwise than by notice on the register. The most obvious example would be equitable easements which qualified for protection under paragraph (g) as part of the rights of a person in actual occupation.

This gave a general protection to the beneficiary of an equitable easement who could therefore in most cases enforce his easement against a purchaser of the servient tenement, without the need to register it. This position has now been reversed, and under the Land Registration Act 2002 no new equitable easement will be an overriding interest either on first registration or on a registered disposition.[398] However, easements that were already overriding interests in relation to a registered estate immediately before the coming into force of the Act (13 October 2003[399]) retain their status as overriding interests[400] and therefore the old law on equitable easements will remain relevant for some time.[401]

Under the Land Registration Act 2002,[402] on a first registration all existing legal easements will override, thus allowing the legal easements that bound the servient tenement automatically under the system of unregistered land[403] to continue to bind the registered estate. However, in relation to new easements created in relation to a registered servient tenement, several distinctions are drawn. The express[404] grant or reservation of a legal easement is a disposition that is required to be completed by registration;[405] and the registration requirement for such easements is that a notice be entered in the register of the servient tenement and also, if it is a registered estate, the dominant tenement.[406] An expressly granted or reserved easement therefore does not

---

[397] [1985] 1 WLR 204, 220; [1986] Conv 31 (MP Thompson); [1999] Conv (J Greed).

[398] LRA 2002, Sch 1, para 3, and Sch 3, para 3 respectively, which are both expressly restricted to legal easements.

[399] SI 2003 No 1725, art 2(1).   [400] LRA 2002, Sch 2, para 9.

[401] The problem should, however, recede over time: on the application to register a registrable disposition the applicant must provide information about interests (such as overriding interests) so that they can be entered onto the register: LRA 2002, s 71(b); LRR 2003, r 57(1); H & B, para 11.17.

[402] On the impact of the changes made by the 2002 Act, see [2003] Conv 304 (P Kenny); [2005] Conv 195 (G Battersby).

[403] Below.

[404] This does not include an easement granted as a result of the operation of LPA 1925, s 62: LRA 2002, s 27(7).

[405] LRA 2002, s 27(2)(e).   [406] Ibid, Sch 2, para 7.

take effect as a legal easement until these registration requirements have been met,[407] and, since there will then be an appropriate notice on the register, there is no question of it being an overriding interest: a purchaser of the servient tenement is bound by virtue of the notice on the register.

Other newly created legal easements—those created by implied[408] grant or prescription—are capable of being overriding interests and therefore of overriding a registered disposition without being protected by notice on the register. However, a further distinction is drawn according to the date of the disposition. Under transitional provisions[409] *all* legal easements were overriding interests for a period of three years from the day on which the Act came into force—that is for the period from 13 October 2003 to 12 October 2006. This therefore continued for this limited period the position that prevailed under the 1925 Act, giving overriding effect to legal easements as a general class. However, since 13 October 2006 the only legal easements that qualify as overriding interests are set out in the Land Registration Act 2002, Schedule 3, paragraph 3:

(1) A legal easement or profit à prendre, except for an easement, or a profit à prendre which is not registered under the Commons Registration Act 1965,[410] which at the time of the disposition—

    (a) is not within the actual knowledge of the person to whom the disposition is made, and

    (b) would not have been obvious on a reasonably careful inspection of the land over which the easement or profit is exercisable.

(2) The exception in sub-paragraph (1) does not apply if the person entitled to the easement or profit proves that it has been exercised in the period of one year ending with the day of the disposition.

The general effect[411] of this provision is that a legal easement or profit à prendre will still be an overriding interest if:

  (i) it is a right of common registered under the Commons Registration Act 1965;[412] or

 (ii) it is within the actual knowledge of the disponee; or

(iii) it would have been obvious on a reasonably careful inspection of the servient tenement; or

---

[407] Above, p 651.

[408] Including those granted as a result of the operation of LPA 1925, s 62: above, n 404.

[409] LRA 2002, Sch 12, para 10.

[410] This reference will be changed to Part I of the Commons Act 2006 once the 2006 Act is brought fully into force: Commons Act 2006, Sch 5, para 8.

[411] The reading of the provision is complicated by its negative formulation, which presumably has an effect on the burden of proof: and so, for example, it will be for the disponee to show that he did *not* have actual knowledge of the easement. The burden of proof in sub-para (2) is explicit.

[412] Or Part I of the Commons Act 2006: above, n 410. For registration of commons, see below, p 708. The registration renders it discoverable by the purchaser.

(iv) the dominant owner proves that it has been exercised within one year of the disposition.

A legal easement will therefore bind a purchaser of the servient tenement, without being protected by a notice on the register of title, if it is, or ought reasonably to have been, known by him; or if it has been exercised within the last year. This has the effect of reintroducing the doctrine of notice into registered land in this context;[413] but also allows legal easements to bind a purchaser that are not patent, but are not dormant (in the sense of having fallen into more than a year's disuse), such as rights of drainage that, by being beneath the surface, are not necessarily obvious on inspection. It is a pragmatic exception to the general principle that a purchaser should be bound only by those rights that he could have discovered, and may not be a significant burden in practice, because pre-contract enquiries will generally seek to identify such rights.[414]

Moreover, as mentioned above, there is a general policy that legal easements should where possible be noted on the register so as to reduce reliance on the category of overriding interests.[415] A person applying either for first registration or to register a registrable disposition—such as the purchaser of the servient tenement—must provide information about overriding interests that affect the estate that are within his actual knowledge;[416] a legal easement that is disclosed under this provision will therefore be noted on the register and bind future purchasers accordingly.[417]

(b) Unregistered land

In unregistered land, in accordance with general principle,[418] the burden of a legal easement is enforceable against all the world, and therefore against all subsequent owners of the servient tenement, or of any interest in it, whether or not they give value for the acquisition of their interest, or have notice of the easement.

An equitable easement, however, does not bind all later owners of the servient tenement. Certain forms of equitable easement are registrable as land charges under the Land Charges Act 1972, and if not registered are void against a purchaser of the legal estate for money or money's worth.[419] This applies to equitable easements that arise under the doctrine of *Walsh v Lonsdale*[420] pursuant to a contract to create a legal easement (registrable as an estate contract[421]); and an 'equitable easement',[422] which is defined as[423] 'any easement, right or privilege over or affecting land created or arising on or after 1st January 1926, and being merely an equitable interest' but which is to

---

[413] See also the similar issue that arises in relation to LRA 2002, Sch 3, para 2; below, p 1110.

[414] H & B, para 11.15. For pre-contract enquiries generally, see Ch 24.

[415] H & B, paras 11.18–11.22.

[416] LRA 2002, s 71(a) (first registration), (b) (registrable disposition); LRR 2003, rr 28 (first registration), 57 (registrable disposition).

[417] In addition, the registrar has a general power to note overriding interests that overrode first registration, and that come to his attention otherwise than through the disclosure requirement: LRA 2002, s 37; LRR 2003, r 89.

[418] Above, p 80.   [419] LCA 1972, s 2(6).   [420] Above, p 653.

[421] LCA 1972, s 2(4)(iv), Class C(iv).   [422] Ibid, s 2(5)(iii), Class D(iii).   [423] Ibid.

be construed more narrowly[424] than might first appear. It has been limited to such proprietary interests in land as would before 1926 have been recognised as capable of being conveyed or created at law, but which since 1925 only take effect as equitable interests, such as an easement granted for the life of the grantee.[425]

An equitable easement that is not capable of registration as a land charge[426] will be void against a purchaser without notice, actual, constructive or imputed, of it.[427]

G REMEDIES FOR INFRINGEMENT OF AN EASEMENT[428]

The dominant owner may seek one or more remedies in order to enforce his rights. Not being in possession of the servient tenement, he cannot maintain an action of trespass for infringement of the easement.[429] However, he may seek a declaration in order to establish the existence and extent of the easement; and since infringement of an easement constitutes the tort of nuisance against the dominant owner,[430] he may seek the usual remedies for nuisance: the self-help remedy of *abatement*; or an action for *damages* or an *injunction*.

(1) Abatement

The party suffering a nuisance may abate it: that is take steps to stop the nuisance—such as by pulling down a physical obstruction to the light to his windows that the servient owner has erected on his land. However, 'the abatement of a nuisance is a remedy that the law does not favour and is not usually advisable',[431] since it involves the party taking matters into his own hands rather than pursuing his remedies through legal action. The party purporting to exercise the right of abatement risks committing

---

[424] *Shiloh Spinners Ltd v Harding* [1973] AC 691, M & B p 68; below, p 1059.

[425] *E R Ives Investment Ltd v High* [1967] 2 QB 379, 395 (Lord Denning); M & B p 1074; (1937) 53 LQR 259 (CV Davidge); (1948) 12 Conv (NS) 202 (JF Garner).

[426] Such as one arising under the doctrine of proprietary estoppel: *E R Ives Investment Ltd v High* [1967] 2 QB 379.

[427] LPA 1925, s 199(1)(ii).   [428] Gale, ch 14.

[429] In this respect an easement differs from a profit à prendre, for which the remedy of trespass may therefore be available: below, p 703; *Paine & Co Ltd v St Neots Gas & Coke Co* [1939] 3 All ER 812, 823 (Luxmoore LJ).

[430] 'Nuisance is a tort against land, including interests in land such as easements and profits': *Hunter v Canary Wharf Ltd* [1997] AC 655, 702 (Lord Hoffmann). The action for infringement (or *disturbance*) of an easement has sometimes been distinguished from the action of nuisance: see, eg, *Colls v Home and Colonial Stores Ltd* [1904] AC 179, 186 (Lord Macnaghten) (right to light); *Aldred's Case* (1611) 9 Co Rep 57b. It requires different elements of pleading, since, not having possession of the property, the dominant owner must plead (and, if put in issue, prove) his title to the easement in order to show his right to claim: *Paine & Co Ltd v St Neots Gas & Coke Co*, above, at 823. However, in substance the same principles apply to the remedies available for nuisance and in an action for disturbance: Gale, para 13–01. For detailed discussion of the law of nuisance, see Buckley, *The Law of Nuisance* (2nd edn, 1996); *Clerk and Lindsell on Torts* (20th edn, 2010), ch 20. An easement may in turn *negative* liability in nuisance: conduct by the dominant owner which would otherwise constitute a nuisance against a neighbour becomes lawful if it is exercised within the scope of a duly created easement: *Hunter v Canary Wharf Ltd*, above, at 685; *Sturges v Bridgman* (1879) 11 Ch D 852.

[431] *Lagan Navigation Co v Lambeg Bleaching, Dyeing and Finishing Co Ltd* [1927] AC 226, 244 (Lord Atkinson).

an actionable wrong himself if he does not act strictly within his rights under the easement and within the limits allowed to the remedy by the courts:[432] abatement is justified only in clear and simple cases, or in an emergency;[433] the action taken must be no more than necessary to stop the nuisance;[434] and notice must in many cases[435] first be given to the occupier of the servient tenement before the dominant owner enters to abate it. However, within these limits, in an appropriate case abatement can be a very useful and efficient remedy to stop the infringement of an easement.

(2) Injunction and/or Damages

More commonly, however, the dominant owner must bring an action[436] to enforce his rights under the easement. In such a case the claimant must establish his title to the easement, and show that the defendant's actual or threatened conduct constitutes an actionable interference with the easement.[437] Actual loss or damage need not be proved: the infringement of the easement is a sufficient violation of a legal right to found an action.[438] However, there must be a substantial interference with the reasonable use of the easement.[439]

The primary remedy for nuisance is an injunction;[440] damages may be awarded, in the court's discretion, in addition to, or in substitution for, an injunction[441] and, in particular, may be awarded where the injury to the claimant's legal rights is small, capable of being estimated in money and can be adequately compensated by a small money payment, and it would be oppressive to the defendant to grant an injunction.[442]

---

[432] *Wheeldon v Burrows* (1879) 12 Ch D 31 (trespass committed by defendant who knocked down obstructions to light where the court held that he had no easement of light).

[433] *Burton v Winters* [1993] 1 WLR 1077, 1082.   [434] *Greenslade v Halliday* (1830) 6 Bing 379.

[435] Notice is not required in an emergency, but is certainly required where the person in occupation did not himself create the nuisance, and may be required where he did: see the authorities cited in Gale, para 14–09. Notice is not required where the dominant owner can abate the nuisance without entering onto the servient tenement.

[436] An action relating to an easement over land is a pending land action within the meaning of LCA 1972, which in registered land must be protected by notice and cannot be an overriding interest: LRA 2002, s 87(1), (3). In unregistered land it must be registered in the register of pending actions: LCA 1972, s 1(1)(b); if it is to bind a purchaser without express notice of it: ibid, s 5(7).

[437] If the defendant denies any of these elements, the claimant must therefore prove that the right he claims is in the nature of an easement (above, pp 636 ff); that it has been created as an easement (above, pp 651 ff); that he has the benefit of it and the defendant the burden of it (above, pp 690 ff); and the extent of the easement, so as to demonstrate its infringement on the facts (above, pp 686 ff).

[438] *Nicholls v Ely Beet Sugar Factory Ltd* [1936] Ch 343.

[439] *Celsteel Ltd v Alton House Holdings Ltd* [1985] 1 WLR 204, 217 (right of way); *West v Sharp* (2000) 79 P & CR 327; *B & Q plc v Liverpool & Lancashire Properties Ltd* [2001] 1 EGLR 92 (right of way): 'the test of an actionable interference is not whether the grantee is left with what is reasonable, but whether his insistence upon being able to continue the use of the whole of what he contracted for is reasonable': Blackburne J at 96; *Perlman v Rayden* [2004] EWHC 2192 (Ch), [2004] 43 EGCS 142 (aggravated damages awarded).

[440] *Shelfer v City of London Electric Lighting Co* [1895] 1 Ch 287.

[441] SCA 1981, s 50, replacing Chancery Amendment Act 1858, s 2 (Lord Cairns' Act).

[442] *Shelfer v City of London Electric Lighting Co*, above, at 322–3 (AL Smith LJ): a 'good working rule', which has been applied in many later cases. The elements of the 'rule' are cumulative, emphasising the narrow practical scope of the remedy of damages as compared with that of injunction. Many cases have

H EXTINGUISHMENT OF EASEMENTS

An easement may be extinguished by statute or by release or as the result of unity of seisin of the dominant and servient tenements. Where the benefit of an easement is given to the tenant under a lease, the determination of the lease does not necessarily extinguish the easement.[443] There is at present no statutory procedure for the discharge or modification of easements as there is in the case of restrictive covenants.[444]

(1) Statute

Easements may be extinguished by statute. Important examples are to be found in the Town and Country Planning Act 1990, under which acquiring authorities are enabled to extinguish 'all private rights of way and rights of laying down, erecting, continuing or maintaining any apparatus on, under or over the land'.[445] Further, local authorities may build or carry out work on land acquired for planning purposes, even though it involves interference with 'any easement, liberty, privilege, right or advantage annexed to land and adversely affecting other land, including any natural right of support'.[446] However, even if works required to be carried out by a defendant pursuant to statute

arisen in relation to rights to light: see eg *Colls v Home and Colonial Stores Ltd* [1904] AC 179, M & B p 728 (injunction refused); *Pugh v Howells* (1984) 48 P & CR 298 (mandatory injunction granted); *Blue Town Investments Ltd v Higgs and Hill plc* [1990] 1 WLR 696; *Marine and General Mutual Life Assurance Society v St James' Real Estate Co Ltd* [1991] 2 EGLR 178 (measure of damages); *Voyce v Voyce* (1991) 62 P & CR 290 (right of light enforceable against equitable owner); *Deakins v Hookings* [1994] 1 EGLR 190; (1994) 144 NLJ 875 (HW Wilkinson); *Midtown Ltd v City of London Real Property Co Ltd* [2005] EWHC 33 (Ch), [2005] 1 EGLR 65 (injunction refused); *Regan v Paul Properties DPF No 1 Ltd* [2006] EWCA Civ 1319, [2007] Ch 135 (injunction granted); [2007] Conv 175 (P Chynoweth); (2006) 156 NLJ 1868 (A Craig); [2007] All ER Rev 256 (PJ Clarke); *Tamares (Vincent Square) Ltd v Fairpoint Properties (Vincent Square) Ltd* [2007] 1 WLR 2148 (injunction would be oppressive and unjust), *Tamares (Vincent Square) Ltd v Fairpoint Properties (Vincent Square) Ltd (No 2)* [2007] EWHC 212 (Ch), [2007] 1 WLR 2167 (assessment of damages in lieu of injunction: 'the court needs to consider whether the "deal feels right"', Moss QC at [22]); [2007] 14 EG 103 (S Murdoch); *Forsyth-Grant v Allen* [2008] EWCA Civ 505, [2008] 2 EGLR 16 (damages awarded on basis of actual loss caused by infringement of right; account of profits by respondent developer refused); (2010) 126 LQR 102 (C Rotherham); *HKRUK II (CHC) Ltd v Heaney* [2010] EWHC 2245 (Ch), [2010] 44 EG 126 (injunction to order cut-back of offending building works where interference with right to light was committed with view to profit); (2010) 160 NLJ 1372 (E Humphreys and M Dowden). See also *Bracewell v Appleby* [1975] Ch 408 (no right of way to newly-built house; injunction would render house uninhabitable: damages awarded); *Heslop v Bishton* [2009] EWHC 607 (Ch), [2009] 2 EGLR 11 at [21] (provision of alternative right of way relevant to whether court would order injunction to enforce original right of way).

443 *Wall v Collins* [2007] EWCA Civ 444, [2007] Ch 390 (merger of residue of 999-year lease into freehold), above, p 634, n 3. Law Com CP No 186, *Easements, Covenants and Profits à Prendre* (2008), paras 5.72–5.5.86, provisionally proposes a reversal of the decision in relation to termination of leaseholds.

444 LPA 1925, s 84; below, p 764. The Law Commission has provisionally proposed that s 84 be extended to include easements: Law Com CP No 186, *Easements, Covenants and Profits à Prendre* (2008), para 14.41; below, p 725.

445 TCPA 1990, s 236.

446 Ibid, s 237. See also HA 1985, s 295; New Towns Act 1981, s 19; *R v City of London Corp and Royal London Mutual Insurance Society, ex p Master of Governors and Commonality of the Mystery of the Barbers of London* (1996) 73 P & CR 59.

necessarily interfere with a claimant's easement, the easement is not extinguished once and for all if there is a possibility, albeit remote, that there may in the future no longer be any statutory impediment to the exercise of the claimant's rights. In *Jones v Cleanthi* Jonathan Parker LJ said:[447]

> I bear in mind the well-known common law principle, variously expressed, that an Act should not be construed so as to injure or interfere with a person's rights without compensation unless the court is obliged so to construe it;[448] that an intention to take away a person's property without compensation should not be imputed to Parliament unless expressed in unequivocal terms;[449] and that if an Act is to have the effect of taking away a property right, 'it must be by plain enactment or necessary intendment'[450]—a principle which largely reflects article 1 of the First Protocol to the European Convention on Human Rights, incorporated into domestic law by the Human Rights Act 1998.

Absent a finding of negligence, however, the statutory authority for such works will constitute a defence to an action in nuisance by the claimant.[451]

(2) Release

An extinguishment may be effected by a release, either express or implied.

(a) Express release

The dominant owner is free to execute a deed of release relieving the servient tenement from the burden of any easement to which it is subject. At common law a deed is necessary,[452] but if the servient owner, in reliance on an agreement to release, has prejudiced his position to such an extent that it would be inequitable and oppressive to treat the easement as still in being, equity will disregard the absence of formalities and will hold the dominant owner to his bargain. If, for example, a person who is entitled to an easement of light orally agrees to an alteration in the servient tenement that must necessarily obstruct the flow of light to the window, he cannot, after expense has been incurred in making the alteration, bring an action in respect of the resulting obstruction.[453]

---

447 [2006] EWCA Civ 1712, [2007] 1 WLR 1604 at [82] (fire precaution works carried out by freeholder as required by HA 1985, s 352, in order to make property fit for multiple occupation); [2007] L&T Rev 75 (J Summers); [2007] All ER Rev 259 (PJ Clarke).

448 See *Attorney General v Horner* (1884) 14 QBD 245, 257 (Brett MR).

449 See *Comr of Public Works (Cape Colony) v Logan* [1903] AC 355, 363–4 (Lord Davey, delivering the judgment of the Privy Council).

450 See *Bond v Norman* [1939] Ch 847, 856 (Simonds J).

451 *Jones v Cleanthi*, above, n 447, at [92]. Statute is construed as authorising a nuisance only if the statutory powers are exercised without negligence; that is with a reasonable regard and care for the interests of other persons: *Geddis v Proprietors of Bann Reservoir* (1878) 3 App Cas 430, 455 (Lord Blackburn); *Allen v Gulf Oil Refining Ltd* [1981] AC 1001, 1011 (Lord Wilberforce).

452 Co Litt 264b.

453 *Davies v Marshall* (1861) 10 CBNS 697; *Waterlow v Bacon* (1866) LR 2 Eq 514. This is, in substance, an application of the principles of proprietary estoppel; below, Ch 22.

(b) Implied release

(1) Abandonment

A more important and at the same time more difficult point is whether in any given case there has been an implied release or abandonment of the easement by the dominant owner.

The onus of proving abandonment lies fairly and squarely on the person who alleges it, and the onus is a very heavy one.[454] Buckley LJ said in *Tehidy Minerals Ltd v Norman*:[455]

Abandonment of an easement or of a profit à prendre can only, we think, be treated as having taken place where the person entitled to it has demonstrated a fixed intention never at any time thereafter to assert the right himself or to attempt to transmit it to anyone else.

The general principle is that whether he intended to abandon his right depends upon the proper inference to be drawn from the circumstances.[456]

No one circumstance necessarily implies an abandonment, and it has been laid down repeatedly that mere non-user is not decisive of the question.[457] If the non-user is explicable only on the assumption that the dominant owner intended to give up his right, it will amount to an abandonment, but not if there are other circumstances that go to show that he regarded the right as still alive. In other words, a cessation may show either an abandonment or a mere abeyance of an easement according to the particular circumstances of each case.

The principle was restated by Pollock MR in *Swan v Sinclair*:[458]

Non-user is not by itself conclusive evidence that a private right of easement is abandoned. The non-user must be considered with, and may be explained by, the surrounding circumstances. If those circumstances clearly indicate an intention of not resuming the user then a presumption of a release of the easement will, in general, be implied and the easement will be lost.

Thus in the leading case of *Moore v Rawson*:[459]

A claimant, who had some ancient windows, pulled down the wall in which they were situated and rebuilt it as a stable with no windows. Some fourteen years later the defendant erected on his adjoining land a building which would have obstructed the flow of light to the windows had they still been there. After another three years the claimant made a

---

[454] *James v Stevenson* [1893] AC 162.
[455] [1971] 2 QB 528, 553, M & B p 697.
[456] *Cook v Bath Corp* (1868) LR 6 Eq 177.
[457] *R v Chorley* (1848) 12 QB 515; *Ward v Ward* (1852) 7 Exch 838; *Crossley & Sons Ltd v Lightowler* (1867) 2 Ch App 478; *Re Yateley Common, Hampshire* [1977] 1 WLR 840, 845; *Gotobed v Pridmore* (1970) 115 SJ 78; *Benn v Hardinge* (1992) 66 P & CR 246 (no abandonment in spite of 175 years' non-user); *Bosomworth v Faber* (1992) 69 P & CR 288; *Snell & Prideaux Ltd v Dutton Mirrors Ltd* [1995] 1 EGLR 259; [1995] Conv 291 (CJ Davis); *CDC2020 plc v Ferreira* [2005] EWCA Civ 611, [2005] 3 EGLR 15; (2005) 155 SJ 969 (A Rosenthal); [2005] Conv 481 (L Landels); *Walker v Bridgewood* [2006] NSWSC 149, discussed in [2007] Conv 87 (H Conway).
[458] [1924] 1 Ch 254, 266; affd [1925] AC 227.
[459] (1824) 3 B & C 332, M & B p 736.

window in the stable in the exact spot where one of the old windows had been, and then proceeded to bring an action against the defendant for obstruction of light.

It was held that he could not succeed, because, in erecting a building entirely different from the old one, he had shown an intention to abandon the enjoyment of his former right. However, as stated by Holroyd J:[460]

> If he had done some act to shew that he intended to build another in its place, then the new house, when built, would in effect have been a continuation of the old house, and the rights attached to the old house would have continued. If a man has a right of common attached to his mill, or a right of turbary[461] attached to his house, if he pulls down the mill or the house, the right of common or of turbary will prima facie cease. If he show an intention to build another mill or another house, his right continues.

The same principle can be seen at work in the case of rights of way. So, where the exercise of a right of way had been discontinued for many years because the dominant owner had a more convenient route over his own land, it was held that the non-user was adequately explained and did not constitute an abandonment.[462]

But any non-user of a right of way caused by something that is adverse to the enjoyment of the right will be regarded as an abandonment. In *Swan v Sinclair*:[463]

> Certain houses were put up for sale in lots in 1871, one of the conditions being that a strip of land running at the back of the houses should be formed into a roadway, and that the purchaser of each lot should have a right of way along the road when made. At the time when the action was brought in 1923 the road had not been constructed, fences lay across its proposed site between each pair of lots, and in 1883 the then owner of lot 1 nearest the exit of the proposed road had levelled up the site, and by so doing had caused a sheer drop of 6 feet to occur between that lot and lot 2. The claimant was now desirous of building a garage on lot 2, and the question arose whether he was still entitled to a right of way over the strip of land at the back of lot 1.

The majority of the court dismissed his claim on the ground that, though as a rule mere non-user is insufficient to extinguish a right of way, yet in this case the continued existence of the dividing fences and the raising of the level of lot 1 were circumstances adverse to a right of enjoyment, sufficient to show an intention on the part of the various owners to abandon the project.

(2) Alterations to dominant tenement

Alterations to the dominant tenement that make the enjoyment of an easement impossible or unnecessary may show an intention to abandon the right. For example, where a right of water is appurtenant to a mill, and the mill is demolished, without any intention of replacing it, the easement is impliedly released.[464] Furthermore, the easement may be extinguished where the dominant tenement is so altered as to

---

460   Ibid, at 338.   461   Below, p 706.
462   *Ward v Ward* (1852) 7 Exch 838.   463   [1924] 1 Ch 254; affd [1925] AC 227.
464   *Liggins v Inge* (1831) 7 Bing 682, 693; *Ecclesiastical Comrs for England v Kino* (1880) 14 Ch D 213; *Scott v Pape* (1886) 31 Ch D 554.

place a substantially increased burden on the servient tenement to the detriment of its owner.[465]

(3) Alterations to servient tenement

A servient owner has no right to alter the route of an easement of way unless such a right is an express or implied term of the grant of the easement or is subsequently conferred on him.[466] However, even if he has no such right, nevertheless such a realignment will not be an actionable interference with the easement if the realigned right is equally convenient, especially where there is no reasonable objection to the realignment. It has been held[467] that where the dominant owner had notice of the proposal and did not object and where the realignment achieved an object of substantial public importance, the dominant owner's remedy, if any, should be restricted to an award of damages.

(3) Frustration

In *Huckvale v Aegean Hotels Ltd*, the Court of Appeal considered a novel claim that an easement can be extinguished by its ceasing to accommodate the dominant tenement. In granting an interlocutory injunction, Slade LJ said:[468]

> In the absence of evidence of proof of abandonment, the court should be slow to hold that an easement has been extinguished by frustration, unless the evidence shows clearly that because of a change of circumstances since the date of the original grant there is no practical possibility of its ever again benefiting the dominant tenement in the manner contemplated by that grant.

(4) Unity of Seisin

Easements are also extinguished by unity of seisin, that is to say, if the fees simple of both the dominant and the servient tenements become united in the same owner, all easements properly so called come to an end, for the owner can do what he likes with his own land, and any right that formerly ranked as an easement because it was exercisable over another's land is now merely one of the ordinary incidents of his ownership.[469] An easement that has been destroyed by this union of title in one hand

---

[465] *Ankerson v Connelly* [1906] 2 Ch 544; affd [1907] 1 Ch 678 (easement of light); *Ray v Fairway Motors (Barnstaple) Ltd* (1968) 20 P & CR 261 (easement of support); *Lloyds Bank Ltd v Dalton* [1942] Ch 466, 471–2 (Bennett J); cf *Graham v Philcox* [1984] QB 747, M & B p 715, above, p 657; Gale, para 12–32. Cf *Atwood v Bovis Homes Ltd* [2001] Ch 379, M & B p 724, above, p 689, n 384, where there was a change in the *extent* of the user of the dominant tenement.

[466] *Deacon v South-Eastern Railway Co* (1889) 61 LT 377; *Heslop v Bishton* [2009] EWHC 607 (Ch), [2009] 2 EGLR 11 (but provision of equally convenient alternative route may lead to award of a declaration or compensation, rather than an injunction: at [24]-[25]).

[467] *Greenwich Healthcare National Health Service Trust v London and Quadrant Housing Trust* [1998] 1 WLR 1749, 1754 (Lightman J), who granted such a declaration in the absence of the dominant owner.

[468] (1989) 58 P & CR 163, 173; [1990] Conv 292 (K Kodilinye).

[469] Co Litt 313a; *Lord Dynevor v Tennant* (1888) 13 App Cas 279.

may, however, be recreated under the doctrine of *Wheeldon v Burrows* if the property is again severed into its original parts.[470] A complete extinguishment occurs when both the tenements become united in one person for an estate in fee simple, but if he acquires only a particular estate in one of them, such as a life interest or a term of years, the easement is merely suspended and will revive again if upon the determination of his particular estate the tenements are once more in different hands.[471]

Unity of seisin without unity of possession does not extinguish an easement of light, such as where the owner of the servient tenement acquires the fee simple in the dominant tenement while the latter is in the possession of a tenant for years.[472] It is doubtful, however, whether this is true in the case of easements other than light.[473]

III PROFITS À PRENDRE

A NATURE OF PROFITS À PRENDRE

(1) General Nature

A profit à prendre consists of the right to enter another's land and to take something off the land.[474] It is this participation in the produce of the soil or in the soil itself that principally distinguishes a profit from an easement. A right is a profit only if the thing to be taken is something that is capable of ownership. Thus the rights to pasture cattle or horses[475] on another's land, or to take sand or fish from another's river, or to take soil, turf, stones or pheasants[476] from another's estate are all examples of profits, for such things are capable of ownership; but a right to collect and carry away water from a spring on another person's land, or to water cattle in another's stream, is not a profit but an easement, since water is not part of the soil like sand, nor the produce of soil like grass, and unless stored in a tank or other receptacle,[477] is not capable of private ownership.[478]

---

[470] (1879) 12 Ch D 31, above, p 662. But not under LPA 1925, s 62, since there would be no diversity of occupation; above, p 657.

[471] *Thomas v Thomas* (1835) 2 Cr M & R 34.

[472] *Lord Richardson v Graham* [1908] 1 KB 39, M & B p 737.

[473] In *Buckby v Coles* (1814) 5 Taunt 311, Macdonald CB was of opinion that a right of way was not extinguished by mere unity of seisin (at 315), but the Court of Common Pleas expressed a 'decided opinion' to the opposite effect (at 315–16) and counsel abandoned the argument.

[474] *Duke of Sutherland v Heathcote* [1892] 1 Ch 475, 484.

[475] *Polo Woods Foundation v Shelton-Agar* [2009] EWHC 1361 (Ch), [2010] 1 P & CR 12.

[476] On sporting rights, see *Peech v Best* [1931] 1 KB 1 at 9; *Pole v Peake* [1998] EGCS 125.

[477] Such as a reservoir: *Mitchell v Potter* [2005] EWCA Civ 88, The Times, 24 January 2005.

[478] Co Litt 4a; Blackstone, vol ii, p 18; *Mason v Hill* (1833) 5 B & Ad 1; *Race v Ward* (1855) 4 E & B 702; *Lowe v J W Ashmore Ltd* [1971] Ch 545, 557. On the landowner's rights to water see generally above, pp 163 ff.

(2) Different Forms of Profit à Prendre

Profits à prendre may take the following forms:[479]

(a) Profit appurtenant

A profit appurtenant is one that exists for the benefit of, and is annexed to, an estate in land. In this respect, such a profit resembles an easement, since, as we have seen,[480] an easement must exist for the benefit of an estate (the dominant tenement). The following forms of profit à prendre, however, are different from easements.

(b) Profit appendant

A profit is appendant if it is annexed to the land by operation of law. If before the passing of the Statute *Quia Emptores* in 1290 the lord of a manor granted arable land to be held of him by a freehold tenant, the common law automatically appended to the grant a right in the tenant to pasture upon the waste lands of the manor such cattle as were necessary to plough and manure the arable land.[481] This right of pasture was held to be appendant, and necessarily appendant, to a grant of arable land within a manor, for the grantee obviously could not till the arable land without beasts of plough, and he would have no means of sustaining the animals unless he could pasture them on the manorial waste.[482] This right, therefore, arose from common right upon the grant of arable land within a manor, and it must be distinguished from profits appurtenant to land, which are opposed to common right and must be deliberately acquired by an actual or presumed grant.[483] Profits appendant are still possible, but they must have come into existence before 1290,[484] since the effect of *Quia Emptores* was that all sales by the lord of the manor since that date take the land out of the manor altogether,[485] so that the grantee does not hold of the manor in the waste of which he claims a right.

(c) Profit in gross

Unlike an easement,[486] a profit may be granted in gross to be held independently of the ownership of land.[487] From early times it was held that an express grant by deed to a man, his heirs and assigns of a perpetual right to a profit was a valid grant,[488] and as the possibility of a grant is the basis of all the methods whereby profits as well as easements may be acquired, it was later held that a profit in gross might be

---

[479] A different classification, into *several profits* and *profits in common*, is discussed below.

[480] Above, p 636.

[481] Co Litt 122a; Blackstone, vol ii, p 33; *Earl of Dunraven v Llewellyn* (1850) 15 QB 791, 810; Holdsworth, *A History of English Law*, vol iii, pp 147 ff; Hall, *Law relating to Profits à Prendre and Rights of Common* (1871), p 224.

[482] Blackstone, vol ii, p 33.

[483] *Tyrringham's Case* (1584) 4 Co Rep 36b; *Warrick v Queen's College, Oxford* (1871) 6 Ch App 716.

[484] See *Davies v Davies* [1975] QB 172.   [485] Above, p 35.   [486] Above, p 636.

[487] *Lord Chesterfield v Harris* [1908] 2 Ch 397, 421 (Buckley LJ).

[488] 1495 YB 11 Hen, fol 8a, cited by Parke B in *Wickham v Hawker* (1840) 7 M & W 63, 79.

prescribed for at common law.[489] Such profits in gross are not common, but once established they may be sold or leased to a third party,[490] and they will pass under a will or intestacy.

(d) Profit *pur cause de vicinage*

A profit *pur cause de vicinage* is restricted to the common[491] of pasturage, and arises where adjacent commons are open and unfenced and there is a custom for the cattle to inter-common, that is for the cattle rightfully put upon the common of one manor to stray and feed on the common of the adjoining manor without being treated as trespassers.[492]

(3) Differences Between Profits and Easements

We have already noted some of the differences between profits à prendre and easements: in particular, that a profit, unlike an easement, carries the right to remove something from the servient tenement; and that a profit can exist in gross. In the following pages we shall see other differences. For example, profits, as well as easements, may be prescribed for under the Prescription Act 1832; but the statutory periods of enjoyment are fixed at 30 and 60 years instead of 20 and 40.[493] The remedies available to the beneficiary of a profit are also more extensive than those of the beneficiary of an easement. Since a profit imports the privilege of carrying away something from the servient tenement, the dominant owner enjoys such possessory rights as will enable him to maintain trespass or nuisance at common law for an infringement of his right, but the owner of an easement is restricted to the remedies of abatement or an action of nuisance.[494]

(4) Similarities between Profits and Easements

Apart from the differences indicated, the nature of a profit is in general similar to that of an easement. Thus, for example, it is necessary that a profit that is *appurtenant* to land should be connected with the dominant tenement in the sense of increasing its beneficial enjoyment.[495] The law does not recognise an unlimited profit appurtenant, such as a right to cut turf[496] or to catch salmon for sale,[497] or to dig clay wherever it is

---

[489] *Welcome v Upton* (1840) 6 M & W 536; *Johnson v Barnes* (1872) LR 7 CP 592; affd (1873) LR 8 CP 527; *Shuttleworth v Le Fleming* (1865) 19 CBNS 687; *Goodman v Saltash Corp* (1882) 7 App Cas 633, 658.

[490] *Goodman v Saltash Corp*, above.   [491] Below, p 705.

[492] Co Litt 122a; *Tyrringham's Case* (1584) 4 Co Rep 36b. See *Newman v Bennett* [1981] QB 726 (three straying cows in the New Forest).

[493] Prescription Act 1832, s 1; below, p 715.

[494] *Fitzgerald v Firbank* [1897] 2 Ch 96; *Peech v Best* [1931] 1 KB 1; *Nicholls v Ely Beet Sugar Factory Ltd* [1936] Ch 343.

[495] *Clayton v Corby* (1843) 5 QB 415, 419; *Bailey v Stephens* (1862) 12 CBNS 91; cf above, p 636.

[496] *Valentine v Penny* (1605) Noy 145.

[497] *Lord Chesterfield v Harris* [1908] 2 Ch 397; affd [1911] AC 623.

required for making bricks.[498] A profit appurtenant must be limited, and the limit is arrived at by estimating the needs of the dominant tenement.[499]

Further, a profit, like an easement, is capable of subsisting as a legal interest;[500] it may also be equitable.[501]

B CLASSES OF PROFITS À PRENDRE

(1) Several Profits and Profits in Common

Profits fall into two classes, namely those enjoyed by their owner to the exclusion of everybody else, and those enjoyed by him in common with other persons including the owner of the servient tenement.

The first are called 'several' profits à prendre, and the latter profits à prendre in 'common', or rights of common, or more often simply *commons*:

> A right of common may be said to exist where two or more take, in common with each other, from the soil of a third person a part of the natural profits thence produced.[502]

Thus, while every common is a profit à prendre, it does not follow that all profits à prendre are commons.[503]

Profits à prendre are rights that have existed from a very early date in the history of this country, and that in their origin[504] were exercised by numbers of persons in common with each other. Moreover, that is the form in which they are most frequently found nowadays. It may of course happen that a person possesses the right to take something off the land of another without affecting the right of the owner to take similar things for his own use; or he may be entitled to the exclusive right of taking something, as often occurs in the case of pasturage rights over the Sussex Downs; but the type of profit that a practising lawyer will most likely have to consider is a right of common properly so called.

---

[498] *Clayton v Corby*, above.

[499] See below, pp 705–6, in reference to common of pasture.

[500] LPA 1925, s 1(2)(a).

[501] *Mason v Clarke* [1955] AC 778; see *Lowe v J W Ashmore Ltd* [1971] Ch 545, esp at 557–8, below, p 712.

[502] Woolrych, *A Treatise on the Law of Rights of Common* (2nd edn, 1850), p 13.

[503] Historically, profits à prendre in common came first, and several profits came second. Common pre-dated the establishment of the system of manors under which the villager came to be regarded as having rights not over something that belonged to himself in common with others, but over the property of the lord of the manor, who could in turn appropriate the common land (by inclosure), as long as he left the tenant sufficient pasturage in waste. See the 11th edn of this book, pp 546–9.

[504] For the history of profits, see the 11th edn of this book, pp 547–8.

(2) Rights of Common

(a) Classification

As we have seen,[505] rights of common may be classified into rights appurtenant; rights appendant; rights in gross; and (in the case of the common of pasturage) rights *pur cause de vicinage*. Rights of common may also be classified according to their subject matter into four kinds, namely, common of pasture, of piscary, of turbary and of estovers.[506]

(1) Common of pasture

This, the most usual common, arises when the owner of cattle is, in common with others, entitled to put his cattle to feed on the land of another.[507] In the case of a common *appendant* the right is limited to 'commonable cattle', that is horses and oxen to plough the land and cows and sheep to manure it.[508] A common *appurtenant* is not limited in this way, but depends upon the extent of the enjoyment proved or upon the terms of the grant if there is one, and so a right may well be established to pasture such animals as hogs, goats and geese.[509] Common in gross may also be enjoyed in respect of any animal. Commons of pasture appendant and appurtenant are also restricted in another manner, as we have already seen, for there is no right to pasture an unlimited number of commonable cattle.[510] The rule at common law was that the right is exercisable only in respect of cattle *levant et couchant* ('getting up and lying down'[511]) on the land, ie the number that the dominant tenement is capable of supporting through the winter.[512] Again a right of pasturage in gross cannot be prescribed for unless it is restricted in the same manner.[513]

This doctrine of *levancy et couchancy* was, however, abolished by the Commons Registration Act 1965,[514] which requires all rights of grazing to be registered, but limits registration to a defined number of animals.[515] In the case of a common in gross there is no objection in principle to the existence of pasture without stint, or, in other words,

---

[505] Above, p 702.

[506] Blackstone, vol ii, p 32; Co Litt 122a. See Williams, *Rights of Common and Other Prescriptive Rights* (1880).

[507] *Tyrringham's Case* (1584) 4 Co Rep 36b, 37.

[508] Ibid. This pasture may be claimed for certain animals only, eg sheep (when it is called 'sheep walk'): *Robinson v Duleep Singh* (1878) 11 Ch D 798; or swine (called common of 'pannage'): *Chilton v Corp of London* (1878) 7 Ch D 562.

[509] *Bennett v Reeve* (1740) Willes 227; *Tyrringham's Case*, above.

[510] *Anderson v Bostock* [1976] Ch 312.

[511] 'The language was picturesque': *Bettison v Langton* [2001] UKHL 24, [2002] 1 AC 27, 31 (Lord Nicholls of Birkenhead).

[512] *Robertson v Hartopp* (1889) 43 Ch D 484, 517; Holdsworth, *A History of English Law*, vol vii, p 320 and authorities there cited; *Re Ilkley and Burley Moors* (1983) 47 P & CR 324. The number of animals in a profit appurtenant is also limited by reference to the needs of the dominant estate: *Polo Woods Foundation v Shelton-Agar* [2009] EWHC 1361 (Ch), [2010] 1 P & CR 12 at [21]-[23], although the 'needs of the estate' are not to be judged by what the estate in fact needs as a matter of practical necessity: ibid, at [50] (several profit, rather than profit in common).

[513] *Mellor v Spateman* (1669) 1 Saund 339.   [514] Below, p 708.   [515] S 15.

to a right to put an unlimited number of cattle on the servient tenement, because, as it is not appurtenant to anything, there is no dominant tenement with reference to the needs of which the content of the right must be proportioned. Thus, as was said by Buckley LJ:[516] 'it may well be that there can exist in law a right in gross to enter and take without limitation—without stint—the profits or proceeds of another's land commercially for the purposes of sale'.

Such an unstinted right might no doubt be granted expressly by deed, but, though there is no objection to it in principle, the case of *Mellor v Spateman*[517] clearly decided that it could not be prescribed for: 'And the court did not dislike any part of the plea, but only it was not said in the plea '*levant et couchant* within the town'. And Kelynge CJ said positively that there cannot be any common in gross without number.' The old expression *common sans nombre* that is met with in earlier cases is not inconsistent with this principle, for it merely meant that the right was for beasts *levant et couchant*, the point being in such a case that the number was not positively fixed at a definite figure.

(2) Common of piscary

A stranger may acquire a right to catch fish in inland waters, such as lakes, ponds and non-navigable rivers, belonging to private owners. This right takes two forms:

(i)   A 'several fishery' or a 'free fishery', which is not a right of common, but is a right to take fish *in alieno solo* and to exclude the owner of the water from the right to take fish himself;[518]

(ii) A 'common of fishery' which is a liberty of fishing in another man's water in common with other persons.[519]

'Common of piscary being given for the sustenance of the tenant's family'[520] must, if appurtenant to a house, be limited to the needs of that house, and the fish cannot be caught for sale.[521] It should be noted that though the fishery in arms of the sea and in tidal rivers is open to all subjects of the realm,[522] a prescriptive right to a several fishery or a common of fishery in it may be established.[523] The presumption, however, is in favour of the public.

(3) Common of turbary

Common of turbary is the right of cutting turf or peat in another man's land to be expended as fuel in the house of the commoner.[524] For the last 400 years this right

---

[516] *Lord Chesterfield v Harris* [1908] 2 Ch 397, 421.   [517] (1669) 1 Saund 339, 346.
[518] *Foster v Wright* (1878) 4 CPD 438, 449. See *Loose v Castleton* (1978) 41 P & CR 19; *Lovett v Fairclough* (1990) 61 P & CR 385 (claim to profit in gross of piscary over Jeffrey's Pool in the River Tweed failed).
[519] Blackstone, vol ii, p 34; *Seymour v Courtenay* (1771) 5 Burr 2814 (Mansfield CJ).
[520] Ibid, p 35.   [521] *Lord Chesterfield v Harris* [1908] 2 Ch 397.
[522] *Fitzwalter's Case* (1674) 1 Mod Rep 105; *Carter v Murcot* (1768) 4 Burr 2162, 2164.
[523] *Carter v Murcot*, above.   [524] Blackstone, vol ii, p 34.

has always been treated as a common appurtenant, with the qualification that it must be appurtenant to an ancient house or to a new house erected in continuance of the ancient one.[525]

It cannot be appurtenant to land,[526] since, as we have seen, a thing that is appurtenant must agree in nature and quality with the thing to which it is attached, and turf is to be used only for a house on the land.

(4) Common of estovers

Blackstone wrote:

> Common of estovers or estouviers; that is necessaries (from *estoffer*, to furnish), is a liberty of taking necessary wood, for the use or furniture of a house or farm, from off another's estate. The Saxon word, *bote*, is used by us as synonymous to the French *estovers*; and therefore house-bote is sufficient allowance of wood to repair or to burn in the house (which latter is sometimes called fire-bote); ploughbote and cart-bote are wood to be employed in making and repairing instruments of husbandry; and hay-bote, or hedge-bote, is wood for repairing hays, hedges or fences.[527]

This right, which very closely resembles common of turbary, is generally appurtenant to a house,[528] though it may be attached to land for the purpose of repairing fences. When it is appurtenant to a house, the wood taken must be expended on that house, and cannot be used for the reparation of new buildings that may have been erected, or as fuel in new fireplaces that have been built in the original house.[529] But when the old dominant house is demolished and replaced by another one, the right continues to exist according to its original extent: 'If an ancient cottage which had common be fallen down, and another cottage be erected in the place where the old cottage stood; this is no new cottage, but it may claim common as an ancient cottage by prescription.'[530]

A right similar to the common of estovers and also called estovers is given at common law to a tenant for life or years enabling him to cut timber that would otherwise be waste.[531] The only difference between the common law right and that which we have just considered is that the former arises in the tenant by virtue of the possession of the land rented and is exercisable over that land, while the latter is a profit to be taken out of somebody else's land.

---

[525] *A-G v Reynolds* [1911] 2 KB 888; *Warrick v Queen's College, Oxford* (1871) 6 Ch App 716, 730.

[526] *Tyrringham's Case* (1584) 4 Co Rep 36b.

[527] Blackstone, vol ii, p 35.   [528] *A-G v Reynolds* [1911] 2 KB 888.

[529] *Luttrel's Case* (1601) 4 Co Rep 86a.

[530] *Bryers v Lake*, cited Hall, *Law relating to Profits à Prendre and Rights of Common*, p 322.

[531] Above, pp 237, 608.

(b) Registration[532]

The policy of the Commons Registration Act 1965[533] was to have a once-for-all nationwide inquiry into common land and town and village greens and rights of common. When the process had been completed, the register was to be conclusive.[534] The Act provided for the registration before August 1970 with registration authorities[535] of common land and town or village greens in England and Wales,[536] of rights of common over such land, and of persons claiming to be or found to be its owners. Separate registers of common land, and of town or village greens, were established, each to be open to public inspection.[537] The Act also applied to waste land of a manor not subject to rights of common.[538]

Registration under the 1965 Act was final or provisional. It was final if no objection was lodged before August 1972;[539] and final registration was conclusive evidence of the matters registered at the date of registration.[540] If there was any such objection, the

[532] See generally *Gadsden on Commons and Greens* (2nd edn, 2005); Ubhi and Denyer-Green, *Law of Commons, Town and Village Greens* (2nd edn, 2006); Jessel, *Law of the Manor* (1998) and *Law of the Manor: the Twenty-First Century* (2004); Oswald, *A Practitioner's Guide to Common Land and the Commons Registration Act 1965* (1989); Harris and Ryan, *An Outline of the Law relating to Common Land and Public Access to the Countryside* (1967); Clayden, *Our Common Land* (6th edn, 2007). Note that only the more recent books cover the Commons Act 2006 as well as the Commons Registration Act 1965.

[533] Report of the Royal Commission on Common Land, 1955–1958 (Cmnd 462). See Commons Registration (General) Regulations 1966 (SI 1966 No 1471), as amended by SI 1968 Nos 658, 989; SI 1980 No 1195; SI 1982 Nos 209, 210; SI 1989 No 2167; SI 1990 No 311; SI 2003 No 2260; SI 2007 Nos 1032 (which was revoked by SI 2007 No 1553 before coming into force), 2404; SI 2010 No 2357. Commons (Registration of Town or Village Greens) (Interim Arrangements) (England) Regulations 2007 (SI 2007 No 457) provide for registration before Commons Act 2006, below, is brought fully into force.

[534] *R v Oxfordshire CC, ex p Sunningwell Parish Council* [2000] 1 AC 355, 348 (Lord Hoffmann); [2000] Conv 21 (JG Riddall). The Act did not apply to the New Forest, Epping Forest or to any land exempted by an order of the Secretary of State: s 11; SI 1965 No 2001. The register is not conclusive, however, as to whether a right is a stand-alone right exercisable only against the registered common, or might be a split right exercisable also over other commons: *Dance v Savery* [2011] EWHC 16 (Ch), [2011] All ER (D) 92 (Jan).

[535] County councils or, in Greater London, the relevant London borough council: s 2, as amended by LGA 1972, s 272(1), Sch 30 and LGA 1985, s 16, Sch 8.

[536] There are 373,570 hectares of registered common land in England (about 3 per cent of the total land area), and 175,000 hectares in Wales (about 8.4 per cent of the total land area). Nearly 55 per cent of common land is designated as a Site of Special Scientific Interest, and over half of England's common land is in Cumbria and North Yorkshire (31 per cent and 21 per cent respectively): statistics taken from the Defra web site, www.defra.gov.uk, in December 2010.

[537] S 3.

[538] S 22(1); *Re Britford Common* [1977] 1 WLR 39; *Re Yateley Common, Hampshire* [1977] 1 WLR 840; *Re Chewton Common, Christchurch* [1977] 1 WLR 1242; *Baxendale v Instow Parish Council* [1982] Ch 14; *Hampshire County Council v Milburn* [1991] 1 AC 325 (waste land of a manor held by HL to mean 'waste land now or formerly of a manor' or 'waste land of manorial origin'); *Lewis v Mid Glamorgan County Council* [1995] 1 WLR 313; [1995] Conv 500 (HW Wilkinson).

[539] SI 1968 No 989, as amended by SI 1970 No 384; *Smith v East Sussex County Council* (1977) 76 LGR 332.

[540] S 10; *New Windsor Corp v Mellor* [1975] Ch 380, 392 (Lord Denning MR); *Cooke v Amey Gravel Co Ltd* [1972] 1 WLR 1310 (provisional registration is itself no evidence of the existence of the right registered); *Corpus Christi College, Oxford v Gloucestershire County Council* [1983] QB 360 (registration conclusive even

registration was provisional, and only became final if it was confirmed after a hearing before a Commons Commissioner.[541] There was a right of appeal from his decision by a person aggrieved to the High Court on a point of law.[542] All provisional registrations to the Commissioners having been determined, the provisions in the 1965 Act relating to provisional registration were repealed by the Commons Act 2006, and the office of Commissioner was abolished, with effect from 1 December 2010.[543]

It was provided by the 1965 Act that, after July 1970, no land then capable of being registered under the Act was to be deemed to be common land unless it was so registered, and no rights of common were exercisable over any such land unless they were registered either under the Act or in the register of title under the Land Registration Act 1925 or 2002.[544] Thus not only were unregistered rights existing before that date extinguished, but there can be no future acquisition of rights over registered commons. New commons could, however, arise, for example, by grant or by prescription, and be registered.[545] In this case the land does not cease to be common land nor do the rights of common cease to be exercisable, if not registered.

where entry on register was wrong); *R v Mid-Sussex DC* [1993] EGCS 183; *R v Norfolk County Council, ex p Perry* (1996) 74 P & CR 1 (power to amend under s 13, below, n 546, only exercisable if land ceased to be village green after date of registration).

[541] Commons Registration Act 1965, ss 4–7; SI 1970 No 1371; SI 1971 No 1727; SI 1972 No 437, as amended by SI 1993 No 1771; SI 1973 No 815. The Commissioners' decisions covering the period from 1965 to 1990 are recorded in 78 bound volumes, in one volume or sometimes two volumes for each county in England and Wales. Most matters were determined by 1990, though any later decisions are all recorded: [1997] Conv 248 (A Samuels). Decisions are reported in Campbell, *Decisions of the Commons Commissioners* (1972), in Current Law, and in the Annual Reports of the Open Spaces Society (formerly known as the Commons, Open Spaces and Footpaths Preservation Society), and on the web site of the Association of Commons Registration Officers, www.acraew.org.uk.

The onus of establishing the validity of the registration was on the person making the registration: *Re Sutton Common, Wimborne* [1982] 1 WLR 647; *Re West Anstey Common, North Devon* [1985] Ch 329; *Re Newton Fell, Newton in Bowland* [1988] CLY 285. When deciding whether to confirm a provisional registration, the Commissioner should consider not only the situation as it was at the date of registration, but also events occurring since that date; *Re Merthyr Mawr Common* [1989] 1 WLR 1014. See also *Dynevor v Richardson* [1995] Ch 173 (provisional registration prevents time running for purposes of lost modern grant, even when registration subsequently rejected).

[542] Commons Registration Act 1965, s 18. See *Wilkes v Gee* [1973] 1 WLR 742; *R v Chief Commons Comr* (1977) 37 P & CR 67; *Re Tillmire Common, Heslington* [1982] 2 All ER 615.

[543] SI 2010 No 2356.

[544] Commons Registration Act 1965, s 1(2), as amended by LRA 2002, s 133, Sch 11; SI 1966 No 1470, as amended by SI 1970 No 383. Applications for registration had to be made before 3 January 1970. *Central Electricity Generating Board v Clwyd County Council* [1976] 1 WLR 151 (right of common not registered by closing date held to be extinguished); *Re Turnworth Down, Dorset* [1978] Ch 251; *Howse v Newbury DC* (1998) 77 P & CR 231 (Greenham Common). For the liability of a solicitor who failed to search the register, see *G & K Ladenbau (UK) Ltd v Crawley and de Reya* [1978] 1 WLR 266.

[545] Ibid, s 13(b) and Commons Registration (New Land) Regulations 1969 (SI 1969 No 1843). See *R (Whitmey) v Commons Commissioners* [2004] EWCA Civ 951, [2005] QB 282 (Commons Commissioners have no jurisdiction in dispute under s 13; the fact that applicant can challenge refusal of registration authority to register land as a green only by way of judicial review does not violate ECHR, art 6); [2005] JPL 159 (J Hilliard).

Provisions were also made in the 1965 Act for amendment of the register where land registered under the Act ceased to be common land or a town or village green; or any rights registered under the Act are apportioned, extinguished, released or varied;[546] or to deal with certain cases of fraud or mistake.[547]

The 1965 Act was found to have deficiencies,[548] and is being replaced by new provisions on Registration in Part I of the Commons Act 2006.[549] The new Act continues the scheme created by the 1965 Act, and so provides for commons registration authorities to continue to keep the same registers of common land, and of towns or village greens.[550] There are, however, some significant changes, including the new provisions that new rights of common can no longer be created by prescription, and may be created only by express grant in accordance with formalities to be provided by regulations, and only if the land over which it is created is not registered as a town or village green;[551] that rights of common that are registered as appurtenant to common land or a town or village green can no longer be severed from the land;[552] and there are new or wider provisions for the amendment of registers to keep them up to date or to correct errors.[553]

The expression 'rights of common' under the 2006 Act[554] includes, as it did under the 1965 Act,[555] 'a cattlegate or beastgate (by whatever name known)[556] and a rights of

---

[546] Commons Registration Act 1965, s 13(a), (c).

[547] Ibid, s 14. See *Betterment Properties (Weymouth) Ltd v Dorset CC* [2010] EWHC 3045 (Ch), [2010] 48 EGCS 84. In addition, the Common Land (Rectification of Registers) Act 1989 provided that land might be removed from the register if it could be shown that at all times since 5 August 1945 (ie 20 years before the passing of the 1965 Act) the land had included or had been ancillary to a dwelling house; applications had to be made before 21 July 1992: Common Land (Rectification of Registers) Regulations 1990 (SI 1990 No 311). The 1989 Act was repealed by Commons Act 2006, Sch 6, Pt 1; SI 2006 No 2504, art 2.

[548] Lord Denning MR said that the 1965 Act 'is ill-drafted and has given rise to many difficulties': *Corpus Christi College, Oxford v Gloucestershire County Council* [1983] QB 360, 370. There were several proposals for reform. In 1978 the Department of the Environment issued a Consultative Document, and in 1986 the Countryside Commission published the Report of the Commons Land Forum. In 2000 the Department of the Environment, Transport and the Regions published a Consultation Paper; and in 2002 its successor, Defra, published the Common Land Policy Statement, which set out the Government's plans for taking forward the proposals in the Consultation Paper. See also the Explanatory Notes to the 2006 Act, M & B p 97.

[549] The 2006 Act is being brought progressively into force: see commencement orders SI 2006 No 2504; SI 2007 Nos 456 and 2584; SI 2008 No 1960; 2010, Nos 61 and 2356. S. 15 was brought into force on 6 April 2007: see below, n 558. The principal sections were brought into force with effect from 1 October 2008 in relation to seven pilot registration authority areas in England, and it was expected that national implementation would commence in stages from October 2010, but the pilot period was extended until September 2010 and the national commencement has been delayed for at least a year: Ministerial Statement, Hansard, HC Deb 4 February 2010, vol 505, col 23WS.

[550] Commons Act 2006, s 1. The content of the registers is defined in s 3; and the commons registration authorities in s 4. The New Forest, Epping Forest and the Forest of Dean continue to be excluded from the registration provisions: s 5 (cf above, n 534).

[551] Ibid, s 6.   [552] Ibid, s 9.

[553] Ibid, ss 18, 19.   [554] S 61(1).   [555] Commons Registration Act 1965, s 22(1).

[556] Cattlegate or beastgate, sometimes called *stinted pasture*, is a right to pasture a fixed number of beasts on the land of another, generally for a part of the year only. See eg *Rigg v Earl of Lonsdale* (1857) 1 H & N 923; *Brackenbank Lodge Ltd v Peart* (1993) 67 P & CR 249.

sole or several vesture[557] or herbage or of sole or several pasture, but does not include rights held for a term of years or from year to year'.

The Commons Act 2006 contains revised provisions for the registration of land as a town or village green. Any person may apply for registration where[558]

a significant number of the inhabitants[559] of any locality, or of any neighbourhood[560] within a locality, have indulged as of right[561] in lawful sports and pastimes[562] on the land for a period of at least 20 years

---

[557] The right of sole vesture, *vestura terrae*, is not merely to graze cattle, but to take away the product of the land, such as grass, corn, underwood, turf, peat, etc.

[558] Commons Registration Act 2006, s 15, which was brought into force on 6 April 2007: SI 2007 No 456. See also Commons (Registration of Town or Village Greens) (Interim Arrangements) (England) Regulations 2007 (SI 2007 No 457), which provide for registration of new greens within the new scheme provided by the Commons Act 2006, but in the registers under the Commons Registration Act 1965 Act until ss 1-3 of the 2006 Act are in force. The 2007 Regulations were revoked and replaced by Commons Registration (England) Regulations 2008 (SI 2008 No 1961), in relation to the registration areas covered by the current pilot implementation of the 2006 Act; above, n 549.

S 15 in many respects reproduces the definition of a 'town or village green' in Commons Registration Act 1965, s 22(1), and therefore the following footnotes include references to authorities on the equivalent language in the 1965 Act.

[559] The 'significant number of inhabitants' need not have set their feet everywhere on the land, nor need their activity have been exclusively referable to indulging in sports and pastimes rather than (eg) exercising or creating rights of way. 'For example, the whole of a public garden may be used for recreational activities even though 75% of the surface consists of flower beds, borders and shrubberies on which the public may not walk': *Oxfordshire County Council v Oxford City Council*, [2006] 2 AC 674 at [63], [67] (Lord Hoffmann).

[560] 'Neighbourhood' may include two or more neighbourhoods: *Leeds Group plc v Leeds CC* [2010] EWCA Civ 1438, [2011] 2 EGCS 74.

[561] *R v Oxfordshire County Council* [2000] 1 AC 355 at 355-6 ('as of right' reflects common law concept of *nec vi nec clam nec precario* and does not require subjective belief in the existence of the right; above, p 668); [1998] Conv 526 (T Sutton); *R (Beresford) v Sunderland City Council* [2003] UKHL 60, [2004] 1 AC 889 (mowing the grass and providing benches not sufficient to render use *precario* so as negative claim to user as of right: for this, landowner's permission, whether express or implied, must be shown to be temporary or revocable); *R (Lewis) v Redcar and Cleveland BC (No 2)* [2010] UKSC 11, [2010] 2 AC 70 (deference by public to owner's activities on the land, used as a golf course, not inconsistent with user as of right: in practice, the respective rights of the owner and of the local inhabitants can coexist with give and take on both sides; doubting *R (Laing Homes Ltd) v Buckinghamshire CC* [2003] EWHC 1578 (Admin), [2003] 3 EGLR 69); [2010] CLJ 238 (R Meager). On steps taken to contest user, see *Betterment Properties (Weymouth) Ltd v Dorset CC* [2010] EWHC 3045 (Ch), [2010] 48 EGCS 84 (sufficient steps without taking legal proceedings); *R (Oxfordshire & Buckinghamshire Mental Health NHS Foundation Trust) v Oxfordshire County Council* [2010] EWHC 530 (Admin), [2010] 2 EGLR 171 (notices insufficient).

[562] Ibid, 356-7 (Lord Hoffmann) ('sports and pastimes' is a not two classes of activities but a single composite class that uses two words in order to avoid arguments about whether an activity is a sport or a pastime); [1999] All ER Rev 223 (PJ Clarke). For examples of pastimes see *Re White Lane Pond, Four Dales and Clay Pits, Thorne and Stainforth, South Yorkshire* [1984] CLY 287 (unaccompanied local children, picnicking, fishing in a pond, collecting bullrushes and picking mushrooms; local children, accompanied by adults, playing, picking blackberries, and studying fish and plant life; local adults picnicking, taking dogs for walks, and fishing in the pond); cf *Re River Don and its Banks* [1984] CLY 284 (walking with or without dogs along the banks of the River was not indulging); *Re Foreshore, East Bank of River Ouse, Naburn, Selby District, North Yorkshire* [1989] CLY 276 (pastime of idling by a river); [1992] Conv 434 (A Samuels).

Once registered, 'land registered as a town or village green can be used generally for sports and pastimes. It seems to me that Parliament must have thought that if the land had to be kept available for one form of and either they continue to do so at the time of the application, or have ceased to do so within the period of two years before the time of the application for registration.[563]

C LEGAL AND EQUITABLE PROFITS À PRENDRE

A profit à prendre, like an easement,[564] is capable of subsisting as a legal interest, and will be legal if (i) it is held for an interest equivalent to an estate in fee simple absolute in possession or a term of years absolute,[565] and (ii) is created by statute, deed or prescription. In the case of the express[566] grant or reservation of a profit over registered land, other than a right of common that is capable of being registered under the Commons Registration Act 1965, the profit is not a legal interest until the registration requirements of the Land Registration Act 2002 have been satisfied.[567] A notice of the interest must be entered in the register of the title of the servient tenement and (if the dominant tenement is also registered) the proprietor of the dominant tenement must be entered in the register as proprietor of the profit[568] However, a profit in gross, other than one created for a term not exceeding seven years, is an independently registrable legal interest; the grantee must be entered in the register as the proprietor of the interest, and a notice in respect of the interest created must be entered in the register of the servient tenement.[569]

A profit à prendre that does not satisfy these requirements may be an equitable profit: eg if it is created informally or by a contract to grant a legal profit.[570]

D ACQUISITION OF PROFITS À PRENDRE

It will not be necessary to consider this topic at any length, for the methods by which easements may be acquired are applicable, with very few exceptions, to the acquisition of profits à prendre, whether rights of common or not. At the outset we can dismiss profits appendant because they have been impossible to acquire since *Quia Emptores*

---

recreation, it would not matter a great deal to the owner whether it was used for others as well. This would be in accordance with the common law, under which proof of a custom to play one kind of game gave rise to a right to use the land for other games': *Oxfordshire County Council v Oxford City Council* above, n 559 at [50] (Lord Hoffmann).

[563] Commons Registration Act 2006, s 15(2), (3). Where the user had already ceased before s 15 came into force, the period is extended to five years: s 15(4). Sub-sections 3 and 4 reverse the effect of the decision of HL in *Oxfordshire County Council v Oxford City Council*, above, n 559, on the interpretation of Commons Registration Act 1965, s 22(1A) (inserted by Countryside and Rights of Way Act 2000, s 98), which required the use necessary for registration as a town or village green to continue to the date of application.

[564] Above, p 650.　　　　　　　　　　　　　　　　　　　　　　[565] LPA 1925, s 1(2)(a).

[566] A profit created by the operation of LPA 1925, s 62, below, p 713, is not an express grant and therefore does not require to be registered: LRA 2002, s 27(7).

[567] LRA 2002, s 27(2)(d).　　　　　　　　　　　　　　　　　　　　[568] Ibid, Sch 2, para 7.

[569] Ibid, s 38; Sch 2, para 6. The substantive registration of a profit in gross was an innovation of LRA 2002.

[570] *Mason v Clarke* [1955] AC 778; *Lowe v J W Ashmore Ltd* [1971] Ch 545, 557–8.

in 1290, and a claimant will be required to prove that he holds arable land that was granted by the lord of a manor to a freehold tenant before that date.[571]

The four possible methods of acquiring easements are set out on page 652. We will take each of these and show to what extent it applies to profits:

(1) Statute

Profits may be acquired by statute. Former examples include Inclosure Acts that conferred new rights upon manorial lords by way of compensation for the interest lost by them in the soil itself.

(2) Express Grant

Profits, whether appurtenant or in gross,[572] may be created by an express grant, which at common law must be made by deed.[573] The lack of a deed, however, is not necessarily fatal to the grantee, for if he can prove a specifically enforceable contract for the grant of the profit, he may invoke the familiar doctrine of equity that the grantor must be regarded as having already done what he ought to have done, and thereby show the grant *in equity* of a profit.[574]

Thus, in an early case,[575] the defendant signed a written memorandum by which he agreed in return for valuable consideration that the claimant should have the exclusive right of sporting over and killing the game on the defendant's lands, but some years later he revoked the agreement. At the instance of the claimant, Wood V-C decreed specific performance by ordering the execution of a formal deed and meanwhile granting an injunction forbidding the defendant to interfere with the enjoyment of the right.

Section 62 of the Law of Property Act 1925, which, as we have already seen, provides that a conveyance of land shall operate to pass rights and advantages appertaining to the land at the time of the conveyance,[576] applies not only to easements but also to profits, such as a right of depasturing sheep on an adjoining mountain.[577]

---

[571] Above, p 35; *Viner's Abridgment*—Common C p 1; *Comyns' Digest*, Tit Covenant B.

[572] A profit à prendre (grazing) appurtenant to land, if limited to a fixed number of animals, can be severed so as to become a profit in gross: *Bettison v Langton* [2001] UKHL 24, [2002] 1 AC 27. However, under Commons Act 2006, s 9, rights of common that are registered as appurtenant to common land or a town or village green can no longer be severed from the land.

[573] Co Litt 9a, b; *Wood v Leadbitter* (1845) 13 M & W 838, 842–3; *Mason v Clarke* [1954] 1 QB 460.

[574] Above, p 653; below, p 978.

[575] *Earl of Frogley v Lovelace* (1859) John 333; *Mason v Clarke* [1955] AC 778 (part performance).

[576] Above, p 655.

[577] *White v Williams* [1922] 1 KB 727; *White v Taylor (No 2)* [1969] 1 Ch 160; *Anderson v Bostock* [1976] Ch 312 (exclusive right of grazing without limit held to be unknown to the law), above, p 705; *Re Yateley Common, Hampshire* [1977] 1 WLR 840, 850; *Re Broxhead Common, Whitehill, Hampshire* (1977) 33 P & CR 451.

(3) Implied Grant

The next method by which easements may be acquired is an implied grant under the doctrine of *Wheeldon v Burrows*, but since this is confined to interests of a continuous and apparent nature, it can have no application to profits, which can possess neither of these characteristics.

(4) Presumed Grant or Prescription

(a) Prescription at common law

Profits can be acquired by prescription at common law, and when this method of claim is adopted it must conform to all those general principles that obtain in the case of easements, so that:

(i) the possibility of a grant must be shown;

(ii) user must be *as of right*; and

(iii) the claim is liable to be defeated by proof of its origin since 1189.

There is this difference, however, between easements and profits, that although a person can only prescribe in a *que estate* for an easement, he may prescribe in himself and his ancestors for a profit.[578] Examples of this personal prescription are rare,[579] since profits in gross themselves are rare, and such cases as are to be found in the Law Reports refer to *several* profits and not to rights of common.[580] Where one does prescribe in the person, he must adduce evidence to show that either he and his ancestors, or some other person and *his* ancestors from whom the claimant acquired the title to the profit, have enjoyed the right from time immemorial.[581]

(b) Lost modern grant

Profits à prendre may be claimed by virtue of a lost modern grant, but instances are not commonly found.[582] If a claim is so made, it must conform to the rules and surmount the objections that apply where an easement is founded on a lost grant.[583] Even though the Prescription Act 1832 requires 30 years' user in respect of a claim to a profit, only 20 years' user is necessary to support a presumption of a lost grant.[584]

---

[578] Co Litt 122a. *Que estate* is Norman French for 'whose estate'; land in which an interest, in the nature of an easement or profit à prendre, has been acquired by prescription.

[579] *Shuttleworth v Le Fleming* (1865) 19 CBNS 687 (Montague Smith J).

[580] *Welcome v Upton* (1840) 6 M & W 536; *Shuttleworth v Le Fleming*, above; *Johnson v Barnes* (1873) LR 8 CP 527.

[581] *Welcome v Upton* (1839) 5 M & W 398; *Lovett v Fairclough* (1990) 61 P & CR 385.

[582] For a modern claim, see *Polo Woods Foundation v Shelton-Agar* [2009] EWHC 1361 (Ch), [2010] 1 P & CR 12.

[583] *Neaverson v Peterborough RDC* [1902] 1 Ch 557; *Mill v New Forest Comrs* (1856) 18 CB 60; *Loose v Castleton* (1978) 41 P & CR 19 (several fishery).

[584] *Tehidy Minerals Ltd v Norman* [1971] 2 QB 528.

(c) Prescription Act 1832

The Prescription Act 1832 treats profits differently from easements in that it requires longer periods of enjoyment. The periods fixed for profits are 30 years and 60 years instead of 20 and 40.

The Act of 1832 applies only to profits appurtenant,[585] not to those in gross, since it requires the claimant to allege in his pleading that the right has been enjoyed 'by the occupiers of the tenement in respect whereof the same is claimed....'[586] As Montague Smith J said in the leading case: 'The whole principle of this pleading assumes a dominant tenement and an enjoyment of the right by the occupiers of it. The proof must of course follow and support the pleading. It is obvious that rights claimed in gross cannot be so pleaded or proved.'[587]

E THE RUNNING OF THE BENEFIT AND THE BURDEN OF A PROFIT À PRENDRE

A profit à prendre, as a property interest, is capable of binding the owner for the time being of the servient tenement. Whether the purchaser of the servient tenement is bound depends on whether the profit is legal or equitable,[588] and whether the land is registered or unregistered, under the same rules as apply to legal and equitable easements.[589]

The benefit of a profit appurtenant to land, whether legal or equitable, will also pass with the dominant tenement in the same manner as an easement.[590]

F EXTINGUISHMENT OF PROFITS À PRENDRE

Several profits and profits in common may be extinguished by any of the following methods:[591]

(1) Unity of Seisin

If the owner of the profit or common also becomes owner of the land over which the right is exercisable, the right is extinguished, provided that his estates in the right and in the land are similar both in quantum and in quality.[592] Thus a profit appurtenant

---

[585] Under Commons Act 2006, s 6(1), a right of common can no longer be created by prescription. For special provisions relating to prescription of rights of common, repealed by the 2006 Act, see Commons Registration Act 1965, s 16.

[586] Prescription Act 1832, s 5.

[587] *Shuttleworth v Le Fleming* (1865) 19 CBNS 687, 711.

[588] Above, p 712.   [589] Above, pp 691 ff.   [590] Above, p 690.

[591] For extinguishment of commons by approvement and by inclosure, which were abolished by Commons Act 2006, ss 47 and 48 respectively, see the 17th edition of this book, pp 652–5.

[592] *Tyrringham's Case* (1584) 4 Co Rep 36b; *White v Taylor* [1969] 1 Ch 150; *Re Yateley Common, Hampshire* [1977] 1 WLR 840; Hall, *Law relating to Profits à Prendre and Rights of Common*, p 335.

is extinguished if one person becomes seised in fee both of the dominant and of the servient tenement, but if the owner of the profit takes a lease of the servient tenement, the result of this unity of possession, as distinguished from unity of seisin in the former case, is that the profit is only suspended and will revive again upon the expiration of the lease.[593]

(2) Release

A release of a profit in favour of the servient owner extinguishes the right in the sense that it ceases to exist as a right *in alieno solo*, since one cannot have a profit or common in one's own land.

(3) Alteration of Dominant Tenement

Although it has been said that 'common is obtained by long sufferance and also it may be lost by long negligence',[594] it is not true that mere non-user of a profit will by itself produce an extinguishment of the right,[595] but if the character of the dominant tenement is so altered as to make any further appurtenancy impossible, a presumption is raised in favour of extinguishment. If, for example, land to which a common of pasture was appurtenant entirely loses its agricultural character by conversion into a building estate, the common is destroyed, but if the conversion is not irrevocable, such as where arable land is turned into an orchard, the profit is merely suspended and is capable of being resumed on the restoration of the land to its original state.[596]

(4) Commons Registration Act 1965 and Commons Act 2006

As we have seen, rights of common are no longer exercisable over land in England and Wales that is common land or a town or village green, unless they have been registered under the Commons Registration Act 1965 or Part I of the Commons Act 2006.[597] Under the 2006 Act, there are provisions for deregistration and exchange of land registered as common land or as a town or village green.[598]

---

[593] Co Litt 313a, 114b.   [594] *Gateward's Case* (1607) 6 Co Rep 596.
[595] *Seaman v Vawdrey* (1810) 16 Ves 390; *Re Yateley Common, Hampshire*, above.
[596] *Carr v Lambert* (1866) LR 1 Exch 168; *Tyrringham's Case* (1584) 4 Co Rep 36b.
[597] Above, p 708.   [598] Ss 16, 18.

IV RIGHTS IN THE NATURE OF EASEMENTS AND PROFITS À PRENDRE ACQUIRED BY FLUCTUATING AND UNDEFINED CLASSES OF PERSONS

Indefinite and fluctuating classes of persons, such as the inhabitants of a village, may acquire rights, analogous in nature to easements, over the land of another.[599] For example, they have succeeded in establishing rights to enter another's close and take water from a spring,[600] to dry their fishing nets on the land of a private person,[601] to hold horse races[602] or a fair[603] on such land, and to pass to church[604] or market over a man's private property.

A RIGHTS IN THE NATURE OF EASEMENTS

Such rights are not easements capable of acquisition by prescription, for all forms of prescription presuppose the possibility of a grant, and no grant can be made to an indefinite body of persons. Nevertheless, to protect the long sustained enjoyment of a privilege, the law has surmounted the technical difficulty incident to prescription by allowing rights of this nature to be established by *custom*. Hence the name *customary* rights. Custom is an unwritten rule of law that has applied from time immemorial in a particular locality and that displaces the common law in so far as that particular locality is concerned.[605] Tindal CJ said:[606]

> A custom which has existed from time immemorial without interruption within a certain place, and which is certain and reasonable in itself, obtains the force of a law, and is, in effect, the common law within that place to which it extends, though contrary to the general law of the realm.

(1) Requisites for Custom

It has been said[607] that a custom must be:

---

[599] *Gateward's Case* (1607) 6 Co Rep 59b; *Race v Ward* (1855) 4 E & B 702.

[600] *Weekly v Wildman* (1698) 1 Ld Raym 405; *Race v Ward*, above.

[601] *Mercer v Denne* [1905] 2 Ch 538.   [602] *Mounsey v Ismay* (1865) 3 H & C 486.

[603] *Tyson v Smith* (1838) 9 Ad & El 406.   [604] *Brocklebank v Thompson* [1903] 2 Ch 344.

[605] See *Termes de la Ley*, 'Custom'; *Tanistry Case* (1608) Dav Ir 28; Litt, s 169; *Hammerton v Honey* (1876) 24 WR 603.

[606] *Lockwood v Wood* (1844) 6 QB 50, 64.

[607] *Mercer v Denne* [1905] 2 Ch 538; *New Windsor Corp v Mellor* [1975] Ch 380 (right to indulge in lawful sports and pastimes).

(1) certain,[608]

(2) not unreasonable,

(3) commencing from time immemorial,[609]

(4) continued without interruption, and

(5) applicable to a particular district.[610]

Strictly speaking, the requirement of existence from time immemorial means that the custom must have existed since 1189 but, although the nature of the right precludes the court from presuming a lost modern grant if enjoyment cannot be proved for so long, the practice is to presume that the right originated at the proper time if it is obviously of respectable antiquity.[611] It is generally enough to show continuous enjoyment going as far back as living testimony can go.

To quote Tindal CJ again:[612]

> As to the proof of the custom, you cannot, indeed, reasonably expect to have it proved before you that such a custom did in fact exist before time of legal memory, that is before the first year of the reign of Richard I; for if you did, it would in effect destroy the validity of almost all customs; but you are to require proof, as far back as living memory goes, of a continuous, peaceable, and uninterrupted user of the custom.

Although the presumption in favour of enjoyment from time immemorial will readily be raised, it can undoubtedly be rebutted by positive evidence showing that it actually began at some later date.[613] The courts are slow, however, to rebut the presumption. In *Mercer v Denne* it was proved by witnesses that for as long as they could remember—a matter of 70 years—the fishing inhabitants of Walmer had used part of the defendant's beach for the purpose of drying their nets. The defendant, having proved that in 1844 a considerable portion of this part of the beach was under water, argued that the custom of using that particular portion must be disallowed as obviously having arisen since 1189.

Rejecting this plea, Farwell J said:[614]

> A defendant may no doubt defeat a custom by shewing that it could not have existed in the time of Richard I, but he must demonstrate its impossibility, and the onus is on him to do so if the existence of the custom has been proved for a long period; this was done, for instance, in *Simpson v Wells*,[615] where the claim of a custom to set up stalls at the Statute Sessions for the hiring of servants was defeated by shewing that such sessions were introduced by

---

[608] Ie, the persons entitled to the right must be certain and not, eg, 'poor householders': *Selby v Robinson* (1788) 2 Term Rep 758.

[609] Blackstone, vol. i. p 76; *Chapman v Smith* (1754) 2 Ves Sen 506.

[610] *R v Rollett* (1875) LR 10 QB 469, 480.

[611] *Mercer v Denne*, above, at 556; *Wolstanton Ltd and A-G of Duchy of Lancaster v Newcastle-under-Lyme Corpn* [1940] AC 860, 876.

[612] *Bastard v Smith* (1838) 2 Mood & R 129, 136.

[613] *Hammerton v Honey* (1876) 24 WR 603, 604 (Jessel MR).　　　　[614] [1904] 2 Ch 534, 555.

[615] (1872) LR 7 QB 214.

the Statutes of Labourers, the first of which was in the reign of Edward III. But no such impossibility is shewn in the present case. If the beach was of its present extent in 1795, why am I bound to infer that it cannot have been the same in 1189 from the mere fact that between 1795 and 1844 the extent diminished and has since again increased? The mere non-user during the period that the sea flowed over the spot is immaterial, for it was no interruption of the right but only of the possession, and an 'interruption of the possession only for ten or twenty years will not destroy the custom'.[616]

A customary right, once acquired, cannot be lost by mere non-user or by waiver.[617]

(2) Custom and Prescription

Custom bears a close and striking resemblance to prescription. Both methods depend on continuous and uninterrupted enjoyment that has lasted for the time whereof the memory of men runneth not to the contrary, and both are liable to be defeated in the same manner. Coke emphasised the resemblance in quaint language: 'Prescription and custom are brothers, and ought to have the same age, and reason ought to be the father, and congruence the mother, and use the nurse, and time out of memory to fortify them both.'[618]

But there is still an important difference between the two methods, for while prescription always connects the right with a definite person, custom connects it with some particular locality. Prescription is personal, custom is local. A right is always prescribed for in the name of a certain person and his ancestors, or of those whose estate he owns, or in the name of corporations and their predecessors.[619] But a right claimed by custom is not alleged to be vested in any definite person or body of persons, but is claimed on the ground that it is vested in the shifting class of persons connected from time to time with the definite locality to which the right is attached.[620] In custom you first prove the attachment of the right to a locality and then prove your connection with that locality; while in prescription you show the existence of the right in some person from whom your title is derived, or else you prove yourself to be the owner of a tenement to which the right is attached.

The importance of the distinction lies in the fact that persons who are quite unable to establish their claim to an easement by means of prescription, because prescription presupposes a grant to some definite person, may very well succeed under the cover of custom. A customary right is part of the general law applicable to a particular locality; and persons resident there, whether capable grantees or not, are entitled to enjoy the benefit of the law that runs throughout the locality.

---

[616] Blackstone, vol 1, p 77; Co Litt 114b.
[617] *Wyld v Silver* [1963] Ch 243; *New Windsor Corp v Mellor* [1975] Ch 380.
[618] *Rowles v Mason* (1612) 2 Brownl 192, 198.   [619] 4 Co Rep 32a (Sir Edward Coke).
[620] Co Litt 113b; Blackstone, vol ii, p 263; *Foiston v Crachroode* (1587) 4 Co Rep 31b; *Gateward's Case* (1607) 6 Co Rep 59b.

B RIGHTS IN THE NATURE OF
PROFITS À PRENDRE

So far our account has been restricted to the capacity of a fluctuating and ever-changing class of persons to establish a claim to quasi-easements, and it remains to be considered whether such persons can sustain a claim to profits à prendre. It has been the law at least since 1607[621] that indefinite persons cannot acquire a profit by custom.[622] James LJ, in one case, said:[623]

> Of course it is settled and clear law that you cannot have any right to a profit *à prendre in alieno solo* in a shifting body like the inhabitants of a town or residents of a particular district.

Were the rule otherwise the result would be to exhaust and destroy the subject matter of the custom. Thus claims by inhabitants or classes of persons equally indefinite have been disallowed where the customs alleged were to enjoy common of pasture,[624] to collect dead wood for fuel,[625] to carry away sand that has drifted from the sea shore,[626] or to take minerals from the soil.[627]

But in all cases where ancient claims are in question we have to reckon with the tendency of the courts to presume everything reasonably possible in order to uphold a right of which there has been long enjoyment, and it is in furtherance of this general principle that two methods have been evolved whereby fluctuating classes can in certain circumstances maintain a claim even to profits *in alieno solo*. These may be termed (1) the 'presumed Crown grant' method and (2) the 'presumed charitable trust' method.

(1) Presumed Crown Grant

Although a private person cannot make a grant to indefinite classes of persons, the Crown may do so. Lord Romilly said:[628]

> The distinction between a grant by a private individual and a grant by the Crown is this, that as the Crown has the power to create corporations, so, if it is necessary for the purpose of establishing the validity of the grant, the grantees will be treated as a corporation *quoad* the grant, which is not the case with a grant by a private individual, because a private individual has no power of creating a corporation.

---

[621]   *Gateward's Case* (1607) 6 Co Rep 59b.

[622]   Ibid; *Race v Ward* (1855) 4 E & B 702; *Chilton v London Corp* (1878) 7 Ch D 735; *Constable v Nicholson* (1863) 14 CBNS 230.

[623]   *Commissioners of Sewers of the City of London v Glasse* (1872) 7 Ch App 456, 465.

[624]   *Grimstead v Marlowe* (1792) 4 Term Rep 717.

[625]   *Selby v Robinson* (1788) 2 Term Rep 758.   [626]   *Blewett v Tregonning* (1835) 3 Ad & El 554.

[627]   *A-G v Mathias* (1858) 4 K & J 579.   [628]   *Willingale v Maitland* (1866) LR 3 Eq 103, 109.

The Crown by virtue of this power may make a grant to the inhabitants of a town, with the result that they become by implication a corporation for the purposes of the grant and, as such, capable of enjoying a profit in the land of another. So in *Willingale v Maitland*,[629] where an actual Crown grant had been made in the time of Elizabeth to the inhabitants of a parish allowing a certain section of the parishioners to lop the branches of trees growing in the waste of a manor, it was held on demurrer that the grant was legal.

Cases where an actual grant can be found must be rare, and the real question is whether the court will presume a grant so as to incorporate the inhabitants and thus render them eligible to take profits. All that can be said is that such a presumption will be raised only where the circumstances that have accompanied the enjoyment go to show that the claimants have always regarded themselves as a corporation and have acted as such.

Such a grant was presumed in the *Faversham Fishery Case*;[630] but in *Lord Rivers v Adams*,[631] where it appeared that the enjoyment of an alleged right of inhabitants to carry away wood from a manorial waste was inconsistent with the fact that the tenants of the manor had openly asserted and exercised control over the wood, the court refused to raise the presumption. Kelly CB in this case said:[632]

> If the inhabitants had held meetings in reference to this right, or appointed any officer to look to the right, or done any act collectively of that description, the case would be different. We should then have the inhabitants acting in a corporate capacity in reference to this right, and from their doing so, and from their existence *de facto* as a corporation, we might according to the ordinary rule find a legal origin by a grant from the Crown.

(2) Presumed Charitable Trust

The second method, whereby uncertain bodies may establish a claim to profits, namely, that of a presumed charitable trust, is very similar to the one just described. It depends upon the decision of the House of Lords in *Goodman v Mayor and Free Burgesses of the Borough of Saltash*,[633] where the principle was in effect established that, where it appears that a definite body capable of taking by grant, such as the corporation of a borough, has enjoyed a profit *in alieno solo* for a great number of years, and where it also appears that an indefinite body has shared in this enjoyment, then the court

---

629 Above.

630 *Re Free Fishermen of Faversham* (1887) 36 Ch D 329; see especially at 343 (Bowen LJ).

631 (1878) 3 Ex D 361.

632 *Lord Rivers v Adams* (1878) 3 Ex D 361, 366–7. This is a most instructive case on the whole subject of claims to profits by fluctuating bodies.

633 (1882) 7 App Cas 633; *Peggs v Lamb* [1994] Ch 172 (charitable trust for freemen and widows of freemen of the ancient borough of Huntingdon).

presumes a lost grant in favour of the corporation, but declares that the corporation must hold the profit in trust for the indefinite body.

In *Goodman v Mayor and Free Burgesses of the Borough of Saltash*:

> Two facts were clearly proved: first, that the Corporation of Saltash had from time immemorial exercised the right of dredging for oysters in the river Tamar; secondly, that the free inhabitants of ancient tenements in the borough had each year from Candlemas (22 February) to Easter Eve exercised a similar right for the previous 200 years. An action was brought by the corporation against two free inhabitants of ancient tenements for trespass committed in the Tamar and for converting to their own use quantities of oysters.

After holding that the free inhabitants could not be presumed to be separately incorporated, the House addressed itself to the task of discovering a legal origin for the right that undoubtedly had been enjoyed for a very considerable time. The majority of the House (Lord Blackburn dissenting) held that the fishery must have originally been granted to the corporation subject to a condition that the free inhabitants were to be allowed to fish for a certain period each year. Lord Cairns said:[634]

> It appears to me that there is no difficulty at all in supposing such a grant, a grant to the corporation before the time of legal memory of a several fishery, a grant by the Crown, with a condition in that grant in some terms which are not before us, but which we can easily imagine—a condition that the free inhabitants of ancient tenements in the borough should enjoy this right, which as a matter of fact the case tells us they have enjoyed from time immemorial.... Such a condition would create that which in the very wide language of our courts is called a charitable, that is to say a public, trust or interest, for the benefit of the free inhabitants of ancient tenements.

For this principle to apply, however, it must be established that the enjoyment of the profit was regarded by the indefinite body of persons as a right to which they were entitled without anyone's permission, not as a privilege of little significance that was tolerated by the indulgence or good nature of the servient owner.[635]

In conclusion, then, we may say that before a fluctuating class can sustain a claim to a profit, they must show either that a grant was probably made in such a way as to incorporate them, or that there is some definite corporation that is capable of taking a grant and of holding the right granted in trust for them.

---

[634] (1882) 7 App Cas 633, 650.
[635] *Alfred F Beckett Ltd v Lyons* [1967] Ch 449.

V LAW REFORM

The Law Commission is undertaking the first comprehensive review of the law of easements and profits à prendre.[636] In 2008 it issued a Consultation Paper[637] containing (amongst others) the following provisional proposals:[638]

(1) The current requirements that an easement cannot exist in gross, and so must be attached to a dominant estate in the land,[639] and that the easement must accommodate and serve the land and have some nexus with the dominant land,[640] should be retained.

(2) An easement must not involve the unrestricted use of the servient land, but the fact that the dominant owner obtains exclusive possession of the servient land should not, without more, preclude it from being an easement, although the right must not be a lease or a tenancy.[641]

(3) Where the benefit and the burden of an easement are registered, there should be no requirement for the owners to be different persons, provided that the dominant and servient estates are registered with separate title numbers.[642]

(4) An expressly reserved easement should not be interpreted (in case of ambiguity) in favour of the person making the reservation.[643]

(5) In relation to implied easements:[644]

---

[636] There was a preliminary consideration of reform in Law Com WP No 36, *Transfer of Land: Appurtenant Rights* (1971), as well as review and recommendations by the Law Reform Committee for reform of the law of prescription in its Fourteenth Report, *Acquisition of Easements and Profits by Prescription* (1966); above, p 683. The 2008 Consultation Paper was long in gestation: in 1999 the Law Commission reported that it would be examining easements and analogous private rights (particularly profits à prendre) with a view to their reform and rationalisation: Law Com No 259, *Seventh Programme of Law Reform* (1999), Item 5.

[637] CP No 186, *Easements, Covenants and Profits à Prendre*; [2008] Conv 269 (M Dixon); [2009] Conv 448 (E Cooke, giving an indication of some of the likely final recommendations of the Law Commission).

[638] CP No 186, paras 16.4 – 16.32. For the proposals in the Consultation Paper in relation to covenants, including the proposal to create a new category of Land Obligation, see below, pp 774–7. The Consultation Paper also asked whether all or some of the rights capable of existing as negative easements (such as rights to light); above, p 645) should be abolished with prospective effect: para 15.42, but it appears that, in the light of the consultation, the Law Commission does not intend to make any recommendations in their final report about negative easements: [2009] Conv 448, 471 (E Cooke).

[639] Para 3.18. Note that the Law Commission rejects the view of the Court of Appeal in *Wall v Collins* [2007] EWCA Civ 444, [2007] Ch 390, that the benefit of an easement attaches to the land rather than to an estate in the land: above, p 634, n 3.

[640] Para 3.33.

[641] Para 3.55. This justifies the recognition of easements to park (above, p 647) even though the exercise of the right is seriously to restrict the use to which the servient land can be put: para 3.51.

[642] Para 3.66; thus reversing, for registered land, the third characteristic of an easement set out in *Re Ellenborough Park* [1956] Ch 131, M & B p 620, above, p 638.

[643] Para 4.24; thus reversing *St Edmundsbury and Ipswich Diocesan Board of Finance v Clarke (No 2)* [1975] 1 WLR 468, M & B p 651, above, p 654.

[644] The proposals for the reform of the acquisition of easements by prescription have been discussed above, p 685.

(a) in determining whether an easement should be implied, it should not be material whether the easement would take effect by grant or reservation, but in either case the person alleging that there is an easement should be required to establish it;[645]

(b) section 62 of the Law of Property Act 1925 should no longer operate to transform precarious benefits, enjoyed with the owner's licence or consent, into legal easements on a conveyance of the dominant estate;[646]

(c) views are invited as to whether the current rules of acquisition of easements by implied grant or reservation are in need of reform, to be replaced by (for example) an approach based on the actual intentions of the parties, or a set of presumptions that would arise from the circumstances, or a rule based on what is necessary for the reasonable use of the land.[647]

(6) In registered land, where an easement or profit has been entered on the register of the servient title, it should not be capable of extinguishment by abandonment.[648] In the case of unregistered land, or where the easement or profit has not been entered on the register, it should be capable of abandonment, and there should be a presumption of abandonment after a specified continuous period of non-exercise.[649]

(7) The court should have a new power, in the case of 'excessive use'[650] of an easement, to extinguish it, or suspend it on terms, or (where the excessive use can be severed) order that the excessive use cease, or award damages.[651]

(8) Where an easement is attached to a leasehold estate, it should be automatically extinguished on termination of the estate.[652]

(9) Profits à prendre should be created only by express grant or reservation or by statute, and expressly reserved profits should not be interpreted in cases of ambiguity in favour of the person making the reservation.[653]

---

[645] Para 4.53; thus changing the general rule that the law is readier to imply a grant than a reservation: *Wheeldon v Burrows* (1879) 12 Ch D 31, 49 (Thesiger LJ); above, p 660.

[646] Para 4.104. For the operation of s 62, see above, pp 654–9. The Consultation Paper also questions whether the doctrine of non-derogation from grant (above, p 663) should give rise to the implied acquisition of an easement: para 4.106.

[647] Para 4.149; and whether it would be desirable to put the rules of implication into a statutory form: para 4.150.

[648] Para 5.30.   [649] Para 5.31.

[650] Defined as where the dominant land is altered so as to undergo a radical change in character or a change in identity, and the changed use of the dominant land will lead to a substantial increase or alteration in the burden over the servient land: para 5.51.

[651] Para 5.63. Where land is *added* to the original dominant land, whether use may be made of the easement for the additional land would also depend on whether the use is excessive: para 5.71.

[652] Para 5.86. Thus reversing the decision in *Wall v Collins* [2007] EWCA Civ 444, [2007] Ch 390; above, p 696.

[653] Para 6.30.

(10) Profits should be capable of extinguishment by express release, by termination of the estate to which the profit is attached, by statute and (where the profit is not entered on the register) by abandonment.[654]

(11) The jurisdiction of the Upper Tribunal to discharge or modify restrictions on land contained in section 84(1) of the Law of Property Act 1925 (which currently applies only to restrictive covenants)[655] should be extended to include easements and profits.[656]

The Law Commission has indicated that it hopes to publish a final report and draft Bill in 2011.[657]

---

[654] Para 6.54. [655] Below, pp 764–72.
[656] Para 14.41. It should also be extended to include the proposed new Land Obligation, below, p 774.
[657] Law Com No 323, *Annual Report 2009-10*, para 2.61.

19

COVENANTS[1]

Summary

I INTRODUCTION

It sometimes happens that a landowner desires to impose a positive or a negative duty on the owner of neighbouring land with the object of preserving the saleable value or the residential amenities of his own property. X, the owner of Whiteacre, for instance, who sells part of his garden (Blackacre) to Y, may wish to control the manner in which Y uses the land. Accordingly X may require Y to covenant that he will not build shops on Blackacre (a negative or a restrictive covenant) or that he will erect and maintain a fence between it and X's retained land (a positive covenant), for the benefit of X and

---

[1] See generally Preston and Newsom, *Restrictive Covenants Affecting Freehold Land* (9th edn, 1998); Scamell, *Land Covenants* (1996); Francis, *Restrictive Covenants and Freehold Land* (3rd edn, 2009); Elphinstone, *Covenants Affecting Land* (1946); Farrand, *Contract and Conveyance* (2nd edn, 1973), pp 404–27; Maitland, *Equity* (revised Brunyate, 1936), pp 162–78; Emmet, ch 19; (1971) 87 LQR 539 (DJ Hayton); M & B ch 9. For a historical account, see Simpson, *History of the Land Law* (2nd edn, 1986), pp 116–18, 140–1, 256–60.

his successors in title. Such a covenant remains binding in contract between X and Y personally, but does its benefit run with Whiteacre and its burden with Blackacre in the sense that it is enforceable by the successors in title of the former against the successors in title of the latter?

If the right granted by the covenant is characterised as an easement, there is generally no difficulty. As we have seen in the previous chapter, an easement, legal or equitable, is capable of binding the servient tenement Blackacre and of enuring for the benefit of the dominant tenement Whiteacre. If the covenant is contained in a lease, again there is no difficulty, for it will normally pass on an assignment of the whole or any part of the premises or of the reversion.[2] However, in other cases the question is whether a person who was not an original party to the covenant can be bound by it, or can enforce it. In this chapter we shall see that, over the years, the courts (both of law and of equity) and statute have intervened to modify the rule of privity of contract in its application to covenants relating to land. At the present day, the law of covenants remains complex and technical, full of detailed rules that are a product of its historical development. There are significant differences in the rules for the passing of the benefit and the passing of the burden of a covenant; and the rules differ between the common law and equity; and between positive covenants and negative covenants. There has, however, been some tendency in the last 40 years to attempt to escape from the technicalities, and to simplify the rules or their application, particularly in relation to the enforcement of the benefit of a restrictive covenant by successors in title.[3] This policy is also a feature of proposals for the reform of covenants; and the Law Commission is now very well advanced in its work towards a general reform that would transform covenants (postive, as well as negative) into legal interests that, alongside easements, would be able to run with the benefited and the burdened land.[4]

For the law as it presently stands, however, it is important to understand that, in order to enforce a covenant, the claimant must show that the defendant has the burden of the covenant, whether as the original covenantor or as owner of the land to which the burden of the covenant is attached; and that the claimant has the benefit of the covenant, whether as an original beneficiary of it or as a successor to the original beneficiary (either his personal successor as beneficiary of the covenant, or his successor as owner of the land to which the benefit of the covenant is attached). We begin with a consideration of the rules governing the passing of the burden of a covenant.

---

[2] Above, pp 320 ff.

[3] See, for example, the simplified approach of the courts to the annexation of the benefit of a covenant: *Federated Homes v Mill Lodge Properties Ltd* [1980] 1 WLR 594, below, p 748; and the less strict approach to schemes of development: *Re Dolphin's Conveyance* [1970] Ch 654, below, p 757. The general relaxation of the contractual rules for the enforcement of third-party rights, achieved by the Contracts (Rights of Third Parties) Act 1999, below, p 743, also opens up a simpler mechanism for the enforcement of a land covenant.

[4] For proposed reform, see below, pp 774 ff.

II THE DEFENDANT MUST HAVE
THE BURDEN OF THE COVENANT

If the defendant is the original covenantor, he has the burden of the covenant and the only question is whether the claimant has the benefit.[5] As we shall see, there is a range of circumstances in which a successor to the original covenantee can enforce the covenant.[6] The law has been much more cautious, however, in allowing a successor to the covenantor to be bound by it. The general rule is that the burden of a covenant, whether positive or negative, does not run with the land at common law. However, the courts of equity devised a mechanism to allow the burden of a negative (restrictive) covenant to run.

A BURDEN DOES NOT RUN WITH
THE LAND AT COMMON LAW

In *Austerberry v Corporation of Oldham*[7] the view was expressed by two Lords Justices that the burden of a positive covenant made between a vendor and a purchaser does not run with the fee simple at common law. This view was reaffirmed by the House of Lords in *Rhone v Stephens*,[8] where:

> Walford House and Walford Cottage were in common ownership until 1960 when Walford Cottage was sold. The vendor covenanted to keep the common roof that covered part of Walford Cottage in wind and water tight condition. Both properties were sold after 1960. The question arose whether the covenant was enforceable against the owners of Walford House.

Holding that the covenant was not enforceable, Lord Templeman said:[9]

> In the *Austerberry* case the owners of a site of a road covenanted that they and their successors in title would make the road and keep it in repair. The road was sold to the defendants and it was held that the repair covenant could not be enforced against them.
>
> For over a hundred years it has been clear and accepted law that equity will enforce negative covenants against freehold land but has no power to enforce positive covenants against successors in title of the land. To enforce a positive covenant would be to enforce a

---

[5] If the claim is against the original covenantor after he has parted with the land, there is also a question about whether the conduct of the successor constitutes a breach of covenant by the original covenantor. This depends on the construction of the covenant, and the scope of the covenantor's obligation may be enlarged by LPA 1925, s 79: *Tophams Ltd v Earl of Sefton* [1967] 1 AC 50 at 81; *Re Royal Victoria Pavilion, Ramsgate* [1961] Ch 581; *Morrells of Oxford Ltd v Oxford United Football Club Ltd* [2001] Ch 459 at [35].

[6] Below, pp 744 ff.   [7] (1885) 29 Ch D 750; *E and G C Ltd v Bate* (1935) L Jo 203.

[8] [1994] 2 AC 310, M & B p 746; [1994] Conv 477 (J Snape); (1994) 110 LQR 346 (NP Gravells); [1994] All ER Rev (PJ Clarke); [1995] CLJ 60 (S Gardner).

[9] At 434.

personal obligation against a person who has not covenanted. To enforce negative covenants is only to treat the land as subject to a restriction.[10]

The House of Lords held further that *Austerberry v Corporation of Oldham* had not been 'reversed remarkably but unremarked' by section 79 of the Law of Property Act 1925 where a covenant was made after 1925. The section provides that:

> A covenant relating to any land of a covenantor or capable of being bound by him, shall, unless a contrary intention is expressed, be deemed to be made by the covenantor on behalf of himself his successors in title and the persons deriving title under him or them, and, subject as aforesaid, shall have effect as if such successors and other persons were expressed.

This is a welcome and restrictive interpretation of the section,[11] which is at variance with the wide construction of the corresponding section 78 on the running of the benefit of a covenant.[12]

(1) Devices to Circumvent Rule

There are, however, 'a number of current techniques and devices by which lawyers attempt to surmount or circumvent the difficulties of enforcing positive covenants'.[13]

(a) Lease instead of sale

The land may be leased instead of sold, and reliance placed upon the enforceability of covenants between landlord and tenant.[14]

(b) Chains of indemnity covenants

As we have seen, an original covenantor remains liable in contract even after he has parted with the land,[15] and so he may protect himself by taking a covenant of indemnity from his purchaser. Each successive purchaser may give a similar covenant to his vendor with the result that a chain of indemnity covenants is created. In theory the original covenantee should be able to secure the indirect enforcement of the

---

[10] Below, pp 732 ff.

[11] For its construction as a word-saving section, see *Tophams Ltd v Earl of Sefton* [1967] 1 AC 50, 73, 81 (Lords Upjohn and Wilberforce respectively); *Federated Homes Ltd v Mill Lodge Properties Ltd* [1980] 1 WLR 594 (Brightman LJ); M & B, pp 777, 783. See Emmet, para 19.008; and the laconic 'No' given as an answer by Sir Benjamin Cherry in his Lectures on the New Property Acts (1926), p 131, to the question 'Is the case of *Austerberry v Corporation of Oldham* overruled by s 79 of the Law of Property Act?' See also *Morrells of Oxford Ltd v Oxford United Football Club Ltd* [2001] Ch 459 at [14], [35]. The approach in the modern law, however, is to favour the running of the burden of positive covenants, and this has been proposed by the Law Commission: below, pp 774 ff.

[12] See below, pp 748 ff.

[13] Report of the Committee on Positive Covenants Affecting Land (1965), Cmnd 2719, para 8, from which the quotations in this paragraph are taken. See also Law Com No 127, *Positive and Restrictive Covenants* (1984), paras 3.19–3.42; Farrand (2nd edn), pp 422–7; (1973) 37 Conv (NS) 194 (AM Prichard); Law Com CP No 186, *Easements, Covenants and Profits à Prendre* (2008), paras 7.46–7.65.

[14] Above, pp 302 ff.   [15] But see above, n 5.

positive covenant by the current owner of the land by suing the original covenantor. 'But in practice this device sooner or later becomes ineffective, either in consequence of the death or disappearance of the original covenantor, or because a break occurs in the chain of indemnities.'[16]

(c) The doctrine of *Halsall v Brizell*[17]

'In some cases a positive covenant can be enforced in practice by the operation of the maxim *"qui sentit commodum sentire debet et onus"*. This obliges a person who wishes to take advantage of a service or facility (eg a road or drains) to comply with any corresponding obligation to contribute to the cost of providing or maintaining it. The maxim cannot, however, be invoked where the burdened owner does not enjoy any service or facility to which his obligations attach or has no sufficient interest in the continuance of these benefits.'[18]

In *Thamesmead Town Ltd v Allotey*,[19] Peter Gibson LJ explained the limits of the doctrine as follows:

> The reasoning of Lord Templeman [in *Rhone v Stephens*] suggests that there are two requirements for the enforceability of a positive covenant against a successor in title to the covenantor. The first is that the condition of discharging the burden must be relevant to the exercise of the rights that enable the benefit to be obtained. In *Rhone v Stephens* the mutual obligation of support was unrelated to and independent of the covenant to maintain the roof. The second is that the successors in title must have the opportunity to choose whether to take the benefit or, having taken it, to renounce it, even if only in theory, and thereby to escape the burden and that the successors in title can be deprived of the benefit if they fail to assume the burden.

It has also been said that the benefit and burden must be conferred in or by the same transaction, which, in the case of land, will almost inevitably be effected by one or more deeds or other documents.[20]

---

[16] See *Radford v de Froberville* [1977] 1 WLR 1262; *TRW Steering Systems Ltd v North Cape Properties Ltd and Cornerstone Estates Ltd* (1993) 69 P & CR 265.

[17] [1957] Ch 169; *ER Ives Investment Ltd v High* [1967] 2 QB 379, M & B p 1074; *Four Oaks Estate Ltd v Hadley* [1986] LS Gaz R 2326 (no benefit to which burden could be attached); *Law Debenture Trust Corp plc v Ural Caspian Oil Corp Ltd* [1993] 1 WLR 138; *Rhone v Stephens* (1993) 67 P & CR 9 (doctrine not invoked where benefit 'technical or minimal'; see also HL at [1994] 2 AC 310, below). For a detailed discussion of the doctrine, see *Tito v Waddell (No 2)* [1977] Ch 106, 289–311, where Megarry V-C held at 303 that it covered not merely successors in title but also 'anybody whose connection with the transaction creating the benefit and burden is sufficient to show that he has some claim to the benefit whether or not he has a valid title to it'. See also (1977) 41 Conv (NS) 432–5 (FR Crane); [1985] Conv 12 (FP Aughterson); Emmet, para 19.020.

[18] *Rhone v Stephens* [1994] 2 AC 310, 322, where Lord Templeman said: 'The condition must be relevant to the exercise of the right. The obligation to repair the roof was an independent provision'.

[19] [1998] 3 EGLR 97, 99.

[20] *Davies v Jones* [2009] EWCA Civ 1164, [2010] 1 P & CR 22 at [27] (Morritt C). A 'clear understanding', without a transaction having legal effect, is insufficient: ibid, at [28].

(d) Enlargement of long leases into freeholds

This is an 'untried and artificial' device, whereby a long lease is enlarged under section 153 of the Law of Property Act 1925, and the freehold is then subject 'to all the same covenants...as the term would have been subject to if it had not been so enlarged'.[21]

(e) Estate rentcharge

An estate rentcharge may be created to secure the payment of money or contribution to the maintenance of property.[22] The Rentcharges Act 1977 makes special provision for this type of rentcharge.[23]

(f) Right of re-entry

A right of re-entry may be reserved, exercisable on events that amount to the breach of a positive covenant. This right of re-entry runs with the land, but is subject to the rule against perpetuities.[24]

(g) Restriction under Land Registration Act

'Where the title to plots on a newly developed estate is going to be registered and the developer is interested in the continuing observance of the covenants, he can insert a covenant in the original conveyances that the plot shall not be sold without his consent. He can then enter a restriction in the register[25] to ensure compliance with the covenant and can refuse to give his consent to any sale under which the purchaser does not assume the appropriate positive obligations.'

(h) Easement of fencing

A right to have a fence or wall kept in repair is a right that is capable of being enforced as an easement. The right is anomalous in the law of easements.[26]

(i) Commonhold

Under the Commonhold and Leasehold Reform Act 2002 the burden of a positive covenant may run by statute as between the unit-holders of commonhold land. Commonhold has already been discussed in detail in Chapter 7.

---

[21] Above, p 343. Restricted to those: (i) which were originally created for at least 300 years of which no less than 200 years is unexpired; (ii) in which no rent of money value is payable; (iii) which are not liable to be determined by re-entry for condition broken; (1958) 22 Conv (NS) 101 (TPD Taylor). Cf Leasehold Reform Act 1967, above, p 394.

[22] *Morland v Cook* (1868) LR 6 Eq 252; *Austerberry v Oldham Corp* (1885) 29 Ch D 750, 782.

[23] S 2(3)(c), (4), (5). See below, p 782.

[24] *Shiloh Spinners Ltd v Harding* [1973] AC 691. The possibility of relief against forfeiture reduces its effectiveness as a device. See (1950) 14 Conv (NS) 350, 354–7 (SM Tolson). The express grant of a legal rentcharge or a legal right of entry exercisable over a legal term of years or annexed to a legal rentcharge is a registrable disposition: LRA 2002 s 27(2)(e); Sch 2, para 6; H & B, paras 8.17–8.20.

[25] LRA 2002, s 40, replacing LRA 1925, s 58, below, p 1099.

[26] *Jones v Price* [1965] 2 QB 618; *Crow v Wood* [1971] 1 QB 77, M & B p 645; above, p 643; *Marlton v Turner* [1998] 3 EGLR 185.

(2) Law Reform

In spite of these methods of circumvention, the burden of a covenant, whether positive or negative, does not run with the servient land upon which it is imposed. As we are about to see, this rule has been radically relaxed by equity in the case of a negative covenant that restricts an owner from making certain defined uses of his land, but it still governs a positive covenant, such as one to contribute towards the cost of constructing and maintaining a private road. That such a covenant should be unenforceable against the successors in title of the covenantor is in many cases unreasonable, such as where the purchaser of a freehold flat has entered into positive covenants that are essential to the comfort of his neighbours in the same building. Where the freehold of flats is registered as a commonhold scheme,[27] this problem is overcome. But the difficulty of enforcing the burden of a positive covenant outside a commonhold scheme remains. 'This rule, whose discovery has shocked more than one eminent judge unversed in the subtleties of property law'[28] was considered in 1965 by the Wilberforce Committee that recommended that, subject to certain conditions, the burden of positive covenants should run, and again in 1984 by the Law Commission on the wider topic of both Positive and Restrictive Covenants.[29] The Law Commission has now again provisionally proposed reform within its general proposals to reform the law of covenants.[30]

B BURDEN OF A RESTRICTIVE COVENANT MAY RUN WITH THE LAND IN EQUITY

(1) General Nature of the Equitable Doctrine

In the historic case of *Tulk v Moxhay*,[31] the common law rule that the burden of a covenant does not run with the land of the covenantor except in the case of a lease was radically modified by equity so far as negative covenants are concerned. The general effect of the doctrine established by this case is that, subject to certain conditions to be discussed at length later, a covenant *negative in substance* entered into by the owner of Blackacre with the neighbouring owner of Whiteacre, imposes an equitable burden upon Blackacre that is enforceable to the same extent as any other equitable interest, such as a contract for a lease. The right to obtain an injunction[32] against a breach of the negative undertaking will pass to the subsequent owners of Whiteacre, and the duty to observe it will pass to all persons who take the burdened Blackacre except a purchaser

---

[27] Above.   [28] *Rhone v Stephens* (1993) 67 P & CR 9 (Nourse LJ).

[29] Report of the Committee on Positive Covenants Affecting Land 1965 (Cmnd 2719); Law Com No 11, *Restrictive Covenants* (1967); Law Com No 127, *Positive and Restrictive Covenants* (1984); (1972) 31 CLJ 157 (HWR Wade).

[30] Law Com CP No 186, *Easements, Covenants and Profits à Prendre* (2008); below, p 774.

[31] (1848) 2 Ph 774, M & B p 754; [1981] Conv 55 (CD Bell); (1982) 98 LQR 279 (S Gardner); [1983] Conv 29 (R Griffith); 327 (CD Bell).

[32] For remedies generally for breach of a restrictive covenant, see below, p 760.

who takes free of equitable interests. At the time of the decision in *Tulk v Moxhay* this meant that a bona fide purchaser for value of the legal estate without notice, actual or constructive, of the covenant, took free of the burden of it. Since 1925, the test is not notice, but whether the burden of the covenant has been registered as a land charge (in unregistered land) or protected by entry on the register (in registered land).[33]

The facts of *Tulk v Moxhay* were as follows:

> In 1808 the claimant, being then the owner in fee of the vacant piece of ground in the middle of Leicester Square, London, sold the ground to one Elms in fee, Elms covenanting for himself, his heirs and assigns that he and they would:
>
>> keep and maintain the said piece of ground and square garden, and the iron railing round the same in its then form, and in sufficient and proper repair as a square garden and pleasure ground, in an open state, uncovered with any buildings in neat and ornamental order.
>
> The piece of ground passed by various conveyances into the hands of the defendant Moxhay, who, although he had made no similar covenant with his immediate vendor, admitted that he took the land with notice of the original covenant. The defendant then openly proposed to erect buildings upon the square.

The claimant, who still remained the owner of several adjacent houses, succeeded in obtaining an injunction to stop the breach of covenant.[34]

This doctrine has been the subject of development, in the course of which the nature of the right and obligation arising from a restrictive covenant has undergone a radical change.[35] The earlier decisions, culminating in *Luker v Dennis* in 1877,[36] proceeded solely upon the fact of notice,[37] since this was the element that Lord Cottenham stressed in *Tulk v Moxhay* in the following words:[38]

> It is said that, the covenant being one which does not run with the land, this court cannot enforce it, but the question is, not whether the covenant runs with the land, but whether a party shall be permitted to use the land in a manner inconsistent with the contract entered into by his vendor, and with notice of which he purchased.

To rest the enforcement of a contract against a third party on this basis, however, is not without its dangers.

First, if the emphasis is laid upon whether the conscience of the third party acquiring the land of the covenantor is affected, instead of upon whether the land itself is affected, there will be certain persons, such as a squatter obtaining a title by 12 years' adverse possession,[39] who will enjoy an immunity that they do not deserve.

Secondly, if notice alone justifies the issue of an injunction, the remedy can hardly be withheld in principle even where the contract is collateral, in the sense that its purpose

---

[33] Below, pp 739–41.

[34] For the continued enforceability of the covenant, see *R v Westminster CC and London Electricity Board* (1989) 59 P & CR 51, where Simon Brown J described Leicester Square as 'one of London's ornaments'.

[35] See especially Behan, *Covenants Affecting Land*, pp 27 ff.   [36] (1877) 7 Ch D 227.

[37] *LCC v Allen* [1914] 3 KB 642, 658–9, 664–6.   [38] (1848) 2 Ph 774, 777–8.

[39] Below, p 738. Under LRA 2002, 12 years' adverse possession no longer of itself gives title to the squatter: below, pp 739, 1160.

is not to protect the covenantee's land against an undesirable use of the covenantor's land but to confer some personal privilege upon the covenantee.

Since the end of the nineteenth century the judicial approach to the matter has altered. The courts, choosing as the appropriate analogy either the negative easement, such as the right to light, or the tenant's covenant that is annexed to the land by virtue of *Spencer's Case*,[40] have required a restrictive covenant to possess what may be called a real, as distinct from a personal, flavour, before it becomes available to and enforceable against third parties. It must, as Vaughan Williams LJ said, 'arise from the relation of two estates one to the other',[41] or, to use more familiar technical language, it must touch and concern the dominant tenement of the covenantee and must be intended to protect that land against certain uses of the servient tenement. But once it satisfies this requirement it creates an equitable right that will run with the dominant tenement and a corresponding equitable obligation binding on the servient tenement. Discussing the passing of both the benefit and the burden in equity, Collins LJ said:[42]

> When the benefit has been once clearly annexed to one piece of land, it passes by assignment of that land, and may be said to run with it ... without proof of special bargain or representation on the assignment. In such a case it runs, not because the conscience of either party is affected, but because the purchaser has bought something which inhered in or was annexed to the land bought. That is the reason why, in dealing with the burden, the purchaser's conscience is not affected by notice of covenants which were part of the original bargain on the first sale, but were merely personal and collateral, while it is affected by notice of those which touch and concern the land. The covenant must be one that is capable of running with the land before the question of the purchaser's conscience and the equity affecting it can come into discussion.

As the law now stands, certain essentials must be satisfied before the burden of a covenant can be laid upon an assignee of the servient tenement or before its benefit can be exploited by an assignee of the dominant tenement. These will now be stated.

(2) Conditions Precedent to the Running of the Burden in Equity

The burden of a restrictive covenant will bind an assignee of the servient tenement if the following essentials are satisfied.

(a) The conditions precedent

(1) The covenant must be negative in nature

It is essential that the covenant should be negative in substance, not a positive one requiring the expenditure of money for its performance.[43] This condition is satisfied if,

---

[40] Above, p 308; *London and South Western Rly Co v Gomm* (1882) 20 Ch D 562, 583, M & B p 758.

[41] *Formby v Barker* [1903] 2 Ch 539, 553. No such relation existed, for example, in *Tophams Ltd v Earl of Sefton* [1967] 1 AC 50.

[42] *Rogers v Hosegood* [1900] 2 Ch 388, 407.

[43] *Haywood v Brunswick Permanent Benefit Building Society* (1881) 8 QBD 403. Positive and negative obligations may be set in a single covenant. 'There cannot be any doctrine of contagious proximity whereby

for example, the owner of the land undertakes to use the premises for private residence only, or to keep certain windows obscured, or not to build, not to open a public house, or not to carry on a business. But in every case it is the substance and not the form of the covenant that must be regarded, for if an undertaking, though couched in affirmative terms, clearly implies a negative, it will be caught by the doctrine of *Tulk v Moxhay*. Indeed, in that case itself, the covenant was not in terms restrictive, but its provision that the piece of ground was to be used only as an ornamental garden implied a prohibition against building.[44] Again, a covenant to give the first refusal of land is regarded as negative in substance, since in effect it is a promise not to sell without giving the covenantee an option to buy.[45]

(2) The covenantee must at the time of the creation of the covenant own land for the protection of which the covenant is made and he (or the person seeking later to enforce the benefit of the covenant) must continue to own it

A restrictive covenant taken from the purchaser of a freehold estate is a mere covenant in gross, personal to the contracting parties, unless it imposes an equitable burden upon the covenantor's land for the protection of land owned by the covenantee. Equity, acting on the analogy of a negative easement, will not regard a restrictive covenant as other than personal, unless there is the relation of dominancy and serviency between the respective properties.

It follows, therefore, that, if the covenantee retains no adjacent land or owns no land capable of being protected by the covenant, the covenant cannot be enforced against a person other than the covenantor, even if he has notice of it.[46] Thus in *London County Council v Allen*:[47]

the presence of the positive inhibits the enforcement of the neighbouring negative': *Shepherd Homes Ltd v Sandham (No 2)* [1971] 1 WLR 1062 (Megarry J).

[44] *Clegg v Hands* (1890) 44 Ch D 503, 519; *Bridges v Harrow London Borough* (1981) 260 EG 284, 288 (covenant to retain trees in hedgerow held to be probably negative in substance); *Bedwell Park Quarry Co v Hertfordshire CC* [1993] JPL 349 ('It is hard to think of an obligation which was more positive in substance as well as in form').

[45] *Manchester Ship Canal Co v Manchester Racecourse Co* [1901] 2 Ch 37.

[46] But a lessor's interest in the reversion suffices to make a covenant touching and concerning the land enforceable against a sub-lessee: *Hall v Ewin* (1887) 37 Ch D 74; *Regent Oil Co Ltd v J A Gregory (Hatch End) Ltd* [1966] Ch 402, 432–3; *Hemingway Securities Ltd v Dunraven Ltd* [1995] 1 EGLR 61.

For statutory exceptions to the rule (some of which are no longer in force), see National Trust Act 1937, s 8; *Gee v The National Trust for Places of Historic Interest or Natural Beauty* [1966] 1 WLR 170, 174; Green Belt (London and Home Counties) Act 1938, s 22; Water Industry Act 1991, s 164(3); National Parks and Access to Countryside Act 1949, s 16(4); Forestry Act 1967, s 5(2); Endowments and Glebe Measure 1976, s 22; Ancient Monuments and Archaeological Areas Act 1979, s 17(5); Wildlife and Countryside Act 1981, s 39(3); Local Government (Miscellaneous Provisions) Act 1982, s 33; TCPA 1990, s 106, as amended by Planning and Compensation Act 1991, s 12 and Planning Act 2008, s 174 (s 106 was due to be replaced by the new scheme of 'planning contribution' under PCPA 2004, s 46, but that section was never brought into force and was repealed by Planning Act 2008, s 225, Sch 13, para 1); *Re Martin's Application* (1988) 57 P & CR 119; and a number of local authorities have power under local Acts. See also *Peabody Donation Fund Governors v London Residuary Body* (1987) 55 P & CR 355 (Artisans and Labourers Dwellings Improvement Act 1875, s 9; 'a valuable site in Covent Garden'). HA 1985, s 609 does not allow local authority to enforce positive covenants: *Cantrell v Wycombe DC* [2008] EWCA Civ 866, [2009] 1 P & CR 12.

[47] [1914] 3 KB 642, M & B p 755; *Formby v Barker* [1903] 2 Ch 539, M & B p 756.

A, a builder, in return for permission to lay out a new street on his land, entered into a covenant with LCC not to build upon a plot of land which lay across the end of the proposed street. The plot was eventually conveyed to Mrs A, who built on it and mortgaged it to B. The Court of Appeal held that the restrictive covenant was not binding on Mrs A and B, even if they had had notice of it.

Buckley LJ in the course of his judgment said:[48]

> In the present case we are asked to extend the doctrine of *Tulk v Moxhay* so as to affirm that a restrictive covenant can be enforced against a derivative owner taking with notice by a person who never has had or who does not retain any land to be protected by the restrictive covenant in question. In my opinion the doctrine does not extend to that case. The doctrine is that a covenant not running with the land, but being a negative covenant entered into by an owner of land with an adjoining owner, binds the land in equity and is enforceable against a derivative owner taking with notice. The doctrine ceases to be applicable when the person seeking to enforce the covenant against the derivative owner has no land to be protected by the negative covenant. The fact of notice is in that case irrelevant.[49]

Again, once a covenantee has assigned the whole of the dominant land, he cannot enforce the covenant against the servient owner. His one remedy is to sue the covenantor personally on the contract, but even so he is entitled only to nominal damages, not to an injunction. The principle of *London County Council v Allen*[50] is that the equitable doctrine ought to be applied with the sole object of protecting the enjoyment of the land that the covenant was intended to protect. If it were possible for a covenantee to enforce a covenant, despite the fact that he never retained any land at all or that he later disposed of the land that he had retained, the result would be to place an unwarranted and useless burden upon subsequent purchasers from the covenantor.[51]

(3) The covenant must touch and concern the dominant land

The covenant must be capable of benefiting the dominant land in the sense that it must be one that touches and concerns that land.[52] To satisfy this condition in the case where a freehold estate is conveyed: 'the covenant must either affect the land as regards mode of occupation, or it must be such as *per se*, and not merely from collateral circumstances, affects the value of the land'.[53]

---

[48] [1914] 3 KB 642, 654.

[49] See, however, above, n 46, as to modern statutory powers of local authorities to enforce restrictive covenants otherwise than for the protection of land.

[50] [1914] 3 KB 642; *Formby v Barker*, above; *Kelly v Barrett* [1924] 2 Ch 379.

[51] *Chambers v Randall* [1923] 1 Ch 149, 157; *Re Union of London and Smith's Bank Ltd's Conveyance, Miles v Easter* [1933] Ch 611, 632.

[52] Cf above, p 304; *Rogers v Hosegood* [1900] 2 Ch 388, 395; *Kelly v Barrett* [1924] 2 Ch 379, 395; *Marquess of Zetland v Driver* [1939] Ch 1, 8. In *Stocks v Whitgift* [2001] EWCA Civ 1732, [2001] 49 EGCS 130 at [8] Parker LJ preferred the expression 'relates to the land' to the 'old expression' of touch and concern.

[53] *Rogers v Hosegood*, above, at 395 (Farwell J), adopting Bayley J in *Congleton Corp v Pattison* (1808) 10 East 130.

Whether the covenant benefits the dominant land is a question of fact to be determined on expert evidence presented to the court.[54] The onus is on the defendant to show that it does not do so, either originally or at the date of the action.[55] This means that, if there were possible opinions either way, the defendant will still fail unless he can show that the opinion that the covenant benefits the land could not reasonably be held.[56]

(4) It must be the common intention of the parties that the burden of the covenant shall run with the land of the covenantor

This intention may appear from the wording of the covenant itself, as, for instance, where the covenant is made by the covenantor 'for himself, his heirs and assigns'. Covenants that are made after 1925 and relate to any land of the covenantor, or are capable of being bound by him,[57] are deemed by section 79 of the Law of Property Act 1925 to be made by the covenantor on behalf of himself, his successors in title and the persons deriving title under him or them, unless a contrary intention is expressed.[58]

(b) Persons against whom burden runs

We must now examine more closely the effect of a covenant that satisfies the four conditions set out above, and in particular consider those persons against whom the covenant is enforceable.

The doctrine of *Tulk v Moxhay* stands on quite a different footing from the rules that regulate the running of covenants at law, and being of a far more elastic nature it affects a more extensive class of persons and embraces a more extensive class of covenants. In essence, when the above conditions are satisfied a restrictive covenant becomes an equitable interest, and as such is enforceable on general principles against all persons who acquire the burdened land.[59] Moreover, the occupier of the burdened land is liable irrespective of the character of his occupation. This is in sharp contrast with the common law and statutory rules that govern covenants contained in a lease. Under these rules, as we have seen,[60] the burden of a covenant, whether positive or negative, passes to an assignee of the tenant, and it is immaterial that the landlord retains no dominant land.[61] But no one is an assignee for this purpose unless there is privity of estate between him and the reversioner. Thus, though the burden is traditionally said

---

[54] *Marten v Flight Refuelling Ltd* [1962] Ch 115, 137; *Earl of Leicester v Wells-next-the-Sea UDC* [1973] Ch 110; *Wrotham Park Estate Co Ltd v Parkside Homes Ltd* [1974] 1 WLR 798.

[55] *Wrotham Park Estate Co v Parkside Homes Ltd*, above.   [56] [1974] JPL 133 (GH Newsom).

[57] *Lynnthorpe Enterprises Ltd v Sidney Smith (Chelsea) Ltd* [1990] 1 EGLR 148, M & B p 762 (land need not belong to covenantor at time of covenant).

[58] *Re Royal Victoria Pavilion (Ramsgate)* [1961] Ch 581, M & B p 762; *Tophams Ltd v Earl of Sefton* [1967] 1 AC 50, 81; above, p 729, n 11; *Rhone v Stephens* [1994] 2 AC 310; *Morrells of Oxford Ltd v Oxford United Football Club Ltd* [2001] Ch 459 (one covenant contained no reference to successors in title, whereas another covenant did: held that the first covenant was intended to be personal: s 79 did not apply because of contrary intention).

[59] For the requirements of registration of the covenant, in both registered and unregistered land, see below, p 739.

[60] Above, p 323.   [61] *Regent Oil Co Ltd v J A Gregory (Hatch End) Ltd* [1966] Ch 402.

to run with the land, what in fact it runs with is the estate created by the lease. Under the developed doctrine of *Tulk v Moxhay*, on the other hand, it runs with the servient land as such, and there is no question of privity of estate.

The effect of this distinction between running with the land and running with the estate may be illustrated by a reference to three classes of persons who are all caught by the doctrine of *Tulk v Moxhay*, but none of whom is liable at common law under the rules derived from *Spencer's Case*.

(1) Sub-lessees

A restrictive covenant imposed upon a lessee binds a sub-lessee, despite the absence of privity of estate between him and the lessor.[62]

(2) Mere occupiers

A person who is merely occupying land without having any definite estate or interest in it is bound by restrictive covenants. Thus in *Mander v Falcke*:[63]

> a lessee who had covenanted not to use the demised premises for purposes which would cause annoyance or inconvenience to adjoining property owned by the lessor granted an under-lease of the premises. The reversion was ultimately assigned to the claimant and the under-lease became vested in X. Apparently X did not occupy the premises himself, but allowed his father to have possession, and the evidence clearly showed that the latter, while purporting to keep an oyster bar, was in fact using the place as a brothel to the great scandal of the neighbourhood.

When an injunction was sought to restrain a breach of the covenant it was argued that such relief could not be granted against the father, as he had no interest whatever, either legal or equitable, in the land. This argument failed, and an injunction was granted against the father. Lindley LJ said:[64]

> I treat him simply as an occupier managing the business. He may be neither an assignee nor purchaser, but he is in occupation, and that is enough to affect him, he having notice of the covenants in the lease.

A restrictive covenant imposed after 1925 is enforceable against a mere occupier under section 79(2) of the Law of Property Act 1925.[65]

(3) Squatters

A person who acquires a title to land through adverse possession is bound by any restrictive covenants that are annexed to the land.

In unregistered land[66] the effect of the Limitation Act 1980 is merely to extinguish the title of the previous owner and not to transfer his identical interest to the adverse

---

[62] *Clements v Welles* (1865) LR 1 Eq 200; *Hall v Ewin* (1887) 37 Ch D 74; *John Bros Abergarw Brewery Co v Holmes* [1900] 1 Ch 188.

[63] [1891] 2 Ch 554.

[64] Ibid, 557.

[65] Above, p 308.

[66] Below, p 1149.

possessor. A covenant in a lease will therefore not bind a person who by long-continued possession of the premises acquires a superior right to the tenant, because he has no privity of estate with the landlord.[67] This lack of privity, however, will not free a squatter on the servient land from a restrictive covenant since it binds the land itself, and therefore (as long as any requirements for registration are satisfied[68]) the squatter. This is illustrated by *Re Nisbet and Potts' Contract*[69] where

> Nisbet had purchased land in 1901 from X and Y, who had themselves purchased in 1890 from H, whose title was based upon occupation since 1878 (ie more than 12 years' adverse possession). Nisbet agreed to accept proof of title commencing at 1878, although he could have insisted on proof of 40 years' title (ie, commencing in 1861).[70] A restrictive covenant had been imposed on the land in 1867; Nisbet knew nothing of it but would have discovered it if he had insisted on proof of 40 years' title. In 1903 Nisbet contracted to sell the land to Potts, who then discovered the covenants. The question was whether Potts, if he took a conveyance of the land, would be subject to the covenant imposed in 1867; and therefore whether the land was already subject to the covenant in the hands of the vendor, Nisbet.

It was argued that the covenant no longer bound assignees of the servient land, because H, who had seized the land in 1878, acquired a title quite independent of any prior holder's title. But it was held that the equitable interest created by the covenant remained enforceable against X and Y, and Nisbet, unless they could satisfy the court that they had acquired the legal estate for valuable consideration without notice. It was held that they had constructive notice, because if they had insisted on proof of a good root of title at least 40 years old, they would have been led back through the squatter H to the original covenantor; but if they chose to accept less than they might have done, they were bound to take the consequences.[71] They were therefore bound by the covenant.

In registered land, under the Land Registration Act 2002 the squatter does not acquire title to the land without being registered as proprietor.[72] Where he is registered, he is the successor in title to the previously registered proprietor, and is bound by any restrictive covenants affecting the registered title.[73]

(c) Registration of restrictive covenants

Even if the conditions precedent to the passing of the burden of a restrictive covenant are satisfied,[74] in many cases the covenant will bind an assignee of the servient tenement only if it has been registered. Different rules apply for unregistered and registered land.

---

[67] *Tichborne v Weir* (1892) 67 LT 735, M & B p 759.   [68] Below.

[69] [1905] 1 Ch 391, affd [1906] 1 Ch 386, M & B p 759.

[70] The period of title that a purchaser can require was later reduced to 30 years: LPA 1925, s 44(1); and then 15 years: LPA 1969, s 23; below, p 1043.

[71] After 1925 the question would be not whether the purchaser had notice, but whether the covenant was registered under LCA 1925 or 1972; below.

[72] For the significant changes made in this respect by LRA 2002, see below, pp 1160 ff.

[73] LRA 2002, s 97, Sch 6, para 9(2); H & B, ch 31.   [74] Above, p 734.

(1) Unregistered land

The requirements of registration in unregistered land depend on whether the covenant was created before 1926 or after 1925.

(i) Covenants created before 1926

Covenants created before 1 January 1926 bind all persons who acquire the burdened land, with the exception of a bona fide purchaser for value of the legal estate in it without notice, actual or constructive, of the covenants. Such a purchaser can, however, pass a title free from the restriction to a purchaser from him, even though the latter has actual notice of the covenant.[75]

(ii) Covenants created after 1925

Covenants created after 1925, except those made between lessor and lessee,[76] are void against a purchaser (including a mortgagee and lessee) of the *legal estate* in the burdened land *for money or money's worth*, unless they are registered as land charges in the appropriate register.[77] If not registered they are void against the purchaser for value of the legal estate even though he had express notice of them. Thus non-registration does not avail an assignee of a mere equitable interest in the burdened land, or an assignee of the legal estate who does not give money or money's worth. The reason why a restrictive covenant between a lessor and lessee cannot be registered, is that it is a simple and normal step for an assignee to inspect the lease that contains the terms of the tenancy.

(2) Registered land

In registered land the burden[78] of a restrictive covenant, except one made between a lessor and lessee,[79] can be protected by the entry of a notice on the register of the servient tenement.[80] According to the usual principles of protection of equitable

---

[75] *Wilkes v Spooner* [1911] 2 KB 473, M & B p 62.

[76] *Dartstone Ltd v Cleveland Petroleum Co Ltd* [1969] 1 WLR 1807; [1956] 20 Conv (NS) 370 (RG Rowley); *Oceanic Village Ltd v United Attractions* [2000] Ch 234.

[77] LCA 1972, ss 2(5), Class D(ii), 4(6), s 17(1), below, p 1059. Positive and negative covenants entered into with a local authority, a Minister of the Crown or Government Department (otherwise than as between landlord and tenant) are registrable as local land charges: LLCA 1975, ss 1, 2, below, p 1066.

For the duty of a solicitor to advise a purchaser on the nature and effect of a restrictive covenant, see *Bittlestone v Keegan Williams* [1997] EGCS 8.

[78] No provision is made by LRA 2002 for recording the benefit of a restrictive covenant on the register of the dominant tenement: H & B, para 25.13; R & R, para 42.019.01; nor for making entries relating to positive covenants since the burden does not run with the land: above, p 728; below, n 85. In practice, however, positive covenants are often intermixed with restrictive covenants, and where this occurs they are not edited out of the restrictive covenant entry.

[79] LRA 2002, s 33(c). This exclusion from registration parallels the position in unregistered land, above.

[80] Ibid, s 32. R & R, paras 9.018–9.021, 42.009. If the restrictive covenant was protected under LCA 1972, above, before first registration it will become unenforceable if no notice is entered on first registration: *Freer v Unwins* [1976] Ch 288; (1976) 40 Conv (NS) 304 (FR Crane); [1976] CLJ 211 (D Hayton); (1976) 92 LQR 338 (RJ Smith); (1976) 126 NLJ 523 (SM Cretney). See (1984) 81 LSG 1723, where the Chief Land Registrar states that on first registration he does not normally enquire whether a covenant has become void for non-registration under LCA 1925; R & R, para 9.020.

interests in registered land,[81] if the covenant is not so protected it will not bind a person taking a registrable disposition[82] of the registered estate for valuable consideration.[83] It cannot be an overriding interest.[84]

The entry of a notice on the register only makes the covenant binding if it satisfies the other conditions necessary for the passing of the burden.[85]

III THE CLAIMANT MUST HAVE THE BENEFIT OF THE COVENANT

We have seen that the courts were reluctant to allow a person to be burdened by a covenant that he had not himself undertaken. There is no such reluctance in the case of the benefit, for which a number of mechanisms have been developed, by statute, by the courts of common law, and by the courts of equity. In some cases the claimant will be able to enforce the covenant by virtue of being the original covenantee, or (if not the covenantee) being a person defined at the outset as a beneficiary of it. Failing that, he may be an assignee at common law of the benefit of the covenant, or he may acquire the right at common law to enforce it as being annexed to the land that he has acquired. Or, failing that, he may be able to use one of three mechanisms developed by the courts of equity to allow him to enforce the covenant. As we shall see, each of these sets of rules has its own limitations, and sometimes the claimant will need to show that he is within one set of rules; sometimes another.

A ENFORCING THE COVENANT AS AN ORIGINAL BENEFICIARY

Apart from the case where the claimant was himself the direct covenantee, there are two cases in which a person may still enforce a covenant as an original beneficiary of it.

(1) Section 56 of the Law of Property Act 1925

Section 56 of the Law of Property Act 1925 provides that:[86]

A person may take an immediate or other interest in land or other property, or the benefit of any condition, right of entry, covenant or agreement over or respecting land or other property, although he may not be named as a party to the conveyance or other instrument.

---

[81] Below, pp 1095 ff.

[82] Including a transfer, the grant of a lease of more than seven years, and a legal charge: ibid, s 27.

[83] LRA 2002, s 29.   [84] *Hodges v Jones* [1935] Ch 657, 671 (LRA 1925, s 70).

[85] Above, p 734; *Cator v Newton* [1940] 1 KB 415 (positive covenant not made binding by registration); LRA 2002, s 32(3).

[86] On the section generally, see Anson, pp 643–3; *Beswick v Beswick* [1968] AC 58, especially Lord Pearce at 93–4 and Lord Upjohn at 102–7; M & B p 992; (1967) 30 MLR 687 (GH Treitel).

This section reproduces and extends section 5 of the Real Property Act 1845, which abrogated the technical rule of common law that a grantee or covenantee, though named as such in an indenture under seal expressed to be made inter partes, could not take an immediate interest as grantee nor the benefit of a covenant as covenantee unless named as a party to the indenture.

It is important to notice that this section is not concerned with the *passing* of the benefit of a covenant. It is concerned with the *giving* of the benefit of a covenant, at the time when the covenant is created, to a person other than the covenantee. The section in effect makes the person claiming the benefit of the covenant an original covenantee, even though he was not named as a party to the deed in which the covenant was created. Once, however, the benefit of a covenant is given to a person by the section, the benefit can then pass to his successors in title by annexation or assignment.[87]

The application of section 56 is not confined to covenants that touch and concern the land,[88] nor is it confined to restrictive covenants in equity. Its application in the latter context may, however, enable an earlier purchaser of a plot of land on an estate, which is not subject to a scheme of development,[89] to enforce a restrictive covenant against a later purchaser of a plot from the common vendor.

The section has been restrictively interpreted in that the covenant must purport to be made with the claimant as covenantee and not be made merely for his benefit. Thus in *Amsprop Trading Ltd v Harris Distribution Ltd*,[90] where there was a covenant between a tenant and a sub-tenant that 'it shall be lawful for the superior landlords ... to enter and to repair at the cost of the sub-tenant', it was held that the covenant did not purport to be made with them, even though they were named as persons for whose benefit the covenant was made. Neuberger J said:[91]

> The true aim of section 56 seems to be not to allow a third party to sue on a contract merely because it is for his benefit; the contract must purport to be made *with* him. Just as, under the first part of the section a person cannot benefit by a conveyance unless it purports to be made *to* him (as grantee), so he cannot benefit by a covenant that does not purport to be made *with* him (as covenantee).

However, in *Re Ecclesiastical Commissioners for England's Conveyance*:[92]

> in 1887, the purchaser of Blackacre entered into restrictive covenants in favour of the Ecclesiastical Commissioners, the vendors. A separate covenant was also included in the conveyance, with the vendors' 'assigns, owners for the time being of the land adjoining

---

[87] Discussed below.

[88] *Re Ecclesiastical Comrs for England's Conveyance* [1936] Ch 430, 438; but see *Grant v Edmondson* [1931] 1 Ch 1.

[89] Below, pp 756 ff.   [90] [1997] 1 WLR 1025; [1997] All ER Rev 288 (PJ Clarke).

[91] At 1032, adopting M & W (5th edn), p 763; See also W & C, 13th edn, vol 1, p 133: 'the condition was propounded only by Lord Upjohn at 106–7, although he largely had the concurrence of Lord Pearce at 94, and can be regarded as obiter dicta (see at 102). Nevertheless, it rests on and clearly will carry, considerable authority.'

[92] [1936] Ch 430, M & B p 765. See also *Forster v Elvet Colliery Co Ltd* [1908] 1 KB 629; affd as *Dyson v Forster* [1909] AC 98.

or adjacent to' Blackacre to observe and perform the restrictive covenants. Prior to 1887, the Commissioners had sold various freehold plots, situated near Blackacre, to different purchasers and these had passed into other hands by the time of the action.

It was held that the successors in title of the adjacent owners were entitled to enforce the covenants although their respective predecessors in title had not joined in the conveyance of 1887. The separate covenant clearly fell within section 56; it purported to be made with the assigns of the vendor.

The section will not avail a person unless he might have been a party to the deed in question. If he is an ascertainable person at the time of the execution of the deed that purports to grant him an interest in property[93] or to make a covenant available to him, he and his successors in title are in as good a position as if he had been one of the original parties. On the other hand, a deed is inoperative in so far as it purports to extend the advantage of a covenant to an unascertainable person, such as the *future* owner of specified land.[94] It will not, therefore, enable a later purchaser to enforce a restrictive covenant against an earlier purchaser from a common vendor. In order to succeed, he must prove that the benefit of the covenant has passed to him by annexation, express assignment or under a scheme of development.

(2) Contracts (Rights of Third Parties) Act 1999

This Act applies to all contracts (including leases and land contracts) entered into on or after 11 May 2000. It was also possible for parties to contract into it during six months before that date.[95]

Under the Act a person who is not a party to the contract may enforce a term of it *in his own right*, either if the contract expressly provides that he may, or if the term purports to confer a benefit on him (unless on a proper construction of the contract it appears that the parties did not intend the term to be enforceable by the third party).[96] In either case, section 1(3) provides that: 'the third party must be expressly identified in the contract by name, as a member of a class or as answering a particular description but need not be in existence when the contract is entered into'.

---

[93] *Stromdale and Ball Ltd v Burden* [1952] Ch 223; *Drive Yourself Hire Co (London) Ltd v Strutt* [1954] 1 QB 250; *Re Foster* [1938] 3 All ER 357, 365; *Lyus v Prowsa Developments Ltd* [1982] 1 WLR 1044, 1049.

[94] *Kelsey v Dodd* (1881) 52 LJ Ch 34, 39; *White v Bijou Mansions Ltd* [1937] Ch 610, 625; affd [1938] Ch 351, 365, M & B p 767. See also *Pinemain Ltd v Welbeck International Ltd* (1984) 272 EG 1166 (benefit of covenant to sue surety on contract of guarantee not within s 56, since plaintiffs were not identifiable when covenant was made); *Re Distributors and Warehousing Ltd* [1986] 1 EGLR 90; cf *Wiles v Banks* (1983) 50 P & CR 80 (plaintiff identifiable).

[95] The Act was passed on 11 November 1999. On the Act generally, see Emmet, paras 2.131–2.135, 19.003A; Blundell Lectures 25th Anniversary Series 2000: *The Contracts (Rights of Third Parties) Act 1999 and Its Implications for Property Transactions* (A Burrows and C Harpum); (1999) 143 SJ 1082 (S Bright and PJG Williams); [2001] CLJ 353 (N Andrews); (2004) 120 LQR 292 (R Stevens); Anson, pp 624–35. The parties may contract out of it. For subsequent variation or rescission of the contract, see s 2. On clauses to deal with aspects of the Act, see Conv Prec 19-B9.

[96] S 1(1), (2).

In so far as this Act applies to the enforcement of a freehold covenant at common law, we can make three observations.[97] First, such phrases as 'successors in title' bring the covenant within section 1(3), enabling them to sue directly the original covenantor on the covenant. Secondly, being a contractual and not a land law right, there is no need to satisfy the common law requirement of touching and concerning the land and of a legal estate to be benefited. And, thirdly, it will only be rarely necessary to invoke the Act, since in most cases the width of section 78(1) of the Law of Property Act 1925[98] will suffice.

Where the Contracts (Rights of Third Parties) Act 1999 applies,[99] there are two differences from section 56 of the Law of Property Act 1925.[100] First, the contract may be so drafted as to give the third party a direct right to enforce the covenant by an express term under section 1(1)(a), or, failing that, by purporting to confer the 'benefit on him' under section 1(1)(b). The test then is whether, on a proper construction of the covenant, the parties have purported to confer a benefit on the third party and not whether they have purported to make the covenant with him. Secondly, there is no need for the third party to be in existence or identifiable at the time of the making of the contract; it is sufficient if he comes within the scope of section 1(3). Accordingly, a later purchaser may be able to enforce a restrictive covenant against an earlier purchaser, without the need for annexation, assignment or a building scheme.

B ENFORCING THE COVENANT AS A SUCCESSOR AT COMMON LAW

(1) Benefit of a Covenant, Positive or Restrictive, may Run at Common Law

The rule at common law for several centuries has been that the *benefit* of covenants, whether positive or negative, that are made with a covenantee, having an interest in the land to which they relate, passes to his successors in title.[101] Thus in *Sharp v Waterhouse*[102] it was admitted that a covenant by the owner of a mill that 'his heirs executors and administrators' would supply pure water to the adjacent land of X, ran with that land and could be put in suit by X's devisee.

The covenantor is liable to the successors in title of the covenantee merely because of the covenant that he has made, not because of his relationship to any servient tenement.[103] He is liable even though he himself owns no land.[104]

Four things, however, are essential to bring this rule into operation:

---

[97] The Act does not affect the running of the burden of a covenant.
[98] Below, p 748.   [99] (1999) 143 NLJ 1082, 1083 (S Bright and PJG Williams).   [100] Above.
[101] *The Prior's Case* (1368) YB 42 Ed 3, Pl 14, fol 3A; Co Litt 385a; *Shayler v Woolf* [1946] Ch 320 (express assignment by covenantee of the benefit of the covenant); *Smith and Snipes Hall Farm Ltd v River Douglas Catchment Board* [1949] 2 KB 500; 1 Smith's Leading Cases (13th edn), pp 51, 65, 73; M & B, p 774.
[102] (1857) 7 E & B 816.
[103] *Smith and Snipes Hall Farm Ltd v River Douglas Catchment Board*, above.   [104] Ibid.

(i) The covenant must 'touch and concern' the land of the covenantee.[105] In general, the test for this requirement is the same as that for covenants in leases granted before 1996.[106]

(ii) There must be an intention that the benefit should run with the land owned by the covenantee at the date of the covenant.[107]

(iii) The covenantee, at the time of making the covenant, must have the legal estate in the land that is to be benefited.[108]

(iv) A successor who seeks to enforce the covenant must have a legal estate in the land.

At common law, in order to satisfy part (iv) of this test, the successor had to have the same legal estate as the original covenantee, for the covenant was incident to that estate:[109] a covenant taken by an owner in fee simple did not therefore avail his lessee. However, this rule was abrogated for covenants made after 1925 by section 78 of the Law of Property Act 1925, which provides that:

> A covenant relating to any land of the covenantee shall be deemed to be made with the covenantee and his successors in title and the persons deriving title under him or them, and shall have effect as if such successors and other persons were expressed.[110]

This provision will avail anyone holding a legal estate, either as a successor to the same estate as the original covenantee or as the holder of a derivative estate, such as a legal lessee or mortgagee.[111]

(2) Assignment under Section 136 of the Law of Property Act 1925

The benefit of a covenant may also be transferred by assignment as a chose in action under section 136 of the Law of Property Act 1925. To be effective at law, the assignment must be in writing, and express notice in writing given to the covenantor.[112]

---

[105] *Rogers v Hosegood* [1900] 2 Ch 388, 395.   [106] Above, pp 304–7.

[107] *Rogers v Hosegood* [1900] 2 Ch 388, 396; *Shayler v Woolf* [1946] Ch 320; *Smith and Snipes Hall Farm Ltd v River Douglas Catchment Board*, above, at 506. This part of the test may be satisfied by the word-saving effect of LPA 1925, s 78: below.

[108] *Webb v Russell* (1789) 3 Term Rep 393.

[109] *Smith and Snipes Hall Farm Ltd v River Douglas Catchment Board*, above, at 516.

[110] Ibid (where one of the claimants was a yearly tenant); *Williams v Unit Construction Co Ltd* (1955) 19 Conv (NS) 262 (where the claimant was a weekly tenant). This wide interpretation of the section was followed in *Federated Homes Ltd v Mill Lodge Properties Ltd* [1980] 1 WLR 594, M & B p 783, below, p 748, where CA was considering the running of the benefit in equity. For a criticism of the CA decision in *Smith and Snipes Hall Farm Ltd v River Douglas Catchment Board*, see 18 Conv (NS) at 553–6. It would seem that the section was intended to abrogate (ii) and not (iv) and thus to be a 'word-saving' section only. See also Wolstenholme and Cherry, vol 1, pp 162–3; (1972B) 31 CLJ, pp 171–5 (HWR Wade).

[111] Thus excluding a squatter who is not a successor in title, an equitable lessee or mortgagee who has no legal estate, and a licensee who has no estate.

[112] See Anson, pp 663–5. The statute does not say who is to give the express notice.

C ENFORCING THE COVENANT AS
A SUCCESSOR IN EQUITY

We have seen that equity, going further than the common law, allowed the burden of a covenant to run with the land, but only where the covenant is *restrictive*.[113] Equity also developed rules that are in many respects more generous than the common law for the passing of the benefit of a covenant—but, again, only if the covenant is restrictive.[114]

> Suppose that on the sale of Whiteacre to X a restrictive covenant has been taken from him for the protection of Blackacre still retained by the vendor, A; and that A has subsequently sold Blackacre, the dominant land, to B. Can B enforce the covenant against X or against Y who is an assignee of X's land?

The answer is that enforcement is not automatic merely because the dominant land has come into the hands of B. B must go further. He must prove, not only that he has acquired the land, but also that he has acquired the benefit of the covenant itself.[115]

We have already seen that the benefit of a covenant runs at common law subject to certain conditions.[116] If B can satisfy these, there is no need for him to rely on the rules evolved by equity for the running of the benefit. There are however circumstances in which the common law rules are inapplicable, and it is then that B must prove that he has satisfied the conditions that equity imposes.

The situations in which B must do this are:

(a) where B is, or A the original covenantee was, a mere equitable owner of Blackacre;[117]

(b) where B does not have the same legal estate in Blackacre as A had (this would only apply to covenants made before 1926[118]);

(c) where Whiteacre has been conveyed to Y and enforcement against Y depends upon the equitable doctrine of *Tulk v Moxhay*;[119]

(d) where B relies upon an express assignment of the benefit of the covenant from A, and the assignment does not comply with section 136 of the Law of Property Act 1925;[120]

---

[113] Above, p 734.

[114] The requirement that the covenant be restrictive under the rules of equity for the passing of the benefit is a limitation. At common law the benefit of a positive covenant can be annexed to the land: *Smith and Snipes Hall Farm Ltd v River Douglas Catchment Board* [1949] 2 KB 500, M & B p 774, above, p 744.

[115] [1938] CLJ 339 (SJ Bailey); [1971] 82 LQR 539 (DJ Hayton); (1982) 2 LS 53 (DJ Hurst); (1982) 98 LQR 279 (S Gardner).

[116] Above, p 744.

[117] *Fairclough v Marshall* (1878) 4 Ex D 37; *Rogers v Hosegood* [1900] 2 Ch 388, M & B p 780 (mortgagor before 1926).

[118] LPA 1925, s 78(1); above, p 745.

[119] *Renals v Cowlishaw* (1878) 9 Ch D 125, M & B p 782; *Re Union of London and Smith's Bank Ltd's Conveyance, Miles v Easter* [1933] Ch 611, 630; M & B p 798; *Marten v Flight Refuelling Ltd* [1962] Ch 115, M & B p 803.

[120] Above, pp 745 ff.

(e) where part only of Whiteacre has been conveyed to B, for 'at law, the benefit could not be assigned in pieces. It would have to be assigned as a whole or not at all';[121]

(f) where B relies upon his land being part of a scheme of development.[122]

In these situations there are only three ways[123] in which B can show that he has acquired the benefit of the covenant itself, namely by proving:

(1) that the benefit of the covenant has been effectively annexed to the dominant land, and that he had acquired the whole of that land, or the part of it to which the covenant was annexed; or,

(2) that the benefit of the covenant was separately and expressly assigned to him at the time of the sale; or,

(3) that both the dominant and servient lands are subject to a scheme of development.

Let us take these methods separately.

(1) Annexation of Covenant to Dominant Land

(a) Intention to annex

Whether or not the benefit of a restrictive covenant runs with the dominant land by virtue of its express annexation to that land depends on the intention of the parties to be inferred from the language that they used in the deed creating the covenant. This intention to annex is commonly inferred when the covenant is made: '"with so and so, owners or owner for the time being of whatever the land may be". Another method is to state by means of an appropriate declaration that the covenant is taken "for the benefit of" whatever the lands may be.'[124]

Thus in *Rogers v Hosegood*[125] the following covenant was held to be annexed to the land:

with intent that the covenants might so far as possible bind the premises thereby conveyed and every part thereof and might enure to the benefit of the vendors…their heirs and assigns and others claiming under them to all or any of their lands adjoining or near to the said premises.

---

[121] *Re Union of London and Smith's Bank Ltd's Conveyance*, above, at 630; *Federated Homes Ltd v Mill Lodge Properties Ltd* [1980] 1 WLR 594, M & B p 796.

[122] Below, pp 756 ff.   [123] *Re Pinewood Estate, Farnborough* [1958] Ch 280, M & B p 778.

[124] *Drake v Gray* [1936] Ch 451, 456 (Greene LJ).

[125] [1900] 2 Ch 388, M & B p 780. Cf *Renals v Cowlishaw* (1878) 9 Ch D 125, M & B p 782 (covenant with the vendors 'their heirs, executors, administrators and assigns' held insufficient to annex, since no dominant land was specified). See also *J Sainsbury plc v Enfield London Borough Council* [1989] 1 WLR 590, M & B p 782; *Re MCA East Ltd* [2002] EWHC 1684 (Ch), [2003] 1 P & CR 9 (no intention to annex).

(b) Dominant land must be ascertainable

Furthermore, the exact land to which the parties intend to annex the benefit of the covenant must be ascertainable. Whether this is so depends primarily upon the construction of the deed of conveyance. A competent draftsman will describe the land in precise terms, as for instance by declaring that the covenant is taken for the benefit of 'the property known as Blackacre'; or for the 'land marked red on the plan'. If the description is more vague, such as 'the land adjoining' the servient land, extrinsic evidence is admissible to identify the particular land that the parties had in mind.[126]

In summary, the land must be clearly,[127] or easily,[128] identified in the conveyance creating the covenant.[129] As we shall see, this is a stricter rule of identification than that which applies in the case of express assignment.[130]

(c) Law of Property Act 1925, section 78

However, the problem of determining whether the language of a conveyance is sufficient to show an intention to annex the covenant has disappeared in respect of a covenant entered into after 1925 since the decision of the Court of Appeal in *Federated Homes Ltd v Mill Lodge Properties Ltd*.[131] In that case:

A owned land for development which was subject to restrictions on the overall number of houses to be built on it. A sold three parts of the land (blue, red and green) to separate purchasers. The blue land was sold to M who covenanted with A that 'in carrying out the development the Purchaser shall not build at a greater density than a total of 300 dwellings so as not to reduce the number of units which the Vendor might eventually erect on the retained land.' The conveyance contained a reference to the retained lands as 'any adjoining or adjacent property retained' by A. It will be seen that the terms of the covenant were not such as, from its express language, to annex the benefit of it to A's land under the rule in *Rogers v Hosegood*.

A then sold the red and green lands to other purchasers, and eventually F became owner of both of them. In the case of the green land, there was a complete chain of assignments of

---

[126] See Preston and Newsom, para 2.19.
[127] *Newton Abbot Co-operative Society Ltd v Williamson and Treadgold Ltd* [1952] Ch 286, 289 (Upjohn J).
[128] *Marquess of Zetland v Driver* [1939] Ch 1, 8 (Farwell J); followed in *Crest Nicholson Residential (South) Ltd v McAllister* [2004] EWCA Civ 410, [2004] 1 WLR 2409 at [30]-[33] (Chadwick LJ), noting that this has not been changed by the decision in *Federated Homes Ltd v Mill Lodge Properties Ltd*, above, in which *Marquess of Zetland v Driver* was not cited.
[129] The relevant date for identifying the benefited land is that of transfer not registration: *Mellon v Sinclair* [1997] CLY 4258.
[130] Below, p 754. Cf, however, *Stocks v Whitgift Homes Ltd* [2001] EWCA Civ 1732, [2001] 48 EGCS 130 (language sufficient to identify land for purposes of annexation under LPA 1925, s 78, but not sufficient to define area for scheme of development, below, p 758).
[131] [1980] 1 WLR 594, M & B p 783; *Robins v Berkeley Homes (Kent) Ltd* [1996] EGCS 75; *Stocks v Whitgift Homes Ltd*, above; *Crest Nicholson Residential (South) Ltd v McAllister*, above; [2004] Conv 507 (J Howell); [2005] Conv 2.

the benefit of the covenant through the various purchasers to A, but not in the case of the red land.

F sought an injunction to restrain M from breaking the restrictive covenant.

Granting the injunction, the Court of Appeal held that F was entitled to the benefit of the covenant in respect of the green land, by reason of the chain of assignments.[132] This was sufficient to entitle F to relief, but the Court then went on to consider whether F also had the benefit of the covenant in his capacity as owner of the red land. It was held that F had that benefit under section 78(1) of the Law of Property Act 1925.[133] The actual wording of the covenant was 'sufficient to intimate that the covenant was one relating to the land of the covenantee',[134] and, therefore, the benefit was annexed to the land without the need to use appropriate language from which an intention to annex might be inferred. Brightman LJ said:[135]

> If the condition precedent of section 78 is satisfied—that is to say, there exists a covenant which touches and concerns the land of the covenantee—that covenant runs with the land for the benefit of his successors in title, persons deriving title under him or them and other owners and occupiers.

This decision simplifies the rules as to the passing of the benefit of a restrictive covenant, but it has been criticised on the ground that a narrow construction of the section is preferable, in other words that it is merely a statutory shorthand for reducing the length of legal documents.[136] On this view the section would only operate when annexation had already been established according to the general rule. There are strong arguments in favour of the narrow view. The Law of Property Act 1925 is a consolidation statute and 'if the words are capable of more than one construction then the Court will give effect to the construction that does not change the law';[137] and the predecessor to section 78, section 58 of the Conveyancing Act 1881, did not have the effect of annexing the benefit of a restrictive covenant to the covenantee's

---

[132] Below, p 753.

[133] Above, p 745. The Court of Appeal found support for this wide construction in *Smith and Snipes Hall Farm Ltd v River Douglas Catchment Board* [1949] 2 KB 500, M & B p 774; above, p 744; *Williams v Unit Construction Co Ltd* (1955) 19 Conv (NS) 262, M & B p 776. John Mills QC had decided in favour of F at first instance, but under LPA 1925, s 62; above, p 655; below, p 750, n 143.

[134] See *Bridges v Harrow LBC* (1981) 260 EG 284; [1982] Conv 313 (F Webb). [135] At 605.

[136] [1980] JPL 371; [1981] 97 LQR 32; [1981] JPL 295; (1982) 98 LQR 202 (GH Newsom); (1980) 43 MLR 445 (DJ Hayton); 130 NLJ 531 (T Bailey); [1985] Conv 177 (PN Todd). And there is no suggestion of a wide construction in Sir Benjamin Cherry's book (*Wolstenholme and Cherry's Conveyancing Statutes* (11th edn, 1925)). See also the 30th Anniversary Blundell Lecture (27 June 2005), where Neuberger LJ, whilst noting that the decision in *Crest Nicholson Residential (South) Ltd v McAllister* [2004] EWCA Civ 410, [2004] 1 WLR 2409, confirms that *Federated Homes* is authority for the wider construction, which renders the law much simpler and clearer, said that 'there do seem to be pretty formidable arguments ... for doubting the correctness of the decision in *Federated Homes*', especially the failure to repeat in s 78 the annexation formulae in the two preceding sections, ss 76 and 77: [1982] JPL 295; (1982) 98 LQR 202 (GH Newsom and EHB).

[137] *Beswick v Beswick* [1968] AC 58, 87 (Lord Guest), 105 (Lord Upjohn). In that case the rule was used to restrict the scope of LPA 1925, s 56; above, p 741.

land.[138] Further, if a far-reaching and substantial alteration to the law had been intended by Parliament, one would expect it to be expressed in unambiguous terms,[139] and a formula was ready to hand to do this; the repetition of the wording in the two immediately preceding sections would have given the effect of the wider construction without any ambiguity.[140] The Court of Appeal's view is also at variance with the narrow interpretation by the House of Lords of the similar but not identical section 79 in respect of the running of the burden of a covenant.[141]

The decision in *Federated Homes Ltd v Mill Lodge Properties Ltd* was further considered in *Roake v Chadha*,[142] where a covenant contained the words 'so as to bind ... the land hereby transferred into whosoever hands the same may come ... but so that this covenant shall not enure for the benefit of any owner or subsequent purchaser of any part of the estate unless the benefit of this covenant shall be expressly assigned'. It was held that the annexation of the benefit under section 78 was not automatic, notwithstanding that section 78, unlike its counterpart, section 79, does not contain the words 'unless a contrary intention is expressed'. Even where a covenant is deemed to be made with successors in title as section 78 requires, 'one still has to construe the covenant as a whole to see whether the benefit of the covenant is annexed'.[143] This was approved by the Court of Appeal in *Crest Nicholson Residential (South) Ltd v McAllister*[144] where Chadwick LJ said that section 78 did not include the words 'unless a contrary intention is expressed' because 'it did not need to'.[145] The effect of the section

---

[138] *Forster v Elvet Colliery Co Ltd* [1908] 1 KB 629, 635 (Cozens-Hardy MR); Neuberger LJ, 30th Anniversary Blundell Lecture, above; *J Sainsbury plc v Enfield LBC* [1989] 1 WLR 590, M & B p 782 (covenant made in 1894).

[139] *Beswick v Beswick*, above at 93 (Lord Pearce).

[140] LPA 1925, ss 76(6) (covenants for title), 77(5) (implied covenants in conveyances subject to rents). The two sub-sections have identical wording: 'The benefit of a covenant implied as aforesaid shall be annexed to, and shall go with, the estate of interest of the implied covenantee, and shall be capable of being enforced by every person in whom that estate or interest is, for the whole or any part thereof, from time to time vested.' See also ss 141(1), 142(1); above, pp 309, 311. Similar language is also used in Rentcharges Act 1977, s 11(3), LT(C)A 1995, s 3(1) and LP(MP)A 1994, s 7.

[141] *Rhone v Stephens* [1994] 2 AC 310, M & B p 746; above, p 728.

[142] [1984] 1 WLR 40, M & B p 787; [1983] All ER Rev 331 (PJ Clarke); [1984] Conv 68 (PN Todd).

[143] Judge Paul Baker QC at 46. He also held that the benefit of the covenant did not pass under LPA 1925, s 62; above, p 655. It was not a right 'appertaining or reputed to appertain' to land. He also thought that the rights in s 62 might be confined to legal rights, thereby excluding the benefit of a restrictive covenant, which is an equitable right. In *Kumar v Dunning* [1989] QB 193 Browne-Wilkinson V-C said at 198: 'A right under covenant cannot appertain to the land unless the benefit is in some way annexed to the land. If the benefit of a covenant passes under s 62 even if not annexed to the land, the whole modern law of restrictive covenants would have been established on an erroneous basis.' See also *Mahon v Sims* [2005] 3 EGLR 67 (requirement that covenantor obtain consent of 'the Transferor' before carrying out work; on construction, this was not personal to the original transferor, but referred to successor in title for the time being); cf *City Inn (Jersey) Ltd v Ten Trinity Square Ltd* [2008] EWCA Civ 156, [2008] 1 P & CR DG22 (on construction, 'Transferor' was personal to original transferor).

[144] [2004] EWCA Civ 410, [2004] 1 WLR 2409 at [37]-[44]; [2004] All ER Rev 244 (PJ Clarke); followed by *Sugarman v Porter* [2006] EWHC 331 (Ch), [2006] 2 P & CR 14 (wording of covenant, which made clear that benefit of covenant lasted only as long as covenantee retained land unsold, displaced statutory annexation of s 78 LPA 1925).

[145] Ibid, at [43].

is to annex the benefit of the covenant to the land in the hands of the covenantee's 'successors in title'—which are defined[146] as 'the owners and occupiers for the time being of the land of the covenantee intended to be benefited'.

> In a case where the parties to the instrument make clear their intention that land retained by the covenantee at the time of the conveyance effected by the transfer is to have the benefit of the covenant only for so long as it continues to be in the ownership of the original covenantee, and not after it has been sold on by the original covenantee—unless the benefit of the covenant is expressly assigned to the new owner—*the land of the covenantee intended to be benefited* is identified by the instrument as (i) so much of the retained land as from time to time has not been sold off by the original covenantee and (ii) so much of the retained land as has been sold off with the benefit of an express assignment, but as not including (iii) so much of the land as has been sold off without the benefit of an express assignment.[147]

Finally, we should notice the proviso to section 78(1):

> For the purposes of this subsection in connexion with covenants restrictive of the user of land 'successors in title' shall be deemed to include the owners and occupiers for the time being of the land of the covenantee intended to be benefited.

The effect is that in the case of restrictive covenants any owner or occupier for the time being can enforce the annexed covenant even though he may be a squatter or licensee.[148]

(d) Annexation to whole of covenantee's land

Even if the language of the covenant indicates an intention to annex the benefit of the covenant to the whole of the land of the covenantee, such annexation will not be effected unless substantially the whole of the land is capable of benefiting. Thus in *Re Ballard's Conveyance*[149] the benefit of a covenant that imposed a restriction on 18 acres was annexed by the conveyance to 'the Childwickbury Estate'. The area of this estate was about 1,700 acres, by far the largest part of which could not possibly be directly affected by a breach of the covenant.

Although it would seem that an injury to a part of any unity is inevitably an injury to the whole, Clauson J held that the covenant was not enforceable by assignees of the whole of the dominant land. Moreover, he refused to sever the covenant and thus to regard it as annexed to the part of the land that was in fact touched and concerned. The decision seems to amount to this: if a covenantee over-estimates to a moderate degree the area of the dominant land capable of deriving advantage from a restrictive covenant, his attempt to preserve the amenities of the neighbourhood and to maintain the selling value of what he retains will fail.[150] Why the doctrine of severance should be excluded from this type of contract is difficult to appreciate.[151]

---

146 LPA 1925, s 78(1), second paragraph.

147 *Crest Nicholson Residential (South) Ltd v Mc Allister* [2004] EWCA Civ 410, [2004] 1 WLR 2409 at [42] (Chadwick LJ).

148 But neither can enforce a positive covenant; above, p 745, n 111.

149 [1937] Ch 473.   150 (1941) 57 LQR pp 210–11 (GRY Radcliffe).

151 See Elphinstone, *Covenants Affecting Land*, p 60, n 10.

On the other hand, a covenant that is annexed to the whole *or any part or parts of* the dominant land is enforceable by a successor in title to any part of that land that is in fact benefited by the covenant. In *Marquess of Zetland v Driver*,[152] for instance:

> The covenant was expressed to be for the benefit and protection of 'such part or parts of the [dominant land] (a) as shall for the time being remain unsold or (b) as shall be sold by the vendor or his successors in title with the express benefit of this covenant.' Certain parts of the unsold land were contiguous to the land of the covenantor, but other parts were more than a mile distant. The covenant, therefore, did not benefit the whole of the dominant land.

It was held that the person who succeeded to the dominant land could enforce the covenant against a purchaser of the servient land. The Court of Appeal, without expressing approbation of *Re Ballard's Conveyance*, distinguished it on the ground that: 'in that case the covenant was expressed to run with the whole estate, whereas in the present case ... the covenant is expressed to be for the benefit of the whole or any part or parts of the unsold settled property'.[153]

Extrinsic evidence is admissible to show whether a covenant is capable of operating to the advantage of the dominant land;[154] and, as we have seen, the onus is on the defendant to show that it does not do so, either originally, or at the date of the action.[155]

(e) Annexation to part of covenantee's land

The benefit of a restrictive covenant, once it has been annexed to the dominant land, runs automatically with that land and is enforceable by the successors in title of the covenantee, even though they do not learn of its existence until after execution of the conveyance.[156] If a successor in title acquires the whole of the land, the benefit passes to him without question; but if he acquires only part he must show that the benefit was annexed to that particular part alone or to each portion of the whole.

> For instance, A, the owner of a large property, sells part of it to Y and takes a covenant that no public house shall be opened on it. This covenant is annexed to A's land. Later A sells part of the dominant land to B. If B seeks to enforce the covenant by virtue of its annexation to A's land, he must prove that its benefit was annexed to each and every part of those lands or to the very part bought by him.

Whether or not there has been effective annexation to each and every part of the land is once again a question of construction of the language of the covenant. Thus in

---

[152] [1939] Ch 1.

[153] *Marquess of Zetland v Driver* [1939] Ch 1, 10.

[154] *Marten v Flight Refuelling Ltd* [1962] Ch 115, M & B, p 803; *Earl of Leicester v Wells-next-the-Sea UDC* [1973] Ch 110 (expert evidence admitted to show that a covenant restricting 19 acres afforded 'great benefit and much needed protection to the Holkham Estate as a whole' ie to 32,000 acres). In *Re Ballard's Conveyance* [1937] Ch 473 no evidence was offered to show benefit to the dominant land as a whole.

[155] *Wrotham Park Estate Co v Parkside Homes Ltd* [1974] 1 WLR 798; above, p 737; *Cryer v Scott Bros (Sunbury) Ltd* (1986) 55 P & CR 183; [1988] Conv 172 (JE Adams).

[156] *Rogers v Hosegood* [1900] 2 Ch 388, M & B p 780.

Re Selwyn's Conveyance[157] it was held that a covenant 'to enure for the protection of the adjoining or neighbouring land part of, or lately part of, the Selwyn Estate' was annexed to each part of the dominant land.

Furthermore, even if the covenant has been annexed only to the whole of the dominant land, a purchaser of part of it will be able to enforce the covenant if the benefit of the covenant has been expressly assigned to him.[158]

Finally, we must notice that this problem of construction will disappear if the approach of the Court of Appeal in *Federated Homes Ltd v Mill Lodge Properties Ltd*[159] is subsequently adopted. In that case the court found it difficult to understand how a covenant, which is annexed to the land as a whole, is not also annexed to the individual parts of that land. It favoured a rule that the benefit of such a covenant annexed to the whole is prima facie annexed to every part thereof, unless a contrary intention clearly appears.

(2) Express Assignment of Covenant

Failure to establish the annexation described above is not necessarily fatal to an assignee of the covenantee's land, for he will succeed in an action for an infringement of the restriction if he shows that he is not only an assignee of the land, but also the express assignee of the *covenant* itself.[160]

Such an express assignment will be necessary in fewer instances in the future, as a result of the decision in *Federated Homes Ltd v Mill Lodge Properties Ltd*,[161] in which, as we have seen, annexation was held to be effected under section 78 of the Law of Property Act 1925 without the need for appropriate language in the deed creating the covenant. Instances may, however, still arise, as for example where there is express provision to the effect that express assignment of the covenant shall be required,[162] or where there is no identification in the conveyance of the land to be benefited.[163]

---

[157] [1967] Ch 674. Cf *Russell v Archdale* [1964] Ch 38, M & B p 795; *Re Jeff's Transfer (No 2)* [1966] 1 WLR 841; *Stilwell v Blackman* [1968] Ch 508. See *Griffiths v Band* (1974) 29 P & CR 243 ('this somewhat muddy corner of legal history': Goulding J at 246). Law Com CP No 186, *Easements, Covenants and Profits à Prendre* (2008), para 10.44, proposes that on a sub-division of the benefited land the benefit of a Land Obligation (their proposed replacement for covenants in registered land: below, p 774) should run with each and every part of the benefited land unless it does not 'relate to', or benefit, that part of the land, or the sub-division increases the scope of obligations, or a contrary intention is expressed.

[158] *Russell v Archdale*, above (against the original covenantor who was still owner of the servient land); *Stilwell v Blackman*, above (against a successor in title of the original covenantor).

[159] [1980] 1 WLR 594, 606, 607, M & B p 796. This would involve reconsideration of the decisions in n 157, above.

[160] *Reid v Bickerstaff* [1909] 2 Ch 305, 320; *Re Union of London and Smith's Bank Ltd's Conveyance, Miles v Easter* [1933] Ch 611.

[161] [1980] 1 WLR 594, M & B p 783; above, p 748.

[162] *Marquess of Zetland v Driver* [1937] Ch 651; *Roake v Chadha* [1984] 1 WLR 40, M & B p 787; above, p 750.

[163] *Newton Abbot Co-operative Society Ltd v Williamson and Treadgold Ltd* [1952] Ch 286, below. But see *Federated Homes Ltd v Mill Lodge Properties Ltd* [1980] 1 WLR 594, 604 (Brightman LJ).

As we have already seen, the benefit of a covenant may be transferred at law by assignment as a chose in action under section 136 of the Law of Property Act 1925.[164] 'Where the defendant is liable at law (as the original covenantor or his personal representative) there is no difficulty peculiar to the case of covenants affecting land: such an action is governed by the ordinary rules as to the assignment of a chose in action. But where the defendant is sued as an assign of the land burdened by the covenant, the plaintiff can only establish the defendant's liability in equity under the rule in *Tulk v Moxhay*.'[165]

The equitable rules under which an express assignment is permissible were crystallised by Romer LJ in *Re Union of London and Smith's Bank Ltd's Conveyance, Miles v Easter*:[166]

> (i) The covenant must have been taken for the benefit of the land of the covenantee and (ii) that land must be indicated with reasonable certainty. This indication need not appear in the conveyance creating the covenant. It is sufficient if in the light of the attendant circumstances the identity of the dominant land is in some other way ascertainable with reasonable certainty. (iii) It must also be retained in whole or part by the plaintiff and (iv) be capable of benefiting from the covenant. (v) The assignment of the covenant and the conveyance of the land to which it relates must be contemporaneous.

Whether the first two requirements were satisfied was neatly raised in *Newton Abbot Co-operative Society Ltd v Williamson and Treadgold Ltd*[167] on the following facts:

> The owner of Devonia, in which she carried on the business of an ironmonger, sold a shop on the opposite side of the street to a purchaser who traded there as a grocer. The purchaser covenanted not to trade as an ironmonger at the premises. The conveyance did not define any dominant land for the benefit of which the covenant was taken, but simply described the vendor as 'of Devonia'.

Upjohn J held in the first place that the covenant was not a mere covenant in gross. Its objects were not only to protect the vendor personally against competition, but also to enhance the selling value of Devonia if sold to someone intending to trade there as an ironmonger. The learned judge further held that the identity of the dominant land was sufficiently clear. The only reasonable inference to draw from the surrounding circumstances, especially from the propinquity of the two shops, was that the covenant was taken for the benefit not only of the vendor's business, but also of the land that she retained.

Nevertheless, in order to appreciate the limits within which assignment is permissible it is essential to stress that the reason why equity allows a restrictive covenant to be enforced against third parties is that the land of the covenantee may be protected, and

---

[164] Above, p 745.
[165] Preston and Newsom, *Restrictive Covenants* (4th edn, 1967), p 30.
[166] [1933] Ch 611, 631–2, M & B p 798.
[167] [1952] Ch 286, M & B p 799, approved by Wilberforce J in *Marten v Flight Refuelling Ltd* [1962] Ch 115, 133. But see (1952) 68 LQR 353 (Sir Lancelot Elphinstone).

in particular, that its sale value shall not be diminished.[168] Such a covenant is not an independent entity having its own intrinsic value. It has no *raison d'être* apart from the land for whose protection it was taken. Therefore, as we have already seen, even the covenantee himself cannot enforce the covenant against an assignee of the covenantor after he has disposed of the whole of his dominant land, for he no longer requires protection.[169] This theory, that the maintenance of the value of the covenantee's land is the sole justification for allowing restrictive covenants to run in favour of his successors in title, leads to the result that the express assignment of the benefit of a covenant is ineffective unless it is contemporaneous with the assignment of the land affected. The covenant has spent its force if the covenantee has not required its aid in disposing of the dominant land.[170]

> if he has been able to sell any particular part of his property without assigning to the purchaser the benefit of the covenant, there seems no reason why he should at a later date and as an independent transaction be at liberty to confer upon the purchaser such benefit. To hold that he could do so would be to treat the covenant as having been obtained, not only for the purpose of enabling the covenantee to dispose of his land to the best advantage, but also for the purpose of enabling him to dispose of the benefit of the covenant to the best advantage.[171]

Subject to these limitations, however, an express assignment of a covenant to a purchaser of the whole or part of the dominant land made at the time of the purchase is effective.

The benefit of a restrictive covenant is also capable of assignment by operation of law. Thus on the death of the covenantee it passes to his executors and is held by them as bare trustees for the devisee of the dominant land and becomes assignable to him.[172]

A final question is whether the express assignment of the benefit of a restrictive covenant annexes it to the dominant land, so that it will thereafter run automatically with that land without the necessity for any further express assignment. There are judicial dicta that support the view that an express assignment has this effect of annexation,[173] but recent cases are against it. The decision in *Re Pinewood Estate*,

---

[168] *Chambers v Randall* [1923] 1 Ch 149; *Re Union of London and Smith's Bank Ltd's Conveyance, Miles v Easter* [1933] Ch 611, 632.

[169] Above, p 735.

[170] *Chambers v Randall*, above; *Re Union of London and Smith's Bank Ltd's Conveyance, Miles v Easter* [1933] Ch 611; *Re Rutherford's Conveyance* [1938] Ch 396.

[171] *Re Union of London and Smith's Bank Ltd's Conveyance, Miles v Easter*, above, at 632 (Romer LJ).

[172] *Newton Abbot Co-operative Society Ltd v Williamson and Treadgold Ltd* [1952] Ch 286, M & B p 799; *Earl of Leicester v Wells-next-the-Sea UDC* [1973] Ch 110 (special executors of settled land held to be bare trustees of benefit of restrictive covenant for beneficiary under SLA 1925, s 7(1)).

[173] *Renals v Cowlishaw* (1878) 9 Ch D 125, 130–1; *Rogers v Hosegood* [1900] 2 Ch 388, 408; *Reid v Bickerstaff* [1909] 2 Ch 305, 320.

Farnborough[174] assumes without argument that a chain of assignments is necessary, and the decision in *Stilwell v Blackman*[175] is inconsistent with the dicta.

This problem disappears if the successor in title of the covenantee is able to enforce the restrictive covenant under the Contracts (Rights of Third Parties) Act 1999.[176] He then bypasses the land law requirements of annexation and assignment and enforces the covenant directly in his own right.

(3) Scheme of Development (or Building Scheme)[177]

The third case in which a restrictive covenant is enforceable by and against persons other than the original covenanting parties is when lands are held by their respective owners under a scheme of development.

(a) Nature of scheme

A scheme of development comes into existence where land is laid out in plots and sold to different purchasers or leased to different lessees, each of whom enters into a restrictive covenant with the common vendor or lessor agreeing that his particular plot shall not be used for certain purposes. In such a case these restrictive covenants are taken because the whole estate is being developed on a definite plan, and it is vital, if the value of each plot is not to be depreciated, that the purchasers or lessees should be prevented from dealing with their land so as to lower the tone of the neighbourhood. When the existence of a scheme of development has been established, the rule is that each purchaser and his assignees can sue or be sued by every other purchaser and his assignees for a breach of the restrictive covenants.[178] In such an action for breach it is immaterial whether the defendant acquired his title before or after the date on which the claimant purchased his plot. In other words, the restrictive covenants constitute a special local law for the area over which the scheme extends, and not only the plot-owners, but even the vendor himself, become subject to that law,[179] provided that the

---

[174] [1958] Ch 280. See the criticism in (1957) CLJ 146 (HWR Wade). See also *Federated Homes Ltd v Mill Lodge Properties Ltd* [1980] 1 WLR 594, 603, where John Mills QC said at first instance: 'I am not satisfied or prepared to hold that there is any such thing as 'delayed annexation by assignment' to which the covenantor is not party or privy.'

[175] [1968] Ch 508; (1968) 84 LQR at 29–32 (PV Baker).   [176] Above, p 743; below, p 986, n 238.

[177] 'Scheme of development is the genus: building scheme a species': *Brunner v Greenslade* [1971] Ch 993, 999 (Megarry J). For successful schemes, see *Baxter v Four Oaks Properties Ltd* [1965] Ch 816, M & B p 811; *Re Dolphin's Conveyance* [1970] Ch 654, M & B p 811; *Eagling v Gardner* [1970] 2 All ER 838; *Brunner v Greenslade*, above; *Texaco Antilles Ltd v Kernochan* [1973] AC 609; *Re 6, 8, 10 and 12 Elm Avenue, New Milton* [1984] 1 WLR 1398; *Clarke v Murphy* [2009] 22 EGCS 118. Cf *Lund v Taylor* (1975) 31 P & CR 167, M & B p 814, esp Stamp LJ at 176; *Kingsbury v L W Anderson Ltd* (1979) 40 P & CR 136; *Allen v Veranne Builders Ltd* [1988] NPC 11; *Emile Elias & Co Ltd v Pine Groves Ltd* [1993] 1 WLR 305. This is in marked contrast to the usual fate of schemes during the previous four decades: Preston and Newsom, paras 2–74 to 2–75.

[178] *Spicer v Martin* (1888) 14 App Cas 12; *Renals v Cowlishaw* (1878) 9 Ch D 125; affd (1879) 11 Ch D 866; *Hudson v Cripps* [1896] 1 Ch 265 (lease).

[179] *Reid v Bickerstaff* [1909] 2 Ch 305, 319; *Brunner v Greenslade*, above, at 1004. The scheme may expressly entitle the vendor to dispose of plots free from its restrictions: *Mayner v Payne* [1914] 2 Ch 555.

area[180] and the obligations to be imposed therein are defined. 'They all have a common interest in maintaining the restriction. This community of interest necessarily requires and imports reciprocity of obligation.'[181] There thus arises what Simonds J has called: 'an equity which is created by circumstances and is independent of contractual obligation'.[182]

(b) Essentials of scheme

Pre-eminent among the essentials for the creation of a scheme of development is proof of a common intention that the restrictive covenants have been taken for the mutual benefit of the respective purchasers.[183] This community of interest and intention may be evidenced by the existence of a deed of mutual covenant to which all the several purchasers are parties,[184] or it may be inferred on the construction of the conveyances of the several parts of the estate.[185] If, however, the necessary intention cannot be derived solely from the formal documents, but extrinsic evidence is also required, a scheme of development may nevertheless come into existence. In these circumstances the conditions formulated by Parker J in *Elliston v Reacher*[186] must exist before the benefit and the burden of the restrictive covenants can pass to the various purchasers and their assignees:

(a) Both the claimant and the defendant to the action for breach of the restrictive covenant must have derived their titles to the land from a common vendor.

(b) Before the sale of the plots to the claimant and the defendant, the common vendor must have laid out his estate for sale in lots[187] subject to restrictions which it was intended to impose on all the lots, and that were consistent only with some general scheme of development.[188]

(c) The restrictions were intended by the common vendor to be and were for the benefit of all the lots sold.[189] This intention is gathered from all the circumstances

---

[180] *Lund v Taylor*, above, where there was no scheme because no area was defined. See also *Harlow v Hartog* (1977) 245 EG 140 (no scheme, because no estate plan).

[181] *Spicer v Martin* (1888) 14 App Cas 12, 25 (Lord Macnaghten).

[182] *Lawrence v South County Freeholds Ltd* [1939] Ch 656, 682.

[183] *Nottingham Patent Brick and Tile Co v Butler* (1885) 15 QBD 261, 268 Wills J); approved in *White v Bijou Mansions Ltd* [1938] Ch 351, 361. See Preston and Newsom, paras 2–53 ff.

[184] *Baxter v Four Oaks Properties Ltd* [1965] Ch 816 (where the common vendor had not laid out the estate in lots before the sale); *Price v Bouch* (1986) 53 P & CR 257 (co-operative scheme on part of 53 Victorian tradesmen in Northumberland).

[185] *Re Dolphin's Conveyance* [1970] Ch 654 (where there was no common vendor and no lotted estate). See (1970) 114 SJ 798 (GH Newsom): (1970) 86 LQR 445 (PV Baker). For the modification of these covenants under LPA 1925, s 84, see *Re Farmiloe's Application* (1983) 48 P & CR 317; below, p 764.

[186] [1908] 2 Ch 374, 384, M & B p 809; for a case in which all these conditions are considered, see *Eagling v Gardner* [1970] 2 All ER 838. For a succinct formulation, see *Briggs v McCusker* [1996] 2 EGLR 197, 199 (Judge Rich QC).

[187] *Lawrence v South County Freeholds Ltd* [1939] Ch 656, 674.

[188] *Willé v St John* [1910] 1 Ch 84; affd [1910] 1 Ch 325.

[189] 'It is not necessary that the covenants entered into should benefit only the defined area:...The mere fact that the covenant is not expressly stated to be for the benefit of the plot holders is in no sense decisive...I

of the case, but if the restrictions are obviously calculated to enhance the value of each lot,[190] the intention is readily inferred.

(d) The original purchasers must have bought their lots on the understanding that the restrictions were to enure for the benefit of the other lots.[191]

(e) The geographical area to which the scheme extends must be ascertained with reasonably clear definitiveness.[192]

To a certain extent the first three conditions overlap, but the basic requirement is the existence of common regulations, obviously intended to govern the area that is to be developed. As Greene MR explained:

> The material thing I think is that every purchaser ... must know when he buys what are the regulations to which he is subjecting himself, and what are the regulations to which other purchasers on the estate will be called upon to subject themselves. Unless you know that, it is quite impossible in my judgment to draw the necessary inference, whether you refer to it as an agreement or as a community of interest importing reciprocity of obligation.[193]

In order to create a valid scheme, the purchasers of all the land within the area of the scheme must also know what that area is.[194]

The conditions in *Elliston v Reacher* are 'a valuable, and perhaps complete guide to what has to be sought in the extrinsic evidence when such evidence is the foundation of the case'.[195] This may include parol evidence from the common vendor[196] or his predecessor in title[197] and evidence of what was said and done before the contracts that preceded the conveyances.

The common vendor may reserve the power to waive or vary the restrictive covenants, especially in the case of land of which he has not yet disposed.[198] Furthermore the restrictions that he imposes may vary in detail.[199] But the variation was held to preclude

---

do not think that it is inconsistent with the existence of a scheme of development that the vendor retains his right to exempt part of the [Wildernesse] Estate from stipulations': *Allen v Veranne Builders Ltd* [1988] NPC 11 (Sir Nicolas Browne-Wilkinson V-C). See also *Jamaica Mutual Life Assurance Society v Hillsborough Ltd* [1989] 1 WLR 1101 (no reciprocity: no building scheme).

[190] 'Enhancement in value ... does not mean merely monetary enhancement, but also enhancement of the ambience in which the residents live': *Allen v Veranne Builders Ltd*, above.

[191] If points (a) to (c) are established, (d) may readily be inferred, provided that the purchasers have notice of the facts involved in the first three points: *Elliston v Reacher*, above, at 375.

[192] *Osborne v Bradley* [1903] 2 Ch 446; *Reid v Bickerstaff* [1909] 2 Ch 305, M & B p 810; *Torbay Hotel Ltd v Jenkins* [1927] 2 Ch 225; *Lund v Taylor* (1975) 31 P & CR 167. See *Jackson v Bishop* (1979) 48 P & CR 57 (developer held liable for breach of covenant of title and negligence where there was a double conveyance due to inaccurate plans of neighbouring plots).

[193] *White v Bijou Mansions* [1938] Ch 351, 362.

[194] *Emile Elias & Co Ltd v Pine Groves Ltd* [1993] 1 WLR 305, 310 (Lord Browne-Wilkinson); *Stocks v Whitgift Homes Ltd* [2001] EWCA Civ 1732, [2001] 48 EGCS 130 (no defined area within which scheme intended to operate).

[195] (1970) 114 SJ at 800 (GH Newsom).   [196] *Kelly v Battershell* [1949] 2 All ER 830, 843.

[197] *Kingsbury v L W Anderson Ltd* (1979) 40 P & CR 136.

[198] *Elliston v Reacher* [1908] 2 Ch 665, 672; *Pearce v Maryon-Wilson* [1935] Ch 188; *Re Wembley Park Estate Co Ltd's Transfer* [1968] Ch 491, 497.

[199] *Collins v Castle* (1887) 36 Ch D 243, 253; *Elliston v Reacher* [1908] 2 Ch 374, 384.

a scheme where covenants imposed on some plots were expressed to be by way of indemnity only, and on others were all by way of absolute covenant.[200]

The subject-matter of a scheme generally consists of freehold land that is to be sold in plots to persons who desire to erect houses, but it may equally well comprise houses or a block of flats that have already been built,[201] and leaseholds as well as freeholds.[202] There may also be a sub-scheme within an area that is itself subject to a scheme of development.[203]

(c) Registration of building schemes

Finally we should notice that there is some controversy over the question whether the registration provisions of the Land Charges Act 1972 apply to restrictive covenants under schemes of development. The better view is that they do.[204] In registered land, similarly, the burden of a covenant under a scheme of development must be registered.[205] The Registrar will not, however, refer on the register to an arrangement as being a scheme of development unless its existence as such is demonstrated to him unequivocally.[206]

IV REMEDIES FOR BREACH OF COVENANT

A POSITIVE COVENANTS

The claim for breach of a positive covenant is generally[207] a claim to enforce an obligation at common law, and so is based on the same principles as are generally applicable for breach of contract.[208] As we have seen, the defendant is liable for breach (actual or threatened) of a positive covenant only if he is the original covenantor,[209] and only at the suit of the original covenantee or a person for whom the benefit of the obligation was initially created;[210] or an assignee from the original covenantee;[211] or a person holding a legal estate in the land to which the benefit of the covenant was

---

[200] *Kingsbury v L W Anderson Ltd*, above. [201] See *Torbay Hotel Ltd v Jenkins*, above, at 241.

[202] See *Spicer v Martin* (1888) 14 App Cas 12; *Hudson v Cripps* [1896] 1 Ch 265.

[203] See *Knight v Simmonds* [1896] 1 Ch 653; *King v Dickeson* (1889) 40 Ch D 596; *Lawrence v South County Freeholds Ltd* [1939] Ch 656; *Brunner v Greenslade* [1971] Ch 993.

[204] (1928) 78 LJ 39 (JML); (1933) 77 SJ 550; (1950) 20 Conv (NS) 370 (RG Rowley); Emmet, para 19.042; Farrand, *Contract and Conveyance* (2nd edn), pp 420–1; Barnsley, *Conveyancing Law and Practice*, p 388; Preston and Newsom, paras 2-80 to 2-83, 3-25.

[205] Above, p 740. [206] R & R, para 42.019.01.

[207] Setting aside claims made under the devices to circumvent the rule against the passing of the burden at common law: above, pp 729 ff.

[208] The defendant's action in breach of covenant may also give rise to other claims, eg in nuisance for building in breach of covenant so as to interfere with the claimant's reasonable enjoyment of his property: cf the discussion in relation to easements, above, pp 694–5.

[209] Above, p 728.

[210] Contracts (Rights of Third Parties) Act 1999, above, p 743; LPA 1925, s 56, above, p 741.

[211] LPA 1925, s 136, above, p 745.

annexed and therefore having the right as estate owner to enforce the covenant at law.[212] Thus, the claim for breach of a positive covenant will generally be for damages for breach of contract,[213] although an injunction may also be sought to restrain a threatened breach and, presumably, the remedy of specific performance is available to the court in an appropriate case.[214]

B RESTRICTIVE COVENANTS

Where the defendant is the original covenantor, the claim for breach of a restrictive covenant may still be simply a claim for breach of contract. However, as we have seen, the great step forward taken by *Tulk v Moxhay*[215] was to allow the burden of a restrictive covenant to bind a successor of the covenantor where he had notice of it. This was an equitable rule, which related only to negative covenants, for breach or threatened breach of which the appropriate remedy was the equitable remedy of injunction. Although the jurisdictions of the common law courts and the courts of equity have now been fused for over 130 years,[216] the claim today to enforce a restrictive covenant against a successor of the covenantor, in so far as it rests on the principles derived from *Tulk v Moxhay*, is still a claim in equity.[217] The primary remedy is therefore the injunction. However, by statute the court has a discretion to award damages in addition to, or in substitution for, an injunction.[218] Questions therefore arise as to when the court will award damages in substitution for an injunction; and the basis on which such damages will be calculated.

(1) Damages in Substitution for an Injunction[219]

The courts are reluctant to refuse an injunction and therefore to allow a defendant, who is bound by the covenant, to act in disregard of it. However, damages may be awarded

---

[212] Above, p 744.

[213] *Smith and Snipes Hall Farm Ltd v River Douglas Catchment Board* [1949] 2 KB 500, M & B p 774. For a discussion of the general principles for assessment of damages for breach of contract, see Anson, ch 17.

[214] The equitable remedies of injunction and specific performance are available for breach of contract: Anson, ch 18. Damages are however the primary remedy. Specific performance is available only where (inter alia) damages cannot adequately compensate the breach, and may not often be awarded in a case of breach of covenant. For the refusal to award specific performance of a tenant's covenant in a lease, see *Co-operative Insurance Society Ltd v Argyll Stores Ltd* [1998] AC 1; below, p 993. An injunction is more readily granted in the case of a breach or threatened breach of a negative (ie restrictive) covenant, but even there damages may be preferred: below.

[215] (1848) 2 Ph 774, M & B p 754; above, p 732.   [216] Supreme Court of Judicature Act 1873, s 3.

[217] Ibid, s 24, which preserved the equitable rights and remedies that existed before the fusion of the jurisdictions.

[218] SCA 1981, s 50. This discretion was originally conferred on the courts of equity, before the fusion of the jurisdictions, by Chancery Amendment Act 1858, s 2 (Lord Cairns' Act). See generally [1975] CLJ 224 (JA Jolowicz). On the jurisdiction of the Court of Chancery to award damages before the 1858 Act, see (1992) 108 LQR 652 (PM McDermott).

[219] Preston and Newsom, paras 8–11 to 8–19; [1996] Conv 329 (J Martin); Jones and Goodhart, *Specific Performance* (2nd edn, 1996), ch 8.

in substitution for an injunction where the injury to the claimant's legal rights is small, capable of being estimated in money and can be adequately compensated by a small money payment, and it would be oppressive to the defendant to grant an injunction.[220] This test was applied in *Jaggard v Sawyer*[221] where

> the plaintiff and defendants each owned one of a development of ten houses, served by a private road which was a cul de sac. All ten houses were subject to restrictive covenants against using their unbuilt land other than as a private garden, and positive covenants to keep the road in good repair. The defendants, in breach of covenant, but in the erroneous belief that the road was public and without appreciating the problem of the covenant, built an additional house on their own unbuilt land. The plaintiff complained to the defendants before the building work started, but brought proceedings only once the building was at an advanced stage.

The trial judge, confirmed by the Court of Appeal, held that an injunction should be refused. Millett LJ said:[222]

> The outcome of any particular case usually turns on the question: would it in all the circumstances be oppressive to the defendant to grant the injunction to which the plaintiff is prima facie entitled? Most of the cases in which the injunction has been refused are cases where the plaintiff has sought a mandatory injunction to pull down a building which infringes his right to light or which has been built in breach of a restrictive covenant.[223] In such cases the court is faced with a fait accompli. The jurisdiction to grant a mandatory injunction in those circumstances cannot be doubted, but to grant it would subject the defendant to a loss out of all proportion to that which would be suffered by the plaintiff if it were refused, and would indeed deliver him to the plaintiff bound hand and foot to be subjected to any extortionate demands the plaintiff might make.

---

220 *Shelfer v City of London Electric Lighting Co* [1895] 1 Ch 287, 322–3 (AL Smith LJ). This is the general test for the application of the court's discretion under the statute, applicable also in relation to the tort of nuisance and the infringement of an easement: above, p 695.

221 [1995] 1 WLR 269; [1995] Conv 141 (T Ingram). Cf *Bracewell v Appleby* [1975] Ch 408 (no right of way to newly-built house: injunction similarly refused).

222 [1995] 1 WLR 269, 288. The judge also held that the injury to the plaintiff's right was small, because the increase in traffic would be minimal, and there would be no significant increase in the cost of upkeep of the road, which the defendants had in any event agreed to pay; the value of the injury to the plaintiff's right could be estimated in money and compensated by a small money payment (see below); and he was influenced by the conduct of the parties, including the plaintiff's failure to apply for interlocutory relief: ibid, at 275, 282–3. The plaintiff's failure or delay in applying for an interim injunction is relevant but not conclusive: *Mortimer v Bailey* [2004] EWCA Civ 1514, [2005] 2 P & CR 9; (2004) 154 NLJ 1896 (M Pawlowski); [2005] Conv 460 (G Watt); distinguishing *Gafford v Graham* (1998) 77 P & CR 73.

223 See also *Wrotham Park Estate Co Ltd v Parkside Homes Ltd* [1974] 1 WLR 798, 811 (Brightman J): 'I cannot close my eyes to the fact that the houses now exist. It would, in my opinion, be an unpardonable waste of much needed houses to direct that they now be pulled down and I have never had a moment's doubt during the hearing of this case that such an order ought to be refused.'

(2) Measure of Damages

Damages awarded under the Senior Courts Act 1981[224] in substitution for, or in addition to, an injunction are measured on the same basis as damages at common law.[225] However, a number of cases have considered the particular difficulties of assessing damages for breach of a restrictive covenant. In *Jaggard v Sawyer*[226] the Court of Appeal reviewed the cases and approved the approach taken by Brightman J in *Wrotham Park Estate Co Ltd v Parkside Homes Ltd.*[227] Damages are calculated to compensate the claimant's injury, not to deprive the defendant of a gain he has made by his breach of covenant.[228] However, in calculating the claimant's loss, the defendant's profit can be a relevant consideration. The defendant might have avoided breaking the covenant by seeking from the claimant a relaxation of it—for which the claimant would have sought payment.

> A just substitute for a mandatory injunction would be such a sum of money as might reasonably have been demanded by the plaintiff from [the defendant] as a quid pro quo for relaxing the covenant.[229]

In calculating this sum, the amount that the defendant might have expected to make by way of profit would be relevant, because it would have been part of the (hypothetical) bargaining that would have been entered into between the parties—the bargain of which the claimant has been deprived.[230]

---

[224] Formerly known as the Supreme Court Act 1981: Constitutional Reform Act 2005, Sch 11, para 1.

[225] *Johnson v Agnew* [1980] AC 367, 400 (Lord Wilberforce).   [226] [1995] 1 WLR 269.

[227] [1974] 1 WLR 798.

[228] In recent years the courts have begun to accept that damages for breach of contract can be calculated so as to deprive the defendant of a profit, rather than to compensate the claimant for a loss: *A-G v Blake* [2001] 1 AC 268. However, such a measure is appropriate only in exceptional circumstances: ibid, 285 (Lord Nicholls of Birkenhead).

[229] *Wrotham Park Estate Co Ltd v Parkside Homes Ltd* [1974] 1 WLR 798, 815 (Brightman J); *Experience Hendrix LLC v PPX Enterprises Inc* [2003] EWCA Civ 323, [2003] 1 All ER (Comm) 830; *WWF—World Wide Fund for Nature v World Wrestling Federation Entertainment Inc* [2007] EWCA Civ 286, [2008] 1 WLR 445.

[230] In *Wrotham Park* the plaintiff was awarded £2,500, being 5 per cent of the defendant's anticipated profits, on the basis that this would have been a fair price to have agreed for the release of the covenant. In *Jaggard v Sawyer* [1995] 1 WLR 269 the plaintiff was awarded her proportionate share (as one of nine beneficiaries of the defendants' covenant) of the price (£6,250) that the judge held the defendants should have been prepared to pay for release of the covenant. See also *Gafford v Graham* (1998) 77 P & CR 73, 86–7; *Amec Developments Ltd v Jury's Hotel Management (UK) Ltd* [2001] 1 EGLR 81; *Lane v O'Brien Homes* [2004] EWHC 303 (QB) (collateral contract; date of assessment is time at which defendants would have sought to be released from their contractual commitment); *Small v Oliver & Saunders (Developments) Ltd* [2006] EWHC 1293 (Ch), [2006] 3 EGLR 141; *Forsyth-Grant v Allen* [2008] EWCA Civ 505, [2008] 2 EGLR 16; *Harris v Williams-Wynne* [2006] EWCA Civ 104, [2006] 2 P & CR 27. For a different approach, see *Surrey County Council v Bredero Homes Ltd* [1993] 1 WLR 1361; [1994] Conv 110 (T Ingram) (nominal damages; disapproved in so far as it may be inconsistent with *Wrotham Park* in *A-G v Blake* [2001] 1 AC 268, 283). See generally Anson, pp 597-603.

V DISCHARGE AND MODIFICATION OF RESTRICTIVE COVENANTS[231]

A POSITION AT COMMON LAW

(1) Express or Implied Release

A covenantee (including his assignees) is deprived of his right to enforce the covenant if he has expressly released it; or if he has submitted to a long course of usage wholly inconsistent with its continuance, such as where he remains inactive for a considerable time while open breaches of the covenant are taking place;[232] or if he disregards breaches in such a way as to justify a reasonable person in believing that future breaches will be disregarded.[233]

(2) Unity of Seisin

A restrictive covenant will be discharged when a person becomes entitled in the same capacity[234] to both the dominant and servient lands to which it relates.[235] This is similar to the extinguishment of an easement by the unity of ownership and possession.[236] In *Texaco Antilles Ltd v Kernochan*,[237] however, the Privy Council held that, if there is a scheme of development, unity of seisin does not automatically discharge a covenant within the area of unity, and that on severance it revives, unless there is evidence from the circumstances surrounding the severance that the parties intended that it should not do so.

---

[231] See generally Preston and Newsom, chs 10–16; Scamell, chs 11–21; (1986) 49 MLR 195 (P Polden).

[232] *Gibson v Doeg* (1857) 2 H & N 615; *Hepworth v Pickles* [1900] 1 Ch 108; *Re Summerson* [1900] 1 Ch 112n; discussed in *Lloyds Bank Ltd v Jones* [1955] 2 QB 298, 320–2. See also *Shaw v Applegate* [1977] 1 WLR 970 (injunction refused against original covenantor on grounds of acquiescence, but damages awarded); *A-G of Hong Kong v Fairfax Ltd* [1997] 1 WLR 149 (covenant in 999-year Crown lease held to be abandoned); *Gafford v Graham*, above.

[233] *Chatsworth Estates Co v Fewell* [1931] 1 Ch 224, M & B p 818. This is 'in many ways analogous to the doctrine of estoppel': Farwell J at 231.

[234] *University of East London Higher Education Corp v Barking and Dagenham LBC* [2004] EWHC 2710 (Ch), [2005] Ch 354 at [57]-[60] (local authority holding dominant and servient land for different statutory purposes: covenant not extinguished, on analogy of trustee holding on different trusts).

[235] *Re Tiltwood, Sussex* [1978] Ch 269; (1980) 54 ALJ 156 (GM Bates); (1982) 56 ALJ 587 (AA Preece); *Re Victoria Recreation Ground, Portslade's Application* (1979) 41 P & CR 119.

[236] Above, p 700.   [237] [1973] AC 609, M & B p 820; *Brunner v Greenslade* [1971] Ch 993.

(3) Change in Circumstances relating to Covenant or in Character of Neighbourhood

A covenant may be so drafted that it ceases to apply in changed circumstances.[238] Furthermore, it will no longer be enforceable if the character of the neighbourhood in which the protected property lies is so entirely altered that it would be inequitable and senseless to insist upon the rigorous observance of a covenant that is no longer of any value.[239]

B SECTION 84 OF THE LAW OF PROPERTY ACT 1925

(1) Power to Discharge or Modify Covenants

Section 84 of the Law of Property Act 1925[240] develops this last ground of extinction, and sets up a new method whereby restrictions may be discharged or modified by the Upper Tribunal.[241]

---

[238] *Dano Ltd v Earl Cadogan* [2003] EWCA Civ 782, [2004] 1 P & CR 13 (covenant for benefit of 'the Cadogan Settled Estate in Chelsea' no longer binding after the Estate ceased to exist on settlement being brought to an end in 1961. However, Etherton J had held at first instance that restriction of use of property to the 'housing of the working classes' would still be enforceable: 'There is no difficulty in conferring on the restrictive covenant today a similar meaning, namely the use of the property for the housing of those who, by virtue of their low incomes, might find it difficult to purchase or rent suitable and appropriate accommodation in the private sector': [2003] EWHC 239 (Ch), [2003] 2 P & CR 10 at [99]); *Crest Nicholson Residential (South) Ltd v McAllister* [2004] EWCA Civ 410, [2004] 1 WLR 2409 at [36]. See also the decision at first instance in *Crest Nicholson* [2002] EWHC 2443 (Ch), [2003] 1 All ER 46, where Neuberger J held that a covenant that imposed a restriction unless the covenantee's approval was obtained was discharged by the dissolution of the covenantor; *Churchill v Temple* [2010] EWHC 3369 (Ch), [2011] 17 EG 72 (death of vendor discharged covenants).

[239] *Chatsworth Estates Co v Fewell* [1931] 1 Ch 224; *Robins v Berkeley Homes Ltd* [1996] EGCS 75 (heavy burden of proof to show change); see generally, Behan, *Covenants Affecting Land*, pp 148 ff; Elphinstone, *Covenants Affecting Land*, pp 110 ff; *Westripp v Baldock* [1938] 2 All ER 779; affd [1939] 1 All ER 279; (1966) 5 Melbourne University Law Review, pp 209–14 (D Mendes da Costa).

[240] As amended by LPA 1969, s 28. See Law Com No 11, *Restrictive Covenants* (1967), pp 21–6. For further provisional proposals for reform of the substance of s 84, as well as its extension to cover easements, profits and the proposed Land Obligations, see Law Com CP No 186, *Easements, Covenants and Profits à Prendre* (2008), Part 14; below, p 772. Applications made under the section are noted in Current Law and in the Journal of Planning and Environment Law. Some are recorded in P & CR, EGLR and the EG. Condensed reports of all applications from 1974–79 appeared in Lands Tribunal Cases, and decisions since 2000 can be found on the Upper Tribunal (Lands Chamber) web site: www.landstribunal.gov.uk.

[241] The Upper Tribunal (Lands Chamber), formerly the Lands Tribunal: s 84(1), amended by Transfer of Tribunal Functions (Lands Tribunal and Miscellaneous Amendments) Order 2009, SI 2009 No 1307, Sch 1, para 5. See also *Richardson v Jackson* [1954] 1 WLR 447; *Re University of Westminster* [1998] 3 All ER 1014 (ultimate discretion of tribunal); *Re Kentwood Properties Ltd's Application* [1987] JPL 137 (discretion to modify not exercised where there had been a flagrant, cynical and continuing breach of the covenant). Statements in cases such as *Re Lee's Application* (1996) 72 P & CR 439 and *Shephard v Turner* [2006] EWCA Civ 8, [2006] P & CR 28 at [10] that there is a greater presumption that restriction under building scheme will be upheld, are apt to mislead; the Tribunal should consider the weight to be attached to objections in the light of the special interest of the beneficiaries of covenants in the building scheme: *Dobbin v Redpath* [2007] EWCA Civ 570, [2007] 4 All ER 465 at [24], followed in *Re Cordwell's Application* [2008] 2 P & CR 26 at [70]. For an unsuccessful application to the European Commission of Human Rights (No 1074/84) on the ground that the Northern

The first point to notice is that the Act mainly applies to restrictions imposed on freehold estates. It has no application to leaseholds that are subject to restrictive covenants, except where the lease was originally made for more than 40 years, and 25 years of this term have expired when the question of extinction arises.[242]

It is then provided that any person interested in any such freehold or leasehold land[243] affected by the restrictive covenant,[244] may apply to the Upper Tribunal to have the restriction either wholly or partially discharged, or modified.[245]

In making an order discharging or modifying a restriction the Tribunal may direct the applicant to pay to any person entitled to the benefit of the restriction such sum by way of consideration[246] as it may think it just to award.[247] This must fall under one of the following heads:

(i) a sum to make up for any loss or disadvantage suffered by that person in consequence of the discharge or modification;[248] or

(ii) a sum to make up for any effect which the restriction had, at the time when it was imposed, in reducing the consideration then received for the land affected by it.[249]

Before making any order the Tribunal must be satisfied:

Ireland equivalent of s 84 violated the ECHR, see [1986] Conv 124 (N Dawson). As to whether s 84 is compatible with the Human Rights Act 1998, see Rook, *Property Law and Human Rights* (2001), pp 208–11.

[242] S 84(12), as amended by LTA 1954, s 52. The 25 years is reckoned from the date of the lease, and not from any earlier date at which the term is expressed in the lease to begin: *Earl of Cadogan v Guinness* [1936] Ch 515.

[243] The Tribunal should be more reluctant to interfere with leasehold than freehold covenants: *Ridley v Taylor* [1965] 1 WLR 611, M & B p 825.

[244] It may be personal only: *Shepherd Homes Ltd v Sandham (No 2)* [1971] 1 WLR 1062; *Gilbert v Spoor* [1983] Ch 27. It must be restrictive, not positive: *Blumenthal v Church Commissioners for England* [2004] EWCA Civ 1688, [2005] 1 EGLR 78.

[245] Tribunal Procedure (Upper Tribunal) (Lands Chamber) Rules 2010 (SI 2010 No 2600), replacing Lands Tribunal Rules 1996 (SI 1996 No 1022); Upper Tribunal (Lands Chamber) Fees Order 2009 (SI 2009 No 1114), amended by SI 2010 No 2601. Where proceedings are taken to enforce a restrictive covenant the defendant may apply to the court to stay the proceedings to allow an application to be made to the Upper Tribunal: s 84(9); *Luckies v Simons* [2002] EWHC 2504 (Ch), [2003] 2 P & CR 30 (court should normally order stay). See also *R (Sinclair Gardens Investments (Kensington) Ltd) v Lands Tribunal* [2005] EWCA Civ 1305 [2006] 1 EGLR 7 (judicial review of decision of Lands Tribunal refused).

On the Upper Tribunal (Lands Chamber) generally, and Practice Directions of the Lands Chamber, see the Upper Tribunal (Lands Chamber) web site, above, n 240.

[246] See *SJC Construction Co Ltd v Sutton London Borough Council* (1975) 29 P & CR 322, where Stephenson LJ said, in argument, that 'consideration' was probably a misprint for 'compensation': Preston and Newsom, para 13-02.

[247] LPA 1925, s 84(1), as amended by LPA 1969, s 28(3). See generally [1976] JPL 18 (WA Leach). Only a person appearing to have the benefit of the covenant by virtue of an interest in the application land (and not person with merely a contractual right) is entitled to be admitted as objector: *Re Hutchinson's Appeal* [2009] UKUT 182 (LC), [2010] 1 EGLR 105.

[248] *SJC Construction Co Ltd v Sutton LBC*, above ('there is no method prescribed by the Act by which it is to be assessed; it is essentially a question of quantum': Lord Denning MR at 326). The basis of an award by the Upper Tribunal is not the same as an award of damages by the court for breach of covenant, above, p 762; *Stockport MBC v Alwiyah Developments* (1983) 52 P & CR 278 (loss of bargaining power not a benefit); [2005] 35 EG 107 (H Williamson).

[249] *Re Davies' Application* [2001] 1 EGLR 111 (reduction in consideration, increased for inflation).

(a) that by reason of changes in the character of the property or the neighbourhood[250] or other circumstances of the case[251] which the Tribunal may deem material, the restriction ought to be deemed obsolete; or

(aa) that the continued existence thereof would impede some reasonable user of the land for public or private purposes or, as the case may be, would unless modified so impede such user.[252]

Under this paragraph the Tribunal must be satisfied that the restriction, in impeding the user, either:

(i) does not secure to persons entitled to the benefit of it any practical benefits of substantial value or advantage to them; or

(ii) is contrary to the public interest;

and that money will be an adequate compensation for the loss or disadvantage (if any) which any such person will suffer from the discharge or modification;[253] or

(b) that the persons of full age and capacity for the time being or from time to time entitled to the benefit of the restriction, whether in respect of estates in fee simple or any lesser estates or interests in the property to which the benefit of the restriction is annexed, have agreed, either expressly or by implication,[254] by their acts or omissions, to the same being discharged or modified; or

(c) that the proposed discharge or modification will not injure the persons entitled to the benefit of the restriction.[255]

---

[250] *Keith v Texaco Ltd* (1977) 34 P & CR 249 (coming of oil industry to Aberdeenshire); *Re Bradley Clare Estates Ltd's Application* (1987) 55 P & CR 126; *Re Quaffers Ltd's Application* (1988) 56 P & CR 142 (advent of motorway network); *Re North's Application* (1997) 75 P & CR 117 (change in neighbourhood not material; house in Winkfield, Berkshire, retained attractive semi-rural character despite infilling).

[251] *Re Cox's Application* (1985) 51 P & CR 335 (covenant requiring occupiers of extension of house in East Sussex to be domestic staff employed for service in the house held obsolete); cf *Re Beechwood Homes Ltd's Application* [1994] 2 EGLR 178 (covenant to prevent cul-de-sac development, involving lopping of trees held not obsolete); *Re Kalsi's Application* (1993) 66 P & CR 313; *Re Wards Construction (Medway) Ltd's Application* (1994) 67 P & CR 379 (green field area now an infill site); *Re Kennet Properties' Application* [1996] 1 EGLR 163 (original purpose of unimpeded views across each neighbour's land no longer possible due to housing development); *Re Nichols' Application* [1997] 1 EGLR 144; *Re Marcello Developments Ltd's Application* [2002] RVR 146 (frontage and building line restrictions obsolete); *Re Davies' Application* [2001] 1 EGLR 111; *Re Broomhead's Application* [2003] 2 EGLR 157 (purpose of covenant to control development and extract premium on release held not to be obsolete).

[252] See *Stannard v Issa* [1987] AC 175, where PC construed a similar but not identical paragraph under the Restrictive Covenants (Discharge and Modification) Act (No 2 of 1960) of Jamaica, s 3(1).

[253] LPA 1925, s 84(1A). For the formulation of the questions to be answered by the Tribunal, see *Re Bass Ltd's Application* (1973) 26 P & CR 156.

[254] See *Re Memvale Securities Ltd's Application* (1974) 233 EG 689; *Re Fettishaw's Application (No 2)* (1973) 27 P & CR 292.

[255] *Re Forestmere Properties Ltd's Application* (1980) 41 P & CR 390 ('replacement of one eyesore (Odeon cinema) by another could hardly be said to be an improvement'); *Re Bailey's Application* (1981) 42 P & CR 108 ('quaint rural backwater' not to be changed into riding school with attendant manure and noise including sound of human voice); *Re Livingstones' Application* (1982) 47 P & CR 462 ('eyesore' carport); *Re Severn Trent Water Ltd's Application* (1993) 67 P & CR 236 (site for sewage disposal works to become leisure centre).

The Upper Tribunal may, however, add further restrictive provisions if it appears to it to be reasonable to do so.[256] This cannot be done unless the applicant accepts them, but, if he does not, the application may be refused.

There may be an appeal to the Court of Appeal from a decision of the Upper Tribunal, but only with the permission of either the Tribunal or the Court of Appeal, and only if the Tribunal or Court considers that the proposed appeal would raise some important point of principle or practice, or there is some other compelling reason for the appeal.[257]

(2) Changes Made to Section 84 by Law of Property Act 1969

The substantive change made by the Law of Property Act 1969 was to widen the scope of section 84 of the Law of Property Act 1925, and, in particular, to redraft paragraph (1)(aa), so as to enable the Lands Tribunal (now the Upper Tribunal)[258] 'to take a broader view of whether the use of land is being unreasonably impeded; and to make clear provision for an award of monetary compensation where the Tribunal thinks that the injury that an objector would suffer by a modification or discharge can be properly compensated in that way'.[259] Carnwath LJ has said:[260]

> The general purpose is to facilitate the development and use of land in the public interest, having regard to the development plan and the pattern of permissions in the area. The section seeks to provide a fair balance between the needs of development in the area, public and private, and the protection of private contractual rights. 'Reasonable user' in this context seems to me to refer naturally to a long term use of land, rather than the process of transition to such a use. The primary consideration, therefore, is the value of the covenant in providing protection from the effects of the ultimate use, rather than from the short-term disturbance which is inherent in any ordinary construction project. There may, however, be something in the form of the particular covenant, or in the facts of the particular case, which justifies giving special weight to this factor.

To enable it to take this broader view the Tribunal must take into account the development plan and any declared or ascertainable pattern for the grant or refusal of planning permissions in the relevant areas, as well as the period at which and

---

[256] *Re Patten Ltd's Application* (1975) 31 P & CR 180; *Re Dransfield's Application* (1975) 31 P & CR 192; *Re Kershaw's Application* (1975) 31 P & CR 187; *Re Banks Application* (1976) 33 P & CR 138; *Re Forestmere Properties Ltd's Application* (1980) 41 P & CR 390; *Re Austin's Application* (1980) 42 P & CR 102; *Re Shah and Shah's Application* (1991) 62 P & CR 450; *Re University of Westminster's Application* [1997] 1 EGLR 191 ('it is a matter of discretion to limit or cut down the form of relief sought').

[257] Tribunals, Courts and Enforcement Act 2007, s 13; SI 2008 No 2834. See also Tribunal Procedure (Upper Tribunal) (Lands Chamber) Rules 2010 (SI 2010 No 2600), r 55. The Tribunal, on receiving an application for permission to appeal may itself review its own decision but only if when making the decision the Tribunal overlooked a legislative provision or binding authority that could have had a material effect on the decision; or, since the Tribunal's decision, a court has made a decision that is binding on the Tribunal and that, had it been made before the Tribunal's decision, could have had a material effect on the decision: SI 2010 No 2600, r 56.

[258] Above, p 764, n 241.   [259] Law Com No 11, *Restrictive Covenants* (1967), p 23.

[260] *Shephard v Turner* [2006] EWCA Civ 8; [2006] 2 P & CR 28 at [58].

context in which the restriction was created or imposed and any other material circumstances.[261]

The statutory provisions apply to restrictive covenants entered into either before or after the commencement of the Act, but do not apply where the restriction was imposed on the occasion of a disposition made gratuitously, or for a nominal consideration, for public purposes.[262]

(a) Public interest

Since 1969 the new paragraph (1)(aa) and the power to award compensation have resulted in an increased number of cases before the Tribunal.[263] Several important criteria have been established for deciding whether a covenant should be modified or discharged. In particular, where the applicant has obtained planning permission for the proposed user, the effect is very persuasive in considering whether that user is reasonable.[264] The proposition that impeding that user is contrary to the public interest may also be aided by a planning permission, but in rather a different way. The question is not whether the proposed user is in the public interest, but whether impeding the proposed user is contrary to it. 'There is here more than a narrow nuance of difference: a planning permission only says, in effect, that a proposal will be allowed; it implies that such a proposal will not be a bad thing, but it does not necessarily imply that it will be positively a good thing.'[265]

Consistently with this restrictive approach, the President of the Lands Tribunal said in 1974:[266]

> For an application to succeed on the ground of public interest it must be shown that that interest is so important and immediate as to justify the serious interference with private rights and the sanctity of contract.

An acute shortage of building land in a particular locality does not establish that any restriction that prevents development of land is in itself contrary to the public interest;[267] nor does a housing need in the area.[268] In only two situations so far has an

---

[261] LPA 1925, s 84(1B). See *Re Collins' Application* (1974) 30 P & CR 527.   [262] Ibid, s 84(7).

[263] See generally Preston and Newsom, chs 10–16; [1974] JPL 72, 130; [1975] JPL 644; [1976] JPL 407; [1979] JPL 64; [1981] JPL 551, 656; [1982] JPL 552; [1984] JPL 847 (GH Newsom); and for a useful summary of the cases (1979) 129 NLJ 523; (2000) 150 NLJ 1525, 1623 (HW Wilkinson); M & B pp 825–32.

[264] *Re Beecham Group Ltd's Application* (1980) 41 P & CR 369 (refusal to differ from very 'closely reasoned decision' of Secretary of State granting planning permission on appeal from inspector); *Gilbert v Spoor* [1983] Ch 27 ('the subsection does not make planning decisions decisive': Eveleigh LJ at 34); *Re Martin's Application* (1988) 57 P & CR 119, M & B p 832; *Re Kennet Properties' Application* [1996] 1 EGLR 163 (development plan); *Re Hextall's Application* (2000) 79 P & CR 382 (planning permission strongly persuasive); *Re Diggens' Application (No 2)* [2001] 2 EGLR 163 (planning permission, but application to modify covenant refused).

[265] *Re Bass Ltd's Application* (1973) 26 P & CR 156, 157.

[266] *Re Collins' Applications* (1974) 30 P & CR 527 (Douglas Frank QC). See also *Re Mansfield District Council's Application* (1976) 33 P & CR 141, 143; *Re Brierfield's Application* (1976) 35 P & CR 124; *Re Solarfilms (Sales) Ltd's Application* (1993) 67 P & CR 110.

[267] *Re Beardsley's Application* (1972) 25 P & CR 233; *Re Gardner's Application* [1974] JPL 728.

[268] *Re New Ideal Homes Ltd's Application* (1978) 36 P & CR 476 (where, however, the covenant was modified on payment by consent of £51,000 compensation because it did not secure practical benefits of

application succeeded on the ground of public interest. The first was where there was a scarcity of land available for building development, and, if the restriction were not modified, building work costing £47,000 would have to be demolished. That was to be avoided in 'the present economic circumstances of the country'.[269] The second was where modification did not involve the demolition of a building.[270] A covenant not to carry on any trade or business in a large house in Worthing was modified to permit use as a community care home for ten psychiatric patients who had been assessed as ready to live independently in the community. The restriction was contrary to the public interest, because government policy was for mental patients to be rehabilitated in the community, and there was a desperate need for such a facility in the area. The restriction did not confer any substantial benefit or advantage because there was already a home for 41 old people that had been built next door in breach of covenant; and planning permission had already been granted.

(b) Practical benefits of substantial value or advantage

Further, in considering whether the restriction secures to the persons entitled to the benefit of the covenant practical benefits of substantial[271] value or advantage,[272] the

substantial value to objecting local authority); *Re Osborn's and Easton's Application* (1978) 38 P & CR 251; *Re Beech's Application* (1990) 59 P & CR 502 (residential enclave in predominantly commercial setting). See also *Re London Borough of Islington's Application* [1986] JPL 214 (covenant forbidding use of land in Islington 'except for open space', purchased from Greater London Council who remitted half of the purchase price, discharged on repayment of that half with adjustments for inflation).

269 *Re SJC Construction Co Ltd's Application* (1974) 28 P & CR 200; affd by CA on method of assessing compensation as *SJC Construction Co Ltd v Sutton LBC* (1975) 29 P & CR 322; *Re Fisher & Gimson (Builders) Ltd's Application* (1992) 65 P & CR 312 (risk of demolition of important housing accommodation against public interest; £6,000 compensation); *Re Bradley Clare Estates Ltd's Application* (1987) 55 P & CR 126. Cf *Re O'Reilly's Application* (1993) 66 P & CR 485; *Re Hounslow and Ealing LBC's Application* (1995) 71 P & CR 100 (part of ground floor of mansion to be used as horticultural training centre); *Re Bromor Properties Ltd's Application* (1995) 70 P & CR 569; *Re Milius's Application* (1995) 70 P & CR 427 (restriction adopted by local authority pursuant to lawful policy approved by Parliament held not contrary to public interest).

270 *Re Lloyd's and Lloyd's Application* (1993) 66 P & CR 112.

271 On the meaning of substantial, see *Re Gaffney's Application* (1974) 35 P & CR 440; *Re Dransfield's Application* (1975) 31 P & CR 192; *Re Jillas' Application* [2000] 2 EGLR 99 (covenant modified to allow for extension of house: reduction in value of adjoining house of £10,000, about 1.5 per cent of its value, was not substantial, so compensation ordered); (2000) 150 NLJ 1523 (HW Wilkinson).

272 *Re John Twiname Ltd's Application* (1971) 23 P & CR 413, 417–18; *Re Wards Construction (Medway) Ltd's Application* (1973) 25 P & CR 223, 231 ('even ordinary people not infrequently value space and quiet and light'); *Re Gossip's Application* (1972) 25 P & CR 215, 220 ('houses built on the application land would overlook the garden and the principal rooms, albeit somewhat screened by a hawthorn, a poor substitute for a covenant'); *Re Ballamy's Application* [1977] JPL 456 (enjoyment of evening sunshine in the sun-lounge); *Re Banks Application* (1976) 33 P & CR 138 ('direct view of the sea is of immense value'); *Re Bovis Homes Southern Ltd's Application* [1981] JPL 368 (beauty and aesthetic and historic interest of National Trust house and its setting); *Gilbert v Spoor* [1983] Ch 27 (magnificent view over Tyne Valley from road adjacent to objector's land); [1984] Conv 429 (P Polden); *Re Burr's Application* [1987] JPL 137 (amenities of a high class development); *Stannard v Issa* [1987] AC 175 ('the privacy and quietude of an enclave of single dwellings in large gardens is going to be adversely affected by the introduction on adjoining lands of no less than 40 additional families': Lord Oliver of Aylmerton at 196); cf *Stockport MBC v Alwiyah Developments* (1983) 52 P & CR 278 (loss of bargaining power not a benefit); *Re Bennett's and Tamarlin Ltd's Applications* (1987) 54 P & CR 378 (loss of ability to extract money for agreeing to modification of restriction not a benefit); *Re Bushell's Application* (1987) 54 P & CR 386 (particularly fine landscape view at Wimbledon 'very unusual so

Lands Tribunal has observed that the words 'value or advantage' are not intended to be assessed in terms of pecuniary value only.[273] It takes account of any matters however unusual or personal they may be.[274]

(c) Thin end of the wedge

In *McMorris v Brown* Lord Cooke of Thorndon explained the argument of the thin end of the wedge:[275]

> A familiar and at times legitimate argument in this branch of the law is known as the thin end of the wedge argument. Other expressions are sometimes coupled with it, such as 'the first is the worst.' ... [Decisions in Jamaica] have accepted that cases may arise in which it is very difficult to say that the particular thing which the applicant wishes to do will of itself cause anyone any harm; but that harm may still come to the persons entitled to the bene-fit of the restriction if it were to become generally allowable to do similar things. Or such harm may flow from the very existence of the order making the modification through the

near the centre of London'); *Re Purnell's Application* (1987) 55 P & CR 133 (large garden providing privacy in Orpington, Kent). See also *Re Crest Homes plc's Application* (1983) 48 P & CR 309 (proposal to build 12 houses to replace neglected Edgware Lawn Tennis Club would cause undesirable increase in housing density and change area from semi-rural to urban); *Re Lake's Application* [1984] JPL 887 (proposal to erect split-level house in Lyme Regis would be design out of character with surroundings); *Re Williams' Application* (1987) 55 P & CR 400 (sense of spaciousness; preventing nuisance of building works); *Re Whiting's Application* (1988) 58 P & CR 321 (natural beauty of Howley, Gloucestershire); *Re Tarhale Ltd's Application* (1990) 60 P & CR 368 (preventing intolerable nuisance during construction work); *Re Sheehy's Application* (1991) 63 P & CR 95 (moral obligation undertaken by the St Aubyn Discretionary Trustees to maintain a scheme of covenants within the Devonport Estate, where cost of administration exceeded total rental income, held to be of practical benefit). See also *Re Edwards' Application* (1983) 47 P & CR 458 (restriction modified to enable house in Mold, North Wales, to be used as a general village store, for 'groceries, sweets, tobacco, cigarettes, cigars, soft drinks, ice cream, newspapers, trinkets, haberdashery, gardening utensils and supplies, tools, nuts and bolts' subject to payment of £500 as compensation to objector for loss of amenity); *Re Shah and Shah's Application* (1991) 62 P & CR 450 (restriction impeding nursing home user so small as to warrant monetary compensation only of £23,000); *Re Hopcraft's Application* (1993) 66 P & CR 475 (pleasant open area to remain open); *Re Hydeshire Ltd's Application* (1993) 67 P & CR 93 (right to build within set limit, provided no one else had done so, not a practical benefit); *Re Cornick's Application* (1994) 68 P & CR 372 (jam factory); *Re Azfar's Application* [2002] 1 P & CR 17 (adverse impact from traffic, parking, access to neighbouring properties and unsightliness of large extension); *Duffield v Gandy* [2008] EWCA Civ 379, [2008] 2 P & CR DG7 (privacy to be protected against erection of a bungalow and from use of an adjoining part of property as a garden ancillary to occupation of the bungalow).

[273] *Re Bass Ltd's Application* (1973) 26 P & CR 156; *Re Diggens' Application (No 2)* [2001] 2 EGLR 163 (practical benefits secured by density restriction were preservation of view, privacy, seclusion and sense of spaciousness and tranquillity in semi-rural atmosphere). Loss of bargaining power is not a proper head of compensation: *Stockport MBC v Alwiyah Developments* (1983) 52 P & CR 278; cf *Re Quaffers Ltd's Application* (1988) 56 P & CR 142 (loss of competition advantage); *Winter v Traditional & Contemporary Contracts Ltd* [2008] EWCA Civ 1088, [2008] 1 EGLR 80 at [26]-[28] (Carnwath LJ: the test is not the 'negotiated share approach ..[which] is well recognised in civil proceedings for breach of restrictive covenants. ... compensation under section 84 is based on the impact of the development on the objectors, not on the loss of the opportunity to extract a share of the development value. Short of intervention by the House of Lords, or the legislature, it is too late to turn the clock back').

[274] *Re Matcham's Application* [1981] JPL 431 (house built on tranquil site because of wife's severe migraine).

[275] [1999] 1 AC 142, 151.

implication that the restriction is vulnerable to the action of the Lands Tribunal in England or the Supreme Court in Jamaica...

Their Lordships find more recent decisions of the Lands Tribunal in England in the same line of cases collected in *Maudsley and Burn's Land Law: Cases and Materials* (7th edn, 1998), p 926.[276]

(3) Registered Land

Where title to the servient estate is registered, any release, discharge or modification of a restrictive covenant should be noted on the register, either by the cancellation of the original notice and the entry of a fresh notice, or by a supplementary notice.[277]

(4) Declaration Whether Restriction Binding

In order to meet the case where it may be doubtful whether an effectual restrictive covenant has been imposed on land and if so what persons it now affects, the Act confers jurisdiction upon the court:[278]

(a) to declare whether or not in any particular case any freehold land is, or would in any given event be, affected by a restriction imposed by any instrument; or

(b) to declare what, upon the true construction of any instrument purporting to impose a restriction, is the nature and extent of the restriction thereby imposed and whether the same is, or would in any given event be, enforceable and if so by whom.

Kitchin J has said[279]

> The procedure under s 84(2) may usefully be invoked where a claimant believes a covenant is, on its proper construction, no longer enforceable and wishes to obtain a clean title, clear of any restrictions. Its value is that it is binding *in rem* on all persons entitled to the benefit of the restriction, whether they are parties to the proceedings or not.[280] Accordingly, it is well established that when an order of this kind is asked for, the court ought to make every effort to see that all persons who may wish to oppose the making of the order have

---

[276] See now 9th edn 2009, p 828. See also *Re Chapman's Application* (1980) 42 P & CR 114; *Re Farmiloe's Application* (1983) 48 P & CR 317; *Re Love's and Love's Application* (1993) 67 P & CR 101; *Re Solarfilms (Sales) Ltd's Application* (1993) 67 P & CR 110; *Re Page's Application* (1995) 71 P & CR 440; *Re Snaith and Dolding's Application* (1995) 71 P & CR 104 ('erection of this house could materially alter the context in which further applications would be considered'); *Re Churchill's Application* (1994) LP/45/94; *Re Hunt's Application* (1996) 73 P & CR 126; *Shephard v Turner* [2006] EWCA Civ 8, [2006] 2 P & CR 28 at [29] ('thin end of the wedge' argument relevant but the issues it raises are ones of fact not law, so limited scope for challenge on appeal).

[277] R & R, para 42.019.02. If the original notice was unilateral, no proof of the release, modification or discharge is required: LRA 2002, s 35(3); but if it was an agreed notice, the Registrar must be satisfied about it: LRR 2003, r 87(2).

[278] LPA 1925, s 84(2), as amended by LPA 1969, s 28(4); *Re Sunnyfield* [1932] 1 Ch 79; *Re Freeman-Thomas Indenture* [1957] 1 All ER 532; *Re MCA East Ltd* [2002] EWHC 1684, [2003] 1 P & CR 9 (application by developer).

[279] *Norwich City College of Further and Higher Education v McQuillin* [2009] EWHC 1496 (Ch), [2009] 2 P & CR 22 at [17]; (2009) 159 NLJ 1535 (A Francis).

[280] LPA 1925, s 84(5).

the opportunity of being heard, stating their objections in argument before the court, and inviting the court to refuse to exercise its powers.

(5) Proposed Further Reform

In making provisional proposals for a general reform of the law of easements, covenants and profits à prendre, the Law Commission has made some specific proposals to change the detail of section 84.[281] Amongst other things, the Commission says that the provisions of section 84(1) are unnecessarily complex and difficult to interpret;[282] reject obsoleteness as a ground in section 84(1)(a);[283] does not consider that the requirement in section 84(1)(aa) that the user should be reasonable is necessary;[284] envisages a greater role for section 84(1)(b) where the party entitled to the benefit of the interest has to all intents and purposes abandoned it;[285] and proposes that an application to the court under section 84(2)[286] should be made only with permission of the Tribunal or the court, in order to limit a party's ability, by making an application to the court, to stop the section 84(1) proceedings in their tracks.[287] The principal provisional proposals of the Law Commission are that:[288]

(1) the Tribunal in exercising its jurisdiction should seek to give effect to the 'purpose' for which the restriction or other interest in land was imposed;

(2) the Tribunal should be able to discharge or modify where

    (a) it is satisfied of one of the statutory grounds, and

    (b) it is reasonable in all the circumstances to discharge or modify the restriction or interest;

(3) the statutory grounds for discharge or modification should be that the discharge or modification:

    (a) would not cause substantial injury to the person entitled to the benefit of the restriction or other interest in land; or

    (b) would enable the land to be put to a use that is in the public interest and that could not reasonably be accommodated on other land;

and that (in either case) money would provide adequate compensation to the person entitled to the benefit of the restriction or other interest in land.

---

[281] Law Com CP No 186 (2008), Part 14. It also proposes extending the scope of application of s 84 (as reformed) to easements and profits (above, p 725), and to the new Land Obligation (which the Law Commission proposes should replace covenants in registered land: below, pp 774–7), and some of the proposed changes to the section follow from its extension to the discharge of modification of these other interests.

[282] Para 14.45.   [283] Para 14.50; above, p 766.   [284] Para 14.53; above, p 766.

[285] Para 14.62.   [286] Above, p 765.

[287] Paras 14.96–14.101.   [288] Paras 14.70–14.71.

C HOUSING ACT 1985

If it is proved that where

(a) owing to changes in the character of the neighbourhood, premises cannot readily be let as a single dwelling-house but could readily be let if converted into two or more dwelling-houses, or

(b) planning permission has been granted for the use of premises as converted into two or more separate dwelling-houses instead of as a single dwelling-house,[289]

and the conversion is prohibited or restricted by a restrictive covenant affecting the premises, section 610 of the Housing Act 1985[290] empowers the county court to vary the restrictive covenant subject to such conditions and upon such terms as the court may think just.

D TOWN AND COUNTRY PLANNING ACT 1990

Under section 106,[291] a local planning authority has power to regulate land use by agreement.[292] It may enter into an agreement with any person interested in land in their area for the purpose of restricting or regulating the development or use of land, either permanently or during such period as may be prescribed by the agreement. Where such an agreement has been made, the authority is said to hold the benefit of the covenant as custodian of the public interest.[293] Such an agreement may be modified or discharged under the Law of Property Act 1925, section 84.[294]

---

[289] *Lawntown Ltd v Camenzuli* [2008] EWCA Civ 949, [2008] 1 WLR 2656 (although triggered by the grant of planning permission, the court's task is separate from the planning process and requires an independent exercise of judgment, including but not limited to factors considered by the planning authority); [2008] Conv 328 (J Morgan).

[290] As amended by Local Government and Housing Act 1989, s 165(1)(e), Sch 9, para 88. See Preston and Newsom, paras 10–20.

[291] S 106 was due to be replaced by the new scheme of 'planning contribution' under Planning and Compulsory Purchase Act 2004, s 46, but that section was never brought into force and was repealed by Planning Act 2008, s 225, Sch 13, para 1.

[292] Replacing TCPA 1971, s 52. Such an agreement is within LP(MP)A 1989, s 2, below, p 966. *Jelson Ltd v Derby City Council* [1999] 3 EGLR 91; [1999] Conv 379 (JEA). See Current Law Statutes TCPA 1990, s 106, annotated by M Grant, paras 8-299 to 8-302.

[293] *Re Abbey Homesteads (Developments) Ltd's Application* [1986] 1 EGLR 24; *Re Martin's Application* (1988) 57 P & CR 119, esp at 125, M & B p 832 (Fox LJ); *Re Houdret & Co Ltd's Application* (1989) 58 P & CR 310; *Re Jones' and White & Co's Application* (1989) 58 P & CR 512; *Re Quartley's Application* (1989) 58 P & CR 518; *Re Beech's Application* (1990) 59 P & CR 502; [1990] Conv 455 (NDM Parry); *Re Wallace & Co's Application* (1993) 66 P & CR 124; *Re Hopcraft's Application* (1993) 66 P & CR 475 (storage of touring caravans refused); *Re Bromor Properties Ltd's Application* (1995) 70 P & CR 569.

[294] For successful modifications, see *Re Cox's Application* (1985) 51 P & CR 335; *Re Towner's and Goddard's Application* (1989) 58 P & CR 316 (tennis court with chain link fencing); *Re Barclays Bank plc's Application* (1990) 60 P & CR 354 (discharge in favour of mortgagee); *Re Poulton's Application* (1992) 65 P & CR 319 (extension of bungalow in Metropolitan Green Belt). *Re O'Reilly's Application* (1993) 66 P & CR 485 (use for car parking only modified to allow erection of six houses on payment of £11,000 compensation);

Under section 237, a local planning authority is authorised, subject to the payment of compensation, to carry out a scheme of development, notwithstanding that it interferes with an easement or infringes a restrictive covenant.[295]

VI LAW REFORM

In 1984, the Law Commission issued a Report on the Law of Positive and Restrictive Covenants, which recommended a comprehensive reform of the law relating to covenants affecting freehold land.[296] That report was never implemented, and the Law Commission has now again considered the options for reform. In 2008 it made provisional proposals in its Consultation Paper on Easements, Covenants and Profits à Prendre.[297]

The key elements of the 2008 scheme are:

(1) There should be a new interest in land, to be called a Land Obligation. However, there should not be separate types of Land Obligation,[298] although for some purposes it would be necessary to distinguish between obligations of a positive or restrictive nature:[299]

Re Williamson's Application (1994) 68 P & CR 384 (granny annexe as a separate dwelling); *Re Bewick's Application* (1996) 73 P & CR 240; *Re Willis' Application* [1997] 2 EGLR 185 (bed and breakfast establishment wholly compatible with surrounding residential area).

[295] *Sutton LBC v Bolton* (1993) 68 P & CR 166. See Local Government Act 1972, ss 120(3), 124(2); *R v City of London Council, ex p Master Governors and Commonality of the Mystery of the Barbers of London* [1996] 2 EGLR 128; *Thames Water Utilities v Oxford City Council* (1998) 77 P & CR D16; cf Scamell, pp 191–3; *Re Wiggins Application* [1998] JPL 599; *Re Caton's Application* [1999] 3 EGLR 121 (changes in planning policy did not render restriction obsolete).

[296] Law Com No 127. For earlier Reports, see Wilberforce Committee on Positive Covenants (1965, Cmnd 2719); Law Com No 11, *Restrictive Covenants* (1967) and WP No 36, *Rights Appurtenant to Land* (1971); Benson Committee on Legal Services 1979 (Cmnd 7648); Second Report of the Conveyancing Committee: *Conveyancing Simplifications* (1985), paras 4.52–4.57, 7.21–7.22. See also [1984] JPL 222, 317, 401, 485 (SB Edell); 134 NLJ 459, 481 (HW Wilkinson); (1984) 47 MLR 566 (P Polden).

Following the 1984 Report the Law Commission also proposed that, after the implementation of the Report, existing restrictive covenants should be phased out: Law Com No 201, *Obsolete Restrictive Covenants* (1991). Since the 1984 Report was never implemented, the 1991 Report was not pursued.

In New Zealand, Property Law Act 2007, s 302, now allows the burden of both negative and positive covenants to run with the land. In Ireland, Land and Conveyancing Law Reform Act 2009, s 49, abolished the rule in *Tulk v Moxhay* and allows all freehold covenants, negative and positive, to run as legal interests in the land: Wiley, *Irish Land Law* (4th edn, 2010), paras 19.49–19.58.

[297] Law Com CP No 186. The scheme proposed in the Consultation Paper in 2008 is in a number of respects a simplified version of the 1984 scheme.

[298] In the 1984 scheme, the Law Commission had proposed distinguishing between a *neighbour obligation* (imposed on one plot for the benefit of another plot) and a *development obligation* (where an area of land is to be divided into separately owned but inter-dependent units): Law Com No 127, *The Law of Positive and Restrictive Covenants* (1984), paras 4.29–4.36, 6.2–6.6, 27.1(3)–(11). The terminology of 'Land Obligation' also derives from the 1984 report.

[299] Law Com CP No 186, para 8.23.

(a) an obligation of a restrictive nature would be an obligation imposing a restriction, which benefits the whole or part of the dominant land, on the doing of some act on the servient land;

(b) an obligation of a positive nature could be a positive obligation (ie an obligation to do something), or a reciprocal payment obligation (ie an obligation requiring the making of payments in a specified manner on account of expenditure that has been or is to be incurred by a person in complying with a positive obligation).

(2) A Land Obligation must be expressly labelled as a 'Land Obligation' in the instrument creating it,[300] and it should only be able to be created expressly over registered title,[301] and in a prescribed form,[302] to be completed by registration against both the the benefited estate and the burdened estate if it is to take effect at law.[303]

(3) Land Obligations must have a dominant and servient tenement[304] and so could not be created in gross,[305] but the Land Obligation must 'relate to', or be for the benefit of, dominant land, ie it must benefit only the dominant owner for the time being, must affect the nature, quality, mode of user or value of the land, and must not be expressed to be personal.[306]

(4) In the event of the introduction of Land Obligations, it should no longer be possible to create covenants that run with the land where both the benefited and burdened estates in the land are registered. The question of whether new covenants could still be created in relation to unregistered land is left open.[307]

(5) In the event of the introduction of Land Obligations, it should no longer be possible to create new estate rentcharges over registered estates.[308]

(6) The rule against perpetuities would not apply to Land Obligations.

(7) The benefit of a Land Obligation would pass to all successors in title of the original owner of the benefited estate or any part of it,[309] or the owner of an estate

---

[300] Para 8.28. [301] Para 8.38.

[302] Para 8.40. It should be possible for parties to create short-form Land Obligations by reference to a prescribed set of statutory words: para 12.25.

[303] Para 8.47. The Law Commission asks for views on whether it should be possible to create equitable Land Obligations (in the same way as expressly granted equitable easements), and (if so) whether equitable Land Obligations should be capable of binding successors in title: paras 8.54 and 8.61.

[304] Although there must be separate registered titles for the benefited and burdened estates, there would be no need for the estates to be owned and possessed by different persons: para 8.88.

[305] Para 8.65.

[306] Para 8.80. The fact that a Land Obligation is to pay a sum of money will not prevent it from relating to the land as long as these conditions are satisfied: ibid.

[307] Paras 8.109–110.

[308] Para 8.119. Such rentcharges are used as a device to circumvent the present rule against the passing of the burden of positive covenants (above, p 731), and would thus no longer be needed.

[309] On sub-division of the dominant land, the benefit would run with each and every part, unless it does not 'relate to' or benefit that part, or the sub-division increases the scope of the obligations to an extent beyond that contemplated by in the Land Obligation deed, or express provision has been made for it not to pass: para 10.44.

derived out of the benefited estate or any part of it, unless express provision has been made for the benefit not to pass.[310]

(8) The burden of a Land Obligation would attach to an estate in the servient land,[311] but distinctions are drawn (and some points not yet settled by way of final proposals) as to what category of person should be bound by different forms of Land Obligation:[312]

   (a) *positive obligations* or *reciprocal payment obligations* might bind (i) those with freehold or long leasehold (terms over 21 years) estates in the servient land or any part of it,[313] as long as they have a right to possession, together with mortgagees and other owners of the burdened estate that were clearly intended to be bound; or only (ii) owners for the time being of the burdened estate; or (iii) owners for the time being together with derivative estates held for at least some specified residual term;

   (b) *restrictive obligations* would bind all persons with an estate or interest in, or in occupation of, the servient land or any part of it.

(9) A squatter in adverse possession of registered land but who has not yet applied successfully to be registered as proprietor[314] should not be able to enforce any Land Obligation, but should be bound by restrictive obligations.[315]

(10) The statutory jurisdiction to discharge or modify restrictive covenants, contained in section 84 of the Law of Property Act 1925,[316] should be extended to include Land Obligations.

The Law Commission has indicated that it hopes to publish a final report and draft bill on the reform of the law of easements, covenants and profits à prendre in early 2011.[317] The Law Commissioner responsible for the project has, however, already given an indication of some of the changes to the provisional proposals that are likely to be made in the final report.[318] It appears that the language of 'Land Obligation' will be abandoned, and the familiar term 'covenant' will be retained. The mechanism for the introduction of the new rules (which, as envisaged by the Consultation Paper, will allow the automatic passing of the benefit of both positive and negative covenants) will also be simpler: the covenant will be added to the list of legal interests in section 1 of

---

[310] Para 9.10.

[311] Thus maintaining consistency with the Law Commission's view that the burden of an easement attaches to an estate in the land, rather than to the land itself: above, pp 634, n 3; 723, n 639.

[312] Paras 9.19-9.23. A mortgagee would not be liable unless he has actually taken possession of the land or has appointed a receiver, and a person should not be liable where contrary provision was made in the insrument creating the Land Obligation: para 9.48.

[313] On sub-division of the servient land, the burden would run with each and every part: para 10.26.

[314] For the acquisition of registered title by adverse possessors, see below, pp 1160-4.

[315] Paras 9.34, 9.36. The question of whether a squatter should be bound by a positive or reciprocal payment obligation is left open: para 9.37.

[316] Above, p 764. There are, however, also proposals to reform s 84: above, p 772.

[317] Law Com No 323, *Annual Report 2009-10*, para 2.61.   [318] [2009] Conv 448 (E Cooke).

the Law of Property Act 1925,[319] and the list of registrable interests in section 2 of the Land Registration Act 2002.[320] Equitable covenants will therefore be possible pending the completion of the formality requirements;[321] but there need be no special rules for formalities for the creation of covenants under the new model:[322]

> With covenants enrolled among the list of interests that can exist at law, s 52 of the 1925 Act and s 27 of the 2002 Act tell us, without further amendment, how they can be created; a deed will suffice in unregistered land, but a covenant like an easement will not take effect at law as a benefit appurtenant to registered land until it is registered.

VII COVENANTS AND PLANNING

Tulk v Moxhay[323] was decided in 1848 and the doctrine to which it gave rise was one of the bases for control of land use by private landowners during the suburban expansion of the nineteenth century. Restrictive covenants and (in so far as they are enforceable between freeholders[324]) positive covenants, and covenants in leases, are fundamental to private planning. So, too, are easements.[325] However, these private law rules can serve only the interests of those who own land that can be benefited by the imposition of covenants, and they may even be an inadequate instrument to serve those private interests since the opportunity to impose covenants can be limited, and the enforcement of covenants requires vigilance and determination on the part of the individual landowner affected by an actual or threatened breach. During the twentieth century, it came to be accepted that there is also a place for the *public* control of the use of land, both in the interests of the individual landowners and other occupiers of property in a neighbourhood, and in order to determine, in the public interest, the limits of the appropriate use of land and to provide public enforcement mechanisms. The first planning statute was passed in 1909,[326] though it only applied to 'town' planning, and planning on the fringes of existing towns at that. Planning control, which was still potential rather than actual, later came to be extended more generally over towns, and then over the countryside also.[327] Finally, in the 1940s, the general extent of control became actual instead of potential and the modern planning era opened.[328] Modern planning control is in the hands of local planning authorities under the Town and Country Planning Act 1990, as further refined by the Planning and Compulsory Purchase Act 2004 and the Planning Act 2008.[329]

---

[319] Above, p 123.

[320] Below, p 1074.

[321] Under the doctrine of *Walsh v Lonsdale* (1882) 21 Ch D; above, p 215; below, pp 978, 1012.

[322] Above, n 318, p 465.

[323] (1848) 2 Ph 774, M & B p 942.

[324] Above, p 728.

[325] Above, Ch 18.

[326] Housing, Town Planning, etc Act 1909.

[327] Hence *town and country* planning.

[328] TCP (Interim Development) Act 1943; TCPA 1947.

[329] See Law Com No 11, *Restrictive Covenants* (1967), paras 16–19 and Law Com No 127, *The Law of Positive and Restrictive Covenants* (1984), paras 2.5–2.7.

It is important to notice that these two methods of control, private and public, are cumulative.[330] A purchaser of land must not only satisfy himself about the existence of private covenants that may bind the land that he is buying, but he must also investigate its planning aspect. Specialist works should be consulted on public planning control.[331]

[330] See (1964) 28 Conv (NS) 190 (AR Mellows).
[331] See Encyclopedia of Planning Law and Practice; Telling and Duxbury, Planning Law and Procedure (14th edn, 2009); Moore, A Practical Approach to Planning Law (11th edn, 2010). On the impact of ECHR on planning law, see Rook, Property Law and Human Rights (2001), section 8.10; Allen, Property Law and the Human Rights Act 1998 (2005), ch 7. See also the 17th edn of this book, chs 29 (planning control) and 30 (compulsory purchase).

20

RENTCHARGES[1]

I NATURE OF A RENTCHARGE

A ORIGIN AND HISTORY

We have already seen that a rent payable by a tenant to a landlord is called rent service because of the tenure that exists between the parties, but that it is called a rentcharge if there is no tenure between the creditor and the debtor from whose land it issues.[2] In former days this lack of tenurial interest between the parties meant that the rent owner had no automatic right at law to distrain upon the land of the debtor for the recovery of arrears, and generally speaking, rentcharges, though of considerable antiquity, were regarded as contrary to the policy of the common law, since the debtor was rendered less able to perform the military service due to his overlord, while the rent owner

---

[1] See generally Preston and Newsom, *Restrictive Covenants Affecting Freehold Land* (9th edn, 1998), ch 7; Easton, *Law of Rentcharges* (2nd edn, 1931); Law Com No 68, *Rentcharges* (1975) on which the Rentcharges Act 1977 is based.

[2] Above, pp 269–71.

himself was free from all feudal obligations in respect of the land.[3] It became usual, therefore, for the parties to enter into an express agreement that the creditor should have a power of distress over the debtor's land. A rent supported in this way by a specially reserved power of distress, as distinct from a rent service where such power existed of common right, was called a rentcharge, since the land liable for payment was charged with a distress.[4] We have seen that there is no longer any necessity to charge the land expressly, since the Law of Property Act 1925, re-enacting the Landlord and Tenant Act 1730, and the Conveyancing Act 1881, confers the right of distress upon all rentcharge owners.[5]

A rentcharge is thus an annual sum of money issuing and payable out of land, the due payment of which is secured by a right of distress that is not the result of tenure between the parties but is either expressly reserved or allowed by statute.[6] It is now defined in the Rentcharges Act 1977[7] as:

any annual or other periodic sum charged on or issuing out of land, except

(a) rent reserved by a lease or tenancy, or

(b) any sum by way of interest.

B LEGAL AND EQUITABLE

A legal rentcharge is an incorporeal interest that may be limited for all the estates recognised at common law.[8] Before 1926, therefore, it could be limited to a person for an estate in fee simple, in tail, for life, for years or in remainder, but under the Law of Property Act 1925, which reduced the estates that could be created at law to the fee simple absolute in possession and the term of years absolute,[9] the interest conferred on the rent owner is a legal interest only where it is in possession and either perpetual or for a term of years absolute.[10] Thus, an annual sum of money granted to a widow for life and charged upon the settled lands by a marriage settlement confers an equitable interest. Furthermore, a rentcharge can only be legal if the proper formalities for its creation have been observed.[11]

---

[3] Cruise, *Digest*, Tit xxvii, c, i, ss 1, 7.   [4] Co Litt 144a.

[5] LPA 1925, s 121; above, p 272. S 121 is to be repealed when the Tribunals, Courts and Enforcement Act 2007 is brought into force: above, p 277.   [6] See Co Litt 143b, 147b.

[7] S 1(1). This includes an annual sum known by a name other than rentcharge, eg chief rent (or chief), fee farm rent and ground rent (a confusing name since it usually means rent payable under a long lease).

[8] Cruise, *Digest*, Tit xxviii, c ii, ss 1–3.

[9] LPA 1925, s 1(1); above, p 123.

[10] S 1(1)(b). A rentcharge, provided that it is not limited to take effect upon the determination of some other interest, is 'in possession' notwithstanding that its payment is to commence at some time subsequent to its creation: Law of Property (Entailed Interests) Act 1932, s 2.

[11] Below, pp 784–6.

C RENTCHARGE ON A RENTCHARGE

As the essence of a rentcharge lies in the power of the owner to distrain upon lands, it follows that, strictly speaking, it can issue only out of corporeal hereditaments. A dominant owner, for example, cannot charge a right of way to which he is entitled, since there is nothing on which the rent owner can distrain, though of course the debtor will be liable for the amount he has agreed to pay.[12] For the same reason at common law a rent cannot be reserved out of a rent,[13] and therefore if A, who is entitled to a rentcharge of £50, grants it to B, but reserves to himself thereout a rentcharge of £25, the reservation is void in the sense that the £25 does not constitute a rentcharge properly so called.

But this rule of the common law was in part abrogated by the Law of Property Act 1925, which enacted that a rentcharge or annual sum of money (not being a rent service) may be reserved out of or charged on another rent charge in the same manner as it could have been charged on land.[14] In such a case the ordinary remedies of distress and entry upon the lands are impossible, and therefore it is provided that where the rent is in arrears for 21 days, the owner of the second rent (£25) shall have power to appoint a receiver of the rent (£50) on which it is charged. The receiver is then entitled to acquire the £50 by action, distress or otherwise, and out of this to pay arrears, expenses and his own remuneration.

II EXAMPLES OF RENTCHARGES

Rentcharges have been used in three main situations:

A SALE OF LAND

On the sale of land a vendor, instead of receiving the purchase money in the form of a lump sum, may reserve to himself a legal rentcharge, under which a sum of money is payable annually to himself and his heirs for ever, and, in addition, receive a capital payment. The rentcharge, being legal, binds all subsequent purchasers of the land. This type of transaction occurred mainly in Manchester and other parts of the North West of England, and in the County of Avon, including Bristol, where some 80 per cent of owner-occupied residential property may be subject to rentcharges.[15]

B SECURED FAMILY ANNUITIES

In this situation, a rentcharge is created voluntarily or in consideration of marriage or by way of family settlement for the life of any person (or for any shorter but indefinite

---

12 Co Litt 47a.
13 *Earl of Stafford v Buckley* (1750) 2 Ves Sen 170, 177.
14 LPA 1925, s 122. This occurs very rarely in practice.
15 Law Com No 68, para 16.

period, such as widowhood) or for providing sums for the advancement, maintenance or benefit of any persons. In this case the rentcharge is equitable and if created before 1997 the land on which the payments are secured became settled land under the Settled Land Act 1925,[16] unless it was already settled land or was held upon trust for sale. If such a rentcharge is created after 1996 the land becomes subject to a trust of land under the Trusts of Land and Appointment of Trustees Act 1996.[17]

C POSITIVE COVENANTS

Where, as a result of a property development, there is a distinct grouping of separate freehold houses or where a single building is divided into separate freehold parts,[18] a rentcharge is sometimes used as a conveyancing device to enable the burden of positive covenants to run against the unit holder for the time being. As we have seen, it was held in *Rhone v Stephens*[19] that the burden of positive covenants on the sale of land by a freeholder does not run at common law, nor does it in equity under the doctrine of *Tulk v Moxhay*,[20] which is confined to restrictive covenants. In *Austerberry v Corporation of Oldham*[21] Lindley LJ expressly mentioned the use of the rentcharge for this purpose.

One scheme in common use for smaller developments has been described as follows:[22]

> a rentcharge affecting each unit will be imposed for the benefit of the other units and this rentcharge will be supported by positive covenants to repair, insure, and so on. The purpose of this scheme is not to procure the actual payment of the rentcharge—its amount may be nominal and the rent owners are unlikely to trouble very much whether it is paid or not—but to create a set of positive covenants that are actually designed to preserve the development as a whole but that are directly enforceable because they happen incidentally to support the rentcharge.

The amount of the rentcharge may, however, not be nominal, but considerable, where the object is to provide funds for a management company to look after the maintenance of a large development as a whole.

III RENTCHARGES ACT 1977

The policy of the Rentcharges Act 1977[23] is to abolish existing rentcharges where possible and to prevent their creation in the future. The creation of a rentcharge under the above example A (sale of land) is void after 21 August 1977, and an existing

---

[16] S 1(1)(v), below, p 435. [17] S 2, Sch 1, para 3; s 25(1), Sch 3, para 15(1), (2).

[18] Since 27 September 2004, however, it has been possible to use a commonhold scheme under CLRA 2002 for the registered freehold owners of two or more units of land, for example, in a block of flats or offices; and positive covenants will be enforceable amongst the owners: above, Ch 7.

[19] [1994] AC 310, M & B p 746; above, p 728. [20] (1848) 2 Ph 774, M & B p 754; above, p 732.

[21] (1885) 29 Ch D 750, 783. [22] Law Com No 68, para 49; [1988] Conv 99 (S Bright).

[23] See generally (1977) 127 NLJ 1042 (HW Wilkinson).

rentcharge will be extinguished 60 years after the date of the passing of the Act (ie 22 July 2037) or 60 years after the date on which it first becomes payable, whichever is the later.[24] Such a rentcharge can cause conveyancing difficulties, especially where the land sold is divided in subsequent sales; the amount of the rentcharge may be very small in relation to the property purchased, and the purchaser may feel that 'a liability to pay an annual sum to a former owner who is not necessarily the vendor is repugnant to the concept of freehold ownership.'[25]

Rentcharges under the above examples B (secured family annuities) and C (positive covenants), however, are expressly preserved by the Rentcharges Act,[26] although the conveyancing device of C will become unnecessary if the provisional proposals contained in the Law Commission's Consultation Paper on Easements, Covenants and Profits à Prendre,[27] allowing for the enforcements of positive covenants between freeholders, are implemented. The Act calls C an estate rentcharge and defines it as follows:[28]

a rentcharge created for the purpose—

(a) of making covenants to be performed by the owner of the land affected by the rentcharge enforceable by the rent owner against the owner for the time being of the land; or

(b) of meeting, or contributing towards, the cost of the performance by the rent owner of covenants for the provision of services, the carrying out of maintenance or repairs, the effecting of insurance or the making of any payment by him for the benefit of the land affected by the rentcharge or for the benefit of that and other land.

A rentcharge of more than a nominal amount is not treated as an estate rentcharge unless it represents a reasonable payment for the performance of covenants in (b) of the definition of an estate rentcharge.[29]

Two other kinds of rentcharge are also preserved by the Act:[30]

(i) a rentcharge under any Act of Parliament providing for the creation of rentcharges in connection with the execution of works on land (whether by way of improvements, repairs or otherwise) or the commutation of any obligation to do any such work; and

(ii) a rentcharge by, or in accordance with the requirements of, any order of a court.

Since the year 2037 is sometime in the future and certain kinds of rentcharge may still exist, it is necessary to set out some details of the law apart from the Act.

IV CREATION OF A RENTCHARGE

A rentcharge may be created by instrument inter vivos, by will, or by statute.

---

[24] Rentcharges Act 1977, ss 2(1), 3.   [25] Law Com No 68, para 26.

[26] Rentcharges Act 1977, s 2(3).

[27] Law Com CP No 186 (2008); above, p 774. The Consultation Paper proposes that positive covenants (in the form of new 'Land Obligations') should run in registered land, and that no new estate rentcharges should be created where title to land is registered, but also asks whether it should no longer be possible to create estate rentcharges over unregistered land: para 8.119.

[28] Rentcharges Act 1977, s 2(4).   [29] Ibid, s 2(5).   [30] Ibid, s 2(3).

A BY INSTRUMENT INTER VIVOS

At common law a rentcharge, if created inter vivos, must be granted by deed.[31] But the equitable principle underlying the doctrine of *Walsh v Lonsdale* applies here just as it does in the case of a contract to grant a term of years[32] or an easement, so that, where one person has made a contract to grant a rentcharge to another, an equitable rentcharge may be created.[33]

The quantum of the interest in a rentcharge depends upon the words of limitation that are inserted in the deed of grant, and the rule is that such words are construed in exactly the same way as in a grant of corporeal hereditaments. Thus before 1926, in order to pass a perpetual rentcharge it was necessary to convey the rent to the grantee *and his heirs*, or to the grantee *in fee simple*, but the changes that were effected by the Law of Property Act 1925 in regard to words of limitation sufficient to pass a fee simple estate in land[34] apply to rentcharges, and at the present day the effect of a grant that contains no technical words of limitation is to give the grantee a perpetual rentcharge, or if that is impossible owing to the grantor only having a smaller estate, then to give him a rentcharge for the whole interest possessed by the grantor. This rule is displaced, however, if a contrary intention is shown in the conveyance, and in such a case the size of the grantee's interest will depend upon the intention of the parties.[35]

B BY WILL

A rentcharge may be validly created by will, and whether it is or not depends upon the intention of the testator. If he directs that an annual sum shall be paid to a donee and uses words that show that the money is to be a charge upon the land and not upon his personal property, it is a rentcharge as distinct from an annuity, such as where he devises land to A:

> subject to and charged and chargeable with the payment of £100 a year to B for twenty-five years.[36]

Section 28 of the Wills Act 1837[37] applies only to the transfer of an existing rentcharge, and not to the creation of a new one. Thus, if a rentcharge is created by will without any words of limitation, the devisee can take it only for life.[38]

---

[31] Co Litt 169a; *Hewlins v Shippam* (1826) 5 B & C 221, 229.   [32] Above, pp 215 ff; below, p 978.

[33] *Jackson v Lever* (1792) 3 Bro CC 605. A contract to grant a rentcharge must comply with the formalities required for a contract for the disposition of an interest in land: below, Ch 24.

[34] LPA 1925, s 60; above, p 156.

[35] Ibid, s 60(1). See Megarry and Wade, *Law of Real Property* (5th edn, 1984), p 823 for an argument that s 60 may not apply to the creation of rentcharges by deed.

[36] *Ramsay v Thorngate* (1849) 16 Sim 575.

[37] Above, p 156.   [38] *Nichols v Hawkes* (1853) 10 Hare 342.

C BY STATUTE

There are two distinct series of enactments under which an owner of land may carry out certain improvements and arrange that the cost shall be charged upon the land and reimbursed in full, together with interest, by a definite number of annual payments. The chief statute of the first class is the Improvement of Land Act 1864, which allows 'landowners' (anyone except a lessee at a rack rent[39] who is in actual possession of the rents and profits) to borrow money for improvements from certain private land improvement companies.

Money may not be borrowed in this way for every improvement, but only for those specified in the Settled Land Act 1925.[40] No rentcharge can be imposed upon the land until the Secretary of State for Environment, Food and Rural Affairs[41] has, on the application of the landowner, satisfied himself that the suggested improvement will permanently increase the yearly value of the land to an extent greater than the annual rentcharge that is contemplated.[42]

If satisfied on this point the Secretary of State issues a provisional order that specifies the sum to be charged upon the land, the rate of interest and the number of years within which it must be paid off. The rate of interest is at the discretion of the Secretary of State,[43] but the period for payments must not exceed 40 years.[44] After the improvements are completed the Secretary of State issues an absolute order imposing the annual sum as a rentcharge upon the fee simple, and this has priority over all existing and future incumbrances affecting the land with the certain specified exceptions.[45] The remedies for its recovery are the same as in the case of other rentcharges,[46] except that the landowner is not personally liable.

The second class of statute is represented by the Settled Land Act 1925, which allows a limited owner to raise money for the purpose of carrying out permanent improvements on the settled land. Prior to 1 January 1926, there was an important difference between the operation of the Improvement of Land Acts and that of the Settled Land Acts in this matter, for, while under the former a tenant for life could raise new money for the purpose, all that the Settled Land Acts did was to authorise the expenditure upon improvements of capital money that happened to be in the hands of the trustees. A tenant for life could not raise new money by mortgage under

---

[39] Ie the full yearly value of the land.

[40] Above, p 447. The improvements specified in the 1864 Act are all covered by those set out in SLA 1925, and the latter are expressly brought within the operation of the earlier Act.

[41] Or, in Wales, the National Assembly for Wales: SI 1999 No 672, art 2, Sch 1.

[42] Improvement of Land Act 1864, s 25. There are certain improvements that may be allowed although they will not permanently increase the yearly value of the land, ie construction of waterworks for the use of residents on the estate (40 & 41 Vict c 31, s 5); erection of mansion house under Limited Owners Residences Acts 1870, 1871; planting, under Improvement of Land Act 1864, s 15; erection or improvement of farmhouse or cottage for use of workers on the land, under Agricultural Credits Act 1923, s 3(3).

[43] Agricultural Credits Act 1923, s 3(1). [44] Improvement of Land Act 1899, s 1(1).

[45] Improvement of Land Act 1864, s 59. [46] Below.

the Settled Land Acts for carrying out improvements, but this power, as we have seen, was expressly conferred upon him by the Settled Land Act 1925.[47]

D REGISTERED LAND

The express grant over a registered estate of a rentcharge in possession that is either perpetual or for a term of years absolute—that is a rentcharge that can exist at law under the Law of Property Act 1925[48]—is a registrable disposition.[49] Such a rentcharge does not therefore take effect at law, but is only equitable, until the registration requirements are met.[50] A legal rentcharge, other than one created for a term not exceeding seven years, is an independently registrable legal interest;[51] the grantee must be entered in the register as the proprietor of the interest, and a notice in respect of the interest created must be entered in the register.[52] In the case of a rentcharge for a term not exceeding seven years, a notice must be entered in the register of the estate affected.[53]

V REMEDIES FOR THE RECOVERY OF A RENTCHARGE

The following remedies are available to a rentcharge owner:

A DISTRESS

A power to distrain upon the land, out of which the rent issues, is, as we have seen, an implicit incident of a rentcharge, though formerly it had to be specifically reserved. Even when the Landlord and Tenant Act 1730 had conferred the power of distress on rent owners, it was the usual practice to insert an express provision to the same effect in all instruments creating rentcharges, but this ceased to be the practice in the case of instruments coming into effect after 31 December 1881. The Conveyancing Act of that year provided that where any rent (not incident to the relationship of landlord and tenant) is in arrears for 21 days, the person entitled to receive it may enter into and distrain upon the land charged or any part thereof, and dispose of any distrainable

---

[47] SLA 1925, s 71(1)(ii); above, p 447.   [48] S 1(2)(b); above, p 124.
[49] LRA 2002, s 27(2)(e).   [50] Ibid, s 27(1).
[51] Cf ibid, s 3(1)(b), (3) (voluntary registration of existing unregistered legal rentcharges except those for a term of which more than seven years are unexpired). See also ibid, s 5(2)(b) (Lord Chancellor's power to make registration compulsory); below, p 1072.
[52] Ibid, Sch 2, para 6.   [53] Ibid, Sch 2, para 7.

objects according to the general law.[54] This remedy is now re-enacted by the Law of Property Act 1925.[55]

B ENTRY UPON THE LAND CHARGED

The Law of Property Act 1925[56] provides that, when a rentcharge is in arrears for 40 days, even though no legal demand has been made for payment, the owner may enter into possession of and hold the land charged or any part thereof, and take the income thereof, until all arrears and costs and expenses occasioned by the non-payment of the rent are satisfied. The Act does not give the owner of the rent a power of entry that will cause a forfeiture of the debtor's interest in the land, as is usual between landlord and tenant, but such a power may be, and generally is, reserved in the instrument of creation.

As we have seen, neither type of power, whether to hold the land until payment or to determine the debtor's interest, is subject to the rule against perpetuities.[57]

C LEASE TO TRUSTEES

When a rentcharge is in arrears for 40 days, the person entitled to payment, whether taking possession or not, may by deed lease the whole or part of the land to a trustee for a term of years, with or without impeachment of waste, on trust to raise and pay the rent together with all arrears, costs and expenses.[58] The trustee may adopt any reasonable means[59] to raise the money, such as by the mortgage, assignment or sub-lease of the term vested in him, or by appropriating the income of the land, but he cannot create a *legal* mortgage unless the rentcharge itself is held for a legal estate.

The above three remedies are not enforceable if a contrary intention is expressed in the instrument under which the annual sum arises,[60] and they are subject to the provisions of such instrument. Moreover, when a rentcharge is charged on another rentcharge, the above remedies are excluded and replaced by a right in the rent owner to appoint a receiver of the annual sum charged whenever payment is in arrears for 21 days.[61]

---

[54] S 44. See above, p 272.

[55] S 121(2). This subsection is to be repealed when the Tribunals, Courts and Enforcement Act 2007 is brought into force and the common law remedy of distress is abolished: above, p 277.

[56] S. 121(3).

[57] For instruments taking effect before 6 April 2010 this was provided by LPA 1925, s 121(6), above, p 554 (right to enter for purpose of distraint or leasing) and PAA 1964, s 11(1), above, p 574 (right to effect forfeiture). S 121(6) was repealed by PAA 2009 in relation to instruments taking effect after 5 April 2010, since such rights of entry are in any event no longer within the rule under the 2009 Act: above, p 575.

[58] LPA 1925 s 121(4).   [59] Ibid.

[60] Ibid, s 121(5).   [61] Ibid, s 122; above, p 781.

D ACTION FOR PAYMENT

(1) Action of Debt

It is well settled that an action of debt for the recovery of arrears lies against the *terre tenant*[62] for the time being of the whole or part only of the land charged,[63] provided that he holds a freehold as distinct from a leasehold interest.[64] It is no defence that the profits of the land do not equal in amount the value of the rentcharge. Thus in *Pertwee v Townsend*:[65]

> Lands were charged with the payment of a rentcharge of £80 a year. A certain portion of these lands was acquired by the defendant's predecessor in title, who released the rest of the land from the burden of the charge and imposed it upon the portion so acquired. At the time of the action for the recovery of £80, being one year's arrears, the defendant was able to show that the annual profits of the portion charged, of which he was tenant for life, amounted only to £7.5s, but nevertheless he was held personally liable for the whole £80.

Collins J said:[66]

> The defendant holds the land subject to a charge, and he cannot keep the land and refuse to pay the charge. If he does refuse, the remedy against him is personal for the amount of the charge itself.

Although the right to sue runs with the rentcharge and the liability to be sued runs with the land, the benefit of a covenant to pay a rentcharge does not run with the rentcharge so as to entitle an assignee to maintain an action *on the covenant* against the covenantor or his assignee.[67] Thus:

> where A granted a fee simple to B on the terms that A his heirs and assigns should be entitled to a rent issuing out of the land, and the conveyance contained a covenant by B to pay the rent to A his heirs and assigns, it was held that X, to whom A had demised the rent for 1,000 years, could not sue B on the covenant.[68]

The technical nature of this rule was demonstrated by Lawrence LJ:[69]

> Whatever may be the foundation of the rule, and whether it rests on the broader principle that (except as between lessor and lessee) no covenant can run with an incorporeal hereditament, or whether it rests on the narrower principle that a covenant to pay a rentcharge is a collateral covenant or a covenant in gross that does not touch or concern the rentcharge, or whether it rests on no principle and is merely arbitrary, I am of opinion that it is too firmly established to be disturbed by this court.

---

[62] A *terre tenant* is the person who has the actual possession or occupation of land.
[63] *Thomas v Sylvester* (1873) LR 8 QB 368.
[64] *Re Herbage Rents, Greenwich* [1896] 2 Ch 811. Distress, however, may be levied on the premises.
[65] [1896] 2 QB 129.   [66] Ibid, 134.   [67] *Grant v Edmondson* [1931] 1 Ch 1.
[68] *Milnes v Branch* (1816) 5 M & S 411.
[69] *Grant v Edmondson* [1931] 1 Ch 1, 26; (1931) 47 LQR 380 (W Strachan).

(2) Apportionment

A purchaser of any part of land that is burdened by a rentcharge is liable for the whole of the rent, unless there has been an apportionment. This may be legal where the owner of the rentcharge has formally severed the rent so as to charge part only of it on the land sold, or so as to exonerate the land from the rent. If, however, the owner of the rentcharge is not a party to the severance, the apportionment is equitable, and he is not bound by it. The person affected by the rentcharge remains liable to him for the whole of the rent, with a right of contribution from the other owners of the land.[70]

Under the Rentcharges Act 1977,[71] subject to small exceptions, a rentcharge may be legally apportioned by the Secretary of State for Environment, Food and Rural Affairs[72] on the application of any landowner whose land is affected by it. The Secretary of State may make an order, with or without conditions, apportioning the rentcharge between the rentpayer's land and the remaining land affected by the rentcharge. The order is made after a draft apportionment order is served on the person who appears to be the rent owner or his agent, and, subject to their rights of appeal to the Upper Tribunal,[73] the order takes effect after 28 days from the date on which it was made. The effect of the order is to release the applicant's land from any part of the rentcharge not apportioned to it and to release the remaining land from such part (if any) of the rentcharge as is apportioned to the applicant's land.[74]

The Law of Property Act 1925 provides[75] that, where equitable apportionment has been made in a conveyance for valuable consideration, then the apportionment, without prejudice to the rights of the rent owner, shall be binding between the grantor and the grantee under the conveyance and their respective successors in title. If the owner of part of the land fails to pay the rentcharge in accordance with the agreement or fails to perform some covenant, and the owner of the other part is in consequence obliged to pay the charges or damages, the latter may distrain upon the land of the former and may also take the income thereof until he has been satisfied.[76]

---

[70] For the problems that arise, see Law Com No 68, paras 12–15, 29–30. In 1982 a consultation paper proposed new arrangements for the apportionment and redemption of rentcharge and ground rents under which they would be primarily operated by the parties themselves: Law Com No 119, Annual Report 1981–1982 (1983), para 2.105.

[71] Ss 4–7. Application for apportionment may also be made under LTA 1927, s 20, as amended by Rentcharges Act 1977, s 17(1), Sch 1, para 3.

[72] Or, in Wales, the National Assembly for Wales: SI 1999 No 672, art 2, Sch 1.

[73] Formerly the Lands Tribunal: Rentcharges Act 1977, s 6, amended by Transfer of Tribunal Functions (Lands Tribunal and Miscellaneous Amendments) Order 2009 (SI 2009 No 1307), Sch 1.

[74] Rentcharges Act 1977, s 7(4).   [75] S 190.

[76] S 190(2); Whitham v Bullock [1939] 2 KB 81. S 190(2) is to be repealed when the Tribunals, Courts and Enforcement Act 2007 is brought into force and the common law remedy of distress is abolished: above, p 277.

VI EXTINCTION OF A RENTCHARGE

There are several ways in which a rentcharge may be extinguished and the land freed from liability.

A RELEASE

If the rent owner releases the whole of the land charged from any further liability to pay, the rent is extinguished. Indeed, on the somewhat questionable ground that a rent, being entire and issuing out of every part of the land, cannot be thrown upon one particular part not apportioned between several parts, the old rule was that a release of *part* of the land discharged the whole land and produced a total extinguishment of the rent.[77] But the Law of Property Act 1925,[78] re-enacting the Law of Property (Amendment) Act 1859, provides that the release from a rentcharge of part of the lands charged shall not extinguish the whole rentcharge, but shall only render it unenforceable against the part released. This provision, however, is not to prejudice the rights of the persons who are interested in the unreleased part of the lands unless they concur in or confirm the release. The effect of this enactment is that where the owner of land that is subject to a rentcharge sells the land in separate portions to different persons, and only one portion is released from the charge by the rent owner, the purchaser of the unreleased portions will be liable for the whole rent if they concur in the release, but will be liable only for an apportioned part if they do not concur.[79]

B MERGER

A rentcharge may also be extinguished by merger.[80] The rigid rule of common law is that, whenever a lesser and a greater estate in the same lands become united in one person in his own right, the lesser estate is merged in the greater and extinguished without regard to the intention of the parties. As we shall see later, however, the equitable view that no merger occurs if it is contrary to the intention of the party in whom the two estates vest now obtains in all courts,[81] and this principle applies to the merger of a rentcharge. Thus, if the absolute owner of a rentcharge also becomes absolute owner in his own right of the land charged, either by grant or by devise, there is prima facie a merger of the rent in the estate because there is no obvious advantage in keeping both the interests alive.[82] But, on the other hand, if the person who is responsible for the rent mortgages the land charged to the rent owner, there is no merger, since the two interests do not unite in one person in the same right.

---

[77] Co Litt 147b.   [78] S 70.   [79] *Booth v Smith* (1884) 14 QBD 318.

[80] As to merger generally, see *Forbes v Moffatt* (1811) 8 Ves 384; Tudor, *Leading Cases on Real Property* (4th edn, 1898), p 244; below, Ch 29.

[81] Below, pp 1124–5.   [82] *Freeman v Edwards* (1848) 2 Exch 732.

C LAPSE OF TIME

The usual provisions relating to limitation periods and adverse possession generally apply to rentcharges.[83]

In unregistered land, if a rentcharge is not paid for 12 years,[84] and no sufficient acknowledgment of the owner's title is made, the rentcharge is extinguished under the Limitation Act 1980.[85] If it is wrongly paid to a third party, after 12 years from the last receipt of rent by the rightful owner the latter's title to the rentcharge is extinguished and the third party acquires a new title to it by adverse possession.

In registered land, as in all cases of adverse possession under the new regime introduced by the Land Registration Act 2002,[86] there is no automatic extinction of the title to a rentcharge by non-payment or by wrongful payment to a third party, however long the period may be. In the case of non-payment for a period of 10 years ending with the date of the application,[87] the proprietor of the land over which the rentcharge exists may apply to the registrar to close the registered title of the rentcharge; and where a third party has been in adverse possession of the rentcharge, by virtue of receipt of the rent under it, for a period of 10 years he may apply to be registered as the proprietor of the registered rentcharge.[88] But notice is then given to the registered proprietor of the rentcharge,[89] who may resist the claim, and has two years to regularise his position. Only after that period does the claimant, if then still in adverse possession, have the right[90] to closure of the title in the case of non-payment,[91] or to registration of himself as proprietor in the case of the third party.[92]

D STATUTE

Lastly, under the Rentcharges Act 1977,[93] the owner of any land affected by a rentcharge may apply to the Secretary of State for Environment, Food and Rural Affairs[94] for a redemption certificate that certifies that the rentcharge has been redeemed.[95] The certificate is issued when the redemption price certified by the Secretary of State has

---

[83] Below, Ch 29. In the case of registered land, the provisions of LRA 2002, Sch 6 are modified to apply to rentcharges by LRR 2003, r 191, Sch 8.

[84] Time runs from the last receipt of rent by the rightful owner: Limitation Act 1980, s 38(8). For the implications of this, see below, p 1140.

[85] Limitation Act 1980, ss 15(1), 38(1); *Shaw v Crompton* [1910] 2 KB 370.   [86] Below, pp 1140 ff.

[87] The rentcharge need not have been registered throughout the whole period of adverse possession: LRA 2002, Sch 6, para 1(3), as substituted by LRR 2003, r 191, Sch 8.

[88] LRA 2002, Sch 6, para 1(1), as substituted by LRR 2003, r 191, Sch 8.   [89] Ibid, Sch 6, para 2.

[90] On making a further application: ibid, para 6.

[91] LRR 2003, r 192. If the registered title also comprises other rentcharges, the Registrar must cancel the particular rentcharge, rather than closing the whole title: ibid, r 192(2).

[92] LRA 2002, Sch 6, para 7, as substituted by LRR 2003, r 191, Sch 8.

[93] Replacing the similar but not identical procedure under LPA 1925, s 191.

[94] Or, in Wales, the National Assembly for Wales: SI 1999 No 672, art 2, Sch 1.

[95] Rentcharges Act 1977, s 8(1); Rentcharges Regulations 1978 (SI 1978 No. 16).

been paid to the rent owner or into court.[96] The price is calculated in accordance with a formula based on the length of time that the rentcharge has still to run.[97] The effect of the certificate is to release the applicant's land from the rentcharge, but it does not affect the rent owner's rights and remedies to recover previous arrears.[98]

This statutory method of redemption does not apply to rentcharges that can still be created, nor to variable rentcharges.[99] It does not, therefore, apply to estate rentcharges,[100] whose attractiveness is thereby enhanced; they had been liable to redemption under the former procedure of the Law of Property Act 1925 for statutory discharge.

---

[96] Ibid, s 9(5).   [97] Ibid, s 10(1).   [98] Ibid, s 10(3).
[99] Ibid, s 8(4), (5). A rentcharge is variable if the amount of the rentcharge will, or may, vary in accordance with the provisions of the instrument under which it is payable: s 8(5).
[100] Above, p 783.

21

MORTGAGES[1]

Summary

I INTRODUCTION

A mortgage is a conveyance or other disposition of an interest in property designed to secure the payment of money or the discharge of some other obligation.[2] The party who conveys the property by way of security is called the *mortgagor*, the lender who obtains an interest in the property is called the *mortgagee*, and the debt for which the security is created is called the mortgage debt. The mortgagee, since he is the grantee of a proprietary interest, acquires a real, not merely a personal, security that prevails

---

[1] See generally Coote, *Law of Mortgages* (9th edn, 1927); Cousins, *Law of Mortgages* (3rd edn, 2010); Fairest, *Mortgages* (2nd edn, 1980); Fisher and Lightwood, *Law of Mortgage* (13th edn, 2010), Waldock, *Law of Mortgages* (2nd edn, 1950); Snell, Part VII; M & B ch 10; (1978) 94 LQR 571 (P Jackson); Council of Mortgage Lenders, *Lenders' Handbook* (revised from time to time: the up-to-date version is available on the CML web site, www.cml.org.uk). The Code of Mortgage Lending Practice, a voluntary code followed by lenders (from 1 July 1997) and mortgage intermediaries (from 31 April 1998) in their relations with personal customers in the United Kingdom, ceased to apply from 31 October 2004, and was superseded by the Mortgages: Conduct of Business requirements published by the Financial Services Authority as statutory regulator of the mortgage industry; below, n 17. See also American Law Institute, *Restatement of the Law, Property 3d, Mortgages* (1997).

[2] See *Santley v Wilde* [1899] 2 Ch 474 (Lindley MR): 'A mortgage is a conveyance of land or an assignment of chattels as a security for the payment of a debt or the discharge of some other obligation for which it is given.'

against the general body of creditors in the event of the mortgagor's bankruptcy. He is not only a creditor of the mortgagor; he is a secured creditor. As long as the mortgaged property remains worth as much as the debt, the mortgagee will receive payment in full; but if it falls in value and becomes worth less than the debt,[3] the mortgagee will only be a secured creditor to the extent of its value, and he must prove in the mortgagor's bankruptcy with the unsecured creditors for the remainder of the debt.

In our present-day society the purchase of a dwelling-house by an individual is a common transaction, and inseparable from the purchase is the mortgage of that house to a bank, building society or other lender. The political economist refers to a property-owning democracy, and, with more particularity, Lord Diplock referred to:[4]

a real-property-mortgaged-to-a-building-society-owning democracy.

There may be other reasons why a loan of money is required, such as where a borrower calculates that he can make more money from the use of borrowed money than the loan will cost him in interest. His capital may be locked up in his business, and he may need a loan in order to expand it.[5] Or a house owner may wish to raise money for a particular project, such as home improvements; or to provide capital or income to spend during retirement. Very significant increases in property values in recent decades have made it particularly attractive for home owners to release capital in this way; several banks and building societies now offer mortgages in the context of 'equity release schemes'.[6]

The mortgage industry is big business. Building societies, banks, insurance companies and local authorities are all substantial lenders of money on mortgage. Until the mid-1990s the building societies[7] were the single most significant sector

---

[3] Commonly known as 'negative equity'. For the scale of negative equity in the residential housing sector in the recession that began in 2008, see Office for National Statistics, *Social Trends 40* (2010), p 151.

[4] *Pettitt v Pettitt* [1970] AC 777, 824. During the period 1971 to 2007 the number of dwellings in Great Britain increased by 38 per cent, from 18.8 million to 25.9 million: Office for National Statistics, *Social Trends 40* (2010), p 140. Between 1971 and 2007 home ownership increased from 49 per cent to 69 per cent, with most of the increase occurring in the 1980s: Office for National Statistics, *Living in Britain, No 31* (2004), p 7; and in 2007 31 per cent of households owned their property outright; 40 per cent owned it on mortgage; 19 per cent rented from the social sector and 9 per cent rented privately: Office for National Statistics, *Social Trends 39* (2009), p 146. For the idea that there should be a *Eurohypothec*—a common mortgage for Europe—see [2005] Conv 32 (S Nasarre-Aznar).

[5] The loan is usually made to the company, but the lender may also insist on a personal guarantee from its directors secured by a charge on their own property. For problems that can arise in practice where a jointly-owned home is mortgaged to support a business loan to only one of the joint owners, see *Royal Bank of Scotland plc v Etridge (No 2)* [2001] UKHL 44, [2002] 2 AC 773, M & B p 902, below, p 830.

[6] Eg the provision of a capital sum (often up to 50 per cent of the market value of the home) or a regular income payment, secured on a 'lifetime mortgage' intended to be called in only on the death of the borrower, thus giving the borrower the freedom to release some of the capital value of his major asset during his lifetime, at the expense of those who would otherwise inherit on his death. See *Unlocking the value of your home—a guide to equity release* in the Consumer Information section of the Council of Mortgage Lenders' web site: www.cml.org.uk.

[7] Building societies have also extended the range of their own activities under reforms introduced by Building Societies Act 1986, as amended by Building Societies Act 1997. A Society may now lend for all forms of housing, rented as well as owner-occupied and, with a few exceptions, may carry on any type of business within the terms of its memorandum. See generally Wurtzburg and Mills, *Building Society Law*; Cousins, *The Law of Mortgages*, ch 17; Fisher and Lightwood, paras 22.60–22.66. Building Societies Act 1986

providing residential mortgages,[8] but thereafter some of the largest societies converted into banks, or were taken over by banks.[9] The Bank of England publishes monthly statistics on lending; these show, for example, that the gross lending secured on dwellings during 2004 was £291,224 million, including lending of £202,756 million by banks, and £46,864 million by building societies;[10] but after the downturn in the housing market during the recession that began in 2008, gross lending by banks in 2009 was £118,561 million, and by building societies was £18,534 million.[11]

When a borrower falls into arrears with his payments, a bank or a building society does all it can to avoid repossession, but if it has to take action to enforce the security, difficult social questions arise.[12] The mortgagor has given as security, not an investment, but his home. And a mortgagor who has defaulted with one lender will have difficulty in borrowing money from another.

The law of mortgages that grew up in the eighteenth and nineteenth centuries has had to be adapted to meet twentieth century circumstances:

> Traditionally, Courts of Equity have looked upon a mortgage transaction as one in which the terms were likely to be dictated by the mortgagee. In early days the mortgagor was at a disadvantage in that he was in need of money and must take it on the mortgagee's terms; it was a lender's market. And, while the law followed the maxim 'caveat emptor' in the affairs of merchants and trade, equity not surprisingly took a different view in the case of

established the Building Societies Commission as the industry regulator. Financial Services and Markets Act 2000, s 336 and SI 2001 No 2617 substituted the Financial Services Authority as regulator. In 2010 the Government proposed that the Financial Services Authority be abolished and replaced by a new Prudent Regulation Authority, as a subsidiary of the Bank of England, which would supervise individual firms, and a consumer protection and markets authority, to be called the Financial Conduct Authority to act as a single integrated regulator focussed on conduct in financial markets. Legislation is expected during 2011, with the new regulatory framework in place by the end of 2012; for developments, see www.hm-treasury.gov.uk.

[8] In 1990 building societies collectively took 75 per cent of the new mortgage market: Annual Report of the Building Societies' Commission 1990–1991, para 2.5; M & B (6th edn, 1992), p 713.

[9] Between 1995 and 1997 seven building societies converted to banks, or were taken over by banks; most significantly, in 1997 five of the eight largest societies converted, accounting for around 60 per cent of the total assets of the sector: see the notes to FSA Building Society Statistics 2007.

[10] Bank of England Monetary and Financial Statistics, August 2005, Table A5.10.

[11] Bank of England Monetary and Financial Statistics, November 2010, Table A5.3. Separate data for banks and building societies have been discontinued from January 2010 onwards.

[12] As interest rates rose during the late 1980s and early 1990s, repayments became increasingly difficult, and arrears and repossessions increased. However, largely owing to lower interest rates, arrears and repossessions later fell. At its peak in 1992, the number of loans in arrears by six to 12 months was 205,000. By 2002 this had fallen to 34,000, and the number of homes repossessed had fallen (from a peak of over 75,000) to 12,000: Office for National Statistics, *Social Trends 34* (2004), p 164. The number of repossessions increased again from 2004 onwards, to 40,000 by 2008, and were forecast by the Council of Mortgage Lenders to rise to 65,000 in 2009 reflecting the impact of the recession that began in 2008: Office for National Statistics, *Social Trends 40* (2010), p 153. In 2009 the Government established two schemes to support homeowners in mortgage arrears: a Homeowners Mortgage Support Scheme, designed to enable households that experience a significant and temporary loss of income as a result of the economic downturn to defer a proportion of the interest payments on their mortgage for up to two years; the Government will guarantee the deferred interest payments in return for the banks' participation in the scheme; and a Mortgage Rescue Scheme under which a household with someone with priority need may obtain advice from the local authority, as well as possible support from a housing association through a shared equity loan or a Government 'mortgage to rent'.

mortgages. The fact that mortgagors were, in the early days, often members of great families and mortgagees were professional money lenders no doubt contributed to some extent to the development. A consideration of the changed position of borrowers and lenders in the capitalist society of the present day will suggest that the old cases should be accepted with some reserve. The cases on this subject show a continual struggle between the principle of binding precedent and the requirements of a changing society; they can only be understood with this in mind. Those which were decided about the turn of the twentieth century do not create the principle they apply. That litigation was a challenge to the validity of the principle laid down in earlier centuries, but generally it succeeded only in reaffirming the old principles; it was not until 1914[13] that substantial progress was made.[14]

The problem at the present day is the extent to which these old rules still hold good. A modern mortgage of land is very commonly, as already discussed, a transaction between a house-buyer and an institutional lender such as a bank or building society; or it may form part of a development project embarked upon by property financiers. In either case the historical concerns of the Courts of Equity hardly find a place in the modern mortgage market. Although there is some statutory protection peculiar to consumers,[15] the terms of mortgages are generally dictated by the market, with significant competition amongst the numerous lenders who seek business from domestic or commercial borrowers. The rate of interest will be set by institutional lenders by reference to the prevailing financial market, and according to the other terms of the mortgage (including the length of the term, and the ratio of the loan to the value of the security). The mortgage may be an instalment, or repayment, mortgage (where the capital is repaid over the life of the mortgage, along with interest on the outstanding balance) or interest-only, or endowment, mortgage (where the capital is paid off at the end of the term, generally timed to coincide with the maturity of a separate investment contract); and the interest may be fixed (either for a particular period or, less commonly, throughout the life of the loan) or variable.[16] Apart from generally having a choice of terms from different mortgage providers in the market, the individual borrower is also protected from unfair pressure by the high standards set by institutional lenders as well as by the regulation of the mortgage industry[17]—and

---

[13] *Kreglinger v New Patagonia Meat and Cold Storage Co Ltd* [1914] AC 25, M & B p 890; below, p 824.

[14] M & B p 852.

[15] See esp CCA 1974, ss 140A-140C, inserted by CCA 2006, ss 19-21, below, pp 827 ff, giving the court a wide power to make orders in connection with credit agreements (including consumer mortgage agreements but not land morgages that are regulated under Financial Services and Markets Act 2000) where the relationship between the creditor and debtor arising out of the agreement is 'unfair'; Unfair Terms in Consumer Contracts Regulations 1999 (SI 1999 No 3159), below, p 828; AJA 1970, below, p 848, giving the court power to restrict the mortgagee's right to possession of dwelling-house.

[16] Office for National Statistics, *Social Trends 34* (2004), pp 162–3. The Bank of England produces statistics giving the average quoted household interest rates for different types of mortgage.

[17] The Financial Services Authority (FSA) is the regulator responsible for the authorisation and regulation of mortgage lending and mortgage advice business in the UK under Financial Services and Markets Act 2000. For proposals to replace the FSA by the end of 2012, see above, n 7. A regulated mortgage contract is a loan to an individual or trustees, secured by a first legal mortgage on land of which at least 40 per cent of that land is used, or is intended to be used, as or in connection with a dwelling by the borrower (or, in

by other statutory protections,[18] the general law of contract[19] and the criminal law,[20] which apply equally, of course, to protect commercial borrowers.

II CREATION OF MORTGAGES

A THE MODERN LAW IN HISTORICAL PERSPECTIVE

If we are to understand the methods of creating mortgages in the modern law, it is first necessary to appreciate something of their history. The nature of a mortgage in the twenty-first century follows from radical changes that were made in the twentieth century to the methods of mortgaging land; and those changes can themselves be understood only by reference to the earlier law.

(1) History of Mortgages before 1926[21]

(a) Mortgages of freehold

(1) At common law

The developed law of mortgages is the joint product of common law, equity and statute. In the earliest days of the common law a mortgage was a mere pledge, which took one of two forms. It might be agreed that the lender should enter into possession of the land, and should take the rents and profits in discharge of both the principal

the case of credit provided to trustees, by an individual who is a beneficiary of the trust, or by a related person): Financial Services and Markets Act 2000 (Regulated Activities) Order 2001 (SI 2001 No 544), art 61(3) as substituted by SI 2001 No 3544, art 8, and amended by SI 2006, No 2383, art 17. This includes business loans to customers under a regulated mortgage contract. The detailed provisions for regulation are set out in the FSA's *Mortgages and Home Finance: Conduct of Business sourcebook* (MCOB), which can be viewed on the FSA web site: www.fsa.gov.uk. Regulation of Financial Services (Land Transactions) Act 2005 amended Financial Services and Markets Act 2000 to bring within the regulatory framework other financial arrangements involving land, and this was designed to include both home reversion plans (a form of equity release product: above, n 6) and home purchase plans (Islamic mortgages); [2005] 34 EG 107 (M Rutter). For the principles of Islamic banking and finance, see Schoon, *Islamic Banking and Finance* (2009); Land Registry Practice Guide 69, *Islamic Financing* (2010). As interest is contrary to Islamic law, a 'home purchase plan' is in essence a sale and lease arrangement: FSA Consultation Paper 06/8, *Regulation of Home Reversion and Home Purchase Plans* (April 2006). At the beginning of 2011 Parliament had not yet approved the proposed new regulatory regime.

18 CCA 1974, amended by CCA 2006, provides protection to consumer mortgagors where the mortgage is not within other regulatory frameworks: below pp 826–8.

19 Below, p 829.

20 On mortgage fraud, see Clarke, *Mortgage Fraud* (1991); Osborn, *Mortgage Fraud* (1995). Theft (Amendment) Act 1996 created two new offences by inserting into the Theft Act 1968, ss 15A (obtaining a money transfer by deception) and 24A (dishonestly retaining a wrongful credit). See Law Com No 243, *Offences of Dishonesty: Money Transfers* (1996). S 15A was repealed and replaced by Fraud Act 2006.

21 Holdsworth, *A History of English Law*, vol iii, p 128; Plucknett, *Concise History of the Common Law* (5th edn, 1956), pp 603–9; Simpson, *A History of the Land Law* (2nd edn, 1986), pp 141–3, 242–7. See also *Modern Studies in Property Law*, vol 4 (2007), 73 (G Watt).

and the interest on the loan. This was called a *vivum vadium*, or living pledge, since it automatically and by its own force discharged the entire debt. But, on the other hand, the arrangement might be that the lender should take the rents and profits of the land in discharge of the interest only, in which case the transaction was called a *mortuum vadium*, a dead pledge,[22] since it did not effect the gradual extinction of the debt.

By the time of Littleton (1402–81), however, a mortgage had become a species of estate upon condition, created by a feoffment[23] defeasible upon condition subsequent. The land was conveyed in fee simple to the mortgagee on condition that if the loan was repaid upon the day that had been fixed by agreement, the conveyance should be defeated, and the mortgagor be free to re-enter. If repayment was not made on the exact date fixed, then the estate of the mortgagee became absolute, and the mortgagor's interest in the land was extinguished. In the words of Littleton:

> If a feoffment be made upon such condition, that if the feoffor pay to the feoffee at a certain day etc 40 pounds of money, that then the feoffor may re-enter, etc, in this case the feoffee is called tenant in mortgage, which is as much to say in French as mortgage, and in Latin *mortuum vadium*. And it seemeth that the cause why it is called mortgage is, for that it is doubtful whether the feoffor will pay at the day limited such sum or not, and if he doth not pay, then the land which is put in pledge upon condition for the payment of the money is taken from him for ever, and so dead to him upon condition etc. And if he doth pay the money, then the pledge is dead as to the tenant.[24]

That a feoffor should be bound to repay the loan on the exact day fixed or be precluded for ever from redeeming his property was a hard rule, and 'what made the hardship on the debtor a glaring one was that the debt still remained unpaid and could be recovered from the feoffor notwithstanding that he had actually forfeited the land to his mortgagee'.[25]

(2) In equity. Equity of redemption

By the time of Charles I, equity had so fundamentally altered this strict legal view that the law of mortgages was transformed. The form indicated by Littleton remained, but equity interfered on the general principle that relief should be granted against forfeiture for breach of a penal condition.[26] No longer was redemption to depend upon a strict compliance with the contract. In the view of equity the essential object of a mortgage is to afford security to the lender, and as long as the security remains intact there is no justification for expropriating the property of the mortgagor merely because of his failure to make prompt payment. Lord Nottingham said:

> In natural justice and equity the principal right of the mortgagee is to the money, and his right to the land is only as a security for the money.[27]

---

[22] In French: *mort* (dead) *gage* (pledge).   [23] Above, p 62.   [24] Litt, s 332.

[25] *Kreglinger v New Patagonia Meat and Cold Storage Co Ltd* [1914] AC 25, 35 (Lord Haldane).

[26] Holdsworth, *A History of English Law*, vol v, p 330; Turner, *The Equity of Redemption* (1931).

[27] *Thornborough v Baker* (1675) 3 Swan 628, 630. For Lord Nottingham's contribution to the development of mortgages, see (1961) 79 Selden Society, pp 7 ff (DEC Yale).

Hence the rule ultimately established by courts of equity was that a mortgagor must be allowed to redeem his fee simple despite his failure to make repayment on the appointed day. Time was not to be of the essence of the transaction. This is still the rule, although a mortgage is no longer created by the conveyance of a fee simple estate. The position, then, is this: that upon the date fixed for repayment[28] the mortgagor has at common law a contractual right to redeem. If this date passes without repayment, he obtains a right to redeem in equity.

However:[29]

> The equity to redeem, which arises on failure to exercise the contractual right of redemption, must be carefully distinguished from the equitable estate, which, from the first, remains in the mortgagor, and is sometimes referred to as an equity of redemption.

This *equity of redemption* is an equitable interest that arises as soon as the mortgage is created, and is an equitable interest owned by the mortgagor. It is an interest in land that may be conveyed, devised or entailed, and it may descend on intestacy or pass as *bona vacantia* to the Crown.[30] It is destructible only by four events: its release by the mortgagor, lapse of time under the Limitation Act 1980,[31] the exercise by the mortgagee of his statutory power of sale,[32] and a foreclosure decree, that is a judicial decree that the subject-matter of the mortgage shall be vested absolutely in the mortgagee free from any right of redemption.[33]

(3) Position prior to 1926

Before 1 January 1926, the normal method by which a mortgage of the fee simple was created was for the mortgagor to convey the legal fee simple to the mortgagee together with a covenant to repay the loan in, say, six months' time, with a proviso, however, that if the loan were repaid at such date, the mortgagee would reconvey the legal estate. Outwardly it still seemed as if the mortgagee became absolute owner failing repayment within six months, but essentially, owing to the doctrine of the equity of redemption, the mortgagor was from the outset the true owner. Technically he was a mere equitable owner, but in the eyes of equity he was the real owner and, on his repaying the principal and interest with costs to the mortgagee, equity was prepared to grant specific performance of the proviso for reconveyance of the legal estate to him.

A still older method of creating a mortgage, used between the thirteenth and fifteenth centuries and worthy of notice because of its revival by the 1925 legislation, was for the mortgagor to lease his land to the mortgagee for a short term of years. If the debt was not repaid at the end of the lease, the right of the mortgagor was extinguished,

---

[28] Traditionally this is six months after the creation of the mortgage, although in most cases neither mortgagor nor mortgagee intends that the loan shall be repaid on that date, and modern mortgages may contain various different provisions for repayment of the capital by instalments, or only at the end of the term under an interest-only mortgage: above, p 796.

[29] *Kreglinger v New Patagonia Meat and Cold Storage Co Ltd*, above, at 48 (Lord Parker).

[30] *Casborne v Scarfe* (1738) 1 Atk 603; *Re Sir Thomas Spencer Wells* [1933] Ch 29, M & B p 868; Waldock, *Law of Mortgages*, pp 202 ff.

[31] Below, p 837. This applies only to unregistered land.   [32] Below, p 854.   [33] Below, p 862.

and the term was automatically enlarged into a fee simple that vested absolutely in the mortgagee.[34] This method, however, went out of use, mainly because the law in its growing strictness could not countenance this mode of enlarging a term of years into a fee. An attempt to resuscitate it was made about the beginning of the nineteenth century, but owing to certain disadvantages, such as the doubt whether the mortgagee was entitled to possession of the title deeds, it failed, and the term of years was used only in family settlements where it was desired to secure money lent for the payment of portions.[35]

(b) Mortgages of leasehold

If the security offered by the borrower was a leasehold interest, not the fee simple, there were two methods before 1926 by which the mortgage might be created. Usually the mortgagor sub-leased his term of years to the mortgagee for a period slightly shorter than the remainder of the term. This was the most desirable method, since the sub-lease did not involve privity of estate between the mortgagee and the superior landlord, and therefore the mortgagee was immune from liability on the covenants contained in the original lease, unless they were negative covenants enforceable under the doctrine of *Tulk v Moxhay*.[36] The alternative method was for the mortgagee to take an assignment of the whole remainder of the term, but in this case he became liable to covenants and conditions under the doctrine of *Spencer's Case*.[37]

(c) Equitable mortgages

In addition to the conveyance of a legal estate, whether a fee simple or a term of years, by way of security, it has long been possible to create an equitable mortgage by the grant of an equitable interest. This is necessarily the method where the borrower himself is an equitable owner, such as where before 1926 a mortgagor created a second mortgage in the same land: the legal estate had been conveyed to the first mortgagee and what the mortgagor conveyed to the second mortgagee was his equity of redemption. A further example of an equitable mortgage, made by a borrower who is an equitable owner, is where a beneficiary under a settlement mortgages his equitable life interest.

On the other hand, it is also possible for an equitable mortgage to be created by the owner of a legal estate, such as where he enters into a contract to create a legal mortgage that entitles the lender in equity to specific performance of the contract, and thereby constitutes the grant of a mortgage in equity. Indeed, without the grant even of an equitable interest, an owner may *charge* his land with the repayment of a loan and so entitle the lender in equity to enforce a sale of the property. These equitable mortgages are considered in more detail later.[38]

---

[34] Holdsworth, *A History of English Law*, vol iii, p 129.   [35] (1925) 60 LJ News 46 (JM Lightwood).
[36] Above, pp 732 ff.   [37] Above, pp 307 ff.   [38] Below, p 807.

(2) Changes Made by the Law of Property Act 1925

The prevailing practice, by which the legal fee simple was conveyed to a mortgagee, presented a difficult problem to the draftsmen of the 1925 legislation. How were they to bring it into line with the principles that they intended to introduce?

The cornerstone of their policy was that the legal fee simple should always be vested in its true owner and that he should be able to convey it free from equitable interests.[39] In the eyes of the law the true owner is the mortgagor. Yet, all that he held before 1926 was an equitable interest, and unless some alteration were made there could be no question of his ability to convey any kind of legal estate during the continuance of the mortgage.

On the other hand it was important to protect the mortgagee in the enjoyment of certain valuable advantages that he derived from his legal ownership. Pre-eminent among these was the priority that, by virtue of the legal fee simple, he obtained over other mortgages created in the same land, for these were necessarily equitable in nature. Moreover, his possession of the title deeds enabled him to control the actions of the mortgagor in his dealings with the land. He also enjoyed the right to take actual possession of the land, and therefore to grant leases; and lastly, when he exercised his power of sale on failure by the mortgagor to repay the loan, he was able to vest the legal estate in the purchaser.[40]

The solution contained in the Law of Property Act 1925 was to revert to the old fifteenth-century method of effecting mortgages by means of a lease for a term of years, commonly known as a mortgage *by demise*.

Mortgages by which the legal fee simple is vested in the mortgagee were prohibited, and a mortgagee who required a legal estate instead of a mere equitable interest became compelled to take either a long term of years or a newly invented interest[41] called a *charge by deed expressed to be by way of legal mortgage*.[42] In the first case both parties have legal estates: the mortgagee has a legal term of years absolute, and the mortgagor has a reversionary and legal fee simple, subject to the mortgagee's term. In the case of a charge by way of legal mortgage, however, the mortgagee does not have a legal estate, but a legal interest in the land[43] which by statute gives him the same protection, powers and remedies as if he had taken a legal term of years.

In this way the principle that the legal fee simple should always remain vested in the true owner was maintained. The mortgagor is owner at law as well as in equity, and the mortgagee has only a right in another's land. The charge expressed to be by way

---

[39] Above, p 129.   [40] (1925) 60 LJ News 91 (JM Lightwood).

[41] Charges over *registered* land were however introduced by Land Transfer Act 1875: Law Com No 271, *Land Registration for the Twenty-First Century* (2001), para 7.2. The 1875 Act gave the registered proprietor of a registered charge the right to enter the land and take its rent and profits: s 25; and the same powers of foreclosure and sale as if the land had been transferred to him by way of mortgage: s 26. But the 1875 Act was not successful, because it provided for only a voluntary system of registration, and by 1885 only 113 titles had been registered under it: Rowton Simpson, *Land Law and Registration* (1976), p 44. For mortgages of registered land in the modern law, see below.

[42] For a precedent of a legal charge, see below, p 804.   [43] LPA 1925, s 1(2)(c).

of legal mortgage at last provided a method reflecting the reality of the transaction. We should also notice two important consequences of the changes made by the 1925 legislation. First, the mortgagor's retention of the legal estate means that any second and subsequent mortgages that he creates may be legal. And secondly, the rights of the parties remain unchanged, and in particular, the mortgagor's equity of redemption is still of importance. This, as before 1926, is an equitable proprietary interest and is in value equal to the value of the land less the amount of the debt secured by the mortgage. The mortgagor retains that interest and keeps a legal estate as well. On the other hand, the mortgagee retains all his remedies, and so, for example, may sell and convey the legal fee simple, if the mortgagor defaults in his obligations.[44]

(3) Changes Made by the Land Registration Act 2002

The Land Registration Act 1925 followed, for registered land, the new scheme of the Law of Property Act 1925 for mortgages; accordingly the proprietor of registered land had in general terms the same powers to mortgage the land as if the land had not been registered;[45] and so a legal mortgage of registered land could be made by a charge by way of legal mortgage, or by demise or (in the case of a mortgage of a leasehold) by sub-demise, although the default position, if no contrary express provision were made in the deed creating it, was that it took effect as a charge.[46] The Land Registration Act 2002, however, took the reforms of 1925 one step further. Now it is no longer possible for the owner of a registered estate to create a mortgage by demise or sub-demise;[47] the legal charge is therefore now the only method of creating a legal mortgage over registered land—a reform made not only to simplify the law but also to reflect reality, mortgages by demise or sub-demise having been obsolete in practice for some time.[48] And the powers of the owner of a registered charge to mortgage his own interest under the charge are now limited: he may not transfer his interest by way of legal mortgage, nor create a mortgage of it by sub-demise, nor grant a legal charge of it; but is limited to charging at law with the payment of money the indebtedness being secured by the registered charge.[49]

(4) Impact of History on the Modern Law

The modern law of mortgages cannot therefore be understood without the perspective of history. The registered proprietor today has the power to make any disposition of his

---

[44] Below, p 854.

[45] LRA 1925, s 106(1). The mortgage could therefore be equitable or (if in proper form and registered) legal: s 106(2).

[46] Ibid, s 27(1), (2).

[47] LRA 2002, s 23(1)(a). Nor may the mortgagee under an existing mortgage by demise be registered as the proprietor of the lease where there is a subsisting right of redemption: ibid, s 3(5); this latter rule was already established in LRA 1925, s 8(1). 'It would make no sense to register a mortgage term where the estate charged was an unregistered freehold or leasehold and the mortgage might still be redeemed': Law Com No 271, *Land Registration for the Twenty-First Century* (2001), para 3.12.

[48] H & B, para 12.2; Law Com No 271, para 7.2; Emmet, para 25.000.   [49] LRA 2002, s 23(2).

estate—including mortgaging it—*except* for the mortgage by demise or sub-demise.[50] To comprehend this, it is necessary to understand the general powers of mortgaging that are still contained in the Law of Property Act 1925. But the principles of mortgages contained in that Act are themselves a development of the pre-1926 law of mortgages and have to be understood in that light. Although the Land Registration Act 2002 has prohibited the creation of mortgages by demise, the form of mortgage that is retained as the universal method of mortgaging registered land—the legal charge—is itself defined in the Law of Property Act 1925, for the purposes of registered land as much as unregistered land,[51] as giving the mortgagee the same protection, powers and remedies as if it had been a mortgage by demise. The 2002 Act does not therefore break with history: the theory of a demise underpins the present day law.

B METHODS OF CREATING MORTGAGES TODAY

(1) Legal Mortgages

(a) Unregistered land

As we have seen, the Law of Property Act 1925 provided that a legal mortgage of an estate in fee simple must be effected by either:

(1) a demise for a term of years absolute, subject to a provision (called a provision for cesser) that the term shall cease if repayment is made on a fixed day; or

(2) a charge by deed expressed to be by way of legal mortgage;[52]

and, similarly, that a legal mortgage of a term of years absolute must be effected by a demise (a sub-lease) for a term of years absolute or by a legal charge.[53] These provisions continue to apply to the creation of a mortgage over land that is, and is to continue for the time being, to be unregistered. In practice, this is therefore limited to the creation of a mortgage by a freeholder or leaseholder of his existing estate in unregistered land, since in the more common case of the conveyance of an estate to a purchaser who is financing the purchase by mortgage, the conveyance will generally trigger the compulsory registration of the estate and of the mortgage—which must therefore comply with the rules for the creation of a legal mortgage of registered land.[54] Moreover, even where the mortgage is of an existing unregistered estate, if it is a legal mortgage protected by the deposit of documents relating to the mortgaged estate, the mortgage triggers the compulsory registration of the title to the estate and the mortgage.[55]

---

[50] Ibid, s 23(1).

[51] LPA 1925, s 87(4), inserted by LRA 2002, s 133, Sch 11, para 2(1), (8), reinforces this by providing that it is not affected by the removal of the registered owner's power to mortgage by demise.

[52] LPA 1925, s 85(1).

[53] Ibid, s 86(1).   [54] LRA 2002, s 4(1)(a); below, pp 806 ff.

[55] Ibid, s 4(1)(g), (8); R & R para 27.019. A legal mortgage over unregistered land that is *not* protected by the deposit of documents should instead be protected by the registration at the Land Charges Registry of a land charge, Class C(i): Land Charges Act 1972, s 2(4)(i); below, pp 885, 1057, 1063.

Although there are no doubt mortgages still in existence at the present time that were created by demise or sub-demise, the creation of new mortgages by this method is in practice obsolete.[56] Instead, for some time it has been usual to create a legal mortgage of unregistered land using the simpler and more realistic method provided by the Law of Property Act 1925: the legal charge.

(1) Precedent of a legal charge

The following simple form of legal charge was provided by the Law of Property Act 1925:[57]

Charge by way of Legal Mortgage.

This Legal Charge is made [etc.] between A. of [etc.] of the one part and B. of [etc.] of the other part.

[*Recite the title of A. to the freeholds or leaseholds in the Schedule and agreement for the loan by B.*]

Now in consideration of the sum of…pounds now paid by B. to A. (the receipt etc.) this Deed witnesseth as follows:—

(1) A. hereby covenants with B. to pay [Add the requisite covenant to pay principal and interest].

(2) A. as Beneficial Owner[58] hereby charges by way of legal mortgage All and Singular the property mentioned in the Schedule hereto with the payment to B. of the principal money, interest, and other money hereby covenanted to be paid by A.

(3) [*Add covenant to insure buildings and any other provisions desired.*]

In witness [etc.] [*Add Schedule*].

This precedent gives the flavour of the simplicity of a legal charge, although in practice legal charges take a more expanded form, containing further appropriate covenants by the borrower.[59]

(2) Effect of charge

The Law of Property Act 1925 does not vest a term of years in the mortgagee,[60] but it provides that he shall have 'the same protection, powers and remedies' as if he had taken a lease of a fee simple or a sub-lease of demised premises.[61] In other words, he

---

[56] Above, p 802, n 48. For an account of the form of a mortgage by demise or sub-demise, and the precedent of a mortgage deed, see the 16th edition of this book, pp 724–7.

[57] S 206, Sch 5, Form No 1; this was repealed in 2004: Statute Law (Repeals) Act 2004, s 1(1), Sch. 1, Part 12. Forms of statutory legal charge are also provided by LPA 1925, s 117, Sch 4, Forms 1 and 4, but these are in practice rarely used: Emmet, para 25.010.

[58] The words 'as beneficial owner' were designed to imply certain covenants; since 30 June 1995 the appropriate wording is 'with full title guarantee': LP(MP)A 1994: below, pp 1089 ff.

[59] For fuller precedents, see *Encyclopaedia of Forms and Precedents*, vol 28(1), Forms 2–5.

[60] *Weg Motors Ltd v Hales* [1962] Ch 49; *Cumberland Court (Brighton) Ltd v Taylor* [1964] Ch 29; *Thompson v Salah* [1972] 1 All ER 530; *Edwards v Marshall-Lee* (1975) 235 EG 901.

[61] LPA 1925, s 87(1).

is in exactly the same position as if the relationship of landlord and tenant existed between him and the mortgagor.[62] If, for example, A has charged his term of years in favour of B and later commits a breach of a covenant contained in the lease by reason of which his landlord starts proceedings for the enforcement of his right of re-entry under a forfeiture clause, B is entitled to claim relief under section 146 of the Law of Property Act 1925.[63]

This method of creating a mortgage steadily gained popularity since its introduction, and at the present day is adopted in preference to the long lease. Its defect is that it does not contain the provision for cesser that always figured in the mortgage by demise. This provision corresponds to the old provision for redemption, the importance of which lay in fixing the date at which the mortgagor's right to redeem and the mortgagee's right to foreclose came into being. Although the right of a legal *chargee* to foreclose probably arises by implication at the date fixed in the covenant for repayment, provided that the mortgagor makes default, it is safer to insert an express provision for redemption or discharge in addition to the covenant for repayment.[64]

(3) Advantages of legal charge

Three advantages may be claimed for the legal charge as compared with the mortgage by demise.

First, its form is short and simple and more intelligible to a mortgagor.

Secondly, the legal charge is as appropriate for leaseholds as it is for freeholds, and therefore it provides a simple method of executing a compound mortgage that relates to both these different interests.

Thirdly, a mortgagor with a leasehold interest who holds his term on condition that he will not sub-lease without the consent of his landlord, must clearly obtain this consent if his mortgage takes the form of a sub-demise,[65] but a legal charge, since it does not create an actual legal estate, is presumably not in breach of a covenant against underletting.[66]

(4) Sub-mortgage

If the legal chargee desires to create a sub-mortgage, he cannot do so by means of a sub-lease, since he himself holds no term of years. He must, therefore, either charge his own interest under the mortgage, or assign the mortgage debt to the sub-mortgagee subject to a right of redemption.

---

[62] *Regent Oil Co Ltd v J A Gregory (Hatch End) Ltd* [1966] Ch 402 at 431, M & B p 858; *Weg Motors Ltd v Hales*, above, 77 (Donovan LJ).

[63] *Grand Junction Co Ltd v Bates* [1954] 2 QB 160; *Church Comrs for England v Ve-Ri-Best Manufacturing Co Ltd* [1957] 1 QB 238. See also above, p 295.

[64] The forms of statutory legal charge provided by LPA 1925, s 117, Sch 4, Forms 1 and 4, above, n 57, contained by statute implied covenants for payment and discharge.

[65] *Matthews v Smallwood* [1910] 1 Ch 777.

[66] *Grand Junction Co Ltd v Bates* [1954] 2 QB 160, 168 (Upjohn J).

(b) Registered land

(1) Mortgages created under Land Registration Act 1925

Under the Land Registration Act 1925 a legal mortgage could be created by registered charge, a legal interest that must be created by deed and completed by the Registrar entering on the charges register the chargee as proprietor of the charge.[67] It could be made by a charge by way of legal mortgage, or it could contain, in the case of freehold land, an express demise, and, in the case of leasehold land, an express sub-demise.[68] Subject to any contrary provision in the charge, however, it would take effect as a charge by way of legal mortgage.[69]

(2) Mortgages created under Land Registration Act 2002

The Land Registration Act 2002 does not permit the owner of a registered estate to create a mortgage by demise or sub-demise.[70] The only method of creating a legal mortgage of registered land, whether freehold or leasehold, is now[71] therefore the charge by way of legal mortgage. As in the case of unregistered land, a legal charge must be executed as a deed,[72] but in registered land the grant of a legal charge is a registrable disposition[73] that therefore does not take effect at law until the registration requirements have been met:[74] the chargee must be entered in the register as the proprietor of the charge.[75] On completion of the registration requirements, the charge has the same effect as a charge by deed by way of legal mortgage in unregistered land, and the proprietor of the charge has, in relation to the property subject to the charge, the powers of disposition conferred by law on the owner of a legal mortgage.[76]

The mortgagor can create a second or further legal mortgages in respect of the same registered estate, following the same rules as to formality and registration as are required for a first legal mortgage. Registered charges on the same registered estate rank in the order shown on the register.[77]

(3) Sub-mortgages under Land Registration Act 2002

The proprietor of a registered charge (the mortgagee) cannot now create a legal sub-mortgage of his own interest under the mortgage by transfer or sub-demise. The only permitted method is to charge at law with the payment of money the indebtedness being secured by the registered charge.[78] The effect of a legal sub-charge is to give the sub-chargee the right to exercise the chargee's rights under the principal charge.[79]

---

[67] LRA 1925, s 26(1).

[68] Ibid, s 27(1), (2); LRR 1925, r 139 and Schedule as substituted by LR (Charges) R 1990 (SI 1990 No 2613), r 2, and LRR 1997 (SI 1997 No 3037) r 2(1), Sch 1, para 32.18.

[69] LRA 1925, s 27(1).   [70] LRA 2002, s 23(1)(a).

[71] Existing mortgages, registered under LRA 1925, are unaffected: LRA 2002, s 134, Sch 12, para 1.

[72] LPA 1925, ss 85(1), 87.   [73] LRA 2002, s 27(2)(f).   [74] Ibid, s 27(1).

[75] Ibid, s 27(4), Sch 2, para 8. For provision for the creation of legal charges in electronic form ('e-charges') using the Land Registry electronic communications network, see LRA 2002, ss 91, 92; above, p 142; below, p 840; LR (Electronic Conveyancing) R 2008 (SI 2008 No 1750). A pilot scheme for e-charges by a small number of lenders and conveyancers was introduced in 2009.

[76] Ibid, ss 51, 52(1).   [77] Ibid, s 48(1); below, pp 897–8.

[78] Ibid, s 23(2).   [79] H & B, paras 7.4, 12.8.

(4) Form of legal charge

Under the Land Registration Act 2002 rules may provide requirements as to the form and content of a charge that must be satisfied before it takes effect.[80] No such mandatory rule has been made, but a form in which a legal charge may be made is provided.[81] In practice, many institutional lenders will have their own form of charge that will have been approved by the Land Registry.[82] The general form provided by the rules (form CH1[83]) is set out on page 808.

(2) Equitable Mortgages

The statutory provisions that have been mentioned so far apply only to the creation of a legal mortgage, and do not affect equitable mortgages and charges. It always has been, and still is, possible to confer upon a lender an equitable right over the land by way of security, instead of passing a legal estate or interest to him.

The commonest examples of equitable mortgages before 1926 were those that followed a legal mortgage in the same land, but, as we have seen, second and subsequent mortgages may now be created so as to give each lender a legal estate or interest. The following forms of equitable mortgages, however, still remain.

(a) Equitable mortgages under the doctrine of Walsh v Lonsdale

(1) Contract to create a legal mortgage

Under the doctrine of *Walsh v Lonsdale*[84] if A enters into a contract that, in consideration of money advanced, he will execute a legal mortgage in favour of B, then as long as the contract is one of which the court would be prepared to grant the equitable remedy of specific performance, it is treated in equity as creating an equitable mortgage in favour of B.[85] But such a contract does not have this effect unless the money has been actually advanced, for a contract to make a loan, whether executed as a deed or not, cannot be specifically enforced by either party.[86] The only remedy is the recovery of damages.

However, it must be remembered that an agreement for the sale or other disposition of an interest in land—which includes a mortgage—is not a contract unless it is in writing, signed by both parties in compliance with section 2 of the Law of Property (Miscellaneous Provisions) Act 1989.[87]

---

[80] LRA 2002, s 25. Cf LRA 1925, s 25(2) (charge could be in any form, subject to certain provisos).

[81] LRR 2003, r 103; Form CH1.

[82] H & B, para 12.14; Land Registry Practice Guide 30, *Approval of Mortgage Documentation* (September 2009).

[83] Source acknowledgement: CH1 produced by Land Registry. © Crown copyright material is reproduced with the permission of Land Registry.

[84] (1882) 21 Ch D 9; below, p 978.   [85] *Tebb v Hodge* (1869) LR 5 CP 73.

[86] *Sichel v Mosenthal* (1862) 30 Beav 371.

[87] Below, pp 966 ff. See also *Kinane v Mackie-Conteh* [2005] EWCA Civ 45; [2005] 2 P & CR DG3 (agreement to create mortgage not in writing as required by LP(MP)A 1989, s 2(1), but enforceable because constructive trust created under s 2(5)). For contracts made before 27 September 1989, the formality requirements of LPA 1925, s 40, apply (sufficient memorandum or part performance): below, pp 961 ff, post; *Re Leathes* (1833) 3 Deac & Ch 112.

Land Registry
Legal charge of a registered estate

This form should be accompanied by either Form AP1 or Form FR1

If you need more room than is provided for in a panel, and your software allows, you can expand any panel in the form. Alternatively use continuation sheet CS and attach it to this form.

'Conveyancer' is a term used in this form. It is defined in rule 217(1) of the Land Registration Rules 2003 and includes, among others, solicitor, licensed conveyancer and fellow of the Institute of Legal Executives.

Leave blank if not yet registered.	1　Title number(s) of the property:
Insert address including postcode (if any) or other description of the property, for example 'land adjoining 2 Acacia Avenue'.	2　Property:
	3　Date:
Give full name(s).	4　Borrower:
Complete as appropriate where the borrower is a company.	For UK incorporated companies/LLPs Registered number of company or limited liability partnership including any prefix: For overseas companies (a) Territory of incorporation: (b) Registered number in the United Kingdom including any prefix:
Give full name(s).	5　Lender for entry in the register:
Complete as appropriate where the lender is a company. Also, for an overseas company, unless an arrangement with Land Registry exists, lodge either a certificate in Form 7 in Schedule 3 to the Land Registration Rules 2003 or a certified copy of the constitution in English or Welsh, or other evidence permitted by rule 183 of the Land Registration Rules 2003.	For UK incorporated companies/LLPs Registered number of company or limited liability partnership including any prefix: For overseas companies (a) Territory of incorporation: (b) Registered number in the United Kingdom including any prefix:
Each proprietor may give up to three addresses for service, one of which must be a postal address whether or not in the UK (including the postcode, if any). The others can be any combination of a postal address, a UK DX box number or an electronic address.	6　Lender's intended address(es) for service for entry in the register:

Place 'X' in any box that applies.	**7**	The borrower with
		☐ full title guarantee
Add any modifications.		☐ limited title guarantee
		charges the property by way of legal mortgage as security for the payment of the sums detailed in panel 9
Place 'X' in the appropriate box(es).	**8**	☐ The lender is under an obligation to make further advances and applies for the obligation to be entered in the register
You must set out the wording of the restriction in full. Standard forms of restriction are set out in Schedule 4 to the Land Registration Rules 2003.		☐ The borrower applies to enter the following standard form of restriction in the proprietorship register of the registered estate:
Insert details of the sums to be paid (amount and dates) and so on.	**9**	Additional provisions
The borrower must execute this charge as a deed using the space opposite. If there is more than one borrower, all must execute. Forms of execution are given in Schedule 9 to the Land Registration Rules 2003. If a note of an obligation to make further advances has been applied for in panel 8 this document must be signed by the lender or its conveyancer.	**10**	Execution

WARNING
If you dishonestly enter information or make a statement that you know is, or might be, untrue or misleading, and intend by doing so to make a gain for yourself or another person, or to cause loss or the risk of loss to another person, you may commit the offence of fraud under section 1 of the Fraud Act 2006, the maximum penalty for which is 10 years' imprisonment or an unlimited fine, or both.

Failure to complete this form with proper care may result in a loss of protection under the Land Registration Act 2002 if, as a result, a mistake is made in the register.

Under section 66 of the Land Registration Act 2002 most documents (including this form) kept by the registrar relating to an application to the registrar or referred to in the register are open to public inspection and copying. If you believe a document contains prejudicial information, you may apply for that part of the document to be made exempt using Form EX1, under rule 136 of the Land Registration Rules 2003.

(2) Imperfect legal mortgage

An imperfect legal mortgage may also be treated in equity as if it were a contract to create a legal mortgage, with similar consequences. This may happen, for example, where A purports to create a legal mortgage in writing without executing it as a deed. However, for the doctrine of *Walsh v Lonsdale* to apply, there must at least be sufficient formality to comply with section 2 of the Law of Property (Miscellaneous Provisions) Act 1989.

(3) Deposit of title deeds

It used to be held, following the case of *Russel v Russel*[88] in 1783, that an equitable mortgage is created by the delivery to the lender of the title deeds relating to the borrower's land, provided that it is intended to treat the land as security. In reality this is a further example of the application of the doctrine of *Walsh v Lonsdale* to mortgages, since the deposit of deeds was evidence of a contract to create a mortgage, or an imperfect legal mortgage.

Before 27 September 1989 this caused no difficulty, since under the formalities then applicable to a contract for an interest in land the deposit ranked as an act of part performance,[89] and so the deposit alone, without writing, was treated as constituting a contract to execute a legal mortgage.[90] Since 26 September 1989, however, the formalities of section 2 of the Law of Property (Miscellaneous Provisions) Act 1989 have to be satisfied.[91]

This is not to suggest that mortgages have commonly been made by deposit of title deeds without any accompanying written document. In practice the borrower would sign a memorandum executed as a deed contemporaneously with the delivery of the title deeds, for such a memorandum makes the transaction a mortgage by deed within the meaning of the Law of Property Act 1925, and entitles the equitable mortgagee to exercise all the powers, including the power of sale,

---

[88] (1783) 1 Bro CC 269. The right to create this kind of equitable mortgage was saved by LPA 1925, s 13. The mortgagee can retain the deeds until he is paid, but has no separate legal lien: *Re Molton Finance Ltd* [1968] Ch 325; see also *Capital Finance Co Ltd v Stokes* [1969] 1 Ch 261, 278.

[89] *Bank of New South Wales v O'Connor* (1889) 14 App Cas 273, 282.

[90] *Carter v Wake* (1877) 4 Ch D 605, 606 (Jessel MR). An actual deposit, though essential, was not in itself sufficient. The depositee must go further, and prove by parol or by written evidence that the deposit was intended to be by way of security, for the mere deposit by a customer of his deeds with a bank would not, for example, constitute the bank an equitable mortgagee in respect of an overdraft: *Dixon v Muckleston* (1872) 8 Ch App 155; *Re Wallis & Simonds (Builders) Ltd* [1974] 1 WLR 391; *Thames Guaranty Ltd v Campbell* [1985] QB 210 (deposit of land certificate to secure a debt by one joint tenant without consent of the other joint tenant not effective to create equitable charge of the jointly owned land; but it could create a charge of the equitable interest of the depositor, if the deposit amounts to an act of severance, above, p 508); *First National Securities Ltd v Hegerty* [1985] QB 850; above, p 508, n 87.

[91] *United Bank of Kuwait plc v Sahib* [1997] Ch 107, 143–4 (Phillips LJ: 'The clear intent of section 2 ... is to introduce certainty in relation to contracts for the disposition of interests in land where uncertainty existed before'); Emmet, para 25.217; (1997) 113 LQR 533 (M Robinson). For the liability of a solicitor for failing to advise (even before *Kuwait*) that the mortgage was required to satisfy s 2, see *Dean v Allin & Watts* [2001] EWCA Civ 758, [2001] 2 Lloyd's Rep 249.

given by the Act.[92] And since an equitable mortgagee cannot convey the legal estate to a purchaser, it is usual to insert a power of attorney or a declaration of trust, or both, in the memorandum, so as to enable the mortgagee to deal with the legal estate. But the significance of the 1989 Act goes beyond this, since it requires all the express terms of the contract to be in writing signed by or on behalf of *both* parties: a memorandum signed only by the borrower will not therefore satisfy the requirements of the Act.

It should be noted that there is now no place for mortgages by deposit in registered land. Although provision was made in the Land Registration Act 1925 for the creation of a charge by deposit of the land certificate or charge certificate,[93] this is not reproduced in the 2002 Act because of the change in formalities for contracts under the Law of Property (Miscellaneous Provisions) Act 1989, and the consequential reassessment of the place of mortgages by deposit.[94] It was a necessary reform, however, because land certificates and charge certificates have themselves now been abolished.[95]

(b) Mortgage of an equitable interest

A mortgage of an equitable interest, such as a life interest arising under a settlement, or a contract for a lease,[96] is itself necessarily equitable. The method of creation corresponds to that employed before 1926 in the case of a legal mortgage of the fee simple, namely the entire equitable interest is assigned to the mortgagee, subject to a proviso for reassignment on redemption.[97]

The assignment, if not made by will, must be in writing signed by the mortgagor or by his agent thereunto lawfully authorised in writing[98] and the mortgagee should protect himself by giving written notice of it to the owner of the legal estate.[99]

(c) Equitable charge

Another form of equitable security, differing from the forms already described in respect of the remedies it confers, is the equitable charge. This arises where, without any transfer of, or agreement to transfer, ownership or possession, property is appropriated to the discharge of a debt or some other obligation.[100]

In *Matthews v Goodday*[101] Kindersley V-C said:

---

[92] Below, p 871.   [93] LRA 1925, s 66.

[94] *United Bank of Kuwait plc v Sahib*, above; H & B, para 12.5; Law Com No 271, para 7.9.

[95] H & B, ch 21; above, p 141. The practice of entering a notice on the register, to support a deposit of the land certificate with the lender, was however already discontinued in 1995, following the decision at first instance in *United Bank of Kuwait plc v Sahib*, above: H & B, para 12.86.

[96] *Rust v Goodale* [1957] Ch 33.   [97] Waldock, *Law of Mortgages*, pp 136–9.

[98] LPA 1925, s 53(1)(c); below, p 1011.   [99] Ibid, s 137.

[100] *London County and Westminster Bank Ltd v Tompkins* [1918] 1 KB 515, 528.

[101] (1861) 31 LJ Ch 282, 282–3; *Swiss Bank Corp v Lloyds Bank Ltd* [1982] AC 584, 594–5 (Buckley LJ); [1982] AC 584, 613 (Lord Wilberforce); *Thames Guaranty Ltd v Campbell* [1985] QB 210. A purported legal charge of jointly owned property by one co-owner without the authority of the other has the effect only of charging in equity the former's interest: *First National Securities Ltd v Hegerty* [1985] QB 850; *Edwards v Lloyds Bank plc* [2004] EWHC 1745 (Ch), [2005] 1 FCR 139 (wife's signature forged).

With regard to what are called equitable mortgages, my notion is this. Suppose a man signed a written contract, by which he simply agreed that he thereby charged his real estate with £500 to A, what would be the effect of it?

It would be no agreement to give a legal mortgage, but a security by which he equitably charged his lands with payment of a sum of money, and the mode of enforcing it would be by coming into a court of equity to have the money raised by sale or mortgage; that would be the effect of such a simple charge. It is the same thing as if a testator devised an estate to A charged with the payment of a sum of money to B. B's right is not to foreclose A, but to have his charge raised by sale or mortgage of the land ... But the thing would be distinctly an equitable charge, and not a mortgage nor an agreement to give one. On the other hand the party might agree that, having borrowed a sum of money, he would give a legal mortgage whenever called upon. That agreement might be enforced according to its terms, and the court would decree a legal mortgage to be given, and would also foreclose the mortgage, unless the money was paid.

An equitable charge does not have to satisfy section 2 of the Law of Property (Miscellaneous Provisions) Act 1989, because it involves the *creation* of a security rather than an *agreement to create* a legal charge. Its validity depends on section 53(1)(a) of the Law of Property Act 1925, which requires the writing to be signed by only the chargor.[102]

The remedies of an equitable chargee will be considered later.[103]

(d) Equitable mortgages in registered land

The registered proprietor has the general power to make any disposition permitted by the general law in relation to the description of interest that he holds,[104] and so he can create an equitable mortgage or charge in the same way as the owner of unregistered land, with two exceptions. First, no mortgage by demise or sub-demise is now permitted in registered land,[105] and so a contract to create a legal mortgage by demise cannot be recognised as creating an equitable mortgage.[106] Secondly, as we have already noted, a mortgage by deposit of title deeds cannot be created since there are no longer documents of title in registered land.[107]

It should be recalled that, until the relevant registration requirements are met,[108] a mortgage over registered land executed as a legal charge does not operate at law, but takes effect only as an equitable mortgage.[109]

If it is to bind a purchaser from the mortgagor, an equitable mortgage requires protection by notice on the register unless it is an overriding interest by virtue of the

---

[102] Emmet, para 25.218.   [103] Below, p 872.
[104] LRA 2002, s 23(1).   [105] Ibid.
[106] The doctrine of *Walsh v Lonsdale*, above, p 807, rests on the basis that the court would order specific performance of the contract, which it could not do in the case of a contract to create a mortgage by demise. The language of LRA 2002, s 23(1)(a) appears in any event sufficient to deprive the registered owner of the power to create an equitable mortgage by demise or sub-demise.
[107] Above, p 811.   [108] Above, p 806.   [109] LRA 2002, s 27(1).

mortgagee being in discoverable actual occupation (for example, where he has taken possession).[110]

(3) Charging Orders

The court has powers under the Charging Orders Act 1979 to impose a charge on the land of a judgment debtor to secure the payment of his judgment debt. Such a charge has the same effect as an equitable charge created by the debtor by writing under his hand.[111]

The Land Charges Act 1972 and the Land Registration Act 2002 apply to charging orders as they apply to other orders or writs made for the purpose of enforcing judgments.[112] Where the interest affected by the order is a beneficial interest under a trust of land, the interest can be overreached on sale,[113] and there is no provision for registration in unregistered land;[114] in registered land the order should be protected by a restriction.[115] All other charging orders should be protected by registration under the Land Charges Act 1972[116] (in the case of unregistered land) or by a notice on the register of the debtor's title[117] (in the case of registered land).

(4) Summary of Forms of Mortgage

If we look back at the different kinds of mortgages, we see that they may be either legal or equitable, and that the same land may be subjected both to several legal and to several equitable mortgages.

For example, the fee simple owner may have entered into the mortgages in the following order:

a legal charge to A;

a contract (not completed) to enter into a legal charge in favour of B;

---

[110] Ibid, s 29; Sch 3, para 2. Where, however, the mortgage is constituted by the transfer by way of charge of an interest that is an overreachable interest (eg a beneficial interest under a trust of land) the mortgage is itself overreachable.

[111] S 3(4); *Ladup Ltd v Williams & Glyn's Bank plc* [1985] 1 WLR 851; *Clark v Chief Land Registrar* [1994] Ch 370; *Yorkshire Bank Finance Ltd v Mulhall* [2008] EWCA Civ 1156, [2009] 1 P & CR 16 (no provision in LA 1980 affecting the enforcement of a charging order). See generally Walker and Buckley, *Charging Orders against Land* (2nd edn, 2004). See CPR r 73.2–73.10.

If a charging order is obtained over land that is subject to a trust of land, the judgment creditor may then apply to the court under TLATA 1996, s 14, above, p 488, for an order for sale of the property. See *Mortgage Corp v Shaire* [2001] Ch 743, 756–1 (Neuberger J) (under TLATA 1996 the interest of the chargee, unlike that of the trustee in bankruptcy, is only one factor to be taken into account in deciding whether to order sale, thus changing the position that formerly applied in cases such as *Lloyds Bank plc v Byrne & Byrne* [1993] 1 FLR 369). A sample form of order for sale following a charging order is set out in Appendix A to CPR, PD73.

[112] Charging Orders Act 1979, s 3, amended by LRA 2002, s 133, Sch 11, para 15.

[113] For overreaching, see above, p 486; below, pp 1068, 1113–17.

[114] LCA 1972, s 6(1A), inserted by TLATA 1996, s 25(1), Sch 3, para 12(1), (3).

[115] LRR 2003, r 91, Sch 4 (Form K), substituted by LR(A)R 2008 (SI 2008 No 1919).

[116] S 6 (register of writs and orders affecting land).   [117] LRA 2002, s 32.

a written agreement charging his land in favour of C;

a legal charge to D.

The mortgages in favour of A and D, so long as they satisfy the necessary formalities,[118] take effect as legal mortgages; those in favour of B and C are only equitable.[119] It can be seen that a legal mortgage may follow an equitable mortgage of the same property.

We shall see later that whether a mortgage is legal or equitable can have significance for the rights it gives to the mortgagee;[120] and for the method—principally, registration—by which it should be protected so as to give the mortgagee's security priority as against later mortgagees and third parties.[121]

III RIGHTS OF THE MORTGAGOR[122]

A THE EQUITY OF REDEMPTION

(1) Protection of the Mortgagor

A mortgagor, as we have seen, is the owner of the equity of redemption.[123] This is fundamental to the law of mortgages. It arises in the case of every conveyance or

---

[118] Execution as a deed and, in the case of registered land, completed by registration: above, pp 803 ff.

[119] Respectively, an equitable mortgage under the doctrine of *Walsh v Lonsdale*: above, p 807; and an equitable charge: above, p 811.

[120] Below, pp 845 ff.   [121] Below, pp 872 ff.

[122] For a mortgagor's action in negligence against:

(a) his solicitor where he enters into a mortgage as a result of the solicitor's failure to give proper advice, see *Forster v Outred & Co* [1982] 1 WLR 86; *Mortgage Express Ltd v Bowerman & Partners* [1996] 2 All ER 836 (duty of solicitor acting for mortgagor and sub-purchaser to inform mortgagor of price increase) [1996] Conv 204 (MP Thompson); *National Home Loans Corpn plc v Giffen Couch & Archer* [1998] 1 WLR 207 (solicitor acting for both mortgagor and mortgagee under a duty to inform mortgagee of mortgagor's default in previous mortgage); *Midland Bank v Cox McQueen* [1999] 1 FLR 1002 (solicitor not liable for loss caused by forged signature of wife executing charge); *Nationwide Building Society v Goodwin Harte* [1999] Lloyd's Rep PN 338 (breach of contract and fiduciary duty). On the duties of a solicitor acting for both mortgagor and mortgagee, see also Solicitors' Practice Rules 1990, r 6(3), as amended; [1999] Conv 2 (PH Kenny).

(b) the mortgagee's surveyor on whose negligent report he relied, see *Smith v Eric S Bush* [1990] 1 AC 831; [1989] Conv 359 (C Francis); [1989] CLJ 306 (WVH Rogers); (1989) 105 LQR 511 (D Allen); (1989) 52 MLR 841 (T Kaye); *Beaumont v Humberts* [1990] 2 EGLR 166; *Roberts v J Hampson & Co* [1990] 1 WLR 94;

(c) a valuer: *South Australian Asset Management Corp v York Montague Ltd* (the *Banque Bruxelles* case) [1997] AC 191 (extent of liability of valuer who provided mortgagee with negligent overvaluation, where mortgagee would not have lent if it had received careful valuation); (1997) 113 LQR 1 (J Stapleton); [1997] CLJ 19 (J O'Sullivan); *Nykredit Mortgage Bank plc v Edward Erdman Group Ltd (No 2)* [1997] 1 WLR 1627; Cartwright, *Misrepresentation, Mistake and Non-Disclosure* (2nd edn, 2006), para 6.41; *Oates v Anthony Pitman & Co* (1998) 76 P & CR 490; *Platform Home Loans Ltd v Oyston Shipways Ltd* [1996] 2 EGLR 110 (Jacob J: 'valuation is an art not a science, but it is not astrology'); on appeal [2000] 2 AC 190; (1999) 115 LQR 527 (J Stapleton) (imprudent lending policy can constitute contributory negligence when loan made in reliance on negligent valuation); *United Bank of Kuwait plc v Prudential Property Services Ltd* [1994] 2 EGLR 100 (criteria for valuation; contributory negligence of mortgagee in making advance); RICS Appraisal and Valuation Standards (8th edn, 2010); *Bristol and West Building Society v Mothew* [1998] Ch 1 (causation and relationship with measure of damages).

[123] Above, pp 798.

other transaction relating to property, whether styled a mortgage or not, in which the true intention of the parties is that the subject matter shall be security for a debt or other obligation. Outwardly a transaction may wear the appearance of an absolute conveyance; it may even be deliberately couched in language calculated to give that appearance, yet evidence is admissible to disclose the true intention of the parties.[124] For example, a transaction that takes the form of a sale by A to B, with a right in B to repurchase upon payment of a given sum on a particular date may or may not be a mortgage. It is a matter of intention. 'The question always is—was the original transaction a bona fide sale with a contract for repurchase, or was it a mortgage under the form of a sale?'[125] If it was the former, there is no right in B to redeem the property after the contract date.

What particularly concerns us here, however, is to notice that equity, in order to ensure that a transaction intended to be by way of mortgage shall afford nothing more than security to the lender, laid down two important rules concerning, first, the inviolability of the right of redemption; and secondly, the limits within which collateral advantages may be reserved to a mortgagee.

It will be seen, as the cases on these two rules are discussed, that in the twentieth century there was a development from a rigid to a more flexible attitude to the relationship between mortgagor and mortgagee, and an increasing awareness that, unless there is evidence of harsh and unconscionable dealing, a bargain freely entered into between the parties must be kept.

Let us consider these rules separately.

(a) The right of redemption is inviolable

Since the object of a mortgage is merely to provide the mortgagee with a security, any provision that directly or indirectly prevents the recovery by the mortgagor of his property upon performance of the obligation for which the security was created, is repugnant to the very nature of the transaction and therefore void, for when performance is completed there is no longer any need or justification for the retention of the security. Romer J said:[126]

> Now there is a principle which I will accept without any qualification ... that on a mortgage you cannot, by contract between the mortgagor and mortgagee, clog, as it is termed, the equity of redemption so as to prevent the mortgagor from redeeming on payment of principal, interest and costs.

---

[124] *Jason v Eyres* (1681) 2 Cas in Ch 33.

[125] *Williams v Owen* (1840) 5 My & Cr 303, 306 (Lord Cottenham); *Greendon Holdings Ltd v Oragwu* [1989] EGCS 100; *Lavin v Johnson* [2002] EWCA Civ 1138, [2002] All ER (D) 501 (Jul) at [82] (Robert Walker LJ): 'to say that the identification of a mortgage is a matter of substance, not form, is not to say that any transaction that is expected to produce the same economic consequences as a mortgage must be a mortgage in the eyes of the law'.

[126] *Biggs v Hoddinott* [1898] 2 Ch 307, 314.

This principle is commonly expressed in the aphorism, *once a mortgage always a mortgage*.[127] There are two aspects of this rule:

(1) The right to redeem must not be excluded

The courts refuse to countenance any provision that unduly restricts, even if it does not altogether prevent, the right of redemption. Each of the following cases exemplifies an agreement that was held void as being inconsistent with or repugnant to the true nature of a mortgage transaction:

(1) An agreement that redemption should be available to the mortgagor and *the heirs of his body*, and not to anyone else.[128]

(2) An agreement that renders part of the mortgaged property absolutely irredeemable.[129]

(3) A covenant by the mortgagor that the mortgagee, if he so desired, should be entitled to a conveyance of so much of the mortgaged estate as should equal the value of the loan at 20 years' purchase.[130]

(4) A covenant that if the borrower died before his father the subject matter of the mortgage should belong absolutely to the mortgagee.[131]

In two cases at the beginning of the last century the House of Lords considered provisions in mortgages that gave to the mortgagee an option to purchase the mortgaged property. In *Samuel v Jarrah Timber and Wood Paving Corp Ltd*,[132] the option was given at the time of the creation of the mortgage and was held to be void; otherwise the mortgagee by exercising the option could exclude the mortgagor's right of redemption. In *Reeve v Lisle*,[133] however, an option to purchase was held to be valid, where it was given by a subsequent and independent transaction, even though the only consideration was the release of the mortgagor from his obligation to pay the original loan. Lord Halsbury and Lord Macnaghten, who delivered speeches in both cases, expressed a lack of enthusiasm for their decision in *Samuel v Jarrah*. Lord Halsbury said:[134]

A perfectly fair bargain made between two parties to it, each of whom was quite sensible of what they were doing, is not to be performed because at the same time a mortgage arrangement was made between them. If a day had intervened between the two parts of the arrangement, the part of the bargain which the appellant claims to be performed would have been perfectly good and capable of being enforced; but a line of authorities going

---

[127] *Samuel v Jarrah Timber and Wood Paving Corp Ltd* [1904] AC 323, 329.

[128] *Howard v Harris* (1682) 1 Vern 33; *Salt v Marquess of Northampton* [1892] AC 1.

[129] *Davis v Symons* [1934] Ch 442.

[130] *Jennings v Ward* (1705) 2 Vern 520, as explained in *Biggs v Hoddinott* [1898] 2 Ch 307, 315, 323.

[131] *Salt v Marquess of Northampton*, above.

[132] [1904] AC 323, M & B p 870. For searching criticisms of this scholastic attitude, see (1903) 18 LQR 359 (Sir Frederick Pollock), M & B p 872; (1944) 60 LQR at 191 (GL Williams).

[133] [1902] AC 461, M & B p 871. See also *Alec Lobb (Garages) Ltd v Total Oil GB Ltd* [1985] 1 WLR 173; below, p 836, n 246.

[134] [1904] AC 323, 325.

back for more than a century has decided that such an arrangement as that which was here arrived at is contrary to a principle of equity, the sense or reason of which I am not able to appreciate, and very reluctantly I am compelled to acquiesce in the judgments appealed from.

And Lord Macnaghten said[135] of the decision:

I should not be sorry if your Lordships could see your way to modify it so as to prevent its being used as a means of evading a fair bargain come to between persons dealing at arms' length and negotiating on equal terms. The directors of a trading company in search of financial assistance are certainly in a very different position from that of an impecunious landowner in the toils of a crafty money-lender.

Samuel v Jarrah was followed in *Lewis v Frank Love Ltd*[136] where, on the transfer of a mortgage, the mortgagor gave to the transferees an option to purchase. There were separate documents for the transfer and the mortgage, but Plowman J held that the loan and the grant of the option were all part and parcel of one transaction.

In two cases the Court of Appeal has recently applied the doctrine set out in *Samuel v Jarrah*, but has expressed some misgivings about it. In one case an option to purchase fell within the doctrine, and was therefore struck down;[137] but in the other the Court emphasised that the court should look at the substance of the transaction, to inquire as to the true nature of the bargain that the parties have made. The mere fact that, contemporaneously with the grant of a mortgage over his property, the mortgagor grants the mortgagee an option to purchase the property does no more than raise the question whether the rule against 'clogs' applies.[138] Lord Phillips MR has said:[139]

The doctrine of a clog on the equity of redemption is ... an appendix to our law that no longer serves a useful purpose;

and Jonathan Parker LJ has added:[140]

it has to be accepted that the 'unruly dog'[141] is still alive (although one might perhaps reasonably expect its venerable age to inhibit it from straying too far or too often from

---

[135] Ibid, 327.

[136] [1961] 1 WLR 261; (1961) 77 LQR 163 (PVB).

[137] *Jones v Morgan* [2001] EWCA Civ 995, [2002] 1 EGLR 125, M & B p 873 (variation of existing mortgage that gave mortgagee right to buy part of property comprised in original mortgage: the right to purchase was an integral part of the financing agreement; Pill LJ dissenting on construction); [2001] Conv 500 (MP Thompson).

[138] *Warnborough Ltd v Garmite Ltd* [2003] EWCA Civ 1544, [2004] 1 P & CR DG8 (where option to purchase is granted against the background of a sale of the property by the grantee of the option, as owner of the property, to the grantor for a price that is to be left outstanding on mortgage, there must be a very strong likelihood that, on an examination of all the circumstances, the court will conclude that the substance of the transaction is one of sale and purchase and not one of mortgage: Jonathan Parker LJ at [76]: case remitted for decision on facts at trial, where judge held that the transaction was sale and purchase: [2006] EWHC 10 (Ch), [2007] 1 P & CR 2). See also *Brighton v Hove CC v Audus* [2009] EWHC 340 (Ch), [2009] 2 EGLR 131 (equitable rule does not apply where the transaction includes a charge but is a composite transaction that in substance is wider than a mortgage), criticised [2009] Conv 490 (A Tanney).

[139] *Jones v Morgan* [2002] 1 EGLR 125, 136.   [140] *Warnborough Ltd v Garmite Ltd*, above, at [72].

[141] *Kreglinger v New Patagonia Meat and Cold Storage Co Ltd* [1914] AC 25, 46 (Lord Mersey); below, p 825.

its kennel); and that however desirable an appendectomy might be thought to be, no such relieving operation has as yet been carried out.

The doctrine of *Samuel v Jarrah Timber and Wood Paving Corp Ltd* is due for reconsideration by the Supreme Court.[142]

(2) The right to redeem may be postponed

(i) Postponement

An important question is whether the postponement for a considerable period of the contractual right to redeem is objectionable as being an unreasonable interference with the rights of the mortgagor. If a mortgage is in essence a mere security, it is arguable that a clause that prolongs the security after the mortgagor is ready and willing to pay all that is due, is one that ought not to be upheld, even though it was accepted by him without objection at the time of the loan. The question was much canvassed by the Court of Appeal in *Knightsbridge Estates Trust Ltd v Byrne*,[143] where the facts were as follows:

> The Knightsbridge Company had mortgaged their property, consisting of 75 houses, eight shops and a block of flats, to the Prudential Assurance Company in return for a loan of £300,000 at 6½ per cent. The loan was liable to be called in at any time, and the mortgagors, desiring to obtain a reduction in the rate of interest and also to spread the repayment of the principal sum over a long term of years, transferred the mortgage to the Royal Liver Friendly Society. This mortgage was for £310,000 at 5¼ per cent, and at the suggestion of the mortgagors it was agreed that the loan should be repaid in 40 years by half-yearly instalments. The mortgagees agreed not to call the money in before the end of this period, provided that the instalments were punctually paid. A few years later, when mortgage interest rates fell again, the mortgagors sued for a declaration that they were entitled, on giving the usual six months' notice, to redeem the mortgage upon payment of principal, interest and costs.

It was argued for the mortgagors that this suspension for 40 years of the contractual right to redeem their property was unreasonable and therefore void. The Court of Appeal, however, upheld the suspension and denied that reasonableness, whether in respect of time or in other respects, is the true criterion of validity in such a case.[144] A

---

[142] See also other developments in other aspects of the equity of redemption, discussed in the following sections; and especially *Knightsbridge Estates Trust Ltd v Byrne* [1939] Ch 441, below; and *Kreglinger v New Patagonia Meat and Cold Storage Co Ltd* [1914] AC 25, below, p 000. See also (1985) Real Property Probate and Trust Journal 821 (LC Prebble and DW Cartwright); (1986–86) 60 St John's Law Review 452 (JL Light).

For proposals to reform the law to abolish the equitable jurisdiction concerned with clogs and fetters on the equity of redemption, see below, p 902. For legislation in the USA removing the mortgagee's option from the purview of the doctrine of clogs, see Uniform Land Security Interest Act 1986, para 211; New York General Obligations Law 1986, para 5.334; California Civil Code (1984), para 2906; cited 60 St John's Law Review at pp 492–7.

[143] [1939] Ch 441, M & B p 882. On appeal, [1940] AC 613, the House of Lords decided the case on an entirely different ground, namely that the mortgage was a valid debenture under the Companies Act 1929, ss 74 and 380 (now 2006, ss 738, 739) and expressed no opinion upon the reasoning of the Court of Appeal.

[144] See *Multiservice Bookbinding Ltd v Marden* [1979] Ch 84, 108, below, p 822.

contract freely entered into after due deliberation by parties dealing with each other at arms' length is not lightly to be interfered with.

Sir Wilfrid Greene MR said:

> The resulting agreement was a commercial agreement between two important corporations experienced in such matters, and has none of the features of an oppressive bargain where the borrower is at the mercy of an unscrupulous lender.[145]

A court of equity is vigilant in its support of the principle that 'redemption is of the very nature and essence of a mortgage',[146] but it does not attempt to reform mortgage transactions.

(ii) Illusory right of redemption

A provision that leaves the mortgagor with nothing more than an illusory right of redemption has, however, been held to be void. In *Fairclough v Swan Brewery Co Ltd*,[147] for example:

> the mortgagor was a tenant of a brewery in Western Australia, with an unexpired lease of seventeen and a half years. The mortgage prevented redemption until a date six weeks before the lease expired. There was no evidence of oppression.

The Privy Council held that this provision rendered the property substantially irredeemable, and therefore the mortgagor was entitled to redeem at an earlier date.

This decision of the Privy Council is in conflict with an earlier decision of the Court of Appeal, which was not cited to the Council. In *Santley v Wilde*:[148]

> S was the lessee of a theatre, the lease still having ten years to run. In return for a loan for the purpose of carrying on the theatre, S mortgaged the lease to W, and covenanted that she would repay the capital by instalments and also that she would 'during the residue of the term, notwithstanding that all principal moneys and interest may have been paid, pay a sum equal to one-third part of the clear net profit rent or rents to be derived' from the lease. There was a provision that the mortgage should determine on payment of the principal sum and interest and 'all other the moneys hereinbefore covenanted to be paid'.

As Lindley MR said, W's 'security depended not only on the solvency of the lady but also on the success of the theatre'. S claimed a declaration that she was entitled to redeem on payment of principal interest and costs and that the provision for a share of the profits was illegal and void. The Court of Appeal held that S could not redeem except by observing all the covenants for which her property was given as security, including the profit-sharing covenant. In effect the mortgage was irredeemable until the end of the lease, since only then could the net profits be earned and calculated.

---

[145] [1939] Ch 441, 455.

[146] *Noakes & Co Ltd v Rice* [1902] AC 24, 30 (Lord Macnaghten).

[147] [1912] AC 565, M & B p 881. Restraint of trade was also pleaded, at 566.

[148] [1899] 2 Ch 474, M & B p 879. It was the view of Dr JHC Morris that 'the transaction was not in essence one of mortgage, but a partnership agreement to share in the profits of the theatre', and therefore valid on that ground: Waldock, *Law of Mortgages*, p 187.

Accordingly, another old rule may come under review in the future, and rather than remorselessly applying the rule in *Fairclough v Swan Brewery Co Ltd* the courts may, in the absence of fraud or oppression, hold the parties to their bargain.

(b) Collateral advantages

A collateral advantage in favour of the mortgagee means something that is granted to him in addition to the return of his loan with interest, such as where a mortgagor agrees that for a given number of years he will purchase beer (or oil and petrol) for sale on the premises only from the mortgagee.

The question whether the reservation of such an advantage is valid is rendered difficult by a number of apparently irreconcilable decisions stretching back for more than a century. Indeed, the case law will be unintelligible unless it is realised that the attitude of the courts towards the matter has changed materially in the course of the last century, and that reliance can no longer be placed upon many of the older decisions. Lord Haldane, in a reference to one of the early cases of the modern era,[149] said:[150]

> In the 17th and 18th centuries a Court of Equity could hardly have so decided, and the judgment illustrates the elastic character of equity jurisdiction and the power of equity judges to mould the rules which they apply in accordance with the exigencies of the time.

In early days the judges frowned upon any attempt by a mortgagee to reap some additional advantage, as is shown by a remark of Trevor MR in 1705 that:

> a man shall not have interest for his money on a mortgage, and a collateral advantage besides for the loan of it.[151]

In a time when there was statutory control of interest rates, through usury laws designed to avoid the exploitation of borrowers, it was natural that the courts should be wary of any attempt by lenders to circumvent the statute by securing an advantage that did not constitute interest. However, in modern times a different note has been struck. The usury laws were repealed in 1854,[152] which therefore removed an objection to collateral advantages in a contact of loan. And the mortgagor is no longer seen as in need of such general special protection.[153] As Lord Haldane said in 1914:[154]

> The rule as to collateral advantages ... has been much modified by the repeal of the usury laws and by the recognition of modern varieties of commercial bargaining.

---

[149] *Biggs v Hoddinott* [1898] 2 Ch 307, M & B p 886.

[150] *Kreglinger v New Patagonia Meat and Cold Storage Co Ltd* [1914] AC 25, 38.

[151] *Jennings v Ward* (1705) 2 Vern 520.   [152] Usury Laws Repeal Act 1854.

[153] Statutory protection against 'harsh and unconscionable transactions' was introduced by Money-Lenders Act 1900; see now CCA 1974, ss 140A–140C, inserted by CCA 2006, ss 19–21, below, p 827. The equitable jurisdiction to relieve against unconscionable bargains, below, was also developed after the repeal of the usury laws as a tool to control unconscionable loans: Ibbetson, *Historical Introduction to the Law of Obligations* (1999), p 254. But these are more flexible rules, capable of discriminating between those borrowers that need protection, and those that can look after themselves.

[154] *Kreglinger v New Patagonia Meat and Cold Storage Co Ltd* [1914] AC 25, 38.

In the eye of the novelist, no doubt, the mortgagor is an impoverished debtor on the brink of ruin, unable to resist the demands of the rapacious lender, and it is perhaps true that the Court of Chancery in its more paternal days tended to take a somewhat similar view of his predicament. In fact, however, the parties to a modern mortgage may be hard-headed businessmen well able to protect their own interests, and in these days, when so much stress is laid upon the sanctity of contracts, it is difficult to appreciate why one of them should be allowed to disregard a bargain freely made, simply because he happens to be a mortgagor. Such maxims as 'Once a mortgage, always a mortgage' and 'A mortgage cannot be made irredeemable', undoubtedly express an important principle, but to apply them in an unbending and inflexible fashion so as to upset an ordinary commercial transaction would be out of keeping with the times. Lord Parker of Waddington said:[155]

> Such maxims, however convenient, afford little assistance where the court has to deal with a new or doubtful case. They obviously beg the question, always of great importance, whether the particular transaction which the court has to consider is, in fact, a mortgage or not, and if they be acted on without a careful consideration of the equitable considerations on which they are based, can only, like Bacon's idols of the market place, lead to misconception and error.

Despite the judicial uncertainties of the past, the modern law on the subject is clear, though its application to particular cases may be a difficult matter. As we shall see, collateral advantages are no longer struck down simply because they are collateral advantages. They are only invalidated where they are either unfair or unconscionable, or where they unfairly restrict redemption.

(1) The collateral advantage must not be unfair or unconscionable

In certain circumstances, a contract may be set aside as an 'unconscionable bargain'.[156] In English law[157] this is not a principle that has been applied generally to all types of contract, nor one that has been applied very often in the modern law;[158] but one area in which it has been applied, both historically[159] and in more recent cases,[160] is that of mortgages.

---

[155] Ibid, 53.   [156] Anson, pp 372–4; Chitty, paras 7–126 to 7–135.

[157] Commonwealth jurisdictions and the courts in the USA have been more favourable to the development of a general doctrine of unconscionability in contract: Chitty, para 7–136.

[158] More commonly claims have been brought under the equitable doctrine of undue influence, below, p 829.

[159] *Earl of Aylesford v Morris* (1873) 8 Ch App 484; *Barrett v Hartley* (1866) LR 2 Eq 789, 795; *James v Kerr* (1889) 40 Ch D 449; Waldock, *Law of Mortgages*, ch 8.

[160] *Cityland and Property (Holdings) Ltd v Dabrah*, below; *Multiservice Bookbinding Ltd v Marden*, below; *Alec Lobb (Garages) Ltd v Total Oil (Great Britain) Ltd* [1985] 1 WLR 173; *Crédit Lyonnais Bank Nederland NV v Burch* [1997] 1 All ER 144 (transaction set aside for undue influence, but was also an unconscionable bargain: at 151 (Nourse LJ); see also at 152–3 (Millett LJ)). See also [1995] LMCLQ 538 (N Bamforth).

In order to invoke this principle, the terms of the transaction must be 'not merely hard or improvident, but overreaching and oppressive'.[161] The court will always be astute to invalidate a mortgage that is unfair and unconscionable. Thus, in *Cityland and Property (Holdings) Ltd v Dabrah*:[162]

the mortgagor was a tenant who was buying the freehold of his house from his landlord and was 'obviously of limited means'; he undertook to pay a premium or bonus which represented either no less than 57 per cent of the amount of the loan or interest at 19 per cent.

Goff J stressed that this was not a 'bargain between two large trading concerns' and held that the mortgagor was entitled to redeem by paying the capital sum borrowed with reasonable interest fixed by the court.

In *Multiservice Bookbinding Ltd v Marden*,[163] Browne-Wilkinson J emphasised that the mortgagor must show that the bargain was unfair and unconscionable and not merely unreasonable and, furthermore,

a bargain cannot be unfair and unconscionable unless one of the parties to it has imposed the objectionable terms in a morally reprehensible manner, that is to say, in a way which affects his conscience.[164]

Not only, therefore, must *terms* of the transaction be unconscionable, but also the mortgage must have been obtained by unconscionable *conduct*. In that case:

the mortgagor was a small but progressive company in need of cash to enable it to expand; it had acted with independent legal advice. The mortgagee was only willing to lend money if he could be safeguarded against a decline in the purchasing power of sterling. The terms of the mortgage were that (i) interest be payable at 2 per cent above bank rate on the full capital sum for the duration of the mortgage, (ii) arrears of interest be capitalised after 21 days (thus providing for interest on interest), (iii) the loan be neither called in nor redeemed for ten years, and (iv) the value of the capital and interest be index-linked to the Swiss franc. When the mortgage became redeemable at the end of ten years in 1976, the total capital repayment had become £87,588 as against £36,000 lent, and the average rate of interest over the ten years would have been 16.01 per cent.

[161] *Alec Lobb (Garages) Ltd v Total Oil (Great Britain) Ltd* [1983] 1 WLR 87, 95 (Peter Millett QC). See also *Crédit Lyonnais Bank Nederland NV v Burch*, above, at 152–3 (Millett LJ).

[162] [1968] Ch 166. See also CCA 1974, ss 140A–140C, inserted by CCA 2006, ss 19–21, below, p 827, replacing the original provisions in CCA 1974, ss 137–40. It would appear that the mortgagor would also have succeeded under these various sections.

[163] [1979] Ch 84, M & B p 894; [1978] Conv 346 (HW Wilkinson), 432 (DW Williams); and for an economist's view (1981) 131 NLJ 4 (RA Bowles). CCA 1974 was not applicable, since the mortgagor was a body corporate. The rate may be linked to 'the base rate of X Bank plc': see Conv Prec 7–A2; or the retail prices index: Conv Prec 7–A3.

[164] Ibid, at 110. See *Boustany v Piggott* (1995) 69 P & CR 288, where PC set aside a lease on the grounds that it was an unconscionable bargain; *Commercial Bank of Australia Ltd v Amadio* (1983) 46 ALR 402, [1996] Conv 434 (M Pawlowski); *Jones v Morgan* [2001] EWCA Civ 995, [2002] 1 EGLR 125, 129–30.

It was held that all the terms of the mortgage were valid. An index-linked money obligation was not contrary to public policy, and the bargain, though hard, was not unfair and unconscionable.[165]

(2) The collateral advantage must not unfairly restrict redemption

We must now turn to the chequered history of collateral advantages. Most of the cases are concerned with an advantage that is to continue *after* redemption. In *Biggs v Hoddinott*,[166] however, where it was designed to cease with redemption, the Court of Appeal had no difficulty in holding it valid. In that case:

> Hoddinott mortgaged his hotel to Biggs, the brewer, in return for an advance of £7,654, and agreed that during the continuance of the mortgage he would sell no other beer than that supplied by B. It was mutually agreed that the mortgage should not be redeemable, nor should the loan be repayable, for five years.

The claim of Hoddinott, made two years later, that he was entitled to be released from the solus agreement and to procure beer elsewhere upon repayment of the loan, was rejected.[167]

Where, however, the advantage was designed to continue after redemption, the House of Lords struck it down in two cases. First, in *Noakes & Co Ltd v Rice*,[168] where:

> the tenant of a public-house, under a lease which had 26 years to run, mortgaged the premises as security for a loan and covenanted that for the duration of the lease, whether he had already repaid the mortgage money or not, he would not sell any malt liquors except those provided by the mortgagees. Three years later he claimed a declaration that he should be released from the covenant upon payment of all moneys due under the mortgage.

It was held by the House of Lords that he was entitled to the release he claimed. His right of redemption was hampered in the sense that after attainment of the object for which the security was created he would not be master in his own house—he would not recover his property as it was before the mortgage. 'The public-house, which was free when mortgaged, would have been tied to the mortgagee when redeemed.'[169]

Secondly, in *Bradley v Carritt*:[170]

---

[165] A building society has power to make an index-linked mortgage: *Nationwide Building Society v Registry of Friendly Societies* [1983] 1 WLR 1226 (decided under Building Societies Act 1962, ss 1, 4). See also Building Societies Act 1986, ss 10(10), 11(2) (repealed by Building Societies Act 1997, s 12(1)), 9A (inserted by Building Societies Act 1997, s 10).

[166] [1898] 2 Ch 307, M & B p 886; approved by the House of Lords in *Noakes & Co Ltd v Rice* [1902] AC 24, M & B p 887.

[167] There was no appeal from the decision of Romer J at first instance, that the postponement of the right to redeem for five years was valid; above, p 818.

[168] [1902] AC 24, M & B p 887. See also *Morgan v Jeffreys* [1910] 1 Ch 620. The discussions in these two cases could not be justified on the ground that the tie imposed upon the publican was void as being in restraint of trade; see *Esso Petroleum Co Ltd v Harper's Garage (Stourport) Ltd* [1968] AC 269, below, p 836.

[169] *Bradley v Carritt* [1903] AC 253, 277–8 (Lord Lindley).   [170] [1903] AC 253, M & B p 889.

the defendant, who owned shares which gave him a controlling interest in a tea company, mortgaged them to the claimant, a tea-broker, and in further consideration for the loan, entered into the following contract:

'I agree... to use my best endeavours as a shareholder to secure that you or any firm of brokers of which you for the time being shall be a partner shall *always hereafter* have the sale of the company's teas as broker, and in the case of any of the company's teas being sold otherwise than through you or your firm, I personally agree to pay you or your firm the amount of the commission which you or your firm would have earned if the teas had been sold through you or your firm.'

The claimant was appointed broker; but the defendant repaid the loan, redeemed his shares and transferred them to another mortgagee, X, who succeeded in ousting the claimant from his appointment.

The House of Lords, reversing by a majority of three to two the court of first instance and the Court of Appeal, held that the agreement set out above was void, and that the defendant was not liable for its breach. Lord Lindley and Lord Shand, however, dissented. What weighed with the majority was that, after redemption, the shares would be more or less frozen assets in the hands of the mortgagor, since, unless he showed great vigilance, their sale would almost certainly result in his being liable to the claimant for loss of brokerage; they gave him a controlling interest in the tea company, and it was only by retaining them that he could ensure the continued employment of the claimant as broker.

In spite of these two decisions, the House of Lords came to a different conclusion in *Kreglinger v New Patagonia Meat and Cold Storage Co Ltd*,[171] where the facts were as follows:

A firm of woolbrokers lent £10,000 to a company which carried on business as meat preservers, the agreement being that the company might pay off the loan at any time by giving a month's notice. The loan was secured, not by an ordinary mortgage, but by an analogous security called a floating charge.[172] It was agreed that for five years from the date of the loan the company would not sell sheepskins to any person other than the lenders, so long as the latter were willing to pay the full market price. It was also agreed that the lenders would not demand repayment before five years had elapsed. The loan was repaid within two and a half years. The point that fell to be decided was whether the option on the sheepskins was enforceable by the lenders after repayment of the loan.

The House held unanimously that the lenders were entitled to an injunction restraining the company from selling skins to third parties during the remainder of

---

[171] [1914] AC 25, M & B p 890.

[172] This, though a charge upon the assets for the time being, does not prevent a company from dealing with its property in the ordinary course of business, but it does so when the chargee takes steps, such as by the appointment of a receiver, to crystallise the security. For the characteristics of the charge, see *Re Yorkshire Woolcombers Association Ltd* [1903] 2 Ch 284, 295 (Romer J); *Re Spectrum Plus Ltd* [2005] UKHL 41, [2005] 2 AC 680; and for crystallisation of a charge, see *Re Woodroffes (Musical Instruments) Ltd* [1986] Ch 366; *Re Brightlife Ltd* [1987] Ch 200; (1976) 40 Conv (NS) 397 (JH Farrar); [1988] CLJ 213 (E Ferran); *William Gaskell Group Ltd v Highley (Nos 1, 2, 3)* [1993] BCC 200. See generally [1994] CLJ 81 (S Worthington); *Re Cosslett (Contractors) Ltd* [1998] Ch 495.

the five years. While it was true that the company would not be as free in the conduct of their business after repayment of the loan as they were before the grant of the charge, the House of Lords unanimously held that the agreement should be upheld, and that it should continue to bind the mortgagor even though it was to continue after redemption. For Viscount Haldane LC the matter was one of construction:[173]

> The question in the present case is whether the right to redeem has been interfered with. And this must…depend on the answer to a question which is primarily one of fact. What was the true character of the transaction? Did the appellants make a bargain such that the right to redeem was cut down, or did they simply stipulate for a collateral undertaking, outside and clear of the mortgage, which would give them an exclusive option of purchase of the sheepskins of the respondents? The question is in my opinion not whether the two contracts were made at the same moment and evidenced by the same instrument, but whether they were in substance a single and undivided contract or two distinct contracts…If your Lordships arrive at the conclusion that the agreement for an option to purchase the respondents' sheepskins was not in substance a fetter on the exercise of their right to redeem, but was in the nature of a collateral bargain the entering into which was a preliminary and separable condition of the loan, the decided cases cease to present any great difficulty.

And their Lordships so concluded. This approach provides the court with a much needed flexibility in the area of collateral advantages and enables it to adapt the earlier strict rules to modern circumstances.

Bradley v Carritt thus represents the high-water mark of the conception of a mortgage as an onerous obligation imposed upon a necessitous borrower, in whose favour the court should therefore intervene.[174] The *Kreglinger* case, on the other hand, reveals a judicial appreciation of a mortgage as a transaction freely concluded by businessmen without colour of oppression, which should therefore form no exception to the maxim *pacta sunt servanda*. This is a more realistic and reasonable approach, and one more compatible with the business conditions of the modern era.

In 1914 Lord Mersey said in the *Kreglinger* case:[175]

> The doctrine itself seems to me to be like an unruly dog, which, if not securely chained to its own kennel, is prone to wander into places where it ought not to be. Its introduction into the present case would give effect to no equity and would defeat justice.

The dog is now under control.

We must now consider further bases of protection of the mortgagor. The first two are statutory, the third equitable and the fourth common law.

---

[173] At 39. See *De Beers Consolidated Mines Ltd v British South Africa Co* [1912] AC 52, M & B p 897; *Re Petrol Filling Station, Vauxhall Bridge Road, London* (1968) 20 P & CR 1, M & B p 898.
[174] Waldock, *Law of Mortgages*, ch viii.   [175] [1914] AC 25, 46.

(c) Consumer Credit Act 1974

(1) Regulated agreements

The Consumer Credit Act 1974[176] established a comprehensive code regulating the supply of credit to an individual.[177] The Act includes provisions on the licensing of credit and hire businesses;[178] advertising and canvassing;[179] all aspects of the agreement; and judicial control over its enforcement.[180]

To come within the Act, a mortgage must constitute a regulated consumer credit agreement, that is to say, an agreement by which a creditor provides a debtor with credit of any amount.[181] There are, however, exempt agreements,[182] of which the most important are consumer credit agreements where the creditor is one of a specified list (including a building society, bank[183] or local authority); and the Act does not regulate a consumer credit agreement if (a) it is secured by a land mortgage; and (b) entering into that agreement as lender is a regulated activity for the purposes of the Financial Services and Markets Act 2000.[184] The effect is that the Act will include consumer mortgage agreements, although not those where there are other regulatory protections in place.[185]

---

[176] See Bennion and Dobson, *Consumer Credit Control*; Lomnicka, *Encyclopedia of Consumer Credit Law*; Goode, *Consumer Credit Law and Practice*; Cousins, *The Law of Mortgages*, ch 16; Fisher and Lightwood, ch 20; [1975] CLJ 79 (RM Goode); (1975) 39 Conv (NS) 94 (JE Adams). The provisions of the 1974 Act have since been amended or superseded in various respects; some of the relevant amendments are noted below. For discussion of the amendments made by CCA 2006, see [2007] Conv 316 (S Brown).

[177] This includes a partnership consisting of two or three persons, and an unincorporated body of persons: s 189(1), substituted by CCA 2006, s 1 (to restrict the protection of the Act to small partnerships).

[178] Part III.

[179] Part IV; Consumer Credit (Advertisement) Regulations 2004 (SI 2004 No 1484); (2004) 148 SJ 1298 (N Chowdhury). Provisions on false or misleading advertisements were replaced by Consumer Protection from Unfair Trading Regulations 2008 (SI 2008 No 1277).

[180] Part IX.

[181] S 8, as amended by CCA 2006. Until that amendment, there was a financial limit on regulated agreements: originally £5,000, raised to £15,000 and finally £25,000 by Consumer Credit (Increase of Monetary Limits) Amendment Order 1998 (SI 1998 No 996).

[182] S 16, as amended. CCA 2006 introduced futher exemptions for (i) high net worth debtors and hirers who sign a declaration agreeing to forgo the Act's protection and remedies: CCA 1974, s 16A, added by CCA 2006, s 3 and (ii) businesses debtors and hirers in relation to agreements exceeding £25,000: CCA 1974, s 16B, added by CCA 2006, s 4. Legislative Reform (Consumer Credit) Order 2008 (SI 2008 No 2826) introduced an exemption for land mortgages where less than 40 per cent of the land is used, or is intended to be used, as or in connection with a dwelling by the debtor, a beneficiary of a trust or a connected person: CCA 1974, s 16C. The exemptions in ss 16A, 16B and 16C do not affect the application of ss 140A to 140C, below.

See also CCA 1974 (Electronic Communications) Order 2004 (SI 2004 No 3236), which makes amendments for the purpose of enabling and facilitating communications for concluding regulated agreements and when sending notices and other documents; Consumer Credit (Enforcement, Default and Termination Notices) (Amendment) Regulations 2004 (SI 2004 No 3237), which amend the Consumer Credit (Enforcement, Default and Termination Notices) Regulations 1983 to ensure that all notices sent under the Regulations are sent in paper format.

[183] 'Deposit-taker': a person with permission under Part 4 of the Financial Services and Markets Act 2000 to accept deposits: CCA 1974, s 16(1)(h), (10), inserted by Banking Act 1987, s 88, and substituted by SI 2001 No 3649, art 165(1), (2)(b), (6).

[184] S 16(6C), inserted by SI 2001 No 544, art 90(2) and substituted by SI 2006 No 2383.

[185] For the significance of regulation of mortgages, see above, p 796.

A security cannot be enforced by reason of any breach of a regulated agreement by the debtor, until the creditor has served a notice under section 87. This is similar to, but not identical with, the notice required by section 146 of the Law of Property Act 1925 in the case of the forfeiture of a lease.[186] Further, a land mortgage securing a regulated agreement is enforceable on an order of the court only.[187] And a regulated agreement that is 'improperly executed' (that is it does not comply with the formalities prescribed in Part V of the Act) can also be enforced only on an order of the court.[188]

There are other provisions that protect a debtor. These include section 93 which prohibits any term requiring the rate of interest to be increased on default; and section 94 under which the debtor has the right, on giving notice to the creditor, to repay prematurely at any time. Any provision in the agreement that limits his rights in this respect is void.[189] It would seem that if a provision to postpone the contractual right to redeem[190] were included in a regulated agreement it would be void. Finally, under section 113, a creditor shall not derive from the enforcement of the security any greater benefit than he would obtain from enforcement of a regulated agreement, if the security were not provided. This would seem to deny the mortgagee the full benefit of foreclosure.[191]

(2) Unfair relationships

The most far-reaching provision for the protection of the debtor is the power given to the court under section 140B,[192] which arises where:[193]

> it determines that the relationship between the creditor and the debtor arising out of the agreement (or the agreement taken with any related agreement) is unfair to the debtor because of one or more of the following–
>
> (a) any of the terms of the agreement or of any related agreement;
>
> (b) the way in which the creditor has exercised or enforced any of his rights under the agreement or any related agreement;
>
> (c) any other thing done (or not done) by, or on behalf of, the creditor (either before or after the making of the agreement or any related agreement).

---

[186] Above, p 288.

[187] S 126. For orders that the court can make, see Part IX of the Act.

[188] S 65. The county court has exclusive jurisdiction: s 141(1). See also s 127 (enforcement orders), amended by CCA 2006, Sch 4, para 1 to remove restrictions on the court's power to allow enforcement; cf *Wilson v First County Trust Ltd (No 2)* [2003] UKHL 40, [2004] 1 AC 816 where HL had held that the original provisions of s 127 were not incompatible with ECHR.

[189] S 173(1).   [190] *Knightsbridge Estates Trust Ltd v Byrne* [1939] Ch 441; above, p 818.

[191] Below, p 862; (1975) 39 Conv (NS) 94, 108.

[192] Ss 140A–140C were inserted with effect from 6 April 2007 by CCA 2006, ss 19–21, to replace earlier provisions set out in CCA 1974, ss 137–140 by which the courts had power to 'reopen' a credit agreement if the credit bargain was 'extortionate'—ie either if the payments to be made under it were 'grossly exorbitant' or if it 'otherwise grossly contravenes ordinary principles of fair dealing' (s 138(1)). For discussion of the old provisions, see the 17th edn of this book, pp 745–8; and for criticism of the old provisions and proposals for reform, see *Unjust Credit Transactions*: Report by the Director General of Fair Trading (1991), paras 1.7, 1.9 and 3.9, set out in the 8th edn of this book at pp 850–1. The original provisions in CCA 1974 replaced Money-lenders Act 1900, s 1, under which a court could reopen a transaction with a money-lender where the interest or other charges were excessive and the transaction was 'harsh and unconscionable'.

[193] S 140A(1).

The application for an order may be made only by the debtor or a surety,[194] but the burden is on the creditor to show that the relationship is not unfair.[195]

The powers of the court under section 140B are wide. It may:[196]

(a) require the creditor, or any associate or former associate of his, to repay (in whole or in part) any sum paid by the debtor or by a surety by virtue of the agreement or any related agreement (whether paid to the creditor, the associate or the former associate or to any other person);

(b) require the creditor, or any associate or former associate of his, to do or not to do (or to cease doing) anything specified in the order in connection with the agreement or any related agreement;

(c) reduce or discharge any sum payable by the debtor or by a surety by virtue of the agreement or any related agreement;

(d) direct the return to a surety of any property provided by him for the purposes of a security;

(e) otherwise set aside (in whole or in part) any duty imposed on the debtor or on a surety by virtue of the agreement or any related agreement;

(f) alter the terms of the agreement or of any related agreement;

(g) direct accounts to be taken...between any persons.

This power extends to all credit agreements, except[197] a land mortgage where the lender is a regulated under the Financial Services and Markets Act 2000.[198]

Where the mortgagor is a company, the court has power to set aside or vary the terms of any extortionate credit transaction entered into within three years before the day on which the company entered administration or went into liquidation.[199]

(d) Unfair Terms in Consumer Contracts Regulations 1999

The Unfair Terms in Consumer Contracts Regulations 1999[200] apply to mortgages entered into by consumers[201]—that is where the mortgagor is a natural person acting

---

[194] S 140A(2), setting out the contexts in which the debtor or surety may raise the point; *Patel v Patel* [2009] EWHC 3264 (QB), [2010] 1 All ER (Comm) 864 at [62]-[66] (claim for relief not barred 12 years after date of credit agreement, because assessment of unfairness of relationship has to be made with regard to entirety of the relationship, and debtor's cause of action accrues from day to day until relationship ends).

[195] S 140B(9).   [196] S 140B(1).
[197] S 140A(5).   [198] S 16(6C); above, n 184.
[199] Insolvency Act 1986, s 244, amended by Enterprise Act 2002, s 248(3), Sch 17, paras 9, 30.

[200] SI 1999 No 2083 reimplementing Council Directive 93/13/EEC, and replacing Unfair Terms in Consumer Contracts Regulations 1994. The Law Commission has proposed the replacement of the Regulations and the Unfair Contract Terms Act 1977 with a single unified legislative regime, which would continue to maintain the control on unfair contract terms in land contracts (including mortgages) in favour of a consumer: Law Com No 292 (2005), paras 3.80, 5.76. However, legislation awaits the outcome of negotiations in Europe on a possible new Directive on consumer rights: Law Com No 323, *Annual Report 2009-10*, para A.21. The FSA considers the fairness under the 1999 Regulations of standard terms in financial services contracts issued by authorised firms and their representatives, including mortgage contracts: OFT and FSE Concordat 2008, available on www.oft.gov.uk.

[201] *Falco Finance Ltd v Michael Gough* (1999) 17 Tr LR 526 (terms providing for (i) higher interest rate payable in case of single default; (ii) flat rate of interest; and (iii) six-month deferment of redemption of

for purposes that are outside his trade, business or profession.[202] An unfair term is not binding on the consumer, but the contract continues to bind the parties if it is capable of continuing in existence without the unfair term;[203] the court therefore has the power to strike out just the unfair clause. A term that has not been individually negotiated is regarded as unfair if, contrary to the requirement of good faith, it causes a significant imbalance in the parties' rights and obligations arising under the contract, to the detriment of the consumer.[204]

(e) Undue influence. Misrepresentation

A mortgage may be set aside for duress,[205] undue influence[206] or misrepresentation,[207] not only where it is exerted by the mortgagee himself on the mortgagor, but also in some circumstances[208] where it is exerted by a third party. In a number of cases the mortgage was given to secure not the mortgagor's own borrowings or business activities but those of another family member. Sometimes the mortgagor has claimed that the mortgagee himself exerted undue influence on him,[209] but more often the

mortgage all unfair within 1994 Regulations, above, n 200); (1999) 143 SJ 572 (C Banks); Emmet, paras 25.260–25.267; [1995] CLJ 235 (J Beatson); (1995) 111 LQR 655 (S Bright and C Bright); (1999) 115 LQR 360 (S Bright); (2000) 4 L & T Rev 38 (J Holbrook). On the Regulations see generally Lawson, *Exclusion Clauses and Unfair Contract Terms* (9th edn, 2008); Anson, pp 206–15.

[202] Unfair Terms in Consumer Contracts Regulations 1999, reg 3(1); *Evans v Cherry Tree Finance Ltd* [2008] EWCA Civ 331 (borrower who took out loan on property that was partly residential and partly commercial was 'consumer' for purposes of the Regulations).

[203] Ibid, reg 8.

[204] Ibid, reg 5(1). An 'indicative and non-exhaustive list of terms that *may* be regarded as unfair' is set out in Sch 2. The list is drafted with contracts of sale or supply of goods in mind, and is not aimed at the terms normally found in a mortgage, but includes such things as (para 1(j), (k), (l)) the power to increase the price or change other terms unilaterally—but with specific exception (para 2(b), (c) and (d)) for interest rate fluctuations in contracts of financial services, as long as the supplier is required to notify the consumer, and the consumer has the right to dissolve the contract; and lawful price indexation clauses, so it appears that an index-linked mortgage (above, p 823, n 165) would not normally be unfair within the meaning of the Regulations. On the application of the test (as set out in the 1994 Regulations: above, n 200) to an unsecured credit agreement regulated under CCA 1974, see *Director General of Fair Trading v First National Bank plc* [2001] UKHL 52, [2002] 1 AC 481. A term of the mortgage that appears unfair might, on proper construction, be limited: *Paragon Finance plc v Pender* [2005] EWCA Civ 760, [2005] 1 WLR 3412 (increase by mortgagee in rate of interest; whether breach of implied obligation not to exercise variation right improperly); leave to appeal to HL refused [2006] 1 WLR 398.

[205] On duress generally, see Anson, pp 350–58; Chitty, paras 7–003 to 7–055.

[206] On undue influence generally, see Anson, pp 359–72; Chitty, paras 7–056 to 7–125; H & M, paras 26–007 to 26–013. On the relationship between the doctrine and unconscionability, see (1997) 113 LQR 10 (H Tjio); [1997] CLJ 71 (E O'Dell); (1998) 114 LQR 479 (D Capper).

[207] On misrepresentation generally, see Anson, pp 300–32; Chitty, ch 6; Cartwright, *Misrepresentation, Mistake and Non-Disclosure*, esp ch 4.

[208] Below, p 831.

[209] See, in particular, *Lloyds Bank Ltd v Bundy* [1975] QB 326 (undue influence presumed where assistant bank manager obtained mortgage guaranteeing £10,000 on property worth only £11,000 from client's aged father to support client's failing company, visiting him at home in presence of his family to obtain his signature on forms already filled in, without leaving them for him to consider or giving him the opportunity of taking independent advice: he 'crossed the line': at 347 (Sir Eric Sachs)); *National Westminster Bank plc v Morgan* [1985] AC 686 (mortgage by wife to support husband's business not entered into under undue influence, even though signed on visit by bank manager to their home, where the 'atmosphere ... was plainly

claim is of undue influence or misrepresentation exerted by the third party for whose benefit the mortgage was entered into: commonly the husband, for whom the wife has agreed to mortgage her interest in the family home.

This area of the law was clarified by the House of Lords in *Royal Bank of Scotland plc v Etridge (No 2)*.[210]

(1) Establishing undue influence or misrepresentation

Whether the claim is that it was exerted by the mortgagee or by a third party, the mortgagor must first establish the undue influence or misrepresentation. Misrepresentation must be proved on the facts.[211] The earlier cases spoke of two distinct categories of undue influence:[212] 'actual undue influence', which can be affirmatively proved on the evidence of the defendant's conduct; and 'presumed undue influence', which cannot be proved affirmatively but is presumed from the relationship of the parties, coupled with a consideration of the terms of the contract.[213] The House of Lords has now made clear that there is just a single doctrine:[214]

> Whether a transaction was brought about by the exercise of undue influence is a question of fact. Here, as elsewhere, the general principle is that he who asserts a wrong has been committed must prove it. The burden of proving an allegation of undue influence rests upon the person who claims to have been wronged. This is the general rule. The evidence required to discharge the burden of proof depends on the nature of the alleged undue influence, the personality of the parties, their relationship, the extent to which the transaction cannot readily be accounted for by the ordinary motives of ordinary persons in that relationship, and all the circumstances of the case.

tense. Mr Morgan was in and out of the room, 'hovering around.': at 701 (Lord Scarman). 'A relationship of banker and customer may become one in which the banker acquires a dominating influence. If he does and a manifestly disadvantageous transaction is proved, there would then be room for the court to presume that it resulted from the exercise of undue influence': ibid, at 707. But the manger did not 'cross the line', nor was the transaction unfair to the wife).

[210] [2001] UKHL 44, [2002] 2 AC 773, M & B p 902; [2002] Conv 174 (MP Thompson); [2002] CLJ 229 (M Oldham); (2002) 65 MLR 435 (R Bigwood); (2002) 118 LQR 337 (D O'Sullivan); [2001] All ER Rev 254 (PJ Clarke). The speech of Lord Nicholls of Birkenhead sets out the view of the House: at [3] (Lord Bingham of Cornhill).

[211] For the elements of the claim to rescission for misrepresentation, see Cartwright, *Misrepresentation, Mistake and Non-Disclosure*, paras 4.21 ff.

[212] 'Class 1' (actual undue influence) and 'Class 2' (presumed undue influence, sub-divided into 2A, where the relationship is in an established category giving rise automatically to a presumption, and 2B, where the relationship has to be shown on the facts to be sufficient to give rise to the presumption): *Bank of Credit and Commerce International SA v Aboody* [1990] 1 QB 923, 953, adopted by Lord Browne-Wilkinson in *Barclays Bank plc v O'Brien* [1994] 1 AC 180, 189. In the case of presumed influence, the presumption could be rebutted by showing that the party was in fact acting independently of any influence, typically by showing that he had advice from a fully informed independent adviser: *Inche Noriah v Shaik Allie Bin Omar* [1929] AC 127.

[213] *National Westminster Bank plc v Morgan*, above, n 209, used the language of (i) a relationship of 'dominating influence' coupled with (ii) a 'manifestly disadvantageous transaction'. This terminology was disapproved in *Royal Bank of Scotland plc v Etridge (No 2)* [2002] 2 AC 773 at [11], [26].

[214] *Royal Bank of Scotland plc v Etridge (No 2)*, above, at [13]-[14] (Lord Nicholls of Birkenhead).

Proof that the complainant placed trust and confidence in the other party in relation to the management of the complainant's financial affairs, coupled with a transaction which calls for explanation, will normally be sufficient, failing satisfactory evidence to the contrary, to discharge the burden of proof. On proof of these two matters the stage is set for the court to infer that, in the absence of a satisfactory explanation, the transaction can only have been procured by undue influence. In other words, proof of these two facts is prima facie evidence that the defendant abused the influence he acquired in the parties' relationship. He preferred his own interests. He did not behave fairly to the other. So the evidential burden then shifts to him. It is for him to produce evidence to counter the inference which otherwise should be drawn.

Even if there is no evidence of actual pressure or the like, the court may therefore still be satisfied, on the balance of probabilities, that the mortgagor was subject to undue influence by a person (either the mortgagee or a third party) in whom he placed trust and confidence, if the terms of the transaction cannot otherwise be explained. The 'presumption' of undue influence is only a rebuttable evidential presumption.[215]

This must, however, be distinguished from a different kind of presumption: in certain types of relationship the law presumes, irrebuttably, that one party had influence over the other, thus dispensing with the necessity of proving on the facts that the claimant actually reposed trust and confidence in the other party.[216] This will not, however, apply in the situations that have commonly arisen in relation to mortgages: the relationship between bank and customer,[217] or between husband and wife,[218] are not without more presumed to be relationships of trust and confidence for this purpose.

(2) Undue influence or misrepresentation by a third party

In recent years many cases[219] have arisen in which the mortgagor has sought to avoid being bound by the mortgage on the basis of undue influence or misrepresentation by

---

[215] Ibid, at [16].

[216] Ibid, at [18]. This was formerly known as 'Class 2A' undue influence: above, n 212. Proof of such a relationship does not establish undue influence: it only establishes the relationship of confidence, or influence; there is no presumption that the confidence has been abused: ibid, at [104] (Lord Hobhouse of Woodborough).

[217] Ibid, at [10]; *Lloyds Bank Ltd v Bundy* [1975] QB 326; *National Westminster Bank plc v Morgan* [1985] AC 686.

[218] Ibid, at [19]; *Leeder v Stevens* [2005] EWCA Civ 50 (where CA assumed that the presumption applies to a relationship between fiancé and fiancée and by analogy between a man and a woman who were not engaged but had talked about getting married); (2005) 121 LQR 567 (N Enonchong). A presumption of undue influence has been considered in *Turkey v Awadh* [2005] EWCA Civ 382, [2005] 2 P & CR 29 (father and his daughter and son-in-law); *Watson v Huber* [2005] All ER (D) 156 (March) (half-sisters); *Hughes v Hughes* [2005] EWHC 469 (Ch), [2005] 1 FCR 679 (loving relationship between mother and son); (2005) 155 NLJ 1579.

[219] In *Royal Bank of Scotland plc v Etridge (No 2)* the House of Lords heard appeals in eight separate cases. In the earlier decision in *Barclay's Bank plc v O'Brien* [1994] 1 AC 180, 185–6 Lord Browne-Wilkinson noted that there had been eleven reported decisions in such cases in the Court of Appeal in the previous eight years. For cases since *Etridge*, see, eg, *National Westminster Bank plc v Amin* [2002] UKHL 9, [2002] 1 FLR 735; [2002] Conv 499 (M Haley); *UCB Corporate Services Ltd v Williams* [2002] EWCA Civ 555, [2003] 1 P & CR 12; *Bank of Scotland v Hill* [2002] EWCA Civ 1081, [2003] 1 P & CR DG 7; *Lloyds TSB Bank plc v Holdgate* [2002] EWCA Civ 1543, [2003] HLR 25; *First National Bank plc v Achampong* [2003] EWCA Civ 487, [2004]

a third party. Lord Nicholls of Birkenhead explained that this is a comparatively recent phenomenon:[220]

> It arises out of the substantial growth in home ownership over the last 30 or 40 years and, as part of that development, the great increase in the number of homes owned jointly by husbands and wives. More than two-thirds of householders in the United Kingdom now own their own homes. For most home-owning couples, their homes are their most valuable asset. They must surely be free, if they so wish, to use this asset as a means of raising money, whether for the purpose of the husband's business or for any other purpose. Their home is their property. The law should not restrict them in the use they may make of it. Bank finance is in fact by far the most important source of external capital for small businesses with fewer than ten employees. These businesses comprise about 95% of all businesses in the country, responsible for nearly one-third of all employment. Finance raised by second mortgages on the principal's home is a significant source of capital for the start-up of small businesses.
>
> If the freedom of home-owners to make economic use of their homes is not to be frustrated, a bank must be able to have confidence that a wife's signature of the necessary guarantee and charge will be as binding upon her as is the signature of anyone else on documents which he or she may sign. Otherwise banks will not be willing to lend money on the security of a jointly owned house or flat.
>
> At the same time, the high degree of trust and confidence and emotional interdependence which normally characterises a marriage relationship provides scope for abuse. One party may take advantage of the other's vulnerability. Unhappily, such abuse does occur. Further, it is all too easy for a husband, anxious or even desperate for bank finance, to misstate the position in some particular or to mislead the wife, wittingly or unwittingly, in some other way. The law would be seriously defective if it did not recognise these realities.

The House of Lords first explored this problem in detail in *Barclay's Bank plc v O'Brien*,[221] in which the wife had joined her husband in mortgaging the matrimonial home as surety for debts owed to the bank by a company in which the husband, but not the wife, had an interest. The wife sought to resist the mortgagor's claim to possession on the basis of the husband's undue influence or misrepresentation in procuring her agreement to the mortgage. The House of Lords held that the wife in such a case could avoid the mortgage as against the bank if (i) the wrongdoing of the husband could be shown, and (ii) *either* the husband was acting as agent for the bank in obtaining the mortgage, *or* the bank had notice, actual or constructive, of the wrongdoing.[222]

The theory that the husband can be treated as acting as agent for the bank when procuring his wife to become surety is highly artificial. In reality the husband is acting on his own behalf and not as agent for the mortgagee. Since *O'Brien* the doctrine of notice has gained the upper hand.[223] *O'Brien* turned on the application of the doctrine

1 FCR 18; [2003] Conv 314 (MP Thompson); *Chater v Mortgage Agency Services Number Two Ltd* [2003] EWCA Civ 490, [2004] 1 P & CR 4; *First Plus Financial Group plc v Hewett* [2010] EWCA Civ 312, [2010] 2 EGLR 51 (husband's concealment of affair amounted to undue influence against wife of which mortgagee had notice).

[220] *Royal Bank of Scotland plc v Etridge (No 2)* [2002] 2 AC 773 at [34]-[36].
[221] [1994] 1 AC 180; (1998)114 LQR 220 (Millett LJ).
[222] [1994] 1 AC 180, 191 (Lord Browne-Wilkinson).
[223] *Royal Bank of Scotland plc v Etridge (No 2)* [2002] 2 AC 773. Before *O'Brien* agency was found in *Kingsnorth Trust Ltd v Bell* [1986] 1 WLR 119; cf *Coldunell Ltd v Gallon* [1986] QB 1184; *Midland Bank plc*

of constructive notice. Lord Browne-Wilkinson said that, unless the creditor who is put on inquiry of the risk of the husband's undue influence or misrepresentation takes reasonable steps to satisfy himself that the wife's agreement to stand surety has been properly obtained, the creditor will have constructive notice of the wife's rights—and therefore the wife will be able to avoid the surety contract with the bank. The bank is put on inquiry by two factors:

(i)   the transaction is on its face not to the financial advantage of the wife and,

(ii) there is a substantial risk in a transaction of that kind that, in procuring the wife to act as surety, the husband has committed a legal or equitable wrong that entitles the wife to set aside the transaction.[224]

His Lordship set out guidelines for the future as to what reasonable steps a bank should take in order to avoid being fixed by constructive notice:[225]

> Unless there are special circumstances, a creditor will have taken reasonable steps…if the creditor warns the surety (at a meeting not attended by the principal debtor) of the amount of her potential liability and of the risks involved and advises the surety to take independent legal advice…I would not exclude exceptional cases where a creditor has knowledge of further facts which render the presence of undue influence not only possible but probable. In such cases the creditor to be safe will have to insist that the wife is separately advised.

In *O'Brien* the bank was put on inquiry, but had failed to warn and advise, and the wife was therefore entitled to avoid the mortgage as against the bank.

The basis of the decision in *O'Brien* was further reviewed by the House of Lords in *Royal Bank of Scotland plc v Etridge (No 2)*.[226] Lord Nicholls of Birkenhead noted that the use of the concept of constructive notice in *O'Brien* was not conventional,[227] and that the decision had made a change in the law:[228]

> The traditional view of equity in this tripartite situation seems to be that a person in the position of the wife will only be relieved of her bargain if the other party to the transaction (the

---

v Perry [1988] 1 FLR 161; *Barclays Bank plc v Kennedy* (1988) 58 P & CR 221. See also *National Westminster Bank plc v Beaton* [1997] EGCS 53 (postscript in letter from bank asking solicitor to advise wife did not make solicitor agent of bank).

224   [1994] 1 AC 180, 196.

225   Ibid, 199. As to past transactions it was said to depend on the facts of each case whether the bank has taken steps to bring home to the wife the risk she is taking by standing as surety and to advise her to take independent advice.

226   Above.

227   'The traditional use of this concept concerns the circumstances in which a transferee of property who acquires a legal estate from a transferor with a defective title may nonetheless obtain a good title, that is a better title than the transferor had. That is not the present case': at [39]. See also [1994] Conv 421 (M Dixon and C Harpum). On the general equitable principle of notice, see above, pp 84–9. The development made by *O'Brien* in England also applies to Scotland: *Smith v Governor & Co of Bank of Scotland* [1997] NPC 94, M & B p 920, although Lord Clyde preferred to base it on the principle of good faith: 'The law already recognises that there may arise a duty of disclosure to a potential cautioner in certain circumstances. As a part of the same good faith that lies behind that duty it seems to me reasonable to accept that there should also be a duty in particular circumstances to give the potential cautioner certain advice'; (1998) 114 LQR 17 (CEF Rickett).

228   [2002] 2 AC 773 at [40]–[42].

bank, in the present instance) was privy to the conduct which led to the wife's entry into the transaction. Knowledge is required ... The law imposes no obligation on one party to a transaction to check whether the other party's concurrence was obtained by undue influence. But *O'Brien* has introduced into the law the concept that, in certain circumstances, a party to a contract may lose the benefit of his contract, entered into in good faith, if he ought to have known that the other's concurrence had been procured by the misconduct of a third party.

There is a further respect in which *O'Brien* departed from conventional concepts. Traditionally, a person is deemed to have notice (that is he has 'constructive' notice) of a prior right when he does not actually know of it but would have learned of it had he made the requisite inquiries. A purchaser will be treated as having constructive notice of all that a reasonably prudent purchaser would have discovered. In the present type of case, the steps a bank is required to take, lest it have constructive notice that the wife's concurrence was procured improperly by her husband, do not consist of making inquiries. Rather, *O'Brien* envisages that the steps taken by the bank will reduce, or even eliminate, the risk of the wife entering into the transaction under any misapprehension or as a result of undue influence by her husband. The steps are not concerned to discover whether the wife has been wronged by her husband in this way. The steps are concerned to minimise the risk that such a wrong may be committed.

These novelties do not point to the conclusion that the decision of this House in *O'Brien* is leading the law astray. Lord Browne-Wilkinson acknowledged he might be extending the law.[229] Some development was sorely needed. The law had to find a way of giving wives a reasonable measure of protection, without adding unreasonably to the expense involved in entering into guarantee transactions of the type under consideration. The protection had to extend also to any misrepresentations made by a husband to his wife. In a situation where there is a substantial risk the husband may exercise his influence improperly regarding the provision of security for his business debts, there is an increased risk that explanations of the transaction given by him to his wife may be misleadingly incomplete or even inaccurate.

The scope of this new application of the principle of constructive notice was also explained. It clearly applies to the case of a wife entering into a contract of surety (including a mortgage) to guarantee her husband's debts.[230] But it also applies between unmarried couples, whether heterosexual or homosexual, where the bank is aware of the relationship; and cohabitation is not essential.[231] In short, the bank is 'put on inquiry' in every case where the relationship between the surety and the debtor is non-commercial.[232]

---

[229] [1994] 1 AC 180, 197.   [230] [2002] 2 AC 773 at [48].

[231] Ibid, at [47]. See also *Massey v Midland Bank plc* [1995] 1 All ER 929 (long-standing emotional and sexual relationship, but not living in same house); *Banco Exterior Internacional SA v Thomas* [1997] 1 WLR 221, 230 (Sir Richard Scott V-C: a bank 'has no business inquiring into the personal relationship between those with whom it has business dealings or as to their personal motives for wanting to help one another. A bank is not to be treated as a branch of the social services agencies'); *Barclays Bank plc v Rivett* [1999] 1 FLR 730 (husband surety); *Northern Rock Building Society v Archer* (1999) 78 P & CR 65 (brother and sister). In *Smith v Bank of Scotland* [1997] NPC 94, above, n 227, Lord Jauncey of Tullichettle said: 'If the creditor has no information to suggest that cautioner and principal debtor are co-habiting I do not consider that he is under any obligation to make enquiries thereanent.'

[232] [2002] 2 AC 773 at [87]. See also *Crédit Lyonnais Bank Nederland NV v Burch* [1997] 1 All ER 144 (relationship between 18-year-old employee and her 28-year-old Italian employer for whom she baby sat

The relationship between the mortgagor and the third party is only half the picture, however. In addition, in the formulation set out in *O'Brien*,[233] the transaction must on its face be not to the financial advantage of the wife. Where, as in *O'Brien*'s case, the wife's mortgage is to support a company in which she has no personal interest, the case is clear. In *CIBC Mortgages plc v Pitt*,[234] however, the result was different. In that case:

> the bank made a loan to the husband and wife jointly. The wife established actual undue influence by the husband. The husband was not acting as agent for the bank, and there was nothing to indicate to the bank that this was anything other than a normal advance to husband and wife for their joint benefit.

What distinguishes the case of the joint advance from that of the surety is that, in the latter, there is not only the possibility of undue influence having been exercised but also the increased risk of it having in fact been exercised, because at least on its face, the guarantee by a wife of her husband's debts is not for her financial benefit. It is the combination of these two factors that puts the creditor on inquiry.[235]

(3) The steps the bank should take

In *Etridge* the House of Lords revised the guidance given in *O'Brien* as to the steps expected of a bank, once put on inquiry, to avoid being fixed with constructive notice of the husband's misrepresentation or undue influence towards the wife. Most significantly, it was made clear that Lord Browne-Wilkinson's suggestion[236] that the bank should hold a private meeting with the wife was not mandatory. It had already become clear that banks were unwilling to hold such a meeting, because they feared that it would increase their liability.[237]

> The furthest a bank can be expected to go is to take reasonable steps to satisfy itself that the wife has had brought home to her, in a meaningful way, the practical implications of the proposed transaction. This does not wholly eliminate the risk of undue influence or misrepresentation. But it does mean that a wife enters into a transaction with her eyes open so far as the basic elements of the transaction are concerned.[238]

To fulfil this duty, the bank is entitled to rely on confirmation from a solicitor, acting for the wife, that he has advised the wife appropriately.[239]

---

at his substantial house in Gerrards Cross and who visited the family on holidays at his large villa in Italy); [1997] CLJ 60 (M Chen-Wishart); discussed in *Etridge* [2002] 2 AC 773 at [83], [86], [89].

[233] Above, p 833.

[234] [1994] 1 AC 200, discussed in *Etridge* at [48]. See also *Britannia Building Society v Pugh* (1996) 29 HLR 423 (wife joint borrower with husband for development intended for their joint benefit); *Barclays Bank plc v Sumner* [1996] EGCS 65 (wife had financial interest in company as great as that of her husband and nothing in her involvement with company to alert bank to make inquiries); cf *Bank of Cyprus (London) Ltd v Markou* [1999] 2 All ER 707; *Dunbar Bank plc v Nadeem* [1998] 3 All ER 876 (joint loan facility for purchase of lease in joint names). The mere fact that the wife holds shares in the company whose debts she guarantees is not conclusive: *Etridge* [2002] 2 AC 773 at [49].

[235] [1994] 1 AC 200, 211 (Lord Browne-Wilkinson).   [236] Above, p 833.

[237] [2002] 2 AC 773 at [51], [55].   [238] Ibid, at [54].

[239] Ibid, at [56]. If, however, the bank knows that the solicitor has not duly advised the wife, or knows facts from which it ought to have realised that the wife has not received the appropriate advice, the bank will

(4) Procedure

In *Barclays Bank plc v Boulter*,[240] the House of Lords held that the wife must adequately plead and discharge the burden of proving that the bank has notice of the misrepresentation or undue influence of the husband. As Lord Hoffmann said:[241]

> In the case of undue influence exercised by a husband over a wife, the burden is prima facie very easily discharged. The wife needs to show only that the bank knew that she was a wife living with her husband and that the transaction was not on its face to her financial advantage. The burden is then on the bank to show that it took reasonable steps to satisfy itself that her consent was properly obtained.

(5) Effect of undue influence or misrepresentation

Undue influence or misrepresentation render the mortgage[242] voidable by the wife. However, the extent of the relief accorded may vary. In *TSB Bank plc v Camfield*:[243]

> The wife charged her interest in the matrimonial home to the bank in order to secure the business debts of her husband, who had innocently misrepresented that her liability under the charge was restricted to £15,000. The bank had constructive notice of the misrepresentation. It was held that the wife's charge should be set aside in its entirety; the bank could be in no better position than the husband.

But if the wife has herself derived some benefit from the transaction, then she can have the guarantee set aside only if she makes counter-restitution in respect of the benefit she has received.[244]

If only part of the charge is voidable for undue influence, the voidable part may be severed, leaving the rest of the charge valid.[245]

(f) Restraint of trade

A mortgage is subject to the common law doctrine that invalidates any contract in restraint of trade that places an unreasonable restriction upon the freedom to pursue a trade or profession.[246] This test is unreasonableness and not unconscionability; it takes

---

proceed at its own risk: at [57]. For a detailed account of what the legal advice should contain in order to satisfy the test, see at [58]-[68]; and for the extent to which the solicitor must be independent of the husband and the bank, see at [69]-[74].

[240] [1999] 1 WLR 1919; [2000] Conv 43 (MP Thompson). [241] Ibid, 1925.

[242] And any replacement mortgage, at any rate if it is taken out as a condition of discharging an earlier voidable mortgage: *Yorkshire Bank plc v Tinsley* [2004] EWCA Civ 816, [2004] 1 WLR 2380; [2004] Conv 399 (MP Thompson); [2005] CLJ 42 (NP Gravells); [2004] All ER Rev 250 (PJ Clarke).

[243] [1995] 1 WLR 430; (1995) 111 LQR 555 (P Ferguson); [1996] RLR 21 (L Proksch).

[244] *Midland Bank plc v Greene* (1993) 27 HLR 350; *Dunbar Bank plc v Nadeem* [1998] 3 All ER 876 (wife would have had to pay half to bank, if there had been undue influence).

[245] *Barclays Bank plc v Caplan* (1997) 78 P & CR 153.

[246] *Esso Petroleum Co Ltd v Harper's Garage (Stourport) Ltd* [1968] AC 269; *Re Petrol Filling Station, Vauxhall Bridge Road, London* (1968) 20 P & CR 1, M & B p 898; *Texaco Ltd v Mulberry Filling Station Ltd* [1972] 1 WLR 814; *Alec Lobb (Garages) Ltd v Total Oil GB Ltd* [1985] 1 WLR 173 (trading restraints in sale and 51-year leaseback of part of property entered into between mortgagor and mortgagee after date of mortgage held to be reasonable). See Anson, pp 396 ff; Heydon, *Restraint of Trade Doctrine* (1971), chs 3, 9.

into account not only the interests of the parties but also the public interest. It may happen, therefore, that a postponement of the right of redemption that is not in itself oppressive may nevertheless become so if it is accompanied by an excessive restraint upon the mortgagor's business activities. Thus where a garage was mortgaged to suppliers of motor fuels, and the mortgagors covenanted that they would not exercise their right of redemption for 21 years and, during the same period, would not buy or sell any fuel other than that supplied by the mortgagees, it was held that the covenant was void as being in restraint of trade, and that the mortgage was redeemable.[247]

(2) Enforcement of the Equity of Redemption

(a) Loss of right of redemption by mortgagor

The right of redemption is lost in the event of (i) the release of the right by the mortgagor to the mortgagee; (ii) (in unregistered land) the lapse of time under the Limitation Act 1980; (iii) the sale of the land by the mortgagee under his statutory power; or (iv) a foreclosure decree obtained by the mortgagee.

The last two methods are discussed later.[248]

(1) Release of right of redemption by mortgagor

Although a provision in the mortgage deed itself giving the mortgagee an option to purchase the land is void as being a clog on the equity,[249] there is nothing to prevent the mortgagor from getting rid of the debt by releasing the equity of redemption to him, provided that it is the result of an independent bargain made subsequently to the mortgage deed.

(2) Lapse of time

In relation to a mortgage of unregistered land, the Limitation Act 1980 provides that:[250]

> When a mortgagee of land has been in possession of any of the mortgaged land for a period of twelve years, no action to redeem the land of which the mortgagee has been so in possession shall be brought after the end of that period by the mortgagor or any person claiming through him.

As to the impact of article 85 of the EEC Treaty (later article 81 of the EC Treaty and now article 101 of the Treaty on European Union), see *Delimitis v Henninger Bräu A-G* [1991] ECR I-935; *Passmore v Morland plc* [1999] 3 All ER 1005 (tie void only during period of invalidity); *Courage Ltd v Crehan* [2002] QB 507; *Crehan v Inntrepreneur Pub Co* [2004] EWCA Civ 637, [2004] 3 EGLR 128 (damages awarded to tenant; rvsd [2006] UKHL 38, [2007] 1 AC 333 on the question whether UK courts are bound by decisions of the European Commission); Anson, pp 408–10.

[247] *Esso Petroleum Co Ltd v Harper's Garage (Stourport) Ltd* [1968] AC 269.

[248] Below, p 854 (sale), 862 (foreclosure).   [249] Above, p 816.

[250] S 16. Under LRA 1925, s 75, the same principle applied to registered land, but LRA 2002, s 96(2), disapplies LA 1980, s 16, in relation to a registered estate in land or rentcharge. LRA 2002 did not, however, change the law in relation to the mortgagee's right to possession or foreclosure against a mortgagor in possession: H & B, paras 29.6, 29.7.

If, however, the mortgagee in possession either receives any sum in respect of principal or interest or signs an acknowledgment of the mortgagor's title, an action to redeem the land may be brought at any time before the expiration of 12 years after the last payment or acknowledgment.[251] An acknowledgment given after the mortgagee has been in possession for 12 years, without receiving a payment in respect of principal or interest, is ineffective.[252]

When a mortgagee has obtained a title to the land free from the mortgage by remaining in possession for 12 years he may by deed enlarge the term of years into a fee simple under the Law of Property Act 1925.[253]

When, as in the ordinary case, a mortgagee does not take possession of the land, the mortgagor can redeem regardless of the lapse of time.

(b) Redemption by mortgagor

In practice, the terms on which the mortgagor may redeem are generally provided for expressly in the contract contained in the mortgage deed.[254] However, in the absence of more specific provision, the mortgagor is entitled to tender the exact amount due,[255] and to claim redemption on the date fixed for repayment. This date is not usually, however, meant to be taken seriously,[256] and if it has elapsed, the mortgagor still has a right in equity to redeem, but must first either give either six months' notice or pay six months' interest.[257] If a notice so given is not followed by repayment upon the date notified, he must give a fresh notice of a reasonable length.[258] Where, however, the mortgage is merely temporary, as in the case of an equitable mortgage by deposit of title deeds,[259] the mortgagee is not entitled to six months' notice or interest in lieu. The mortgagor must give him a reasonable time, though it may be short, to look up the deeds.[260]

(1) Form of discharge: unregistered land

Before 1926, a reconveyance by the mortgagee was necessary to revest the legal estate in the mortgagor upon redemption, but now, when redemption has been effected, there is no need for the mortgagee to execute a deed surrendering the term. A receipt written at the foot of the mortgage deed will be sufficient to extinguish the mortgage, provided that it states the name of the person who pays the money and is executed by

---

[251] LA 1980, ss 29(4), 30.   [252] Ibid, s 17.

[253] LPA 1925, ss 88(3), 153, as amended by TLATA 1996, s 25(1), Sch 3, para 4(1), (16); above, p 343.

[254] See, eg, *Enyclopaedia of Forms and Precedents*, vol 28, Form 5, cl 3.1.2. Such provision is usual in a domestic mortgage, to enable the borrower to redeem at relatively short notice if he sells the property on moving house. However, there may be enforceable contractual restrictions on the time within which redemption may take place: above, p 818.

[255] In an action for redemption the mortgagor must pay all that is due in respect of principal and interest, including interest that is statute-barred: *Holmes v Cowcher* [1970] 1 WLR 834. Any person entitled to redeem must pay full amount of debt and interest even if in right of only part of the property: *Carroll v Manek* (2000) 79 P & CR 173.

[256] Above, p 799.

[257] *Cromwell Property Investment Co Ltd v Western and Toovey* [1934] Ch 322.   [258] Ibid.

[259] Which takes effect now only in unregistered land, and only if accompanied by a document that satisfies the formality requirements of a valid contract to create a legal mortgage: above, p 810.

[260] *Fitzgerald's Trustee v Mellersh* [1892] 1 Ch 385.

the person in whom the mortgage is vested.[261] In the case of a mortgage by demise this receipt effects a surrender of the term and merges it in the reversion held by the mortgagor.[262] If a person, such as a second mortgagee, to whom the immediate equity of redemption does not belong, pays the money that is due, the benefit of the mortgage passes to him by virtue of the receipt,[263] and thus his incumbrance is kept alive. But where there are two mortgages of the same land and the mortgagor pays off the first, the receipt does not transfer the first mortgage term to him so as to enable him to keep it alive against the second mortgagee.[264] Moreover, it is enacted that a mortgage term shall, after repayment of the money, become a satisfied term, and shall cease.[265]

It is the duty of a mortgagee, upon receiving repayment of the loan, to deliver the title deeds to the person who has the best right to them: that is the mortgagor if there is only one incumbrance, or the next mortgagee if the land has been subjected to more incumbrances than one.[266] A mortgagee will not, however, incur liability to a later mortgagee for delivering the deeds to the mortgagor, unless he has actual notice of the later mortgage.[267] Mere registration of a mortgage as a land charge under the Land Charges Act 1972[268] does not in this case constitute notice, but nevertheless he is for several reasons well advised to search at the Registry before handing over the deeds to the mortgagor.[269] If the mortgagee has lost the deeds, the mortgagor has an equitable right to compensation on redemption.[270]

(2) Form of discharge: registered land[271]

The provisions set out above do not apply to the discharge of a registered charge.[272] Instead, three methods of discharge are provided. Under the first method, the mortgagee must execute a statutory form of discharge in documentary form,[273] and the mortgagor then makes application to the Registrar to cancel the entries relating to the charge.[274] The second and third methods involve the notification of the discharge

---

[261] See *Erewash BC v Taylor* [1979] CLY 1831 (receipt valid in spite of miscalculation of redemption figure by mortgagee).

[262] LPA 1925, s 115(1). A building society may use either a reconveyance or a special statutory receipt: Building Societies Act 1986, s 6C and Sch 2A, inserted by Building Societies Act 1997, s 7.

[263] Ibid, s 115(2); *Cumberland Court (Brighton) Ltd v Taylor* [1964] Ch 29.

[264] LPA 1925, s 115(3); *Otter v Lord Vaux* (1856) 6 De GM & G 638; *Parkash v Irani Finance Ltd* [1970] Ch 101.

[265] Ibid, s 116; *Edwards v Marshall-Lee* (1975) 235 EG 901; (1976) 40 Conv (NS) 102.

[266] *Re Magneta Time Co Ltd* (1915) 84 LJ Ch 814.

[267] LPA 1925, s 96(2), as amended by LP(A)A 1926, Sch.   [268] Below, p 885.

[269] See (1926) 61 LJ News pp 431, 471, 488, 519 (T Cyprian Williams).

[270] *Browning v Handiland Group Ltd* (1976) 35 P & CR 345.

[271] See generally Land Registry Practice Guide 31: Discharge of Charges (revised January 2010).

[272] LPA 1925, s 115(10), as amended by LRA 2002, s 133, Sch 11, para 2(1), (11).

[273] LRR 2003, r 114: Form DS1 (discharge of registered charge) or DS3 (release of part of a registered estate from a registered charge). It must be executed as a deed, or authenticated in such other manner as the registrar may approve: ibid, r 114(3). However, the Registrar has power to accept other proof of satisfaction of a charge: ibid., r 114(4).

[274] Ibid, r 114(5); there is a prescribed form. Until 3 January 2010 certain lenders had the right to transmit electronic notices of discharge (ENDs) to the Registrar instead of completing form DS1.

or release of a charge delivered in electronic form.[275] Under the second method, the discharge of a registered charge is sent electronically, by the mortgagee's computer system, directly to the Registrar.[276] It cancels the charge automatically (and, generally, immediately). Under the third method, an electronic form of discharge[277] is submitted by lenders or their authorised agents, which acts as both the evidence of discharge and the application to remove the charge from the register. The second and third methods will in due course form part of the integrated e-conveyancing system.

(3) Sale in lieu of redemption

The mortgagor may commence proceedings to enforce redemption, and if he is successful, an order will be made directing the mortgagee to surrender or give a statutory receipt upon receiving payment within six months. But where such proceedings are taken, the mortgagor may have a judgment for sale instead of for redemption, and the court may, on the request either of the mortgagor or of the mortgagee, and despite the dissent of the other party, direct a sale on such terms as it thinks fit.[278]

(4) Transfer of mortgage

Finally, upon payment of the amount due, a mortgagor is entitled to require the mortgagee to transfer the debt and the property to a third person and the mortgagee, unless he is or has been in possession, is bound to comply.[279] This is the procedure adopted where a third person pays the amount of the loan to the mortgagee, and then himself assumes the position of mortgagee.[280]

(5) Subrogation

A person whose money has been used to discharge a mortgage may be entitled to that mortgage by way of subrogation, or substitution, even though there has been no assignment of any rights or remedies. In a classic statement of the doctrine Lord Diplock said:[281]

> One of the sets of circumstances in which a right of subrogation arises is when a liability of a borrower B to an existing creditor C secured on the property of B is discharged out of moneys provided by the lender L and paid to C either by L himself at B's request and on B's behalf or directly by B pursuant to his agreement with L. In these circumstances L is

---

[275] LRR 2003, r 115. See Land Registry Practice Guide 31, sections 7 and 8.

[276] ED (electronic discharge).   [277] e-DS1 (electronic form of discharge).

[278] LPA 1925, s 91; *Palk v Mortgage Services Funding plc* [1993] Ch 330, below, p 861.

[279] Ibid, s 95. The reason for the exception is that a mortgagee, having once been in possession, remains liable to account for the profits that the transferee has, or ought to have, received after the transfer. He should, therefore, never transfer the security without an order of the court: *Hall v Heward* (1886) 32 Ch D 430, 435.

[280] For transfer of a registered charge, see H & B, paras 12.42–12.47.

[281] *Orakpo v Manson Investments Ltd* [1978] AC 95, 104. On subrogation generally, see Emmet, paras 25.0194–25.198; Mitchell and Watterson, *Subrogation: Law and Practice* (2007). For a critical analysis of the doctrine and its relation to restitution, see *Boscawen v Bajwa* [1996] 1 WLR 328, 334–5, 338–41 (Millett LJ); *Banque Financière de la Cité v Parc (Battersea) Ltd* [1999] 1 AC 221, 231–4 (Lord Hoffmann); [1998] Conv 113 (D Wright); reviewed and explained by Jonathan Parker LJ in *Halifax plc v Omar* [2002] EWCA Civ 121, [2002] 2 P & CR 26.

prima facie entitled to be treated as if he were the transferee of the benefit of C's security on the property to the extent that the moneys lent by L to B were applied to the discharge of B's liability to C. This subrogation of L to the security upon the property of B is based upon the presumed mutual intentions of L and B; in other words where a contract of loan provides that moneys lent by L to B are to be applied in discharging a liability of B to C secured on property, it is an implied term of that contract that L is to be subrogated to C's security.

Subrogation is especially relevant to a prospective mortgagee who has advanced money in order to discharge an existing mortgage but has failed to obtain a valid security for himself. Thus in *Penn v Bristol and West Building Society*[282] a mortgage advance was used to redeem the vendor's mortgage. The transfer of title to the purchaser was held to be a sham and his mortgagee therefore failed to acquire any interest on completion. It was held that the purchaser's mortgagee was entitled to the vendor's mortgage by subrogation.

(3) Effect of Death of Mortgagor

On the death of a mortgagor the equity of redemption passes through his personal representatives to the persons entitled on intestacy if he dies without leaving a will, and to his devisee if he leaves a will. Under the law as it existed prior to 1854, such an heir or devisee was entitled to have the mortgage debt paid out of the personal estate of the deceased, and to take the property free from the mortgage burden, but, in accordance with the general principle that he who has the benefit ought to have the burden, this rule was reversed by the Real Estate Charges Acts of 1854, 1867 and 1877. These statutes have now been repealed, although their general tenor is retained, and it is enacted that property, whether land or not, which at the time of the owner's death is charged with the payment of money, whether by way of legal mortgage, equitable charge or otherwise, shall, as between the different persons claiming through the deceased, be primarily liable for the payment of the charge.[283] This rule is not to apply, however, if the deceased has expressed a contrary intention by will, deed or other document, but such intention must be clear and unambiguous, and is not to be implied merely because the deceased has directed that his debts are to be paid out of his personal estate or his residuary estate.[284]

---

[282] [1995] 2 FLR 938. See also *Halifax plc v Omar*, above; *Cheltenham & Gloucester plc v Appleyard* [2004] EWCA Civ 291, [2004] 13 EGCS 127 (subsequent mortgagee paid off first legal mortgage but was unable to obtain registration of its own charge, so held only an equitable mortgage: entitled to be subrogated as a legal chargee to the value of the legal mortgage at the time it was paid off); *Anfield (UK) Ltd v Bank of Scotland plc* [2010] EWHC 2374 (Ch), [2011] 1 All ER 708 (subrogation even where equitable mortgage followed from lender's own failure to register legal charge).

[283] AEA 1925, s 35(1).

[284] Ibid, s 35(1), (2): *Re Neeld* [1962] Ch 643; *Re Wakefield* [1943] 2 All ER 29.

B RIGHTS OF A MORTGAGOR WHO
REMAINS IN POSSESSION

In the eyes of equity the mortgagor remains the true beneficial owner of the property, and as long as he remains in possession he is entitled to appropriate the rents and profits to his own use without any liability to account for them, even though he may be in default in the payment of interest. As we shall see, the mortgagee has the right to enter into possession of the land, independently of any default on the part of the mortgagor,[285] but in normal circumstances the mortgagor remains in possession. Provided that the mortgagee has not given notice of his intention to take possession or to enter into receipt of the rents and profits, the mortgagor in possession may sue in his own name for the recovery of possession and for the rents and profits. He may bring an action to prevent, or recover damages for, any trespass or other wrong done to the land.[286]

Where a mortgagor retained possession, it was formerly a common practice to include in the mortgage deed a clause by which he *attorned* to the mortgagee, that is acknowledged that he held the land as a tenant at will or from year to year of the mortgagee. The chief advantages were that it enabled the mortgagee to pursue the remedies available to a landlord for the recovery of arrears of rent, and also to obtain a summary judgment for possession if the need arose.

These two advantages no longer exist, however, since the mortgagee cannot distrain upon the premises for arrears unless the attornment clause has been registered as a bill of sale;[287] and a summary judgment is available to him independently of attornment.[288] Nevertheless, an attornment clause is not altogether superfluous, since it enables a covenant by a mortgagor to be enforced against his successors in title.[289]

A mortgagor, *while in actual possession*, is given the following statutory powers:

(1) Right to Grant Valid Leases

(a) At common law

At common law a mortgagor is entitled to grant a lease binding between him and the lessee, and his power in this respect has not been affected by statute.[290] But if granted

---

[285] Below, p 847.   [286] LPA 1925, s 98.

[287] *Re Willis, ex p Kennedy* (1888) 21 QBD 384. For the abolition of distress when the Tribunals, Courts and Enforcement Act 2007, Sch 14, is brought into force, see above p 277.

[288] CPR, Part 24. See generally (1969) 22 CLP, pp 143–6 (EC Ryder).

[289] *Regent Oil Co Ltd v J A Gregory (Hatch End) Ltd* [1966] Ch 402, where the covenant was included in a charge by way of legal mortgage. For mortgages entered into before 1996, the fact that the mortgage takes effect as a lease should make the covenant run even in the absence of attornment: (1966) 82 LQR 21. However, the LT(C)A 1995, s 28(1), excludes a mortgage term from the definition of tenancy for the purposes of the running of covenants in leases entered into after 1995.

[290] *Iron Trades Employers Insurance Association Ltd v Union Land and House Investors Ltd* [1937] Ch 313.

without the concurrence of the mortgagee[291] it confers only a precarious title upon the lessee, since the paramount title of the mortgagee may be asserted against both him and the mortgagor.[292]

(b) By statute

The Conveyancing Act 1881 expanded the power of the mortgagor in this particular by allowing him to grant leases for limited periods that would be binding upon the mortgagee. The present position is governed by the Law of Property Act 1925, which confers upon a mortgagor *in possession* a statutory right to grant the following leases that will be binding upon all incumbrancers:

(1) Agricultural or occupation leases for any term not exceeding 21 years, or, if the mortgage was made after 1925, 50 years.

(2) Building leases for any term not exceeding 99 years, or, in the case of a mortgage made after 1925, 999 years.[293]

Such a lease must be made to take effect in possession not later than 12 months after its date; it must reserve the best rent that can reasonably be obtained, and no fine must be taken;[294] it must contain a condition of re-entry in the event of rent being in arrears for 30 days,[295] and the mortgagor is bound to deliver to the mortgagee within one month a counterpart of the lease executed by the lessee.[296]

Thus when a mortgagor makes a lease to A for 50 years, the effect is that the mortgagee is not entitled to actual possession during the continuance of A's term; but if he is driven to pursue his remedies, he is entitled to receipt of the rent paid by A.

These statutory powers of leasing may be, and in practice frequently are, excluded or abridged by the mortgage deed,[297] but no such exclusion or abridgement is allowed in the case of a mortgage of agricultural land made after 1 March 1948, but before 1

---

[291] The mortgage deed itself may confer leasing powers within defined limits upon the mortgagor: LPA 1925, s 99(14). There is no implied term that the mortgagee should not unreasonably withhold consent: cf LTA 1927, s 19(1), above, p 259: nor is the condition contrary to article 48 of the EC Treaty (now article 45 of the Treaty on the Function of the European Union): *Citibank International plc v Kessler* [1999] Lloyd's Rep Bank 123. Nor is the mortgagee under a duty in equity properly to consider any request for permission: *Starling v Lloyds TSB Bank Ltd* [2000] 1 EGLR 101 (in extreme circumstances there might be scope for a complaint of bad faith).

[292] *Corbett v Plowden* (1884) 25 Ch D 678, 681 (Lord Selborne LC).

[293] LPA 1925, s 99(1), (3).

[294] Ibid, s 99(5), (6). See, for example, *Rust v Goodale* [1957] Ch 33, 39, where the consideration for a sub-lease was an immediate payment of £2,260 and a rent of £5.

[295] Ibid, s 99(7). It is doubtful whether this requirement must be satisfied in the case of an oral tenancy: *Pawson v Revell* [1958] 2 QB 360; *Rhodes v Dalby* [1971] 1 WLR 1325, 1331–2.

[296] Ibid, s 99 (11). But not in the case of an oral tenancy: *Rhodes v Dalby*, above. A lease that fails to comply with one or more of these requirements may be validated under s 152, if it has been made in good faith and if the lessee has entered. It then takes effect in equity as a contract for the grant of a valid lease. See eg, *Pawson v Revell*, above.

[297] Ibid, s 99(13).

September 1995.[298] Exclusion is permitted in the case of a mortgage made on or after that date. Thus the power to grant a farm business tenancy,[299] which can only begin on or after that date, may be validly excluded.

(c) Effect of unauthorised lease

If a mortgagor in possession grants a lease that does not satisfy the provisions of the Law of Property Act 1925 or the terms of the mortgage deed, the lease may be binding on both the mortgagor and the tenant under the doctrine of estoppel.[300] Thus the mortgagor may sue or distrain for the rent.[301] The mortgagee, however, is not bound by the lease. As between the lessee and the mortgagee and his successors in title the lease granted by the mortgagor is void,[302] and the lessee is not protected against the mortgagee by the Rent Acts.[303] The mortgagee has an option. He may either treat the lessee as a trespasser or accept him as his own tenant.[304] If, for example, he demands that the rent be paid direct to him instead of to the mortgagor, the original tenancy is destroyed and replaced by a yearly tenancy between the mortgagee and the lessee.[305] Moreover, the acceptance of rent without any such demand raises the implication of a yearly tenancy.[306] This implication, however, does not arise merely because the mortgagee, being aware of the lease, allows the tenant to remain in possession.[307]

If a mortgagee refuses to recognise an unauthorised lease, the tenant may redeem the mortgage and thus secure himself against eviction.[308]

---

[298] LPA 1925, s 99(13A), inserted by Agricultural Tenancies Act 1995, s 31. See *Pawson v Revell*, above; *Rhodes v Dalby*, above.

[299] Above, p 420.

[300] *Cuthbertson v Irving* (1860) 6 H & N 135; *Church of England Building Society v Piskor* [1954] Ch 553; above, p 208.

[301] *Trent v Hunt* (1853) 9 Exch 14.

[302] *Rust v Goodale* [1957] Ch 33; cf *Lever Finance Ltd v Trustee of Property of LN and HM Needleman and Kreutzer* [1956] Ch 375 (mortgagee's assignee estopped from asserting invalidity of lease).

[303] *Dudley and District Benefit Building Society v Emerson* [1949] Ch 707; *Sadiq v Hussain* (1997) 73 P & CR D44. Section 98 of the Rent Act 1977 prohibits the court from ordering possession of a dwelling house subject to a statutory tenancy unless certain criteria are met: it does not prohibit a prior mortgagee with title paramount from recovering possession (i) from a protected contractual tenant; *Dudley and District Benefit Building Society v Emerson*, above; (ii) from a statutory tenant; *Britannia Building Society v Earl* [1990] 1 WLR 422; [1990] Conv 450 (S Bridge) but it does prohibit a mortgagee in all cases where the tenancy predates the mortgagee's mortgage: *Woolwich Building Society v Dickman* [1996] 3 All ER 204, [1996] All ER Rev 254 (PJ Clarke); 279 (PH Pettit); cf *Barclays Bank plc v Zaroovabli* [1997] Ch 321 (tenancy predated registration but not grant of bank's charge); (1997) 113 LQR 390 (M Robinson). Mortgage Repossessions (Protection of Tenants etc) Act 2010, however, allows unauthorised tenants to apply for postponement of execution of possession orders for up to two months: below, p 852. See also *Quennell v Maltby* [1979] 1 WLR 318, below, p 851, for the court's discretion in equity to protect a lessee where possession is sought, but not in good faith to protect the security.

[304] *Stroud Building Society v Delamont* [1960] 1 WLR 431, 434; *Chatsworth Properties Ltd v Effiom* [1971] 1 WLR 144.

[305] *Taylor v Ellis* [1960] Ch 368, 375–6.   [306] Above, p 207.   [307] *Taylor v Ellis*, above.

[308] *Tarn v Turner* (1888) 39 Ch D 456.

(2) Right to Accept Surrenders of Leases

The Law of Property Act 1925, authorises a mortgagor to accept a surrender of any lease, if, and only if, his object in doing so is to grant a new lease that falls within his statutory powers.[309] Such a surrender is not valid, however, unless a new lease is granted within one month, for a period not shorter than the unexpired term of the surrendered lease, and at a rent not less than the old rent.[310] These provisions are subject to the terms of the mortgage deed, or of any other written agreement between the parties.[311]

IV RIGHTS OF THE MORTGAGEE

A RIGHTS OF LEGAL MORTGAGEE

We now come to the five remedies that are available to a legal mortgagee for enforcing the payment of what is due to him under the mortgage:[312] the action on the personal covenant to repay the principal with interest; entry into possession of the mortgaged premises; the appointment of a receiver; sale and foreclosure. The first three of these remedies do not involve the realisation of the mortgaged property, but as a result of sale and foreclosure the mortgage is terminated.

These several remedies may all be pursued concurrently as soon as the mortgagor is in default, so that, for example, the mortgagee at one and the same time may sue upon the personal covenant and begin foreclosure proceedings. They are generally also cumulative. Thus if the mortgagee exercises his power of sale and the purchase price is less than the mortgage debt, he may sue the mortgagor for the balance on the covenant to pay.[313] Foreclosure, however, puts an end to other remedies; a mortgagee who has foreclosed can sue on the covenant to pay only if he reopens the foreclosure,[314] so that the mortgagor may redeem. If, therefore, the mortgagee sells the mortgaged property after foreclosure, he has put it out of his power to reopen the foreclosure and so can no longer sue the mortgagor[315] or his guarantor[316] on the personal covenant.

---

[309] LPA 1925, s 100(1). [310] Ibid, s 100(5). [311] Ibid, s 100(7).

[312] A mortgagee may also have an action against a valuer for a negligent valuation that causes him loss: *Coris and Investments Ltd v Druce & Co* (1978) 248 EG 315, 407; *Mount Banking Corp Ltd v Brian Cooper & Co* [1992] 2 EGLR 142. For a similar action against a surveyor, see *London and South of England Building Society v Stone* (1981) 261 EG 463; *Anglia Hastings & Thanet Building Society v House & Son* (1981) 260 EG 1128, and for an action in the tort of deceit against a surveyor who overvalued the property, see *Cheshire Building Society v Dunlop Haywards (DHL) Ltd* [2008] EWHC 51 (Comm); [2008] PNLR 19.

[313] *Rudge v Richens* (1873) LR 8 CP 358; *Gordon Grant & Co Ltd v Boos* [1926] AC 781. See also *Alliance & Leicester plc v Slayford* [2001] 1 All ER (Comm) 1 (mortgagee not prevented from pursuing money judgment after failure to realise security through possession proceedings).

[314] *Perry v Barker* (1806) 13 Ves 198.

[315] *Palmer v Hendrie* (1859) 27 Beav 349. See *Kinnaird v Trollope* (1888) 39 Ch D 636, 642 (Stirling LJ), M & B p 977.

[316] *Lloyds and Scottish Trust Ltd v Britten* (1982) 44 P & CR 249.

(1) Action on the Personal Covenant

(a) Personal remedy

A mortgage deed contains an express covenant whereby the mortgagor covenants to repay the principal sum, and interest at a certain rate per cent. The date at which the mortgagor becomes liable to pay is a question of construction of the deed.[317] The moment that date has passed, the mortgagee can sue on this personal covenant for the recovery of the principal sum and any interest that may be in arrear, and can have the judgment satisfied out of any property belonging to the mortgagor, though it is not comprised in the mortgage. Further, the mortgagor remains liable on the covenant to the mortgagee, even though he has transferred his interest in the mortgaged property.[318] He usually takes a covenant of indemnity from the transferee.[319]

(b) Effect of lapse of time

An action to recover the principal sum is barred unless it is brought within 12 years from the date when the right to receive the money accrued.[320] This date is that which is fixed by the mortgage deed for repayment, and is not affected by the mortgagee's subsequent exercise of his power of sale;[321] but on each occasion that some part of the principal or interest is paid or a written acknowledgment of his liability to pay is given by the mortgagor, the period of 12 years begins to run afresh.[322] In the case of interest, only six years' arrears are recoverable.[323]

---

[317] *Wilkinson v West Bromwich Building Society* [2005] UKHL 44, [2005] 1 WLR 2303; [2005] Conv 566 (T Prime); [2005] All ER Rev 267 (PJ Clarke); *Gotham v Doodes* [2006] EWCA Civ 1080, [2007] 1 WLR 86. Traditionally, the mortgage deed provided for the repayment of the whole of the principal sum on a specified date, and to pay interest in the mean time: above, p 799. However, a modern domestic mortgage (above, p 796) may contain detailed provisions for repayment of the capital by instalments, with interest on the capital left outstanding from time to time: eg *Encyclopaedia of Forms and Precedents*, vol 28(1) (2006), Form 5; or may provide for repayment of capital at the end of the term under an interest-only mortgage: ibid, Form 2. Such forms will generally make the whole of the principal sum repayable on demand in the event of certain specified events of default; the action on the covenant is available whenever any sum has become due under the contract and is unpaid, whether the whole or any instalment of the capital, or any arrears of interest.

[318] *Kinnaird v Trollope* (1888) 39 Ch D 636.

[319] A transferee for value is under an implied obligation to indemnify: *Bridgman v Daw* (1891) 40 WR 253.

[320] LA 1980, s 20(1); *Bristol & West plc v Bartlett* [2002] EWCA Civ 1181, [2003] 1 WLR 284 (even if mortgagee has exercised power of sale before issuing proceedings for recovery of principal and interest); *Scottish Equitable plc v Thompson* [2003] EWCA Civ 225, [2003] HLR 48; *Gotham v Doodes*, above, n 317 (charge under s 313 Insolvency Act 1986 did not create a present right to receive money, so time did not start to run until order for sale); *Yorkshire Bank Finance Ltd v Mulhall* [2008] EWCA Civ 1156, [2009] 1 P & CR 16 (s 20(1) does not apply to defeat creditor's claim to enforce charging order, following *Ezekiel v Orakpo* [1997] 1 WLR 340 (s 20(5)).

[321] *Wilkinson v West Bromwich Building Society* above, n 317, at [10] (Lord Hoffmann: 'It would be strange if the lender could then stop time running by his own act in exercising the power of sale. If, therefore, the cause of action when it arose was a claim to a debt secured on a mortgage, I do not think s 20 ceases to apply when the security is subsequently realised').

[322] LA 1980, ss 29(3), (5), 30; *Ashcroft v Bradford & Bingley plc* [2010] EWCA Civ 223, [2010] 2 P & CR 13.

[323] Ibid, s 20(5)–(7); *Barclays Bank plc v Walters* The Times, 20 October 1988.

(2) Entry into possession

(a) Right to take possession

A legal mortgagee has the right to enter into possession of the mortgaged property. As Harman J said:

> The right of the mortgagee to possession in the absence of some contract has nothing to do with default on the part of the mortgagor. The mortgagee may go into possession before the ink is dry on the mortgage unless there is something in the contract, express or by implication,[324] whereby he has contracted himself out of that right. He has the right because he has a legal term of years in the property.[325]

It is not usual, however, for a mortgagee, despite his legal right, to enter into possession of the mortgaged property, unless he wishes to do so as a preliminary to exercising his statutory power of sale, when the mortgagor is in default. As Harman J went on to say:

> An application for possession has become a very fashionable form of relief, because, owing to the conditions now prevailing, if it is desired to realise a security by sale, vacant possession is almost essential.

In other words, entry into possession is a necessary preliminary to sale. It is important for the mortgagee to enter, so that he can evict the mortgagor and offer vacant possession to a purchaser. Otherwise, the property might be difficult to sell, or, if sold, its price might be depressed, if the sale took place with the mortgagor in possession and the purchaser had to evict him after the sale.

(b) Liability of mortgagee to account strictly

It is, in theory at least, possible for a mortgagee to enter into possession to ensure the payment of interest, but a formidable deterrent to this course is the strict supervision that equity exercises over a mortgagee in possession. The rule is that he must get no advantage out of the mortgage beyond the payment of principal, interest and costs, and he is made to account not only for what he has actually received, but also for what he might have received but for his own wilful default or neglect.[326] Thus he is liable for voluntary waste, and if he allows property to remain vacant that might have been let, he is personally liable to pay an occupation rent.[327] In *White v City of London Brewery Co*[328] mortgagees, who happened to be brewers, took possession of the mortgaged

---

[324] See *Esso Petroleum Co Ltd v Alstonbridge Properties Ltd* [1975] 1 WLR 1474, 1484; *Western Bank Ltd v Schindler* [1977] Ch 1.

[325] *Four-Maids Ltd v Dudley Marshall (Properties) Ltd* [1957] Ch 317, 320, M & B p 929. See generally Fisher and Lightwood, ch 29; [1979] Conv 266 (RJ Smith); [1983] Conv 293 (A Clarke); [1997] LS 483 (M Haley). Where the mortgage is created by a legal charge under LPA 1925, s 87, the mortgagee has the same protection, powers and remedies *as if* he had a legal term of years: above, p 804.

[326] *Chaplin v Young* (1864) 33 Beav 330; *White v City of London Brewery Co* (1889) 42 Ch D 237, 243.

[327] *Gaskell v Gosling* [1896] 1 QB 669, 691.

[328] (1889) 42 Ch D 237, M & B p 930; see also *Hughes v Williams* (1806) 12 Ves 493; (1979) 129 NLJ 334 (HE Markson); [1982] Conv 345, 346–8 (JE Stannard).

premises and leased them to a tenant, subject to a restriction that he should take his supply of beer entirely from them. It was held that they must account for the additional rent that they would have received had they let the premises as a 'free' instead of a 'tied' house.

(c) Relief of mortgagor

(1) Statutory

If a mortgagee seeks possession he will usually take proceedings in the county court.[329] Unless the mortgagee agrees, the court has no jurisdiction to decline the order or to adjourn the hearing. But it may adjourn the application for a short time to enable the mortgagor to pay off the whole of the mortgage debt.[330]

Where, however, a mortgagee brings an action for possession of a *dwelling-house*,[331] wide discretionary powers are given to the court by the Administration of Justice Act 1970.[332] The Act does not abrogate the common law right of the mortgagee to take possession; it supplies, as a procedural measure, a judicial discretion.[333] The court may

---

[329] CPR, r 55.3. Part 55 came into force on 15 October 2001 and changed radically the traditional jurisdiction of the Chancery Division in respect of mortgages: *Chancery Guide 2009*, ch 21. Only exceptional circumstances now justify starting a claim in the High Court, eg there are complicated disputes of fact, or points of law of general importance. The value of the property and the amount of any financial claim may be relevant circumstances, but these factors alone will not normally justify starting the claim in the High Court. If, however, the claim is brought in the High Court, it will be assigned to the Chancery Division: CPR, PD 55A, para 1.6. For details that must be set out in the particulars of claim, see PD 55A, para 2.5. For enforcement of a judgment or order for possession, see RSC Ord 45, r 3. For possession claims online, see PD 55B.

Repossession in accordance with the terms of the loan and the domestic law is necessary for the protection of the rights and freedoms of others, namely the lender, and does not contravene ECHR, art 8. To the extent that the mortgagor is deprived of his possessions by the repossession, this deprivation is in the public interest, that is the public interest in ensuring payment of contractual debts, and is also in accordance with the rules provided for by law: *Wood v UK* (1997) 24 EHRR CD69.

[330] *Birmingham Citizens Permanent Building Society v Caunt* [1962] Ch 883. A mortgagor's counterclaim or set off against mortgagee for sum exceeding debt is not in itself a reason for an adjournment: *Samuel Keller (Holdings) Ltd v Martins Bank Ltd* [1971] 1 WLR 43; *Mobil Oil Co Ltd v Rawlinson* (1981) 43 P & CR 221, M & B p 931; *Citibank Trust Ltd v Ayivor* [1987] 1 WLR 1157 (right to possession not affected where mortgagor's counterclaim for damages greater than arrears due under mortgage); *First National Bank plc v Syed* [1991] 2 All ER 250; (1991) 141 NLJ 793 (HW Wilkinson); (1994) 110 LQR 221 (N Hickman); *National Westminster Bank plc v Skelton* [1993] 1 WLR 72n; *Ashley Guarantee plc v Zacaria* [1993] 1 WLR 62 (no distinction in principle where mortgagor is principal debtor and where he is only guarantor); [1993] All ER Rev 253 (PJ Clarke); *Midland Bank plc v McGrath* [1996] EGCS 61. See Derham, *The Law of Set Off* (4th edn, 2010), paras 4.125–4.148.

[331] The fact that part of it is used for business purposes does not prevent a house from being a dwelling-house: AJA 1970, s 39(2). The relevant date for determining whether premises consist of a dwelling-house is the date when the mortgagee brings the action for possession: *Royal Bank of Scotland plc v Miller* [2001] EWCA Civ 344, [2002] QB 255.

[332] AJA 1970, s 36.

[333] *Ropaigealach v Barclays Bank plc* [2000] QB 263; [1999] Conv 263 (A Dunn); [1999] CLJ 281 (M Dixon). See Law Com WP No 99, *Land Morgages* (1996), para 3.69. As to the compatibility of the right to peaceable re-entry and its exclusion from AJA 1970, s 36, with ECHR, see Rook, *Property Law and Human Rights*, pp 199–203. See also *Horsham Properties Group Ltd v Clark* [2008] EWHC 2327 (Ch), [2009] 1 WLR 1255, M&B 937, below, p 855, at [45].

adjourn the proceedings, or suspend or postpone the possession order for such period or periods as the court thinks reasonable[334]

> if it appears to the court that in the event of its exercising the power the mortgagor is likely to be able within a reasonable period[335] to pay any sums due under the mortgage or to remedy a default consisting of a breach of any other obligation arising under or by virtue of the mortgage.[336]

Where the mortgagor is entitled to pay the principal sum by instalments, or otherwise to defer the payment of it in whole or in part, the court may treat as sums due only those instalments that are actually in arrear, even if the mortgage makes the whole of the balance outstanding payable on any default by the mortgagor.[337] But the court may only exercise its discretion if the mortgagor is likely to be able within a reasonable period also to pay any further instalments then due.[338]

The period within which the arrears had to be paid used to be usually an automatic two years. However, in *Cheltenham and Gloucester Building Society v Norgan*,[339] the Court of Appeal held that the court should take the full term of the remainder of the mortgage as its starting point in deciding what period is reasonable. Evans LJ set out a practical summary of the relevant considerations:[340]

---

334 *National & Provincial Building Society v Ahmed* [1995] 2 EGLR 127; *Cheltenham and Gloucester Building Society v Obi* (1994) 28 HLR 22 (after mortgagee has obtained possession order, court cannot suspend effect of order unless the order itself can be set aside); *Cheltenham and Gloucester Building Society v Grattidge* (1993) 25 HLR 454; *Cheltenham and Gloucester Building Society v Johnson* (1996) 73 P & CR 293 (when a mortgagee is entitled to a money judgment, this may be suspended on same terms as, and in line with, the possession order itself). For the inter-relation between s 36(1) and LPA 1925, s 91(2), see *Cheltenham and Gloucester plc v Krausz* [1997] 1 WLR 1558, below, p 862.

335 *Royal Trust Co of Canada v Markham* [1975] 1 WLR 1416 (an order for suspension must be for a fixed period).

336 AJA 1970, s 36(1). The section does not apply to a mortgage that is within CCA 1974: s 38A, added by CCA 1974, s 192, Sch 4, para 30.

337 AJA 1973, s 8(1), reversing the effect of *Halifax Building Society v Clark* [1973] Ch 307. But the grant of the statutory discretion was unnecessary: *First Middlesbrough Trading and Mortgage Co Ltd v Cunningham* (1974) 28 P & CR 69. See (1973) 37 Conv (NS) 213; (1974) 38 Conv (NS) 1.

338 AJA 1973, s 8(2); *Centrax Trustees Ltd v Ross* [1979] 2 All ER 952 (principal to be repaid at indeterminate future date held to be within the section); cf *Habib Bank Ltd v Tailor* [1982] 1 WLR 1218 (overdraft secured by charge to be repaid on demand in writing held to be not within the section, since there was no agreement as to deferred payment); [1983] Conv 80 (PH Kenny); [1982] All ER Rev 117 (PJ Clarke); [1984] Conv 91 (S Tromans). In instalment mortgages, the discretionary powers extend to foreclosure actions, whether or not possession is claimed in the same proceedings: s 8(3). See *Lord Marples of Wallasey v Holmes* (1975) 31 P & CR 94.

339 [1996] 1 WLR 343, M & B p 945; (1996) 146 NLJ 252 (HW Wilkinson); [1996] Conv 118 (MP Thompson); (1996) 112 LQR 553 (J Morgan); [1996] All ER Rev 260 (PJ Clarke).

For postponement to enable sale to take place, see *National & Provincial Building Society v Lloyd* [1996] 1 All ER 630 (sale by part disposals); *Bristol & West Building Society v Ellis* (1996) 73 P & CR 158, M & B p 947; [1998] Conv 125 (MP Thompson). For retention by mortgagor while mortgagee sells, see *Target Homes Loans Ltd v Clothier* [1994] 1 All ER 439 (three months' postponement; mortgagor had better prospect of achieving earlier sale if in possession); [1993] Conv 62 (J Martin); *Cheltenham & Gloucester plc v Booker* (1996) 73 P & CR 412, 415 (Millett LJ: possible if mortgagor's presence will not depress sale price, and mortgagor will complete sale and give up possession to purchaser on completion).

340 Ibid, 357.

(a) How much can the borrower reasonably afford to pay, both now and in the future? (b) If the borrower has a temporary difficulty in meeting his obligations, how long is the difficulty likely to last? (c) What was the reason for the arrears which have accumulated? (d) How much remains of the original term? (e) What are the relevant contractual terms, and what type of mortgage is it, i.e. when is the principal due to be repaid? (f) Is it a case where the court should exercise its power to disregard accelerated payment provisions (section 8 of the Act of 1973)? (g) Is it reasonable to expect the lender, in the circumstances of the particular case, to recoup the arrears of interest (1) over the whole of the original term, or (2) within a shorter period, or even (3) within a longer period, i.e. by extending the repayment period? Is it reasonable to expect the lender to capitalise the interest or not? (h) Are there any reasons affecting the security which should influence the length of the period for payment? In the light of the answers to the above, the court can proceed to exercise its overall discretion, taking account of any further factors which may arise in the particular case.

This statutory relief may be given to a mortgagor,[341] whether or not he is in default under the mortgage,[342] and is available in the case of both instalment and endowment mortgages.[343]

In 2008 a new Pre-Action Protocol was introduced for Possession Claims based on Mortgage or Home Purchase Plan Arrears in Respect of Residental Property,[344] which applies to all residential mortgages and home purchase plans[345] and is designed to provide further protection to the mortgagor. It prescribes steps that the parties should take to ensure that the lender and the borrower act fairly and reasonably with each other in resolving matters relating to arrears, and is designed to encourage more pre-action contact between the parties to seek agreement. In particular, it requires the parties to discuss proposals for the payment of arrears, and generally to use alternative dispute resolution mechanisms to seek to settle disputes rather than having a possession claim brought to the court; and it requires the lender to provide information and advice to the borrower (eg to seek assistance from third parties, such as the local authority and independent debt advisers), to consider a reasonable request from the borrower for changes to payment dates and to consider a proposal from the borrower for payment,

---

[341] Mortgagor and mortgagee includes any person deriving title under the original mortgagor or mortgagee: AJA 1970, s 39(1); *Britannia Building Society v Earl* [1990] 1 WLR 422 (statutory tenant of mortgagor whose tenancy was not binding on mortgagee, above, p 844, was not such a person and court had no jurisdiction to adjourn proceedings); (1990) 140 NLJ 823 (HW Wilkinson). For protection of other occupiers, such as a spouse, see below, p 852.

[342] *Western Bank Ltd v Schindler* [1977] Ch 1 (Goff LJ expressed doubts); (1977) 40 MLR 356 (C Harpum).

[343] *Bank of Scotland (Governor & Co) v Grimes* [1985] QB 1179, M & B p 943. AJA 1973, s 8 is infelicitously drafted and was interpreted 'so as to give effect to the general tenor of the language in a purposive way': Sir John Arnold P at 1188. See also *Royal Bank of Scotland plc v Miller* [2001] EWCA Civ 344, [2002] QB 255. For instalment (repayment) and endowment (interest only) mortgages, see above, p 796.

[344] (2009) 106(2) LSG 18 (C Atkinson), 24 (P Jolly); [2008] Conv 474 (M Dixon, discussing the draft Protocol); (2009) 72 MLR 793 (L Whitehouse, criticising the reduced protection for mortgagors in the final text of the Protocol).

[345] Above, p 796, n 17.

and to postpone the start of a possession claim where the borrower is pursuing a claim for support under the Government's mortgage support scheme, or mortgage rescue scheme,[346] or under a mortgage protection policy, or is actively marketing the property. The Protocol does not alter the parties' rights and obligations, but the court may take into account compliance or non-compliance with it when giving directions for the management of proceedings[347] and when making orders for costs.[348]

(2) In equity

In addition to the statutory relief, equity may have a wide discretion to restrain any unjust use of the right to possession. In *Quennell v Maltby*:[349]

> Q mortgaged his house to a bank. The mortgage deed prohibited the creation of a tenancy without the bank's consent. In breach of that covenant Q let the house to M, who became a statutory tenant protected by the Rent Act. This tenancy was binding on Q but not on the bank.[350] Q, who wanted to sell the house with vacant possession, asked the bank to bring an action for possession against M. On the bank's refusal, Q's wife then paid off the mortgage debt, took a transfer of the mortgage from the bank and claimed possession against M as mortgagee.

The Court of Appeal held that she was not entitled to possession. According to Bridge and Templeman LJJ, she was to be treated as acting as agent for Q, who, as mortgagor, could not obtain possession. Lord Denning MR however stated a wider principle:[351]

> The objective is plain. It was not to enforce the security or to obtain repayment or anything of the kind. It was in order to get possession of the house and to overcome the protection of the Rent Acts... Equity can step in so as to prevent a mortgage, or a transferee from him, from getting possession of a house contrary to the justice of the case. A mortgagee will be restrained from getting possession except when it is sought bona fide and reasonably for the purpose of enforcing the security, and then only subject to such conditions as the court thinks fit to impose.

It is difficult to reconcile this wider principle with previous authority, and it would render unnecessary the protection accorded to the mortgagor by the Administration of Justice Act 1970.

---

[346] For these Government schemes, see above, p 795, n 12. The Protocol was amended in 2009 to include reference to the schemes.

[347] CPR, rr 3.1(4), (5), 3.9(1)(e).   [348] CPR, r 44.3(5)(a).

[349] [1979] 1 WLR 318, M & B p 933; (1979) 129 NLJ 624 (HW Wilkinson); (1979) 38 CLJ 257 (RA Pearce).

[350] *Dudley and District Benefit Building Society v Emerson* [1949] Ch 707, above, p 844.

[351] [1979] 1 WLR 318, 322; applied in *Albany Home Loan Ltd v Massey* [1997] 2 All ER 609, 612–13; both cases were distinguished in *Abbey National v Tufts* [1999] 2 FLR 399, 405–7.

(d) Protection of other occupiers[352]

(1) Person with right of occupation under Family Law Act 1996

A present or former spouse, civil partner or cohabitant of the mortgagor, who has a right of occupation of a dwelling-house under the Family Law Act,[353] does not thereby have any larger right of occupation than the mortgagor as against the mortgagee,[354] but may have a right to be joined as party to an action by the mortgagee to enforce his security if he is able to meet the mortgagor's liabilities under the mortgage.[355]

(2) Unauthorised tenant of mortgagor

Where a mortgagee of land that consists of or includes a dwelling-house brings an action for possession, there may be an unauthorised tenant in possession of all or part of the property—that is a person who has an assured tenancy or a protected or statutory tenancy that is not binding on the mortgagee's interest in the property.[356] The Mortgage Repossessions (Protection of Tenants etc) Act 2010[357] introduced protection for such a tenant against immediate eviction: he may apply for a postponement of the date for delivery of possession for a period not exceeding two months,[358] thus allowing him time to find alternative accommodation. In exercising its powers, the court has regard to the tenant's circumstances, and any outstanding breach of his tenancy by the tenant, but may make its order conditional on the tenant making payments to the mortgagee in respect of his occupation during the period of postponement.

(e) Effect of lapse of time

Where the mortgagor remains in possession for 12 years without making any payment under the terms of the mortgage and without the mortgagee enforcing his right to possession, the mortgagee's right to take possession, and his title to the mortgage, are extinguished.[359]

---

[352] See also CPR, r 55.10 (mortgagee seeking possession must send notice to (inter alia) the property addressed to 'the tenant or the occupier'); Mortgage Repossessions (Protection of Tenants etc) Act 2010, s 2 (notice to be given at the property before a possession order can be executed); Dwelling Houses (Execution of Possession Orders by Mortgagees) Regulations 2010 (SI 2010 No 1809).

[353] Family Law Act 1996, s 30; above, pp 522–4.

[354] Ibid, s 54(3).

[355] Ibid, s 55. If he has registered his right of occupation (above, p 523) he must be served with notice of any action by the mortgagee to enforce his security: ibid, s 56.

[356] Mortgage Repossessions (Protection of Tenants etc) Act 2010, s 1(8). For assured tenancies under Housing Act 1988, and protected or statutory tenancies under Rent Act 1977, see above, Ch 11. For the circumstances in which a tenancy granted by a mortgagor is authorised or unauthorised, see above, pp 842–4.

[357] [2010] L & T Rev 225 (D Dovar).

[358] Ibid, s 1(2). If the order for possession has already been made but not executed, the tenant may apply for a stay or suspension of execution of the order for a period not exceeding two months: s 1(4).

[359] LA 1980, ss 15, 17; *Ashe v National Westminster Bank plc* [2008] EWCA Civ 55, [2008] 1 WLR 710. The mortgagor in possession is in 'adverse possession' within the meaning of LA 1980 Sch 1, para 8: *Ashe v National Westminster Bank plc* at [73]-[88], applying *JA Pye (Oxford) Ltd v Graham* [2002] UKHL 30, [2003] 1 AC 419; below, p 1132. These provisions of LA 1980 apply to the rights of mortgagors as against mortgagees in relation to registered land, as well as in unregistered land: below, p 1161, n 245.

(3) Appointment of a Receiver

We have seen that, owing to the strict supervision that the court exercises over a mortgagee, it is undesirable for him to take possession of the land, but, on the other hand, there are cases where it is essential that he should be able to intercept the rents and the profits, and employ them in keeping down the interest. The mortgaged property may have been leased by the mortgagor to third parties under his statutory powers or the property may consist not of land but of a rentcharge, so that there is an annual sum that can be prevented from reaching the mortgagor and can be set against interest. In such cases the most effective procedure is to appoint a receiver of the income of the property.

The mortgage deed may contain special provisions with regard to this matter, and in some cases, such as where the property is already let to tenants, it is not uncommon to appoint a receiver from the moment when the mortgage is created. But apart from this a mortgagee has a statutory power of appointing a receiver in the case of every mortgage created by deed,[360] even though he has already gone into possession before the appointment.[361] The appointment and removal of a receiver must be effected in writing.[362]

Although this statutory power arises as soon as the mortgage money has become due, it cannot be exercised until one of the three events that qualify a mortgagee to exercise his power of sale has occurred.[363]

The advantage of such an appointment from the mortgagee's point of view is that the receiver is deemed to be the agent of the mortgagor,[364] and that the sole responsibility for his acts and defaults falls on the latter.[365] The receiver is not entitled to grant leases without the sanction of the court,[366] but he has power to recover the income of the property by action or distress or otherwise, and to give effectual receipts,[367] and he is bound to apply any money received by him in the following order:[368]

(1) In discharge of rents, taxes,[369] rates and outgoings.

---

[360] LPA 1925, s 101(1)(iii). *Shamji v Johnson Matthey Bankers Ltd* [1991] BCLC 36 (mortgagee owes no duty of care to mortgagor or guarantor in deciding whether or not to appoint a receiver).

[361] *Refuge Assurance Co Ltd v Pearlberg* [1938] Ch 687.

[362] LPA 1925, s 109(1), (5). In registered land the power to appoint a receiver is not exercisable until the mortgage is registered: *Lever Finance Ltd v Trustee of the Property of Needleman and Kreutzer* [1956] Ch 375.

[363] LPA 1925, s 109 (1), below, p 854.

[364] For the peculiar incidents of this agency, see *Silven Properties Ltd v Royal Bank of Scotland plc* [2003] EWCA Civ 1409, [2004] 1 WLR 997 at [21]–[29] (Lightman J).

[365] LPA 1925, s 109(2). See *Chatsworth Properties Ltd v Effiom* [1971] 1 WLR 144; *Standard Chartered Bank Ltd v Walker* [1982] 1 WLR 1410; *American Express International Banking Corp v Hurley* [1985] 3 All ER 564; below, p 860, n 411. See *Lever Finance Ltd v Trustee of the Property of Needleman and Kreutzer*, above (receipt by receiver as agent of mortgagor does not create tenancy by estoppel binding on mortgagee): *Mann v Nijar* (2000) 32 HLR 223.

[366] *Re Cripps* [1946] Ch 265.

[367] LPA 1925, s 109(3). The reference to distress will be replaced by a reference to commercial rent arrears recovery under Tribunals, Courts and Enforcement Act 2007, s 72(1), when that Act is brought into force and distress is abolished: above, p 277.

[368] Ibid, s 109(8).   [369] *Sargent v Customs and Excise Comrs* [1993] EGCS 182 (VAT).

(2) In keeping down payments that rank before the mortgage.

(3) In paying his own commission, fire and other insurance premiums and, if so directed in writing by the mortgagee, the cost of repairs. His commission is at a rate not exceeding five per cent on the gross sum received; if no rate is specified, then at five per cent, or at such other rate as the court thinks fit to allow.[370]

(4) In payment of the mortgage interest.

(5) In discharging the principal sum if so directed in writing by the mortgagee. A breach of this direction renders him liable to an action for an account.[371]

Any residue that remains must be paid to the mortgagor.

A receiver, when managing the mortgaged property, owes not only a duty of good faith to the mortgagor and anyone else with an interest in the equity of redemption, but also a duty to manage the property with due diligence. The extent of the duty depends on the facts and circumstances of the case.[372]

(4) Sale[373]

(a) Power of sale

(1) When power arises

As soon as the mortgage money has become due, that is as soon as the date fixed for repayment has passed, the legal mortgagee or chargee has a statutory power, which may be varied or extended by the parties or excluded altogether,[374] to sell the mortgage property *provided that the mortgage has been made by deed*.[375] If the money secured by the mortgage is payable by instalments, the power of sale arises as soon as an instalment is due and unpaid.[376]

(2) When power exercisable

Although the power of sale *arises* as soon as the mortgage money becomes due, it nevertheless does not become *exercisable* until one of the following events has occurred:

(i) Notice requiring payment of the mortgage money has been served on the mortgagor or one of two or more mortgagors, and default has been made in payment of the mortgage money, or of part thereof, for three months after such service.[377]

---

[370] *Marshall v Cottingham* [1982] Ch 82.

[371] *Leicester Permanent Building Society v Butt* [1943] Ch 308.

[372] *Medforth v Blake* [2000] Ch 86; [1999] Conv 434 (A Kenny); [2000] CLJ 31 (LS Sealy). On the receiver's duty of care in selling the property, see [2010] Conv 369 (KCF Loi).

[373] See generally Fisher and Lightwood, ch 30; (1976) 73 LSG 92, 654; (1977) 74 LSG 493 (HE Markson).

[374] *Alliance Building Society v Shave* [1952] Ch 581.   [375] LPA 1925, s 101(1)(i).

[376] *Payne v Cardiff RDC* [1932] 1KB 241; cf *Twentieth Century Banking Corp Ltd v Wilkinson* [1977] Ch 99.

[377] LPA 1925, s 103(i).

This notice, which must be in writing,[378] may demand payment either immediately or at the end of three months, and if it is drafted in the latter form, the mortgagee need not wait for a further three months before selling, but can exercise his power after the lapse of three months from the service of notice.[379]

If there are more mortgages than one, the notice should also be served upon the later mortgagees.

(ii) Some interest under the mortgage is in arrear and unpaid for two months after becoming due.[380]

(iii) There has been a breach of some provision contained in the mortgage deed or in the Law of Property Act 1925, and on the part of the mortgagor, or of some person concurring in making the mortgage, to be observed or performed, other than and besides a covenant for payment of the mortgage money or interest thereon.[381]

For example, if the mortgagor has broken a covenant to keep the premises in repair, the mortgagee can exercise his power of sale immediately, despite the fact that no interest is in arrear and that he has not demanded repayment of the loan.

Sections 101–107 of the Law of Property Act 1925 contain detailed provisions dealing with the power of sale.[382] The mortgagee may sell the mortgaged property, or any part of it, either subject to prior charges or not, and either together or in lots, by public auction or by private contract. He may sell the land either with or apart from the minerals, and may impose either on the sold or on the unsold part of the mortgaged land such conditions or restrictive covenants as seem desirable.[383]

(3) Exercise of power of sale not regulated by Human Rights Act 1998

In *Horsham Properties Group Ltd v Clark*[384] Briggs J held that the exercise by the mortgagor of his power of sale without first obtaining a court order for possession, or an order for sale, did not infringe the mortgagor's rights under the European Convention on Human Rights. The mortgagor's equity of redemption is a 'possession' within article 1 of the First Protocol,[385] but in the case in hand the mortgagor lost her equity of redemption by virtue of the contract of sale that was entered into by the mortgagee's receiver, and the powers for the mortgagee to appoint a receiver, and for the receiver to sell, were conferred by contract in the mortgage itself. Strictly, therefore, given that no statutory power was exercised, the mortgagor lost the equity of redemption without any state intervention and therefore the case fell outside the scope of protection of the Human Rights Act 1998.[386] However, the judge went on to consider the case where a sale is pursuant to the statutory power of sale under section 101 of the Law of Property

---

378 Ibid, s 196.

379 *Barker v Illingworth* [1908] 2 Ch 20.

380 LPA 1925, s 103(ii).

381 LPA 1925, s 103(ii), s 103(iii).

382 See also CCA 1974, s 126; above, p 827.

383 LPA 1925, s 101(2).

384 [2008] EWHC 2327 (Ch), [2009] 1 WLR 1255, M&B 937; [2009] Conv 283 (M Dixon), 516 (S Greer). Cf Rook, *Property Law and Human Rights*, pp 199–203.

385 Ibid, at [25]; for the text of the relevant provisions of the ECHR, see above, p 23.

386 For the scope of the Act, see above, pp 22–4.

Act 1925, and held that in such a case there would still be no relevant deprivation of possessions within the meaning of the Convention:[387]

> My primary reason for that conclusion is that section 101 serves to implement rather than override the private bargain between mortgagor and mortgagee.... its history, going back to 1860,[388] is that it supplies a convenient power of sale out of court to mortgagees in substitution for the parties having (as they routinely did before 1860) to spell out such a power in every legal mortgage. It is in substance a form of conveyancing shorthand designed to implement the ordinary expectations of mortgagors and mortgagees while reducing the costs and delays of conveyancing...
>
> Furthermore, all the statutory powers in section 101 are expressed to be subject to contrary intention. Section 101(4) provides: 'This section applies only if and as far as a contrary intention is not expressed in the mortgage deed, and has effect subject to the terms of the mortgage deed and to the provisions therein contained.' That subsection on its own demonstrates that section 101 serves rather than overrides the parties' bargain. It is in my judgment as far removed from the concept of state intervention into private rights through overriding legislation, which lies behind article 1, as it is possible for legislation to get. It is neither rigid, arbitrary or discriminatory, and its effect is not only apparent on the face of section 101, but (in the present case) spelt out in terms in the mortgage itself.

Moreover, the judge held that, even if he was wrong in holding that the Convention was not engaged, any deprivation of possession constituted by the exercise by a mortgagee of its powers under section 101 of the LPA after a relevant default by the mortgagor is justified in the public interest:[389]

> it reflects the bargain habitually drawn between mortgagors and mortgagees for nearly 200 years, in which the ability of a mortgagee to sell the property offered as a security without having to go to court has been identified as a central and essential aspect of the security necessarily to be provided if substantial property based secured lending is to be available at affordable rates of interest. That it is in the public interest that property buyers and owners should be able to obtain lending for that purpose can hardly be open to doubt, even if the loan-to-value ratios at which it has recently become possible have now become a matter of controversy.

This robust decision confirms the traditional rule that the mortgagee may exercise a contractual or statutory power of sale without prior authorisation from the court. It should be remembered that, in the case of residential mortgages, the mortgagee will generally need first to obtain vacant possession in order to maximise the opportunities of sale, and the action for possession will be subject to the control of the court under the Adminstration of Justice Act 1970[390] and the Pre-action Protocol for Possession Claims.[391] However, the *Horsham* case was seen as having brought to light a 'loophole' and in 2009 the Government provisionally proposed that the power of sale in residential

---

[387] Above, n 384, at [35]-[36].

[388] Ibid, at [17]: Lord Cranworth's Act 1860, repeated in Conveyancing Act 1881, s 19(1) and now found in LPA 1925, s 101(1)(i).

[389] Ibid at [44].   [390] Above, p 848.   [391] Above, p 850.

owner-occupier cases should in general only be exercisable with the approval of the court or by the agreement of the parties.[392]

(b) Effect of Sale

If a mortgagee realises his security by exercising the statutory power of sale, the effect is to extinguish the mortgagor's equity of redemption. It is, however, the contract to sell and not the subsequent conveyance that represents the effective exercise of the mortgagee's power; and, providing that there is no impropriety in the sale, the mortgagor's equity is extinguished as soon as the contract of sale is made.[393]

(1) Fee simple

A mortgagee, although he holds only a term of years or, more commonly, a charge by way of legal mortgage, is given express statutory power to vest the fee simple in the purchaser. The conveyance may be made in the name of the mortgagor as estate owner, and it operates to pass his legal fee simple to the purchaser and to extinguish the mortgage terms vested both in the selling mortgagee and in any subsequent mortgagees.[394] If the person exercising the power of sale is not the first mortgagee, then the purchaser takes the fee simple subject to prior mortgages.

(2) Leasehold

Where a term of years has been mortgaged by a sub-lease, the effect of a sale by the mortgagee is to convey to the purchaser both the mortgage sub-term and the residue of the term vested in the mortgagor.[395] The sub-term is extinguished, since it merges in the mortgagor's reversion that thus passes to the purchaser. The conveyance, however, does not have this effect if the mortgage term does not comprise the whole of the land included in the mortgagor's term, unless the rent and the covenants have been apportioned, or unless the land excluded from the mortgage term bears a rent of no money value.[396] The acquisition of the reversion by the purchaser results in his becoming liable, in his capacity as assignee, upon the covenants contained in the lease from the lessor to the mortgagor. The Act, therefore, provides that if the leave of the court is obtained the sub-term alone may be conveyed to the purchaser to the exclusion of the mortgagor's reversion.[397]

---

[392] MoJ Consultation Paper CP55/09, *Mortgages: Power of Sale and Residential Property*. The consultation period closed on 28 March 2010 but at the beginning of 2011 no response to the consultation had yet been announced.

[393] *Lord Waring v London and Manchester Assurance Co Ltd* [1935] Ch 310, M & B p 954; *Property and Bloodstock Ltd v Emerton* [1968] Ch 94; *Horsham Properties Group Ltd v Clark*, above, p 855. For the effect of a contract of sale by the mortgagor upon the powers of the mortgagee, see *Duke v Robson* [1973] 1 WLR 267.

[394] LPA 1925, ss 88(1), 113.   [395] Ibid, s 89(1).

[396] Ibid, s 89(6). 'Apportionment' includes an equitable apportionment, ie one made without the consent of the lessor: LP(A)A 1926, Sch, amending LPA 1925, s 89.

[397] LPA 1925, s 89(1)(a).

These provisions also apply where the owner of a charge over a leasehold by way of legal mortgage exercises his power of sale.

(c) Position of purchaser from mortgagee

It is clear, therefore, that there is no difficulty in transferring to a purchaser a valid legal title to the whole interest vested in the mortgagor. Such a purchaser takes the estate freed from all estates, interests and rights to which the mortgage has priority;[398] but if he buys from a second mortgagee he will take the fee simple subject to the term vested in the first mortgagee, and he will himself be deprived of the fee simple if such a first mortgagee exercises his powers of sale or foreclosure. A sale that is made in the professed exercise of the statutory power of sale (and after 1925 every sale made by a mortgagee is deemed so to have been made unless a contrary intention appears) cannot be impeached on the ground that no case has arisen to authorise the sale, or that the power has been improperly exercised. If either of these facts is proved, then the injured person has his remedy against the mortgagee who exercised the power, not against the purchaser.[399]

A purchaser is thus only concerned to see that the power of sale has arisen, and this he can discover merely by examining the mortgage deed. He need not satisfy himself that the power of sale has become exercisable or that it has been properly exercised. If, however, he 'becomes aware...of any facts showing that the power of sale is not exercisable, or that there is some impropriety in the sale, then, in my judgment, he gets no good title on taking the conveyance'.[400]

(d) Application of purchase money

The money received from a purchaser is held by the mortgagee, after any prior mortgages have been paid off, on trust:

First, to pay all expenses incidental to the sale.

Secondly, to pay to himself the principal, interest and costs due under the mortgage, and

Thirdly, to pay the surplus, if any, to the person entitled to the mortgaged property.[401]

The words 'person entitled to the mortgaged property' include subsequent mortgagees, and the rule is that where there are several mortgagees interested in the same land, a prior mortgagee holds any surplus proceeds on trust for those later

---

[398] LPA 1925, s 104(1).   [399] Ibid, s 104(2), (3).
[400] *Lord Waring v London and Manchester Assurance Co Ltd* [1935] Ch 310, 318 (Crossman J). See *Jenkins v Jones* (1860) 2 Giff 99; *Selwyn v Garfit* (1888) 38 Ch D 273; *Bailey v Barnes* [1894] 1 Ch 25; *Price Bros (Somerford) Ltd v J Kelly Homes (Stoke-on-Trent) Ltd* [1975] 1 WLR 1512; *Northern Development (Holdings) Ltd v UDT Securities Ltd* [1976] 1 WLR 1230; *Forsyth v Blundell* (1973) 129 CLR 477; *Pasquarella v National Australia Finance Ltd* [1987] 1 NZLR 312 and generally Emmet, para 25.115; [1988] Conv 317; [1989] Conv 412 (S Robinson); *Corbett v Halifax Building Society* [2002] EWCA Civ 1849, [2003] 1 WLR 964.
[401] LPA 1925, s 105; *Weld-Blundell v Synott* [1940] 2 KB 107.

If the mortgagor does not pay, the court issues an order for *foreclosure nisi*, the effect of which is that the mortgagor loses his property unless he pays upon a certain date (generally six months later) specified by the Master's certificate. The judgment orders that an account shall be taken of what is due to the claimant for principal, interest and costs, and directs that if this amount is paid within six months, the mortgage term shall be surrendered to the defendant, but that if default in payment is made, the defendant shall stand absolutely debarred and foreclosed of and from all right, title, interest and equity of redemption in and to the mortgaged premises. The mortgagee then proves in chambers what is due to him for principal, interest and costs, and the Master draws up a certificate of what is due and fixes a day and an hour for repayment (usually six months from then). On that day the mortgagee attends, and waits for the mortgagor, and if the latter does not appear, an affidavit is sworn in proof of non-payment either prior to or at the appointed time, and an order is made for *foreclosure absolute*.

(b) Effect of foreclosure order

The effect of the order absolute is to vest in the mortgagee the fee simple absolute (or, in the case of a mortgage of a leasehold, the leasehold reversion affected by the mortgage), and to extinguish his mortgage term and all subsequent mortgage terms or legal charges.[432] In registered land, in order to perfect his title the mortgagee will apply to be registered as proprietor of the registered estate in respect of which the charge is registered. The registrar must then cancel the registration of the charge, cancel all entries in respect of interests over which the charge has priority, and enter the applicant as proprietor of the registered estate.[433]

(1) Foreclose down

The rights of prior mortgagees are not affected. If there are more mortgagees than one interested in the same land, an order absolute obtained by the first mortgagee forecloses all subsequent incumbrancers while if, for example, the second mortgagee obtains such an order, its effect is to foreclose the third and later mortgagees, but to leave untouched the rights of the first mortgagee. The rule is 'foreclose down'.[434]

Where there are in this way several mortgagees and the first brings an action for foreclosure, not only the mortgagor, but also each of the subsequent mortgagees must be given an opportunity to redeem, and the ordinary practice is to direct in the order *nisi* that any of the subsequent incumbrancers may repay the amount due to the first

---

432 LPA 1925, ss 88(2) (freehold mortgages), 89(2) (leasehold mortgages).   433 LRR 2003, r 112.

434 From this must be distinguished the maxim 'Redeem up, foreclose down'. This applies where there are several mortgagees and in a redemption action one of them seeks to redeem a prior mortgage. Thus, if there are five mortgages and the fourth seeks to redeem the second mortgage, he must redeem up, ie redeem the third as well as the second, and foreclose down, ie foreclose the fifth mortgage and the mortgagor. The first mortgage is unaffected. See Waldock, *Law of Mortgages*, p 337.

mortgagee on the date appointed.[435] If subsequent mortgagees are not made parties they are not foreclosed.

(2) Sale in lieu of foreclosure

The court has statutory jurisdiction in a foreclosure action to order a sale instead of a foreclosure on the request of the mortgagee or mortgagor, or of any person interested in the mortgage money or the equity of redemption, notwithstanding the dissent of any other person.[436]

(3) Lapse of time

An action for foreclosure is an action to recover land,[437] and must therefore be brought within 12 years from the date on which the right of recovery accrues.[438] The right accrues at the date fixed for payment of the principal,[439] but there is a fresh accrual, and the 12 years begin to run again, from any payment of principal or interest by the mortgagor or from a written acknowledgment by him of the mortgagee's title.[440]

(c) Revival of equity of redemption

But it must not be thought that a foreclosure absolute irrevocably passes the mortgagor's interest to the mortgagee, although it appears on the surface to do so: there are certain circumstances in which the foreclosure may be reopened and the equity of redemption revived. This reopening takes place if the mortgagee, after obtaining an order absolute, proceeds to sue on the personal covenant,[441] but in addition to this case the court has a discretion to reopen a foreclosure if such relief appears in the special circumstances of the case to be due to the mortgagor. Moreover, the foreclosure may be reopened against one who has purchased the estate from the mortgagee. It is impossible to lay down a general rule as to when the relief will be granted, since everything turns upon the particular circumstances of each case, although such a reopening of the foreclosure is very rare.

In *Campbell v Holyland*,[442] Jessel MR enumerated those factors that might influence the court in reopening the foreclosure: the promptness of the mortgagor's application, his failure to redeem being due to an accident that prevented him from raising the money, the difference between the value of the property and the loan,[443] and any

---

[435] If subsequent mortgagees request that they be granted successive periods for repayment, an order to that effect is generally issued: *Platt v Mendel* (1884) 27 Ch D 246.

[436] LPA 1925, s 91(2); *Silsby v Holliman* [1955] Ch 552; *Twentieth Century Banking Corp Ltd v Wilkinson* [1977] Ch 99. See also *Palk v Mortgage Services Funding plc* [1993] Ch 330, above, p 861; *Arab Bank plc v Mercantile Holdings Ltd* [1994] Ch 71; *Halifax Building Society v Thomas* [1996] Ch 217, 226 (Peter Gibson LJ, noting the modern preference to order sale under s 91(2) rather than foreclosure).

[437] LA 1980, s 20(4).

[438] Ibid, s 15(1).

[439] *Purnell v Roche* [1927] 2 Ch 142; *Lewis v Plunket* [1937] Ch 306.

[440] LA 1980, s 29; *Harlock v Ashberry* (1882) 19 Ch D 539.

[441] *Perry v Barker* (1806) 13 Ves 198; above, p 845.

[442] (1877) 7 Ch D 166, 172–5, M & B p 975.

[443] *Lancashire & Yorkshire Reversionary Interest Co Ltd v Crowe* (1970) 114 SJ 435 (foreclosure decree made absolute in respect of mortgage of reversionary interest, and re-opened after the interest fell in

special value that the property had to the parties. Further the court may still reopen the foreclosure, even if the mortgagee has sold the property after the foreclosure absolute, such as where a purchaser bought the property within 24 hours after the order and with notice of the fact that it was of much greater value than the amount of the mortgage debt.[444]

(6) Restitution

The law of restitution may provide a remedy for the mortgagee. Thus in *Goss v Chilcott*,[445] the mortgagee was held to be able to recover the amount of an advance made to the defendants that was secured by a mortgage over their property. The mortgage deed was subsequently altered by a solicitor, as a result of which the defendants were discharged from liability as from the date of alteration. Lord Goff of Chieveley said:[446]

> The effect of the alteration was that their contractual obligation to repay the money was discharged; but they had nevertheless been enriched by the receipt of the money, and prima facie were liable in restitution to restore it.

(7) Further Rights of Legal Mortgagees

(a) Grant and acceptance of surrender of leases

If a mortgagee takes possession of the land with a view to utilising the profits in satisfaction of the money due to him, he is authorised by statute to grant leases, and to accept surrenders of leases, within the limits made applicable to a mortgagor who is in actual possession.[447] He is also permitted, where the mortgage is made by deed, to cut and sell timber and other trees if they are ripe for cutting and are not planted for shelter or ornament.[448]

(b) Insurance of the mortgaged property

Where a mortgage is made by deed, the mortgagee has statutory authority to insure the property against loss or damage by fire, and to charge the premiums on the mortgaged property.[449] But the amount of the insurance must not exceed the amount specified in the mortgage deed, or, if no amount is specified, must not exceed two-thirds of the sum

---

possession on death of the tenant for life. The sum due was £3,000, and the fund £6,100). This is a very rare case in the modern law. There appears to be no case reported in the Law Reports since the beginning of the twentieth century in which a foreclosure was re-opened, the last such case in which a claim to re-open was made being *Pennington v Cayley* [1912] 2 Ch 236.

[444] *Campbell v Holyland*, above.

[445] [1996] AC 788, M & B p 974.

[446] Ibid, at 792; Goff and Jones, *The Law of Restitution* (7th edn, 2007), paras 19-007 to 19-008. See also *Portman Building Society v Hamlyn Taylor Neck* [1998] 4 All ER 202 (mortgagee's loss arising from mistake induced by solicitor: no restitution because solicitor not enriched).

[447] LPA 1925, ss 99(2), 100(2); above, pp 842–5; *Berkshire Capital Funding Ltd v Street* [1999] 2 EGLR 92 (interests of prior lender unaffected by loan).

[448] Ibid, s 101(1)(iv).   [449] Ibid, s 101(1)(ii).

it would take to restore the premises in the event of their total destruction. Moreover, the mortgagee does not possess this statutory right where the mortgage deed contains a declaration that no insurance is required, or where an insurance is kept up by the mortgagor according to the mortgage deed, or where that deed contains no provision and the mortgagor himself insures up to the statutory amount.[450] Insurance money, when received, may be applied at the instance of the mortgagee in the discharge of the mortgage debt.[451]

(c) Possession of the title deeds

A legal mortgagee takes a lease or, if he is a chargee, is in the same position as if he had done so, and the ordinary rule is that a leaseholder is not entitled to hold title deeds appertaining to the fee simple of the lessor. But, since the continued possession of the deeds by the mortgagor involves considerable risk to one who has advanced money on the security of the land, it is enacted that a first mortgagee shall have the same right to possession of documents as if his security included the fee simple.[452] This is relevant only to unregistered land.

At law the mortgagee becomes the absolute owner of the title deeds, and is therefore under no duty of care in respect of them. He is subject only to pay compensation in equity for their loss on redemption.[453]

(d) Fixtures

Fixtures pass with the land to the mortgagee even though not mentioned in the deed,[454] as also do those that are added later by the mortgagor himself while in possession. Moreover, a mortgagor in possession is not entitled to remove 'tenant's' fixtures, whether they have been annexed to the land before or after the mortgage transaction.[455] These rules apply whether the mortgage is legal or equitable, and whether it affects freehold or leasehold premises. Where, however, fixtures have been annexed to land by a *third party* under an agreement between him and the mortgagor that permits him to remove them in certain circumstances, his right of removal cannot in general be defeated by the mortgagee. The mortgagee, by allowing the mortgagor to remain in possession, implicitly authorises him to make agreements usual and proper in his particular trade.[456]

(e) Tacking of further advances

We shall see later that a mortgagee who makes a further loan to the mortgagor is allowed, in certain circumstances, to demand that both loans shall be paid out of the

---

[450] LPA 1925, s 108(1), (2); *Colonial Mutual General Insurance Co Ltd v ANZ Banking Group (New Zealand) Ltd* [1995] 1 WLR 1140.

[451] Ibid, s 108(4).   [452] Ibid, ss 85(1), 86(1).

[453] *Browning v Handiland Group Ltd and Bush Investments Trust Ltd* (1976) 35 P & CR 345.

[454] *Vaudeville Electric Cinema Ltd v Muriset* [1923] 2 Ch 74; LPA 1925, ss 62(1), 205(1)(ii).

[455] *Longbottom v Berry* (1869) LR 5 QB 123.   [456] *Gough v Wood & Co* [1894] 1 QB 713.

land in priority to loans made by other mortgagees, although the latter may have taken their securities before the date of such further loan.[457]

(f) Consolidation

Consolidation is the right[458] of a person who holds two or more mortgages granted by the same mortgagor on different properties to refuse in certain circumstances to be redeemed as to one, unless he is also redeemed as to the other or others.[459]

The mortgages in actual fact are quite separate, having been given on different properties and perhaps at different times, but none the less the mortgagee is allowed in certain cases to consolidate them and treat them as one. The right is based upon the doctrine that *he who comes to equity must do equity*; for a mortgagor who is seeking to redeem is asking a favour in the sense that he is petitioning equity for the restoration of his property after the date fixed by the mortgage deed for redemption has passed, and this being so, he must himself be prepared to act equitably.

Suppose, for example, that:

> A has mortgaged Blackacre to B for £10,000 and Whiteacre to B for £10,000. If Blackacre diminishes, while Whiteacre appreciates, in value, it is unethical that A should be allowed to redeem the latter unless he is also prepared to repay the loan of £10,000 on Blackacre. In such a case B can insist that both properties shall be treated as one and redeemed together.

This example illustrates the primary meaning and the simplest application of consolidation, but the doctrine has been developed further and extended to cases where the mortgages were originally made to different mortgagees. In such a case if the mortgages ultimately become vested in one person, that is in one mortgagee, he possesses the right of consolidation.[460] Thus, if:

> A mortgages W to B,
> A mortgages X and Y to C,
> B and C transfer their mortgages to D,

A cannot redeem any one of the properties W, X, Y, unless, if called upon, he pays the amount due on the other two.

But consolidation extends even further than this, and applies to a case where the person who is entitled to redeem is not the original mortgagor, but a transferee of one or more of the equities. There are two different cases to be considered, since the law differs according as the equities of redemption have all become united in one person, or have become separated so that the person claiming to redeem, that is the person

---

[457] Below, pp 878, 893.   [458] The right must be expressly reserved: below, p 870.

[459] *Jennings v Jordan* (1881) 6 App Cas 698, 700; White and Tudor, *Leading Cases in Equity*, vol ii, p 129. For a criticism of the doctrine, see Waldock, *Law of Mortgages*, pp 293–5. As to whether the right amounts to a general equitable charge within LCA 1972, s 2(4), Class C(iii), see (1948) 92 SJ 736; Wolstenholme and Cherry, vol 1, p 189. For registered land, see LRA 2002, s 57 and LRR 2003, r 110, under which a right of consolidation may be entered on the register.

[460] *Vint v Padget* (1858) 2 De G & J 611; *Pledge v White* [1896] AC 187, M & B p 978.

against whom the doctrine of consolidation is invoked, is not the owner of all the equities.

(1) Where all equities transferred to one person

If a person acquires the equities on all the properties, whether as trustee in bankruptcy, purchaser or second mortgagee, the mortgages can in all cases be consolidated against him, even though the mortgage terms did not become vested in one mortgagee until after the person seeking to redeem had obtained the equities.

An illustration may elucidate this:

> 2004 A mortgages U and V to B.
> 2006 A mortgages W to C.
> 2007 A mortgages X, Y and Z to D.
> 2009 A sells the *equities* on U, V, W, X, Y and Z to F.
> 2011 E acquires all the mortgages from B, C and D.

Here all the mortgages are vested in one person, E, and, although he knew, when he bought out B, C and D, that the equities were not vested in the original mortgagor, he can require F to redeem all the properties or none. Lord Davey said in *Pledge v White*:[461]

> It appears to me, my Lords, that an assignee of two or more equities of redemption from one mortgagor stands in a widely different position from the assignee of one equity only. He knows, or has the opportunity of knowing, what are the mortgages subject to which he has purchased the property, and he knows they may become united by transfer in one hand. If the doctrine of consolidation be once admitted it appears to me not unreasonable to hold that a person in such a position occupies the place of the mortgagor or assignor to him towards the holders of the mortgages, subject to which he has purchased.

(2) Where equities separated

Turning now to the case where the equities are separated and do not all pass to one person, it will be useful, before stating the general principle, to present an illustration showing how the purchaser of a single equity of redemption may find himself saddled with the burden of redeeming other mortgages of whose very existence he was unaware:

> If at different times A mortgages X, Y and Z to B, and then later transfers the fee simple of X to C, who gives full value and knows nothing of the other two properties which have been mortgaged, C, on tendering the amount of the loan due on X, may be unable under the doctrine of consolidation to redeem X unless he also pays what is due on Y and Z.

Where the mortgage transactions entered into by the original mortgagor are many, and where dealings have taken place both in the equities and in the mortgages, the question whether in any particular case consolidation is enforceable appears at first sight to be both difficult and complicated. But all difficulty disappears if attention is

---

[461] [1896] AC 187, 198.

paid to the cardinal rule. This rule covers all cases of separation of equities, and clearly defines the limits within which consolidation is applicable. Consolidation is allowed only if, at the date when redemption is sought, all the mortgages, having originally been made by one mortgagor, are vested in one mortgagee and all the equities are vested in one person, or if, *after these two things have once happened, the equities of redemption have become separated.*[462]

If all the mortgages are in one hand and all the equities in another, it is clear that the right of consolidation exists against the mortgagor. It is equally clear that, *once this right has been established in respect of all the properties*, a transferee of one or more of the equities cannot stand in a better position than the mortgagor from whom he took the transfer. The principle of law involved here is that a person who buys an equity of redemption from a mortgagor takes it subject to all liabilities to which it was subject at the time of the sale; one of these is the liability to have certain other mortgages consolidated with it, provided, however, that the consolidation was enforceable against that particular equity *at the time of the purchase.*[463] In the words of Lord Selborne:

> The purchaser of an equity of redemption must take it as it stood at the time of his purchase, subject to all other equities which then affected it in the hands of his vendor, of which the right of the mortgagee to consolidate his charge on that particular property with other charges *then* held by him on other property at the same time redeemable under the same mortgagor was one.[464]

But on no principle of law would it be justifiable to hold the purchaser of an interest bound by equities that were not enforceable against that interest at the time of its sale. It follows from this that the assignee of an equity does not become subject to consolidation in respect of mortgages created *after* the sale to him, nor in respect of mortgages that, though created before that date, became united in one mortgagee afterwards.[465] Suppose, for example, that the following transactions successively occur:[466]

A mortgages X to B,
A mortgages Y to B,
A sells the equity of redemption in Y to C,
A mortgages Z to B.

When C seeks to redeem his own property Y, he can be compelled by B to redeem X, because, at the time when he bought his equity, the equities on X and Y were vested in one person, and the mortgages were vested in one person. But he cannot be compelled to redeem Z, for the mortgage on it was created only after the sale of the equity on Y to C, so that the right to have Z consolidated with X and Y obviously did not exist at that time.

---

[462] *Pledge v White* [1896] AC 187, 198 (Lord Davey).
[463] *Cummins v Fletcher* (1880) 14 Ch D 699, 712, M & B p 980.
[464] *Jennings v Jordan* (1881) 6 App Cas 698, 701.   [465] *Harter v Colman* (1882) 19 Ch D 630.
[466] *Hughes v Britannia Permanent Benefit Building Society* [1906] 2 Ch 607, M & B p 981.

The holder of an equity of redemption who is compelled under the doctrine of consolidation to redeem some other mortgage steps into the shoes of the mortgagee, and can demand payment from the mortgagor in respect of the mortgage he has had to redeem.

(3) Mortgages must be by same person

No right to consolidation arises if the mortgages were originally made by different mortgagors, even though the equities subsequently become united in one hand.[467]

(4) Reservation of right

The right of consolidation does not exist as a matter of course, but only where it is expressly reserved in the various deeds *or in one of them*. When the right is not so reserved, it is enacted that:[468]

> A mortgagor seeking to redeem any one mortgage is entitled to do so without paying any money due under any separate mortgage made by him, or by any person through whom he claims, solely on property other than that comprised in the mortgage which he seeks to redeem.

This is a re-enactment of the Conveyancing Act 1881, and it does not apply where all the mortgages were made before 1882. In mortgages made before that date the right of consolidation existed as a matter of course.

B RIGHTS OF EQUITABLE MORTGAGEE

The remedies of an equitable mortgagee vary according as the security is a mortgage in the strict sense, namely a contract to create a legal mortgage or a mortgage of an equitable interest;[469] or is a charge upon property.[470] We will take these two classes separately.

(1) Equitable Mortgagee

If the mortgage falls within the first class the general principle is that the remedies available to the lender correspond as nearly as possible with those available to a legal mortgagee.

(a) Foreclosure

Thus the remedy of foreclosure applies where a deposit of title deeds with the lender has been accompanied by a contract by the borrower to give a legal mortgage if required to do so.[471] When such an equitable mortgagee takes foreclosure proceedings to enforce

---

[467] *Sharp v Rickards* [1909] 1 Ch 109.   [468] LPA 1925, s 93(1).
[469] Above, pp 807, 811.   [470] Above, p 811.
[471] *York Union Banking Co v Artley* (1879) 11 Ch D 205.

his security, the decree of the court declares that the deposit operated as a mortgage, that in default of payment the mortgagor is trustee of the legal estate for the mortgagee and that he must convey that estate to him.[472]

(b) Sale

The general rule is that foreclosure and not sale is the proper remedy for an equitable mortgagee.[473] But if the mortgage is made in a form that entitles him to require the execution of a mortgage containing a power of sale, he can exercise the statutory power of sale that is given by the Law of Property Act 1925.[474] This statutory power, however, is exercisable only when the mortgage is made by deed, and therefore the proper course is for an equitable mortgagee not to be content with a mere contract, but to take a memorandum executed as a deed. If this is done he can sell the property subject to the conditions specified by the Act. The memorandum should also give the mortgagee a power of attorney authorising him, upon exercising the power of sale, to convey the mortgaged property in the name of the mortgagor to the purchaser.[475] This enables the mortgagee, though only an equitable incumbrancer, to convey the legal estate in the property to the purchaser.[476] The same result may be achieved by inserting in the memorandum a declaration of trust, stating that the mortgagor holds the legal estate on trust for the mortgagee and empowering the mortgagee to appoint someone, including himself, as trustee in place of the mortgagor. The mortgagee can thus vest the legal estate in himself or the purchaser.

Again, the statutory power of the court to order a sale instead of foreclosure, which we have already noticed,[477] is exercisable in favour of an equitable mortgagee even though he has taken a mere contract without a deed.

(c) Appointment of receiver

If an equitable mortgage is created by deed, the statutory power of appointing a receiver is available to the mortgagee,[478] but in the absence of a deed the appointment must be made by the court.[479]

(d) Entry into possession

An equitable mortgagee is not entitled to take possession of the land unless the right to do so has been expressly reserved[480] or unless the court makes an order to that effect. Though this is the prevalent view, it has been argued with considerable force that it is justified neither on principle nor on the authorities.[481]

---

[472] *Marshall v Shrewsbury* (1875) 10 Ch App 250, 254.

[473] *James v James* (1873) LR 16 Eq 153. For the preference for sale over foreclosure in the modern law, however, see above, p 864, n 436.

[474] S 101(1)(i), above, p 854.   [475] See Powers of Attorney Act 1971, ss 4(1), 5(3).

[476] *Re White Rose Cottage* [1965] Ch 940, M & B p 971.   [477] LPA 1925, s 91; above, p 864.

[478] Ibid., s 101(1)(ii); above, p 853.   [479] *Meaden v Sealey* (1849) 6 Hare 620.

[480] *Finck v Tranter* [1905] 1 KB 427, 429; *Barclays Bank Ltd v Bird* [1954] Ch 274, 280.

[481] (1955) 72 LQR 204 (HWR Wade).

(e) Further rights of equitable mortgagee

An equitable mortgagee can sue the mortgagor personally for recovery of the money lent.

Finally, where, in unregistered land, an equitable mortgage is accompanied by the deposit of title deeds, the mortgagee has the right to retain the deeds under the mortgage until he is paid, but he has no separate legal lien.[482]

(2) Equitable Chargee

The second class of equitable security is the charge, which involves no transfer of a legal or equitable interest to the lender, but entitles him to have the debt discharged out of the land. His sole remedies in this respect are to have the charge satisfied by the sale of the land or by the appointment of a receiver under the direction of the court. He has no right to take possession of the land nor may he foreclose. In the words of Lord Hatherley:

> Although some of the authorities appear to conflict with each other, it seems, on the whole, to be settled that if there is a charge *simpliciter*, and not a mortgage, or an agreement for a mortgage, then the right of the parties having such a charge is a sale and not foreclosure.[483]

From a mere equitable charge must be distinguished the *charge by deed expressed to be by way of legal mortgage* introduced by the legislation of 1925, for as we have seen such a chargee has the same remedies as if he held a term of years absolute;[484] and a *registered charge* is the equivalent in registered land.[485]

V PRIORITY OF MORTGAGES[486]

If two or more mortgagees have advanced money on the security of the same land and if the land is of insufficient value when realised to satisfy the claims of all, it is vital to know in what order they are entitled to be paid out of the land. The mortgagor has, let us say, granted separate and successive mortgages on Blackacre to A, B, C and D. Owing to unforeseen circumstances Blackacre has depreciated in value and its sale will produce sufficient money to repay only one or perhaps two of the mortgagees the amount of their advances. This does not mean that mortgagees who fail to get satisfaction out of the land are remediless, for they can of course sue the mortgagor on

---

[482] *Re Molton Finance Ltd* [1968] Ch 325. See also *Capital Finance Co Ltd v Stokes* [1969] 1 Ch 261, 278. The beneficiary of a charging order has only the rights of an equitable chargee: Charging Orders Act 1979, s 3(4); *Yorkshire Bank Finance Ltd v Mulhall* [2008] EWCA Civ 1156, [2009] 1 P & CR 16 at [14].

[483] *Tennant v Trenchard* (1869) 4 Ch App 537, 542; *Re Owen* [1894] 3 Ch 220.   [484] Above, p 804.

[485] Above, p 806.

[486] See generally Fisher and Lightwood, Part VI, and for a closely reasoned study [1940] CLJ 243 (RE Megarry); Waldock, *Law of Mortgages*, pp 381–435.

his personal covenant, but since his other property may be of little value it will be their object to proceed against the land if the law allows them to do so. A knowledge of the former rules that governed this matter, although they are substantially affected by the legislation of 1925, is essential to an understanding of the modern law on this subject; and, as we shall see, there are situations in which they may still be applicable.[487]

The rules for the priority of mortgages, both before 1926 and after 1925, are subject to variation by the mortgagees amongst themselves without the mortgagor's consent, unless the mortgages otherwise provide.[488]

A PRIORITY OF MORTGAGES BEFORE 1926

(1) The Priority of the Legal Mortgagee of Land

To understand the order in which mortgages ranked for repayment out of the land before 1926 we must recall that under the practice then prevailing it was usual in the case of a mortgage of the fee simple to convey the legal estate in fee simple to the mortgagee.[489] There might be several mortgages of Blackacre, but there could be only one *legal* mortgage, and all the others, whether created before or after the legal mortgage, were necessarily equitable in nature.

(a) Where equities are equal the law prevails

The fundamental rule before 1926, based upon the maxim 'where the equities are equal the law prevails', was that the mortgagee who held the legal estate ranked, for the purpose of obtaining satisfaction out of the land, before all other mortgagees of whose securities he had no notice at the time when he made his advance.[490] Equity respected the legal title, and it was a rule without exception that a court of equity took away from a purchaser for value without notice nothing that he had honestly acquired.[491] Lord Hardwicke said:

> As courts of equity break in upon the common law, where necessity and conscience require it, still they allow superior force and strength to a legal title to estates; and therefore where there is a legal title and equity on one side, this court never thought fit that by reason of a prior equity against a man, who had a legal title, that man should be hurt, and this by reason of that force this court necessarily and rightly allows to the common law and to legal titles.[492]

If, therefore, a mortgagor granted an equitable mortgage to A and later conveyed the legal estate to B by way of mortgage, the latter had the better right to the land provided that, when he made his own advance, he had no notice of the earlier mortgage to A. The onus lay on B to prove this affirmatively.[493] As the legal mortgagee, B had an even

---

[487] Below, pp 883 ff.   [488] *Cheah Theam Swee v Equiticorp Finance Group Ltd* [1992] 1 AC 472.

[489] Above, p 799.   [490] *Plumb v Fluitt* (1791) 2 Anst 432.

[491] *Heath v Crealock* (1874) 10 Ch App 22, 33.   [492] *Wortley v Birkhead* (1754) 2 Ves Sen 571, 574.

[493] *A-G v Biphosphated Guano Co* (1879) 11 Ch D 327.

stronger case against mortgagees who obtained their securities at a date *later* than his own, for not only did he alone hold the legal title, but having acquired it first in order of time he could invoke the maxim *qui prior est tempore potior est jure*: the first in time has the stronger right.

This rule giving priority to the legal mortgagee, however, applied only where the equities were equal, that is where the legal mortgagee had as good a moral right as the equitable mortgagees, and in the following cases he was displaced in favour of equitable mortgagees.

(b) Cases where equities are not equal

(1) Where legal mortgagee had notice of earlier mortgage

If, at the time when he advanced his money, the legal mortgagee had actual or constructive notice of an earlier incumbrance, he was postponed to the earlier incumbrancer. A legal mortgagee who failed to investigate his mortgagor's title according to the usual practice or who abstained from investigation altogether, was affected with notice of, and therefore postponed to, any earlier mortgage that he would have discovered had he followed the customary practice.[494]

(2) Where legal mortgagee was negligent with regard to title deeds

The obvious duty of a person who acquired a legal estate by conveyance by way of legal mortgage before 1926 was to obtain and to keep possession of the title deeds, or, if for some reason this was impossible, to make inquiries for them. Title deeds are in unregistered land the symbol of ownership, and if they were not produced by a mortgagor the suspicion naturally arose that they had been utilised by him in order to vest some right in a third person, and that he was deliberately concealing this transaction from the mortgagee.

There were two indiscretions in this connection that a mortgagee could commit: failure to obtain the deeds at the time of the transaction, and failure to retain deeds of which he had once had possession.

(i) Postponement owing to failure to obtain deeds

It was well established before 1926 that a legal mortgagee who made no inquiries whatever for the deeds must be postponed to a prior equitable incumbrancer who had already secured them, and even to a later innocent incumbrancer who was more diligent in getting them into his custody.[495] On the other hand, if he made inquiry and yet failed to obtain them, it depended upon the circumstances whether he was postponed to an earlier equitable incumbrancer in whose possession they were. Postponement was not an automatic result of failure to obtain possession, for it was always held that in addition there must have been some degree of negligence. The cases show a growing severity against the legal mortgagee. At first it was laid down that he must not be postponed unless he had been guilty of fraud in the transaction under

---

[494] *Berwick & Co v Price* [1905] 1 Ch 632.   [495] *Walker v Linom* [1907] 2 Ch 104.

which he acquired the legal estate, or unless he had shown such wilful negligence as to indicate complicity in the fraud.[496] But a new rule more favourable to an earlier equitable mortgagee was pronounced by the Court of Appeal in 1899 in the case of *Oliver v Hinton*.[497] This may be stated in the words of Lindley LJ:

> To deprive a purchaser for value[498] without notice of a prior incumbrance of the protection of the legal estate it is not, in my opinion, essential that he should have been guilty of fraud; it is sufficient that he has been guilty of such gross negligence as would render it unjust to deprive the prior incumbrancer of his priority.[499]

The case related to a purchaser of a legal estate, but the result would have been the same had the person who acquired the legal estate been a mortgagee. The facts were as follows:

> A, the owner of the legal estate, deposited the title deeds with X as security for advances to the value of £400 made by the latter. Some two years later A conveyed the legal estate to the purchaser, P, in consideration of £320. P inquired about the deeds, but was told that they could not be delivered as they related also to some other property. This answer was accepted, and A was not even asked to produce the deeds for inspection. It was held that P, though entirely innocent of fraud or of any complicity in fraud, must be postponed to X.

Epithets such as 'gross' are unreliable guides, and the rule as stated by the Court of Appeal left open in each case the question whether the requisite degree of negligence had been shown, but the expression 'gross negligence' was described in a later case as meaning something more than mere carelessness. Eve J said:[500]

> It must at least be carelessness of so aggravated a nature as to amount to the neglect of precautions which the ordinary reasonable man would have observed and to indicate an attitude of mental indifference to obvious risks.

(1) Postponement to earlier incumbrancers

If, therefore, a mortgagee had inquired for the title deeds and had been given a reasonable excuse for their non-delivery, he would not be postponed to an earlier equitable mortgagee. An extreme case, perhaps, is *Hewitt v Loosemore*,[501] where the defendant, who had taken a legal mortgage of a leasehold interest from a solicitor by way of assignment, failed to obtain possession of the lease, which, as a matter of fact, had already been deposited with the claimant. Part of the answer made by the defendant to the bill that the claimant brought against him was as follows:

---

[496] *Hunt v Elmes* (1860) 2 De GF & J 578; *Ratcliffe v Barnard* (1871) 6 Ch App 652; see *Hudston v Viney* [1921] 1 Ch 98, 103–4; *Northern Counties of England Fire Insurance Co v Whipp* (1884) 26 Ch D 482.

[497] [1899] 2 Ch 264.   [498] This includes a mortgagee.

[499] It would have been simpler to apply the doctrine of the bona fide purchaser for value without notice and to postpone the later legal mortgagee unless he satisfies that test. See Romer J at first instance in *Oliver v Hinton* [1899] 2 Ch 264, 268; and Parker J in *Walker v Linom*, above, at 114.

[500] *Hudston v Viney* [1921] 1 Ch 98, 104.

[501] (1851) 9 Hare 449. See also *Agra Bank Ltd v Barry* (1874) LR 7 HL 135.

> The defendant...was a farmer and unacquainted with legal forms; but upon the said indenture of assignment being handed to him as aforesaid, he inquired of [the mortgagor] whether the lease of the premises ought not to be delivered to him as well; when [the mortgagor] replied that it should, but that, as he was rather busy then, he would look for it and give it to the defendant when he next came to market.

It was held that in the circumstances the claimant had failed to make out a sufficient case for postponing the defendant.

(2) Postponement to later incumbrancers

Likewise failure to obtain the deeds might entail postponement of a legal mortgagee to a *later* equitable incumbrancer. Again, however, nothing short of gross negligence was sufficient to produce this result. Thus in *Grierson v National Provincial Bank of England Ltd*:[502]

> A mortgagor, having already deposited the deeds with a bank as security for a loan, executed a legal mortgage in favour of the claimant. The claimant had actual notice of this earlier equitable mortgage, but he neither informed the bank of his legal mortgage, nor instructed them to deliver the deeds to him should the mortgagor repay their loan. The mortgagor later paid off the bank, obtained the deeds and deposited them with the defendant as security for an advance. The defendant was ignorant of the claimant's legal mortgage.

It was held that the claimant had not been sufficiently negligent to justify his postponement to the defendant.

(ii) Postponement due to subsequent negligence

It was also the case before 1926 that the conduct of the legal mortgagee in dealing with the title deeds *after* he had obtained them might be such as to justify his postponement to subsequent equitable mortgagees.

In the first place the principle of *Oliver v Hinton* applied, and any conduct on the part of the legal mortgagee in relation to the deeds that would have made it inequitable for him to claim priority over an earlier equitable mortgagee was sufficient to postpone him to a subsequent mortgage the creation of which was due entirely to his own conduct.[503] There need not have been fraudulent conduct, but there must have been 'gross negligence'. Thus in a leading case[504] the priority of the legal mortgagee was not displaced where a company took a legal mortgage from its manager, and the manager, having stolen the deeds from a safe to which he had access, used them to create another mortgage in favour of an innocent person. The following remarks were made by the court upon the arguments that had been advanced in favour of postponement:

> The case was argued as if the legal owner of land owed a duty to all other of Her Majesty's subjects to keep his title deeds secure; as if title deeds were in the eye of the law analogous

---

[502] [1913] 2 Ch 18.

[503] *Walker v Linom* [1907] 2 Ch 104, 114; *Northern Counties of England Fire Insurance Co v Whipp* (1884) 26 Ch D 482. Cf *Re King's Settlement* [1931] 2 Ch 294.

[504] *Northern Counties of England Fire Insurance Co v Whipp*, above.

to fierce dogs or destructive elements, where from the nature of the thing the courts have implied a general duty of safe custody.[505]

In the second place a legal mortgagee was postponed if he constituted the mortgagor his agent with authority to raise more money on the security of the land. This postponement occurred, for example, where the mortgagor, having been entrusted with the deeds for the purpose of obtaining a further loan of a given amount, procured one of a greater amount without disclosing to the lender the existence of the first mortgage. In such a case the legal mortgagee was postponed on the ground that, having enabled the mortgagor to represent himself as unincumbered owner, he was estopped from asserting that the actual authority had been exceeded.[506]

(2) Priority as Between Equitable Mortgagees of Land

(a) First made, first paid

Where the legal estate was outstanding and a conflict arose between incumbrancers who all held equitable mortgages, the rule was that the several mortgagees must be paid according to their priority of time, *qui prior est tempore potior est jure*.[507]

If, therefore, a mortgagor subjected his land to equitable charges first in favour of A and then in favour of B, or if, after granting a legal mortgage to X, he made subsequent equitable mortgages first to A and then to B, A had the prior right as against B to receive payment out of the land. He had a better and superior equity because it was an earlier equity. This rule was based upon the principle that: 'An owner of property, dealing honestly with it, cannot confer upon another a greater interest in that property than he himself has.'[508]

All that the mortgagor had to dispose of when he had once made a legal mortgage was the equitable interest, and it had long been the rule that: 'Every conveyance of an equitable interest is an innocent conveyance, that is to say, the grant of a person entitled merely in equity passes only that which he is justly entitled to, and no more.'[509]

(b) Exceptions

The rule that priority of time gave the better right to payment might, however, be excluded in two cases: first, where the equities were in other respects not equal; and secondly, where the doctrine of tacking operated.

---

[505] Ibid, at 493.

[506] *Perry Herrick v Attwood* (1857) 2 De G & J 21; *Northern Counties of England Fire Insurance Co v Whipp*, above, at 493; *Brocklesby v Temperance Permanent Building Society* [1895] AC 173.

[507] Above, p 874; *Brace v Duchess of Marlborough* (1728) 2 P Wms 491, 495; *Willoughby v Willoughby* (1756) 1 Term Rep 763.

[508] *West v Williams* [1899] 1 Ch 132, 143 (Lindley MR).

[509] *Phillips v Phillips* (1861) 4 De GF & J 208, 215 (Lord Westbury).

(1) Where equities are not equal. negligence of prior mortgagee

In a contest between equitable claimants, the court had to be satisfied that the party with the earlier equity had acted in such a way as to justify his retention of priority over the later incumbrancer.[510] Thus, he lost the protection that was normally due to him if his negligent failure to obtain or to retain the title deeds had misled the later mortgagee into believing that no earlier equity existed. The question as to what degree of negligence sufficed to produce this result hardly admits of a dogmatic answer, since the judges expressed varying opinions, and one view was that the priority of an equitable mortgage was more easily displaced than that of a legal mortgage.[511] No decision has been found, however, in which the negligence held sufficient to postpone an equitable mortgagee would not also have defeated a legal mortgagee.[512] In the case before 1926 of a legal mortgage to A, followed by equitable mortgages to B and C, the question could arise only exceptionally, since A would normally hold the deeds, but it would arise in an acute form if the only transactions effected by the mortgagor were of an equitable nature. In this connection, two rules were definitely established.

(i) Failure to obtain deeds

First, if an incumbrancer was entitled to have the deeds as part of his security but did not insist upon his right, he was postponed to a later equitable incumbrancer who obtained them without notice of the earlier equity. This occurred in *Farrand v Yorkshire Banking Co*,[513] where the mortgagor agreed to deposit the deeds relating to the mortgaged property with A, but the deposit was never made. A year later he handed the deeds to a bank with which he had made a similar agreement.

It was held that A must be postponed, for it was entirely due to his inactivity that the bank had been defrauded into advancing a second loan.

(ii) Failure to retain deeds

Secondly, if an equitable incumbrancer obtained the deeds but later delivered them to the mortgagor, he was postponed to a later lender to whom they had been delivered as security.[514]

> It is an elementary principle that a party coming into equity in such a case is bound to show that he has not been guilty of such a degree of neglect as to enable another party so to deal with that which was the plaintiff's right, as to induce an innocent party to assume that he was dealing with his own.[515]

(2) Tacking

The general rule that equitable mortgagees ranked for payment according to the dates at which they took their mortgages was also liable to be displaced by the operation of the doctrine of tacking, or 'the creditor's *tabula in naufragio*' ('the plank in the

---

[510] *National Provincial Bank of England v Jackson* (1886) 33 Ch D 1, 13 (Cotton LJ).
[511] *Taylor v Russell* [1891] 1 Ch 8, 17; affd [1892] AC 244, 262.
[512] See the discussion in Waldock, *Law of Mortgages*, pp 397–8.   [513] (1888) 40 Ch D 182.
[514] *Waldron v Sloper* (1852) 1 Drew 193.   [515] Ibid, at 200 (Kindersley V-C).

shipwreck').[516] This doctrine, which is founded on technical and suspect reasoning, is an example of the superiority attached by courts of law and of equity to the legal estate. Equitable owners who were equally meritorious in regard to honesty of dealing might compete for the legal estate, and the one who succeeded in obtaining it won the right to rank before an earlier equitable mortgagee despite the maxim *qui prior est tempore potior est jure*.[517] The reason was that, having obtained the legal estate, he could take advantage of that other and more potent maxim 'where equities are equal, the legal title prevails'.[518]

There were two distinct branches of tacking before 1926, and we must consider these separately.

(i) Where equitable mortgagee acquired legal estate
The first form consisted of joining an equitable mortgage to the legal mortgage in order to squeeze out and gain priority over an intermediate mortgage. If a legal mortgage to A was followed by equitable mortgages first to B and secondly to C, then C would gain priority of payment over B if he paid off A and took a conveyance of his legal estate. C now had the prior right to recover from the land not only the amount that A had advanced on the first mortgage, but also the amount that C himself had advanced to the mortgagor. But he could not tack his own advance to the legal estate and squeeze out B unless he had an equal equity with B; and the equities were not equal unless, *at the time when he made his advance*, he was without notice that B had made an earlier advance.

(ii) Where legal mortgagee made further advance
The second form of tacking was available only to a *legal* mortgagee who had made a further advance. It was not available to equitable mortgagees before 1926. If a legal mortgagee, subsequently to his original loan, made a further advance to the mortgagor without at that time having notice of equitable mortgages created after the legal mortgage, he could, by virtue of his ownership of the legal estate, tack the second to the first advance and recover the whole amount due to him in priority to all other incumbrancers.[519]

If, for example:

The mortgagor made a legal mortgage to A for £2,000, a second mortgage to B, a third mortgage to C, and then a further mortgage to A for £500, A was entitled to be paid £2,500 out of the land before B and C received anything.

But this right did not avail the legal mortgagee if, at the time when he made his further advance, he knew that other persons had already lent money on the security of the land. Thus in *Freeman v Laing*:[520]

---

516 *Brace v Duchess of Marlborough* (1728) 2 P Wms 491. On tacking generally, see *Macmillan Inc v Bishopsgate Investment Trust plc (No 3)* [1995] 1 WLR 978, 1002–5 (Millett J). The doctrine is of reduced importance after 1925. In relation to registered land, see LRA 2002, s 49; below, p 898.

517 Above, p 874.   518 Above, p 873; *Bailey v Barnes* [1894] 1 Ch 25, 36 (Lindley LJ).

519 *Brace v Duchess of Marlborough*, above.   520 [1899] 2 Ch 355.

Three trustees advanced money jointly on a legal mortgage of land and subsequently made a further advance. At the time of this second advance one alone of the trustees had notice of an intermediate mortgage. It was held that the successors in title of the trustees could not tack the second loan to the first, for since each of them was individually entitled to the entire security, notice to one was notice to all.

An important application of this rule, that notice excluded the right to tack, occurred where land was mortgaged by way of security not only for the original loan, but also for such future advances as might be made. A mortgagee likes to know that he can have recourse to the land in respect of any money he may advance later, and when such further loans are contemplated it has always been customary to provide expressly in the deed that they, equally with the original loan, shall be secured by the land. But it was laid down in *Hopkinson v Rolt*[521] that, notwithstanding such an express provision, the right to tack was excluded by notice of other incumbrances. This principle was carried further by the case of *West v Williams*[522] and made applicable where the legal mortgagee had not (as in *Hopkinson v Rolt*) taken security merely for such further advances as he might *voluntarily* make, but had entered into a binding covenant to make further advances upon the security of the land, if called upon to do so. The fact that he was under a contractual obligation to increase his original loan did not entitle him to priority in respect of a further advance made with notice of a later incumbrance.

The doctrine of tacking was abolished in 1874 by the Vendor and Purchaser Act, but as this prejudiced the ability of mortgagors to obtain further advances from first mortgagees, it was restored by the Land Transfer Act of 1875.

(3) Priority between Assignees and Mortgagees of an Equitable Interest in Pure Personalty

(a) The Rule in *Dearle v Hall*

Priority between mortgagees of pure personalty has been governed since 1823 by the rule in *Dearle v Hall*.[523] This rule, which is of greater importance now than formerly because of its extension by the Law of Property Act 1925,[524] applied whenever successive mortgages or assignments were made of an equitable interest in pure personalty, as distinct from an interest, whether legal or equitable, in freeholds or leaseholds. To make the rule applicable, the mortgagor or assignor must have had an equitable interest in a debt or fund and he must have made two or more successive assignments

---

[521] (1861) 9 HL Cas 514.   [522] [1899] 1 Ch 132.

[523] (1823) 3 Russ 1, M & B p 912. For comment on the rule (mostly adverse), see *Ward v Duncombe* [1893] AC 369; *B S Lyle Ltd v Rosher* [1959] 1 WLR 8; *E Pfeiffer Weinkellerei-Weineinkauf GmbH & Co v Arbuthnot Factors Ltd* [1988] 1 WLR 150; *Rhodes v Allied Dunbar Pension Services Ltd* [1987] 1 WLR 1703; (1989) 9 OJLS 513 (F Oditah); *Compaq Computer Ltd v Abercorn Group Ltd* [1991] BCC 484, [1992] CLJ 19 (LS Sealy); *Australian Guarantee Corp (NZ) Ltd v CFC Commercial Finance Ltd* [1995] 1 NZLR 129; (1996) 112 LQR 215 (AJ Oakley). For an analysis of the rule, see [1999] Conv 311 (J de Lacey).

[524] Below, p 895.

of that subject matter in favour of different persons.[525] It is chiefly remarkable as being a departure from the fundamental principle that equities are entitled to rank according to the order of time in which they have been created.

The rule laid down that as between mortgagees or assignees of an equitable interest in pure personalty (ie excluding leaseholds, but including an interest under a trust for sale[526]) priority depended upon the order in which notice of the mortgages or assignments was received[527] by the legal owner of the personalty (ie in most cases by the trustees). However, a later mortgagee or assignee, who had actual or constructive notice of a prior mortgage or assignment at the time when he lent his money, could not gain priority by giving notice first.[528] The headnote to the report of *Dearle v Hall* makes the general position clear:

> A person having a beneficial interest in a sum of money invested in the names of trustees, assigns it for valuable consideration to A, but no notice of the assignment is given to the trustees; afterwards, the same person proposes to sell his interest to B, and B, having made inquiry of the trustees as to the nature of the vendor's title, and the amount of his interest, and receiving no intimation of the existence of any prior incumbrance, completes the purchase, and gives the trustees notice: B has a better equity than A to the possession of the fund, and the assignment to B, though posterior in date, is to be preferred to the assignment to A.

Thus in equitable mortgages of personalty notice to the trustees supplants order of time as the determining factor in the question of priorities.

(b) Principle of rule

Although the principle upon which *Dearle v Hall* was decided has been obscured by later cases, it would appear to be simply this, that in order to perfect his title a mortgagee of equitable personalty must do that which in equity is the nearest approach to the delivery of a personal chattel.[529] Plumer MR explained this as follows:[530]

> They say that they were not bound to give notice to the trustees, for that notice does not form part of the necessary conveyance of an equitable interest. I admit, that, if you mean to rely on contract with the individual, you do not need to give notice; from the moment of the contract, he, with whom you are dealing, is personally bound. But if you mean to go further, and to make your right attach upon the thing which is the subject of the contract, it is necessary to give notice; and, unless notice is given, you do not do that which is essential in all cases of transfer of personal property. The law of England has always been, that personal property passes by delivery of possession; and it is possession which determines the

---

[525] *B S Lyle Ltd v Rosher* [1959] 1 WLR 8, 16, 19.

[526] *Lee v Howlett* (1856) 2 K & J 531; below, p 883. For the doctrine of conversion in relation to the trust for sale before TLATA 1996, see above, pp 465 ff.

[527] *Calisher v Forbes* (1871) 7 Ch App 109.

[528] *Spencer v Clarke* (1878) 9 Ch D 137; *Re Holmes* (1885) 29 Ch D 786.

[529] *Meux v Bell* (1841) 1 Hare 73, 85; *Foster v Cockerell* (1835) 3 Cl & Fin 456, 476; but see Lord Macnaghten in *Ward v Duncombe* [1893] AC 369, 392–3.

[530] *Dearle v Hall* (1823) 3 Russ 1, 22.

apparent ownership. If, therefore, an individual, who in the way of purchase or mortgage contracts with another for the transfer of his interest, does not divest the vendor or mortgagor of possession, but permits him to remain the ostensible owner as before, he must take the consequences which may ensue from such a mode of dealing.

(c) Rule extended by judicial interpretation

It is in fact the duty of an assignee or mortgagee to affect the conscience of the trustees, for by doing so he acquires a better equity than a prior mortgagee who has failed to act likewise, and where one of two innocent parties must suffer through the fraud of the mortgagor, it certainly should not be the one who has done all in his power to prevent any fraudulent dealing. But this consideration was lost sight of in later years, and instead of the principle being that priority should depend upon the diligence of the claimants in perfecting their title, it was gradually made dependent upon the bare fact of notice, it being held that it was immaterial whether notice was given with the deliberate intention of completing the title or whether it was purely informal or even accidental.[531] The following will serve to illustrate this fact and, at the same time, to state the main rules that have grown up in the application of *Dearle v Hall*.

(1) Notice may be informal

It is not necessary, in order to gain priority, that a mortgagee should give express notice to the trustees with the intention of doing all that is possible to perfect his title. In fact it is not necessary that *he* should give notice at all, provided that the trustees have notice. It is enough if he can prove that the mind of the trustee has in some way been brought to an intelligent apprehension of the existence of the incumbrance, so that a reasonable man or an ordinary man of business would regulate his conduct by that knowledge in the execution of the trust.[532] Thus, notice that a trustee obtained from reading a newspaper has been held to be sufficient,[533] and in a later case it was held that where a trustee *before* his appointment acquired knowledge of an incumbrance on the trust estate in such a way that when appointed he would normally act on the information, the priority thereby attached to the incumbrance was not displaced by an express formal notice given after his appointment by another incumbrancer.[534]

(2) Effect of notice not given to all trustees

The course that a diligent mortgagee should pursue is to give notice to each trustee, since a failure to do so may cause his postponement to a later mortgagee who has been more careful. The two principles relevant to the situation are, first, that a notice given to one alone of several trustees is effective against later mortgages created while that one trustee remains in office, but is ineffective against mortgages created after he vacates office;[535] secondly, that a notice to all existing trustees

---

[531] See (1895) 11 LQR 337 (ECC Firth).
[532] *Lloyd v Banks* (1868) 3 Ch App 488, 490 (Lord Cairns).   [533] *Lloyd v Banks*, above.
[534] *Ipswich Permanent Money Club Ltd v Arthy* [1920] 2 Ch 257.
[535] *Smith v Smith* (1833) 2 Cr & M 231.

remains effective even after they have vacated office. The result may be appreciated from three examples.

(1) A, B and C are the trustees. Mortgagee X notifies A only. A later mortgagee, Y, notifies A, B and C. A dies.

X ranks before Y, for when Y took his mortgage X's notice to A was still effective.[536]

(2) A, B and C are the trustees. Mortgagee X notifies A only. A dies. A later mortgagee, Y, notifies B and C.

Y ranks before X, since the effectiveness of X's notice ceased with the death of the one person to whom he gave it.[537]

(3) A, B and C are the trustees. Mortgagee X notifies A, B and C. A, B and C retire in favour of D, E and F, who are not informed of X's mortgage. A later mortgagee, Y, notifies D, E and F.

X ranks before Y.[538]

(d) Limits of rule

We must finally observe that before 1926 the rule in *Dearle v Hall* was restricted to the assignment of choses in action, of which an equitable interest in pure personalty is an example, and to assignments of such interests in real estate as could reach the hands of the assignor only in the shape of money, such as a beneficial interest given to him by a trust for sale.[539] The rule did not apply to mortgages or assignments of equitable interests in *land*, whether freehold or leasehold. Thus in a case where a testator, having bequeathed a leasehold interest to trustees, charged it with the payment of an annuity of £45 to his daughter, and the daughter mortgaged the annuity first to A and then to B, it was held that A had the prior claim against the land, although B alone had given notice to the trustees.[540]

Having thus reviewed the rules that obtained before the legislation of 1925, we are in a position to examine the existing law governing the priorities between mortgages in general.

B PRIORITY OF MORTGAGES AFTER 1925

(1) Unregistered Land

The Law of Property Act 1925 and the Land Charges Act 1925 (now replaced by the Land Charges Act 1972) introduced a new system for the determination of priorities. The apparent design of this is to fix the priority of a mortgage according to the time

---

536 *Ward v Duncombe* [1893] AC 369.
537 *Timson v Ramsbottom* (1837) 2 Keen 35; *Re Phillips' Trusts* [1903] 1 Ch 183.
538 *Re Wasdale* [1899] 1 Ch 163.
539 *Lee v Howlett* (1856) 2 K & J 531; *Re Wasdale*, above; *Ward v Duncombe*, above.
540 *Wiltshire v Rabbits* (1844) 14 Sim 76.

of its creation, provided that the mortgagee has taken steps to render the completion of the transaction easily ascertainable by persons who later have dealings with the mortgagor.[541] There are three ways of doing this that vary with the circumstances.

First, by obtaining possession of the title deeds. This will put a later mortgagee upon inquiry and will normally affect him with notice of the earlier incumbrance.

Secondly, if possession of the deeds is unobtainable and if the property given as security is a *legal* estate, by recording the mortgage, whether legal or equitable, in a public register.

Thirdly, if the property given as security is an *equitable* interest in land or pure personalty, by notifying the mortgage to the owner of the legal interest, thereby putting it on record.

Such is the design in outline, but it is not fully worked out by the Acts and we shall see that certain doubts and complexities remain. The paucity of litigation on priorities may suggest that the new system has worked reasonably well, but that may be due more to the considerable rise in the value of land than to the merits of the system.

The modern rules vary not with the nature of the mortgage as under the pre-1926 law, but with the nature of the mortgaged property, and we must therefore consider:

first, legal and equitable mortgages of a *legal estate*; and

secondly, mortgages of an *equitable interest*, whether in land or in personalty.

(a) Priority as between legal and equitable mortgagees of a legal estate

We have seen that before 1926 a legal mortgagee who had not been guilty of gross negligence in respect of the title deeds enjoyed priority over the other mortgagees (necessarily equitable) of the same land of which he had no notice. It is obvious that the introduction of the new method of creating mortgages, under which there may be several *legal* mortgages and not one only as before 1926,[542] precluded the retention of the old rule that the legal estate as such gave priority. Some substitute had to be found. The other rule of the pre-1926 law, that equitable mortgages ranked according to the order of their creation, could hardly be made universally applicable, since it would render it difficult for a mortgagee to ascertain by inquiry the true state of the mortgagor's commitments. The Acts of 1925, therefore, attempted to introduce a new scheme, the motif of which apparently was that priorities should depend upon the order of registration, though whether in the actual result registration is as important as it was intended to be is, perhaps, a little doubtful.

(1) Statutory provisions

It is necessary to set out the relevant statutory provisions in order that the matter may be viewed in the right perspective.

---

[541] Waldock, *Law of Mortgages*, pp 409–10.   [542] Above, p 802.

(i) Law of Property Act 1925

The Law of Property Act 1925, section 97, provides in relation to mortgages of unregistered land as follows:

> Every mortgage affecting a legal estate in land made after the commencement of this Act, whether legal or equitable (not being a mortgage protected by the deposit of documents relating to the legal estate affected) shall rank according to its date of registration as a land charge pursuant to the Land Charges Act, 1925.[543]

The same statute, in section 198(1),[544] provides that registration shall constitute notice:

> The registration of any instrument or matter on any register kept under the Land Charges Act 1972 or any local land charges register shall be deemed to constitute actual notice of such instrument or matter, and of the fact of such registration, to all persons and for all purposes connected with the land affected, as from the date of registration or other prescribed date and so long as the registration continues in force.

(ii) Land Charges Act 1972. Registrable mortgages

The Land Charges Act 1972 contains two relevant sections. Section 2(4)[545] specifies the two kinds of mortgages that are registrable,[546] namely:

> A 'puisne mortgage',[547] ie a *legal* mortgage that is not protected by a deposit of documents relating to the legal estate affected (Class C (i)).

> A 'general equitable charge', ie any equitable charge that is not secured by a deposit of documents relating to the legal estate affected, does not arise, or affect an interest arising, under a trust of land[548] or a settlement, and is not included in any other class of land charge (Class C (iii)).

The Land Charges Act 1972 states what the effect shall be of a failure to register. Section 4(5)[549] provides that a Class C land charge created or arising after 1925 shall:

> be void as against a purchaser of the land charged with it, or of any interest in such land, unless the land charge is registered in the appropriate register before the completion of the purchase.

Section 17(1) defines 'purchaser' as:

> any person (including a mortgagee or lessee) who, for valuable consideration, takes any interest in land or in a charge on land.

A mortgagee does not pay the amount of the loan until the transaction has been completed by the execution of the deed. There is a danger, therefore, that after X, a

---

543 Or LCA 1972. See LCA 1972, s 18(6).
544 As amended by Local Land Charges Act 1975, s 17, Sch 1.
545 S 2(4), Class C(i), (iii), replacing LCA 1925, s 10(1).
546 For registration of charges created by companies, see below, p 1067.
547 'Puisne' is derived from the old French, *puis* (after) *né* (born); hence a later or subsequent mortgage.
548 As amended by TLATA 1996, s 25(1), Sch 3, para 12(1), (2).
549 Replacing LCA 1925, s 13(2). See *Midland Bank Trust Co Ltd v Green* [1981] AC 513; below, p 1065.

mortgagee, has searched the register, another mortgage of the same land may have been registered in favour of Y, the effect of which will be to render X's mortgage at the moment of its completion void against Y. X is, therefore, allowed to protect himself by registering a *priority notice*, giving notice of his contemplated mortgage.[550]

(2) Mortgage accompanied by deeds is not registrable

One outstanding feature, then, of this legislation is that no mortgage, legal or equitable, under which the mortgagee obtains the title deeds, is capable of registration. The principal reason for this exclusion is to avoid the inconvenience that would arise if the efficacy of temporary advances that are so frequently made in unregistered land[551] against a deposit of deeds were to be affected by a failure to register. Section 2 of the Land Charges Act 1972, however, provides that an estate contract shall be registrable as a land charge Class C(iv). An estate contract is a contract by an estate owner to convey or create a legal estate.[552] The normal example is a contract for the sale of a legal fee simple or for the grant of a term of years absolute, but it also includes a contract to create a legal mortgage, that is to grant a mortgage term. Further, it would seem to include the equitable mortgage that arises from a contract to create a legal mortgage, which is accompanied by a deposit of title deeds, for as we have already seen the deposit does not of itself create an equitable mortgage, but constitutes an implicit agreement to create a legal mortgage that has effect as an equitable mortgage under the doctrine of *Walsh v Lonsdale* only if it satisfies the formality requirements of a valid contract to create a legal mortgage.[553] It has therefore been suggested that an express contract, accompanied by the title deeds, to create a legal mortgage, and a deposit of title deeds by way of security accompanied by a written agreement between the parties that satisfies the formality requirements for a contract, are registrable as estate contracts, in spite of the fact that because accompanied by the deeds they are excluded from registration by the paragraph that deals specifically with mortgages.[554] It is submitted, however, that the correctness of this view is at least doubtful. If the sub-section that explicitly defines what mortgages shall be registrable deliberately excludes those that are accompanied by a deposit of documents, it seems inconsistent with the policy underlying the Act to permit their registration in their other capacity as estate contracts. The result of doing so would be to render void against a subsequent incumbrancer an unregistered mortgage to which the sub-section concerned with mortgages denies the possibility of registration for the very reason that registration ought not to be necessary. To put this construction upon the statute would prejudice the commercial practice by which deeds are deposited with bankers to secure a temporary loan, for the result of invalidating against later lenders an arrangement that is often only transient would be

[550] LCA 1972, s 11; for details, see below, p 1062.

[551] Since 2002 mortgages of registered cannot be made involving the deposit of a land certificate since land certificates have been abolished: above, p 811.

[552] Below, p 1058.   [553] Above, p 807.

[554] (1940) CLJ pp 250–1 (RE Megarry); (1962) 26 Conv (NS) pp 446–9 (RG Rowley); Fairest, *Mortgages* (2nd edn, 1980), pp 133–6; Fisher and Lightwood, *Law of Mortgage* (10th edn, ed ELG Tyler, 1988), p 72; Waldock, *Law of Mortgages*, pp 425–8.

(5) Tacking

(i) *Partial abolition*

The doctrine of tacking was materially affected by the Law of Property Act 1925.[574] One branch of that doctrine was abolished, the other was retained. The first branch, which under the pre-1926 law[575] comprised the right of a later mortgagee to buy in the legal estate from the first incumbrancer and to squeeze out an intermediate mortgage, has been abolished.[576] The second branch has been retained, for it is important that a mortgagee should be at liberty to tack further advances to his first loan. In fact, the preservation of this right is essential where a bank takes a mortgage from a client as security for his current account, since a further advance is made whenever his cheque is honoured. It was therefore enacted in relation to unregistered land[577] that in certain cases, which will be given in a moment, a prior mortgagee shall have a right to make further advances to rank in priority to subsequent mortgages (whether legal or equitable).[578]

(ii) *Tacking of further advances*

It will be noticed that this enactment does not confine the right to the first mortgagee or to a legal mortgagee, but grants it to any prior mortgagee, legal or equitable, against every later mortgagee. But it is only in the three following cases that the right may be exercised.

(1) *When later mortgagees agree*[579]

This is an obvious and not an unusual case. After mortgages of Blackacre have been granted to A, B and C, the mortgagor may seek a further advance from B on the same security. B will rank for payment of both his loans before C if he makes an arrangement to that effect with C before advancing further money. C is not likely to agree unless the land is sufficient cover for all the money with which it is charged.

(2) *When there is no notice of later mortgages*[580]

A mortgagee who has no notice of subsequent mortgages at the time when he makes his further advances may claim priority for both his loans over subsequent mortgagees. This is the same rule as applied before 1926,[581] with this important difference, however, that registration of a later mortgage as a land charge is deemed to constitute *actual* notice of that mortgage.[582] A mortgagee therefore who contemplates a further advance should not make it until he has ascertained by a search at the Land Registry that no later mortgages have been made.

There is, however, an important exception to this rule that the mere registration of a mortgage will prevent a prior mortgagee from tacking later advances. It is enacted that in the case of a mortgage made expressly for securing:

---

574 S 94. See (1958) 22 Conv (NS) 44 (RG Rowley).   575 Above, p 878.

576 LPA 1925, s 94(3). Tacking by purchase of the legal estate survives in other contexts: *McCarthy & Stone Ltd v Julian S Hodge & Co Ltd* [1971] 1 WLR 1547, above, p 84, n 93.

577 LPA 1925, s 94(4), amended by LRA 2002, s 133, Sch 11, para 2(1), (9).   578 Ibid, s 94(1).

579 Ibid, s 94(1)(a).   580 Ibid, s 94(1)(b).   581 Above, p 879.

582 LPA 1925, s 198(1), as amended by LLCA 1975, s 17, Sch 1.

(a) a current account, or

(b) other further advances,

the mere registration of a subsequent mortgage shall not constitute notice sufficient to deprive the earlier mortgagee of his right to tack. In those two cases the rule is that:

> A mortgagee shall not be deemed to have notice of a mortgage merely by reason that it was registered as a land charge, if it was not so registered at the time when the original mortgage was created or when the last search (if any) by or on behalf of the mortgagee was made, whichever last happened.[583]

Thus registration of a subsequent mortgage constitutes actual notice of that mortgage to a prior incumbrancer and necessarily displaces his right to tack, except where the prior mortgage was taken not merely as security for the original loan, but as security either for the original loan and further advances or for a current account. In either of these cases registration will be notice only if it was in being when the prior mortgage was created (which might of course be before any money was actually advanced by the prior mortgagee, as often happens where a current account is secured), or when the prior mortgagee last made a search at the Land Registry. Failing registration at one of these dates a prior mortgagee will not be deprived of the right to tack unless, at the time of the further advance, he had notice, in the old sense of actual or constructive notice, of the later mortgage.

This exception to the rule that registration is equivalent to actual notice has been made in the interest of bankers, for were the rule unqualified it would be impracticable to take a mortgage as security for a current account. An illustration will make this clear. If A mortgages his land to a bank in order to secure an overdraft that at the time of the mortgage is £3,000, and if he subsequently grants a mortgage of the same land to B, notice of which is given to the bank, the rule as laid down in *Hopkinson v Rolt*[584] is that the bank obtains priority only for the amount due from the mortgagor at the time when the second mortgage to B was made. If the overdraft at that moment is £4,000, then £4,000 is the amount with which the land is charged in favour of the bank. When, moreover, A from time to time pays sums into his account, and the overdraft is thus reduced below £4,000, only the reduced amount is recoverable under the mortgage;[585] and although, after notice of the second mortgage, the actual overdraft may be increased as a result of drawings out, the payments or further advances by the bank in respect of these drawings cannot be tacked to the loan as it stood at the time when notice of the second mortgage was received.[586] To fix the mortgage at £4,000 is equitable if the bank has actual notice of the second mortgage, but it would make this side of banking business impossible if mere registration constituted notice, for it

---

[583] LPA 1925, s 94(2), as amended by LP(A)A 1926, Sch.   [584] (1861) 9 HL Cas 514; above, p 880.
[585] *Clayton's Case* (1816) 1 Mer 572; *Russell-Cooke Trust Co v Prentis* [2003] 1 All ER 478; [2005] CLJ 45 (M Conaglen).
[586] *Deeley v Lloyds Bank Ltd* [1910] 1 Ch 648, reversed [1912] AC 756.

would be unsafe to honour the customer's cheques unless on each occasion a search were made at the Land Registry.

Two practical results emerge from this legislation.

First, a mortgage will generally provide expressly that the land shall be security for further advances, since this will enable a further advance to be made without a search at the Land Registry; secondly, a mortgagee who searches and discovers the existence of a prior mortgage expressly made to secure a current account or further advances will be careful to notify his mortgage to the prior mortgagee.

(3) When the mortgage imposes an obligation on the mortgagee to make further advances

When the provision in the prior mortgage is not that the land shall be security for any further advances that *may* be made, as in the case (b) just considered, but that the mortgagee shall be bound to make further advances if called upon to do so, the new rule is[587] that the doctrine of tacking shall apply to such advances notwithstanding the fact that at the time of making them the prior mortgagee had notice of a later mortgage. The law as laid down in *West v Williams*[588] is therefore reversed.

(b) Priority as between mortgagees of an equitable interest in land or personalty

(1) Extension of rule in *Dearle v Hall*

We have already seen that under the law before 1926 the priority as between mortgagees of an equitable interest in pure personalty depended, in accordance with the rule in *Dearle v Hall*, upon the order in which the trustees had received notice from the mortgagees, but that this principle did not apply to mortgages of freeholds or of leaseholds.[589] The innovation made by the 1925 legislation is the extension of the rule in *Dearle v Hall* to mortgages of *all* equitable interests, realty being put on the same footing as personalty. This assimilation is accomplished by section 137(1) of the Law of Property Act 1925:

> The law applicable to dealings with equitable things in action which regulates the priority of competing interests therein, shall, as respects dealings with equitable interests in land, capital money, and securities representing capital money effected after the commencement of this Act, apply to and regulate the priority of competing interests therein.[590]

This extension of the rule to all mortgages and assignments of equitable interests in freeholds and leaseholds is of special importance owing to the increased number of interests that are necessarily equitable since 1925. Thus, the purchaser or mortgagee of an interest arising under a strict settlement, such as a life interest, an entailed interest or any species of future interest, must protect himself by giving the necessary notice. In effect the priority of mortgages of equitable beneficial interests under strict settlements and trusts of land is now determined by the same rule.

---

587 LPA 1925, s 94(1)(c). 588 [1899] 1 Ch 132; above, p 880. 589 Above, p 880.
590 For an analysis of the section, see [1993] Conv 22 (J Howell).

(2) Rules regarding notice

The rules that existed before 1926 with regard to the nature of the notice still hold good,[591] subject to one exception. This is that a notice given otherwise than in writing in respect of any dealing with an equitable interest in real or personal property shall not affect the priority of competing claims of purchasers or mortgagees.[592]

(i) Persons to whom notice must be given

The Law of Property Act 1925 contains the following rules with regard to the persons upon whom the written notice must be served.

(1) Where the equitable interest is in settled land or capital money.[593]

Where dealings take place with such an interest, notice must be given to the *trustees of the settlement*. If the interest in question has been created by a derivative settlement (ie one by which an interest already settled is resettled), then notice must be given to the trustees of the derivative settlement.

(2) Where the equitable interest is in land held on a trust of land.

In this case notice must be given to the *trustees* of such land.[594]

(3) Where the equitable interest is neither (1) nor (2).[595]

If, for example, the subject of the transaction is a life annuity charged on land by a tenant in fee simple, it is provided that notice shall be given to the *estate owner*.

It will be remembered that certain complexities had arisen before 1926 with regard to a notice served on a single trustee.[596] The proper course, which, however, is not always adopted, is to serve the notice on each of the trustees and to take a receipt from each, and it is perhaps regrettable that the Act did not made this practice compulsory. No statutory direction has, however, been given, and it therefore appears that in this regard the old decisions continue to represent the law.[597]

(ii) Notice by way of endorsed memorandum

To meet any difficulty that may arise in identifying the appropriate person to receive notice, the Act provides that where:

(a) the trustees are not persons to whom a valid notice can be given; or

(b) there are no trustees to whom a valid notice can be given; or

(c) for any other reason a valid notice cannot be served, or cannot be served without unreasonable cost or delay,

---

[591] Above, p 882.   [592] LPA 1925, s 137(3).
[593] Ibid, s 137(2)(i).   [594] Ibid, s 137(2)(ii), as amended by TLATA 1996, s 25(1), Sch 3, para 4(15).
[595] Ibid, s 137(2)(iii).   [596] Above, p 882.
[597] See (1925) 60 LJ News 264 (JM Lightwood); Wolstenholme and Cherry (13th edn), vol 1, p 246.

the assignee may require that a memorandum of the transaction be endorsed on, or permanently annexed to, the instrument that creates the trust.[598] Such a memorandum, as respects priorities, operates in like manner as if a written notice had been given to trustees. Thus if the land in which the equitable interest exists is subject to a strict settlement, the memorandum will be annexed to the trust instrument; if it is land belonging to an owner who has died intestate, the memorandum will be annexed to the letters of administration. The objection to a memorandum of this nature is that trust instruments may become overladen with endorsements of charges and assignments. Therefore an alternative method of registering a notice has been provided.[599]

(iii) Notice to nominated trust corporation

It is provided that a settlor when drafting a settlement, or the court at a later date, may nominate a trust corporation to whom notice of dealings affecting real or personal property may be given. Where such a nomination has been made, notice of any dealings with the equitable interest must be given to the trust corporation, and if given to the trustees must be transmitted by them to the corporation. A notice that is not received by the corporation has no effect on priorities.

(iv) Right to production of notice

The object of the rule in *Dearle v Hall* is to enable a person to discover by inquiries addressed to the trustees whether the owner of an equitable interest has created any earlier incumbrances. But this object was not always attained under the law before 1926, for since, in the language of Lindley LJ: 'it is no part of the duty of a trustee to assist his *cestui que trust* in selling or mortgaging his beneficial interest and in squandering or anticipating his fortune',[600] it was held that a trustee owed no greater duty to a person who was proposing to deal with a *cestui que trust*.[601] Thus a trustee might refuse to answer inquiries, and even if he gave an answer that contained wrong information, he was not liable for the consequences unless he had been guilty of fraud or had made such a clear and categorical statement that he was estopped from denying its truth.[602] A prospective assignee, however, is given at least this advantage by the Act, that he may demand production of any written notice that has been served on the trustees or their predecessors.[603]

(2) Registered Land

The rules governing the priority of mortgages over unregistered land are therefore extremely complex—for a number of reasons: the fact that in unregistered land some, but not all, mortgages are capable of protection by registration—and, in particular, that a mortgage protected by deposit of title deeds with the mortgagee is not capable of

---

[598] LPA 1925, s 137(4).
[599] Ibid, s 138. See also Law Reform Committee 23rd Report, *The Powers and Duties of Trustees* (1982, Cmnd 8733), paras 2.17–2.24.
[600] *Low v Bouverie* [1891] 3 Ch 82, 99. [601] *Burrowes v Lock* (1805) 10 Ves 470. [602] Ibid.
[603] LPA 1925, s 137(8).

registration;[604] the different (historically grounded[605]) rules for the priority as between legal and equitable mortgages;[606] and difficulties that follow from the registration provisions of the Land Charges Act and their relationship to the equitable rules for notice.[607] These complexities are not, in general, reproduced in relation to registered land.

(a) Priority of charges

Registered charges on the same registered estate rank for priority between themselves in the order shown in the register.[608] This therefore means that in the normal course the order of priority is the order of registration, although the chargees may decide on a different order of priority and apply for the order shown on the register to be altered.[609]

The priority as between equitable charges depends on the general rules of priority of interests under the Land Registration Act 2002—that is the order in which they are created.[610]

The priority as between a legal charge and an equitable charge also depends on the general rules of priority: and so the registration of a legal charge made for valuable consideration gives it priority over a prior equitable charge entered into before the legal charge was created that has not been protected by entry of a notice at the time of registration.[611]

(b) Tacking

Section 94 of the Law of Property Act 1925[612] does not apply to registered land.[613] The Land Registration Act 2002,[614] however, provides that the proprietor of a registered charge may make a further advance on the security of his charge, which will rank in priority to a subsequent charge, if

    (a) he has not received from the subsequent chargee notice of the creation of the subsequent charge;[615] or

---

[604] Above, p 888.   [605] Above, p 873.
[606] Above, pp 872–897.   [607] Above, p 891.
[608] LRA 2002, s 48(1), LRR 2003, r 101; R & R, paras 27.008–27.009. Certain statutory charges, such as the charge in favour of the Legal Services Commission under Access to Justice Act 1999, s 10(7), may however take overriding priority: LRA 2002, s 50, LRR 2003, rr 105, 106; H & B, paras 12.51–12.58.
[609] LRR, 2003, r 102. See also *Scottish & Newcastle Plc v Lancashire Mortgage Corp Ltd* [2007] EWCA Civ 684, [2007] NPC 84 (one legal charge ranked behind another by virtue of estoppel).
[610] LRA 2002, s 28. Until 1987 such priorities in registered land were in some cases governed by the order in which 'priority cautions' or 'priority inhibitions' had been lodged in the Minor Interests Index: LRA 1925, s 102; LRR 1925, r 229. The Index was abolished by the Land Registration Act 1986. See H & B, para 12.59, noting that, when electronic conveyancing is fully introduced, it will not be possible to create equitable charges without simultaneously registering them, and therefore the register will determine the priority for equitable, as well as legal, charges.
[611] Ibid, s 29.   [612] Above, p 893.
[613] LPA 1925, s 94(4), amended by LRA 2002, s 133, Sch 11, para 2(1), (9).
[614] S 49. Under LRA 1925 the common law rule applied, but by s 30, before making any entry on the register that would prejudicially affect the priority of any further advances, the Registrar had to give notice by registered post to the proprietor of the charge, who could tack any advances made by him up to the time when he received or ought to have received the notice in due course of post.
[615] S 49(1). Notice is treated as received when, in accordance with rules, it ought to have been received: s 49(2); LRR 2003, r 107.

(b) the further advance is made in pursuance of an obligation and at the time of the creation of the subsequent charge the obligation was entered in the register;[616] or

(c) the parties to the prior charge have agreed a maximum amount for which the charge is security and at the time of the subsquent charge the agreement was entered into the register.[617]

Apart from these situations, tacking in relation to a charge over registered land is only possible with the agreement of the subsequent chargee.[618]

VI LAW REFORM

A LAW COMMISSION REPORT ON LAND MORTGAGES 1991

In 1991 the Law Commission recommended that all existing methods of consensually mortgaging or charging interests in land should be abolished and replaced by a new form of mortgage to be used for mortgaging any interest in land whether legal or equitable.[619] 'The present complex mortgage structure would be replaced by a new simplified structure.' It also proposed a new class of 'protected mortgages' by an individual of property that includes a dwelling-house, and wider powers of intervention against unfair mortgages. The rights, remedies and powers of a mortgagee would be exercisable only in good faith for the purpose of protecting or enforcing the security.

In 1998 the Government decided not to implement the Report due to lack of support, but invited the Law Commission to reconsider its proposals.[620] However, the Report contains a useful discussion of the merits and demerits of the current law on mortgages. The main recommendations were:

---

[616] S 49(3); LRR 2003, r 108.

[617] S 49(4); LRR 2003, r 109. Rules may disapply this subsection in relation to particular types of charge, but no such rules have been made; H & B, para 12.78.

[618] S 49(6).

[619] Law Com No 204, *Land Mortgages* (1991); [1992] Conv 69 (HW Wilkinson); (1992) 136 SJ 267, 292 (G Frost). A summary of the recommendations is contained in Part X of the Report; M & B pp 991–8.

In March 1989 the Law Commission's Conveyancing Standing Committee published a consultation document suggesting the use of a new form of mortgage called a flexi-mortgage as a means of avoiding chains, cutting out delays and defeating gazumping. Its unique feature would be that for a limited time it gives the borrower the right to extend the period of the mortgage on a property he is buying and increase the amount he borrows to cover the cost of an overlapping sale and purchase. Payments under his old mortgage would be suspended. This would allow the house-owner to agree to buy a new property before selling his own by incurring only a small increase in mortgage interest and without increasing his capital repayments: Fourth Annual Report of the Conveyancing Standing Committee 1989, para 2.2, annexed to Law Com No 190, *Twenty-Fourth Annual Report 1989*.

[620] Law Com No 258, *Thirty-Third Annual Report 1998*, para 1.10. The invitation was to return to the topic when its then current work on land registration was finished, but there has not yet been any proposal from the Law Commission to work further on it.

(1) Creation of Mortgages

There should be only two methods of creating a mortgage: the formal and the informal land mortgage.

(a) The formal land mortgage would not be valid unless it was created by deed, whether the property mortgaged was a legal estate or an equitable interest. It would require registration under the Land Registration Act 1925 if any part of the mortgagor's title was itself registered; and in the case of unregistered land, it would be registrable as a land charge, Class C (i), under the Land Charges Act 1972.

(b) The informal land mortgage would not be valid unless it was made by deed or satisfied the requirements of section 2 of the Law of Property (Miscellaneous Provisions) Act 1989.[621] A mortgagee under an informal land mortgage would have no right to enforce the security, nor to take any other action in relation to the mortgaged property, but would have a right to have the mortgage perfected by the grant of a formal land mortgage.

(2) Overriding Provisions

Certain provisions would be overriding in that they cannot be varied or excluded. In particular:

(a) The mortgagor would have the right to possession unless the mortgagee took possession in order to sell or to prevent a fall in the value of the property.

(b) The power of sale would only be exercisable if the mortgagor was in arrears or there was an outstanding breach of covenant substantially prejudicing the mortgagee's security or an event had occurred that substantially reduced the mortgagor's ability to meet his financial obligations or which prejudiced the value of the property as security.

(c) There would be no right of consolidation.

(3) Protected Mortgages

A distinction was drawn between commercial and non-commercial mortgages.

> The most important differences lie in the extent to which the law needs to interfere with the parties' freedom of contract. If all provisions have to apply equally to all types of mortgage, it is difficult to reconcile the need to allow maximum flexibility to commercial transactions entered into between parties of equal bargaining power, with the need to provide adequate protection for vulnerable mortgagors who in a wholly free market would have no real choice but to accept whatever terms lenders may choose to dictate. The obvious way of reconciling these conflicting needs is to have a protected class of mortgage (para. 4.1).

---

[621] Below, p 966.

(a) Definition

A protected mortgage would consist of all formal and informal land mortgages of any interest in land that included a dwelling-house except those where either (i) the mortgagor was a body corporate, or (ii) enforcement of the mortgage would not affect enjoyment of the dwelling-house, or (iii) the dwelling-house was occupied under a service tenancy.

(b) Protection

The main protection afforded to the mortgagor under a protected mortgage would be:

(1) Possession

The mortgagee would not be entitled to take possession without serving an enforcement notice in the prescribed form on the mortgagor and obtaining a court order. The court would have power to order that interest payable under the mortgage should cease to accrue after 12 weeks of possession or such other period as the court should decide.

(2) Sale

Similarly, before exercising the power of sale under a formal land mortgage, the mortgagee must serve an enforcement notice and obtain a court order.

   If the mortgagee applied to the court for possession or sale, the court would have powers equivalent to those applicable to residential mortgages under the Administration of Justice Acts 1970 and 1973 and the Consumer Credit Act 1974. In addition it would have power to order the debt to be rescheduled.

(3) Foreclosure

There is a general recommendation that the remedy of foreclosure should be abolished and replaced by the power of the mortgagee to sell to himself provided leave of the court is first obtained.

(4) Revision of Mortgage Terms

Credit bargains made by land mortgage would be removed from the Consumer Credit Act 1974 and instead be protected under a comprehensive code affecting all land mortgages. Under this the court should have power to set aside or vary any terms of a mortgage

> with a view to doing justice between the parties if (a) principles of fair dealing were contravened when the mortgage was granted, or (b) the effect of the terms of the mortgage is that the mortgagee now has rights substantially greater than or different from those necessary to make the property adequate security for the liabilities secured by the mortgage, or (c) the mortgage requires payments to be made which are exorbitant, or (d)

the mortgage includes a postponement of the right to redeem, or a provision intending to impede redemption (para. 8.5).[622]

This new jurisdiction would be in addition to the court's general powers to set aside on grounds such as fraud, mistake, rectification, estoppel, undue influence, or restraint of trade. The equitable jurisdiction concerned with clogs or fetters on the equity of redemption would be abolished.

B LIMITATION OF ACTIONS

In 2001 the Law Commission[623] recommended significant reforms to the law on limitation of actions in many areas of private law. Certain specific proposals are made in relation to land mortgages.[624] A long-stop limitation period of 10 years should apply to claims to enforce a mortgage or charge over land, running from the date on which the mortgagee's or chargee's right to enforce the mortgage or charge accrues;[625] and the long-stop period should also apply to claims to enforce an obligation secured by a mortgage or charge by suing on the covenant to repay.[626] Where a prior mortgagee is in possession of the mortgaged property, the limitation period applicable to a claim by the subsequent mortgagee to recover arrears of interest (or damages in lieu) should, if necessary, be extended so that it does not end until a year after the prior mortgagee ceases to be in possession;[627] and the limitation period applying to foreclosure proceedings should be suspended during the period that the mortgagee is in possession of the mortgaged property.[628] No limitation period should apply to a claim by the mortgagor to redeem a mortgage over land;[629] and the expiry of the limitation period applying to claims to enforce a mortgage should extinguish the claimant's interest in the mortgaged property.[630]

The Government accepted the report in principle in July 2002, and in 2008 it was announced that provisions on the subject would be included within a proposed Civil Law Reform Bill. However, in 2009 the Government announced that the limitation reforms would not, after all, be taken forward.[631]

---

[622] For a more limited reforms made by Consumer Credit Act 2006, see above, pp 826–8.

[623] Law Com No 270, *Limitation of Actions*.   [624] Paras 4.158–4.196.

[625] Para 4.166; similarly, for a mortgages over land and personal property together: para 4.173.

[626] Para 4.177.   [627] Para 4.184.   [628] Para 4.185.

[629] Para 4.186. At present, the limitation period for unregistered land is 12 years from the date on which the mortgagee takes possession of the land: LA 1980, s 16, but this has now been disapplied for registered land by LRA 2002, s 96; below, p 1160, thus implementing this proposal in Law Com No 270.

[630] Para 4.196.

[631] Law Com No 323, *Annual Report 2009–10*, paras 3.12–3.15. The general regime governing limitation of actions was substantially modified in relation to registered land by LRA 2002; below, pp 1160 ff. There is no change to the position of *mortgagors* in possession: the mortgagee's rights to possession or foreclosure as against the mortgagor in possession remain subject to the limitation provisions of LA 1980: below, p 1161, n 245. The provisions of LA 1980 are however disapplied in relation to the *mortgagee* in possession: below, pp 1160–1; above, n 610; Law Com No 271, *Land Registration for the Twenty-First Century* (2001), paras 14.12–14.18.

22

EQUITIES AND PROPRIETARY ESTOPPEL

Summary

I   MERE EQUITIES

In the preceding chapters we have discussed those estates and interests in land that are recognised as subsisting at law or in equity. An equitable interest is distinguishable from an 'equity' or, as it is often called for emphasis, a 'mere equity'.

A   NATURE OF AN EQUITY

The courts have never found a satisfactory definition of an equity.[1] But, it is generally taken to refer to an equitable right of a procedural nature. It includes a right to enforce an equitable remedy, such as specific performance, rescission for misrepresentation or undue influence, rectification for mistake, and the rights to consolidation of mortgages or to reopen a foreclosure.[2]

The right to an equitable remedy is generally only characterised as an 'equity' where it is ancillary to some right of property,[3] and where the remedy, if granted, would change the

---

[1] *National Provincial Bank Ltd v Ainsworth* [1965] AC 1175, 1238 (Lord Upjohn), 1252–3 (Lord Wilberforce); *Shiloh Spinners Ltd v Harding* [1973] AC 691, 721 (Lord Wilberforce); (1976) 40 Conv (NS) 209 (AR Everton); (1955) 71 LQR 480 (RE Megarry); Law Com No 271, *Land Registration for the Twenty-First Century* (2001), para 5.33; [2010] L & T Rev 100 (M Pawlowski and J Brown).

[2] For consolidation of mortgages, and foreclosure, see above, Ch 21.

[3] [1965] AC 1175, 1238 (Lord Upjohn); Snell, para 2–006.

property rights. For example, where freehold property passes under a deed that could be rescinded by the transferor for fraud,[4] incapacity or undue influence,[5] or where a transfer is executed under a mistake as to the scope of the property it includes that renders it liable to rectification,[6] it is said that the party with the right to the remedy has, respectively, an 'equity to rescind', or an 'equity to rectify'. If granted, the remedy of rescission would restore the property rights to the claimant; and the remedy of rectification would change the terms of the deed and therefore the respective property rights of the parties to the deed.

B PROPRIETARY CHARACTERISTICS OF EQUITIES

There is some controversy over the exact proprietary status of an equity,[7] but it can at least be said that 'mere equities' are those rights in equity that subsist in relation to an estate or interest in property, and are recognised as having proprietary characteristics, but that have not been recognised as full equitable interests.[8] We have seen[9] that the most significant characteristic of a property right is that it is inherently capable of both benefiting and binding parties who were not involved in its original creation; and so the acquisition of the land brings with it the burden of property rights that are in law recognised as attaching to the land.

(1) Passing the Benefit of an Equity

The benefit of an equity, in relation to land, is capable of passing with the land.[10]

---

[4] Cf *Phillips v Phillips* (1861) 4 De G F & J 208, 218 (Lord Westbury). The same principle applies to chattels: *Car and Universal Finance Co Ltd v Caldwell* [1965] 1 QB 525.

[5] *Link Lending Ltd v Bustard* [2010] EWCA Civ 424, [2010] 2 EGLR 55.

[6] *Blacklocks v J B Developments (Godalming) Ltd* [1982] Ch 183; [1983] Conv 169, 257 (JTF), 361 (DG Barnsley). See also *Smith v Jones* [1954] 1 WLR 1089, M & B p 82 (equity to rectify lease). For rectification generally, see below, pp 988–9.

[7] In particular, there is some disagreement about the nature of the rights of the party who has an equity to *rescind*—whether the right to rescind constitutes a retained (and therefore continuing) equitable interest in the property: Cartwright, *Misrepresentation, Mistake and Non-Disclosure* (2nd edn, 2006), para 4.10, M & B p 1004.

[8] Some equitable interests have come to be recognised even though they too depend on, or originate in, the theory that a personal remedy in equity can create an interest in property that is then capable of binding a successor to the property who takes with notice of it: eg an estate contract, arising from a specifically enforceable contract under the doctrine of *Walsh v Lonsdale* (1882) 21 Ch D 9, M & B, p 30, below, p 978; the burden of a restrictive covenant, arising from an injunction under *Tulk v Moxhay* (1848) 2 Ph 774, M & B, p 754, above, p 732; the equity of redemption, arising from equity's willingness to enforce the mortgagor's right to redeem in spite of his having no legal remedy: above, p 799.

[9] Above, pp 4–5 ff.

[10] LPA 1925, s 63; *Boots the Chemist Ltd v Street* (1983) 268 EG 817 (rectification of conveyance); *Berkeley Leisure Group Ltd v Williamson* [1996] EGCS 18 (rectification of lease).

(2) Passing the Burden of an Equity

(a) Unregistered land

In relation to unregistered land, the courts recognised that certain equities could have the status of proprietary rights, in the sense that they could bind successors to the property against which the beneficiary of the equity had a claim to a remedy; but they placed the mere equity below equitable interests in the hierarchy of property rights in land. We have seen that, before 1926, the rule was that a legal estate or interest bound all those who acquired any interest in the property; and an equitable interest bound all except the bona fide purchaser of the legal estate without notice.[11] In the case of a mere equity, however, the rule was that it was not binding on a bona fide purchaser of *an equitable interest* without notice.[12] A purchaser of an equitable interest therefore took subject to prior equitable interests, whether or not he had notice of them; but not mere equities *unless* he had notice. This not only restricts the capacity of a mere equity to bind a purchaser, but also—in those limited cases where an equity *can* bind a purchaser (that is the purchaser of an equitable interest)—rests the actual binding force of an equity in any particular case on the application of the principles of notice. No provision was made in the 1925 legislation for the registration of equities in relation to unregistered land, and therefore their enforceability still depends on the doctrine of notice.[13] However, it can be difficult for the beneficiary of a mere equity to establish that the purchaser ought to have been aware of his interest.[14]

(b) Registered land

The position in registered land, however, is different. Even before the Land Registration Act 2002, it had been established that a mere equity was an interest subsisting in reference to the land and therefore capable of binding a purchaser of the land;[15] and that, since the doctrine of notice has no place in registered land, the purchaser could be bound by an equity of which he did not have notice (and in respect of which there was no entry on the register) if the beneficiary was in actual occupation.[16]

This is confirmed by section 116 of the 2002 Act, which provides that:

> It is hereby declared for the avoidance of doubt that, in relation to registered land...
>
> (b) a mere equity
>
> has effect from the time the equity arises as an interest capable of binding successors in title (subject to the rules about the effect of dispositions on priority).

---

[11] Above, pp 80 ff.   [12] *Phillips v Phillips* (1861) 4 De GF & J 208, 218.

[13] As now contained in statutory form in LPA 1925, s 199(1)(ii); above, p 85.

[14] *Smith v Jones* [1954] 1 WLR 1089, 1092 (Upjohn J) (purchaser entitled to take lease as containing correct terms, and not bound by equity to rectify it).

[15] *Blacklocks v J B Developments (Godalming) Ltd* [1982] Ch 183.

[16] LRA 1925, s 70(1)(g); *Nurdin & Peacock plc v D B Ramsden & Co Ltd* [1999] 1 EGLR 119, 125 (Neuberger J), distinguishing *Smith v Jones*, above, on the basis that it was a case on unregistered land; [1998] Conv 421 (S Pascoe).

In effect, therefore, no distinction is now made between an equitable interest and a mere equity for the purposes of registered land. A transferee of the land will be bound by it on the same basis as any other proprietary interest: that is it will retain its priority on the disposition of the registered estate, except against a disponee of the estate for valuable consideration where the equity has not been protected at the time of the registration of the disposition—and it may be protected either by entry of a notice in the register, or as an overriding interest.[17]

II PROPRIETARY ESTOPPEL[18]

A particular form of 'equity' is that which arises under the doctrine of proprietary estoppel. Again, we are concerned with the right of a person to seek a remedy in equity in relation to property; and the question arises as to whether that right can bind a purchaser of the property. The doctrine of proprietary estoppel has undergone very significant development in recent years, to the point where it can be recognised as a basis for the informal creation of interests in land. It has been used in particular in order to give protection to a licensee, but it is not confined to licences. In this chapter we shall explain the background to the doctrine, its elements, and its status as a property right. In Chapter 23 we shall see its operation in the context of licences; and in Chapter 25 we shall see its more general significance as an informal means of creating rights in land.

A DIFFERENT FORMS OF ESTOPPEL

There are several varieties of 'estoppel' in English law,[19] and there is some debate as to whether all (or at least some of them) are species of the same genus, or should be regarded as so different in principle as to be wholly independent.[20] But the common

---

[17] LRA 2002, ss 28, 29, Sch 3; *Link Lending Ltd v Bustard* [2010] EWCA Civ 424, [2010] 2 EGLR 55 (equity to rescind transfer: overriding interest by virtue of actual occupation). For a detailed discussion of these provisions, see below, pp 1095 ff. See also H & B, para 9.17.

[18] Finn, *Essays in Equity* (1985), pp 59–94; Pawlowski, *The Doctrine of Proprietary Estoppel* (1996); Wilken, *Waiver, Variation and Estoppel* (2nd edn, 2002); Spencer Bower and Turner, *Estoppel by Representation* (4th edn, 2003) throughout, and especially ch 12; Cooke, *The Modern Law of Estoppel* (2000); Dawson and Pearce, *Licences Relating to the Occupation or Use of Land* (1979), pp 29–36, 97–9, 144–5, 161–3; Snell, ch 12; [1981] Conv 347 (PN Todd); [1983] CLJ 257 (MP Thompson); (1986) 49 MLR 741 (J Dewar); (1984) 100 LQR 376 (S Moriarty); (1994) 14 LS 147 (S Baughen); (1995) 58 MLR 637 (G Battersby); (1997) 17 LS 258 (E Cooke); [1998] 18 LS 360 (A Robinson); (1998) 58 MLR 637 (G Battersby); Sir Christopher Slade, *The Informal Creation of Interests in Land* (1984) Child & Co Oxford Lecture.

[19] See Halsbury, vol 16(2) (2003 reissue); Cooke, *The Modern Law of Estoppel*.

[20] *Crabb v Arun District Council* [1976] Ch 179, 193 (Scarman LJ); *Amalgamated Investment and Property Co Ltd v Texas Commerce International Bank Ltd* [1982] QB 84, 103 (Robert Goff J); affd [1982] QB 84; (1982) 79 LSG 662 (P Matthews); *Pacol Ltd v Trade Lines Ltd and R/I Sif IV* [1982] 1 Lloyd's Rep 456; for Australian developments, see *Waltons Stores (Interstate) Ltd v Maher* (1988) 164 CLR 387; (1988) 104 LQR 362 (A Duthie); *Commonwealth of Australia v Verwayen* (1990) 95 ALR 321, 331–2 (Mason CJ), 333 (Deane J), discussed by Hobhouse LJ in *Sledmore v Dalby* (1996) 72 P & CR 196, 208, M & B p 1045.

underlying idea behind them all can be understood by the very choice of the word 'estoppel'. This was explained by Lord Denning:[21]

> The word 'estoppel' only means stopped. You will find it explained by Coke in his *Commentaries on Littleton*.[22] It was brought over by the Normans. They used the old French 'estoupail.' That meant a bung or cork by which you stopped something from coming out. It was in common use in our courts when they carried on all their proceedings in Norman-French. Littleton writes in the law-French of his day (15th century) using the words 'pur ceo que le baron est estoppe a dire,' meaning simply that the husband is *stopped* from saying something.

From an early date the common law recognised forms of estoppel by which a person who had made a statement of fact, on which the other had relied, was estopped from denying the truth of his statement in his dealing with that other: it was often described as a rule of evidence,[23] by which a party would not be permitted to lead evidence to contradict his own representation in an action by or against the party to whom he had made the representation and who had relied on it—had changed his position in some way, on the faith of the representation, to his detriment. *Estoppel by deed*[24] and *estoppel by representation* are ancient forms of estoppel within this principle. However, the common law only recognised an estoppel based on a representation, or assumption,[25] of present fact, and not of intention or promise,[26] but equity has extended the principles of estoppel into a wider arena. Early authority can be found for *promissory estoppel*,[27] but it was not generally recognised until the judgment of Denning J in the *High Trees* case in 1947.[28] However, the role played by promissory estoppel in English law is still limited: it can be used to vary an existing contract, but not to create new obligations.[29] By contrast, *proprietary estoppel* has been actively developed by the courts and is

---

[21] *McIlkenny v Chief Constable of the West Midlands* [1980] QB 283, 316–17. The case itself raised a question about estoppel *per rem judicatam*.

[22] 19th edn, 1832, vol II, s 667, 352a.

[23] *Low v Bouverie* [1891] 3 Ch 82, 105, 112.

[24] A statement of fact made by a party in a deed cannot be challenged by that party as against the other party to the deed. Cf a 'tenancy by estoppel', where a person purports to grant a lease when he has no legal estate; once both parties have acted on the assumption that the deed created a tenancy, neither is allowed to deny to the other that their relationship has all the incidents of the lease: above, p 208.

[25] *Estoppel by convention*: where parties to a transaction act on an assumed state of facts or law, the assumption being either shared by them both or made by one and acquiesced in by the other, but as long as the assumption is communicated by each party to the other, then each is estopped from denying the assumed facts or law if it would be unjust to allow him to go back on the assumption: *Republic of India v Indian Steamship Co Ltd (No 2)* [1998] AC 878, 913. This bears a strong similarity to the equitable principles of the 'common intention' constructive trust: above, pp 512 ff.

[26] *Jordan v Money* (1854) 5 HL Cas 185, 214–15, 226–7.

[27] *Hughes v Metropolitan Rly Co* (1877) 2 App Cas 439.

[28] *Central London Property Trust Ltd v High Trees House Ltd* [1947] KB 130.

[29] *Combe v Combe* [1951] 2 KB 215; *Baird Textiles Holdings Ltd v Marks and Spencer plc* [2002] 1 All ER (Comm) 737 at [55]; it can be used only as a 'shield'. By contrast, it has been used to found a cause of action to remedy the non-performance of a promise unsupported by consideration—as a 'sword'—in the law of the United States: American Law Institute, *Restatement of the Law (2d), Contracts* (1981), para 90; and Australia: *Waltons Stores (Interstate) Ltd v Maher* (1988) 164 CLR 387. See generally Anson, pp 116–29.

now recognised as a mechanism through which property rights can be created and enforced.

B THE DEVELOPMENT OF PROPRIETARY ESTOPPEL

The courts of equity recognised a doctrine of 'encouragement and acquiescence' that has recently been treated as a type of estoppel and is now called proprietary estoppel. The early cases dealt almost exclusively with situations in which a landlord encouraged the occupier of his land to believe that the latter held under a lease.[30] The principle was explained in a well-known and generally accepted dictum in a dissenting speech of Lord Kingsdown:[31]

> If a man, under a verbal agreement with a landlord for a certain interest in land, or, what amounts to the same thing, under an expectation, created or encouraged by the landlord, that he shall have a certain interest, takes possession of such land, with the consent of the landlord, and upon the faith of such promise or expectation, with the knowledge of the landlord, and without objection by him, lays out money upon the land, a court of equity will compel the landlord to give effect to such promise or expectation.

In *Willmott v Barber*[32] Fry J set out five elements of a claim to proprietary estoppel, which have come to be referred to as the 'five probanda':

> It has been said that the acquiescence which will deprive a man of his legal rights must amount to fraud, and in my view that is an abbreviated statement of a very true proposition. A man is not to be deprived of his legal rights unless he has acted in such a way as would make it fraudulent for him to set up those rights.
>
> What, then, are the elements or requisites necessary to constitute fraud of that description? In the first place the plaintiff must have made a mistake as to his legal rights. Secondly, the plaintiff must have expended some money or must have done some act (not necessarily upon the defendant's land) on the faith of his mistaken belief. Thirdly, the defendant, the possessor of the legal right, must know of the existence of his own right which is inconsistent with the right claimed by the plaintiff. If he does not know of it he is in the same position as the plaintiff, and the doctrine of acquiescence is founded upon conduct with a knowledge of your legal rights. Fourthly, the defendant, the possessor of the legal right, must know of the plaintiff's mistaken belief of his rights. If he does not, there is nothing which calls upon him to assert his own rights. Lastly, the defendant, the possessor of the legal right, must have encouraged the plaintiff in his expenditure of money or in the other acts which he has done, either directly or by abstaining from asserting his legal right. Where all these elements exist, there is fraud of such a nature as will entitle the Court to restrain the possessor of the legal right from exercising it, but, in my judgment, nothing short of this will do.

---

[30] *Huning v Ferrers* (1710) Gilb Ch 85; *Stiles v Cowper* (1748) 3 Atk 692; *East India Co v Vincent* (1740) 2 Atk 83; *Jackson v Cator* (1800) 5 Ves 688.

[31] *Ramsden v Dyson and Thornton* (1866) LR 1 HL 129, 170.   [32] (1880) 15 Ch D 96, 105–6.

C THE MODERN LAW OF PROPRIETARY ESTOPPEL

Building on these early cases, the courts have constructed a modern doctrine of proprietary estoppel. In *Crabb v Arun District Council*[33] Scarman LJ made clear that the issues in such a claim must be addressed systematically:

> If the plaintiff has any right, it is an equity arising out of the conduct and relationship of the parties. In such a case I think it is now well settled law that the court, having analysed and assessed the conduct and relationship of the parties, has to answer three questions. First, is there an equity established? Secondly, what is the extent of the equity, if one is established? And, thirdly, what is the relief appropriate to satisfy the equity?

(1) Establishing the Equity

The first question, in a claim based on proprietary estoppel, is therefore whether the claimant can establish an equity. The general principle is that where one party (A) makes a representation or promise to another party (B) to the effect that B has or shall have an interest in, or right over, A's property, or acquiesces in B's mistaken belief that he has or shall have such an interest or right, then if in the circumstances B is reasonably entitled to act[34] in reliance to his detriment on the representation, promise or mistaken belief, and B does so act in reliance, equity may intervene to prevent (*estop*) A from asserting his own strict legal rights to his property. The key elements in a typical claim are therefore:[35]

> a representation or assurance made to the claimant; reliance on it by the claimant; and detriment to the claimant in consequence of his (reasonable) reliance.

(a) Unconscionability

In deciding whether an equity is established, the five probanda set out in *Willmott v Barber*[36] have been listed and applied in some cases[37] and ignored in others. The

---

[33] [1976] Ch 179, 193, M & B p 1051.

[34] This has often been described in terms that A must *intend* B to act in reliance on the representation, but this can be misleading in suggesting that A must subjectively so intend; the test is objective: *Thorner v Major* [2009] UKHL 18, [2009] 1 WLR 776 at [5] (Lord Hoffmann: 'It was enough that the meaning [A] conveyed would reasonably have been understood as intended to be taken seriously as an assurance that could be relied upon. If [B] did then rely upon it to his detriment, the necessary element of the estoppel is in my opinion established. It is not necessary that [A] should have known or foreseen the particular act of reliance'). See also below, p 913.

[35] *Thorner v Major*, above, at [29] (Lord Walker of Gestingthorpe).   [36] Above.

[37] *E and L Berg Ltd v Grey* (1979) 253 EG 473 (plaintiff failed because he was unable to satisfy the first and fifth requirements); *Crabb v Arun District Council* [1976] Ch 179, M & B p 1051. See also the approval of the probanda in *Kammins Ballrooms Co Ltd v Zenith Investments (Torquay) Ltd* [1971] AC 850, 884 (Lord Diplock), and their application in detail by Jonathan Parker QC in *Coombes v Smith* [1986] 1 WLR 808; *Matharu v Matharu* (1994) 68 P & CR 93 (where majority of CA somewhat liberally applied the five probanda); (1995) 58 MLR 412 (P Milne). See also *Gloucestershire County Council v Farrow* [1983] 2 All ER 1031; *Jones v Stones* [1999] 1 WLR 1739 (no acquiescence where delay in complaining about acts of trespass in using wall to place flower pots thereon and to support an oil tank).

modern cases show a preference for a much broader approach based on the defendant's *unconscionable* behaviour. In *Taylors Fashions Ltd v Liverpool Victoria Trustees Co Ltd*,[38] Oliver J held that, contrary to the requirements of Fry J, proprietary estoppel is not restricted to cases where the defendant knows his rights, and that it is not possible to formulate strict and rigid rules:[39]

> The more recent cases indicate that the application of the *Ramsden v Dyson* principle—whether you call it proprietary estoppel, estoppel by acquiescence or estoppel by encouragement is really immaterial—requires a very much broader approach that is directed rather at ascertaining whether, in particular individual circumstances, it would be unconscionable for a party to be permitted to deny that which, knowingly, or unknowingly, he has allowed or encouraged another to assume to his detriment than to inquiring whether the circumstances can be fitted within the confines of some preconceived formula serving as a universal yardstick for every form of unconscionable behaviour.

The effect of this approach is that the court now regards the five probanda no longer as rigid criteria to be satisfied, but as being 'guidelines which will probably prove to be the necessary and essential guidelines, to assist the court to decide the question whether it is unconscionable for the plaintiffs to assert their legal rights by taking advantage of the defendant'.[40] Oliver J suggested that the five probanda might be necessary where the defendant has done no positive act, and merely 'stands by without protest'.[41]

Unconscionability is the underlying principle;[42] the representor will be held to his representation only if it would be unconscionable for him to go back on it. However, the courts have emphasised that unconscionability is not an independent test, and that the uncertainty of palm tree justice[43] must be avoided. Lord Walker of Gestingthorpe has said:[44]

---

[38] [1982] QB 133n, M & B p 1012. Oliver J approved at 151 the broad test (applied by CA in *Shaw v Applegate* [1977] 1 WLR 970) of 'whether in the circumstances the conduct is unconscionable without the necessity of forcing those circumstances into a Procrustean bed constructed from some unalterable criteria'. The statement in the text was approved by Oliver LJ in *Habib Bank Ltd v Habib Bank AG Zurich* [1981] 1 WLR 1265, 1285; (1981) 97 LQR 513; *Pridean Ltd v Forest Taverns Ltd* (1998) 75 P & CR 447. See also Scarman LJ in *Crabb v Arun District Council* [1976] Ch 179, 195; (2004) 20 JCL (N Hopkins).

[39] At 151.

[40] *Swallow Securities Ltd v Isenberg* [1985] 1 EGLR 132, 134 (Cumming-Bruce LJ: no evidence to induce in the defendant an expectation that she had legal rights more extensive than was in fact the case).

[41] *Taylors Fashions Ltd v Liverpool Victoria Trustees Co Ltd* [1982] QB 133n, 146.

[42] [2010] LS 408 (M Dixon).

[43] In *Taylor v Dickens* [1998] 1 FLR 806, Judge Weeks QC said: 'There is no equitable jurisdiction to hold a person to a promise simply because the court thinks it unfair, unconscionable or morally objectionable to go back on it. If there were such a jurisdiction, one might as well forget the law of contract and issue every civil judge with a portable palm tree. The days of justice varying with the size of the Lord Chancellor's foot would have returned.'

[44] *Cobbe v Yeoman's Row Management Ltd* [2008] UKHL 55, [2008] 1 WLR 1752 at [46]. See further *Jennings v Rice* [2002] EWCA Civ 159, [2003] 1 P & CR 8, below, p 917; *Knowles v Knowles* [2008] UKPC 30 at [27] (Sir Henry Brooke): 'While recourse to the doctrine of estoppel provides a welcome means of effecting justice when the facts demand it, it is equally important that the courts do not penalise those who through acts of kindness simply allow other members of their family to inhabit their property rent free'; (2006) 122

equitable estoppel is a flexible doctrine which the court can use, in appropriate circumstances, to prevent injustice caused by the vagaries and inconstancy of human nature. But it is not a sort of joker or wild card to be used whenever the court disapproves of the conduct of a litigant who seems to have the law on his side. Flexible though it is, the doctrine must be formulated and applied in a disciplined and principled way

The claimant must still show the key elements of representation, reliance and detriment,[45] although they must be treated as one:[46]

It is important to note at the outset that the doctrine of proprietary estoppel cannot be treated as subdivided into three or four watertight compartments ... in the course of the oral argument in this court it repeatedly became apparent that the quality of the relevant assurances may influence the issue of reliance, that reliance and detriment are often intertwined, and that whether there is a distinct need for a 'mutual understanding' may depend on how the other elements are formulated and understood. Moreover the fundamental principle that equity is concerned to prevent unconscionable conduct permeates all the elements of the doctrine. In the end the court must look at the matter in the round.

(b) The representation

It has been emphasised that a key element of proprietary estoppel is a proprietary claim: that is the claim that the defendant is estopped from denying that the claimant has, or should be granted, an interest in property.[47] In some cases the estoppel has been based on a representation that the representee already has an interest in land; and it is upon the belief in that *existing* right that the representee has incurred some detriment in reliance on it.[48] The doctrine is not, however, limited to acts done in reliance on a belief relating to an existing right, but extends to acts done in reliance on a belief that *future* rights will be granted, such as where a step-daughter acted to her detriment in reliance on her belief that she would ultimately benefit by receiving the deceased's property under his will.[49] However, not every idle statement of intention by

LQR 492 (S Gardner, arguing that the remedial discretion as actually exercised by the courts cannot be sufficiently reconciled with the Rule of Law).

[45] *Thorner v Major* [2009] UKHL 18, [2009] 1 WLR 776 at [29] (Lord Walker of Gestingthorpe).

[46] *Gillett v Holt* [2001] Ch 210, 225 (Walker LJ).

[47] *Cobbe v Yeoman's Row Management Ltd*, above, n 44, at [14] (Lord Scott of Foscote: 'usually a right to or over land but, in principle, equally available in relation to chattels or choses in action'). See also *Western Fish Products Ltd v Penwith DC* [1981] 2 All ER 204; below, p 919.

[48] *Pascoe v Turner* [1979] 1 WLR 430, M & B, p 1056 ('the house is yours and everything in it'); [1979] Conv 379 (FR Crane); (1979) 42 MLR 574 (B Suffrin); below, p 939. See also *ER Ives Investment Ltd v High* [1967] 2 QB 379, M & B p 1074 (garage built by landowner on own land but in belief, acquiesced in by neighbour, that he had a right of way over neighbour's land). Sometimes the belief can be characterised either as one of a present right, or of a future right: see, eg, *Taylors Fashions Ltd v Liverpool Victoria Trustees Co Ltd* [1982] QB 133n (expenditure on property by tenants in the erroneous belief that an option to renew the lease was valid—or, in other words, that they *would* be entitled to renew), but nothing turns on this distinction.

[49] *Re Basham* [1986] 1 WLR 1498; [1987] Conv 211 (JE Martin); [1987] CLJ 215 (DJ Hayton); [1987] All ER Rev 156 (PJ Clarke), 260 (CH Sherrin); (1988) 8 LS 92 (M Davey); *Jennings v Rice* [2002] EWCA Civ 159], [2003] 1 P & CR 8, M & B p 1040, below, p 917). Cf *Thorner v Major*, above, n 45, at [20], where Lord Scott of Foscote preferred to restrict proprietary estoppel to representations of immediate, or more or less immediate, interests in the property, and to view representations of future benefits, such as inheritances, as

the testator or assumed expectation of inheritance by the beneficiary will give rise to an estoppel. In the context of wills, which by their nature are revocable at any time by the testator, Robert Walker LJ said in *Gillett v Holt*:[50]

> The inherent revocability of testamentary dispositions (even if well understood by the parties...) is irrelevant to a promise or assurance that 'all this will be yours'... Even when the promise or assurance is in terms linked to the making of a will... the circumstances may make clear that the assurance is more than a mere statement of present (revocable) intention, and is tantamount to a promise. *A-G of Hong Kong v Humphreys Estate (Queen's Gardens) Ltd*[51]... is essentially an example of a purchaser taking the risk, with his eyes open, of going into possession and spending money while his purchase remains expressly subject to contract...
>
> It is notorious that some elderly persons of means derive enjoyment from the possession of testamentary power, and from dropping hints as to their intentions, without any question of an estoppel arising. But in this case Mr Holt's assurances were repeated over a long period, usually before the assembled company on special family occasions and some of them (such as 'it was all going to be ours anyway'...) were completely unambiguous.

The claimant must therefore have a sufficiently certain belief that he has or will have a right before it is unconscionable to deny it to him.[52]

The question of how clear and unequivocal the representation must be in order to found an estoppel was considered by the House of Lords in *Thorner v Major*:[53]

> From 1976 to 1995, the claimant, David Thorner, did substantial work without payment on the farm of his father's cousin, Peter Thorner. Peter (a 'man of few words', according to the trial judge) never made an express representation that he would leave the farm to David, but from oblique remarks, and certain actions (in particular, handing to David documents in 1990 relating to Peter's life insurance, and saying 'that's for my death duties'), David understood Peter as giving an assurance that he would inherit the farm.

The trial judge held that it was reasonable for David to understand Peter to this effect, and that he relied on the assurance by continuing to work without remuneration on the farm, and that he therefore had a claim to the farm on the basis of proprietary estoppel.

---

falling within the principles of remedial constructive trusts; but cf [2009] CLJ 537, 549 (Lord Neuberger of Abbotsbury).

[50] [2001] Ch 210, 227–8; [2000] CLJ 453 (M Dixon); [2000] All ER Rev 244 (PJ Clarke), 370 (CH Sherrin); [2001] Conv 78 (MP Thompson). See also *Taylor v Dickens* [1998] 1 FLR 806, where the claimant failed (his wife told him not to count his chickens before they were hatched); *Murphy v Burrows* [2004] EWHC 1900 (Ch), [2005] 1 P & CR DG 3 (not unconscionable for deceased to have changed will).

[51] [1987] AC 114, M & B p 27.

[52] *Parker v Parker* [2003] EWHC 1846 (Ch), [2003] All ER (D) 421 (Jul) at [213] (9th Earl of Mansfield could not establish estoppel entitling him to possession for life of Shirburn Castle, Oxfordshire, based only on a false tradition that the right to live in the castle went with the Earldom); *Keelwalk Properties Ltd v Waller* [2002] EWCA Civ 1076, [2002] 3 EGLR 79 (long-standing practice cannot justify assumption that it will continue in perpetuity); *MacDonald v Frost* [2009] EWHC 2276 (Ch), [2010] 1 P & CR DG14.

[53] [2009] UKHL 18, [2009] 1 WLR 776; (2009) 125 LQR 535 (B McFarlane and A Robertson); [2009] Conv 260 (M Dixon); [2009] CLJ 537 (Lord Neuberger of Abbotsbury).

The Court of Appeal reversed the trial judge on the basis that, in order to found an estoppel, there must be a clear and unequivocal representation, which the representor intended the representee to act upon, and there was no sufficient representation here, nor was there evidence that Peter intended David to act upon it. However, the House of Lords rejected this. The question was not what Peter subjectively intended David to understand. The test is objective:[54]

> Even though clear and unequivocal statements played little or no part in communications between the two men, they were well able to understand one another. So, however clear and unequivocal his intention to assure David that he was to have the farm after his death, Peter was always likely to have expressed it in oblique language. Against that background, respectfully adopting Lord Walker's formulation,[55] I would hold that it is sufficient if what Peter said was 'clear enough'. To whom? Perhaps not to an outsider. What matters, however, is that what Peter said should have been clear enough for David, whom he was addressing and who had years of experience in interpreting what he said and did, to form a reasonable view that Peter was giving him an assurance that he was to inherit the farm and that he could rely on it.

The sufficiency of the content of the representation was also discussed in *Thorner v Major*.[56] Although there was no clear statement about the property that David was to inherit, and the extent of the farm varied over the years as parcels were sold off or added, this did not prevent a valid claim based on proprietary estoppel. There was no doubt as to what was the subject of the assurance, namely the farm as it existed from time to time:[57]

> the nature of the interest to be received by David was clear: it was the farm as it existed on Peter's death. As in the case of a very different equitable concept, namely a floating charge, the property the subject of the equity could be conceptually identified from the moment the equity came into existence, but its precise extent fell to be determined when the equity crystallised, namely on Peter's death.

---

[54] Ibid, at [26] (Lord Rodger of Earlsferry).

[55] Ibid, at [56] ('I would prefer to say (while conscious that it is a thoroughly question-begging formulation) that to establish a proprietary estoppel the relevant assurance must be clear enough. What amounts to sufficient clarity, in a case of this sort, is hugely dependent on context').

[56] See also *Orgee v Orgee* [1997] EGCS 152 (claim to agricultural tenancy on basis of estoppel refused in the absence of details as to crucial terms on which tenancy was expected to be based, for example, provisions for repairs and rent and rent review regime); cf *JT Developments Ltd v Quinn* (1990) 62 P & CR 33; (1998) 114 LQR 351 (M Pawlowski); *Parker v Parker* [2003] EWHC 1846 (Ch), [2003] All ER (D) 421 (Jul) (expectation too vague and indefinite); [2004] Conv 516 (MP Thompson); *Sutcliffe v Lloyd* [2007] EWCA Civ 153, [2007] 2 EGLR 13 at [38] (promisor need not make clear that promise is irrevocable).

[57] [2009] UKHL 18, [2009] 1 WLR 776, at [95] (Lord Neuberger of Abbotsbury), contrasting (at [94]) the different situation that arose in *Cobbe v Yeoman's Row Management Ltd* [2008] UKHL 55, [2008] 1 WLR 1752, below, p 976, where there was 'total uncertainty as to the nature or terms of any benefit (property interest, contractual right, or money), and, if a property interest, as to the nature of that interest (freehold, leasehold, or charge), to be accorded to Mr Cobbe'. See also *Jennings v Rice* [2002] EWCA Civ 159], [2003] 1 P & CR 8, M & B p 1040, below, p 917 (estoppel, although no specific promise as to the property the claimant would receive).

(c) Reliance. Detriment

In *Crabb v Arun District Council*:[58]

> C owned a two acre plot of land which had access in the northern part (at point A) onto a lane owned by the defendants and thence along a right of way over that lane to the highway. In 1967 C decided to sell the northern and southern parts of the plot separately. Since he had no means of access from the southern part to the highway (except over the northern part), he made an oral agreement with the defendants under which they would give to him a further point of access (point B) together with a further right of way along the lane. No formal grant of the right of access or easement was made. As a result of the agreement, the defendants erected a fence between their land and C's land, and gates at the two access points. C, relying on this agreement, sold the northern part with the point A access to X, without reserving a right of way over it in favour of the retained southern part. In 1969 the defendants removed the gate at point B, and fenced the gap, thus making C's southern plot land-locked; further, they asked C to pay 'close on £4,000 in order to provide him with that which their representative had undertaken to provide'.[59]

The Court of Appeal held that the defendants were estopped from denying C's right of access at point B and the right of way from there to the highway, and, in view of the sterilisation of his land for a considerable period, the rights would be granted without any payment by him to the defendants.[60] This case shows a shift of emphasis from the paradigm case, where the representee has spent money on the land of the representor, to one where he has suffered detriment arising from some activity or inactivity on his part. The detriment to C was that, in reliance on the agreement with the defendants that he would have an access to and a right of way over the defendants' land, he refrained from expressly reserving an easement of way over the northern plot when he sold and conveyed it to X.[61]

The doctrine was also widened in *Greasley v Cooke*[62] in connection with the burden of proof. In that case the Court of Appeal held that, once there is proof that a representation has been made that was likely to influence the representee, and made with the intention that it should influence him, the onus shifts to the representor to

---

[58] [1976] Ch 179, 193, M & B p 1051; (1976) 40 Conv (NS) 156 (FR Crane); (1976) 92 LQR 174 (PS Atiyah); 342 (PJ Millett); (1995) 58 MLR 637, 640 (G Battersby).

[59] [1976] Ch 179, 191 (Lawton LJ).

[60] See *Crabb v Arun District Council (No 2)* (1976) 121 SJ 86 where C was refused an inquiry as to damages. See also *Salvation Army Trustee Co Ltd v West Yorkshire Metropolitan County Council* (1980) 41 P & CR 179 (where proprietary estoppel was extended to the *disposal* of an interest in land where the disposal was closely linked by an arrangement that also involved the acquisition of an interest in land); discussed in *A-G of Hong Kong v Humphreys Estate (Queen's Gardens) Ltd* [1987] AC 114, 126, 127.

[61] See also *Lloyd v Dugdale* [2001] EWCA Civ 1754, [2002] 2 P & CR 13 at [36]-[38] (detriment consisted in lost opportunity to purchase alternative premises).

[62] [1980] 1 WLR 1306, M & B p 1036. This test was taken from the similar rule elsewhere, under which the court is entitled to infer, as a matter of *fact*, the representee's reliance from the (objective) materiality of the statement—that it was 'calculated' to induce reliance; see, eg, *Smith v Chadwick* (1882) 20 Ch D 27, 44 (Jessel MR) (proof of reliance in the tort of deceit).

prove that the representee did not rely on it.[63] It spite of this rule, however, the basic requirement of detriment remains unimpaired. As Dunn LJ said in that case:[64]

> There is no doubt that for proprietary estoppel to arise the person claiming must have incurred expenditure or otherwise have prejudiced himself or acted to his detriment.

And there must be a sufficient link between the detrimental reliance and the interest which is claimed. In *Brinnand v Ewens*,[65] Nourse LJ said:

> The acting [to the detriment] must have taken place in the belief either that the claimant owned a sufficient interest in the property to justify the expenditure or that he would obtain such an interest.[66]

But it must always be remembered that the purpose of identifying the detrimental reliance by the claimant is to justify finding that it would be inequitable for the defendant to insist on his strict rights to the property and thereby to deny the claimant the right to it that he believed he had, or would obtain. Robert Walker LJ said in *Gillett v Holt*:[67]

---

[63] *Watts v Story* [1983] CA Transcript 319, (1983) 134 NLJ 631, M & B p 1037, where Dunn LJ explained the observations of Lord Denning MR in *Greasley v Cooke*; *Wayling v Jones* (1993) 69 P & CR 170; [1994] LS 15 (M Halliwell) (requirement of promise and 'conduct of such a nature that inducement may be inferred': Balcombe LJ at 175); (1995) 111 LQR 389 (E Cooke); [1995] Conv 409 (CJ Davis); *Thompson v Foy* [2009] EWHC 1076 (Ch), [2010] 1 P & CR 16 at [93].

[64] At 1313. See *Dann v Spurrier* (1802) 7 Ves 231, 235–6 (Lord Eldon LC), cited in *Taylors Fashions Ltd v Liverpool Victoria Trustees Co Ltd* [1982] QB 133n, 156; *Christian v Christian* (1981) 131 NLJ 43; *Watkins v Emslie* (1982) 261 EG 1192; *Coombes v Smith* [1986] 1 WLR 808 (no detriment where wife left husband and went to live with lover and their child); [1986] CLJ 394 (DJ Hayton); *Hammersmith and Fulham London Borough Council v Top Shop Centres Ltd* [1990] Ch 237 (failure to negotiate for grant of new lease or to apply for relief against forfeiture held to be detriment; reliance presumed); *Matharu v Matharu* (1994) 68 P & CR 93 (son's expenditure in improving property held to be detrimental reliance on part of his wife); [1995] 7 CFLQ 59 (G Battersby); [1995] Conv 61 (M Welstead); *Gan v Wood* [1998] EGCS 77 (expenditure not amounting to more than minor detriment held not to suffice); *Century (UK) Ltd SA v Clibbery* [2004] EWHC 1870 (Ch), [2004] All ER (D) 541 (Jul) (household chores of answering telephone calls and video-recording programmes not sufficient detriment); *Holmes v South Yorkshire Police Authority* [2008] EWCA Civ 51, [2008] HLR 33 (police constable occupying job-related accommodation had not acted in reliance on being able to stay there).

[65] [1987] 2 EGLR 67 (expenditure incurred on work 'done to make the home more comfortable'). See also *Bristol and West Building Society v Henning* [1985] 1 WLR 778, where, in a case concerning the priority between the beneficial interest of a spouse and the rights of a mortgagee, Browne-Wilkinson LJ said at 782, that 'in the absence of express agreement, an intention or assumption [that a party other than the legal owner should have a beneficial interest in the property] must be proved in order to found the lesser interest of an irrevocable licence conferring a property interest: see *Re Sharpe* [1980] 1 WLR 219 [below, p 934]'. See also *Paddington Building Society v Mendelsohn* (1985) 50 P & CR 244; [1985] CLJ 354 (M Welstead); *Grant v Edwards* [1986] Ch 638, 657.

[66] Adapted from *Snell's Equity* (28th edn, 1982), p 559.

[67] [2001] Ch 210, 232, referring to the judgment of Slade LJ in *Jones v Watkins* (CA, 26 November 1987); and applied by Sir Christopher Slade in *Lloyd v Dugdale* [2001] EWCA Civ 1754, [2002] 2 P & CR 13 at [31]. See also *Lim Teng Huan v Ang Swee Chuan* [1992] 1 WLR 113, 117 (Lord Browne-Wilkinson: 'it is not essential that the representor should have been guilty of unconscionable conduct in permitting the representee to assume that he could act as he did: it is enough if, in all the circumstances, it is unconscionable

The authorities show that detriment is not a narrow or technical concept. The detriment need not consist of the expenditure of money or other quantifiable financial detriment, so long as it is something substantial. The requirement must be approached as part of a broad inquiry as to whether repudiation of an assurance is or is not unconscionable in all the circumstances. ... There must be sufficient causal link between the assurance relied on and the detriment asserted. The issue of detriment must be judged at the moment when the person who has given the assurance seeks to go back on it. Whether the detriment is sufficiently substantial is to be tested by whether it would be unjust or inequitable to allow the assurance to be disregarded—that is, again, the essential test of unconscionability. The detriment alleged must be pleaded and proved.

(2) Satisfying the Equity. The Remedy

In *Crabb v Arun District Council*[68] Scarman LJ's second and third questions were: what is the extent of the equity? And what is the relief appropriate to satisfy it? These two questions can be taken together, since they both concern the question of what remedy the courts should award in an established case of proprietary estoppel.

(a) The range of available remedies

As we shall see in the context of licences,[69] the remedies awarded by the court have ranged from simply negative protection, preventing the licensor from revoking a licence,[70] to positive protection through the transfer of the fee simple to the licensee.[71] The courts have also ordered that the party in whose favour an equity arises by estoppel be granted other interests in land, such as an easement[72] or a lease;[73] or that his expenditure be reimbursed rather than that he be given a positive interest in the land;[74] and have also on occasion held that, although the equity was established, it had either expired before the hearing or for other reasons no remedy was necessary or appropriate.[75] The range of remedies that the courts have at their disposal in the case of

for the representor to go back on the assumption that he permitted the representee to make'); [1993] Conv 173 (SK Goo); M & B p 1060.

[68] [1976] Ch 179, above, p 914.

[69] Below, pp 937 ff. For a useful account of examples of remedies, see Snell, paras 12–026 to 12–030.

[70] *Inwards v Baker* [1965] 2 QB 29, M & B p 1049.

[71] Either without compensation: *Pascoe v Turner* [1979] 1 WLR 431, M & B p 1056, above; *Dillwyn v Llewelyn* (1862) 4 De GF & J 517; *Voyce v Voyce* (1991) 62 P & CR 290; or with compensation: *Lim Teng Huan v Ang Swee Chuan* [1992] 1 WLR 113, M & B p 1060.

[72] *Crabb v Arun District Council*, above; *ER Ives Investment Ltd v High* [1967] 2 QB 379, M & B p 1074; *Bexley LBC v Maison Maurice Ltd* [2006] EWHC 3192 (Ch), [2007] 1 EGLR 19.

[73] *Griffiths v Williams* (1977) 248 EG 947, M & B p 1061.

[74] *Dodsworth v Dodsworth* (1973) 228 EG 1115; M & B p 1068, below, p 940.

[75] *Sledmore v Dalby* (1996) 72 P & CR 196, M & B p 1045 (equity had expired where licensee had enjoyed 18 years' free occupation, had little need for the property and the licensor was in serious financial difficulty); *Appleby v Cowley*, The Times, 14 April 1982, M & B p 1069 (by the time the claim was made, plaintiff barristers had had sufficient satisfaction for their expenditure on property occupied as chambers: 'it may be a nice academic point whether the result is that no case of proprietary estoppel has been established, or whether it is that such a case has been established but no remedy should be granted': Megarry V-C); *Savva*

an established equity by estoppel is very wide, including the award of both proprietary and personal rights.[76] It is therefore important to know by what principles they will select the appropriate remedy.

(b) Selecting the appropriate remedy[77]

In selecting the remedy, the court asks what is now 'the minimum equity to do justice to the plaintiff?'[78] And in doing so, the court has a discretion. But the fact that the courts have adopted a flexible approach in their selection of remedies does not mean that the discretion is not based on principle:[79]

the court must take a principled approach, and cannot exercise a completely unfettered discretion according to the individual judge's notion of what is fair in any particular case.

The principles underlying the exercise of discretion, and their application in earlier cases, were reviewed by the Court of Appeal in *Jennings v Rice*.[80] In that case:

J began to work as a part-time gardener for Mrs Royle in 1970. Over the years he did more for her, including taking her shopping and running errands. In the late 1980s Mrs Royle stopped paying him, but she provided a deposit of £2000 to enable J and his wife to buy a house, and told him that 'he would be alright' and she would 'see to it'. J believed that he was going to receive all or part of Mrs Royle's property on her death, although nothing was put in writing, and none of Mrs Royle's assurances were specific. Mrs Royle became increasingly dependent on J, and from 1994 until her death in 1997 J spent almost every night on a sofa in her sitting room, and provided personal care for her and cared for the house and garden. Mrs Royle died intestate, with an estate worth £1.285m, including her house worth £435,000.

The trial judge awarded J £200,000 out of Mrs Royle's estate, on the basis of proprietary estoppel, holding that it was not appropriate to award him the full value of the benefit he expected to receive (the house and its furniture) because it was disproportionate and excessive. The cost of full-time nursing care of the kind provided by J was around

---

v Costa [1980] CA Transcript 723, (1981) 131 NLJ 1114, M & B p 1070 (claim based on proprietary estoppel premature because defendant was not (yet) seeking to disturb her enjoyment of the property); *Uglow v Uglow* [2004] EWCA Civ 987, [2004] All ER (D) 472 (Jul); *Horton v Brandish* [2005] EWHC 3423 (Ch), [2005] All ER (D) 460 (Jul) (equity excluded by representee's failure to pay agreed rent to representor, and his exclusion of representor from the property); *Clarke v Swaby* [2007] UKPC 1, [2007] 2 P & CR 2 at [18].

[76] [2005] CLJ 449 (S Bright and B McFarlane). The grant of a property right might be accompanied by compensation; and for an interim award of compensation where the extent of the disturbance to the occupation (as compared with the represented occupation rights) was not yet certain, see *Brightlingsea Haven Ltd v Morris* [2009] EWHC 3061 (QB), [2009] 48 EGCS 103.

[77] (1999) 115 LQR 438 (S Gardner), M & B p 1039, setting out four hypotheses for the court's discretion, and discussed in *Jennings v Rice*, below; (1997) 17 LS 258 (E Cooke). See further (2006) 122 LQR 492 (S Gardner); *Modern Studies in Property Law*, vol 5 (2009), ch 16 (J Mee).

[78] *Crabb v Arun District Council* [1976] Ch 179, 198 (Scarman LJ). The court considers the facts at the date of the hearing, and does not limit its inquiry to what would have been unconscionable when the representation was made: above, n 75.

[79] *Jennings v Rice*, below, at [43] (Robert Walker LJ).

[80] [2002] EWCA Civ 159, [2003] 1 P & CR 8, M & B p 1040; (2002) 118 LQR 519 (M Pawlowski); [2003] Conv 225 (MP Thompson).

£200,000; and he would probably need £150,000 to buy a home. The judge concluded that[81]

> I do not think that he could complain that he had been unfairly treated if he had been left £200,000 in Mrs Royle's will. Most people would say that she would, at least, then have performed her promise to see him all right. The quality of her assurance affects not only questions of belief, encouragement, reliance and detriment, but also unconscionability and the extent of the equity.

This was affirmed by the Court of Appeal, which took the opportunity to review the question of when it is appropriate to award a remedy which gives the claimant the full value of his expectation, and when it is appropriate to depart from that. The starting-point is the expectation, and not simply the value of the detrimental reliance incurred by the claimant in order to establish the equity.[82] But the court will not simply order a remedy that protects the expectation; it will consider also the value of the claimant's reliance, and whether an award of the expectation would be disproportionate. As Aldous LJ said:[83]

> reliance and detriment are two of the requirements of proprietary estoppel and that the basis of the estoppel is, as Lord Denning MR said in *Crabb*'s case, the interposition of equity: thus the requirement of unconscionability. If the conscience of the court is involved, it would be odd that the amount of the award should be set rigidly at the sum expected by the claimant.

Where the claimant's expectation is specific, the court may well order that the expectation be fulfilled.[84] But in a case where the expectation is uncertain, or

---

[81]   Quoted by Aldous LJ: ibid, at [15].

[82]   Ibid, at [30] (Aldous LJ) and [54] (Robert Walker LJ), contrasting the preference shown by the Australian courts for compensating only the reliance loss. See also [2008] Conv 295 (A Robertson, comparing the English and Australian courts' approaches).

[83]   Ibid, at [21]. See also at [49] (Robert Walker LJ). *Commonwealth of Australia v Verwayen* (1990) 95 ALR 321, 331 (Mason CJ); followed in *Sledmore v Dalby* (1996) 72 P & CR 196, 208 (Hobhouse LJ, suggesting that 'in many of its applications the equitable doctrine of proprietary estoppel bears a close relationship to restitutionary principles', under which the remedy is awarded to prevent unjust enrichment of the defendant at the claimant's expense).

[84]   Or even exceeded: ibid, at [21] (Aldous LJ), referring to *Crabb v Arun District Council* [1976] Ch 179 (claimant expected to receive easement in return for payment; court ordered easement without payment); but the expectation is normally the maximum extent of the equity: *Parker v Parker* [2003] EWHC 1846 (Ch), [2003] All ER (D) 421 (Jul) at [210], and the claimant cannot be compensated for losses that do not flow from the reliance on the representation: *Wormall v Wormall* [2004] EWCA Civ 1643, The Times, 1 December 2004 (representation that daughter could occupy property as long as it continued to be family farm; disturbance costs of moving earlier than expected could not be compensated because the relocation 'was always on the cards': at [39] (Jonathan Parker LJ)). Where 'the assurances, and the claimant's reliance on them, have a consensual character falling not far short of an enforceable contract … the consensual element of what has happened suggests that the claimant and the benefactor probably regarded the expected benefit and the accepted detriment as being (in a general, imprecise way) equivalent, or at any rate not obviously disproportionate': at [45] (Robert Walker LJ). This is close to the principle of contract law that the courts will not investigate the adequacy of consideration as long as there is a bargain between the parties: Anson, pp 99–101.

disproportionate, it may well be appropriate to depart from that and to order a more limited remedy:[85]

> there is a category of case in which the benefactor and the claimant have reached a mutual understanding which is in reasonably clear terms but does not amount to a contract. I have already referred to the typical case of a carer who has the expectation of coming into the benefactor's house, either outright or for life. In such a case the court's natural response is to fulfil the claimant's expectations. But if the claimant's expectations are uncertain, or extravagant, or out of all proportion to the detriment which the claimant has suffered, the court can and should recognise that the claimant's equity should be satisfied in another (and generally more limited) way.

D THE LIMITS OF PROPRIETARY ESTOPPEL

In English law the doctrine of proprietary estoppel has been limited to land. In *Western Fish Products Ltd v Penwith District Council*, Megaw LJ said:[86]

> We know of no case, and none has been cited to us, in which the principle set out in *Ramsden v Dyson* ... has been applied otherwise than to rights and interests created in and over land. It may extend to other forms of property[87] ... In our judgment there is no good reason for extending the principle further.

It may well be related to other doctrines of equity under which property rights are created in one who does not have legal ownership;[88] but the English courts have not

---

[85] Ibid, at [50] (Robert Walker LJ). His Lordship declined to give a comprehensive list, or hierarchy, of factors relevant to the court's discretion, but included (at [52]) the claimant's misconduct; particularly oppressive conduct on the part of the defendant; the court's recognition that it cannot compel people who have fallen out to live peaceably together, so that there may be a need for a clean break; alterations in the benefactor's assets and circumstances, especially where the benefactor's assurances have been given, and the claimant's detriment has been suffered, over a long period of years; the likely effect of taxation; and (to a limited degree) the other claims (legal or moral) on the benefactor or his or her estate; see (2006) 122 LQR 492 (S Gardner). See also *Ottey v Grundy* [2003] EWCA Civ 1176, [2003] All ER (D) 05 (Aug), [2004] Conv 137 (MP Thompson); *Murphy v Burrows* [2004] EWHC 1900 (Ch), [2005] 1 P & CR DG 3 (lack of proportionality); *Powell v Benney* [2007] EWCA Civ 1283, [2008] 1 P & CR DG12 (claimants' expectations to receive properties worth £280,000 were out of all proportion to the detriment that they suffered: £20,000 ordered); [2008] Conv 253 (M Pawlowski); *Henry v Henry* [2010] UKPC 3, [2010] 1 All ER 988 at [65] ('Proportionality lies at the heart of the doctrine of proprietary estoppel and permeates its every application').

[86] [1981] 2 All ER 204 at 218 (no estoppel where owner spent money on his own land in the expectation encouraged by a local authority that he would acquire a planning permission); *West Middlesex Golf Club Ltd v Ealing London Borough Council* (1993) 68 P & CR 461, 468; *Newport CC v Charles* [2008] EWCA Civ 1541, [2009] 1 WLR 1884 at [27] (*proprietary* estoppel does not apply to local housing authority's claim to possession under HA 1985, Sch 2, ground 16 because the claim has no proprietary element). Cf *Lester v Woodgate* [2010] EWCA Civ 199, [2010] 2 P & CR DG 14 at [43] (Patten LJ: proprietary estoppel capable of equal application to estop party from complaining about nuisance interfering with easement).

[87] *Re Foster* [1938] 3 All ER 610 (life insurance policy); *Moorgate Mercantile Co Ltd v Twitchings* [1976] QB 225, 242 (Lord Denning MR). See also *Cobbe v Yeoman's Row Management Ltd* [2008] UKHL 55, [2008] 1 WLR 1752 at [14] (Lord Scott of Foscote); above, p 911, n 47.

[88] See esp *Re Basham* [1986] 1 WLR 1498, 1503–4 (Nugee QC, comparing proprietary estoppel to secret trusts and mutual wills); J Cartwright, in Getzler (ed) *Rationalizing Property, Equity and Trusts: Essays in*

absorbed it into a larger general doctrine within the law of property; nor have they absorbed it into a larger general doctrine of estoppel.[89]

E PROPRIETARY ESTOPPEL AS AN INTEREST IN LAND

We have seen that there are two stages in the doctrine of proprietary estoppel. First, the equity arises, as a result of one party's representation (or acquiescence) and the other party's reliance to his detriment; and secondly, the court grants a remedy to satisfy the equity.

There has been controversy as to the status of the right before the court decides on the remedy and makes the order.[90] It may be either inchoate, that is to say it is not a property right until the court makes the order, and therefore cannot bind third parties until that happens. Or it may be choate and is a property right at the earlier stage.

There is authority in favour of the second view. In *ER Ives Investment Ltd v High*:[91]

the defendant, High, built a house on his own land. His neighbour then erected a block of flats whose foundations encroached on High's land. They agreed orally that the foundations should remain and that High should have a right of way across the neighbour's yard. High, relying on this agreement, built a garage on his own land so sited that it could only be approached across the yard. The neighbour sold the block of flats to a purchaser, who resold it to the claimants, expressly subject to High's right of way. The right of way was not a legal interest since it had not been formally created; nor had it been registered as an equitable easement under the Land Charges Act 1925.[92]

The Court of Appeal held that High had a right by estoppel, which, not being registrable as a land charge, was binding on the claimants who had purchased the legal estate of the licensor with actual notice.[93]

Honour of Edward Burn (2003), ch 3. The relationship between proprietary estoppel and constructive trusts is considered below, pp 1015–17.

[89] For such a development in Australia, see *Waltons Stores (Interstate) Ltd v Maher* (1988) 164 CLR 387 (assimilating proprietary and promissory estoppel, which in England are still kept separate: above, p 907, n 29).

[90] (1990) 106 LQR 87, 97; [1990] Conv 370, 380 (D Hayton); [1991] Conv 36, 45; (1995) 58 MLR 637, 642 (G Battersby); (1992) 22 Fam Law 72 (P Clarke); [1994] 14 LS 147, 154 (S Baughen); [1996] Conv 34 (J Howell), 193 (C Davis); [2003] CLJ 661 (B McFarlane). On the question of whether the equity is overreachable, see below, pp 941, 944.

[91] [1967] 2 QB 379, M & B p 1074; (1967) 31 Conv (NS) 332 (FR Crane).

[92] Land Charges Act 1972, s 2(5), Class D (iii); below, p 1059.

[93] The CA also relied on the doctrine of *Halsall v Brizell* [1957] Ch 169, that he who takes the benefit must accept the burden; above, p 730.

In unregistered land the right has been held to bind a purchaser with notice,[94] or a donee whether he has notice or not.[95] In registered land under the Land Registration Act 1925 it was held to be an interest capable of being an overriding interest under section 70(1)(g) as long as the person with the benefit of the equity was in actual occupation.[96] This is confirmed by section 116 of the Land Registration Act 2002,[97] which provides that:

It is hereby declared for the avoidance of doubt that, in relation to registered land, ...

(a) an equity by estoppel...

has effect from the time the equity arises as an interest capable of binding successors in title (subject to the rules about the effect of dispositions on priority).

The equity, if it is to have priority over a registered disposition for valuable consideration, must therefore be protected by notice in the register[98] or, if it is not registered, it may take effect as an overriding interest if the beneficiary is in discoverable actual occupation.[99]

But what the purchaser is bound by—in the sense of the scope of the claimant's rights (if any) to the land—is not yet at that moment capable of being ascertained. The remedy might be the grant of an estate or interest in the land; but it might not be.[100] And the nature of the discretion exercised by the court in deciding on the remedy, although a principled discretion,[101] emphasises the uncertainty in the remedy until the court has considered the facts at the time of the hearing. Almost all cases that have come before the courts have involved the original parties; we therefore await further clarification of the position of the claimant as against the purchaser.[102]

---

[94] *Duke of Beaufort v Patrick* (1853) 17 Beav 60, 78; *Inwards v Baker* [1965] 2 QB 29, 37; *ER Ives Investment Ltd v High* [1967] 2 QB 379. In *Lloyds Bank plc v Carrick* [1996] 4 All ER 630, 642, Morritt LJ commented that '[i]n the circumstances it is unnecessary to consider further the submission ... to the effect that a proprietary estoppel cannot give rise to an interest in land capable of binding successors in title. This interesting argument will have to await another day, though it is hard to see how in this court it can surmount the hurdle constituted by the decision of this court in *Ives v High*'.

[95] *Voyce v Voyce* (1991) 62 P & CR 290, 296 (claimant equitable owner before the conveyance); see also *Sen v Headley* [1991] Ch 425, 440.

[96] *Brocket Hall (Jersey) Ltd v Clague* [1998] CLY 4367; *Habermann v Koehler (No 2)*, The Times, 22 November 2000; *Lloyd v Dugdale* [2001] EWCA Civ 1754, [2002] 2 P & CR 13; (2002) 146 SJ 90 (M Pawlowski).

[97] See Law Com No 254, *Land Registration in the Twenty-First Century – A Consultative Document* (1998), paras 3.33–3.36; [2003] CLJ 661 (B McFarlane).

[98] LRA 2002, s 29.   [99] Ibid, Sch 3, para 2.   [100] Above, pp 916–17.

[101] *Jennings v Rice*, above, p 917.

[102] It is likely, however, that a court will take into account the particular circumstances of the purchaser—now the defendant in the claim—where such a case arises. It is already clear that the change in the original representor's circumstances is a relevant factor in determining the remedy to be awarded against him, and so the position of the purchaser as the present owner of the land should equally be relevant: *Sledmore v Dalby* (1996) 72 P & CR 196, M & B p 1045. Cf *Redstone Mortgages plc v Welch* [2009] 36 EG 98 at [73] (county court judge took into account that the chargee bound by the estoppel was an innocent party, but still awarded remedy to give effect to representations: at [78]; the case was disapproved on other grounds by *Re North Eastern Property Buyers Litigation* [2010] EWHC 2991 (Ch), [2010] All ER (D) 275 (Nov)). For discussion of

It is clear, however, that an equity by estoppel is treated as having the character of an interest in property; and, at least in relation to registered land, the equity by estoppel and the 'mere equity'[103] are treated identically in this respect by section 116 of the Land Registration Act 2002.[104] It may well be that an equity by estoppel is in the process of being accepted not simply as an equity—the right to an equitable remedy[105]—but as a new form of property in its own right. This, together with the conveyancing difficulties that arise from the acceptance of the proposition that an equity by estoppel can bind successors, are discussed later.[106]

---

whether the original representor remains personally liable after disposal of the land, see [2005] Conv 14 (S Bright and B McFarlane).

[103] Above, p 905.

[104] In this respect, the fact that an equity arising by estoppel can bind a purchaser is more problematic than the fact that a 'mere equity' can. For in the case of a mere equity the nature of the right to which the purchaser is subject is more closely circumscribed, since an equity is generally defined by reference to the right to a particular equitable remedy (such as rescission or rectification) above, p 903.

[105] Above, p 903.   [106] Below, pp 942 ff.

E LICENCES

Summary

23

LICENCES[1]

Summary

As we have seen, a licence is essentially a permission to enter upon the land of another for an agreed purpose.[2] The permission justifies what would otherwise have been a trespass.[3] The main issues through the years have been whether the licensee is entitled to protection against eviction by the licensor, and, if so, whether that protection is effective also against third-party transferees from the licensor. In both these issues, the availability of equitable remedies after the passing of the Supreme Court of Judicature Act 1875 played an important part, and in more recent years the development of the doctrine of proprietary estoppel has revolutionised the position of the licensee. Under that doctrine a licensee may be entitled, not only to protection from eviction, but also to a transfer of the interest or estate in the land that the licensor, by his acts or statements, had led the licensee to expect to receive.[4] Further, licensees have sometimes been protected by finding that a constructive trust arises in their favour, and this jurisdiction to find a constructive trust has been widened and developed in recent years.[5]

---

[1] See generally Dawson and Pearce, *Licences Relating to the Occupation or Use of Land* (1979); Sharples, *Land Licences* (2011); M & B pp 1080–116, (1954) 70 LQR 326 (Lord Evershed).

[2] Above, p 649.

[3] *Thomas v Sorrell* (1673) Vaugh 330, 351 (Vaughan CJ).

[4] Above, pp 916–19; below, pp 937–40.

[5] Below, pp 933 ff.

The facts in the cases will show the wide variety of circumstances in which questions of the protection of licensees can arise. They range from a visit to the grandstand at Doncaster race-course in 1845[6] to the provision of a house for a mistress in more modern times.[7] The courts have been astute to adapt the law of licences to solve problems arising from the occupation of a quasi-matrimonial home.

I THE LICENSEE AT COMMON LAW

Licences at common law may be divided into three categories:

A BARE OR GRATUITOUS LICENCE

A bare or gratuitous licence is a mere permission for the licensee to enter upon the licensor's land, such as when permission is given to play cricket on a field. This permission may be withdrawn at any time by the licensor, although the licensee cannot be treated as a trespasser until a reasonable time after notice that the licence has been or will be withdrawn.[8]

B LICENCE COUPLED WITH A GRANT OR INTEREST

A licence *coupled with a grant or interest*, on the other hand, may be irrevocable. It is said to be coupled with a grant or interest when the licensee, having been granted a definite proprietary interest in the land or in chattels lying on the land, is given permission to enter in order that he may enjoy or exploit the interest. Such a licence, as distinct from a *bare* licence, is of this nature if given to one who is entitled to chattels,[9] or to growing timber[10] or to game on the land.[11] There are here two separate matters—the grant and the licence: 'a licence to hunt in a man's park and to carry away the deer killed to his own use; to cut down a tree in a man's ground and to carry it away the next day after to his own use, are licences as to the acts of hunting and cutting down the tree; but as to the carrying away of the deer killed and the tree cut they are grants.'[12]

---

[6] *Wood v Leadbitter* (1845) 13 M & W 838, below, p 928, n 23.

[7] There are many cases; see, eg, *Chandler v Kerley* [1978] 1 WLR 693, below, p 929 (contractual licences); *Pascoe v Turner* [1971] 1 WLR 431, below, p 939 (proprietary estoppel).

[8] *R v Doncaster MBC ex p Braim* (1989) 57 P & CR 1, 15–16; *E & L Berg Homes Ltd v Grey* (1979) 253 EG 473, applying to a bare licence the principles applicable in this respect to contractual licences in *Minister of Health v Bellotti* [1944] KB 298, below, p 927, n 21.

[9] *Wood v Manley* (1839) 11 Ad & El 34.

[10] *James Jones & Sons Ltd v Earl of Tankerville* [1909] 2 Ch 440.

[11] *Frogley v Earl of Lovelace* (1859) John 333. See also *Vaughan v Hampson* (1875) 33 LT 15 (right of solicitor to attend a creditors' meeting), described as a 'curiosity' in *Hounslow LBC v Twickenham Garden Developments Ltd* [1971] Ch 233, 254.

[12] *Thomas v Sorrell* (1673) Vaugh 330, 551 (Vaughan CJ).

Such a licence is not effective at common law unless the grant is formally valid. Thus a grant merely by writing of a right to shoot and carry away game, coupled with a licence to enter the land, is ineffective, since a deed is necessary at common law for the grant of a profit à prendre.[13] But under the doctrine of *Walsh v Lonsdale*[14] a specifically enforceable contract to grant an interest is treated in equity as if the formalities required by law had been observed. Thus a contract to grant a right of shooting over land is as effective, as between the parties, as an actual grant by way of deed;[15] to be enforceable against third parties it must be protected by a notice in the register[16] or, in unregistered land, registered as an estate contract under the Land Charges Act 1972.[17]

Where the licence is coupled with a grant or interest, the licensor cannot revoke it if the licensee is thereby prevented from exploiting the interest that the licensor has granted to him.[18] The revocability of the licence therefore depends upon the construction and enforceability of the grant.

C CONTRACTUAL LICENCE

A contractual licence is a licence supported by consideration, such as where the licensee buys a ticket for a race meeting or a theatre,[19] or where he is contractually entitled to the exclusive privilege of supplying refreshment in a theatre.[20] Even when it is revoked in accordance with the terms of the contract, the licensee must be given a reasonable time to leave the premises.[21]

D REMEDIES FOR WRONGFUL REVOCATION

In considering the effect of these licences as between licensor and licensee, the common law drew a distinction between a mere licence, whether gratuitous or contractual, and a licence coupled with a grant.[22] We have seen that a licence coupled with a grant

---

[13] *Wood v Leadbitter* (1845) 13 M & W 838, M & B p 1083. For the formalities for the grant of a profit à prendre, see above, p 713.

[14] Below, p 978.

[15] *Frogley v Earl of Lovelace* (1859) John 333.

[16] LRA 2002, s 32; below, p 1097.

[17] LCA 1972, s 2(4) Class C(iv); below, pp 1058.

[18] *Australian Blue Metal Ltd v Hughes* [1963] AC 74, 94.

[19] *Wood v Leadbitter* (1845) 13 M & W 838; *Hurst v Picture Theatres Ltd* [1915] 1 KB 1.

[20] *Frank Warr & Co Ltd v LCC* [1904] 1 KB 713.

[21] *Minister of Health v Bellotti* [1944] KB 298; *Greater London Council v Jenkins* [1975] 1 WLR 155, 158 (Lord Diplock); *Canadian Pacific Rly Co v R* [1931] AC 414; *Australian Blue Metal Ltd v Hughes* [1963] AC 74; *Wallshire Ltd v Advertising Sites Ltd* [1988] 2 EGLR 167; *Express Newspapers plc v Silverstone Circuits Ltd,* The Times, 20 June 1989 (right to place advertisements on bridge at Woodcote Corner); *Re Hampstead Garden Suburb Institute,* The Times, 13 April 1995 (nine months' notice given to school 'for all purposes from four to four score' held to be inadequate by any standards of reasonableness; public nature of licensee's function, known to the licensor, taken into account); [1996] CLJ 229 (T Kerbal). For the abandonment of a licence, see *Bone v Bone* [1992] EGCS 81 (no formalities are necessary: 'it is enough that the parties have so conducted themselves that it ought to be inferred that they have mutually agreed to bring the contract to an end').

[22] For a doctrine of long standing, but little relied on, that a licence is irrevocable if it has been acted on, see *Webb v Paternoster* (1619) Palm 71; *Hounslow LBC v Twickenham Garden Developments Ltd* [1971] Ch 233, 255; (1965) 29 Conv (NS) 19 (MC Cullity).

may be irrevocable. On the other hand the early cases[23] held that a mere licence may, at common law, be revoked at any moment, even where the licensee had entered by contract, and the revocation of the licence by the licensor was in breach of contract. The licence itself did not endure beyond the (wrongful) revocation: the licensee became a trespasser, and liable to be evicted. He had to be satisfied with a financial remedy for breach of contract.[24]

II CONTRACTUAL LICENCE: THE INTERVENTION OF EQUITY

The tide turned with the availability of equitable remedies after 1875. In *Hurst v Picture Theatres Ltd*:[25]

> Hurst purchased a ticket to attend the cinema. The proprietors, erroneously thinking that he had not paid for the ticket, evicted him, using no more force than was reasonably necessary. Hurst successfully sued for damages for assault.

The matter was authoritatively settled by the House of Lords in *Winter Garden Theatre (London) Ltd v Millennium Productions Ltd*.[26] This case finally established that the rights of the parties to a contractual licence must be determined upon the proper construction of the contract. Their Lordships favoured the argument that, if on its construction a contractual licence is irrevocable, then, even though it is not coupled with a grant, its revocation in breach of the contract should be prevented where possible[27] by the grant of an injunction.[28] In other words, equity does what it

---

[23] *Wood v Leadbitter* (1845) 13 M & W 838; *Thompson v Park* [1944] KB 408.

[24] *Kerrison v Smith* [1897] 2 QB 445 (the first case to decide that an action will lie for damages for revoking a licence); *Tanner v Tanner* [1975] 1 WLR 1346, below, p 929.

[25] [1915] 1 KB 1, M & B p 1083. See also *Cowell v Rosehill Racecourse Co Ltd* (1937) 56 CLR 605, M & B p 1084.

[26] [1948] AC 173, M & B p 1088; for a critique of this case, see *Hounslow LBC v Twickenham Garden Developments Ltd* [1971] Ch 233, 245 ff; (1971) 87 LQR 309; *Mayfield Holdings Ltd v Moana Reef Ltd* [1973] 1 NZLR 309.

[27] *Thompson v Park* [1944] KB 408 (where an injunction was refused to a licensee who 'had been guilty at least of riot, affray, wilful damage, forcible entry and, perhaps, conspiracy': Goddard LJ at 409); *Brynowen Estates Ltd v Bourne* (1981) 131 NLJ 1212; cf *Williams v Staite* [1979] Ch 291 (effect of misbehaviour by estoppel licensee); *J Willis & Son v Willis* [1986] 1 EGLR 62, below, p 942. See also *Ivory v Palmer* [1975] ICR 340 (licensee, whose occupation of premises was dependent on his employment, not protected when dismissed in breach of contract).

For a possession action by a licensee against a trespasser on the land that the licensee occupies, even though not in de facto occupation of it, see *Manchester Airport plc v Dutton* [2000] QB 133; [1999] Conv 535 (E Paton and G Seabourne); cf *Countryside Residential (North Thames) Ltd v Tugwell* [2000] 2 EGLR 59.

[28] The House of Lords construed the licence as being revocable by the licensor, and so their views were obiter. The Court of Appeal, however, had construed it as irrevocable and had protected the licensee by granting an injunction against the licensor: [1946] 1 All ER 678, 684 (Lord Greene MR), M & B p 1089. For a full discussion of contractual licences, see Megarry J in *Hounslow LBC v Twickenham Garden Developments Ltd* [1971] Ch 233, where this approach was followed.

can by means of a decree of injunction to preserve the sanctity of a bargain[29] and by that remedy it is prepared to restrain a revocation that would derogate from the right of occupation conferred by the contract. If the contract does not expressly state the time for which the licence is to last, a promise by the licensor must be implied that he will not revoke the permission in a manner contrary to the intention of the parties.[30] The exact scope of the implied promise, if any, must be ascertained in each case, for it will, of course, vary with the circumstances. For example, a spectator who buys a ticket for a theatre is a licensee with a right to occupy his seat until the spectacle is over;[31] a licence of the 'front of the house rights' at a theatre cannot be revoked until a reasonable time has been afforded to the licensee for his withdrawal.[32] In those cases such as *Hurst v Picture Theatres Ltd*, where there is no time or opportunity to obtain an injunction, the court will presumably give judgment on the basis of what the rights of the parties would have been, had the grant of this remedy been practicable.

The injunction will last for the period of the contract or for such other period as the court thinks appropriate. The situation is simpler where, as in the *Winter Garden* case, there is an express contract. But the courts have, in some cases, including family or 'mistress' situations, found the existence of a contractual licence where the evidence of the contract was of the flimsiest. Indeed, in *Tanner v Tanner*,[33] where the mistress had vacated the premises in obedience to an order of the lower court, and an injunction would have been sterile, Lord Denning went so far as to say that the court should 'imply a contract by him ... or if need be impose the equivalent of a contract by him'.[34] Similarly, in *Hardwick v Johnson*[35] and *Chandler v Kerley*[36] contractual licences were found. In the latter case:

> Mr and Mrs K jointly purchased a house intending it to be their matrimonial home, the mortgage payments being made by Mr K. On the breakdown of the marriage, Mr K left, never to return, and Mrs K remained with their two children. She became the mistress of C, who moved into the house with her. Mr K then ceased to pay the mortgage instalments, and Mrs K and he tried without success to sell the house for £14,300. Finally C purchased it from them for £10,000, out of which the mortgagee was repaid and the balance divided

[29] *Winter Garden Theatre (London) Ltd v Millennium Productions Ltd*, above, at 202 (Lord Uthwatt).

[30] *Errington v Errington and Woods* [1952] 1 KB 290. See also *Roach v Johannes* [1976] CLY 1549 (licence of 'paying guest' terminable on giving reasonable notice, which in the circumstances was not less than 21 days).

[31] *Hurst v Picture Theatres Ltd*, above.

[32] *Winter Garden Theatre (London) Ltd v Millennium Productions Ltd*, above.

[33] [1975] 1 WLR 1346; cf *Horrocks v Forray* [1976] 1 WLR 230 where no contract was implied in similar circumstances (described in (1976) 40 Conv (NS) 362 (M Richards) as '*Tanner v Tanner* in a middle class setting'); *Coombes v Smith* [1986] 1 WLR 808, above, p 915, n 64 (no contract implied that man would provide mistress with house for rest of her life).

[34] At 1350.

[35] [1978] 1 WLR 683, M & B p 1093 (mother purchased house for son and his bride, who were to pay her £7 a week; on breakdown of marriage son left bride, now pregnant, for another woman. Mother sued for possession. Daughter-in-law held entitled to protection as contractual licensee for indefinite period on payment of £7 a week). Lord Denning at 688 would have preferred to find a personal 'equitable licence', following his own decision in *Errington v Errington and Woods* [1952] 1 KB 290, below, p 931.

[36] [1978] 1 WLR 693, M & B p 1090.

between Mr and Mrs K. Six weeks later C terminated the relationship with Mrs K and claimed possession of the house. Mrs K claimed that she was a licensee for life or for so long as the children remained in her custody. The Court of Appeal held that she was a contractual licensee for a period terminable on twelve months' notice.

It is possible even for the contractual licensee to obtain specific performance of the contractual licence. In *Verrall v Great Yarmouth Borough Council*:[37]

The Conservative council granted a licence to the National Front to hold its annual conference at the Wellington Pier Pavilion for £6,000. After the local government elections, the new Labour council purported to revoke the licence.

Granting specific performance of the contractual licence, Lord Denning MR said:[38]

Since the *Winter Garden* case, it is clear that once a man has entered under his contract of licence, he cannot be turned out. An injunction can be obtained against the licensor to prevent his being turned out. On principle it is the same if it happens before he enters. If he has a contractual right to enter, and the licensor refuses to let him come in, then he can come to the court and in a proper case get an order for specific performance to allow him to come in.

III CONTRACTUAL LICENCE AND THIRD PARTIES

Once the courts had given specific protection to a contractual licensee against the licensor, the next question inevitably arose—whether that protection was good against a third party. On the one hand, protection of a licensee may be of little value if the licensor can defeat him by transfer to a third party. On the other hand, protection of the licensee against third parties goes a long way towards the recognition of a licence as an interest in land.[39]

A bare licence is revocable by the licensor at any time. It clearly, therefore, does not bind his successors in title. If, however, the licence is coupled with a grant or interest, it is irrevocable by the licensor as long as the grant or interest is irrevocable. If, therefore, the interest binds a third party, the licence will bind him also.

The main controversy has been in relation to contractual licences and third parties. On principle, a contract between A and B is not capable of imposing a burden on C.[40] Nor is it an answer to say that, on the principle of *Tulk v Moxhay*,[41] the fact that A has

---

[37] [1981] QB 202, M & B p 609. For the reasons given by the court for exercising its discretion to grant specific performance in the interests of freedom of speech, see at 216–18.

[38] At 216.

[39] On the nature of an interest in land, see above, p 4; and (in the context of licences) *National Provincial Bank Ltd v Ainsworth* [1965] AC 1175, 1248 (Lord Wilberforce: a property right must be 'definable, identifiable by third parties, capable in its nature of assumption by third parties, and have some degree of permanence or stability'); below, p 943.

[40] Anson, pp 652 ff.

[41] Above, p 732.

to the rights of Mrs Evans, were bound by a constructive trust and so could not ignore them; and, on the other hand, on the wider ground that the contractual licence gave rise at the outset to an equitable interest that bound the claimants to permit her to reside in the cottage during her life or as long as she wished. It is submitted that the former view is preferable. It is difficult to see how the wider view is consistent with earlier authority on contractual licences, and the expressions of opinion in the House of Lords in *National Provincial Bank Ltd v Ainsworth*.

Clearly these cases provide no support for the view that contractual licences generally are binding on third parties.[54] Moreover, in *Ashburn Anstalt v Arnold*[55] the Court of Appeal held, obiter, that, where land was conveyed to a purchaser expressly 'subject to' a contractual licence, the licence was not a property interest and therefore not enforceable against the third party. In rejecting the wide implications of *Errington v Errington and Woods* and *Binions v Evans*, Fox LJ emphasised that there was no other case in which a contractual licence had been held to bind a third party in the absence of a finding that the third party took the land as a constructive trustee:

> The far-reaching statement of principle in *Errington* was not supported by authority, not necessary for the decision of the case and *per incuriam* in the sense that it was made without reference to authorities which, if they would not have compelled, would surely have per-suaded the court to adopt a different ratio. Of course, the law must be free to develop. But as a response to problems which had arisen, the *Errington* rule (without more) was neither practically necessary nor theoretically convincing. By contrast, the finding on appropriate facts of a constructive trust may well be regarded as a beneficial adaptation of old rules to new situations.[56]

IV LICENCE PROTECTED BY CONSTRUCTIVE TRUST

We have seen that gratuitous licences and contractual licences do not of themselves constitute interests in land, and so do not bind third parties. The analysis of a person's occupation of land as constituting a gratuitous or contractual licence does not however preclude the finding that some other interest has also been created that is an interest in land and that is therefore capable of binding a third party. In particular, the courts will consider whether the person is in occupation of the land pursuant to a constructive trust or has an interest protected under the doctrine of proprietary estoppel.[57]

---

54 Nor does *Midland Bank Ltd v Farmpride Hatcheries Ltd* (1980) 260 EG 493, where the issue was not raised; above, p 88, n 117.

55 [1989] Ch 1, M & B p 1104. The case was decided against the purchaser on the ground that the agreement created a tenancy that was binding on him. See also *Patel v Patel* (CA, 30 June 1983), where Slade LJ said: 'A mere licence to occupy land, albeit of a contractual nature, as opposed to a lease, does not confer any interest on the licensee in the land'.

56 [1989] Ch 1, 22.

57 In *Ashburn Anstalt v Arnold* [1989] Ch 1, for example, the Court of Appeal held that the contractual licence did not create an interest in land; they went on however to consider whether the facts also gave rise

A few cases have been decided on the basis of a constructive trust. Such a trust arises by operation of law when the court is of the opinion that it is in the interests of justice or for the prevention of unjust enrichment that such a trust should be found.[58]

The first, *Bannister v Bannister*,[59] could more appropriately have been decided under the doctrine of proprietary estoppel;[60] but the protection of licences by proprietary estoppel had not generally been recognised in 1948. In that case:

> the defendant, who owned two cottages, sold them in 1943 to her brother-in-law, the claimant, for £250 (which was £150 below market price). They made an oral agreement under which the brother-in-law would let her stay in one of the cottages 'as long as you like, rent free'. In 1945 the defendant gave up possession of the cottage except for one room. In 1947 the brother-in-law claimed possession of the room on the ground that she was a tenant at will.

The defendant was unable to rely on an express trust, because that was required to be in writing.[61] The Court of Appeal, however, held that it would be a fraud to disregard the oral trust and that she was entitled under a constructive trust to a life interest determinable upon her ceasing to reside in the cottage.

Re Sharpe[62] could likewise have been decided under the doctrine of proprietary estoppel. In that case:

> an elderly aunt lent money to her nephew to purchase and improve a house on the understanding that she would live there and be looked after by the nephew and his wife for the rest of her life. The aunt moved in, and the nephew went bankrupt. His trustee in bankruptcy then entered into a contract to sell the house with vacant possession to a purchaser, and sought to recover possession of the house from the aunt.

Holding that the aunt was entitled under a constructive trust as against the trustee to remain in the house until she was repaid[63] the sums she advanced, Browne-Wilkinson J said:[64]

> In my judgment, whether it be called a contractual licence or an equitable licence or an interest under a constructive trust, the aunt would be entitled as against the nephew to

to a constructive trust, which would have created such an interest. They found that, on the facts, there was no constructive trust.

[58] See generally Oakley, *Constructive Trusts* (3rd edn, 1997), pp 53 ff; H & M, ch 12, esp pp 337–43; Maudsley and Burn, *Trusts and Trustees* (7th edn, 2008), ch 7; Snell, paras 26–009 to 26–010 (trust to prevent wrongdoing by the trustee).

[59] [1948] 2 All ER 133, M & B p 1101; *Hussey v Palmer* [1972] 1 WLR 1286.   [60] Below, p 936.

[61] LPA 1925, s 53(1); below, p 1010.

[62] [1980] 1 WLR 219, M & B p 1109; [1980] Conv 207 (J Martin); (1980) 96 LQR 336 (G Woodman). In *Bristol and West Building Society v Henning* [1985] 1 WLR 778, Browne-Wilkinson LJ said at 783 that 'nothing in this judgment should be taken as expressing any view on the question … whether the decision in *Re Sharpe* was correct.'

[63] The purchaser was not a party to the action, and it was left open whether he was also bound.

[64] [1980] 1 WLR 219, 224, 225. See *Re Basham* [1986] 1 WLR 1498, 1504, where Edward Nugee QC, holding that a claim for proprietary estoppel succeeded, treated it 'as giving rise to a species of constructive trust'; [1981] Conv 211 (J Martin); [1987] CLJ 215 (D Hayton). See also Sir Christopher Slade, *The Informal Creation of Interests in Land* (1984) Child & Co Oxford Lecture, 12.

stay in the house… The introduction of a constructive trust is an essential ingredient if the plaintiff has any right at all.

In *Hussey v Palmer*[65] and *Binions v Evans*[66] (where the constructive trust was relied on as a second ground) the constructive trust was described as an available remedy in the widest terms. Such a remedy is both too wide and too severe. 'The dicta are… certainly fine sounding, but one needs more guidance as to when such trusts will be implied.'[67]

In *Ashburn Anstalt v Arnold*[68] the Court of Appeal took the view that the mere fact that land is expressed to be conveyed 'subject to' a contract does not necessarily imply that the grantee is to be under an obligation, not otherwise existing, to give effect to the provisions of the contract:

The Court will not impose a constructive trust unless it is satisfied that the conscience of the estate owner is affected… The words 'subject to' will, of course, impose notice. But notice is not enough to impose on somebody an obligation to give effect to a contract into which he did not enter.[69]

Binions v Evans was regarded as a legitimate application of the doctrine of constructive trusts, since the facts that the Tredegar Estate provided the purchasers with a copy of the agreement with Mrs Evans, and that the purchasers paid a reduced purchase price, indicated that the intention of the Estate and the purchasers was that the purchasers should give effect to Mrs Evans's agreement. If they had failed to do so, the Estate would have been liable in damages to Mrs Evans.[70]

---

[65] [1972] 1 WLR 1286 (elderly widow, invited to live with daughter and son-in-law, paid cost of extra bedroom built onto house for her accommodation; held entitled to recover money when she left). See also *DHN Food Distributors Ltd v Tower Hamlets LBC* [1976] 1 WLR 852 (irrevocable contractual licence that gave rise to constructive trust, under which DHN had 'a sufficient interest in the land to qualify them for disturbance' upon compulsory purchase by local authority); (1977) 93 LQR 170 (D Sugarman and F Webb); (1977) 41 Conv (NS) 73; *Sparkes v Smart* [1990] 2 EGLR 245 (collusive transaction between purchaser of freehold farm and ageing tenant, purchaser's father-in-law, with object of destroying youngest son's tenancy; CA held, obiter, constructive trust in favour of the son).

[66] [1972] Ch 359.   [67] [1973] CLJ 142 (RJ Smith).

[68] [1989] Ch 1, M & B p 1104. The Appellate Committee dismissed a petition for leave to appeal [1989] Ch 32; [1988] CLJ 353 (AJ Oakley); 104 LQR 175 (P Sparkes); 51 MLR 226 (J Hill); Conv 201 (MP Thompson); All ER Rev 176 (PJ Clarke).

[69] Ibid, 25 (Fox LJ). See also *IDC Group Ltd v Clark* [1992] 1 EGLR 187, where Sir Nicolas Browne-Wilkinson V-C said at 189: 'The Court of Appeal put what I hope is the *quietus* to the heresy that a mere licence creates an interest in land. They also put the *quietus* to the heresy that parties to a contractual licence necessarily become constructive trustees'. See also *Canadian Imperial Bank of Commerce v Bello* (1991) 64 P & CR 48, 51–2; *Lloyd v Dugdale* [2001] EWCA Civ 1754, [2002] 2 P & CR 13 at [52] (Sir Christopher Slade). A purchaser may, however, make a bargain with the vendor that he undertakes *de novo* to honour existing contractual obligations: *IDC Group Ltd v Clark* [1992] 1 EGLR 187, 190, approving the analysis of Dillon J in *Lyus v Prowsa Developments Ltd* [1982] 1 WLR 1044; *Chattey v Farndale Holdings Inc* (1996) 75 P & CR 298, 313, 317. Such a bargain may now be enforceable by the licensee *in contract* under the Contracts (Rights of Third Parties) Act 1999: see above, p 743; p 932, n 53.

[70] In *Ashburn Anstalt v Arnold* the purchaser had not paid a reduced price, nor would the licensor have been liable in damages to the licensee.

The remedy of the constructive trust is also too severe. For if it creates undocumented proprietary interests in land,[71] it can cause difficulties for the conveyancing system. If the constructive trust creates an equitable fee simple, it will be one that is not registrable, though it may be overreachable;[72] and if it creates an interest for life, in the case of trusts created before 1997[73] it could bring the provisions of the Settled Land Act 1925 into operation. The problem will be discussed in more detail below,[74] where it will be seen that a similar problem arises on the application of the doctrine of proprietary estoppel.

V LICENCE PROTECTED BY PROPRIETARY ESTOPPEL

The doctrine of proprietary estoppel has undergone a remarkable development over the last 50 years; and this has occurred largely in the context of licences. We have already seen in Chapter 22 the circumstances in which proprietary estoppel will arise, and the principles by which the courts will remedy it. We shall here explain something of the use that can be made of it in order to protect a licensee who is not otherwise adequately protected under a bare licence, a licence coupled with an interest, or a contractual licence.[75]

A THE DOCTRINE IN OUTLINE

As we have seen,[76] the general principle of proprietary estoppel is that where one party (A) makes a representation or promise to another party (B) to the effect that B has or shall have an interest in, or right over, A's property, or acquiesces in B's mistaken belief that he has or shall have such an interest or right, then if in the circumstances B is reasonably entitled to act in reliance to his detriment on the representation, promise or mistaken belief, and B does so act in reliance, equity may intervene to prevent (*estop*) A from asserting his own strict legal rights to his property. The doctrine can be traced back to older cases, in a wide range of situations.[77] But much of its revival and development during the twentieth century occurred in licence cases. We have already noted that in some cases courts strove to find other principles to protect the licensee, which might now better be decided under the developed doctrine of proprietary

---

[71] For the view that a constructive trust in this situation creates a personal right, rather than an interest in the property, see (2004) 120 LQR 667 (B McFarlane).

[72] See *Hodgson v Marks* [1971] Ch 892.   [73] TLATA 1996, s 2(1).   [74] Below, p 944.

[75] On the relationship between contractual licences and proprietary estoppel, see the controversy between [1981] Conv 212; [1983] Conv 285 (A Briggs) and [1983] Conv 50, 471 (MP Thompson).

[76] Above, p 909.   [77] Above, p 908.

estoppel.[78] The advantage of proprietary estoppel is its great flexibility.[79] Once it is established that an estoppel is working in favour of a licensee—that is an equity has arisen[80]—the court will decide which of the available remedies is most appropriate.[81] As has been said many times in the cases:

> The court must look at the circumstances in each case to decide in what way the equity can be satisfied.[82]

Moreover, the remedy may be negative or positive; personal to the licensee or an interest in the property that will protect him against third parties; the enforcement of the licence by means of a right of occupation, or only the right to reimbursement of expenditure incurred by the licensor.[83] Some examples will be given here.

B ILLUSTRATIONS OF THE REMEDIES AVAILABLE TO PROTECT LICENSEE

(1) Negative Protection to Prevent Revocation of Licence

Once an equity arising by estoppel is established, the court may grant a remedy that is, essentially, negative: preventing the licensor from revoking the licence by refusing his claim for possession, or perhaps by granting to the licensor an injunction to prevent revocation. In *Inwards v Baker*:[84]

---

[78] *Bannister v Bannister* [1948] 2 All ER 133, M & B p 1101, above, p 934 (constructive trust); *Errington v Errington and Woods* [1952] 1 KB 290, above, p 931 (contractual licence); *Re Sharpe* [1980] 1 WLR 219, M & B p 1109, above, p 934 (constructive trust).

[79] This flexibility is also, however, a disadvantage of the doctrine, at least as regards third-party purchasers who can be bound by the equity before knowing what remedy the court may attach to it: below, p 945.

[80] Above, pp 909 ff.

[81] Above, pp 917 ff; Pawlowski, *The Doctrine of Proprietary Estoppel*, pp 43–71. See *Lord Cawdor v Lewis* (1835) 1 Y & C Ex 427, 433; *Plimmer v Wellington Corp* (1884) 9 App Cas 699, 713, 714, M & B p 1065.

[82] *Plimmer v City of Wellington Corp*, above, at 713. See also, in particular, *Crabb v Arun DC* [1976] Ch 179, 193 (Scarman LJ: 'what is the relief appropriate to satisfy the equity?'). For the nature and scope of the court's discretion, see *Jennings v Rice* [2002] EWCA Civ 159, [2003] 1 P & CR 8, above, p 917.

[83] Sometimes, by the time the case is heard, the facts are such that no substantive award is appropriate: above, p 916, n 75.

[84] [1965] 2 QB 29, M & B p 1049; (1965) 81 LQR 183 (RH Maudsley). Cf *Sledmore v Dalby* (1996) 72 P & CR 196, M & B p 1045; [1997] CLJ 34 (P Milne); [1997] Conv 458 (JE Adams), in which the trial judge held that the defendant had a personal licence to occupy; reversed by CA on the basis that the equity arising by estoppel had expired; *Parker v Parker* [2003] EWHC 1846 (Ch), [2003] All ER (D) 421 (Jul) (9th Earl of Mansfield could not establish estoppel entitling him to possession for life of Shirburn Castle, Oxfordshire, a 'sleeping beauty of a castle', but had licence terminable on two years' notice once negotiations for his long-term occupation broke down); [2004] Conv 516 (MP Thompson); *Clark v Clark* [2006] EWHC 275 (Ch), [2006] 1 FCR 421 at [43]-[45] (company to be allowed to use accessway for purpose of business, but not for an indefinite period: it would no longer be unconscionable for landowner to claim back his land if company ceased to carry on same business, or ceased to provide a living for landowner and his brother, its sole and equal shareholders); *Stallion v Albert Stallion Holdings (Great Britain) Ltd* [2009] EWHC 1950 (Ch), [2010] 2 FLR 78 (wife induced to consent to divorce and not seek ancillary relief: residence rent free for life but without exclusive possession, unless and until property sold).

B's son wished to build a bungalow on land which he had hoped to purchase, but the project was beyond his means. B then said to his son 'Why not put the bungalow on my land and make the bungalow a little bigger?' The son did so, building it mainly through his own labour and expense. He lived there continuously until B died in 1951, and then from B's death until the proceedings began in 1963. B had left the land elsewhere in a will dated 1922 to trustees on trust for sale in favour of others. When the trustees sought possession, the Court of Appeal held that the son 'can remain there as long as he desires to use it as his home'.[85]

In this case, therefore, the son was given a remedy that vindicated his expectation:[86] he claimed that he was given an oral licence for his lifetime, and relied to his detriment accordingly; and the court used a negative remedy to give effect to that licence, by refusing to grant possession of the property to the legal owner. The court had to have recourse to the principles of equity because there was here no contract on which a remedy could be based.[87] But finding an equity, and not simply a contract, moves the protection for the licensee into the realm of property, since it can be enforced against a purchaser from the licensor. In *Inwards v Baker* itself, the licence was enforceable against the volunteer trustees who took under the licensor's will. But Lord Denning MR made clear that the equity was also capable of binding a purchaser with notice.[88]

(2) Positive Protection by the Grant of a Property Right

In some cases the courts have gone further, and have held that the proper remedy to satisfy the equity is the grant to the licensee of a particular right in the property. Most such cases[89] have not involved simple licences: the court orders the grant of a property right because that is what the representee was reasonably led to believe that he had, or would obtain—that is the claim is not based on a licence to occupy the land, but on the representation that an interest in the property itself (beyond the licence to occupy) was granted or promised by the legal owner.

---

[85] [1965] 2 QB 29, 37 (Lord Denning MR).

[86] On the general question of when the courts will think it appropriate to grant a remedy to protect the representee's expectation, or only the value of his reliance, see above, pp 917–19. In *Inwards v Baker* the son claimed only that he had been promised a licence for life, and did not pursue a claim that he had been promised or given the fee simple: [1965] 2 QB 29, 30–1. Contrast, however, *Dillwyn v Llewelyn* (1862) 4 De GF & J 517 where the father had signed an unexecuted and gratuitous memorandum of conveyance in favour of his son, and the son had spent no less than £14,000 in building himself a home, with his father's knowledge and approval. The House of Lords ordered a conveyance of the land without payment. It might be thought, in either of the cases, that a better solution, to balance the positions of the licensee and the licensor (or his successor), would have been to give the son the option of taking a conveyance of the land on payment of site value or of receiving compensation for the value of his expenditure on the land.

[87] [1965] 2 QB 29, 37 (Lord Denning MR).

[88] Ibid, 37. For further discussion of the proprietary effect of proprietary estoppel, see above, pp 920–2; below, pp 941–2.

[89] See above, pp 916 ff.

However, there are cases in which the remedy has been awarded in order to protect what might otherwise have been simply a licence to occupy. In *Pascoe v Turner*:[90]

> In 1963 P, a businessman, and T, a widow with an invalidity pension and a small amount of capital, lived together in his house. In 1965 P purchased another house, into which they moved and lived as man and wife. In 1973 P started an affair with another woman. T remained in the house and was told by P that the house and everything in it was hers. In reliance on this statement, T spent, to P's knowledge, her own money on repairs and improvements, and also on furniture. P moved out in 1973 when the relationship ended, and in 1976 he gave T two months' notice to determine the licence.

In defence to P's claim for possession, T sought a declaration that the house and its contents were hers, and that P held the house on trust for her; alternatively, that P had given her a licence to occupy the house for her lifetime, and that P was estopped from denying the licence. The Court of Appeal held that there was a gift of the contents, since T was in possession of them as a bailee when P declared the gift. As far as the house was concerned, there was no valid declaration of trust,[91] but an estoppel arose in her favour. However, the court rejected a solution that would give T a licence to occupy the house for her lifetime, and ordered that the fee simple be conveyed to her. Only in this way could the defendant be 'assured of security of tenure, quiet enjoyment, and freedom of action in respect of repairs and improvements without interference from the plaintiff'.[92] Instead of granting a life interest to T, as a result of which she might have become tenant for life under the Settled Land Act 1925,[93] and leaving her to her remedies in tort against P, if necessary, the Court awarded T the fee simple of a house worth £16,000 at the time of the judgment for an outlay of less than £1,000. It may be thought that this solution was extreme.

In *Sledmore v Dalby*,[94] by contrast, the Court of Appeal rejected a claim for the conveyance of the fee simple.

> The licensee had carried out substantial works to a house, on the encouragement of the licensor, in order to improve it as a family home. He had enjoyed 18 years' free occupation, had little need for the property, and the licensor was in serious financial difficulty; she was on income support and her mortgage interest, which was in arrears, was being paid by the Department of Social Security.

The Court held that the licensee's equity had now expired and therefore the owner was entitled to possession of the house. Hobhouse LJ[95] adopted the approach of the

90 [1979] 1 WLR 431, M & B p 1056; [1979] Conv 379 (FR Crane); (1979) 42 MLR 574 (B Sufrin). Cf *Dillwyn v Llewelyn* (1862) 4 De GF & J 517, above, n 86; *Voyce v Voyce* (1991) 62 P & CR 290 (donee of farm and cottage from licensor ordered to convey fee simple to licensee).

91 It was not evidenced in writing as required by LPA 1925, s 53(1)(b), below, p 1010.

92 [1979] 1 WLR 431, 438.

93 For the powers of a tenant for life, see above, p 443. And for the problem that, before 1997, a settlement might have been created by awarding a licence for life, see below, p 944.

94 (1996) 72 P & CR 196, M & B 1045; [1997] CLJ 34 (P Milne); [1997] Conv 458 (JE Adams).

95 Ibid, 208.

High Court of Australia in *Commonwealth of Australia v Verwayen* where Mason CJ said:[96]

> A central element of the doctrine of estoppel is that there must be a proportionality between the remedy and the detriment that is its purpose to avoid. It would be wholly inequitable and unjust to insist upon a disproportionate making good of the relevant assumption.

(3) Licence to Occupy until Expenditure Reimbursed

In some cases the courts have held that the equity arising by estoppel can most appropriately be satisfied by ordering that the licensor repay the expenditure incurred by the licensee in reliance on the representation that he had a licence to occupy. For example, in *Dodsworth v Dodsworth*:[97]

> the claimant lived alone in a bungalow. Her younger brother and his wife, the two defendants, returned to England from Australia and were looking for a home. The claimant persuaded them to join her in her bungalow. They did so, and spent some £700 on improvements to the bungalow, in the expectation, encouraged and induced by the claimant, that the defendants and the survivor of them would be able to remain in the bungalow as their home for as long as they wished to do so. Nine months later, the claimant repented of her invitation and started proceedings for possession; she died before the hearing in the Court of Appeal.

The Court of Appeal held that the equity would best be satisfied by securing the occupation of the defendants until the expenditure had been reimbursed.[98]

---

[96] (1990) 95 ALR 321, 331. The English courts have now adopted this approach generally in proprietary estoppel, and therefore consider whether an award of the expectation would be disproportionate to the value of the claimant's reliance: *Jennings v Rice* [2002] EWCA Civ 159, [2003] 1 P & CR 8, M & B p 1040, above, p 917. For a creative solution to the problems of over-compensation (by ordering the fee simple) or under-compensation (by ordering only repayment of the expenditure incurred), whilst still avoiding the problems of SLA 1925, below, p 944, see *Griffiths v Williams* (1977) 248 EG 947, M & B p 1061 (with the consent of the parties, the grant of a long, non-assignable lease, determinable on the death of the licensee, at a nominal rent).

[97] (1973) 228 EG 1115, M & B p 1068; *Burrows and Burrows v Sharpe* (1991) 23 HLR 82 (clean break only proper and fair solution in view of breakdown between parties; compensation in return for loss of accommodation); [1992] Conv 54 (JE Martin); *Baker v Baker* (1993) 25 HLR 408 (granny flat); *McGuane v Welch* [2008] EWCA Civ 785, [2008] 2 P & CR 24 (agreement to transfer lease: equity satisfied by charge on the lease to compensate for expenditure incurred in reliance; the detriment was quantifiable in financial terms and could be completely reversed; 'to order the transfer of the lease ... would enforce the performance of a transaction, which was not a binding contract for sale, at a price that was at a substantial undervalue and in respect of which the transferor had received no independent advice': Mummery LJ at [44]); *Clarke v Swaby* [2007] UKPC 1, [2007] 2 P & CR 2 at [18] (Lord Walker of Gestingthorpe: 'often the equity can best be satisfied by a monetary award'). Cf *Campbell v Griffin* [2001] EWCA Civ 990, (2001) 82 P & CR DG23 (family carer ordered to vacate property to enable it to be sold, but granted a charge over the property to secure the interest (£35,000) he was held to have by way of proprietary estoppel); [2002] Conv 519 (M Pawkowski); [2003] Conv 157 (MP Thompson).

[98] A principal concern of the Court in awarding this remedy was to avoid the operation of the Settled Land Act 1925, below, p 944, if a life interest were instead ordered.

C THIRD PARTIES

(1) The Burden of a Licence Protected by Proprietary Estoppel

We have already seen that, both in unregistered land and in registered land, the burden of an equity by estoppel has been recognised as being proprietary in character.[99] A licence that is protected by proprietary estoppel is therefore capable of binding the licensor's successor, and in accordance with the general principles can bind a purchaser of unregistered land if he has notice of it,[100] or a purchaser of registered land if the right is protected by a notice in the register[101] or as an overriding interest if the licensee is in discoverable actual occupation.[102]

A further question arises that is critical to the analysis of the licensee's rights against the purchaser. Even if the equity by estoppel is recognised as having a sufficiently proprietary quality to bind the purchaser, can the purchaser overreach it by paying the purchase money to two trustees[103] and thereby transfer the burden of the equity to the purchase money? It has been said that the equity cannot be overreached.[104] However, in a case where the equity is to be satisfied by the grant of an interest that would itself be overreachable, it has been suggested that the equity arising by estoppel should also be overreachable.[105] This only adds to the controversy as to the nature of the equity before it is satisfied.

Once the court has awarded the remedy to give effect to the equity, however, its status is crystallised and, if a proprietary interest is awarded, its priority over future registered dispositions will depend on the nature of the interest in question.

(2) The Benefit of a Licence Protected by Proprietary Estoppel

There is no English authority on the transfer of the benefit of a licence protected by proprietary estoppel. In New South Wales, however, the Supreme Court held in *Hamilton v Geraghty*[106] that the benefit of an estoppel based on passive acquiescence was assignable and in fact had been assigned. The estoppel was not a personal right to sue that could not be assigned, but an interest in the land itself.[107]

---

[99] *ER Ives Investment Ltd v High* [1967] 2 QB 379 (unregistered land); LRA 2002, s 116(a) (registered land); above, pp 920–2.

[100] *ER Ives Investment Ltd v High*, above (since the equity by estoppel cannot be registered as a land charge).

[101] LRA 2002, s 29.   [102] Ibid, Sch 3, para 2.

[103] Or a trust corporation: LPA 1925, s 2; below, pp 1113–17.

[104] *Shiloh Spinners Ltd v Harding* [1973] AC 691, 720–1 (Lord Wilberforce), approving the approach of CA in *ER Ives Investment Ltd v High* [1967] 2 QB 379 (unregistered land); *Sweet v Sommer* [2005] EWCA Civ 227, [2005] All ER (D) 162 (Mar) at [26] (Morritt VC) (registered land).

[105] *Birmingham Midshires Mortgage Services Ltd v Sabherwal* (2000) 80 P & CR 256 at [24] (Robert Walker LJ).

[106] (1901) 1 SRNSW Eq 81; *Lands Comr v Hussein* [1968] EA 585; (1969) ASCL 354 (EH Burn).

[107] (1901) 1 SRNSW Eq 81, 89 (Owen J).

Whether a licence is transferable depends on the circumstances and in particular on its construction. In *Inwards v Baker*,[108] where the son's licence was to remain in the bungalow as long as he desired to use it as his home, the right was clearly personal and not transferable. In *ER Ives Investment Ltd v High*,[109] however, the benefit of High's licence would run with the land.

D TERMINATION OF LICENCE

A licence is revocable when it is not binding on the licensor or his successors in title in accordance with the rules stated in this chapter. A question has arisen whether a licence, irrevocable under the doctrine of proprietary estoppel, can be made revocable by the serious misconduct of the licensee. In *Williams v Staite*,[110] where the licensee announced that the successor in title of the licensor was in for 'bloody trouble' and blocked the entrance to the house that he had purchased, the Court of Appeal held that the licence did not thereby become revocable. As Goff LJ said:[111]

> Excessive user or bad behaviour towards the legal owner cannot bring the equity to an end or forfeit it. It may give rise to an action for damages for trespass or nuisance or to injunctions to restrain such behaviour, but I see no ground on which the equity, once established, can be forfeited.

Lord Denning MR thought that, in an extreme case, the licence might be revocable.

The effect of serious misconduct may, however, prevent an equity from arising in the first place, for example, where a forged document is used to bolster the claim. This is a simple application of the equitable maxim that 'he who comes to equity must come with clean hands'.[112]

VI CONVEYANCING DIFFICULTIES

Sufficient has been said to demonstrate the dramatic development of the law of licences in the past 60 years or so. *Hurst v Picture Theatres Ltd*[113] was then the only glimmer of hope for the contractual licensee. Now, as has been seen, through the

---

[108] [1965] 2 QB 29; above, p 937.

[109] [1967] 2 QB 379, above, p 920.

[110] [1979] Ch 291.

[111] Ibid, 300. See also *Manton Securities Ltd v Nazam* [2008] EWCA Civ 805, [2008] 2 P & CR DG19 (late payment record not a bar to award of tenancy). Cf, however, (1) a contractual licence where misconduct may be a breach of an implied term, and so prevent the licensee from relying on equitable relief against revocation: *Brynowen Estates Ltd v Bourne* (1981) 131 NLJ 1212 (driving car at speed along roads of caravan park with sounding of horn at night; and swearing at and making obscene gestures at visitors to it); and (2) an equitable interest arising under the doctrine of *Walsh v Londsale* (1882) 21 Ch D 9, below, p 978, which can be lost by misconduct of the beneficiary sufficient to remove his entitlement to claim specific performance of the contract: *Coatsworth v Johnson* (1886) 55 LJQB 220, above, p 218.

[112] *J Willis & Son v Willis* [1986] 1 EGLR 62; *Gonthier v Orange Contract Scaffolding Ltd* [2003] EWCA Civ 873, [2003] All ER (D) 332 (Jun).

[113] [1915] 1 KB 1, M & B p 1083; above, p 928.

intervention of equity he not only has stronger protection against the licensor,[114] but his licence might even be protected in some circumstances by the mechanism of the constructive trust or proprietary estoppel so as to be recognised as having the quality of an interest in land; and property interests such as a life interest[115] and a fee simple[116] have been awarded to licensees even though they were volunteers and had no documentary title to such estate or interest. But this progress has produced a number of problems.

In the 1950s there grew up the concept of the deserted wife's licence. A husband who deserted his wife could not turn her out of the home, even though he owned it. And this protection was extended through a series of cases[117] to protect the deserted wife against third parties to whom the home might be transferred. This situation created conveyancing complications, and the doctrine was disapproved by the House of Lords in *National Provincial Bank Ltd v Ainsworth* in 1965,[118] on the ground that the wife held no proprietary interest recognised by the law. The deserted wife was thus left unprotected against third parties. The criticism that followed led to the registration of a deserted wife's 'right of occupation' under the Matrimonial Homes Act 1967 (now Family Law Act 1996).[119]

The problem presented in *National Provincial Bank Ltd v Ainsworth* is a very real one in the context of the conveyancing system, and is relevant throughout the law of licences. One basic principle of the 1925 legislation was to provide for the document-ation of all dealings with the legal estate and for equities and equitable interests to be either overreachable or registrable.[120] The principle is all the more obvious with registered land, when the intention is to record everything except overriding interests. From a conveyancer's point of view, these are good principles, but the system has not remained intact either in the case of unregistered land,[121] or in the case of registered land because of the wide provision for the protection of overriding interests of a person

---

[114] *Winter Garden Theatre (London) Ltd v Millennium Productions Ltd* [1948] AC 173; above, p 928 (injunction).

[115] *Inwards v Baker* [1965] 2 QB 29; above, p 937. See *Griffiths v Williams* (1977) 248 EG 947, above, p 940, n 96.

[116] *Pascoe v Turner* [1979] 1 WLR 431, above, p 939; *Voyce v Voyce* (1991) 62 P & CR 290.

[117] *Bendall v McWhirter* [1952] 2 QB 466; *Ferris v Weaven* [1952] 2 All ER 233; *Street v Denham* [1954] 1 WLR 624; *Lee v Lee* [1952] 2 QB 489n; *Jess B Woodcock & Son Ltd v Hobbs* [1955] 1 WLR 152; *Westminster Bank Ltd v Lee* [1956] Ch 7; *Miles v Bull* [1969] 1 QB 258.

[118] [1965] AC 1175, M & B p 1002. See also *Hall v King* [1987] 2 EGLR 121, 122 (Sir John Donaldson MR): 'A wife's right to occupy the matrimonial home is of a very special nature, depending upon her status as a wife and not upon any leave or licence of her husband... This accords with common sense and experience. Whoever heard of a husband expressly or impliedly saying to his wife "Do come and stay with me in the matrimonial home, dear".'

[119] Above, p 522.   [120] Above, pp 122–3.

[121] *ER Ives Investment Ltd v High* [1967] 2 QB 379, M & B p 1074 (proprietary estoppel), above; *Poster v Slough Estates Ltd* [1969] 1 Ch 495 (right of entry to remove a fixture on termination of lease); *Caunce v Caunce* [1969] 1 WLR 286; *Kingsnorth Finance Co Ltd v Tizard* [1986] 1 WLR 783, M & B p 216; above, p 88, n 112 (beneficial interest of wife who had contributed towards purchase price); *Shiloh Spinners Ltd v Harding* [1973] AC 691, M & B p 68 (equitable right of entry on breach of covenant); above, p 130.

in actual occupation of the land.[122] A very significant inroad into these principles of conveyancing is found in the modern development of licences. If the licence has a sufficiently proprietary quality that it can bind a third party, then, even where only negative protection is given to the licensee,[123] a purchaser is faced with the interest of the licensee as a blot on his title. The licensee may be in possession, and the purchaser may thus have what would be considered to be constructive notice under the pre-1926 cases.[124] But these rules are now taken over by provisions for registration, and licences are not registrable under the Land Charges Act 1925. Indeed, it would be a disaster for the licensee if they were; for many of the licence situations arise in connection with personal family affairs, without legal advice, and as a matter of practice would hardly ever be registered; and, further, if they were registrable and not registered, they would in unregistered land be void even against a purchaser who actually knew of the licence.

The difficulties are even greater where the licensee receives an award of an undocumented proprietary interest or estate. Once the case has been determined, the proper documentation can be prepared, but the licensee's protection cannot depend upon the trial of the action. The protection is given in equity, and not by the court's decision; and, as we have seen,[125] it has been recognised that an equity arising by estoppel already has a sufficiently proprietary quality to bind the purchaser before the court's decision if (in unregistered land) he has notice of it or (in registered land) it is protected by notice or as an overriding interest. And it is not at all clear whether the purchaser can overreach the equity.[126] Before 1997 there was a particular danger attached to the court's decision to award the licensee a life interest, since it was arguable that the licensee would thereby become a tenant for life under the Settled Land Act 1925. The point was first noticed by Scott LJ in *Bannister v Bannister*,[127] a case decided on the theory of constructive trust. The point was overlooked in many of the licence cases.[128] The view has been expressed that the Settled Land Act 1925 would not apply.[129] Russell LJ, on the other hand, noted in *Dodsworth v Dodsworth*,[130] that the award of a life interest would 'lead, by virtue of the provisions of the Settled Land Act, to a greater and more extensive interest than was ever contemplated by the plaintiff and the defendants'. Since the Trusts of Land and Appointment of Trustees Act 1996 came into force on 1 January 1997,[131] however, settlements can no longer be created under the Settled Land Act 1925, and so the award of a life interest no

[122] LRA 1925, s 70(1)(g); *Hodgson v Marks* [1971] Ch 892; *Williams and Glyn's Bank Ltd v Boland* [1981] AC 487, M & B p 203; below, p 1106; LRA 2002, s 29, Sch 3, para 2; s 116.

[123] *Inwards v Baker* [1965] 2 QB 29.

[124] *Hunt v Luck* [1901] 1 Ch 45; above, p 88.   [125] Above, p 941.

[126] Above, p 941.   [127] [1948] 2 All ER 133, M & B p 1101; above, p 934.

[128] Cf *Inwards v Baker*, above.

[129] *Binions v Evans* [1972] Ch 359, 366 (Lord Denning MR) (unintended settlement), above, p 932. See also *Ivory v Palmer* [1975] ICR 340, 347 (Cairns LJ): '*Binions v Evans* stretched to the very limit the application of the Settled Land Act'. See (1977) 93 LQR 561 (JA Hornby).

[130] (1973) 228 EG 1115, M & B p 1068.   [131] Above, Ch 13.

longer gives the licensee a statutory fee simple and the wide powers of a tenant for life. However, an even more serious problem arises for the purchaser where a fee simple is awarded to the licensee, as in *Pascoe v Turner*.[132] The licensor holds the legal estate, and the licensee has an equity entitling him to the fee simple: he is the equitable owner.[133] In registered land the licensee in actual occupation who had not protected his interest by a notice in the register would be held to have an overriding interest,[134] and therefore the purchaser is bound by the equity and liable to be deprived of his title—and without any way of having been able to determine with certainty at the time of his purchase what rights were held by the licensee, given the inchoate nature of the equity before the court order. In unregistered land the old principle of notice presumably applies;[135] and its application must be particularly difficult where, as in *Pascoe v Turner*, the licensee had not the slightest idea that she was entitled to a fee simple.

The question is sometimes asked as to whether these developments show that a licence should now be regarded as an interest in land. At an early stage the courts took the view that a licence coupled with a grant under seal was irrevocable,[136] from which one might conclude that if a licence was granted under seal, it must be the subject matter of a grant, and that makes it look like an interest in land. That theory, however, was largely exploded once it was decided that there could be no easement in gross, for that, at best, is what a licence granted under seal could claim to be.[137] From the 1940s, the doctrine has been accepted that a contractual licensee or licensee holding an equity by estoppel may be protected by injunction. And although the courts flirted with the idea that, in consequence of this protection in equity, the contractual licence can bind a third party,[138] this has been rejected.[139] Licences protected by estoppel have been held to be binding on third parties,[140] and the Land Registration Act 2002[141] has declared that an equity by estoppel is an interest capable of binding successors in title. But in none of these cases can it properly be said that the licence is itself an interest in land. The licence coupled with a grant is not irrevocable on its own account, but only by virtue of the irrevocability of the grant to which it was coupled. A licence protected only by contract carries only the benefits that the law of contract gives: and since contracts are personal, the contractual licence does not of itself create an interest in land. However, if the licensee is protected by constructive trust, or by proprietary estoppel, then the interest held by the licensee under

---

[132] [1979] 1 WLR 431; above, p 939.   [133] *Voyce v Voyce* (1991) 62 P & CR 290, 294 (Dillon LJ).

[134] LRA 2002, s 30, Sch 3, para 2, replacing LRA 1925, s 70(1)(g); above, pp 139–40, below, pp 1105–11.

[135] *ER Ives Investment Ltd v High* [1967] 2 QB 379; above, p 920.   [136] Above, p 926.

[137] See *Cowell v Rosehill Racecourse Co Ltd* (1937) 56 CLR 605, 616, M & B p 1084, (Latham CJ): 'the right to see a spectacle cannot, in the ordinary sense of legal language, be regarded as a proprietary interest. Fifty thousand people who pay to see a football match do not obtain fifty thousand interests in the football ground'.

[138] *Errington v Errington and Woods* [1952] 1 KB 290; above, p 931; *Binions v Evans* [1972] Ch 359; above, p 932.

[139] *Ashburn Anstalt v Arnold* [1989] Ch 1; above, p 933.   [140] Above, pp 920, 941.

[141] S 116 ('for the avoidance of doubt'); above, p 921.

the trust, or his equity by estoppel, may themselves have proprietary consequences. In ascertaining, therefore, the nature and strength of the licensee's rights, both against the licensor and against a third party, one must consider not just the licence itself—the permission to enter upon the land—but the circumstances surrounding the giving of the licence, and the continuing exercise of it by the licensor, to see whether there are factors to justify the analysis that the licensor has an interest in the land.[142]

---

[142] See, eg, *Re Sharpe* [1980] 1 WLR 219, where Browne-Wilkinson J analysed the nature of a licensee's rights on multiple bases (contractual licence, equitable licence and constructive trust) in order to find a basis on which they would bind the licensor's trustee in bankruptcy.

PART IV

THE CREATION, TRANSFER AND EXTINCTION OF ESTATES AND INTERESTS IN LAND

Summary

It may be said that what we have described so far is the law at rest. Our attention has been directed to the actual rights that can be enjoyed in land. We have taken each estate and interest that is capable of subsisting, either at law or in equity, and have explained what incidents are applicable to it when it exists. It now remains to consider the law in motion, that is to show how estates and interests may be validly created, transferred and dealt with generally, and how they may be extinguished.

24

THE CONTRACT[1]

Summary

The creation or transfer of an estate or interest in land will often be preceded by a contract. A contract for the sale of land usually precedes the conveyance of the legal estate to the purchaser; and this is so whether the land is already registered[2] or is still unregistered.[3] Similarly, a contract for a lease may be made first, and then followed at a later date by a formal grant of the legal term of years absolute.[4] Moreover, the owner of an estate in land may contract to create an interest in it, such as an easement or a charge, the actual creation of the interest to follow later. The formalities required for

---

[1] See generally Barnsley, *Conveyancing Law and Practice* (4th edn, 1996); Sweet & Maxwell's *Conveyancing Practice*; Silverman, *Conveyancing Handbook* (17th edn, 2010); Emmet; M & B pp 16–41.

[2] LRA 2002, s 23(1)(a); R & R, para 13.004.03.

[3] Most dispositions of unregistered land will now trigger compulsory registration: above, pp 132, 140; below, p 1073.

[4] Above, p 210.

the creation and transfer of estates and interests in land, and certain aspects of the law and practice governing the creation and transfer, will be considered in Chapters 25, 27 and 28. In this Chapter we are concerned with the contract.

I FORMATION OF THE CONTRACT

Apart from the requirement of formality,[5] a contract for the sale or other disposition of an interest in land is created in the same way as any other contract.[6] There must be final and complete agreement between the parties on its essential terms,[7] that is to say, the parties, the property (and the interest to be granted in it[8]) and the consideration. However, certain particular issues arise in connection with the negotiation and formation of a contract relating to land, which are considered in this section. The formality requirements will be discussed in the following section.

A PRE-CONTRACT ENQUIRIES AND DISCLOSURE

The general position taken by the English law of contract is *caveat emptor*: in a contract of sale it is for the purchaser to satisfy himself about what he is buying, and the vendor has no general duty of disclosure, not even a duty to disclose facts relating to the property that he knows the purchaser would regard as significant, nor to disabuse the purchaser of mistakes that the vendor realises he is making.[9] The vendor may be liable if he makes a misrepresentation, or if he gives a contractual undertaking (express or implied) about the property.[10] But otherwise the purchaser generally has no remedy against him. The vendor under a contract for the sale of land therefore has no general duty of disclosure, and no duty to disclose defects in the quality of the property,[11]

---

[5] Below, pp 959 ff.   [6] Anson, Part I.

[7] *Rossiter v Miller* (1878) 3 App Cas 1124, 1135 (Lord Blackburn). See *Gibson v Manchester City Council* [1979] 1 WLR 294, 297 (bipartite contract must normally be formed by offer and acceptance); *Fletcher v Davies* (1980) 257 EG 1149 (flat in Inner Temple).

[8] In the case of a lease, this includes the commencement and the period of the tenancy: above, p 197.

[9] *Smith v Hughes* (1867) LR 6 QB 597, 606–7; Cartwright, *Misrepresentation, Mistake and Non-Disclosure* (2nd edn, 2006), ch 16.

[10] For the purchaser's remedies, see below, pp 986 ff.

[11] Emmet, para 4.020; Farrand, *Contract and Conveyance* (4th edn, 1983), pp 67–8; Barnsley, *Conveyancing Law and Practice*, pp 178–80; Cartwright, *Misrepresentation, Mistake and Non-Disclosure*, paras 17.29, 17.31; *Terrene Ltd v Nelson* (1937) 157 LT 254, 256–7. In this respect the purchaser under a contract relating to land is even less protected than the purchaser under a contract for the sale or supply of goods, since by statute a business seller or supplier of goods impliedly guarantees such things as the quality of the goods and their fitness for purpose: Sale of Goods Act 1979, s 14; Supply of Goods and Services Act 1982, ss 4, 9, all as amended by Sale and Supply of Goods Act 1994, s 7(1), Sch 2 and Sale and Supply of Goods to Consumers Regulations 2002 (SI 2002 No 3045). However, in a contract to build and sell a house the builder-vendor impliedly promises that the house will be constructed in a good and workmanlike manner, with good and proper materials, and will be fit for habitation: *Hancock v B W Brazier (Anerley) Ltd* [1966] 1 WLR 1317; and builders of new houses may provide guarantees under schemes run by the National House-Building Council, and may owe duties in tort under Defective Premises Act 1972 (but cf above, p 233, n 81).

although in the absence of express provision to the contrary he does have certain implied obligations at common law under the contract of sale relating to the proof of his title to the property.[12] There is some uncertainty about the scope of these implied obligations,[13] and therefore it is in the interests of both parties to a contract for the sale of land to make express provision. Moreover, since in general the purchaser's remedies in the event of his discovering a problem with his purchase are limited to claims for the vendor's misrepresentation or breach of contract, it became established practice for the party negotiating for the purchase of land to ask questions not only of the vendor personally but also through his solicitor or other agent; and to ask for certain matters to be covered explicitly in the terms of the contract. This practice grew over the years to the point where there were numerous so-called 'standard' forms of enquiry used by purchasers' solicitors, and 'standard' forms of contract terms that allocated to one or other party the risk of certain matters relating to the property.[14]

In relation to residential conveyancing[15] this standard practice has been simplified and taken further by professional regulation. In 1990 the Council of the Law Society issued the National Conveyancing Protocol[16] designed for use in domestic conveyancing of freehold and leasehold property, setting out the steps to be followed by solicitors acting for vendors and purchasers; its aim was to provide the purchaser's solicitor with as much information as possible about the property at the outset, as well as to simplify the existing practice by providing a single standard form of pre-contract enquiries and a single standard form of contract.[17]

A further attempt was made in the Housing Act 2004 to relax the *caveat emptor* rule[18] through the introduction of compulsory 'home information packs', a collection of documents relating to the property or the terms on which it is or may become available for sale. This was a controversial scheme, which was revised significantly during its short lifetime,[19] and has now been suspended. In the case of a sale of residential

---

[12] Below, p 1043; Emmet, para 4.023; Farrand, *Contract and Conveyance* (4th edn), pp 62–75; Barnsley, *Conveyancing Law and Practice*, p 266. For the landlord's obligation (in the absence of contrary stipulation) to disclose information about his own title to the party negotiating to take a new lease, and the tenant's obligation to disclose information about the superior title to the assignee of his lease, see below, pp 1046–7.

[13] In particular, the duty to disclose latent defects in the title, and the purchaser's remedies in the case of a defect that was not in fact known to the vendor: Cartwright, *Misrepresentation, Mistake and Non-Disclosure*, para 17.40.

[14] Barnsley, *Conveyancing Law and Practice*, pp 188–9.

[15] For non-residential conveyancing, see Standard Commercial Property Conditions of Sale (2nd edn, 2004); Silverman, *Conveyancing Handbook*, Appendix III.6.

[16] [1990] Conv 137 (HW Wilkinson); Barnsley, *Conveyancing Law and Practice*, pp 188–93; Silverman, *Conveyancing Handbook*, section A19. The sixth edition of the Protocol was published by the Law Society in April 2011. It is specified by the Council of the Law Society as 'preferred practice' for solicitors, but is not mandatory under the rules of professional conduct.

[17] The Standard Conditions of Sale: below, p 954.

[18] See, however, *Reforming the home buying and selling process in England and Wales: Contents of the home information pack* (Consultation Paper, Office of the Deputy Prime Minister, March 2003), para 7.5 'We do not intend, however, to change the principle of *caveat emptor* (let the buyer beware). We are not suggesting that sellers should be under a legal obligation to answer questions set out in a property information form included in the home information pack.'

[19] Below, n 22.

property with vacant possession, the Housing Act 2004 placed a statutory duty[20] on the seller or his estate agent to have a home information pack in his possession. A copy of the home information pack had to be provided to a potential buyer on request,[21] and the documents that it had to contain were prescribed in regulations: some were mandatory, others were optional, but an earlier plan to make a 'home condition report' compulsory within the pack were abandoned.[22] The duties under the 2004 Act relating to home information packs were suspended on 21 May 2010;[23] formal repeal is expected in due course.[24] However, one duty remains from the original scheme: an 'energy performance certificate' must be made available to any prospective buyer and, in the case of residential property, the seller must secure that a certificate is commissioned before the property is put on the market.[25]

We are left, then, with the general position as it stood before the intervention of the Housing Act 2004: good conveyancing practice was already well-established under the National Conveyancing Protocol, for example, in relation to the provision of information about the property in the form of answers to standard pre-contract enquiries. But the general rule remains *caveat emptor*. Unless the vendor made a misrepresentation in his reply the purchaser has no remedy; and the courts have

---

[20] HA 2004, s 155. Home information packs were phased in from 1 August 2007: SI 2007 No 1668 (1 August 2007 for properties with four bedrooms or more); SI 2007 No 2471 (10 September 2007 for properties with three bedrooms); SI 2007 No 3308 (14 December 2007 for properties with fewer than three bedrooms); SI 2008 No 898 (6 April 2008 for all remaining provisions). The duty was imposed only on either the seller or the estate agent, depending on which was for the time being responsible for marketing the property: ss 151–153; and was enforceable not directly by the purchaser but through an enforcement authority that could require production of the pack and issue penalty charge notices for failure to comply: ss 167–168; Sch 8. The purchaser's remedy against the seller or his estate agent was only for recovery of fees paid to commission documents that should have been supplied in a home information pack: s 170.

[21] Ibid, s 156. For circumstances where the request could properly be refused, see s 156(4). The purchaser could insist on receiving a paper copy of the pack, rather than an electronic copy (s 156(11)), but could be required to pay for a paper copy and to accept conditions relating to the use or disclosure of the copy (s 157).

[22] Home Information Pack Regulations 2007 (SI 2007 No 992), reg 10(a), replacing Home Information Pack Regulations 2006 (SI 2006 No 1503). A home condition report was a survey prepared by a qualified home inspector. It was a central document in the original scheme for home information packs.

The 2007 Regulations were then revoked and replaced by Home Information Pack (No 2) Regulations 2007 (SI 2007 No 1667), which were further amended : SI 2007 No 3301, SI 2008 Nos 572, 1266 and 3107 (introducing the requirement of a 'property information questionnaire' with effect from 6 April 2009: regs 9, 10); SI 2009 No 34.

[23] SI 2010 No 1455.

[24] The repeal of HA 2004, Part 5 (home information packs) is contained in the Localism Bill, which was published in December 2010 and will be passing through Parliament during 2011.

[25] SI 2007 No 991, amended by SI 2010 No 1456; giving effect to Directive 2002/91/EC on the energy performance of buildings (later recast as Directive 2010/31/EU). Before marketing the property, a person acting on behalf of the seller must be satisfied that the certificate has been commissioned, and he and the seller must use all reasonable efforts to secure that a valid certificate is obtained within 28 days of the property being put on the market: reg 5A, inserted by SI 2010 No 1456. Once a certificate has been obtained, a copy must be attached to any written marketing particulars: reg 6. For the required contents of a certificate, see reg 11. The Regulations apply to lettings as well as sales. See generally Silverman, *Conveyancing Handbook*, section A27. An energy performance certificate was one of the mandatory documents within a home information pack: SI 2007 No 1667, reg 8(b).

construed the enquiries put by prospective purchasers strictly so as not to impose an inappropriate obligation of disclosure on vendors.

A striking example is *Sykes v Taylor-Rose*[26] in which the vendors of a house, who had recently discovered that a horrific murder had been committed in the house some years earlier, answered their purchaser's question,[27] 'Is there any other information that you think the buyer might have a right to know?' with a simple 'No'. Holding that this question required only an honest answer, and noting that the vendors had been acting on the advice of their solicitor to the effect that they had no duty of disclosure, the trial judge[28] rejected the purchaser's claims based on non-disclosure and misrepresentation. The Court of Appeal upheld the judge. Peter Gibson LJ said:[29]

> Because the *caveat emptor* rule can work harshly on purchasers, whose knowledge of material facts affecting the property they are purchasing is almost certain to be considerably less than that of the vendors, the practice of sending pre-contract enquiries has become standard and the scope of the enquiries has been extended over a period of time. It is for the buyer to decide what enquiries to raise and in what form. It cannot be doubted that a more specific and less subjective question going to the value of the property or to the ability of the purchaser to enjoy the property could have been asked. Unhappily, question 13 in the Law Society's form at that time (we are told that it is no longer in use) did allow the answer to be given in a way which only required, in my view, the vendor to answer the question honestly.

B TERMS OF THE CONTRACT. 'OPEN CONTRACT' AND SPECIAL CONDITIONS OF SALE

If a contract for the sale of land specifies merely the names of the parties, a description of the property and a statement of the price, it is called an *open contract*. As has already been mentioned,[30] when this form of contract is made the parties are bound by certain obligations implied by the law, and it is in both parties' interest to include special stipulations in the contract to modify their implied obligations, as well as to make specific provision for matters on which the contract would otherwise be silent. The parties may incorporate into their contract such terms as they think fit, as long as they do not contravene any common law or statutory rule.[31] In practice contracts for

---

[26] [2004] EWCA Civ 299, [2004] 2 P & CR 30; (2004) 148 SJ 497 (M Pawlowski).

[27] Question 13 in the Law Society's standard form of pre-contract enquiries in use at the time within the National Conveyancing Protocol.

[28] Judge Langan QC, Leeds County Court (8 July 2003). Counsel for the claimants had argued that, although there is no general duty on a vendor to disclose defects in the quality or expected enjoyment of land that he is selling, or matters that may affect the value of the land, the particular facts of the case were so heinous that they could not be withheld because there is no other way by which the reasonably prudent purchaser would be able to discover them; and that the principle of *caveat emptor*, hallowed though it may have been in the past, is nearing the end of its useful life. This was firmly rejected by the Judge, and there was no appeal on this point: [2004] 2 P & CR 30 at [15].

[29] [2004] 2 P & CR 30 at [50].   [30] Above, pp 950–1.

[31] Eg a stipulation that the conveyance to, or the registration of title of, the purchaser shall be prepared or carried out at the expense of the purchaser by a solicitor appointed by the vendor is void: LPA 1925, s 48(1). See also s 42, as amended by TLATA 1996, s 25(1), Sch 3, para 4(1), (11). The general statutory controls on the

the sale of land are generally in standard form. For most residential sales and small commercial property sales the Standard Conditions of Sale[32] are usually employed; for more complex commercial sales the Standard Commercial Property Conditions are often used.[33] In both cases the parties will generally make amendments to the standard forms, or add their own particular terms.[34]

Further, if the contract is made by correspondence, the Statutory Form of Conditions of Sale 1925 applies, except in so far as there is any modification or intention to the contrary expressed in the correspondence.[35]

The terminology of 'conditions' of sale can be misleading. Danckwerts LJ has referred to

> the long-standing practice which has arisen among conveyancers of referring to the provisions in a contract for the sale of land as 'conditions of sale', whether special or general (such as those provided by the common forms produced under the name of the National Conditions of Sale, or those produced by the Law Society). The word 'condition' is traditional rather than appropriate, and these provisions are not so much concerned with the validity of the contract of sale as with the production of the title and the performance of the vendor's and purchaser's obligations leading up to completion by conveyance. Shortly, they are no more than the terms of the contract.[36]

---

fairness of exclusion and limitation clauses in the Unfair Contract Terms Act 1977, ss 2–4 do not apply to a contract so far as it relates to the creation, transfer or termination of an interest in land: Sch 1, para. 1(b). The Unfair Terms in Consumer Contracts Regulations 1999 do however apply to land contracts: *R (Khatun) v Newham LBC* [2004] EWCA Civ 55, [2005] QB 37. The Law Commission's proposals to replace the 1977 Act and the 1999 Regulations with a single unified legislative regime would continue to maintain the control on unfair contract terms in land contracts in favour of a consumer: Law Com No 292 (2005), paras 3.80, 5.76. A contract term that excludes or restricts liability for misrepresentation is subject to Misrepresentation Act 1967, s 3, as substituted by Unfair Contract Terms Act 1977, s 8; there is no exclusion for contracts relating to land; see *Walker v Boyle* [1982] 1 WLR 495, 507–8 (condition in National Conditions of Sale, 19th edn, unreasonable and therefore of no effect).

[32] The current edition is the 5th edn 2011. The 4th edn 2003, which came into effect with the implementation of LRA 2002, is reproduced with explanatory notes in *Silverman*, Conveyancing Handbook, Appendix III.5. Sweet and Maxwell's, *Conveyancing Practice*, reproduces the 1st to 4th edn at B001–B030/3; *Encyclopedia of Forms and Precedents*, vol 38(1) (2006), para 2001. See also (sometimes on earlier editions of the Conditions), Aldridge, *Companion to the Standard Conditions of Sale* (3rd edn, 2003), Silverman, *Standard Conditions of Sale* (6th edn, 1999), Wilkinson, *Standard Conditions of Sale of Land* (1989); [1990] Conv 179, [1992] Conv 316 (JE Adams).

[33] 2nd edn, 2004, reproduced with explanatory notes in Silverman, *Conveyancing Handbook*, Appendix III.6; Sweet and Maxwell's *Conveyancing Practice*, B030/4–B033. [2004] 23 LSG 37 (M Waters); *Encyclopedia of Forms and Precedents*, vol 38(1) (2006), para 2051; [2004] Conv 260 (E Slessenger, comparing the 1st and 2nd edns).

[34] Generally termed 'special conditions', to distinguish them from the 'general conditions' contained in the standard forms.

[35] LPA 1925, s 46; SR & O 1925 No 779; *Stearn v Twitchell* [1985] 1 All ER 631 (contract arising out of acceptance by single letter of oral offer to buy or sell land held to be contract by correspondence). See (1974) 90 LQR 55 (AM Prichard). This section was not repealed by LP(MP)A 1989, below, p 966. It may have been overlooked or left on the statute book out of an abundance of caution: *Commission for the New Towns v Cooper (Great Britain) Ltd* [1995] Ch 259, 287 (Stuart-Smith LJ), although it may well have a reduced application now, given that an exchange of correspondence will often not fulfil the formality requirements of s 2 LP(MP)A 1989; below, p 971.

[36] *Property and Bloodstock Ltd v Emerton* [1968] Ch 94, 118.

C NEGOTIATIONS OR AGREEMENT 'SUBJECT TO CONTRACT'

It is common practice in sales of land for the parties to agree a price 'subject to contract'.[37] The object of this procedure, 'though it has drawbacks and is capable of being abused in certain circumstances, is based on a sound concept, namely, that the buyer should be free from binding commitment until he has had the opportunity of obtaining legal and other advice, arranging his finance and making the necessary inspections, searches and enquiries'.[38] In 1975 the Law Commission recommended that there should be no change in this practice, even though one consequence is that the purchaser may be 'gazumped' (that is the vendor may withdraw from the bargain or threaten to do so, in the expectation of receiving a higher price).[39]

The effect of such phrases as 'subject to contract',[40] or 'subject to a formal contract to be drawn up by our solicitors' is that there is no contract, unless there are some very exceptional circumstances necessitating a different construction.[41] Either party is free to repudiate the bargain until a formal contract has been made.[42]

[37] See [1984] Conv 173, 251 (RW Clarke), comparing English and Irish law. For its continued use in contracts after 26 September 1989, see below, p 973.

[38] Law Com No 65, 'Subject to Contract' Agreements (1975), para 13. See Cohen v Nessdale Ltd [1981] 3 All ER 118, 127–8; affd [1982] 2 All ER 97.

[39] See the Law Commission Conveyancing Standing Committee's suggestion of a standard form of Pre-Contract Deposit Agreement, which would go some way towards deterring gazumping. It was called a paper-tiger: The Times, 17 January 1987, and was abandoned: [1988] Conv 79. See also the Committee's House Selling the Scottish Way for England and Wales (1987). See generally Barnsley: Conveyancing Law and Practice, pp 216–19. The converse of 'gazumping' is 'gazundering': the corresponding freedom of the purchaser to withdraw in order to achieve a lower price. The state of the sales market dictates which is the more likely practice. One of the Government's purposes in introducing home information packs, above, was to reduce gazumping.

[40] Tiverton Estates Ltd v Wearwell Ltd [1975] Ch 146; Munton v Greater London Council [1976] 1 WLR 649; Sherbrooke v Dipple (1980) 41 P & CR 173; [1981] Conv 165.

[41] Chillingworth v Esche [1924] 1 Ch 97; Alpenstow Ltd v Regalian Properties plc [1985] 1 WLR 721 (words 'subject to contract' meaningless); Westway Homes Ltd v Moores [1991] 2 EGLR 193 (notice served by grantee of option to purchase headed 'subject to contract' held to be surplusage and of no effect); Farah v Moody [1998] EGCS 1; Prudential Assurance Co Ltd v Mount Eden Land Ltd [1997] 1 EGLR 37 (subject to licence).

See Wilkinson, Standard Conditions of Sale of Land (2nd edn, 1974), ch 5 for a useful summary of standard conditional phrases; Barnsley, Conveyancing Law and Practice, pp 135–9, (1975) 39 Conv (NS) 229–36, 311–13; Emmet, paras 2.016–2.019. See, for examples of valid phrases, Janmohamed v Hassam (1976) 241 EG 609 ('subject to purchaser obtaining mortgage on terms satisfactory to himself within one month'); Meehan v Jones (1982) 56 ALJR 813; [1984] Conv 243; cf Lee-Parker v Izzet (No 2) [1972] 1 WLR 775; (1976) 40 Conv (NS) 37 (B Coote); Ee v Kakar (1979) 40 P & CR 223 ('subject to survey'); (1981) 131 NLJ 771 (HW Wilkinson); Duttons Brewery Ltd v Leeds City Council (1981) 43 P & CR 160 ('at a price of £15,000 subject to a contract to be approved by me'); Heron Garage Properties Ltd v Moss [1974] 1 WLR 148 ('conditional on purchaser obtaining detailed town planning consent'); cf Balbosa v Ayoub Ali [1990] 1 WLR 914 ('subject to obtaining from the Town and Country Planning Department of all the necessary approvals for the transfer of the premises'); Graham v Pitkin [1992] 1 WLR 403 ('subject to the purchaser obtaining a mortgage from [a building society] of $19,000 for 10 years'); [1992] Conv 318 (C Harpum); [1995] Conv 83 (C Harpum and G Barnsley). See also Provost Developments Ltd v Collingwood Towers Ltd [1980] 2 NZLR 205 ('subject to a solicitor's approval'); [1981] Conv 90 (HW Wilkinson).

[42] Usually by exchange of contracts: below, p 971.

Thus in *Winn v Bull*:[43]

a written agreement was entered into whereby the defendant agreed to take from the claimant a lease of a house for a certain time at a certain rent, 'subject to the preparation and approval of a formal contract'. No formal or other contract was ever entered into between the parties. It was held that there was no contract.

The parties may, however, be bound at once, although they intend to make a more formal contract later on. In *Branca v Cobarro*,[44] for example,

a written agreement to sell the lease and goodwill of a mushroom farm ended as follows: 'This is a provisional agreement until a fully legalised agreement, drawn up by a solicitor and embodying all the conditions herewith stated, is signed'. It was held by the Court of Appeal[45] that the parties, by using the word 'provisional' had intended the document to be immediately binding and to remain so until superseded by a more formal document.

Once applied, the words 'subject to contract' are very difficult to displace except by the formal contract that the parties envisaged. Where the parties have started their negotiations under a 'subject to contract' formula, their later negotiations, and any apparently final (but not yet formalised) agreement, will continue to be qualified by it, unless and until they agree expressly or by necessary implication that the qualification should be expunged.[46] It is even more difficult to displace a 'subject to contract' qualification that the parties have expressly applied to a concluded agreement in principle. It has been said that a party might possibly be estopped from relying on a 'subject to contract' clause, but that this is rarely likely to occur.[47] For an estoppel, one party must have created or encouraged the other party's belief or expectation that it would not withdraw from the agreement, and the latter party must have relied on that belief or expectation.[48] But the very purpose of having expressed the agreement to be 'subject to contract' is to indicate that it is not to be binding until the exchange of formal contracts. If the parties have not agreed to lift the 'subject to contract' restriction on their agreement—in which case there would be no need to rely on an estoppel—the continuing force of that restriction will normally preclude any assertion by one party that the other has encouraged him to believe that he will be bound unconditionally.[49]

---

[43] (1877) 7 Ch D 29.   [44] [1947] KB 854.

[45] Reversing Denning J, who construed 'provisional' as equivalent to 'tentative'.

[46] *Tevanan v Norman Brett (Builders) Ltd* (1972) 223 EG 1945, 1947 (Brightman J); *Sherbrooke v Dipple* (1980) 41 P & CR 173; *Cohen v Nessdale Ltd* [1981] 3 All ER 118.

[47] *A-G of Hong Kong v Humphreys Estate (Queen's Gardens) Ltd* [1987] AC 114, 127–8 (Lord Templeman), M & B p 27.

[48] Ibid, at 124.

[49] Ibid; *James v Evans* [2000] 3 EGLR 1, 4; *Edwin Shirley Productions Ltd v Workspace Management Ltd* [2001] 2 EGLR 16 at [50]; *Secretary of State for Transport v Christos* [2003] EWCA Civ 1073, [2004] 1 P & CR 17 at [41]-[44]; [2003] Conv 360. See also *Cobbe v Yeoman's Row Management Ltd* [2008] UKHL 55, [2008] 1 WLR 1752 at [25] (Lord Scott of Foscote: 'The reason why, in a "subject to contract" case, a proprietary estoppel cannot ordinarily arise is that the would-be purchaser's expectation of acquiring an interest in the property in question is subject to a contingency that is entirely under the control of the other party to the negotiations ... The expectation is therefore speculative').

It should be noted, however, that the words 'subject to contract' only prevent an executory contract from coming into existence. If the parties perform the obligations contemplated by the 'subject to contract' agreement, they may be held to have entered into an implied binding contract on the terms of the agreement.[50]

D LOCK-OUT AGREEMENT

As we have seen, a purchaser may be gazumped by a vendor (or a vendor gazundered by a purchaser) at any stage before completion. However he may seek to avoid this hazard by entering into a 'lock-out' agreement with the vendor, that is by making an agreement with him not to enter into a contract with, or not to negotiate with,[51] any third party, which will be contractually binding provided that it is made for good consideration and a specified period of time. Lord Ackner said in *Walford v Miles*:[52]

I stress that this is a negative agreement—B, by agreeing not to negotiate for a fixed period, locks himself out of such negotiations. He has in no legal sense locked himself into negotiations with A. What A has achieved is an exclusive opportunity, for a fixed period, to try to come to terms with B, an opportunity for which he has, unless he makes his agreement under seal, to give good consideration.

However, the commercial usefulness of a lock-out agreement can be limited. All the lock-out does is to prohibit the vendor from contracting with, or negotiating with, other parties during the lock-out period. He can decline to take further the negotiations with the purchaser, and simply wait until the end of the period and then remarket the property: the agreement may therefore give little comfort to the purchaser unless in addition to the lock-out it provides for reimbursement of the purchaser's expenditure, such as legal and surveying fees, should the vendor pull out of the transaction for no good reason.[53] Moreover, even if the vendor breaches the agreement, the courts

---

[50] *Rugby Group Ltd v Proforce Recruit Ltd* [2005] EWHC 70, [2005] All ER (D) 22 (Feb) (not a contract relating to land, and rvsd on different grounds [2006] EWCA Civ 69, [2006] All ER (D) 247 (Feb)); *RTS Flexible Systems Ltd v Molkerei Alois MüllerGmbH & Co Kg (UK Production)* [2010] UKSC 14, [2010] 1 WLR 753 (where work begins before formal contract executed, it will depend on the circumstances whether the parties have waived the subject-to-contract term). For the question of whether LP(MP)A 1989, s 2 applies to an executed agreement relating to land, see below, p 969, and for the relevance of the 'subject to contract' qualification under that section, see below, p 973); *Bryen & Langley Ltd v Boston* [2005] EWCA Civ 973, [2005] All ER (D) 507 (Jul) (parties proposed in letter that agreement shall be contained in later formal contract; this did not preclude conclusion that they had informally already contractually bound themselves on exactly the same terms).

[51] The scope of the (negative) undertaking depends on the terms of the agreement: eg *Encyclopedia of Forms and Precedents*, vol 4(3) (2008), para [178]; vol 38(1) (2006), paras [1241], [1244].

[52] [1992] 2 AC 128, 139. In this case the agreement was void since it did not say for how long it was to last. Cf *Pitt v PHH Asset Management Ltd* [1994] 1 WLR 327 (agreement whereby vendor agreed for valuable consideration not to negotiate with anyone else for fourteen days held valid); [1993] CLJ 392 (C MacMillan); [1994] Conv 58 (MP Thompson). A lock-out agreement does not have to satisfy the formalities required by LP(MP)A 1989, below, p 966.

[53] *Moroney v Isofam, Investments SA* [1997] EGCS 178. For precedents, see Conv Prec 19-I6, I7 which do not, however, contain express provision for reimbursement of expenditure; *Encyclopedia of Forms and Precedents*, vol 38(1) (2006), para [1244] (which does). On the courts' reluctance to award compensation for

will not normally enforce it by way of injunction, since damages are said to be an adequate remedy;[54] and even so the purchaser may have some difficulty in establishing the loss that flowed from the vendor's breach. In principle, the damages will cover the purchaser's loss of opportunity to purchase the property.[55] But to do this he has the burden of showing that he lost a real or substantial, not merely a speculative, chance of purchasing the property.[56] Lord Woolf has said:[57]

> Even though you can now arrange a 'lock-out' if you are sufficiently knowledgeable to do so, that only provides partial compensation. Much more extensive protection is needed. It should be axiomatic that, once you have made an offer to purchase, you can be released from the transaction only in restricted circumstances; likewise if you have accepted an offer to purchase, subject to contract. If you withdraw, without cause, you should be liable to pay compensation on a basis that recognises that the loss that you have caused to the other party is not confined to financial loss.

E EXCHANGE OF CONTRACTS

Where a formal contract is drawn up, two identical copies[58] are usually made, and each of the parties signs one of them. In such a case there is no binding contract until the copies have been exchanged.[59] It used to be common practice for exchange

expenditure incurred under a 'subject to contract' agreement in the absence of express contractual provision, see *Regalian Properties plc v London Docklands Development Corp* [1995] 1 WLR 212; [1995] Conv 135 (MP Thompson); [1995] CLJ 243 (G Virgo).

[54] *Tye v House* (1998) 76 P & CR 188 (purpose of lock-out is to protect purchasers against costs incurred by losing contract to another party at the last minute); [1998] PLJ 1, 21 (F Richards).

[55] In *Walford v Miles*, above, the trial judge made clear that the breach of a lock-out agreement would give rise to an assessment of damages for the loss of opportunity, although no assessment was in fact made because the Court of Appeal and the House of Lords held that there was no binding lock-out contract. The assessment of damages in *Pitt v PHH Asset Management Ltd*, above, is not reported.

[56] *Dandara Holdings Ltd v Co-operative Retail Services Ltd* [2004] EWHC 1476 (Ch), [2004] 2 EGLR 163 at [13]-[14] (breach of lock-out did not cause purchaser's loss, because there was a strong probability the vendor would have remarketed the property anyway); [2004] EG 151 (J Murdoch).

[57] EG Millennium Issue, p 70.

[58] Cf *Smith v Mansi* [1963] 1 WLR 26 (exchange unnecessary where there is only one document, signed by both parties, and the same solicitor acts for both); *Storer v Manchester City Council* [1974] 1 WLR 26 (exchange not necessary where informal agreement intended to be binding. This would not now satisfy LP(MP)A 1989, s 2, below, p 966). For a statement of the features of exchange of contracts, the 'well-recognised concept understood by both lawyers and laymen', see *Commission for the New Towns v Cooper (Great Britain) Ltd* [1995] Ch 259, 285 (Stuart-Smith LJ), following propositions submitted by counsel (see Evans LJ at 294–5).

[59] This was already well-established conveyancing practice before 1989, being the formality contemplated by the parties as giving binding effect to their agreement 'subject to contract': *Trollope & Sons v Martyn Bros* [1934] 2 KB 436, 455; *Eccles v Bryant and Pollock* [1948] Ch 93; *Harrison v Battye* [1975] 1 WLR 58 (no exchange if documents not identical); *Longman v Viscount Chelsea* (1989) 58 P & CR 189, 190 (Nourse LJ). Under LP(MP)A 1989, s 2, however, the contract cannot come into existence unless both parties sign the same document or separate, identical documents that are exchanged: below, pp 970–1; *Commission for the New Towns v Cooper (Great Britain) Ltd* [1995] Ch 259. See generally Barnsley, *Conveyancing Law and Practice*, pp 219–26.

to be effected in person or by post,[60] but other methods are now frequently used; in particular, where the contract is not an isolated transaction but part of a chain, as often in the case of contracts for the sale of residential property, speedier methods of exchange are necessary. The Council of the Law Society has given advice on how exchange may be effected by the parties' solicitors by telephone, telex or fax, including the method to be used in the case of a chain of transactions.[61]

When electronic contracts are introduced, the practice of exchange of physical copies of identical documents will be superseded by the (electronic) signature of a single copy by or on behalf of each party, which will take effect at such time as the parties have agreed.[62]

II FORMALITIES REQUIRED FOR CONTRACTS FOR THE SALE OR OTHER DISPOSITION OF AN INTEREST IN LAND

Unlike most other contracts,[63] contracts for the sale or other disposition of an interest in land are subject to formality requirements. A contract for the sale or other disposition of land or an interest in land made before 27 September 1989 is valid, even

---

[60] There is some uncertainty about the time at which the contract will be formed when exchange takes place by post. If the sending of the two copies is seen as analogous to, respectively, an offer and an acceptance, the normal rules of contract formation should apply, and so the posting of the later copy will conclude the contract if the parties so intended (expressly or impliedly): cf Anson, p 46–9. The Standard Conditions of Sale make express provision to that effect: condition 2.1.1. However, in the absence of express provision judges have been divided over whether it should be implied that posting is sufficient to conclude the contract: *Domb v Isoz* [1980] Ch 548, 564 (Templeman LJ); or whether each party expects not to be bound until he has actual or constructive possession of the other party's signed copy: *Eccles v Bryant and Pollock* [1948] Ch 93, 108 (Asquith LJ); *Domb v Isoz* at 557 (Buckley LJ).

[61] Formulas A (where one solicitor already holds both signed copies), B (where each solicitor still holds his own client's signed copy) and C (chains of transactions), reproduced in Silverman, *Conveyancing Handbook*, Appendix IV.11. The Law Society's guidance was issued in the light of a suggestion by Lord Templeman in *Domb v Isoz* [1980] Ch 548, 564; (1981) 78 LSG 961 (PV Baker and G Woolf). A physical exchange of documents must follow to comply with LP(MP)A 1989, s 2: [2005] 09 LSG 32; below, p 971.

On the duties of solicitors, see Solicitors' Code of Conduct 2007 (as amended) Rules 3.07–3.22 (conflicts of interest in conveyancing, property selling and mortgage related services), reproduced in Silverman, *Conveyancing Handbook*, Appendix I.1; *Clarke Boyce v Mouat* [1994] 1 AC 428 (where solicitors wrongly acted for both sides in a property development transaction, the fact that they could not perform their duties to both sides did not mean that their duty to one client was impliedly modified or that they were exonerated from liability for breach of contract); [1994] Conv 404 (R Tobin).

[62] LCD Consultation Paper, *Electronic Conveyancing—A draft order under s 8 Electronic Communications Act 2000*, March 2001, paras 53–55. LP(MP)A, s 2, will be amended: below, p 972.

[63] Statute of Frauds 1677, s 4, required five types of contract to be either in writing or evidenced by a written memorandum. Most of s 4 was repealed by LR (Enforcement of Contracts) Act 1954, s 1; the only remaining formality requirements in relation to contracts are land contracts and (under the only words of s 4 Statute of Frauds still in force) for contracts of guarantee. On s 4 generally, see Williams, *The Statute of Frauds: Section Four, in the Light of its Judicial Interpretation* (1932); Law Reform Committee First Report 1953 (Cmnd 8809).

if not made in writing, but will only be enforceable by action if evidenced by a signed memorandum in writing that complies with section 40 of the Law of Property Act 1925 or, failing that, if there is a sufficient act of part performance by the party seeking to enforce it. After 26 September 1989 this was superseded by section 2 of the Law of Property (Miscellaneous Provisions) Act 1989, under which there can be *no* contract unless it is in writing signed by or on behalf of both parties. Although the doctrine of part performance cannot now render enforceable an agreement that fails to comply with the 1989 Act, we shall see that other doctrines might sometimes have a similar effect.

Although section 40 of the Law of Property Act 1925 was repealed in 1989,[64] we shall first consider it briefly[65] because even now a claim might still occasionally turn on the enforceability of a contract made before 27 September 1989;[66] and in any event it will assist in understanding some aspects of section 2 of the Law of Property (Miscellaneous Provisions) Act 1989, which replaced it. However, it is important to keep the two provisions separate. There are some similarities in their wording, and it might be thought that decisions on the wording of section 40 would be relevant to the interpretation of section 2. But, rejecting the view that the word 'signed' in section 2 should be interpreted on the basis of cases concerning a sufficient signature for the purposes of section 40, Peter Gibson LJ said:[67]

> Prior to the Act of 1989 the courts viewed with some disfavour those who made oral contracts but did not abide by them. The courts were prepared to interpret the statutory requirements generously to enable contracts to be enforced and in relation to the question whether there was a sufficient memorandum evidencing an agreement extrinsic evidence was admissible....
>
> The Act of 1989 seems to me to have a new and different philosophy from that which the Statute of Frauds 1677 and section 40 of the Act of 1925 had. Oral contracts are no longer permitted. To my mind it is clear that Parliament intended that questions as to whether there was a contract, and what were the terms of the contract, should be readily ascertained by looking at the single document said to constitute the contract.

This highlights a question of policy that, in other contexts, we have seen already and will see again:[68] where the law prescribes a particular formality for a transaction, how strict is the rule? And can ways properly be found around the formality rule, consistently with the policy underlying the rule, in order to give some effect to the transaction that failed to comply with it? As we shall see, the courts have found ways around the statutory rules governing the formalities for contracts for the sale or other

---

[64] LP(MP)A 1989, s 4, Sch 2.

[65] For a more detailed discussion, see the 16th edn of this book, pp 116–26.

[66] See, eg, *Inglorest Investments Ltd v Campbell* [2004] EWCA Civ 408, [2004] 2 P & CR DG7; *Coaten v PBS Corp* [2006] EWHC 1781 (Ch), [2006] EGLR 43.

[67] *Firstpost Homes Ltd v Johnson* [1995] 1 WLR 1567, 1575–6. Balcombe LJ said at 1577 that there was 'every reason for consigning [the old law] to the limbo where it clearly belongs'. See below, pp 970–1.

[68] Below, pp 1011–17.

disposition of an interest in land, but at the highest level caution has recently been expressed in this respect; and in relation to the avoidance of formalities the approach taken under section 40 of the 1925 Act was different from that now taken under section 2 of the 1989 Act.

A CONTRACTS MADE BEFORE 27 SEPTEMBER 1989.
EVIDENCE OF CONTRACT

Section 40 of the Law of Property Act 1925[69] provided that:

(1) No action may be brought upon any contract for the sale or other disposition of land or any interest in land, unless the agreement upon which such action is brought, or some memorandum or note thereof, is in writing, and signed by the party to be charged or by some other person thereunto by him lawfully authorised.

(2) This section...does not affect the law relating to part performance...

This provision did not require writing as a condition of validity of the contract; it only provided that certain contracts relating to land should be unenforceable by either party in the absence of a sufficient written memorandum.[70] However, it expressly allowed the law relating to part performance to continue to provide an exception to the requirement of a memorandum.

(1) Contracts within Section 40

The section applied to any contract for the sale or other disposition of land or any interest in land. This covered not only a contract for the sale of freehold land, but also included a contract for the grant of a mortgage, lease, easement or profit.[71] It applied to a contract for the creation of a new interest in land as well as to a contract for the disposition of an existing interest; it also applied to a concluded unilateral contract to enter into a written contract for the sale of land.[72] Land is given a very wide definition in the Law of Property Act,[73] and has been held to include an interest in the proceeds of sale under a trust for sale of land.[74]

---

[69] Replacing (in part) Statute of Frauds 1677, s 4: LPA 1925, s 207, Sch 7; above, p 959, n 63. Farrand, *Contract and Conveyance* (4th edn), pp 321 ff; Barnsley, *Conveyancing Law and Practice*, pp 111–13. LPA 1925, s 40 was repealed by LP(MP)A 1989, s 4, Sch 2.

[70] *Leroux v Brown* (1852) 12 CB 801; *Maddison v Alderson* (1883) 8 App Cas 467, 474.

[71] LPA 1925, s 205(ii).

[72] *Daulia v Four Millbank Nominees Ltd* [1978] Ch 231. But it did not apply to compulsory purchase: *Munton v Greater London Council* [1976] 1 WLR 649.

[73] LPA 1925, s 205(ix); above, p 6.

[74] *Cooper v Critchley* [1955] Ch 431; *Steadman v Steadman* [1974] QB 161, followed on this point without argument [1976] AC 536; *Thompson's Trustee in Bankruptcy v Heaton* [1974] 1 WLR 605, 610.

(2) The Memorandum

The contract itself did not have to be in writing. All that was required was that, before any action could be brought,[75] there should be a written memorandum. In furtherance of the policy underlying the statute, the courts gave a rather generous interpretation to the question of whether there was a sufficient memorandum.[76] The question was whether a written document, signed by or on behalf of the party against whom the contract was sought to be enforced, constituted sufficient evidence against him of the contract. This in turn required the document relied on as a memorandum to satisfy two conditions: it must contain the terms of the contract; and it must constitute an express or implied recognition that a contract[77] had been entered into.

The memorandum had to contain a sufficient written statement of the terms of the contract of which it purported to be evidence: that is, as in the case of all contracts for the sale of land,[78] the parties, the property[79] (and the interest to be granted in it) and the consideration, together with any special terms regarded by the parties as essential.[80] However, the courts qualified this strict rule by holding that if a term that was not evidenced by the memorandum was exclusively for the benefit of one party, he might waive the benefit of it and sue for the enforcement of the other terms;[81] and that if an oral term not contained in the memorandum was beneficial to the defendant, the claimant could perform it and so cure its omission from the memorandum.[82] Where a term was required to be recorded in the memorandum, it had to be mentioned with sufficient certainty to satisfy the normal rules for the formation of a contract,[83] and to do so without resorting to parol evidence on the very point on which the statute required written evidence.[84] However, as long as the memorandum contained something definite to go on, the courts were prepared to admit extrinsic evidence to

---

[75] The memorandum could be created after the contract: *Barkworth v Young* (1856) 4 Drew 1 (more than 14 years after the contract); and might even be made before the contract, where a written offer was accepted orally but unconditionally: *Reuss v Picksley* (1866) LR 1 Exch 342; *Parker v Clark* [1960] 1 WLR 286; *Tiverton Estates Ltd v Wearwell Ltd* [1975] Ch 146, 166.

[76] *Firstpost Homes Ltd v Johnson* [1995] 1 WLR 1567, 1575–6 (Peter Gibson LJ), above, p 960.

[77] A document expressed to be 'subject to contract' could not be a sufficient memorandum: *Tiverton Estates Ltd v Wearwell Ltd*, above, the Court of Appeal not following the own previous decision in *Law v Jones* [1974] Ch 112 (which had held that 'subject to contract' was a suspensive condition capable of subsequent oral waiver). On 'subject to contract' agreements generally, see above, p 955.

[78] Above, pp 950, 953.

[79] The whole of the property had to be described in the memorandum, otherwise the entire contract would be unenforceable unless it could be severed: *Ram Narayan s/o Shankar v Rishad Hussain Shah s/o Tasaduq Hussain Shah* [1979] 1 WLR 1349 (oral agreement for sale of land and chattels unenforceable where memorandum only related to land and the price was indivisible: decision on Fiji statute in identical terms to LPA 1925, s 40).

[80] *Tiverton Estates Ltd v Wearwell* [1975] Ch 146, 161; *Tweddell v Henderson* [1975] 1 WLR 1496.

[81] *Hawkins v Price* [1947] Ch 645, 659 (Evershed J).

[82] *Martin v Pycroft* (1852) 2 De GM & G 785; *Scott v Bradley* [1971] Ch 850.   [83] Anson, pp 61–9.

[84] Eg if the intending vendor is not named but referred to only as 'the vendor': *Potter v Duffield* (1874) LR 18 Eq 4.

explain incomplete references such as the identity of the vendor[85] or the property to be sold.[86] Moreover, where all the terms of the agreement were not contained in a single document that satisfied section 40, but the signed document expressly or impliedly referred to another document that was necessary to complete the statement of terms, parol evidence could be given to identify the other document and all the documents formed together a sufficient memorandum for the purposes of the statute.[87]

The memorandum need not be in any particular form: even a document that had been drawn up with the express intention of repudiating the oral agreement was held to suffice.[88] The memorandum had, however, to bear the signature of the 'party to be charged'—in other words, the defendant in the action—or his agent.[89] If, therefore, in an agreement between A and B the memorandum was signed by A only, it follows that B could enforce the contract but A could not.[90] However, again, the courts construed the statute quite liberally in its requirement as to the existence of a signature.[91] It did not need to be written at the foot of the agreement, but could appear anywhere, provided that it was written with the view to governing the whole instrument;[92] and it could consist merely of the defendant's intials,[93] or even of his printed name,[94] provided that the intention was clearly to authenticate the document.

(3) Part Performance

Even if there was no memorandum sufficient to satisfy section 40 of the Law of Property Act 1925, the agreement embodied in an oral contract could be enforced in equity by a

---

[85] *Sale v Lambert* (1874) LR 18 Eq 1, 3 (Jessel MR): 'The question is, can you find out from the memorandum who the vendor is? The property is stated to be put up for sale "by direction of the proprietor." ... What more do you want? It is said that the term "proprietor" is not a sufficient description; I think that it is an excellent description; certainly in Acts of Parliament the proprietor or owner is frequently mentioned as the person on whom notices are to be served, and the like.'

[86] *Plant v Bourne* [1897] 2 Ch 281. This is an application of the general principle *id certum est quod certum reddi potest*: ibid, at 288; Lewison, *Interpretation of Contracts*, para 11.03.

[87] *Timmins v Moreland Street Property Co* Ltd [1958] Ch 110, 130. For this difficult question see further the 16th edn of this book, pp 120–1. The courts' generous interpretation of this rule again contrasts with the strict approach to joinder of documents under LP(MP)A 1989, s 2, below, p 970.

[88] *Bailey v Sweeting* (1861) 9 CBNS 843; *Dewar v Mintoft* [1912] 2 KB 373.

[89] An agent is 'lawfully authorised' if his authority has been conferred in writing or orally, or if it is reasonably inferable from the attendant circumstances: *Davies v Sweet* [1962] 2 QB 300, 305. An estate agent has no authority to contract on behalf of his client unless he is instructed to sell at a definite price and to enter into the necessary agreement: *Keen v Mear* [1920] 2 Ch 574, 579. In the case of a sale by auction, the auctioneer becomes the agent of both parties on the fall of the hammer, and so has the authority to sign a memorandum: *Bell v Balls* [1897] 1 Ch 663; *Chaney v Maclow* [1929] 1 Ch 461; *Phillips v Butler* [1945] Ch 358. LP(MP)A 1989, s 2(5)(b) excludes a contract made in the course of a public auction from the requirement of a written contract, below, p 967.

[90] *Laythoarp v Bryant* (1836) 2 Bing NC 735.

[91] *Firstpost Homes Ltd v Johnson* [1995] 1 WLR 1567, 1575–6 (Peter Gibson LJ), above, p 960, below, p 971, contrasting the requirement of signature under LP(MP)A 1989, s 2.

[92] *Johnson v Dodgson* (1837) 2 M & W 653, 659; *Caton v Caton* (1867) LR 2 HL 127.

[93] *Hill v Hill* [1947] Ch 231.   [94] *Cohen v Roche* [1927] 1 KB 169; *Leeman v Stocks* [1951] Ch 941.

party who could show a sufficient act of part performance on his own side. The policy underlying this was stated by Lord Bingham of Cornhill:[95]

> Section 4 of the Statute of Frauds was enacted in 1677 to address a mischief facilitated, it seems, by the procedural deficiencies of the day (*Holdsworth, A History of English Law*, vol VI, pp 388–390): the calling of perjured evidence to prove spurious agreements said to have been made orally. The solution applied to the five classes of contract specified in section 4 was to require, as a condition of enforceability, some written memorandum or note of the agreement signed by the party to be charged under the agreement or his authorised agent.
>
> It quickly became evident that if the 17th century solution addressed one mischief it was capable of giving rise to another: that a party, making and acting on what was thought to be a binding oral agreement, would find his commercial expectations defeated when the time for enforcement came and the other party successfully relied on the lack of a written memorandum or note of the agreement.
>
> In one of the five specified classes of agreement, relating to contracts for the sale or other disposition of land, this second mischief was mitigated by the doctrine of part performance. Implementation of an agreement (even if partial) could be relied on to prove its existence. This doctrine was expressly preserved by section 40(2) of the Law of Property Act 1925, when section 4 of the Statute of Frauds (in its application to real property) was effectively re-enacted in section 40(1).

It should be noticed that the act of part performance was not simply evidence of the contract in place of the written memorandum required by the statute, otherwise an act by either party should logically suffice. Rather, the doctrine of part performance was a creation of the courts of equity, which took the view that it would be fraudulent for a defendant to take advantage of the absence of a signed memorandum if he had stood by and allowed the claimant to alter his position for the worse by carrying out acts in performance of the contract.[96] In such a case the defendant was really 'charged' upon the equities resulting from the acts done in execution of the contract, and not (within the meaning of the statute) upon the contract itself.[97]

We have seen already[98] that the general approach of the courts was to construe the statutory requirement of a written memorandum under section 40 of the Law of Property Act 1925 rather generously, so as to seek to find, if possible, a sufficient memorandum. The doctrine of part performance was developed to allow a contract to be enforced even in the absence of a written memorandum; and the courts[99] tended again to interpret, or develop, the requirements of the doctrine so as to enable the

---

[95] *Actionstrength Ltd v International Glass Engineering IN.GL.EN SpA* [2003] UKHL 17, [2003] 2 AC 541 at [1]-[3].

[96] *Steadman v Steadman* [1976] AC 536, 540 (Lord Reid). There is a marked similarity between the doctrine of part performance and other equitable doctrines that allow statutory formalities to be avoided: see below, pp 973–8 (LP(MP)A 1989, s 2: constructive trust), 1015–17 (LPA 1925, s 53: constructive trust and proprietary estoppel).

[97] *Maddison v Alderson* (1883) 8 App Cas 467, 475 (Lord Selborne).   [98] Above, p 962.

[99] In particular, the majority in *Steadman v Steadman* [1976] AC 536. For a more detailed discussion of that case, and examples of the operation of the doctrine of part performance, see the 16th edn of this book, pp 122–5.

contract to be enforced rather than not. However, although one of the parties may have done several things towards performing his side of the agreement, it did not follow that they would amount to part performance. The act must of itself on a balance of probability[100] establish the existence of the oral contract, although it was sufficient that it proved *a* contract, and need not refer to the precise terms of *the* contract on which the claimant relied.[101] It must be an act intelligible only on the assumption that some such contract as that alleged had been made, and if it were explicable on some other equally good ground,[102] it did not satisfy the test. Further, there might be more than one act, and the acts when joined together 'may throw light on each other; and there is no reason to exclude light'.[103]

(4) Remedies at Law or in Equity

If a party to a contract relating to land relied on a memorandum and proved his case, he was entitled to the usual range of remedies for enforcement of his contractual rights:[104] he would be entitled as of right to an award of damages at common law for breach of contract; and he might also be able to obtain a decree of specific performance in equity. However, if he was compelled to base his action on part performance, he was not in such a favourable position. He could not enforce the contract at law, and therefore had no entitlement to damages. His remedy was in equity, and therefore hinged in the first place on his showing that the contract was one for which the court had jurisdiction to grant specific performance. As long as this was the case—even if no

---

[100] [1976] AC 536, 564–5 (Lord Simon of Glaisdale), 541–2 (Lord Reid).

[101] *Kingswood Estate Co Ltd v Anderson* [1963] 2 QB 169, 189 (Upjohn LJ), approving a statement in *Fry on Specific Performance* (6th edn, 1921), p 278, and modifying the earlier strict view that the act must be unequivocally referable to the particular contract. Upjohn LJ's statement was approved unanimously by the House of Lords in *Steadman v Steadman*, above. However, the House was divided on whether the act must refer to a contract relating to land.

[102] Eg entry into possession by the claimant was very commonly the act of part performance: *Kingswood Estate Co Ltd v Anderson*, above (entry into possession of flat sufficient act of part performance to enforce oral contract of tenancy). But *remaining* in possession, without additional circumstances, would not be sufficient because it was equivocal: cf *Nunn v Fabian* (1865) 1 Ch App 35 (contract for new lease to tenant already in possession; payment of increased rent constitutes the act of part performance). Payment of money posed a particular difficulty, since it will often be equivocal; but a majority of the House of Lords in *Steadman v Steadman*, above, decisively rejected the argument that it could never be a sufficient act of part performance. For insufficient acts of part performance, see *New Hart Builders Ltd v Brindley* [1975] Ch 342 (submission by purchasers of application for planning permission); *Re Gonin* [1979] Ch 16 (unmarried daughter's returning home after compassionate release from wartime service to look after ageing parents); *Daulia v Four Millbank Nominees Ltd* [1978] Ch 231 (purchasers' tender of draft contract together with banker's draft for deposit). For sufficient acts of part performance, see *Liddell v Hopkinson* (1974) 233 EG 513 (vacation of matrimonial home by divorced wife so that husband could sell it, in return for his offer of two-thirds of proceeds of sale if she would give up her right of occupation); *Sutton v Sutton* [1984] Ch 184 (wife's consent to divorce on terms that matrimonial home be conveyed to her); *Dakin v Dakin* [1990] EGCS 45 (father's signing of draft conveyance as a result of son's deceit); *Morritt v Wonham* [1993] NPC 2 (extensive work to farm), [1994] Conv 233 (MP Thompson).

[103] *Steadman v Steadman* [1976] AC 536, 564 (Lord Simon of Glaisdale). The flexibility of this approach is enhanced when 'even spoken words may themselves be part performance of a contract': ibid.

[104] For further discussion of remedies for breach of contract, see below, pp 990 ff.

damages would be available at common law, or a decree of specific performance would be refused on some discretionary ground—the court had power to award damages either in addition to, or in substitution for, specific performance.[105] Such damages are assessed in the same way as they would be at common law.[106]

B CONTRACTS MADE AFTER 26 SEPTEMBER 1989. REQUIREMENT OF WRITING

Section 2(1) of the Law of Property (Miscellaneous Provisions) Act 1989[107] provides that:

> A contract for the sale or other disposition of an interest in land can only be made in writing and only by incorporating all the terms which the parties have expressly agreed in one document or, where contracts are exchanged, in each.

It follows, therefore, that if the requirements as to writing are not complied with, there is *no* contract. This is a major change from the position under section 40 of the Law of Property Act 1925 where, as we have seen, non-compliance meant that the contract was merely unenforceable by action.[108] Under section 2, there must of course still be an agreement between the parties that satisfies the general rules governing the formation of contracts.[109] But that agreement does not become a contract until the additional requirement of writing set out in section 2 is satisfied.

(1) Contracts within Section 2

Section 2, like section 40, applies to any contract for the sale or other disposition of an interest in land. 'Interest in land' is widely defined as meaning any estate, interest or

---

[105] SCA 1981, s 50. See *Lavery v Pursell* (1888) 39 Ch D 508, 519 (Chitty J) (Chancery Amendment Act 1858, s 2, the predecessor of SCA 1981, s 50, 'did not give the old Court of Chancery a general jurisdiction to give damages whenever it thought fit, it was only in that kind of case where specific performance would have been the right decree and there were reasons why it would be better to substitute damages, but that could not apply to a case where you could not have given specific performance').

[106] *Johnson v Agnew* [1980] AC 367, below, p 992.

[107] Based on Law Com No 164, *Formalities for Contracts of Sale etc of Land* (1987); [1987] Conv 313. The section does not apply to contracts made before it came into force: s 2(7). LPA 1925, s 40, ceased to have effect: s 2(8). For the changes see Emmet, paras 2.030-2.030.13; Sweet and Maxwell's *Conveyancing Practice*, paras 4.040–4.046; and generally (1989) 105 LQR 555 (RE Annand); [1989] Conv 431 (PH Pettit); (1990) LS 325 (L Bently and P Coughlan). See also Requirements of Writing (Scotland) Act 1995, which has not followed the English approach to formalities.

[108] Ignorance of the change is professional negligence: for a solicitor or barrister *Green v Collyer-Bristow* [1999] Lloyd's Rep PN 798.

[109] Final and complete agreement on the parties, the property (and the interest to be granted in it) and the consideration, together with any special terms regarded by the parties as essential: above, p 950. Section 2 therefore contemplates offer and acceptance between the parties, before the agreement so formed is put into writing to form the contract: *Commission for the New Towns v Cooper (Great Britain) Ltd* [1995] Ch 259, 293 (Evans LJ).

charge in or over land.[110] However, three types of contract are expressly excluded:[111] (a) a contract to grant a lease for a term not exceeding three years to which section 54(2) of the Law of Property Act 1925 applies;[112] (b) a contract made in the course of a public auction; and (c) certain contracts regulated under the Financial Services and Markets Act 2000.[113]

In interpreting section 2 the courts have noted that, although it represents a radical change in the law, the change relates to the substance of the law rather than to its scope:[114]

The expression 'a contract for the sale or other disposition of an interest in land' is clearly modelled on s 40(1) of the Law of Property Act 1925, 'any contract for the sale or disposition of land, or any interest in land…'. There is nothing in the 1989 Act, or in the Law Commission report which preceded it, which suggests any intention to widen the category of transactions to which the special law was applicable.

The section therefore includes contracts to sell the freehold or to assign a lease, and other contracts relating to an existing estate or interest in land, such as a contract to surrender a lease,[115] or to grant a new lease or mortgage, easement or profit, and applies whether the title to the land in question is already registered or not.

A number of cases have arisen in which the limits of application of section 2 have been tested. The section has been held to apply to:

(a) An existing contract for sale where the vendor does not at the time of the contract have an interest in land but proposes to acquire it in order to complete the sale.[116]

(b) An agreement to enter into a formal legal mortgage;[117] and, likewise, an equitable charge by deposit of title deeds, since it is construed as an agreement to create a charge and therefore the deposit must be accompanied by a document that

---

[110] S 2(6), as amended by TLATA 1996, s 25(2), Sch 4 (deleting the words 'or in or over the proceeds of sale of land'). 'Disposition' has the same meaning as in the Law of Property Act 1925: see LPA 1925, s 205(1)(ii).

[111] S 2(5), which also provides that nothing in the section affects the creation or operation of resulting, implied or constructive trusts: see below, pp 974 ff.

[112] Above, p 212; *Parc Battersea Ltd v Hutchinson* [1999] 2 EGLR 33. Such a contract was within LPA 1925, s 40.

[113] As amended by SI 2001 No 3649, art 317(1), (2). Otherwise, some forms of investment that include interests in land, such as unit trusts, would be within s 2. FSA-regulated mortgage contracts, home reversion plans, home purchase plans and sale and rent back agreements are, however, included within s 2: ibid; SI 2009 No 1342, art 24(a). For home reversion plans and home purchase plans, see above, p 796, n 17.

[114] *Nweze v Nwoko* [2004] EWCA Civ 379, [2004] 2 P & CR 33 at [34] (Carnwath LJ). See also Sedley LJ at [31]: 'A requirement for writing in a legal system that ordinarily recognises parol contracts as valid and enforceable is an exception to a rule and as such should be construed no more widely than is necessary.' See also *Kilcarne Holdings Ltd v Targetfollow (Birmingham) Ltd* [2004] EWHC 2547 (Ch), [2005] 2 P & CR 8 at [194] (Lewison J: fixed charge over a lease is an interest in land within s 2 because it was under the old law).

[115] *Commission for the New Towns v Cooper (Great Britain) Ltd* [1995] Ch 259, 283.

[116] *Singh v Beggs* (1995) 71 P & CR 120.

[117] *Murray v Guinness* [1998] NPC 79; *Kinane v Mackie-Conteh* [2005] EWCA Civ 45, [2005] 6 EGCS 140 (agreement saved by constructive trust under s 2(5)).

satisfies the requirements of the section.[118] However, section 2 does not apply to the *grant* of an equitable charge, because it takes immediate effect from the date of the grant.[119]

(c) The variation of a material term in an existing contract that was itself subject to the requirements of section 2.[120]

On the other hand, the section has been held *not* to apply to:

(a) The exercise of an option to purchase land.[121] If the agreement under which the option is granted itself satisfies the requirements of the section, then the notice that exercises the option need not do so.[122]

(b) A collateral contract. In *Record v Bell*:[123]

before signed contracts were exchanged, the vendor offered to the purchaser a warranty as to the state of his title in order to induce him to exchange. This warranty was referred to in a side-letter which was attached to the contract, but which was only signed by the purchaser. It was held that the side-letter had not been incorporated into the main contract (there was no reference to it there), but that there was a collateral contract which fell outside section 2.

However:[124]

---

[118] *United Bank of Kuwait plc v Sahib* [1997] Ch 107, above, p 810; [1998] Conv 502 (P Critchley).

[119] *Murray v Guinness*, above; cf *Target Holdings Ltd v Priestley* (2000) 79 P & CR 305 (agreement to vary mortgage also held to be outside s 2 because mortgage was a disposition, not a contract for the disposition of land); [1999] Conv 414 (MP Thompson). See also *Helden v Strathmore Ltd* [2011] EWCA Civ 542, [2011] All ER (D) 92 (May) at [27]-[28].

[120] *McCausland v Duncan Lawrie Ltd* [1997] 1 WLR 38, M & B, p 20; [1996] Conv 366 (MP Thompson); (1992) 147 NLJ 219 (HW Wilkinson).

[121] *Spiro v Glencrown Properties Ltd* [1991] Ch 537, M & B, p 34; below, p 984 ('call option', ie, the right to call for a conveyance of the property); *Active Estates Ltd v Parness* [2002] EWHC 893 (Ch), [2002] 3 EGLR 13, 18 ('put option', ie the right to require the other party to take a conveyance). For options generally, see below, pp 983 ff.

[122] There are practical difficulties, however, with the application of s 2 to a right of pre-emption. Since the grant of the right of pre-emption does not itself create an interest in land, below, p 985, the contract to purchase can arise only at a later date when the right is exercised, and commonly that is not done by a document signed by both parties: *Bircham & Co Nominees (No 2) Ltd v Worrell Holdings Ltd* [2001] EWCA Civ 775, (2001) 82 P & CR 34; cf *Butts Park Ventures (Coventry) Ltd v Bryant Homes Central Ltd* [2003] EWHC 2487 (Ch), [2004] BCC 207 (both grant of pre-emption and exercise complied with s 2). For the application of s 2 to declarations relating to the disposition of land contained in two wills (which could not, because of the failure to comply with s 2, take effect as mutual wills) see *Healey v Brown* [2002] 19 EGCS 147.

[123] [1991] 1 WLR 853; (1992) 108 LQR 217 (RJ Smith); [1991] CLJ 399 (C Harpum); [1991] Conv 471 (M Harwood); [1991] All ER Rev 201 (PJ Clarke). See also *Pitt v PHH Asset Management Ltd* [1994] 1 WLR 327; *Lotteryking Ltd v AMEC Properties Ltd* [1995] 2 EGLR 13 (collateral agreement to remedy defects outside s 2).

[124] *Kilcarne Holdings Ltd v Targetfollow (Birmingham) Ltd* [2004] EWHC 2547 (Ch), [2005] 2 P & CR 8 at [189] (Lewison J). See also *Business Environment Bow Lane Ltd v Deanwater Estates Ltd* [2007] EWCA Civ 622, [2007] 2 EGLR 51 at [42] (Morritt C: 'the law relating to collateral contracts is well-established but in connection with sales or leases of land needs to be applied with caution if not ... suspicion'). Cf *Hanoman v Southwark LBC (No 2)* [2008] EWCA Civ 624, [2009] 1 WLR 374 at [56] (Arden LJ: 'on general principle the court should so far as possible interpret [a collateral contract] so that it can be enforced and party autonomy respected); *North Eastern Properties Ltd v Coleman* [2010] EWCA Civ 277, [2010] 1 WLR 2715 (appropriately worded 'entire agreement' clause can be of assistance in showing that the terms of the land contract are complete in themselves).

Although it may be possible for parties to hive off parts of their arrangements into separate and distinct contracts,[125] the court should be wary of artificially dividing what is in truth a composite transaction.[126] If part of a composite transaction is a contract for the sale or other disposition of an interest in land, then the contract as a whole must satisfy the statutory requirements.[127]

(c) An agreement, not itself a contract for the sale or other disposition of land, which is supplemental to a land contract that has been duly carried out, and is therefore no longer executory.[128]

(d) A contract to put property on the market and to sell to a third party if such a purchaser were found.[129]

(e) An agreement by which neighbours settled a boundary dispute; section 2 did not apply either (i) because the agreement was not one 'for' the disposition of an interest in land, even if its effect was that land was to be conveyed in consequence of it; or (ii) because Parliament could not have intended the section to apply to demarcating agreements under which trivial transfers of land were involved.[130]

(2) The Writing Required

The writing requirements are[131] as follows:

2.—(1) A contract for the sale or other disposition of an interest in land can only be made in writing and only by incorporating all the terms that the parties have expressly agreed in one document or, where contracts are exchanged, in each.[132]

---

125 *Tootal Clothing Ltd v Guinea Properties Ltd Management Ltd* (1992) 64 P & CR 452.

126 *Grossman v Hooper* [2001] EWCA Civ 615; [2001] 3 FCR 662. [See Sir Christopher Staughton at [35]-[36], doubting *Tootal Clothing Ltd v Guinea Properties Management Ltd* on this point.]

127 *Godden v Merthyr Tydfil Housing Association* (1997) 74 P & CR D1.

128 *Tootal Clothing Ltd v Guinea Properties & Management Ltd*, above; [1993] Conv 89 (P Luther); (1993) 109 LQR 191 (D Wilde).

129 *Nweze v Nwoko* [2004] EWCA Civ 379, [2004] 2 P & CR 33; [2004] Conv 323 (MP Thompson) distinguishing *Jelson Ltd v Derby City Council* [1999] 3 EGLR 91, in which the judge had held that a contract between A and B under which A has the right without more to call for the property to be transferred to a buyer whom he nominates on terms set out in the contract was a contract to which s 2 applied, because it was in effect an option contract relating to the land. The further decision of the judge, to the effect that the contract failed because s 2 required the signature of the third party, rather than just of the two contracting parties, was however not approved. See also *RG Kensington Management Co Ltd v Hutchinson IDH Ltd* [2002] EWHC 1180 (Ch), [2003] 2 P & CR 13 at [57] (Neuberger J): closing words of s 2(3) require the contract to be signed by 'each party to the contract'; not by 'each party to the prospective conveyance or transfer' (applied to agreement under s 106 TCPA 1990 in *Milebush Properties Ltd v Tameside MBC* [2010] EWHC 1022 (Ch), [2010] 2 EGLR 93).

130 *Joyce v Rigolli* [2004] EWCA Civ 79, [2004] 1 P & CR DG22; [2004] Conv 224 (MP Thompson); [2007] Conv 544 (T Watkin).

131 For a proposal to introduce electonic contracts, see below, p 972.

132 *Milton Keynes Development Corp v Cooper (Great Britain) Ltd* [1993] EGCS 142 (exchange of faxes held not to be a contract or exchange of contracts). On the meaning of 'exchange', see above, p 971; below.

This refers only to express terms, and therefore does not extend to implied terms, such as a term that where there is a sale with vacant possession, vacant possession must be given on completion. However, *all* the expressly agreed terms must be incorporated in the document if the contract is to be valid.[133]

> 2.—(2) The terms may be incorporated in a document either by being set out in it or by reference to some other document.

This provision differs from that for joinder of documents under section 40 of the 1925 Act, where there could be joinder if there was an express or implied reference in a signed memorandum to some other document or transaction. The rule under section 2 is narrower in that it requires reference to some other *document*. It is not clear whether that reference must be express or whether it can be implied, although it is likely that a court will take a stricter view than used to be taken under section 40.[134] If another document is incorporated by reference, it is the incorporating document that must be signed so as to satisfy section 2:[135] it is insufficient that one party's signature appears only on the incorporated document.[136]

> 2.—(3) The document incorporating the terms or, where contracts are exchanged, one of the documents incorporating them (but not necessarily the same one) must be signed by or on behalf of each party to the contract.

There are several points to notice about this provision. First, *each* party to the contract must sign for the contract to come into existence. This is a marked change from the position under section 40, where, if there was a memorandum signed by only one party, the oral contract could be enforced but only by the *other* party. However, as under section 40, if a party does not himself sign the document, someone else may be authorised to sign on his behalf.[137]

There is then a question about what constitutes 'signature'. It has been held that, for the purposes of section 2, the signer of the document must sign his own name with his own hand upon it. In *Firstpost Homes Ltd v Johnson*[138]

> X, who had orally agreed to purchase land from Mrs F prepared a typewritten letter addressed to himself by name, including the words 'I now agree to sell to you the above

---

[133] *Rudra v Abbey National plc* (1998) 76 P & CR 537 (failure to state name of vendor; section not satisfied). For rectification to bring the document within s 2, see below, pp 971, 988–9.

[134] *Firstpost Homes Ltd v Johnson* [1995] 1 WLR 1567, 1571 (Peter Gibson LJ).

[135] *Courtney v Corp Ltd* [2006] EWCA Civ 518; [2006] All ER (D) 16 (Mar).

[136] Ibid, at 1573 (Peter Gibson LJ, discussing also the meaning of 'document').

[137] If the contract is signed by an agent, the agent's authority need not itself be conferred in writing: *McLaughlin v Duffill* [2008] EWCA Civ 1627, [2010] Ch 1 (CA left open the question of which party has the burden of proof that the agent had (or had no) authority). See also *Orton v Collins* [2007] EWHC 803 (Ch), [2007] 1 WLR 2953 (court has power to order parties to sign single document containing terms of settlement that would otherwise not be compliant with s 2 because concluded only by acceptance of offer under CPR Part 36 during settlement negotiations).

[138] [1995] 1 WLR 1567; [1996] CLJ 192 (AJ Oakley); [1995] Conv 319 (MP Thompson).

land shown on the enclosed plan'. X signed the plan but not the letter; Mrs F signed the letter and counter-signed the plan.

Holding that there was no contract satisfying the requirements of section 2, the Court of Appeal held, first, that the letter and the plan were not self-evidently a single document for the purposes of section 2(1); and, second, that the typing of X's name and address in the letter was not a signature. Peter Gibson LJ said:[139]

> it is an artificial use of language to describe the printing or the typing of the name of an addressee in the letter as the signature by the addressee when he has typed that document. Ordinary language does not, it seems to me, extend that far.

The section also provides that the parties' signatures can be on separate documents, if the contract is formed by exchange of contracts. The practice of 'exchange of contracts' was well established before 1989,[140] but it has acquired a new significance as a result of section 2. It was held by the Court of Appeal in *Commission for the New Towns v Cooper (Great Britain) Ltd*[141] that 'exchange of contracts', whilst not a term of art, is none the less a well-recognised concept that is to be construed in a technical sense. Each party, in the expectation that the other would do likewise and intending to bring about a binding contract, must sign a contractual document incorporating all the agreed terms and intended to take effect as a formal document of title, neither party being bound until each had delivered his part into the other's possession in a manner to be mutually agreed. The concluding stages of correspondence between the defendant and the claimant by which agreement had been reached could not therefore constitute an exchange of contracts for the purposes of section 2.

> 2.—(4) Where a contract for the sale or other disposition of an interest in land satisfies the conditions of this section by reason only of the rectification of one or more documents in pursuance of an order of a court, the contract shall come into being, or be deemed to have come into being, at such time as may be specified in the order.

Although the statute requires that the parties have incorporated all their expressly agreed terms in the written document, it also contemplates that the court might rectify a document that fails to comply with section 2 and thereby to bring it into compliance. The philosophy behind section 2 is that questions as to whether there is a contract,

---

139 Ibid, at 1575, rejecting analogies from cases on LPA 1925, s 40, above, p 963, and adopting a general statement of the normal meaning of 'signature' from *Goodman v J Eban Ltd* [1954] 1 QB 550, 561 (Denning LJ). See also *Butts Park Ventures (Coventry) Ltd v Bryant Homes Central Ltd* [2003] EWHC 2487 (Ch), [2004] BCC 207 (on balance of probabilities, lost document bore signatures of both parties, rather than the signature of one on a document that contained only the photocopy signature of the other).

140 Above, p 958.

141 [1995] Ch 259, refusing to follow its own previous decision in *Hooper v Sherman* [1994] NPC 153 that had held that an exchange of letters of offer and acceptance, each signed by one party, could satisfy s 2. The actual decision in *Hooper v Sherman* was distinguishable, since the exchange of letters were no more than confirmation of an oral agreement that the parties had already reached: [1995] Ch 259, 289 (Stuart-Smith LJ), 295 (Evans LJ). But the general approach of the earlier decision was rejected as being wrongly based on Law Com No 164, para 4.15, since the drafting of s 2 had not in this respect followed the Law Commission's proposal.

and what are the terms of the contract, should be readily ascertained by looking at the single document said to constitute the contract, without resort to parol evidence.[142] However, one general exception to the parol evidence rule is where a party seeks to show that that a written contract does not properly reflect the parties' agreement and should therefore be rectified in equity.[143] This may therefore equally apply to a written contract for the sale of land.[144]

(3) Electronic Contracts

Under the Land Registration Act 2002, electronic conveyancing is now gradually being introduced.[145] As part of this change, it is inevitable that parties will wish their contract, as well as the later disposition of the interest in land, to be effected electronically. However, the Land Registration Act did not make provision for electronic contracts, which were intended to be introduced through other provisions. In 2001 the Lord Chancellor's Department published draft proposals[146] for the introduction of electronic contracts. A new section 2A would be inserted into the Law of Property (Miscellaneous Provisions) Act 1989 to enable an 'electronic contract' to be as effective for the purposes of section 2 (and any other enactment) as an equivalent paper contract if it meets certain conditions: all the terms that the parties have expressly agreed are incorporated in the electronic document (or by reference to some other document); the document makes provision for the time and date when the contract takes effect; the document has the electronic signature of each person by whom it purports to be authenticated; and each electronic signature is certified.[147]

It is proposed that the change be implemented through secondary legislation.[148] Electronic contracts will obviate the need for exchange of contracts. The contract will be made on a secure electronic communications network,[149] to which only authorised persons have access; and each party (or their respective agents) will sign the contract

---

[142] *Firstpost Homes Ltd v Johnson* [1995] 1 WLR 1567, 1576 (Peter Gibson LJ).

[143] Treitel, para 6.025; below, pp 988–9.

[144] *Wright v Robert Leonard (Developments) Ltd* [1994] EGCS 69 (contract that referred only to land rectified to include furniture as agreed before exchange of contracts took place); cf *Oun v Ahmad* [2008] EWHC 545 (Ch), [2008] 2 P & CR DG3 (no rectification: term omitted by express agreement).

[145] See generally above, pp 141–3; p 1122, below.

[146] LCD Consultation Paper, *Electronic Conveyancing—A draft order under s 8 Electronic Communications Act 2000*, CP 05/2001, March 2001. The paper also contained certain proposals relating generally to electronic conveyancing that are superseded by the provisions of LRA 2002.

[147] References of an electronic signature and to the certification of a signature are to be read in accordance with Electronic Communications Act 2000, s 7(2), (3). For a worked example of the operation of the proposed form of electronic contract, contrasted with the operation of the current law, see LCD Consultation Paper, above, n 146, paras 53–55; Mason, *Electronic Signatures in Law* (2nd edn, 2007).

[148] An order to be made by the Lord Chancellor under Electronic Communications Act 2000, s 8. Such an order can only make electronic communications or storage *possible*; to make it compulsory would require primary legislation: ibid, s 8(6)(a).

[149] A land registry network, which is to be put in place for electronic conveyancing: LRA 2002, s 92 and Sch. 5.

electronically. The contract will be made at the time and date that has been agreed between the parties.

In 2007 the Land Registry published a revised version of the proposed section 2A, which would apply only to contracts relating to registered land.[150] However, it has now been decided that the facility to use electronic contracts will not be introduced until later in the incremental programme by which electronic conveyancing is to be introduced.[151] It has even been questioned whether there is any need for such legislative change, or whether an electronic contract can already satisfy the requirements of writing and signature in section 2 of the Law of Property (Miscellaneous Provisions) Act 1989.[152] It seems, however, preferable to introduce new express provisions to deal with electronic contracts since they do not fit comfortably with the language of section 2.[153]

(4) Continued Use of 'Subject to Contract'

It would seem at first sight that the practice of heading pre-contract correspondence with the phrase 'subject to contract' is no longer necessary, since no contract can come into existence until a document is signed by both parties. However, in practice it is still used in order to draw a clear distinction between the communications preparatory to the contract and the contract itself; and it also thereby makes clear that the parties do not yet intend their communications to have any binding force, not only as a contract but also outside the contract, such as through a constructive trust or estoppel.[154]

(5) Proprietary Estoppel and Constructive Trust

We saw[155] that when a signed memorandum was required by statute for the enforcement of a contract for the sale of land, the courts developed a doctrine under which the contract, although not complying with the statutory formality, could be enforced by a party who could show a sufficient act of *part performance*;[156] and that this doctrine was rooted in the desire not to permit a defendant fraudulently to take advantage of the absence of a signed memorandum if he had stood by and let the claimant alter his position for the worse by carrying out acts in performance of the contract. The doctrine of part performance was therefore, at least in part, a form of estoppel.[157]

---

[150] Land Registry Consultation paper, *E-conveyancing Secondary Legislation Part 1* (February 2007), pp 95–102.

[151] Land Registry *Report on Responses to E-conveyancing Secondary Legislation Part 1* (2007), p 26.

[152] *Electronic Commerce: Formal Requirements in Commercial Transactions: Advice from the Law Commission* (2001), discussed H & B, p 329.

[153] H & B, pp 329–30.   [154] Above, p 955; below.   [155] Above, pp 963–5.

[156] LPA 1925, s 40, re-enacting Statute of Frauds 1677, s 4, expressly retained the exception of part performance that had been developed by the courts: s 40(2).

[157] *Actionstrength Ltd v International Glass Engineering IN.GL.EN SpA* [2003] UKHL 17, [2003] 2 AC 541 at [22]-[23] (Lord Hoffmann).

The doctrine of part performance, as such, is no longer relevant to contracts for the sale of land: under section 2 of the Law of Property (Miscellaneous Provisions) Act 1989 an agreement that does not comply with the statutory formalities does not constitute a contract that can be partly performed.[158] However, there are two bases on which it can be argued that an agreement that fails to comply with section 2 might none the less be enforced: either under the doctrine of proprietary estoppel; or under a constructive trust. The latter is expressly provided for in section 2(5) by the words 'nothing in this section affects the creation or operation of resulting, implied or constructive trusts'.

The policy arguments in relation to section 2 are not, of course, identical to those for the old formality rule under section 40.[159] There, the contract was not void but unenforceable; it may have seemed a smaller step to allow parol evidence to be given to prove the contract where it would otherwise be fraudulent to allow the defendant to rely on the statute. Under section 2, there is no contract if it is not in the required written form. However, the courts have started to apply the doctrine of proprietary estoppel, and the saving for constructive trusts contained in section 2(5), to further the same policy as that which lay behind the doctrine of part performance; and they have recognised the similarity between them although, as we shall see, in *Cobbe v Yeoman's Row Management* Ltd[160] the House of Lords has narrowed the circumstances in which proprietary estoppel can be used in this context, and dicta of Lord Scott of Foscote even cast coubt on whether it can be used at all.

In *Yaxley v Gotts*:[161]

Y, a builder, agreed orally with a friend, BG, that he would carry out work on a building that BG was buying, in order to convert it into flats, and would manage the property thereafter, in return for being given the ground floor flats of the converted property. The property was in fact bought by AG, BG's son; but AG adopted the arrangement made by his father. After Y had done the building work, the parties fell out and AG excluded him from the property.

The Court of Appeal held that, although the agreement could not be enforced as a contract because it was not in writing for the purposes of section 2(1) of the Law of Property (Miscellaneous Provisions) Act 1989, Y was entitled to a rent-free 99-year lease of the ground floor flats, either under the doctrine of proprietary estoppel, as held by the judge, or under a constructive trust. Robert Walker LJ said:[162]

---

[158] Above, p 966. For a suggestion that part performance has not been abolished but may survive as an equitable doctrine, see *Singh v Beggs* (1995) 71 P & CR 120, 122 (Neill LJ); [1997] Conv 293 (SIA Swann); cf however *Yaxley v Gotts* [2000] Ch 162, 172 (Robert Walker LJ). The New Zealand Property Law Act 2007 requires a contract for the disposition of land to be in writing (s 24), but retains the doctrine of part performance (s 26).

[159] Above, p 960.   [160] [2008] UKHL 55, [2008] 1 WLR 1752, below, p 976.

[161] [2000] Ch 162, M & B p 22; [2000] CLJ 23 (L Tee); (2000) 116 LQR 11 (RJ Smith); (2000) 63 MLR 912 (I Moore); [2000] Conv 245 (MP Thompson); [2000] All ER Rev 242 (PJ Clarke).

[162] [2000] Ch 162, 176. See also at 189–90 (Beldam LJ), drawing attention to the links between the old law of part performance and the use of estoppel and constructive trust under s 2, by reference to Law Commission's report on which s 2 was based; below, n 163. See also *Kinane v Mackie-Conteh* [2005] EWCA

At a high level of generality, there is much common ground between the doctrines of proprietary estoppel and the constructive trust, just as there is between proprietary estoppel and part performance. All are concerned with equity's intervention to provide relief against unconscionable conduct, whether as between neighbouring landowners, or vendor and purchaser, or relatives who make informal arrangements for sharing a home, or a fiduciary and the beneficiary or client to whom he owes a fiduciary obligation.

The Court inferred from the Law Commission's report on which section 2 was based,[163] and from the express saving for constructive trusts in section 2(5), that the policy behind section 2 was not to prevent the court from giving effect in equity to the principles of proprietary estoppel and constructive trusts. Beldam LJ said:[164]

> I cannot see that there is any reason to qualify the plain words of section 2(5). They were included to preserve the equitable remedies to which the Commission had referred. I do not think it inherent in a social policy of simplifying conveyancing by requiring the certainty of a written document that unconscionable conduct or equitable fraud should be allowed to prevail.
>
> In my view the provision that nothing in section 2 of the Act of 1989 is to affect the creation or operation of resulting, implied or constructive trusts effectively excludes from the operation of the section cases in which an interest in land might equally well be claimed by relying on constructive trust or proprietary estoppel.

It has been emphasised that to use proprietary estoppel in this context is not simply to give effect to the contract:[165]

> reliance on the unenforceable agreement only takes the claimant part of the way: he must still prove all the other components of proprietary estoppel. In particular, the requirement that the defendant encouraged or permitted the claimant in his erroneous belief is not satisfied simply by the admission of the invalid agreement in evidence. In this sort of case, the claimant has to show that the defendant represented to the claimant, by his words or conduct, including conduct in the provision or delivery of the agreement, that the agreement created an enforceable obligation. The cause of action in proprietary estoppel is thus not founded on the enforceable agreement but upon the defendant's conduct which, when viewed in all relevant respects, is unconscionable.

Civ 45, [2005] 06 EGCS 140 at [32] (Arden LJ): 'section 2(5) plays a similar role to that of part performance, although it operates more flexibly than that doctrine'.

[163] Law Com No 164, *Formalities for Contracts for Sale etc of Land* (1987), Part V, relied on by Clarke LJ at 182, and Beldam LJ at 188–90.

[164] [2000] Ch 162, 193. For discussion of the relationship between proprietary estoppel and constructive trust, see ibid, 176–7, 180 (Robert Walker LJ) and 191–3 (Beldam LJ), both relying on, inter alia, *Grant v Edwards* [1986] Ch 638, 656 (Sir Nicolas Browne-Wilkinson); above, p 514; cf *Stack v Dowden* [2007] UKHL 17, [2007] 2 AC 432 at [37] (Lord Walker of Gestingthorpe: 'I am now rather less enthusiastic about the notion that proprietary estoppel and "common interest" constructive trusts can or should be completely assimilated'). Whether proprietary estoppel is to be seen technically as separate from, or a particular manifestation of, constructive trust, both judges held that the saving in LP(M)A 1989, s 2(5) was sufficient to support the judge's decision on the basis of proprietary estoppel. For further discussion of proprietary estoppel, see above, pp 904–22, 936–46; below, pp 1014–27; and for constructive trusts, see above, pp 512–19, 933–6; below, pp 1012–14.

[165] *Kinane v Mackie-Conteh*, above, at [29] (Arden LJ).

The approach taken in *Yaxley v Gotts* has been followed in a series of cases in the Court of Appeal.[166] However, in *Cobbe v Yeoman's Row Management Ltd*[167] the House of Lords appears to have narrowed the scope for the operation of proprietary estoppel as a means of saving an agreement that fails to comply with section 2.[168] In *Cobbe*:

> C, an experienced property developer, reached an oral agreement in principle with YRM Ltd, owner of a block of flats, under which C would at his own expense obtain planning permission for a development of the property, and YRM Ltd would obtain vacant possession of the property and transfer it to C, for development and subsequent sale, the profits to be distributed between the parties. Many details were settled, including the price for the transfer of the building to C, and the share of the profit on sale that C was to pay to YRM Ltd, but the oral agreement did not cover some terms that would have been expected in the final agreement, and no written contract was ever finalised in compliance with section 2 of the Law of Property (Miscellaneous Provisions) Act 1989. The trial judge held that L-M, a director of YRM Ltd, had encouraged C's belief that if he succeeded in obtaining planning permission, the oral agreement would be honoured. C obtained the planning permission.

The trial judge, followed by the Court of Appeal,[169] held that C was entitled to a lien for 50 per cent of the increase in value of the property in consequence of the grant of planning permission, under the doctrine of proprietary estoppel. The House of Lords reversed the Court of Appeal, and held that C had no interest in the property on the basis of either proprietary estoppel or constructive trust, although it did award him a quantum meruit for the value of his services that YRM Ltd knew he was not providing gratuitously.

Lord Scott of Foscote and Lord Walker of Gestingthorpe, giving the two reasoned opinions in the House of Lords,[170] emphasised that both parties were experienced in commercial transactions, who knew that there was not yet a legally binding contract and that each therefore undertook the risk of whether a contract would ultimately be concluded.[171] A claim based on proprietary estoppel arises where one party has led

---

[166] *James v Evans* [2000] 3 EGLR 1 (no estoppel); [2001] Conv 86 (L McMurtry); *Joyce v Rigolli* [2004] EWCA Civ 79 at [35]-[36], [2004] 1 P & CR DG22 (Arden LJ); *Kinane v Mackie-Conteh* [2005] EWCA Civ 45, [2005] 06 EGCS 140; [2005] Conv 247 (M Dixon), 501 (B McFarlane); *Oates v Stimson* [2006] EWCA Civ 548, [2006] All ER (D) 219 (May); *McGuane v Welch* [2008] EWCA Civ 785, [2008] 2 P & CR 24 at [37] (Mummery LJ); *Cobbe v Yeoman's Row Management Ltd* [2006] EWCA Civ 1139, [2006] 1 WLR 2964, rvsd by HL, below. See also *Representative Body of the Church in Wales v Newton* [2005] EWHC 631 (QB), [2005] 16 EGCS 145 (no constructive trust where condition of contract (landlord's giving consent to assignment) had not been satisfied).

[167] [2008] UKHL 55, [2008] 1 WLR 1752; (2008) 158 NLJ 1171 (M Dowden), 1629 (K Chambers); [2009] CLJ 37 (A Goymour); [2009] Conv 141 (G Griffiths).

[168] For suggestions that the decision narrowed the doctrine of proprietary estoppel *in general* to an unacceptable degree, see [2008] LMCLQ 449 (B McFarlane and A Robertson); [2009] Conv 104 (T Etherton); but cf *Thorner v Major* [2009] UKHL 18, [2009] 1 WLR 776 at [31] (Lord Walker of Gestingthorpe), [92]–[100] (Lord Neuberger of Abbotsbury), above, p 912; [2009] Conv 260 (M Dixon); (2009) 125 LQR 535 (B McFarlane and A Robertson); (2009) 72 MLR 998 (N Piska).

[169] [2006] EWCA Civ 1139, [2006] 1 WLR 2964; above, n 166.

[170] Lord Hoffmann and Lord Mance agreed with Lord Scott; Lord Brown of Eaton-under-Heywood agreed with both Lord Scott and Lord Walker.

[171] Above, n 167, at [27] (Lord Scott); [71], [91] (Lord Walker).

the other to believe that he has or shall have an interest in, or right over, the other's property.[172] But no claim to proprietary estoppel could arise in *Cobbe*:[173]

Mr Cobbe did not spend his money and time on the planning application in the mistaken belief that the agreement was legally enforceable. He spent his money and time well aware that it was not. Mrs Lisle-Mainwaring did not encourage in him a belief that the second agreement was enforceable. She encouraged in him a belief that she would abide by it although she was not. Mr Cobbe's belief, or expectation, was always speculative. He knew she was not legally bound. He regarded her as bound 'in honour' but that is an acknowledgement that she was not legally bound.

The claim here was to give effect by proprietary estoppel to an agreement that did not yet constitute a concluded contract: an agreement that lacked both certainty of terms and compliance with the required formality of section 2. Proprietary estoppel does not assist a claimant in such a case,[174] and should not be allowed to undermine the risk allocation of contractual negotiations before they reach their conclusion, particularly between commercial parties.[175] A claim to a constructive trust was rejected on similar grounds.[176]

It can therefore be said that the effect of the decision of the House of Lords in *Cobbe* is that[177]

if the parties intend to make a formal agreement setting out the terms on which one or more of the parties is to acquire an interest in property, or, if further terms for that acquisition remain to be agreed between them so that the interest in property is not clearly identified, or if the parties did not expect their agreement to be immediately binding, neither party can rely on constructive trust as a means of enforcing their original agreement. In other words, at least in those situations, if their agreement (which does not comply with s 2(1)) is incomplete, they cannot utilise the doctrine of proprietary estoppel or the doctrine of constructive trust to make their agreement binding on the other party by virtue of s 2(5) of the 1989 Act.

However, in an obiter dictum, Lord Scott of Foscote went one step further and doubted whether the doctrine of proprietary estoppel could ever be relied upon where a contract fails to comply with section 2:[178]

Section 2 of the 1989 Act declares to be void any agreement for the acquisition of an interest in land that does not comply with the requisite formalities prescribed by the section. Subsection (5) expressly makes an exception for resulting, implied or constructive trusts. These may validly come into existence without compliance with the prescribed

---

[172] Ibid, at [18], [28] (Lord Scott). See generally above, pp 911–13.

[173] Ibid, at [27] (Lord Scott). See also at [71]-[72] (Lord Walker).

[174] Ibid, at [18] (Lord Scott). See also at [87] (Lord Walker).   [175] Ibid, at [85] (Lord Walker).

[176] Ibid, at [38] (Lord Scott: 'a claim for the imposition of a constructive trust in order to provide a remedy for a disappointed expectation engendered by a representation made in the context of incomplete contractual negotiations is, in my opinion, misconceived').

[177] *Herbert v Doyle* [2010] EWCA Civ 1095, [2010] All ER (D) 126 (Oct) at [57] (Arden LJ).

[178] Above, n 167, at [29]. Cf, however, Lord Walker at [93] ('I do not think it is necessary or appropriate to consider the issue on section 2 of the Law of Property (Miscellaneous Provisions) Act 1989').

formalities. Proprietary estoppel does not have the benefit of this exception. The question arises, therefore, whether a complete agreement for the acquisition of an interest in land that does not comply with the section 2 prescribed formalities, but would be specifically enforceable if it did can become enforceable via the route of proprietary estoppel. It is not necessary in the present case to answer this question … My present view, however, is that proprietary estoppel cannot be prayed in aid in order to render enforceable an agreement that statute has declared to be void. The proposition that an owner of land can be estopped from asserting that an agreement is void for want of compliance with the requirements of section 2 is, in my opinion, unacceptable. The assertion is no more than the statute provides. Equity can surely not contradict the statute.

In making this statement, however, Lord Scott made no reference to the decision in *Yaxley v Gotts*[179] or the arguments discussed in that and other cases in the Court of Appeal[180] that have held that proprietary estoppel can operate outside the statute.[181]

III EFFECT OF CONTRACT

A CONTRACT EQUIVALENT TO CONVEYANCE IN EQUITY. THE DOCTRINE OF *WALSH V LONSDALE*

If the contract for the sale or other disposition of an interest in land is one of which the court would be prepared to grant the equitable remedy of specific performance, it is treated in equity as creating the equivalent interest to that which, if the contract were performed, would be created at law. Generally known as the doctrine of *Walsh v Lonsdale*,[182] after the case in which it was applied in the context of leases, this is an application of the maxim that 'equity looks on that as done which ought to be done':[183] the contract to convey is treated as already having the same effect as the conveyance,[184] so far as equity can permit.[185] Thus an enforceable contract for the

---

[179] Above, p 974.   [180] Above, n 166.

[181] The dictum of Lord Scott has had a mixed reception: it was followed by Peter Smith J in *Hutchison v B & DF Ltd* [2008] EWHC 2286 (Ch), [2009] L & TR 12 at [68], but was not followed by Jack J in *Brightlingsea Haven Ltd v Morris* [2008] EWHC 1928 (QB), [2009] 2 P & CR 1 at [47]; [2009] Conv 85 (J de Souza). See also, *Herbert v Doyle* [2008] EWHC 1950 (Ch), [2008] All ER(D) 40 (Aug) at [15] (Mark Herbert QC): 'Lord Scott's statement of his present view was avowedly obiter, and in my view it remains the case that, if all the requirements are otherwise satisfied for a claim based on proprietary estoppel to succeed, the claim will not fail solely because it also consists of an agreement that falls foul of section 2. The analysis of such a case may be that the court gives effect to the proprietary estoppel by recognising or imposing a constructive trust, and it is this that enables section 2(5) to apply'; this issue was not addressed in CA, above, n 177.

[182] (1882) 21 Ch D 9, M & B p 30; above, p 215.   [183] Snell, para 5–030.

[184] Ie, the document required at law to perfect the contract, whether a conveyance of the unregistered freehold (below, p 1052), the transfer of a registered estate (below, p 1085), or any other transaction designed to create or dispose of a legal estate or interest; cf LPA 1925, ss 52(1), 205(1)(ii).

[185] The conveyance in equity is in many circumstances not as good as the conveyance at law: see, eg, the differences between a legal lease and an equitable lease: above, pp 217–20.

sale of the legal estate creates an equivalent equitable estate;[186] a contract for a legal lease creates an equivalent equitable lease;[187] a contract for a legal mortgage creates an equivalent equitable mortgage;[188] and a contract for a legal easement creates an equivalent equitable easement;[189] and similarly any contract to convey or create any legal estate or interest. The equitable interest so created is precarious, however, in that, since it depends on the contract being specifically enforceable, the equitable interest can be created by the contract, and will continue to subsist once created, only as long as there is no obstacle to the remedy of specific performance being available on the facts of the case.[190]

The following section will consider the particular application of this doctrine to the vendor and purchaser under a contract of sale. The application to contract for dispositions of other interests in land is considered in the relevant chapters in this book.[191]

B CONTRACT OF SALE. VENDOR AS TRUSTEE FOR PURCHASER[192]

If a contract for sale is capable of specific performance, an immediate equitable interest in the land passes to the purchaser, who retains it for as long as the contract remains enforceable.[193] The legal estate remains in the vendor until the conveyance has been executed or, in registered land, the transfer is completed by registration,[194] but meanwhile equity regards the vendor as a trustee for the purchaser, and is prepared to decree specific performance at the instance of the latter.[195] In the words of Jessel MR:[196]

The moment you have a valid contract for sale the vendor becomes in equity a trustee for the purchaser of the estate sold, and the beneficial ownership passes to the purchaser, the

---

[186] Below. *Industrial Properties (Barton Hill) Ltd v Associated Electrical Industries Ltd* [1977] QB 580, M & B p 31 (double application of the doctrine of *Walsh v Londsale*).

[187] *Walsh v Lonsdale*, above; above, p 215.   [188] Above, p 807.   [189] Above, p 653.

[190] *Coatsworth v Johnson* (1886) 55 LJQB 220, M & B p 32; above, p 218 (contract for lease); *Warmington v Miller* [1973] QB 877, 887 (Stamp J) (contract for lease); *Sookraj v Samaroo* [2004] UKPC 50, [2005] 1 P & CR DG11 at [15] (Lord Scott of Foscote) (contract of sale). For the remedy of specific performance in relation to land contracts, see below, pp 992–5.

[191] Above, pp 215–20 (leases); 653–4 (easements); 807 (mortgages).

[192] H & M, para 12.035; Farrand, *Contract and Conveyance* (4th edn), pp 163–73; Barnsley, *Conveyancing Law and Practice*, pp 245–50; Oakley, *Constructive Trusts* (3rd edn, 1997), ch 6.

[193] *Sookraj v Samaroo* [2004] UKPC 50, (2004) 148 SJLB 1244 at [15] (Lord Scott of Foscote: 'a fairly fundamental principle').

[194] LRA 2002, s 27(1); below, p 1093. In the absence of express or implied contractual provision, the purchaser is entitled to require the vendor to transfer the property on completion to a third party of its own choosing: *Pittack v Naviede* [2010] EWHC 1509 (Ch), [2010] 43 EG 100; [2010] 43 EG 97 (S Murdoch).

[195] *Shaw v Foster* (1872) LR 5 HL 321, 333, 338; *Howard v Miller* [1915] AC 318, 326. There may be a decree even though, between contract and completion, a compulsory purchase order has been made by a local authority: *Hillingdon Estates Co v Stonefield Estates Ltd* [1952] Ch 627.

[196] *Lysaght v Edwards* (1876) 2 Ch D 499, 506; *Lake v Bayliss* [1974] 1 WLR 1073.

vendor having a right to the purchase money, a charge or lien[197] on the estate for the security of that purchase money, and a right to retain possession of the estate until the purchase money is paid, in the absence of express contract as to the time of delivering possession.

Thus, for example, pending completion, the purchaser may dispose of his equitable interest by sale or otherwise; he becomes owner of the rents and profits that fall due after the time fixed for completion; and he can demand an occupation rent if the vendor remains in possession after that time.

On the other hand, as from the date of the contract, unless it otherwise provides, the purchaser must bear the risk of any loss or damage suffered by the property, such as from an accidental fire or from a fall in price; and from the date fixed for completion he must meet the cost of all necessary outgoings.

(1) Vendor's Rights and Duties. Qualified Trusteeship

Pending the completion of the sale, the vendor occupies a fiduciary position, and therefore he must manage and preserve the property with the same care as a trustee must show with regard to trust property. He must, for example, relet the premises if an existing lease runs out, but before doing so he must consult the purchaser.[198] Nevertheless, the vendor is not an ordinary trustee, since he possesses certain rights of a valuable nature in the land, which he is entitled to protect on his own behalf:

(i)   he has a right to remain in possession until the purchase money is paid, and to protect that possession, if necessary, by the maintenance of an action, though while in possession he is under a duty to maintain the property in a reasonable state of preservation and so far as may be in the state in which it was when the contract was made;[199]

(ii) he is entitled to take the rents and profits of the land[200] until the time fixed for completion; and

(iii) he possesses an equitable lien on the property for the amount of the purchase money. An equitable lien is in the nature of a charge on land and entitles the person in whom it resides to apply to the court for a sale of the property in satisfaction of his claim. Unlike a common law lien, it is not dependent on possession.[201]

---

[197] The purchaser's lien arises from his equitable interest the land, and is not dependent on his having a right to immediate specific performance of the contract: *Chattey v Farndale Holdings Inc* (1998) 75 P & CR 298.

[198] *Earl of Egmont v Smith* (1877) 6 Ch D 469; *Abdulla v Shah* [1959] AC 124.

[199] *Clarke v Ramuz* [1891] 2 QB 456 (removal of soil by trespasser); *Phillips v Lamdin* [1949] 2 KB 33 (removal of door); *Berkley v Poulett* (1976) 241 EG 911, 242 EG 39 (discussing the rights of a sub-purchaser); *Ware v Verderber* (1978) 247 EG 1081 (duty of vendor to take reasonable care of property); *Englewood Properties Ltd v Patel* [2005] EWHC 188 (Ch), [2005] 1 WLR 1961 (duty does not extend to dealing with vendor's adjoining or neighbouring premises).

[200] Or dividends in the case of shares: *J Sainsbury plc v O'Connor* [1991] STC 318.

[201] See generally [1994] CLJ 263 (S Worthington); [1997] Conv 336 (DG Barnsley); *Barclays Bank plc v Estates and Commercial Ltd* [1997] 1 WLR 415, 419 (Millett LJ); *Uziell-Hamilton v Keen* (1971) 22 P & CR 655; White and Tudor, *Leading Cases in Equity* (9th edn, 1928), vol ii, p 857.

Although the equitable ownership has passed to the purchaser, the vendor retains a substantial interest in the land, and for that reason is generally called a qualified trustee.[202] Lord Cairns, dealing with a case where a valid contract had been made for the sale of a London theatre, said:[203]

> There cannot be the slightest doubt of the relation subsisting in the eye of a Court of Equity between the vendor and the purchaser. The vendor was a trustee of the property for the purchaser; the purchaser was the real beneficial owner in the eye of a Court of Equity of the property, subject only to this observation, that the vendor, whom I have called the trustee, was not a mere dormant trustee, he was a trustee having a personal and substantial interest in the property, a right to protect that interest, and an active right to assert that interest if anything should be done in derogation of it. The relation, therefore, of trustee and *cestui que trust* subsisted, but subsisted subject to the paramount right of the vendor and trustee to protect his own interest as vendor of the property.

Thus, the trusteeship relates only to the property sold, which, failing express agreement, is confined to vacant possession of the land together with any physical accretions.[204] Therefore the vendor is entitled to retain compensation money payable in respect of the requisitioning of the property and falling due between the date of the contract and the date of the conveyance.[205]

(2) Insurance by Purchaser

Likewise, if between these dates the premises are damaged by fire, the former rule was that the money paid by the insurance company in respect of the loss belonged to the vendor, not to the purchaser, for the policy of insurance was not part of the property sold.[206] This, however, was reversed by section 47 of the Law of Property Act 1925 which provides:

> Where after the date of any contract for sale or exchange of property, money becomes payable under any policy of insurance maintained by the vendor in respect of any damage to or destruction of property included in the contract, the money shall, on completion of the contract, be held or receivable by the vendor on behalf of the purchaser and paid by the vendor to the purchaser on completion of the sale or exchange, or so soon thereafter as the same shall be received by the vendor.

This obligation may be varied by the contract; it is subject to the liability of the purchaser to pay the premiums falling due after the date of the contract, and is also subject to any requisite consents of the insurers.[207]

---

[202] *Rayner v Preston* (1881) 18 Ch D 1, 6 (Cotton LJ).   [203] *Shaw v Foster* (1872) LR 5 HL 321, 338.
[204] Including fixtures: below, p 982.   [205] *Re Hamilton-Snowball's Conveyance* [1959] Ch 308.
[206] *Rayner v Preston*, above. See also *Re Watford Corp's and Ware's Contract* [1943] Ch 82.
[207] This would appear to put the purchaser in a doubtful position. If the house that is the subject of the sale is burnt down, the purchaser is nevertheless obliged to pay the purchase money, and if the insurance company refuses to give the requisite consent to the transfer of the insurance money, he will be unable to obtain payment of that money under the section. On the other hand, having regard to the nature of fire insurance, it seems clear that the vendor is not entitled both to the insurance money and to the purchase

(3) Standard Conditions of Sale

The Standard Conditions of Sale are usually incorporated into the contract.[208] When they were first introduced in 1990, a radical change was made in the rules for the passing of risk. Condition 5 provided[209] that the vendor retained the risk until completion, that he was under no duty to the purchaser to insure the property, and that the provision for taking over the benefit of the vendor's insurance policy under section 47 was excluded. The purchaser had the right to rescind the contract if the physical state of the property had made it unusable for its purpose at the date of the contract, as a result of damage against which the vendor could not reasonably have insured or which it was not legally possible for him to make good. In the light of this condition, the Law Commission recommended[210] that it would be inappropriate to propose any legislative change.

The 5th edition of the Standard Conditions of Sale (2011), however, has reversed the allocation of risk, but condition 5 still provides that the seller is generally under no obligation to insure, and section 47 is still excluded.

(4) Fixtures

A conveyance of land, in the absence of express reservation, passes fixtures, but not chattels,[211] to the purchaser without special mention,[212] and they cannot be removed by a vendor who remains in possession between the contract of sale and the completion of the transaction, even though they consist of articles that, as between landlord and tenant, would be 'tenant's fixtures'.[213] The fixtures are deemed to have been paid for by the price fixed for the land, and if the vendor desires to remove them or to receive an additional sum in respect of them a clause to that effect must be inserted in the contract.[214]

C REGISTRATION OF CONTRACT

Since the enforceable contract for the sale or other disposition of an interest in land creates an equitable interest in favour of the purchaser, the purchaser must protect his interest if it is not to be overridden by a subsequent dealing with the legal title before he acquires the legal title himself.

---

money. A purchaser is well advised to insure the property himself immediately after the contract and not to rely on this section. See [1984] Conv 43 (MP Thompson). On the insurer's potential liability both to the assured and to a third party, see *Lonsdale & Thompson Ltd v Black Arrow Group plc* [1993] Ch 361; [1993] Conv 472 (M Haley); [1993] CLJ 387 (AJ Oakley).

208 The current edition is the 5th edn, 2011: above, p 954, n 32.

209 For a critical analysis of Condition 5, see [1989] Conv 1 (HW Wilkinson); Emmet, para 6.002.

210 Law Com No 191, *Risk of Damage after Contract for Sale* (1990).

211 *Moffatt v Kazana* [1969] 2 QB 152; *H E Dibble Ltd v Moore* [1970] 2 QB 181; *Deen v Andrews* (1986) 52 P & CR 17. See also *Berkley v Poulett* [1977] 1 EGLR 86 (sub-purchaser).

212 LPA 1925, s 62(1). The section is set out above, p 655.

213 *Gibson v Hammersmith & City Rly Co* (1863) 32 LJ Ch 337; *Phillips v Lamdin* [1949] 2 KB 33.

214 On hire-purchase agreements and fixtures, see (1963) 27 Conv (NS) 30 (AG Guest and J Lever); [1990] Conv 275 (G McCormack).

If the land is already registered, he should enter a notice in the register,[215] although if he is in actual occupation of the land his interest, if not protected by notice, might be protected as an overriding interest.[216] In the case of a contract for the sale of the land, it has not normally been the practice for the purchaser to enter a notice of his contract, since if he has applied for an official search of the register with priority before entering into the contract, his search gives him priority against other entries on the register for a period of 30 business days, within which period he will take the transfer and apply for its registration.[217] The Land Registration Act 2002 now makes specific provision for priority to be given by the noting of a contract for the making of a registrable disposition of a registered estate or charge, since, when electronic conveyancing is introduced, the formation of the electronic contract will necessarily be entered on the register.[218]

In unregistered land, a contract to convey or create a legal estate or interest is registrable as an estate contract under the Land Charges Act 1972.[219] If not registered it is void against later purchasers for money or money's worth of a legal estate in the land.[220]

IV OPTION TO PURCHASE AND RIGHT OF PRE-EMPTION

We must now consider two special cases: an option to purchase, and a right of pre-emption.

A OPTION TO PURCHASE

An option to purchase[221] creates an immediate equitable interest in favour of the grantee as soon as it is granted. The grantee's right to call for a conveyance of the land is an equitable interest; as far as the grantor is concerned, 'his estate or interest is taken away from him without his consent, and the right to take it away being vested in

---

[215] LRA 2002, s 32; below, p 1097.

[216] Ibid, s 29(2), Sch 3, para 2; below, p 1104. A contract for the grant of lease or an easement will create an equitable lease or an equitable easement, but only legal leases and legal easements can take effect as overriding interests under Sch 3, paras 1 and 3; below, p 1104.

[217] Ibid, s 72 and LRR 2003, rr 148(3), 131, replacing LR (Official Searches) R 1990 (SI 1993 No 3276); below, p 1085.

[218] Ibid, s 72(6)(a)(ii); H & B, para 19.5. For detail on official searches and priority protection, see generally H & B, ch 19.

[219] LCA 1972, s 2(4), Class C(iv). The contract must be registered against the name of the owner of the legal estate: s 3(1); Barrett v Hilton Developments Ltd [1975] Ch 237.

[220] Ibid, s 4(6); Midland Bank Trust Co Ltd v Green [1981] AC 513, M & B p 72; below, p 1065.

[221] See generally Barnsley, Land Options (5th edn, 2009); (1974) 38 Conv (NS) 8 (A Prichard); [1984] CLJ 55 (S Tromans); (1991) Can BR (PM Perell); Blundell Memorial Lecture 1996 (T Etherton and D Beales).

another, the covenant giving the option must give that other an interest in the land'.[222] Since an option creates an equitable interest in favour of the grantee from the moment of the contract, the grantee must protect his interest by registration (unless, in the case of registered land, it is protected as an overriding interest).[223]

We have seen[224] that section 2 of the Law of Property (Miscellaneous Provisions) Act 1989 provides that a contract for the sale or other disposition of an interest in land must be made in writing that incorporates all the agreed terms and is signed by both parties. A question that has arisen is whether the contract to which section 2 applies is formed when the option is granted, or when it is exercised. In some contexts the grant of an option has been analysed as a conditional contract,[225] in which case section 2 would be satisfied as long as the grant of the option was in writing, incorporating all the terms and signed by both parties. Other authorities support the view that the grant of an option is an irrevocable offer, resulting in a contract only when accepted by the notice exercising the option.[226] If this is the proper analysis for the purposes of section 2, the section would not be satisfied unless the grantor signed the notice of exercise, which he could not be compelled to do.

In *Spiro v Glencrown Properties Ltd*:[227]

an option to purchase was granted by documents satisfying section 2 of the 1989 Act. The purchaser gave written notice to exercise it but failed to complete. When the vendor sued for damages for breach of contract, the purchaser claimed that there was no contract

---

[222] *London and South Western Rly Co v Gomm* (1882) 20 Ch D 562, 581 (Jessel MR); *Griffith v Pelton* [1958] Ch 205, 225; *Webb v Pollmount* [1966] Ch 584, 597; *Mountford v Scott* [1975] Ch 258; *George Wimpey & Co Ltd v IRC* [1974] 1 WLR 975, 980; affd [1975] 1 WLR 995; *Pritchard v Briggs* [1980] Ch 338, 418. For the application of the rule against perpetuities, see above, pp 553–4, 564, 577. An option must be exercised strictly in accordance with its terms, and time is of the essence: *Di Luca v Juraise (Springs) Ltd* [1998] 2 EGLR 125; it does not however follow that time is of the essence for the compliance with any conditions in the option as to the manner in which the option, once exercised, is to be carried to completion: *Allardyce v Roebuck* [2004] EWHC 1538 (Ch), [2005] 1 WLR 815. See also *BP Oil UK Ltd v Lloyds TSB Bank plc* [2004] EWCA Civ 1710, [2005] 1 EGLR 61 (option for three joint assignees to require assignor to take reassignment of lease not exercisable by only two); *Sainsbury's Supermarkets Ltd v Olympia Homes Ltd* [2005] EWHC 1235 (Ch), [2006] 1 P & CR 17.

[223] Above, pp 982–3 (protection by a notice in registered land; as a land charge, Class C(iv), in unregistered land: LCA 1972, s 2(4) expressly includes option to purchase within the definition of estate contract). If the option is registered, there is no need to register the ensuing contract when the option is exercised: *Armstrong & Holmes Ltd v Holmes* [1993] 1 WLR 1482 (unregistered land); [1994] Conv 483 (NP Gravells). See *Freeguard v Royal Bank of Scotland plc* (1998) 79 P & CR 81 (unregistered option to purchase lost priority against later registered charge in 'a thoroughly artificial transaction' involving a ransom strip). The benefit of an option may be assigned; for the mechanisms contemplated for the compliance of such an assignment with LPA 1925, s 136 (legal assignment requires writing) under electronic conveyancing, see LRA 2002, s 91; H & B, paras 26.14–26.18.

[224] Above, p 966.

[225] *Helby v Matthews* [1895] AC 471, 482 (Lord Macnaghten); *Re Mulholland's Will Trusts* [1949] 1 All ER 460; *Griffith v Pelton* [1958] Ch 205; *Armstrong & Holmes Ltd v Holmes* [1993] 1 WLR 1482.

[226] *Helby v Matthews*, above, 477 (Lord Herschell), 479–80 (Lord Watson); *Beesly v Hallwood Estates Ltd* [1960] 1 WLR 549; affd [1961] Ch 105.

[227] [1991] Ch 537, M & B p 34; [1991] Conv 140 (P Smith); [1993] Conv 13 (P Jenkins); [1990] Conv 9 (JE Adams); [1990] 47 EG 48 (C Sydenham and M Rodrigues); [1991] Conv 140 (PF Smith); [1991] CLJ 236 (AJ Oakley); Emmet, para 2.080.

because the notice of exercise, which was not signed by the vendor, did not satisfy section 2. Hoffmann J held that the grant of the option, and not its exercise, was the contract to which section 2 applied.

Strictly speaking the grant of an option was neither a conditional contract nor an irrevocable offer, but created a relationship *sui generis*. The conditional contract was the more appropriate analogy in the context of section 2, as the purpose of an option would be destroyed if the purchaser had to obtain the vendor's signature to the notice of exercise, a result that had not been intended by the legislature. Thus the purchaser was liable to damages.

B   RIGHT OF PRE-EMPTION

In *Pritchard v Briggs*, Templeman LJ distinguished an option from a right of preemption as follows:[228]

> Rights of option and rights of pre-emption share one feature in common: each prescribes circumstances in which the relationship between the owner of the property which is the subject of the right and the holder of the right will become the relationship of vendor and purchaser. In the case of an option, the evolution of the relationship of vendor and purchaser may depend on the fulfilment of certain specified conditions and will depend on the volition of the option holder. If the option applies to land, the grant of the option creates a contingent equitable interest ... In the case of a right of pre-emption, the evolution of the relationship of vendor and purchaser depends on the grantor, of his own volition, choosing to fulfil certain specified conditions[229] and thus converting the pre-emption into an option. The grant of the right of pre-emption creates a *mere spes* which the grantor of the right may either frustrate by choosing not to fulfil the necessary conditions or may convert into an option and thus into an equitable interest by fulfilling the conditions.

The Court of Appeal held unanimously that, unlike an option, a right of pre-emption did not confer an equitable interest in the land on the holder of the right.[230] One difficulty

---

[228] [1980] Ch 338, 418. See also *Brown v Gould* [1972] Ch 53, 58. A right of pre-emption is sometimes referred to as a right of first refusal but 'in so far as there is a distinction, the expression "right of first refusal" is commonly used to describe the position (as in the present case) where the grantee has the first right to refuse an offer to purchase at the price at which the grantor is willing to sell; and the expression "right of preemption" is commonly used to describe the position (as in *Pritchard v Briggs*) where the grantee has the right to purchase at a fixed price (or at a price that is not chosen by the grantor) before the grantor is free to sell to anyone else': *Bircham & Co Nominees (No 2) Ltd v Worrell Holdings Ltd* [2001] EWCA Civ 775, (2001) 82 P & CR 34 at [31] (Chadwick LJ). See further *Speciality Shops v Yorkshire and Metropolitan Estates Ltd* [2002] EWHC 2969 (Ch), [2003] 2 P & CR 31 at [25]-[29], (Park J), identifying three forms of right of pre-emption; 'more may exist'.

[229] *Tuck v Baker* [1990] 2 EGLR 195 (pre-emption clause provided that there should be two months for acceptance of an offer of first refusal: the owner could change his mind about selling and withdraw the offer before acceptance within the two months).

[230] See also *Manchester Ship Canal Co v Manchester Racecourse Co* [1901] 2 Ch 37; *Murray v Two Strokes Ltd* [1973] 1 WLR 823; (1973) 89 LQR 462 (MJ Albery); *First National Securities Ltd v Chiltern DC* [1975] 1 WLR 1075; cf *Birmingham Canal Co v Cartwright* (1879) 11 Ch D 421; *Bircham & Co Nominees (No 2) Ltd v Worrell Holdings Ltd*, above; *Speciality Shops v Yorkshire and Metropolitan Estates Ltd*, above; *Dear v Reeves*

was that many statutory provisions assumed that a right of pre-emption was a proprietary interest.[231] Goff LJ held that these provisions were framed on a mistaken view of the law and were, therefore, of no effect.[232] A right of pre-emption was therefore not a proprietary interest capable of binding a successor in title, and could never be converted to such an interest, even if registered as an estate contract.[233] Templeman and Stephenson LJJ, on the other hand, held that a right of pre-emption, while not initially an interest in land, was converted to an equitable interest as soon as the grantor fulfilled the condition on deciding to sell. If registered as an estate contract, either before or after fulfilment of the condition, the interest would be binding on the grantor's successors in title.[234]

Neither view is free from difficulties, and the precise effect of a right of pre-emption remains uncertain in unregistered land.[235] In relation to registered land, however, the Land Registration Act 2002[236] resolved the matter by providing that, subject to the rules about the effect of dispositions on priority, a right of pre-emption has effect from the time of creation as an interest capable of binding successors in title.

V REMEDIES OF PARTIES TO THE CONTRACT[237]

Various remedies are available to the parties[238] to the contract. Some relate to the formation of the contract; others to a breach of the contract itself.

A REMEDIES RELATING TO THE FORMATION OF THE CONTRACT

Of the claims that might arise in relation to the formation of the contract, the most common are for misrepresentation and mistake.[239] In practice, a misrepresentation

---

[2002] 1 Ch 1; *Tiffany Investments Ltd v Bircham & Co Nominees (No 2) Ltd* [2003] EWCA Civ 1759, [2004] 2 EGLR 31.

[231] LCA 1972, s 2(4), where it is registrable as an estate contract; LPA 1925, ss 2(3)(iv), 186; SLA 1925, ss 58(2), 61(2); PAA 1964, s 9(2).

[232] [1980] Ch 338, 399. [233] Ibid, 396.

[234] [1980] Ch 338, 418, 423, followed in relation to registered land in *Kling v Keston Properties Ltd* (1983) 49 P & CR 212, M & B p 38.

[235] (1980) 96 LQR 488 (HWRW); [1980] Conv 433 (J Martin).

[236] S 115(1). The section has effect only in relation to rights of pre-emption created on or after 13 October 2004: s 115(2); SI 2003 No 1725. What is meant, however, by a 'right of pre-emption' for the purposes of s 115 has still to be addressed; cf *Speciality Shops v Yorkshire and Metropolitan Estates Ltd* [2002] EWHC 2969 (Ch), [2003] 2 P & CR 31 at [25]-[29], above, n 228.

[237] See generally Emmet, ch 7; Annand and Cain, *Remedies under the Contract* (1988).

[238] Under the Contracts (Rights of Third Parties) Act 1999 a third party may now sometimes be able to enforce a term of the contract, and obtain the remedies that would have been available to him in an action for breach of contract if he had been a party to the contract: s 1(5). On the Act generally, see Emmet, paras 2.091–2.095, 19.004; Blundell Lectures 25th Anniversary Series 2000: The Contracts (Rights of Third Parties) Act and its Implications for Property Transactions (A Burrows and C Harpum); Anson, pp 624–35.

[239] For rescission for undue influence that, in the context of contracts relating to land, has most commonly been claimed in the case of mortgage transactions, see above, pp 829–36.

might give rise to claims for rescission *ab initio* of the contract, or for damages—most commonly, in the case of a contract of sale, these are claims made by the purchaser against the vendor. A mistake might give rise to a claim by either party to rectify the contract.[240]

(1) Remedies for Pre-contractual Misrepresentation[241]

(a) Rescission *ab initio*[242]

A party to the contract may rescind if he can show that a false representation was made to him, by or on behalf of the other party,[243] on which he relied in entering into the contract; and as long as there is no bar to his obtaining the remedy—such as the fact that rescission would prejudice an innocent third party.[244] The remedy is available whether the misrepresentation was fraudulent or innocent;[245] and the fact that the contract has been completed is not a bar to rescission.[246] Rescission is available as of right, although in the case of a non-fraudulent misrepresentation the court has discretion to refuse it, to declare the contract subsisting, and to order damages in lieu of rescission.[247] If rescission is available the contract is voidable; the remedy of rescission for misrepresentation renders the contract a nullity *ab initio*, and restitution must be made between the parties in respect of any performance already made under the contract.[248]

(b) Damages

The misrepresentation may give rise to a claim for damages. An action in the tort of deceit may lie if the misrepresentation was made fraudulently;[249] and damages on the

---

[240] A contract might sometimes be void for a common (shared) mistake, but not voidable: *Great Peace Shipping Ltd v Tsavliris Salvage (International) Ltd* [2002] EWCA Civ 1407, [2003] QB 679. For mistake in contract generally, see Anson, ch 8.

[241] Cartwright, *Misrepresentation, Mistake and Non-Disclosure* (2nd edn, 2006), Part I; Anson, ch 9.

[242] Snell, ch 15.

[243] A misrepresentation by a third party is normally insufficient to give rise to rescission; see, however, *Royal Bank of Scotland v Etridge (No 2)* [2001] UKHL 44, [2002] 2 AC 773 at [40] (Lord Nicholls), [144] (Lord Scott of Foscote) (knowledge of the third party's misrepresentation is required; but constructive notice is sufficient in a case covered by the principle of *Barclays Bank plc v O'Brien* [1994] 1 AC 181, above, pp 832–3); Anson, pp 369–372. A different remedy, eg damages in the law of tort, must therefore normally be sought directly against the third party.

[244] The misrepresentation gives rise to an equity to rescind that, in the case of a contract for the sale of land, will be defeated by certain later dispositions to third parties: see below. For other bars to rescission, see Anson, pp 314–19.

[245] *Redgrave v Hurd* (1881) 20 Ch D 1, 12 (Jessel MR); *Derry v Peek* (1889) 14 App Cas 337, 359 (Lord Herschell).

[246] Misrepresentation Act 1967, s 1(b). The Law Reform Committee, which proposed the Act, had proposed that contract for the sale or other disposition of an interest in land, apart from contracts for short leases, should not be capable of rescission after execution: Tenth Report, Innocent Misrepresentation, Cmnd 1782 (1962), paras 6, 7. This was not, however, implemented in the Act.

[247] Misrepresentation Act 1967, s 2(2); *William Sindall plc v Cambridgeshire CC* [1994] 1 WLR 1016.

[248] For some problems in this respect associated with rescission, see Cartwright, *Misrepresentation, Mistake and Non-Disclosure*, paras 4.05–4.16.

[249] *Derry v Peek* (1889) 14 App Cas 337.

tort measure[250] may be recovered under section 2(1) of the Misrepresentation Act 1967 for non-fraudulent misrepresentation, unless the party making the misrepresentation can prove that he had reasonable ground to believe and did believe up to the time the contract was made that the facts represented were true. The measure of damages in tort does not give recovery for loss of bargain;[251] it puts the claimant in the position he would have been in had the tort not been committed—typically, therefore, placing the purchaser in the financial position as if he had not entered into the contract at all in reliance on the misrepresentation. Damages may also be claimed in the tort of negligence, although the purchaser is more likely to rely on his claim under section 2(1) of the Misrepresentation Act if seeking a remedy against the vendor.[252]

(2) Rectification of the Contract

If, as the result of a mistake common to both parties, the written evidence omits some material term and therefore does not express the true bargain between the parties, the court has jurisdiction to rectify the contract.[253] In such a case it first rectifies the written contract by adding the oral omission or variation, and then decrees specific performance of the contract as rectified. At one and the same time it reforms and enforces the contract.[254] This remedy may be granted even where the mistake is embodied in the final deed of conveyance.[255]

In *Agip SpA v Navigazione Alta Italia SpA*,[256] Slade LJ summarised the conditions that must be satisfied for rectification on the grounds of common mistake:

> First, there must be a common intention[257] in regard to the particular provisions of the agreement in question, together with some outward expression of accord. Secondly, this

---

[250] Damages are assessed on the same basis as in the tort of deceit: *Royscot Trust Ltd v Rogerson* [1991] 2 QB 297; see however *Smith New Court Securities Ltd v Citibank NA* [1997] AC 254, 267, 282–3; Anson, pp 327–8.

[251] *McConnel v Wright* [1903] 1 Ch 546, 554–5 (Collins MR). The loss recoverable in deceit may, however, include the lost opportunity of making profits from *other* contracts: *East v Maurer* [1991] 1 WLR 461.

[252] Under s 2(1) the burden of proof of honest and reasonable belief in the truth of the statement lies on the defendant. The tort of negligence must be used if the claim is against a third party to the contract, because the Misrepresentation Act 1967, s 2(1) does not cover that case: *Resolute Maritime v Nippon Kaiji Kyokai* [1983] 1 WLR 857. The tort of negligence may also be used by either party to impose liability in damages on their own advisers: *Smith v Eric S Bush* [1990] 1 AC 831 (surveyor's duty to mortgagee and also to mortgagor to whom contents of survey were communicated); *Hilton v Barker Booth and Eastwood* [2005] UKHL 8, [2005] 1 WLR 567 (solicitor's breach of duty in acting for both parties); and sometimes even the other party's advisers: *McCullagh v Lane Fox & Partners Ltd* [1996] 1 EGLR 35 (vendor's estate agent; but no duty on facts). Under the Property Misdescriptions Act 1991 it is an offence to make false or misleading statements about property matters in the course of estate agency or property development business; Property Misdescriptions (Specified Matters) Order 1992 (SI 1992 No 2834); *Lewin v Barratt Homes Ltd* [2000] 1 EGLR 77; *Dacre Son & Hartley Ltd v North Yorkshire Trading Standards* [2004] EWHC 2783 (Admin), [2005] 1 EGLR 11 (conviction for false or misleading statement on dampness); although the contract is not void or unenforceable, and no right of civil action arises in respect of any loss, by reason only of the commission of an offence s 1(4).

[253] *United States of America v Motor Trucks Ltd* [1924] AC 196; *Joscelyne v Nissen* [1970] 2 QB 86.

[254] [1924] AC 196, 201 (Lord Birkenhead).

[255] *Craddock Bros Ltd v Hunt* [1923] 2 Ch 136. See also *Riverlate Properties Ltd v Paul* [1975] Ch 133.

[256] [1984] 1 Lloyd's Rep 353, 365.

[257] For the view that this 'common intention' is to be tested objectively rather than, as generally assumed, subjectively, see *Chartbrook Ltd v Persimmon Homes Ltd* [2009] UKHL 38, [2009] 1 AC 1101 at [60] (Lord Hoffmann); cf Anson, p 263, n 80.

common intention must continue up to the time of execution of the instrument. Thirdly, there must be clear evidence that the instrument as executed does not accurately represent the true agreement of the parties at the time of its execution. Fourthly, it must be shown that the instrument, if rectified as claimed, would accurately represent the true agreement of the parties at that time...

The standard of proof required in an action of rectification to establish the common intention of the parties is the civil standard of balance of probability.

Unilateral mistake may also give rise to a claim for rectification if the mistaken party can show that it would be unconscionable for the other party to insist on the document as drafted. Normally this is satisfied by proof that the other party knows of the mistake, would benefit by it, and failed to draw it to the attention of the mistaken party.[258] For this purpose 'knowledge' is not limited to actual knowledge, but extends to wilfully shutting one's eyes to the obvious, and wilfully and recklessly failing to make such inquiries as an honest and reasonable man would make.[259]

In *Commission for the New Towns v Cooper (GB) Ltd*, Stuart-Smith LJ said:[260]

Where A intends B to be mistaken as to the construction of the agreement, so conducts himself that he diverts B's attention from discovering the mistake by making false and misleading statements, and B in fact makes the very mistake that A intends, then notwithstanding that A does not actually know, but merely suspects that B is mistaken, and it cannot be shown that the mistake was induced by any misrepresentation, rectification may be granted. A's conduct is unconscionable and he cannot insist on performance in accordance with the strict letter of the contract; that is sufficient for rescission. But it may also not be unjust or inequitable to insist that the contract be performed according to B's understanding, where that was the meaning that A intended that B should put upon it.

Whether the mistake was common or unilateral, the fact that it arose through the negligence of the claimant or his legal advisers is normally no bar to rectification.[261]

The mistake must be as to the effect of the document that it is sought to rectify; a mistaken belief as to its relation to another document is not sufficient.[262]

(3) Passing of the Benefit and Burden of Equities to Rescind or Rectify

We saw in Chapter 22 that the right to rescind and the right to rectify are 'mere equities', which are not equitable interests in the property, but have proprietary characteristics.

---

258 *A Roberts & Co Ltd v Leicestershire County Council* [1961] Ch 555; *Thomas Bates & Son Ltd v Wyndham's (Lingerie) Ltd* [1981] 1 WLR 505; *Kemp v Neptune Concrete Ltd* [1988] 2 EGLR 87; *Huber (Investments) Ltd v Private DIY Co Ltd* (1995) 70 P & CR D33; *Coles v William Hill Organisation Ltd* [1998] EGCS 40; *Nurdin & Peacock plc v Ramsden & Co Ltd* [1999] 1 EGLR 119; *Oceanic Village Ltd v United Attractions Ltd* [2000] Ch 234 (London Aquarium); *George Wimpey UK Ltd v VI Construction Ltd* [2005] EWCA Civ 77, [2005] BLR 135; *Littman v Aspen Oil (Broking) Ltd* [2005] EWCA Civ 1579, [2006] 2 P & CR 2 at [18]-[26].

259 *Commission for the New Towns v Cooper (GB) Ltd* [1995] Ch 259, 280–1. 260 Ibid, 280.

261 *Weeds v Blaney* (1977) 247 EG 211; *Central and Metropolitan Estates Ltd v Compusave* (1982) 266 EG 900; *Boots the Chemist Ltd v Street* (1983) 268 EG 817.

262 *London Regional Transport v Wimpey Group Services Ltd* [1986] 2 EGLR 41 (rent review).

The benefit, in cases concerning land, is capable of passing with the land.[263] The burden is capable of binding successors to the property against which the beneficiary of the equity had a claim to a remedy. In unregistered land the equity can be defeated not only by a conveyance of the legal estate, but also by a conveyance of an equitable interest, to a bona fide purchaser without notice of the equity; in registered land, however, a mere equity is now[264] treated from the time it arises as being an interest capable of binding successors—and therefore as having the same protection as an equitable interest, as long it is either protected by notice on the register, or takes effect as an overriding interest by virtue of the claimant's discoverable actual occupation.[265]

B REMEDIES FOR BREACH OF CONTRACT

The remedies available for breach of the contract are damages, specific performance, rescission and vendor and purchaser summons.

(1) Damages

In the event of a breach of any contract the general rule that governs the measure of damages is that the claimant is to be placed, so far as money can do it, in the same situation as if the contract had been performed.[266] This is subject, however, to the rule relating to remoteness of damage, which limits the defendant's liability to such losses as he ought reasonably to have contemplated as likely to occur, having regard to the knowledge, actual or constructive, possessed by him at the time of the contract.[267] The defendant is therefore liable only for loss of a kind he could foresee might occur in the usual course of things, unless he knows of special circumstances by which it may be increased.[268]

(a) Damages recoverable by vendor

In the case of a contract for the sale of land this general rule applies when it is the vendor who brings the action. The loss caused to the vendor in the usual course of things by the failure of the purchaser to complete is the deprivation of the purchase price diminished by the value of the land that he still holds, and he is therefore entitled to recover by way of damages the difference, if any, between the value of the land that remains in his possession and the price he would have received had the contract been

---

[263] LPA 1925, s 63; *Boots the Chemist Ltd v Street* (1983) 268 EG 817; *Berkeley Leisure Group Ltd v Williamson* [1996] EGCS 18.

[264] LRA 2002, s 116 ('declared for the avoidance of doubt').   [265] Above, pp 904–6.

[266] *Robinson v Harman* (1848) 1 Exch 850, 855 (Parke B); Anson, p 539. For difficulties in applying this rule to a claim for breach of a restrictive covenant, see above, p 762.

[267] *Hadley v Baxendale* (1854) 9 Exch 341; *Victoria Laundry (Windsor) Ltd v Newman Industries Ltd* [1949] 2 KB 528; *Koufos v C Czarnikow Ltd, The Heron II* [1969] 1 AC 350; cf *Transfield Shipping Inc v Mercator Shipping Inc, The Achilleas* [2008] UKHL 48, [2009] 1 AC 61; Anson, pp 543–55.

[268] *Cottrill v Steyning and Littlehampton Building Society* [1966] 1 WLR 753 (defendant knew claimant intended to develop the land for profit: 'special circumstances' established); dist. *Diamond v Campbell-Jones* [1961] Ch 22.

completed,[269] giving credit also for any deposit that he received that is forfeited upon the purchaser's failure to complete.[270] If he resells, he is entitled to recover both the difference in price and the expenses attending the resale.[271]

(b) Damages recoverable by purchaser

The general rule of assessment of damages now applies where it is the purchaser who sues for breach. Until it was abolished by the Law of Property (Miscellaneous Provisions) Act 1989,[272] there was a rule[273] that the general principle—that damages are recoverable for loss of bargain—was excluded in a case where the vendor was unable to complete the conveyance owing to a defect in his title; he was instead limited to the recovery of his deposit, if any, and of the expenses he had incurred in investigating title. Now, however, a purchaser is entitled in all cases to damages for loss of bargain. If the value of the property is greater than the purchase price, the claimant recovers the difference, though in this case he cannot recover his conveyancing costs.[274] If the value of the property is less than the purchase price, he is entitled to a return of the deposit with interest and also to damages in respect of the cost of investigating the title.[275]

(c) Date for assessment of damages

It was at one time thought that, while the general rule at common law requires damages to be assessed as at the date of the breach of contract, that is the date fixed for completion, a greater measure of damages, based on the value of the land at the date of the judgment, would be recoverable where the damages were awarded in substitution for specific performance under Lord Cairns' Act (Chancery Amendment Act 1858).[276] Lord Cairns' Act gave the Court of Chancery discretionary power to award damages either in addition to or in substitution for specific performance (in cases where the court had jurisdiction to award specific performance), the damages to be assessed in such manner as the court shall direct. Since the Judicature Act 1873, making the common law remedy of damages available in the Chancery Division, it is only necessary to invoke Lord Cairns' Act in a case where common law damages would

---

269 *Laird v Pim* (1841) 7 M & W 474; *Harold Wood Brick Co Ltd v Ferris* [1935] 1 KB 613; affd [1935] 2 KB 198.

270 *Ng v Ashley King (Developments) Ltd* [2010] EWHC 456 (Ch), [2010] 3 WLR 911.

271 *Noble v Edwardes* (1877) 5 Ch D 378; *Keck v Faber, Jellett and Keeble* (1915) 60 SJ 253.

272 Ss 3, 5(3), adopting the recommendations in Law Com No 166, *The Rule in* Bain v Fothergill (1987).

273 Known as the rule in *Bain v Fothergill* (1874) LR 7HL 158. For further details of this rule, see the 16th edn of this book, pp 137–8.

274 *Re Daniel* [1917] 2 Ch 405. The loss for which compensation is recoverable is the difference between the purchase price and the value of the property if it had been conveyed in accordance with the contract. But if the property had in fact been so conveyed, the conveyancing costs would have fallen on the purchaser, and therefore he cannot recover both the difference and the costs: ibid, 412 (Sargant J).

275 *Wallington v Townsend* [1939] Ch 588; *Lloyd v Stanbury* [1971] 1 WLR 535.

276 Now SCA 1981, s 50. *Wroth v Tyler* [1974] Ch 30; *Grant v Dawkins* [1973] 1 WLR 1406; (1975) 34 CLJ 224 (JA Jolowicz); [1981] Conv 286 (T Ingman and J Wakefield); (1981) 97 LQR 445 (SM Waddams). On the jurisdiction of the court to award damages before Lord Cairns' Act, see (1992) 108 LQR 652 (PM McDermott).

not be available.[277] The position as to the time at which damages are to be assessed was clarified by the House of Lords in *Johnson v Agnew*.[278] Subject to the point that in some cases damages would be available under Lord Cairns' Act where none at all would be available at common law, the Act does not permit a departure from the common law rule on the quantum of damages. But there is no inflexible rule at common law that damages must be assessed as at the date of the breach of contract.[279] The principle is that the claimant should be put in the same position as if the contract had been duly performed. Where, after the breach, the innocent party has reasonably continued to try for completion, the damages, however awarded, should be assessed as at the date when the contract was lost.[280] This will normally be the date of the hearing, but an earlier date will be substituted if the claimant has delayed.[281]

Damages recoverable where completion is delayed, or where specific performance is ordered but enforcement subsequently proves impossible, are dealt with below.[282]

(2) Specific Performance

The most effective remedy available to either party is to sue for specific performance, that is to demand that the contract be completed according to its terms. One of the general principles established by equity is that this relief should be given only where damages do not afford an adequate remedy. But the subject matter of a contract for the sale of land[283] is of unique value, so that specific performance of the contract is available to a purchaser as a matter of course. Furthermore, even though a vendor could be adequately compensated by damages for the failure of a purchaser to complete, yet, in pursuance of the doctrine that remedies should be mutual, equity grants specific performance to a vendor as well as to a purchaser.[284]

A full discussion of specific performance is outside the scope of this book,[285] but it may be noticed that the remedy is discretionary, though the discretion is not exercised in an arbitrary or capricious manner, but according to the rules that have been

---

[277] Such as, perhaps, where the case is based on proprietary estoppel, which gives rise to no action at law: *Crabb v Arun DC (No 2)* (1976) 121 SJ 86. See also *Oakacre Ltd v Claire Cleaners (Holdings) Ltd* [1982] Ch 197 (action for damages at law not accrued at date of writ).

[278] [1980] AC 367.

[279] Ibid. See also *Wroth v Tyler*, above, at 57; *Radford v de Froberville* [1977] 1 WLR 1262; *Malhotra v Choudhury* [1980] Ch 52; *Techno Land Improvements Ltd v British Leyland (UK) Ltd* (1979) 252 EG 805; *Forster v Silvermere Golf and Equestrian Centre Ltd* (1981) 42 P & CR 255, (1979) 95 LQR 270 (D Feldman and DF Libling); *Suleman v Shahsavari* [1988] 1 WLR 1181; Treitel, paras 20.063 ff.

[280] In *Johnson v Agnew*, this was the date on which the vendor's mortgagees contracted to sell the property, thus preventing completion of the vendor's contract with the claimant.

[281] *Radford v de Froberville*, above; *Malhotra v Choudhury*, above.   [282] Below, pp 993 ff.

[283] Specific performance may also be granted of a contractual licence to occupy land; *Verrall v Great Yarmouth BC* [1981] QB 202, M & B p 1094; above, p 930.

[284] *Kenney v Wexham* (1822) 6 Madd 355, 357 (Leach V-C).

[285] See generally H & M, ch 24; Snell, ch 17; Jones and Goodhart, *Specific Performance* (2nd edn, 1996); White and Tudor, *Leading Cases in Equity*, vol ii, pp 372 ff; Burrows, *Remedies for Torts and Breach of Contract* (3rd edn, 2004), ch 20. On the availability of specific performance under the Contracts (Rights of Third Parties) Act 1999, see Emmet, para 2.093.

established by the judges. If the defendant can show any circumstances independent of the written contract that make it inequitable to decree specific performance, such as where the claimant has delayed, or in certain cases of mistake, misrepresentation and misdescription, or where the vendor or the purchaser has not acted fairly,[286] or where the completion of the contract would cause hardship to an innocent vendor or purchaser,[287] the court will not grant the remedy.[288]

(a) Specific performance when completion delayed

Where a contract for the sale of land is not completed upon the date fixed in the contract, specific performance may still be available, even at the instance of the delaying party.[289] *At law* time was always considered to be of the essence of the contract, and a party who failed to complete upon the agreed date was without remedy. If the vendor failed to complete, the purchaser could therefore terminate the contract and recover the deposit and the costs of investigating the title. Equity, however, taking a different view that now prevails in all courts,[290] did not regard time as necessarily of the essence, and has always been prepared to decree specific performance notwithstanding failure to observe the exact date fixed for completion, *provided that this will not cause injustice to either party*.

But it must be emphasised that, even where time is not of the essence of a contract, failure to complete on the contractual date is a breach of contract, both at law and in equity. The contractual duty of the parties is not merely to complete on that date or within a reasonable time thereafter.[291] The fact that time is not of the essence merely means that the delaying party does not lose the right to specific performance, nor will he forfeit his deposit, provided that he is ready to complete within a reasonable time. If completion does not occur on the contractual date, the delaying party will be liable to pay damages, such as where the innocent party incurs hotel or storage expenses as a result of the breach.

---

[286] *Sang Lee Investment Co Ltd v Wing Kwai Investment Co Ltd* (1983) 127 SJ 410.

[287] *Patel v Ali* [1984] Ch 283, 288 (Goulding J: specific performance would inflict on vendor 'a hardship amounting to injustice'); (1984) 100 LQR 337. But ECHR, art 8 cannot be successfully prayed in aid to prevent a contractual purchaser from obtaining specific performance of a contract for the purchase of the house that is the vendor's home; art 8 does not diminish the purchaser's rights under domestic law: *Harrow LBC v Qazi* [2003] UKHL 43, [2004] 1 AC 983 at [136] (Lord Scott of Foscote).

[288] *Co-operative Insurance Society Ltd v Argyll Stores (Holdings) Ltd* [1998] AC 1 (covenant by tenant to keep a Safeway supermarket 'open for retail trading during the usual hours of business' held not enforceable by specific performance). But damages are available: *Costain Property Developments Ltd v Finlay & Co Ltd* (1988) 57 P & CR 345; *Transworld Land Co Ltd v J Sainsbury plc* [1990] 2 EGLR 255 (loss caused on neighbouring property); (1998) 61 MLR 421 (A Phang); [1998] Conv 396 (P Luxton); [1997] CLJ 458 (G Jones); (1997) 147 NLJ 1281 (HW Wilkinson).

[289] See generally Farrand, *Contract and Conveyance* (4th edn), pp 208–10; Barnsley, *Conveyancing Law and Practice*, pp 420–34. For the position where the claimant delays in enforcing the order for specific performance, see *Easton v Brown* [1981] 3 All ER 278.

[290] LPA 1925, s 41, re-enacting Judicature Act 1873, s 25(7). See generally (1980) 39 CLJ 58 (AJ Oakley).

[291] *Raineri v Miles* [1981] AC 1050; *Oakacre v Claire Cleaners (Holdings) Ltd* [1982] Ch 197. See also *Inns v D Miles Griffiths, Piercy & Co Ltd* (1980) 255 EG 623.

While the general position is that the party in breach of contract remains entitled to specific performance, that remedy will not be decreed if the parties have expressly stipulated that time shall be essential, or if there is something in the nature of the property or in the surrounding circumstances that renders it inequitable to treat the appointed date as non-essential.[292]

So, if the nature of the property is such as to make its conveyance at the agreed date imperative, for example, when the contract is for the sale of licensed premises,[293] or of a shop as a going concern, specific performance, even with compensation, will not be decreed; but if there is nothing special in the nature of the property or in the purposes for which it is required, the court will decree specific performance, subject to the condition that the defaulting party pay compensation for the delay. The principle in such a case is that specific performance will be awarded unless the claimant has delayed unreasonably. There is no statutory period of limitation barring claims to specific performance,[294] and no rule to lay down what is meant by unreasonable delay.

It used to be thought that the claimant must normally seek specific performance well within one year,[295] but it now seems that this approach is too strict.[296] An exceptional case where delay will not be a bar is where the claimant has taken possession under the contract, so that the purpose of specific performance is merely to vest the legal estate in him.[297]

A new contract cannot be made at the will of one of the parties and therefore, where time is not initially essential, one party cannot make it so of his own volition.[298] Nevertheless, there must be some limit to delaying tactics, and it is established that after the date fixed for completion has passed one party may serve a notice on the other requiring completion within a specified time.[299] The notice will be valueless unless the time allowed is reasonable,[300] but if satisfactory in this respect it will bind both parties.[301]

(b) Specific performance with abatement

There are other circumstances where the court will decree specific performance in favour of the claimant subject to the condition that compensation is paid in respect

---

[292] *Stickney v Keeble* [1915] AC 386, 415–16 (Lord Parker). See also *Rightside Properties Ltd v Gray* [1975] Ch 72; *Dean v Upton* [1990] EGCS 61; *Union Eagle Ltd v Golden Achievement Ltd* [1997] AC 514 (time of the essence: no decree where purchaser tendered purchase price ten minutes late); [1997] Conv 382 (MP Thompson).

[293] *Lock v Bell* [1931] 1 Ch 35.　　　　　　　　　　　　　　[294] Limitation Act 1980, s 36(1).

[295] See Farrand, *Contract and Conveyance* (4th edn), p 216.

[296] *Lazard Bros & Co Ltd v Fairfield Properties Co (Mayfair) Ltd* (1977) 121 SJ 793; [1978] Conv 184.

[297] *Williams v Greatrex* [1957] 1 WLR 31 (delay of ten years no bar in such a case).

[298] *Green v Sevin* (1879) 13 Ch D 589, 599.

[299] *Finkielkraut v Monohan* [1949] 2 All ER 234; *Dimsdale Developments (South East) Ltd v De Haan* (1983) 47 P & CR 1; [1984] Conv 34 (MP Thompson).

[300] *Smith v Hamilton* [1951] Ch 174; *Re Barr's Contract* [1956] Ch 551; *Ajit v Sammy* [1967] 1 AC 255.

[301] *Finkielkraut v Monohan*, above; *Quadrangle Development and Construction Co Ltd v Jenner* [1974] 1 WLR 68; *Oakdown Ltd v Bernstein & Co* (1984) 49 P & CR 282; *Behzadi v Shaftesbury Hotels Ltd* [1992] Ch 1; [1991] CLJ (C Harpum); [1991] 107 LQR 534 (PV Baker).

of some term of the contract that has not been literally fulfilled. Such cases of specific performance with an abatement of the purchase price are primarily concerned with misdescription of the property.[302] Subject to any conditions of sale applying to the contract, the general rule is that if the misdescription is substantial, the vendor cannot obtain specific performance even subject to an abatement, while the purchaser may enforce the contract if he so chooses.[303] But if the misdescription is not substantial either party may obtain specific performance subject to compensation.[304]

(c) Where defendant fails to comply with decree of specific performance

Where the claimant obtains a decree of specific performance, but the defendant fails to comply with it, the claimant may apply either to enforce[305] or to dissolve the contract. The contract still exists after the grant of specific performance and does not merge into the decree; thus the claimant is not precluded in such a case from seeking damages at common law.[306] But any subsequent performance of the contract is regulated by the provisions of the order of specific performance and not by those of the contract.[307] If the order for specific performance is not complied with, the claimant, having elected to affirm the contract, cannot then unilaterally terminate it for breach. He must apply to the court either for further enforcement measures or for a dissolution of the order and termination of the contract;[308] in which case he may claim for damages.

(3) Rescission for Breach of Contract[309]

(a) Terminology

A distinction must be drawn between rescission *ab initio*[310] and rescission in the sense of discharging the contract by accepting the repudiation of the other party. Where rescission *ab initio* occurs, such as in cases of misrepresentation, the contract is treated as if it had never existed; the innocent party cannot therefore recover damages for breach of contract. Where, however, the vendor fails to show a good title[311] or to deliver

---

302 See Farrand, *Contract and Conveyance* (4th edn), pp 52–5; (1980) 40 CLJ 47 (C Harpum).

303 *Flight v Booth* (1834) 1 Bing NC 370; *Rutherford v Acton-Adams* [1915] AC 866, 870; *Rudd v Lascelles* [1900] 1 Ch 815. It is otherwise if the compensation cannot be assessed, or if the subject matter is entirely different from that contracted for; see below, p 1050.

304 *Jacobs v Revell* [1900] 2 Ch 858. This principle cannot be used so as to increase the price: *Re Lindsay and Forder's Contract* (1895) 72 LT 832.

305 See *Easton v Brown* [1981] 3 All ER 278, above, p 993, n 289.

306 *Johnson v Agnew* [1980] AC 367, confirming the views expressed in (1975) 91 LQR 337 (MJ Albery) and (1977) 93 LQR 232 (F Dawson) (enforcement impossible because after date of contract with purchaser, vendor's mortgagees contracted to sell the property).

307 *Singh v Nazeer* [1979] Ch 474 (contractual completion notice served after decree of specific performance invalid); (1980) 96 LQR 403 (M Hetherington).

308 *GKN Distributors Ltd v Tyne Tees Fabrication Ltd* (1985) 50 P & CR 403.

309 For solicitors' liability in negligence for failing to advise purchaser of lease of his right to rescind, see *Peyman v Lanjani* [1985] Ch 457.

310 Above, p 987.

311 A purchaser can rescind as soon as he discovers that the vendor has no title, ie before date fixed for completion: *Pips (Leisure Productions) Ltd v Walton* (1980) 43 P & CR 415 (contract to sell leasehold that was already forfeited); *Pinekerry Ltd v Needs (Kenneth) (Contractors) Ltd* (1992) 64 P & CR 245.

the actual land or interest described in the contract, or where the vendor or purchaser fails to complete after time has been made of the essence,[312] or commits a repudiatory breach of contract,[313] it is commonly said that the innocent party may rescind. This is not rescission *ab initio*, but acceptance of a repudiation of the contract, discharging both parties from further performance. In such a case damages are recoverable at common law for breach of contract.[314] As discussed below, the terms of the contract may also confer a right to rescind in specified circumstances, and provide for the consequences. In the absence of any such terms, the innocent party may either accept the repudiation and proceed to claim damages (in which case he cannot later seek specific performance), or he may seek specific performance.[315] If an order for specific performance is made, but not complied with, he may apply to the court to enforce or to dissolve the order,[316] damages being recoverable in the latter case.[317]

(b) Contractual right to rescind

The right to rescind may also be conferred by the express terms of the contract.[318] There used commonly to be found in a contract of sale a condition that allows the vendor to rescind if the purchaser should insist on any requisition that the vendor is unable or unwilling to comply with.[319] But 'a vendor, in seeking to rescind, must not act arbitrarily, or capriciously, or unreasonably. Much less can he act in bad faith... Above all, perhaps, he must not be guilty of 'recklessness' in entering into his contract.'[320] Thus, in *Baines v Tweddle*,[321] a vendor was unable to exercise a contractual right to rescind because he had failed to seek the concurrence of his mortgagees before contracting to sell free from the mortgage.

---

[312] Time is not normally of the essence unless made so by the contract: above, p 994; cf *Allardyce v Roebuck* [2004] EWHC 1538 (Ch), [2005] 1 WLR 815 (completion following exercise of option).

[313] Whether a contract has been repudiated depends on whether, from the perspective of a reasonable person in the position of the innocent party, the contract-breaker has clearly shown an intention to abandon and refuse to perform the contract; a mistaken communication by the contract-breaker might not satisfy this test: *Eminence Property Developments Ltd v Heaney* [2010] EWCA Civ 1168, [2010] 3 EGLR 165; *Hooper v Oates* [2010] EWCA Civ 1346, [2010] 48 EGCS 85.

[314] *Johnson v Agnew* [1980] AC 367, overruling *Henty v Schröder* (1879) 12 Ch D 666, and many other authorities. See *Tilcon Ltd v Land and Real Estate Investments Ltd* [1987] 1 WLR 46.

[315] If he proceeds for these remedies in the alternative, he must elect at the trial: *Meng Leong Development Pte Ltd v Jip Hong Trading Co Pte Ltd* [1985] 1 AC 511.

[316] *Hillel v Christoforides* (1991) 63 P & CR 301 (where vendor has sought dissolution, purchaser cannot complete unless vendor has acted unconscionably).

[317] *Meng Leong Development Pte Ltd v Jip Hong Trading Co Pte Ltd*, above; *GKN Distributors Ltd v Tyne Tees Fabrication Ltd* (1985) 50 P & CR 403.

[318] Emmet, paras 7.004–7.006.

[319] See, eg Condition 4.5.2 of the Standard Conditions of Sale (1st edn, 1990) This right to rescind is no longer contained in the Standard Conditions of Sale; there are, however, other express rights to rescind such as on the purchaser's or the vendor's failure to complete the contract: conditions 7.4.2, 7.5.2; Emmet, para 7.006.

[320] *Selkirk v Romar Investments Ltd* [1963] 1 WLR 1415, 1422 (Lord Radcliffe).

[321] [1959] Ch 679; *Re Des Reaux and Setchfield's Contract* [1926] Ch 178. See also, on misdescription, *Topfell Ltd v Galley Properties Ltd* [1979] 1 WLR 446.

(c) Forfeiture of deposit

Where the purchaser defaults, the vendor is entitled to retain any deposit that the purchaser may have paid. Thus in *Howe v Smith*,[322]

£500 was paid as deposit and part payment of the purchase money. The purchaser, who was in default in completing the contract, sued to recover the £500, but it was held that, since it was the intention of the parties that this sum should be deposited as a guarantee for the due performance of his obligations, it must be forfeited to the vendor.

Where a defaulting purchaser has not yet paid over the whole of the deposit, the whole or any unpaid part is recoverable by the vendor.[323] Similarly, where the vendor is in default, the purchaser may recover any deposit that he has paid. But whether the rule as to retention of the deposit applies or not is in each case a matter of construction, and if the terms show that the money has not been paid as a guarantee of performance, but solely by way of part payment, it is recoverable by the purchaser even though the contract is rescinded owing to his own default.[324]

A purchaser may be able to secure the return of his deposit under section 49(2) of the Law of Property Act 1925, which provides that:

where the court refuses to grant specific performance of a contract, or in any action for the return of a deposit, the court may, if it thinks fit, order the repayment of any deposit.

Considering this provision, Buckley LJ said that it was designed simply to do justice between vendor and purchaser:[325]

---

[322] (1884) 27 Ch D 89. On deposits generally, see Farrand, *Contract and Conveyance* (4th edn), pp 203–8; Barnsley, *Conveyancing Law and Practice*, pp 233–43; [1994] Conv 41, 100 (AJ Oakley). For the position where an estate agent holds the pre-contract deposit of a prospective purchaser, see *Sorrell v Finch* [1977] AC 728; *Ramsden v James Bennett* [1993] NPC 91 (£6,000 deposit for option to purchase villa in Spain); cf *Ojelay v Neosale Ltd* [1987] 2 EGLR 167 and on stakeholders generally: *Sorrell v Finch*; *Tudor v Hamid* [1988] 1 EGLR 251; (1988) 138 NLJ 40 (HW Wilkinson); *Rockeagle Ltd v Alsop Wilkinson* [1992] Ch 47.

[323] *Dewar v Mintoft* [1912] 2 KB 373, 387–8; *Millichamp v Jones* [1982] 1 WLR 1422 (where the authorities were fully reviewed by Warner J); *Damon Cia Naviera SA v Hapag-Lloyd International SA* [1985] 1 WLR 435 (applied by CA in a case relating to ships); *John Willmott Homes Ltd v Read* (1985) 51 P & CR 90; cf *Lowe v Hope* [1970] Ch 94; Farrand, *Contract and Conveyance* (4th edn), p 206.

[324] *Mayson v Clouet* [1924] AC 980.

[325] *Universal Corp v Five Ways Properties Ltd* [1979] 1 All ER 552, 555 (deposit of £88,500). Where the court orders the return of the deposit, the vendor is left to his remedy in damages. See also *James Macara Ltd v Barclay* [1944] 2 All ER 31, 32; affd on other grounds [1945] KB 148; *Charles Hunt Ltd v Palmer* [1931] 2 Ch 287; *Finkielkraut v Monohan* [1949] 2 All ER 234; *Schindler v Pigault* (1975) 30 P & CR 328; *Faruqi v English Real Estates Ltd* [1979] 1 WLR 963, 968; *Cole v Rose* [1978] 3 All ER 1121; *Maktoum v South Lodge Flats Ltd*, The Times, 22 April 1980; 130 NLJ 668 (HW Wilkinson); *Dimsdale Developments (South East) v De Haan Ltd* (1983) 47 P & CR 1; *McGrath v Shah* (1987) 57 P & CR 452 (where no reference was made to LPA 1925, s 49(2)); *Country and Metropolitan Homes Survey Ltd v Topclaim Ltd* [1996] Ch 307. See also Estate Agents Act 1979, ss 12–17.

On the principles governing relief against forfeiture of deposit, see *Stockloser v Johnson* [1954] 1 QB 476; *Linggi Plantations Ltd v Jagatheesan* [1972] 1 MLJ 89; *Windsor Securities Ltd v Loreldal and Lester Ltd*, The Times, 10 September 1975; *Workers Trust & Merchant Bank Ltd v Dojap Investments Ltd* [1993] AC 573 (relief possible where deposit is a penalty and not a true deposit; deposit exceeding 10 per cent held not to be a true 'reasonable' deposit); [1989] Conv 377 (HW Wilkinson); [1993] CLJ 389 (C Harpum); (1993) 109 LQR 524 (H Beale); *Safehaven Investments Inc v Springbok Ltd* (1995) 71 P & CR 59 (repayment of deposit

It confers on the judge a discretion, which is unqualified by any language of the subsection, to order or refuse repayment of the deposit, a discretion which must, of course, be exercised judicially and with regard to all relevant considerations, including the very important consideration of the terms of the contract into which the parties have chosen to enter...repayment must be ordered in any circumstances which make this the fairest course between the two parties.

(4) Vendor and Purchaser Summons

The Vendor and Purchaser Act 1874 introduced a new method whereby parties to a contract of sale, whose disagreement upon some matter prevents the completion of the contract, may apply in a summary way to a judge in chambers, and obtain such an order as may appear just. This summary proceeding is termed a vendor and purchaser summons, and is now governed by the Law of Property Act 1925.[326] Typical questions that lead to a summons are the sufficiency of the title shown by the vendor,[327] the sufficiency of an answer made to a requisition,[328] the construction of the contract, and the question whether a vendor is entitled to rescind.

The Act expressly excludes the possibility of raising any question that affects the existence or the validity of the contract, such as the question whether the formalities of the contract have been complied with.

Not only may the court decide the question submitted to it, but it may also grant consequential relief, that is may order such things to be done as are the natural consequence of the decision. For example, it may order rescission in favour of a purchaser, together with the return of his deposit.

refused where contract concerning commercial property made between capable businessmen with access to best professional advice. Purchaser was experienced property dealer well aware of the function of a deposit and the risks of losing it); *Union Eagle Ltd v Golden Achievement Ltd* [1997] AC 514 (10 per cent deposit not a penalty), above, p 994, n 292; *Omar v El-Wakil* [2001] EWCA Civ 1090, [2002] 2 P & CR 3 at [36] (Arden LJ: 'I would start from the position that a deposit should not normally be ordered to be repaid'), followed in *Midill (97PL) Ltd v Park Lane Estates Ltd* [2008] EWCA Civ 1227, [2009] 1 WLR 2460. See generally Goff and Jones, *The Law of Restitution* (7th edn, 2007) paras 20-035 to 20-046; Emmet, paras 7.017–7.020; [1994] Conv 41, 100 (AJ Oakley).

[326] LPA 1925, s 49(1). The county court has jurisdiction where the capital value of the land does not exceed £30,000: s 49(4); County Courts Act 1984, s 148(1), Sch 2, para 2; SI 1991 No 724. For the suggestion that this procedure is today of limited usefulness and continuing efficacy, see [2001] Conv 301 (G Griffiths); cf [2010] Conv 308 (M Merry) (vendor and purchaser summons 'alive and well in Hong Kong').

[327] See *MEPC Ltd v Christian-Edwards* [1981] AC 205, illustrating that such proceedings are not necessarily expeditious or cheap.

[328] See *Faruqi v English Real Estate Ltd* [1979] 1 WLR 963.

25

FORMALITIES REQUIRED FOR THE CREATION AND TRANSFER OF ESTATES AND INTERESTS IN LAND

Summary

I INTRODUCTION

The law prescribes formalities for certain transactions. Sometimes compliance with the formality is a condition of validity of the transaction; sometimes it is only a condition of legal enforceability.[1] But in any case in which a formality is prescribed, a question may arise as to how strict the formality rule is. One might begin by assuming that, if the formality is not complied with, the transaction is ineffective, or unenforceable, as the case may be. It is not, however, always quite so straightforward. In assessing the significance of a particular requirement of form, it is important to bear in mind the

---

[1] Under LPA 1925, s 40, the written memorandum was a condition of enforceability of a contract relating to land; now LP(MP)A 1989, s 2, makes a written contract a condition of validity: above, Ch 24.

purposes for which formality may in general be required. Three aims of formalities are commonly identified:[2]

(a) *cautionary*: that is trying to ensure that the maker does not enter into the transaction without realising what he is doing;

(b) *evidential*: providing evidence that the maker did enter into a transaction, and evidence of its terms;

(c) *labelling*: making it apparent to third parties what kind of a document it is and what its effect is to be.

The courts will sometimes look at the underlying purpose of the particular formality for the particular type of transaction that is before them, in order to decide how strictly they should interpret the statute that requires it.

In the context of land law, a number of formality requirements are laid down by statute. This is not perhaps surprising. For most individuals, land is their most significant asset—significant not only in financial terms, if they own their own home, but also in functional terms: it is their home.[3] As we have seen in Chapter 24, the law now requires a contract for the sale or other disposition of an interest in land to be in writing, signed by both parties. In this chapter we shall see the formality requirements that are prescribed for the creation and transfer of estates and interests in land. But we shall also need to consider the law's response to the failure to comply with particular formality requirements. Sometimes the statute that sets out the formality required for a transaction gives an indication of the consequences of the failure to comply. But sometimes not; and cases often arise in which parties have quite innocently failed to comply with the requirements, and the courts have had to consider whether the law should assist them by admitting the creation or transfer of property rights in spite of the statute.

'Under a legal system recognizing the individualistic institution of private property and granting to the owner the power to determine his successors in ownership, the general philosophy of the courts should favor giving effect to an intentional exercise of that power.'[4] The conflict between the certainty of a strict requirement of form, and the desire to do justice for individuals in particular cases, is at the heart of some

[2] Law Com WP No 93, *Transfer of Land: Formalities for Deeds and Escrows* (1985), para 3.2, discussing the aims of formalities for making a deed, but drawing on the analysis of the aims of formalities in general in (1941) 41 Colum L Rev 799, 800–1 (LL Fuller: 'evidentiary', 'cautionary', 'channeling' functions); (1941) 51 Yale LJ 1, 3–5 (AG Gulliver and CJ Tilson: 'ritual', 'evidentiary', 'protective' functions); (1975) 88 Harv L Rev 489, 492–7 (JH Langbein: 'evidentiary', 'channeling', 'cautionary', 'protective' functions); (1974) 43 Fordham L Rev 39 (JM Perillo: 'magical, sacramental and psychological', 'earmarking and classifying', 'cautionary', 'clarifying', 'managerial', 'publicity', 'educational', 'regulatory and taxation', 'evidentiary' functions); [1984] CLJ 306 (TG Youdan).

[3] 'Forms must be reserved for relatively important transactions. We must preserve a proportion between means and end; it will scarcely do to require a sealed and witnessed document for the effective sale of a loaf of bread': (1941) 41 Colum L Rev 799, 805 (LL Fuller).

[4] (1941) 51 Yale LJ 1, 2 (AG Gulliver and CJ Tilson).

significant developments in recent years in land law. As we shall see,[5] the development of proprietary estoppel and the use of constructive trusts as means of creating interests in land are the prime examples of this.

II THE FORMALITIES

A FORMALITIES FOR THE CREATION AND TRANSFER OF LEGAL ESTATES AND INTERESTS

(1) Necessity for a Deed

(a) Forms of alienation before 1926

The appropriate form at the present day for the conveyance of any interest in land is a deed of grant, but this form, though always required for the transfer of incorporeal hereditaments, was not extended to freehold estates in possession until 1845. Before that date the distinction drawn by the law was that freehold estates in possession *lay in livery*, that is they were transferable by delivery of possession, and that incorporeal interests *lay in grant*, that is they must be conveyed by deed of grant.[6] The Real Property Act of 1845,[7] however, provided that all corporeal hereditaments should, as regards the conveyance of the immediate freehold, be deemed to lie in grant as well as in livery. This Act did not, however, abolish the old forms of conveyance, and although it led to the general use of a deed of grant as a means of transferring all kinds of landed interests, there were still occasions upon which such forms as the feoffment and the bargain and sale[8] were used.

(b) Forms of alienation after 1925

The Law of Property Act 1925 simplified practice by providing that:[9]

> All lands and all interests therein lie in grant and are incapable of being conveyed by livery or livery and seisin, or by feoffment, or by bargain and sale; and a conveyance of an interest in land may operate to pass the possession or right to possession thereof, without actual entry, but subject to all prior rights thereto.

This section, which shows that a grant is the usual method of conveying any interest in land, is followed by another that provides that:[10]

> all conveyances of land or of any interest therein are void for the purpose of conveying or creating a legal estate unless made by deed.

---

[5] Below, pp 1011 ff.

[6] For the history of the forms of alienation, see Holdsworth, *A History of English Law*, vol iii, pp 217–46; vol vii, pp 357–62. See above, p 69, n 29.

[7] S 2.   [8] Above, p 69.   [9] LPA 1925, s 51(1).   [10] Ibid, s 52(1).

This enactment, if unqualified, would cause inconvenience in certain cases, and it is therefore subject to exceptions. These are as follows:[11]

(2) Exceptions to Necessity for a Deed

(a) Assent by personal representative

The land of a deceased person vests in his personal representatives for the purposes of administration, and any devises he may have made are suspended until the administration is completed.[12] Upon such completion the land does not pass automatically to a devisee, but only when the assent of the personal representatives has been given. An assent to the vesting of a legal estate must be *in writing*, signed by the personal representatives, and must name the person in whose favour it is given; it operates to vest in that person the legal estate to which it relates. An assent not in writing or not in favour of a named person is ineffectual to pass a legal estate.[13] An implied assent, that is one inferred from conduct, may be effective to pass a title to equitable interests or to choses in action and personal chattels.[14]

(b) Disclaimer by trustee in bankruptcy

When any part of the estate of a bankrupt consists of land that is burdened with onerous covenants and is therefore unsaleable, the trustee in bankruptcy may, by writing, disclaim the property. Such a disclaimer operates to determine the rights and the liabilities of the bankrupt in respect of the property, but it does not affect the rights of third parties. The court may, on the application of any person who is interested in the disclaimed property, make an order vesting the property in him, and the effect of such an order is that the property vests in that person without any conveyance.[15]

(c) Surrender by operation of law

Surrender is not an instrument, but means that the owner of a smaller estate yields up that estate to the person who is entitled in reversion or remainder to the larger estate in the same lands, such as where the tenant for life of Blackacre surrenders his life interest to the person who is entitled to the fee simple in the land. In such a case the life interest is merged in the fee simple.

---

[11] LPA 1925, s 52(2).   [12] AEA 1925, ss 1(1), 3(1), (3)–(5); below, pp 1053, n 78; 1121.

[13] AEA 1925, s 36(1), (4); *Re King's Will Trusts* [1964] Ch 542; (1964) 28 Conv (NS) 298 (JF Garner); (1976) CLP 60 (EC Ryder); Farrand, *Contract and Conveyance* (4th edn), p 106; Barnsley, *Conveyancing Law and Practice*, p 321. See Law Com WP No 105, *Title on Death* (1987), paras 4.19–4.28; Law Com No 184, *Title on Death* (1989), paras 1.5–1.6. *Re King's Will Trusts* was not followed in *Mohan v Roche* [1991] 1 IR 560; [1992] Conv 383 (JA Dowling).

[14] *Re Hodge* [1940] Ch 260; *Re Edwards' Will Trusts* [1982] Ch 30; [1982] Conv 4 (PW Smith).

[15] Insolvency Act 1986, s 315; *Eyre v Hall* [1986] 2 EGLR 95.

Surrenders are either express or implied, and when implied they are said to arise by operation of law. An express surrender is void at law unless it is made by deed, but an implied surrender is effectual without any formality.[16]

(d) Lease for term not exceeding three years

A lease that is to take effect in possession reserves the best rent that can be reasonably obtained without taking a fine, and is for a term not exceeding three years need not be created by deed, but can be created by writing or even orally. This has been discussed already.[17]

(e) Receipt not required to be under seal

An example of this before 1926 was where the legal estate of a mortgagee was revested in the mortgagor upon redemption not by a reconveyance under seal, but by an endorsed receipt.[18]

(f) Vesting order of the court

A vesting order is an order made by the court that may operate to vest, convey or create a legal estate in the same way as if a conveyance had been executed by the estate owner.[19] If, for example, an equitable chargee applies for a sale of the land, the court may make an order vesting the land for a legal estate in the purchaser.[20]

(g) Conveyance taking effect by operation of law

Examples of these are grants of probate or of letters of administration and adjudications in bankruptcy.

(3) Form of Deeds, and Methods of Execution

In order to take effect as a deed, a document must comply with certain requirements as to its form and its method of execution. The requirements vary according to whether the document is to be executed by an individual or a company; but in both cases the formalities, originally prescribed by the common law, have been changed in recent years by statute.

(a) General nature of a deed

A deed of grant is a formal written instrument that is signed and delivered by the grantor as his act, and in which he expresses an intention to pass an interest to the grantee.

The common law prescribed certain formalities for a deed:[21] 'There are but three things of the essence and substance of a deed, that is to say, writing in paper or parchment, sealing and delivery.' Section 1 of the Law of Property (Miscellaneous

---

16 Above, pp 340–1.   17 LPA 1925, s 54(2); above, p 212.   18 Above, p 838.
19 LPA 1925, s 9.   20 LPA 1925, s 90.   21 *Goddard's Case* (1584) 2 Co Rep 4b, 5a.

Provisions) Act 1989,[22] which applies to deeds executed on and after 31 July 1990, made the following general changes to the requirements to the form of a deed:

(1) Any rule of law which—

    (a)   restricts the substances in which a deed may be written…

       is abolished.

(2) An instrument shall not be a deed unless—

    (a)   it makes it clear on its face that it is intended to be a deed by the person making it or, as the case may be, by the parties to it (whether by describing itself as a deed or expressing itself to be executed or signed as a deed or otherwise); and

    (b)   it is validly executed as a deed…

(1) Physical form of a deed

Before 31 July 1990 a deed had to be written on paper or parchment. Section 1(1) of the Act abolishes any rule of law that restricts the substance on which a deed may be written. Hence a deed may now be written on more durable material than paper, for example, fire- and flood-proof metal.[23]

Section 1(2) requires, however, that in its form the deed be 'clear on its face' that it is intended to be a deed. This is a strict requirement: an instrument is not to be taken to make it clear on its face that it is intended to be a deed merely because it is executed under seal.[24] The simplest form will be the reference to 'This deed…' at the head of the document. The particular requirements of valid execution are discussed below.

(2) Delivery

(i) General requirement of delivery

A deed must be 'delivered'.[25] This requirement was not changed by the 1989 Act. However, delivery does not mean a mere physical delivery, but a delivery accompanied by words or conduct signifying the grantor's intention to be bound by the provisions in the deed. The most apt and expressive mode of acknowledging this liability is for the grantor to hand the deed over, saying, 'I deliver this as my deed', but any other

---

[22] This section is based on Law Com No 163, *Deeds and Escrows* (1987). It came into force on 31 July 1990 and is not retrospective: Law of Property (Miscellaneous Provisions) Act 1989 (Commencement) Order 1990 (SI 1990 No 1175); [1990] Conv 1, 90. See [1991] LMCLQ 209 (G Virgo and C Harpum) for a trenchant criticism of 'the recent reforms which have left the law of deeds both more complex and less rational than it was hitherto'. The section was further amended by Regulatory Reform (Execution of Deeds and Documents) Order 2005, SI 2005 No 1906, and Legal Services Act 2007, Sch 21, para 81.

[23] Emmet, para 20.002.

[24] S 1(2A), added by SI 2005 No 1906. See also *HSBC Trust Co Ltd v Quinn* [2007] EWHC 1543 (Ch), [2007] All ER (D) 125 (Jul) (formal language of agreement and witnessed signatures not sufficient).

[25] *Bolton MBC v Torkington* [2003] EWCA Civ 1634, [2004] Ch 66; [2004] Conv 9 (JE Adams).

words or acts that show an undoubted acknowledgment of immediate liability will suffice.[26]

(ii) Escrow

A physical delivery, however, unaccompanied by this express or implied acknowledgment, is insufficient. If, for example, the grantor signs and seals the deed and then delivers it to his solicitor to be dealt with according to instructions to be given later, it does not operate as an immediate grant of the interest.

There are two kinds of delivery recognised by the law in this connection, one absolute and the other conditional.[27] If a document is delivered, either to a party to it or to a stranger,[28] with an intimation, express or implied, that it is not to become effective until some condition has been performed, it is called an escrow (or scroll). In such a case the deed is inoperative until the condition is performed, but upon performance it takes effect as a deed without further delivery, and, if necessary, relates back to the time when it was delivered as an escrow.[29] Lord Cross of Chelsea said:[30]

> On fulfilment of the condition subject to which it was delivered as an escrow, a deed is not taken to relate back to the date of its delivery for all purposes, but only for such purposes as are necessary to give efficacy to the transaction—*ut res magis valeat quam pereat*.[31] Thus the fact that the grantor has died before the condition of an escrow is fulfilled does not entail the consequence that the disposition fails.

> If and when the condition is fulfilled the doctrine of relation back will save it, but notwithstanding the relation back for that limited purpose the grantee is not entitled to the rents of the property during the period of suspense or to lease it or to serve notices to quit.[32]

A delivery of a deed as an escrow is a final delivery in the sense that it cannot be withdrawn by the grantor before the grantee has had an opportunity to decide whether to fulfil the condition or not. A deed delivered subject to a condition and subject to such a right of withdrawal is not an escrow, but merely an undelivered deed.[33]

---

[26] *Xenos v Wickham* (1866) LR 2 HL 296, 312. In the case of a deed executed by a company incorporated under the Companies Act, or a corporation aggregate, there is a presumption that the document is delivered upon its being executed; but this is now only a rebuttable presumption: LPA 1925, s 74A(2), as inserted by SI 2005 No 1906; CA 2006, s 46(2). The presumption for companies under the Companies Act was formerly irrebuttable: CA 1995, s 36A(6), as inserted by CA 1989, s 130.

[27] *Foundling Hospital v Crane* [1911] 2 KB 367, 377.

[28] *London Freehold and Leasehold Property Co v Baron Suffield* [1897] 2 Ch 608, 621–2.

[29] *Vincent v Premo Enterprises (Voucher Sales) Ltd* [1969] 2 QB 609; *Alan Estates Ltd v WG Stores Ltd* [1982] Ch 511; *Dyment v Boyden* [2005] 1 WLR 792 (party to lease not treated as bound from date when other party had delivered the lease in escrow where escrow conditions subsequently satisfied).

[30] *Security Trust Co v Royal Bank of Canada* [1976] AC 503, 517; [1982] Conv 409 (PH Kenny).

[31] *Butler and Baker's Case* (1591) 3 Co Rep 25a.

[32] Sheppard's Touchstone (7th edn, 1830), p 60; *Thompson v McCullough* [1947] KB 447. See also *Terrapin International Ltd v IRC* [1976] 1 WLR 665; *Venetian Glass Gallery Ltd v Next Properties Ltd* [1989] 2 EGLR 42.

[33] *Beesly v Hallwood Estates Ltd* [1961] Ch 105; *Windsor Refrigerator Co Ltd v Branch Nominees Ltd* [1961] Ch 88, rvsd on a different point [1961] Ch 375; *D'Silva v Lister House Development Ltd* [1971] Ch 17; *Longman v Viscount Chelsea* (1989) 58 P & CR 189.

A common example of delivery as an escrow occurs where a vendor executes a deed of conveyance and gives it to his solicitor for transfer to the purchaser upon payment by the latter of the purchase money. If the sale is not completed in due course, the vendor is released, and the solicitor has no authority to hand over the conveyance.[34] Another example of delivery as an escrow occurs where a landlord executes a deed creating a lease, and the condition of the escrow is the execution of a counterpart by the tenant.[35]

(3) Deeds poll and indentures

Deeds are either deeds poll or indentures. A deed poll is one that is executed by a party of one part, an indenture is a deed (such as a conveyance by way of sale) to which there are parties of two or more parts.

In earlier days, when deeds were more concise than they are at present, it was usual, when they were made between two parties, to write two copies on the same parchment with some words written in the middle through which the parchment was cut in acute angles or indentations.[36] These two parts were called 'counterparts', and, when put together so that the indentations fitted into each other, constituted the complete deed. Hence the name 'indenture'. Counterparts are not nowadays written on the same paper, but the part that is executed by the grantor of an interest is commonly called the *original*, while that which is executed by the party to whom the interest passes—for example, a lessee—is called the *counterpart*.[37] The custom of indenting deeds gradually died out, and all that the term 'indenture' came simply to indicate is that the deed in question involved parties of more than one part.

A deed poll is so called because, unlike an indenture, it was formerly polled (or cut even) at the top.

(4) Description of deeds in the modern law

Despite the provision of the Real Property Act 1845 that a deed should have the effect of an indenture although not actually indented, it remained customary to introduce every deed that involved more than one party by the expression 'This Indenture...' But it is now provided by section 57 of the Law of Property Act 1925 that:

Any deed, whether or not being an indenture, may be described (at the commencement thereof or otherwise) as a deed simply, or as a conveyance, deed of exchange, vesting deed, trust instrument, settlement, mortgage, charge, transfer of mortgage, appointment, lease or otherwise according to the nature of the transaction intended to be effected.

---

[34] *Kingston v Ambrian Investment Co Ltd* [1975] 1 WLR 161; *Glessing v Green* [1975] 1 WLR 863. As to the time limit for the performance of this condition, see [1975] 39 Conv (NS) 430 (FR Crane).

[35] *Beesly v Hallwood Estates Ltd*, above, n 33; *Alan Estates Ltd v WG Stores Ltd*, above, n 29 (both lease and counterpart executed in escrow).

[36] Blackstone, vol ii, p 295.   [37] Elphinstone, *Introduction to Conveyancing* (7th edn, 1918), p 60.

(b) Deed executed by individual[38]

Section 1(3) of the Law of Property (Miscellaneous Provisions) Act 1989 lays down a new rule for the execution of a deed by an individual:

> (3) An instrument is validly executed as a deed by an individual if, and only if—
>
> (a) it is signed[39]—
> (i) by him in the presence of a witness who attests the signature; or
> (ii) at his direction and in his presence and the presence of two witnesses who each attest the signature; and
>
> (b) it is delivered as a deed.[40]

(1) Sealing

Before 31 July 1990 a deed had to be sealed; that is to say, it had to bear wax, or a wafer, or some other indication of a seal.[41] Section 1(1) abolishes the requirement of a seal for the valid execution of a deed by an individual.

(2) Attestation

Section 1 makes new and precise attestation provisions for the valid execution of a deed by an individual. The signature must be attested by a witness who is present at the time of the signature. If the deed is not signed by a party (for example, where he is physically incapable of doing so) then it must be signed at his direction and in his presence and there must be *two* witnesses who each attest the signature.

(c) Deed executed by company[42]

In 1989 the requirements for the valid execution of a deed by companies incorporated under the Companies Act were also amended.[43] For such companies a document is executed by a company either by affixing the common seal of the company,[44] or by

---

[38] See generally Barnsley, *Conveyancing Law and Practice*, pp 446–56.

[39] Signing includes making one's mark on the instrument: s 1(4).

[40] A lawyer (or his agent or employee) who, in the course of a transaction purports to deliver a deed on behalf of a party is conclusively presumed in favour of a purchaser to be authorised to deliver the deed: s 1(5), amended by SI 2005 No 1906 and Legal Services Act 2007, Sch 21, para 81.

[41] *Stromdale and Ball Ltd v Burden* [1952] Ch 223; *First National Securities Ltd v Jones* [1978] Ch 109 (legal charge without wax or wafer, but with attestation clause and signature across printed circle containing letters LS [*locus sigilli*: the 'place of the seal'] held duly executed); (1980) 43 MLR 415 (DC Hoath). See also *Commercial Credit Services v Knowles* [1978] CLY 794; *TCB Ltd v Gray* [1986] Ch 621 (deed not sealed, but grantor estopped from denying that it was).

[42] For reforms designed to standardise in certain respects the formal requirements for companies, corporations and individuals, see Regulatory Reform (Execution of Deeds and Documents) Order 2005, SI 2005 No 1906.

[43] Companies Act 1985, s 36A, as added by Companies Act 1989, s 130. S 36A was amended by SI 2005 No 1906, and the amended section was replaced by CA 2006, s 44. For execution by foreign companies, see Overseas Companies (Execution of Documents and Registration of Charges) Regulations 2009 (SI 2009 No 1917), Part 2.

[44] A company may have a common seal, but need not have one: CA 2006, s 45.

being expressed to be executed by the company and signed either by one director in the presence of a witness who attests the signature, or by two directors or by a director and the company secretary.[45]

No change, however, was then made to the requirements of execution by corporations sole, and by corporations aggregate that are not companies within the Companies Act 1985; sealing therefore remains a requirement.[46]

(4) Electronic Documents

The strict formalities discussed above cannot be maintained for transactions effected under electronic conveyancing.[47] The Land Registration Act 2002 has made provision for this, not by disapplying the requirement of a deed for the conveyance or creation of a legal interest in land; nor by making a general change to the requirements of a valid deed; but by providing that certain types of document in electronic form, when used to effect certain types of transaction, will be regarded for the purposes of any enactment as a deed.[48]

Where the disposition is of a registered estate or charge, or of an interest that is the subject of a notice in the register, or a disposition that triggers the requirement of registration, and if it is of a kind specified by the rules, then a document in electronic form that purports to effect the disposition is to be regarded as a deed if it makes provision for the time and date it is to take effect, has the certified electronic signature of each person by whom it purports to be authenticated, and it satisfies any other conditions as are provided by rules.[49]

(5) Registration Requirements

In the case of registered land, certain dispositions are required to be completed by registration, and do not operate at law until the relevant registration requirements are met. In the case of a registered estate, these dispositions are the following:[50]

---

[45] CA 2006, s 44. See *Redcard Ltd v Williams* [2011] EWCA Civ 466, [2011] 25 EG 106 at [25] (not necessary that there be words on the document spelling out that signatures are 'by or on behalf of' the company where document makes clear it is executed by the company).

[46] In favour of a purchaser an instrument shall be deemed to have been duly executed by a corporation aggregate if a seal purporting to be the corporation's seal purports to be affixed to the instrument in the presence of and attested by (a) two members of the board of directors, council or the governing body of the corporation, or (b) one such member and the clerk, secretary or other permanent officer of the corporation or his deputy: LPA 1925, s 74(1) as substituted by SI 2005 No 1906, art 3.

[47] On electronic conveyancing generally, see above, pp 141–3; below, p 1122. On contracts in electronic conveyancing, see above, pp 972–3.

[48] Such an electronic document will therefore satisfy LPA 1925, s 52(1).

[49] LRA 2002, s 91; H & B, pp 329–35. References to an electronic signature and to the certification of a signature are to be read in accordance with Electronic Communications Act 2000, s 7(2), (3): LRA 2002, s 91(10). The document is also to be regarded as in writing, and signed by each individual and sealed by each corporation whose electronic signature it has: s 91(4).

[50] Ibid, s 27(1). In the case of a registered charge, the dispositions required to be completed by registration are a transfer and the grant of a sub-charge: ibid, s 27(2). These provisions apply also to dispositions by

(a) a transfer,[51]

(b) where the registered estate is an estate in land, the grant of a term of years absolute—

   (i) for a term of more than seven years from the date of the grant,

   (ii) to take effect in possession after the end of the period of three months beginning with the date of the grant,

   (iii) under which the right to possession is discontinuous,

   (iv) in pursuance of Part 5 of the Housing Act 1985 (the right to buy), or

   (v) in circumstances where section 171A of that Act applies (disposal by landlord which leads to a person no longer being a secure tenant),

(c) where the registered estate is a franchise or manor, the grant of a lease,

(d) the express grant or reservation of an interest of a kind falling within section 1(2)(a) of the Law of Property Act 1925,[52] other than one which is capable of being registered under Part 1 of the Commons Act 2006,[53]

(e) the express grant or reservation of an interest of a kind falling within section 1(2)(b) or (e) of the Law of Property Act 1925,[54] and

(f) the grant of a legal charge.

Thus, for example, the transfer of a registered estate, the grant of a legal lease for more than seven years,[55] the express grant of a legal easement,[56] or the grant of a legal charge[57] cannot be effected simply by deed. The deed is necessary in order to satisfy section 52 of the Law of Property Act 1925. But the grant takes effect only in equity[58] until it is perfected by registration.[59]

B FORMALITIES FOR THE CREATION AND TRANSFER OF EQUITABLE INTERESTS

Finally we must consider the formalities necessary for the creation of a trust and for the disposition of an equitable interest. In neither case is a deed required.

---

operation of law, except for a transfer on death or bankruptcy of an individual proprietor, or on dissolution of a corporate proprietor, and the creation of a local land charge: s 27(5).

[51] For the prescribed form of transfer, see below, p 1086.

[52] Legal easements and profits. This does not include a grant as a result of the operation of LPA 1925, s 62; above, p 654.

[53] Amended by Commons Act 2006, Sch 5, para 8. Until the 2006 Act is brought into force, the reference is to the Commons Registration Act 1965.

[54] Rentcharges and rights of entry.

[56] Above, pp 650–1, 691.

[55] Above, p 220.

[57] Above, p 806.

[58] If it is to bind a purchaser it therefore requires protection by notice on the register unless it is an overriding interest (eg, in the case of a lease, by virtue of the tenant being in discoverable actual occupation). Under LRA 1925, s 123A(5), as substituted by LRA 1997, s 1, dispositions that were subject to compulsory registration under LRA 1925, s 123, were effective at law but became void as regards the transfer, grant or creation of legal estate if not registered within two months, and thereafter took effect as (in the case of a purported transfer) a bare trust for the transferee or (in the case of a purported grant of a legal estate or mortgage) a contract to grant the estate or mortgage.

[59] The registration requirements are set out in LRA 2002, Sch 2.

(1) Creation of a Trust

There are very few rules restricting the method by which a trust must be created. The trust is the successor of the old use,[60] and for the raising of a use no formalities were necessary. Spoken words were as effectual as written instruments, and according to the preamble to the Statute of Uses bare signs and gestures seem to have been sufficient. The one guiding principle was that effect should be given to the intention of the settlor, no matter how it had been indicated by him. The same is generally true with the modern trust.

A trust may be created either by an instrument inter vivos or by will. If it is created inter vivos and if it relates to land, it must conform to the Law of Property Act 1925.[61]

If it is created by will, then, whether it relates to real or to personal property, the instrument of creation must be made in accordance with the Wills Act 1837, which prescribes the manner in which all wills must be made.[62]

If neither the Law of Property Act 1925 nor the Wills Act 1837 applies—if, that is to say, the trust relates neither to freeholds nor to leaseholds, and if it is not contained in a will—it may be created by word of mouth or by some other indication of intention, and without any kind of formality. A clear oral declaration by the owner of pure personalty that he is a trustee of that property for another person constitutes a valid trust and can be enforced by the volunteer in whose favour it was declared.[63]

But it was found in the case of land that oral declarations of trusts led to disputes and inconvenience, and therefore the Statute of Frauds in 1677[64] required for the first time that the creation of a trust of real estate should be manifested and proved by some writing signed by the settlor. This provision is now contained in section 53(1)(b) of the Law of Property Act 1925 in the following words:

> A declaration of trust respecting any land or any interest therein must be manifested and proved by some writing signed by some person who is able to declare such trust or by his will.

There are several points that should be noticed about this enactment.

First, it is confined to land and does not interfere with the rule that a trust of pure personalty may be constituted by an oral declaration.

It does not require a deed, but only writing, and even so it does not require that the trust should have been declared by writing in the first place. The statute uses the words 'manifested and proved', and it is sufficient if the trust can be proved by some writing signed by the settlor no matter what the date of the writing may have been.[65]

---

[60] Above, pp 65 ff.   [61] S 53(1)(b), below.

[62] See the 16th edn of this work, ch 25.

[63] *Jones v Lock* (1865) 1 Ch App 25; *Richards v Delbridge* (1874) LR 18 Eq 11; *Middleton v Pollock* (1876) 2 Ch D 104; *Paul v Constance* [1977] 1 WLR 527; see generally Maudsley and Burn, *Trusts and Trustees* (7th edn, 2008), pp 111 ff.

[64] S 7.   [65] *Rochefoucauld v Boustead* [1897] 1 Ch 196, 206.

The writing is to be signed by 'some person who is able to declare such trust', that is the person who is the owner of the property in respect of which the trust is declared.[66] No provision is made for signature by an agent.

The statutory provisions apply only to express trusts, and not to the creation or operation of resulting, implied or constructive trusts.[67] This is very significant for the informal creation of interests in land, discussed later in this chapter.

(2) Disposition of Equitable Interest

Section 53(1)(c) of the Law of Property Act 1925 provides that:

> a disposition of an equitable interest or trust subsisting at the time of the disposition must be in writing signed by the person disposing of the same, or by his agent thereunto lawfully authorised in writing or by will.

In this context the word 'disposition' must be given the wide meaning that it bears in normal usage, and therefore, for example, an oral direction by a beneficiary to trustees to hold an equitable interest upon new trusts is a disposition that is ineffective for lack of writing.[68]

III FAILURE TO COMPLY WITH THE REQUIRED FORMALITIES. THE INFORMAL CREATION OF INTERESTS IN LAND

A GENERAL

We now need to consider how the law responds to cases in which one or both parties have not complied with the rules prescribed for the creation of an interest in land.[69] A strict line might be taken: the law requires a formality, and so failure to comply means that the transaction is simply not effective. However, this strict line has often not found favour with the courts, particularly where one party is acting inequitably, or 'unconscionably', in resisting the enforcement of a property right on the basis that the

---

66 *Tierney v Wood* (1854) 19 Beav 330.

67 LPA 1925, s 53(2); *Hodgson v Marks* [1971] Ch 892; *Ottaway v Norman* [1972] Ch 698.

68 *Grey v IRC* [1960] AC 1; *Oughtred v IRC* [1960] AC 206; *Neville v Wilson* [1997] Ch 144; *Bishop Square Ltd v IRC* (1997) 78 P & CR 169; *Vandervell v IRC* [1967] 2 AC 291; *Re Tyler* [1967] 1 WLR 1269; *Re Danish Bacon Co Ltd Staff Pension Fund* [1971] 1 WLR 248; *Re Vandervell's Trusts (No 2)* [1974] Ch 269. See generally Maudsley and Burn, *Trusts and Trustees*, pp 112 ff; H & M, para 3.008; [1979] Conv 17 (G Battersby). S 53(1)(c) is not limited to equitable interests or trusts *of land*.

69 For the use of similar doctrines of equity to allow a party to enforce an *agreement* for the sale or other disposition of an interest in land which does not satisfy the formality requirements for a contract, see above. pp 963–5 (part performance, where no sufficient written memorandum as required by LPA 1925, s 40); 973–8 (proprietary estoppel and constructive trust where no written contract as required by LP(MP)A 1989, s 2).

formalities required for its creation or transfer were not properly complied with. The informal creation of interests in land is within the traditional domain of equity. For the most part, the courts have not been prepared to allow legal estates and interests to be created where the required statutory formalities have not strictly been followed.[70] But they have sometimes found that the failure to comply with legal formalities can be solved by the safety-net of equity.[71] We have seen the following examples earlier in this book, but they are briefly gathered here to demonstrate their common links.

B THE DOCTRINE OF *WALSH V LONSDALE*

The attempt to create a legal estate or interest in land, which fails for lack of formality, might sometimes be held to create the equivalent equitable interest. This is generally known as the doctrine of *Walsh v Lonsdale*,[72] after the case in which it was applied in the context of leases. The doctrine does not, however, allow for the creation of an equitable interest in the absence of all formality; but it requires the formality of a *contract*, although not the deed of conveyance. If there is a valid contract for the sale or other disposition of an interest in land, of which the court would be prepared to grant the equitable remedy of specific performance, it is treated in equity as creating the equivalent interest to that which, if the contract were performed, would be created at law. This doctrine has been discussed already in the context of contracts relating to land.[73]

C RESULTING OR CONSTRUCTIVE TRUST

(1) Resulting and Constructive Trusts as Statutory Exceptions to the Formality Requirements

Certain statutory provisions relating to formalities contain an exception for resulting, implied or constructive trusts. In the context of contract formalities, we have already seen that section 2 of the Law of Property (Miscellaneous Provisions) Act 1989, which requires a contract for the sale or other disposition of an interest in land to be in writing, provides[74] that the section does not affect the creation or operation of such trusts; and that in *Yaxley v Gotts*[75] this provision was applied to give effect to the parties'

---

[70] Cf, however, *Shah v Shah* [2001] EWCA Civ 527, [2002] QB 35 (deed signed and delivered, but attested by a person who was not present when party signed as required by LP(MP)A 1989, s 1; held, party estopped from denying validity of the deed; following *Yaxley v Gotts* [2000] Ch 162, above, p 974).

[71] Cf *Bexley LBC v Maison Maurice Ltd* [2006] EWHC 3192 (Ch), [2007] 1 EGLR 19 at [55]-[64] (reliance on estoppel cannot validate what would otherwise be an *ultra vires* act, but if the Council could lawfully have exercised a power, the principles of estoppel as they apply to the Council are the same as would apply to a private landowner).

[72] (1882) 21 Ch D 9, M & B p 30; above, p 215.   [73] Above, p 978.   [74] S 2(5).

[75] [2000] Ch 162, M & B p 22; above, p 974. Cf, however, *Cobbe v Yeoman's Row Management Ltd* [2008] UKHL 55, [2008] 1 WLR 1752, M & B p 1021, above, pp 976–8, and esp at [29] (Lord Scott of Foscote), above, p 977, and cases noted above, p 978, n 181.

intentions that one should have an interest in property where their agreement did not satisfy the formality requirements for a contract. Similarly, the general requirements for formality contained in section 53 of the Law of Property Act 1925—that (a) no interest in land can be created or disposed of except by writing; (b) a declaration of trust respecting land must be proved by writing; and (c) a disposition of a subsisting equitable interest or trust must be in writing—do not apply to the creation or operation of resulting, implied or constructive trusts.[76]

This last provision has opened the way for the courts to find—and, sometimes, to impose—a solution under which one party who does not have an estate or interest in the property at law has an equitable interest under a resulting or constructive trust.

(2) Co-ownership in Equity on the Basis of Resulting or Constructive Trusts

One context in which the courts have made particular use of resulting and constructive trusts is in co-ownership of property: the creation of concurrent equitable interests, often in the family home.[77] This has already been discussed in detail in Chapter 14,[78] where we saw that the courts can find a constructive trust to give effect to the parties' common intention that the one who has no legal title should share the beneficial interest in the property with the paper owner where the latter has not made an express declaration of trust to satisfy the formality requirements of section 53 of the Law of Property Act 1925, but where the party without legal title has acted to his or her detriment in reliance on the agreement. Similarly, where there is neither an express trust, nor a constructive trust based on the parties' evidenced common intentions, the court may find a resulting trust under which the paper owner holds the property on trust for the other to the extent of the latter's contribution to the purchase price.

(3) Licences Protected by Constructive Trust

In Chapter 23[79] we saw another species of constructive trust, used to give protection in equity to a licensee. Where a purchaser of property has undertaken to the vendor to give effect to the licence and where, in addition,[80] the facts are such as to bind the

---

[76] LPA 1925, s 53(2); above, p 1011. On constructive trusts, see Oakley, *Constructive Trusts* (3rd edn, 1997), pp 53 ff; H & M, ch 12; Maudsley and Burn, *Trusts and Trustees*, chs 7 and 8; Snell, paras 24–041 to 24–056. On resulting trusts generally, see H & M, ch 10; Maudsley and Burn, *Trusts and Trustees*, ch 6. An express declaration of trust can be superseded by a constructive trust or proprietary estoppel: *Clarke v Meadus* [2010] EWHC 3117 (Ch), [2010] All ER (D) 08 (Dec) at [83].

[77] For non-family cases (such as the '*Pallant v Morgan* equity') see above, p 520, n 142.

[78] Above, pp 512 ff.   [79] Above, pp 933 ff.

[80] Notice by the purchaser, and even his undertaking to the vendor, are not of themselves sufficient to create a trust; more is necessary to affect the purchaser's conscience: *Ashburn Anstalt v Arnold* [1989] Ch 1, 25, M & B, p 1104, above, p 935. A contract between the vendor and purchaser which expressly identifies the licensee and is (expressly or impliedly) intended to be enforceable by him, may now, however, be enforceable by the licensee *in contract* under the Contracts (Rights of Third Parties) Act 1999: above, p 932, n 53.

vendor's conscience to give effect to the licence, the court may find that the purchaser is a constructive trustee for the benefit of the licensee, and is therefore bound to give effect to the terms of the licence.[81]

D PROPRIETARY ESTOPPEL

We have already seen the general principles applicable to the doctrine of proprietary estoppel,[82] and how the doctrine can be used to protect a licensee.[83] Here we shall consider its relationship to the constructive trust discussed in the previous section.

Under the doctrine of proprietary estoppel, an 'equity by estoppel' arises—without any requirement of writing or other formality—in favour of the claimant, by virtue of the defendant's representation or acquiescence, combined with the claimant's reasonable reliance upon his belief that he has, or will acquire, a right in or over the defendant's land.[84] At a later stage, the court may order a remedy to give effect to that equity.

Even before the court order, the equity has a sufficiently proprietary character to be capable of binding a purchaser.[85] Proprietary estoppel can therefore be seen as a method of creating rights in land without complying with the formalities usually required for their creation. Much depends, however, on how we analyse the rights that arise at the two stages of the application of the doctrine. Section 53 of the Law of Property Act 1925 provides that:

(1) Subject to the provisions hereinafter contained with respect to the creation of interests in land by parol[86]—

    (a) no interest in land can be created or disposed of except by writing signed by the person creating or conveying the same, or by his agent thereunto lawfully authorised in writing, or by will, or by operation of law...

(2) This section does not affect the creation or operation of resulting, implied or constructive trusts.

If the equity arising by estoppel is itself an interest in land, then it appears not to comply with this requirement, unless it can be brought within the exception of subsection (2)—that is it takes effect as a constructive trust.

---

[81] *Binions v Evans* [1972] Ch 359, M & B p 1102, above, p 932; *Bannister v Bannister* [1948] 2 All ER 133, M & B p 1101, above, p 934; *Re Sharpe* [1980] 1 WLR 219, M & B p 1109, above, p 934; *Lyus v Prowsa Developments Ltd* [1982] 1 WLR 1044, M & B p 223.

[82] Above, pp 904 ff.   [83] Above, pp 936 ff.   [84] Above, p 909.

[85] LRA 2002, s 116(a) (registered land); *E R Ives Investment Ltd v High* [1967] 2 QB 379 (unregistered land). To bind a purchaser it must also be protected by notice in the register or as an overriding interest (registered land) or the purchaser must have notice of it (unregistered land); and it is not clear whether the equity can be overreached by the purchaser; see generally above, pp 920–2, 941–2.

[86] S 54(2): leases in possession for a term not exceeding three years at the best rent which can reasonably be obtained without taking a fine.

The close relationship between the doctrines of proprietary estoppel and constructive trust has been discussed by judges in a number of cases;[87] and some cases arise on facts that might equally well be analysed as a constructive trust based on the common intention of the parties, or proprietary estoppel.[88] Some recent developments might appear to have brought these doctrines even closer together. We have seen that the Court of Appeal in *Oxley v Hiscock*[89] has emphasised the court's discretion in deciding the value of the parties' respective interests under a constructive trust based on their common intention to share property; and *Jennings v Rice*[90] has also emphasised the courts' discretion in deciding on the remedy to be awarded in a case of proprietary estoppel. However, this similiarity can be deceptive.[91] The court in *Oxley v Hiscock* described the discretion only in a case in which the parties had agreed to share but had not agreed on the value of their respective shares, and as we have seen, the House of Lords in *Stack v Dowden*[92] sought to emphasise that the court's task in valuing the interest is not to decide simply what is 'fair' but rather to search for the intention of the parties. In a case of proprietary estoppel, however, the court in *Jennings v Rice* made clear that, even if there is a clearly evidenced representation as to the interest to be conferred, the court will not necessarily order it; the remedy is still at the discretion of the court.[93] This emphasises that the nature of the claimant's right under the equity arising by estoppel is more uncertain, more precarious than that arising under a constructive trust that gives effect to the parties' common intention. It also shows that, in the case of such a constructive trust, the right is from the beginning an interest in land—a beneficial interest in the land itself, albeit to a share that the court may not yet have quantified, if the parties did not agree it. However, in the case of proprietary estoppel, the right is only an 'equity'—the right to seek a remedy; but it is not yet a full interest in the land. Indeed, it may never be, if the court does not order a property interest as

---

[87] Sir Nicolas Browne-Wilkinson V-C in *Grant v Edwards* [1986] Ch 638, 656–7; Lord Bridge of Harwich in *Lloyds Bank plc v Rosset* [1991] 1 AC 107, 132; Chadwick LJ in *Oxley v Hiscock* [2004] EWCA Civ 546, [2005] Fam 211, below, at [70]-[71]; Robert Walker LJ in *Birmingham Midshires Mortgage Services Ltd v Sabherwal* (2000) 80 P & CR 256 at [24], *Yaxley v Gotts* [2000] Ch 162, 176–7 and *Jennings v Rice* [2002] EWCA Civ 159, [2003] 1 P & CR 8 at [45]; cf, however, *Stack v Dowden* [2007] UKHL 17, [2007] 2 AC 432 at [37] (Lord Walker of Gestingthorpe: 'I have to say that I am now rather less enthusiastic about the notion that proprietary estoppel and "common interest" constructive trusts can or should be completely assimilated'). See also Sir Christopher Slade, *The Informal Creation of Interests in Land* (1984) Child & Co Oxford Lecture.

[88] See, eg, *Jennings v Rice*, above, at [45] (Robert Walker LJ), discussing *Yaxley v Gotts* [2000] Ch 162; *Kinane v Mackie-Conteh* [2005] EWCA Civ 45, [2005] 2 P & CR DG 3. The requirement of reliance by the claimant on the parties' common intention to share—which resonates with the language of estoppel—reinforces this analogy.

[89] [2004] EWCA Civ 546, [2005] Fam 211, M & B p 578; above, p 516.

[90] [2002] EWCA Civ 159, [2003] 1 P & CR 8, M & B p 1040; above, p 917.

[91] (2004) 120 LQR 541 at 545–6 (S Gardner); [2004] Conv 496 (MP Thompson).

[92] [2007] UKHL 17, [2007] 2 AC 432, above, p 518; but note the difficulty with the formulation by Baroness Hale of Richmond at [60], that 'the search is to ascertain the parties' shared intentions, actual, inferred *or imputed*, with respect to the property in the light of their whole course of conduct in relation to it' (emphasis added): above, p 517.

[93] Above, p 918.

the remedy. Lord Walker of Gestingthorpe, who had commented in earlier cases on the apparent similarity between constructive trust and proprietary estoppel,[94] has also now expressed some reservations about the link between the doctrines:[95]

> I have to say that I am now rather less enthusiastic about the notion that proprietary estoppel and 'common interest'[96] constructive trusts can or should be completely assimilated. Proprietary estoppel typically consists of asserting an equitable claim against the conscience of the 'true' owner. The claim is a 'mere equity'. It is to be satisfied by the minimum award necessary to do justice,[97] which may sometimes lead to no more than a monetary award. A 'common intention' constructive trust, by contrast, is identifying the true beneficial owner or owners, and the size of their beneficial interests.

An alternative analysis would be that the equity arising by proprietary estoppel is indeed an interest in land, but one that is not simply to be classified as a form of constructive trust, but is a new form of property in its own right.[98] In the nineteenth century a new equitable property right—the restrictive covenant—emerged as the consequences of *Tulk v Moxhay*[99] became fully recognised. Perhaps proprietary estoppel is in a similar process of development into a new equitable property right.[100] There are certain technical difficulties presently standing in the way of this analysis: the prima facie limitation in the Law of Property Act 1925 on the creation of new equitable rights in land;[101] and the absence of any provision in that Act to exempt proprietary estoppel from the requirement of writing to create an interest in land.[102] However, the modern statutory recognition of the equity by estoppel as having effect as an interest capable of binding third parties[103] may show that the proprietary status of proprietary estoppel is now being recognised and that it should be assimilated into the list of known property rights.

A third possibility, however, is that the equity is not to be characterised as an interest in land, but more akin to a mere equity.[104] This gives certain proprietary characteristics

---

[94] Above, p 1015, n 87.   [95] *Stack v Dowden*, above, at [37].

[96] Presumably this should read 'common intention'.

[97] *Crabb v Arun District Council* [1976] Ch 179, 198.

[98] For the view that proprietary estoppel does not need a constructive trust to protect it, but is independently based on the unconscionability involved in going back on an assurance about formality, see (2010) 30 LS 408 (M Dixon).

[99] (1848) 2 Ph 774, M & B p 754; above, p 732.

[100] For the development of other equitable property rights, see above, p 904, n 8.

[101] LPA 1925, s 4(1).

[102] Cf LPA 1925, s 55, which contains savings which were known to be required in 1925—including (para (d)) the law relating to part performance. There is a close similarity between part performance and proprietary estoppel, in that both involve an equity arising outside the statutory formality relating to land, to prevent a party from relying on the absence of formality: above, p 973; cf *Crabb v Arun District Council* [1976] Ch 179 at 195 (Scarman LJ).

[103] LRA 2002, s 116 (although it is expressed to be only 'for the avoidance of doubt'); above, p 921. However, s 116 gives the same force to a mere equity (which is not generally recognised as an interest in land itself; below).

[104] Above, p 903; *Stack v Dowden*, above, at [37] (Lord Walker of Gestingthorpe).

to the right;[105] but the effect of proprietary estoppel is not then to create an interest in the land itself, and so there is no conflict with the formality requirements for the creation of an interest in land. The interest in the land itself, if such is the remedy ordered by the court, is created only by the court's order,[106] or by the grant of the interest, in accordance with the proper formalities, by the defendant pursuant to the court order.

---

[105] LRA 2002, s 116, above.

[106] Even if it is a legal estate, this does not require a deed for its creation or transfer, since the court order suffices: LPA 1925, s 52(2)(f); above, p 1003. It will, however, require registration in registered land.

26

CAPACITY TO ACQUIRE, HOLD AND TRANSFER ESTATES AND INTERESTS IN LAND

Summary

I MINORS

A TERMINOLOGY. 'INFANT' AND 'MINOR'

In this section we are concerned with persons who are not of full age. Before 1970 it was common to describe such a person as an 'infant'. The Family Law Reform Act 1969,[1] however, provided that 'a person who is not of full age may be described as a minor instead of as an infant'.

---

[1] S 12. Statutes passed before 1970 continue to use the old language. Cf Limitation Act 1980, s 38(2) (although this was derived from Limitation Act 1939, s 31(2)).

In this chapter the term 'minor' is generally used, in accordance with modern usage.

B DEFINITION OF MINORITY

A minor is a person, whether male or female, who has not attained full age. As from 1 January 1970, a person attains full age at the first moment of the 18th anniversary of his birth.[2] Before then, the age of majority had been the first moment of the day preceding the 21st anniversary.[3]

C MINOR MAY NOT HOLD LEGAL ESTATE

In accordance with the fundamental principle of the legislation of 1925, a minor can never hold a legal estate in land.[4] He cannot be an estate owner nor, therefore, can he be registered as proprietor.[5] This restriction, which is imposed in the interests of a simplified system of conveyancing, does not mean that he cannot hold and enjoy beneficially an equitable interest[6] and there is nothing to prevent land being transferred to him by way of gift, sale, settlement or lease. In such a case, the statutory policy before 1997 was to treat the land as settled land, and during the minority to vest the legal estate in trustees whose identity will depend upon whether the minor comes to his interest as grantee, devisee, heir on intestacy, beneficiary under a settlement, mortgagee, or trustee of the land for the benefit of another person. The Trusts of Land and Appointment of Trustees Act 1996, in accordance with the general policy of the Act, replaced the mechanism of the strict settlement with the new trust of land in relation to settlements created after 31 December 2006.[7] There is simplification without the introduction of any substantive changes.

[2] Persons of 18 or over, but under 21, attained full age on that date: Family Law Reform Act 1969, ss 1(1), 9. See Report of the Committee on the Age of Majority (the Latey Report) 1967 (Cmnd 3342); (1979) 120 NLJ 144 (SM Cretney). S 1(2) provides that for the 'construction of "full age", "infant", "infancy", "minor", "minority" and similar expressions' in any statutory provision, whenever passed or made, the references shall be deemed to be references to the age of majority as amended by the Act. Where, however, a statutory provision refers to a specified age, s 1(3), Sch 1, sets out those statutes in which references to 21 are changed to 18. S 1(4), Sch 2 excepted from s 1(2) the Regency Acts 1937–1953; Representation of the People Act 1969 and tax statutes. For subsequent changes in fiscal legislation, however, see FA 1969, s 16, and, in the age of franchise, Representation of the People Act 1983, s 1. In the case of private transactions the Act is not retrospective, eg 'to X on attaining his majority', if made in a will or settlement before 1970, X takes at 21; if made after 1969, X takes at 18.

[3] See Report of the Committee on the Age of Majority (1967), paras 37–42; *Re Shurey* [1918] 1 Ch 263.

[4] LPA 1925, s 1(6).

[5] If a minor is registered in error, the register is conclusive and therefore the legal estate is deemed to be vested in the minor, although it is liable to be rectified: LRA 2002, ss 58(1), 65, Sch 4. See generally R & R, para 13.005.01.

[6] *Kingston upon Thames Royal LBC v Prince* [1999] 1 FLR (minor succeeds to secure tenancy held by her grandfather, holding equitable interest during her minority) (before 1997); applied in *Newham LBC v R* [2004] EWCA Civ 41 (after 1996).

[7] TLATA 1996, s 2; above, p 475.

Since, however, settlements created before 1997 can still exist, we must first set out the position before the Trusts of Land and Appointment of Trustees Act 1996 came into force on 1 January 1997.

(1) Before 1997

(a) Grant inter vivos to minor

A conveyance of a legal estate in land to a minor alone, or to two or more persons jointly, both or all of whom are minors, for his or their own benefit, operated before 1997 only as an agreement for valuable consideration to execute a settlement in his or their favour.[8] This means that the grantor had as soon as possible to execute a principal vesting deed and a trust instrument,[9] meanwhile holding the land in trust for the minor. In this case, however, the legal estate would be transferred by the vesting deed not to the minor as tenant for life, but to the trustees when they were appointed, who then became the statutory owners.[10]

If a legal estate was conveyed to a minor jointly with one or more other persons of full age, the person or persons of full age took the legal estate on trust for sale.[11] In this case the persons of full age held upon the statutory trusts applicable to a joint tenancy, that is upon trust to sell the land and to hold the proceeds and the profits until sale for the benefit of themselves and the minor.[12] If, however, life interests were given, there was a settlement and the adults were tenants for life under the Settled Land Act 1925.[13]

(b) Devise to minor

In the case of a devise to a minor the legal estate vested at first in the personal representatives of the deceased by virtue of the Administration of Estates Act 1925, but in considering the ultimate destination of the legal estate we must distinguish between a devise of an absolute interest, and a devise by way of settlement in which trustees of the settlement have been appointed.

Where the land was devised to the minor for an estate in fee simple or for a term of years absolute, or where it was settled upon him for life and no trustees were appointed, the personal representatives could retain the land until the minor attained his majority, and until that time they possessed all the powers of a tenant for life under a settlement,[14] and also the powers of trustees for sale.[15] If, however, they did not desire to retain the land, they could appoint trustees to be trustees of the land for the purposes

---

[8] LPA 1925, s 19(1); SLA 1925, s 27(1). This can be protected (in registered land) by a notice in the register or (in unregistered land) by registration as an estate contract under LCA 1972; above, pp 982–3. On the grant of a lease to a minor, see Law Com No 134, *Minors' Contracts* (1984), paras 5.13–5.16, explaining supposed difficulties.

[9] Above, pp 436 ff. Or he could execute a confirmatory conveyance to the minor after the minor attains majority: *Darvell v Basildon Development Corp* (1969) 211 EG 33, 37.

[10] Above, p 442.   [11] LPA 1925, s 19(2).

[12] Ibid, s 35.   [13] S 19(3).   [14] SLA 1925, s 26(1).   [15] AEA 1925, s 39(1).

of the Settled Land Act and for the purposes of the statutory provisions relating to the management of land during a minority.[16]

Where the land was devised by way of settlement to a minor for a limited interest and the testator had appointed trustees of the settlement, the Settled Land Act directs that the personal representatives should, when their administration duties are completed, transfer the legal estate to the trustees if they are required to do so.[17]

(c) Descent of land to minor

(1) Fee simple

In the case of deaths occurring after 1925 it is impossible for a minor to become entitled to a fee simple estate by descent. The residuary estate of the intestate is held by the administrator upon trust to sell and to divide the proceeds among the relatives entitled under the Administration of Estates Act 1925. If a minor is the sole relative so entitled, he will become entitled absolutely to the fee simple when he either marries or forms a civil partnership or attains his majority. But as we have seen, a minor cannot hold a legal estate in land, and therefore, the land remains settled land until he attains his majority.[18]

(2) Entailed interest

The old law of descent, however, still applies to the entailed interest, but if the heir is a minor the legal estate must be vested in the trustees of the settlement until he attains his majority. If money is required during his minority for his maintenance, education or benefit, the court if necessary may make an order under the Trustee Act 1925,[19] appointing a person to execute a disentailing assurance that will bar the issue and remaindermen as completely as if it were effected by the minor after attaining his majority.[20]

(d) Settlement of land in favour of minor

Before 1997, a person who desired to settle land in favour of a minor could create either a strict settlement under the Settled Land Act 1925 or a trust for sale.

In the case of a strict settlement, the statutory powers of a tenant for life and the trustees of a settlement, together with any additional powers that may be conferred by the settlement, become exercisable by the trustees,[21] who, in their capacity as 'statutory owners',[22] are entitled to have the legal estate transferred to them by a vesting deed. If the settlor adopted the method of a trust for sale, the trustees not only obtain the legal estate but they also possess all the statutory powers under the Settled Land Act 1925, so long as the land remains unsold.[23]

---

[16] Ibid, s 42.   [17] SLA 1925, ss 6, 26.
[18] AEA 1925, s 47, as amended by Civil Partnership Act 2004, s 71, Sch 4, para 8.
[19] TA 1925, s 53.   [20] Re Gower's Settlement [1934] Ch 365.   [21] SLA 1925, s 26(1)(b).
[22] Ibid, s 117(1)(xxvi).   [23] LPA 1925, s 28(1).

If a tenant for life under an existing settlement is succeeded by a minor as tenant for life, the latter is not entitled to the legal estate until he attains his majority. In the meantime the legal estate and the statutory powers will be held by the trustees of the settlement.[24]

Where a minor becomes absolutely entitled under a settlement, such as where there is a grant or a devise:

> to A for life, remainder to B (a minor) in fee simple, and A dies during the minority of B,

the settlement continues until B attains his majority,[25] the legal estate in the meantime being vested in the trustees of the settlement. In a case such as this, statutory provision is made to meet the contingency of the minor dying under age: unless he marries or forms a civil partnership before reaching his majority, he is deemed to have had a life interest at the time of his death.[26] In other words, the fee simple of B, in the above example, though potentially absolute,[27] is cut down to a life interest until he marries or forms a civil partnership or reaches 18. Therefore, if at his death he is still a minor, unmarried and has not formed a civil partnership, the estate will revert to the settlor if the settlement was by deed, or will pass to the residuary devisee in the case of a testamentary settlement. It is better that there should be this reversion to the settlor, rather than that the estate should enure for the benefit of some distant relative of the minor, which would be the result if he were to die owning an absolute interest.

(e) Mortgage to minor

Before 1997, section 19(6) of the Law of Property Act 1925 provided that a legal estate could not be conveyed to a minor by way of mortgage. A grant of a legal mortgage of land to a minor merely operated as an agreement for valuable consideration that the grantor would execute a proper conveyance when the minor attained full age, and that in the meantime he would hold the beneficial interest on trust for the minor.[28] If, however, the conveyance was made to the minor and to another person of full age, it operated as if the minor had not been named, though of course his beneficial interest was not prejudiced.[29]

(f) Conveyance to minor as trustee

A minor cannot be appointed a trustee.[30] A conveyance that purported to convey land to a minor as trustee did not transfer the legal estate, but operated as a declaration of trust in favour of the beneficiaries designated.[31] In such a case the person who

---

[24] SLA 1925, s 26(1).   [25] Ibid, s 3(b).

[26] AEA 1925, s 51(3), as amended by TLATA 1996, s 25(1), Sch 3, para 6(1), (4) and Civil Partnership Act 2004, s 71, Sch 4, Pt 2, para 11. Before the amendment in 1996, the minor's interest was deemed to be an entailed interest, not a life interest, and entails thus created before 1997 are unaffected: TLATA 1996, s 25(4). The effect, however, of the death of the minor is the same since an unmarried minor cannot have heirs capable of taking an estate tail.

[27] *Re Taylor* [1931] 2 Ch 242, 246.

[28] LPA 1925, s 19(6). The minor's interest can be protected (in registered land) by a notice in the register or (in unregistered land) by registration as an estate contract under LCA 1972.

[29] Ibid, s 19(6).   [30] Ibid, s 20.   [31] Ibid, s 19(4).

is empowered by the trust instrument to appoint new trustees may make a new appointment,[32] or, if there is no such person, the court may do so.[33]

Similarly, the legal estate cannot pass to a minor who is appointed executor by the will of a testator.[34]

(2) After 1996

Under the Trusts of Land and Appointment of Trustees Act 1996 a purported conveyance after 1996 to a minor takes effect as a declaration of trust, the land being held by the relevant trustees under the new system.[35] Where the conveyance is made inter vivos, the grantor holds the land as a trustee for the minor. Where it is conveyed to a minor jointly with a person of full age, the person of full age holds the land on trust for himself and the minor as joint tenants or as tenants in common according to the terms of the conveyance.[36] Where there is a devise to a minor, the personal representatives act as trustees for the minor.

As we have seen, section 19 of the Law of the Property Act 1925[37] made provision for conveyances on trust or by way of mortgage. Since a conveyance of a legal estate in land to a minor creates a trust in favour of the minor, these provisions are no longer necessary and are repealed.

D ACQUISITION AND ALIENATION BY MINOR OF EQUITABLE INTERESTS IN LAND

(1) Conveyance to Minor

An equitable interest, as distinct from a legal estate, may be effectively transferred to a minor, but since the ownership of an interest in land may occasionally prove to be more of a burden than a benefit, especially in the case of a leasehold containing onerous covenants, the long-established rule is that the transfer is voidable at the option of the minor on attaining his majority or within a reasonable time thereafter.[38] In the event of his death his personal representatives may exercise the same power within a reasonable time.[39] But repudiation must not be unduly delayed. Where a minor bought land at a price payable by instalments, and continued to pay them for some time after he reached full age, it was held that

---

[32] TA 1925, s 36.   [33] Ibid, s 41.
[34] SCA 1981, s 118. Nor can a minor be an administrator: *Re Manuel* (1849) 13 Jur 664.
[35] TLATA 1996, s 2(1), Sch 1, paras 1 and 2; Law Com No 181, *Trusts of Land* (1989), para 5; W & H, paras 6.31–6.33.
[36] SLA 1925, s 27 was ambiguous in that it did not expressly provide for the conveyance to minors as tenants in common. It was repealed by TLATA 1996, s 25(2), Sch 4.
[37] Repealed by TLATA 1996, s 25(2), Sch 4.   [38] *Ketsey's Case* (1613) Cro Jac 320.
[39] Blackstone, vol ii, p 292; *North Western Rly Co v M'Michael* (1850) 5 Exch 114, 123.

his procrastination had defeated his right of avoidance and that he must pay the instalments that remained due.[40]

(2) Conveyance by Minor

A minor cannot make an irrevocable disposition of his interest, for the rule is that any disposition is voidable and can be repudiated by him during his minority or within a reasonable time after he attains full age.[41] So the disability is not absolute. It goes no further than is necessary for the protection of the minor. It leaves him the power to act during his minority, but in order that he may have protection, it permits him to avoid the transaction when he comes of age if he finds it right and proper to do so.[42] The tendency of the courts, however, is to regard very slight acts, such as the receipt of rent in the case of a lease, as amounting to a ratification of the conveyance.[43]

(3) Will of Minor

A minor cannot make a will, either of real or of personal property.[44]

(4) Settlement by Minor

In accordance with the principle applicable to alienation in general, a settlement made by a minor in contemplation of marriage is voidable, but it becomes binding upon him or her unless it is repudiated within a reasonable time after the attainment of majority.[45] The reasonable time is calculated from the attainment of majority, and not, as was once thought, from the moment when the property falls into possession.[46] If, for example, a minor settles a reversionary interest, consisting of a fee simple estate that will come to him on the death of his mother, he will lose his right to repudiate unless he takes the necessary steps soon after he reaches full age, notwithstanding that it may be many years before possession of the land becomes available by the death of his mother.

His ignorance of the right of repudiation does not absolve him from the obligation to take steps within a reasonable time.[47]

---

[40] *Whittingham v Murdy* (1889) 60 LT 956; *Davies v Beynon-Harris* (1931) 47 TLR 424 (lease). If the minor repudiates the lease, he cannot recover rent already paid: *Valentini v Canali* (1889) 24 QBD 166.

[41] Co Litt 171b. The Infant Settlements Act 1855, which enabled a male infant over 20 and a female infant over 17 to make a binding marriage settlement of property with the consent of the Chancery Division, was repealed by the Family Law Reform Act 1969, s 11(a), as from 1 January 1970, 'except in relation to anything done before' that date.

[42] *Burnaby v Equitable Reversionary Interest Society* (1885) 28 Ch D 416, 424. This parallels the general (protective) approach in respect of minors' contracts: Anson, pp 232 ff.

[43] *Slator v Brady* (1863) 14 ICLR 61.

[44] Wills Act 1837, s 7. There is an exception for soldiers and airmen on active military service, and sailors at sea: Wills Act 1837, s 11; Wills (Soldiers and Sailors) Act 1918, s 3(1).

[45] *Edwards v Carter* [1893] AC 360.   [46] *Carnell v Harrison* [1916] 1 Ch 328.   [47] Ibid.

E MANAGEMENT OF MINOR'S PROPERTY

(1) Powers of Trustees

Land to which a minor is beneficially entitled, either absolutely or for a lesser interest (such as a life interest) must be held by trustees. Where the interest was created before 1997 and the land is deemed to be settled land, the trustees have all the ordinary powers conferred on a tenant for life and upon settlement trustees by the Settled Land Act 1925.[48] They may also enter into and continue in possession of the land on behalf of the minor, and if they do, they are directed to manage or superintend the management of the land, with full power, inter alia:

(1) to fell timber in the usual course for sale or for repairs;

(2) to erect, pull down, rebuild and repair buildings;

(3) to work mines that have usually been worked;

(4) to drain or otherwise improve the land;

(5) to deal generally with the land in a proper and due course of management.[49]

These powers are also exercisable, subject to any prior interests or charges, where a minor is contingently entitled to land.[50]

After 1996 the trustees have all the powers of an absolute owner, under section 6 of the Trusts of Land and Appointment of Trustees Act 1996, for the purpose of exercising their functions as trustees.[51]

(2) Application of Surplus Income

As regards the use that must be made of surplus income during the minority, it is provided[52] that the trustees may, at their sole discretion, apply a reasonable part of the income of the property for the maintenance, education or benefit of the minor, notwithstanding that some other fund may be applicable to those purposes, or that some other person, such as a parent, may be legally bound to provide for the minor's maintenance or education. But in deciding whether income shall be used for such purposes, the trustees must have regard to the age and requirements of the minor and to the circumstances of the case in general. In particular they must, in spite of the latitude allowed them, take into account whether some other fund may be used for the purpose.

The residue of the income is to be accumulated by way of compound interest, and the accumulations are to be paid over to the minor when he attains 18 years or marries or forms a civil partnership under that age, provided that his interest is vested. If the minor has a merely contingent interest, or if he dies under 18 years of age and without having married or formed a civil partnership, the accumulations must be added to

---

[48] SLA 1925, s 26; above, pp 443 ff.   [49] Ibid, s 102.   [50] Ibid, s 102(5).
[51] Above, p 479.   [52] TA 1925, s 31(1).

capital.[53] Where land to which a minor is entitled is subject to a trust of land, the trustees are empowered to use the capital to an amount not exceeding one-half of his presumptive or vested share for his advancement or benefit.[54]

II MARRIED WOMEN

In the twenty-first century, it seems hardly credible that a married woman should have any proprietary disability by virtue simply of her status. However, this used to be the case; and the history of this area forms an illuminating chapter in the growth of English law—and an understanding of it is necessary to be able fully to appreciate the context in which some of the older cases were decided.

A COMMON LAW

At common law husband and wife are one person.[55] The general result of this merger of the wife's status in that of her husband was that he became absolute owner of her personal chattels, he might dispose of her leaseholds and take the proceeds, and he had the sole right of controlling and managing her freehold estates. If she predeceased him, he became absolutely entitled to any personal property of which she died possessed, and to a life estate by curtesy in her freehold estates of inheritance provided that a child had been born.[56] In addition, a man could not make a grant to his wife directly or enter into a covenant with her, for to allow either of these things would have been to suppose her separate existence. In short, the effect of marriage at common law was to make a man complete master of his wife's property and to deprive her of contractual capacity.

B EQUITY

Gradually, however, and quite apart from legislation, wives were placed by the courts of equity in an even more favourable position than men or unmarried women, a

---

[53] TA 1925, s 31(2), amended by Family Law Reform Act 1969, Sch 1; Civil Partnership Act 2004, Sch 27, para 5.

[54] Ibid, s 32. The section does not apply to capital money arising under SLA 1925: s 32(2) as substituted by TLATA 1996, s 25(1), Sch 3, para 3(1), (8).

[55] For a history of the rule, see *Midland Bank Trust Co Ltd v Green (No 3)* [1979] Ch 496, 512 ff, where Oliver J traces its origin to Genesis chapter 2, verse 24 and then refers to chapter 3, verses 12–13: 'The common law was a trifle selective in its application of biblical doctrine. Adam after all was treated as a competent witness against Eve and his evidence was accepted and acted upon.' For the 'Green saga', see below, p 1066, n 176. The decision was affirmed [1982] Ch 529, where Sir George Baker referred at 542 to 'the erudite and so felicitously expressed judgment of Oliver J'. See also *Routhan v Arun DC* [1982] 1 QB 502, 506–7 (Lord Denning MR: 'the doctrine of unity ... says that in law "husband and wife are one and the husband is that one." I remember well that it was invoked when I used to prosecute in the magistrates' courts. A wife was travelling on the railway using her husband's ticket. When she put forward the excuse: "We are one in the eyes of the law," the collector replied: "But not in the eyes of the Southern Railway"').

[56] Above, p 589.

result that was due to the invention by the Court of Chancery of the doctrine of equitable separate estate. If property was given to a married woman by words that indicated either expressly or by implication that she was to enjoy it for her sole and separate use, equity removed that property from the control of the husband by regarding him as trustee, and conferred upon the wife full powers of enjoyment and disposition. But equity went even further than this: perceiving the danger that a husband might over-persuade his wife to sell her separate property and hand the proceeds to him, it permitted the insertion in marriage settlements of what was known as a restraint upon anticipation. The effect of such a restraint was that a woman, while possessing full enjoyment of the income, was prevented during her coverture[57] from alienating or charging the corpus of the property. She could devise, but could not sell or mortgage it.

C STATUTE

The next step in the emancipation of married women came with the enactment from 1870 onwards of various Married Women's Property Acts.[58] The principle of these was not to let the existence of separate property depend upon the intention of the donor, but to provide that in all cases property of married women should be separate property. Thus the intervention of the court of equity was no longer needed, for all property belonging to a married woman became her statutory separate property over which she had sole control and power of disposition.

The final stage in the emancipation of married women came with the Law Reform (Married Women and Tortfeasors) Act 1935. This provides that so far as concerns the acquisition, holding and disposition of any property a married woman shall be in the same position as if she were a *feme sole* (that is, a single woman). This Act also forbade the imposition of restraints upon anticipation after 1935, while preserving those already in existence, but in 1949 all restrictions upon anticipation or alienation, whether already imposed or not, were totally abolished.[59] Thus in future any restriction that it is proposed to place upon the enjoyment of property by a married woman must take the form of a protective trust, which is the only form of restriction applicable to a man or a *feme sole*.[60]

The position of a married woman has, indeed, been improved in a more positive sense by a statute that entitles her to an equal share in any property acquired out of money given to her for household expenses.[61]

---

[57] Ie, during the marriage, when she was under the authority and protection of her husband.
[58] See Dicey, *Law and Opinion in England* (2nd edn, 1962), pp 371–95.
[59] Married Women (Restraint upon Anticipation) Act 1949.   [60] Above, p 615.
[61] Married Women's Property Act 1964, s 1. See Cretney, *Principles of Family Law* (8th edn, 2008), para 3.007. Equality Act 2010, s 200 (if brought into force) will apply the rule also to husbands who receive money from their wives, and so will rename the Act the Matrimonial Property Act 1964.

D THE MODERN LAW

In the modern law, therefore, a married woman is under no legal disability. Moreover, the social changes that occurred in relation to property ownership during the second half of the last century have radically changed the position of the wife's rights in relation to the matrimonial home. This has already been discussed.[62] But it must be remembered that the significance of these changes has been fully recognised only relatively recently. As late as 1968 a judge could hold that a wife was not in apparent occupation or possession of the matrimonial home that she shared with her husband.[63] But this was finally rejected in 1980. As Lord Wilberforce then said:[64]

> it was suggested that the wife's occupation was nothing but the shadow of the husband's—a version I suppose of the doctrine of unity of husband and wife. This expression and the argument flowing from it was used by Templeman J in *Bird v Syme-Thomson*,[65] a decision preceding and that he followed in the present case. The argument was also inherent in the judgment in *Caunce v Caunce*[66] which influenced the decisions of Templeman J. It somewhat faded from the arguments in the present case and appears to me to be heavily obsolete.

III PERSONS LACKING MENTAL CAPACITY[67]

A JURISDICTION

The law relating to mentally incompetent persons, originally styled 'lunatics' by the legislature,[68] then 'persons of unsound mind' and now 'patients' suffering a 'mental disorder', was codified and radically altered by the Mental Health Act 1959, later consolidated in the Mental Health Act 1983. Amongst other things, those Acts contained provisions relating to the management of property and affairs of patients,[69] the jurisdiction in respect of which was vested in the Lord Chancellor and one or more judges of the Chancery Division, called 'nominated judges', whose functions were usually exercised by the Master or a nominated officer of the Court of Protection or by the Public Trustee,[70] subject to an appeal to a nominated judge.[71] These provisions were

---

[62] Above, pp 522–4, 832, 943.   [63] *Caunce v Caunce* [1969] 1 WLR 286 (Stamp J).

[64] *Williams & Glyn's Bank Ltd v Boland* [1981] AC 487, 505.   [65] [1979] 1 WLR 440, 444.

[66] Above.

[67] See generally Heywood and Massey, *Court of Protection Practice*; and on the new regime under the Mental Capacity Act 2005, Jones, *Mental Capacity Act Manual* (4th edn, 2010); *Blackstone's Guide to the Mental Capacity Act 2005* (2nd edn, 2008). A solicitor is generally required to make inquiries as to his client's capacity to contract (and therefore owes a duty of care to the client in that respect) only if there are circumstances such as to raise doubt as to his capacity in the mind of a reasonably competent practitioner: *Thorpe v Fellowes Solicitors LLP* [2011] EWHC 61 (QB), [2011] All ER (D) 157 (Jan) at [75].

[68] Prescription Act 1832, s 7, still refers to 'idiot' and 'non compos mentis'.

[69] Mental Health Act 1983, Part VII.

[70] Ibid, s 94, amended by Public Trustee and Administration of Funds Act 1986, s 2.

[71] Ibid, s 105.

repealed and replaced by the Mental Capacity Act 2005,[72] which gives a new definition of the lack of capacity, and provides a new framework within which the court itself or designated persons (either a deputy appointed by the court or an attorney appointed by the person himself under a lasting power of attorney) can take decisions on behalf of someone who lacks capacity, and a new structure for the regulation and supervision of such persons and of the operation of the Act generally by a newly constituted Court of Protection and a Public Guardian. The Court of Protection is now a superior court of record,[73] whose jurisdiction is exercisable by a judge nominated by the Lord Chief Justice, and that has the same authority and powers as the High Court.[74] The functions of the Public Guardian include establishing and maintaining a register of lasting powers of attorney, and supervising deputies appointed by the court.[75]

B DEFINITION OF LACK OF CAPACITY

The lack of capacity is now defined not as a general disability, but as the inability to make a decision on a particular matter, at a particular time, because of an impairment of, or a disturbance in the functioning of, the mind or brain.[76] A person is unable to make a decision for himself if he is unable to understand the information relevant to the decision, to retain that information, to use or weigh the information, or to communicate his decision.[77]

C DECISIONS TAKEN BY THE COURT OR A DEPUTY APPOINTED BY THE COURT

If a person lacks capacity to make a decision, the court may make it on his behalf, or may appoint a deputy to make decisions on his behalf.[78] The court's powers are to

---

[72] Law Com No 231, *Mental Incapacity* (1995). The Act was brought fully into force on 1 October 2007: SI 2007 No 1897. It did not replace other provisions of the Mental Health Act 1983, such as those relating to the compulsory admission to hospital and guardianship of patients suffering a mental disorder, although there have been further amendments to those provisions by Mental Health Act 2007. For Court of Protection Rules, made under s 51 of the 2005 Act, see SI 2007 No 1744, amended by SI 2009 No 582.

[73] The old Court of Protection was not in fact a court, but an office of the Supreme Court: SCA 1981, ss 88, 89(1), Sch 2; it ceased to exist by virtue of Mental Capacity Act 2005, s 45(6).

[74] Mental Capacity Act 2005, ss 45–47, as amended by Lord Chancellor (Transfer of Functions and Supplementary Provisions) (No 2) Order 2006 (SI 2006 No 1016). S 53 provides for appeals to the Court of Appeal, or (if so provided by Court of Protection Rules) to higher judges of the Court of Protection. See Court of Protection Rules 2007 (SI 2007 No 1744), Part 20, esp rr 180–182.

[75] Ibid, s 58.

[76] Ibid, s 2. A person is assumed to have capacity unless it is established on the balance of probabilities that he does not: s 1(2), 2(4).

[77] Ibid, s 3(1).

[78] Ibid, s 16. The predecessor of the deputy was the receiver: Mental Health Act 1983, s 99. Under the general law, a contract made during mental incapacity in voidable at the instance of the person making it, if the other party knows or ought to know of the incapacity: *Molton v Camroux* (1849) 4 Exch 17; *Beavan v M'Donnell* (1854) 9 Exch 309; *Imperial Loan Co v Stone* [1892] 1 QB 599; *Hart v O'Connor* [1985] AC

be exercised subject to overriding principles set out in the Act that are designed to protect the individual concerned, and must be done in his best interests,[79] and the appointment of a deputy is not to be made lightly: a decision by the court is preferable, and if a deputy is appointed, his powers must be as limited in scope and duration as is reasonably practicable.[80] Moreover, even if appointed, a deputy has no power to make a decision on behalf of a person if he knows or has reasonable grounds for believing that the person has capacity in relation to the matter,[81] nor can he be given power to make a decision inconsistent with a decision made by the person's own attorney.[82]

In relation to the property and affairs of the person lacking capacity, the powers exercisable by the court (or that may be conferred on a deputy where appointed) are very wide, and extend to, amongst other things, the control and management of the person's property; the sale, exchange, charging, gift or other disposition of it; the acquisition of property in his name or on his behalf; the settlement of any of his property, whether for his benefit or for the benefit of others; and (as long as the person has reached the age of 18) the execution for him of a will.[83] This will apply equally to registered and unregistered land.[84]

The paramount consideration of the judge in his exercise of these powers is the interest of the patient, even though this may mean changing the nature of his property to the detriment of those who would otherwise have been entitled to it on his death. The Act, therefore, includes provisions designed to preserve the interests of such persons. It provides in effect that where any of the patient's property has been disposed of by sale, exchange, charging or other disposition or where money has been spent on

---

1000; [1986] Conv 178 (AH Hudson). Cf *Re Sutton (Deceased)* [2009] EWHC 2576 (Ch), [2010] 1 P & CR DG20 at [29]-[51] (Christopher Nugee QC, leaving open the question whether incapacity makes a voluntary disposition void or voidable).

[79] Mental Capacity Act 2005, ss 1, 4, 16(3).

[80] Ibid, s 16(4). The deputy is treated as the person's agent: s 16(6), and therefore has the corresponding general duties to him by virtue of his agency.

[81] Ibid, s 20(1). Under the law before the 2005 Act, once a receiver had been appointed, the patient lost all legal capacity to exercise any powers of disposition inter vivos over his property: *Re Walker* [1905] 1 Ch 160; *Re Marshall* [1920] 1 Ch 284.

[82] Ibid, s 20(4).

[83] Ibid, ss 18(1), (2); 19(8), broadly repeating the wide powers already conferred by Mental Health Act 1983, s 96(1). Since 1969 the judge has had power to direct or authorise the execution of a will or codicil, provided that the patient is of full age and the judge has reason to believe that the patient is incapable of making a valid will himself. See *Re D (J)* [1982] Ch 237, 243 where Megarry V-C set out the principles to be followed in making a will for a patient; *Re C* [1991] 3 All ER 866 (patient mentally disabled from birth who had never enjoyed a rational mind: Hoffmann J held that 'the court must assume that she would have been a normal decent person, acting in accordance with contemporary standards of morality'); [1991] All ER Rev 340 (CH Sherrin). See also Cross J in *Re L (WJG)* [1966] Ch 135, 145 (the making of a settlement). On the exercise of a power of appointment, see *Re B* [1987] 1 WLR 552.

[84] A squatter may not, however, make a valid application to be registered as proprietor during any period in which the existing registered proprietor is unable because of mental disability to make decisions about issues of the kind to which such an application would give rise, or unable to communicate such decisions because of mental disability or physical impairment; and the Registrar may include a note to that effect in the register: LRA 2002, Sch 6, para 8(2); R & R, para 33.031. On squatters in registered land generally, see below, pp 1158 ff.

the purchase of property, then the proprietary rights of the persons entitled under his will or intestacy shall attach to that property in its new form. If the property was real property, any property representing it shall so long as it remains part of his estate be treated as real property.[85]

As regards conveyances of property, when a legal estate in land (whether settled or not) is vested, either solely or jointly with any other person or persons, in a person lacking capacity to convey or create a legal estate, a deputy or some other person authorised by the Court of Protection may make all requisite dispositions for conveying or creating a legal estate in his name and on his behalf.[86] Again, if land is vested in such a person on trust, a new trustee must be appointed in his place.[87]

D LASTING POWER OF ATTORNEY[88]

In order to avoid the subsequent necessity and expense of an application to the Court of Protection, a person may decide to grant a power of attorney to manage his affairs during mental incapacity. At common law a power of attorney is automatically revoked when the donor becomes mentally incapable. The Enduring Powers of Attorney Act 1985, however, established a procedure for the creation of an 'enduring power of attorney' that would continue to be effective notwithstanding the incapacity of the donor. Certain statutory conditions had to be complied with; for example, the power had to be in a prescribed form, executed by both donor and donee, and be registered with the Court of Protection in the event of the actual or impending mental incapacity of the donor. Notice of the intention to register had first to be given to the donor and to certain of his relatives who could then make objections.[89]

The 1985 Act was repealed by the Mental Capacity Act 2005, which replaced enduring powers with 'lasting powers of attorney', following the same basic scheme: the power must be in a prescribed form, and must be registered with the Public Guardian before it confers authority to act.[90] Enduring powers of attorney that had already been

---

[85] Mental Capacity Act 2005, Sch 2, para 8, replacing Mental Health Act 1983, s 101(1).

[86] LPA 1925, s 22(1), as substituted by Mental Health Act 1959, s 149(1), Sch 7, Part I and amended by Mental Health Act 1983, s 148, Sch 4, para 5, TLATA 1996, s 25(1), Sch 3, para 4 (1), (6), and Mental Capacity Act 2005, s 67(1), Sch 6, para 4(1), (2).

[87] Ibid, s 22(2), as substituted by Mental Health Act 1959, s 149(1), Sch 7, Part I, and amended by TLATA 1996, s 25(1), Sch 3, para 4(6), and Mental Capacity Act 2005, s 67(1), Sch 6, para 4(1). As regards the descent of land on intestacy, the rule under the Administration of Estates Act 1925 is that, where a person of unsound mind was living and already of full age on 1 January 1926 and was before that date entitled to a beneficial interest in freehold property, such interest shall in the event of his intestacy descend according to the old canons of descent applicable to freeholds of inheritance before 1926: AEA 1925, s 51(2); above, pp 117, 589. See Re Gates [1930] 1 Ch 199; Re Sirett [1969] 1 WLR 60. This provision must be of limited scope today: such a person would be aged at least 106 on 1 January 2011.

[88] Law Com No 122, The Incapacitated Principal (1983); Cretney and Lush on Lasting and Enduring Powers of Attorney (6th edn, 2009).

[89] S 4(3), Sch 1.

[90] Mental Capacity Act 2005, ss 9–14, Sch 1, Pt 1 (formalities for creating the power), Pt 2 (registration). The lasting power of attorney can be wider in scope than the enduring power of attorney under the 1985

executed when the new Act came into force were preserved and integrated into the new scheme.[91]

IV CORPORATIONS

A NATURE OF CORPORATIONS

One of the reasons for the existence of corporations is the principle of law that rights of property can be vested only in definite persons. It often occurs that a body of persons desires to hold and enjoy land, but apart from the case where a fluctuating class of persons acquires rights in the nature of easements by custom,[92] there are only two methods by which effect can be given to this. Either the land must be vested in trustees upon trust to hold and manage the land for the benefit of the proposed beneficiaries,[93] or the indefinite body of persons must be turned into a definite, though artificial, person called a corporation; and this must be done by Royal Charter or by the authority of Parliament, either by a special statute or, more commonly, by incorporation as a company under the Companies Acts[94] or, since 2001, as a limited liability partnership under the Limited Liability Partnerships Act 2000. The effect of this latter method is that the corporation becomes in the eye of the law a separate person, distinct from the member of which it is formed, and capable of acquiring, holding and alienating land.

The modern limited liability company is not, like a partnership,[95] a mere collection or aggregate of the shareholders, but is a metaphysical entity, a legal persona with many of the rights and powers of a human person.

B CLASSIFICATION OF CORPORATIONS

Corporations may be classified in several ways. The main classification is into aggregate and sole.

Act, because it can extend to matters about the person's personal welfare, as well as his property and affairs: s 9(1)(a). See also Lasting Powers of Attorney, Enduring Powers of Attorney and Public Guardian Regulations 2007 (SI 2007 No 1253), amended by SI 2007 No 2161, SI 2009 No 1884 and SI 2010 No 1063.

[91] Mental Capacity Act 2005, s 66(3), Sch 4.   [92] Above, pp 717 ff.

[93] On the holding of property by *unincorporated* associations, see Warburton, *Unincorporated Associations* (2nd edn, 1990), ch 5; Baxendale-Walker, *Purpose Trusts* (1999); Conv Prec, section 15; Maudsley and Burn, *Trusts and Trustees* (7th edn, 2008), pp 378–99; *Conservative and Unionist Central Office v Burrell* [1982] 1 WLR 522, 525 (Lawton LJ).

[94] The present Act is CA 2006, which replaced CA 1985.

[95] A *limited liability* partnership, however, is a body corporate with legal personality separate from that of its members: Limited Liability Partnerships Act 2000, s 1(2).

(1) Aggregate and Sole

A corporation aggregate is a collection of several persons who are united together into one body and who are followed by a perpetual succession of members, so that the corporation is capable of existing for ever.[96] Examples are:

the mayor and corporation of a city;

the dean and chapter of a cathedral;

a limited liability company incorporated under the Companies Act 2006;

a limited liability partnership under the Limited Liability Partnerships Act 2000; and

national corporations, such as the BBC.

A corporation sole consists of a single person occupying a particular office and each and several of the persons in perpetuity who succeed him in that office, such as the Crown, the vicar of a parish, the Secretary of State for Environment, Food and Rural Affairs, and the Public Trustee.

(2) Ecclesiastical and Lay

Another division of corporations is into ecclesiastical and lay.

Ecclesiastical corporations are those that exist for upholding religion and perpetuating the rights of the church, such as bishops, vicars, and deans and chapters, and the abbot and monks of an earlier age.

Lay corporations may be either trading or non-trading corporations.

Trading corporations are those that have been incorporated by charter, by special Act of Parliament or under the provisions of the Companies Acts, and whose main object is trade.

Non-trading corporations are those that have no concern with commerce, but that exist either for the better government of a town or district, such as urban district councils and municipal corporations, or for charitable purposes, such as St Thomas's Hospital and the colleges of Oxford and Cambridge.

C METHODS OF CREATION

A corporation can in general exist only if it has been formed under the authority of the State, and the two methods of creation in use at the present day are by charter from the Crown or by the authority of Parliament. If, for example, a town wishes to become a borough, application must be made for a charter; while persons who wish to form themselves into a trading corporation must either secure the passing of a private Act of Parliament or (more simply, and so more commonly) take advantage of the

---

[96] Blackstone, vol i, p 469.

Companies Act 2006, which contains provisions enabling companies to be formed without the necessity of a special statute.

But in addition to those that are incorporated by charter or by statute, corporations may also exist by common law and prescription.

Examples of common law corporations are a parson, a bishop, and the Crown. Corporations by prescription are those that have existed so long that the law presumes that they received from the Crown a grant or charter that has been lost.[97]

D DOCTRINE OF ULTRA VIRES

Statutory corporations are subject to the ultra vires doctrine.[98] At common law a corporation that has been created by charter has power to deal with its property and to bind itself by contract to the same extent as a private person, and even if the charter imposes some direction that would have the effect of limiting its natural capacity, the legal power of the corporation is not affected, though the direction may be enforced by the Attorney-General.[99]

But the case of a statutory corporation is very different.[100] Such a body exists for certain purposes that are defined in the statute to which it owes its origin, and the powers of a statutory corporation are limited to those that are reasonably necessary to the realisation of the purposes for which it is incorporated. The corporation possesses its own constitution, which has statutory effect. Anything that the constitution authorises, either expressly or by implication, can be done, but what is not so authorised is ultra vires and cannot be done.

Before the passing of the Companies Act 2006, a company incorporated under the Companies Acts was limited to the purposes set out in its memorandum of association. The operation of the doctrine of ultra vires was restricted in practice by the drafting of the terms of the memorandum of association in very wide and general terms,[101] as well as formally by the Companies Act 1989,[102] which restricted the doctrine to the internal management of the company. The 2006 Act went further, however, and provided that the principal document within a company's constitution should now be the articles of association, and that, unless a company's articles specifically restrict the objects of the company, its objects are unrestricted.[103]

---

[97] Re Free Fishermen of Faversham (1887) 36 Ch D 329; above, p 721.   [98] Anson, pp 228–30.

[99] Baroness Wenlock v River Dee Co (1883) 36 Ch D 675n, 685 (Bowen LJ).

[100] A limited liability partnership, however, has unlimited capacity: Limited Liability Partnerships Act 2000, s 1(3).

[101] See Bell Houses Ltd v City Wall Properties Ltd [1966] 2 QB 656; Re Introductions Ltd [1969] 1 All ER 887, 888 (Harman LJ): 'The little man starting a grocery business usually combines groceries with the power to bridge the Zambezi.'

[102] S 108, amending CA 1985, s 35, and inserting ss 35A and 35B; 'the validity of an act done by a company shall not be called into question on the ground of lack of capacity by reason of anything in the company's memorandum' and third parties who deal with a company were no longer bound to make inquiries about its capacity or the authority of its directors.

[103] CA 2006, ss 17, 31(1). The memorandum of association is now a much simpler document: s 8. Provisions of the memorandum of a company that already existed when the 2006 Act came into force are to be treated as provisions of the company's articles: s 28.

E CAPACITY TO DEAL WITH LAND

Corporations, whether aggregate or sole, have the same capacity as natural persons to acquire, hold and dispose of land. Where land is registered, the application to register a corporation as proprietor of a registered estate or charge must be supported by evidence of its status and powers in relation to the transaction.[104] If the powers of alienation are limited in a way that would affect a purchaser the corporation should apply for the entry of a restriction on the register.[105]

(1) Abolition of Technicalities

The Law of Property Act 1925 has removed certain conveyancing difficulties. There were rules at common law that leaseholds could not be granted to a corporation sole in such a way as to make them vest in the successive holders of the office; and that a grant of land to a corporation sole made at a time when the office was vacant was void. If leaseholds were granted to a parson in his capacity as parson, and he died before the term had run out, his personal representatives and not his successor in the office became entitled to the residue of the lease.[106]

The 1925 Act provided,[107] however, that where any property or any interest in property is or has been vested in a corporation sole, whether before or after the commencement of the Act, it shall pass to the successors from time to time of such corporation; and that where property is granted to a corporation sole during a vacancy of the office, or to a corporation aggregate during a vacancy of the headship, the property shall, notwithstanding such vacancy, vest in the successor of the corporation sole, or in the corporation aggregate, as the case may be.

(2) Words of Limitation

The rule was formerly that, unless a grant was made to a corporation sole and his successors, the grant operated to confer a life estate upon the actual holder of the office in his natural capacity; but now, as we have already seen, a conveyance of freehold land to a corporation sole by his corporate designation even without the word 'successors' passes to the corporation the fee simple or other the whole interest that the grantor has power to convey in such land, unless a contrary intention appears in the conveyance.[108]

---

[104] LRR 2003, rr 182 (corporation or trustees holding on charitable, ecclesiastical or public trusts: trust document), 183 (other corporation aggregate except, inter alia, companies incorporated under the Companies Acts or limited liability partnerships: evidence of powers in relation to land, including the documents constituting the corporation). Rule 181, requiring a company incorporated under the Companies Acts or a limited liability partnership to provide its registered number, was revoked by LR(A)R 2008 (SI 2008 No 1919), Sch 1, para 54, but its effect is retained by requiring the information to be provided in relevant prescribed Land Registry forms.

[105] R & R, para 41.006.   [106] Co Litt 46b.   [107] S 180.   [108] Above, p 157.

(3) Dissolution of Corporation

The rule at common law is that when a corporation is dissolved, any land that it may have held does not escheat to the Crown, but reverts to the original donor,[109] but after 1925 when a legal estate determines for this reason, the court is empowered to vest a corresponding estate in the person who would have been entitled to the estate had it not determined.[110] This power is apparently meant to be used when the corporation has been holding land as a trustee.

(4) Repeal of Law of Mortmain

Until 1 January 1961, when the Charities Act 1960 came into force, the long-established rule was that no land could be assured to or for the benefit of, or acquired by or on behalf of, any corporation unless the corporation was authorised, either by some statute or by a licence from the Crown, to hold land. If land was transferred by way of gift, sale, mortgage, settlement or devise to a corporation that had no such authority, the land was liable to be forfeited to the Crown.[111] The explanation of this disability lies far back in history and is to be found in the exigencies of the feudal system.[112]

    With the progress of time the restrictions imposed by the Mortmain and Charitable Uses Act 1891 had become of little significance, for the vast majority of corporations were for one reason or another exempt from the necessity to obtain a licence from the Crown. The subject, however, requires no further elaboration, since the Act was repealed by the Charities Act 1960,[113] and so the law of mortmain is now defunct.

V CHARITIES

Before 1997 all land that was vested in trustees[114] for charitable, ecclesiastical or public purposes was deemed to be settled land under the Settled Land Act 1925, and the trustees had all the powers conferred by that Act on a tenant for life and on the trustees of the settlement, subject to obtaining any consents or orders required apart from the Act.[115] The land did not, however, become settled land for all purposes; for example, a conveyance to a charity did not have to be made by a vesting deed and a

---

[109] Co Litt 13b; Blackstone, vol i, pp 484–5; *Hastings Corp v Letton* [1908] 1 KB 378; *Re Woking UDC (Basingstoke Canal) Act 1911* [1914] 1 Ch 300, 310.

[110] LPA 1925, s 181.   [111] Mortmain and Charitable Uses Act 1888, s 1.

[112] See Simpson, *A History of the Land Law* (2nd edn, 1986), pp 53–6, 183–4.   [113] S 38.

[114] The right of a charity to acquire land was severely restricted by Mortmain and Charitable Uses Acts 1888 and 1891, above. Subject to many exceptions, an assurance of land inter vivos was void unless it was irrevocable and gave the charity the right to take immediate possession; and, if not made for valuable consideration, unless it was executed at least 12 months before the death of the alienor. Charitable devises were not generally permitted before the 1891 Act, but even then the land had to be sold within one year from the testator's death unless the High Court or the Charity Commissioners decided otherwise. These restrictions, however, disappeared with the repeal of the 1888 and 1891 Acts by Charities Act 1960, s 38, above, n 113.

[115] SLA 1925, s 29, as amended by Charities Act 1960, Sch 7.

trust instrument, and a sole trustee might receive capital money if the trust deed for the charity allowed him to do so.[116]

After 1996 charity land is no longer settled land[117] but is held on a trust of land under the Trust of Land and Appointment of Trustees Act 1996. In the case of registered land,[118] the managing trustees of the charity, or, if there are no managing trustees and the land is vested in a corporation, the corporation, will be the registered proprietors, unless the legal estate is vested in the Official Custodian for Charities,[119] who will then be registered as proprietor, notwithstanding that the powers of disposition are vested in the managing trustees.

A RESTRICTIONS ON DISPOSITION

(1) Before 1993

The freedom of charities to alienate or deal with their land has long been restricted by a series of Charitable Trusts Acts and then by the Charities Act 1960. The latter, replacing the former statutes, provided that no property forming part of the permanent endowment[120] of a charity should, without an order of the court or of the Charity Commissioners, be mortgaged or charged by way of security for the repayment of money borrowed, nor, in the case of land in England or Wales, be sold, leased or otherwise disposed of.[121] Similar restrictions applied to land that was or had at any time been occupied for the purposes of a charity, even though it did not form part of the permanent endowment; but if a transaction in respect of such land was entered into without the required order, it would nevertheless be valid in favour of a person who in good faith acquired an interest in or charge on the land for money or money's worth.[122] An order was not, however, required for a charity to grant a lease for a term ending not more than 22 years after it was granted, provided that it was not granted wholly or partly in consideration of a fine.[123]

(2) After 1992

The Charities Act 1992 made important changes.[124] The distinction between permanent endowment property and charity occupied property has been abolished,

---

[116] *Re Booth and Southend-on-Sea Estates Co's Contract* [1927] 1 Ch 579.

[117] TLATA 1996, s 2(5), Sch 1, para 4. SLA 1925, s 29 was repealed by TLATA s 25(2), Sch 4, and with effect from 1 January 1997 all existing settled charity land became held on trust for sale.

[118] See generally Land Registry Practice Guide 14; R & R, ch 38; H & B, paras 13.38–13.41.

[119] A public official in whom the property of a charity may be vested as a custodian trustee: Charities Act 1993, ss 2, 21, 22 (as now amended by Charities Act 2006, Sch 8); LRR 2003, r 178.

[120] Ie property held subject to a restriction on the expenditure of capital: Charities Act 1960, s 45(3).

[121] Charities Act 1960, s 29(1); *Michael Richards Properties Ltd v Corp of Wardens of St Saviour's Parish, Southwark* [1975] 3 All ER 416 (contract for sale of charity land made expressly subject to approval of Charity Commissioners held valid); *Haslemere Estates Ltd v Baker* [1982] 1 WLR 1109; *Hounslow LBC v Hare* (1990) 24 HLR 9; [1993] Conv 224 (J Martin).

[122] Ibid, s 29(2).   [123] Ibid, s 29(3)(b).

[124] Repealed and consolidated in Charities Act 1993, ss 36–40, further amended by Charities Act 2006 (inter alia, to replace references to the 'Charity Commissioners' by 'Charity Commission' on the creation of

and the trustees of a charity may sell, lease or otherwise dispose of its land without an order of the court or of the Charity Commission, provided that certain procedural steps are taken.

In the case of a sale or lease, the trustees must take advice from a qualified surveyor, and, having considered that advice, decide that the terms are the best that can reasonably be obtained for the charity, and normally advertise the proposed transaction.[125] In the case of a mortgage, the trustees must take advice on its necessity, its terms and the charity's ability to repay on those terms.[126] The disposition to a charity must also contain a statement in a prescribed form that will identify whether the charity is exempt.[127] If it is not exempt, in the case of registered land a restriction must be entered on the register when the title is registered.[128] Similarly, a statement in a prescribed form must be made in a disposition by a charity.[129]

A disposition not complying with these requirements is valid in favour of a purchaser in good faith.[130]

The Charity Commission has a general power to authorise dealings with charity property, whether or not it would otherwise be within the powers of the charity trustees.[131]

B EXEMPT CHARITIES

The restrictions upon disposition do not affect exempt charities, a list of which is given in the Act.[132] The list includes, inter alia, the universities of Oxford, Cambridge, London, Durham, Newcastle and Manchester; any university or similar institution declared by an Order in Council to be an exempt charity, the boards of trustees of a number of national museums and galleries, including the Victoria and Albert Museum, the Science Museum, the British Museum and the Tate Gallery, and the British Library Board.

---

the Commission as a body corporate and the abolition of the office of Charity Commissioner: s 6, inserting s 1A into the 1993 Act).

[125] Charities Act 1993, s 36(3). Advertisement is not necessary for a lease of seven years or less (other than one granted wholly or partly in consideration of a fine): ibid, s 36(5).

[126] Ibid, s 38.   [127] Ibid, s 37(5); LRR 2003, r 179.

[128] LRR 2003, r 176(4), Sch 4 (Form E).   [129] Ibid, r 180.

[130] Charities Act 1993, ss 37(4), 39(4); *Bayoumi v Women's Total Abstinence Educational Union Ltd* [2003] EWCA Civ 1548, [2004] Ch 46.

[131] Ibid, s 26.

[132] Ibid, ss 36(10), 38(7); 96(1), Sch 2, amended by Charities Act 2006 and SI 2010 No 500 (which removed exempt charity status from, inter alia, the colleges and halls in the Universities of Cambridge, Durham and Oxford). The Charity Commission does not generally have jurisdiction over ecclesiastical corporations or trusts: s 96(2).

27

UNREGISTERED CONVEYANCING[1]

Summary

I INTRODUCTION

As we have already seen in outline,[2] there are two quite separate and distinctive methods of conveyancing in operation in England and Wales at the present day; that relating to unregistered land and that relating to registered land. During the twentieth century there was a transition from unregistered to registered conveyancing, from the old to the modern: compulsory registration of title was gradually extended across the country, and was finally extended to the whole of England and Wales from 1 November 1990.[3] The former is the development of techniques that reach back to mediaeval times.

---

[1] See generally Barnsley, *Conveyancing Law and Practice* (4th edn, 1996); *Emmet and Farrand on Title*; Farrand, *Contract and Conveyance* (4th edn, 1983); Silverman, *Conveyancing Handbook* (17th edn, 2010); *Storey's Conveyancing* (5th edn, 2001). For the liability of professional advisers, such as solicitors, surveyors, valuers and estate agents, for negligence during the course of conveyancing transactions, see Emmet, paras 1.018–1.031; *Sweet and Maxwell's Conveyancing Practice*, paras 1–001 to 1–019; Jackson and Powell, *Professional Negligence* (6th edn, 2009); Cartwright, *Misrepresentation, Mistake and Non-Disclosure* (2nd edn, 2006), paras 6.30–6.32, 6.40–6.41

[2] Above, pp 119–46.

[3] Registration of Title Order 1989 (SI 1989 No 1347).

The system of unregistered conveyancing in essence is one whereby the estate owner proves his title to land by showing from deeds and documents in his possession that he derives his title lawfully from some person or persons who have been in peaceful possession for a long period of time. In the nature of things, the title to his estate can never be proved absolutely, for there may have been an interference with the rights of the true owner many years back. However, with the assistance of the Limitation Acts,[4] proof of title during the last 15 years is, for practical purposes, sufficient; and a purchaser is now required to trace the title back to a good root of title at least 15 years old.[5] In unregistered land, before registration of title became compulsory, the deeds were handed over to the purchaser on completion of the purchase, and he then made title in a similar manner when he decided to sell. Under compulsory registration of title, completion of the purchase is followed by registration of the title at the Land Registry and transfers of title thereafter are effected under the system of registered conveyancing.

Registration of the title in a central registry is a much more satisfactory system of proof of title. New countries and states commonly use such a system. The practical difficulties, however, of changing over from a system of unregistered conveyancing to one of registered conveyancing are great. The change involves the recording of all interests in land that need to be placed on the register. In England and Wales, a system of registration of title introduced in 1862[6] was superseded by more comprehensive legislation in the Land Registration Act 1925. This provided for registration of title following the first conveyance of land after the Act had been made applicable to the district in question. The 1925 Act has now itself been superseded by the Land Registration Act 2002.

Although the unregistered system is obsolescent, it is not yet obsolete, and it will remain necessary to investigate the title to every parcel of unregistered land for at least one final time when it is next transferred, before it is placed on the register. A substantial task remains, and no date can yet be given for the completion of the register.[7] The conveyancer must therefore not only fully understand the system of registration of title, its limitations as well as its strengths, but must also still be able to work within the old system of unregistered land. Moreover, as we shall see, many of the rules and principles of registered conveyancing, and the form of instruments used within it, cannot be properly understood without a prior understanding of their traditional equivalents within unregistered conveyancing. We shall therefore begin

---

[4] Below, Ch 29.   [5] LPA 1969, s 23; below, p 1043.

[6] Land Registry Act 1862; above, p 131.

[7] From 2002 until 2005 the Land Registry had as a strategic objective the creation of a Land Register with comprehensive content and national coverage by 2012, although this has now been replaced by the setting of annual targets for increasing the total area of freehold land that is on the register. By 2010 the freehold title to 73 per cent of the area of England and Wales had been registered, comprising 22.5 million titles: Land Registry Annual Report 2009–10, p 12; above, p 132.

by considering in this chapter the principles of unregistered conveyancing, before discussing in Chapter 28 registration of title in some detail.

The creation or transfer of an estate or interest in land may take place inter vivos or on the death of the holder. And a transfer inter vivos may be either by act of parties or by act of law, that is either due to the deliberate intention of the estate owner or in spite of his intention. The discussion in this chapter and the following chapter will focus on voluntary transfer inter vivos. Succession (testate or intestate) to property on death, and the special rules and practices relating to transfer by personal representatives (executors or administrators) to whom the property of a deceased owner passes, will not be considered in detail here.[8] Nor will involuntary transfer inter vivos, where the owner of an estate or interest is sued to judgment for non-payment of a debt, or made bankrupt, or dies insolvent, and the land is liable to be seized in satisfaction of the debts.[9]

II STAGES IN A CONVEYANCING TRANSACTION

The first formal stage in a conveyancing transaction, at least where the transaction consists in the sale of the freehold estate,[10] is commonly the contract of sale. The creation, enforceability and effect of a contract of sale has been considered in detail in Chapter 24. A vendor and a purchaser of land generally desire that a binding contract should be concluded at the earliest possible moment, subject to the purchaser's right to rescind (in the sense of accepting repudiation[11]) if the vendor cannot show a good unincumbered title. The purchaser therefore usually does not have the opportunity to investigate the vendor's title before entering into the contract.[12] Once a binding contract has been made, however, the purchaser of unregistered land follows a series of steps through investigating the title, to the execution of the conveyance.

---

[8] For transfers by personal representatives in unregistered and registered land, see the 17th edn of this book, pp 988–91; and for the rules governing testacy, intestacy and succession generally, see the 16th edn of this book, chs 25 and 26; *Theobald on Wills* (17th edn, 2010); *Williams on Wills* (9th edn, 2008); Miller, *The Machinery of Succession* (2nd edn, 1996); Parry and Kerridge, *The Law of Succession* (12th edn, 2009); Sherrin and Bonehill, *Law and Practice of Intestate Succession* (3rd edn, 2004); Law Com No 184, *Title on Death* (1989).

[9] Reference should be made to specialist works on insolvency, such as *Muir Hunter on Personal Insolvency*; Schaw Miller and Bailey, *Personal Insolvency Law and Practice* (4th edn, 2008).

[10] Where the transaction consists in the grant of a lease, a contract for the lease may be made first, followed at a later date by a formal grant of the legal term of years absolute. This is common, however, only in relation to the grant of longer, commercial leases. A mortgage of the legal estate, and the grant of other limited interests in land (such as an easement) will not generally be preceded by a contract. In this chapter and Chapter 28 the paradigm conveyancing transaction is taken to be the sale of the freehold.

[11] Above, p 996.   [12] For enquiries that are usually made before contract, see above, pp 950–3.

A DELIVERY OF ABSTRACT

The vendor is bound to show a good title[13] to the interest that he has contracted to sell, and to this end, and with a view to simplifying the purchaser's task, he must at his own expense deliver to the purchaser an abstract of title, that is a summary of all the documents, such as wills and deeds of conveyance, that have dealt with the interest during the period for which his ownership has to be proved, and of all the events, such as deaths, that have affected the devolution of the ownership during that period. The period is either the 15 years fixed by statute, or that which is prescribed by a special stipulation in the contract of sale, though, as we shall see, the period will generally in fact be longer than 15 years since the period must begin with a good root of title.

B PERUSAL OF ABSTRACT

The vendor verifies the abstract by producing evidence of the accuracy of the statements that he has made in the course of setting out his title. The purchaser's solicitor, at the expense of the purchaser, peruses the abstract, requisitions (ie addresses inquiries to) the vendor about any defects he may observe, satisfies himself that the property described in the contract is identical with that which has been dealt with in the documents abstracted, calls for evidence (such as death certificates) of any events material to the title that have not yet been provided by the vendor, and finally advises the purchaser whether he can accept the title offered.

C CONVEYANCE

The vendor must then convey the property in accordance with the terms of the contract, and so he must execute a deed of conveyance and must hand over to the purchaser at the completion of the transaction all the title deeds relating to the property. The expense of preparing the deed of conveyance falls upon the purchaser.

III RIGHTS AND DUTIES OF THE PARTIES

The exact obligations of a vendor and purchaser may be either specified or unspecified by their contract. If they are unspecified, and so left to be implied by law, the vendor is said to sell under an *open contract*.[14] Although in practice contracts for the sale of land are generally made in standard form, and most of these forms contain detailed

---

[13] On the meaning of 'good marketable title' in an undertaking by the purchaser's solicitors to his mortgagee, see *Barclays Bank plc v Weeks Legg & Dean* [1999] QB 309. The title to be shown by the vendor to the purchaser in any particular case may be limited or otherwise defined by the terms of the contract.

[14] Above, p 953.

provisions that cover the matters that will be discussed in the following paragraphs, it is important first to understand the rights and duties of the parties under an open contract, so as to be able to identify whether (and, if so, to what extent) specific terms in the contract vary them.

A RIGHTS AND DUTIES UNDER AN OPEN CONTRACT

The rights and the duties of the parties under an open contract are as follows:

(1) Duty of Vendor to Show Title for 15 years[15]

(a) Period of title to be shown

Since the obligation of the vendor is to convey to the purchaser the interest that he has agreed to sell, free from incumbrances and competing interests, it follows that he must disclose and verify the state of his title to the land. Save in the rare case where he has been invested with an absolute title by Act of Parliament, he cannot show that he is entitled to an interest good against the whole world, for, however long he and his predecessors may have possessed and administered the land, the existence of some adverse claimant, such as a remainderman or reversioner, is always a possibility. But possession is prima facie evidence of seisin in fee[16] and if he shows that he and his predecessors have been in possession for a considerable time, the existence of an earlier and therefore better title is at least improbable. On this assumption, the practical rule was ultimately evolved that proof of the exercise of acts of ownership over the land by the vendor and his predecessors for a period of not less than 60 years was prima facie evidence of his right to convey what he had agreed to sell. 'It is a technical rule among conveyancers to approve a possession of sixty years, as a good title to a fee simple.'[17] This period was reduced by statute to 40 years in 1874,[18] to 30 years in 1925,[19] and to 15 years in 1969.[20]

(b) Good root of title

Enjoyment for this period is not, however, conclusive evidence of a good title, and if it appears from the information supplied by the vendor or if it can be shown from other evidence that the title falls short of what is required by the contract, the purchaser is not bound to complete. Possession by the vendor is no doubt evidence of seisin in fee, but nevertheless he must show its origin, for though it is probably attributable to his position as freehold owner, there is always the possibility that he is a tenant for life or years. As Lord Erskine once said:[21] 'No person in his senses would take an offer of a purchase from a man, merely because he stood upon the ground.' Even the rule under the Limitation Act 1980, that a person's title to unregistered

---

[15] Barnsley, *Conveyancing Law and Practice*, pp 272–4.   [16] Above, p 51.
[17] *Barnwell v Harris* (1809) 1 Taunt 430, 432 (Heath J).   [18] Vendor and Purchaser Act 1874, s 1.
[19] LPA 1925, s 44(1).   [20] LPA 1969, s 23.   [21] *Hiern v Mill* (1806)13 Ves 114, 122.

land is extinguished after 12 years' adverse possession by a disseisor, does not in itself enable a disseisor to show a good title by proving possession in himself for even 15 years, since possession for the statutory period does not bar the rights of remaindermen and reversioners entitled to the land upon the determination of the disseisee's interest. He must go further and show what persons were entitled to the land when he took possession and prove that their claims have been barred by his continuance in possession.[22]

The usual way, therefore, in which the vendor proves his title is to produce the deeds or other documents by which the land has been disposed of in the past in order to show that the interest that he has agreed to sell has devolved upon him. In the normal case, the evidence of his title is documentary and is set out in the abstract of title that he delivers to the purchaser. This abstract must start with a *good root of title*, that is a document that deals with the legal estate in the land, which is valid without requiring a reference to any earlier document, which adequately identifies the land,[23] and that contains nothing to cast doubt on the title of the disposing party.

A conveyance by way of sale or of legal mortgage[24] effected at least 15 years ago is a perfect root of title, since it may be presumed that the purchaser or mortgagee was satisfied at that time with the state of the vendor or mortgagor's title, and if the intervening dispositions have been satisfactory, the present purchaser will acquire a good title. An assent[25] can be a good root of title,[26] but a *general*, as distinct from a *specific*, devise of land is not, since it does not identify the property and therefore does not show that the will passed the ownership of the same land as the vendor has now agreed to sell.

The obligation to begin the abstract with a good root of title may, of course, necessitate going back to some document more than 15 years old. North J said:[27]

> And when I say a [15] years' title, I mean a title deduced for [15] years, and for so much longer as it is necessary to go back in order to arrive at a point at which the title can properly commence. The title cannot commence in nubibus at the exact point of time which is

---

[22] *Games v Bonnor* (1884) 54 LJ Ch 517; *Scott v Nixon* (1843) 3 Dr & War 388 (Ireland); below, Ch 29.

[23] See *Re Stirrup's Contract* [1961] 1 WLR 449, 454 (Wilberforce J): the vendor must be 'in the position, without the possibility of dispute or litigation, to pass the fee simple to the purchaser'; *Barclays Bank plc v Weeks Legg & Dean* [1999] QB 309, 324 (Millett LJ).

[24] Even though a post-1925 mortgage does not take effect as a conveyance of the fee simple; above, p 801; Barnsley, *Conveyancing Law and Practice*, pp 275–7.

[25] A document in writing by which personal representatives vest the estate in the person entitled under the will or on intestacy: AEA 1925, s 36(2), (4).

[26] In favour of a purchaser for money or money's worth, an assent is sufficient evidence that the beneficiary is entitled to have the legal estate conveyed to him, unless notice of a previous assent or conveyance has been endorsed on the probate copy or letters of administration: AEA 1925, s 36(7), (11). But an assent will not avail a purchaser if his investigation of title discloses that the person in whose favour it was given was not entitled to the legal estate: *Re Duce and Boots Cash Chemists (Southern) Ltd's Contract* [1937] Ch 642.

[27] *Re Cox and Neve's Contract* [1891] 2 Ch 109, 118. North J's judgment referred to 40 years' title. The period was later reduced: above.

represented by 365 days multiplied by [15]. It must commence at or before the [15] years with something which is in itself... a proper root of title.

There are a few cases in which the period for which title must be shown is longer than 15 years.[28] Upon the sale of a leasehold, an abstract or copy of the lease, however old, must be produced with proof of dealings with the lease from a disposition at least 15 years old,[29] but the purchaser is not entitled to call for the title to the reversion;[30] if the subject-matter of the sale is a reversionary interest, an abstract of the instrument that created the interest must be produced, with proof of 15 years' title back from the date of purchase.

(2) Duty of Vendor to Abstract and Produce Documents[31]

The vendor must at his own expense abstract and, if under his own control, produce the document that forms the root of his title, and all subsequent documents that affect the legal estate. In addition he must state and prove all facts that have affected the legal estate in the last 15 years. There are certain things, however, that must not be abstracted, and certain titles and documents that cannot be called for.

(a) Certain equitable interests not to be abstracted

Before 1926, a purchaser who took a conveyance of the legal estate was bound by any equitable interests affecting that estate of which he had notice. If, for example, the abstract showed that the legal estate was held by the vendor as trustee, then, provided that he was an express trustee for sale, the equitable interests were notified to the purchaser. It was necessary for the vendor to abstract the title to the equitable interests, and to obtain the concurrence of the beneficiaries in the conveyance.

But, as we have seen,[32] one of the chief objects of the legislation of 1925 was to enable a purchaser to acquire the legal estate from the estate owner without being required to concern himself with equitable interests enforceable against the land. In general pursuance of this idea the Law of Property Act 1925[33] provides that in certain cases it shall not be necessary or proper to mention equitable interests in the abstract that will be overreached by the conveyance.[34] Therefore, for example, when a trustee of land contracts to sell trust land, he is not required to abstract the equitable interests of the beneficiaries. These are overreachable and are therefore of no concern to a purchaser. Similarly, and because the beneficial interests under a strict settlement are

---

[28] LPA 1925, s 44(1). See Emmet, paras 5.018, 5.034–5.035. Until 1988, where an advowson (the right to present to or bestow any ecclesiastical benefice) was sold, title had to be shown for at least a hundred years with a list of presentations during that period: Benefices Act 1898, s 1; Benefices Act 1898 (Amendment) Measure 1923; Dart, *Vendors and Purchasers of Real Estate* (8th edn, 1929), vol i, p 292. These provisions were repealed by Patronage (Benefices) Measure 1986 under which, with effect from 1 January 1989, the right of presentation may be exercised only if it is registered in a register held by the diocese in question.

[29] *Frend v Buckley* (1870) LR 5 QB 213; *Williams v Spargo* [1893] WN 100.

[30] LPA 1925, s 44(2)–(4).   [31] Barnsley, *Conveyancing Law and Practice*, pp 281–5.

[32] Above, p 122–3.   [33] S 10(1).   [34] For overreaching, see below, pp 1068–9, 1113–22.

overreachable, on the sale of land subject to a settlement under the Settled Land Act 1925, the trust instrument is not disclosed; it is not allowed to appear on the title and with a few exceptions[35] the purchaser is not entitled to call for it or to make it the subject of interrogatories. Moreover, once satisfied that the vesting deed was executed by a party competent to execute it, 'a purchaser of a legal estate in settled land'[36] must take it at its face value and make the following assumptions:

that the estate owner named in the vesting deed is the tenant for life or statutory owner and entitled to exercise the statutory powers;

that the trustees named in the deed are the properly constituted trustees;

that the settlements contained in the deed in accordance with the requirements of the Settled Land Act 1925 are correct;

that a later deed appointing new trustees is correct.[37]

(b) Freehold title not to be abstracted on sale of leasehold

If the subject-matter of the sale is a term of years (that is where the transaction constitutes the assignment of the lease), the vendor is bound, as we have seen, to abstract and produce the lease under which he holds the land; but the Law of Property Act 1925[38] provides that in an open contract he shall not be required to prove the title to the freehold. This latter rule also applies where a fee simple owner agrees to *grant* a lease. Thus:

If A is fee simple owner of the land, and if he agrees to grant a lease to B for 5 years, B is not entitled to call for proof of A's title to the fee simple, unless he has inserted an express stipulation to that effect in the contract. Again, if B agrees later to sell his lease to C, the latter is precluded from calling for the title of A.

Similar rules apply to an agreement to sell a leasehold interest that is derived out of a leasehold interest, or to an agreement to grant such a lease.[39] If, for example:

---

[35] SLA 1925, s 110(2)(a), (b), (c), (d). For example, where a settlement inter vivos has not been created by the proper method or where there is a pre-1926 settlement, whether made inter vivos or by will. See Emmet, paras 23.042–23.043.

[36] For the problems that arise when a purchaser takes a conveyance of settled land

    (a) under the mistaken impression that the vendor is still tenant for life, whereas in fact he is no longer so, see Megarry and Wade, *Law of Real Property* (7th edn. 2008), para A-013; [1984] Conv 354 (PA Stone); [1985] Conv 377 (R Warrington);

    (b) under the mistaken impression that the vendor is an absolute owner in fee simple when he is in fact a tenant for life of settled land, see *Weston v Henshaw* [1950] Ch 510 (SLA 1925, s 110(1) protects purchaser only where he knows other party is tenant for life and deals with him on that footing); cf *Re Morgan's Lease* [1972] Ch 1 (s 110 applies whether ot not the purchaser knows that the other party is tenant for life). The latter interpretation of s 110(1) seems preferable; *Weston v Henshaw* appears to be the only decision in unregistered land that is an exception to the immunity of the bona fide purchaser for value of the legal estate without notice: (1971) 87 LQR 338 (DW Elliott); (1973) 36 MLR, p 28 (RH Maudsley).

[37] Ibid, s 110(2); but the proviso to the section contains exceptions.

[38] S 44(2).

[39] Ibid, s 44(3), (4).

A leases to B, and B under-leases to C, and C agrees to sell his underlease to D, then D is entitled to production of the under-lease,[40] but he cannot call for the lease to B.

However, these rules precluding the tenant from calling for title to the reversion do not apply to a contract to grant a term of years if the grant will be an event that triggers compulsory first registration of the title to the estate out of which the grant is made.[41]

These rules were formerly contained in the Vendor and Purchaser Act 1874, and the Conveyancing Act 1881, and it was held under those statutes that, failing their express exclusion by the contract, a lessee or a purchaser of a term of years was bound by equities affecting the legal estate that would have come to his notice had he expressly required the freehold title to be disclosed. This was decided in *Patman v Harland*:[42]

> The plaintiff sold land to A subject to a restrictive covenant. A sold to B, and B leased part of the land to the defendant, who committed a breach of the covenant. The defendant had no knowledge of the existence of the restrictive covenant, and, in an action brought against her for an injunction, it was argued that, as in an open contract she was debarred by the statute from inquiring into the title to the freehold out of which her lease was derived, she had no notice, actual or constructive, of the restrictive covenant, and therefore was not liable for its breach.

This argument was rejected by the Court of Appeal.

It is now, however, provided that, in contracts made after 1925, a person who, under the above rules, is not entitled to call for the title to the freehold or the leasehold reversion shall not be deemed to be affected with notice of any matter or thing of which, if he had contracted that such a title should be furnished, he might have had notice.[43] The doctrine of *Patman v Harland* is therefore abolished in cases where a purchaser of a leasehold interest has no right to call for the freehold title, but the alteration is subject to the qualification that the lessee remains bound by any incumbrances that have been registered under the Land Charges Act 1972.[44]

There is also a more general enactment to the effect that a purchaser shall not be deemed to have notice of any matter or thing of which, if he had investigated the title

---

[40] *Gosling v Woolf* [1893] 1 QB 39. C is, however, entitled to call for B's lease. This is not precluded by s 44, and, therefore, an under-lessee has constructive notice of the restrictive covenants in a lease: *Clements v Welles* (1865) LR 1 Eq 200. See Farrand, *Contract and Conveyance*, p 131.

[41] LPA 1925, s 44(4A), inserted by LRA 2002, Sch 11, para 2(2). For leases triggering compulsory first registration of the reversion, see LRA 2002, s 4(1), below, p 1074 (leases of more than seven years, or taking effect in possession more than three months after the grant, or pursuant to the right to buy under HA 1985, Part 5, or where HA 1985, s 171A applies (disposal by landlord that leads to a person no longer being a secure tenant)).

[42] (1881) 17 Ch D 353. See (1950) 56 LQR 361 (DW Logan).   [43] LPA 1925, s 44(5).

[44] *White v Bijou Mansions Ltd* [1937] Ch 610, 619. See *Shears v Wells* [1936] 1 All ER 832, M & B p 461; [1956] CLJ pp 230–4 (HWR Wade). Where the land is already registered, LPA 1925, s 44 does not apply because the register of the landlord's title is open to inspection: below, p 1073; LPA 1925, s 44(12), inserted by Land Registration Act 2002, s 133, Sch 11, para 2(1), (4).

prior to the beginning of the 15 years' period, he might have had notice, unless he actually makes the investigation.[45]

(3) Purchaser to Bear the Cost of Producing Certain Documents

We have seen that one of the duties of a vendor is to produce a perfect abstract of title; it is incidental to this that he must produce at his own expense the documents that go to prove the title. If these are not in his possession, he must arrange for the production of those dated after the period of 15 years began in so far as they are material.[46] But as regards the expense of producing documents, the rule varies according to whether they are in the possession of the vendor.

At common law a vendor was bound to bear the cost of producing documents whether in his own possession or not, but the Conveyancing Act 1881 provided that the expenses of the production and of the inspection of documents *not in the vendor's possession*, the expenses of all journeys incidental to such production or inspection, and the expenses of procuring all evidences and information not in the vendor's possession, should be borne by the purchaser.[47]

It was held under this section that where the vendor had mortgaged his property, the purchaser must pay the mortgagee's solicitor a fee for producing the deeds relating to the property.[48] This was a harsh application of the rule, and therefore the Law of Property Act 1925, while re-enacting the provisions of the Conveyancing Act, expressly excludes from the costs to be borne by the purchaser the expense of producing deeds that are in the possession of the vendor's *mortgagee or trustee*.[49] If, however, the mortgagee retains possession of a document, the purchaser must pay for any copy that he desires to have.

(4) Purchaser to Examine the Abstract at his Own Expense

The perusal of the abstract is carried out by the purchaser's solicitor, whose duty to his client is to advise whether the vendor has shown a good title to the exact interest that he has agreed to sell. The solicitor must satisfy himself that the abstract exhibits an ordered sequence of all the documents and events that have disposed of or affected the interest during the last 15 years, and if he observes defects or omissions, he must requisition the vendor on the matter. He must compare the abstract with the original deeds that are produced by the vendor's solicitor, and put in requisitions on points of discrepancy.

---

[45] LPA 1925, s 44(8). Purchaser in this connection means one who acquires an interest for money or money's worth, and includes a lessee and a mortgagee: ibid, s 205(1)(xxi). The expression money's worth excludes the consideration of marriage.

[46] *Re Stamford, Spalding and Boston Banking Co and Knight's Contract* [1900] 1 Ch 287.   [47] S 3(6).

[48] *Re Willett and Argenti* (1889) 60 LT 735.   [49] LPA 1925, s 45(4).

The solicitor must, for instance, require proper evidence of facts that affect the interest, ascertain that the abstracted documents bear stamps of the proper value, and inquire concerning the existence of tenancies and easements.

(5) Purchaser to Search Registers of Incumbrances

One of the first essentials in the investigation of an abstract of title is that a purchaser should search for incumbrances and interests that affect the land to be sold, and that may have been registered by their owners in a public register. This will be seen to be of great importance when we come to examine whether the purchaser of a legal estate takes the estate free from interests charged on the estate. There are two main registers to be noticed:

(1) the land charges register, a central register kept by the Land Charges Department of the Land Registry at Plymouth;[50]

(2) the various local land charges registers kept in London by each London borough or the City of London, and elsewhere by each district council.[51]

These are discussed in more detail later in this chapter.[52]

(6) Duty of Vendor to Convey the Identical Property that he has Agreed to Sell

The vendor must prove that the property that he is able to convey is substantially the same in nature, situation and quantity as that which he has agreed to sell, and it is advisable, when a contract for the sale of land is drafted, to obtain a description of the land from the 'parcels' clause of the last conveyance.[53]

---

[50] LCA 1972, replacing LCA 1925.

[51] LLCA 1975, s 3(1); or a Welsh county or county borough council: added by Local Government (Wales) Act 1994, Sch 16, para 49. Such registers need not be kept in documentary form: s 3(3), substituted by Local Government (Miscellaneous Provisions) Act 1982, s 34(a).

[52] Below, pp 1054–66 (land charges), 1066–7 (local land charges). There are other registers that a purchaser may have to search. There is a register of company charges kept by the Registrar of Companies (below, p 1067); registers of common land and town or village greens under Commons Act 2006, s 1 (formerly Commons Registration Act 1965, s 3; above, p 708); and of agricultural charges under Agricultural Credits Act 1928, s 5 (charge created by a farmer on his farming stock and other agricultural assets as security for sums advanced to him by a bank: this register is kept at the Land Registry at Plymouth: in 2009–10 there were 917 new registrations, 737 cancellations and rectifications, and 3,405 searches: Land Registry Annual Report and Accounts 2009–10, p 16). On searches for and information on contaminated land, see Tromans and Turrall-Clarke, *Contaminated Land* (2nd edn, 2007); (2001) 145 SJ 827; Silverman, *Conveyancing Handbook*, para B10.5.10. For other registers maintained by local authorities, see Garner, *Local Land Charges* (14th edn, 2010), ch 20. On searches generally, see Silverman and Hewitson, *Conveyancing Searches and Enquiries* (3rd edn, 2006); Silverman, *Conveyancing Handbook*, section B10. For the liability of a solicitor who failed to search the Commons Register, see *G & K Ladenbau (UK) Ltd v Crawley and de Reya* [1978] 1 WLR 266.

[53] Williams, *Vendor and Purchaser* (4th edn, 1936), p 36. The 'parcels clause' contains a description of the property sold, which may be accompanied by a plan.

If, in the case of an open contract, the property is not identical in quantity or quality with that agreed to be sold, the vendor cannot compel specific performance of the contract subject to compensation, unless the difference is insignificant and his conduct has been honest:[54]

> If a vendor sues and is in a position to convey substantially what the purchaser has contracted to get, the court will decree specific performance with compensation for any small and immaterial deficiency, provided that the vendor has not, by misrepresentation or otherwise, disentitled himself to his remedy.

If a contract for sale is made, and investigation of the title shows that the property is subject to restrictive covenants, the vendor cannot therefore force the title on the purchaser subject to compensation,[55] but he can do so, for example, if the sole mistake is that a right of common attached to the land extends only to sheep instead of being, as represented, unlimited.[56]

A purchaser, on the other hand, is in a more favourable position, for as a general rule he is allowed to take all that he can get, and to subject the vendor to a proportionate diminution of the purchase money. But specific performance will not be decreed at the suit of the purchaser if the property that the vendor is in a position to convey is entirely different from that which he agreed to sell, or if the difference is one for which it is impossible to fix pecuniary compensation, or if the effect of decreeing specific performance would be to cause injustice to third parties.[57]

(7) Duty of Purchaser to Complete the Contract

After the purchaser has investigated the abstract, it is his duty either to accept or to reject the title offered to him. If he takes the latter course, the parties are left to their remedies under the contract.[58] If, however, the purchaser is satisfied with the title, then the contract must be completed in accordance with its terms. Completion of a contract means that the purchaser must at his own expense prepare a proper deed of conveyance that is effectual to pass the interest to be sold and that contains the usual covenants for title by the vendor.[59] He must also tender the price that he has agreed to pay. On the vendor's side completion involves the execution of the conveyance and the delivery of possession of the land to the purchaser.[60]

---

[54] *Rutherford v Acton-Adams* [1915] AC 866, 869–70 (Viscount Haldane); *Cox v Coventon* (1862) 31 Beav 378; *Re Arnold* (1880) 14 Ch D 270, 279; above, p 995.

[55] Cf *Rudd v Lascelles* [1900] 1 Ch 815.   [56] *Howland v Norris* (1784) 1 Cox Eq Cas 59.

[57] *Willmott v Barber* (1880) 15 Ch D 96; *Rudd v Lascelles*, above, at 819.   [58] Above, pp 990 ff.

[59] For covenants for title, see below, pp 1089–93.

[60] Williams, *Vendor and Purchaser*, p 37; [1991] Conv 15, 81, 185 (DG Barnsley); Silverman, *Conveyancing Handbook*, section F.

(8) Duty of Vendor to Deliver the Title Deeds[61]

The vendor must deliver to the purchaser all title deeds that relate solely to the property sold, though he may retain such documents where he retains any part of the land to which they relate, or where the document consists of a trust instrument creating a trust that is still subsisting.[62] Where the documents that are necessary to show a good title remain in the vendor's possession, or where their custody belongs to some person other than the vendor, it is the vendor's duty to give a written acknowledgment of the purchaser's right to their production and to delivery of copies and a written undertaking for their safe custody. The effect of such an acknowledgment is that the purchaser, or persons claiming under him, can, at their own expense, demand to see the documents, or claim to be supplied with copies.[63]

(9) Duty of Vendor to Deliver Vacant Possession

Lastly, it is an implied term of a contract of sale that vacant possession shall be given to the purchaser on completion.[64] Therefore a refusal by the purchaser to complete is justified if the land is subject to an unexpired tenancy, or if it has been lawfully requisitioned by a public authority.[65]

B CONTRACTS CONTAINING SPECIAL STIPULATIONS

We have described in outline the nature of the parties' obligations under an open contract. Land is not, however, usually sold in this manner. As we have seen,[66] in practice it is usual for the parties to regulate their rights and duties by *special conditions* in the contract of sale. A professionally drawn contract will generally incorporate the terms of Standard Conditions of Sale with variations to meet the particular case. Reference must be made to the standard textbooks on conveyancing for full treatment.[67]

Matters that are commonly the subject of special conditions are the root of title and the length of title (although this is less important as a result of the Law of Property Act 1969);[68] the date upon which possession is to be given, and the consequences if default is made; interest to be payable by the purchaser on the purchase price, if the sale is not completed on the stipulated date; the restriction of the purchaser's remedies for minor misdescriptions; and planning matters.

---

61 As to the right to possession of title deeds, see *Clayton v Clayton* [1930] 2 Ch 12.

62 LPA 1925, s 45(9).

63 Ibid, s 64.

64 *Cook v Taylor* [1942] Ch 349; *Sheikh v O'Connor* [1987] 2 EGLR 269. See Farrand, *Contract and Conveyance* (4th edn), pp 174–8; [1988] Conv 324, 400 (C Harpum).

65 *Cook v Taylor*, above; *James Macara Ltd v Barclay* [1945] KB 148; cf *Re Winslow Hall Estates Co and United Glass Bottle Manufacturers Ltd's Contract* [1941] Ch 503; *Hillingdon Estates Co v Stonefield Estates Ltd* [1952] Ch 627; *Topfell Ltd v Galley Properties Ltd* [1979] 1 WLR 446.

66 Above, p 953–4.   67 See above, p 954, nn 32 and 33.   68 Above, p 1043.

IV THE CONVEYANCE

A NECESSITY FOR A DEED

We have already seen that a deed is necessary for the creation and transfer of legal estates and interests.[69] A conveyance in unregistered land must therefore be by deed.[70]

B CONVEYANCE BY A PERSON TO HIMSELF

It is sometimes necessary that an interest shall be conveyed by the grantor to himself jointly with another person, such as where a surviving trustee wishes to vest the legal estate in himself and a new trustee. At common law this could not be done by one deed, for the effect of a grant by A to A and B was to vest the whole estate in B. The only solution was that A should convey to X, who would then convey to A and B, though an alternative method became available, and in fact general, under the doctrine of uses, for if A conveyed to X *to the use* of himself and B, the effect of the Statute of Uses[71] was to vest an immediate legal estate in A and B jointly. It has been possible, however, since August 1859 in the case of leaseholds, and since 1881 in the case of freeholds, for a person to convey land to himself jointly with another person by a direct deed of grant and, as the Statute of Uses has been repealed, this is now the only method.[72]

There are also occasions when it is necessary that a person should convey land to himself, such as where personal representatives assent to the land vesting in themselves as trustees of land.[73] Although it could be effected directly under statutory provisions, it remained generally true, prior to 1926, that a conveyance by a person to himself required a grant to uses. It is now provided, however, that 'a person may convey land to or vest land in himself'.[74] This does not, however, enable an owner to grant a tenancy to himself, for a lease, though it falls within the statutory definition of a 'conveyance' and vests a legal estate in the lessee, is essentially a contractual transaction. At the lowest it creates a number of implied obligations and liabilities, a situation that is impossible where only one person is involved. A man cannot contract with himself.[75] However, in spite of these limitations, a person who holds land as a nominee for his principal may grant a valid lease to that principal.[76]

---

[69] LPA 1925, s 52(1); above, pp 1001 ff. For the form of a deed, and its method of execution, see above, pp 1003–8.

[70] In registered land, the deed is not sufficient of itself to pass the legal title where the disposition is required to be completed by registration: above, pp 1008–9, below, pp 1093–5.

[71] Above, p 73.

[72] LPA 1925, s 72(1), (2), replacing LP(A)A 1859, s 21, and Conveyancing Act 1881, s 50.

[73] *Re King's Will Trusts* [1964] Ch 542.

[74] LPA 1925, s 72(3).   [75] *Rye v Rye* [1962] AC 496, M & B p 355; (1962) 78 LQR 175 (PV Baker).

[76] *Ingram v IRC* [2000] 1 AC 293 (as part of an inheritance avoidance scheme HL held that Lady Ingram's solicitor, as nominee for her, granted a valid lease to her. The tax advantage has been negatived by FA 1999, s 104); (1999) 115 LQR 351 (R Kerridge). The convincing dissenting judgment of Millett LJ in CA was approved: [1997] STC 1234, 1255.

Two or more persons, whether trustees or personal representatives or not, may convey any property vested in themselves to any one or more of themselves, though if the conveyance amounts to a breach of trust, it is liable to be set aside.[77]

C THE FORM OF A DEED OF CONVEYANCE ON SALE

The deed used for the conveyance on sale of freehold land has taken a traditional form, an example of which was set out and explained in some detail in the 16th edition of this book.[78] The conveyancer will need to understand such a form of conveyance when he is investigating the title to unregistered land, since the title will generally be constituted by documents that were drafted in that form. However, although the traditional form of deed of conveyance may still be used, a simpler form may now be employed. Since the conveyance on sale of unregistered land will trigger the compulsory registration of the title,[79] it is possible to use one of the standard Land Registry forms of transfer.[80] Where, for example, the conveyance is by the freehold owner, and of the whole of the title comprised in the previous conveyance to him, Form TR1 can be used. An example of this form, together with an explanation of some of its key provisions, and an account of the procedures that are necessary for the first registration of the title, are set out in the following chapter on registered conveyancing.[81]

V THE PRIORITY OF COMPETING INTERESTS IN UNREGISTERED LAND

We have already seen in outline that, in unregistered land after 1925, as regards third-party rights in or over the land, the position of a transferee of the land depends on whether the third-party right is registrable under the Land Charges Act (and, if so, whether it is registered and whether the transferee is a 'purchaser'); and whether it is overreachable (and, if so, whether it is overreached by the conveyance).[82] If the right is

---

See Lord Radcliffe in *Rye v Rye*, above, at 511: 'In effect, putting aside conveyancing forms, a man was able to convey to himself before the 1925 Act. He could, of course, put land in trust for himself by conveying it to a nominee, and, I suppose, if there was any conceivable point in the operation, he could similarly demise land to a nominee.' Cf *Kildrummy (Jersey) Ltd v IRC* [1990] STC 657, where it was held by the Court of Session that land could not be demised to a nominee. *Rye v Rye* was not cited.

[77] LPA 1925, s 72(4).

[78] Pp 847–55. The transfer of land by personal representatives may be effected by an *assent* (AEA 1925, s 36); and on the death of a tenant for life under a strict settlement the legal estate devolves upon his special personal representatives, ie the trustees of the settlement (AEA 1925, s 22(1)), who may convey the legal estate to the next tenant for life either by a vesting deed or by a vesting assent, which contains the particulars set out above at pp 436–7.

[79] Below, p 1074.

[80] Land Registry Practice Guide 1, section 7; Silverman, *Conveyancing Handbook*, para E1.3.6.

[81] Below, pp 1085 ff.

[82] Above, pp 121–31, 143; see in particular the summary set out in the diagram on p 144.

not registrable, and is not overreachable or (if overreachable) has not been overreached, the old doctrine of the bona fide purchaser[83] still applies to determine whether the transferee is bound. In this section we consider in more detail the circumstances in which a third-party right in unregistered land can be protected by registration. The doctrine of overreaching, which also applies in registered land, will be discussed in more detail in the following chapter.

A PROTECTION OF INTERESTS BY REGISTRATION

(1) Land Charges Register[84]

(a) Registrable interests

Under the Land Charges Act 1972, the Registrar of the Land Registry keeps five separate registers,[85] namely:

    (a) a register of land charges;

    (b) a register of pending actions;

    (c) a register of writs and orders affecting land;

    (d) a register of deeds of arrangement affecting land; and

    (e) a register of annuities.

We shall take these registers separately, and notice what kind of right or interest in land may be registered in each. Since, however, the principal register is of land charges, we shall briefly first discuss the other four registers and then discuss land charges in some detail.

(1) Register of pending actions

It is obviously impossible to bring an action relating to land to a successful termination if alienation is permissible during the course of the litigation, and therefore, in order that a claimant may not lose the fruits of his action, the law provides him with the means of protecting himself. This is afforded by the right to register a pending land

---

[83] Above, pp 83–91.

[84] In 2009-10, there were 204,235 new registrations, rectifications and renewals of land charges, and 2,272,546 searches of the Register (492,207 full searches, and 1,780,339 searches limited to insolvency). There were 15,781 applications for cancellation of charges. 81.4 per cent of search requests were made by telephone, direct electronic access and fax, and 94 per cent of official copy applications were delivered in those ways: Land Registry Annual Report 2009–10, pp 15-16.

[85] LCA 1972, s 1(1). The original order, as set out in LCA 1925, s 1(1), was pending actions, annuities, writs and orders, deeds of arrangement, and land charges. See generally Barnsley, *Conveyancing Law and Practice*, pp 189–96, 333–66; Land Registry Practice Guide 63. On the history of registration, see *Ministry of Housing and Local Government v Sharp* [1970] 2 QB 223, 280 (Cross LJ).

action, that is any action, information or proceeding that is pending in court, and that relates to land or to any interest in, or charge on, land.[86]

If a creditor wishes to make his debtor's property available for distribution among creditors generally, he may register in the same register the petition in bankruptcy that is the first step in setting bankruptcy proceedings in motion.[87]

If a pending action (ie either an action relating to land or a petition in bankruptcy) is registered, the registration remains effective for five years, but it may be renewed for successive periods of five years.[88] A purchaser for value (which includes a mortgagee or lessee) of any interest in the land takes free from an *unregistered* pending action unless he has express, as distinct from constructive, notice of it.[89] In the case of an unregistered bankruptcy petition, however, this protection avails him only if he is a purchaser of a *legal* estate in good faith for money or money's worth.[90]

(2) Register of writs and orders affecting land

Any writ or order affecting land issued by a court for the purpose of enforcing a judgment or recognisance (eg an order of the court charging the land of a judgment debtor with payment of the money due[91]), any order that appoints a receiver[92] or sequestrator of land, any bankruptcy order, whether it is known to affect land or not, and any access order under the Access to Neighbouring Land Act 1992[93] is void against a purchaser for value of the land unless it is registered.[94] The registration remains effective for five years, but it may be renewed for successive periods of five years.[95]

The title of a trustee in bankruptcy, however, is void only against a purchaser of a legal estate in good faith for money or money's worth unless the bankruptcy order is registered.[96]

---

[86] Ibid, s 5(1), (4A) as added by LP (Miscellaneous Provisions) Act 1994, s 15(3) (registration after death), s 17(1); see *Taylor v Taylor* [1968] 1 WLR 378; *Calgary and Edmonton Land Co Ltd v Dobinson* [1974] Ch 102; *Whittingham v Whittingham* [1979] Fam 9; *Greenhi Builders Ltd v Allen* [1979] 1 WLR 156; *Selim Ltd v Bickenhall Engineering Ltd* [1981] 1 WLR 1318; *Regan & Blackburn Ltd v Rogers* [1985] 1 WLR 870; *Sowerby v Sowerby* (1982) 44 P & CR 192; *Haslemere Estates Ltd v Baker* [1982] 1 WLR 1109; [1983] Conv 69 (JEM); *Perez-Adamson v Perez-Rivas* [1987] Fam 89; [1987] Conv 58 (JE Martin); *Kemmis v Kemmis* [1988] 1 WLR 1307; *Willies-Williams v National Trust for Places of Historic Interest or Natural Beauty* (1993) 65 P & CR 359. See generally (1986) 136 NLJ 157 (HW Wilkinson); [1995] Conv 309 (J Howell).

[87] Ibid, s 5(1).   [88] Ibid, s 8.   [89] Ibid, s 5(7).

[90] Ibid, ss 5(8), 6(5), as amended by Insolvency Act 1985, s 235, Sch 8, para 21 and Sch 11.

[91] Charging Orders Act 1979, s 1; above, p 813. A freezing order (formerly called a Mareva injunction) prohibiting a party from disposing of his assets is not registrable: *Stockler v Fourways Estates Ltd* [1984] 1 WLR 25.

[92] *Clayhope Properties Ltd v Evans* [1986] 1 WLR 1223 (receivership order made against landlord for specific performance of repairing covenants held registrable).

[93] See above, p 652. No will or order affecting an interest under a trust of land may be registered under s 6(1A), inserted by TLATA 1996, s 21(1), Sch 3, para 12(3).

[94] LCA 1972, s 6(1), (4), as amended by SCA 1981, s 152(1), Sch 5 and County Courts Act 1984, s 148(1), Sch 2, para 18.

[95] Ibid, s 8.   [96] Ibid, s 6(5) as amended by Insolvency Act 1985, s 235, Sch 8, para 21(3) and Sch 10.

(3) Register of deeds of arrangement affecting land

An insolvent debtor sometimes comes to an arrangement with the general body of his creditors whereby, although he does not pay his debts in full, he obtains a release from the claims of the creditors. As a rule the debtor either compounds with his creditors, or assigns his property to a trustee for distribution among the creditors.

If such an arrangement is reduced to writing, it is called a deed of arrangement whether it is made by deed or not.[97] Such an arrangement is void against a purchaser for value of the debtor's land unless it is registered in the register of deeds of arrangement affecting land. Registration ceases to have any effect after five years unless it is renewed.[98]

(4) Register of annuities

Before 1926 annuities or rentcharges did not affect purchasers of the land upon which they are charged unless they were registered in the register of annuities. No annuity can be entered in this Register after 1925, and it will be closed as soon as the annuities registered before 1 January 1926 have been worked off.[99]

Annuities, being interests for life, are necessarily equitable in nature after 1925, and they may now be registered as *general equitable charges* in the register of land charges, provided that they do not arise under a settlement or a trust of land.[100]

(5) Register of land charges

The term *land charge* is comprehensive; it includes a number of different rights and interests affecting land. The Land Charges Act 1925, which made considerable additions to this part of the law, divided land charges into five classes, denominated A, B, C, D, and E; a further Class F was added by the Matrimonial Homes Act 1967.[101] The whole has now been consolidated in the Land Charges Act 1972.[102]

Class A[103]

This comprises a rent or a sum of money that is charged upon land, *pursuant to the application of some person*, under the provisions of any Act of Parliament, and with the object of securing money that has been spent on the land under the provisions of such Act. It also comprises a rent or a sum of money charged upon land in accordance with, for example:

the Land Drainage Act 1991, section 34(2);[104]

---

[97] Deeds of Arrangement Act 1914, s 1.
[98] LCA 1972, ss 7, 8.   [99] Ibid, s 1(4), Sch 1.
[100] Ibid, s 2(4), Class C (iii), as amended by TLATA 1996, Sch 3, para 12(1), (2), below, p 1058.
[101] Now Family Law Act 1996; above, p 522.
[102] See Land Charges Rules 1974 (SI 1974 No 1286), amended by Land Charges (Amendment) Rules in 1990 (SI 1990 No 485), 1995 (SI 1995 No 1355) and 2005 (SI 2005 No 1981); Land Charges Fees Rules 1990 (SI 1990 No 327), amended by Land Charges Fees (Amendment) Rules 1994 (SI 1994 No 286).
[103] LCA 1972, s 2(2).
[104] Ibid, Sch 2, para 1(d) (charge in respect of sum paid in commutation of certain obligations to repair banks, water-courses etc), amended by Land Drainage Act 1976, s 117(2), Sch 7, para 8; Water Consolidation (Consequential Provisions) Act 1991, Sch 1, para 21.

the Agricultural Holdings Act 1986, sections 85 and 86;[105] and

the Landlord and Tenant Act 1927, Schedule 1, paragraph 7.[106]

Thus, if a tenant for life has to pay compensation to an outgoing tenant of an agricultural holding, he may obtain an order charging the holding with the repayment of the amount, and may have the charge registered. A land charge of this class is void against a purchaser unless it is registered before the completion of the purchase.[107]

Class B[108]

This comprises a charge on land (not being a local land charge) of any of the kinds described in Class A, which has not been created 'pursuant to the application of any person', and is imposed automatically by statute. An example is a charge on property recovered or preserved for an assisted litigant arising under the Access to Justice Act 1999,[109] in respect of unpaid contributions for services received from the Criminal Defence Service.

Charges of this class, however, are not important as regards searches in the Land Registry: they mostly arise under the Public Health Act 1936 and, being in the majority of cases of a local nature (such as those arising in respect of paving expenses), they are *local land charges* and must therefore be registered locally.[110]

Failure to register such a charge (not being a local land charge) at the Land Registry renders it void as against a purchaser of the land or of any interest in the land:

(i)   if it arises after 31 December 1925, and has not been registered;

(ii) if it arose before that date and has not been registered within a year from the first conveyance of the charge made after 31 December 1925.[111]

Class C[112]

This class is important in that it creates a system of registration of mortgages of land, and provides for the registration of estate contracts. It comprises four different land charges (not being local land charges), namely:

(i)   *Puisne mortgage* This is a *legal* mortgage not protected by a deposit of documents relating to the legal estate affected.[113]

---

[105] Ibid, Sch 2, para 1(i) (charges in respect of sums due to tenant of agricultural holding and in favour of landlord of agricultural holding in respect of compensation for or cost of certain improvements), inserted by Agricultural Holdings Act 1986, s 100, Sch 14, para 51. The 1986 Act does not apply to tenancies beginning on or after 1 September 1995: above, p 417. In the case of a farm business tenancy (above, p 420) such sums are payable out of capital money; Agricultural Tenancies Act 1995, s 33(3).

[106] Ibid, Sch 2, para 1(c) (charge in respect of improvements to business premises). For other examples, see LCA 1972, s 2, Sch 2.

[107] Ibid, s 4(2). For 'purchaser' see s 17(1); below, p 1063.

[108] Ibid, s 2(3) as amended by LLCA 1975, s 19, Sch 2.   [109] S 17(3)(g).   [110] Below, p 1066.

[111] LCA 1972, s 4(5), (7). For 'purchaser' see s 17(1); below, p 1063.

[112] Ibid, s 2(4), as amended by LLCA 1975, s 17(1)(b).

[113] Above, pp 810–11, 885. It should be noticed that, by requiring registration of this form of legal mortgage, the land charges legislation departed from the pre-1925 rule that legal estates and interests automatically bind a subsequent purchaser: above, p 80.

(ii) *Limited owner's charge* This is an equitable charge acquired under any statute by a tenant for life or statutory owner by discharging inheritance tax or other liabilities, and to which special priority is given by the statute. Thus a charge may arise under the Inheritance Tax Act 1984,[114] in favour of a tenant for life who pays inheritance tax in respect of the estate out of which his life interest is carved.

(iii) *General equitable charge* This is a comprehensive expression that includes any equitable charges that[115]

(a) is not secured by a deposit of documents relating to the legal estate affected; and

(b) does not arise or affect an interest arising under a trust of land or a settlement; and

(c) is not a charge given by way of indemnity against rents equitably apportioned or charged exclusively on land in exoneration of other land and against the breach or non-observance of covenants or conditions; and

(d) is not included in any other class of land charge.

In particular, it includes an equitable mortgage of a legal estate that is not secured by a deposit of the title deeds; but it also comprises a rentcharge for life and a vendor's lien for unpaid purchase money.[116] To be registrable, the charge must be on land, and not (for example) upon the purchase money that will arise from the sale of land.[117]

(iv) *Estate contract* This is the only item included within Class C which is not in the nature of a mortgage. It is defined as being:[118]

a contract by an estate owner or by a person entitled at the date of the contract to have a legal estate conveyed to him to convey or create a legal estate, including a contract conferring either expressly or by statutory implication a valid option to purchase, a right of pre-emption[119] or any other like right.[120]

This means in practice a contract for the sale of a legal fee simple, a contract for the grant of a term of years absolute,[121] or an option to acquire either of these interests[122] or

---

[114] LCA 1972, s 2(4), as amended by FA 1975, s 52, Sch 12, para 18; ITA 1984, s 276, Sch 8, para 3(1)(a); FA 1986, s 100(1)(b). See ITA 1984, ss 2(2), 237, 238.

[115] Ibid, s 2(4) as amended by TLATA 1996, s 25(1), Sch 3, para 12(2).

[116] See *Uziell-Hamilton v Keen* (1971) 22 P & CR 655; *Property Discount Corp Ltd v Lyon Group Ltd* [1981] 1 WLR 300, 313.

[117] *Georgiades v Edward Wolfe & Co Ltd* [1965] Ch 487. Report of Committee on Land Charges (1956 Cmnd 9825), para 13 suggested that Class C(iii) might be abolished, except as regards mortgages.

[118] LCA 1972, s 2(4).

[119] See above, pp 985 ff.   [120] *Shiloh Spinners Ltd v Harding* [1973] AC 691, 719.

[121] *Sharp v Coates* [1949] 1 KB 285 (contract by estate owner to convey an estate greater than he was entitled to at the time of the contract). It also includes a contract by which A agrees with B to create a legal estate in favour of such third person as B may nominate: *Turley v Mackay* [1944] Ch 37; but not a contract by which A agrees that B has the power to accept offers to purchase made by third persons: *Thomas v Rose* [1968] 1 WLR 1797.

[122] *Beesly v Hallwood Estates Ltd* [1960] 1 WLR 549. The decision was affirmed on another point: [1961] Ch 105; *Taylors Fashions Ltd v Liverpool Victoria Trustees Co Ltd* [1982] QB 133n; and approved in *Phillips*

a contract to grant any other legal interest, such as a mortgage or easement.[123] We have already seen that the effect of such a contract is to confer an equitable interest upon the intending purchaser or tenant under the doctrine of *Walsh v Lonsdale*.[124] The effect of the Land Charges Act is to make it capable of registration.[125]

Class D[126]

This comprises the three following different land charges (not being local land charges):

(i) *Inland Revenue charge* The Commissioners of Her Majesty's Revenue and Customs may register a charge on the occasion of the transfer of land that gives rise to the liability for inheritance tax under the Inheritance Tax Act 1984.[127]

(ii) *Restrictive covenant* This has already been described.[128] It should be noted that restrictive covenants made between a lessor and a lessee are expressly excluded, and are not capable of registration.

(iii) *Equitable easement* This is defined as[129]

an easement, right or privilege over or affecting land created or arising on or after 1 January 1926, and being merely an equitable interest.

An easement held for some smaller interest than a fee simple absolute in possession or for a term of years absolute, or an easement that has been informally created, satisfies this definition and is therefore registrable.

The three charges in Class D are not registrable unless they have arisen after 1925.

v Mobil Oil Co Ltd [1989] 1 WLR 888; [1990] Conv 168, 250 (J Howell); [1989] All ER Rev 193 (PH Pettit). A notice to treat served under a compulsory purchase order is not a contract (although it may lead to one) and therefore is not registrable: *Capital Investments Ltd v Wednesfield UDC* [1965] Ch 774. Cf Leasehold Reform Act 1967, s 5(5) (notice given by tenant of his desire to acquire the freehold or an extended lease registrable as estate contract); above, p 394.

123 'Legal estate' in LCA 1972, as in LPA 1925, is not limited to the legal estates properly so-called, but extends to all estates, interests and charges that can be conveyed or created at law: LCA 1972, s 17(1); LPA 1925, s 1(4).

124 Above, p 978.

125 *Universal Permanent Building Society v Cooke* [1952] Ch 95, 104. See *Barrett v Hilton Developments Ltd* [1975] Ch 237 (registration against the name of a person who has contracted to purchase the legal estate in land is not sufficient).

126 LCA 1972, s 2(5), as amended by LLCA 1975, s 17(1)(b).

127 Ibid, s 2(5), as amended by FA 1975, s 52, Sch 12, para 18; ITA 1984, s 237, Sch 8, para 3(1)(b); FA 1986, s 100(1)(b); Commissioners for Revenue and Customs Act 2005, ss 5(2), 50(1). See ITA 1984, ss 2(2), 237, 238.

128 Above, pp 732 ff.

129 For a discussion of this class, see *Shiloh Spinners Ltd v Harding* [1973] AC 691, M & B p 68 (equitable right of re-entry on breach of contract not registrable as Class D(iii) land charge); (1973) 32 CLJ 218 (PB Fairest); above, pp 693–4. Report of the Committee on Land Charges (1956 Cmnd 9826), para 16 suggested that Class D(iii) might be abolished. Law Com No 18, *Land Charges Affecting Unregistered Land* (1969), para 65, recommended its retention. Registrations in that class were then running at an annual rate of 2,500–3,500; there were 829 registrations during the year ended 31 March 1993: Report on HM Land Registry 1992–93, p 21.

Class E[130]

This class comprises annuities created before 1926 and not registered in the register of annuities. That register, as we have seen, was closed to new entries as from 1 January 1926,[131] but annuitants who omitted to register before that date may register under Class E.

Class F[132]

This is the right of occupation of a dwelling-house given to a spouse or civil partner by Part IV of the Family Law Act 1996.[133]

(b) Effect of registration

The effect of registration is set out in section 198(1) of the Law of Property Act 1925:[134]

> The registration of any instrument or matter in any register kept under the Land Charges Act 1972 or any local land charges register shall be deemed to constitute actual notice of such instrument or matter, and of the fact of such registration, to all persons and for all purposes connected with the land affected, as from the date of registration...and so long as the registration continues in force.

As we have seen,[135] this makes a substantial inroad on the doctrine of the bona fide purchaser for value without notice: that doctrine no longer operates in respect of land charges that are registrable.

(1) Registration against name of estate owner

It is important to notice that land charges affecting unregistered land are registered, not against the burdened *land*, as is the case with registered land, but against the *name* of the estate owner of the land at the time when the land charge was created.[136] The name of the estate owner means the name as disclosed by the conveyance.[137]

Where a person has died and a land charge created before his death would (apart from his death) have been registered in his name, it should be so registered notwithstanding his death.[138] If, therefore, a purchaser wishes to make a complete search at the Land Registry, he will have to discover the names of every owner of a legal estate in the land since 1 January 1926.[139] Even though this may be impossible, he will nevertheless be

---

[130] LCA 1972, s 2(6).   [131] Above, p 1056.

[132] LCA 1972, s 2(7), amended by Family Law Act 1996, s 66(1), Sch 8, para 47.   [133] Above, p 522.

[134] As amended by LLCA 1975, s 17, Sch 1. For an exception in the case of tacking, see LPA 1925, s 198(2), above, p 893. See also s 96(2), as amended by LP(A)A 1926, Sch; above, p 839.

[135] Above, pp 127–8.

[136] LCA 1972, ss 3(1), 17(1). On the mechanics of the register see *Oak Co-operative Building Society v Blackburn* [1968] Ch 730, 741 (Russell LJ).

[137] *Standard Property Investment plc v British Plastics Federation* (1985) 53 P & CR 25; [1987] Conv 135 (JEA). A person entitled to have the legal estate conveyed to him is not an estate owner: *Barrett v Hilton Developments Ltd* [1975] Ch 237; *Property Discount Corp Ltd v Lyon Group Ltd* [1981] 1 WLR 300.

[138] LCA 1972, ss 3(1A), 5(4A), 6(2A), inserted by LP(MP)A 1994, s 15(2). See Law Com No 184, *Title on Death* (1989), paras 2-2 to 2-9; [1995] Conv 476 (L Clements).

[139] Since January 1889 in respect of Class A land charges.

bound by a registered land charge. This causes difficulty to a purchaser and led to statutory intervention in 1969.[140]

(i) Land charge discovered between contract and completion

As we have seen, a purchaser does not normally investigate the vendor's title before contract.[141] In *Re Forsey and Hollebone's Contract*,[142] Eve J took the view that by virtue of section 198 of the Law of Property Act 1925, a purchaser has notice at the date of the contract of land charges that are then on the register, whether he knows of them or not. The difficulty for a purchaser under an open contract is that at the pre-contract stage he will not normally know the names of all the estate owners, and so he may be compelled to take a conveyance of the land subject to land charges on the register that he cannot discover. Section 24 of the Law of Property Act 1969 amended the law so as to ensure that in respect of contracts entered into after 1 January 1970, *as against the vendor*, a purchaser will only be deemed to have notice of those registered land charges of which he has actual or imputed knowledge at the date of the contract.[143] Consequently, a purchaser will no longer be prevented from rescinding the contract on the ground of an undisclosed land charge merely because it has been registered. The owner of the registered land charge, however, remains protected: here registration still constitutes notice to all the world.

Section 24 does not apply to local land charges,[144] and, where they are concerned, the rule in *Forsey and Hollebone's Contract* may still apply. In this case, however, the problem for the purchaser is different. He does not need to know the names of the estate owners; the charges are registered against the land.[145] But the need to search the register before contract rather than at the same time as the other registers, that is to say, shortly before completion, is inconvenient and entails a delay that can put the contract at risk. The correctness of the rule continues to be questioned.[146]

(ii) 'Old land charge' discovered after completion

A purchaser, who has carried out a full and proper investigation of title, may discover after completion that he is bound by land charges registered before the commencement of the vendor's title. He can, of course, stipulate for a list of all estate owners since 1 January 1926,[147] but this may be impracticable. The risk that he may be caught by an 'old land charge' is increased by the reduction of the minimum period of investigation of title to 15 years.

---

[140] LPA 1969, ss 24, 25. See generally Report of the Committee on Land Charges 1956 (Cmnd 9825); Law Com No 18, *Land Charges affecting Unregistered Land* (1969); (1970) 34 Conv (NS) 4 (FR Crane).

[141] Above, p 1041.   [142] [1927] 2 Ch 379.

[143] The parties cannot contract out of the section: LPA 1969, s 24(2).

[144] LRA 1969, s 24(1), (3). Nor does it apply to registered land.   [145] Below, p 1067.

[146] *Rignall Developments Ltd v Halil* [1988] Ch 190, 200–1 'This part of Eve J's judgment…was greeted at the time by conveyancers with consternation and incredulity…It has since been subjected to severe criticism by the editors of Emmet on Title and other eminent conveyancers' (Millett J); [1987] Conv 291 (C Harpum); (1987) 137 NLJ 1178 (HW Wilkinson). See also *Citytowns Ltd v Bohemian Properties Ltd* [1986] 2 EGLR 258.

[147] And perhaps should, where he purchases land for development: see (1969) 113 SJ 930 (SM Cretney).

The Law of Property Act 1969 preserves the validity of the registered land charge against the purchaser, but provides that where he has suffered loss as a result of its existence he is entitled to compensation.[148] This is payable if (a) his purchase was completed after 1 January 1970, (b) he purchased without actual or imputed[149] knowledge of the land charge[150] and (c) the charge was registered against the name of a person who did not appear as an estate owner in the relevant title.[151] Relevant title means either the statutory period of 15 years under an open contract, or the period of title in fact contracted for, whichever is the longer.[152]

(iii) Land charge discovered after grant or assignment of lease

As we have seen, in the case of an open contract for the grant or assignment of a lease or underlease, the lessee or assignee is not entitled to call for the superior reversionary titles.[153] He may, however, be bound by registered land charges affecting those titles, even though he is unable to discover the names of the estate owners that are concealed in those titles.[154]

(2) Priority notices

The fact that a charge cannot be registered until it has actually been created occasioned some difficulty after the Land Charges Act 1925 came into operation. The provision of the Act that a charge on land, such as a restrictive covenant, shall be void against a subsequent purchaser of the legal estate for money or money's worth unless it is registered before *completion* of that purchase, creates a problem in certain cases, for it is sometimes impossible to effect registration before completion. A common example of this arises where:

> X agrees to sell Blackacre to Y and takes a restrictive covenant from Y. Y funds the purchase with the assistance of a loan from Z, who requires a mortgage of Blackacre. The conveyance from X to Y which creates the restrictive covenant, and the mortgage from Y to Z are in practice completed at the same time, so that it is practically impossible for X to register his restrictive covenant before it is rendered void under the Act by the completion of the purchase in favour of Z.

The Law of Property (Amendment) Act 1926[155] removed this difficulty by providing that any person *intending* to apply for the registration of any *contemplated* charge may register notice of his intention at the Land Registry. This *priority notice* must be given at least 15 days before the registration is to take effect.[156] When the contemplated charge is actually created and later registered, then, provided that it is registered within 30

---

[148] LPA 1969, s 25. This does not apply to local land charges.   [149] Ibid, s 25(11).

[150] LPA 1925, s 198, is disapplied for the purpose of determining whether the purchaser had actual knowledge, and therefore the actual notice normally deemed by that provision to be constituted by registration under LCA 1972 or in a local land charges register does not apply: LPA 1969, s 25(2).

[151] LPA 1969, s 25(1). It is payable by the Chief Land Registrar out of public funds.

[152] Ibid, s 25(10).   [153] Above, p 1046.

[154] See also Law Com No 18, *Land Charges Affecting Unregistered Land* (1969), para 37.

[155] S 4(1); now LCA 1972, s 11(1). See (1977) 74 LSG 136 (P Freedman).

[156] LCA 1972, s 11(3), (6). Days when the registry is not open to the public are excluded.

days after the priority notice, it takes effect as if registration had been made at the time when it was created.[157]

(3) Official searches

Although a purchaser may search in a register himself,[158] it is usual to obtain an official search.[159] Upon receipt of a requisition (as it is called) the registrar, after making the search, issues an official certificate, which is conclusive in favour of the purchaser.[160] If another charge is registered by a third person between the time when the certificate is issued and the time when the purchase is completed by the certificate holder, the registration does not affect the latter, provided that he completes his purchase within 15 days of the issue of the certificate.[161]

(c) Effect of failure to register

The failure to register a land charge does not affect the original parties to the transaction; as between them it remains valid. The effect as far as third parties are concerned is not, however, uniform. We have already seen the effect in connection with Classes A and B.

Classes C, D and F merit more detailed treatment. The effect of a failure to register these classes of land charges is as follows:

(a) Puisne mortgages (C(i))

Limited owners' charges (C(ii))

General equitable charges (C(iii))

Spouse or civil partner's right of occupation (F)

are void against:

a purchaser of the land charged with it, or of any interest in such land, unless the land charge is registered in the appropriate register before the completion of the purchase.[162]

'Purchaser' is defined in the Land Charges Act 1972[163] as:

unless the context otherwise requires, ... any person (including a mortgagee or lessee) who, for valuable consideration, takes any interest in land or in a charge on land.

---

[157] Ibid, s 11(3).   [158] Ibid, s 9.   [159] Ibid, s 10.

[160] Ibid, s 10(4). To be effective, registration must be in the correct full name of the estate owner. If it is not, a clear certificate as a result of an official search against the correct name will not bind a purchaser. 'But if there be registration in what may fairly be described as a version of the full names of the vendor, albeit not a version that is bound to be discovered on a search in the correct full names, we would not hold it a nullity against someone who does not search for all, or who (as here) searches in the wrong name': *Oak Co-operative Building Society v Blackburn* [1968] Ch 730, 743 (Russell LJ); (1968) 31 MLR 705. See too *Du Sautoy v Symes* [1967] Ch 1146; *Horrill v Cooper* (1998) 78 P & CR 336. On liability where an erroneous certificate is issued, see *Ministry of Housing and Local Government v Sharp* [1970] 2 QB 223; *Coats Patons (Retail) Ltd v Birmingham Corp* (1971) 69 LGR 356; *Diligent Finance Co Ltd v Alleyne* (1972) 23 P & CR 346; LCA 1972, s 10(6). In 2009–10 the Land Registry met one claim (for £74,889.68) from its indemnity fund for a land charges error: Land Registry Annual Report 2009–10, p 20.

[161] Ibid, s 11(5), (6)(a).   [162] Ibid, s 4(5), (8).   [163] Ibid, s 17(1).

'Valuable consideration' is widely interpreted and includes the consideration of marriage, and may be inadequate or even nominal.[164] The effect of the words 'any interest' is that a purchaser even of an equitable interest in the land affected takes free from these charges if unregistered, irrespective of whether he has actual notice or not.

(b) Estate contracts (C(iv))
    Restrictive covenants (D(ii))
    Equitable easements (D(iii))

are void against:

> a purchaser for money or money's worth...of a legal estate in the land charged with it, unless the land charge is registered in the appropriate register before the completion of the purchase.[165]

(c) Inland Revenue charge (D(i)) is void, as in the case of charges listed in (b) above, against

> a purchaser for money or money's worth...of a legal estate in the land charged with it, unless the land charge is registered in the appropriate register before the completion of the purchase

but in this case the definition of 'purchaser' is significantly narrower:[166]

> a purchaser in good faith for consideration in money or money's worth other than a nominal consideration and includes a lessee, mortgagee or other person who for such consideration acquires an interest in the property in question.

The purchaser here must be in good faith; the consideration of marriage is excluded, and so is nominal consideration.

It therefore follows that the four charges in (b) and (c), even if unregistered, bind a purchaser of an equitable interest whether he has notice or not.[167] Again, a purchaser even of a legal estate whose title is supported only by a marriage consideration, cannot rely upon the omission to register.

Subject to these distinctions, the general effect of the non-registration of an interest that is registrable as a land charge is that it is void against a purchaser for value of an interest in the land. It is immaterial that a purchaser has actual knowledge of the

---

[164] *Midland Bank Trust Co Ltd v Green* [1981] AC 513, 532; *Nurdin & Peacock plc v D B Ramsden & Co Ltd* [1999] 1 EGLR 119.

[165] LCA 1972, s 4(6).

[166] Ibid, s 4(6), as amended by FA 1975, s 52, Sch 12, para 18(5); ITA 1984, s 276, Sch 8, para 3(2); FA 1986, s 100(1)(b); incorporating the definition of 'purchaser' from ITA 1984, s 272.

[167] *McCarthy and Stone Ltd v Julian S Hodge & Co Ltd* [1971] 1 WLR 1547, M & B p 76 (unregistered estate contract held to have priority over subsequent equitable mortgage).

unregistered interest, and this is so even if the land is conveyed to him expressly subject to it.[168] As Harman J said in *Hollington Bros Ltd v Rhodes*:[169]

> It appears at first glance wrong that a purchaser, who knows perfectly well of rights subject to which he is expressed to take, should be able to ignore them ... It seems to me, however, that this argument cannot prevail having regard to the words in section 13(2) of the Land Charges Act 1925[170] ... The fact is that it was the policy of the framers of the 1925 legislation to get rid of equitable rights of this sort unless registered.[171]

The House of Lords adopted a similar approach in *Midland Bank Trust Co Ltd v Green*,[172] when considering the effect of failure to register an estate contract. Lord Wilberforce said:[173]

> The case is plain. The Act is clear and definite. Intended as it was to provide a simple and understandable system for the protection of title to land, it should not be read down or glossed: to do so would destroy the usefulness of the Act. Any temptation to remould the Act to meet the facts of the present case on the supposition that it is a hard one and that justice requires it, is, for me at least, removed by the consideration that the Act itself provides a simple and effective protection for persons in [the son's] position—viz—by registration.

In that case:

> a father granted to his son a 10-year option to purchase the farm of which the son was his tenant. The option was not registered as an estate contract. Later the father, wishing to deprive the son of his option, conveyed the farm, then worth about £40,000 to the mother for £500. When the son found this out, he registered the option and purported to exercise it.

It was held that the mother was a purchaser for money or money's worth and therefore the option was void against her.[174] It was immaterial that she had given inadequate (or even nominal) consideration and might have intended to defeat the unregistered interest. There was no requirement of good faith in the definition of a purchaser in the Land Charges Act, and, even though it existed in other definitions in

---

168 LPA 1925, s 199(1)(i).

169 [1951] 2 TLR 691, 695, M & B p 81. An unregistered registrable interest is not always void and unenforceable owing to lack of registration (eg a pending land action: LCA 1972, s 5(7): in such case a purchaser with express notice is bound; above, p 1055). Such an interest may also be binding (a) by estoppel: *Taylors Fashions Ltd v Liverpool Victoria Trustees Co Ltd* [1982] QB 133n, M & B p 1012; above, p 910; (b) by failure to plead the non-registration when sued: *Balchin v Buckle*, The Times, 1 June 1982 ('One would have thought that the purchaser could waive its effect and agree to be bound by the covenant (Class D(ii)). If he chose, whether from incompetence of his own or his legal advisers or from gentlemanly consideration for the rights or convenience of others, to be bound by the covenant or not to raise the point that it was void, there was no reason why the court should raise the point for him': Stephenson LJ). But he is not bound by a bare trust 'which is merely an equitable consequence of a specifically enforceable contract of sale': *Lloyds Bank plc v Carrick* [1996] 4 All ER 630; (1996) 112 LQR 549 (P Ferguson); [1996] Conv 295 (MP Thompson); [1997] CLJ 32 (M Oldham); [1996] All ER Rev 257 (PJ Clarke); (1998) 61 MLR 486 (N Hopkins).

170 Now LCA 1972, s 4(6).   171 See, however, [1982] Conv 213 (M Friend and J Newton), 215–17.

172 [1981] AC 513, M & B p 72.   173 Ibid, 528.

174 *Lloyds Bank plc v Carrick* [1996] 4 All ER 630, above, p 146.

the 1925 legislation,[175] it should not be imported into that Act. There was no need to analyse a purchaser's motives.[176]

(d) Summary[177]

In unregistered conveyancing the Land Charges Act 1972 therefore plays a major part in enabling a purchaser to discover whether certain rights will bind him. The effect of the Act is automatic: if a registrable interest is registered, it binds; if not, in general a purchaser for value of an interest in the land takes free from it. The system of registration of charges has largely superseded the old doctrine of the bona fide purchaser,[178] and therefore many of the risks for the purchaser that would arise from the doctrine of constructive notice have been mitigated. But because the list of charges that are registrable under the Land Charges Act is specific and not comprehensive, there is still a residual category of equitable interests that are not registrable. As we shall see below, some of these will be overreachable and, if overreached, will thereby not bind a purchaser. But if the interest is not overreachable or, if overreachable, not in fact overreached, it will bind a purchaser unless he is a bona fide purchaser for value of the legal estate without notice.[179] Interests that are not overreachable, but for which no provision is made in the Land Charges Act for registration, include a restrictive covenant entered into before 1926[180] and an equity by estoppel.[181]

The importance of the Land Charges register is declining now that the system of registration of title under the Land Registration Acts 1925 and 2002 has been extended throughout the country. But its importance will continue until the title to every parcel of land in England and Wales has been registered.

(2) Other Registers

(a) Local land charges registers

These are maintained under the Local Land Charges Act 1975[182] by all district councils in England and county or county borough councils in Wales, and also by London

---

[175] LPA 1925, s 205(1)(xxi); SLA 1925, s 117(1)(xxi); AEA 1925, s 55(1)(xviii); LRA 1925, s 3(xxi).

[176] [1981] AC 513, 530. The 'Green saga', which 'bids fair to rival in time and money the story of *Jarndyce v Jarndyce*' (see [1980] Ch 590, 622 (Lord Denning MR)), continued. For the liability of the solicitor for failing to advise the son to register the option and for failing to register it, see *Midland Bank Trust Co Ltd v Hett, Stubbs & Kemp* [1979] Ch 384; and for conspiracy between husband and wife, see *Midland Bank Trust Co Ltd v Green (No 3)* [1982] Ch 529. For a full review of all three cases by Sir Peter Oliver, who tried them at first instance, see *The Green Saga* (1983) Child & Co Oxford Lecture. See also [1981] CLJ 213 (C Harpum); (1981) 97 LQR 518 (B Green).

[177] For a diagram summarising the circumstances in which third-party rights will bind a transferee in unregistered land, and therefore showing the place of the registration of land charges under the Land Charges Act 1972, see above, p 144.

[178] Above, pp 83–91.   [179] Above, p 130.

[180] Above, p 740.   [181] Above, p 920.

[182] LLC Rules 1977 (SI 1977 No 985), as amended by LLC(A) Rules 1978 (SI 1978 No 1638); 1995 (SI 1995 No 260); 2003 (SI 2003 No 2502); Transfer of Tribunal Functions (Lands Tribunal and Miscellaneous Amendments) Order 2009 (SI 2009 No 1307). The Act came into force on 1 August 1977 and replaced LCA

boroughs and the Common Council of the City of London.[183] They differ from those kept at the Land Registry in that the charges are registered against the land and not against the name of the estate owner; they relate both to registered and to unregistered land[184] and are of public rather than a private nature.[185] Local land charges are a heterogeneous collection[186] and include charges for securing money recoverable by local authorities under public health legislation, and prohibitions of or restriction on the user of land imposed by a local authority, Minister of the Crown or a Government department.

The Act made a significant change in the effect of the non-registration of a local land charge. Section 10[187] provides that failure to register such a charge in the local land charges register shall not affect the enforcement of the charge, but that a purchaser[188] shall be entitled to compensation[189] for any loss suffered by him by reason that the charge was not registered, or was not shown as registered by an official search certificate.[190] This follows a recommendation by the Law Commission that observed that the overwhelming majority of local land charges are created in the public interest, and that it is usually inappropriate that lack of registration or non-disclosure in an official certificate of search should affect their enforceability.[191]

(b) Companies register

This is a register maintained under the Companies Act 2006, by the Registrar of Companies, of charges created by a company on land or any interest in land (other than a charge for any rent or other periodical sum issuing out of land).[192] Registration

---

1925, s 15 and other sections set out in LCA 1972, s 18, Sch 4. See Law Com No 62, *Local Land Charges* (1974); Garner, *Local Land Charges*, which has a useful table of all local land charges arranged alphabetically (pp 183–205). For local authority search forms, see CON 29R and 29O, printed in Silverman, *Conveyancing Handbook*, Appendix III. Forms CON 29DW (standard drainage and water enquries) and 29M (coal mining and brine subsidence claim search) may be addressed to the water company and the Coal Authority respectively.

[183] LLCA 1975, s 3(1), amended by Local Government (Wales) Act 1994, Sch 16, para 49. The area of the Common Council of the City of London includes the Inner Temple and the Middle Temple: s 3(4).

[184] Below, pp 1102, 1103.

[185] For an exception, see the notice under the Rights of Light Act 1959, s 2; above, p 681.

[186] LLCA 1975, ss 1, 2. A condition or limitation subject to which planning permission is granted is excluded: s 2(e). See the recommendation of the Second Report of the Conveyancing Committee (1985) for a more comprehensive Local Land Charges Register by consolidating the Commons Register with it.

[187] As amended by Local Government (Miscellaneous Provisions) Act 1982, s 34.

[188] LLCA 1975, s 10(3)(a) defines a purchaser as a person who, for valuable consideration, acquires any interest in land or the proceeds of sale of land; and this includes a lessee or mortgagee.

[189] *Pound v Ashford BC* [2003] EWHC 1088 (Ch), [2004] 1 P & CR 2 (criteria for awarding compensation).

[190] Under LCA 1925, s 15, a local land charge was void against a purchaser for money or money's worth of a legal estate in the land affected, unless registered before completion of the purchase.

[191] Law Com No 62, *Local Land Charges* (1974), para 90. See also paras 52–4.

[192] CA 2006, s 860(7)(a). The main office of Companies House is at Crown Way, Cardiff. Records can also be searched in the public search room at the Companies House London Information Centre at Bloomsbury Street, London. Between 1999 and 2005 there was a very significant shift to electronic searches of the register (eg by e-mail or online viewing): Companies House Annual Report and Accounts 2004/05, p 34, and almost 100 per cent of company searches are now made electronically: Companies House Annual Report and Accounts 2008/9, p 48. All documents filed since April 1995 are available electronically (in the case of

on this register of a charge created by a company before 1970, or so created at any time as a floating charge, is sufficient in place of registration in the Land Charges Register and has the same effect. A charge created by a company on or after 1 January 1970, other than a floating charge, must be registered at the Land Charges Registry if it is to bind a purchaser.[193] If it is to bind a liquidator, administrator or creditor of the company it must also be registered in the Companies Charges Register within 21 days of its creation.[194] These provisions also apply with appropriate modifications to similar charges created by a limited partnership.[195]

B OVERREACHING

In certain circumstances, the conveyance will overreach equitable interests. The detail of overreaching, which applies in both unregistered land and registered land, will be considered in detail in Chapter 28.[196] Here it is sufficient to notice that overreachable interests include equitable beneficial interests arising under a strict settlement under the Settled Land Act 1925 or under a trust of land under the Trusts of Land and Appointment of Trustees Act 1996;[197] and that as long as the statutory mechanism for overreaching is followed, the conveyance of the legal estate overreaches the equitable interests: that is the transferee takes the legal estate free of the interests, even if he knows about them; and the interests of the beneficiaries exist only in the capital money paid by the transferee as the price of the transfer. The statutory mechanism for overreaching depends upon the circumstances. In the case of settled land, the tenant for life in whom the legal estate is vested has the power to convey it and so to overreach interests under the settlement, but any capital money arising on the sale must be paid to the trustees of the settlement or into court; and (except were the trusteeship of

hard copy documents, scanned copies or microfiches are available). A company must also keep available for inspection a copy of every instrument creating a registrable charge, and every limited company must keep available for inspection a register of charges: CA 2006, ss 875, 876. See generally McCormack, *Registration of Company Charges* (3rd edn, 2009); *Gore-Browne on Companies*, ch 31.

[193] LCA 1972, s 3(7), (8), as amended by SI 2009 No 1941, Sch 1, para 23. See *Property Discount Corp Ltd v Lyon Group Ltd* [1981] 1 WLR 300 (registration in companies register held sufficient, even though it was not in name of estate owner as required by LCA 1972, s 3(1)); above, p 1060; [1982] Conv 43 (DM Hare and T Flanagan).

[194] CA 2006, ss 860, 870, 874. Failure to register is a criminal offence committed by the company and every officer of it who is in default: s 860(4). On the registration of charges on property of overseas companies, see CA 2006, s 1052 and Overseas Companies (Execution of Documents and Registration of Charges) Regulations 2009 (SI 2009 No 1917), Part 3.

[195] Limited Partnerships Regulations (Application of Companies Act 2006) Regulations 2009 (SI 2009 No 1804), Part 9.

[196] Below, pp 1113–22.

[197] Some legal interests arising under a strict settlement may be overreached by a conveyance of the settled land: below, p 1117, n 302; but many equitable interests in the land that is subject to a strict settlement or a trust of land (eg leases, easements, profits, estate contracts, and restrictive covenants—which cannot be effectively transferred into money) are not overreachable: below, pp 1114, 1118, 1120.

the settlement is held by a trust corporation) there must be at least two trustees.[198] In the case of a trust of land, it is the trustees who hold the legal estate and therefore have the power to overreach on a conveyance, but again the statutory overreaching mechanism requires any capital money arising to be paid to at least two trustees (or a trust corporation), or into court.[199] Mortgagees exercising their power of sale, and personal representatives acting under a will or intestacy, also have statutory powers to overreach by their conveyances, although in such cases it is not necessary, as in the case of strict settlements and trusts of land, that there should be at least two mortgagees or personal representatives to enter into the conveyance or receive any capital money.[200]

[198] LPA 1925, s 2(1)(i); SLA 1925, ss 18(1)(b), 117(1)(xxx); below, pp 1118–19.
[199] Ibid, s 2(1)(ii), (2), 27; below, p 1114.   [200] Ibid, s 2(1)(iii), 27(2); below, p 1121.

28

REGISTERED CONVEYANCING[1]

Summary

---

[1] For the current regime in relation to registered land under LRA 2002, see Ruoff and Roper, *Registered Conveyancing* (2003 looseleaf edn); Harpum and Bignell, *Registered Land: The New Law* (2002) and *Registered Land: Law and Practice under the Land Registration Act 2002* (2004); Wolstenholme and Cherry's *Annotated Land Registration Act 2002* (2004), which contains LRA 1925 and 2002, and LRR 1925 and 2003; Wontner's *Guide to Land Registry Practice* (22nd edn, 2009); *Blackstone's Guide to the Land Registration Act 2002* (2002); Cooke, *The New Law of Land Registration* (2003); Current Law Statutes 2002 (ch 9) annotated by PH Kenny; [2002] Conv 11 (E Cooke); [2003] Conv 136 (M Dixon); Law Com No 254, *Consultative Document on Land Registration for the Twenty-First Century* (1998); Law Com No 271, *Land Registration for the Twenty-First Century—a Conveyancing Revolution* (2001). The Land Registry produces Practice Guides on many aspects of its practice and procedure, and the Chief Land Registrar publishes an Annual Report; the current versions can be viewed on the Land Registry web site: www.landreg.gov.uk. For the Land Registry, see LRA 2002, Part 10 and Sch 7; R & R, paras 2.001–2.002; H & B, Part 8; and for the new office of Adjudicator, whose function is to determine contested applications to the registrar that cannot be disposed of by agreement between the parties, see LRA 2002, Part 11 and Sch 9; Adjudicator to Her Majesty's Land Registry (Practice

I INTRODUCTION

We have already considered the system of registered conveyancing in outline.[2] We must now discuss it in more detail. This chapter explains the current regime under the Land Registration Act 2002 and the Land Registration Rules 2003, which came into force on 13 October 2003,[3] although reference will be made where appropriate to the earlier regime under the Land Registration Act 1925, either by way of comparison and contrast, or because the new regime carries over principles from the old that render decisions on the 1925 Act still relevant to the interpretation of the new Act. For a detailed discussion of the 1925 Act, however, reference must be made to the 16th edition of this book.[4]

II THE REGISTER

A SCOPE OF TITLE REGISTRATION

The Land Registration Act 2002 carries over the register that had been built up under the 1925 Act,[5] although it redefines the scope of titles that may now be registered. No

---

and Procedure) Rules 2003 (SI 2003 No 2171), amended by SI 2008 No 1731; R & R, para 2.004; H & B, Part 7; *Jayasinghe v Liyanage* [2010] EWHC 265 (Ch), [2010] 1 WLR 2106 (reviewing the jurisdiction of the Adjudicator); *Silkstone v Tatnall* [2010] EWHC 1627 (Ch), [2010] 3 EGLR 25 (objector cannot withdraw objection unilaterally once dispute referred to Adjudicator).

For the law as it used to be under LRA 1925 and before LRA 2002, see Ruoff and Roper, *Law and Practice of Registered Conveyancing* (1991 looseleaf edn, updated to 2002 before its replacement by the new 2003 looseleaf edn); Ruoff and Pryer, *Concise Land Registration Handbook* (1990); Wolstenholme and Cherry, *Conveyancing Statutes* (13th edn, 1972), vol 6; Barnsley, *Conveyancing Law and Practice* (4th edn, 1996), chs 2, 3, 4, 11, 15; Potter, *Principles and Practice of Conveyancing under the Land Registration 1925* (1934; 2nd edn, 1948); Brickdale and Stewart-Wallace, *The Land Registration Act 1925* (4th edn, 1939).

For earlier Reports of the Law Commission on Land Registration, see Law Com No 125, *First Report: Identity and Boundaries, Conversion of Title, the Treatment of Leases and the Minor Interests Index* (1983); Law Com No 148, *Second Report: Inspection of the Register* (1985); Law Com No 158, *Third Report: Overriding Interests, Rectification and Indemnity and Minor Interests* (1987); [1987] Conv 334 (RJ Smith). The recommendations on the last three topics of the 1983 Report were implemented in LRA 1986, and the 1985 Report was implemented in LRA 1988. Law Com No 173, *Fourth Report on Land Registration* (1988) presented a Land Registration Bill incorporating the recommendations of the third report and 'is a modern, and we hope, simpler version of the 1925 Act'. In advance of this, the Law Commission published in 1995 a *First Report on the Implementation of its Third and Fourth Reports* (Law Com No 235); and this was implemented in LRA 1997.

[2] Above, pp 131 ff.   [3] SI 2003 No 1725; SI 2003 No 1417, r 1.   [4] Pp 100–8, 855–76.
[5] LRA 2002, s 1(1). The register may be kept in electronic and/or paper form: LRR 2003, r 2(1), although the last uncomputerised register was converted in 2003–04, and the Land Register is now fully electronic: Land Registry, Annual Report 2004–05, p 53.

change is made to the principle that only legal estates and interests may be registered with an individual register. But now the list of registrable estates is:[6]

    (i) a legal estate in land (the fee simple and certain leases);

    (ii) a rentcharge;[7]

    (iii) a franchise;[8]

    (iv) a profit à prendre in gross.[9]

Franchises and profits à prendre are now registrable for the first time with separate titles. Manors, which were registrable under the 1925 Act, are no longer registrable.[10] In the following sections we shall focus on the registration of freehold and leasehold estates in land, which form the vast majority of registered titles.

B ARRANGEMENT OF THE REGISTER

The individual register for each registered estate has a separate title number, and is divided into three parts.[11] The *property register* must contain a description of the registered estate, by reference to a plan,[12] together with certain other matters such as

---

[6] LRA 2002, s 2(a), 3(1); LRR 2003, r 2(2). A legal charge over a registered estate can also be registered but not as a separate title.

[7] Above, Ch 20.

[8] A 'royal privilege or branch of the royal prerogative subsisting in the hands of a subject by grant from the King': *Spook Erection Ltd v Secretary of State for the Environment* [1989] QB 300, 305 (Nourse LJ). The most important franchise is that of the market. See Land Registry Practice Guide 18; *R (Corporation of London) v Secretary of State for the Environment, Food and Rural Affairs* [2006] UKHL 30, [2006] 1 WLR 1721 (Covent Garden market, now operated under statutory authority).

[9] Ie a profit without a dominant tenement: above p 702.

[10] LRR 1925, rr 50, 51. A manor that was registered under LRA 1925 may now be removed from the register on the application of the proprietor: LRA 2002, s 119. See generally Land Registry Practice Guide 22.

[11] LRR 2003, r 4(1), (2). If an entry in the register refers to a plan or other document the registrar must keep the original or a copy: ibid, r 4(3). The tripartite register follows the pattern set by LRA 1925; above, p 135. There is also (a) an index that records all registered estates and land affected by any caution against first registration: LRA 2002, s 68; LRR 2003, r 10; (b) an index of proprietors' names: LRR 2003, r 11; (c) the day list showing the date and time at which every pending application was made and of every application for an official search with priority under LRR 2003, r 147: ibid, r 12; (d) a register of cautions against first registration: LRA 2002, s 19. For a specimen extract from the register, see M & B pp 127–30.

[12] Ibid, r 5(1)(a). No plan is required for a registered profit à prendre. See also LRA 2002, s 60: boundary shown for purposes of the register is a general boundary and does not determine the exact line of the boundary, which may, however, be fixed in accordance with s 60(3), (4); LRR 2003, rr 117–123, amended by LR(A)R 2008, SI 2008 No 1919, Sch 1, para 44; R & R, ch 5; Law Com No 271, *Registered Land for the Twenty-First Century* (2001), paras 9.9–9.15; *Chadwick v Abbotswood Properties Ltd* [2004] EWHC 1058 (Ch), [2005] 1 P & CR 10 (reviewing the authorities). See also s 61 (accretion and diluvion; on which, see *Southern Centre of Theosophy Inc v State of South Australia* [1982] AC 706, 716 (Lord Wilberforce)).

See *Alan Wibberley Building Ltd v Insley* [1999] 1 WLR 894, 895 (Lord Hoffmann): 'boundary disputes are a particularly painful form of litigation. Feelings run high and disproportionate amounts of money are spent. Claims to small and valueless pieces of land are pressed with the zeal of Fortinbras's army'.

easements benefiting the registered estate.[13] The *proprietorship register* must state the class of title,[14] the name and address of the proprietor, and certain other matters such as restrictions affecting the disposition of the estate, a note of positive or indemnity covenants affecting the estate, and (where practicable) the price paid on the most recent change of proprietor.[15] The *charges register* must contain, where appropriate, details of leases, charges and any other interests that adversely affect the registered estate, as well as a range of other matters.[16]

C INSPECTION OF THE REGISTER

The registers of title, documents that are referred to in the registers, and the register of cautions against first registration[17] are open to the public. Any person may inspect them and make copies of them, although certain documents that contain prejudicial information may be excluded.[18] A purchaser may make an application for an official search with priority: in this case, any entry made in the register during the priority period relating to his application is postponed to any entry made in pursuance of it.[19]

III FIRST REGISTRATION OF TITLE

A COMPULSORY REGISTRATION

We have seen[20] that in 1990 compulsory registration was at last extended to the whole of England and Wales; and that, in pursuance of the policy of eventually producing a complete register of the title to the whole of the territory, certain transactions with unregistered land have been defined by successive enactments as requiring the title

---

[13] LRR 2003, r 5(1)(b), as amended by LR(A)R 2008, Sch 1, para 1. The property register of a registered leasehold estate must contain particulars of the lease to enable it to be identified, and any registered rentcharge, franchise or profit à prendre that was created by an instrument must, where practicable, contain particulars to enable the instrument to be identified: rr 6, 7, amended by LR(A)R 2008, Sch 1, para 3.

[14] Below, p 1076.

[15] LRR 2003, r 8, amended by LR(A)R 2008, Sch 1, para 4. The reference to the price is removed if there is a change in the register of title that the registrar considers would result in the entry being misleading: r 8(3).

[16] Ibid, r 9, amended by LR(A)R 2008, Sch 1, para 5.   [17] Above, n 1079.

[18] LRA 2002, ss 66–7; LRR 2003, rr 133–8, amended by LR(A)R 2008, Sch 1, paras 46–48; Land Registry Practice Guide 11. For the problems of potential fraud arising from the right for the public to inspect the register, see (2008) 124 LQR 351 (P Matthews); Land Registry Practice Guide 67.

[19] LRA 2002, ss 70, 72; LRR 2003, rr 147–154. An official search may also be made without priority: r 155. For the priority period, see r 131 (broadly, 30 business days excluding weekends). Searches may be made by post, telephone, fax, electronically or orally at a Land Registry Customer Information Centre. See generally Land Registry Practice Guide 12.

[20] Above, p 131.

to be placed on the register. Under the Land Registration Act 2002, these triggers for compulsory registration are:[21]

(a) the transfer[22] of a 'qualifying estate'—that is an unregistered legal freehold or leasehold that (at the time of the transfer, grant or creation) has more than seven years to run;[23]

(b) the transfer of an unregistered legal estate in land in circumstances where section 171A of the Housing Act 1985 applies (disposal by landlord that leads to a person no longer being a secure tenant);

(c) the grant out of a qualifying estate of an estate in land (i) for a term of years absolute of more than seven years from the date of the grant, and (ii) for valuable or other consideration, by way of gift or in pursuance of an order of any court;[24]

(d) the grant out of a qualifying estate of an estate in land for a term of years absolute to take effect in possession after the end of the period of three months beginning with the date of the grant;

(e) the grant of a lease in pursuance of Part 5 of the Housing Act 1985 (the right to buy) out of an unregistered legal estate in land;

(f) the grant of a lease out of an unregistered legal estate in land in such circumstances as are mentioned in paragraph (b) above;

(g) the creation of a protected first legal mortgage of a qualifying estate.[25]

From 2002 until 2005 the Land Registry had as a strategic objective the creation of a Land Register with comprehensive content and national coverage by 2012,[26] although this has now been replaced by the setting of annual targets for increasing the total area of freehold land that is on the register.[27] The operation of these triggers for compulsory registration will not alone achieve a comprehensive register, since there are very many

[21] LRA 2002, s 4(1).

[22] This includes a transfer for valuable or other consideration, by way of gift or in pursuance of an order of any court, or by means of an assent (including a vesting assent), or giving effect to a partition of land subject to a trust of land, and certain transfers by a deed or vesting order on the appointment of a new trustee: s 4(1)(a), (aa), amended by LRA 2002 (Amendment) Order 2008 (SI 2008 No 2872), art 2; but does not include a transfer by operation of law: s 4(3); nor the assignment of a mortgage term, nor the assignment or surrender of a lease to the owner of the immediate reversion where the term is to merge in that reversion: s 4(4). On 'valuable consideration', see s 4 (6), 132(1). A transfer by way of gift includes a transfer or grant (a) constituting a trust under which the settlor does not retain the whole of the beneficial interest (thus excluding a transfer to trustees on bare trust), or (b) uniting the bare legal title and the beneficial interests under a trust that was so constituted: s 4(7).

[23] LRA 2002, s 4(2).   [24] But not including the grant of an estate by way of mortgage: s 4(5).

[25] Ie, a mortgage that takes effect on its creation as a mortgage to be protected by the deposit of documents relating to the mortgaged estate, and that ranks ahead of any other mortgages then affecting the mortgaged estate: s 4(8).

[26] Land Registry Annual Reports 2001–02, p 89; 2004–05, p 50.

[27] By 2010 the freehold title to 73 per cent of the area of England and Wales had been registered, comprising 22.5 million titles: Land Registry Annual Report 2009–10, p 12.

estates in land that are still unregistered and that, if not registered voluntarily,[28] are unlikely to be subject to any disposition triggering compulsory registration before then—such as land held by companies or by charities.[29] To this end, section 5 of the Land Registration Act empowers the Lord Chancellor by order to add further events as triggers for compulsory registration.[30]

B VOLUNTARY REGISTRATION

Even if no event occurs in relation to an unregistered estate that triggers compulsory registration, the owner[31] of a registrable estate[32] may apply to be registered as its proprietor.[33] To encourage voluntary registration, the fees payable to the Land Registry on first registration are reduced.[34]

C DEMESNE LAND OF THE CROWN. SPECIAL RULES[35]

The principles of registered conveyancing apply to the registration of legal *estates* in land. It will be recalled that, under the doctrine of estates peculiar to English land law, the holder of the estate does not own the land as such, but holds as tenant of the Crown.[36] A corollary of this is that the Crown does not hold an estate in 'demesne land'—land that it holds in its capacity as ultimate feudal overlord. Before the 2002 Act demesne land could not therefore be registered. Now, however,[37]

> Her Majesty may grant an estate in fee simple absolute in possession out of demesne land to Herself

---

[28] Below.

[29] In 2004–05 the Land Registry met with a number of large landholders, including the Crown Estate, Port of London Authority, Imperial College, a number of utility companies, Peak District National Park, Highways Agency, Blenheim Estate, Christ Church Oxford, and Boots plc to encourage them to consider the benefits of voluntary registration: Annual Report 2004–05, p 50. Since 2008–09 the Land Registry has set targets for voluntary registrations. The targets in 2008–09 (325 hectares of freehold land) and 2009–10 (310,000 hectares) were exceeded (633,316 and 456,534 hectares respectively), including the registration of Lincoln's Inn, Hereford Cathedral, Ironbridge, the 2012 Olympics site, and Salisbury Plain: Annual Reports 2008-09, pp 10, 13; 2009-10, pp 11, 15.

[30] The power is to be exercised by statutory instrument: s 128. Such an addition was made by Land Registration Act 2002 (Amendment) Order 2008 (SI 2008 No 2872), adding to the list a transfer giving effect to a partition of land subject to a trust of land, and a certain transfers by a deed or vesting order on the appointment of a new trustee: above, n 22.

[31] Or a person entitled to require the estate to be vested in him: s 3(2)(b).

[32] The fee simple absolute or a leasehold with more than seven years still to run (and as long as the right to possession is not discontinuous); or a rentcharge, franchise or profit à prendre in gross (in each case granted for an interest equivalent to a fee simple absolute or for a term of years with more than seven years still to run).

[33] LRA 2002, s 3.   [34] LR Fee Order 2009 (SI 2009 No 845), art 2(6), 6(3).

[35] R & R, ch 40; H & B, ch 6; Law Com No 271, *Registered Land for the Twenty-First Century* (2001), paras 11.2–11.38. See also LRA 2002 ss 81 (demesne land: cautions against first registration); 82 (escheat etc); 83 (Crown and Duchy land: representation); 84 (disapplication of requirements relating to Duchy land); 85 (bona vacantia).

[36] Above, pp 33 ff.   [37] LRA 2002, s 79(1).

and this will then be capable of being registered.[38]

D CLASSES OF TITLE[39]

As under the Land Registration Act 1925,[40] there are four different classes of title that may be entered on the proprietorship register; absolute, qualified, possessory and good leasehold.[41]

(1) Absolute Title

(a) Freehold estates

In the case of a freehold estate, a person may be registered with absolute title if the registrar is of the opinion that the person's title to the estate is such as a willing buyer could properly be advised by a competent professional adviser to accept, and in applying this test the registrar may disregard the fact that the title appears to be open to objection if he is of the opinion that the defect will not cause the holding under the title to be disturbed.[42] The registrar must therefore carry out a full investigation of the title as it exists under the old system of unregistered conveyancing for one last time before it is placed on the register, since he will be acting on behalf of the State in giving the guarantee of the status of the title by accepting it for registration.

The effect of first registration with absolute title is[43] to vest the freehold estate in the proprietor together with all interests subsisting for the benefit of the estate, and subject only to the following interests affecting the estate at the time of registration:

(a) interests that are the subject of an entry in the register in relation to the estate—notices, restrictions, or registered charges. If, on investigating the title to the (unregistered) estate, the registrar discovers that there are third party interests affecting the title, he will make such entries as are appropriate to protect the interest of the third party, so that the registered title continues to reflect the state of the title as it existed before registration;[44]

---

[38] This is a form of voluntary registration, since it takes effect only if Her Majesty then applies for registration within a prescribed period (normally two months): s 79(2)–(5). Other grants of a fee simple or of a leasehold for more than seven years out of demesne land are subject to compulsory registration: ibid, s 80. Cf [2010] Conv 300 (A Lyall) at 305 ('All that was necessary in order to provide for the registration of land in the royal demesne was to provide for it to be registered directly, as the sole exception to the registration of estates. That would be a more pragmatic and sensitive response to a purely technical problem, paying proper regard to the theory of tenure and the unique position of the monarch within it, rather than the meaningless gobbledegook of s 79(1)').

[39] On classes of title, see R & R, ch 6; H & B, ch 3; Law Com No 271, *Registered Land for the Twenty-First Century* (2001), paras 3.42–3.52; and on the effect of registration with each class of title, see R & R, paras 3.007–3.008; H & B, ch 4.

[40] Above, p 136.   [41] LRA 2002, ss 9, 10.

[42] Ibid, s 9(2), (3).   [43] Ibid, s 11(2)–(4).

[44] For details of entries on the register, see below, p 1097.

(b) unregistered interests that fall within any of the paragraphs of Schedule 1 to the Land Registration Act 2002 (unregistered interests that override first registration);[45] and

(c) interests acquired under the Limitation Act 1980[46] of which the proprietor has notice.[47]

If the proprietor is not entitled to the estate for his own benefit, or at least not solely for his own benefit—for example, if he is holds the legal estate on trust for himself and his wife[48]—then as between himself and the person(s) beneficially entitled to the estate, the estate is vested in him subject to their interests of which he has notice.[49]

(b) Leasehold estates

In the case of a leasehold, an absolute title may be registered only if the registrar approves not only the title to the leasehold itself, but also the lessor's title to grant the lease.[50]

The effect of first registration with absolute title is[51] to vest the leasehold estate in the proprietor together with all interests subsisting for the benefit of the estate, and subject to the same interests as in the case of the registration of the freehold with absolute title, but subject also to implied and express covenants, obligations and liabilities incident to the leasehold estate.[52]

(2) Good Leasehold Title

Good leasehold title is available only for leaseholds. Where a leaseholder cannot produce the title to the reversion,[53] he may be registered as the owner of a good leasehold title. The title to the leasehold interest is alone investigated and guaranteed by the Land Registry, if the registrar is of the opinion that the person's title to the estate is such as a willing buyer could properly be advised by a competent professional adviser to accept.[54]

---

[45] Below, pp 1100 ff. [46] Below, Ch 29.

[47] This is a significant change from LRA 1925, under which the rights of squatters bound the registered proprietor whether or not he had notice: H & B, paras 4.5–4.6; Explanatory Notes on the Land Registration Bill, cited Wolstenholme and Cherry, *Annotated Land Registration Act 2002*, para 3–011.

[48] It may also include a case where another party has an equity arising by proprietary estoppel: H & B, para 4.7.

[49] LRA 2002, s 11(5).

[50] Ibid, s 10(2). Again, the registrar may disregard possible objections if of the opinion that the defect will not cause the holding under the title to be disturbed: s 10(4).

[51] Ibid, s 12(2)–(5).

[52] The details of the covenants in the lease are not entered onto the register, but the lease itself (or a copy) forms part of the register and so can be inspected.

[53] If the reversion is already registered with absolute title, this will suffice. If not, the registrar must examine the title to the reversion if absolute title is sought to the leasehold estate.

[54] LRA 2002, s 10(3). Again, the registrar may disregard possible objections if of the opinion that the defect will not cause the holding under the title to be disturbed: s 10(4).

Registration with good leasehold title has the same effect as registration with absolute title, with the important exception that registration does not affect the enforcement of any estate, right or interest affecting, or in derogation of, the title of the lessor to grant the lease.[55]

(3) Qualified Title

Where the registrar is of the opinion that the person's title to the freehold estate can be established only for a limited period or subject to certain reservations that cannot be disregarded, he may register the person with qualified title.[56] Qualified title may also be registered in respect of a leasehold estate, when the examination of the title either of the lessor to the reversion, or of the lessee to the leasehold interest, discloses similar problems to those described above.[57]

Registration has the same effect as registration with absolute title, except that it does not affect the enforcement of any estate, right or interest that appears from the register to be excepted from the effect of registration.[58]

(4) Possessory Title

Possessory titles usually arise out of claims by squatters, and also where a title is lodged that is too weak for a better kind of title but not deserving of outright rejection—for example, where the owner has lost the title deeds. Possessory titles are mainly freeholds, although possessory leaseholds do exist. In either case, a person may be registered with possessory title if the registrar is of the opinion that the person is in actual possession of the land, or in receipt of the rents and profits of the land, by virtue of the estate, and that there is no other class of title with which be may be registered.[59]

The guarantee is a limited one, as the registration, whilst in other respects having the same effect as registration with absolute title, does not affect the enforcement of any estate, right or interest adverse to, or in derogation of, the proprietor's title subsisting or capable of arising at the time of the first registration.[60] In the case of a freehold or leasehold interest registered with a possessory title the guarantee covers, therefore, only dealings that take place after the registration and does not extend to the title prior to registration.

(5) Upgrading of Titles

The Land Registration Act 2002 provides for the upgrading of inferior titles to absolute or good leasehold titles, and of good leasehold to absolute.[61] If at any time the registrar

---

[55] Ibid, s 12(6).   [56] Ibid, s 9(4).   [57] Ibid, s 10(5).
[58] LRA 2002, ss 11(6) (freehold), 12(7) (leasehold).   [59] Ibid, ss 9(5) (freehold), 10(6) (leasehold).
[60] Ibid, ss 11(7) (freehold), 12(8) (leasehold); *Spectrum Investment Co v Holmes* [1981] 1 WLR 221; below, p 1159.
[61] LRA 2002, s 62. The effect of registration is not retrospective: s 63.

is satisfied as to the title to the estate, to the same standard as he is required to be satisfied on first registration,[62] then he may enter it as the superior title. In addition, where the title to a freehold or leasehold estate has been entered as possessory for at least 12 years,[63] the registrar may enter it as absolute or good leasehold if he is satisfied that the proprietor is in possession of the land. This reflects the idea that any existing rights adverse to the proprietor will have become barred under the Limitation Act 1980 no later than 12 years from the date of registration.[64]

E CAUTIONS AGAINST FIRST REGISTRATION

Any person who claims to have an interest in an unregistered legal estate[65] may apply for a caution against first registration of title to the estate.[66] The object is to ensure that on first registration his interest will be protected on the register. The caution gives the cautioner the right to be notified of the application and to object to it. It is a procedural device, and gives no substantive right.[67]

IV CONCLUSIVENESS OF THE REGISTER. ALTERATION AND RECTIFICATION

The fundamental principle of the system of registration of title is that the register is conclusive as to the legal title of the registered proprietor to the estate that is registered in his name. If the person registered as proprietor would not (apart from the registration) be the owner of the legal estate, the estate is deemed to be vested in him as a result of the registration.[68]

If, therefore, a person is registered by mistake, or if a transaction by which he claims to have acquired the estate is a nullity, the defect is cured by registration. As long as his name appears as registered proprietor, in the eyes of the law (and as far as third parties

---

[62] Ibid, s 62(8).

[63] The Lord Chancellor has power to amend the number by statutory instrument: ibid, ss 62(9), 128.

[64] Although the Limitation Act 1980 does not apply to registered land under LRA 2002, it does apply to matters excepted from the effect of registration (such as rights then existing superior to the possessory title of the registered proprietor). On adverse possession generally, see below, Ch 29.

[65] Ie an estate that qualifies for individual registration: an estate in land, a rentcharge, franchise, or profit à prendre in gross: LRA 2002, s 15(2).

[66] LRA 2002, s 15.

[67] LRR 2003, rr 39–53, amended by LR(A)R 2008, Sch 1, paras 11, 12; R & R, ch 11; H & B, ch 5; Law Com No 271, *Land Registration for the Twenty-First Century* (2001), paras 3.54–3.65. See also LRA 2002, ss 19 (register of cautions against first registration), 20, 21 (alteration of cautions register by court and by registrar). For transitional provisions, see Sch 12, paras 4, 14–17.

[68] LRA 2002, s 58(1), replacing LRA 1925, s 69(1). All the registration requirements must be met before the registration has effect: s 58(2); eg the registration of person as proprietor of a registered lease is not effective until a note has been entered also on the title to the reversion, if it is registered. Until satisfaction of the registration requirements, the transaction has effect only in equity: s 27(1); below, p 1093.

are concerned, who search the register) he is proprietor. However, this provision deals only with the legal estate, and does not determine to what equitable rights the registered owner's title may be subject.[69] Moreover, the Land Registration Act 2002 provides for the register to be altered in certain circumstances, to correct errors.

A RECTIFICATION UNDER THE 1925 ACT

The Land Registration Act 1925 made detailed provision for *rectification* of the register.[70] Under section 82 of the Land Registration Act 1925, the register could be rectified, inter alia, where the court so ordered upon deciding that any person was entitled to any estate, right or interest in the land,[71] where an entry had been obtained by fraud,[72] where two or more persons were by mistake registered as proprietors of the same property, where a legal estate had been registered in the name of a person who, if the land had not been registered, would not have been the estate owner,[73] or where, because of any error or omission in the register or because of any entry made under a mistake it would be deemed just to rectify it.[74] The *proprietor in possession*, however, was protected by the provision that rectification could only take place against him if:

(a) it was to give effect to an overriding interest,[75] or an order of the court,[76] or

---

[69] In *Malory Enterprises Ltd v Cheshire Homes (UK) Ltd* [2002] EWCA Civ 151, [2002] Ch 216 the CA went so far as to say that transfer that is a nullity was not a 'disposition' for the purposes of LRA 1925, s 20, and therefore the registration of the transferee as proprietor, though vesting the legal estate in him under LRA 1925, s 69 (the predecessor to LRA 2002, s 58), only vested the bare legal title on trust for the person entitled. See criticism by Harpum in Getzler (ed), *Rationalizing Property, Equity and Trusts: Essays in Honour of Edward Burn* (2003), ch 9; H & B, ch 15; [2009] Conv 127 (A Hill-Smith).

[70] See *Norwich and Peterborough Building Society v Steed* [1993] Ch 116, M & B p 145 for a full examination of the eight statutory grounds; Ruoff and Roper (1991 edn), ch 40; Farrand, *Contract and Conveyance* (2nd edn), pp 209–20; Barnsley, *Conveyancing Law and Practice*, ch 4. For further powers of rectification under LRR 1925, see rr 13 (clerical errors), 14 (registration in error of too much land), 131 (where power of disposing of registered land has become vested in some person other than the proprietor), 283 (correction of particulars of addresses), 284 (corrections of plans), 285 (alterations to resolve conflicting descriptions). See also Law Com No 271, *Land Registration for the Twenty-First Century* (2001), para 10.1; *Malory Enterprises Ltd v Cheshire Homes (UK) Ltd*, above, at [79] (there is no jurisdiction to order rectification with retrospective effect: Arden LJ); (2004) 119 LQR 31 (D Sheehan).

[71] *Chowood Ltd v Lyall (No 2)* [1930] 2 Ch 156; *Calgary and Edmonton Land Co Ltd v Discount Bank (Overseas) Ltd* [1971] 1 WLR 81; *Proctor v Kidman* (1986) 51 P & CR 67. See also *Spectrum Investment Co v Holmes* [1981] 1 WLR 221, below, p 1159; *Orakpo v Manson Investments Ltd* [1977] 1 WLR 347; affd on other grounds [1978] AC 95.

[72] *Argyle Building Society v Hammond* (1984) 49 P & CR 148 (transfer void for forgery); [1985] Conv 135 (A Sydenham); LRA 1925, s 114; cf *Norwich and Peterborough Building Society v Steed* [1993] Ch 116 (transfer voidable for fraud); (1993) 109 LQR 187 (RJ Smith); [1992] Conv 293 (C Davis). See also *Re Leighton's Conveyance* [1936] 1 All ER 667; affd [1937] Ch 149 (fraudulent misrepresentation and undue influence).

[73] *Chowood Ltd v Lyall (No 2)* [1930] 2 Ch 156.

[74] *Re Dances Way, West Town, Hayling Island* [1962] Ch 490 (notice of adverse easement cancelled).

[75] *Re Chowood's Registered Land* [1933] Ch 574, M & B p 160; *Epps v Esso Petroleum Co Ltd* [1973] 1 WLR 1071, M & B p 152.

[76] As added by AJA 1977, s 24(a); *Hayes v Nwajiaku* [1994] EGCS 106 (proprietor means proprietor of land, not of charge).

(b) he had caused or substantially contributed to the error or omission by fraud or lack of proper care,[77] or

(c) for any other reason, it would be unjust not to rectify the register against him.[78]

The principle that emerges is that a *purchaser* who bought registered land and remained in *possession* of it was guaranteed his possession, and rectification would only be ordered against him in exceptional circumstances.

B ALTERATION AND RECTIFICATION UNDER THE 2002 ACT[79]

The provisions have been recast under the Land Registration Act 2002 so as to reflect the modern practice in relation to rectification and amendment of the register. The essentials of the scheme of the 1925 Act are, however, maintained.

The basic concept is now *alteration* of the register; rectification is one form of alteration. The court may make an order for the alteration of the register for the purpose of correcting a mistake, bringing the register up to date, or giving effect to any estate, right or interests excepted from the effect of registration.[80] The registrar has similar powers, and may also alter the register to remove a superfluous entry.[81] It can therefore be seen that alteration of the register is a very general term that embraces both major changes and minor corrections to tidy up the register.

Rectification is defined[82] as an alteration that:

(a) involves the correction of a mistake; and

(b) prejudicially affects the title of a registered proprietor.[83]

In such a case, the court may not order, nor may the registrar make, any alteration to the register without the proprietor's consent in relation to land in his possession unless he has by fraud or lack of proper care caused or substantially contributed to the

---

[77] As substituted by AJA 1977, s 24(b). The original statutory provision had produced the undesirable result of rectification being ordered against a purchaser who innocently put forward a misleading description of property when applying for first registration of his title: *Re Deptford High Street (No 139)* [1951] Ch 884. See also *Re Seaview Gardens* [1967] 1 WLR 134.

[78] *Epps v Esso Petroleum Co Ltd*, above; *Hounslow LBC v Hare* (1990) 24 HLR 9; [1993] Conv 224 (J Martin); *Horrill v Cooper* (1998) 78 P & CR 336.

[79] R & R, ch 46; H & B, ch 22; Law Com No 271, *Land Registration for the Twenty-First Century* (2001), Part X; Land Registry Practice Guide 39.

[80] LRA 2002, Sch 4, para 2. The effect of alteration on priorities is prospective, not retrospective: ibid, para 8.

[81] Ibid, para 5. [82] Ibid, para 1.

[83] *Derbyshire CC v Fallon* [2007] EWHC 1326 (Ch), [2007] 3 EGLR 44 (not a case for rectification because no prejudice where boundary on land registry plan showed wrong title; correcting the plan would only give effect to actual property rights); criticised [2007] Conv 238.

mistake, or it would for any other reason be unjust for the alteration not to be made.[84] The protection of the proprietor in possession is therefore maintained.

C INDEMNITY[85]

Under the 1925 Act[86] right of indemnity—payment of compensation—was available to anyone suffering loss by reason of any rectification of the register, an error or omission on the register that was not rectified, the loss or destruction of any document lodged at the registry for inspection or safe custody, or an error in any official search.

Again, the Land Registration Act 2002 maintains the essential elements of the scheme, although the provisions are recast. Schedule 8, paragraph 1, sets out the eight grounds on which an indemnity may be paid for loss suffered by reason of:

(a) rectification of the register,

(b) a mistake whose correction would involve rectification of the register,

(c) a mistake in an official search,

(d) a mistake in an official copy,

(e) a mistake in a document kept by the registrar which is not an original and is referred to in the register,

(f) the loss or destruction of a document lodged at the registry for inspection or safe custody,

(g) a mistake in the cautions register, or

(h) failure by the registrar to perform his duty under section 50 (duty to give notice of the creation of a statutory charge).

It is important to notice that, compensation is paid when someone *suffers loss by reason of* a rectification, etc. Hence, when a purchaser bought registered land on part of which, unknown to the purchaser, a squatter had already established a title by adverse possession and rectification was ordered (because the right was an overriding interest), the purchaser was unable to obtain an indemnity under the 1925 Act because

---

[84] LRA 2002, Sch 4, paras 3, 6; *Sainsbury's Supermarkets Ltd v Olympia Homes Ltd* [2005] EWHC 1235 (Ch), [2006] 1 P & CR 17, M & B p 157; *James Hay Pension Trustees Ltd v Cooper Estates Ltd* [2005] EWHC 36 (Ch), [2005] All ER (D) 144 (Jan) (proprietor in possession was accidental owner of small piece of land it never intended to acquire, useful only to extract ransom payment: transfer and register rectified); *Barclays Bank plc v Guy* [2008] EWCA Civ 452, [2008] 2 EGLR 74 at [23] (charge properly executed and registered, but proprietor of charged land was itself not entitled to be registered as proprietor: claim by person entitled to be registered as proprietor for rectification of register by removal of the charge refused: no 'mistake' because mortgagee had no actual or 'Nelsonian' notice of the defect in mortgagor's title); *Baxter v Mannion* [2011] EWCA Civ 120, [2011] 2 All ER 574 (registration of squatter as proprietor reversed where adjudicator found 'mistake' in that occupier had not in fact been in adverse possession for the ten-year period required under LRA 2002, Sch 6, para 1, below, p 1161).

[85] R & R, ch 47; H & B, ch 23; Law Com No 271, *Land Registration for the Twenty-First Century* (2001), Part X; Land Registry Practice Guide 39.

[86] LRA 1925, s 83, as substituted by Land Registration Act 1997, s 2; (1997) 147 NLJ 925 (HW Wilkinson).

his loss was not 'by reason of the rectification' but had resulted from the purchase itself,[87] that is because he had purchased land from a vendor against whom a squatter had already obtained title so that the rectification made him no worse off than before. If someone still suffers loss, even though the register has been rectified in his favour, he can claim an indemnity.[88] If, however, a proprietor of a registered estate or charge claims in good faith under a disposition that is forged and the register is rectified against him, he is deemed to have suffered loss by reason of the rectification.[89] But no compensation is payable on account of any loss suffered by a claimant wholly or partly as a result of his fraud or wholly as a result of his own lack of proper care.[90] Where any loss is suffered by a claimant partly as a result of his own lack of proper care 'any indemnity payable to him is to be reduced to such extent as is fair having regard to his share in the responsibility for the loss'.[91]

Any fraud or lack of proper care on the part of a person from whom the claimant derives title (except by a disposition for valuable consideration that is registered or protected by an entry on the register) is to be treated as if it were that of the claimant.[92] An example is a donee or a devisee under a will.

For the purposes of limitation, the period under the Limitation Act 1980 is six years; the cause of action arises when the claimant knows, or but for his own default, might have known, of the existence of his claim.[93]

Finally, where indemnity has been paid in respect of any loss, the registrar is given rights to recover the amount paid from any person who caused or substantially contributed to the loss by his fraud and to enforce any right of action that the claimant would have had.[94]

A macabre example of a refusal to rectify leading to a true owner being given indemnity is provided by the case of the acid bath murderer, John Haigh.[95] Haigh forged the signature of a registered proprietor, was registered in his name and then, in that name, sold to an innocent purchaser for value. Rectification was not ordered as the purchaser was in possession. But the personal representatives of the real proprietor were compensated in full.

---

[87] *Re Chowood's Registered Land* [1933] Ch 574, M & B p 160; applied in *Re Boyle's Claim* [1961] 1 WLR 339. The Limitation Act 1980 is now, however, disapplied in relation to registered land: LRA 2002, s 96; below, p 1160.

[88] LRA 2002 Sch 8, para 1(1)(b), (3); H & B, para 23.4. The predecessor to this provision, LRA 1925, s 83(1)(b), was introduced by LRA 1997 so as to avoid a potential injustice arising from *Freer v Unwins Ltd* [1976] Ch 288 (where it was held that the rectification of the register of title to servient land by the entry of a notice of restrictive covenants does not operate retrospectively so as to bind a person taking under a prior registered disposition for valuable consideration). See (1976) 40 Conv (NS) 304 (FR Crane); 126 NLJ 523 (SM Cretney).

[89] Ibid, Sch 8, para 1(2)(b).   [90] Ibid, para 5(1).

[91] Ibid, para 5(2): in effect, contributory negligence, similar to the test under the Law Reform (Contributory Negligence) Act 1945.

[92] Ibid, para 5(3).   [93] Ibid, para 8.   [94] Ibid, para 10.

[95] Recounted in Ruoff and Roper (5th edn, 1986), p 71.

V DISPOSITIONS OF REGISTERED LAND

Once the title to an estate has been registered, the rules of unregistered conveyancing[96] become irrelevant, and the estate will thereafter be transferred or otherwise disposed of under the provisions of the Land Registration Act 2002.

A OWNER'S POWERS IN RELATION TO A REGISTERED ESTATE

The Act provides[97] that 'owner's powers' in relation to a registered estate consist of

(a) power to make a disposition of any kind permitted by the general law in relation to an interest of that description, other than a mortgage by demise or sub-demise, and

(b) power to charge the estate at law with the payment of money.

In other words, the registered proprietor has the same general powers of disposition as an unregistered estate owner—with the single exception that he cannot create a mortgage by demise.[98] The proprietor's right to exercise these powers is to be taken to be free from any limitation affecting the validity of the disposition, unless the limitation is reflected by an entry in the register or otherwise imposed by or under the Act.[99] This follows from the fundamental basis of the registration system that those who rely on the register can assume that its contents are true.

B THE MACHINERY OF TRANSFER OF REGISTERED LAND

(1) Pre-transfer Machinery

The preliminary inquiries and the contract of sale follow the pattern of unregistered conveyancing,[100] but the investigation of the title is radically different. No longer does the vendor need to trace the history of the transactions in which the estate has been involved, for the register is conclusive on the question of ownership.

The Land Registration Act 2002 makes no specific provision about the documents that the vendor must supply to the purchaser,[101] but the standard forms of contract

---

[96] Above, Ch 27.

[97] LRA 2002, s 23(1). See also s 23(2) (owner's powers in relation to a registered charge). The person entitled to exercise these powers is the registered proprietor or a person entitled to be registered as the proprietor of the estate: s 24.

[98] For the abolition in registered land of the (already obsolescent) mortgage by demise, see above, p 802.

[99] LRA 2002, s 26. This does not affect the lawfulness of any disposition (eg if it is in breach of trust, the trustee may be personally liable to the beneficiaries), but has effect to prevent the title of a disponee being questioned: s 26(3); H & B, paras 7.7, 7.8.

[100] Above, pp 950 ff.

[101] LRA 2002, Sch 10, para 2, provides that rules may make provision about the obligations with respect to proof of title, or perfection of title, of the seller under a contract for the transfer, or other disposition, for

conditions in common use[102] require the vendor at his own expense to supply official copy entries of the individual register, title plan and any other documents referred to in the register and kept by the registrar.

Requisitions on title follow the usual form[103] but where the title is absolute or good leasehold, they are limited to overriding interests[104] and other matters in respect of which the register is not conclusive. Possessory or qualified titles will require more careful investigation. Searches must be made of local land charges registers, because local land charges are overriding interests. But it will not be necessary to search the register of land charges under the Land Charges Act 1972,[105] as third-party rights that would appear there if the land were unregistered will appear on the register under the Land Registration Act 2002. The main search will therefore be of the register itself, through the official copy entries supplied by the vendor, or by the purchaser himself undertaking an official search with priority.[106]

(2) Form of Transfer

The Land Registration Act 2002[107] provides that a registrable disposition of a registered estate or charge only has effect if it complies with such requirements as to form and content as rules may provide. The Land Registration Rules 2003[108] prescribe a great many forms for particular purposes, including several forms for the transfer. The form to be used for the transfer of whole of a registered title is reproduced on pages 1086–8;[109] the following paragraphs explain certain of its provisions.

(a) Section 1: title number

The title number is the unique reference number for the individual register comprising the title. A registered lease has a different title number from the registered freehold out of which the lease was granted, because they are separate registered titles.

It should be noted that the section can be left blank, if the title is not yet registered—because the transfer form TR1 may be used for the conveyance of unregistered land that will be then subject to registration, as well as for the transfer of land that is already on the register.[110]

---

valuable consideration of a registered estate or charge. No such rules have, however, been made. LRA 1925, s 110, made detailed provision about the documents that a purchaser could require the vendor to produce.

[102] Standard Conditions of Sale (5th edn), para 4.1.2; Standard Commercial Property Conditions of Sale (2nd edn), para 6.1.2: above, p 954.

[103] Silverman, *Conveyancing Handbook*, paras D2.3; D3.   [104] Below, p 1100.

[105] Above, pp 1054 ff.   [107] S 25.

[106] On the effect of the search with priority, see above, p 1073.

[108] R 206, Sch 1, substituted by LR(A)R 2008, Sch 2. The forms are also available for downloading from the Land Registry web site. The prescribed form of wording and layout must be used, but the Regulations permit certain variations: rr 209–11, amended by LR(A)R 2008, Sch 1, paras 70–71. See generally Land Registry Practice Guide 46.

[109] Source acknowledgment: TR1 produced by Land Registry. © Crown copyright material is reproduced with the permission of Land Registry.

[110] Above, p 1053.

Land Registry
Transfer of whole of registered title(s)

If you need more room than is provided for in a panel, and your software allows, you can expand any panel in the form. Alternatively use continuation sheet CS and attach it to this form.

Leave blank if not yet registered.	**1** Title number(s) of the property:
Insert address including postcode (if any) or other description of the property, for example 'land adjoining 2 Acacia Avenue'.	**2** Property:
	3 Date:
Give full name(s).	**4** Transferor:
Complete as appropriate where the transferor is a company.	For UK incorporated companies/LLPs Registered number of company or limited liability partnership including any prefix: For overseas companies (a) Territory of incorporation: (b) Registered number in the United Kingdom including any prefix:
Give full name(s).	**5** Transferee for entry in the register:
Complete as appropriate where the transferee is a company. Also, for an overseas company, unless an arrangement with Land Registry exists, lodge either a certificate in Form 7 in Schedule 3 to the Land Registration Rules 2003 or a certified copy of the constitution in English or Welsh, or other evidence permitted by rule 183 of the Land Registration Rules 2003.	For UK incorporated companies/LLPs Registered number of company or limited liability partnership including any prefix: For overseas companies (a) Territory of incorporation: (b) Registered number in the United Kingdom including any prefix:
Each transferee may give up to three addresses for service, one of which must be a postal address whether or not in the UK (including the postcode, if any). The others can be any combination of a postal address, a UK DX box number or an electronic address.	**6** Transferee's intended address(es) for service for entry in the register:
	7 The transferor transfers the property to the transferee

Place 'X' in the appropriate box. State the currency unit if other than sterling. If none of the boxes apply, insert an appropriate memorandum in panel 11.	**8**	**Consideration**
		☐ The transferor has received from the transferee for the property the following sum (in words and figures):
		☐ The transfer is not for money or anything that has a monetary value
		☐ Insert other receipt as appropriate:
Place 'X' in any box that applies. Add any modifications.	**9**	**The transferor transfers with** ☐ full title guarantee ☐ limited title guarantee
Where the transferee is more than one person, place 'X' in the appropriate box. Complete as necessary.	**10**	**Declaration of trust. The transferee is more than one person and** ☐ they are to hold the property on trust for themselves as joint tenants ☐ they are to hold the property on trust for themselves as tenants in common in equal shares ☐ they are to hold the property on trust:
Insert here any required or permitted statement, certificate or application and any agreed covenants, declarations and so on.	**11**	**Additional provisions**

The transferor must execute this transfer as a deed using the space opposite. If there is more than one transferor, all must execute. Forms of execution are given in Schedule 9 to the Land Registration Rules 2003. If the transfer contains transferee's covenants or declarations or contains an application by the transferee (such as for a restriction), it must also be executed by the transferee.

12	Execution

WARNING
If you dishonestly enter information or make a statement that you know is, or might be, untrue or misleading, and intend by doing so to make a gain for yourself or another person, or to cause loss or the risk of loss to another person, you may commit the offence of fraud under section 1 of the Fraud Act 2006, the maximum penalty for which is 10 years' imprisonment or an unlimited fine, or both.

Failure to complete this form with proper care may result in a loss of protection under the Land Registration Act 2002 if, as a result, a mistake is made in the register.

Under section 66 of the Land Registration Act 2002 most documents (including this form) kept by the registrar relating to an application to the registrar or referred to in the register are open to public inspection and copying. If you believe a document contains prejudicial information, you may apply for that part of the document to be made exempt using Form EX1, under rule 136 of the Land Registration Rules 2003.

© Crown copyright (ref: LR/HO) 07/09

(b) Section 7: the transfer

This provision is deceptively simple. It is the principal provision of the form, which by its express terms transfers the title to the property to the transferee, although the legal title will pass only when the relevant registration requirements are satisfied.[111] However, by statute it has a larger effect.

A grant operates to pass the rights incidental to the land, such as easements and profits which have become attached to it. But since rights such as quasi-easements that have not become legally appurtenant to the land would not pass without special mention, it was usual, prior to 1882, to insert *general words*, which were framed widely enough to include all rights actually enjoyed by the vendor in respect of the land. Since 1881, however, unless a contrary intention is expressed, such *general words* are implied in every conveyance. Thus a conveyance[112] of land now operates, by virtue of the Law

---

[111] Below, p 1094.

[112] Defined at LPA 1925, s 205(1)(ii) in terms sufficiently wide to include a transfer by deed in registered land.

of Property Act 1925, to convey[113] 'all buildings, erections, fixtures, commons, hedges, ditches, fences, ways, waters, watercourses, liberties, privileges, easements, rights and advantages whatsoever, appertaining or reputed to appertain to the land or any part thereof'.

An equally wide implication is raised with regard to rights appertaining to buildings.[114]

It was also usual before 1882 to add what was called an *all estate clause* with the object of ensuring that the entire interest of the grantor should be transferred. This was as a matter of fact quite ineffective to transfer anything that would not pass automatically, and it is now omitted in reliance on the enactment that, unless a contrary intention is expressed, every conveyance is effectual to pass all the estate, right, title, interest, claim, and demand that the conveying parties respectively have in, to, or on the property.[115]

(c) Section 8: consideration

The statement in section 8 that the consideration has been received is a sufficient discharge to the purchaser without any further receipt being indorsed on the deed.[116] Again, such a receipt is sufficient evidence of the payment to a subsequent purchaser, provided that he has no notice that the money was not actually paid.[117]

One function of section 8 is to indicate whether stamp duty land tax is payable on the transfer. This topic is outside the scope of this book,[118] but it should be noted that most transactions, for consideration in money or money's worth, relating to estates and interests in land[119] are subject to tax, payable by the purchaser. The rate of tax payable depends on the consideration for the transaction (and any linked transaction). A land transaction, or a document effecting or evidencing a land transaction, must not be registered, recorded or otherwise reflected in the land register unless the application is accompanied by a certificate about the compliance with the statutory requirements as to the tax.[120]

(d) Section 9: title guarantee

Section 9 calls for some explanation, and can be understood only in the light of the history of conveyancing practice.

(1) History of covenants for title

In former days a deed of conveyance ran to considerable length since it usually contained elaborate *covenants for title*, the object of which was to render the vendor liable in covenant if a flaw were later discovered in his title. Although titles were

---

[113] LPA 1925, s 62(1); above, p 655.   [114] Ibid, s 62(2).   [115] Ibid, s 63.
[116] LPA 1925, s 67.   [117] Ibid, s 68.
[118] See Silverman, *Conveyancing Handbook*, section A14; FA 2003, Part 4.
[119] A licence to use or occupy land is not a chargeable interest for the purpose of this tax; nor (in England, Wales and Northern Ireland) is a tenancy at will: FA 2003, s 48(2); this therefore gives a reason to prefer a licence to the grant of a lease; cf above, pp 185 ff.
[120] FA 2003, s 79(1), amended by Finance (No 2) Act 2005, s 47(2).

traditionally investigated with such care that a purchaser would seldom need to enforce this contractual liability, it was usual before 1882 to set out the appropriate undertakings at length,[121] a practice that, while it militated against simplicity and brevity, increased the profits of solicitors, whose remuneration in those days depended upon the length of the documents they prepared. Since 1881, however, covenants for title need not be expressly stated, because statute provides a mechanism for covenants to be implied by the use of simple words and phrases inserted into conveyances and transfers of land.

Before 1 July 1995[122] the appropriate words to imply these covenants upon sale of land were 'as beneficial owner'. If the conveyance was for valuable consideration, and if the vendor 'conveyed and was expressed to convey as beneficial owner',[123] and if in fact he possessed that status,[124] the effect was that four covenants were implied: that the vendor had a good right to convey; that the purchaser should have quiet enjoyment; that the property was free from incumbrances; and a covenant for further assurance that obliged the vendor to execute assurances and to do everything that is right and possible in order to perfect the conveyance.[125]

(2) Current law on implied covenants for title

The Law of Property (Miscellaneous) Provisions Act 1994,[126] which came into force on 1 July 1995, repealed the existing law on the implied covenants for title, and the key words that trigger them (such as 'beneficial owner') are no longer effective. Instead, there are two new key words; either covenants 'with full title guarantee' or covenants 'with limited title guarantee'. Use of the covenants remains a matter of contract between the parties, but depends on the new key words being expressed in the instrument.[127] Their effect can be limited or extended by the terms of the instrument.[128]

The archaic wording of the covenants has been shortened and modernised, and some changes of substance have been made.

---

[121] See (1962) 26 Conv (NS) 45 (MJ Russell).

[122] LPA 1925, s 76, Sch 2. The language to be used to imply the covenants, and the content of the covenants themselves, varied according as the grantor conveyed freeholds or assigned leaseholds for valuable consideration, or by way of mortgage or settlement, or as trustee, mortgagee, personal representative, etc.

[123] Ibid, s 76(1)(A).

[124] *Fay v Miller, Wilkins & Co* [1941] Ch 360, 362; *Pilkington v Wood* [1953] Ch 770, 777; *Re Robertson's Application* [1969] 1 WLR 109, 111–12.

[125] LPA 1925, Sch 2, Part I. The covenants could be varied or extended. The benefit of the covenants implied by the Act ran with the land, so as to entitle each person in whom the land is vested to enforce them: ibid, s 76(6). For further detail, see the 16th edn of this book, pp 848–50; Farrand, *Contract and Conveyance* (4th edn), pp 258 ff; Barnsley, *Conveyancing Law and Practice*, ch 23; (1968) 32 Conv (NS) 123; (1970) 34 Conv (NS) 178 (MJ Russell).

[126] Based on Law Com No 199, *Implied Covenants for Title* (1991). See generally *Blackstone's Guide to Covenants for Title*; Barnsley, *Conveyancing Law and Practice*, pp 683–6; Emmet, ch 16. In registered land, see LRR 2003, rr 67, 68 amended by LR(A)R 2008, Sch 1, paras 18, 19; H & B, para 25.3.

[127] These may be in Welsh: LP (MP) A 1994, s 8(4).   [128] S 8(1).

(3) Changes from the previous law

First, the covenants are now to be implied on the disposition of property on the part of the person making the disposition.[129] Disposition is defined so as to include the creation of a lease.[130] This is an important change; before then only the disposition of a lease had attracted the covenants. Property includes a thing in action, and any interest in real or personal property;[131] for example, sales and acquisitions of companies and sales of chattels are now included.

Secondly, the new covenants may be implied into a disposition, even though there is no consideration.[132] The old covenants could only be implied in a conveyance for valuable consideration.

Thirdly, there are now only three covenants, which are common to the new types of guarantee:

(1) The right to dispose of the property.

(2) Further assurance.

(3) Freedom from charges, incumbrances and third party rights.

The old covenant that a purchaser shall have quiet enjoyment has disappeared. It has no place in freehold conveyancing, and is unnecessary in leasehold conveyancing, where the covenant is implied at common law.[133] The detail of the new covenants is discussed below.

Fourthly, the implied covenants for right to dispose and freedom from charges, etc, do not apply to any particular matter to which the disposition is expressly made subject.[134] Under the Standard Conditions of Sale,[135] property is sold expressly subject, for example, to the covenants mentioned in the agreement, to those discoverable by inspection of the property before the contract, and to those that the vendor does not and could not reasonably know about.

Fifthly, it would be unfair if the disponor were to be liable on the implied covenants if the disponee knew of the defects. Section 6(2) provides that the covenants for right to dispose and freedom from charges, etc, will not apply to anything (even if the disposition is not expressly made subject to it)

(a) which at the time of the disposition is within the actual knowledge, or

(b) which is a necessary consequence of facts that are then within the actual knowledge of the person to whom the disposition is made.

---

[129] Ss 1(1), (4). For specified covenants implied under statutes, see s 21, Sch 1, amending Leasehold Reform Act 1967, Rentcharges Act 1977, HA 1985 and Leasehold Reform, Housing and Urban Development Act 1993.

[130] S 1(1). For implied covenants in leases, see ss 4 (validity of lease); 5 (discharge of obligations when property subject to rentcharge or leasehold land or a commonhold unit: amended by CLRA 2002, Sch 5, para 7).

[131] S 1(4). [132] S 1(1).

[133] Above, p 224. The effect of this omission is that the limitation period for all implied covenants runs from the date of the conveyance.

[134] S 6(1).

[135] 5th edn, condition 3. See also Standard Commercial Property Conditions, 2nd edn, condition 3.

Knowledge does not include deemed notice by virtue of registration under the Land Charges Act 1972, although in registered land the disponor of an interest is not liable in respect of matters entered on the register of title of the interest.[136]

Sixthly, the annexation of the benefit of the implied covenants to the estate or interest of the disponee is repeated in section 7.[137]

(4) The implied covenants

We must now consider briefly the content of the new covenants.

(i) The right to dispose of the property

Under section 2(1)(a) there is implied a covenant that the person making the disposition has the right (with the concurrence of any other person conveying the property) to dispose of the property as he purports to.

A disponor is thus liable for breach of this covenant where he has never had title to the property described in the conveyance, or where[138] he has lost it by having been dispossessed under the Limitation Act 1980.

(ii) Further assurance

Under section 2(1)(b) there is also implied a covenant by the person making the disposition that he will at his own cost do all that he reasonably can to give the person to whom he disposes of the property the title he purports to give.

Section 2(2) extends this duty to ensuring that the disponee of registered land is registered with at least the class of title registered immediately before the disposition.

These two covenants are implied whether the disposition is expressed to be made with full title guarantee or with limited title guarantee. The difference between these two guarantees occurs only in the third implied covenant.

(iii) Freedom from charges, incumbrances and third party rights

Under section 3, if there is a *full title guarantee*, there is also implied a covenant that the property is disposed of free:

    (a) from all charges and incumbrances (whether monetary or not); and

    (b) from all other rights exercisable by third parties.

This covenant is more onerous than the similar one under the old law; the disponor is now made liable for charges etc that have been created by his predecessor in title. However, the scope of the covenant is narrowed in that it does not extend to any charges etc that the disponor does not and could not reasonably be expected to know about.

---

[136] S 6(4), inserted by LRA 2002, s 133, Sch 11, para 31. No reference is made on the register to the implied covenants for title, unless they are limited or extended under s 4: LRR 2003, rr 67(5), (6).

[137] The suggestion of Lord Brightman in HL to adopt the wording of LPA 1925, s 78(1) was not followed in spite of its wide interpretation in *Federated Homes Ltd v Mill Lodge Properties Ltd* [1980] 1 WLR 594, above, p 748. See the Proceedings of the Special Standing Committee of the House of Lords (7 June 1994 HL Paper 62).

[138] In unregistered land, or in registered land before LRA 2002: below, Ch 29.

If there is *limited title guarantee*, only a qualified covenant is implied and the disponee has less protection. Under section 3(3) the limitation is that the person making the disposition has not, since the last disposition for value, created or suffered any subsisting charges etc to be created and that he is not aware that anyone else has done so.

(e) Section 10: declaration of trust

If there is more than one transferee, they are required to declare the basis on which they are to hold the property: whether on trust for themselves as joint tenants or tenants in common, or otherwise.[139]

(f) Section 12: execution

The transfer must be executed as a deed, to comply with the requirements of section 52 of the Law of Property Act 1925.[140]

(3) *Registrable Dispositions*[141]

Certain dispositions are required by the Land Registration Act 2002 to be completed by registration. Until the relevant registration requirements are met, the disposition does not operate at law,[142] although it will still take effect between the parties within the law of contract, and may also take effect in equity as a property right capable of binding a third party who takes a subsequent registered disposition for value, if it is protected in the manner required by the Act.[143]

(a) Dispositions required to be registered

The following dispositions relating to a registered estate are required to be completed by registration:[144]

    (a) a transfer,

    (b) where the registered estate is an estate in land, the grant of a term of years absolute—

        (i)   for a term of more than seven years from the date of the grant,

---

[139] Above, pp 493, 513.   [140] Above, p 1001.   [141] H & B, ch 8.

[142] LRA 2002, s 27(1). The importance of this provision will be diminished when electronic conveyancing is introduced, because dispositions will then occur and be registered simultaneously. Hence s 27(1) is disapplied by s 93(4); below, p 1122.

[143] By entry of a notice, or as an overriding interest: s 29(2); below. The unregistered disposition of a legal estate takes effect in equity under the doctrine of *Walsh v Lonsdale*, above, p 978. For the effect in equity of a transfer before registration under LRA 1925, see *Mascall v Mascall* (1984) 50 P & CR 119; *E S Schwab & Co Ltd v McCarthy* (1975) 31 P & CR 196, 212; *Brown & Root Technology Ltd v Sun Alliance and London Assurance Co Ltd* [1996] Ch 51 (rvsd on other grounds (1996) 75 P & CR 223; above, p 135, n 144.

[144] LRA 2002, s 27(2). For registrable dispositions relating to a registered charge, see s 27(3). The section applied to dispositions by operation of law, except for a transfer on death or bankruptcy of an individual proprietor, a transfer on the dissolution of a corporate proprietor, or the creation of a local land charge: s 27(5).

(ii) to take effect in possession after the end of the period of three months beginning with the date of the grant,

(iii) under which the right to possession is discontinuous,

(iv) in pursuance of Part 5 of the Housing Act 1985 (the right to buy), or

(v) in circumstances where section 171A of that Act applies (disposal by landlord which leads to a person no longer being a secure tenant),

(c) where the registered estate is a franchise or manor, the grant of a lease,

(d) the express grant or reservation of an interest of a kind falling within section 1(2)(a) of the Law of Property Act 1925,[145] other than one which is capable of being registered under Part I of the Commons Act 2006,[146]

(e) the express grant or reservation of an interest of a kind falling within section 1(2)(b) or (e) of the Law of Property Act 1925,[147] and

(f) the grant of a legal charge.

Thus the most common transactions—the transfer of the freehold, the grant of most leases for longer than seven years, and the creation of a charge by way of legal mortgage—must be registered if they are to take effect at law.

(b) Registration requirements

The registration requirements are set out in Schedule 2 to the Land Registration Act 2002, and vary according to the nature of the disposition. But the general principle is that, where the disposition transfers or creates a registrable estate,[148] the disponee must be entered in the individual register as the proprietor of the estate, and if the interest subsists in relation to another registered estate, a notice must be entered on the register of the latter estate. In the case of a transfer of a registered freehold estate, therefore, the transferee must be entered in the register as the proprietor;[149] and in the case of a grant of a lease the tenant must be entered in the register as the proprietor of the lease, and a notice in respect of the lease must be entered in the register of the title to the reversion.[150] If the disposition does not create an estate that is individually registrable, such as a legal easement, a notice must be entered in the register of the estate in respect of which the interest subsists (the servient tenement) and if the interest is created for

---

[145] Ie, an easement or profit à prendre for an interest equivalent to the fee simple or a term of years absolute. 'Express grant' does not include a grant as a result of the operation of LPA 1925, s 62: LRA 2002, s 27(7); easements implied by s 62 can therefore be legal without registration and take effect as overriding interests under LRA 2002, Sch 3, para 3(1); above, pp 691–3.

[146] Amended by Commons Act 2006, Sch 5, para 8. Until the 2006 Act comes into force (above, p 708) the reference is to the Commons Registration Act 1965.

[147] Ie, a legal rentcharge or right of entry.

[148] Ie, an interest or estate that is substantively registrable with its own individual register: a legal estate in land (fee simple and certain leases), rentcharge, franchise, or profit à prendre in gross: above, p 1072.

[149] LRA 2002, Sch 2, para 2(1).

[150] Ibid, para 3. For the registration of an independently registrable rentcharge or profit à prendre, see para 6.

the benefit of a registered estate an entry must be made in the individual register for that estate to indicate that the proprietor has the benefit.[151]

VI THE PRIORITY OF COMPETING INTERESTS IN REGISTERED LAND[152]

The Land Registration Act 2002 lays down a new, simple, statutory scheme of priorities for competing interests in registered land.

A THE BASIC RULE: DATE OF CREATION

The basic rule is that the priority of any interest is determined by the date of its creation. This is the effect (although not the literal language) of section 28, which provides that:

(1) Except as provided by sections 29 and 30, the priority of an interest affecting a registered estate or charge is not affected by a disposition of the estate or charge.

(2) It makes no difference for the purposes of this section whether the interest or disposition is registered.

This is a much more straightforward rule than that which existed before the Act in registered land, or that exists in unregistered land, and applies to all interests affecting registered land, whether legal or equitable,[153] and whether (or when) registered.[154]

B EXCEPTIONS TO THE BASIC RULE

Sections 29 to 31 of the Act set out two important exceptions to this basic rule: where there is a registered disposition for valuable consideration, and in the case of an Inland Revenue charge. In addition, the doctrine of overreaching[155] protects a purchaser against being bound by certain equitable interests.

---

151 Ibid, para 7. If the dominant tenement is not yet registered, there will be no individual register of title against which the benefit can be noted. In the case of a registered charge the chargee is entered as proprietor of the charge in the register of the estate that has been charged: ibid, para 8. On transfer of charges, see para 10; and on sub-charges, see para 11.

152 R & R, ch 15; H & B, chap. 9; Law Com No 271, *Land Registration for the Twenty-First Century* (2001), Part V. For a useful example of the operation of the principal rules, see R & R, paras 15.032–15.039; [2006] Conv 111.

153 It applies to rights of pre-emption from the time of creation: LRA 2002, s 115; above, p 986; and mere equities and equities by estoppel from the time the equity arises: LRA 2002, s 116; above, pp 905, 921.

154 For criticism of the law under LRA 1925, see Law Com No 254, *Consultative Document on Land Registration for the Twenty-First Century* (1998), paras 7.15–17.19; H & B, para 9.1. For the position in unregistered land, see above, pp 121–31; and for a comparison between registered land and unregistered land, see above, pp 143–6.

155 Below, pp 1113 ff.

(1) Registered Disposition for Valuable Consideration

The main exception is where a registrable disposition of a registered estate[156] is made for valuable consideration,[157] and is completed by registration. Registration has the effect of postponing to the interest under the disposition any interest affecting the estate immediately before the disposition whose priority is not protected at the time of registration.[158] In other words, prior interests affecting the estate continue to bind successors to the estate and others whose interests in or over the estate are created later; but a *purchaser for value* of the legal estate takes it free of prior interests whose priority is not protected *at the time of his registration as proprietor*.[159] The burden of establishing that priority under the basic rule has been displaced in favour of a prior interest lies on the party who wishes to rely on the prior interest.[160]

A prior interest will be protected if it is:[161]

(a) a registered charge;

(b) the subject of a notice in the register;[162]

(c) an unregistered interest that overrides a registered disposition under Schedule 3;[163]

(d) an interest that appears from the register to be excepted from the effect of registration—such as an interest to which registration of the title as possessory, rather than absolute, is subject;[164] or

(e) in the case of a disposition of a leasehold estate, an interest that is incident to the estate, such as restrictive covenants in a lease that do not have to be protected by a notice on the register.

The protection of interests by means of entries on the register, and overriding interests, are considered in detail below. But it should be noted that, as in unregistered conveyancing, actual notice of what should be protected in the register, but is not so protected, is immaterial.[165]

---

[156] Or charge: LRA 2002, s 30.

[157] 'Valuable consideration' does not include marriage consideration or a nominal consideration in money: LRA 2002, s 132 (cf LRA 1925, s 3(xxxi), which did not exclude marriage consideration). *Halifax plc v Curry Popeck* [2009] 1 P & CR D7 (fraudulent transaction not for valuable consideration so did not defeat bank's prior charge).

[158] LRA 2002, s 29(1).

[159] The purchaser may also be protected by having made a priority search of the register that prevents his being affected by any interests entered on the register during the priority period: above, p 1073.

[160] *Halifax plc v Curry Popeck*, above, at [30] (Norris J: bank could not show that the disposition was made for valuable consideration).

[161] LRA 2002, s 29(2) (disposition of registered estate). See also s 30(2) (disposition of registered charge).

[162] Below, pp 1097 ff.   [163] Below, pp 1100 ff.   [164] Above, p 1078.

[165] See, however, two decisions at first instance under LRA 1925, where the constructive trust was used to avoid the consequences of failure to register a right as a minor interest, but that have been much criticised: (a) *Peffer v Rigg* [1977] 1 WLR 285, M & B p 222, where Graham J treated a transferee under s 20(1) and a purchaser, defined in s 3(xxi) as 'bona fide purchaser for value', as synonymous, and held that, where an ex-wife purchased a house from her former husband, with actual knowledge that he held it on trust for himself and her brother-in-law, she was not a bona fide transferee under s 20(1), and therefore was bound by the trust. He also held that she was a constructive trustee of the house: (1977) 41 Conv (NS) 207 (FR Crane); (1977) 93 LQR 341 (RJ Smith); [1977] CLJ 227 (DJ Hayton); (1977) 40 MLR 602 (S Anderson); [1978] Conv 52 (J Martin); and, after LRA 2002, (2004) 120 LQR 640 (E Cooke and P O'Connor). (b) *Lyus v Prowsa Developments Ltd* [1982] 1 WLR 1044, M & B p 223, where a purchaser, who agreed to take part of a building

(2) Inland Revenue Charge

The second exception to the basic rule concerns the Inland Revenue charge for unpaid tax, which has a separate priority rule under the Inheritance Tax Act 1984.[166]

C PROTECTION OF INTERESTS BY ENTRY ON THE REGISTER[167]

We have seen[168] that the Land Registration Act 1925 designated as 'minor interests' those unregistrable interests that needed to be protected by entry on the register in order to give them priority against later purchasers; and that there were four categories of entry on the register: notices, restrictions, cautions and inhibitions. The scheme of the Land Registration Act 2002 is simpler. The language of 'minor interests' is not used: the rules of priority of interests[169] apply generally to all interests affecting a registered estate. And there are now only two forms of entry on the register: notices and restrictions.[170]

(1) Notices[171]

(a) Nature and effect

A notice is an entry in the register in respect of the burden of an interest affecting a registered estate or charge. The entry of a notice does not, however, mean that the interest is valid; only that, if valid, its priority is protected against a later disposition of the estate for value.[172] The registrar does not therefore enquire into the validity of the claim to the interest when the application is made to enter it on the register.

(b) Interests that may be protected by entry of a notice

The Act requires or permits the registrar to enter a notice in certain cases where it appears to him that a registered estate is burdened by an interest.[173] But it does not

---

estate expressly 'subject to and with the benefit of' an existing contract for the sale of one plot, was held bound by that contract under a constructive trust, on the ground that the LRA was not to be used as an instrument of fraud; approved in *Ashburn Anstalt v Arnold* [1989] Ch 1, 25. For criticism, see (1983) 46 MLR 96 (PH Kenny); [1982] All ER Rev (PJ Clarke); [1983] CLJ 54 (C Harpum); [1983] Conv 64 (P Jackson); (1983) 133 NLJ 798 (CT Emery and B Smythe); cf (1984) 47 MLR 476 (P Bennett); [1985] CLJ 280 (MP Thompson). See also *Du Boulay v Raggett* (1988) 58 P & CR 138; Emmet, para 9.016. For the use of Contracts (Rights of Third Parties) Act 1999 to solve by contract the problem addressed in *Lyus v Prowsa*, see above, p 932, n 53.

[166] Ss 237, 238; LRA 2002, s 31.

[167] R & R, chs 42 (notices), 43 (cautions against dealings), 44 (restrictions), 45 (matrimonial and civil partnership homes); H & B, ch 10; Land Registry Practice Guide 19.

[168] Above, p 137. For detail, see the 16th edn of this book, pp 870–6.

[169] Above.

[170] Cautions against dealings and inhibitions are abolished: the former are subsumed under notices, the latter under restrictions. Entries on the register made before LRA 2002 came into force continue to have effect: Sch 12. For the vacation of cautions entered under LRA 1925, see above, p 137, n 165.

[171] LRA 2002, ss 32–9; LRR 2003, Part 7 (as amended). [172] Ibid, s 32(1), (3).

[173] Ibid, ss 37 (permissive: entry of matters that, on first registration, would constitute overriding interests, if not otherwise excluded from protection by notice; this is in furtherance of the policy of making

define exhaustively the interests that can be protected by notice;[174] rather, it lists five interests that *cannot* be so protected. These are:[175]

    (a) an interest under—

        (i) a trust of land, or

        (ii) a settlement under the Settled Land Act 1925.

A beneficial interest under a trust of land or a strict settlement cannot be protected by entry of a notice because, as long as it is overreached,[176] it is of no concern to a purchaser. The appropriate entry on the register is therefore a restriction, to ensure that the overreaching machinery is adopted on any sale.[177]

    (b) a leasehold estate in land which—

        (i)   is granted for a term of years of three years or less from the date of the grant, and

        (ii)   is not required to be registered.

A lease granted for more than seven years must be registered;[178] the effect of this provision is therefore to permit a notice to be entered on the title to the reversion only in respect of a lease granted for more than three years but not more than seven years. The period of three years was chosen here because it was envisaged that, when electronic conveyancing is fully introduced, the seven-year period for registration of leases will be reduced to three years,[179] and therefore the periods will be brought into line.

    (c) a restrictive covenant made between a lessor and lessee, so far as relating to the demised premises.

The purchaser of land will be able to inspect the lease, and therefore discover the covenants.[180]

    (d) an interest which is capable of being registered under Part 1 of the Commons Act 2006,[181] and

    (e) an interest in any coal or coal mine, the rights attached to any such interest and the rights of any person under section 38, 49 or 51 of the Coal Industry Act 1994.[182]

the register as complete as possible, rather than relying on overriding interests); 38 (mandatory: entry on the register of the burdened estate where a person is registered as proprietor of a lease, easement, profit à prendre, rentcharge or right of entry).

[174] Numerous other statutes make explicit provision for notices to be (or not to be) used to protect particular interests; eg a spouse or civil partner's rights of occupation under Family Law Act 1996, s 31; above, pp 522–3. For a detailed list, see Wolstenholme and Cherry, *Annotated Land Registration Act 2002*, para 3-037.

[175] LRA 2002, s 33.   [176] Below, pp 1113–21.

[177] Below. This reproduces the position under LRA 1925, s 49(2).

[178] Above, p 1093. And most leases granted for a term not exceeding seven years are overriding interests: Sch 3, para 1; below, pp 1102–3.

[179] H & B, para 10.8.

[180] The burden of covenants incident to the leasehold estate have priority in any event: LRA 2002, s 29(2)(b).

[181] Amended by Commons Act 2006, Sch 5, para 8. Until the 2006 Act comes into force (above, p 708) the reference is to the Commons Registration Act 1965.

[182] Such interests are overriding interests: Sch 1, para 7 (first registration); Sch 3, para 7 (registered dispositions).

(c) Agreed and unilateral notices

Under the 2002 Act notices are of two kinds: agreed notices and unilateral notices.[183] An agreed notice will be entered on the application of or with the agreement of the registered proprietor of the land affected. A unilateral notice, however, may be entered without the consent of the proprietor, but the registrar must inform him of the entry so that he may exercise his right to apply for its cancellation.[184]

(2) Restrictions[185]

(a) Nature and effect

A restriction is an entry in the register regulating the circumstances in which a disposition of a registered estate or charge may be the subject of an entry in the register. It may prohibit the making of an entry in respect of any particular disposition, or kind of disposition; for a defined period or indefinitely; and subject or not to particular conditions.[186] Its effect is to prevent any entry being made in the register in contravention of the terms of the restriction, unless the registrar disapplies or modifies the restriction.[187]

(b) Entry of a restriction

A restriction may be entered by the registrar if it appears to him to be necessary or desirable for the purpose of:[188]

    (a) preventing invalidity or unlawfulness in relation to dispositions of a registered estate or charge,

    (b) securing that interests which are capable of being overreached on a disposition of a registered estate or charge are overreached, or

    (c) protecting a right or claim in relation to a registered estate or charge.[189]

Restrictions can therefore be used for a variety of situations, and the Land Registration Rules 2003[190] contain numerous standard forms of restriction for particular types of

---

[183] LRA 2002, s 34. These reflect the differences between notices and cautions against dealings under LRA 1925.

[184] Ibid, ss 35–6. This is more effective than the old caution under LRA 1925 (above, pp 137–8) since, in the absence of an objection, a unilateral notice will protect the interest in the same way as an agreed notice does. A caution only recorded the cautioner's claim, and did not give priority as such: above, p 137, n 165.

[185] Ibid, ss 40–47; LRR 2003, Part 8 (as amended).

[186] Ibid, s 40.　　　　　　　　　　　　　　　　　　　　　　　　　[187] Ibid, s 41.

[188] Ibid, s 42(1). Application may be made by or with the consent of the registered proprietor, or by any person with a sufficient interest in the making of the entry: s 43; LRR 2003, rr 91–4. See *Croatia v Serbia* [2009] EWHC 1559 (Ch), [2010] Ch 200 at [46]-[63] (person can have a 'sufficient interest' without having, or even claiming, a proprietary interest in the estate; Croatia had arguable claim to property interest, although the claim would not be justiciable in the English courts). If the registrar makes an entry other than in pursuance of such an application, he must give notice to the proprietor of the registered estate or charge: s 42(3). For entry of a restriction on the order of the court see s 46.

[189] But not for the purpose of protecting a right of claim that is or could be the subject of a notice: ibid, s 42(2). If priority is sought, a notice should be used.

[190] Sch 4, as substituted by LR(A)R 2008, Sch 4, para 1, and further amended by Housing and Regeneration Act 2008 (Consequential Provisions) (No 2) Order 2010, (SI 2010 No 671), Sch 1, para 33.

case. The most common case, however, is the restriction to protect the beneficiary under a trust of land or strict settlement, to ensure that the requirements for overreaching are complied with. Where two or more persons are entered as the proprietor of a registered estate the legal title will necessarily be subject to a trust,[191] and it is mandatory for the registrar to enter an appropriate restriction.[192]

(3) Anti-abuse Provision

Under section 77 of the Land Registration Act 2002, a person must not exercise the right to apply for the entry of a notice or restriction[193] without reasonable cause. This creates a statutory duty, breach of which is actionable in tort by any person who suffers damage in consequence of it.[194]

D OVERRIDING INTERESTS[195]

Overriding interests are unregistered interests to which a registered title is subject. On first registration, certain unregistered interests will bind the registered proprietor.[196] On a subsequent registered disposition of the registered estate for value, certain unregistered interests will have priority against the disponee even though they have not been protected by the entry of a notice on the register.[197]

Overriding interests thus detract from the principle that the register should be a mirror of title. They consist of third party rights that on policy grounds should bind the registered proprietor, and a purchaser from him, even though they have not been entered on the register. The Land Registration Act 1925 listed overriding interests in section 70(1), and further additions were made by later enactments.[198] The wide scope

---

[191] Above, pp 501, 505, 513.   [192] LRA 2002, s 44; above, p 478.

[193] Or to lodge a caution against first registration, or to object to an application to the registrar.

[194] *Anderson Antiques (UK) Ltd v Anderson Wharf (Hull) Ltd* [2007] EWHC 2086 (Ch), [2007] All ER (D) 409 (May) (company that could not establish interest in registered land by virtue of oral agreement to purchase made application for notices to be entered against title. Held, declaration under s 77 that notices had been applied for without reasonable cause; liability for damages (if loss established) would attach primarily to company but also to sole director and shareholder of the company who had procured the application for notices against claimant's title).

[195] R & R, chs 10, 17; H & B, ch 11; Land Registry Practice Guide 15. 'Overriding interests' was a defined term under LRA 1925, s 3(xvi). It is no longer so used under LRA 2002, although the concept is the same, and the Land Registry still uses the old terminology: Practice Guide 15. On overriding interests under the LRA 1925, see R & R (1991 edn), ch 6; Wolstenholme and Cherry, vol 6, pp 63–7; Farrand, *Contract and Conveyance* (2nd edn), pp 184–209; Barnsley, *Conveyancing Law and Practice*, pp 50–69; Hayton, *Registered Land*, ch 6; M & B pp 182–9.

[196] LRA 2002, ss 11(4)(b) (freehold), 12(4)(c) (leasehold), Sch 1: unregistered interests that override first registration.

[197] LRA 2002, ss 29(2)(a)(ii) (registered disposition of registered estate), 30(2)(a)(ii) (registered disposition of registered charge), Sch 3: unregistered interests that override registered dispositions.

[198] LRR 1925, r 258; Coal Act 1938, s 41; Tithe Act 1936, s 13(11); Leasehold Property (Temporary Provisions) Act 1951, s 2(4); Coal Industry Act 1987, s 1; Coal Industry Act 1994, Sch 9, para 1(2); Greater London Authority Act 1999, s 219(7).

of overriding interests was subject to criticism,[199] and the Land Registration Act 2002 reduced their number and extent in pursuance of its policy of creating as complete a register of land as possible. Some of the old categories of overriding interests were abolished; others will be phased out after ten years;[200] others are reduced in extent or otherwise modified.[201] The basic principle is now said to be that[202] 'the *only* overriding interests should be those where protection against purchasers is needed, yet it is either not reasonable to expect nor sensible to require any entry on the register'.

(1) Unregistered Interests Which Override First Registration

When a person becomes proprietor of a registered estate on first registration, he takes the estate subject to those overriding interests that are set out in Schedule 1 to the 2002 Act. These are:[203]

1. A leasehold estate in land granted for a term not exceeding seven years from the date of the grant, except for a lease the grant of which falls within section 4(1)(d), (e) or (f).[204]

2. An interest belonging to a person in actual occupation, so far as relating to land of which he is in actual occupation, except for an interest under a settlement under the Settled Land Act 1925.

3. A legal easement or profit à prendre.

4. A customary right.

5. A public right.[205]

---

[199] See esp Law Com No 158, *Third Report on Land Registration* (1987), Part II; Law Com No 254, *Consultative Document on Land Registration for the Twenty-First Century* (1998), Part IV; *Overseas Investment Services Ltd v Simcobuild Construction Ltd* [1996] 1 EGLR 49, 51 (Peter Gibson LJ): 'As they constitute an exception [to the mirror of title principle], the court should, in my opinion, not be astute to give a wide meaning to any item constituting an overriding interest'.

[200] Ie, with effect from 13 October 2013, 10 years after the Act came into force: above, p 139.

[201] There are transitional provisions that preserve any overriding interests acquired under the 1925 Act: LRA 2002, Sch 12, paras 7–13. Cases on LRA 1925, s 70(1) may still be relevant to the interpretation of the equivalent provisions of LRA 2002.

[202] Law Com No 254, *Consultative Document on Land Registration for the Twenty-First Century* (1998), para 4.17, adopting Law Com No 158, *Third Report on Land Registration* (1987), para 2.6. See also Law Com No 271, *Land Registration for the Twenty-First Century* (2001), para 8.6. An earlier rationale for overriding interests was that the system of registration of title was designed to replace the title deeds; and so it was still to be expected that a purchaser should make enquiries outside the register for those 'various minor liabilities which are not usually, or at any rate not invariably, shown in title-deeds or mentioned in abstracts of title, and as to which, therefore, it is impracticable to form a trustworthy record on the register': Brickdale and Stewart Wallace, *Land Registration Act 1925*, p 190, quoted and criticised in Law Com No 254, para 4.4.

[203] See also s 90(5), adding PPP leases relating to transport in London. S 134(2), Sch 12, para 7, inserted para 15 into Sch 1, with effect only until 13 October 2006, to preserve the overriding status of rights acquired under the Limitation Act 1980 before the coming into force of the Schedule.

[204] That is, a legal lease not exceeding seven years, which is not required to be registered with its own individual title. For LRA 2002, s 4(1)(d), (e) and (f) see above, p 1074.

[205] *Secretary of State for the Environment, Transport and the Regions v Baylis* [2000] 2 EGLR 13 (dedication to the public accepted by highway authority rather than by public use); *Overseas Investment Services Ltd v Simcobuild Construction Ltd* [1996] 1 EGLR 49 (right to have road constructed under Highways Act 1980, s 38) (LRA 1925, s 70(1)(a)).

6. A local land charge.[206]

7. An interest in any coal or coal mine, the rights attached to any such interest and the rights of any person under section 38, 49 or 51 of the Coal Industry Act 1994.

8. In the case of land to which title was registered before 1898, rights to mines and minerals (and incidental rights) created before 1898.

9. In the case of land to which title was registered between 1898 and 1925 inclusive, rights to mines and minerals (and incidental rights) created before the date of registration of the title.

10. A franchise.[207]

11. A manorial right.

12. A right to rent which was reserved to the Crown on the granting of any freehold estate (whether or not the right is still vested in the Crown).

13. A non-statutory right in respect of an embankment or sea or river wall.

14. A right to payment in lieu of tithe.

16. A right in respect of the repair of a church chancel.[208]

The detail of some of these categories will be explained in relation to Schedule 3 (unregistered interests that override registered dispositions), below.[209]

(2) Unregistered Interests Which Override Registered Dispositions

Schedule 3 to the Land Registration Act lists the interests that will override a registered disposition of a registered estate or charge. They are:[210]

1. A leasehold estate in land granted for a term not exceeding seven years from the date of the grant, except for—

[206] This is a very important category of overriding interests. The Local Land Charges Act 1975, above, pp 1066–7, applies to both unregistered and registered land. A purchaser must therefore search in the local authority's register whether or not the land is registered.

[207] Paras 10–14 and 16 are all repealed with effect from 13 October 2013. Those with the benefit of such rights may protect them on the register before then, without payment of fees, by a caution against first registration: LRA 2002, s 117.

[208] Inserted by SI 2003 No 2431, art 2(1), to continue the position under LRA 1925, s 70(1)(c), after decision of HL in *Aston Cantlow Parochial Church Council v Wallbank* [2003] UKHL 37, [2004] 1 AC 546 that the recovery of costs of chancel repair is not contrary to HRA 1998. Law Com No 152, *Liability for Chancel Repairs* (1985) recommended that liability should be abolished after ten years; but, if not abolished promptly, it should be registered in Local Land Charges registers, and failure to register would exonerate a purchaser of the land; (1984) 100 LQR 185 (JH Baker). For the liability in unregistered land, see *Hauxton Parochial Church Council v Stevens* [1929] P 240; *Chivers & Sons Ltd v Air Ministry* [1955] Ch 585.

[209] The categories of interest listed in Schs 1 and 3 are the same, although the detail of their operation is in some respects different because first registration does not presuppose a disposition of the land—and therefore it is not necessary or appropriate for the test of overriding interests on first registration to include reference to inquiries to be made of the occupier at the time of disposition to the proprietor.

[210] See also s 90(5), adding PPP leases relating to transport in London. Sch 12, para 8, inserted para 2A into Sch 3, with effect only until 13 October 2006, to preserve the overriding status of the rights of an individual who was in receipt of rents and profits under LRA 1925, s 70(1)(g); and LRA 2002 Sch 12, para 11, inserted para 15 into Sch 3, with effect only until 13 October 2006, to preserve the overriding status of a person who had acquired the right to be registered as proprietor following the completion of the period of limitation under LRA 1925, s 75(1).

(a) a lease the grant of which falls within section 4(1)(d), (e) or (f);[211]

(b) a lease the grant of which constitutes a registrable disposition.

2. An interest belonging at the time of the disposition to a person in actual occupation, so far as relating to land of which he is in actual occupation, except for—

(a) an interest under a settlement under the Settled Land Act 1925;

(b) an interest of a person of whom inquiry was made before the disposition and who failed to disclose the right when he could reasonably have been expected to do so;

(c) an interest—
(i) which belongs to a person whose occupation would not have been obvious on a reasonably careful inspection of the land at the time of the disposition, and
(ii) of which the person to whom the disposition is made does not have actual knowledge at that time;

(d) a leasehold estate in land granted to take effect in possession after the end of the period of three months beginning with the date of the grant and which has not taken effect in possession at the time of the disposition.

3. (1) A legal easement or profit à prendre, except[212] for an easement, or a profit à prendre which is not registered under the Commons Act 2006,[213] which at the time of the disposition—

(a) is not within the actual knowledge of the person to whom the disposition is made, and

(b) would not have been obvious on a reasonably careful inspection of the land over which the easement or profit is exercisable.

(2) The exception in sub-paragraph (1) does not apply if the person entitled to the easement or profit proves that it has been exercised in the period of one year ending with the day of the disposition.

4. A customary right.

5. A public right.[214]

6. A local land charge.[215]

7. An interest in any coal or coal mine, the rights attached to any such interest and the rights of any person under section 38, 49 or 51 of the Coal Industry Act 1994.

8. In the case of land to which title was registered before 1898, rights to mines and minerals (and incidental rights) created before 1898.

---

[211] That is, a legal lease not exceeding seven years, which is not required to be registered with its own individual title. For LRA 2002, s 4(1)(d), (e) and (f) see above, p 1074.

[212] The exception was omitted until 13 October 2006: LRA 2002, Sch 12, para 10.

[213] Amended by Commons Act 2006, Sch 5, para 8. Until the 2006 Act comes into force (above, p 708) the reference is to the Commons Registration Act 1965.

[214] See above, n 205.   [215] See above, n 206.

9. In the case of land to which title was registered between 1898 and 1925 inclusive, rights to mines and minerals (and incidental rights) created before the date of registration of the title.

10. A franchise.[216]

11. A manorial right.

12. A right to rent which was reserved to the Crown on the granting of any freehold estate (whether or not the right is still vested in the Crown).

13. A non-statutory right in respect of an embankment or sea or river wall.

14. A right to payment in lieu of tithe.

16. A right in respect of the repair of a church chancel.[217]

The first three paragraphs merit closer attention. Paragraphs 1 (legal leases) and 3 (legal easements and profits à prendre arising by implied grant or prescription) have already been discussed in detail.[218] We must now consider paragraph 2, which constitutes the most significant qualification to the general principle that the register should be a mirror of the title.

(a) The principle of paragraph 2

Paragraph 2 is the successor to section 70(1)(g) of the Land Registration Act 1925. These provisions show that the legislature has accepted a compromise in respect of its replacement of the old doctrine of notice by the system of registration. A purchaser should inspect the premises, and he should ask anyone in occupation on what grounds he is there. He will thereby be able to discover the rights and interests of persons in occupation, and it seemed right therefore to subject a purchaser to those rights and interests rather than to let him disregard them because someone had failed to enter them on the register. The paragraph thus operates as a safety-net. Some of these rights may, however, be capable of being protected by notice on the register of the title affected, and if they are, a notice should be applied for by the person entitled. Moreover, as we shall see,[219] there is a duty on the person applying for registration of an estate to disclose certain unregistered interests to the registrar so that they can be recorded on the register. In short, the general policy of the Land Registration Act 2002 is that all claims, rights and interests should be protected by entry on the register as far as possible. This special exception of paragraph 2 is made in the case of an interest belonging to a person in actual occupation. The purchaser should get to know what the rights of such a person are, and, on balance, it is better that he should take subject to them, even at the expense of the doctrine of completeness of the register.

---

[216] Paras 10–14 and 16 are all repealed with effect from 13 October 2013. Those with the benefit of such rights may protect them on the register before then, without payment of fees, by a notice: LRA 2002, s 117.

[217] Inserted by SI 2003 No 2431, art 2(2). See above, n 208.

[218] Above, pp 220 ff (leases); 691–3, 715 ff (easements and profits).

[219] Below, p 1112.

(b) The scope of paragraph 2

Paragraph 2 is different in character from the other paragraphs of Schedule 3. Each of the other paragraphs relates to a particular kind of interest in land: a lease, an easement, a local land charge, and so forth. Paragraph 2, however, is general. It is not limited to any particular kind of interest in land; but it covers any kind of 'interest belonging at the time of the disposition to a person in actual occupation, so far as relating to land of which he is in actual occupation' with certain exceptions. We shall consider the exceptions shortly. First, we should notice the range of interests that are covered by these opening words of the paragraph.

(1) 'Interest' within paragraph 2

Section 70(1)(g) of the 1925 Act referred to the 'rights' of a person in actual occupation, rather than his 'interest', but it appears that no change of substance is intended. Paragraph 2 is certainly not confined to an interest that confers the right to occupy, for it extends to the *interests belonging to a person in actual occupation*. It is the interests of the occupier and not the occupation itself that are crucial. As Russell LJ put it, when discussing the 1925 Act:[220]

> It seems to me that section 70 in all its parts is dealing with rights in reference to land which have the quality of being capable of enduring through different ownerships of the land, according to normal conceptions of title to real property…It is the rights of such a person which constitute the overriding interest and must be examined, not his occupation.

The question, therefore, is whether the person in actual occupation has a proprietary right in respect of the registered estate. The deserted wife in occupation of the matrimonial home has no right affecting property entitling her to claim an overriding interest,[221] while the owner of an option to purchase a freehold contained in a lease has, since it 'affects the reversion…and subsists in reference to the registered land'.[222]

Other examples of rights that were held to be sufficient within section 70(1)(g) of the 1925 Act, and that would now constitute 'interests' within paragraph 2 of Schedule 3 to the 2002 Act, are a right of pre-emption,[223] an unpaid vendor's lien where the vendor

---

[220] *National Provincial Bank Ltd v Hastings Car Mart Ltd* [1964] Ch 665, 696, a dissenting judgment that was upheld (with special reference to this passage) in the House of Lords; [1965] AC 1175, 1226, 1228, 1240 and 1261–2.

[221] *National Provincial Bank Ltd v Ainsworth* [1965] AC 1175, M & B p 199; above, p 943.

[222] *Webb v Pollmount* [1966] Ch 584, 595–6, 597–9 (Ungoed-Thomas J), M & B p 200. Cf *Ferrishurst Ltd v Wallcite Ltd* [1999] Ch 355, 372 (Robert Walker LJ): 'the rights of an occupier of registered land are to be distinguished from the fact of his occupation. The capacity in which a person occupies, for example as a tenant, need not be indicative of the right that he claims, such as an option to purchase the freehold reversion or an unpaid vendor's lien' (the effect of the actual decision is reversed by LRA 2002: below, n 1109).

[223] *Kling v Keston Properties Ltd* (1983) 49 P & CR 212, M & B p 38; above, pp 995–6. Under LRA 2002, s 115, the right of pre-emption has effect as an interest capable of binding successors in title from the time of its creation.

remains in occupation under a lease-back by the purchaser,[224] an equity by estoppel,[225] a right to rectify an instrument,[226] the right to seek rectification of the register,[227] and the right of a beneficiary under a bare trust to the fee simple in equity. In *Hodgson v Marks*:[228]

> Mrs H, an elderly widow, voluntarily transferred the registered title to her house to E, who was her lodger. She intended that the house, though it was in E's name, should remain hers, and she continued to reside there. E then sold it to M who became the registered proprietor and executed a mortgage in favour of a building society. Mrs H claimed that E held the house as a bare trustee for her, that she was entitled to the beneficial interest in it, and that M and his mortgagee took subject to her rights 'as a person in actual occupation' when M became the registered proprietor.

The Court of Appeal held that Mrs H was in actual occupation within the meaning of section 70(1)(g) of the 1925 Act and ordered rectification of the register in her favour as M had not made any enquiries of Mrs H prior to registration of the transfer to him.[229]

Further, in *Williams and Glyn's Bank Ltd v Boland*:[230]

> a husband and wife each contributed to the purchase of a matrimonial home. The husband was registered under the Land Registration Act 1925 as the sole proprietor. By virtue of her contribution the wife had an equitable interest in the house, and the husband held the legal title upon trust for sale for himself and his wife as equitable tenants in common.
>
> Later the husband, without the wife's consent, created a legal charge on the house in favour of the bank. On default being made in the mortgage payments, the bank brought an action for possession of the house.

---

[224] *London and Cheshire Insurance Co Ltd v Laplagrene Property Co Ltd* [1971] Ch 499, M & B p 217. Cf *Nationwide Anglia Building Society v Ahmed and Balakrishnan* (1995) 70 P & CR 381 (vendor of premises who remained in possession of part under contractual licence after completion held not to have overriding interest).

[225] *Habermann v Koehler* (1996) 73 P & CR 515. Under LRA 2002, s 116, an equity by estoppel has effect as an interest capable of binding successors in title from the time the equity arises: above, p 921.

[226] *Blacklocks v JB Developments (Godalming) Ltd* [1982] Ch 183. Cf *Smith v Jones* [1954] 1 WLR 1089, where Upjohn J held that a right to rectify a tenancy agreement would not be enforceable by a tenant against a purchaser of the reversion who had inspected the agreement; [1983] Conv 169, 257 (JTF), 361 (DG Barnsley); distinguished in *Nurdin & Peacock plc v Ramsden & Co Ltd* [1999] 1 EGLR 119 as being a case on unregistered land; [1999] [Conv] 421 (S Pascoe). Under LRA 2002, s 116, a mere equity has effect in relation to registered land as an interest capable of binding successors in title from the time the equity arises: above, p 905.

[227] *Malory Enterprises Ltd v Cheshire Homes (UK) Ltd* [2002] EWCA Civ 151, [2002] Ch 216.

[228] [1971] Ch 892; *Collings v Lee* [2001] 2 All ER 332 (rights of beneficiary under bare trust arising as a result of transfer induced by fraudulent misrepresentation); [2001] CLJ 477 (R Nolan); [2001] All ER Rev 253 (PJ Clarke).

[229] See (1971) 35 Conv (NS) 255, 268–276 (I Leeming): Law Com WP No 37 (1971), paras 56–77.

[230] [1981] AC 487, M & B p 203; above, p 466; [1980] Conv 361; [1981] Conv 84 (J Martin); (1979) 95 LQR 501; (1982) 97 LQR 12 (RJ Smith); (1980) 130 NLJ 896 (RL Deech); *City of London Building Society v Flegg* [1988] AC 54, M & B p 551; below, p 1115 (equitable interests of parents as tenants in common arising from contribution to purchase price of house registered in names of their daughter and son-in-law held to be overreachable by payment to two trustees, even though the parents were in actual occupation). Cf *Winkworth v Edward Baron Development Co Ltd* [1986] 1 WLR 1512. A beneficial interest under a strict settlement is not capable of being an overriding interest: LRA 2002, Sch 3, para 2(a), below; above, p 1103.

The question was whether the wife's interest was valid against the bank; it could only be so if it was an overriding interest due to her actual occupation of the house under section 70(1)(g) of the Land Registration Act 1925.

The House of Lords held that the beneficial interest of a wife as tenant in common with her husband of the matrimonial home under a statutory trust for sale[231] was an interest that subsists in reference to registered land; and that, being in actual occupation, she had an overriding interest that bound the bank to which her husband had mortgaged the house.

(2) 'Belonging at the time of the disposition'

The 2002 Act appears[232] to apply the same rule as had been settled under the 1925 Act: that the date for deciding whether there is actual occupation is the date for completion of the purchase (the disposition), when the transfer is executed and exchanged for the purchase money, rather than the (later) date of registration of the transferee as proprietor.[233] This makes practical sense, since it is at that date that the purchaser can make enquiries of those in occupation; he has no control over the timing of registration. The time gap between the disposition and its registration will, however, disappear once electronic conveyancing is fully introduced.[234]

If, however, there has been an overriding interest by virtue of actual occupation on the relevant date, it is not lost if its holder subsequently goes out of occupation.[235]

(3) 'In actual occupation'

Using the same language as under the Land Registration Act 1925, the paragraph protects an interest belonging to a person 'in actual occupation'.[236] As Lord Wilberforce said in *Williams and Glyn's Bank Ltd v Boland*:[237]

---

[231] Since 1997, a trust of land under TLATA 1996: above, pp 477 ff.

[232] For a different view, based on the assumption that the 'time of the disposition' is registration because under LRA 2002, s 27(1), the disposition does not operate at law until registration, see Wolstenholme and Cherry, *Annotated Land Registration Act 2002*, para 3–173A; rejected by Lewison J in *Thompson v Foy* [2009] EWHC 1076 (Ch), [2010] 1 P & CR 16 at [121] (leaving open, however, at [126] whether there must be actual occupation both at the date of the disposition and also at the date of registration); [2010] Conv 285.

[233] *Abbey National Building Society v Cann* [1991] 1 AC 56, M & B p 214; (1990) 106 LQR 32, 545 (RJ Smith); [1990] CLJ 397 (AJ Oakley); (1990) 87 LSG 19–24, 34–19 (M Beaumont, junior counsel for Mrs Cann); [1991] Conv 116 (S Baughen), 155 (PT Evans). The date for other overriding interests is the date of registration, except for para 3 of Sch 3 (legal easements and profits à prendre) where the discoverability test is applied at the time of the disposition. Under Sch 1 (first registration), all overriding interests (including actual occupation under para 2, and easements and profits under para 3), are tested at the date of registration because first registration does not presuppose any disposition: above, p 1102, n 209. For a disagreement at first instance as to whether the vendor/tenant's rights under a sale and lease-back arrangement were binding as overriding interests on the purchaser's mortgagee, see *Redstone Mortgages plc v Welch* [2009] 3 EGLR 71 (Cty Ct); *Re North East Property Buyers Litigation* [2010] EWHC 2991 (Ch), [2010] All ER (D) 275 (Nov).

[234] Below, p 1122.

[235] *London and Cheshire Insurance Co Ltd v Laplagrene Property Co Ltd* [1971] Ch 499, M & B p 217.

[236] LRA 1925, s 70(1)(g) also protected a person not in actual occupation, but 'in receipt of the rents and profits thereof', which meant that a landlord's rights were protected by his tenant's actual occupation. This is not reproduced in LRA 2002.

[237] [1981] AC 487, 504–5, M & B p 203; *Bhullar v McArdle* [2001] EWCA Civ 510, (2001) 82 P & CR 38 at [36] (actual occupation must be by the relevant party of the relevant land; no concept of constructive or 'transferred' actual occupation).

These words are ordinary words of plain English, and, should, in my opinion, be interpreted as such ... Given occupation, ie presence on the land, I do not think that the word 'actual' was intended to introduce any additional qualification, certainly not to suggest that possession must be 'adverse': it merely emphasises that what is required is physical presence, not some entitlement in law.

The occupation must involve some degree of permanence and continuity that would rule out mere fleeting presence. In *Abbey National Building Society v Cann*,[238] the House of Lords held that there was no actual occupation where carpets were laid and furniture moved into a dwelling-house with the vendor's consent. Lord Oliver of Aylmerton said:[239] 'These were acts of a preparatory character carried out by the courtesy of the vendor prior to completion.'

Similarly, in *Epps v Esso Petroleum Co Ltd*, the parking of a car at night on an undefined strip of land did not suffice;[240] and in *Strand Securities Ltd v Caswell*,[241] it was held that the tenant of a flat was not in actual occupation, even though the tenant and members of his family used it as a London rendezvous, and he had a key to the flat that contained some of his furniture.[242]

The nature and state of the property may also be relevant. In *Lloyds Bank plc v Rosset*,[243] the Court of Appeal held that, in the case of a semi-derelict farmhouse:

there was physical presence on the property by the wife and her agent of the nature, and the extent, that one would expect of an occupier having regard to the then state of the property, namely, the presence involved in actively carrying out the renovation necessary to make the house fit for residential use.

On the other hand, it has been suggested that 'physical presence' does not connote continued and uninterrupted presence: 'such a notion would be absurd'. Nor is the requisite presence negatived by repeated and regular absence. Thus a wife would be in actual occupation of a matrimonial home where she spent virtually some part of every day in order to discharge her duties as housewife and mother, but where she did not usually sleep.[244] A person has also been held to have been in actual occupation of property when she was involuntarily absent by being detained in a residential care institution under the Mental Health Act, but where her furniture and personal effects

---

[238] Above.   [239] [1991] 1 AC 56, 94.   [240] [1973] 1 WLR 1071, M & B p 152.
[241] [1965] Ch 958, M & B p 212.
[242] In *Chhokar v Chhokar* [1984] FLR 313, M & B p 217, furniture was held to be relevant.
[243] [1989] Ch 350, M & B p 209; [1988] Conv 453 (MP Thompson); [1989] CLJ 180 (PG McHugh); [1988] All ER Rev 163 (PJ Clarke); (1988) 104 LQR 507 (RJ Smith); [1989] Conv 342 (P Sparkes). HL reversed CA on the ground that Mrs Rosset had no beneficial interest under a trust; no views were expressed on the question of her actual occupation: [1991] 1 AC 107. See also *Goodger v Willis* [1999] EGCS 32 (demolition of buildings and laying of concrete base held to be actual occupation); *Malory Enterprises Ltd v Cheshire Homes (UK) Ltd* [2002] EWCA Civ 151, [2002] Ch 216 (derelict block of flats only used for temporary storage; gates in fence kept locked and ground floor windows blocked up; held to be actual occupation).
[244] *Kingsnorth Finance Co Ltd v Tizard* [1986] 1 WLR 783, 788, M & B p 216; [1987] CLJ 28 (PC McHugh); [1986] Conv 283 (MP Thompson). This was a case on unregistered land. See also *Chhokar v Chhokar*, above (wife evicted by fraudulent purchaser of matrimonial home from husband held to be in actual occupation).

remained at the property and she made relatively brief supervised visits about once a week to check the property and collect the post.[245]

A person may be in actual occupation through the agency of another, such as his caretaker or employee, but not through his gratuitous licensee acting on his own account.[246] However, the Court of Appeal has held that minors aged one and three, who had equitable beneficial interests under a trust for sale, were not capable of being in actual occupation. 'They were there because their parent is there. They have no right of occupation of their own: they are only there as shadows of their parents.'[247]

(4) 'So far as relating to land of which he is in actual occupation'

This is a change from the law as it stood before the Land Registration Act 2002. Under the 1925 Act it was held[248] that a person who had an option to purchase the leasehold interest in the whole of a building comprising offices and a garage, but occupied only part of it, had an overriding interest in respect of the whole. Now, however, the overriding interest—and therefore the priority afforded by it—can exist only in relation to the part actually occupied.

(5) Exceptions from paragraph 2

We now come to the exceptions contained within paragraph 2.[249]

Two of them relate to particular types of interests in land. An interest under a settlement under the Settled Land Act 1925 cannot be an overriding interest, even if the beneficiary is in actual occupation.[250] Nor can[251]

---

[245] *Link Lending Ltd v Bustard* [2010] EWCA Civ 424, [2010] 2 EGLR 55.

[246] See *Strand Securities Ltd v Caswell*, above; *Lloyd v Dugdale* [2001] EWCA Civ 1754, [2002] 2 P & CR 13 (where D Ltd was in occupation as licensee of D, major shareholder and managing director of D Ltd, D was not in actual occupation. Nor did D's regular presence help, since he was there as managing director and not on his own account).

[247] *Hypo-Mortgage Services Ltd v Robinson* [1997] 2 FLR 71 (Nourse LJ, citing *Bird v Syme Thomson* [1979] 1 WLR 440). The view that a *wife* is there only as a shadow of her husband, without a right of occupation of her own, was rejected in *Williams and Glyn's Bank Ltd v Boland* [1981] AC 487, 505; above, p 1028.

[248] *Ferrishurst Ltd v Wallcite Ltd* [1999] Ch 355; [1999] Conv 144 (S Pascoe); [1999] CLJ 483 (L Tee); (2000) 63 MLR 113 (J Hill).

[249] In addition, certain interests are excluded by other statutes from being overriding interests under LRA 2002, Schs 1 and 3: the spouse or civil partner's rights of occupation under Family Law Act 1996, s 31(10)(b) (above, p 523); the right of a tenant arising from a notice under the Leasehold Reform Act 1967 of his desire to acquire the freehold or an extended lease: Leasehold Reform Act 1967, s 5(5) (above, p 394); the secure tenant's 'right to buy' under Part V of the Housing Act 1985: Housing Act 1985 Sch 9A, para 6(1), inserted by Housing and Planning Act 1986, s 8(2), Sch 2 (above, p 389); the rights conferred by or under an access order under the Access to Neighbouring Land Act 1992: Access to Neighbouring Land Act 1992, s 5 (above, p 652); the right to an overriding lease under LT(C)A 1995, s 20(6) (above, p 319).

[250] LRA 2002, Sch 3, para 2(a). This follows the position under LRA 1925, s 86(2). It must therefore be protected by the entry of a restriction on the register: above, p 1099. An interest under a trust of land should also be protected by the entry of a restriction, although if not so protected it can take effect as an overriding interest under para 2: *Williams and Glyn's Bank Ltd v Boland*, above.

[251] Ibid, para 2(d). It is perhaps a rather unlikely scenario for the tenant under a lease that has not yet taken effect in possession, to be in actual occupation.

a leasehold estate in land granted to take effect in possession after the end of the period of three months beginning with the date of the grant and which has not taken effect in possession at the time of the disposition.

Such leases are required to be registered.[252]

Of more general significance, however, are the other two. First, a purchaser is not bound by[253]

an interest of a person of whom inquiry was made before the disposition and who failed to disclose the right when he could reasonably have been expected to do so.

This is quite straightforward. If the purchaser has in fact asked questions of a person in actual occupation, the latter's interest is not given priority over the purchaser's disposition, once it is registered, if he failed to disclose his rights, as long as he could reasonably[254] have been expected to do so. In effect, once the question is asked, the person in actual occupation has a duty of disclosure—or, at least, he will lose his priority if he does not disclose his interest.

But we then find a final exception, new in the 2002 Act, which has the effect of reintroducing the doctrine of notice into this category of overriding interests.[255] A purchaser is not bound by[256]

an interest—

(i)   which belongs to a person whose occupation would not have been obvious on a reasonably careful inspection of the land at the time of the disposition, and

(ii) of which the person to whom the disposition is made does not have actual knowledge at that time.

This exception allows a purchaser to say that, although a person who had in interest in the property was in actual occupation, he is not bound by it because (i) that *occupation* would not have been *obvious*[257] *on a reasonably careful inspection*, and (ii) he did not *in fact* know about the *interest*. The first limb of the test is objective; the second subjective. In effect, it is a test based on (i) constructive notice of the occupation and (ii) actual notice of the interest. But although this introduction of the doctrine of notice appears at first sight to undermine the purposes of the system of registered land, where notice is normally irrelevant,[258] it should be realised that it does not

---

[252] LRA 2002, s 4(1)(d).   [253] Ibid, Sch 3, para 2(b).

[254] This is in fact more favourable to the occupier than LRA 1925, s 70(1)(g), which only excluded the overriding interest where 'enquiry is made of such person ... and the rights are not disclosed'—there was no test of reasonableness in failing to disclose.

[255] LRA 2002 also introduces the principles of notice into the category of overriding interests relating to legal easements and profits à prendre: Sch 3, para 3(1); above, p 693.

[256] LRA 2002, Sch 3, para 2(c).

[257] 'Obviousness' may be a rather generous test in the purchaser's favour, less demanding than constructive notice of the occupation: Law Com No 271, *Land Registration for the Twenty-First Century* (2001), Explanatory Notes, para 617.

[258] *Williams and Glyn's Bank Ltd v Boland* [1981] AC 487, 503-4 (Lord Wilberforce): 'the system is designed to free the purchaser from the hazards of notice—real or constructive ... The only kind of notice recognised is by entry on the register'. See however *Peffer v Rigg* [1977] 1 WLR 285, M & B p 222; *Lyus v Prowsa Developments Ltd* [1982] 1 WLR 1044, M & B p 223; above, p 1096, n 165.

reintroduce the doctrine as it existed in unregistered land, under which the question whether a purchaser is bound by a third party's interest depended on whether he had notice of it.[259] Instead, in registered land, in the absence of the entry of a notice on the register, it is the fact of the third party's actual occupation that renders his interest binding on the purchaser; but not if the purchaser did not in fact know about the interest and the occupation was not reasonably obvious. It is not notice that binds the purchaser, but his *lack* of notice that can *prevent* him being bound by the third party's right.[260] This therefore further favours the purchaser over the person in actual occupation.

(6) Practical solutions to the problems of paragraph 2

The decision in *Williams and Glyn's Bank Ltd v Boland*[261] highlighted a real difficulty caused by the category of overriding interests based on actual occupation—and, in particular, a difficulty for institutional lenders, who naturally sought ways in which to avoid the consequence of being bound by such an overriding interest. They had to make more careful inquiries of the mortgagor[262] and of the property, and, if they discovered an actual occupant who had a beneficial interest in the property, they resorted to forms of consent or waiver to be signed by the occupant. But difficulties still exist. The waiver may be invalid if there is undue influence either on the part of the lender (or of an agent acting on his behalf), or of a third party, such as the husband against the wife, and the bank has not fulfilled its duty to ensure that the wife is entering into the transaction properly informed and without undue pressure.[263]

Another possibility is to insist on the appointment of an additional trustee (there was only one trustee in *Boland*) so that the mortgage money can be paid to two trustees, thereby overreaching the beneficial interest of the occupant and attaching it to the equity of redemption in the hands of the mortgagor and the money paid to him.[264]

On the other hand, if the occupant knows that the property is being acquired by the registered proprietor with the aid of a mortgage, the occupant's interest may not bind the mortgagee, either by virtue of estoppel,[265] or by virtue of an imputed intention that his interest is subject to the rights of the mortgagee.[266]

---

[259] Above, pp 84 ff.

[260] It has been said, however, that whether the person is in fact in actual occupation is to be decided by reference to the discoverability of it: *Malory Enterprises Ltd v Cheshire Homes (UK) Ltd* [2002] EWCA Civ 151, [2002] Ch 216 at [81] (Arden LJ): 'The requisite physical presence must, as it seems to me, in fairness be such as to put a person inspecting the land on notice that there was some person in occupation.' This was a decision on LRA 1925, s 70(1)(g), and at least in relation to the interpretation of LRA 2002, Sch 3, para 2, must be doubted given that the discoverability of the occupation is dealt with explicitly by the statute.

[261] Above.

[262] 'Reliance on the true ipse dixit of the vendor will not suffice': *Hodgson v Marks* [1971] Ch 892, 932 (Russell LJ).

[263] *Royal Bank of Scotland plc v Etridge (No 2)* [2001] UKHL 44, [2002] 2 AC 773, M & B p 902; above, pp 830 ff.

[264] *City of London Building Society v Flegg* [1988] AC 54, below, p 1115.

[265] *Spiro v Lintern* [1973] 1 WLR 1002; Emmet, para 12.075.

[266] *Bristol and West Building Society v Henning* [1985] 1 WLR 778; *Paddington Building Society v Mendelsohn* (1985) 50 P & CR 244; [1986] Conv 57 (MP Thompson); *Abbey National Building Society v Cann* [1991] 1 AC 56, 94; *Equity and Law Home Loans Ltd v Prestridge* [1992] 1 WLR 137 (a person who consented to

(3) Duty to Disclose Overriding Interests

The Land Registration Act 2002[267] introduced a new duty on the person applying for registration to provide to the registrar certain information about overriding interests affecting the estate to which the application relates. The duty arises in the case of both first registration and registration of subsequent dispositions.

There is no specific penalty for failure to disclose, but the object of the provision is to ensure that as many rights as possible are brought onto the register: the registrar may enter a notice in the register in respect of overriding interests that are disclosed.[268]

(4) Criticism of Overriding Interests

The effect of overriding interests is, as we have seen, to bind a transferee from a registered proprietor, whether he knows about them or not—although we have seen that the Land Registration Act 2002 has protected the transferee against certain undiscoverable interests.[269] They detract from the principle that the register should be a mirror of the title, and so it is important that they should be able to justify their existence as a separate category within the system of registered conveyancing. A balance has to be struck between the protection of the person enjoying the interest and the inconvenience to a purchaser. Sympathy for the latter leads to a plea for as complete an abolition of the category as is feasible.

Criticism of overriding interests must, however, be tempered by four considerations. First, although the range of overriding interests has been reduced by the 2002 Act,[270] the category cannot be abandoned completely, however desirable it is that the register should be a complete mirror of the title. It is impossible to enter on the register easements and profits being acquired by prescription. Secondly, as we have seen, the legislature has decided as a matter of policy that protection should be accorded to the rights of a person in actual occupation, even if he has failed to register his interest. This

---

a mortgage was deemed to consent to a later mortgage replacing the earlier mortgage, even if it was obtained without consent, to the extent of the amount secured by the first mortgage plus interest); *Locabail (UK) Ltd v Waldorf Investment Corp,* The Times, 31 March 1999; *Woolwich Building Society v Dickman* [1996] 3 All ER 204; [1996] All ER Rev 254 (PJ Clarke); [1998] CLJ 328 (L Tee); *Bank of Scotland v Hussain* [2010] EWHC 2812 (Ch), [2010] All ER (D) 95 (Nov) at [105] (principle applies even where there is no direct relationship between the person asserting rights and the mortgagee). And the mortgage itself may be invalid if the registered proprietor has no power to create it.

[267] S 71; LRR 2003, rr 28, 57; Land Registry Practice Guide 15. There is no requirement to disclose interests that cannot be protected by notice on the register, public rights, local land charges and leases that have one year or less still to run and, in the case of first registration, interests that are apparent from the deeds and documents of title accompanying the application.

[268] LRR 2003, rr 28(4), 57(5). Under LRA 1925 the applicant had no duty of disclosure, but the registrar has a mandatory duty to enter a notice on first registration of 'any easement, right, privilege, or benefit created by an instrument' which appeared on the title and adversely affected the land: LRA 1925, s 70(2).

[269] LRA 2002, Sch 3, paras 2(c) (interest belonging to person whose occupation not discoverable), 3 (easement or profit not discoverable); above, p 1103.

[270] From 13 October 2013 the only overriding interests that will remain are: most leases granted for three years or less; interests of a person in actual occupation; legal easements and profits that have arisen by implied grant or prescription; customary and public rights; local land charges; and certain mineral rights: *Blackstone's Guide to the Land Registration Act 2002,* para 12.6; above, nn 207, 216.

is most desirable in those situations where the holder of the right might not consult a solicitor and therefore be unaware of the need for entry on the register, such as a contract for a lease. It is the opposite to the Draconian policy of the Land Charges Act 1972 for unregistered conveyancing.[271] 'The rule for registered land is much more reasonable, for possession is the strongest possible title to security.'[272] It should, however, also be remembered that the balance as between the purchaser and the person in actual occupation has been tilted in favour of the purchaser by the 2002 Act, which provides that the purchaser is not bound by the interest of which he has no knowledge, of a person whose occupation would not have been obvious on a reasonably careful inspection of the land.[273] Thirdly, it is impracticable to require the registration of all short tenancies. Fourthly, overriding interests appear frequently on the register—and, since the introduction of the duty of disclosure under the Land Registration Act 2002,[274] more overriding interests will be entered on the register. Even before the 2002 Act the registrar had a duty to enter a note of interests on the register, and in 1969 the then Registrar was able to write:[275]

The plain fact is…that there are mandatory provisions requiring most [overriding interests] to be entered on the register, which operate either on first registration,[276] or on a dealing with registered land,[277] or at any time on proof of their being furnished,[278] and so ensure that, save for squatters' rights,[279] which cannot be recorded, or rights of occupiers or lessees, which are discoverable, under the rule in *Hunt v Luck*,[280] from a proper inspection and inquiry, or local land charges which, obviously, must be recorded locally,[281] they are all entered on the register.

E OVERREACHING[282]

As in unregistered land,[283] a disposition of a registered estate may overreach certain interests with the result that the disponee takes the estate free of the interests, even if he knows about them and even if they would (in the absence of the operation of overreaching) have constituted overriding interests. After the disposition has overreached the interests, they exist only in any capital money paid by the disponee as the price of the disposition. As we shall see, the doctrine of overreaching applies mainly

---

[271] This aspect of the LCA 1925 may have been due to an error on the part of the draftsman of the 1925 legislation: (1977) 41 Conv NS p 419, n 31 (C Harpum); [1982] Conv pp 215–17 (M Friend and J Newton).

[272] (1956) CLJ 228 (HWR Wade).

[273] Above, p 1110.   [274] Above, p 1112.

[275] (1969) 32 MLR at 129 (TBF Ruoff) (some footnotes abbreviated).   [276] LRA 1925, s 70(2).

[277] Ibid, ss 19(2), 22(2).   [278] Ibid, s 70(3). [This was in fact discretionary only.]

[279] Ibid, s 70(1)(f).   [280] [1902] 1 Ch 428 [above, p 88].   [281] LRA 1925, s 70(1)(i).

[282] Smith, *Plural Ownership* (2005), pp 184–92. For a critical analysis of the statutory provisions on overreaching, see [1990] CLJ 277, 287–310 (C Harpum); [1998] Conv 168; [2000] Conv 221 (G Ferris and G Battersby); [2007] Conv 120 (N Jackson); W & H, para 2.175. See also (2003) 119 LQR 94, 125 (G Ferris and G Battersby): 'When viewed as a whole the statutory reforms contained in TLATA 1996, TA 2000, and LRA 2002 create a legal environment in which the law of overreaching will continue to operate as a central support to the marketability of land.'

[283] Above, p 1068.

in relation to a limited category of equitable interests,[284] often termed 'family' interests (such as the beneficial interests of successive owners or co-owners), by contrast with 'commercial' interests (such as leases, estate contracts, easements and profits) that cannot appropriately be substituted by money. Today the principal context in which overreaching operates is on a disposition by trustees of land. We must also consider, however, overreaching on a disposition by the tenant for life or statutory owners under a strict settlement, and by personal representatives and mortgagees.

(1) Trustees of Land

(a) The principle

As we have already seen, a virtue long possessed by the trust for sale[285] or, since 1997, the trust of land,[286] is that upon a sale of the land, the equitable interests of the beneficiaries are kept off the title to the legal estate and are not disclosed to the purchaser, who takes the legal estate free from the beneficial interests.[287] The conveyance by the trustees overreaches the beneficial interests that arise *under* the trust.[288] The purchaser does not enjoy this immunity, however, unless he pays the purchase money to at least two trustees or to a trust corporation, if one has been appointed.[289]

In *State Bank of India v Sood*,[290] the Court of Appeal interpreted the doctrine widely, holding that the interests of beneficiaries were overreached even when no capital money had been advanced at the time when a mortgage (which is a purchase[291]) was created. Peter Gibson LJ said:

> The exercise intra vires of a power of disposition which does not give rise to any capital money, such as an exchange of land, overeaches just as much as a transaction which does. There is every reason to think that the draftsman of the 1925 property legislation fully appreciated the true nature of overreaching. A principal objective of the 1925 property legislation was to simplify conveyancing and the proof of title to land. To this end equitable interests

---

[284] In the case of a strict settlement under the Settled Land Act 1925 certain legal interests can be overreached: below, p 1117, n 302.

[285] For the trust for sale before 1997, see above, pp 103 ff.   [286] Above, Ch 13.

[287] Above, pp 104–5. The 'conveyance to a purchaser of a legal estate in land' (LPA 1925, s 2(1)) includes, eg, the creation of a legal mortgage, and 'purchaser' means a purchaser in good faith for valuable consideration: s 205(1)(ii), (xxi); *HSBC Bank plc v Dyche* [2009] EWHC 2954 (Ch), [2010] 2 P & CR 4.

[288] LPA 1925, ss 2(1)(ii), as amended by TLATA 1996, s 25(1), Sch 3, para 4(1), (2); 27(1), as amended by TLATA 1996, s 25(1), Sch 3, para 4(1), (8); TA 1925, s 14(1), as amended by TA 2000, s 40(1), Sch 2, Pt II, para 19. The extent of overreaching in the case of a trust of land would appear to be less than that accorded to a purchaser from a tenant for life under SLA 1925, s 72(2), (3), below, p 1117, since there is no power to overreach any interests that arise *prior to* the trust of land, apart from the creation of an ad hoc trust of land: below, p 1119. As to whether ordinary trustees of land can overreach interests arising prior to the trust, see Emmet, para 5.152; Megarry and Wade, *Law of Real Property* (5th edn), p 404, n 64, citing *Re Ryder and Steadman's Contract* [1927] 2 Ch 62, 82.

[289] LPA 1925, s 27(2), as amended by TLATA 1996, s 25(1), Sch 3, para 4(1), (8). For a definition of trust corporation see LPA 1925, s 205(1)(xxviii), as extended by LP(A)A 1926, s 3; and below, p 1118, n 315.

[290] [1997] Ch 276, 281; [1997] CLJ 494 (M Oldham); [1997] Conv 134 (MP Thompson); [1997] All ER Rev 267 (PJ Clarke).

[291] Above, n 287.

were to be kept off the title to the legal estate and could be overreached on a conveyance to a purchaser who took free of them.

(b) Bare trusts

The only change made to the doctrine by the Trusts of Land and Appointment of Trustees Act 1996 was to bring bare trusts within its scope. Before 1997 a bare trust fell outside the dual system of trust for sale and strict settlement, and, accordingly, interests under it could not be overreached. After 1996 a bare trust comes within the definition of a trust of land, and accordingly the doctrine of overreaching applies.[292]

(c) Beneficiaries in occupation

In registered land payment to at least two trustees or to a trust corporation overreaches the beneficial interests under a trust of land, even though the beneficiaries are in actual occupation.

In *City of London Building Society v Flegg:*[293]

Mr and Mrs M-B purchased Bleak House and were registered as proprietors. The house was conveyed to them upon trust for sale as beneficial joint tenants, with an express declaration that the trustees should have all the powers of mortgaging of an absolute owner. Part of the purchase price was provided by Mr and Mrs F (the parents of Mrs M-B) who thereby became beneficial tenants in common in respect of their contribution; their interests were not entered on the register. Mr and Mrs M-B raised their part of the purchase price on mortgage with the consent of Mr and Mrs F. Later, without telling Mr and Mrs F, they mortgaged Bleak House by way of second and third charges, and finally they mortgaged it to the Building Society for £37,500, again without the knowledge of Mr and Mrs F, using the proceeds to repay the three earlier loans. At all material times Mr and Mrs F were in actual occupation of the house. When Mr and Mrs M-B defaulted and were made bankrupt, the Building Society sued for possession. The House of Lords held that the society succeeded; the payment of the mortgage money had been made to two trustees, thereby overreaching the equitable interests of Mr and Mrs F, whose interests were transferred to the equity of redemption vested in Mr and Mrs M-B and to the £37,500 received by them.

Mr and Mrs F claimed that, by virtue of their actual occupation, they were entitled to an overriding interest under section 70(1)(g) of the Land Registration Act 1925[294] and that this prevented the overreaching of their interests, unless they had given their consent. Rejecting this argument, Lord Templeman said:[295]

The interests of the respondents cannot at one and the same time be overreached and overridden and at the same time be overriding interests ... There must be a combination of

---

[292] S 1(2)(a), above, p 478. See Law Com No 158, *Overreaching: Beneficiaries in Occupation* (1989), paras 2.17, 3.10, 4.27.

[293] [1988] AC 54, M & B p 551; [1987] All ER Rev 149 (PJ Clarke); (1988) 51 MLR 365 (S Gardner); [1988] Conv 108 (MP Thompson), 141 (P Sparkes) (2006) 69(2) MLR 214 (N Jackson). The decision in *Flegg* is not affected by TLATA 1996: *Birmingham Midshires Mortgage Services Ltd v Sabherwal* (2000) 80 P & CR 256, M & B p 555; (2000) 116 LQR 341 (C Harpum); [2000] Conv 267 (M Dixon); [2001] Conv 221 (G Ferris and G Battersby).

[294] Now LRA 2002, Sch 3, para 2; above, p 1103.   [295] [1988] AC 54, 73, 74.

an interest which justifies continuing occupation plus actual occupation to constitute an overriding interest. Actual occupation is not an interest in itself.

And Lord Oliver of Aylmerton said:[296]

Section 70(1)(g) protects only the rights in reference to the land of the occupier whatever they are at the material time—in the instant case the right to enjoy in specie the rents and profits of the land held in trust for him. Once the beneficiary's rights have been shifted from the land to capital monies in the hands of the trustees, there is no longer an interest in the land to which the occupation can be referred or which it can protect. If the trustees sell in accordance with the statutory provisions and so overreach the beneficial interests in reference to the land, nothing remains to which a right of occupation can attach and the same result must, in my judgment, follow vis-à-vis a chargee by way of legal mortgage so long as the transaction is carried out in the manner prescribed by the Law of Property Act 1925, overreaching the beneficial interests by subordinating them to the estate of the chargee which is not longer 'affected' by them so as to become subject to them on registration pursuant to section 20(1) of the Land Registration Act 1925. In the instant case, therefore, I would, for my part, hold that the charge created in favour of the appellants overreached the beneficial interests of the respondents and that there is nothing in section 70(1)(g) of the Land Registration Act 1925 or in *Boland's* case which has the effect of preserving against the appellants any rights of the respondents to occupy the land by virtue of their beneficial interests in the equity of redemption which remains vested in the trustees.

Any other decision would have undermined the main object of the doctrine of overreaching whereby a compromise is effected between, on the one hand, the interests of the public in securing that land held in trust is freely marketable and, on the other hand, the interests of the beneficiaries in preserving their rights under the trusts.[297]

If, however, the mortgage moneys had been paid to only *one* trustee, as in *Williams & Glyn's Bank Ltd v Boland*,[298] then the interests of Mr and Mrs F would not have been overreached, and they would have had an overriding interest by virtue of their actual occupation, which would have given them an effective defence against the society's claim for possession.

It was further held that their interests were not affected by section 14 of the Law of Property Act 1925, which says:

---

[296] Ibid, 91.

[297] Similarly in unregistered land, the possession of Mr and Mrs F would not have prevented their interests from being overreached; Lord Oliver of Aylmerton at 84. See Law Com No 188, *Overreaching: Beneficiaries in Occupation* (1989), which recommended that there should be no overreaching without the consent of every occupying beneficiary of full age irrespective of registration. This would in effect reverse the decision in *City of London Building Society v Flegg*; [1990] CLJ 277 at pp 311–33 (C Harpum); (1988) OJLS 367 (S Gardner). No such change was implemented, however, by LRA 2002. See also *National Westminster Bank plc v Malhan* [2004] EWHC 847 (Ch), [2004] 2 P & CR DG9 (no decision on whether doctrine of overreaching, and especially the requirement of two trustees, is contrary to HRA 1998). In Ireland, Land and Conveyancing Law Reform Act 2009, s 21, introduced the general concept of overreaching of equitable interests in the land but excluded the operation as against an equitable interest that has been protected by registration, or that belongs to a person in actual occupation: s 21(3)(b)(iii); Wiley, *Irish Land Law* (4th edn, 2010), para 3.110.

[298] [1981] AC 487, M & B p 203; above, p 1106.

This Part of this Act [Part I] shall not prejudicially affect the interest of any person in possession or in actual occupation of land to which he may be entitled in right of such possession or occupation.

The overreaching provisions are to be found in Part I. Lord Templeman said:[299]

Section 14 is not apt to confer on a tenant in common of land held on trust for sale, who happens to be in occupation, rights which are different from and superior to the rights of tenants in common, who are not in occupation on the date when the interests of all tenants in common are overreached by a sale or mortgage by trustees for sale.

(2) Tenant for Life and Statutory Owners

A conveyance by the tenant for life or statutory owners[300] under the powers conferred by the Settled Land Act 1925 or any additional powers conferred by the settlement overreaches the equitable interests of the beneficiaries and also certain other interests, as long as the statutory requirements for the payment of any capital money arising are complied with.[301] More precisely, the position is set out in the Settled Land Act as follows.

The conveyance by the tenant for life passes to the purchaser a title to the legal estate discharged from the following:

(i)   All estates, interests and charges arising *under* the settlement.[302]

(ii) Limited owner's charges,[303] general equitable charges[304] and certain annuities.[305]

These three interests are overreached even if they have been registered as land charges and even though they were created prior to the settlement.[306] The reason is that they lose nothing in value or protection by their conversion into claims against the purchase money.

---

[299] [1988] AC 54, 72. See Lord Oliver of Aylmerton at 80: 'The ambit of section 14 is a matter that has puzzled conveyancers ever since the Law of Property Act was enacted...What section 14 does not do, on any analysis, is to enlarge or add to whatever interest it is that the occupant has in right of his occupation.' He then agreed with Wolstenholme and Cherry (13th edn), vol i, p 63, that s 14 was designed to preserve the principle of *Hunt v Luck* [1902] 1 Ch 428; above, p 88. See [1982] Conv 213 (M Friend and J Newton). See also *Lloyds Bank plc v Carrick* [1996] 4 All ER 630, 642.

[300] Above, p 442.   [301] LPA 1925, s 2(1)(i).

[302] SLA 1925, s 72(2). Before 1926, interests under a settlement might be legal or equitable, and therefore the overreaching machinery in SLA 1882 applied to both legal and equitabe interests. Since 1925, however, there are no legal life estates, entails, etc, and so the interests of beneficiaries under a settlement (to which overreaching applies) are equitable. For a rare exception of an overreachable legal interest (a rentcharge to discharge instalments of capital money expended by the tenant for life), see SLA 1925, s 85.

[303] Above, p 1058.   [304] Above, p 1058.

[305] Ie, under LCA 1972, s 1(4), Sch 1, in unregistered land. 'Annuity' is here limited to annuities for one or more life or lives created after 25 April 1855, and before 1 January 1926. The register in which they might formerly have been entered was closed as from 1 January 1926. All annuities created after 1925 are registrable as general equitable charges.

[306] SLA 1925, s 72(3); see (1934) 77 LJ News 3, 21, 39, 57 (JML).

On the other hand the conveyance by the tenant for life does *not* overreach the following (broadly, 'commercial' interests, which cannot be adequately protected by conversion into money):

(i) Legal estates and charges by way of legal mortgage having priority to the settlement.[307]

(ii) Legal estates and charges by way of legal mortgage to secure money that has been actually raised before the date of the conveyance.[308] An example is a mortgage created before the conveyance by which money has been raised for the payment of portions.

(iii) Terms of years, easements and profits granted for money or money's worth under the settlement.[309]

(iv) Estate contracts, restrictive covenants and equitable easements created after 1925,[310] if registered as land charges.[311]

(v) Restrictive covenants and equitable easements created before 1926, but only if the purchaser has actual or constructive notice of them.[312]

(vi) Estate contracts created before 1926 if the purchaser has actual or constructive notice of them, or if they are capable of registration and have been registered. Such a contract becomes capable of registration upon its assignment after 1925.[313]

For the overreaching provisions to apply, it is essential that upon a sale of the land by the tenant for life or the statutory owner, the purchase money is paid either to the trustees or into court;[314] moreover, except where the trusteeship is held by a trust corporation,[315] there must be at least two trustees to whom this payment is

---

[307] SLA 1925, s 72(2)(i).

[308] Ibid, s 72(2)(ii). See *Re Mundy and Roper's Contract* [1899] 1 Ch 275, 289 (Chitty LJ).

[309] Ibid, s 72(2)(iii)(a).   [310] Above, pp 940, 941.   [311] SLA 1925, s 72(2)(iii)(a), (b).

[312] Above, p 740.   [313] LCA 1972, s 4(7).

[314] SLA 1925, s 18(1)(b).

[315] Ibid, s 117(1)(xxx). 'Trust corporation' means, 'The Public Trustee or a corporation either appointed by the court in any particular case to be a trustee or entitled by rules made under sub-s (3) of s 4 of the Public Trustee Act 1906, to act as custodian trustee.'

Corporations that are entitled under the Public Trustee Rules 1912 (SI 1912 No 348), r 30, as substituted by the Public Trustee (Custodian Trustee) Rules 1975 (SI 1975 No 1189, as amended by SI 1976 No 836; SI 1981 No 358; SI 1984 No 109; SI 1985 No 132; SI 1987 No 1891; SI 1994 No 2519; SI 2002 No 2469), include 'any corporation constituted under the law of the United Kingdom ... or of any other Member State of the European Economic Community ... empowered by its constitution to undertake trust business [and having] one or more places of business in the United Kingdom', and being a company registered in the United Kingdom or another Member State of the European Economic Community 'having a capital (in stock or shares) for the time being issued of not less than £250,000 ... of which not less than £100,000 ... has been paid up in cash'.

The definition was extended by LP(A)A 1926, s 3 to include the 'Treasury Solicitor, the Official Solicitor, and any person holding any other official position prescribed by the Lord Chancellor, and, in relation to the property of a bankrupt and property subject to a deed of arrangement, includes the trustee in bankruptcy and the trustee under the deed respectively, and, in relation to charitable, ecclesiastical and public trusts, also includes any local or public authority so prescribed, and any other corporation constituted under the laws of the United Kingdom or any part thereof that satisfies the Lord Chancellor that it undertakes the administration of any such trusts without remuneration, or that by its constitution it is required to apply made.[316] In registered land the operation of the overreaching machinery is secured by the registrar entering on the register a restriction where he registers the tenant for life or statutory owners as registered proprietor of settled land.[317]

(3) Approved Trustees. Ad hoc Trust of Land or Settlement

The overreaching effect of a conveyance either by trustees of land or by a tenant for life under a strict settlement is limited in the sense that it does not extend to equitable interests that were in existence before the creation of the trust or settlement.[318] If, for example, a fee simple owner charges his land with the payment of a sum of money, and later subjects it to a trust, the normal rule is that a purchaser from the trustees takes the legal estate burdened by the equitable charge.

(a) Ad hoc trust of land

The Law of Property Act 1925 introduced what is variously called an *ad hoc*, or a *special* or an *approved* trust for sale that enables the trustees to overreach even prior interests.[319] Whether it is of this special nature depends entirely upon the character of the trustees. They must be either:

(a) two or more individuals approved or appointed by the court or the successors in office of the individuals so approved or appointed; or

(b) a trust corporation.[320]

(b) Ad hoc Strict Settlement

Before 1997, an alternative open to an estate owner whose land was already subject to an equitable interest was to create an *ad hoc* strict settlement under the Settled Land Act. If he executed a vesting deed, declaring the legal estate to be vested in him upon trust to give effect to equitable interests to which it was subject, and if at the same time he named as trustees either a trust corporation or two persons appointed or approved by the court,[321] the result was that the land became settled land and he acquired the statutory powers of a tenant for life, including the power of sale.[322] It would seem that this alternative is no longer open under the Trusts of Land and Appointment of Trustees Act 1996.

---

the whole of its net income after payment of outgoings for charitable, ecclesiastical or public purposes, and is prohibited from distributing, directly or indirectly, any part thereof by way of profits amongst any of its members, and is authorised by him to act in relation to such trusts as a trust corporation'. A trust corporation must be authorised to act (and give a good receipt) in respect of private trusts, and not only in respect of charitable, ecclesiastical and public trusts: *Fraser v Canterbury Diocesan Board of Finance* [2007] EWHC 1590 (Ch), [2007] 28 EG 121 (CS). See also LPA 1925, s 205(1)(xxviii); TA 1925, s 68(18); AEA 1925, s 55(1)(xxvi); SCA 1981, s 128.

[316] Ibid, s 18(1)(c).
[317] LRA 2002, s 40; LRR 2003, r 91, Sch 4, forms G, H and I (substituted by LR(A)R 2008, Sch 4); Sch 7, paras 2, 4(2), 5(b), 6(2), 7(1), 10(3), 12(1)(a), 13(1)(c).
[318] Except in three cases under SLA 1925, s 72(2), (3); above, p 1118.   [319] LPA 1925, s 2(2).
[320] Defined above, p 1118, n 315.   [321] SLA 1925, s 21.   [322] Ibid, s 21(1)(a).

(c) Overreachable interests

The *ad hoc* trust of land and the *ad hoc* strict settlement are similar in their effects. The land will be conveyed by the estate owner—by the trustees in the one case, by the tenant for life in the other—and, though the equitable charge will be overreached by the conveyance to the purchaser, it will be the duty of the trustees to see that it is paid out of the proceeds of sale to which it has now become attached.

Neither device, however, is of great practical use, for the number of equitable interests capable of being overreached is severely limited. It is enacted that a conveyance, whether under the trust of land or under the strict settlement, shall not affect the following interests:[323]

(i)   Equitable interests protected by a deposit of documents, relating to the legal estate affected, eg where title deeds are deposited with a bank to secure an overdraft.

(ii) Certain equitable interests that cannot be represented in terms of money, namely:

    (a) restrictive covenants;

    (b) equitable easements; and

    (c) estate contracts.[324]

(iii) Any equitable interest that has been registered in accordance with the Land Charges Act 1972,[325] *except*

    (a) certain annuities;[326]

    (b) limited owner's charges;[327] and

    (c) general equitable charges.[328]

Registration of these three interests does not prevent them from being overreached, since they are adequately protected if enforceable against the money instead of against the land.

Thus, if land held by a beneficial owner in his own right, that is land that is subject neither to a trust of land nor a strict settlement, is burdened with the payment of, for example, a general equitable charge that impedes the transfer of an absolute title to a purchaser, there are four possible methods of clearing off the incumbrances, namely:

(i)   The creation of an *ad hoc* trust of land.

(ii) The creation of an *ad hoc* strict settlement.

---

[323] LPA 1925, s 2(3); SLA 1925, s 21(2).

[324] Above, pp 1058–9. These three interests, however, if created after 1925, will be void in unregistered land as against a purchaser of the legal estate for money or money's worth, unless they are registered under the Land Charges Act 1972; or require to be protected by entry of a notice on the register in registered land. If they were created before 1926, they do not bind a purchaser unless he has actual or constructive notice of them: LPA 1925, s 2(5).

[325] Above, p 1054.   [326] Ie, annuities created and registered before 1926; above, p 1056.

[327] Above, p 1058.   [328] Above, p 1058.

(iii) A conveyance of the land to the purchaser by the beneficial owner with the concurrence of the incumbrancer.

(iv) An application for leave to pay into court a sum of money in discharge of the incumbrance.[329]

(4) Personal Representatives

A disposition by personal representatives of the legal estate may become necessary in two types of cases; where they transfer the land to a beneficiary; or where, in order to raise money for the payment of debts, they convey to a purchaser in the ordinary course of administration. Section 18 of the Trusts of Land and Appointment of Trustees Act 1996 confers on personal representatives, subject to suitable modifications, all the powers of trustees of land.[330]

Personal representatives have the overreaching powers of trustees of land including, if the occasion arises, overreaching by approved trustees under an *ad hoc* trust of land.[331] Thus, even equities charged on the land prior to the death of the deceased may be overreached. A conveyance of a legal estate to a purchaser by a personal representative overreaches equitable interests affecting the estate (such as the equitable interets of beneficiaries under the will or intestacy), as long as any capital money arising is paid to the personal representative.[332] No approval by the court is necessary; nor is it necessary, as it is in the case of trustees of land, that there should be at least two personal representatives.[333]

(5) Mortgagors

A conveyance of a legal estate to a purchaser by a mortgagee in the exercise of his power of sale[334] overreaches equitable interests affecting the estate (such as the mortgagor's equity of redemption), as long as any capital money arising is paid to the mortgagee.[335] It is not necessary, as it is in the case of trustees of land, that there should be at least two mortgagors.[336]

---

[329] LPA 1925, s 50.

[330] AEA 1925, s 39(1)(ii), as amended by TLATA 1996, s 25(1), Sch 3, para 6(1), (2); W & H, paras 2.180–2.188. Three sections of the Act are excluded: section 10 on consents, section 11 on consultation with beneficiaries, and section 14 on power to apply to the court: above, pp 483, 484, 488.

[331] Above, p 1119.   [332] LPA 1925, s 2(1)(iii).

[333] LPA 1925, s 27(2), as amended by TLATA 1996, s 25(1), Sch 2, para 4(8). But, if there are two or more personal representatives, a contract or conveyance of land cannot be made without the concurrence of all of them (or, in the case of executors, all the proving executors), or a court order: AEA 1925, s 2(2), as amended by LP(MP)A 1994, s 16(1). See Law Com No 184, *Title on Death* (1989), paras 2.13–2.19.

[334] Above, p 854.   [335] LPA 1925, s 2(1)(iii).

[336] LPA 1925, s 27(2), as amended by TLATA 1996, s 25(1), Sch 2, para 4(8). But, if there are two or more personal representatives, a contract or conveyance of land cannot be made without the concurrence of all of them (or, in the case of executors, all the proving executors), or a court order: AEA 1925, s 2(2), as amended by LP(MP)A 1994, s 16(1). See Law Com No 184, *Title on Death* (1989), paras 2.13–2.19.

A conveyance by a mortgagee under the power of sale conferred by the Law of Property Act 1925 has by statute the effect of overreaching the mortgagor's legal estate as well as other legal mortgages to which the mortgage has priority.[337]

VII ELECTRONIC CONVEYANCING[338]

As we have seen[339] the changes made by the Land Registration Act 2002 prepare the way for the move from a paper-based system of conveyancing to one that is entirely electronic. The enabling provisions for its introduction are set out in Part 8 of the Act, and Schedule 5 sets out the details for the Land Registry network under which electronic conveyancing will take place.

When electronic conveyancing is fully introduced,[340] it will only be possible to make transfers of land and to create many rights and interests in and over land by their electronic registration. The effect will be to move from the present three-stage process, under which a document is executed in the form prescribed by the Land Registration Rules, is then lodged with the appropriate district land registry, and, after the transaction has been processed, the appropriate entry is made on the register. Under the new scheme there will be only a one-stage process by which the completion of a transaction and its registration take place simultaneously. The so-called registration gap will be eliminated.[341]

---

[337] LPA 1925, s 104(1). The conveyance is subject, however, to all estates, interests and rights that have priority over the mortgage: ibid.

[338] R & R, ch 19; H & B, Part 5; Law Com No 271 (2001), Part XIII; Land Registry Consultations on E-conveyancing 2002 (on general principles of e-conveyancing), 2006 (on electronic funds transfer), 2007 (with draft Land Registration (Network Access) Rules and draft Land Registration (Electronic Communications) Order), 2010 (secondary legislation, with draft Land Registration (Electronic Conveyancing) R 2011). The responses to the Consultations are available in the E-conveyancing section of the Land Registry web site: www.landregistry.gov.uk. Land Registration (Network Access) Rules 2008 (SI 2008 No 1748); Land Registration (Electronic Conveyancing) Rules 2008 (SI 2008 No 1750). See also above, pp 839–40 (electronic discharge of registered charges); 972–3 (electronic contracts).

[339] Above, pp 141–3.

[340] It is being introduced incrementally; there is already provision for certain electronic searches and the lodgement of certain documents, and the discharge of registered charges. See above, p 142. The current state of progress can be discovered by consulting the E-conveyancing section of the Land Registry web site.

[341] For an illustration of how the Law Commission thought that a typical conveyancing transaction might operate under electronic conveyancing, see Law Com No 271, *Land Registration for the Twenty-First Century* (2001), paras 2.52–2.55.

29

EXTINCTION OF ESTATES AND INTERESTS IN LAND

Summary

A person's estate is *extinguished* where it is terminated, other than by its natural ending (such as a lease, by effluxion of time) or by its transfer (such as a transfer of the freehold or the assignment of a lease). This may happen in certain circumstances by merger; or by virtue of adverse possession.

I MERGER

A MEANING OF MERGER

The term *merger* means that, where a lesser and a greater estate in the same land come together and vest, without any intermediate estate, in the same person and in the same right, the lesser is immediately annihilated by operation of law. It is said to be 'merged', ie sunk or drowned, in the greater estate.[1]

B MERGER AT COMMON LAW

At common law the doctrine of merger has nothing to do with the intention of the parties, and provided that certain essentials are satisfied, the effect is automatically to

---

[1] Blackstone, vol 11, p 177; Cruise, *Digest,* Tit xxxix, s 1.

annihilate the smaller estate. The essentials are that the estates shall unite in the same person without any intervening estate, and that the person in whom they unite shall hold them both in the same right.

Since 1926, the only estates that can subsist at law are the fee simple absolute in possession and the term of years absolute,[2] and so the modern application of the doctrine of merger of legal estates is limited to the case where the leasehold interest and its immediate reversion are united. This may occur where the tenant acquires the freehold from his immediate landlord; or where a sub-tenant acquires the leasehold estate held by his landlord. But it must be remembered that the merger is not effected if the person holding the two interests does so in different capacities. For example, if an executor takes, under the Administration of Estates Act 1925, a term of years that belonged to the testator, and then purchases the freehold reversion on his own behalf, the term that the executor holds for the purposes of administration does not merge in the freehold that he owns beneficially.[3]

One effect of the common law doctrine was that the merger of a term of years in the reversion destroyed the covenants contained in any sub-lease that has been carved out of the term. For example:[4]

A, who held the fee simple, leased the land to T who sub-leased it to S. If T were to surrender his interest to A, the covenants contained in the sub-lease would become unenforceable, since the reversion to which they were formerly attached no longer existed.

To remedy this, it was enacted in effect by the Real Property Act 1845,[5] in a section reproduced in the Law of Property Act 1925,[6] that where the reversion on a lease is destroyed by surrender or merger, the next vested interest in the land shall be deemed to be the reversion for the purpose of preserving the incidents and obligations of the defunct reversion. In the example given above, therefore, the covenants entered into between T and S are enforceable by and against A and S respectively.

C MERGER IN EQUITY

Equity has taken a different view of merger. At common law merger results automatically from the union of two estates in the circumstances we have mentioned, and intention does not affect the result. But equity looks to the intention and to the duties of the parties. If an intention is expressly declared to the effect that the lesser

---

[2] Above, p 123.   [3] *Chambers v Kingham* (1878) 10 Ch D 743.

[4] *Webb v Russell* (1789) 3 Term Rep 393. Cf *Wall v Collins* [2007] EWCA Civ 444, [2007] Ch 390 at [16] (Carnwath J: 'merger of lease into larger interest in the dominant tenement is not in itself fatal to the continuance of the easement, for the period for which it was granted. The dominant tenement remains unchanged and there is no legal impediment to the continued enjoyment of the easement by by the occupier for the time being of that tenement'); above, p 634, n 3.

[5] S 9; *Bromley Park Garden Estates Ltd v George* [1991] 2 EGLR 95.

[6] S 139; *Electricity Supply Nominees Ltd v Thorn EMI Retail Ltd* [1991] 2 EGLR 46, 48 (Fox LJ).

estate shall be kept alive, there is no difficulty;[7] but, even in the absence of such an express declaration, equity will presume an intention against merger if it is clearly advantageous to the person in whom the estates are united, or if it is consistent with his duty, that the lesser interest shall not be destroyed.[8] This view now prevails: the Law of Property Act 1925 provides that[9]

> there is no merger by operation of law only of any estate the beneficial interest in which would not be deemed to be merged or extinguished in equity.

In *Ingle v Vaughan Jenkins*, for example:[10]

> X, the first tenant for life under a settlement, agreed to let three acres of the land for 99 years to Y, the second tenant for life, at an annual ground rent of £9, in consideration that Y would erect a house on the land at a cost of £1,500. After the house had been erected, X died, with the result that at common law Y's term of years was merged in the life interest to which he now became entitled.

On the death of Y, the remainderman contended that Y's executor was prevented by this merger from claiming any further leasehold interest in the land. The contention failed. The court's one concern is the benefit of the person in whom the two interests unite, and in the instant circumstances it was obviously to the advantage of Y that the term of years should be kept separate from the life interest.

II ADVERSE POSSESSION

An estate in unregistered land may be extinguished[11] at the expiration of the period prescribed by the Limitation Act 1980 for the estate owner to bring an action to recover land.[12] That period is normally 12 years.[13]

In the case of registered land, under the Land Registration Act 1925 the passage of the time prescribed by the Limitation Act 1980 did not extinguish the registered proprietor's legal title, but he held it on trust for the adverse possessor until the register was rectified to reflect the underlying rights that followed from the expiration of the

---

[7] *Golden Lion Hotel (Hunstanton) Ltd v Carter* [1965] 1 WLR 1189. See also *Belaney v Belaney* (1867) 2 Ch App 138 (no merger where conveyance contained recital that purchaser did not wish the term to merge).

[8] *Ingle v Vaughan Jenkins* [1900] 2 Ch 368; *Re Fletcher* [1917] 1 Ch 339; *EDF Energy Networks (EPN) Ltd v BOH Ltd* [2011] EWCA Civ 19, [2011] 5 EGCS 104 (where original reversion had been split, and there are co-reversioners, it is irrelevant that it might be in the co-reversioners interests for there to be no merger).

[9] S 185, replacing Supreme Court of Judicature Act 1873, s 25(4).

[10] [1900] 2 Ch 368. See also *Snow v Boycott* [1892] 3 Ch 110.

[11] There is no Parliamentary conveyance of the title of the dispossessed person to the squatter: below, p 1150.

[12] LA 1980, s 17; below, pp 1149 ff. For an exception for settled land and land held on trust, see s 18; below, p 1142.

[13] Ibid, s 15. For extension of the time because of disability, fraud or deliberate concealment, or mistake, see ss 28, 32; below, pp 1153 ff.

limitation period.[14] Now, under the Land Registration Act 2002, the position is different again: the passage of time does not of itself affect the estate of the registered proprietor, but the adverse possessor may apply to be registered in place of the existing proprietor if he has been in possession for ten years; and although he may not often be entitled to be registered unless the proprietor then consents or fails to object, if he retains possession for a further two years after his first application has been unsuccessful, he is then entitled as of right to be registered.[15]

The effect of both Land Registration Acts is not simply to extinguish the former owner's title, but to transfer it to the adverse possessor. However, the effect of adverse possession on title to registered land, as well as unregistered land, is discussed in this chapter. First, we consider some preliminary matters relating to the nature of possession and its effect on title to land.

A THE SIGNIFICANCE OF POSSESSION IN THE MODERN LAW

We saw in Chapter 2 that the common law developed the doctrine of the *estate*: the 'owner' of land was not absolute owner of the land itself in the manner recognised by the civil law. Rather, he held an estate in the land: the right to seisin, or possession,[16] of the land for a period. The fee simple owner, for example, had the right to possession—and was therefore entitled to exercise proprietary rights over the land—for as long as he or his successors had heirs. The holder of a life estate had the similar right, but only for his own life. The tenant under a lease had the right to possession for the term of the lease. Since the enactment of the Law of Property Act 1925, the estates that can exist at common law are limited to the fee simple absolute in possession, and the term of years absolute.[17] But that Act did not change the nature of land ownership or of the doctrine of the estate. From 1926 in English law the 'ownership' of land was still based on the doctrine of the estate, which is itself inextricably linked to the notion of the right to possession of the land.

We also saw[18] that this reliance on possession as the basis of land ownership resulted in the common law taking the view that the acquisition of possession of the land was itself the acquisition of a title to the land. Possession was a *root of title*. From the first day of his possession, the disseisor had full beneficial rights over the land, holding a fee simple estate—although this was only a *relative* title, since if anyone could show a better right to possession, he could recover the land.[19]

Two separate issues arise from this view, taken by the common law, of the significance of possession.[20] First, if possession is a root of title, how, in practice,

---

[14] LRA 1925, s 75; below, p 1158.   [15] Below, pp 1160 ff.

[16] For the technical usage of 'seisin' (for freeholds) and 'possession' (for leaseholds), see above, p 53.

[17] LPA 1925, s 1(1); above, p 123.   [18] Above, p 51.   [19] Above, pp 49–50.

[20] Possession, or the right to possession, of land also has other significance; eg in the law of tort it gives standing to sue in trespass, or in nuisance: *Powell v McFarlane* (1977) 38 P & CR 452, 469 (Slade J); *Malory*

will a vendor of land in the modern law establish his title to sell? We have seen the answer to this in Chapter 27, in relation to unregistered conveyancing.[21] Secondly, what is the significance of the loss of possession: in what circumstances does a squatter not only oust the owner from possession of his land, but also deprive him of the right any longer to claim that he is owner? This is the question for the present chapter. The answer tells us much about the contemporary development of land law, and completes the picture of the nature of land ownership as it stands at the start of the twenty-first century—because the changes made in this area by the Land Registration Act 2002 have fundamentally changed the significance of possession in the modern law.

B LAPSE OF TIME, PRESCRIPTION AND LIMITATION OF ACTIONS

Most systems of law have realised the necessity of fixing some definite period of time within which persons who have been unlawfully dispossessed of their land must pursue their claims. It is, no doubt, an injustice that after this period has elapsed the wrongdoer should be allowed to retain the land against the person whom he has ousted, but it would be an even greater injustice to the world at large if the latter were allowed after any interval of time, however long, to commence proceedings for recovery of possession. If A, having ejected B, is allowed to remain in long and undisturbed possession of the land, the impression will grow that his title is superior to B's, and the public should be allowed to deal safely with him on that footing. Lord St Leonards said:[22]

> All statutes of limitation have for their object the prevention of the rearing up of claims at great distances of time when evidences are lost; and in all well-regulated countries the quieting of possession is held an important point of policy.

(1) Limitation and Prescription

The effect of a person remaining in possession of the land of another for the period of time fixed by law varies in different countries and in different ages. Thus the effect of *usucapio* in Roman law was to confer a positive title to the land upon a person who had remained in possession for a certain time.[23] Under the Statutes of Limitation,

---

Enterprises Ltd v Cheshire Homes (UK) Ltd [2002] EWCA Civ 151, [2002] Ch 216; *Hunter v Canary Wharf Ltd* [1997] AC 655. Cf [2010] Conv 426 (M Dixon) ('"possession" continues to enjoy a jack-of-all-meanings status in modern property law').

[21] Above, pp 1043–5. In registered land, the register itself establishes the title: above, p 1079.

[22] *Dundee Harbour Trustees v Dougall* (1852) 1 Macq 317. See also *R B Policies at Lloyd's v Butler* [1950] 1 KB 76, 81; [1985] Conv 272 (M Dockray).

[23] Similarly, modern French law adopts the Roman principle, and allows a possessor to acquire a positive title by *usucapion*—after a period (between 10 and 30 years) that depends on whether the acquisition of possession was in good faith, and whether the previous owner is still living in the same district: Bell, Boyron

which were in force in England prior to 1833, the effect of remaining in possession for the prescribed period was to bar only the remedy of the person dispossessed, not his right. His *title* remained intact, and, if he came lawfully into possession of the land again, his title might prevail against the possessor.[24] Under the statutes that have been in force from time to time since 1833[25] the effect of remaining in possession for the statutory period of 12 years in unregistered land is still merely negative, but in the sense that the right as well as the remedy of the person dispossessed is extinguished. The *usucapio* of Roman law exemplified what is sometimes called acquisitive prescription in the sense that possession of another's land for a given period conferred a positive title upon the occupier, but English law has never adopted this theory in its treatment of corporeal hereditaments and chattels, though it has done so in the case of easements and profits.[26]

(2) The Modern Acts

The English law relating to the period within which an action for the recovery of land must be brought was recast and simplified by the Real Property Limitation Act of 1833; was consolidated and amended by the Limitation Act 1939; and, after further amendment by the Limitation Amendment Act 1980, was again consolidated by the Limitation Act 1980. In relation to registered land, this has now been further changed by the Land Registration Act 2002. Originally the period was fixed at the discretion of individual judges. Later, certain dates (such as the first coronation of Henry II) were chosen from time to time by the legislature. Then in 1623 the Limitation Act introduced the modern principle that actions must be brought within a fixed number of years. But even so the state of the law was unsatisfactory owing to the variety of remedies that lay for the recovery of land, and to the fact that the period of limitation varied according to the nature of the remedy adopted. An account of the old law must be sought in works on legal history.[27] We confine ourselves to describing the current law as it has been established by the Limitation

---

and Whittaker, *Principles of French Law* (2nd edn, 2008), pp 277–9. See also *International Encyclopedia of Comparative Law*, vol VI, *Property and Trust*, ch 2, para 2–23 (JH Beekhuis), discussing the role of possession and ownership in modern civil law jurisdictions.

[24] Lightwood, *Possession of Land* (1894), p 153. See *Buckinghamshire County Council v Moran* [1990] Ch 623, 644 (Nourse LJ); *R v Oxfordshire County Council, ex p Sunningwell Parish Council* [2000] 1 AC 335, 349 (Lord Hoffmann).

[25] Real Property Limitation Act 1833; Real Property Limitation Act 1874; LA 1939; Limitation Amendment Act 1980; LA 1980, as amended by Latent Damage Act 1986.

[26] Above, pp 666 ff.

[27] See especially Hayes, *Introduction to Conveyancing* (5th edn, 1840), vol i, pp 222 ff; Holdsworth, *A History of English Law*, vol iv, p 484;vol vii, pp 29 ff; Simpson, *A History of the Land Law* (2nd edn, 1986), pp 151–5.

Act 1980[28] and now varied, in relation to registered land, by the Land Registration
Act 2002.[29]

C UNREGISTERED LAND. LIMITATION ACT 1980

(1) Period of Limitation for Actions to Recover Land

Under the Limitation Act 1980, which applies in relation to unregistered land,[30] no
action can be brought to recover any land after the expiration of 12 years from the date
on which the *right of action accrued* to the claimant,[31] or to the person through whom
he claims.[32] This limitation applies to a foreclosure action.[33]

Land is defined in wide terms. It includes:[34] 'corporeal hereditaments, tithes[35] and
rentcharges[36] and any legal or equitable estate or interest therein,...but except as
provided above in this definition does not include any incorporeal hereditament.'

There are certain exceptional cases[37] in which the ordinary period of 12 years is
increased.

---

[28] Based on the Law Reform Committee 21st Report (Final Report on Limitations of Actions) 1977
(Cmnd 6923), which contains a valuable discussion of all aspects of limitation. The Act came into force on 1
May 1981. See the annotation in Current Law Statutes 1980 (D Morgan); and generally McGee, *Limitation
Periods* (6th edn, 2010); Preston and Newsom, *Limitation of Actions* (3rd edn 1953; 4th edn 1989); Prime
and Scanlan, *Modern Law of Limitation* (1993); Redmond-Cooper, *Limitation of Actions* (1992); Josling,
Periods of Limitation (7th edn, 1989); Oughton, Lowry and Merkin, *Limitation of Actions* (1998); Jourdan
and Radley-Gardner, *Adverse Possession* (2011).

Law Com No 270, *Limitation of Actions* (2001) proposed the repeal of the 1980 Act, and its replacement by
a new, simplified regime for limitation periods. It included proposals relating to land, although substantial
reforms were later made in relation to registered land by the Land Registration Act 2002; below, pp 1160 ff.
The Government accepted the Report in principle in July 2002, and in 2008 it was announced that provisions
on the subject would be included within a proposed Civil Law Reform Bill. However, in 2009 the Government
announced that the limitation reforms would not, after all, be taken forward: Law Com No 323, *Annual
Report 2009–10*, paras 3.12-3.15.

[29] Below, pp 1160 ff.   [30] Below, p 1160.

[31] After a judgment for possession has been obtained in an action begun in due time, the successful
claimant has 12 years from the date of judgment: *BP Properties Ltd v Buckler* (1987) 55 P & CR 337.

[32] LA 1980, s 15(1). Action means proceedings in court for possession, but not an application to the Land
Registry to rectify the register: *JA Pye (Oxford) Ltd v Graham* [2000] Ch 676 (this point was not further
argued on appeal to CA or HL). For possession claims generally, see CPR Pt 55, Part I; and (for summary
proceedings for possession) CPR Sch 1 RSC Ord 113; Sch 2 CCR Ord 24. An appointee under a special power
is not deemed to claim through the appointor: s 38(6).

[33] Ibid, s 20(4). There can be adverse possession of a party wall: *Prudential Assurance Co Ltd v Waterloo
Real Estate Inc* [1999] 2 EGLR 85.

[34] Ibid, s 38(1), as amended by TLATA 1996, s 25(2), Sch 4.   [35] Above, p 124, n 77.

[36] The reference to rentcharges will be removed by Tribunals, Courts and Enforcement Act 2007, Sch 14,
when that Act is brought into force: see above, p 277.

[37] The special period of limitation in respect of an advowson (the right to present to or bestow any
ecclesiastical benefice) was repealed by Patronage (Benefices) Measure 1986, s 4(3); above, p 1045, n 28.

(a) Actions by the Crown

The Crown Suits Act 1769, generally called the *Nullum Tempus* Act, altered the ancient rule that Statutes of Limitations do not bind the Crown and prescribed a period of 60 years in the case of an action to recover land. This period is now 30 years,[38] and there is a general provision that the 'Act shall apply to proceedings by or against the Crown in like manner as it applies to proceedings between subjects'.[39] An action to recover land brought *against* the Crown, however, is subject to the 12 years' period.

(b) Action by corporation sole

An action to recover land by a spiritual or an eleemosynary corporation sole, such as a bishop, dean or master of a hospital, must be brought within 30 years after the date on which the right of action accrued to the corporation or to the person through whom the corporation claims.[40] The ordinary period of 12 years applies in the case of a charitable corporation aggregate, such as one of the colleges of Oxford or Cambridge.

In the case of the Crown or a spiritual or eleemosynary corporation the position with regard to *claiming through a person* may be illustrated by examples:

The Crown purchased from A in 2005 land which was then in the wrongful possession of a third party, X.

If a right of action to recover the land from the wrongful possessor accrued to A more than 12 years before 2005, A's title is extinguished and the Crown acquires nothing. If, however, A's right of action accrued less than 12 years before 2005, say in 2000, then the Crown can sue the wrongdoer at any time within 30 years after 2000.[41]

The reverse case arises where a person claims through the Crown or a corporation sole after a cause of action has already accrued, as for example where:

In 2005 the Crown conveyed to A land which had been in the wrongful possession of X since 1985.

The statutory rule here is that A's remedy against X is barred either 30 years after 1985, when the cause of action accrued to the Crown, or 12 years after the cause of action accrued to himself, *whichever period expires first.*[42] The cause of action

---

[38] LA 1980, s 15(7), Sch 1, para 10. It remains 60 years where foreshore is owned by the Crown: para 11; *Secretary of State for Foreign and Commonwealth Affairs v Tomlin*, The Times, 4 December 1990 (former embassy of Government of Cambodia in St John's Wood, London).

[39] Ibid, s 37(1); *Roberts v Swangrove Estates Ltd* [2008] EWCA Civ 98, [2008] Ch 439. This applies to proceedings by or against the Duke of Cornwall or the Duchy of Lancaster.

[40] Ibid, s 15(7), Sch 1, para 10.   [41] Ibid, s 15(7), Sch 1, paras 10, 13.

[42] Ibid, para 12. This provision applies whether or not the Crown was the owner when the adverse possessor first took possession; the Crown's 30-year period is available from the moment when it acquires the title as long as the title has not already been extinguished by adverse possession (above), and this longer period can then benefit a successor to the Crown: *Hill v Transport for London* [2005] EWHC 856 (Ch), [2005] Ch 379.

accrued to A by virtue of the conveyance of 1985, but nevertheless his remedy is barred in 2015.

(2) The Date from which Time Begins to Run

(a) The general rule

(1) Accrual of right of action

Time begins to run against a claimant only from the date on which the right of action accrued to him or to the person through whom he claims. In the case of land, as distinct from other cases such as contract or tort, the Act lays down specific rules fixing the date at which in varying circumstances this accrual occurs.[43] It deals separately with present interests, future interests, settled land, land held on trust, tenancies and forfeiture or breach of condition.

(2) 'Adverse possession'

Before dealing with these different cases, however, it is necessary to notice an overriding provision of the greatest importance: that time does not begin to run from the specified dates unless there is some person in 'adverse possession' of the land. It does not run merely because the land is vacant.[44] There must be both absence of possession by the claimant and adverse possession by the defendant.

This rule, founded on the obvious reason that a right of action cannot accrue unless there is somebody against whom it can be asserted, was well established after the Real Property Limitation Act 1833, in the case where an *actual possessor* left possession vacant, though there was some doubt whether it applied where the land of a deceased owner remained vacant owing to the failure of the person entitled to the land to take possession. All doubts are now removed, for each statutory rule fixing the date at which the right of action accrues is subject to the overriding condition that there must be some person in possession of the land in whose favour time can run:[45]

No right of action to recover land shall be treated as accruing unless the land is in the possession of some person in whose favour the period of limitation can run (referred to below in this paragraph as 'adverse possession'); and where ... any such right of action is treated as accruing on a certain date and no person is in adverse possession on that date, the right of action shall not be treated as accruing unless and until adverse possession is taken of the land.[46]

---

[43] For accrual in negligence cases in respect of latent damage to property, see the Latent Damage Act 1986, which is based on the recommendations of the Law Reform Committee 24th Report on Latent Damage (1984 Cmnd 9390); McGee, *Limitation Periods* (6th edn), ch 6; (1991) 54 MLR 345 (NJ Mullany); Emmet, para 1.025.

[44] *M'Donnell v M'Kinty* (1847) 10 ILR 514; *Smith v Lloyd* (1854) 9 Exch 562.

[45] LA 1980, s 15(6), Sch 1, para 8(1).

[46] *Moses v Lovegrove* [1952] 2 QB 533. The mere fact that the premises become subject to the Rent Acts, so that possession cannot be recovered without a court order, does not prevent the tenant's possession from being adverse. See too *Hughes v Griffin* [1969] 1 WLR 23.

The term 'adverse possession' must not, however, be misunderstood. It does not mean that the possessor must act adversely to the paper title owner, or 'oust' him, or intend to exclude the whole world including the true owner, or that his use of the land has to be inconsistent with any present or future use by the true owner.

In *JA Pye (Oxford) Ltd v Graham*[47]

P was the registered proprietor of land which it intended to develop. In February 1983 P entered into a contract with G to allow G to use a portion of the land, which was adjacent to G's farm, and was accessible only through G's own land, for the purposes of grazing. This grazing contract ended on 31 December 1983, and P required G to vacate the land but G continued to use it for grazing and P took no steps to evict him. G knew of P's intention to develop the land, and continued to use it knowing that he might be requested to vacate it or to pay for its continued use for grazing, but no such request was made by P. In August 1984 P allowed G to cut and remove hay, in return for payment. In December 1984 G asked P whether he might have a further formal grazing contract, but P did not reply. G made no further attempts to contact P, but would have been prepared to pay for occupation if asked. In 1997 G registered a caution at the Land Registry claiming that he had obtained title by adverse possession. On 30 April 1998 P brought an action challenging this.

The question was whether, by that date, G had been in adverse possession for a period of 12 years. It was held that he had; and that P's title to the land had therefore been extinguished.[48] Lord Browne-Wilkinson said:[49]

> much confusion and complication would be avoided if reference to adverse possession were to be avoided so far as possible and effect given to the clear words of the Acts. The question is simply whether the defendant squatter has dispossessed the paper owner by

---

[47] [2002] UKHL 30, [2003] 1 AC 419; [2003] CLJ 36 (L Tee).

[48] LA 1980, s 17, below, p 1149; LRA 1925, s 75, below, p 1158. For subsequent proceedings arising from this case in which the ECtHR held by a majority that the operation of these statutory provisions was incompatible with Article 1 of the First Protocol to ECHR, see below, pp 1165–6.

[49] [2002] UKHL 30, [2003] 1 AC 419 at [36] (Lord Browne-Wilkinson). 'Adverse possession' bore a technical meaning before the Real Property Limitation Act 1833. Before that date wrongful possession did not ripen into a claim to bar the owner's remedy unless there had been ouster of the seisin in one of five ways (for which see Carson, *Real Property Statutes* (3rd edn, 1927, notes to RPLA 1833, s 2). Moreover, possession where possible was referred to a lawful title, and there were several cases where possession obviously held without title was held not to be 'adverse'. For example, possession of a younger brother was possession of the heir; possession of one co-parcener, joint tenant or tenant in common was the possession of all, unless an intention to claim the whole was expressed; a tenant for years continued to hold for the landlord after the lease ended; if a squatter was entitled to an interest in the land less in extent than that which he claimed under the statute, his possession was referred to his lawful title: see *Lightwood on Possession*, pp 159 ff. Lord St Leonards described the effect of the 1833 Act in these words: 'It is perfectly settled that adverse possession is no longer necessary in the sense in which it was formerly used, but that mere possession may be and is sufficient under many circumstances to give a title adversely': *Dean of Ely v Bliss* (1842) 2 De GM & G 459, 476–7. The effect of the Act was 'to substitute for a period of adverse possession in the old sense a simple period of time calculated from the accrual of the right of action': Preston and Newsom, *Limitation of Actions* (3rd edn), p 87. So 'adverse possession' is now used by the statute simply to describe the possession of those against whom a right of action has accrued to the owner.

going into ordinary possession of the land for the requisite period without the consent of the owner.

(3) Successive adverse possessors

This general principle may be illustrated by the case where the adverse possessor (let us call him X) fails for one reason or another to occupy for the full period of 12 years. In this connection there are four possible situations that must be considered separately.

(i) X dies or transfers his interest to another person before the lapse of 12 years

The principle obtaining here is that since possession is prima facie evidence of seisin in fee,[50] X holds a transmissible interest in the land. The time during which he has possessed is available to his successor in title, and therefore a purchaser or devisee who immediately follows him into possession and holds for the remainder of the 12 years acquires as good a right to the land as if he himself had been in possession for the whole period.[51]

(ii) Possession is abandoned by X and is not retaken by another person

After this abandonment the dispossessed person is in the same position as if he had never been deprived of possession by X. There is no one whom he can now sue. There is no need for him to perform some act or ceremony in order to rehabilitate himself. The former possession of X, as Lord Macnaghten said, is not available to 'some casual interloper or lucky vagrant'.[52] This rule is now statutory:

> Where a right of action to recover land has accrued and after its accrual, before the right is barred, the land ceases to be in adverse possession, the right of action shall no longer be treated as having accrued and no fresh right of action shall be treated as accruing unless and until the land is again taken into adverse possession.[53]

(iii) Possession is abandoned by X and after an interval of time is taken by Y

It follows that in this case the time during which X has occupied is not available to Y, for during a distinct and definite period there was no person against whom the person ousted by X could bring an action for the recovery of the land. Y is not a successor in title of X, and his intrusion causes a fresh right of action to accrue in favour of the person dispossessed by X.

(iv) X loses possession and is followed by a succession of trespassers each claiming adversely to the others

Here there is no distinct interval of time during which the possession is vacant. X, for instance, ejects V, Y ejects X, Z ejects Y, and is in actual possession when the statutory period of 12 years has run from the time of V's ejectment. Who is entitled to succeed

---

[50] Above, p 51.

[51] *Asher v Whitlock* (1865) LR 1 QB 1, M & B p 251; *Mount Carmel Investments Ltd v Peter Thurlow Ltd* [1988] 1 WLR 1078.

[52] *Trustees, Executors and Agency Co Ltd v Short* (1888) 13 App Cas 793, 798; explained by Parker J in *Samuel Johnson & Sons Ltd v Brock* [1907] 2 Ch 533, 538; (1956) 19 MLR p 22, n 11 (AD Hargreaves).

[53] LA 1980, s 15(6), Sch 1, para 8(2).

in an action to recover the land?[54] Objection may be taken to the title of each of these persons, for V has been out of possession for more than 12 years, and yet none of the trespassers has been in possession for that period. Nevertheless, V is barred: 'A continuous adverse possession for the statutory period, though by a succession of persons not claiming under one another, does, in my opinion, bar the true owner.'[55] As for the trespassers, something might be said by the moralist for the earliest possessor, also for the one who has possessed for the longest period, and again for the latest possessor,[56] but it is clear that these conflicting claims must be decided in accordance with the general principle that possession is evidence of title.[57] X, while in possession, is ejected by Y. His possession, therefore, entitles him to recover the land from the wrongdoer, Y. If he takes no proceedings, then Y, upon being ejected by Z, may recover upon the strength of his existing possession: 'Possession being once admitted to be a root of title, every possession must create a title that, as against all subsequent intruders, has all the incidents and advantages of a true title.'[58]

We are now in a position to deal with the accrual of the cause of action in the different cases described by the statute.

(b) Accrual of Rights of Action

(1) Present interests

Time does not begin to run against a person in present possession of land until possession has been taken by another person. The Act states the rule in this way:[59]

> Where the person bringing an action to recover land, or some person through whom he claims, has been in possession of the land, and has while entitled to the land been dispossessed or discontinued his possession, the right of action shall be treated as having accrued on the date of the dispossession or discontinuance.

(i) Discontinuance or dispossession

The language of the above paragraph is not altogether happy, for it might be thought that a mere abandonment of possession is sufficient to set time running. This is not so, however, for the factor common to dispossession and discontinuance is entry upon the land by a stranger.[60] And there will be a 'dispossession' of the paper owner whenever the squatter takes possession:[61]

---

[54] See Pollock and Wright, *Possession in the Common Law* (1888), pp 95 ff; Lightwood, *Possession of Land*, pp 275 ff.

[55] *Willis v Earl Howe* [1893] 2 Ch 545, 553 (Kay LJ).

[56] *Dixon v Gayfere* (1853) 17 Beav 421, 430 (Lord Romilly).

[57] *Asher v Whitlock* (1865) LR 1 QB 1, 6, M & B p 251; approved *Perry v Clissold* [1907] AC 73; Pollock and Wright, p 98.

[58] Pollock and Wright, p 95.   [59] LA 1980, s 15(6), Sch 1, para 1.

[60] Preston and Newsom, *Limitation of Actions* (3rd edn), p 99. See *Rains v Buxton* (1880) 14 Ch D 537; *Tecbild Ltd v Chamberlain* (1969) 20 P & CR 633.

[61] *J A Pye (Oxford) Ltd v Graham* [2002] UKHL 30, [2003] 1 AC 419 at [38] (Lord Browne-Wilkinson). See also *Powell v McFarlane* (1977) 38 P & CR 452, 470 (Slade J).

Except in the case of joint possessors, possession is single and exclusive. Therefore if the squatter is in possession the paper owner cannot be. If the paper owner was at one stage in possession of the land but the squatter's subsequent occupation of it in law constitutes possession the squatter must have 'dispossessed' the true owner for the purposes of Schedule 1, paragraph 1.[62]

(1) 'Possession'

'Possession' requires both the *fact* of possession, and the *intention* to possess. As Lord Browne-Wilkinson has said:[63]

> there are two elements necessary for legal possession: (1) a sufficient degree of physical custody and control ('factual possession'); (2) an intention to exercise such custody and control on one's own behalf and for one's own benefit ('intention to possess') ...
>
> ... there has always, both in Roman law and in common law, been a requirement to show an intention to possess in addition to objective acts of physical possession. Such intention may be, and frequently is, deduced from the physical acts themselves. But there is no doubt in my judgment that there are two separate elements in legal possession. So far as English law is concerned intention as a separate element is obviously necessary. Suppose a case where A is found to be in occupation of a locked house. He may be there as a squatter, as an overnight trespasser, or as a friend looking after the house of the paper owner during his absence on holiday. The acts done by A in any given period do not tell you whether there is legal possession. If A is there as a squatter he intends to stay as long as he can for his own benefit: his intention is an intention to possess. But if he only intends to trespass for the night or has expressly agreed to look after the house for his friend he does not have possession. It is not the nature of the acts which A does but the intention with which he does them which determines whether or not he is in possession.

(2) Factual possession

Leaving aside for the moment the 'special type of case', the question whether there is factual possession does not always admit of a ready answer. The test was put by Lord O'Hagan:[64]

> As to possession, it must be considered in every case with reference to the peculiar circumstances. The acts, implying possession in one case, may be wholly inadequate to prove it in another. The character and value of the property, the suitable and natural mode of using it, the course of conduct which the proprietor might reasonably be expected to follow with a due regard to his own interests—all these things, greatly varying as they must, under various conditions, are to be taken into account in determining the sufficiency of a possession.

---

62 *Treloar v Nute* [1976] 1 WLR 1295, 1300 (Sir John Pennycuick); [1982] Conv 256 (M Dockray).

63 *J A Pye (Oxford) Ltd v Graham*, above, at [40]. In this context the word 'possession' has its ordinary meaning, which is the same as in the law of trespass or conversion: ibid, at [42]. For a useful summary of the general propositions, see *Topplan Estates Ltd v Townley* [2004] EWCA Civ 1369, [2005] 1 EGLR 89 at [70]-[76] (Jonathan Parker LJ).

64 *Lord Advocate v Lord Lovat* (1880) 5 App Cas 273, 288; cited in *Treloar v Nute* [1976] 1 WLR 1295, 1299.

Some cases, of course, may be obvious, as for instance, where a stranger occupies the house of another or encloses and cultivates a strip of his neighbour's land.[65] It must be a very exceptional case in which enclosure will not demonstrate the relevant adverse possession required for a possessory title;[66] but enclosure is not necessarily conclusive.[67] And cultivation without fencing may amount to adverse possession.[68]

---

[65] *Marshall v Taylor* [1895] 1 Ch 641.

[66] *George Wimpey & Co Ltd v Sohn* [1967] Ch 487, 512 (Russell LJ).

[67] Ibid (where the stranger had an easement over the land in question). See also *Littledale v Liverpool College* [1900] 1 Ch 19; *Hughes v Cork* [1994] EGCS 25.

[68] *Seddon v Smith* (1877) 36 LT 168. See also *Tecbild Ltd v Chamberlain*, above, n 60 (playing by children and tethering of ponies held to be acts too trivial for adverse possession); *Basildon DC v Manning* (1975) 237 EG 879 (erecting fence and dumping poultry manure held not to be adverse possession); *Red House Farms (Thorndon) Ltd v Catchpole* (1976) 244 EG 295 (shooting over marshy ground held to be adverse possession); *Treloar v Nute* [1976] 1 WLR 1295 (grazing of two cows and a yearling, storing timber and stone and filling in a gully held to be adverse possession); *Hyde v Pearce* [1982] 1 WLR 560 (continued occupation by purchaser, after termination of licence to occupy pending completion, held not to be adverse possession since 'he had at no time made it clear that he was no longer bound by the contract of sale'); cf *Bridges v Mees* [1957] Ch 475 (contracting purchaser having equitable ownership was in adverse possession); [1982] Conv 383 (JEM); 46 MLR 89 (M Dockray); *Bills v Fernandez-Gonzalez* (1981) 132 NLJ 60 (compost pens, bonfires, free-ranging chickens and planting trees and shrubs, together with adjoining owner's walking along line of fence for purposes of *his* garden, held not to be adverse possession); *Williams v Usherwood* (1983) 45 P & CR 235 (enclosure of land by fence, parking of three cars in enclosed curtilage of private dwelling house and paving of driveway with decorative crazy-paving stones held to be adverse possession); [1983] Conv 398 (M Dockray); 134 NLJ 144 (H Wilkinson); *Dear v Woods* [1984] CA Transcript 318 (playing of children, single perambulation by male claimant and laying of tar macadam on strip half the width of a brick held not to be adverse possession; this note was cited by Sir David Cairns as containing examples of trivial acts that will not suffice); *Boosey v Davis* (1987) 55 P & CR 83 (grazing of goats, cutting down of scrub and erection of secondary wire mesh fence held not to be adverse possession); *Buckinghamshire County Council v Moran* [1990] Ch 623 (placing of new lock and chain on access gate held to be adverse possession); *Bladder v Phillips* [1991] EGCS 109 (cleaning of ditch at defendant's request ('thinking it was my ditch') held not to be adverse possession); *Ellett-Brown v Tallishire Ltd* (CA 29 March 1990) (clipping of hedge, filling in ditch, planting of daffodils and building of brick pillar to serve as gatepost held not to be adverse possession); *Marsden v Miller* (1992) 64 P & CR 239 (erection of fence for 24 hours held not to be adverse possession by person having no documentary title against another such person); *Wilson v Martin's Executors* [1993] 1 EGLR 178 (walking boundary, cutting chestnuts for repair of fence, clearing fallen timber for firewood, repairing wire fence and cutting trees for sale held not to be adverse possession); *Stacey v Gardner* [1994] CLY 568 (incinerator on concrete base on small part of land held not to be adverse possession, even though it was a substantial piece of machinery and a prominent feature); *Hughes v Cork* [1994] EGCS 25 (enclosure of triangular shaped plot 'most cogent evidence' of adverse possession); *Basildon DC v Charge* [1996] CLY 4929 (keeping of geese within chestnut paling fence, digging of vegetable patch and storage of sawed wood held not to be adverse possession); *London Borough of Hounslow v Minchinton* (1997) 74 P & CR 221 (keeping of compost heap, trimming of hawthorn and elderberry hedges and erection of fencing to prevent dogs from escaping held to be adverse possession); (1997) 147 NLJ 1662 (HW Wilkinson); *Prudential Assurance Co Ltd v Waterloo Real Estate Inc* [1998] EGCS 51, affd [1999] 2 EGLR 85 (adverse possession of one face of a divided wall); *Central Midlands Estates Ltd v Leicester Dyers Ltd* [2003] 2 P & CR DG1 (no possession where car parking was on an unenclosed strip of land with no erection of car parking signs; cf above, p 646, for the relationship between taking possession and the enjoyment of an easement); *Inglewood Investment Co Ltd v Baker* [2002] EWCA Civ 1733, [2003] 2 P & CR 23 (erection of portakabins for use as lavatories for those attending car boot sales; shooting of rabbits and foxes; children playing and deposit of rubbish held not to be adverse possession; nor was the erection of a fence, the object of which was to keep sheep in and not to keep the paper owner out); *Purbrick v Hackney LBC* [2003] EWHC 1871 (Ch), [2004] 1 P & CR 34 (placing makeshift door with two locks on entrance to dilapidated 'burnt-out shell' held to be adverse possession, even though squatter was aware that he was liable to be dispossessed); *Topplan Estates Ltd v Townley* [2004] EWCA Civ 1369, [2005] 1 EGLR 89 (no obligation in law on squatter to alert owner that time is running against him); *Ashe v National Westminster*

Once he has taken possession, the adverse possessor can still exclude himself from possession, and thereby lose his claim; but there must be an exclusion from possession, as opposed merely to a temporary absence.[69]

(3) Intention to possess

Not only must the stranger establish factual possession; he must also show that he has the requisite intention to possess (*animus possidendi*). It used to be said that the stranger must take occupation with the intention of excluding the owner as well as others,[70] but this has now been disapproved. Instead, what is required is an[71]

> intention, in one's own name and on one's own behalf, to exclude the world at large, including the owner with the paper title if he be not himself the possessor, so far as is reasonably practicable and so far as the processes of the law will allow.

It is therefore not inconsistent with the squatter's possession that he knows that, until the full time has run, the paper owner can recover the land from him; nor that he would be willing to pay the paper owner if asked. An admission of title by the squatter is not inconsistent with his being in possession in the meantime.[72]

In *Powell v McFarlane*[73] Slade J's elaboration of the requirement of intention shows how heavy the burden of proof is on a stranger whose alleged possession originates in a trespass:

Bank plc [2008] EWCA Civ 55, [2008] 1 WLR 710 (adverse possession by mortgagor against mortgagee); *Port of London Authority v Ashmore* [2010] EWCA Civ 30; [2010] 1 All ER 1139 (acquisition of title to tidal foreshore and river bed by mooring; see also *Roberts v Swangrove Estates Ltd* [2008] EWCA Civ 98, [2008] Ch 439).

69 *Generay Ltd v Containerised Storage Co Ltd* [2005] EWCA Civ 478, [2005] 2 EGLR 7 (three months' exclusion from part of land by erection of line of rods and orange tape).

70 *Littledale v Liverpool College* [1900] 1 Ch 19, 23 (Lindley MR).

71 *Powell v McFarlane* (1977) P & CR 452, 471–2 (Slade J), approved in *JA Pye (Oxford) Ltd v Graham* [2002] UKHL 30, [2003] 1 AC 419 at [43] (Lord Browne-Wilkinson).

72 *JA Pye (Oxford) Ltd v Graham*, above, at [46].

73 Above, n 71 (infant who at age of 14 began to graze the cow, Kashla, otherwise known as Ted's cow, held not to have requisite intent); (1980) 96 LQR 333 (P Jackson); [1982] Conv 256, 345 (M Dockray); *Lodge v Wakefield Metropolitan City Council* [1995] 2 EGLR 124 (occupier who wrongly believed that he was a rent paying tenant held to have necessary animus possidendi); *Ellis v Lambeth LBC* (2000) 32 HLR 596 (squatter not estopped by failure to return community charge form); *Battersea Freehold and Leasehold Property Co Ltd v Wandsworth LBC* [2001] 2 EGLR 75 (distribution of access keys to other persons entitled to use land indicates lack of animus); *Wretham v Ross* [2005] EWHC 1259 (Ch), [2006] 1 P & CR DG2 at [41] (David Richards J): 'erroneous belief by the occupier that he has the consent of the owner does not mean that he is not in possession of the property'; *Clowes Developments (UK) Ltd v Walters* [2005] EWHC 669 (Ch), [2006] 1 P & CR 1 (daughter and son-in-law of former licensee had no intention to possess; intention to remain in factual possession only for so long as the true owner continues so to permit not sufficient animus), disapproved in *J Alston & Sons Ltd v BOCM Pauls Ltd* at [100] (Judge Marshall: 'in finding that the two occupants "never intended to dispossess the true owner", Hart J [in *Clowes*] was, again, reintroducing extraneous notions of confrontation that are inappropriate, and was converting the requirement of an "intention to possess" into one of "an intention to dispossess", which is incorrect and unnecessary', but the decision in the case could be supported on other grounds); *Tennant v Adamczyk* [2005] EWCA Civ 1239; [2006] 1 P & CR 28 (mere intention to use own land and to make additional use of other land only so far as necessary for parking and unloading not sufficient); *Ofulue v Bossert* [2009] UKHL 16, [2009] 1 AC 990 at [67] (fact that person wrongly believes he is in possession as tenant, in law or or equity, does not prevent the possession having been 'adverse').

An owner or other person with the right to possession of land will be readily assumed to have the requisite intention to possess, unless the contrary is clearly proved. This, in my judgment, is why the slightest acts done by or on behalf of an owner in possession will be found to negative discontinuance of possession. The position, however, is quite different from a case where the question is whether a trespasser has acquired possession. In such a situation the courts will, in my judgment, require clear and affirmative evidence that the trespasser, claiming that he has acquired possession, not only had the requisite intention to possess, but made such intention clear to the world.[74] If his acts are open to more than one interpretation and he has not made it perfectly plain to the world at large by his actions or words that he has intended to exclude the owner as best he can, the courts will treat him as not having had the requisite *animus possidendi* and consequently as not having dispossessed the owner.[75]

In the absence of concealed fraud,[76] it is irrelevant that the true owner is ignorant that he has been dispossessed. As Slade J said:[77]

In view of the drastic results of a change of possession, a person seeking to dispossess an owner must at least make his intentions sufficiently clear so that the owner, if present at the land, would clearly appreciate that the claimant is not merely a persistent trespasser, but is actually seeking to dispossess him.[78]

(4) Intention of true owner

Difficulties have arisen where the owner of a strip of land who has no immediate use for it, retains it for some specific purpose in the future, and meanwhile some other person has physical possession of it. Until recently the owner was not treated as dispossessed. In *Leigh v Jack*,[79] for instance, where a stranger deposited heavy factory materials on a strip of land that the owner intended to dedicate as a highway at a future date, it was held that there was neither discontinuance nor dispossession. Bramwell LJ said:[80]

In order to defeat a title by dispossessing the former owner, acts must be done which are inconsistent with his enjoyment of the soil for the purposes for which he intended to use it: that is not the case here, where the intention of the plaintiff and her predecessor in title was not either to build upon or to cultivate the land, but to devote it at some future time to public purposes.

However, this has been doubted at first instance,[81] and rejected by the Court of Appeal,[82] and again most recently in very firm terms by the House of Lords:[83]

---

[74] This requirement applies to an unconscious as well as to a conscious trespasser: *Prudential Assurance Co Ltd v Waterloo Real Estate Inc* [1999] 2 EGLR 85.

[75] *Morrice v Evans* [1989] EGCS 26 (claimant accepted an assertion by the true owner of a right to restrict the claimant's activities on the land); *Pavledes v Ryesbridge Properties Ltd* (1989) 58 P & CR 459 (claimant of land for car-parking asked the true owner 'to do its duty as the person entitled to possession to keep out trespassers').

[76] Below, p 1154.   [77] *Powell v McFarlane* (1977) 38 P & CR 452, 480.

[78] *Wilson v Martin's Executors* [1993] 1 EGLR 178.   [79] (1879) 5 Ex D 264.   [80] Ibid, 273.

[81] *Powell v McFarlane* (1977) 38 P & CR 452, 469 (Slade LJ).

[82] *Buckinghamshire County Council v Moran* [1990] Ch 623, 645 (Nourse LJ). See also *London Borough of Hounslow v Minchinton* (1997) 74 P & CR 221.

[83] *JA Pye (Oxford) Ltd v Graham*, above, n 47, at [45] (Lord Browne-Wilkinson). For the re-introduction, however, of this 'heresy' in relation to the acquisition of title by a trespasser between October 2000 and

The suggestion that the sufficiency of the possession can depend on the intention not of the squatter but of the true owner is heretical and wrong. It reflects an attempt to revive the pre-1833 concept of adverse possession requiring inconsistent user. ... The highest it can be put is that, if the squatter is aware of a special purpose for which the paper owner uses or intends to use the land and the use made by the squatter does not conflict with that use, that may provide some support for a finding as a question of fact that the squatter had no intention to possess the land in the ordinary sense but only an intention to occupy it until needed by the paper owner. For myself I think there will be few occasions in which such inference could be properly drawn in cases where the true owner has been physically excluded from the land. But it remains a possible, if improbable, inference in some cases.

(5) Implied licence

If the owner gives permission to a stranger to commit the acts of possession upon which he seeks to rely, then the latter cannot succeed, because time does not run in favour of a licensee.[84] The reliance in some earlier cases on a doctrine of an implied or hypothetical licence[85] was rejected by the Limitation Act 1980. The doctrine was explained by Slade J as follows:[86]

Very broadly ... it would appear that in any case where the acts of an intruder, however continuous and far-reaching, do not substantially interfere with any present or future plans which the owners may have for the use of unbuilt land, the court will not treat the intruder as having dispossessed the owner for the purpose of the Limitation Act 1939 because it will treat him as having been there under some implied or hypothetical licence.

The Limitation Act 1980 rejected this doctrine while preserving the possibility of a licence being implied where the actual facts of the case warrant it:[87]

For the purpose of determining whether a person occupying any land is in adverse possession of the land it shall not be assumed by implication of law that his occupation is by permission of the person entitled to the land merely by virtue of the fact that his occupation is not inconsistent with the latter's present or future enjoyment of the land.

This provision shall not be taken as prejudicing a finding to the effect that a person's occupation of any land is by implied permission of the person entitled to the land in any case where such a finding is justified on the actual facts of the case.

October 2003, in order to construe the provisions of LA 1980 and LRA 1925 as compatible with HRA 1998, see *Beaulane Properties Ltd v Palmer* [2005] EWHC 817 (Ch), [2006] Ch 79; below, p 1165.

[84] *BP Properties Ltd v Buckler* [1987] 2 EGLR 168 (possession ceased to be adverse when claimant occupied by unilateral licence from true owner), [1994] Conv 196 (H Wallace); *Sze To Chun Keung v Kung Kwok Wai David* [1997] 1 WLR 1232 (licence from someone other than the dispossessed) (the last appeal to PC from Hong Kong); *Smith v Lawson* (1997) 75 P & CR 466 (time held not to run against freeholder in favour of occupier of land protected by promissory estoppel).

[85] *Wallis's Cayton Bay Holiday Camp Ltd v Shell-Mex and BP Ltd* [1975] QB 94, 103 (Lord Denning MR); *Gray v Wykeham-Martin and Goode* [1977] Bar Library Transcript No 10A (where there had first been an express licence); *Powell v McFarlane* (1977) 38 P & CR 452. The contrary approach along traditional lines was demonstrated in *Treloar v Nute* [1976] 1 WLR 1295. See (1980) 77 LSG 270 (PA Kay).

[86] *Powell v McFarlane*, above, at 484. See also *JA Pye (Oxford) Ltd v Graham*, above, at [32].

[87] S 15(6), Sch 1, para 8(4), replacing Limitation Amendment Act 1980, s 4. Implied licences were found on the facts in *Colin Dawson Windows Ltd v King's Lynn and West Norfolk BC* [2005] EWCA Civ 9, [2005] 2 P & CR 19; *Batsford Estates (1983) Co Ltd v Taylor* [2005] EWCA Civ 489, [2005] 2 EGLR 12.

(ii) Deceased person in possession at death

When A, the person entitled to land, dies while still in possession, and a stranger seizes possession after his death, time begins to run from the date of his death, not from the wrongful seizure, against those who claim under his will or upon his intestacy.[88] The same rule applies to a rentcharge created by will or taking effect upon death.[89]

(iii) Grant of present interest

Where an interest in possession has been granted to A, or where the land has been charged in his favour with the payment of a rentcharge, and he has not taken possession or has not received the rent, time begins to run against him from the date of the grant.[90]

So far as a rentcharge is concerned this rule meets the case where the rent payer has never made a payment of the money due.

Where, however, he wrongfully makes payment to a stranger,[91] the statutory rule is that time shall begin to run against the owner of the rentcharge from 'the date of the last receipt of rent' by him.[92] The result of this is to reduce the limitation period of 12 years, for normally a right of action would accrue and time would begin to run, not from the last receipt of rent, but from the date when the rent again became due. If, for example, the rent is payable annually on 29 September and payment is duly made on that date in 2005, no *right of action or of distraint* accrues until 29 September 2006. Nevertheless time begins to run under the statute on 29 September 1999, so that in effect the period of limitation is reduced to 11 years.[93]

(2) Future interests

(i) Alternative periods

The date upon which time begins to run against the owner of a future interest depends upon whether the person entitled to the preceding estate was in possession when it came to an end. Suppose that there is a:

grant to A for life, remainder to B in fee simple,

and that B fails to take possession on the death of A. In such a case the statute enacts alternative rules.

(i) If A dies while still possessed of the land, B's right of action accrues upon the determination of the life interest, ie he must sue within 12 years from the death of A.[94]

(ii) If A is not in possession at death, eg where he has been dispossessed by a stranger, B has the longer of two alternative periods within which he may bring

---

[88] LA 1980, Sch 1, para 2; *James v Williams* [2000] Ch 1 (executor de son tort).

[89] Ibid, Sch 1, para 2.   [90] Ibid, Sch 1, para 3.

[91] See generally Preston and Newsom, *Limitation of Actions* (4th edn 1989), para 6.6.4.

[92] LA 1980, s 38(8).   [93] *Owen v De Beauvoir* (1847) 16 M & W 547.

[94] LA 1980, s 15(6), Sch 1, para 4.

his action, namely, 12 years from the time when the cause of action accrued to A, or six years from the death of A.[95]

This second rule does not apply where the preceding estate is a term of years absolute.[96] Therefore time does not begin to run against a landlord until the lease determines, even though the tenant may have been ejected before that date.[97]

(ii) Entailed interest

Neither rule applies to an interest limited after an entailed interest that is capable of being barred by the tenant in tail.[98] In this case the remainderman 'claims through' the tenant in tail, so that if time has commenced running against the latter it continues to run against the remainderman, and does not start afresh upon the determination of the entail.

(iii) Settlement made by person out of possession

Future interests created by a settlor after time has commenced to run against him are subject to a different rule. The second case given above contemplates that *after* the settlement in favour of B has been made, a right of action accrues to A, the owner of the preceding estate, against an adverse possessor. In those circumstances, as we have seen, B may recover the land within six years from the death of A, though it may be more than 12 years since A was wrongfully dispossessed. But if time begins to run against a settlor, no *subsequent* alteration in his title, for example, by the later creation of future interests, will prevent the bar from operating after the lapse of 12 years. The persons deriving title from the settlor cannot be in a better position than he is:[99]

> Thus, if A, seised in fee in possession, were dispossessed by X, and were afterwards to settle the estate upon B for life, remainder to C in fee, the time would run from the dispossession, in the same manner as if no such settlement had been made.[100]

(iv) Same person entitled to successive interests

Where a person is entitled to successive interests in land, one present, the other future, the general principle is that, if his present interest is barred, the bar shall extend also to his future right.[101] Thus if land stands limited:

> to A for life, remainder to B for life, remainder to A in fee simple,

and A is dispossessed for 12 years, he and those claiming under him lose the right to recover both the life interest and the fee simple in remainder. The right to recover the fee simple, however, is not barred if, to quote the words of the Act, 'possession has been recovered by a person entitled to an intermediate estate or interest'.[102] If, for instance, in the example just given, B were to recover possession after A had been dispossessed

---

[95] Ibid, s 15(2). The corresponding periods are 30 years and 12 years where the Crown or a spiritual or eleemosynary corporation is entitled to the future interest: s 15(6), Sch 1, para 13.

[96] Ibid.   [97] Below, p 1145.   [98] LA 1980, s 15(3).   [99] Ibid, s 15(4).

[100] Hayes, *Introduction to Conveyancing*, vol I, p 257.   [101] LA 1980, s 15(5).

[102] Ibid.

for 12 years, a right of recovery in respect of the fee simple would accrue to A and those claiming under him, upon the death of B.

(3) Forfeiture or breach of condition

A right of action to recover land by virtue of a forfeiture or breach of condition accrues on the date on which the forfeiture was incurred or the condition broken. If, however, a reversioner or remainderman fails to take advantage of the forfeiture or breach of condition he still retains the right of recovery that accrues to him when his estate falls into possession.[103] So if A, tenant for years, subject to a condition of re-entry, breaks the condition, the time runs against the reversioner in respect of his right of entry for the breach from its occurrence; but a bar to such right of entry will not affect his right to enter on the expiration of the lease by effluxion of time.[104]

(4) Settled land and land held on trust

Equitable interests in land, such as a life interest under a strict settlement and equitable interests under a trust of land, are land within the meaning of the Limitation Act 1980.[105] In general, the provisions of the Act apply to these interests in like manner as they apply to legal estates, and the right to sue for the recovery of the land is deemed to accrue to the person entitled in possession on the date on which it would accrue if his interest were a legal estate.[106] Where such equitable interests exist the legal estate will, according to the circumstances, be vested in a tenant for life or statutory owner, or in personal representatives or in trustees of land, all of whom are trustees for the purposes of the Act.[107]

There are two circumstances in which the beneficiaries entitled to the equitable interests may be affected by wrongful possession:

(1)   The trustee in possession may disregard the rights of the beneficiaries.

(2)   A stranger may seize possession and hold it adversely to the beneficiaries.

(i) Adverse possession by trustee

The first case raises no difficulty, for a trustee cannot obtain a title to the land by adverse possession against the beneficiaries. It is expressly enacted that no period of limitation shall apply to an action brought by a beneficiary:[108]

(a)   in respect of any fraud or fraudulent breach of trust to which the trustee was a party or privy;

In the context of this paragraph, fraud and fraudulent breach of trust are limited to cases involving dishonesty. The result is that in the absence of deliberate concealment,[109]

---

[103]   LA 1980, s 15(6), Sch 1, para 7.
[104]   Hayes, *Introduction to Conveyancing*, vol I, p 252.
[105]   LA 1980, s 38(1), as amended by TLATA 1996, s 25(2), Sch 4.
[106]   Ibid, s 18(1), as amended by TLATA 1996, s 25(2), Sch 4.
[107]   Ibid, s 38(1).
[108]   Ibid, s 21(1).
[109]   Below, p 1154.

liability for an honest breach of trust is statute-barred after six years, but liability for a dishonest breach of trust endures without limitation of time.[110]

    (b) to recover from the trustee trust property or the proceeds of trust property in the possession of the trustee or previously received by the trustee and converted to his use.

Thus, if a person, who is in possession of land as trustee for A and B, pays the whole of the profits to A, time does not run against B.[111] Even a notional receipt of property may come within this enactment. Thus, a trustee who remains in occupation of trust land for his own benefit is deemed to have received profits belonging to the beneficiaries, since in the circumstances he is chargeable with an occupation rent. Therefore, he can never escape liability for payment of this by pleading lapse of time, unless, under the equitable doctrine of laches, a beneficiary has been so late in bringing his action that it would be practically unjust to grant him relief.[112]

The statutory provision (b) has an important effect upon tenancies in common. Where land is limited to A and B as tenants in common in fee simple, the beneficiaries become joint tenants and trustees of the legal estate upon trust to give effect to their own beneficial interests.[113] If, therefore, A appropriates the whole of the rents and profits to himself for many years, he does not acquire a title against B, for, since the land is in his possession as trustee, time does not run in his favour.[114]

If a beneficiary is entitled to a future interest in the trust property, his right of action does not accrue until the interest falls into possession; otherwise he would be compelled to litigate in respect of any injury to an interest that he may never live to enjoy.[115]

Where the claim is not comprised in provisions (a) and (b), such as where it concerns an unauthorised investment, the beneficiary must sue the trustee within six years from the accrual of his cause of action.[116]

In one case a trustee who is *also a beneficiary* under the trust is entitled to some relief from the effect of these provisions. If he distributes the trust property amongst himself and, for example, A and B, two other beneficiaries under the trust, and then another beneficiary C appears more than six years after the distribution, under these provisions C would be able to claim from the trustee the full amount of the share of the trust property to which he would have been entitled if all the beneficiaries had claimed in time. The law was amended in 1980 to limit the liability of a trustee who has acted

---

[110] *Armitage v Nurse* [1998] Ch 241, 260.

[111] *Knight v Bowyer* (1858) 2 De G & J 421; see Preston and Newsom, *Limitation of Actions* (3rd edn), pp 148, 169.

[112] *Re Howlett* [1949] Ch 767; below, p 1147.   [113] Above, p 501.

[114] *Re Landi* [1939] Ch 828; *Re Milking Pail Farm Trusts* [1940] Ch 996; Preston and Newsom, *Limitation of Actions* (3rd edn), pp 149–51. See (1941) 57 LQR 26 (REM); (1971) 35 Conv (NS) 6 (G Battersby).

[115] *Armitage v Nurse* [1998] Ch 241, 261.

[116] LA 1980, s 21(3). The section does not apply to an action by the Attorney-General to enforce a charitable trust, because there is no relevant beneficiary: *A-G v Cocke* [1988] Ch 414.

honestly and reasonably in making the distribution: he has to pay to C only the excess over his, the trustee's, proper share.[117]

(ii) Adverse possession by stranger

Where a stranger seizes possession, the rule stated above, that the statutory provisions apply to equitable interests as well as to legal estates, if it stood alone, would mean that 12 years' possession held by the stranger adversely to the trustee would extinguish the legal estate and bar the remedy of the beneficiaries. This is not so. It is provided by another section[118] that where possession of land has been held for 12 years adversely to the trustee (ie adversely to a tenant for life or statutory owner of settled land, or to trustees of land), the legal estate shall not be extinguished so long as the right of a beneficiary to recover the land has not accrued or has not been barred.

Thus the legal estate is not extinguished until the right of action of the *beneficiary* is barred. There is a further provision that a statutory owner or a trustee may sue for the recovery of the land on behalf of a beneficiary whose title to the equitable interest has not been barred.[119] By way of illustration:

> Suppose that land is settled under a strict settlement upon A for life with remainder to B in fee simple, and that a stranger seizes the land in A's lifetime and remains in adverse possession for 12 years.

In these circumstances the *beneficial* life interest of A is extinguished, with the result that the adverse possessor acquires an equitable interest *pur autre vie*. Nevertheless the *legal fee simple*, held by A under the provisions of the Settled Land Act 1925, remains intact, and therefore B, as the owner of a future interest, will be able to enforce his right of action when it accrues to him upon the death of A. When that event occurs, the representatives of A, upon whom his legal fee simple devolves, may recover the land on behalf of B.[120]

(iii) Adverse possession by beneficiary

The only case remaining for consideration is where a *beneficiary* claims title by virtue of adverse possession for 12 years. Under the law as it stood before the Limitation Act 1939, such a person, although he was ordinarily regarded as tenant at will of the trustee, acquired a title by 12 years' possession if he occupied the land to the exclusion of the trustees and the other beneficiaries.[121] Now, however, his possession cannot be adverse to these persons, for it is enacted that during his occupation of the land time shall not run against a tenant for life, statutory owner, trustee or beneficiary.[122]

---

[117] LA 1980, s 21(2), replacing Limitation Amendment Act 1980, s 5.   [118] Ibid, s 18(2), (3).
[119] Ibid, s 18(4).
[120] See generally Preston and Newsom, *Limitation of Actions* (3rd edn), pp 143–6.
[121] *Burroughs v M'Creight* (1844) 1 Jo & Lat 290 (Ireland).
[122] LA 1980, s 15(6), Sch 1, para 9, as amended by TLATA 1996, s 25(1), (2), Sch 3, para 18, Sch 4. But see Preston and Newsom, *Limitation of Actions* (3rd edn), p 148.

(5) Tenancies

(i) Recovery of possession from the tenant

The right of action of a landlord to recover the land from the tenant accrues when the lease determines.[123] He must, therefore, sue within 12 years from this date. The mere fact that he has received no rent for many years does not affect his right to recover the land within this period.[124]

(1) Encroachment

If a tenant avails himself of the opportunity afforded him by his tenancy to encroach on other land (whether belonging to the landlord or to a third party), he is presumed to have done so for the benefit of his landlord.[125] But this presumption may be rebutted by showing that there are circumstances pointing to an intention to take the land for his own benefit exclusively. Although a tenant may thus acquire a title by adverse possession over other land, he must give it up to the landlord at the end of his lease.[126]

(2) Forfeiture

If the lease contains a clause providing for the forfeiture of the premises upon non-payment of the rent, and if the rent is not paid within the stipulated period, the landlord acquires by virtue of this clause a right to recover the land during the continuance of the tenancy.[127] This right accrues to him, as we have seen, when the forfeiture is incurred,[128] but the fact that he fails to enforce it does not affect his right to recover the land within 12 years after the determination of the term. Moreover, his failure to enforce one forfeiture does not prejudice him with regard to the future. A fresh right of re-entry accrues to him on each occasion that the tenant defaults in payment.[129]

(ii) Recovery of possession from a stranger

If a stranger enters upon land that is held by lease, time begins to run in his favour against the *tenant* from the moment when the latter is dispossessed; but it does not begin to run against the *landlord* until the end of the lease, for it is only then that the landlord's right of action arises. The landlord must sue within the next 12 years, even though the existing lease is renewed in favour of the tenant while the stranger is still in possession.[130]

---

[123] Ibid, para 4.   [124] *Doe d Davy v Oxenham* (1840) 7 M & W 131.

[125] A 'rather esoteric doctrine', but too well established to be overruled by CA: *Tower Hamlets LBC v Barrett* [2005] EWCA Civ 923, [2006] 1 P & CR 9 at [21], [30] (Neuberger LJ, who at [31] was 'sceptical about the application of the doctrine (especially in relation to land owned by a third party), unless the land to which possessory title is acquired is very close to the demised land and occupied by the tenant together with that demised land').

[126] *Kingsmill v Millard* (1855) 11 Exch 313; *Whitmore v Humphries* (1871) LR 7 CP 1; *Smirk v Lyndale Developments Ltd* [1975] Ch 317, M & B p 257; *Kensington Pension Developments Ltd v Royal Garden Hotel (Oddenino's) Ltd* [1990] 2 EGLR 117.

[127] Above, p 279.   [128] Above, p 1142.

[129] *Barratt v Richardson and Cresswell* [1930] 1 KB 686.

[130] *Ecclesiastical Commrs of England and Wales v Rowe* (1880) 5 App Cas 736; *Gray v Wykeham-Martin and Goode* [1977] Bar Library Transcript No. 10A, M & B p 259.

But since the receipt of rent is the only fact that symbolises the landlord's title to the land, and since an adverse receipt by a stranger is really tantamount to dispossession, it is enacted that:[131]

Where—

(a) any person is in possession of land by virtue of a lease in writing by which a rent of not less than ten pounds a year is reserved; and

(b) the rent is received by some person wrongfully claiming to be entitled to the land in reversion immediately expectant on the determination of the lease; and

(c) no rent is subsequently received by the person rightfully so entitled;

the right of action to recover the land of the person rightfully so entitled shall be treated as having accrued on the date when the rent was first received by the person wrongfully claiming to be so entitled and not on the date of the determination of the lease.

Thus, if the rent is wrongfully received by a stranger for 12 years, both the right of action and the title of the landlord are irretrievably barred, but if before the 12 years have elapsed rent is once more received by him, his right of action revives. If the lease is not in writing or if the annual rent is less than £10, adverse receipt of the rent does not set time running against the landlord.

(iii) Tenancies at will, from year to year and at sufferance

Tenancies at will and from year to year have received special treatment.

(1) Tenancy at will[132]

Time begins to run against the landlord from the determination of the tenancy. The landlord may determine the tenancy either by demanding possession or by exercising some act of ownership on the land that is inconsistent with the right of the tenant.

Until the rule was abolished in 1980,[133] in the absence of determination, time began to run against the landlord at the end of one year from the beginning of the tenancy.[134] If, therefore, the landlord did nothing that constituted a positive determination, his title was extinguished in 13 years from the commencement of the tenancy.

This rule was confined to a tenancy at will properly so called. If, for instance, A were given exclusive occupation of the land of B for an indefinite period and the circumstances showed that all that was intended was that he should have a personal privilege with no interest in the land, he was not a tenant at will, but a licensee, and time did not run against B while the licence subsisted.[135]

A tenancy at will and a licence are in this respect now on the same footing.

---

[131] LA 1980, s 15(6), Sch 1, para 6. Limitation Amendment Act 1980, s 3(2) had substituted £10 for twenty shillings.

[132] Above, pp 201–3.

[133] Limitation Amendment Act 1980, ss. 3(1), 13(2), Sch 2.

[134] LA 1939, s 9(1).

[135] *Cobb v Lane* [1952] 1 All ER 1199; *Hughes v Griffin* [1969] 1 WLR 23; *Heslop v Burns* [1974] 1 WLR 1241.

(2) Tenancy from year to year[136]

In the case of a tenancy from year to year or other period *without a lease in writing*,[137] the right of the landlord to recover the land accrues either at the end of the first of such years or other period, or at the last receipt of rent, whichever shall last occur.[138] If the tenant remains in possession without paying rent for 12 years after the right of action has arisen, and without giving a written acknowledgment of the landlord's title, the cause of action is effectually barred,[139] and subsequent acknowledgment or payment of rent does not start time running afresh.[140]

If the lease is in writing the present rule does not apply, and the landlord's right of action accrues when he determines the tenancy by notice to quit.

(3) Tenancy at sufferance[141]

In the case of a tenancy at sufferance, time runs from the beginning of the tenancy.

(c) The Doctrine of Laches

Despite the general rule that the provisions of the Limitation Act apply to equitable interests in land,[142] there are certain cases in which an equitable claim is unaffected by the statutory bars just discussed. Thus, as we have seen, a claim by a beneficiary to recover trust property retained by a trustee or to recover damages from a fraudulent trustee is subject to no period of limitation.[143] Again, the statutory bars do not apply to any claim for specific performance, an injunction or other equitable relief, except in so far as they may be applied by analogy to the Act.[144]

Nevertheless, whenever a claimant seeks to enforce an equitable right to which no statute of limitation applies or to obtain a form of relief unknown to the common law, courts of equity have always required him to prosecute his claim with due diligence. In pursuance of the maxim *vigilantibus non dormientibus iura subveniunt*—'equity aids the vigilant, not those who sleep over their rights'—they discourage *laches*, a word that signifies the negligent failure of a claimant to take proceedings for the enforcement of his claim within a reasonable time after he has become aware of his rights.[145] But the

---

[136] Above, p 204.

[137] The possession by the tenant of a rent book does not covert an oral into a written lease: *Moses v Lovegrove* [1952] 2 QB 533. A document is not a lease in writing unless it is dispositive, that is a document that at law creates, of and by itself, a leasehold estate in land. A document that is merely a contract for a lease, or merely evidential of the terms of a lease is not a lease in writing: *Long v Tower Hamlets LBC* [1998] Ch 197, 208.

[138] LA 1980, s 15(6), Sch 1, para 5(1).

[139] *Hayward v Chaloner* [1968] 1 QB 107, M & B p 256; *Jessamine Investment Co v Schwartz* [1978] QB 264; *Lodge v Wakefield Metropolitan City Council* [1995] 2 EGLR 124, above, p 1137, n 73; *Price v Hartley* [1995] EGCS 74 (weekly tenant, who remained in occupation without paying rent, held to be a trespasser for purposes of Limitation Act only and therefore extinguished his landlord's title).

[140] *Nicholson v England* [1926] 2 KB 93.   [141] Above, p 203.

[142] LA 1980, s 18(1), as amended by TLATA 1996, s 25(2), Sch 4.   [143] Ibid, s 21(1); above, p 1142.

[144] Ibid, s 36(1).

[145] For a detailed discussion, see Brunyate, *Limitation of Actions in Equity* (1932), pp 185 ff; Preston and Newsom, *Limitation of Actions* (3rd edn), pp 256–64; Snell, paras 5–016 to 5–019.

application of the doctrine of laches has always depended upon whether or not the suit in equity corresponds to an action at law that is within a statute of limitation.

If the equitable claim is substantially similar to a legal right that is subject to a statutory bar, the courts act by analogy to the statute and enforce the same bar upon the equitable right of action.[146] Thus an action by a widow for the assignment to her of specific land in satisfaction of her right to dower, which lay in Chancery before the abolition of dower, would fail unless she started proceedings within the statutory period prescribed for an action of ejectment.[147] The court will not, however, adopt the analogous statutory bar if the equitable claim has been deliberately omitted from the Act as a matter of policy. Relevant examples are the right of a mortgagor to redeem a mortgage of personalty,[148] or of a beneficiary to recover trust property retained by a trustee.

This principle of analogous application is now of much diminished importance, for the legislation of the nineteenth century, fortified by the Limitation Act 1980, has imposed a statutory bar upon most equitable claims.

If there is no corresponding claim or remedy at common law, or if, despite such correspondence, the equitable claim has been omitted from the statutory limitation as a matter of policy, equity applies its own test of unreasonable delay. Mere delay is seldom sufficient to constitute laches. It must be considered in the light of the circumstances.

The modern approach to laches or acquiescence has been set out by the Court of Appeal:[149]

It should not require an exhaustive enquiry into whether the circumstances could fit within the principles established in previous cases. Instead a broader approach should be adopted, namely whether it was unconscionable for the party concerned to be permitted to assert his beneficial rights.

And in *Nelson v Rye*[150] Laddie J indicated some of the factors to be considered in deciding whether this defence runs:

Those factors include the period of the delay, the extent to which the defendant's position has been prejudiced by the delay, and the extent to which that prejudice was caused by the actions of the plaintiff. I accept that mere delay alone will almost never suffice, but the court has to look at all the circumstances, including in particular those factors set out above, and then decide whether the balance of justice or injustice is in favour of granting the remedy or withholding it. If substantial prejudice will be suffered by the defendant, it is not necessary for the defendant to prove that it was caused by the delay. On the other hand, the plaintiff's knowledge that the delay will cause such prejudice is a factor to be taken into account.

---

[146] *Knox v Gye* (1872) LR 5 HL 656, 674 (Lord Westbury).   [147] *Williams v Thomas* [1909] 1 Ch 713.

[148] Waldock, *Law of Mortgages* (2nd edn, 1950), p 199. LA bars after 12 years an action to foreclose a mortgage of personalty, but not an action to redeem such a mortgage.

[149] *Frawley v Neill*, The Times, 5 April 1999 (Aldous LJ); *Patel v Shah* [2005] EWCA Civ 157, [2005] 8 EGCS 190.

[150] [1996] 1 WLR 1378, 1382, citing *Lindsay Petroleum Co v Hurd* (1874) LR 5 PC 221, 239, 240, and *Erlanger v New Sombrero Phosphate Co* (1878) 3 App Cas 1218, 1279–80 (Lord Blackburn).

Such will be the nature of the inquiry if laches is pleaded as a defence to an action by a beneficiary to recover property retained by a trustee;[151] by a mortgagor, to redeem a mortgage of pure personalty.[152] The doctrine of laches, which is of ancient origin, is preserved by the Limitation Act 1980 which provides that:[153]

> Nothing in this Act shall affect any equitable jurisdiction to refuse relief on the ground of acquiescence or otherwise.

(3) Nature of Title Acquired under the Limitation Act 1980

(a) Title to Land

It is necessary to consider what effect the expiration of the statutory period produces upon the title to the land: first, the title of the person dispossessed, secondly, the title of the person who has held adverse possession for 12 years.

(1) Title of person dispossessed

When time has run against a claimant, the effect in every case, no matter whether his claim is founded on tort, breach of contract, dispossession of land or some other wrong, is to bar his *remedy*. As a general rule, however, his *right* is not barred. He is precluded by the extinction of his remedy from a resort to legal proceedings, but he is free to enforce his still-existent right by any other method that may be available. Before 1833 this was the effect of adverse possession of land for the required period, but the Real Property Limitation Act[154] of that year provided that at the end of the statutory period the right, as well as the remedy, of the dispossessed owner should be extinguished. This rule is retained by the Limitation Act 1980, which provides that:[155]

> At the expiration of the period prescribed by this Act for any person to bring an action to recover land (including a redemption action) the title of that person to the land shall be extinguished.

There is an exception, however, in the case of settled land and land held on trust where, as we have already seen, the title of the trustee to the legal estate is not extinguished until all the beneficiaries have been barred.[156]

---

151 See eg *Baker v Read* (1854) 18 Beav 398; *Re Jarvis* [1958] 1 WLR 815.

152 *Weld v Petre* [1929] 1 Ch 33.

153 S 36(2); *Filross Securities Ltd v Midgeley* [1998] 3 EGLR 43 (equitable set-off held to be within s 36(2) and not statute-barred).

154 S 34.

155 S 17 (disapplied in relation to registered land by LRA 2002: below, p 1160). Similarly for an action to enforce an advowson: s 25(3). The extinguishment of title also extinguishes the rights to claim rent and mesne profits during the period of adverse possession: *Mount Carmel Investments Ltd v Peter Thurlow Ltd* [1988] 1 WLR 1078; and adverse possession by the mortgagor extinguishes the mortgagee's right to take possession of the land, as well as his right to payment of the mortgage debt: *Ashe v National Westminster Bank plc* [2008] EWCA Civ 55, [2008] 1 WLR 710.

156 Above, p 1143.

In considering the extent to which the existing rights of the parties are affected by the statutory extinguishment of the right of action, we will deal first with the former possessor and then with the squatter.

The dispossessed person and those who claim through him lose the title to possession that he could previously have enforced against the squatter. To that extent, his title is finally destroyed and there is no method by which it can be revived, not even by a written acknowledgment given by the squatter.[157]

But the effect of the extinguishment is limited. It extinguishes nothing more than the title of the dispossessed *against the squatter*.[158] Thus, the dispossession of a tenant does not destroy his lease. His title against the landlord remains good, so that, for example, he is entitled to resume possession if the land is vacated by the squatter. Likewise, the landlord remains entitled to sue the tenant on the covenants or indeed to re-enter the land for a forfeiture committed by the squatter if the lease contains a proviso for forfeiture.[159]

A fortiori, the titles of third parties who have enforceable interests in the land, such as those entitled to the benefit of an easement or a restrictive covenant, are unaffected by the adverse possession of the land, for no remedy accrues to them until *their* rights have been infringed.[160]

(2) Title of squatter

It follows from what has been said, that the sole, though substantial, privilege acquired by a squatter is immunity from interference by the person dispossessed. In other words, the statutory effect of 12 years' adverse possession is merely negative; not, as Baron Parke once said,[161] 'to make a parliamentary conveyance to the person in possession'. This judicial heresy has long been exploded and it is now recognised that we must not confound the negative effect of the statute with the positive effect of a conveyance.[162]

There is no transfer, statutory or otherwise, to the squatter of the very title held by the dispossessed person. As Lord Radcliffe said:[163]

He is not at any stage of his possession a successor to the title of the man he has dispossessed. He comes in and remains in always by right of possession, which in due course becomes incapable of disturbance as time exhausts the one or more periods allowed by statute for

---

[157] *Nicholson v England* [1926] 2 KB 93.

[158] *Fairweather v St Marylebone Property Co Ltd* [1963] AC 510, 539 (Lord Radcliffe); M & B p 269.

[159] Ibid, 545 (Lord Denning). See also *Jessamine Investment Co v Schwartz* [1978] QB 264 (sub-tenant, protected as statutory tenant under Rent Act 1968, acquired title by adverse possession against his immediate landlord. Held (1) title of immediate landlord not extinguished as against the freeholder until head-lease expired; (2) when it did expire, sub-tenant still protected against freeholder under the Rent Act).

[160] *Re Nisbet and Potts' Contract* [1905] 1 Ch 391, M & B p 273; above, p 739. It is in principle possible for title to land to be acquired by adverse possession notwithstanding that it is a public highway (cf *JA Pye (Oxford) Ltd v Graham* [2002] UKHL 30, [2003] 1 AC 416), but where a highway is maintainable at public expense, under s 263 Highways Act 1980 no title can be obtained by adverse possession: *R (Smith) v Land Registry (Peterborough)* [2010] EWCA Civ 200, [2010] 3 WLR 1223.

[161] *Doe d Jukes v Sumner* (1845) 14 M & W 39, 42.

[162] Hayes, *Introduction to Conveyancing*, vol i, p 269.

[163] *Fairweather v St Marylebone Property Co Ltd* [1963] AC 510, 535.

successful intervention. His title, therefore, is never derived through but arises always in spite of the dispossessed owner.

Therefore if a man ejects a tenant for years and remains in possession for the statutory period, he cannot be sued for breach of a repairing covenant contained in the lease, for there has been no transfer to him of the tenant's estate.[164] Again, any right enjoyed by the dispossessed person that is based upon an implied grant, such as a way of necessity, will not avail an adverse possessor, for the doctrine of implication cannot be imported into a statutory provision that is purely negative.[165]

(i) Dispossession of tenant

The decision of the House of Lords in *Fairweather v St Marylebone Property Co Ltd*,[166] is a further illustration of the rule that there is no transfer to a squatter of an interest commensurate with that held by the person dispossessed. The facts relevant to the present inquiry may be stated in a much simplified form as follows:

> A house and garden containing a shed were leased by X to Y for 99 years. The shed was occupied by a neighbour, Z, for more than 12 years adversely to Y. While the lease was still running, Y surrendered it to the freeholder, X.
>
> The question was whether, X, as freeholder, could resume possession immediately or whether he had no such right until the lease determined by effluxion of time.

The majority of the House of Lords, overruling *Walter v Yalden*,[167] gave judgment for X. Despite the title acquired by the squatter against Y the tenant, the relationship between X and Y still continued with all its implications, including the right of Y to retain possession as against X. By surrendering the lease, Y had abandoned the right to possession, with the result that his tenancy had merged in the freehold and had disappeared. Therefore, the landlord could recover the shed on the strength of his own right to immediate possession of the freehold.[168]

The earlier decision of *Taylor v Twinberrow*[169] was approved. In that case, the facts were in effect as follows:

> X, a yearly tenant, allowed Y to occupy a cottage for more than 13 years as a tenant at will. X then bought the fee simple, with the result that the yearly tenancy was determined by its merger in the freehold. It was argued that the title acquired by Y was commensurate with that lost by X and that therefore he was entitled to the half a year's notice to quit appropriate to a yearly tenancy.

---

164 *Tichborne v Weir* (1892) 67 LT 735, M & B p 272; above, p 318.

165 *Wilkes v Greenway* (1890) 6 TLR 449.   166 [1963] AC 510, M & B p 269.

167 [1902] 2 KB 304.

168 Lord Morris dissented. He took the view that the tenant could not surrender what he had not himself got, namely, a right to immediate possession: *nemo dat quod non habet*. For a criticism of the decision, see (1962) 78 LQR 541 (HWR Wade). For a discussion of the difficulty of terminology in this context, see (1964) 80 LQR 63 (B Rudden). See also (1973) 37 Conv (NS) 85 (JA Omotola).

169 [1930] 2 KB 16.

This argument was fallacious. All that the squatter had acquired was a title to possession indefeasible by the yearly tenant. With the disappearance of the yearly tenancy, the former yearly tenant had become the freeholder, and as such he had an immediate right to recover possession.

In *Chung Ping Kwan v Lam Island Development Co Ltd*,[170] the Privy Council held that, where a tenant has been dispossessed, he cannot recover possession against the squatter, if the tenant exercises an option to renew the lease. The tenant's right of action is not revived by his exercise of the option because he acquires a new legal estate by virtue only of a right included in the lease whose title has been extinguished as against the trespasser.[171]

If, however, the landlord grants a new lease even to the original tenant the new tenant is entitled to recover possession from the squatter by virtue of the landlord's title.

One effect of these decisions is that the landlord and tenant can combine to defeat the squatter. If the landlord accepts a surrender of the term, he is then able to grant a new lease to the tenant.[172]

(ii) Subsequent improvement of title

Nevertheless, despite the negative operation of the Limitation Act, the title to possession acquired by a squatter against the person dispossessed may ultimately ripen into an indefeasible title to the fee simple. Cozens-Hardy MR said:

> Whenever you find a person in possession of property, that possession is prima facie evidence of ownership in fee, and that prima facie evidence becomes absolute once you have extinguished the right of every other person to challenge it.[173]

In other words, a squatter, though a wrongdoer, acquires by virtue of his possession a new independent title to the fee simple that prevails against all persons except those who can rely on an earlier and therefore a better title. Moreover, it is a title that will prevail against those with better titles if they fail to assert their rights within the period prescribed by the Limitation Act. Thus, a title originally defeasible may in course of time become indefeasible.[174]

For example:

> X dispossesses W, the fee simple owner of Blackacre, and remains in possession for eight years when he himself is dispossessed by Y.

As between X and Y, X's is the earlier and therefore the stronger title of the two, but he must assert it against the weaker within the statutory period. If Y is allowed to remain in possession for 12 years without being challenged either by W or by X, his title to possession of the fee simple becomes indefeasible. It rests on the infirmity of the right of others to eject him.[175]

---

[170] [1997] AC 38, M & B p 266. *Taylor v Twinberrow*, above, was expressly approved at 47.
[171] Ibid, 48 (Lord Nicholls of Birkenhead).
[172] *Fairweather v St Marylebone Property Co Ltd* [1963] AC 510, 547 (Lord Denning).
[173] *Re Atkinson and Horsell's Contract* [1912] 2 Ch 1, 9.
[174] *St Marylebone Property Co Ltd v Fairweather* [1962] 1 QB 498, 513 (Holroyd Pearce LJ).
[175] Darby and Bosanquet, *Statutes of Limitations* (1867), p 493, adopted by Bowen LJ in *Tichborne v Weir* (1892) 67 LT 735.

Again, if some lesser title than that to the fee simple is destroyed, as when a tenant is ejected, the squatter may still be challenged by the landlord, the freeholder. So, if the lease terminates by effluxion of time or becomes forfeitable for breach of condition,[176] the freeholder's right to recover possession accrues and prevails over that of the squatter. Relatively to the tenant, the squatter's right is the stronger; relatively to the freeholder, it is the weaker. But if the freeholder does not pursue his remedy within 12 years from the end of the lease, the squatter's title to the fee simple becomes indefeasible.

(b) Proof of title

A consequence of the negative effect of the Limitation Act 1980 is that as between vendor and purchaser a title based on adverse possession alone for the limitation period or longer is not necessarily a good title. The claims of a reversioner or a remainderman may have yet to be extinguished;[177] the reversion may be on a 99-year lease; the remainderman's interest may not vest in possession for over 100 years.[178] But if a vendor can establish that the flaw in an otherwise good title is one that can be cured by the running of time in his favour under the Act, he can force a purchaser of unregistered land to take the title.[179] Proof that rival claims have been extinguished by the lapse of time may be very difficult, and in practice a purchaser often agrees to accept an imperfect title.[180]

(4) *Circumstances in which the Statutory Period is Extended*

In three cases, namely:

(1) where the person entitled to recover land is under a disability;

(2) where there has been fraud or deliberate concealment of a cause of action; and

(3) where a person seeks relief from the consequences of a mistake;

the period of 12 years within which an action must normally be brought is lengthened.

(a) Disability

A person is deemed to be under a disability for the purposes of the Act while he is a minor or lacks capacity (within the meaning of the Mental Capacity Act 2005[181]) to conduct legal proceedings.[182]

---

[176] *Tickner v Buzzacott* [1965] Ch 426.   [177] LA 1980, ss 15, 18.

[178] *Cadell v Palmer* (1833) 1 Cl & Fin 372; vesting postponed for over 100 years (note to *Re Villar* [1928] Ch 471, 478); above, p 536.

[179] *Re Atkinson and Horsell's Contract* [1912] 2 Ch 1; *Re Spencer and Hauser's Contract* [1928] Ch 598; distinguished in *George Wimpey & Co Ltd v Sohn* [1967] Ch 487.

[180] Farrand, *Contract and Conveyance* (4th edn), pp 108–9.

[181] Above, p 1028.

[182] LA 1980, s 38(2), amended by Mental Capacity Act 2005, Sch 6, para 25(a); *Kirby v Leather* [1965] 2 QB 367. The terminology of 'infant' remains in LA 1980, s 38(2), although the usual term is now 'minor'; above, p 1018.

If, on the date when a right of action for the recovery of land accrues, the person to whom it has accrued is under a disability, the action may be brought at any time within six years from the removal of the disability or from his death, whichever event first occurs, notwithstanding that the period of limitation has expired.[183] No action, however, to recover land or money charged on land may be brought after the expiration of 30 years from the date on which the right accrued.[184] A disability that begins *after* the accrual of a right of action does not prevent time from continuing to run against the disabled person.[185]

If before the cessation of one disability another one supervenes, time does not begin to run until both have ceased.[186] For example:

> A dispossesses B, who is six years of age. When 15 years old B becomes under a lack of mental capacity, and is still in this state upon the attainment of his majority. Time does not begin to run until he recovers his capacity.

If the person entitled to the right of action dies while still under a disability, his successor in title must sue within six years even if he himself is under a disability.[187]

(b) Fraud or deliberate concealment of right of action

Section 32(1) of the Limitation Act 1980 provides that where:

(a) the action is based upon the fraud of the defendant; or

(b) any fact relevant to the plaintiff's right of action has been deliberately concealed from him by the defendant

time shall not begin to run until the plaintiff has discovered the fraud or concealment, or could with reasonable diligence have discovered it.[188] The defendant includes the defendant's agent and any person through whom the defendant claims and his agent.[189]

The section provides, however, that the enactment shall not enable a person to recover the land or its value from a purchaser for valuable consideration who was not a party to the fraud or to the concealment, and who at the time of the purchase did not know and had no reason to believe that the fraud or concealment had taken place.[190]

'Fraud' in paragraph (a) bears its usual meaning,[191] but deliberate concealment in paragraph (b) is more difficult. It is presumably intended to take account of the restrictive interpretation placed by the courts on the words 'concealed fraud' in the corresponding section of the Limitation Act 1939.[192] The word 'deliberate' is not defined, but section 32(2) provides that: 'deliberate commission of a breach of duty in circumstances in

---

[183] LA 1980, s 28(1).   [184] Ibid, s 28(4).   [185] Ibid, s 28(1), (2).
[186] *Borrows v Ellison* (1871) LR 6 Exch 128.   [187] LA 1980, s 28(3).
[188] *Peco Arts Inc v Hazlitt Gallery Ltd* [1983] 1 WLR 1315, 1323 (drawing *Études Pour le Bain* by Ingres).
[189] *Eddis v Chichester Constable* [1969] 2 Ch 345 (painting attributed to Caravaggio).
[190] LA 1980, s 32(3), (4).
[191] See *Beaman v ARTS Ltd* [1949] 1 KB 550, 558 (Lord Greene).
[192] S 26. See *Applegate v Moss* [1971] 1 QB 406, 413; *Clark v Woor* [1965] 1 WLR 650, 654; *King v Victor Parsons & Co* [1973] 1 WLR 29, 33; *Tito v Waddell (No 2)* [1977] Ch 106, 224–5; *Lewisham London Borough v Leslie & Co Ltd* (1978) 250 EG 1289; *Bartlett v Barclays Bank Trust Co Ltd* [1980] Ch 515, 537.

which it is unlikely to be discovered for some time amounts to deliberate concealment of the facts involved in that breach of duty'. Deliberate concealment is clearly less than fraud, and in essence[193] 'denotes conduct by the defendant or his agent such that it would be "against conscience" for him to avail himself of the lapse of time.' Thus, wrongfully to enter land without the knowledge of the owner would not constitute deliberate concealment.[194] It would, however, be deliberate concealment in the context of adverse possession where a person, knowing that the land belongs to X, conceals from X the circumstances that confer the right upon him, and thus enables himself to enter and hold.[195] Examples are the destruction of title deeds,[196] the intentional concealment of a voluntary conveyance to the claimant,[197] the passing off of an illegitimate son as the eldest legitimate son,[198] the procuring of a conveyance from a person of unsound mind,[199] and where a builder covers up what he knows to be inadequate foundations and does not tell the owner anything about it.[200]

Finally, even though time has started to run after a cause of action has arisen, subsequent concealment starts time running again.[201]

(c) Mistake

Similar provisions apply where the action is for relief from the consequences of a mistake.[202] The period of limitation does not begin to run until the claimant has discovered the mistake or could with reasonable diligence have discovered it. The relief, however, is only available 'where the mistake is an essential ingredient of the cause of action',[203] such as where the action is to recover money paid under a mistake. There is no general rule that a mistake prevents time from running under the Act.

In *Kleinwort Benson Ltd v Lincoln City Council*,[204] the House of Lords held that this provision applies where the claim is for recovery of money paid under a mistake of law, including the case where the claimant's mistake was based on a settled understanding of the law that is shown by a later judicial decision to have been mistaken. The effect is that rent paid under a mistake (even a mistake of law[205]) made many years ago may be recoverable well beyond the normal limitation period.

---

[193] *Applegate v Moss*, above, at 413 (Lord Denning MR); *Westlake v Bracknell DC* [1987] 1 EGLR 161; *Johnson v Chief Constable of Surrey*, The Times, 23 November 1992; *Sheldon v RHM Outhwaite (Underwriting Agencies) Ltd* [1996] AC 102. Cf *Cave v Robinson Jarvis & Rolf* [2002] UKHL 18, [2003] 1 AC 384 (deliberate concealment does not include failure to disclose a negligent breach of duty that the actor was unaware of committing). See Emmet, para 1.026.

[194] *Rains v Buxton* (1880) 14 Ch D 537.   [195] *Petre v Petre* (1853) 1 Drew 371, 397 (Kindersley V-C).

[196] *Lawrance v Lord Norreys* (1890) 15 App Cas 210.   [197] *Re McCallum* [1901] 1 Ch 143.

[198] *Vane v Vane* (1873) 8 Ch App 383.   [199] *Lewis v Thomas* (1843) 3 Hare 26.

[200] *Applegate v Mossi*, above; *King v Victor Parsons & Co*, above.

[201] *Sheldon v RHM Outhwaite (Underwriting Agencies) Ltd* [1996] AC 102. 'In the case of subsequent concealment, the clock is turned back to zero': Lord Nicholls at 152; criticised by Law Com CP No 151, *Limitation of Actions* (1998), paras 8.17–8.20.

[202] LA 1980, s 32(1)(c).   [203] *Phillips-Higgins v Harper* [1954] 1 QB 411, 419 (Pearson J).

[204] [1999] 2 AC 349; [1999] CLJ 478 (G Virgo).

[205] *Nurdin & Peacock plc v D B Ramsden & Co Ltd* [1999] 1 WLR 1249.

(5) Methods by which Time may be Prevented from Running

Time that has begun to run under the Act is stopped, either when the owner asserts his right or when his right is admitted by the adverse possessor.

(a) Assertion of owner's right

Assertion of right occurs when the owner takes legal proceedings or makes an effective entry onto the land.

(b) Admission of owner's right

An admission of the right of the person entitled occurs when the adverse possessor acknowledges the right, or, if the right is to the payment of money, where he makes a part payment.

(1) Acknowledgment

Where a right of action to recover land or an advowson or to foreclose a mortgage has already accrued to X and his title is later acknowledged by the person in possession, his right is treated as having accrued on and not before the date of the acknowledgment.[206] The effect is that the owner's right of action recommences, not only against the person who makes the admission, but also against all later possessors, and remains effective until there has been adverse possession for a further period of 12 years.[207] An acknowledgment, however, has no effect if it is given after the period of limitation has run its full course.[208]

Every acknowledgment must be in writing and signed by the person by whom it is made.[209] It must be made to the person whose title or claim is being acknowledged or to his agent.[210] Any written statement is sufficient that implicitly recognises the title of the person to whom it is made, such as an offer by a squatter to purchase the land from the freeholder;[211] or a request for further time within which to pay made by

---

[206] LA 1980, s 29(1), (2)(a).

[207] Ibid, s 31(1).

[208] Ibid, s 29(7), below; *Sanders v Sanders* (1881) 19 Ch D 373.

[209] Ibid, s 29(1). See *Browne v Perry* [1991] 1 WLR 1297, 1301 (Lord Templeman); *Archangel v Lambeth LBC* [2002] 1 P & CR 18 at [14] (effect of signature by individual not negatived by fact that he wrote on notepaper, or signed as chief executive, of organisation he had founded and ran from the property); *Rehman v Benfield* [2006] EWCA Civ 1392, [2007] 2 P & CR 16 (document that purported to be a lease of the property, signed by possessors as 'tenants' but without paper owner's knowledge, constituted acknowledgment when signed by possessors or when sent to paper owner's solicitor). The acknowledgment must be by the person in possession of the land: s 29(2); *Allen v Matthews* [2007] EWCA Civ 216, [2007] 2 P & CR 21 (acknowledgment by solicitors acting not for person in possession but for his company).

[210] Ibid, s 29(2).

[211] *Edginton v Clark* [1964] 1 QB 367 (letter to owner's agent offering to purchase land held to be effective acknowledgment); *Ofulue v Bossert* [2009] UKHL 16, [2009] 1 AC 990 (acknowledgment in defence and implied admission in offer to purchase); *Re Compania de Electricidad de la Provincia de Buenos Aires Ltd* [1980] Ch 146 (balance sheet effective acknowledgment if received by creditor). But an offer to purchase is not a sufficient acknowledgment where it is made by the landlord of the person in possession, even though the tenant was by his possession acquiring title for the landlord: the acknowledgment must be made by the person in possession: *Tower Hamlets LBC v Barrett* [2005] EWCA Civ 923, [2006] 1 P & CR 9 at [95].

the possessor of land in response to a demand for rent.[212] An acknowledgment made during the course of proceedings normally operates only at the date of the document in which it is contained, unless it is later affirmed or repeated; and it will not amount to an acknowledgment for the purposes of the Limitation Act if it is contained in a 'without prejudice' document during settlement negotiations.[213]

(2) Part payment

If, after a right of foreclosure or other cause of action has accrued to a mortgagee, the possessor of the land or the person liable for the mortgage debt makes any payment of principal or interest, there is a fresh accrual of the right of action from the date of payment.[214]

Where a right of action has accrued to recover any debt or other liquidated pecuniary claim, as for instance rent due under a lease, and the person liable acknowledges the claim or makes any payment in respect of it, the right is treated as accruing on and not before the date of the acknowledgment or payment.[215] A payment of part only of rent does not, however, enable the remainder then due to be recovered more than six years after it became due.[216] An acknowledgment to be effective for this purpose must admit the existence of the debt, but it need not state its precise amount, provided that this is ascertainable by extrinsic evidence,[217] and it includes the admission of a debt even though its quantum is disputed.[218]

(3) Persons bound by acknowledgment and part payment

There is a distinction between acknowledgment and part payment with regard to the persons upon whom they are binding. An acknowledgment binds only the acknowledgor and his successors,[219] in other words, persons who claim through him, such as a trustee in bankruptcy or an executor.[220] A part payment of a debt or other liquidated money claim, on the other hand, binds all persons liable in respect of it,[221] for since they derive advantage from the payment it is only just that they should share the disadvantage of a fresh accrual of a right of action to the creditor. Thus a part payment of rent by a tenant revives the landlord's right of action against a surety.[222]

(4) Acknowledgment or part payment after time has run

No acknowledgment or part payment can revive any right to recover land if it is made after the full period of limitation has run. The reason is that the effect of the Limitation Act is to bar not only the remedy of an owner for recovering the land but also his right

---

[212] *Fursdon v Clogg* (1842) 10 M & W 572.
[213] *Ofulue v Bossert*, above, n 211.
[214] LA 1980, s 29(3).
[215] Ibid, s 29(5).
[216] Ibid, s 29(6).
[217] *Dungate v Dungate* [1965] 1 WLR 1477, explaining *Good v Parry* [1963] 2 QB 418; *Surrendra Overseas Ltd v Government of Sri Lanka* [1977] 1 WLR 565; *Kamouh v Associated Electrical Industries International Ltd* [1980] QB 199; *Re Overmark Smith Warden Ltd* [1982] 1 WLR 1195.
[218] *Bradford & Bingley plc v Rashid* [2006] UKHL 37, [2006] 1 WLR 2066.
[219] LA 1980, s 31(6).
[220] Ibid, s 31(9).
[221] Ibid, s 31(7).
[222] *Re Powers* (1885) 30 Ch D 291; *Re Frisby* (1889) 43 Ch D 106.

to it;[223] and, since the right as well as the remedy is barred, there is nothing left to acknowledge. Where, however, the remedy alone is barred, for example, in the case of an action for the payment of a debt, the rule used to be that an acknowledgment or part payment was effective even if given after the period had elapsed.[224] This rule was changed in the Limitation Act 1980[225] under which: 'a current period of limitation may be repeatedly extended by further acknowledgments or payments, but a right of action, once barred by this Act, shall not be revived by any subsequent acknowledgment or payment'.

D REGISTERED LAND.
LAND REGISTRATION ACTS 1925 AND 2002

(1) Land Registration Act 1925

(a) Title of person dispossessed

Before the Land Registration Act 2002,[226] the Limitation Act 1980 applied to registered land, and a title to a registered estate could be acquired by adverse possession,[227] as long as the required period had already been completed by the date on which the 2002 Act came into force.[228] There was, however, one important difference that sprang from the mechanics of registration. When a squatter acquires a legal title to unregistered land by adverse possession, the former owner's estate is automatically extinguished. With registered land, however, there was no automatic extinction of the proprietor's title but under section 75 of the Land Registration Act 1925 it was deemed to be held by the proprietor in trust for the squatter.

This was without prejudice to the rights of any other person interested in the land whose estate or interest was not extinguished by the operation of the Limitation Act. Anyone claiming to have acquired a title to registered land under the Act could apply to be registered as proprietor and he could be registered with an absolute, good leasehold, qualified or possessory title, as the case may be, but his registration would have the same effect as that of a first proprietor.[229]

Rights acquired or in the course of being acquired under the Limitation Act were overriding interests under the Land Registration Act 1925,[230] and therefore a registered purchaser for value could never be in a better position than his predecessor in title and must take subject to the rights of the squatter.[231] The purchaser's registered title, even

---

[223] Above, p 1128.   [224] See LA 1939, s 25(5), (6).

[225] S 29(7), replacing Limitation Amendment Act 1980, s 6. A squatter may be estopped from asserting his title: *Colchester BC v Smith* [1991] Ch 448.

[226] Below, p 1160.   [227] See generally R & R (1991 edn), ch 32.

[228] 13 October 2003; below, n 243.

[229] LRA 1925, s 75; *Fairweather v St Marylebone Property Co Ltd* [1963] AC 510, 541, 548; *Spectrum Investment Co v Holmes* [1981] 1 WLR 221, 229; (1981) 131 NLJ 718 (PF Smith); 774 (EG Nugee); [1981] Conv 155 (RE Annand); [1982] Conv 201 (PH Kenny).

[230] Ibid, s 70(1)(f); *Bridges v Mees* [1957] Ch 475; ibid, s 70(1)(g).   [231] *Bridges v Mees*, above.

if absolute, could be rectified in favour of the squatter,[232] but the purchaser would not be entitled to an indemnity, as he had only lost thereby a valueless asset, that is a title barred by adverse possession on the part of the squatter.[233]

(b) Dispossession of tenant

The rule in *Fairweather* did not, however, apply to registered land. This was decided twice at first instance.

First, where the squatter had acquired a title as against the tenant and had then been registered under section 75 as proprietor in place of the tenant. It was then no longer possible for the tenant 'to do a Marylebone',[234] and thereby enable the freeholder to dispossess the squatter.

In *Spectrum Investment Co v Holmes*[235] the question arose whether the rule in *Fairweather v St Marylebone Property Co Ltd*[236] applied to registered land:

> In 1902 a registered freeholder granted a registered lease of a house to T. In 1968 H acquired a title by adverse possession against D, a registered assignee of T, under the Limitation Act 1939. H applied for and obtained registration as proprietor of the leasehold interest with possessory title, and the title under which D was registered was closed. In 1975 D 'woke up' and purported to surrender the lease to S the freeholder's successor in title, who was then the registered proprietor with absolute title to the freehold. S then claimed possession against H, the registered squatter.

Browne-Wilkinson J held that the rule in *Fairweather* did not apply to registered land. Since D's title had been closed, D was no longer the registered proprietor of the lease, and was therefore unable to surrender it. In any event the surrender itself was invalid as not having been effected by a registered disposition.[237]

Secondly, where the squatter had acquired a title as against the tenant but had not yet exercised his right to register it in his place. In *Central London Commercial Estates Ltd v Kato Kagaku Ltd*,[238]

> a freeholder granted a long lease in 1935 of land forming part of Bush House in the Strand. Both titles were registered. The squatter had been in continuous adverse possession of a courtyard for more than 12 years before 1996, using it as a paying car park. The lease was surrendered by a successor in title of the tenant to the freeholder.

---

232 *Chowood Ltd v Lyall (No 2)* [1930] 2 Ch 156.

233 See *Re Chowood's Registered Land* [1933] Ch 574, M & B p 160.

234 Christopher Nugee QC, counsel in *Central London Commercial Estates Ltd v Kato Kagaku Ltd* [1998] 4 All ER 948.

235 [1981] 1 WLR 221; (1981) 131 NLJ 718 (PF Smith); 774 (EG Nugee); [1981] Conv 155 (RE Annand); [1982] Conv 201 (PH Kenny); [1984] LS 1 (CE Cooke).

236 [1963] AC 510; above, p 1151.

237 LRA 1925, ss 21, 22, 69(4). D's claim to rectification of the register to enable her to executed a valid surrender was rejected. H was properly registered under the mandatory requirements of s 75(5). See also *Mount Carmel Investments Ltd v Peter Thurlow Ltd* [1988] 1 WLR 1078, 1089 (original squatter forged a long lease from the registered freeholder and assigned it to another squatter).

238 [1998] 4 All ER 948; (1999) 115 LQR 187 (C Harpum); [1999] 149 NLJ 118 (HW Wilkinson); [1999] Conv 136 (EJ Cooke), 329 (S Pascoe); [1998] All ER Rev 272 (PJ Clarke).

Sedley J held that here too the tenant cannot do a Marylebone. He held his estate in trust for the squatter under section 75, and the squatter's rights under the trust were overriding interests under section 70(1)(f) or (g), or both, of the Land Registration Act 1925. Therefore, any disposition by the tenant (and surrender is a disposition) was ineffective to override the rights of the squatter.

We have seen that in unregistered land there is no Parliamentary conveyance of the title of the dispossessed person to the squatter. In registered land, however, the wording and operation of section 75 of the 1925 Act could not be reconciled with that view. Under section 75(1) the estate of the registered proprietor was not extinguished, but was deemed to be held in trust for the squatter. And section 75(2) assumed that the squatter acquired title under the Act to a 'registered estate'—in other words, the estate of the registered proprietor against whom he had been adversely dispossessing. Both subsections suggested that the squatter succeeded to the title of the dispossessed proprietor.[239] As Sedley J said in *Kato*:[240]

> In relation to a registered leasehold, section 75 lifts the extinguishing effect of the Limitation Acts and substitutes a trust of the leasehold title. The squatter becomes entitled, without regard to merits, to be placed in the same relationship with the freeholder as had previously been enjoyed by the leaseholder. The trust preserves not the squatter's common law title but a new statutory right to be substituted by registration for the leaseholder—carrying with it an obligation to indemnify the leaseholder against outgoings. This is to all appearances a statutory conveyance of the entire leasehold interest.

(2) Land Registration Act 2002[241]

The Land Registration Act 2002 changed fundamentally the position of the squatter in relation to registered land. In short, it disapplies the law of adverse possession described earlier in this chapter, and substitutes a new scheme that reflects the fact that the basis of title to registered land is registration, not possession.[242] In so doing, the Act also makes a fundamental change to the role of possession in the modern land law.

(a) Disapplication of the limitation periods

In relation to registered estates and rentcharges in land, section 96 of the Land Registration Act 2002 disapplies the limitation periods that apply to unregistered land:[243]

---

[239] (1999) 115 LQR 187, 189 (C Harpum).   [240] [1998] 4 All ER 948, 959.

[241] LRA 2002, ss 96–98 and Sch 6; LRR 2003, rr 187–194, amended by LR(A)R 2008 (SI 2008 No 1919); R & R, ch 33; H & B, Part 6; Law Com No 271, *Land Registration for the Twenty-First Century* (2001), Part XIV; Land Registry Practice Guide 4.

[242] Law Com No 271, para 1.13.

[243] Where the limitation period running under the old law had already expired before the 2002 Act came into force (13 October 2003) the position of the parties under LRA 1925 is preserved: ie, the registered estate is held in trust (indefinitely) for the adverse possessor: LRA 2002, Sch 12, para 18. An adverse possessor's right remained an overriding interest until 13 October 2006: ibid, para 7, but since that date the right will be protected as an overriding interest only if the adverse possessor is in discoverable actual occupation: LRA 2002, Sch 3, para 2; above p 1105.

(1) No period of limitation under section 15[244] of the Limitation Act 1980 (time limits in relation to recovery of land) shall run against any person, other than a chargee,[245] in relation to an estate in land or rentcharge the title to which is registered.

(2) No period of limitation under section 16[246] of that Act (time limits in relation to redemption of land) shall run against any person in relation to such an estate in land or rentcharge.

Since no limitation period runs against the paper owner in these circumstances, there can be no automatic extinction of his title.[247] In other words, adverse possession of registered land, for however long, does not of itself extinguish the paper owner's title, nor confer any title on the adverse possessor.

(b) Registration of adverse possessor as proprietor

This does not, however, mean that an adverse possessor cannot acquire title to registered land. A new regime is laid down by the 2002 Act.

A person who has been in adverse possession of the estate for a period of ten years may apply to the Registrar to be registered as proprietor.[248] This still requires the possessor to prove his adverse possession; and 'adverse possession' has the same meaning as under the Limitation Act 1980.[249] But the applicant must normally still be in possession on the date of his application in order to qualify.[250]

The Registrar must give formal notice of the adverse possessor's application to the registered proprietor.[251] Once the registered proprietor has been served with the notice, he may consent to the application, and the applicant will then be registered as the new proprietor.[252] However, he may oppose the application by serving a

---

[244] Above, p 1129.

[245] The exclusion of a chargee in sub-s (1) avoids any change to the position of mortgagors in possession: the mortgagee's rights to possession or foreclosure as against the mortgagor in possession remain subject to the limitation provisions of LA 1980: H & B, para 29.6.

[246] Above, p 859.   [247] LRA 2002, s 96(3).

[248] LRA 2002, Sch 6, para 1(1). The estate need not have been registered throughout the ten-year period, as long as it is registered by the time the application is made: para 1(4).

[249] Ibid, para 11(1). A possessor can include in the calculation periods of adverse possession by his predecessor in title, and any period within the ten-year period when he was himself dispossessed by an adverse possessor: para 11(2). For the meaning of 'adverse possession', see pp above, pp 1131 ff.

[250] He still qualifies, however, if he has been evicted by the paper owner, without a judgment for possession, within the last six months: ibid, para 1(2). But he may not make application if he is defendant in proceedings for possession of the land: para 1(3). These rules encourage the paper owner to use the legal process to recover his land, to bar the squatter's right to apply for registration.

[251] And to certain others, such as registered chargees, and the proprietor of the superior estate if the estate in question is leasehold: ibid, para 2(2). In practice, however, the registered proprietor is given an earlier, informal notice because the Land Registry, before accepting that the applicant has an arguable case for registration, will normally require one of its own surveyors to inspect the land; both the registered proprietor and the applicant are notified of the inspection: Land Registry Practice Guide 4, para 5.1.

[252] If he does not serve a counter-notice, below, the applicant is entitled to be registered: LRA 2002, Sch 6, para 4. Any person on whom the notice of application is served may, however, dispute the applicant's right to make the application, and such a dispute may be referred to the Adjudicator: LRA 2002, s 73(1); Land Registry Practice Guide 4, para 6.

counter-notice.[253] In such a case, the applicant will be registered as proprietor only if one of three conditions is met:[254] (i) that the applicant has the benefit of an equity by estoppel by virtue of which he should be registered as proprietor;[255] (ii) that he is for some other reason entitled to be registered; or (iii) that the land in question is involved in a boundary dispute in relation to adjacent land belonging to the applicant, and the applicant is in adverse possession on the basis of a reasonable mistake as to title. These grounds are very limited, and only the third is based on the applicant's adverse possession. It will therefore be evident that the mere fact of adverse possession will rarely result in the squatter acquiring the registered estate after ten years' adverse possession if the paper owner does not consent to it.

Where the proprietor fails to serve a counter-notice and the squatter is wrongly registered because he had not in fact been in possession for the requisite ten-year period, there is a mistake in the register that can be rectified.[256]

However, where the proprietor does object, the squatter may have a further opportunity to acquire the registered title. If he has made a first application to be registered, which has been opposed by the proprietor and rejected, he may make a further application if he is in adverse possession of the estate from the date of the first application for a period ending two years after the date of the rejection, and as long as he is not then a defendant in proceedings for possession of the land, and no judgment for possession has been given against him.[257] In such a case he is entitled to be entered in the register as the new proprietor of the estate, and the paper owner has no further right to object.[258]

The purpose of this provision is to allow the registered proprietor to take steps to recover possession of the land once the first application has been rejected. But if he takes no steps for a further period of two years, he loses his right to recover possession, and also loses his registered title.

(c) Effect of Registration of Adverse Possessor

Where the adverse possessor is registered under these provisions, he becomes the new registered proprietor of the estate, as the successor in title to the previous proprietor.[259] As with the position in relation to registered land under the Land Registration Act 1925,[260] therefore, and unlike the position in unregistered land,[261] he takes in effect a Parliamentary transfer of the title, rather than simply having a new, original title.

---

[253] LRA 2002, Sch 6, para 3.   [254] Ibid, para 5.   [255] [2004] Conv 123 (S Nield).
[256] LRA 2002, Sch 4, para 5; *Baxter v Mannion* [2011] EWCA Civ 120, [2011] 2 All ER 574.
[257] Ibid, Sch 6, para 6.   [258] Ibid, para 7.
[259] His own former title based on possession is extinguished: ibid, para 9(1).
[260] Above, p 1160.
[261] Above, p 1150. Where the estate is a lease, the effect of registration is an assignment of the lease, but as an assignment by operation of law, it will be an 'excluded assignment' under LT(C)A 1995, above, p 326, and so the former tenant will remain liable on the covenants: H & B, para 31.3.

Registration of the adverse possessor as proprietor does not affect the priority of any interest affecting the estate,[262] and so he takes it subject to the estates and interests that bound the original paper owner. He is not, however, normally bound by any registered charge affecting the estate immediately before his registration.[263]

(d) Impact of Changes made by Land Registration Act 2002

The changes to the law of limitation of actions made by the Land Registration Act 2002, therefore, are of immense significance.

Most obviously, they significantly reduce the ability of a squatter to obtain title to the land. The mere passage of time does not give a person in adverse possession of the land the right to an estate. At most, it gives him the right to *apply* to be registered—an application that then necessarily alerts the registered proprietor to the claim that is being asserted. With limited exceptions[264] the registered proprietor can resist the application, and take steps to recover possession against the squatter. Only if he does not do so within a further period does the squatter acquire an indefeasible right to the transfer of the registered estate.

The corollary of this is that the registered proprietor's estate is more secure.[265] Under the Land Registration Act 1925,[266] to which the same essential rules of limitation of actions applied as in unregistered land, the register could fail to reflect the underlying rights to the estate, in the sense that the registered proprietor could (even without his own knowledge) be holding the registered estate on trust for the adverse possessor who had the right to be substituted as proprietor. Now, however, the registered proprietor is and remains the estate owner vis-à-vis an adverse possessor of the estate, both at law and in equity, unless and until the adverse possessor is registered. The register is a more complete mirror of the title to the estate.[267]

A further consequence of this change is that it encourages the owners of unregistered land to register their title. Since the new rules apply to all registered estates, whether or not they have been registered throughout the period of the squatter's adverse possession,[268] the effect of registration of an unregistered estate is now to defeat the potential title of a squatter, even if he is already in adverse possession. As we have already seen,[269] a principal aim of the Land Registration Act 2002 was to facilitate the completion of the register of title, in order to allow the introduction in due course of electronic conveyancing. The provisions on adverse possession are designed to further this aim.

---

262 LRA 2002, Sch 6, para 9(2).

263 Ibid, para 6(3). This is because the chargee will have received notice of the squatter's application and could himself have taken steps to obtain possession: H & B, para 31.6. There is an exception where he is registered on one of the three grounds in the paper owner's counter-notice, above: para 6(4).

264 Ibid, para 5; above.

265 This as a further consequence in relation to the protection of the registered proprietor's human rights: below.

266 Above, p 1158.   267 Above, pp 135 ff.   268 LRA 2002, Sch 6, para 1(4).

269 Above, p 141.

At a more fundamental theoretical level, however, the effect of the new regime for adverse possession and limitation of actions is to change the very basis of title to land. We have already seen in Chapter 5 that the introduction of registration of title, coupled with the State guarantee of the title, has shifted the basis of land ownership to the fact of registration. The Land Registration Act 1925 took this a long way forward, but still left unchanged the basic principle: that the underlying estate in the land, which is subject to registration, is based on possession, and therefore a registered estate could still be defeated by adverse possession. The Land Registration Act 2002, however, has taken this still further. Relativity of seisin, or possession, is no longer the test for title to land. The registered proprietor cannot lose his title without having the opportunity to take steps to recover possession; in that sense, registration is everything.

E ADVERSE POSSESSION AND HUMAN RIGHTS

In recent years questions have been asked about the compatibility of the rules on adverse possession of land with the European Convention on Human Rights. This issue came into sharp focus with the enactment of the Human Rights Act 1998.

(1) Limitation Act 1980 and Land Registration Act 1925

We have seen that, both in relation to unregistered land, and in relation to registered land where the period of adverse possession was completed under the Land Registration Act 1925,[270] the paper owner could lose his title in favour of an adverse possessor. There is no requirement for the adverse possessor to give him any formal notice of his possession, or that he is approaching the completion of the limitation period;[271] nor is there any provision for the paper owner to be compensated for his loss of title. These features of the law have prompted the question whether the statutory provisions constitute an interference with the paper owner's rights under article 1 of the First Protocol to the European Convention, which, as we have seen, provides:[272]

> Every natural or legal person is entitled to the peaceful enjoyment of his possessions. No one shall be deprived of his possessions except in the public interest and subject to the conditions provided for by law and by the general principles of international law.

---

[270] Ie, before 13 October 2003, when the Land Registration Act 2002 came into force: above, p 1160.

[271] *Topplan Estates Ltd v Townley* [2004] EWCA Civ 1369, [2005] 1 EGLR 89 at [85] (Jonathan Parker LJ). It would be otherwise if the squatter had acted dishonestly: ibid.

[272] Above, p 23. For further discussion, see Rook, *Property Law and Human Rights* (2001), esp ch 4 and section 8.5 (written before the development of the case law set out below); Allen, *Property and the Human Rights Act 1998* (2005).

The preceding provisions shall not, however, in any way impair the right of a State to enforce such laws as it deems necessary to control the use of property in accordance with the general interest or to secure the payment of taxes or other contributions or penalties.

The most likely challenge is based on the second rule within this article: the *deprivation of possessions*.

The first indications were that the courts would not hold that the statutory provisions relating to adverse possession were contrary to this rule.[273] However, in *Beaulane Properties Ltd v Palmer*[274] Nicholas Strauss QC held that the effect of section 17 of the Limitation Act 1980[275] is to deprive the owner of the land of all his right to it, and therefore is a deprivation of his possessions;[276] and even if there might be an argument in relation to unregistered land that the effect of section 17 is merely to enlarge the adverse possessor's (relative) title rather than to deprive the paper owner of his property, this cannot apply in registered land, where the basis of title is registration, rather than simply relative possession.[277] The loss of registered title in favour of an adverse possessor under section 75 of the Land Registration Act 1925[278] was therefore contrary to article 1. Rather than simply declaring the domestic statutory provision incompatible with the Convention, however, the judge reinterpreted[279] it so as to make it compatible—and held that 'adverse possession' should be construed as covering only the case where the possession is inconsistent with the use or intended use of the land by the registered proprietor. The effect of this, as the judge noted, was to reintroduce the test of 'adverse possession' that was rejected by the House of Lords in *JA Pye (Oxford) Ltd v Graham*.[280]

The final word, however, came from the European Court of Human Rights, which examined the issue in relation to the *Pye* case itself. Pye, who had lost its title by the operation of adverse possession under section 75 of the Land Registration Act 1925,[281] brought a claim for compensation against the UK Government on the basis that the Government had failed to ensure that section 75 protected Pye's rights under the European Convention on Human Rights. At first the Court held by a majority of four to three that the combined operation of the Limitation Act 1980 and the Land

---

[273] *Family Housing Association v Donnellan* [2002] 1 P & CR 34, following the approach taken (obiter) by CA in *JA Pye (Oxford) Ltd v Graham* [2001] Ch 804.

[274] [2005] EWHC 817 (Ch), [2006] Ch 79; [2005] Conv 345 (M Dixon). An 'impressive judgment': *Tower Hamlets LBC v Barrett* [2005] EWCA Civ 923, [2006] 1 P & CR 9 at [120] (Neuberger LJ).

[275] Above, p 1149.   [276] At [136].

[277] At [139]-[140], relying on the difference between registered and unregistered land set out in Law Com No 254, Consultative Document on *Land Registration for the Twenty-First Century* (1998), para 10.3.

[278] Above, p 1158.   [279] HRA 1998, s 3.

[280] Above, p 1139. The judge (at [214]) thought that this interpretation would be necessary only in relation to the acquisition of title by a trespasser between October 2000 (when HRA came into force) and October 2003 (when LRA 2002 superseded LRA 1925). For a contrary view, see [2005] Conv 345, 350-1 (M Dixon). HL in *JA Pye (Oxford) Ltd v Graham* did not consider the matter because the facts arose before HRA 1998 came into force, and they found no ambiguity in LA 1980: [2002] UKHL 30, [2003] 1 AC 419 at [65].

[281] Above, p 1158.

Registration Act 1925 was incompatible with article 1 of the First Protocol.[282] However, following a request by the Government, the case was referred to the Grand Chamber of the European Court of Human Rights, which held[283] by a majority of ten to seven that article 1 of the First Protocol was engaged, but that the 12-year limitation period for actions for recovery of land pursues a legitimate aim in the general interest, and there is also a general interest in the extinguishment of title at the end of the period. A fair balance has been struck between the demands of the general interest, and the interest of the individuals concerned, within the margin of appreciation of the State. Pye's claim therefore failed. There can now be no challenge to the rules on adverse possession based on the European Convention on Human Rights.[284]

(2) Land Registration Act 2002

Given the view taken by the Grand Chamber of the European Court of Human Rights about the law on adverse possession in unregistered land, there can be no doubt that the provisions of the 2002 Act comply with the Convention. The Grand Chamber itself said:[285]

> since the entry into force of the Land Registration Act 2002, the paper owner of registered land against whom time has been running is in a better position than were the applicant companies at the relevant time. The 2002 Act requires, in effect, the giving of notice to a paper owner before the expiry of the limitation period, to give him time, if he wishes, to take action to deal with the adverse possessor. It improves the position of the paper owner and, correspondingly, makes it more difficult for an adverse possessor to acquire a full 12 years' adverse possession.

---

[282] *J A Pye (Oxford) Ltd v United Kingdom* (2006) 43 EHRR 3, [2005] 3 EGLR 1; [2006] Conv 179 (M Dixon).

[283] (2008) 46 EHRR 45, [2008] 1 EGLR 111; [2007] Conv 552; [2007] 0737 EG 228 (O Radley-Garder and J Small); (2008) 71 MLR 878 (L Fox O'Mahony and N Cobb).

[284] *Ofulue v Bossert* [2008] EWCA Civ 7, [2009] Ch 1 at [52] (the determination of the Grand Chamber in *Pye* applies to all decisions on adverse possession and it is not open to the English court not to follow it because the case is distinguishable on its facts; this position was not challenged on appeal to HL: [2009] UKHL 16, [2009] 1 AC 990 at [72]-[73]); [2008] Conv 160 (M Dixon). At first, even after the decision of the Grand Chamber, the Land Registry still regarded the decision in *Beaulane Properties Ltd v Palmer* [2006] Ch 79 as reflecting English law in the interpretation of s 75 LRA 1925 in relation to applications made under LRA 2002, Sch 12, para 18 (transitional provisions): Land Registry Additional Practice Guide affecting Practice Guide 5 (2007), criticised in [2007] Conv 552 at 557–8 and [2008] Conv 160 at 165 (M Dixon); but it retreated from this and Practice Guide 5 now makes clear that a claimant must meet the *Pye* criteria for adverse possession: [2009] Conv 169.

[285] Above, n 283, at [81]. In *Beaulane Properties Ltd v Palmer* [2005] EWHC 817 (Ch), [2006] Ch 79, above, p 274, Nicholas Strauss QC expressed the view (obiter) at [198]-[200] that the new regime for adverse possession under the Land Registration Act 2002 is not open to the same objections as he had found in relation to unregistered land and the Land Registration Act 1925.

SELECT BIBLIOGRAPHY

AIGLER, RW, AF SMITH, AND S TEFFT *Cases and Materials on the Law of Property*, St Paul: West, 1960

ALDRIDGE, TM *Commonhold Law* (looseleaf), London: Sweet & Maxwell

ALDRIDGE, TM *Companion to the 4th edition of the Standard Conditions of Sale*, 3rd edn, London: Sweet & Maxwell, 2003

ALDRIDGE, TM *Leasehold Law* (looseleaf), London: Sweet & Maxwell

ALDRIDGE, TM *Letting Business Premises*, 8th edn, London: Sweet & Maxwell, 2004

ALDRIDGE, TM *Privity of Contract: Landlord and Tenant Covenants Act 1995*, London: FT Law and Tax, 1995

ALLEN, T *Property and the Human Rights Act 1998*, Oxford: Hart Publishing, 2005

American Law Institute *Restatement of the Law: Property 3d: Mortgages*, 1997; *Servitudes*, 2000; Philadelphia: American Law Institute, 1997

ANDERSON, JS *Lawyers and the Making of English Law 1832–1940*, Oxford: Clarendon Press, 1992

ANNAND, R AND B CAIN *Remedies under the Contract*, London: Sweet & Maxwell, 1988

Anson's Law of Contract, by J Beatson, A Burrows, and J Cartwright, 29th edn, Oxford: Oxford University Press, 2010

AUSTIN, J *Lectures on Jurisprudence*, 5th edn by R Campbell, London: John Murray, 1885

BACON, F *Reading on the Statute of Uses* in *The Works of Francis Bacon*, London: J Stephens, 1892; reprinted New York: Garland, 1979

Bacon's New Abridgement of the Law, 7th edn by Sir Henry Gwilliam and CE Dodd, 7th edn, London, 1832

BAKER, JH *An Introduction to English Legal History*, 4th edn, London: Butterworths, 2002

BARNES, DMW *Leasehold Reform Act 1967*, London: Butterworths, 1968

Barnsley's Conveyancing Law and Practice, by MP Thompson, 4th edn, London: Butterworths, 1996

Barnsley's Land Options, by M Dray, A Rosenthal, and C Groves, 5th edn, London: Sweet & Maxwell, 2009

BARRACLOUGH, H AND P MATTHEWS *The Trusts of Land and Appointment of Trustees Act 1996*, Sutton Coldfield: CLT Professional Publishing, 1996

BATES, JH *Water and Drainage Law* (looseleaf), London: Sweet & Maxwell

BAXENDALE-WALKER, P *Purpose Trusts*, London: Butterworths, 1999

BEAN, JMW *The Decline of English Feudalism*, Manchester: Manchester University Press, 1968

BEHAN, JCV *The Use of Land as Affected by Covenants*, London: Sweet and Maxwell, 1924

BELL, J, S BOYRON, AND S WHITTAKER *Principles of French Law*, 2nd edn, Oxford: Oxford University Press, 2008

BENNION, FAR AND P DOBSON *Consumer Credit Control* (looseleaf), London: Sweet & Maxwell

BERNSTEIN, R AND K REYNOLDS *Essentials of Rent Review*, London: Sweet and Maxwell, 1995

BICKFORD-SMITH, S AND C SYDENHAM *Party Walls—Law and Practice*, 3rd edn, Bristol: Jordan, 2009

BICKFORD-SMITH, S AND A FRANCIS *Rights of Light. The Modern Law*, 2nd edn, Bristol: Jordan, 2007

BLACKSTONE, SIR WILLIAM *Commentaries on the Laws of England*, by E Christian, 15th edn, London: Cadell and Davies, 1809

Blackstone's Guide to Covenants for Title, by P Kenny, London: Blackstone, 1995

Blackstone's Guide to the Land Registration Act 2002, by R Abbey and M Richards, Oxford: Oxford University Press, 2002

Blackstone's Guide to the Mental Capacity Act 2005, by P Bartlett, 2nd edn, Oxford: Oxford University Press, 2008

Blackstone's Statutes on Planning Law, 3rd edn edited by V Moore and D Hughes, 3rd edn, London: Blackstone, 2000

BONFIELD, L *Marriage Settlements, 1601–1740*, Cambridge: Cambridge University Press, 1983

BRAND, CM *Compulsory Purchase and Compensation* (looseleaf), London: Sweet & Maxwell

BRAND, CM *Mobile Homes and the Law*, London: Sweet & Maxwell, 1986

BRICKDALE, CF AND JS STEWART-WALLACE *The Land Registration Act 1925*, 4th edn, London: Stevens, 1939

BRIDGE, S *Assured Tenancies*, London: Blackstone Press, 1999

BRIGHT, S *Landlord and Tenant Law in Context*, Oxford: Hart, 2007

BRIGHT, S (ed) *Landlord and Tenant Law Past Present and Future*, Oxford: Hart, 2006

BRIGHT, S AND J DEWAR (eds) *Land Law. Themes and Perspectives*, Oxford: Oxford University Press, 1998

BRIGHT, S AND G GILBERT *Landlord and Tenant Law*, Oxford: Clarendon Press, 1995

Bromley's Family Law, by NV Lowe and G Douglas, 10th edn, Oxford: Oxford University Press, 2006

BRUNYATE, JB *Limitation of Actions in Equity*, London: Stevens, 1932

BUCKLAND, WW *Textbook of Roman Law*, 3rd edn, revised by P Stein, Cambridge: Cambridge University Press, 1963

BUCKLEY, RA *The Law of Nuisance*, 2nd edn, London: Butterworths, 1996

BURNETT, JFR *The Elements of Conveyancing*, 8th edn, London: Sweet & Maxwell, 1952

BURROWS, A *Remedies for Torts and Breach of Contract*, 3rd edn, Oxford: Oxford University Press, 2004

BURTON, WH *An Elementary Compendium of the Law of Real Property*, 8th edn by EF Cooper, London: Stevens & Norton, 1856

CAFFYN, DJM *The Right of Navigation on Non-Tidal Rivers*, Eastbourne: Caffyn, 2004

Carson's Real Property Statutes, edited by HW Law, 3rd edn, London: Sweet & Maxwell, 1927

CARTWRIGHT, J *Misrepresentation, Mistake and Non-Disclosure*, 2nd edn, London: Sweet & Maxwell, 2006

Challis's Law of Real Property, 3rd edn by C Sweet, London: Butterworths, 1911

CHERRY, SIR BENJAMIN *The New Property Acts. Series of Lectures with Questions and Answers*, London: Solicitors' Law Stationery Society, 1926

Cheshire, Fifoot and Furmston's Law of Contract, 15th edn by MP Furmston, Oxford: Oxford University Press, 2006

Chitty on Contracts, edited by HG Beale (general editor), 30th edn, London: Sweet & Maxwell, 2009

Clarke on Commonhold: Law, Practice and Precedents, by D Clarke, L Crabb, and N Roberts, Bristol: Jordans, 2004

CLARKE, DN *Commonhold: The New Law*, Bristol: Jordans, 2002

CLARKE, M *Mortgage Fraud*, London: Chapman & Hall, 1991

CLAYDEN, P *Our Common Land. The Law and History of Commons and Village Greens*, 6th edn, Henley-on-Thames: Open Spaces Society, 2007

CLAYDEN, P *The Law of Mobile Homes and Caravans*, 2nd edn, Crayford: Shaw, 2003

Clerk & Lindsell on Torts, edited by MA Jones and AM Dugdale (general editors), 20th edn, London: Sweet & Maxwell, 2010

COKE, SIR EDWARD *Complete Copyholder*, London, 1641

COKE, SIR EDWARD *Institutes of the Laws of England*, Part IV, 1644 [Co Fourth Inst.]

Coke's Commentary upon Littleton, 19th edn, with notes by F Hargrave and C Butler, London, 1832 [Co Litt]

COMYNS, SIR JOHN *A Digest of the Laws of England*, London, 1822

COOKE, E (ed) *Modern Studies in Property Law*, Oxford: Hart Publishing, 2001 (vol 1), 2003 (vol 2), 2005 (vol 3), 2007 (vol 4)

COOKE, E *The Modern Law of Estoppel*, Oxford: Oxford University Press, 2000

COOKE, E *The New Law of Land Registration*, Oxford: Hart Publishing, 2003

Coote's Treatise on the Law of Mortgages, 9th edn by RL Ramsbotham, London: Stevens, 1927

Council of Mortgage Lenders *Lenders' Handbook for England and Wales*, 2nd edn, 2002 (revised from time to time: the up-to-date version is available on the CML web site, www.cml.org.uk)

COUSINS, EF *The Law of Mortgages*, 3rd edn, by EF Cousins and I Clarke, London: Sweet & Maxwell, 2010

COWEN, G, J DRISCOLL, AND L TARGET *Commonhold Law and Practice*, London: Law Society, 2005

CRABB, L *Leases Covenants and Consents*, 2nd edn, London: Sweet & Maxwell, 2008

Cretney, and Lush on Lasting and Enduring Powers of Attorney, 6th edn by D Lush, Bristol: Jordans, 2009

CRETNEY, SM AND JM MASSON *Principles of Family Law*, 6th edn, London: Sweet & Maxwell, 1996

CRETNEY, SM *Principles of Family Law*, 8th edn, eds JM Masson, R Bailey-Harris, and R Probert, London: Sweet & Maxwell, 2008

Cruise's Digest of the Laws of England, 4th edn by HH White, London, 1835

CYPRIAN WILLIAMS, T AND JM LIGHTWOOD *A Treatise on the Law of Vendor and Purchaser of Real Estate and Chattels Real*, 4th edn, London: Sweet & Maxwell, 1936

DARBY, JGN AND FA BOSANQUET *A Practical Treatise on the Statutes of Limitations in England and Ireland*, 1st edn, London: W. Maxwell, 1867; 2nd edn by FA Bosanquet and JRV Marchant, London: W Clowes and Sons Ltd, 1893

Dart's Vendors and Purchasers of Real Estate, 8th edn by EP Hewitt and MRC Overton, London: Stevens, 1929

DAWSON, IJ AND RA PEARCE *Licences Relating to the Occupation or Use of Land*, London: Butterworths, 1979

DENYER-GREEN, B *Compulsory Purchase and Compensation*, 9th edn, London: Estates Gazette, 2009

DERHAM, R *The Law of Set-off*, 4th edn, Oxford: Oxford University Press, 2010

DICEY, AV *Lectures on the Relation between Law and Public Opinion in England during the Nineteenth Century*, 2nd edn (reissued) with a preface by ECS Wade, London: Macmillan, 1962

DIGBY, KE AND WM HARRISON *An Introduction to the History of Law of Real Property*, 5th edn, Oxford: Clarendon Press, 1897

Digest of Justinian, edited by T Mommsen and P Krueger and translated by A Watson, Philadelphia: University of Pennsylvania Press, 1985

DOWDING, N AND K REYNOLDS *Dilapidations. The Modern Law and Practice*, 4th edn, London: Sweet & Maxwell, 2008

DUXBURY, RMC *Telling & Duxbury's Planning Law and Procedure*, 14th edn, Oxford: Oxford University Press, 2009

EASTON, HC *The Law of Rentcharges (commonly called chief rents) mainly from a conveyancing standpoint*, 2nd edn, London: Sweet & Maxwell, 1931

EEKELAAR, J AND J BELL (eds) *Oxford Essays in Jurisprudence: Third Series*, Oxford: Clarendon Press, 1987

ELLIS, P *Rights to Light*, London: Estates Gazette, 1989

ELPHINSTONE, SIR LANCELOT *Covenants affecting Land*, London: Law Stationery Society, 1946

ELPHINSTONE, SIR LANCELOT *Introduction to Conveyancing*, 7th edn by FT Maw, London: Sweet & Maxwell, 1918

Emmet and Farrand on Title, by J Farrand and A Clarke (looseleaf), London: Longman

Encyclopedia of Consumer Credit Law, edited by E Lomnicka (looseleaf), London: Sweet & Maxwell

Encyclopedia of Environmental Law, edited by R Wald (general editor) (looseleaf), London: Sweet & Maxwell

Encyclopaedia of Forms and Precedents, 5th edn (1985) edited by Sir Raymond Walton, and since 1985 by Lord Millett, London: LexisNexis Butterworths

Encyclopedia of Planning Law and Practice, edited by C Lockhart-Mummery, J Harper, D Elvin, and M Grant (looseleaf), London: Sweet & Maxwell

Encyclopedia of the Law of Compulsory Purchase and Compensation, edited by HJJ Brown (general editor) (looseleaf), London: Sweet & Maxwell

ENGLISH, B AND J SAVILLE *Strict Settlement*, Hull: Hull University Press, 1985

EVANS AND SMITH: *The Law of Landlord and Tenant*, 6th edn by PF Smith, London: Butterworths, 2002

FAIREST, PB *Mortgages*, 2nd edn, London: Sweet & Maxwell, 1980

FANCOURT, TM *Enforceability of Landlord and Tenant Covenants*, 2nd edn, London: Sweet & Maxwell, 2006

FARRAND, JT *Contract and Conveyance*, 2nd edn, London: Oyez Longman, 1973; 4th edn, 1983

Farwell on Powers, 3rd edn by CJW Farwell and FK Archer, London: Stevens, 1916

FEARNE, CHARLES *An Essay on the Learning of Contingent Remainders and Executory Devises*, 10th edn, with notes by C Butler, with *An Original View of Executory Interests in Real and Personal Property*, by Josiah W Smith, London: Stevens & Norton, 1844

FETHERSTONHAUGH, G, M SEFTON AND E PETERS *Commonhold*, Oxford: Oxford University Press, 2004

FINN, PD *Essays in Equity*, Sydney: Law Book Co, 1985

Fisher and Lightwood's Law of Mortgage, 13th edn edited by W Clarke and others, London: LexisNexis Butterworths, 2010

Foa's General Law of Landlord and Tenant, 8th edn by H Heathcote-Williams, Ipswich: Thames Bank Publishing Co, 1957

FRANCIS, A *Restrictive Covenants and Freehold Land*, 3rd edn, Bristol: Jordans, 2009

FREEDMAN, PE SHAPIRO, AND B SLATER *Service Charges: Law and Practice*, 4th edn, Bristol: Jordans, 2007

FROUDE, JA *History of England, from the Fall of Wolsey to the Defeat of the Spanish Armada*, new edn, London: Longmans, Green and Co, 1893

FRY, SIR CHARLES *A Treatise on the Specific Performance of Contracts*, 6th edn by GR Northcote, London: Sweet & Maxwell/Ashford Press, 1921

FURBER, J, J KARAS, J EVANS, AND T SCOTT *The Commonhold and Leasehold Reform Act 2002*, London: Butterworths, 2002

Gadsden on Commons and Greens, by E Cousins and N de Poidevin, 2nd edn, London: Sweet & Maxwell, 2005

GAIUS *The Institutes of Gaius*, Part I, translated by F de Zulueta, Oxford: Clarendon Press, 1946

Gale on Easements, 11th edn, edited by G Glover, London: Sweet & Maxwell, 1932

Gale on Easements, 12th edn, edited by DH McMullen, London: Sweet & Maxwell, 1950

Gale on Easements, 18th edn, edited by J Gaunt and Mr Justice Morgan, London: Sweet & Maxwell, 2008

Garner's Local Land Charges, by JE Boothroyd, 14th edn, London: Sweet & Maxwell Ltd, 2010

GETZLER, J *A History of Water Rights at Common Law*, Oxford: Oxford University Press, 2004

GETZLER, J (ed.) *Rationalizing Property, Equity and Trusts: Essays in Honour of Edward Burn*, London: LexisNexis UK, 2003

GILBERT, SIR JEFFREY *A Treatise on Rents*, London, 1758

Gilbert on Uses and Trusts, 3rd edn by EB Sugden, London, 1811

GOFF (Lord Goff of Chieveley) and G Jones *The Law of Restitution*, 7th edn, London: Sweet & Maxwell, 2007

GOODE, RM (general editor) *Consumer Credit Law and Practice* (looseleaf), London: LexisNexis Butterworths

Gore-Browne on Companies, 45th edn by AJ Boyle, Bristol: Jordans, 2004 (looseleaf)

GRAY, CM *Copyhold, Equity and the Common Law*, Cambridge, Mass: Harvard University Press, 1963

GRAY, JC *The Rule against Perpetuities*, 4th edn by R Gray, Boston: Little Brown, 1942

GRAZIADEI, M, U MATTEI, AND L SMITH, *Commercial Trusts in European Private Law*, Cambridge: Cambridge University Press, 2005

Hague's Leasehold Enfranchisement, by A Radevsky and D Greenish, 5th edn, London: Sweet & Maxwell, 2009

HALEY, M *Statutory Regulation of Business Tenancies*, Oxford: Oxford University Press, 2000

HALL, JE *A Treatise of the Law relating to Profits à Prendre and Rights of Common*, London: Sweet, 1871

Halsbury's Laws of England, editor in chief Lord Hailsham of St Marylebone LC, and since 1998 Lord Mackay of Clashfern LC: 4th edn, 1973-87 (reissues 1988-2008); 5th edn 2008 onwards, London: LexisNexis Butterworths

HANBURY AND MARTIN, *Modern Equity*, 18th edn by JE Martin, London: Sweet & Maxwell, 2009

HARGREAVES, AD *An Introduction to the Principles of Land Law*, 4th edn by GA Grove and JF Garner, London: Sweet & Maxwell, 1963

HARPUM, C AND J BIGNELL *Registered Land: Law and Practice under the Land*

Registration Act 2002, Bristol: Jordans, 2004

HARPUM, C AND J BIGNELL *Registered Land: The New Law*, Bristol: Jordans, 2002

HARRIS, B AND G RYAN *An Outline of the Law Relating to Common Land and Public Access to the Countryside*, London: Sweet & Maxwell, 1967

HARRIS, J *Property and Justice*, Oxford: Clarendon Press, 1996

HARRIS, J *Variation of Trusts*, London: Sweet & Maxwell, 1975

HARVEY, BW *Settlements of Land*, London: Sweet & Maxwell, 1973

Hawkins and Ryder on the Construction of Wills, edited by EC Ryder, London: Sweet & Maxwell, 1965

HAYES, WILLIAM *An Introduction to Conveyancing*, 5th edn, London: H Sweet, 1840

HAYTON, DJ *Registered Land*, 3rd edn, London: Sweet & Maxwell, 1981

HEWITSON, R *Business Tenancies*, London: Cavendish, 2005

Heywood and Massey: Court of Protection Practice, edited by D Lush and D Rees (looseleaf), London: Sweet & Maxwell

HILL, SIR GEORGE *Treasure Trove in Law and Practice from the Earliest Time to the Present Day*, Oxford: Clarendon Press, 1936

Hill and Redman's Guide to Landlord and Tenant Law, edited by J Furber (general editor), London: Butterworths, 1999

Hill and Redman's Guide to Rent Review, by M Barnes, London: Butterworths, 2001

Hill and Redman's Landlord and Tenant, edited by J Furber and J Moss (general editors) (looseleaf), London: LexisNexis Butterworths

HOLDSWORTH, SIR WILLIAM *A History of English Law*, London: Methuen, 1903–1972

HOLDSWORTH, SIR WILLIAM *An Historical Introduction to the Land Law*, Oxford: Clarendon Press, 1927

HOLYOAK, JH AND DK ALLEN *Civil Liability for Defective Premises*, London: Butterworths, 1982

HUGHES, D AND S LOWE *Public Sector Housing Law*, 3rd edn, London: Butterworths, 2000

IBBETSON, D *A Historical Introduction to the Law of Obligations*, Oxford: Oxford University Press, 1999

International Encyclopedia of Comparative Law, vol VI, *Property and Trust*, edited by FH Lawson (general editor), Tübingen: JCB Mohr (Paul Siebeck), 1973

Jackson and Powell on Professional Negligence, by J Powell, R Stewart, and R Jackson, 6th edn, London: Sweet & Maxwell, 2009

JACKSON, P *The Law of Easements and Profits*, London: Butterworths, 1978

JACKSON, P AND DC WILDE (eds) *Reform of Property Law*, Aldershot: Dartmouth, 1997

Jarman on Wills, 8th edn by RW Jennings and JC Harper, London: Sweet & Maxwell, 1951

JENKS, E *Modern Land Law*, Oxford: Clarendon Press, 1899

JESSEL, C *Law of the Manor*, Chichester: Barry Rose Law, 1998

JESSEL, C *Law of the Manor: the Twenty-First Century*, Chichester: Barry Rose Law, 2004

JONES, G AND W GOODHART *Specific Performance*, 2nd edn, London: Butterworths, 1996

JONES, JHE *The Lands Tribunal—a Practitioner's Guide*, London: Hubert Bewlay Fund, 1932

JONES, R *Mental Capacity Act Manual*, 4th edn, London: Sweet & Maxwell, 2010

JOSLING, JF *Periods of Limitation*, 7th edn, London: Longman, 1989

JOURDAN, S AND O RADLEY-GARDNER, *Adverse Possession*, 2nd edn, London: Bloomsbury, 2011

Keating on Construction Contracts, 8th edn by V Ramsey and S Furst, London: Sweet & Maxwell, 2008

KENNY, A *Forfeiture of Tenancies*, London: Blackstone, 1999

KENNY, P AND A KENNY *The Trusts of Land and Appointment of Trustees Act 1996*, London: Sweet and Maxwell, 1997

LAWSON, FH *The Rational Strength of English Law*, London: Stevens, 1951

LAWSON, FH AND B RUDDEN *The Law of Property*, 3rd edn, Oxford: Clarendon Press, 2002

LAWSON, RG *Exclusion Clauses and Unfair Contract Terms*, 9th edn, London: Sweet & Maxwell, 2008

LEAKE, SM *A Digest of the Law of Uses and Profits of Land*, London: Stevens, 1888

LEWISON, K *Drafting Business Leases*, 7th edn, London: Sweet & Maxwell, 2006

LEWISON, K *Interpretation of Contracts*, 4rd edn, London: Sweet & Maxwell, 2007

LEWISON, K *Lease or Licence: The Law after Street v Mountford*, London: Longman Professional, 1985

LIGHTWOOD, JM *A Treatise on Possession of Land*, London: Stevens, 1894

Littleton's Tenures (1481). See *Coke's Commentary upon Littleton* (Co Litt)

MACLEAN, DM *Trusts and Powers*, London: Sweet and Maxwell, 1989

MAITLAND, FW *Equity*, revised by John Brunyate, Cambridge: Cambridge University Press, 1936

MAITLAND, FW *Forms of Action at Common Law*, edited by AH Chaytor and WJ Whittaker, Cambridge: Cambridge University Press, 1936

MAITLAND, FW *The Collected Papers of Frederick William Maitland*, edited by HAL Fisher, Cambridge: Cambridge University Press, 1911

MAITLAND, FW *The Constitutional History of England*, Cambridge: Cambridge University Press, 1908

MARKBY, W *Elements of Law*, Oxford: Clarendon Press, 1905

MARTIN, JE *Residential Security*, 2nd edn, London: Sweet & Maxwell, 1995

MASON, S *Electronic Signatures in Law*, 2nd edn, London: Bloomsbury, 2007

MAUDSLEY, RH *The Modern Law of Perpetuities*, London: Butterworths, 1979

Maudsley and Burn's Land Law: Cases and Materials, 9th edn by EH Burn and J Cartwright, Oxford: Oxford University Press, 2009

Maudsley and Burn's Trusts and Trustees: Cases and Materials, 7th edn by EH Burn and G Virgo, Oxford: Oxford University Press, 2008

MCAUSLAN, P *Land, Law and Planning: Cases, Materials and Text*, London: Weidenfeld & Nicolson, 1975

MCCORMACK, G *Registration of Company Charges*, 3rd edn, Bristol: Jordans, 2009

MCCRACKEN, R, G JONES, J PEREIRA, AND S PAYNE *Statutory Nuisance Law and Practice*, 2nd edn, London: Bloomsbury, 2008

McCutcheon on Inheritance Tax, 5th edn by Withers LLP, A Nathan, and M Lemos, London: Sweet & Maxwell, 2009

MCGEE, A *Limitation Periods*, 6th edn, London: Sweet & Maxwell, 2010

MCNAIR, SIR ARNOLD *The Law of the Air*, 3rd edn by MRE Kerr and AHM Evans, London: Stevens, 1964

MEGARRY, SIR ROBERT *The Rent Acts*,
11th edn, London: Stevens; vols 1 and
2 by general editors JS Colyer and Sir
Robert Megarry, 1988; vol 3 by Sir Robert
Megarry and A Arden, 1989

MEGARRY, SIR ROBERT AND HWR
WADE *The Law of Real Property*, 5th edn,
London: Sweet & Maxwell, 1984; 7th edn,
edited by C Harpum, S Bridge, and
M Dixon, 2008

MILLER, JG *The Machinery of Succession*,
2nd edn, Aldershot: Dartmouth, 1996

MOORE, V *A Practical Approach to
Planning Law*, 11th edn, Oxford: Oxford
University Press, 2010

MORRIS, JHC AND W BARTON LEACH
The Rule Against Perpetuities, 2nd edn,
London: Stevens, 1962; with supplement,
1964

Muir Hunter on Personal Insolvency by
J Briggs and C Brougham (looseleaf),
London: Sweet & Maxwell

MUIR WATT. See Watt, J Muir

NICHOLAS, B *An Introduction to Roman
Law*, Oxford: Clarendon Press, 1962

OAKLEY, AJ *Constructive Trusts*, 3rd edn,
London: Sweet & Maxwell, 1997

OSBORN, C *Mortgage Fraud*, Birmingham:
CLT Professional Publishing, 1995

OSWALD, R *A Practitioner's Guide to
Common Land and Commons Registration
Act 1965*, Oxford: ESC, 1989

OUGHTON, DW, JP LOWRY, AND RM
MERKIN, *Limitation of Actions*, London:
LLP, 1998

Parry and Kerridge on the Law of Succession,
12th edn by R Kerridge, London: Sweet &
Maxwell, 2009

PARTINGTON, M *Landlord and Tenant:
Cases, Materials, and Text*, London:
Weidenfeld & Nicolson, 1975

PAWLOWSKI, M *The Doctrine of Proprietary
Estoppel*, London: Sweet & Maxwell, 1996

PAWLOWSKI, M *The Forfeiture of Leases*,
London: Sweet & Maxwell, 1993

PLATT, THOMAS *A Practical Treatise on the
Law of Covenants*, London: Saunders &
Benning, 1829

PLATT, THOMAS *A Treatise on the Law of
Leases*, London: A Maxwell, 1847

PLUCKNETT, TFT *A Concise History of
the Common Law*, 5th edn, London:
Butterworths, 1956

PLUCKNETT, TFT *Legislation of Edward I*,
Oxford: Clarendon Press, 1949

POLLOCK, SIR FREDERICK *The Land Laws*,
3rd edn, London: Macmillan, 1896

POLLOCK, SIR FREDERICK AND FW
MAITLAND *The History of English Law
before the time of Edward I*, 2nd edn,
Cambridge: Cambridge University Press,
1898, revised with introduction and
bibliography by SF Milsom, 1968

POLLOCK, F AND RS WRIGHT *An Essay on
Possession in the Common Law*, Oxford:
Clarendon Press, 1888

POTTER, H *Principles and Practice of
Conveyancing under the Land Registration
Act 1925*, London: Sweet & Maxwell, 1934;
2nd edn, 1948

PRESTON, RICHARD *An Elementary
Treatise on Estates*, 2nd edn, London,
1820–7

PRESTON, RICHARD *An Essay in a Course
of Lectures on Abstracts of Title*, 2nd edn,
London, 1823

*Preston and Newsom on Limitation of
Actions*, by GH Newsom and L Abel-
Smith, 3rd edn, London: Solicitors' Law
Stationery Society, 1953

*Preston and Newsom on Limitation of
Actions*, by S Weeks, 4th edn, London:
Longman, 1989

*Preston and Newsom's Restrictive Covenants
Affecting Freehold Land*, 4th edn by
GH Newsom, London: Sweet & Maxwell, 1967

Preston and Newsom's Restrictive Covenants Affecting Freehold Land, 9th edn by GL Newsom, London: Sweet & Maxwell, 1998

PRIME, T AND G SCANLAN *The Modern Law of Limitation*, London: Butterworths, 1993

REDMOND-COOPER, R *Limitation of Actions*, London: Sweet & Maxwell, 1992

REID, K *Abolition of Feudal Tenure in Scotland*, Edinburgh: Butterworths Scotland, 2003

REYNOLDS, K AND W CLARK *Renewal of Business Tenancies*, 3rd edn, London: Sweet & Maxwell, 2007

REYNOLDS, K AND G FETHERSTONHAUGH *Handbook of Rent Review* (looseleaf), London: Sweet & Maxwell

ROBINSON, SS *Law of Game, Salmon and Freshwater Fishing in Scotland*, Edinburgh: Butterworths, 1990

RODGERS, CP *Agricultural Law*, 3rd edn, Haywards Heath: Tottel, 2008

RODGERS, CP *Housing Law Residential Security and Enfranchisement*, revised edn, London: Butterworths, 2002

ROOK, D *Distress for Rent*, London: Blackstone, 1999

ROOK, D *Property Law and Human Rights*, London: Blackstone, 2001

ROSS, MURRAY J *Drafting and Negotiating Commercial Leases*, by T Bell and others (looseleaf), 5th edn, London: Butterworths, 1988

ROUND, JH *Feudal England*, London: Swan Sonnenschein, 1895

ROWTON SIMPSON, S *Land Law and Registration*, Cambridge: Cambridge University Press, 1976

RUBIN, GR AND DAVID SUGARMAN (eds) *Law, Economy and Society, 1750–1914: Essays in the History of English Law*, Abingdon: Professional Books, 1984

RUDALL, AR *Party Walls*, 3rd edn, London: Jordan & Sons, 1922

RUOFF, TBF *Rentcharges in Registered Conveyancing*, London: Sweet & Maxwell, 1961

RUOFF, TBF AND EJ PRYER *Concise Land Registration Handbook Forms and Practice*, London: Sweet & Maxwell, 1990

RUOFF, TBF, RB ROPER, EJ PRYER, C WEST, R FEARNELY, AND J DONALDSON *The Law and Practice of Registered Conveyancing* (looseleaf edn), London: Sweet & Maxwell, 1991

Ruoff & Roper: Registered Conveyancing by D Cavill, S Wheeler, M Dixon, D Fox, S Coveney, and P Timothy (looseleaf; 2003 onwards)

Sanders on Uses and Trusts, 5th edn by GW Sanders and J Warner, London: A Maxwell, 1844

SARA, C *Boundaries and Easements*, 4th edn, London: Sweet & Maxwell, 2007

SAUVAIN, S *Highway Law*, 4th edn, London: Sweet & Maxwell, 2009

SCAMELL, EH *Land Covenants, Restrictive and Positive, relating to Freehold Land, including Covenants for Title*, London: Butterworths, 1996

Scamell and Densham's Law of Agricultural Holdings, by PR Williams, MN Cardwell, and V. Williams, 9th edn, London: Butterworths, 2007

SCHAW MILLER, S AND E BAILEY *Personal Insolvency Law and Practice*, 4th edn, London: LexisNexis Butterworths, 2008

SCHOON, N *Islamic Banking and Finance*, London, Spiramus, 2009

SCOTT, SIR LESLIE *The New Law of Property Explained*, with annotations by BB Benas, London: H Sweet, 1925

SCRIVEN, J *A Treatise on the Law of Copyholds*, 7th edn by A Brown, London: Butterworth & Co, 1896

SCRUTTON, TE *Land in Fetters*, Cambridge: Cambridge University Press, 1886

SHARPLES, J *Land Licences*, Bristol: Jordan, 2011

Sheppard's Touchstone of Common Assurances, 8th edn by EG Atherley, London, 1826

SHERRIFF, G *Service Charges in Leases: A Practical Guide*, London: Waterlow, 1989

SHERRIN, CH AND RC BONEHILL *The Law and Practice of Intestate Succession*, 3rd edn, London: Sweet & Maxwell, 2004

SILVERMAN, F *Standard Conditions of Sale*, 6th edn, Croydon: Tolley, 1999

SILVERMAN, F *Conveyancing Handbook*, 17th edn, London: Law Society, 2010

SILVERMAN, F AND R HEWITSON, *Conveyancing Searches and Enquiries*, 3rd edn, Bristol: Jordans, 2006

SIMES, LEWIS M *Public Policy and the Dead Hand*, Ann Arbor: University of Michigan Law School, 1955

SIMPSON, AWB *A History of the Land Law*, 2nd edn, Oxford: Clarendon Press, 1986

SIMPSON, S ROWTON *Land Law and Registration*, Cambridge: Cambridge University Press, 1976

SLADE, SIR CHRISTOPHER *The Informal Creation of Interests in Land* (public lecture given by the Rt Hon Sir Christopher Slade, Lord Justice of Appeal, on 2 March 1984, Child & Co. Oxford lecture), Oxford, 1984

SMITH, JC *Liability in Negligence*, London: Sweet & Maxwell, 1984

SMITH, RJ *Plural Ownership*, Oxford: Oxford University Press, 2005

SMITH, RJ *Property Law*, 6th edn, Harlow, 2009

Smith's Leading Cases, 13th edn by Sir Thomas Chitty, AT Denning and CP Harvey, London: Sweet & Maxwell, 1929

Snell's Equity, 32nd edn by J McGhee, London: Sweet & Maxwell, 2010

SPARKES, P *A New Landlord and Tenant*, Oxford: Hart, 2001

SPEAIGHT, A AND G STONE *The Law of Defective Premises*, London: Pitman, 1982

SPENCER BOWER, G AND AK TURNER *Estoppel by Representation*, 4th edn by P Feltham, D Hochberg, and T Leech, London: Lexis Nexis UK, 2003

SPRING, E *Law, Land and Family: Aristocratic Inheritance in England, 1300 to 1800*, London: Chapel Hill, 1993

STENTON, FM *William the Conqueror and the Rule of the Normans*, new edn, London: Putnam, 1925

Storey's Conveyancing, by IR Storey, S Peaple, and A Hunjan, 5th edn, London: Butterworths, 2001

STUBBS, W *The Constitutional History of England in its Origin and Development*, 3 vols, Oxford: Clarendon Press, 1874 (vol i), 1875 (vol ii), 1878 (vol iii)

SUGDEN, EDWARD *A Practical Treatise of Powers*, 9th edn, London: H Sweet, 1861

SUGDEN, EDWARD, *The Law of Vendors and Purchasers of Estates*, 14th edn, London: H Sweet, 1862

SUTHERLAND, DW *The Assize of Novel Disseisin*, Oxford: Clarendon Press, 1973

Sweet and Maxwell's Conveyancing Practice, by J Alexander and S Spurgeon (looseleaf), London: Sweet & Maxwell

SYDENHAM, A AND V MAINWARING *Farm Business Tenancies—The Agricultural Tenancies Act 1995*, Bristol: Jordans, 1995

SYDENHAM, A AND C SYDENHAM *Trusts of Land—The New Law*, Bristol: Jordans, 1996

TANNEY, A AND I TRAVERS *Distress for Rent*, Bristol: Jordans, 2000

TEE, L *Land Law Issues, Debates, Policy*, Cullompton: Willan, 2002

Thomas on Powers, by G Thomas, London: Sweet & Maxwell, 1998

THOMPSON, MP *Co-ownership*, London: Sweet & Maxwell, 1988

TREITEL, GH *The Law of Contract*, 12th edn by E Peel, London: Sweet & Maxwell, 2007

TROMANS, S *Commercial Leases*, 2nd edn, London: Sweet & Maxwell, 1996

TROMANS, S AND K FULLER *Environmental Impact Assessment Law and Practice*, London: LexisNexis UK, 2003

TROMANS, S AND R TURRALL-CLARKE *Contaminated Land*, 2nd edn, London: Sweet & Maxwell, 2007

Tudor's Leading Cases on Real Property Conveyancing, and the Construction of Wills and Deeds, 4th edn by TH Carson and HB Bompas, London, 1898

TURNER, RW *The Equity of Redemption*, Cambridge: Cambridge University Press, 1931

UBHI, N AND B DENYER-GREEN *Law of Commons, Town and Village Greens*, 2nd edn, Bristol: Jordans, 2006

UNDERHILL, A *A Century of Law Reform*, 1911

UNDERHILL, A *A Concise Explanation of Lord Birkenhead's Act (the Law of Property Act 1922) in Plain Language*, London: Butterworths, 1922

UNDERHILL, A AND DJ HAYTON, *Law relating to Trusts and Trustees*, 18th edn by DJ Hayton, P Matthews, and C Mitchell, London: LexisNexis Butterworths, 2010

VAIZEY, JS *A Treatise on the Law of Settlements of Property*, London: H Sweet, 1887

VINER, CHARLES *A General Abridgement of Law and Equity*, 2nd edn, London: GGJ and J Robinson, 1791

VINOGRADOFF, P *Villainage in England*, Oxford: Clarendon Press, 1892

WAITE, A AND T JEWELL *Environmental Law in Property Transactions*, 3rd edn by A Waite, T Jewell, G Jones, and V Fogleman, London: Bloomsbury, 2009

WALDOCK, CHM *The Law of Mortgages*, 2nd edn, London: Stevens, 1950

WALKER, GCP AND M BUCKLEY, *Charging Orders Against Land*, 2nd edn, Chichester: Barry Rose, 2004

WARBURTON, J *Unincorporated Associations: Law and Practice*, 2nd edn, London: Sweet & Maxwell, 1990

WATT, J MUIR AND JR MOSS *Agricultural Holdings*, 14th edn, London: Sweet & Maxwell, 1998

WEBBER, G *Business Premises: Possession and Lease Renewal*, 4th edn, London: Sweet & Maxwell, 2009

WEBBER, G AND D DOVAR, *Residential Possession Proceedings*, 8th edn, London: Sweet & Maxwell, 2008

West and Smith's Law of Dilapidations, edited by PF Smith, 11th edn, London: Estates Gazette, 2001

White and Tudor's Leading Cases in Equity, 9th edn by EP Hewitt and JB Richardson, London: Sweet & Maxwell, 1928

WHITEHOUSE, C AND N HASSALL *Trust of Land, Trustee Delegation and the Trustee Act 2000*, 2nd edn, London: Butterworths, 2001

WILKEN, S *The Law of Waiver, Variation and Estoppel*, 2nd edn, Oxford: Oxford University Press, 2002

WILKINSON, HW *The Standard Conditions of Sale of Land*, 4th edn, London: Longman, 1990

WILLIAMS, D, CM BRAND, AND C
   HUBBARD *Handbook of Business Tenancies*
   (looseleaf), London: Sweet & Maxwell

WILLIAMS, D, *Handbook of Dilapidations*
   (looseleaf), London: Sweet & Maxwell

WILLIAMS, JAMES *The Statute of Frauds:
   Section Four, in the Light of its Judicial
   Interpretation*, Cambridge: Cambridge
   University Press, 1932

WILLIAMS, JOSHUA *Principles of the Law of
   Real Property*, 13th edn, London: H Sweet,
   1880

WILLIAMS, JOSHUA *Rights of Common and
   Other Prescriptive Rights*, London:
   H Sweet, 1880

Williams on Wills, 9th edn by RFD Barlow,
   CH Sherrin, RA Wallington, SL Meadway,
   and MC Waterworth, London: LexisNexis
   Butterworths, 2008

*Wolstenholme and Cherry's Annotated Land
   Registration Act 2002*, by I Clarke and
   J Farrand, London: Sweet & Maxwell, 2004

*Wolstenholme and Cherry's Conveyancing
   Statutes*, 11th edn by Sir Benjamin Cherry,
   J Chadwick, and JRP Maxwell, London:
   Stevens, 1925–7

*Wolstenholme and Cherry's Conveyancing
   Statutes*, 12th edn by Sir Benjamin
   Cherry, DH Parry and JRP Maxwell,
   London: Stevens, 1932

*Wolstenholme and Cherry's Conveyancing
   Statutes*, 13th edn by JT Farrand, London:
   Oyez, 1972

Wontner's Guide to Land Registry Practice,
   22nd edn by D Rees, London: Sweet &
   Maxwell, 2009

Woodfall: Landlord and Tenant, edited by
   K Lewison and others (looseleaf), London:
   Sweet & Maxwell

WOOLRYCH, HW *A Treatise on the
   Law of Rights of Common*, 2nd edn by
   HW Woolrych, London: Benning, 1850

*Wurtzburg and Mills: Building Society
   Law*, edited by M Waters, E Ovey, and
   K Selway (looseleaf), London: Sweet &
   Maxwell

WYLIE, JCW *Irish Land Law*, 4th edn,
   Dublin: Bloomsbury, 2010

ZIMMERMANN, R, D VISSER, AND K REID
   (eds) *Mixed Legal Systems in Comparative
   Perspective*, Oxford: Oxford University
   Press, 2004

INDEX

Introductory Note

References such as '178–9' indicate (not necessarily continuous) discussion of a topic across a range of pages. Wherever possible in the case of topics with many references, these have either been divided into sub-topics or only the most significant discussions of the topic are listed. Because the entire work is about 'land law', the use of this term (and certain others which occur constantly throughout the book) as an entry point has been minimised. Information will be found under the corresponding detailed topics.